second edition

O9-ABH-016

ST. MARY'S COLLEGE OF
ST. MARY'S CITY, MARYLAND 20686

Modern Christian Thought

Volume II
The Twentieth Century

JAMES C. LIVINGSTON
The College of William and Mary

FRANCIS SCHÜSSLER FIORENZA
Harvard University

WITH

SARAH COAKLEY
Harvard University

JAMES H. EVANS, JR.
Colgate Rochester Divinity School
Bexley Hall/Crozer Theological Seminary

Prentice Hall
Upper Saddle River, New Jersey 07458

Library of Congress Cataloging-in-Publication Data
LIVINGSTON, JAMES C.
    MODERN CHRISTIAN THOUGHT / JAMES C. LIVINGSTON.—2nd ed.
        p.   cm.
    Includes bibliographical references and index.
    Contents: v. II The twentieth century.
    ISBN 0-02-371410-7 (alk. paper)
    1. Theology, Doctrinal—History—Modern period, 1500–.   I. Title.
BT27.L58   1997
230'.09'03—dc20   96-3409

Editorial director: *Charlyce Jones Owen*
Acquisitions editor: *Karita France*
Editorial/production supervision: *Edie Riker*
Copy editor: *Nancy Marcello*
Buyer: *Benjamin D. Smith*
Cover director: *Jayne Conte*
Marketing manager: *Audra Silverie*
Editorial assistant: *Jennifer Ackerman*

This book was set in 10/12 Goudy by East End Publishing Services, Inc.
and was printed and bound by Quebecor Printing. The cover was
printed by Phoenix Color Corp.

Text and photo credits appear on pages 535–536, which constitute
a continuation of the copyright page

© 2000 by Prentice-Hall, Inc.
Upper Saddle River, New Jersey 07458

All rights reserved. No part of this book may be
reproduced, in any form or by any means,
without permission in writing from the publisher.

Printed in the United States of America

10   9   8   7   6   5   4   3   2   1

ISBN   0-02-371410-7

Prentice-Hall International (UK) Limited, *London*
Prentice-Hall of Australia Pty. Limited, *Sydney*
Prentice-Hall Canada Inc., *Toronto*
Prentice-Hall Hispanoamericana, S.A., *Mexico*
Prentice-Hall of India Private Limited, *New Delhi*
Prentice-Hall of Japan, Inc., *Tokyo*
Pearson Education Asia Pte. Ltd., *Singapore*
Editora Prentice-Hall do Brasil, Ltda., *Rio de Janeiro*

Brief Contents

Volume I: The Enlightenment and the Nineteenth Century

Contents

Chapter Three
The Dialectical Theology: Karl Barth, Emil Brunner, and Friedrich Gogarten   62

Chapter Four
The Theologies of Karl Barth and Dietrich Bonhoeffer   96

Preface

This is the second volume of a two-volume revised edition of the text *Modern Christian Thought*, first published over a quarter of a century ago. Both the sustained interest in the first edition and its need for a substantial revision and expansion led to the decision to publish this new version in a two-volume paperback edition. This second volume covers the twentieth century and includes chapters on the important movements, theologians, and religious writers of the century, including developments in the last years of the century.

In teaching modern Christian thought for many years, it was evident that a text was needed that covers in some depth the important intellectual developments in the history of modern Western Christianity, including movements and thinkers in both the Catholic and Protestant traditions. There are texts that survey the history of Christianity, including the modern period, and there are others that deal with Protestant or Catholic thinkers, but there is no other text that attempts a thorough exploration of the major thinkers and movements in both traditions in Europe and North America since the eighteenth-century Enlightenment.

Each chapter concerns itself with a distinctive movement or school of thought and is relatively independent. The chapters follow essentially the same format. First, the context or historical setting of the movement or group of thinkers is briefly traced—for example, the background of Dialectical theology and Transcendental Thomism—followed by a longer exposition of the distinctive ideas of the movement *as exemplified in the thought of a few representative thinkers*. The goal has been the selection of exemplary figures—Karl Barth, Paul Tillich, Karl Rahner, Gustavo Gutiérrez, John B. Cobb, Jr., Wolfhart Pannenberg—rather than a comprehensive, and necessarily cursory, survey of numerous thinkers.

Second, the text makes extensive use of important and illustrative quotations from primary sources so that the reader can be engaged by a seminal thinker's own ideas. The reader is then assisted in understanding the particular writer's meaning and import through further elucidation and critical analysis. An effort has been made to include figures—e.g., H. N. Wieman, Friedrich Gogarten, Joseph Maréchal, Schubert Ogden, Johann Metz, Elisabeth Schüssler Fiorenza—who have made important contributions to modern Christian thought but who have not always received their due.

The book gives special attention to developments in constructive, historical, philosophical, political, and apologetical theology; that is, with the encounter between Christian ideas and modern philosophy, history, and the social and natural sciences. This is why the book gives special attention to such movements as American Empirical Theology, Christian Existentialism, Transcendental Thomism, History and Hermeneutics, and Political Theology. It also explains the inclusion of such figures as William James, Alfred North Whitehead, Gabriel Marcel, Hans-Georg Gadamer, and Luce Irigaray. The text endorses Nikolai Berdyaev's judgment that many of the great modern philosophers are "Christian" philosophers in the sense that without Christianity much of their philosophical work would have been very different and that, without such thinkers, Christian thought would not be exactly where it finds itself today.

There now is widespread conviction that in the latter decades of the twentieth century we have moved into a new postmodern era and that Christianity in the new millennium will adopt thought-forms and ways of doing theology that will be radically different from the forms that we have come to identify with either the medieval or modern periods. The authors do, however, see the Enlightenment and modernity as a watershed in Christian history that has continued to have a profound influence in the twentieth century. For Christian thought, modernity represents a series of severe crises marked by creative responses and advances. The last three hundred years have witnessed some of the most serious intellectual assaults against Christianity in its history—challenges that, nevertheless, have been met with extraordinary resilience. In the twentieth century this renewal is evident in such movements as the Dialectical theology, Christian Existentialism, the Roman Catholic *aggiornamento* following the Second Vatican Council, feminist theology, the variety of political and liberationist theologies since the 1960s, in hermeneutics, and some of the recent developments explored in Chapter Sixteen.

Twentieth-century Christian thought cannot, of course, be understood without an appreciation of the nineteenth century. It was in that century that the problems posed by modernity were confronted head-on. Theology itself—the very question of the knowledge of God—was challenged by the British empiricist tradition, by Kant's great critique, and later in the century by a self-confident scientific naturalism. The nineteenth century also saw the emergence of our modern historical consciousness, which raised new questions about the nature and authority of the Bible, about the historical development of dogma, and most strikingly, about Christology and the questions surrounding the quest of the historical Jesus. The nineteenth century also produced the great deconstructive critics of Christianity: Strauss, Feuerbach, Marx, and Nietzsche. Although there were theological movements that dismissed the challenges of modern thought, they did not prevail. The legacy of the nineteenth-century to twentieth-century Christian thought is a condition of creative tension between Christ and modern culture. In the first half of the twentieth century, Protestant theology in particular can be viewed as an ongoing dialogue with the nineteenth century, for example, in the work of Albert Schweitzer, Karl Barth and the dialectical theologians, Rudolf Bultmann, and Paul Tillich. The continuities are pronounced, even when couched in the form of opposition.

While the nineteenth-century heritage of Kant, Schleiermacher, Hegel, Kierkegaard, and Nietzsche remains a force in Christian theology in the latter decades of the twentieth, a shift both in thought and cultural sensibility characterizes these years. A convenient cover term for these winds of change is postmodernism. The following are especially significant for Christian thought: First, a deep questioning of the West's superiority, technical mastery, and moral virtue in light of the horrors of the Holocaust and Hiroshima. The other side of this negative verdict is the discovery of *difference*, diversity, and pluralism. This new sensibility has radicalized the issue of Christianity's relation to other religious faiths and has relativized or seriously moderated the traditional emphasis on doctrine and exclusivist notions of truth. A related feature of these decades is the heightened consciousness of issues relating to gender, race, and ethnicity. The effect, in some Christian communities, has been a deepened commitment to action, to praxis—the recognition that the meaning and truth of Christian theology are found in the practice, not in theological speculation. The response has been the various movements of Feminist, Latin American, and Black liberation.

Another feature of the late twentieth century is a new crisis of knowledge due, in part, to an awareness of cultural diversity, but also to the suspicions of contemporary philosophy and critical theory about the Enlightenment's claims regarding the "foundations" of knowledge. The significance of this critique is evident in the sophisticated way that theologians are engaged in the issues raised by hermeneutics and critical theory. The ecology movement also has had a profound influence on theology in the latter decades of the century, especially in the reexamination of the doctrine of Creation and in a rethinking of the entire question of God's relation to the natural world. Christology is increasingly explored "from below"—that is, from reflection on the person and activity of Jesus rather than from a study of church creedal traditions—by theologians working within a political, liberationist, and postmodernist context. This move began earlier in, for example, the work of the Ritschlian theologians, as well as in the later writings of Karl Barth and the reflections of Dietrich Bonhoeffer.

Undertaking a project that covers such a range and variety of movements and thinkers in the twentieth century required a collaborative effort. Responsibility for the individual chapters are as follows: James C. Livingston, Introduction and Chapters 1–6, 10, 12, 15, 16; Francis Schüssler Fiorenza, Chapters 7–9 and 11; Sarah Coakley, Chapter 13; and James H. Evans, Jr., Chapter 14. The authors are acutely aware of the difficulties involved in the selection of representative figures and, at the same time, that a wholly comprehensive coverage was neither feasible nor wise. Our indebtedness is great to the many scholars whose valuable studies of particular movements and thinkers are the foundation of this book. Unfortunately, they are too many to mention here. Specialists in the field will easily recognize their presence in the notes and bibliographies.

We are immensely obliged to several colleagues who read penultimate drafts of chapters. These include Darrell Jodock, John T. Ford, Douglas Jacobsen, Anne E. Carr, and Samuel K. Roberts. The meticulous care for detail that was undertaken by these readers proved invaluable. Some fine suggestions for the inclusion of additional thinkers or themes had to be resisted due to constraints of space. The authors also wish to thank others who assisted with the production of this book: Tammy Cooper at William and Mary and Suzanne Hevelone at Harvard Divinity School, who prepared several of the final drafts of chapters on the word processor; Aylin An and Jackie Livingston, who helped with editorial details; and, finally, the editors for Prentice Hall, especially Maggie Barbieri for her initial support of this two-volume project, Karita A. France who has guided this volume through its publication, Edie Riker, production editor, Joanne Riker, and Nancy Marcello, copy editor.

J.C.L.

Chapter One

❦

The Legacy of Modernity and the New Challenges of Historical Theology

Ernst Troeltsch

THE LEGACY OF MODERNITY

In the preface to Volume I of this text, the claim was advanced that the modern history of Christian thought began not with the Protestant Reformation but with the revolutionary intellectual and social movements of the eighteenth and nineteenth centuries. The influence of advances in science, philosophy, and historical research on Christianity during these two centuries of the modern era was profound and enduring. While Christian thought in the twentieth century has taken new directions, especially in the latter half of the century, many of the questions that emerged during the Enlightenment, and often were pursued more deeply in the nineteenth century, remain vital issues today.

In many respects contemporary discussions of these matters have reached a level of sophistication and a sense of complexity that were not always present earlier. Yet many of the fundamental theological concerns that occupied the Deists, Immanuel Kant, J. G. Herder, D. F. Strauss, the early Romantics, and Kierkegaard remain crucial questions today. Cases in point are the epistemological and the metaphysical issues having to do with our knowledge of God and God's relation to the world, and the hermeneutical or interpretive questions involving the reading of a sacred text such as the Bible. The discussions of these matters in the late twentieth century often disclose extraordinary intellectual dexterity, but to the discerning reader it is also clear that the substantive issues have not always advanced very far beyond the Deists, Kant, Herder, Hegel, Schleiermacher, Kierkegaard, or Nietzsche.

This is not to say that new questions and concerns have not emerged. We are today far more conscious of the limits of reason, more suspicious of metaphysics and of claims to any impregnable foundations of knowledge or truth. We are more sensitive to "otherness" and to the distinctive qualities and claims of other cultures, religions, and groups. The discussion of Christianity's uniqueness and its relationship to other religions thus has been raised to a new level. But the issue itself was already a crucial theme in the writings of the Deists and the early Romantics. Our religious life and thought has been largely shaped by "modernity," and we remain preoccupied with its concerns. It is, therefore, appropriate to begin this volume, concerned with movements of Christian thought in the twentieth century, with a brief overview of those religious issues that contemporary Christian thought has, in large measure, inherited from the Enlightenment and the nineteenth century.

The Question of Authority

The issue of authority is not a modern problem in Christianity. It was a vital question in the primitive Christian Church, and it was a contentious subject of debate during the Protestant and Catholic Reformations of the sixteenth century. However, traditional assumptions about the authority of both the Bible and the Church were profoundly questioned in the modern era, and new claimants for religious authority challenged the traditional sources. Deists such as Anthony Collins and Voltaire, and the great German biblical critics J. S. Semler and J. G. Eichhorn, raised troubling questions about the factual accuracy of the Bible and, by extension, about its inspiration and authority. The Wars of Religion and the competing doctrinal claims of the Lutherans, Calvinists, Anabaptists, and Roman Catholics raised doubts about which ecclesial body, if any, could make good its claim to authoritative teaching. The doctrinal bickering and recriminations provoked William Chillingworth and others to seek

a common religious authority by appeal to the Bible. But, as the Roman theologians justly pointed out, disputes over the interpretation of the Bible were the very cause of the divisions among the Protestants. Subjective appeals to the testimony of the Holy Spirit and to the heart were no solution—they only gave license to the Spiritualists and to the Protestant radicals to deny that the Bible taught such things as the doctrine of the Trinity and other orthodox teachings.

It was, however, the modern "turn to the subject" that proved decisive. Kant's call for "autonomy," for the individual's "release from a self-incurred tutelage" to such heteronomous authorities as the Bible and the Church, embodied the spirit of the Enlightenment. Increasingly, individual reason and conscience became the arbiters of religious truth. Although the Romantics rejected the appeal to autonomous "reason alone," they nevertheless shifted the source of spiritual authority to the "religious self-consciousness," that is, to religious experience. The entire nineteenth century can be viewed as an effort to resolve the increasingly problematic issue of authority. In their different ways, Hegel, Johann Möhler, and F. R. Lamennais looked for authority in a dynamic, developing spiritual tradition, in the working of the "Divine Spirit" immanent in the world and in the Christian community itself. Other writers and movements considered an appeal either to individual reason or religious experience, or to the concept of a *sensus communis* or a communal *Geist,* or tradition, as too subjective. The Anglo-Catholic Oxford Movement appealed rather to antiquity: to the early Church and to the Church Fathers through the fifth century as possessing a unique authority. And it regarded the doctrine of apostolic succession as the guarantor of these traditions of the ancient and undivided Church.

The Roman Catholic Traditionalists and Ultramontanists—e.g., Joseph de Maistre and Henry Manning, as well as John Henry Newman—recognized the Anglican appeal to antiquity as strangely arbitrary. Is the Holy Spirit any less present in guiding the Church and protecting the Catholic faith from error at the third Council of Constantinople in 680 or at the Council of Trent in the sixteenth century? In 1870 the Roman Catholic Church determined that only the infallible authority of the Pope in matters of faith and morals could secure the Church against modern rationalism, subjectivism, and ecclesial chaos and schism. But, as we will see later, papal infallibility has not wholly resolved the problem of authority for Roman Catholicism in the twentieth century.

The Princeton Theology illustrates the response of orthodox Protestantism to the problem of authority in the second half of the nineteenth century. Theologians such as Charles Hodge and Benjamin Warfield regarded the Enlightenment and Romanticism as having a corrosive effect on traditional biblical and ecclesial authority. They insisted on a return to the normative authority of the confessional standards of the seventeenth century and offered new and shrewd arguments in defense of biblical inerrancy. The Princeton doctrine of biblical inspiration and inerrancy did not prove influential in the more progressive and liberal mainline denominations, but it has had a profound influence in both conservative evangelical and in fundamentalist Protestant churches to the present day. The question of the nature and authority of the Bible remains an urgent and persistent issue, and one that likely will not be resolved to the satisfaction of the various Christian churches and groups.

Liberal and Modernist theological movements in the latter decades of the nineteenth century searched for a principle of authority that would be free of claims of inerrancy and infallibility for either the Bible or the Church. They considered such claims to be historically unwarranted, but they also wished to avoid the errors of modern rationalism and subjectivism. Protestant scholars such as Albert Ritschl and Adolf von Harnack and Catholics like George Tyrrell and Alfred Loisy sought to discover in the history of the Church itself a normative Christian principle or idea, one that was both grounded in the New Testament sources and mediated through the historical and communal life of the Christian Church. Ritschl rejected both Schleiermacher's appeal to

the authority of religious feeling and experience and the orthodox rationalists' confident appeal to reason and rational proofs. Ritschl grounded Christian authority in the historical Jesus Christ as mediated through the Christian community—not simply in a Jesus of history reconstructed by "neutral" historians independent of the judgment of religious faith. Harnack called this authoritative norm "the Gospel of Jesus Christ." The Catholic Modernists Tyrrell and Loisy discovered this normative authority in a similar developing idea mediated through the developing life of the Church. Tyrrell, for example, located the norm in what he called the *consensus fidelium,* in the collective mind of "the people of God" as it discerns the "Spirit of Christ." Although these new efforts avoided many of the problems inherent in the more traditional claims for biblical and ecclesiastical authority, there is a noticeable vagueness in appeals to "the Gospel of Jesus," "the Christian idea," or a "consensus fidelium." The problem of authority remains a critical issue for Christian theology, as we will see.

The Development of Doctrine and the Essence of Christianity

In the nineteenth century an issue of considerable importance, and closely related to that of authority, was the problem of the historical development of Church doctrine and the search for an unchanging and unifying essence of Christianity. The problem engaged the best theological minds of the nineteenth century. It emerged as a critical issue in the aftermath of the Wars of Religion when efforts were undertaken to find some principles or theological teachings on which all Christian groups might agree, and that could serve as the basis for religious unity and concord. Once raised, the issue opened up a host of related questions. On the one hand there were the obvious doctrinal differences between the numerous Christian communities, all claiming to represent orthodox Christian belief—and implicitly raising the possibility of multiple Christian "truths," that is, the modern problem of religious pluralism and the relativism of dogmatic traditions. Are there no shared theological norms? Is there no common essence of Christianity? And if so, what is it?

The Deists viewed with repugnance the doctrinal quarreling and intolerance and, like Lord Herbert of Cherbury, searched for certain "immutable" truths that could be agreed upon and shared by all theists. But in this pursuit the Deists raised a different problem. It became clear that their search for a common faith resulted in a considerable reduction in the substance of orthodox Christian belief. The Deists' rationalist presuppositions not only entailed a denial of miracles and a special providence but also such cardinal Christian doctrines as the Incarnation and the Trinity. It was obvious that certain modern preconceptions had entered materially into their assessment of which Christian doctrines could or could not reasonably be retained. Later, other critics of Christian orthodoxy were to argue that there were, in fact, no unchanging, normative doctrines of Christianity that were capable of capturing its essence. All doctrines are shaped by the needs of a particular historical context. For some this seemed to imply that if there are no "immutable" doctrines then Christian belief was at the mercy of the ever-changing *Zeitgeist*, or spirit of the age.

In the nineteenth century the problem of achieving agreement on the common essentials (the "essence") of Christianity was complicated by the emergence of the scientific study of history. This brought with it a new awareness that *Christian doctrine itself had a complex and ever-developing history.* Thus was raised the troubling questions as to whether Christianity possessed any shared essence, or whether there was any original or "classical" expression of Christianity. Was not Christianity, from its very New Testament beginnings, shaping itself into strikingly different forms that, in time, have had little in common? Or is there, beneath these cultural and historical differences, some common denominator, some enduring Christian essence?

At the beginning of the nineteenth century, one of the important features of Friedrich Schleiermacher's influential theology was his recognition of the significance of the plurality of religious communities: that it was a critical task of modern theology to attempt to define the distinctive nature (*das eigentümliche Wesen*) of Christianity. For Schleiermacher what distinguishes the various world faiths are those primal religious feelings or affections from which arise the doctrines and practices that give shape to a particular religious community. And the essence of any positive religion is that element that underlies and gives characteristic shape to all of the religious affections and doctrines that constitute that religious communion. According to Schleiermacher, the unique feature of Christianity, its normative essence that is shared by all Christian groups, is the sense of redemption that is accomplished by Jesus of Nazareth. Schleiermacher further sees this distinctive essence of Christianity as expressing itself most purely and clearly in the earliest life of the Christian Church as that is illuminated in the exegesis of the New Testament documents.

In the immediate decades following Schleiermacher, John Henry Newman and the Catholic Tübingen theologians struggled similarly with the problem of Christianity's identity in light of the obvious development and diversity of Christian creeds and communions. However, they approached the problem somewhat differently. As Catholics they were not preoccupied, as were many Protestants, with restoring Christianity's earliest form, nor were they concerned with the problem of the essence of Christianity as such. Rather, they were absorbed with a related issue made urgent by modern historical research, namely, the problem of a continuity within change in the history of Christianity; that is, with explaining and even justifying the development of dogma. As God is one, so must his revelation and truth be one. There cannot be two or more disparate creeds, for God's truth cannot be divided against itself.

Both Newman and Möhler went to history itself to attempt to discover the idea or the principle that would show that in Roman Catholicism a genuine continuity inheres within and throughout the complex and protean developments that are so prominent in Catholic history. Both the Tübingen theologians and Newman rejected a return to the Bible alone, as if everything after the first century is to be viewed as a corruption of the essential apostolic witness. They also rejected the views of Lessing and Herder that God has offered humanity many revelations, each meant to meet the distinct needs of a historical epoch. They considered the latter idea as contrary to belief in a divine revealed truth. For these Catholic thinkers, neither a concept of a pure, normative antiquity, nor a doctrine of progressive revelations, nor a belief in the immutability of doctrine could adequately account for the *historical identity of Christianity over the centuries*. For Newman only a theory of the development of doctrine, or a full elucidation of "the essential Christian idea" through time, could show the enduring coherence of Christianity as it absorbs, changes, and takes on new forms over the centuries. As Newman argued, here on earth "to live is to change, and to be perfect is to have changed often." What initially may appear to be "corrupting additions" can on inspection be seen as organic components that unite, restore, preserve, and make intelligible the essential Christian truths.

For Johann Adam Möhler the essence of Christianity was similarly to be found in and through its historical development, not in a return to an ideal or classical past nor in appeal to some abstract immutable dogma. For Möhler, this essence of Christianity is discovered in its living, organic tradition present in the unbroken life of the Christian community itself as it is guided by the Holy Spirit. To him, it is only natural that the Christian *sensus communis* unfolds historically, that it develops like any organic body. And so, like the life of the individual, the Christian tradition maintains a continuity of identity as its body undergoes development. Development is simply the embodiment of the interior, spiritual tradition in an external bodily tradition, an embodiment that not only safeguards and passes on the interior spiritual truth, but also protects it against the isolation and the limitations of a narrow, individual judgment. Tradition, then, is perpetuated in and through the whole body of believers, the Church, which for Möhler includes the apostolic testimony revealed in the Scriptures, the development of doctrine, the liturgy and worship, and the priestly hierarchy. It is in this fullness of living tradition, and not in any single aspect of it, that the *norma*, the rule of Christian faith, is to be found. With both Newman and Möhler we can observe a spiritual, in contrast to a largely statutory and juridical, understanding of tradition or the essential Christian idea and norm, with all the attractions and complications attending such a conception.

At the end of the nineteenth century, the issue of the development of dogma and the question of the essence of Christianity were central themes in the work of both the Catholic Modernists and the Liberal Protestants, perhaps best seen in the often misrepresented controversy betweem Adolf von Harnack and Alfred Loisy. Harnack and Loisy shared much regarding the development of dogma. Both were historical theologians and together recognized the critical importance of understanding Christianity historically, that is, in light of its development. Both saw Christian dogma as emerging *out of* the religious life of Jesus and the early Christian community. Therefore, they viewed dogma as secondary, not primary. And yet both saw the development of the Church and its dogma as absolutely indispensable to the protection and vitality of Christianity through the ages. However, they also agreed that over the centuries the Church had embraced dogmas that proved to be corruptions of the true Christian idea and that these dogmas must be corrected or repudiated. The question on which they disagreed was by what true idea or essential criterion should the long development of dogma be measured and judged?

Harnack called this essence or identity of Christianity "the Gospel of Jesus Christ," and he identified it with Jesus's profoundly simple teaching about the Kingdom of God, the infinite value of the human soul, and the commandment of love. Loisy, on the contrary, was closer to the Tübingen theologians in his discovery that the essence of Christianity is "in the fullness and totality of its life," a life that discloses, as Newman also observed, not only development but also variety.

But this variety of elements reveals an underlying generative idea or law, the preservation of type, that governs Christianity's evolution. The problem with such a conception for both Loisy and Newman is that it demands trust that most dogmatic developments do in fact serve to balance and preserve the "living being" of Christianity. But because these elements together constitute the essence, should not Loisy have been required, as was Newman, to make a retrospective case for their indispensable role? This Loisy refused to do. What is striking, however, about both Harnack and Loisy is their very modern conclusion that Christianity does *not* admit to any uniform historical development, that there are corrupting doctrines that require pruning, and, most important, that there is no final or perfect development of historical Christianity. As we will see, the issues of doctrinal development and the identity or essence of Christianity in a pluralistic context will continue to occupy theologians as radically different as Ernst Troeltsch and Karl Rahner.

Knowledge of God and God and World

In an increasingly secular Western culture, the crucial religious issue for many in the modern era is the very reality of God, the possibility of belief in the Christian God. Since the Enlightenment, this radical question has assumed two principal forms: "Can we know God?" and "How are we to understand God's relation to and action in the world?" The first is an epistemological question, and it arises from the compelling critique of metaphysics and natural theology in the work of David Hume and Immanuel Kant and the aftereffects of their writings. The second question has to do with God's being or attributes and activity in the world and in human history. The issue often focuses on an understanding of God's transcendence of and immanence in the world as this bears on questions about the nature of God's creative activity and providential agency.

For many philosophers and theologians, Kant's critique of natural theology made it impossible to claim a knowledge of God through experience of the phenomenal world. In this regard,

Kant largely set the agenda for theology for the next two hundred years. Protestant thought in particular was profoundly shaped by Kant's critique. But the Kantian revolution in knowledge was also instrumental in recasting Roman Catholic apologetics in the nineteenth century. This can be observed both in the movement of French Traditionalism and in the Catholic Tübingen theology in Germany. Both movements show little interest in the older tradition of natural theology and its rational proofs of the existence and nature of God. Rather, God is disclosed in revelation and in historical tradition, which are corroborated in the common experience and testimony of the race. Catholic philosophy in nineteenth-century France experienced a significant revival of interest in the Augustinian tradition. A Christian philosophy must attend to human feeling and action, and to the role of the will and conscience if one is to cultivate a knowledge of God.

Nineteenth-century Protestant Liberal theology is characterized by an even more thoroughgoing "turn to the subject." Two directions are especially prominent. One is the Romantic emphasis on religious experience, on feeling and intuition, important features in the writings of the theologian Friedrich Schleiermacher, the English poet Coleridge, and American writers such as Horace Bushnell and Ralph Waldo Emerson. God is apprehended in the self's receptive communion with nature, and especially in the self's deepest human companionship and nurture. The second route to a knowledge of God—the one taken by Kant himself—was appeal to the moral conscience or "practical reason." Theologians as different as the Catholic John Henry Newman and the Protestant Albrecht Ritschl found a bulwark for belief in God in the demands of our practical reason for belief in freedom, moral obligation, and the reality of the world of Spirit.

Whereas the nineteenth century often is viewed as an era of optimism and great confidence in the advances of science, the latter half of the century was, in fact, a time of profound doubt and radical agnosticism. New misgivings were voiced about scientific knowledge and uncertainties raised about the trustworthiness of reason itself. German historicism and the sociological and psychological critique of knowledge, first by Karl Marx and later by Friedrich Nietzsche, fueled this skeptical temper of mind. It was in this context in the latter decades of the century that new voluntaristic and pragmatic philosophies of belief flourished, challenging not only scientific positivism and materialism but also the older and optimistic Idealistic religious apologetic. The Neo-Kantian theologians' separation of knowledge and moral faith, Nietzsche's preoccupation with the "will to power," Henri Bergson's vitalism, Maurice Blondel's philosophy of *L'Action,* and William James's pragmatic "will to believe" all reflect this new intellectual ethos.

There were counter-movements, of course, that reacted against what they saw as dangerous agnostic, fideistic, and pragmatic tendencies that supported a theological irrationalism and subjectivism. Both the Princeton Theology and the Roman Catholic Neo-Thomistic revival specifically directed their attacks against the religious agnosticism and the subjectivism that they traced back to Kant and his influence. Both of these movements repudiated Idealism and appealed to realist doctrines of knowledge—in the one case to the Scottish "commonsense" empiricist philosophy and, in the other, to the inductive, scientific realism of Aristotle. Both movements opposed what they perceived as the skepticism implicit in the Idealist dualism of mind and matter, self and world, and defended the view that true science and theology were not only compatible but mutually supportive. They insisted that knowledge of God is possible on the solid evidence of scientific induction, whether it be applied to the natural world or to the facts of the Bible. These same issues of faith and reason and of the knowledge of God preoccupy theological discussion today—albeit in somewhat altered formulations.

Both nineteenth-century natural and revealed theology were haunted by a related problem concerning the knowledge of God, namely the use of personalistic, i.e., anthropomorphic, language in speaking about God. This pertained to questions having to do with God's attributes and with conceptions of divine providence, a God who "acts" and intervenes in both nature and human history. The protracted debate over miracles that engaged the Deists and the orthodox theologians during the Enlightenment had fundamentally to do with the Christian doctrine of God's personal, providential action in history. This Enlightenment debate animated a new and lively discussion of theodicy and the problem of evil. Were the classical attributes of God's omnipotence, love, and personal providence compatible with the new awareness of human autonomy and the terrible realities of evil; and with the growing feeling of unease in the face of a "blind nature" devoid of any parental care? The Deists were willing to pay a large price to solve the problem: They simply denied God's providential, superintending presence in the world. Nineteenth-century theology can be viewed from one perspective as the effort to think through problems posed by the Christian understanding of God's transcendence and immanence, and to steer a way between both Deism and Pantheism. This entailed a reconsideration of the classical conceptions of God's being and relation to the world.

Hegel was the first great modern thinker to tackle the implications of God's real presence in time and history for a rethinking of the classical Western conception of God. For Hegel the world was essential to God's own full actualization; God and the world are in a real sense interdependent. This implied some conception of God's temporality and finitude or, alternately as worked out by A. E. Biedermann in Germany and by the *Lux Mundi* theologians in England, a restatement of the doctrine of the divine *kenosis,* or God's "self-emptying" and self-limitation as made manifest in God's taking on flesh in the human person of Jesus. These explorations of the interdependence of God and the world and of God's self-limitation played a crucial role in the emergence of *panentheistic** doctrines of God in the twentieth

---

* Pantheism argues that the world is included in God's being—as cells in a body—but this does not exhaust God's being or activity. God and the world are interdependent, so God is in some sense temporal and not omnipotent in the traditional sense.

century, especially in Process theology as it developed in the work of A. N. Whitehead, Charles Hartshorne, John B. Cobb, Jr., and others (see Chapter Ten). Indeed, nineteenth-century evolutionary and organismic modes of thought are taken for granted in most theistic discussion today, well beyond the circle of those who accept a strict panentheism. It has prompted Christian rethinking of the doctrines of divine omnipotence and providence, of evil, freedom, and eschatology.

Christianity and Other World Faiths

The modern fascination with history, well established by the late eighteenth century, not only stimulated an interest in the recovery of the past and in exotic contemporary foreign cultures. It shaped a whole new perspective on all cultures and historical periods. Each culture was to be seen in its own unique linguistic and historical context. The Bible and Christianity, too, must be understood as having been shaped and developed by the languages and the environments of its time, as well as by untold contingent historical events. The Deists generally agreed with Voltaire's remark that all religions really are "of the same opinion"; that is, they share certain "natural beliefs" such as the existence of a Supreme Being. But writers in the eighteenth century also used this claim both to insist on the need for toleration and to relativize the absolute claims of Christianity. They pointed to the sublime teachings of other religions, teachings that they considered equal to, indeed superior to the doctrines of Christianity. Islam, for example, was viewed by some as a far purer religion than Christianity, free of all the contentious dogmas that did violence to reason and divided Europe. The impressive doctrines of Hinduism, it was pointed out, predated the giving of the commandments to Moses.

This new "historicist" perspective on religion became more firmly established during the Romantic period, as is evident in the writings of Herder and the young Schleiermacher, both of whom exulted in the rich diversity of humanity's spiritual life. Herder stressed the fact that human consciousness develops primarily through language and, therefore, that our perceptions of reality are shaped by our linguistic forms and conventions. These diverse languages and cultures meet the distinctive needs of particular human communities at particular times. The world religions are then the many rooms in "the palace of God," the developing spiritual educators of the human race. But that very fact insists that they are not to be compared in terms of their beauty or their worth, because each spiritual dispensation is an end in itself, to be judged on its own terms, in its own context, and by its own fruits.

In view of what has just been said, it is surprising that the "science of religion," or the comparative study of religion, came to maturity only in the latter half of the nineteenth century. It owed much to German Romanticism and to developments in archaeology and philology, as well as to the new sciences of anthropology and sociology. Britain led the way. The German philologist Friedrich Max Müller, often referred to as the "father" of the new science of religion, spent most of his career in Oxford. He was a liberal churchman, a communicant in the Church of England. But, like Herder, he felt a deep empathy for all religions and called for a disinterested study of them all, including Christianianity. He wished to bracket invidious distinctions between "true" and "false" and "revealed" and "natural" religions. To Müller, religion is a human *a priori*, the essence of which he found in the human feeling or intuition of the Infinite. Howsoever infantile a religion may appear, it is to be revered as sacred because it places the simplest of human souls in the presence of the Infinite or God. A community's religion represents its highest spiritual reach, its ideal of perfection.

As a Christian, Müller was willing to make common cause with Hindus and other theists. He also proposed that Christianity should claim no immunity in the comparative study of religion. Rather, he believed, such a study would shed light both on Christianity's unique character and on what it shares in common with other religions. Müller's liberality of mind was attractive and his articles and books were widely read.

A younger contemporary of Max Müller was the great Scottish Old Testament scholar and Semiticist, William Robertson Smith. He was the first biblical scholar to take serious account of the new work of the social anthropologists and to apply this research to his study of the Bible. Smith is an interesting study in the changing view of Christianity's relation to other faiths that was taking place in the late nineteenth century. He was an ordained minister in the Free Church of Scotland. He first taught in the Free Church College in Aberdeen and later became professor of Arabic in Cambridge University. Today he is known as the founder of the comparative sociology of religion. His work had a profound influence on Emile Durkheim, perhaps the greatest of the modern sociologists of religion. The focus of Smith's work was on ancient sacrifice, totemism, and ritual—all of which illustrate the central *leitmotiv* of his work, namely, the essentially social character of religion. Smith believed in Christianity's absoluteness, Protestantism being for him the acme of the divine education of the human race. But this belief did not appear to square easily with his scholarship which—with its relativistic implications—viewed all religions as mirrors of the social structure of their particular tribe or group. The point of significance here is that Smith's ambiguities and ambivalence are characteristic of many devout Christian scholars and thinkers who wrestled with the question of Christianity's uniqueness and absoluteness in the latter years of the nineteenth century. We will return to this subject in Chapter Fifteen, "Theology of Religions: Christian Responses to Other Faiths." There we will discuss more recent debates regarding Christianity's uniqueness and its relation to the other world religions. I suspect that it will be apparent to the reader that on the substantive issues these current discussions will sound like echoes of a debate that took place a century earlier.

History, the Historical Jesus, and Christology

Many scholars of the history of modern theology would say that it was the "historicizing" of modern consciousness in the early nineteenth century that was the decisive factor in the changes that have occurred in Christian theology in the past two centuries. However, this emergence of a thoroughly historical way of thinking has proven to be a double-edged sword for Christian theology. On the one hand, Christianity has always thought of itself as a historical religion, by which it has meant a religion based on real events that have occurred in history. Unlike some religions, e.g., those of ancient Greece, Christianity has insisted that it is not based on purely "mythical" stories. On the other hand, the claims and benefits of historicity have borne with them a responsibility to substantiate Christianity's historical foundations. This has proved to be a large and complex challenge for modern theologians and historians. Some scholars were emboldened to use the new historical sciences in an attempt to *establish* Christianity's claims, to prove historically "what really happened." Others found that genuine historical inquiry disclosed that the *historical* foundations of their faith were problematic, or worse, unreliable. Lessing had posed the problem: How can contingent events of history serve as the basis for claims of absolute and eternal significance? We noted earlier that historical science had posed a related question: How can we be sure that Christianity today is the same religion as that founded by Jesus and the apostles?

The historical question, proved especially crucial *and* problematic with regard to Christology. Jesus of Nazareth is a historical figure, a human being present at a certain time and place. But Jesus Christ is the Incarnate God, eternally one with the Father, beyond time and space—a supernatural, divine being. Is it possible that empirical, historical research can uncover or distinguish the New Testament figure of Jesus from the earliest community's picture of him as the divine Christ and Son of God? The fact is that the credibility of certain historical traditions in the Bible had long been challenged by scholars such as J. S. Semler and J. G. Eichhorn in the late eighteenth century and later by H. S. Reimarus. But the crucial event was the appearance of D. F. Strauss's *Life of Jesus* in 1835. Strauss's purpose was to test the *historical* claims of the New

Testament concerning Jesus against the theological presuppositions of both the early Jewish messianic traditions applied to him and the preconceptions of later interpreters. Strauss was the first to insist on the importance of the fact that the earliest Christians lacked our modern historical consciousness. They interpreted Jesus in mythopoetic imagery drawn from the Hebrew Scriptures—the natural mode of perception in a pre-scientific culture. Jesus was understood in the earliest community in the terms of the current Jewish legends that told of the immanent expectation of the coming Messiah.

With Strauss was launched the nineteenth-century "quest of the historical Jesus." For after Strauss it was no longer possible to assume that the Gospel traditions could be taken for granted as historical sources for the reconstruction of the life of Jesus. More significantly, Strauss had raised the question whether it was even possible to clearly distinguish the historical Jesus from the theological interpretations of him as the Christ. Strauss, in fact, believed that his ruthless historical criticism had left unscathed the supernatural Christ portrayed in the Gospels—but, of course, also a Christ severed from history.

Later in the nineteenth century sophisticated theologians, such as the German Wilhelm Herrmann, were confident that the essential historical personality or "inner life" of Jesus was historically recoverable, despite the work of historical criticism that had taken place since Strauss. As we will see, however, New Testament historians working with the new tools of Form criticism were to raise new doubts about the use of the Gospel sources for biographical purposes. They were to raise the question whether it was possible to recover the personality or the inner psychological life of Jesus. This work of New Testament historical scholarship in the last years of the nineteenth century was to have a significant impact on the christological thinking of preeminent twentieth-century theologians such as Rudolf Bultmann, Karl Barth, Paul Tillich, and Edward Schillebeeckx. The nineteenth-century legacy of New Testament criticism also was the point of departure for a movement of the 1950s and 1960s

known as the "new quest of the historical Jesus," and it remains the *desideratum* for theologians who today continue to seek to recover the figure of Jesus in the historical context of Judaism and Hellenism in late antiquity.

THE NEW CHALLENGES OF HISTORICAL THEOLOGY

A characteristic of Protestant Liberal theology in the last years of the nineteenth century, especially in its Ritschlian form, was its appeal to history. The British Hegelians, the Neo-Thomists, and even some of the Catholic Modernists found the truth in Christianity in its doctrines or its sublime ideas. They frequently either merely assumed that these truths were anchored in history or remained unconcerned about their historical basis. The Ritschlian theologians, on the contrary, believed that the uniqueness of Christianity lay in its claim to a *historical* revelation and that its truth could be shown by an appeal to history, an appeal that would rescue Christianity from the wild fancies of pious mystics and speculative theologians. As Adolf Harnack asked: How does one gain a basis for a reliable knowledge of Jesus Christ except through historical-critical research—in order not to exchange a dreamed-up Christ for the real one? Recalling this great undertaking of historical theology in the nineteenth century, Albert Schweitzer observed that many of these Protestant scholars "were eager to picture [Jesus] as truly and purely human, to strip from him the robes of splendor with which he had been apparelled, and clothe him once more with the coarse garments in which he had walked in Galilee."[1]

The quest of the historical Jesus was to prove, as Schweitzer himself demonstrated, a far more difficult task than these historical theologians imagined. Some would argue that, ironically, the fading influence of Protestant Liberal theology between the two world wars could be attributed largely to the work of historical criticism itself. Between roughly 1870 and 1920 there appeared a great outpouring of historical and social-scientific research on religion and on Christianity in particular. The various directions of research often took on the character of a self-conscious movement or school. Here we will explore the distinctive contributions of four of these movements and attempt to indicate their significance for Christian theology. They were to change the shape of Christian thinking on a range of crucial matters: on the understanding of the nature of the New Testament documents themselves, and of early Christianity in its Jewish and Hellenistic context; on the question as to whether the historical Jesus was recoverable, and the theological consequences of the inquiry; and on Christianity's relationship to other religions and its claims to uniqueness and finality.

Religionswissenschaft

Throughout the nineteenth century the science of archaeology was uncovering the religious treasures of lost or little-known religions, especially in the Near East. At the same time, advances in the study of Oriental languages were shedding new light on the sacred texts of the great Indian and Asian religions. Accompanying this vast new accumulation of information was the development of new critical methodologies such as social anthropology, sociology, phenomenology, and what the Germans called *Religionswissenschaft,* the new science of the "history of religions" or "comparative religions."

As mentioned earlier, the beginning of this new science often is associated with Friedrich Max Müller's (1833–1900) influential London lectures of 1870, entitled "Introduction to the Science of Religion."

In these lectures Müller protested the ignorant and prejudiced treatment of other religions by Christian historians and theologians: "Every doctrine . . . is interpreted in the worse sense that it will bear; every act of worship that differs from their way of serving God is held up to ridicule and contempt."[2] What also disturbed the Christian Müller was that this depreciating of other religions had torn Christianity out of the sacred contexts from which it had grown, and that it ignored the "sundry times and divers manners" in which in past times God had spoken to the human race.

Müller's lectures were soon followed by a number of valuable works outlining the aims and methods of the new science. These included the Sanscrit scholar Emile Louis Burnouf's (1801–1852) *La Science des Religions,* 2nd ed. (1872); Albert Réville's (1826–1906) (the first incumbent in the chair of the science of religion at the Collège de France) *Prolégomènes de L'histoire des Religions* (1881); P. D. Chantepie de la Saussaye's (1848–1920) *Lehrbuch des Religionsgeschichte* (1887), which established an elaborate classification of religious phenomena (sacred places, times, persons, writings, etc.) and laid the foundation for the field of religious phenomenology; and Cornelius Tiele's (1830–1902) *Kompendium der Religionsgeschichte* (1880) and his widely used two-volume *Elements of the Science of Religion* (1897–1899). These manuals were followed by a great many, often massive, research and reference works that were devoted to the methods and results of the new science; for example, the extensive editing and translating of the fifty volumes of *The Sacred Books of the East* (1879–1904) under the leadership of Max Müller; the *Encyclopedia of Religion and Ethics,* 13 vol. (1908–1921); and *Religion in Geschichte und Gegenwart,* 5 vols. (1908–1913).

Christian scholars and laypersons often were at the forefront of the effort to disseminate better information about the non-Christian religions. In 1877 the Society for the Propagation of Christian Knowledge initiated a series of popular, well-informed primers on the *Non-Christian Religious Systems,* which ran to eleven volumes. At the turn of the century there was a flood tide of similar projects. In 1878 a group of progressive Christian theologians and philosophers helped to establish the famous Hibbert Lectures, which produced a series of scholarly and influential books on the history of religions by world experts. This inexpensive, uniform series on the "origin and growth of religions" included works on India, ancient Egypt, Indian Buddhism, ancient Babylonia, the religions of Mexico and Peru, and so on.

One of the effects of all this new interest was the effort to discover the *primordia* of all religion; that is, religion's historical origin, its most elementary forms, its essential nature or root in human experience, and the laws of its development. For Christian thinkers this, of course, hastened new thinking about Christianity's place in the divine education of the human race. The work of the comparativists also raised questions about Christianity's claim to uniqueness and finality. Some of the important theorists and comparativists, although not overtly hostile to Christianity, were critical of many of Christianity's dogmas and of its claim to absoluteness. The significance of their theories for Christian belief was not lost on the educated public. The prodigious researches of those devoted to the new *Religionswissenschaft* left an indelible impression of the extraordinary multiplicity of religious life worldwide, and the striking commonalities and analogies, the implications of which would require deeper reflection.

Three other movements of historical critical work at the turn of the nineteenth century also focused attention on the beginnings of Christianity in the religious context of late antiquity, as well as on the historical figure of Jesus. But the three movements emerged from *within* the Christian community of scholarship, and all three were focused specifically on the study of the New Testament and Christian origins. In some quarters their conclusions were felt to be more perilous to the faith than was the work of the earlier comparativists. The first movement was the thoroughgoing eschatological interpretation of Jesus carried out by Johannes Weiss and Albert Schweitzer.

The Eschatological Interpretation of Weiss and Schweitzer

There were theologians at the close of the nineteenth century who saw Harnack's portrayal of Jesus as the mirror image of his own bourgeois moral idealism and the embodiment of his own liberal worldview. These theologians were aware of the great distance that separated the world of first-century Palestine from that of nineteenth-century Europe. As historians they were concerned to put aside their own modern preconceptions and to place Jesus squarely in *his* own time

and environment. They believed that when this was done Jesus and his message could be properly understood only in the context of late Jewish apocalypticism. Assuming such a perspective, the liberal version of Jesus's message of the Kingdom of God was judged historically untenable. This point of view was first put forward by Johannes Weiss (1863–1914) in a pamphlet entitled "Jesus' Preaching of the Kingdom of God" (1892). According to Weiss, there is no evidence that Jesus conceived of the Kingdom of God as an enduring and progressively extended earthly ethical community. Rather, Jesus's preaching reflected the radical Jewish apocalyptical eschatology of his own day—the worldview reflected in such literature as the Book of Daniel, the *Assumption of Moses,* and the *Book of Enoch* that speaks of a mysterious Son of Man through whom God will carry out his plan. According to Weiss, Jesus looked to an imminent and catastrophic end of the present age and to the inauguration of a supernatural new creation. Jesus did not inaugurate the Kingdom but heralded its coming and finally, in desperation, gave his life to hasten its arrival in the expectation that he would return again to rule as the apocalyptical Son of Man. Weiss's Jesus lives in a world wholly foreign to our own—a figure who truly is a stumbling block to modern faith.

Weiss's depiction of the mission and message of Jesus led to the thoroughgoing or "consistent eschatological interpretation" of the New Testament that received its classic expression in Albert Schweitzer's (1875–1965) *The Quest of the Historical Jesus* (1906). In the words of a contemporary New Testament scholar, Schweitzer's book proved to be both the "memorial" to the liberal lives of Jesus and their "funeral oration."[3] Noble and sincere as were the modern efforts to depict the historical Jesus, they were, nevertheless, a failure. In each case the Jesus who emerges from the quest was portrayed largely in terms reflecting the historians' own modern philosophy of life. Each historian created Jesus in accordance with his own character. Schweitzer concludes his great work with the following pronouncement:

The Jesus of Nazareth who came forward publicly as the Messiah, who preached the ethic of the Kingdom of God, who founded the Kingdom of Heaven on earth, and died to give His work its final consecration, never had any existence. He is a figure designed by rationalism, endowed with life by liberalism, and clothed by modern theology in an historical garb. . . .

Whatever the ultimate solution may be, the historical Jesus of whom the criticism of the future . . . will draw the portrait . . . will not be a Jesus Christ to whom the religion of the present can ascribe . . . as it did with the Jesus of its own making. Nor will He be a figure which can be made by a popular historical treatment so sympathetic and universally intelligible to the multitude. The historical Jesus will be to our own time a stranger and an enigma. . . . He passes by our time and returns to his own.[4]

Albert Schweitzer

Like Weiss, Schweitzer saw Jesus as a man of his own time, a product of Jewish apocalypticism who mistakenly conceived of the end of the world as imminent and who saw in his own death the beginning of the long-expected apocalyptical tribulations. Such a Jesus is totally foreign to our modern world, and it was the great mistake of Ritschlian theology "to suppose that Jesus could come to mean more to our time by entering into it as a man like ourselves."[5] Indeed, the whole liberal appeal to the court of historical confirmation was both impossible and misguided. It was impossible because the Jesus they portrayed never existed; misguided because, in Schweitzer's opinion, the foundation of Christianity is independent of any historical warrant. According to Schweitzer, "Jesus means something to our world because a mighty spiritual force streams forth from Him and flows through our time also. This fact can neither be shaken nor confirmed by an historical discovery."[6] The historical Jesus must remain for us an enigma, but His message of active love calls us, as of old it called those by the lakeside.

He speaks to us the same word: "Follow thou me!" and sets us the tasks which He has to fulfill for our time. He commands and to those who obey Him, whether they be wise or simple, He will reveal himself in the toils, the conflicts, the sufferings which they shall pass through in His fellowship, and, as an ineffable mystery, they shall learn in their own experience Who He is.[7]

Such was Schweitzer's response to the liberal quest of the historical Jesus. It was an appeal to a form of Christ-mysticism that was freed from the outmoded apocalyptical worldview of the historical Jesus and the early Christian community.

The *Religionsgeschichtliche Schule*

The historians who opposed the liberal "lives of Jesus" argued that those selective reconstructions of Jesus's life were governed by presuppositions of the historian's own time and culture. A new generation of historical critics now sought to explain Jesus solely in terms of his own time. As we have seen, Weiss and Schweitzer viewed Jesus from the perspective of late Jewish apocalypticism. The historians who came to be identified with the movement known as the "History of Religions" school generally sought to interpret Jesus and early Christianity by reference to the beliefs and practices of late Hellenism. The Ritschlians had appealed to history but, in the judgment of scholars such as Hermann Gunkel (1862–1932) and Wilhelm Bousset (1865–1920), to a limited conception of history. Ritschl and his followers were charged with viewing Christianity as an isolated phenomenon, emphasizing its historical uniqueness. For the scholars of the History of Religions school, such a conception of Christianity was singularly unhistorical. In their opinion, early Christianity, when examined in the context of its environment, does not emerge as an absolutely unique reality but as a complex "syncretistic religion," the product of Late Judaism, Oriental eschatology, the Greek mysteries, Gnosticism, and Stoicism. It was Christianity's good fortune to come at a time when these Western and Oriental ideas were converging and in need of a fresh synthesis. Christianity served this purpose.

The *Religionsgeschichtliche Schule* received its name about 1903 when it became identified as a specific school within the larger movement of the history of religions. It had its beginnings at Göttingen University and consisted of a group of younger Protestant scholars who were dedicated to applying the methods of the new science of religion to the Bible, and especially to the New Testament. The group consisted of the Old Testament scholars Gunkel and Hugo Gressmann and the New Testament scholars Bousset, Johannes Weiss, Wilhelm Wrede, and later Rudolf Bultmann. The historian and theologian Ernst Troeltsch was the school's most brilliant theoretician and theologian. It was he, as we will see later in this chapter, who wrestled with the historical and theological problems posed by the school's radical historicism.

The *Religionsgeschichtliche Schule* drew on the vast new archaeological sources from the Near East, on the new developments in textual and literary criticism of the Bible, and on the work of scholars such as F. Max Müller, J. G. Frazer, C. P. Tiele, and others. All of this was applied to a new historical view of early Christianity as a complex mixture of late Jewish apocalyptic eschatology, Hellenistic Judaism, the Greek and Oriental mystery cults, Stoicism, and Gnosticism. This new portrayal of early Christianity also transformed the view of Jesus that had dominated earlier Protestant scholarship. A sharp disjunction now was made between Jesus the Jewish prophet and

teacher and Jesus the *Kyrios*, the supernatural Lord and redeemer worshiped as a new cult deity, similar to the Hellenistic worship of Mithras or Dionysus. Emphasis was placed not on early Christian theology and ethics but on popular Christian piety, on worship, and on cultic practices. The so-called Jesus of history faded from view; in his place emerged the heavenly being, Christ the divine Lord and Savior of the cult of early Catholicism (*Frühkatholizismus*).

In his book *Kyrios Christos,* Bousset developed the thesis that Jesus came to be called *Kyrios* or Lord only when Christianity left Palestine and entered the environment of Hellenism. There Jesus was worshiped like the pagan cult deities, fulfilling a similar function. Bousset stressed the similarities between the Christian rites and those of the Mystery religions. The result was to call into question the distinctive character of Christianity and, particularly, its unique revelatory claims. Christianity was to be assigned its place in the natural evolution of human beliefs and practices. The Bible was to be investigated with the same tools as any other historical document. And yet several members of the school retained their ties with the Protestant community and its theological concerns. Men like Bousset and Troeltsch earnestly sought to discover some unique essence both in Christianity and in the figure of Jesus, despite what they had demonstrated to be the syncretistic and, by inference, the relativistic character of early Christianity. This sort of effort by Bousset and Troeltsch revealed the perplexity and the pathos of the new historical theologian. Why, the critics of the *Religionsgeschichtliche Schule* asked, did Christianity win out over all its rivals and why did it become the worldwide religion that it has become? History itself, of course, could supply reasons, but they could not fully satisfy the theologian or the believer, including Bousset and Troeltsch. The influence of the *Religionsgeschichtliche Schule* declined after World War I. Its early leaders had died, but more significantly the war had brought in its wake a cultural and theological revolution that was expressed most ironically in the new "theology of crisis" (see Chapter Three), a movement that declared the historical approach of the likes of Bousset and Troeltsch to be theologically bankrupt and exhausted.

Form Criticism

Form criticism, or the *Formgeschichtliche Schule*, appeared in the years immediately after World War I, partly in response to the impasse of the *Religionsgeschichtliche* method of New Testament research. The History of Religions school had questioned, at least tacitly, the historicity of the Gospel accounts and had concentrated on the symbolic and cultic meaning of the New Testament traditions. Due largely to disinterest, the question of the history and reliability of the Gospel traditions concerning Jesus was not pursued. The Form critics, on the other hand, addressed themselves to the very question of the origin and historical growth of the layers of literary tradition that make up the Gospels. They were raising in a new way the question of the historical authenticity of the Jesus tradition.

The Form critics took their lead from the Old Testament researches of Hermann Gunkel and Hugo Gressmann. These scholars had shown that the ancient folk literature of the Hebrews had originally circulated as oral traditions in certain limited fixed forms or categories, and that these preliterary units of tradition were the product of the daily life of the Israelite community. That is, they served a practical purpose in the religious life of the people, in worship, instruction, and preaching.

Because it was clear that the Gospels contained tradition that was originally oral, the Form critics sought to apply these same assumptions to the study of this literature in the hope that such a method would help answer the question of the origin and growth of the Gospel traditions. The basic tenets of the Form critical school are nicely summarized by R. H. Lightfoot, the leading English exponent of Form criticism:

The Form critics remind us that the early Church is by no means likely to have expressed itself at once in a literary way, and they believe, first, that in the earliest years memories and traditions of the words and deeds of Jesus were only handed from mouth to mouth, and secondly, that they were valued not so much . . . in and for themselves, as for their importance in solving problems connected with the life and needs of the young churches. These needs, they think, would be chiefly concerned with mission preaching, catechetical teaching . . . and perhaps above all, worship. They believe, further, that these memories and traditions . . . would gradually assume a more or less fixed shape, through constant repetition in the churches. . . . And, finally they suggest that many of these preliterary traditions are still discernible in our written Gospels . . . and that to some extent they can be classified according to their type or form.[8]

In the brief period between 1919 and 1921, three distinguished New Testament scholars applied the Form critical method to the study of the Gospels and published their results. In 1919 K. L. Schmidt (1891–1956) published *Der Rahmen der Geschichte Jesu* (*The Framework of the Story of Jesus*), in which he demonstrated the artificial and arbitrary order of the traditions in Mark and how such details as time and place represented the later additions of the evangelist, who was himself responsible for the historical order and contexts of the separate traditions.

At approximately the same time Martin Dibelius (1883–1947) published *Die Formgeschichte des Evangeliums* (1919; E. T., *From Tradition to Gospel*, 1934). In this important work, Dibelius attempted to trace the growth of the various oral traditions that lay behind the written Gospels and to seek out the influences that determined the different forms. Dibelius found that the *Sitz im Leben*, or life situation out of which the Gospel traditions arose, was principally traceable to the preaching and worship of the early Christian congregations. He divided these early units of tradition (pericopes) into five "forms": paradigm, *novelle* or tales, legend, *parenesis*, and myth. According to Dibelius, the most important of these forms are the paradigms or brief, striking sayings or deeds attributed to Jesus. These paradigms were preserved because of their continuous use in preaching but, because they exhibit the least elaboration, are the surest source of information about the historical Jesus. The tales and legends, although not unhistorical, reflect considerable editorial addition, whereas myth shows little if any interest in history at all.

The most radical approach to Form criticism was developed by Rudolf Bultmann (1884–1966) in *Die Geschichte der Synoptischen Tradition* (1921). Bultmann divided the forms into several classes, somewhat analogous to those of Dibelius. However, Bultmann was more hesitant than Dibelius in recognizing material that could with certainty give historical information about Jesus. This is evident, for example, in the fact that Bultmann made no distinction between "legend" and "historical narrative."

What was relatively new, and to many unsettling, in the work of the Form critics was their evidence that the evangelists were editors whose redactions were clearly discernible in the Gospels, and that these collected traditions were not meant to serve principally an historical or biographical purpose; rather, the persistence of the Jesus traditions was traceable to the ultrapractical needs of the early Church. This discovery raised the specter that even the earliest Gospel traditions were rooted not in the hard rock of historical fact but on the shifting ground of religious need—that is, that the Christian community constructed a portrait of Jesus to serve its purpose and, therefore, the figure portrayed in the Gospels is not the Jesus of history but the Christ of faith. The Gospels are not historical chronicles but religious confessions.

All the Form critics were agreed that the reminiscences of Jesus preserved in the Gospels were refracted through the events of the crucifixion and resurrection. The Jesus preaching in Galilee, for example, is envisioned in the tradition through the eyes of the Easter faith. Fact and faith are indissolubly joined. As the Form critics expressed it, the only Jesus to be found in the Gospels is the Jesus of the *kerygma*, of the preaching of the early community.

To the question of what we have left of the historical life of Jesus, the Form critics proffered very negative replies. This was especially true of Bultmann. In his book *Jesus and the Word* (1934), he disclaimed all interest in the *life* and *personality* of Jesus and asserted:

I do indeed think that we can now know almost nothing concerning the life and personality of Jesus, since the early Christian sources show no interest in either, are moreover fragmentary and often legendary; and other sources about Jesus do not exist.[9]

Bultmann regarded such a state of affairs as a great boon to faith. In Bultmann's view, genuine faith cannot be dependent on the contingencies of historical-critical research. To follow such a path is to seek after a "worldly" proof and security. The only Jesus Christ found in the New Testament is the kerygmatic Christ, the proclaimed Christ.

So we may not go behind the kerygma, using it as a "source" . . . to reconstruct an "historical Jesus." This would be precisely the "Christ according to the flesh" who is gone. It is not the historical Jesus, but Jesus Christ, the Proclaimed One, who is the Lord.[10]

The Christ that is met in the New Testament *kerygma* is Christ as the living Word of God.

Christ meets us in the preaching (kerygma) as one crucified and risen. He meets us in the word of preaching and nowhere else. . . . It would be wrong at this point to raise again the problem of how this preaching arose historically, as though that could indicate its truth. That would be to tie our faith in the word of God to the results of historical research. The word of preaching confronts us as the word of God. It is not for us to question its credentials. It is we who are questioned, we who are asked whether we will believe the word or reject it.[11]

For Bultmann the reliability of the *kerygma* must not be questioned, for to try to confirm it by some historical-critical test is the very sign of unbelief. He was convinced that there was an identity between the historical Jesus and the kerygmatic Christ, but he believed that the proof of such a link was both historically impossible and theologically dubious. As we shall see in Chapter Three, the *kerygmatic theology* of Bultmann was taken up by Dialectical theology and was to resolve for many the historical question initially raised by Schweitzer's *The Quest of the Historical*

Jesus. For many others, however, kerygmatic theology remained unsatisfactory, because it left unresolved the gnawing question of whether the Christ of the Church's faith rested in fact on the historical Jesus of Nazareth.

The work of historians like Schweitzer, Weiss, Bousset, Troeltsch, and Bultmann raised in new and radical ways the question of the historical bases of Christian faith. It is interesting to observe that the radical historical conclusions of these scholars did not lead them to a repudiation of Christian faith but to responses that tended to neutralize the historical questions that they raised in such a radical fashion. For example, Schweitzer resolved the problem through a Christ mysticism of active love. Bultmann appealed to an existential decision of faith in response to the New Testament proclamation.

We now turn to explore in greater detail how Ernst Troeltsch, at the time one of Europe's most learned and brilliant scholars, sought to reconcile Christian belief with the new challenges of historical research.

ERNST TROELTSCH

Ernst Troeltsch (1865–1923) often is referred to as "the theologian of the *Religionsgeschichtliche Schule*," not because he was an especially noted constructive theologian in his own time, but rather because he explored more persistently than any of his contemporaries the philosophical and theological implications of applying a thoroughgoing historical perspective to the study of Christianity. With the decline of interest in historical theology after World War I, due in large part to the impact of the Dialectical theology of Karl Barth, little was written about the work of Ernst Troeltsch for almost forty years. Since the 1960s there is evidence of considerable new interest in Troeltsch, not only as historian and sociologist of religion, but also as theologian. Karl Barth had declared that with Troeltsch it was impossible for theology to advance any further along his "dead-end street."[12] Yet despite the limitations of his tacit philosophical idealism, Troeltsch's work is commanding the attention of Christian thinkers

because many of the issues that he struggled with now require renewed reflection.

Troeltsch was born near Augsburg, Germany, the son of a well-to-do physician who stimulated his son's interest in scientific questions. Troeltsch attended the gymnasium in Augsburg and then in 1884 entered the University of Erlangen to study theology primarily because the subject afforded him the opportunity to explore important metaphysical and historical questions. The conservative theological faculty at Erlangen did not, however, suit him, and he transferred to Berlin for a year and then, with his friend Wilhelm Bousset, to Göttingen, where both came under the influence of Albrecht Ritschl. It was also at Göttingen that Troeltsch's interest in historical study was shaped by Paul de Lagarde, who was committed to the newer methods of the History of Religions school. Troeltsch thus came to see Ritschl's historical theology as a halfway measure, one that was willing to examine other religions from a radical historical perspective but had exempted Christianity from the same historical contextualization.

In 1890 Troeltsch began his academic career as *Privatdozent* or lecturer in Göttingen. There he joined a small circle of like-minded scholars, including Bousset, Wrede, Gunkel, Eichhorn, and later Weiss, Wilhelm Heitmüller, and Paul Wernle. They called themselves "the little theological faculty at Göttingen," and they all were committed to the newer historical and sociological methods of studying religion, especially primitive Christianity. In 1892, Troeltsch moved to Bonn as associate professor, but two years later was appointed to the chair of systematic theology at Heidelberg, where he remained until 1915. He was not a conventional professor of theology, because much of his work was devoted to philosophical and historical investigations.

Troeltsch was deeply occupied with the rise of modern civilization and its implications for Christianity. He saw a fundamental shift taking place between the old Protestantism of the sixteenth and seventeenth centuries and the new Protestantism that had emerged out of the political and intellectual revolutions of the European

Enlightenment. This theme was summarized in his essay "The Significance of the Reformation for the Rise of the Modern World" (1906), published in English under the misleading title *Protestantism and Progress*. Earlier, Troeltsch had similarly disturbed some of his theological colleagues with the short programmatic essay "On Historical and Dogmatic Method in Theology" (1898), in which he distinguished the truly historical method of theology from the dogmatic method that continued to inform the work of the Ritschlian theologians. No historical event, even those associated with the figure of Jesus, should stand in isolation from others by appealing to some miraculous or supernatural agency. Every religious event must be seen in relation to its entire historical context. In this sense all historical occasions are singular and relative. We will return shortly to Troeltsch's central theme of *historicism*, or radical historical contextualization, as it bears on Christianity.

In 1902 Troeltsch published his important long essay on "The Absoluteness of Christianity and the History of Religions," his first extended exploration of this question, with which he continued to wrestle until the end of his life. It was the theme of one of his last lectures, "The Place of Christianity Among the World Religions," prepared to be delivered in Oxford early in 1923. Among Troeltsch's other critically important theological writings are "What Does 'Essence of Christianity' Mean?" (1903); "The Significance of the Historical Existence of Jesus for Faith" (1911); his massive sociological study, *The Social Teachings of the Christian Churches and Groups* (1912), which he saw as the social-ethical parallel to Harnack's *History of Dogma;* "The Dogmatics of the History of Religions School" (1913); and his constructive theological essays on faith, faith and history, redemption, grace, predestination, and eschatology for the encyclopedia *Die Religion in Geschichte und Gegenwart* (1910), which should be read in conjunction with his posthumously edited lectures on *Die Glaubenslehre* (1925) (*The Christian Faith*).

In 1915 Troeltsch moved to the University of Berlin, where he occupied a special chair in the faculty of philosophy as professor in religious, social, and historical philosophy and the history of the Christian religion. While in Heidelberg he had represented the university in the lower chamber of the parliament of the duchy of Baden, but in Berlin his involvement in politics intensified. After the First World War he was active as one of the founders of the new liberal Democratic Party, and for a period he served as undersecretary of state in the Ministry of Education and Public Worship. He had an influence on the shaping of aspects of the Constitution of the Weimar Republic. And he was mentioned as a possible candidate for president.

In Berlin Troeltsch lectured on a wide range of historical, philosophical, religious, ethical, and cultural subjects, often before an audience of a thousand students. His deepest concern remained, however, the questions posed by historicism and the philosophy of history. And his great work of this Berlin period was the unfinished *Der Historismus und Seine Probleme* (1923) (*Historicism and Its Problems*).

It was often said that Troeltsch joined the philosophy faculty in Berlin because he thought his theological work was a failure. Yet he wrote at the time that he would like "to return to the study of religion in order to complete my philosophy of religion. This is my first love."[13] It is also true, however, that at the end of his life he was filled with pessimism and dark forebodings about European civilization. He held out no hope for the future of the institutional church. He continued to believe that the profound personalism of Christianity would remain "a unique and independent source of life and power," at least for the culture of the West. And his own historicism proved to be the source of his measured hope because, he believed, a truth *for us* did not for that reason cease "to be very Truth and Life."[14] Troeltsch died of heart trouble on February 1, 1923.

Troeltsch's scholarly output was enormous, but even more striking is its wide-ranging character. Scholars have had difficulty interpreting and giving a clear shape to his prodigious *oeuvre* as philosopher of religion, theologian, historian of religion and culture, sociologist, and, during the Berlin period, political writer and analyst. Here we will attempt to deal only with Troeltsch's writings that bear most profoundly on issues of Christian theology: radical historical consciousness; the science of religion and theology; the absoluteness of Christianity; development and the question of the essence of Christianity; and the historical Jesus and Christology.

Historicism, the Science of Religion, and Theology

The thread that runs through Troeltsch's work is the problem of how and from whence one derives norms and values when one accepts the fact of radical historical and cultural change, individuality, and relativity. Specifically, how does one who is committed to *historical* theology determine the normativity and absoluteness of Christianity? As was noted earlier, according to Troeltsch it was the Enlightenment that had introduced our modern historical mode of thinking, the historicizing of all thought about history, culture, ethics and religion—a fact that called into question the traditional dogmatic method in theology. In the essay on "Historical and Dogmatic Method in Theology," Troeltsch contrasts the new historical method, which he associates with the History of Religions school, and the dogmatic method that continued to inform the work of Ritschlians such as Wilhelm Herrmann and Julius Kaftan. What is distinctive of all forms of the latter method is that

it starts from a firm point of origin completely beyond the relativity of historical scholarship. . . . Its essence is that it possesses an authority that, by definition, is separate from the total context of history, not analogous to other happenings, and therefore not subject to historical criticism . . . they are safeguarded, rather, by a miraculous transmission and sealed by an inward testimony in the heart.[15]

Troeltsch chided many contemporary theologians for appealing to such a *sui generis Heilsgeschichte* (history of salvation), "a nexus of saving facts" knowable or provable only to the believer.

Progressive theologians did not, of course, reject historical method wholesale. Rather, they applied it in an *ad hoc* way to particular problems that then were resolved or deemed harmless. They also were willing to acknowledge that historical context played a conditioning role in Christianity but denied that it had a substantive influence. The historical method proposed by Troeltsch was not intended to address particular problems, such as the New Testament birth stories. Rather he wished to consider "the effect of modern historical methodology on the interpretation of Christianity itself." Once applied to the study of the Bible, church history, and dogma, "the historical method acts as a leaven, transforming everything and ultimately exploding the very form of earlier theological methods."[16]

What is it about the new historical method that entails such extraordinary consequences for theology? Troeltsch outlines the three principal aspects. First is the principle of *criticism* that is based on the contingent and probable nature of all historical events and judgments. No *historical* event or tradition, no matter how sacrosanct, is free of historical-critical treatment. Second, such criticism is possible because of the principle of *analogy*. Whereas all events are in one sense unique, the historian must assume genuine analogies between the events of the past and those of the present. Present experience must serve as a guide to interpreting the past. Unless such a mental unity or analogy is recognized, there can be no means of discriminating between fact and wild fancy. Third, there is the principle of *correlation*. That is, "the connections between faith and fact are themselves not isolated and unconditioned but are most closely correlated with a much larger historical context; they arise out of this context, they share its substance, and they must be understood in relation to it."[17] This means that no just estimate of Christianity can be made except by reference to this larger context, and not simply by the self-judgment of the Christian community itself.

Troeltsch acknowledges that commitment to such a historical method "relativizes everything." Not that it ends in a nihilistic skepticism, "but rather in the sense that every historical structure and moment can be understood only in relation to others and ultimately to the total context, and that standards and values cannot be derived from isolated events, but only from an overview of the historical totality."[18] The consequence of such a *theological* method is revolutionary, for it refuses to remain simply in the domain of philological and historical research and description but actively undertakes the theological task of enquiring into Christianity's normativity or absoluteness and its essence. Here is where the ground of Christian faith can be found without recourse to isolated, miraculous events or experiences. In the introduction to his lectures on *Glaubenslehre*, or the doctrines of Christian faith, Troeltsch contrasts the new method with the old. Previously theology

started either with a brief discussion of a presupposed universal rational belief in God, or else with a brief natural theology; in either case, the introduction quickly moved on to affirm the exclusive supernatural revelation of the Bible. . . . Instead of constructing a natural theology we now conduct a general investigation into the phenomena and essence of religion; and while an exclusive, supernatural authority was once claimed, we now assess the place of Christianity in the history of religions with reference to the philosophy of history. Hence the Bible is now viewed as a human document, an artifact of Christianity.[19]

The Absoluteness of Christianity

Before attempting to determine the essence of Christianity or the Christian principle by which the precise conceptions of God, world, humanity, redemption, and eschatology can be formulated, Troeltsch insists that the first task of theology is to establish Christianity's "universal supremacy for our own culture and civilization," and to measure the other religions against the Christian standard. This question of the absolute validity of Christianity in relation to the other religions occupied Troeltsch throughout his career. It had been raised by Locke and the Deists and in the most systematic way by Hegel. But Hegel's metaphysical approach to the problem was now discredited. Troeltsch's numerous explorations of the problem

during different stages in his career have been shown to be inconsistent and incompatible. And many critics will argue that his final position on the subject is in accord neither with basic Christian claims nor with the historical and cultural situation in which we find ourselves in the late twentieth century. His two major statements on the question are set forth in his monograph *The Absoluteness of Christianity and the History of Religions* (1901) and in the short lecture prepared for delivery in 1923 and entitled "The Place of Christianity Among the World Religions."

What Troeltsch finds true in Hegel and his followers is the claim that Christianity's truth or validity is shown historically to be the fulfillment of the evolution of religion itself. Hegel appeals neither to authority nor to miracle but to historical development itself. "It includes the horizons of the history of religion generally, the acknowledgment of all non-Christian religions as relative truths, and the interpretation of Christianity in relation to these relative truths as the absolute and completed form of religion." It represents the modern consciousness "conditioned by a levelling process in which all human events are drawn into the modern understanding of history."[20]

It is clear in *Die Absolutheit* that while the Christian theologian must be entirely open to the non-Christian religions, a comparison between them does not lead to a complete value relativism. In broadening the horizon to "the whole historical context" and comparing these vast developments, the purpose is not to discover "a universal principle of law like that at work in concepts employed in the natural sciences but *a principle suggestive of tendencies toward a common goal*."[21] (Italics added.) It is clear that Troeltsch's search for "tendencies" pointing to a "common goal" involves the imposition of a normative principle into his historical, *a forteriori* exploration. He acknowledges that the task of surveying the total religious development of humankind is out of the question and that what is required is "to draw together *the most outstanding* results in man's spiritual development" (italics added)— and this, Troeltsch judges, means that we are faced, not with a "profusion of powerful religious forces . . . but only by a few great orientations." "Polytheism and the numerous religions of uncivilized peoples are," Troeltsch asserts, "irrelevant to the problem of highest religious values."

As it turns out, the religions of "ethical and spiritual greatness" are narrowed to, at most, a half dozen, which Troeltsch divides into two types: "the religions that sprang from a common stock—Judaism, Christianity, and Islam—and . . . the great religions of the East, namely Hinduism and especially Buddhism." In Troeltsch's estimation, when we consider the really powerful religious world orientations, "we have to do with the rivalry between the prophetic Christian, Platonic, and Stoic world of ideas on the one hand, and the Buddhist or Eastern world of ideas on the other."[22]

Another feature of the historical method of proceeding is that it "by no means excludes the possibility of comparing the most important elements and values of the main religious orientations, ranking them in accordance with a criterion of value, and subsuming them under the idea of a common goal." Today Troeltsch's peremptory reduction of the world's religions to a very few "great" types and his judgment that these sublime cultural orientations see "the ultimate problems of life . . . in essentially similar ways" strikes us as naive and profoundly unhistorical. The criterion by which Troeltsch ranks the "values" and the "common goal," while critical of Hegel's *a priorism*, is itself blatantly *a priori*. Troeltsch is, nevertheless, entirely forthright about his judgment: "We cannot," he acknowledges, "regard the criterion as an entity that hangs in midair above the historical religions but as something that requires us to choose among them." It is, in the last resort, "a matter of personal conviction and . . . admittedly subjective."[23]

Troeltsch's ultimate choice is between the highest forms of the personal and the impersonal types of religion—and he opts for the former:

It is necessary to make a choice between redemption through meditation on Transcendent Being or non-Being and redemption through faithful, trusting participation in the person-like character of God, the ground of all life and of all genuine value. This is a choice that depends on religious conviction, not scientific demonstration. The higher goal and the greater profundity of life are found on the side of personalistic religion.[24]

And so, Troeltsch concludes, it is "the personalistic redemption-religion of Christianity [that] is the highest and most significantly developed world of religious life that we know—"[25] and it is to be favored over what he sees as the quietism and pessimism of the highest Oriental religious type.

In the second edition of *Die Absolutheit* (1912), and in other essays written at this time, it is clear that Troeltsch's historical relativism has by now made him less certain of Christianity's destiny as the absolute goal of humanity's spiritual evolution. In the second edition he admits that Christianity may be superseded and "for this reason it cannot be proved with absolute certainty that Christianity will always remain the final culmination point, that it will never be surpassed. . . . We cannot and must not regard it as absolute, perfect, immutable."[26] Troeltsch's final position is outlined in his 1923 lecture on Christianity's place among the world's religions. It is essentially consistent with the principles enunciated in his last great but unfinished work, *Der Historismus und Seine Probleme* (1922). It represents a more radical statement of cultural-religious relativity (*Relativität*) without, as we will see, espousing a thoroughgoing relativism or subjectivism.

In these last writings Troeltsch no longer speaks of the common features in the various Western and Oriental religions, nor of any world-historical trend toward Christian personalistic religion. He now sees "irresolvable contradictions"[27] between the great world faiths. "The question of their several relative values will never be capable of objective determination, since every proof thereof will presuppose the special characteristics of the civilization in which it arises."[28] Moreover, Christianity itself presents no historical uniformity; rather, it displays a widely different character in every age and place. Christianity, like all movements of history, reveals its own complex diversity, particularity, and independence. History, like the development of Christianity,

is an immeasurable, incomparable profusion of always-new, unique, and hence individual tendencies, welling up from undiscovered depths, and coming to light in each case in unsuspected places and under different circumstances. Each process works itself out in its own way, bringing ever-new series of unique transformations in its train, until its powers are exhausted, or until it enters as component material into some new combination. Thus the universal law of history consists precisely in this, that the Divine Reason or the Divine Life, within history, constantly manifests itself in always-new and always-peculiar individualizations—and hence that its tendency is not towards unity or universality at all, but rather towards the fulfillment of the highest potentialities of each separate department of life. It is this law which beyond all else makes it quite impossible to characterize Christianity as the reconciliation and goal of all the forces of history, or indeed to regard it as anything else than a historical individuality.[29]

Christianity as we observe it "could only have arisen in the territory of the classical culture and among Latin and Germanic races."[30] It is indissolubly bound up with elements of Greco-Roman and European culture and is not conceivable when extracted from its cultural matrix. "It stands or falls with European civilization."[31]

Troeltsch thus was forced to give up his earlier contention that Christianity possessed "the loftiest and most spiritual revelation" of all the religions. Rather, Christianity's primary claim to validity must be seen to lie in the fact that only through it have we of the West become what we are, and that only through it can we preserve those values and forces which we require. "We cannot live without a religion, yet the only religion that we can endure is Christianity, for Christianity has grown up with us and has become a part of our very being."[32]

Of course, Christianity could not have endured if it were not possessed of great spiritual power and truth. But, Troeltsch reminds us, it is a power and a truth *for us.* Christianity

is God's countenance as revealed to us; it is the way in which being what we are, we receive, and react to, the revelation of God. It is binding upon us and brings us deliverance. It is final and unconditional for us, because we have nothing else, and because in what we have we can recognize the accents of the divine voice. But this does not preclude the possibility that other racial groups living under entirely different cultural conditions may experience their contact with the Divine Life in quite a different way.[33]

The emphasis in the History of Religions school on the environmental factors in the development of religious beliefs and practices gave impetus to a strong element of cultural determinism in Troeltsch's historicism. He believed that the great world religions were actually "crystallizations of the thought of great races," which were themselves the product of various biological and anthropological types. As a result, Troeltsch maintained that there could be "no conversion or transformation of one into the other, but only a measure of agreement and of mutual understanding."[34]

The implication of such a position for the worldwide mission of Christianity is plain; i.e., such a missionary endeavor to the non-Western peoples should be brought to an end. Troeltsch, we can now appreciate, failed to see the incredible possibilities of cultural adaptability and change that we have observed in more recent years, and he was apparently blind to the remarkable adaptive powers of Christianity in cultures outside Europe during his own lifetime. This is especially surprising in light of Troeltsch's own stress on the unpredictability of historical development, and his view that history is capable of ever new individualizations. Nevertheless, his conception of culture was consistent with his radical historicism.

Troeltsch ended his famous essay on "The Place of Christianity Among the World Religions" by denying that his views constituted a position of skepticism. "A truth which . . . is *a truth for us* does not cease, because of this, to be very Truth and Life."[35] What we must learn is that in this earthly experience "the Divine Life is not

One but Many" but also that "to apprehend the One in the Many constitutes the special character of love."[36] Here we see interjected into Troeltsch's cultural and value relativity (*Relativität*) a metaphysical claim that is prominent in *Der Historismus*. The great religious traditions are, after all, "tending in the same direction" and they "all seem *impelled by an inner force to strive upward toward some unknown final height,* where alone the ultimate unity and the final objective validity can lie."[37] (Italics added.)

Despite Troeltsch's disclaimers, his position did appear to many to relativize Christianity in such a way as to challenge fundamental Christian claims of uniqueness and absoluteness. Prominent theologians over the next half century concluded that Troeltsch's historical method and conclusions meant the dissolution of Christian dogmatics. The judgment of Hermann Diem, "that Troeltsch marked a terminal point in the history of theology from which there could be no further progress in the same line of development,"[38] was widely shared, especially in Europe. However, it is crucial to emphasize that Troeltsch never advocated a value relativism that involved a skepticism that assumed entirely incommensurate worldviews or the impossibility of making normative judgments. All value and truth are necessarily mediated through and conditioned by particular historical contexts. But Troeltsch always concluded that "relativity does not mean denial of the values that appear in these individual configurations," nor does it forbid comparative normative judgments, despite the fact that they, too, are necessarily perspectival; that is, "perceived only in the presentiment of faith."[39]

What Does "Essence of Christianity" Mean?

When Troeltsch outlined the distinctive tasks of a Christian theology, he emphasized that the question "What do we mean by Christianity?" should follow the determination of the validity of Christianity only by juxtaposing it—in all the rich content of its development—in relation to the other great religious-cultural configurations, such as Buddhism. He was convinced that such a historical-comparative undertaking would establish the supremacy of Christianity, or at least its abiding validity for Western civilization. Only then should the theologian turn to the second task of theology: establishing historically the essence of Christianity. And here he found not only the conclusions of the older dogmaticians but also those of "moderns," such as Schleiermacher and Harnack, to be historically insufficient halfway measures.

Troeltsch recognized that, due to our modern historical consciousness, the question of the "essence" of Christianity was now a dominant preoccupation of the theologians. Christianity had developed; the question is, what is the essential element in it that abides in its various historical configurations? The issue absorbed the attention of Schleiermacher, Drey and Möhler, the Idealists, Newman, Harnack, and Loisy. The extraordinary response to Harnack's lectures on the *Essence of Christianity* (translated as *What Is Christianity?*) prompted Troeltsch to reply in an article entitled "What Does 'Essence of Christianity' Mean?" (1903). A revised version appeared in 1913 at about the time that the "Dogmatics of the 'Religionsgeschichtliche Schule'" article appeared in *The American Journal of Theology*. The treatment of the "essence" question in both of these 1913 essays shows the influence of Troeltsch's researches on *The Social Teaching of the Christian Churches* (1912).

Harnack's *What is Christianity?* symbolized the historicizing trend of modern theology, but the criticisms of Alfred Loisy and others demonstrated that a truly adequate account of Christianity's essence could not focus on the teachings of Jesus alone but would "have to be a history of Christianity which placed its object much more firmly in the general history of culture and in intellectual history, but also in the history of the real and material presuppositions of thought."[40] This is because the idea of the "essence of Christianity" is itself "linked to modern, critical and evolutionary history." Catholicism speaks of "the faith of the Church" and orthodox Protestantism refers to "the revelation of the Bible," whereas Enlightenment rationalism searches for the "rationality of Christianity." Only with Chateaubriand's *Génie du Christianisme* and German Idealism does the concept of the "essence of Christianity" truly emerge and refer specifically to "the totality of Christian life."[41] And it is *modern* theology's task "to grasp the decisive and driving religious idea and power" out of this totality and thus give an account of Christianity's essence.

Although the definition of this essence is a matter of critical history, it "at the same time . . . goes beyond the ordinary accounts of inductive-empirical history," for it has "a higher order task"[42] that involves a transition to philosophy of history and its presuppositions. Troeltsch discusses three principles involved in this task: criticism, development, and the ideal concept. Criticism points to the fact that a Neo-Protestant theology can neither ground the essence of Christianity in an authoritative Bible or dogma nor, like Catholicism and Hegelianism, consider the evolution of Christianity from the primitive church to the present to be a teleologically necessary development. Within the history of Christianity there is that which is essential but also that which is contingent and nonessential. The concept of essence entails *criticism:*

Thus it is clear that the essence cannot be simply abstracted from the overall sequence and the totality of the manifestations, but that it is necessary to distinguish here between manifestations which give expression to the essence and those which obscure it, or even distort it.[43]

But such a criticism cannot be external; it must be an *immanent criticism,* "the historical measured by the historical, the individual formation measured against the spirit of the whole conceived intuitively and imaginatively." Troeltsch does not shy away from calling such a criticism "moralizing." "The definition of the essence does not only involve imaginative abstraction, but also, with it and as part of it, a criticism grounded in personal, ethical judgment."[44]

Where, then, is the essence to be found? Not, as Harnack and others have claimed, in the teachings of Jesus or even in Christianity's ori-

gins. Christianity is a *developing* reality, but it is not a dialectical and rational development, as the Hegelians assume. The origin of Christianity is important as its "seminal form," but its essence can be understood only from the *totality* of its development in history, including the medieval, Reformation, and modern Neo-Protestant eras. Early Christianity already, in Jesus and Paul, reveals different developmental trends. The essence, then, cannot be formulated in a static doctrine but only in a rich and flexible concept: *"It must be a developing spiritual principle . . . a driving spiritual force."*[45]

Furthermore, conceptions of this "spiritual force" will vary.

That which for one person belongs to the development of the essence is for another a disruption of the continuity. These are difficulties which will always remain with us. . . . On the other hand real historical mastery . . . can display a continuity which is not visible to the crude observer, and in this way history can seriously advance our insight into the essence of Christianity.[46]

However, defining the essence will always be a difficult task and it will always be "influenced by personal and subjective factors."[47] That is, it is a task that not only is rooted in historical-empirical science but is a matter for the philosophy of history. Most importantly, the conception of Christianity's essence will depend on "whether one takes Christianity to be a religious force which is not yet exhausted . . . and will persist indefinitely to influence the future or a transient formation of the religious life."[48] In other words, the essence is an "ideal concept." To define Christianity's essence is also then to shape it in terms of its future—what it *ought to be.* Determining the essence is a *"creative act."* And therefore, "the definition of the essence for a given time is the new historical formulation of Christianity for that time . . . *a new vouch-safing of revelation in the present."*[49] (Italics added.)

Troeltsch recognizes that such an open, developing, and varied conception of Christianity's essence will raise the specter of subjectivism and the charge that it will lead to the splintering of the Christian community. To potential critics he replies that, of course, there are no guarantees against such an outcome, but he also points out that there are intersubjective checks on arbitrary subjectivism, for example, both in serious historical work itself and "in a continued more or less close relationship to the [Christian] congregation."[50] In the final analysis, however, the criterion for maintaining the continuity of Christianity cannot be given in advance; it is a "continuous new formative process." Troeltsch concludes that the continuity or essence of Christianity is affirmed "when one has the Father of Jesus Christ present in one's daily struggles and labours, hopes and sufferings, when one is armed with the strength of the Christian Spirit for the great decisions to be taken in the world and for the victory of all the eternal, personal values of the soul." But whether these spiritual realities are present can be "decided only by one's own experience and inward certainty."[51] This personal confession can stand as Troeltsch's own Neo-Protestant "ideal concept" of the essence of Christianity, shaped by his own engagement with the totality of Christian history, contemporary experience, and his own courageous judgment of faith.

The Historical Jesus, Faith, and Christology

Troeltsch further pursued his concerns about history, faith, and the essence and absoluteness of Christianity in his writings about the historical Jesus. And scattered throughout his mature writings after 1909 are his reflections on Christology, although he did not regard a modern reconception of Christology to be an important part of his own constructive lectures on *Glaubenslehre* in 1911 or 1912.

Critical to Troeltsch's view of the complex of issues that converge on the question of the historical Jesus is his 1911 lecture, "The Significance of the Historical Existence of Jesus for Faith."[52] The provocation for the lecture was Arthur Drews's *The Christ Myth* (1909), which claimed that all the important religious features of the New Testament picture of the historical Jesus were mythical. The so-called "historical Jesus" of the Gospels, Drews asserted, is simply the product of the religious imaginings of the early Christian community. A religion based on faith in Jesus therefore should be abandoned.[53] Drews's book was dismissed by leading experts from a variety of persuasions; a rationalist critic as averse to Christianity as Sir James Frazer considered Drews's denial of the historicity of Jesus to be entirely groundless. The book nevertheless provoked a series of important debates that renewed the questions posed earlier by Reimarus and Strauss and more recently by Herrmann, Kähler, Harnack, Loisy, and Schweitzer. There were contemporary Christian thinkers, such as the British Hegelians, Wilhelm Bousset, and the American theologian Douglas Clyde Macintosh, who believed that Jesus Christ could be divorced from history without serious loss to Christian belief. For Troeltsch, however, it was important to raise once again the question of the importance of the historical Jesus for faith, and how much can really be known about the historical Jesus. The question raised was: Must not Christian faith "be made internally independent of all necessary connection with historical elements which are always subject to science," as Troeltsch's friend Bousset insisted?

Troeltsch developed his own position in response to three contemporary options. One was that of traditional orthodoxy, which refused to take historical criticism seriously and fell back on biblical authority. A second position was represented by a variety of Neo-Hegelians and Idealists who wished to free Christ from any necessary connections with the contingencies of historical research. The third and popular option, what Troeltsch called "a half-way house," was represented by the Ritschlians. The latter rejected pure appeals to authority or to historical miracle, but held to the unique religious personality and teachings of the *historical* Jesus as normative and essential. But for Troeltsch it was "anything but obvious that the religious personality of the historical Jesus can be fully and clearly known and made directly and personally effective, just like the immediately operative influence of one man upon another."[54] For Troeltsch such an assumption had been rendered impossible by modern criticism. The burden for Christian faith posed by the negative results and constant oscillations of biblical scholarship is "more likely to shatter faith than protect it. It is rather that our souls are overcome by the grandeur of prophetic Christian faith in God and that *this* leads to acknowledgment of Jesus, than vice versa."[55]

Troeltsch is one with the Ritschians in insisting on the necessity of the historical Jesus for Christian faith, but the argument he offers is similar to the one proposed by some of the Idealists: an appeal to the Christian community. Rather than appeal to the New Testament texts alone, Troeltsch stresses the mediation of Jesus "through the community and the living effect by means of subsequent Christian personalities." One is not dealing with an isolated historical fact "but with its infinitely modified and enriched continuing effects." And in such an appeal it "is impossible to say for certain what comes from Jesus and what comes from the later period and the present. Even if one considers the main lines of Jesus' preaching to be fully knowable, that still does not give direct contact between one man and another."[56]

Troeltsch is arguing that the historical Jesus can no longer be guaranteed, either through the imposition of biblical or ecclesial authority or by salvaging some certain core of Jesus's preaching or personality by means of New Testament research. The "inner necessity" of the *historical* person of Christ for redemption is no longer clear to those committed to historical-critical research. "Herrmann's talk about the 'fact of Christ' which cannot be established like other facts . . . is incomprehensible."[57] Yet Troeltsch does not reject the necessity of a connection between the historical Jesus and salvation for the Christian. It is perhaps not surprising that, in the light of his research in preparing *The Social Teaching of the Christian Churches and Groups,* he found the clue to that link in the sociopsychological laws of the religious life, more specifically in an appeal to the Christian community and its cult or worship. Troeltsch had come to see the source of the feebleness of contemporary Christianity in its solitary individualism and its lack of interest in the religious com-

munity and its cult. He recognized that such an individualism is susceptible to the vagaries of personal feelings and enthusiasms and, therefore, is anarchic and schismatic. But what the history and psychology of religion have shown "is that in all religion what really counts is not dogma and idea but cult and community."[58] And in the primitive Christian community, it is entirely clear that the community and the cult had no other means or purpose "than the gathering to worship Christ as the revelation of God."[59] Unlike the nature religions, the great historical religions look to "the prophets and founder personalities who serve as archetypes, authorities, sources of power and rallying-points. As images of personal concrete life they can be interpreted with versatility and flexibility possessed by no mere doctrine or dogma."[60] It is in the community and cult alone, Troeltsch argues, that the Christian idea or essence is handed on because both serve to gather the community around its head who is present to it in the image, symbol, or picture of the historical Christ.

Troeltsch, of course, acknowledges that the picture or image of Jesus Christ is "modified" and "enriched." But he believes that there is support for confidence in the fact of the historical Jesus, and his reality as a total historical phenomenon, in the laws of sociopsychology.

Someone who really belongs in his heart to the world of Christian experience will never be able to see in the centre and head of the congregation, the focal point of the cult and vision of God, a mere myth—no matter how beautiful. For him God is not an idea or possibility but a holy reality. He will therefore insist upon standing with this symbol of his on the solid ground of real life. It is for him a truly significant fact that a real man thus lived, struggled, believed, and conquered, and from this real life a stream of strength and certainty flows down to him.[61]

For the Christian, certainty of redemption and a strengthening of life must be grounded in the real, vivid life of Jesus. And, therefore, it is impossible to ignore historical-critical research. "Faith can interpret facts; it cannot establish them."[62] However, Troeltsch insists, it is not a question of individual details but of the factuality of the total historical phenomenon of Jesus and the basic outline of his teaching and his religious personality. This must be capable of being established by means of historical criticism as historical reality if the "symbol of Christ" is to have a firm and strong inner basis in the "fact" of Jesus.[63]

If a negative verdict were to be decided against the historicity of Jesus or the possibility of our knowing about him that "would be the beginning of the end of the Christ symbol."[64] Troeltsch declared his confidence that "the decisive chief facts can here be ascertained with certainty."[65]

Troeltsch believed, of course, that the New Testament's historical picture of Jesus is not the Christian community's sole source. The picture of Jesus must be set in its wider context of the preparation of the prophets and Jesus's effect on Paul and numerous other religious personalities such as Augustine, Luther, and Schleiermacher and down to the present day. Granted the confident presupposition about our historical knowledge of Jesus, the Christian community "can interpret the picture of Christ in practical proclamation very freely and flexibly, using everything that flowed into him and everything which in the course of thousands of years has been accommodated and loved in him."[66]

Troeltsch concludes his own resolution of the question of the significance of the historical existence of Jesus for Christian faith by acknowledging that his own solution is similar to that of Ritschl and Herrmann. However, his argument is based on fundamentally different theological grounds. First, Troeltsch bases Christianity's confidence in its knowledge of the historical Jesus on an appeal neither to faith, nor to theological norms, nor to historical research *per se*, but to what he calls a universal law of social psychology. Now it would appear that the universality of this law as it applies to the higher "spiritual" religions is highly suspect. For it is clear that religions such as Judaism, Islam, and Theravada Buddhism, while venerating their leaders, do not worship them as divine beings in their cult. Neither do other great religions, for example, Mahayana

Buddhism, demand that their founders or teachers be real, certifiable historical figures. They are not consumed by the same historical anxieties regarding their teachers and gods as is Christianity. Troeltsch's sociopsychological law does, however, illuminate the Christian case, and his all-too-brief discussion anticipates interesting ideas soon to be advanced by the sociologist Emile Durkheim and the psychotherapist Carl Jung.[67] Troeltsch's position differs from the latter, and from the Neo-Hegelians, by his insistence on the crucial place of the *historical* figure of Jesus. But this raises other problems.

Troeltsch's wrestling with the problems surrounding the quest of the historical Jesus underlines the realism of his historical reconception of Jesus Christ and his opposition to the solutions of the Rationalists and the Idealists. This is especially evident in his correspondence with his friend Bousset. In his own response to the challenge of Drews's *The Christ Myth*, Bousset had written the following:

Jesus did not only create the symbols of the Gospel in essentials, but became a symbol Himself. . . . But this symbolic aspect enables us now also to dispose of all difficulties which resulted especially on the part of exact historical enquiry. . . . We need no longer fear the eventual result of historical investigation that this reality [the characterization of Jesus] will remain irrevocably and irretrievably lost. At this point . . . all depends on the symbol and the picture. . . . The symbol serves as illustration not as demonstration.[68]

Troeltsch rejects Bousset's rationalist position because, for Troeltsch, history not only "illustrates" but, more importantly, "confirms," whereas for Bousset it becomes "passing chance that connects rational truths with the person of Jesus."[69]

Troeltsch's historical realism regarding the historical Jesus has its own problems, however. In the last analysis, it appears that his confidence in the reliability of the New Testament reports regarding Jesus's personality and teachings is assumed as established for the future of Christianity. Critics such as Bousset and Bultmann found this a far too sanguine judgment. But equally critical for contemporary theologians—who were committed to the application of historical-critical methods—are two other issues that are raised by Troeltsch's discussion. Both bear on the question of Christology.

While committed to a historical approach, both Schleiermacher and Ritschl were able to construct bridges with the ancient Christologies of Nicaea and Chalcedon. Troeltsch concludes that a theology committed to the principles and methods of the History of Religions school makes the idea of Jesus as a deified *world* redeemer impossible. Based on the sociopsychological necessities of Western culture, it is likely that this culture's religion "will be tied to the central position of Christ for faith." But it is quite another question "whether this culture itself will last forever and extend to the whole world. . . . It is therefore impossible either to affirm or deny that Christianity will last forever and community and cult remain bound to the historical personality of Jesus." In other words, "God in Christ" can only mean that Christians now revere Jesus "as the highest revelation of God accessible to us," but it would be well "not to emphasize too much the eternal dependence of millions yet unborn upon the person of Jesus."[70] Troeltsch's sociopsychological approach has fundamentally weakened the orthodox doctrine of the two natures of Christ. For he believes that the modern rejection of geocentric and anthropocentric views of the world have made it impossible "to deify Jesus and to assign to him an absolutely central position." The efforts of modern liberal theologians to transfer to the human Jesus "the role of a universal world-redeemer . . . is wholly impossible and fraught with difficulties." Future historical contexts may "not need to be connected with the person of Jesus but would link up with other symbols and paradigmatic figures."[71]

For Troeltsch the Christian conception of God will, indisputably, remain inseparable from the figure of Jesus. Yet that connection will not be expressed in metaphysical dogmas but in a "Christ-mysticism" that makes manifest the indwelling of Christ in God. Here again one must pose the question to Troeltsch. The Christ-mysti-

cism that is the source and bond of the Christian community is given to us in a variety of images and pictures embellished in ever new ways in subsequent history. That latter history is especially crucial for Troeltsch. What is critical is Jesus's historical and psychological effects and their significance for religious life. For example, "the only meaning that can be attached to his suffering and death will be historical and psychological—the effect it has on believing souls."[72] Here we note that "history" refers to the variety of spiritually rich images or pictures of Jesus. Now Troeltsch has insisted that these images of Christ do have a correspondence with the actual life of Jesus, but this appears to his critics to be merely assumed and asserted. Like Herrmann, Troeltsch is not interested in carrying out a new search for the historical Jesus; nevertheless, he confidently and persistently speaks of Jesus's personality and teachings in a manner that is rejected by his New Testament colleagues in the History of Religions school. Troeltsch gives the impression of hovering uncertainly between the realism of the older effort to recover the life and personality of Jesus and the Neo-Idealist's "Spirit" of Christ. Neither Troeltsch's reliance on his social-psychological argument about the *need* for the historical figure of Jesus, nor his very creative insight into the ways in which the image of Christ has been read, embellished, and enriched in the history of the community, establishes the logical connection with the earthly life of Jesus that he assumes. Now Troeltsch does rightly see the theological importance of ongoing historical research into the life of Jesus. Christian belief hinges on this particular historical actuality. The problem is that the very accounts of Jesus that believers have found spiritually and psychologically most compelling are, in the judgment of many of Troeltsch's New Testament colleagues, the least certain in view of recent historical-critical research. Both Troeltsch's complacency and his radicalness on the issue of the significance of Jesus for faith and Christology are indicated in passages such as the following:

Research will make advances and when the dust has settled enough will remain of the old picture for Jesus at any rate still to be seen as the source and power of faith in Christ and so of Christianity—even if the historian as such can no longer describe him as "absolute central personality" or "opening up a new stage of humanity."[73]

In the last analysis, Troeltsch sees a viable reconception of the Christological question as resting neither in the latest findings of the biblical scholar nor in some supratemporal idea of Christ, but in "the total conception and evolution of the position of Christianity as part of the history of religion." And, therefore,

one's judgment upon Jesus and evaluation of him will always depend essentially upon our answer at this point. *Someone who sees in Christianity the permanent utmost plateau of man's religion will naturally also see and seek in its founding personality deeper forces than someone who sees in it nothing but a passing phase of religious formation.*[74] (Italics added.)

This represents an interesting theological inversion. Despite the insistence that believers return to "the original source," it is the "total conception," the cumulative power of the Christian tradition and its "developing spiritual principle," that becomes for Troeltsch the prism through which the Christian perceives and interprets the figure of Jesus Christ. "While Jesus maintains the central position [for Christians] each age interprets him really quite differently and puts its own ideas under his protection."[75] And so, as with the essence of Christianity, there will be "many Christs." But, contrary to Troeltsch's supposition, these "many Christs" do not, most critics agree, guarantee continuity with the earthly Jesus, only a loose connection with the earliest portraits.

As mentioned previously, Troeltsch wrote little on Christology, and what he wrote was largely critical of classical christological doctrine. He was dismissive of the metaphysical efforts of the fathers at Nicaea and Chalcedon to describe adequately the relations between God and Jesus. He thought that such doctrines as Jesus's preexistence and his divine omnipotence and omniscience were impossible doctrines in an age dominated by a historical way of thinking. Nevertheless, Troeltsch does not wholly reject a Christian "incarnational" theology, for he often uses language such as "God made visible" in Jesus, Jesus being "the living guarantee of the grace of God in his personality," and "Jesus as the one who reveals God . . ." and "mediates salvation." Thus, as Sarah Coakley has shown, it is quite wrong for critics of Troeltsch to charge him with advocating a "Christless Christianity," or with substituting the Christian "idea" or "principle" for the person of Jesus, or with judging Jesus as dispensable (because he simply "illustrates" a rational ideal), or with having minimized Jesus as one who truly reveals God and brings salvation.[76]

It must also be said, of course, that for Troeltsch Jesus *cannot* be claimed as the decisive, exclusive, or final revelation of God, as his many essays testify. And for most Christians belief that God's revelation in Jesus Christ is decisive and normative is essential to the doctrines of the Incarnation and Trinity; it defines what it means to be a Christian monotheist rather than a theist of some other sort. These critics contend that Troeltsch's historicism and doctrinal relativism are fatal to a Christian theology—what Karl Barth will call Troeltsch's "dead-end street."

Despite the critics, much recent theology reveals a greater appreciation of Troeltsch's work and contribution. In large measure this is because the problems that face Christian theology in the late twentieth century are the issues that Troeltsch recognized as inescapable. Therefore, Troeltsch is seen as important and extraordinarily farsighted in recognizing the issues with which Christian thought would have to wrestle in the decades ahead. One, of course, was the persistent pressures of historical criticism and of historicism's attendant ideological and moral relativism. Other issues include the growth of scientific rationalization and the intensification of autonomy and individualization, and with these the decline of traditional church authority, the expanding horizons of the life sciences and cosmology, which put the human story in a radically new perspective; and the question of the truth and future of Christianity in its relation to the other great world faiths. How does Christian theology develop its truth claims, its norms and standards of value in such an increasingly secular, global, pluralistic, and relativized cultural context? Troeltsch recognized these cultural determinants and, unsuccessful though he may have been, sought to reconceive theology so that it might address the issues encompassed by what he called the problems of historicism. In the words of a discerning commentator, for Troeltsch "historicism is not to be overcome by being abolished, but by our discovery of how to live creatively with a permanent problem. How to do this is the question that Troeltsch left as an inescapable legacy to the theology of the twentieth century."[77]

NOTES

1. Albert Schweitzer, *The Quest of the Historical Jesus* (New York, 1964), p. 4.
2. Friedrich Max Müller, *Lectures on the Science of Religion* (London, 1873), p. 148.
3. Günther Bornkamm, *Jesus of Nazareth* (New York, 1960), p. 13.
4. Schweitzer, op. cit., pp. 398–99.
5. Ibid., p. 399.
6. Ibid.
7. Ibid., p. 403.
8. R. H. Lightfoot, *History and Interpretation in the Gospels* (London, 1935), pp. 30–31.
9. Rudolf Bultmann, *Jesus and the Word* (New York, 1934), p. 8.
10. R. Bultmann, *Glauben und Verstehen*, I (Tübingen, 1933), p. 208.
11. R. Bultmann, *Kerygma and Myth*, I, ed. H. W. Bartsch (London, 1953), p. 41.
12. Karl Barth, *Theology and Church* (London, 1962), p. 60f.
13. Ernst Troeltsch, *Gesammelte Schriften*, IV (Tübingen, 1925), p. 12. For this statement and other biographical information on Troeltsch, I am indebted to Wilhelm Pauck's valuable essay on Troeltsch in W. Pauck, *Harnack and Troeltsch* (New York, 1968), pp. 43–94.
14. E. Troeltsch, *Christian Thought: Its History and Application*, ed. Baron F. von Hügel (New York, 1957), p. 63.
15. E. Troeltsch, *Religion in History*, trans. James Luther Adams and Walter F. Bense (Minneapolis, 1991), p. 20.
16. Ibid., p. 12.
17. Ibid., p. 17.
18. Ibid., p. 18.
19. E. Troeltsch, *The Christian Faith* [*Glaubenslehre*, 1925], trans. Garrett Paul (Minneapolis, 1991), p. 9.
20. E. Troeltsch, *The Absoluteness of Christianity and the History of Religions*, 2nd ed., trans. David Reid (Richmond, Va., 1971), p. 51.
21. Ibid., p. 91.
22. Ibid., pp. 91–93.
23. Ibid., p. 96.

24. Ibid., p. 112.
25. Ibid., p. 117.
26. Ibid., pp. 114–115. See "The Dogmatics of the History-of-Religions School," in Troeltsch, *Religion in History*, p. 95.
27. E. Troeltsch, "The Place of Christianity Among the World Religions," in Troeltsch, *Christian Thought: Its History and Application*, p. 43.
28. Ibid., p. 62.
29. Ibid., pp. 44–45.
30. Ibid., p. 52.
31. Ibid., p. 54.
32. Ibid., p. 55.
33. Ibid., pp. 55–56.
34. Ibid., pp. 58–59.
35. Ibid., p. 63.
36. Ibid.
37. Ibid., p. 61.
38. Hermann Diem, *Dogmatics* (Edinburgh, 1959), pp. 8–9.
39. Troeltsch, *The Absoluteness of Christianity*, pp. 89–90. The finest treatment of the ambiguities and problems in Troeltsch's historicism is Sarah Coakley's discussion in *Christ Without Absolutes: A Study of the Christology of Ernst Troeltsch* (Oxford, 1988), Ch. I, "The Nature of Troeltsch's Relativism," pp. 5–44.
40. E. Troeltsch, "What Does 'Essence of Christianity' Mean?" in *Ernst Troeltsch: Writings on Theology and Religion*, trans. and ed. Robert Morgan and Michael Pye (Atlanta, 1977), p. 127.
41. Ibid., p. 129.
42. Ibid., p. 134.
43. Ibid., p. 140.
44. Ibid., p. 145.
45. Ibid., p. 151.
46. Ibid., p. 152.
47. Ibid., p. 153.
48. Ibid., p. 156.
49. Ibid., p. 163.
50. Ibid., p. 170.
51. Ibid. In "Dogmatics of the 'Religionsgeschichtliche Schule,'" Troeltsch offers this definition of the essence of Christianity: "Christian religious faith

is faith in the divine regeneration of man who is alienated from God—a regeneration effected through the knowledge of God in Christ. The consequence of this regeneration is union with God and social fellowship so as to constitute the kingdom of God" (p. 13). See also Troeltsch, *The Christian Faith*, p. 62 ff.

52. For a thorough analysis of Troeltsch's position on the historical Jesus and Christology, and how his position differs from that of figures such as Schleiermacher, Strauss, Ritschl, Herrmann, and Bousset, see Coakley, op. cit., esp. Ch. 4–6.

53. For an excellent account of the background and of Troeltsch's response to Drews's *The Christ Myth*, see B. A. Gerrish, "Jesus, Myth, and History: Troeltsch's Stand in the 'Christ-Myth' Debate," in *The Old Protestantism and the New: Essays on the Reformation Heritage* (Chicago, 1982).

54. E. Troeltsch, "The Significance of the Historical Existence of Jesus for Faith," in *Ernst Troeltsch: Writings on Theology and Religion*, p. 188.

55. Ibid., p. 189.
56. Ibid.
57. Ibid., p. 192.
58. Ibid., p. 194.
59. Ibid., p. 195.
60. Ibid.
61. Ibid., p. 197.
62. Ibid., p. 198.
63. Ibid.
64. Ibid.

65. Ibid., p. 200.
66. Ibid., p. 201.
67. On the creative potential of these sociopsychological insights, see Coakley, op. cit., pp. 143–145.
68. Wilhelm Bousset, *The Significance of the Personality of Jesus for Belief: Reprinted from the Report of the Fifth International Congress for Free Christianity and Religious Progress* (Berlin, 1910), p. 15. Cited in Coakley, op. cit., p. 157.
69. E. Dinkler-von Schubert, "Ernst Troeltsch: Briefe aus der Heidelberger Zeit an Wilhelm Bousset 1894–1914," *Heidelberger Jahrbücher*, 20 (1976), 46. Cited in Coakley, op. cit., p. 158. I am dependent on Coakley for these references to the Troeltsch-Bousset discussion.
70. Troeltsch, "Significance of the Historical Existence of Jesus," pp. 205, 206.
71. E. Troeltsch, "On the Possibility of a Liberal Christianity," in Troeltsch, *Religion in History*, pp. 348, 350.
72. Troeltsch, *The Christian Faith*, p. 89.
73. E. Troeltsch, "Half a Century of Theology: A Review," in *Ernst Troeltsch Writings on Theology and Religion*, p. 72.
74. Ibid.
75. Troeltsch, "What Does 'Essence of Christianity' Mean?" p. 147.
76. See Coakley, op. cit., p. 188.
77. Claude Welch, *Protestant Thought in the Nineteenth Century*, II (New Haven, 1985), p. 301.

SUGGESTIONS FOR FURTHER READING

The New Science of Religion

The following are excellent guides to the beginnings and development of the new science of religion, the major scholars, theorists, and movements:

Capps, Walter H. *Religious Studies: The Making of a Discipline* (Minneapolis: Fortress Press, 1995). Describes the work of the major scholars from the nineteenth century to the present.

Sharpe, Eric J. *Comparative Religion: A History* (New York: Charles Scribner's Sons, 1975). This is the best one-volume study.

Vries, Jan de. *The Study of Religion: A Historical Approach*, trans. Kees W. Bolle (New York: Harcourt, Brace and World, 1967).

Waardenburg, Jacques. *Classical Approaches to the Study of Religion*, 2 vols. (The Hague: Mouton 1973–1974). Also see the articles on "Comparative Religion," "History of Religions," "Religionsgeschichtliche Schule," and on scholars such as F. Max Müller, E. B. Tylor, J. G. Frazer, Robertson Smith, etc., in *The Encyclopedia of Religion*, 15 vol. (New York: Macmillan, 1987).

The Historical Jesus

For accounts of the issues raised for theology by historical research, especially on the question of the historical Jesus, consult the following:

Harvey, Van A. *The Historian and the Believer* (New York: Macmillan, 1966). Although not focused directly on the debates at the turn of the century, this book analyzes in a profound way the issues posed for Christian theology by modern developments in historical knowledge.

Kissinger, W. S. *The Lives of Jesus: A History and Bibliography* (New York: Garland, 1985).

Robinson, J. M. *A New Quest of the Historical Jesus* (London: SCM Press, 1959).

Schweitzer, Albert. *The Quest of the Historical Jesus* (New York: Macmillan, 1964). The classic study of the nineteenth-century effort to get back to the real historical Jesus—its importance and its failure.

Welch, Claude. *Protestant Thought in the Nineteenth Century*, II (New Haven: Yale University Press, 1985). Ch. 3 and 4 are brief but helpful accounts of developments in the new science of religion and their effect on theology. Ch. 5 is an excellent account of the theological debate over "The Jesus of History and the Christ of Faith," including discussions of Harnack, Herrmann, Kähler, Loisy, Schweitzer, and Weiss.

Zahrnt, Heinz. *The Historical Jesus*, trans. J. S. Bowden (New York: Harper and Row, 1963). A popular but informative account of the discussion from the late nineteenth century through the era of Dialectical and kerygmatic theology to the "new quest" of the 1950s.

Ernst Troeltsch

The new interest in Troeltsch has produced a number of fine book-length studies in English in recent years. There are also several brief studies that are valuable. See, for example, Claude Welch, *Protestant Thought in the Nineteenth Century*, II (New Haven, 1985), Ch. 8, "Ernst Troeltsch: Faith, History, and Ethics in Tension"; Trutz Rendtorff and Friedrich Wilhelm Graf, "Ernst Troeltsch," in Ninian Smart et al., *Nineteenth Century Religious Thought in the West*, III (Cambridge, 1985), Ch. 9. Also see the several valuable essays by Gerrish and Morgan below.

Coakley, Sarah. *Christ Without Absolutes: A Study of the Christology of Ernst Troeltsch* (Oxford: Clarendon Press, 1988). By far the best account of Troeltsch's treatment of the historical Jesus and Christology. However, this study also includes valuable analyses of Troeltsch's historicism and relativism and his views on the "essence" and the "absoluteness" of Christianity.

Clayton, John Powell, ed. *Ernst Troeltsch and the Future of Theology* (Cambridge: Cambridge University Press, 1976). This is an important collection of studies by Troeltsch scholars. Includes a helpful bibliography of Troeltsch's writings in English and studies of Troeltsch's thought to 1976.

Drescher, Hans-Georg. *Ernst Troeltsch: His Life and Work*, trans. John Bowden (Minneapolis: Fortress Press, 1993). The only full-length biographical study of Troeltsch in English. Not a distinguished study of the man and his writings but a good source of information not otherwise available in English studies.

Gerrish, B. A. *The Old Protestantism and the New: Essays on the Reformation Heritage* (Chicago: University of Chicago Press, 1982).

———. *Continuing the Reformation: Essays on Modern Religious Thought* (Chicago: University of Chicago Press, 1993). These two collections of essays include five studies on Troeltsch. Especially valuable on Troeltsch as historical and systematic theologian. Also see Gerrish's study of Troeltsch in Clayton above, Ch. 4.

Morgan, Robert, and Michael Pye, trans. and ed. *Ernst Troeltsch: Writings on Theology and Religion* (Atlanta: John Knox Press, 1977). Excellent translations of four of Troeltsch's important essays, with valuable essays on Troeltsch by the editors.

Pauck, Wilhelm. *Harnack and Troeltsch: Two Historical Theologians* (Oxford: Oxford University Press, 1968). A brief but lively, informative, and sympathetic biographical sketch of these two great historians and their distinctive contributions.

Reist, Benjamin A. *Toward a Theology of Involvement: The Thought of Ernst Troeltsch* (Philadelphia: Westminster Press, 1966). One of the earliest general studies of Troeltsch's theology in English. Reist's conclusion that Troeltsch's theology failed is rather characteristic of these earlier assessments.

Rubanowice, Robert J. *Crisis in Consciousness: The Thought of Ernst Troeltsch* (Tallahassee: University Presses of Florida, 1982). A fine study from the perspective of intellectual history that portrays Troeltsch as a pivotal representative of the crisis felt at the turn of the century through a convergence of sociological, political, philosophical, and religious changes.

Wyman, Walter E., Jr. *The Concept of Glaubenslehre: Ernst Troeltsch and the Theological Heritage of Schleiermacher* (Chico, Calif.: Scholars Press, 1983). Countering a long-standing view of Troeltsch's "dissolution" of Protestant dogmatic theology, Wyman offers a sympathetic study of Troeltsch as a systematic theologian in the tradition of Schleiermacher.

Yasukata, Toshimasa. *Ernst Troeltsch: Systematic Theologian of Radical Historicality* (Atlanta: Scholars Press, 1986). A broad, reliable overview of the thought of Troeltsch as it developed during the three dominant periods of his career, and arguing for the continuing centrality of theology in Troeltsch's later Berlin period.

Chapter Two

American Empirical and Naturalistic Theology

Henry Nelson Wieman

When one compares the movements of conservative Protestantism in America at the end of the nineteenth century with the movements of Liberal and Modernist theology, the influence of the latter appears relatively slight. However, after about 1890 progressive and even radical ideas gained momentum and influence in some of the mainstream Protestant denominations, especially in the Methodist, Northern Baptist, Congregational, and Episcopal churches. One group of moderately liberal theologians—which included Walter Rauschenbusch at Rochester Theological Seminary and William Adams Brown at Union Theological Seminary in New York City—identified themselves with the German Ritschlian theology, especially with the work of Albrecht Ritschl, Julius Kaftan, and Adolf von Harnack.*

There was, however, another American theological movement that also had its beginnings at the turn of the century that did not look to Germany but to native American resources for its inspiration and guidance. It also proved to be a more radical movement. It became associated with scholars at the Divinity School of the newly founded University of Chicago (1892), and therefore came to be called the "Chicago School." We earlier explored the major themes of the Ritschlian theology, and here we will examine the sources, the leaders, and the principal interests of this distinctive movement of American empirical religious thought and theology.

* On the Ritschlian school and Rauschenbusch, see Vol. I, Ch. 11.

INTRODUCTION

Although there were significant differences in the movements of American Liberal and Modernist theology between 1890 and 1940, historians have pointed to a discernible common theme that runs through American theology generally from Jonathan Edwards through Horace Bushnell and Ralph Waldo Emerson to men like Walter Rauschenbusch, W. A. Brown, and the members of the Chicago School. What they share is the attention that they give to religious experience.[1] It is this emphasis on experience that gives to American theology a distinctive empirical stamp and style. It also gives the various strands of Protestant Liberal and Modernist theology a shared temper and spirit. Although they may disagree on the importance and the interpretation of specific doctrinal beliefs, these empirically oriented theologies share an openness and a liberality of spirit; a commitment to reason and to scientific inquiry; a confidence in the use of religious and moral experience as authentic sources of a knowledge of God and the criticism and the reconstruction of traditional Christian beliefs. Also, they share an emphasis on divine immanence and on the moral imperative of Christianity to achieve practical moral ends.

What especially distinguishes this empirical movement of American religious thought is its joining of an empiricist interest in religious experience with a self-conscious commitment to the application of scientific methods in the study of religious phenomena. This is particularly crucial to the program of the Chicago School. It directed its defense of theism and of Christianity against a growing secularism and humanism not through appeals to doctrinal or church authority, but by an appeal to human experience and scientific evidence itself. The scientific ideal embraced by these theologians was not, however, the recently dominant scientific positivism that had its roots in British empiricism, but rather the broader "radical empiricism" that was currently advanced by the Harvard psychologist-philosopher William James and by the philosopher John Dewey. The latter chaired the philosophy, psychology, and education departments at Chicago during the crucial decade 1894–1904. Many of the empirical theologians associated with the Chicago School, including Gerald Birney Smith (1868–1929), Edward Scribner Ames (1870–1958), Douglas Clyde Macintosh (1877–1948), Shailer Mathews (1863–1941), and Henry Nelson Wieman (1884–1975), were deeply influenced by the new empiricism and pragmatism of either James or Dewey, or both. Again, what these theologians owed to these two seminal American philosophers was a commitment to a scientific study of religious experience and the development of a Christian theology *as an empirical science*. The two theologians whose work we will examine in some detail can only be fully understood when seen in relation to the revolution in philosophy carried out first by James and then by Dewey.

RADICAL EMPIRICISM AND RELIGION: WILLIAM JAMES

William James (1842–1910) is one of the great modern philosophers. His interests in philosophy reflect his early training in medicine at Harvard Medical School and his work as a psychologist. His masterpiece, *The Principles of Psychology*, 2 vol. (1890), remains today one of the classics in the field. James is perhaps best known as a founder, with Charles Peirce and John Dewey, of the philosophical movement known as pragmatism. What is striking, in view of his valuable contributions as a scientist and philosopher, is that James admitted in 1897 that "religion is the great interest of my life."[2] It is not surprising then that anticipations of his pragmatism and radical empiricism can be found in his own early religious experience and writings on religious belief. James is not unique in this regard among important thinkers in the last years of the nineteenth century. A diverse group of scientists and philosophers, including Alfred Russel Wallace, Henri Bergson, Henry Sidgwick, Charles Renouvier, James Ward, and Maurice Blondel, came to see scientific naturalism and positivism as the great threat to the spiritual life and its ideals. Yet they also rejected traditional defenses of religion and were committed to discovering empirical evidence for the reality of a spiritual world.

As a result of his early medical studies and scientific explorations, James came to believe that humans were mere automatons caught in a closed, mechanical world. This led to a personal crisis during 1869–1870 that left him in a state of depression and fearing the possibility of insanity or suicide. An entry in his diary reveals how he emerged from this crisis by a decisive commitment to live despite his uncertainty. It also reflects the deeply personal roots of his later philosophical pragmatism and his writings on religious belief:

I think that yesterday was a crisis in my life. I finished the first part of Renouvier's second "Essais" and see no reason why his definition of Free Will—"the sustaining of a thought *because I choose to* when I might have other thoughts"—need be the definition of an illusion. At any rate, I will assume for the present—until next year—that it is no illusion. My first act of free will shall be to believe in free will. For the remainder of the year I will . . . voluntarily cultivate the feeling of moral freedom, by reading books favorable to it, as well as by action. . . . My belief, to be sure, *can't* be optimistic—but I will posit life (the real, the good) in the self-governing *resistence* of the ego to the world. Life shall be built in doing and suffering and creating.[3]

James' early pragmatic affirmation saved his life. He soon after became an instructor in anatomy, physiology, and psychology at Harvard. In 1879 he began teaching philosophy and became professor in that department in 1885 and then professor of psychology in 1889. In 1897 his famous but controversial *The Will to Believe and Other Essays* was published and in 1901–1902 he delivered the Gifford Lectures in Edinburgh—the basis of his *The Varieties of Religious Experience* (1902). Among his later philosophical works are *Pragmatism* (1907), and *The Meaning of Truth: A Sequel to "Pragmatism"* and *A Pluralistic Universe* (1909), both published the year before his death. Our interest here is to show how James's empiricism and pragmatism were used in the service of religion and thereby how his philosophy opened

William James

up new avenues of empirical religious exploration and theological apologetic.

Experience, Pragmatism, and the "Will to Believe"

James's early reflections on knowledge, belief, and truth were closely tied to his own personal crisis, the incipient pragmatism that emerged out of this experience, and his reading of Renouvier and especially Darwin. From the latter James learned to perceive the knower as an actor and to see thought as a complex of perception, conception, and *action*. Fundamentally, he wrote, "perception and thinking are only there for behavior's sake."[4] For James this implied that interests, expectations, and faith are essential components of human thought. He came to realize that faith, and especially religious faith, is key to understanding human behavior from a scientific, Darwinian perspective. "For again and again success depends on faith that we shall not fail; and that faith in turn on the faith that we are right—which faith thus verifies itself."[5] Thought thereby ultimately ministers to "higher mental powers—the powers of the will."[6] In *The Principles of Psychology* James developed his theory of the emotions, attention, habit, belief, and the will. He concluded that we humans "give what seems to us a still higher degree of reality to whatever things we select and emphasize and turn to WITH A WILL."[7] Not that we can simply believe at will, but rather that

gradually our will can lead us to the same results by a very simple method: *we need only in cold blood ACT as if the thing in question were real, and keep acting as if it were real, and it will infallibly end by growing into such a connection with our life that it will become real.* It will become so knit with habit and emotion that our interests in it will be those which characterize belief.[8]

Assuming that James is correct in his psychological analysis of the actual role of the will in believing, he obviously has offered us no help in judging when such believing is right or logically or morally responsible. After all, people do believe things that are illusory and evil. James was challenged by his critics to address the question as to when it is *right* to believe. This he did in "The Will to Believe," a lecture delivered before a student audience at Brown University in 1896. The lecture was proposed as "a defense of our right to adopt a believing attitude in religious matters, in spite of the fact that our merely logical intellect may not have been coerced."[9] Because it was proposed as a defense of the *right* to believe, the use of the word "will" in the title caused much mischief, and James admitted that "will" was misleading.

James begins by suggesting that whatever is proposed to our belief may be thought of as a hypothesis. And when we are faced with competing beliefs or hypotheses, we note that these alternatives possess certain affective qualities for the individual. First, persons respond to certain beliefs as either *live* or *dead*. A live hypothesis "is one that appeals to us as a real possibility."[10] If James were to have asked the students at Brown to believe in the Mahdi (the Islamic Messiah), he suggests that they would have found the belief "completely dead." To a Muslim, however, the hypothesis "is among the mind's possibilities; it is alive."[11] This shows that deadness and liveliness are not intrinsic properties in beliefs but are rel-

ative to particular individuals. They are measured by one's willingness to attend to the possibility, to act.

Second, James sees a decision between two hypotheses as being either *forced* or *avoidable*. To be told to choose between leaving the house with or without your umbrella is not forced since you may not have to go out at all. If, however, a person says "accept this truth or live without it" the option is forced.[12] There is no option beyond the alternative. Finally, hypotheses or beliefs can be *trivial* or *momentous*. An option is trivial when it is not unique and there is nothing to lose by not acting. Life is filled with these options. However, a momentous option involves a one and only chance when the stakes are high. And "he who refuses to embrace a unique opportunity loses the prize as surely as if he tried and failed."[13] Of course, a momentous decision, though live, need not be forced. A genuine religious decision, James proposes, is live, forced, and momentous.

James proceeds to argue that our thinking and believing proceed from the outset in a selective manner. That is, we always proceed with certain "doctrines assumed as facts," preconceptions, or "preexistent tendencies to believe." Thus it would seem wrong to talk of our beliefs being modified by our will. We cannot "by just willing it, believe that Abraham Lincoln's existence is a myth."[14] There has to be some live, preexisting tendency to believe. This is what James finds wrong with Pascal's famous "wager argument" in which he tries to force belief in Christianity in a manner similar to our mode of reasoning in a game of chance. For Pascal, a person faced with the option of believing or not believing in God is in a situation similar to playing a game "which at the day of judgment will bring you either heads or tails."[15] Since the stakes in this wager are very high, even if there were countless chances but only one for God, "you ought to stake your all on God" for a finite loss resulting from error would be real but reasonable, but the possible gain would be "eternal beatitude." So, Pascal argues, "Go, then, and take holy water, and have masses said; belief will come and stupify your scruples. . . . At bottom what have you to lose?"[16]

The problem with this type of argument is that for many, say for the Muslim, or the Protestant for that matter, there is no preexisting tendency to believe in masses or holy water; there is no living option. "The talk of believing by our volition seems, then, from one point of view simply silly. From another point of view it is worse than silly, it is vile." This has been the response of science to such subjective "voluntary smoke-wreaths."[17]

Unfortunately, many individuals caught up in the rugged, unsentimental new ethic of science had, James observed, passed over to the opposite extreme. They assumed that they had put their faith in reason alone. The English mathematician W. K. Clifford summarized this new rationalist ethic of belief when he robustly laid it down that "It is wrong always, everywhere, and for everyone, to believe anything on insufficient evidence."[18] James finds Clifford's demand to be all too sweeping and, as a scientist, he finds that Clifford had overlooked an obvious fact. Clifford falsely assumes that pure reason is what settles our opinions.[19] Furthermore, Clifford comes loaded with preconceptions about knowledge and truth and, like the rest of us, he disbelieves all facts and theories for which he has no use. "Clifford's cosmic emotions find no use for Christian feelings."[20] Scientists refuse even to consider evidence for telepathy, for example, and even if it were true they would bond together to conceal it, because "it would undo the uniformity of Nature . . . without which scientists cannot carry on their pursuits."[21]

James's argument with Clifford is not meant to dismiss or even minimize the work and results of science but, rather, only to insist that it is an evident fact that our nonintellectual natures do influence our beliefs.[22] James sets down the following thesis:

Our passional nature not only lawfully may, but must, decide an option between propositions, whenever it is a genuine option that cannot by its nature be decided on intellectual grounds; for to say, under such circumstances, "Do not decide, but leave the question open," is itself a passional decision—just like deciding yes or no—and is attended with the same risk of losing the truth.[23]

James points out that numerous great philosophers have proposed different foundational doctrines and tests for what is true. But no test of these various claims have ever been agreed upon. Yet the dogmatist claims not only that he or she can attain the truth but *can know when* it is attained. So when the Cliffords of this world say how immoral it is to believe in Christianity on "'insufficient evidence,' insufficiency is really the last thing they have in mind. For them the evidence is absolutely sufficient, only it makes the other way. They believe so completely in an antichristian order of the universe that there is no living option."[24] James, too, believes that we can attain the truth, but not based on some *a priori* absolutist conception of what constitutes objective evidence.

A further moral consideration of some importance regarding the duty of believing requires comment. James distinguishes between two separate laws that govern one's duty in this regard:

We must know the truth; and we must avoid error. . . . Clifford . . . exhorts us to the latter course. Believe nothing . . . keep your mind in suspense forever, rather than by closing it on insufficient evidence incur the awful risk of believing lies."[25]

James finds it impossible to follow Clifford. "For my own part," he writes, "I have also a horror of being duped; but I believe that worse things than being duped can happen to a man in this world."[26] Clifford's exhortation "is like a general informing his soldiers that it is better to keep out of battle forever than to risk a single wound."[27] Both options are, in any case, based on our passional life and not on reason alone. To those who may demur at James's insistence on the determination of our passional nature, he offers a clarification before proceeding to his conclusion. Of course, he acknowledges, that when an option between losing or gaining the truth is trivial and not momentous, we can easily forego the chance of gaining truth and save ourselves from the chance of believing falsehoods.[28] In such cases—and it often is the rule in science—when there is no forced option, dispassion should be the ideal. But moral and religious questions often present us with situations in which we are forced to act without complete evidence. In such instances the belief can only be verified *through* an initial trust and belief. Take personal relationships. *Do you like me or not?* . . . Whether you do or not depends, in countless instances, on whether I meet you half-way, am willing to assume that you like me, and show you trust and expectation. . . . But if I stand aloof, and refuse to budge an inch until I have objective evidence . . . ten to one your liking never comes.[29]

So there are cases *"where faith in a fact can help create the fact."*[30] And it would be insane in such instances to say that belief running ahead of objective evidence was immoral. Where truths are dependent on your action in the "laboratory of life," belief or faith is not only lawful but may be indispensable. In view of such a shocking claim, it needs to be stressed that James is talking about moral and religious truth, existential truth that is urgent but seldom or never reaches complete certitude. James is not talking about faith creating a fact in the choosing of a model of automobile. Nor can belief in God make God exist. Yet belief in God might make *possible* the verification of God's reality just as a scientist's belief in some reality might make possible the scientist's discovery or verification of that reality. Evidence will be withheld from us until our attention and action are engaged.

The religious hypothesis says two things: (1) "that the best things are the more eternal things" and (2) "that we are better off even now if we believe her first affirmation to be true."[31] Assuming that the religious hypothesis is a live option, we recognize that religion is a *momentous* option, because by it we gain or lose "a vital good." Second, it is a *forced* option in regard to that good. We cannot escape by remaining in doubt and waiting for more evidence, for one loses the good. It is like the man who refuses to ask a woman to marry him because he is not absolutely sure that she will prove to be the perfect wife.[32] Reason alone cannot resolve the question because the available evidence is never entirely unambiguous.

To preach skepticism to us as a duty until "sufficient evidence" for religion be found is, tantamount therefore to telling us . . . that to yield to our fear of its being error is wiser and better than to yield to our hope that it may be true. . . . Dupery for dupery, what proof is there that dupery through hope is so much worse than dupery through fear?[33]

James, for one, can see no proof of the skeptic's claim—and insists that we have the right to believe at our own risk any hypothesis that is live, forced, and momentous enough to engage our will.

James's "Will to Believe" was not well received by his philosophical colleagues, including Josiah Royce and George Santayana. The general complaint was that James was legitimizing "wishful thinking" and a "will to deceive." An analysis of many of the critiques shows, however, that they ignored the careful limitations that James had placed on the role of the will in believing. James, for example, insisted that the "liveness" of any proposal must be "among the mind's possibilities," and that implied for him certain socially shared agreements on what experience is in accord with reality, as well as the verdict of an individual's other broad range of experiences. James believed that all of this served as both a measure of and a control against sheer emotional anarchy. Furthermore, critics both then and now fail to take seriously the limited scope that James intended for the application of his proposal, namely, situations in which an individual feels absolutely *compelled* to decide between two disjunctive beliefs when the evidence for either is ambiguous and does not allow for a purely rational settlement. To reply that most cases allow for a tentative belief that may be further tested is to miss the distinctive point of James's entire argument.

"The Varieties of Religious Experience": An Empirical Exploration

In 1901–1902 James delivered the twenty Gifford Lectures that became *The Varieties of Religious Experience*—what one historian has called "the most famous of all American treatises on religion."[34] James sought to appeal "directly to the concrete facts"; that is, to what could be observed biologically, psychologically, and morally in the life of religious individuals. The work is striking for its time because James claims that what makes an experience religious is not in the nature of the person—for example, psychological—but something in the nature of the object and the reactions to that object. Pursuing something of a phenomenological method, James wishes initially to "bracket" the question of the existence of the object—God, the Infinite, and so on—and to concentrate on the meaning and value of religious experience, the phenomena as it is empirically exhibited. Although some important things may be learned about religious experience from the search for origins, James opposed the reductionism that was evident in theories such as those proposed by E. B. Tylor or J. G. Frazer. On the other hand, he rejected the idea of a single spiritual essence or a unique religious *a priori* that is present in all humans and is not available to scientific investigation, as was claimed by some theologians and religious philosophers.

James refers to the reductionists as "medical materialists" who "finish up Saint Paul by calling his vision on the road to Damascus a discharging lesion of the occipital cortex, he being an epileptic."[35] To reduce spiritual experience solely to physiological causes, in an effort to deny the experience's value, is arbitrary, unless we are willing to do the same for all other states of consciousness. All states of mind, whether they be healthy or morbid, scientific or religious, are, of course, organically conditioned, but that does not explain (or explain away) their full significance. For that "one must always look to [a subject's] more completely evolved and perfect form."[36] A scientific study of religion will not, then, focus its attention on stunted or secondhand religious life, but rather on "original experiences which were pattern-setters"—that is, "on geniuses in the religious line," persons who "have been creatures of exalted emotional sensibility."[37] And in the end the test of their experience and belief will be to

apply the empiricist criterion: "By their fruits ye shall know them, not by their roots."[38]

James limits his exploration to the personal dimensions ("inner dispositions") of religious experience, ignoring the various institutional forms of religious expression that increasingly engaged contemporary social scientists. He also was concerned to avoid a conception or definition of religion that would be too narrow. He did not perceive any single essence of religion or any elementary religious sentiment or emotion. "There is religious fear, religious love, religious awe, religious joy, and so forth. But religious love is only man's natural emotion of love directed to a religious object . . . and similarly of all the various sentiments which may be called into play in the lives of religious persons." Specific religious states of mind are simply psychic emotions attached to a specific sort of object, the supernatural or divine. For James, religion means "the feelings, acts, and experiences of individual men in their solitude, so far as they apprehend themselves to stand in relation to whatever they may consider divine."[39] Religious experience is also distinctive in its being something serious and solemn, not trivial. "If glad it must not grin or snicker, if sad, it must not scream or curse."[40]

In the essays that follow in the *Varieties*, James offers a series of typologies of the religious personality. The first is the contrast between the "healthy-minded" person and the "sick soul." Happiness in the deeper sense of joy is the mark of religion, for it is connected with a sense of the presence of the abiding and eternal. But it takes different forms. One form is associated with the healthy-minded person. This type of individual is congenitally happy and naturally optimistic and dwells on the beauty and goodness of life, despite all the counter evidence of evil and sorrow that surrounds them. Such persons feel a deep communion with the Divine, which they experience as beneficent, kind, and merciful. Their own limitations or faults do not weigh heavily on them, and therefore they do not dwell on a sense of sin or unrighteousness. Evil is for them an unreality—it is merely the way that one thinks of an experience. Evil can be "converted into a bracing and tonic good" by a change of attitude. James sees examples of the healthy-minded religion in New England Transcendentalism, and in some forms of liberal Christianity, but it is most evident in Indian Vedantism and in "New Thought" and "Mind-Cure," the latter movements then prevalent in America. Christian Science is, perhaps, the best known of this type. These sects tend to be pantheistic, in that they experience the Divine as present within the self.[41]

The religion of the healthy-minded rejects the fervent moral pulse taking of the Calvinist Puritans, their intensity and strenuous religious mood. Rather, it teaches surrender and passivity, resigning the care of one's being and destiny to higher powers within—to a greater Self. James was struck by the considerable appeal of healthy-minded religious belief, but also by its optimism, its confidence in the powers of the mind, its appeal to a trusting resignation—beliefs that bore fruit in the bodily and mental experience of these people. For others, however, the facts of experience are radically different; they would claim that the healthy minded are living in a fools' paradise. That is the judgment of the "sick soul."

The sick soul is a person possessed of a morbid and pessimistic temperament, one persuaded of the intractable reality of sin and evil. Some people see evil as a maladjustment that is curable by modifying one's behavior. The sick soul sees sin as "something ineradicable ingrained in our natural subjectivity and never to be removed by any superficial piecemeal operations."[42] The experiences of fear and danger, of the emptiness and weariness of life, of the precariousness of fame, health, and life's joys can overwhelm the sick soul unexpectedly at any moment. Many of our geniuses have been plagued by these morbid feelings: Luther, Goethe, Bunyan, Tolstoy—and James himself, who writes of the sick soul as one who knows the experience firsthand. Tolstoy typifies the profound sadness and malaise brought on by a sense of life's meaninglessness. What terrified Tolstoy was that the experience struck him when his life was at the flood tide of success, wealth,

fame, and domestic happiness. All at once he saw all of life as "a stupid cheat."[43]

Another type of the sick soul is burdened by a profound sense of unworthiness, of failure and sin. John Bunyan typifies this temperament, a person "sensitive of conscience to a diseased degree": "My original and inward pollution, that was my plague and my affliction. By reason of that I was more loathsome in my own eyes than was a toad; and I thought I was in God's eyes too. . . . Sure, thought I, I am forsaken of God; and thus I continued for some years together."[44]

The sick soul requires more than a mental "analgesic" proffered by an optimistic mind-curist. What the sick soul requires is a "second birth," a liberation from a form of death that can be wrought only by a power outside the feeble and ineffectual self. James thought that both types of religious experience were genuine and appropriate for different natures. The healthy minded refuses, however, to face the facts of radical evil, a reality that James believed is often the only thing that can open "our eyes to the deepest levels of truth." Morbid-mindedness also "ranges over the wider scale of experience." Therefore, the completest religions seem to James to be those like Buddhism and Christianity, which "are essentially religions of deliverance: the man must die to an unreal life before he can be born into the real life." The religious theme of deliverance leads James to the subject of conversion or the second birth.

Conversion is the process, sudden or gradual, in which a divided self gains unity, regeneration, assurance, stability, and happiness after a period of disunity and distress. James describes the process in terms of the psychological function of human aims and interests. As life proceeds we all experience a change of interests. Some interests become central and vital; toward others we become indifferent and dead. Our vital interests serve as "the centres of our dynamic energy." When one aim displaces all its rivals as our "vital centre," we speak of it as a "transformation"[45]; if the change is a religious one, we call it a *conversion*. How these changes come about and act so decisively is never wholly explainable, either to the subject or to the outside observer. Often the most important influences work unconsciously. Frequently a perception or an emotional shock will bring about the transformation and with it a new sense of stability and security.

James believed that many conversion experiences were due "to 'uprushes' into the ordinary consciousness of energies originating in the subliminal parts of the mind"—in the subconscious life. But the value and significance of such inexplicable events must not be dismissed because of their psychic origin. They, too, must be decided on empirical grounds exclusively: "If the *fruits for life* of the state of conversion are good, we ought to idealize and venerate it, even though it be a piece of natural psychology; if not, we ought to make short work with it, no matter what supernatural being may have infused it." After all, they may come only by way of nature, "or worse still, be counterfeited by Satan."[46] In any case, James is unwilling to judge the *spiritual significance* of regenerative experiences by their natural, e.g., psychological, mechanisms or forms.

James was personally drawn to the accounts of the religious conversions of the great geniuses of history, and he deeply empathized with these "sick souls." Because of his own spiritual crisis and regenerative experience, James trusted the religious testimonies of a Luther and a Tolstoy. The spiritual effects they reported—despite the absurdity of much religiosity—still made religion "mankind's most important function." Religious conversion brought with it a "joyous conviction . . . the assurance that all is well." For the regenerates, the world takes on a new and beautiful aspect.

James uses the word "saintliness" (perhaps not the best term, due to its negative moralistic connotations in our culture) as "the collective name for the ripe fruits of religion." In the saint we see that the "spiritual emotions are the habitual centre of the personal energy," and that this energy, this "expulsive power of a higher affection," is marked by certain features, certain "ripe fruits" that distinguish the genuine religious life:

1. The feeling of being in a wider life than that of this world's selfish little interests . . . of the existence of an Ideal Power.
2. A sense of the friendly continuity of the ideal power with our own life, and a willing self-surrender to its control.
3. An immense elation and freedom, as the outlines of the confining self melt down.
4. A shifting of the emotional centre towards loving and harmonious affections towards "yes, yes," and away from "no," where the claims of the non-ego are concerned.[47]

The life of the person possessed of these religious characteristics will manifest certain practical effects and virtues. Among these are a willingness to surrender the self to the point of ascetic sacrifice; an enlarged capacity for patience and fortitude; an increase of charity and tenderness toward one's fellows; a greater feeling of equanimity, receptivity, and peace. Of course, all of these positive qualities can be, and sadly often are, taken to their spiritual extremes and perversions. Many critics of James's book thought it dwelt excessively on the hysterical and aberrant aspects of religious life. George Santayana spoke of it as "a slumming tour of the New Jerusalem."[48]

Most readers, however, commended James for his religious insight, his fellow feeling and impartiality. Ernst Troeltsch's assessment of the significance of James's work for Christian theology is especially foresighted.[49] He pointed out that James's pluralism and his rejection of any single root or essence of religion rightly opposed both the lingering vestiges of nineteenth-century Idealism and the confident reductionism of recent rationalism and scientism. James's investigations also sharpened and helped to reshape the question of the absoluteness of Christianity by focusing appreciatively on the rich variety of religious experience and belief. Finally, his scientific exploration of actual religious experience—again without reductive preconceptions—gave further impetus to a thoroughgoing empirical approach to a Christian theology in America. One of the earliest theologians to take up James's empiricist challenge was D. C. Macintosh of Yale. In 1910 he published an article entitled "Can Pragmatism Furnish a Philosophical Basis for Theology?" and he answered "yes," so long as pragmatism is based on a truly scientific empiricism, what he called a "critical realism." Both orthodox rationalism and Idealism were, in Macintosh's judgment, now antiquated and undermined, and the theologies of Schleiermacher and the Ritschlians, although an improvement, had proved too subjective and unscientific.

AMERICAN EMPIRICAL THEOLOGY: DOUGLAS CLYDE MACINTOSH

D. C. Macintosh (1877–1948) devoted his career to reinterpreting Christian theology in terms of an empirical, critical realism. In 1909, William James remarked: "Let empiricism once become associated with religion, as hitherto, through some strange misunderstanding, it has been associated with irreligion, and I believe that a new era of religion, as well as philosophy, will be ready to begin."[50] Macintosh took James's counsel and made it the motto of his first theological work, *Theology as an Empirical Science* (1919).

Macintosh was born in Breadalbane, Ontario, and graduated from McMaster University in Toronto. He did graduate work in philosophy and theology at the University of Chicago, where he came under the influence of the Chicago School in the persons of Edward Scribner Ames, Shailer Mathews, G. B. Foster, and G. B. Smith. Foster and Smith weaned Macintosh away from his youthful idealism and toward Ritschlianism and pragmatism. He was never entirely comfortable in these latter theological positions, however, because he felt it imperative that theology take up the metaphysical task. It was only after moving to Yale in 1909 that Macintosh began developing in earnest his own realistic empirical theology. In 1916 he became Dwight Professor of Theology, and in 1933 professor of theology and philosophy of religion. He also served as chairman of the Department of Religion in the Yale Graduate School from 1920 to 1938. Macintosh's most important theological works include *Theology as an Empirical Science* (1919), *The Reasonableness of Christianity* (1925), *The Pilgrimage of Faith* (1931),

"Experimental Realism in Religion," in *Religious Realism* (1931), and *The Problem of Religious Knowledge* (1940).

Macintosh's Method

Macintosh's theology developed out of his encounter with the empirical and experiential methods of the Chicago School and his reflections on James's writings on belief, but, like James, his own early religious experience was most decisive. He was raised in an orthodox and strongly evangelical home and, at the age of fourteen, at an evangelistic meeting, he experienced a deep sense of "assurance" that was "fundamentally determinative" in shaping his enduring faith.[51]

In his maturity, Macintosh was to leave behind the dogmatic method of traditional orthodoxy, but religious experience remained the groundwork and the criterion of religious truth. He saw theology as divided into two main types, the *conservative* and the *radical*. Conservative theology depends on an external authority, and it begins with the teaching of this authority, be it that of the Bible, or the Church, or some individual leader. It seeks to conserve the entire contents of this received doctrine.[52]

Macintosh regarded such a method as perilous, for if on the basis of reason or experience, it is not possible to hold to all of this traditional doctrinal content, the method requires a progressive substraction from it.[53] The radical theologian begins quite otherwise but may well end up with orthodox doctrines more reasonably and thus more firmly held.

The radical theologian, interested primarily in religious and theological certainty, refuses to begin with a docile acceptance of any doctrinal content . . . no matter how great the prestige of that authority. . . . Moreover, if the radical method has been happily chosen, it may lead in the end to a system containing all the vital truths to which the traditionalist clings so tenaciously, but often with so little final certainty.[54]

Empirical theology begins with religious experience but, unlike the psychology of religion, it is not interested in the subjective states of personal consciousness but, rather, in that which is experienced, in *knowledge of God*. Therefore, an empirical theology presupposes some type of realistic epistemology that can overcome the subjectivism that has plagued modern theology since Schleiermacher and Feuerbach, without at the same time falling into the dogmatic objectivism of traditional orthodoxy. Macintosh devotes much of his effort to developing and defending just such an epistemology, which he calls a "critical monistic realism." Critical monistic realism recognizes that the character of human knowledge conditions the nature of the object as known, and yet affirms that

there may still be such an existential unity or identity between them as to enable one to say with truth that an object which is real independently of our conscious experience has been presented in experience and directly known, even though not all the qualities of the object as presented need be thought of as belonging to it in its independent existence.[55]

Macintosh acknowledges that among the basic assumptions of an empirical or scientific theology is the claim to a genuine knowledge of reality in general—an assumption common to all science. Such a theology also presupposes the methods, principles, and established results of all the empirical sciences and this includes the results of historical, literary, and scientific criticism of sacred books, such as the Bible, and the reliable evidence regarding the great religious leaders, such as the historic Jesus.[56]

Another presupposition peculiar to empirical theology is the existence of God. In the physical sciences "one does not assume the physical world and then become sure of it, but assumes it because one is already practically sure of it." So in empirical theology, it may be expected that the theologian

will posit the existence of God—defined, to be sure, in preliminary fashion—because he is already practically sure, on the basis of religious experience, that God really exists. . . . On the basis of knowledge of God

through religious experience, one can scientifically assume *that* God is, although he may have as yet very little knowledge as to *what* God is. It is just this latter, viz., what God is, that is to be investigated through scientific theological observation and experiment under the guidance of definite working hypotheses.[57]

It should be emphasized again that for Macintosh theology is no different than other sciences in making this kind of foundational assumption.

Having established the presuppositions of a scientific theological inquiry, Macintosh proceeds to set apart the religious data with which an empirical theology must work. These data are *revelations* or the recognizable facts of the divine presence in the field of of our human experience. The criterion for discerning the real presence of the divine reality, that is, revelation, is that factor in the world that is value-producing in that it contributes to the right adjustment of human persons. Revelation is then the individual's perception of the religious value issuing in the right adjustment to the religious object or Divine Reality. "It is in this ethically holy human spirit, and in the process of making it more so, that we find the presence, or revelation, of the divine."[58]

It is clear that Macintosh simply assumes certain absolute and universal values and that human beings can discern them. As an ethical intuitionist, he holds that such values as rationality, righteousness, and unselfish love are "intuitively appreciable as intrinsic, ultimate, and universally valid, whether universally appreciated or not."[59] It follows that revelation, or the perception of religious value, is not restricted to Christian sources or experience, a point that Macintosh readily acknowledges.

In a scientific theology, naturally, other religions besides the Christian may present whatever universally valid empirical revelation they possess, and their contributions will be welcomed. Revelation is presumably as universal as experimental religion of any spiritual value.[60]

We are surprised, then, to hear Macintosh continue that, despite his understanding of revelation, our attention will naturally be directed to the data found in the Christian religion for "within the limits of experimental religion the *most normative* revelation of the divine is to be found, *apparently*, in the personal life and character of Jesus," because in the Bible we encounter "the most original available record of what *seems undoubtedly* to be the most significant progressive revelation in the history of experimental religion."[61] (italics added). Macintosh's criteria of normativeness are set forth here without any substantiation. Here, clearly, we encounter a curious blindspot in Macintosh's empirical method. He simply assumes the Christian system of values to be universally normative in any examination of humanity's religious experience. In fact, what Macintosh's empirical theology amounts to is a defense of the Christian religion on radically empirical grounds.

From his analysis of the distinctive data of an empirical theology, Macintosh next turns to the formulation of a body of empirically verified laws based on these data. As in the formulation of any scientific laws, certain constants and variables must be recognized. The constants in theology include the uniformity of nature, certain aspects of the social environment and of human nature in general, but most important "the being and character of God. This is *the Constant* of empirical theological laws."[62] Theology assumes the dependability of God to respond to the right religious adjustment by humans.

The variables in the formulation of theological laws include aspects of the social environment and the individual's training and capacity. In the light of the many unknown factors involved, theology can never claim to be an *exact* science. Nevertheless, Macintosh is assured that the value and direction that are the inherent features of the Constant's action may be discerned through empirical investigation.[63]

It is evident that Macintosh is opposed to those traditional theologies that give little or no place to the human response to the divine action. For Macintosh, God's positive action is contingent upon the right human religious adjustment. Such adjustment includes (1) concentration of

attention on God as the object of religious dependence and on those moral ends of which He is the source; (2) a wholehearted self-surrender to God and consecration of one's self to be worked upon and through by the divine power in the fulfillment of those morally desired ends; (3) a willed responsiveness to the divine guidance; and (4) a steady persistence in this religious attitude.

On the basis of such a religious adjustment, additional "elemental" and "composite" theological laws can be discovered. The laws of elemental religious experience include the receiving of moral aspiration for self-control and courage and for victory over temptation. The law of such elemental experiences may be stated in abbreviated form as follows:

"On condition of the right religious adjustment with reference to desired truly moral states of the will . . . God the Holy Spirit produces the specific moral results desired."[64]

Laws concerning what Macintosh calls "composite experiences" cover such traditional Christian experiences as "regeneration," "perseverance," "fullness of the Spirit," and "sanctification." Macintosh states the laws of regeneration and sanctification as follows:

The theological law of regeneration, or of the genesis of the new or essentially Christian life may be formulated thus: On condition of the right religious adjustment with a view to being turned permanently from sin and to God and the Christian way of life, God the Holy Spirit works primarily in the will and ultimately in the nature more generally the definite and manifest beginning of a new and specifically Christian spiritual life.[65]

The question that begs to be answered at this point, of course, is how does Macintosh know that these laws refer to the working of an external Reality—that is, God—and are not merely a description of the inner workings of the human psyche. The philosopher James Bissett Pratt raised just this question about Macintosh's theology:

It is probably a verifiable fact that when persons of a certain disposition and temperament and with proper training enter into and persist in a certain describable attitude toward a religious object regarded as real, differences of a certain describable sort in their spiritual experience may be depended upon to follow. This is probably a fact and a scientific fact—scientific because repeatable and verifiable. But it is a fact not of theology but of the psychology of religion.[66]

Macintosh's not very satisfactory reply to this kind of criticism is simply that, although such laws can be formulated as psychological laws, they are also justifiable evidences of the existence of God or a dependable factor *in* Reality, which is the real God of experimental religion.[67]

On the basis of the scientific laws of empirical theology, Macintosh believed we could claim scientific knowledge about what God *does*.

We may say that the Divine Reality is a reality that dependably responds to the right religious adjustment, that answers true prayer, that regenerates the human spirit, that maintains the regenerate life, that promotes the health of the spiritual life and develops essentially Christian ethico-religious character. Furthermore, this same Divine Reality convicts of sin, gives peace and joy, and "sheds abroad the love of God," in human hearts. . . .[68]

Normative Theology and Christian Belief

In Macintosh's view, all the above actions of God in the world can be known as strict scientific fact. However, scientific empirical theology is not the whole of theology and knowing what God *does* is not to know fully who God *is*. There are questions—for example, the oneness or unity of God—which lie outside the province of empirical theology. Scientific theology alone gives us *knowledge*, but it cannot answer all the legitimate questions of the theologians. In addition to scientific theology, there is a place for what Macintosh calls *normative theology*. Whereas scientific theology is based on perceptual intuitions, normative theology is grounded in strong subjective convictions concerning the nature of God that transcend our empirical experience. Macintosh believed it was entirely legitimate to hold beliefs

that are in accord with and support the realization of our highest ideals. Therefore, he was willing to accept a critical pragmatic criterion of belief similar to that of William James. Macintosh formulates this criterion as follows: "We have the right to believe that those theological doctrines are true which are necessary for . . . the maintenance of the morality which is necessary for the maintenance of the highest well-being of humanity."[69]

A theological belief is permissible if it accords with our scientific knowledge, does not contradict our empirical religious experience, appears at the same time practically necessary for the realization of our purposes or, in other words, appears to us as "reasonable." Macintosh was insistent that there was a vast difference between a crude utilitarian test and a reasonable will to believe. Special care must be taken to guard against any easy "rationalization" of one's own religious beliefs. To avoid such false rationalizations of Christian belief, certain procedures must be followed. These include assurance that our basic beliefs are not contradicted by known fact, that they are bound up with our critically examined values, and seen as essential to religion at its best, Christian or not. It is then necessary to see if this universal religion is also congruent with Christianity. If so, "we shall ask what additional content of historic Christianity seems essential, either because of its value in facilitating the realization of the true ideal of humanity or for any other reason, and we shall finally inquire whether this further content is reasonable and therefore presumably true."[70] On the basis of such a critical pragmatism, Macintosh believed that certain normative theological beliefs could be affirmed. These would include the belief that God is one, personal, and purposeful, as well as belief in human freedom and immortality.

All that is established so far about the action and being of God in empirical and normative theology is accomplished without any reference to the person or work of Jesus Christ—despite the fact that Macintosh thought of Christ as theologically "normative" in important ways. And this is perfectly consistent with Macintosh's intention, for *God* and *not* Christ is the final criterion of any theology. Our knowledge of God is fundamentally scientific (i.e., universal) and must not be tied to the contingencies of a particular historical revelation. In fact, Macintosh believes that apologetically there is considerable advantage in showing how much can be scientifically established as consistent with positive Christianity, thereby demonstrating Christian belief to be both scientifically verifiable and rationally justifiable, without reference to past historical authority:

We escape the danger of infecting the entire content of essential Christian belief with the necessary incertitude of historical opinion. All that has been said of the reasonableness and truth of Christianity is demonstrably valid, whether we have any Christology or not, and whatever we may or may not believe about the historic Jesus. It would still be valid if it should turn out that Jesus was essentially different from what has been commonly believed, or even that he was not truly historical at all.[71]

The reason for this is that the Christian moral ideal is true apart from the historical question as to how far it was realized or taught by the historical Jesus.[72]

All this is not to say that Jesus is unimportant. First of all, belief in the historical Jesus has proven psychologically valuable in the Christian nurture of countless millions, and appeal to the historic Jesus Christ has had tremendous pedagogical value, the moral example of Jesus being the pivotal influence in the lives of many in the experience of redemption and reconciliation. All Macintosh wants to assert is that belief in the historicity of Jesus is not *logically* indispensable to the exercise of an essentially Christian faith. Nevertheless, while not indispensable, the logical value of the historic Jesus is very great indeed. For if we acknowledge the distinction between historical and scientific fact and can *assume* the historical fact of Jesus, "we can point to a more impressive instance of individual verification of the Christian type of faith in his experience than is to be found anywhere. . . . In his experience the reality of an uplifting power, able to deliver from evil on condition of the right reli-

gious adjustment, was amply demonstrated."[73] Jesus is the perfect exemplification of the right religious adjustment to God.[74]

It must be stressed, however, that such a doctrine does not require the denial of the divine immanence elsewhere. Quite the contrary. The Christian doctrines of Christ and the Holy Spirit

taken with the evolutionary concept, suggest once more a wider divine immanence as the necessary precondition of the specialized immanence in Christ and the Christlike. But the acme of immanence is incarnation. God was in Christ, and it is there that we most surely and satisfactorily find him.[75]

As in the case of the person of Christ, so in our understanding of Christ's work: We begin first with his example and proceed to a deeper conception.

In so far as man is led by this inspiring moral *example* to adopt Jesus' principle and imitate from the heart his way of life, he is *at one* with God.

But the moral example of Jesus brings to sinful man a feeling of self-condemnation, and not inspiration alone. When Jesus is viewed not as human simply but as divine . . . when the pure self-giving love of Christ is taken as *revelation* of the love and grace of God, then sinful man is impelled to come to God in repentence and trust, in self-surrender and love. Thus, through responding to the love and grace of God, man becomes reconciled to God at heart and fulfils, in sincere repentence, the necessary moral condition of forgiveness, or what is called in less personal terms justification.[76]

Macintosh agreed with Liberal theology in rejecting a purely objective and individualistic view of substitutionary atonement. With the Ritschlians, he saw redemption in social terms: "Full atonement is impossible without the at-one-ment, or unification of man with man in a universal brotherhood. Full atonement is thus not a fact of past history, but an ideal for the future."[77]

From this analysis of Macintosh's theology, it is clear that although his *method* is radically different from that of the Ritschlians, the *content* of his theology is at many points hardly distinguishable from that of evangelical liberalism. His concentration on Jesus as moral exemplar, as having the value of God, his conception of Christ's person as being different from that of other humans in degree only, and his conception of the work of Christ are in all essentials consistent with Ritschlian theology. Where Macintosh's radical modernism is most evident is in his commitment to a strictly scientific method and in his assurance that the essentials of Christian belief could be established quite independently of any appeal to special revelation. The latter, especially, separated Macintosh from the Ritschlians, all of whom *began* with the Christocentric principle and held firmly to the interdependence of Christian experience *and* positive historical revelation. The evangelical liberals were fundamentally opposed to Macintosh's logical separation of Christian belief from knowledge of the *historical* Jesus Christ.

In a more pluralistic context one reads Macintosh with considerable bafflement, for it is impossible to shake the conviction that, despite his scientific and empirical pretensions, his theology is built on a specious circular argument. He begins by claiming that our knowledge of God is derived from "universal" religious experience of the "right religious adjustment." But how does one judge a "right religious adjustment"? How does one make a proper selection from the vast data of religious experience? Macintosh blithely informs us that such a selection "presupposes sufficient progress in religious discrimination to be able to distinguish the distinctly divine elements within the human experience" and then, presumably on the basis of his own intuitions, sets it down that

within the limits of experimental religion the most normative revelation of the divine is to be found, apparently, in the personal life and character of Jesus . . . in the resultant Christian experience of "salvation," and in the developing "Kingdom of God."[78]

Why Macintosh accepts Jesus's "religious adjustment" as normative is never clarified. On the one hand, Jesus gives us the supreme example of the "right religious adjustment"; on the other hand, Jesus's adjustment is "right" because it encourages those values that Christians "perceive" to be divine. What he sets out to prove experimentally is predetermined by his commitment to a given religious tradition.[79] Macintosh's empirical theology lacks conviction because his Christian commitments put very obvious limits on what he claims are the "universal" and "objective" standards of his "scientific" theology.

AMERICAN THEOLOGICAL MODERNISM AND NATURALISM: HENRY NELSON WIEMAN

Background: John Dewey and the Chicago School

It was noted that, while radical in his commitment to scientific method, D. C. Macintosh was evangelical both in spirit and in his defense of several traditional Christian doctrines. A number of the scholars at the Divinity School at the University of Chicago were more radically freed from traditional Christian doctrine in formulating their own versions of an empirical and Modernist Christian theology. This was true of Shailer Mathews, but especially of Edward Scribner Ames and Henry Nelson Wieman, the latter representing the farthest extreme of American theological modernism and naturalism. All three of these men were deeply influenced by the philosopher John Dewey's commitment to scientific inquiry and to his instrumentalism; that is, to the process of achieving creative human ideals and values—although as theologians they emphasized the religious significance of Dewey's instrumentalism.

For Dewey the self is a social self and exists only in the context of its social relatedness. Following the lead of Darwin, Dewey believed that we should study human life in terms of the ways an organism adjusts to its environment. Ideas and values, e.g., truth, beauty, and so on, are not to be viewed as immutable, transcendently grounded truths, but rather should be understood in the way in which they *function* and enhance creative human interchange. Truth is not something absolute; there are only "truths" that must be tested by inquiry and experience. So the meaning of a thing is the way it functions. The value of an idea or action is to be discovered in the way it serves the process of individual or social adjustment. Human beings and their communities are organisms confronted with problems and they seek adjustment and the satisfaction of their needs. Science, philosophy, and even religion are communities of persons seeking certain ideals or goals. Now this can be done by appeal to outworn traditions and dogmas or by open, cooperative inquiry guided by the scientific method. Dewey believed that dogmas and traditions inhibited the necessary process of creative encounter with new problems and needs. The Chicago theologians agreed. It was only through devotion to the modern spirit of scientific inquiry that Christianity could continue to function in the contemporary world.

Shailer Mathews, who served as dean of the University of Chicago Divinity School from 1908 to 1933, always insisted that the starting point of a Modernist Christianity must be "Jesus Christ as the revelation of a Savior God." "The Modernist," he wrote, "knows no other center for his faith." He also believed, however, that the Modernist is not to be tied to outworn forms and dogmas. Just as the Church Fathers used Hellenistic philosophy and the medieval Schoolmen followed Aristotle, so the Modernist Christian must use the "*scientific, historical, social method in understanding and applying evangelical Christianity to the needs of living persons.*" Mathews's struggle against the rising tide of Fundamentalism in America in the 1920s convinced him that the older orthodoxy had failed and, if allowed to prevail, would lead Christianity to extinction.

The world needs new control of nature and society and is told that the Bible is verbally inerrant. It needs a means of composing class strife, and is told to believe in the substitutionary atonement. It needs a spirit of love and justice and is told that love without orthodoxy will not save from hell. . . . It needs to find God in the processes of nature and is told that he who believes in evolution cannot believe in God. It needs faith in the divine presence in human affairs and is told it must accept the virgin birth of Christ.[80]

Mathews believed that only a Modernist Christianity could restore Christian faith to what he understood as its evangelical message and could preserve it for the future. This theme is set forth in his most popular book, *The Faith of Modernism* (1924). In this work one can observe Mathews balancing precariously between what he considered his loyalty to the truths of "evangelical Christianity" and his allegiance to the modern scientific *Zeitgeist*. Other representatives of the Chicago School—Edward Scribner Ames and, most notably, Henry Nelson Wieman—were willing to move beyond the orbit of a normative Christian position and to develop a new naturalistic theology.

Henry Nelson Wieman

H. N. Wieman (1884–1975) was forthright in asserting that the Christian *theological tradition* is not an adequate guide for humanity. He believed that scientific inquiry and not tradition is the constructive principle and power that will shape our lives in this modern technological age. "The bomb that fell on Hiroshima," he wrote, "cut history in two like a knife. Before and after are two different worlds. That cut is more abrupt, decisive, and revolutionary than the cut made by the star over Bethlehem."[81] Many critics have held that Wieman's relationship to the Christian tradition is so tenuous that referring to him as a *Christian* theologian is confusing in the extreme. Wieman was constantly questioned as to whether he considered himself a Christian theologian or a philosophical theist freed from the perspective of any positive tradition. He had little patience with this kind of query, and he had no desire to appropriate for himself the name of Christian if anyone was eager to question his right to do so. The ambivalent answer that he gave to the philosopher Edwin A. Burtt perhaps expresses most accurately Wieman's view of his vocation as a theologian:

I find it difficult to answer this question without causing misunderstanding. Certainly I am shaped and biased by the tradition in which I was reared. *The Christian tradition with its error, its evil and its truth, is my chief source. Yet I strongly resent the current practice of appealing to the Christian and Jewish tradition as being the guide to life and identifying this tradition with God rather than seeking what operates in all human life to create, save, and transform.*[82](italics added)

Henry Nelson Wieman graduated from Park College in Missouri in 1907. Three years later he completed his seminary course at San Francisco Theological Seminary. This was followed by two years of study in Germany at Jena and Heidelberg under the philosopher Wilhelm Windelband and Ernst Troeltsch. Neither Harnack nor Troeltsch awakened any interest in Wieman, who remarked at the time that "history cannot tell us how to live." Like John Dewey, Wieman felt that we were living in a new period and that the past could help us very little. This bias against history remained with Wieman and it cut his theology loose from any historical tradition. If anything, his religious language is reminiscent of the now-quaint psychological terminology of the 1920s and 1930s.

Upon his return to this country, Wieman served four years in a Presbyterian pastorate in California. In 1915 he moved to Harvard to work toward the doctorate in the Department of Philosophy. His teachers, William Ernest Hocking and Ralph Barton Perry, had considerable influence on Wieman at this time, and Perry's concern with the theory of value remained for Wieman a lifelong interest.

While at Harvard Wieman became acquainted with the work of John Dewey and it was Dewey who forced Wieman to see something that became for him an enduring commitment:

Inquiry concerning what makes for the good and evil of human life must be directed to what actually and observably operates in human life. Otherwise, the inquiry will produce misleading illusions. . . . The transcendent, the supernatural, the ineffable, the infinite, the absolute being itself, and other such ideas inevitably lead inquiry astray unless they can be identified with something which observably operates in human life.[83]

Bergson's and Whitehead's concern with process and creativity also had a formative influence on Wieman. Through the years, however, Wieman became less and less interested in process metaphysics and showed an ever-increasing affinity with Dewey's experimentalism and instrumentalism in his own delineation of the creative process.

Wieman began his teaching career at Occidental College. In 1927 he moved to the Divinity School of the University of Chicago, where he remained as professor of the philosophy of religion until his retirement in 1949. Among his most important theological writings are *Religious Experience and Scientific Method* (1926), *The Wrestle of Religion with Truth* (1927), *The Source of Human Good* (1946), *The Directive in History* (1949), and *Man's Ultimate Commitment* (1958).

When Wieman arrived at Chicago, Ritschlian theology was in decline in American Protestantism and what was to be called Neo-Orthodoxy had not yet made its impact on this side of the Atlantic. The disaster of World War I had called into question the social idealism of Walter Rauschenbusch and the Social Gospel. The Christocentric emphasis in Ritschlian theology long had left unanswered many searching questions about the doctrine of God. Protestant liberalism in the 1920s was marked by a subjectivism that was hardly distinguishable from religious humanism. Wieman wanted to break through this subjectivism and humanism and to restore the objective reference (i.e., God) within religious experience. And it was during the 1920s through the 1940s that he provided a distinctly American theistic answer to an advancing humanism. Wieman was to do for a Modernist Christian theology in America what Karl Barth was doing for Continental theology; that is, directing the attention of the theologians from subjective religious feelings to the sovereign objectivity of God. Speaking of Wieman's place in the religious history of this time, a student and colleague of Wieman's has written:

He spoke out of the American experience at a specific time in our history when the fate of the liberal era hung in the balance. In many respects, he bypassed the main concerns of liberal theology; yet at a time when liberalism in America was being threatened by its own logic—a logic which led to humanism—Wieman proved a formidable antagonist to religious humanism. For many American liberals during the 1920's, particularly in the Middle West and Southwest, he reopened the way to a theistic faith.[84]

Wieman's Radical Modernism

Wieman wanted to insist on the absolute priority of God, but he refused to do so by turning back to the theological tradition, to the Bible, to the Fathers, or the Reformers, as was being done by theologians such as Karl Barth. Wieman regarded these traditions as no longer adequate. In his view, tradition was the repository of evocative words and symbols that confused desires and sentiments with reality. For Wieman there was only one kind of knowledge that could free us from subjective illusion—the knowledge achieved by scientific method, by experience and testing. Theology thus required a complete reconstruction based on the model of John Dewey's *Reconstruction in Philosophy*.

Two views have been held concerning the way we know God. One has asserted that we must know God just as we know any other object; that there are no other powers or faculties of knowledge except those by which we know ordinary objects; and that we must know God as we know trees and houses and men or else not know Him at all. The other view has tried to show that knowledge of God is a special kind of knowledge; that there is a certain feeling, inner sense . . . instinct or intuition, faith, spiritual organ, moral will or what not, which has God as its special object. . . . We hold this view wrong . . . because it resorts to a peculiar and mysterious faculty. . . . These mysterious faculties of discernment have long since been regarded as mythical by psychology and epistemology. . . . To cling still to such a view with respect to discernment of God is to put the knowledge of God outside the field of scientific knowledge, where it can be neither examined nor tested.[85]

According to Wieman, knowledge of God must be subjected to the scientific method of experiment and this means that God, like any other being, must be perceptible in experience.

Surely any object that sustains human life must affect our senses. Since God is that something that sustains human life he sustains the senses and hence affects the senses. . . . But anything that affects the senses is an object that may be perceived when men learn to note and interpret its sensuous effect. Hence God is an object to be perceived through sense experience. We do not mean that he must necessarily have a certain spatial magnitude. . . . But we do mean that there must be ways of apprehending sense experience which would reveal to a competent observer the presence and character of that Something upon which human life is ultimately dependent for its maximum security and abundance. When this way of apprehending becomes established as a form of habitual reaction rendered accurate through experimental tests, we perceive God.[86]

In the above statement, and elsewhere in his writings, Wieman makes it clear that an empirical knowledge of God includes two factors. First, all perceptual knowledge involves certain requisite habits. We have developed those habits necessary to perceive trees and houses. The trained scientist is disciplined to perceive things not observed by the untrained layman. And so it is with our knowledge of God. Such knowledge comes only through the development of certain habits such as worship, prayer, the cultivation of certain values and openness to new values. Through these habits new awareness and new visions of possible good can be opened up. But the rich increment of these data of religious experience does not give us knowledge by itself. Second, it must be tested by critical analysis and shown to be consistent with the whole range of scientifically verified knowledge, and then further tested in ongoing experience. Knowledge of God requires an alternation between creative, new experience and critical test.

Unlike Macintosh's theology, Wieman's empirical theism demands a thoroughgoing naturalistic worldview. This means that there can be no ultimate separation of God from nature. God, however finally defined, must be a natural process or structure that can be known like any other natural entity. Wieman speaks of his doctrine as the "newer naturalism" to distinguish it not only from supernaturalism but also from the older naturalism, which tended toward a reductionistic materialism. Although the newer naturalism holds that all reality consists basically of spatiotemporal events, it does not deny that this reality includes qualities and values that make life infinitely rich. What naturalism does assert is

that there is nothing in reality accessible to the human mind more basic than events and their qualities and relations. ("Relations" is another word for structure.) No knowable cause or explanation for anything that happens can reach deeper than events and their structure and qualities.[87]

This is to demand that an empirical theology have no recourse to any "transcendental grounds, orders, causes, or purposes" beyond events, their qualities, and relations.

We ignore the transcendental affirmation in the Jewish Christian tradition of a creative God who not only works in history but resides beyond history. The only creative God we recognize is the creative event itself. So also we ignore the transcendental affirmation in the Greek Christian tradition of the reality of Forms of value, uncreated and eternal. . . . The only forms of value we recognize are produced by the creative event. . . . The form of the creative event itself at our higher levels of existence is determined by the creative process at more elementary levels. . . .

These claims rest upon an analysis of our experience, revealing that no transcendental reality could ever *do* anything. It could not make the slightest difference in our lives except in the form of something happening, some event. . . . But when the transcendental becomes an event it is no longer transcendental.[88]

Wieman is convinced that of all the factors presently obstructing the creative advance of human life, theologies based on faith in a transcendent, supernatural God are among the most dangerous to humanity's future. There are two types of theological transcendence that Wieman rejects as imperiling human salvation. One is a theology transcendent of time; the other is a theology transcendent of reason. Of the former he writes:

To set up any eternal, superhistorical, time-transcending reality as the ground and goal of our existence, the meaning and purpose of all we do, the recipient and fulfiller of our sacrifice, is to throw us back helplessly into the temporal process, for there alone can any difference be made. It throws us back *helplessly* because, having put all our faith and hope upon the eternal, we are incapacitated for seeking out and finding in the temporal world that creative event which does, in fact, find progressive fulfilment in and through our lives when we meet the conditions demanded.[89]

Wieman believes that twentieth-century existentialist and Neo-Orthodox theologies, exemplified in the work of Paul Tillich and Karl Barth, are especially pernicious because of their emphasis on a theism that transcends human reason. Tillich speaks of God as "Being-itself" or "the power of being," transcending all cognitive symbols and structures. God, therefore, does not exist, because existence presupposes some definite, limiting structure or form. Wieman asserts that Tillich's talk of God's mystery and nonexistence courts harmful illusions and opens the way for the helpless play of the emotions.

What commands our faith has a structure by which it can be known and distinguished from other kinds of being. To know this structure we must have cognitive symbols. In opposition to Tillich, I contend that God is not the unknowable mystery.[90]

In a different fashion, Barth is charged with placing our knowledge of God beyond any empirical or rational test.

The truth about God as set forth by Barth is beyond the reach of all the powers of human knowledge. Only by a special gift of God can one believe and know it. This truth cannot be found in holy scriptures unless God has given you the freedom to know and believe. But how can anyone detect what is error and what is truth if all the ordinary tests are repudiated save only the freedom to believe given by God?[91]

The Doctrine of God

If Wieman rejects any conception of God as independent of temporal events, and thus independent of human experience and reason, how does he conceive of the reality of God? Does God's radical immanence in nature mean that God lacks transcendence and sovereignty over humans? What of the traditional attributes of God? What of God's self-relevation in Christ?

To understand Wieman's doctrine of God, it is imperative that we recognize his basic ontological assumptions. With the process philosophers (e.g., Henri Bergson and Alfred North Whitehead), Wieman holds that ultimate reality does not consist of levels or orders of disconnected atomic objects and agents but, rather, of an organic *process of events and their qualities*. Wieman begins with the immediacy of events, their felt qualities, and their relations or conjunctions. On this fundamental ontology, he builds his theory of value and his doctrine of God. In analyzing the qualities, events, and processes that make up reality, what is the absolute good—that is, that factor that is the source of creative human good—that produces and sustains value? According to Wieman, quality is the root of any value theory. Value grows through increasing the extent to which a life is able to experience the manifold qualities of the world. The more qualities we take in, the more worth our lives take on. However, the felt quality of life is enhanced by meaning. Meaning joins or relates the parts of experience so that something experienced in the present can convey qualities of past events and potential values. The world takes on more qualitative meaning. It is this qualitative meaning that Wieman identifies with the *created good* of life. Qualitative meaning or created good is *intrinsic good*, for it is not simply instrumental to the achievement or some other good.

Is there any good that is greater than the created good of qualitative meaning? There is, says Wieman, and it is that which produces qualitative meaning. It is *creative good* or the *creative event*. If there is anything better than created good it is the process, the event, that continues,

through all frustrations and destructive conflicts, to produce qualitative meaning. *God is this creative event.*

Here again, we see Wieman's break with the theological tradition. The tradition conceived of God as a being transcendent of the world. But, if reality consists of events and their qualities, then God must be that process or event that is the source of all our created good. God must be thought of functionally, not substantially. And to ask what produces human good or how the growth of qualitative meaning occurs is to ask an empirical question that can be answered only by experience that is open to all who would take the proper care. What we can thereby know about God may not wholly encompass the divine reality but it will be genuine knowledge.

Wieman has described the working of God or the creative event in slightly different ways,[92] but his fullest analysis is given in *The Source of Human Good* in terms of a fourfold event.[93] The four subevents are described as follows:

(1) *The emerging awareness of qualitative meaning derived from other persons through communication*; (2) *integrating these new meanings with others previously acquired*; and (3) *expanding the richness of quality in the appreciable world by enlarging its meaning.* This third subevent leads to the increase and variety of qualities of experience, including new reaches of ideal possibility that were never before perceived. Such an expansion of one's appreciable world may, however, make a person more unhappy and dissatisfied than he or she was before. The person now knows that there are possibilities of good that might be achieved though they are not yet actualized. It is such an expansion of consciousness and craving for genuine community that "would drive a man to that desperate madness in which he dreamed that by dying on a cross he could somehow bring this kingdom of love into existence."[94] (4) The *fourth* subevent involves "*deepening the community among those who participate in this total creative event of intercommunication.*"[95] (Italics added.) As in the case of the third subevent, so is it true of the fourth that creative interaction and the deepening of community do not imply all sweetness and light.

Increase in genuine community, which is not mere increase in backslapping geniality, will include all this discernment of illness and evil in one another. Increase in community is not necessarily pleasant; the good produced by the creative event brings increase in suffering as well as increase in joy; community brings a burden as well as a release. Those who cannot endure suffering cannot endure the increase of human good.[96]

Wieman points out that the creative event is constituted by the four subevents working together and that the fourfold distinction is made solely for the purpose of analysis. Each event may occur separately, but in that case it is not creative. The unitary fourfold combination is necessary to the creativity.[97]

It might appear from Wieman's description of the creative event that this most worthful event (i.e., God) is so identified with human interaction as to be indistinguishable from human creativity itself. Is not Wieman's doctrine a form of religious humanism? Wieman's reply is an unqualified no. First, it must be kept in mind that Wieman has quite intentionally limited himself to a description of God at the level of human experience and not at other levels of existence. But even on the plane of human existence, humans *cannot do what the creative event does*. Wieman analyzes why this is so:

Human effort cannot accomplish anything which the human mind cannot imagine. If something results from human effort which was not intended and which the human mind could not imagine prior to its occurrence, it is an accident relative to human effort. It is not, of course, an accident in the absolute sense of being without cause. But, even though the existence and labors of men are part of the many causes issuing in this consequence, the consequence is not the work of man if the human intent sought a result different from this consequence. . . . The structure of value produced by the creative event cannot be caused by human intention and effort, because it can be produced only by a transformation of human intention and effort. . . . Man's creative ability is something produced in him as a consequence of the prior working of the creative event. . . . The creative event is suprahuman, not in the sense that it works outside the human life, but in the sense that it creates the good of the world in a way that man cannot do. . . . The work of the creative event is different in kind from the work of man.[98]

Humans do not create their own good. Rather, we are called upon to commit ourselves to this process of continuous creative transformation.

Here, then, we have the one master reality which will always be beyond man's control and yet which determines a destiny more glorious than anything else in the universe. [Man's] greatness is attained by giving himself over to be controlled, shaped, and progressively created by it.[99]

If humanity's highest devotion is to the creative event, evil and sin are what obstruct the process of creative growth. For Wieman, evasion, inertia, and complacency are the great evils, because they block the creative event. When individuals become satisfied with things as they are, they are in danger of committing the greatest sin for "sin is any resistance to creativity for which man is responsible."[100] Sin is rebellion against the will of God, the creature turning away from the creator. This sin often manifests itself in the form of idolatry, of giving to some created good our absolute commitment. All created goods can turn demonic: patriotism, education, democracy, technology.

Like so many of the early Christian symbols, the "devil" is illuminating if properly demythologized. Wieman's devil is that which tempts us to the beatific vision.

The devil is the most glorious vision of good that our minds can achieve at any one time when *that vision refuses to hold itself subject to creativity*. This is the most subtle and dangerous and obstructive sin that man can sin.[101]

Similarly, the notion of "original sin" is meaningful if properly interpreted. Original sin is not a condition of the newborn infant, but rather "the inability of men to give themselves completely to what saves and transforms."[102]

The religious problem is to be saved from that sin that obstructs commitment to the creative event. But human beings cannot be freed from the evil that vitiates human life until they acknowledge that they cannot commit themselves perfectly to creative interchange and cannot free themselves from their personal resistance to such a commitment. Before salvation can come, humans must, in Wieman's view, despair of finding any hope in any created good. "If one clings to something as though it were the source of all good when it is not, then the true source cannot dominate and penetrate and so cannot do what is called the 'forgiving of sin.'"[103]

Wieman's conception of the forgiveness of sin and spiritual growth in grace are traditionally orthodox on at least two points. He recognizes that the total eradication of sin from human life is impossible—human beings remain sinners despite the fact that the absolute grip of sin can be broken. Wieman also maintains that the forgiveness of sins cannot be brought about by human effort alone. Wieman describes, as follows, the process of overcoming those barriers to what can save:

The forgiveness of sin refers to what causes that change in the sinner which enables him to confess freely and fully his guilt and unfaithfulness, condemning them as evil, and doing it in such a way that this repentance intensifies his devotion and the completeness of his commitment. His unfaithfulness and his sin continue; but his confession of it and his condemnation of it serve to make his commitment more complete. . . . In this manner his unfaithfulness ceases to be a barrier between himself and what commands his ultimate commitment. By the ardor and sincerity of his confession and repentance he has nullified its power to separate him from what saves.[104]

The question of what causes this change in the sinner can, in Wieman's view, be found only by empirical inquiry. Therefore, he rejects traditional theological answers, especially

the claim that a declaration of forgiveness by a supernatural person can bring about such a change, whether that declaration is granted freely or must be purchased by the blood and suffering and death of Christ or by any other kind of sacrifice practiced in the various religions.[105]

Clinical studies in psychology and reports of cases of religious conversion give evidence that the change that enables an individual to recognize and repent of guilt and unfaithfulness is what Wieman calls *creative interchange* between individuals in openness and acceptance. The process of creative interchange, which leads to forgiveness of sins and spiritual growth, is an entirely natural process, but the cause of this change is not within the individuals themselves. "It resides in the creativity of this interchange . . . the forgiveness of sins is the work of God and not of man."[106]

At this point, it should be clear that Wieman's naturalistic theism differs in marked ways from traditional Christianity. This becomes even more evident in Wieman's rejection of such doctrines as the personality and omnipotence of God and his conception of God's transcendence.

As we have seen, Wieman prefers not to think of God as a being, but as an event or process that reveals a certain structure or pattern. According to Wieman's ontology, persons are not the most basic reality; persons are abstracted from events. Creativity is ontologically prior to personality, and it should be evident that our devotion must be directed to the creator and not to the creatures. Wieman believes that it can be clearly shown that God is not a personality.

A personality can only exist in a society. Personality is generated by interaction between individuals. Now if personality is thus absolutely dependent upon such social interaction, if it is generated, sustained, enriched, ennobled by social interaction, and is degraded, impoverished and perverted when social interaction goes wrong, it is plain that God cannot be a personality.[107]

Wieman believes that the Christian tradition has held to the doctrine of God as a person for purely anthropocentric reasons. For instance, we argue that God must be a person because personality is the highest form of existence *we* know, or because we cannot commune with God if God is not a person. This, says Wieman, is anthropocentric religion with a vengeance. The creative event creates, sustains, and transforms as no mere person could ever do. Of course, we can say that God is a person or mind unlike any person or mind that we know, but then we might as well be saying that a circle is a square.

If we resort to empirical inquiry, there is also no clear evidence that God is omnipotent. Wieman's view of the universe is pluralistic. The creative event is one event or process among many, and we cannot be certain that it is the most powerful. The creative event, like all other processes, is characterized by a distinctive pattern. Among all the innumerable, diverse, and interacting processes of existence, it is this one that works to save humans from evil and to make for the greater good. But God is not absolute in power, and evil may well become regnant. In Wieman's view, God is absolute only in the sense that creative good is trustworthy under all conditions and circumstances.

What cannot be claimed is that "absolute good means all-powerful good"; that is, that the creative event

overrules all evil so that in the end everything will come out all right, no matter how long and how great the intervening evils may be . . . (that) nothing can prevent ultimate, absolute, and complete regnancy of supreme value, somehow, sometime, somewhere, although the human mind cannot know how this may be.[108]

We should keep in mind that our ultimate faith is not in this earth or even in the continuance of the human species—at least as we know it. One's ultimate commitment is to creative good.

With this commitment, he does not depend ultimately upon any known structure of the universe nor any known structure of human personality or society, because he is committed to a creativity transforming all of these. The structures not in existence may destroy his body, but they cannot destroy his faith and his hope, because he looks beyond this universe to

other universes to be brought forth by creativity if required conditions are provided for its effective operation.[109]

We have already stressed Wieman's rejection of any theism that posits a God transcendent of space and time. It must be emphasized, however, that despite his rejection of several traditional attributes of God, Wieman insists that God's transcendence must be viewed axiologically and functionally. The creative event is axiologically transcendent in that this event has an *absolute* goodness, irrespective of time or place, which is not possible with the created good of humanity. For Wieman, the contrast between "creative good" and "created good" is the same as that between God and humanity in the Bible. The creative event is also functionally suprahuman. God works in ways that humans cannot foresee, ahead of and often contrary to human desires and purposes. This means, moreover, that God is transcendent in the sense that the creative event is beyond or more than our knowledge can comprehend.

Jesus and the Creative Event

All that we have said so far about God and the divine saving activity has been free of any mention of the person or work of Jesus Christ. In one sense this is perfectly logical, for Wieman's theism is not dependent on special biblical revelation. Yet, it is also unquestionable that central to Wieman's discussion of the creative event and creative interchange are the events surrounding Jesus and the birth of the primitive Christian community. Where then is the place of Jesus Christ in Wieman's theology?

First, Wieman repudiates any notion that the man Jesus is God. The revelation of God in Christ should not be identified with the man Jesus.[110] In Wieman's opinion, we do not know enough about the facts of Jesus's life and personality to make such a judgment about his person but even if we did, "we still do not have that supernatural knowledge of God which would be required to say that any feature pertaining to Jesus exemplifies a feature essential to the being of God."[111]

Nevertheless, the events surrounding the life and ministry of Jesus constitute one of the unique creative thrusts in the history of life as we know it. The Christ event marks a breakthrough in creative interchange. "This reversal in the direction of human devotion is not new," says Wieman. "It is, we believe, the very substance of the original Christian faith."[112]

What Wieman finds significant about Jesus is not his person but the fact that in the events of his life, death, and resurrection, the work of the creative event was *definitely* present in history. Wieman describes the "work" of Christ in the following way:

Jesus engaged in intercommunication with a little group of disciples with such depth and potency that the organization of their several personalities was broken down and they were remade. They became new men, and the thought and feelings of each got across to the others. . . . *It was not something Jesus did.* It was something that happened when he was present like a catalytic agent. . . . Something about this man Jesus broke the atomic exclusiveness of those individuals so that they were deeply and freely receptive and responsive each to the other. . . . Thus, each was transformed, lifted to a higher level of human fulfilment. Each became more of a mind and a person, with more capacity to understand, to appreciate, to act with power and insight. . . . The appreciable world expanded round about those men . . . the world was more rich and ample with meaning and quality. . . . The disciples found themselves living in a community of men vastly deeper and wider than any before accessible to them.[113]

Wieman is here describing the fourfold creative event as occurring in the interchange between Jesus and his disciples. He sees the crucifixion and resurrection of Jesus as essential to this creative event, for in these occasions the creative interchange broke the narrow bounds of established Jewish expectations and universalized its scope.

What happened after the death of Jesus was the release of this creative power from the constraints and limitations previously confining it. . . . After about

the third day, however, when the numbness of the shock had worn away, something happened. The life-transforming creativity previously known only in fellowship with Jesus began again to work in the fellowship of the disciples. It was risen from the dead. . . . What rose from the dead was not the man Jesus; it was creative power. It was the living God that works in time. It was the Second Person of the Trinity. It was Christ the God, not Jesus the man.[114]

It is important to recognize that for Wieman the creative event is not confined to Jesus's person, for the creative event involves human interaction. Jesus is a *participant* (albeit the catalyst) in the event.

The creative transformative power was not in the man Jesus. . . . Rather he was in it. It required many other things besides his own solitary self. It required the Hebrew heritage, the disciples . . . and doubtless much else of which we have little knowledge.[115]

What the Christ event did was to reverse "the order of domination in the life of man *from* domination of human concern by created good *over to* domination by creative good."[116] The event included the establishment of a community, which has continued down through the centuries, dedicated to this creative exchange. For this reason, Wieman believes the Christ event can be considered "ultimate" or "final." Because of this battle and this victory, we can have hope that the gates of hell will not prevail against the advance of creative good.

Wieman is loath, however, to claim that it is in the Christ event that the redemptive creative event is "uniquely" or most fully revealed. It is unjustifiably dogmatic to make such a claim. Whether or not it is true would have to be discovered by empirical inquiry, but it is extremely difficult to judge such things in traditions alien to one's own. Like Ernst Troeltsch, Wieman believes it is enough to say that "for us, in our tradition, Christ alone is our salvation."[117]

Christianity is final if through it man attains to the last freedom and the unconquerable hope through ultimate commitment to creative good. If other religions also open the way to this salvation, it should be cause for great rejoicing.[118]

Wieman's modernism is once again clearly evident in his Christology. Although his theology gives a significant place to Jesus Christ, that significance is found in the fact that the Christ event *illustrates* or *exemplifies* the creative interchange, which is the cardinal doctrine of Wieman's religious philosophy. What is revealed in Jesus may have reached a peak or dominance in his life not observable elsewhere in our history, but that creative transformation is not unique in kind in the Christ event nor is it limited to that event. It is universal in its work wherever the proper conditions are met. Had Jesus not lived, the creative event would have been redemptively at work, creating the greatest good possible and, at other times and in other worlds, has and will continue to do so.

Despite its severe reduction of traditional Christian substance, Wieman's radical reconception of Christian theology is rich in provocative insights that should be explored more carefully by Christian thinkers. The reason for this failure is due, in part, to the difficulty one encounters in attempting to relate Wieman's doctrine to the mainstream of the Christian theological tradition. Many would say that Wieman's theology stands as a bold alternate to that tradition. To underscore the issue, only a few of the difficulties encountered in Wieman's thought by Christian theologians need be mentioned.

First, there are several problems that emerge in reflecting on Wieman's doctrine of God. Is Wieman's God one? Is the creative event always the same event? Is it not difficult for an empiricist to claim that all the creative events are one metaphysically? For Wieman, God's unity is a unity of structure, not of mind or substance. All creative events exemplify a single structure. But is this an empirical judgment or a metaphysical intuition? And, if *all* creative events exemplify a particular structure, then is there not one structure that is primordial and eternal through and in time? Does not the First Person of the traditional Trinity have to be examined more carefully by Wieman?

Wieman says that human beings do not produce emerging good because they do not foresee or intend the good that is created. Good is the work of God. Yet, Wieman says that God is not a person, is not conscious, does not have memory or purpose. God does not foresee value, nor appreciate and enjoy it. Only humans can do this and, apparently, make the judgment that God is infinitely greater for not being able to do so! On the other hand, the Christian tradition has held that God is personal and conscious, God's redemptive love revealed in Christ being a *conscious* act of will.

Wieman's view of history appears to be tragic, for in Wieman's doctrine of creativity there is little interest in the preservation of the past or in the cumulative historical achievement of value. The future is radically open, and evil might win out. In any case, there is no hope for any redemption "beyond history" in any eschatological new creation or Kingdom of God. Wieman's realism wisely repudiates any simple perfectionism or notion of historical progress, but it also negates the Christian hope as it is expressed in the eschatological symbols of the New Testament. For Wieman, our hope should not go beyond the evidence, that is, the present innovating activity of creative interchange, if it is to avoid illusion.

Finally, Wieman's picture of Jesus and the primitive Christian community would raise serious questions for many biblical scholars and theologians. Is Wieman's demythologization of the Christ event tenable or is it a simple fitting of his own scheme onto the rich complexity of the New Testament? The Christian community of which Wieman speaks was not so much a reality as a possibility from which the disciples, and believers since, are estranged and whose realization is—then, as now—sadly obstructed.

Despite the several problems raised by Wieman's theology, it must be kept in mind that he has always seen his radical reinterpretation of Christian belief as central to his philosophical work and as desperately needed in these days of magnified technological power and social revolution. However, his theology and influence were almost wholly in eclipse after the Second World War, and in an interview in 1968 he judged that his work had been a failure and that it had not had the effect that he had hoped it would have.[119] It is unfortunate that Wieman's writings have not had a wider reading, because many aspects of his thought deserve serious consideration, even if it is unlikely that some of his theological formulations can be considered congruent with a Christian theology. Nonetheless, like Karl Barth, Wieman was concerned to free theology from the worship of human ideals and subjective values. His critique of anthropomorphism and of careless God-talk—e.g., easy appeals to God's "mystery"—is salutary. So is his analysis of God's omnipotence and his attention to how God does in fact "act" in nature and history—a subject about which, many feel, contemporary theologians are able to offer little help. In a secular culture it is doubtful if a sense of God's reality can be sustained when individuals are left ignorant or perplexed about how

God "acts" in and through the events of natural and human history. Here, perhaps, a more empirical theology, one more deeply engaged in dialogue with the natural and social sciences, can best contribute to a reconstructed Christian theology in the decades ahead. There are some signs that developments in this direction are already under way. It is unlikely, however, to proceed on the lines taken by Macintosh and Wieman, for their empiricism, though beginning with the immediacy of experience, moves rapidly to intuitive or metaphysical assumptions and claims that are not shared by either philosophers or most theologians today. A future *empirical* Christian theology likely will be more modest. As one commentator has suggested, it will have "to begin with immediate experience and to show therein the *possibility* of metaphysics. It cannot begin with the easy assumption that a metaphysics, merely because it begins with experience, is to be dubbed 'empirical.'"[120]

NOTES

1. On this theme see, Daniel D. Williams, "Tradition and Experience in American Theology," in *The Shaping of American Religion*, ed. James Ward Smith and Leland Jamison (Princeton, 1961), pp. 443–95.

2. *Letters of William James*, II, ed. Henry James (Boston, 1920), p. 58.

3. *Letters of William James*, I, ed. Henry James (Boston, 1920), pp. 147–148.

4. William James, *The Will to Believe and Other Essays* (Cambridge, 1897), p. 92.

5. Ibid., p. 82.

6. Ibid., p. 83.

7. William James, *The Principles of Psychology*, II (New York, 1890), p. 297.

8. Ibid., p. 231.

9. William James, *The Will to Believe* (New York, 1911), p. 1.

10. Ibid., p. 2.

11. Ibid.

12. Ibid., p. 3.

13. Ibid., p. 4.

14. Ibid.

15. Ibid., p. 5.

16. Ibid., pp. 5–6.

17. Ibid., p. 7.

18. Ibid., p. 8.

19. Ibid.

20. Ibid., p. 10.

21. Ibid.

22. Ibid., p.11.

23. Ibid.

24. Ibid., p. 14.

25. Ibid., pp. 17–18.

26. Ibid., pp. 18–19.

27. Ibid., p. 19.

28. Ibid., pp. 19–20.

29. Ibid., pp. 23–24.

30. Ibid., p. 25.

31. Ibid., pp. 25–26.

32. Ibid., p. 26.

33. Ibid., pp. 26–27.

34. William A. Clebsch, *American Religious Thought: A History* (Chicago, 1973), p. 153.

35. William James, *The Varieties of Religious Experience* (New York: Macmillan, 1961), p. 29.

36. Ibid., p. 22.

37. Ibid., pp. 24–25.

38. Ibid., p. 34.

39. Ibid., p. 42.

40. Ibid., p. 48.

41. Ibid., p. 95.

42. Ibid., p. 119.

43. Ibid., p. 133.

44. Ibid., p. 136.

45. Ibid., p. 163.

46. Ibid., p. 195.

47. Ibid., pp. 220–221.

48. Daniel Cory, ed., *The Letters of George Santayana* (New York, 1955), p. 394.

49. Ernst Troeltsch, "Empiricism and Platonism in the Philosophy of Religion: To the Memory of William James," *Harvard Theological Review*, 5, no. 4 (1912), 401–422.

50. William James, *A Pluralistic Universe* (New York, 1909), p. 314.

51. D. C. Macintosh, "Toward a New Untraditional Orthodoxy", in *Contemporary American Theology*, ed. Vergilius Ferm (New York, 1932), pp. 277–319.

52. D. C. Macintosh, *Theology as an Empirical Science* (New York, 1919), p. 7.

53. Ibid., p. 8.

54. Ibid., pp. 8–9.

55. D. C. Macintosh, *The Reasonableness of Christianity* (New York, 1925), p. 198.

56. Macintosh, *Theology as an Empirical Science*, p. 28.

57. Ibid., p. 29.

58. Ibid., p. 108.

59. D. C. Macintosh, *The Problem of Religious Knowledge* (New York, 1940), p. 374.

60. Macintosh, *Theology as an Empirical Science*, p. 109.

61. Ibid.

62. Ibid., p. 140.

63. Ibid.

64. Ibid., p. 148.

65. Ibid., pp. 148–150.

66. *American Journal of Theology*, XXIV (1920), 185; cited in Macintosh, *The Problem of Religious Knowledge*, p. 198.

67. Macintosh, *The Problem of Religious Knowledge*, p. 198.

68. Ibid., p. 209.

69. Macintosh, *Theology as an Empirical Science*, p. 22.

70. Macintosh, *The Reasonableness of Christianity*, pp. 24–25.

71. Ibid., pp. 135–136.

72. Ibid., p. 138.

73. Ibid., pp. 140–141.

74. Ibid., p. 150.

75. Ibid., p. 154.

76. Ibid., pp. 157–158.

77. Ibid., p. 159.

78. Macintosh, *Theology as an Empirical Science*, p. 109.

79. See James Alfred Martin, Jr., *Empirical Philosophies of Religion* (New York, 1945).

80. Shailer Mathews, *The Faith of Modernism* (New York, 1924), pp. 10, 34, 35, 146.

81. H. N. Wieman, *The Source of Human Good* (Chicago, 1946), p. 37.

82. H. N. Wieman, "Reply to Burtt," in *The Empirical Theology of Henry Nelson Wieman*, ed. Robert W. Bretall (New York, 1963), p. 388.

83. H. N. Wieman, "Intellectual Autobiography," in *The Empirical Theology of Henry Nelson Wieman*, p. 9.

84. Bernard E. Meland, "The Root and Form of Wieman's Thought," in *The Empirical Theology of Henry Nelson Wieman*, p. 45.

85. H. N. Wieman, *Religious Experience and Scientific Method* (New York, 1927), pp. 21–22.

86. H. N. Wieman, *The Wrestle of Religion with Truth* (New York, 1929), pp. 94–95.

87. Wieman, *Source of Human Good*, p. 6.

88. Ibid., pp. 7–8.

89. Ibid., p. 36.

90. Wieman, "Intellectual Autobiography," p.14.

91. Ibid., pp. 16–17.

92. See Wieman, *Intellectual Foundation of Faith* (New York, 1961), pp. 125–126; and Wieman, *Source of Human Good*, pp. 58–65.

93. Wieman, *Source of Human Good*, pp. 58–65.

94. Ibid., p. 63.

95. Ibid., p. 58.

96. Ibid., p. 65.

97. Ibid, p. 58.

98. Ibid., pp. 75–76.

99. H. N. Wieman, *Man's Ultimate Commitment* (Carbondale, Ill., 1958), p. 77.

100. Wieman, *Source of Human Good*, p. 126.

101. Ibid., pp. 128–129.

102. Wieman, *Man's Ultimate Commitment*, p. 133. Ch. 1 of this title contains Wieman's most concise reinterpretation of many of the traditional Christian symbols.

103. Wieman, *Source of Human Good*, pp. 278–279.

104. Wieman, *Man's Ultimate Commitment*, pp. 15–16.

105. Ibid., p 16.

106. Ibid.

107. "Theocentric Religion," in *Contemporary American Theology*, ed. Vergilius Ferm (New York, 1932), pp. 349–350.

108. Wieman, *Source of Human Good*, p 81–82.

109. Wieman, *Intellectual Foundation of Faith*, p 79.

110. *The Empirical Theology of Henry Nelson Wieman*, pp. 191, 365, 373.

111. Ibid., p 365.

112. Wieman, *Source of Human Good*, p 39.

113. Ibid., pp. 39–41.

114. Ibid., pp. 41, 44.

115. Ibid., p. 41.

116. Ibid., p. 269.

117. Ibid., p. 287.

118. Ibid. In *Man's Ultimate Commitment,* Wieman indicates that "whatever has come from Jesus Christ and the early Christians did not complete the work of establishing the conditions which must be present for creativity to operate widely and securely throughout human life" (p. 303). A creative modern technology and the change of institutions and individuals to the dominance of creativity are also required if human salvation is to be achieved. In Wieman's writings since

The Source of Human Good, less attention is given to the ultimate victory achieved in the Christ event.

119. See "A Dialogue with Henry N. Wieman" in Creighton Peden, *Wieman's Empirical Process Theology* (Washington, D.C., 1977).

120. Langdon Gilkey, "New Modes of Empirical Theology" in *The Future of Empirical Theology,* ed. Bernard Loomer (Chicago, 1969), p. 349. Gilkey's essay is a fine analysis of the problems and a possible direction of an empirical theology.

SUGGESTIONS FOR FURTHER READING

William James

Overall studies of James the person and thinker:

Allen, Gay Wilson. *William James* (New York: Viking Press, 1967). Regarded by many as the best biography.

Myer, Gerald E., *William James: His Life and Thought* (New Haven: Yale University Press, 1986). A thorough critical study of James's major ideas and contributions. A valuable study.

Perry, Ralph Barton. *The Thought and Character of William James,* 2 vol. (Boston: Little, Brown, 1936). An important, sympathetic study of James the person and thinker.

On aspects of James as religious thinker:

Levinson, Henry Samuel. *The Religious Investigations of William James* (Chapel Hill: University of North Carolina Press, 1981). A fine study of the full sweep of James's reflections on religion from 1870 to 1910 with extensive treatment of *The Varieties of Religious Experience.*

Smith, John E. *The Spirit of American Philosophy* (New York: Oxford University Press, 1963); *Themes in American Philosophy* (New York: Oxford University Press, 1970); *Purpose and Thought: The Meaning of Pragmatism* (New Haven: Yale University Press, 1978). All of these works by Smith include thoughtful discussions of James's religious thought.

On the "Will to Believe":

There is a vast literature, especially in philosophical journals, on this subject. Among the many studies that represent different perspectives and that include references to some of the best earlier literature, see:

Evans, C. Stephen. *Subjectivity and Religious Belief,* Ch. 4 (Grand Rapids: William B. Eerdmans, 1978).

Hick, John. *Faith and Knowledge,* 2nd ed. (Ithaca: Cornell University Press, 1966).

O'Connell, Robert J., S.J. *William James on the Courage to Believe* (New York: Fordham University Press, 1984).

Wernham, James C. S. *James's Will-to-Believe Doctrine: A Heretical View* (Kingston and Montreal: McGill-Queen's University Press, 1987).

The Empirical Movement in American Theology

Bixler, J. S., R. L. Calhoun, and H. R. Niebuhr, ed. *The Nature of Religious Experience* (New York: Harper and Brothers, 1937).

Frankenberry, Nancy *Religion and Radical Empiricism* (Albany: State University of New York Press, 1987). Also see Frankenberry's essay, "Major Themes in Empirical Theology," in R. C. Miller below.

Macintosh, D. C., ed. *Religious Realism* (New York: Macmillan, 1931). This book and Bixler, Calhoun, and Niebuhr contain essays expounding, defending, and criticizing empirical theology.

Martin, James Alfred, Jr. *Empirical Philosophies of Religion* (New York: Kings Crown Press, 1945).

Meland, Bernard E., ed. *The Future of Empirical Theology* (Chicago: University of Chicago Press, 1969).

Miller, Randolph Crump, ed. *Empirical Theology: A Handbook* (Birmingham, Ala.: Religious Education Press, 1992). An excellent comprehensive treatment of empirical theology.

Peden, Creighton. *The Chicago School: Voices in Liberal Religious Thought* (Bristol, Ind.: Wyndham Hall Press, 1987). Brief studies of S. Mathews, G. B. Foster, G. B. Smith, E. S. Ames, A. E. Haydon, H. N. Wieman, and B. E. Meland.

Douglas Clyde Macintosh

There are no extensive studies of Macintosh's theology available. In addition to the Martin book cited above, the following contain helpful brief studies of Macintosh's thought:

Cauthen, Kenneth. *The Impact of American Religious Liberalism* (New York: Harper and Row, 1962).

Peerman, Dean, and Martin E. Marty, ed. *A Handbook of Christian Theologians* (Cleveland: World Publishing, 1965).

Henry Nelson Wieman

In addition to the Cauthen and Martin books cited above, the following studies are recommended:

Bretall, Robert W., ed. *The Empirical Theology of Henry Nelson Wieman* (New York: Macmillan, 1963). This work contains a wide range of interpretations and criticisms of Wieman's thought by outstanding theologians and philosophers.

Cobb, John B., Jr. *Living Options in Protestant Theology: A Survey of Methods* (Philadelphia: Westminster Press, 1962).

Hardwick, Charley D. *Events of Grace: Naturalism, Existentialism, and Theology* (Cambridge: Cambridge University Press, 1996).

Hutchison, William R. *The Modernist Impulse in American Protestantism* (Oxford: Oxford University Press, 1976).

Peden, Creighton. *Wieman's Empirical Process Theology* (Washington, D.C.: University Press of America, 1977).

Shaw, Marvin C. *Nature's Grace: Essays on H. N. Wieman's Finite Theism* (New York: Peter Lang Publishers, 1995).

Shailer Mathews and the Chicago School

Arnold, Charles Harvey. *Near the Edge of Battle* (Chicago: Divinity School Association, 1966).

Aubrey, Edwin E. "Theology and the Social Process." In *The Process of Religion*, ed. Miles Krumbine (New York: Macmillan, 1933), pp. 17–52.

Cauthen, Kenneth. *The Impact of American Religious Liberalism* (New York: Harper, 1962), Ch. 8.

———. "The Life and Thought of Shailer Mathews." In Shailer Mathews, *Jesus on Social Institutions*, ed. Kenneth Cauthen (Philadelphia: Fortress Press, 1971).

Lindsey, William D. *Shailer Mathews's Lives of Jesus: The Search for a Theological Foundation for the Social Gospel.* (Albany: State University of New York Press, 1997). Sees Mathews's books on Jesus as prefiguring political and liberation theologies.

Chapter Three

The Dialectical Theology: Karl Barth, Emil Brunner, and Friedrich Gogarten

Karl Barth, 1925

The First World War began on August 1, 1914. Years later the most influential Protestant theologian of the twentieth century reflected on the significance of that day from a personal perspective: "Ninety-three German intellectuals issued a terrible manifesto, identifying themselves before all the world with the war policy of Kaiser Wilhelm II and Chancellor Bethmann-Hollweg. . . . And to my dismay, among the signatories I discovered the names of all my German teachers."[1] The theologian was Karl Barth. Although the accuracy of his recollection has been questioned, the manifesto itself was like "the twilight of the gods." For many of his great teachers—among them Adolf von Harnack and Wilhelm Herrmann—had, in Barth's estimation, "hopelessly compromised" their theology by this ethical failure. Thus, Barth

wrote, "a whole world of exegesis, ethics, dogmatics and preaching, which I had hitherto held to be essentially trustworthy, was shaken to the foundations, and with it, all the other writings of the German theologians."[2]

For Karl Barth the theology of the nineteenth century no longer had a future. He soon found himself cast in the role of leader of a theological revolution that, for a relatively brief period of time, brought together in a common cause a remarkable group of theologians whose program came to be called the "Dialectical theology." It also was referred to as the "Theology of Crisis" and the "Theology of the Word of God." Included in the group with Barth were Edward Thurneysen, Friedrich Gogarten, Rudolf Bultmann, Emil Brunner, and Günther Dehn. An early sympathizer was the theologian Paul Tillich. A journal for this new theological program was begun in 1922 by Barth, Thurneysen, Gogarten, and Georg Merz, who served as its supervisor. It was entitled *Zwischen den Zeiten* (*Between the Times*) after an article by Gogarten. This journal published important articles by Barth and other members of the group until 1933, when it was discontinued due to disagreements among the contributors, especially over National Socialist policies in Germany.

The Dialectical theology was relatively short-lived, and from the very beginning there were differences between Barth, Gogarten, Bultmann, Brunner, and the others. By the early 1930s many of these disagreements were pronounced. Nevertheless, the aftereffects of this theological revolution were to prove momentous, and they are reflected in theological debates even today. The creative ferment of the years 1910 to 1930 produced a number of theological trajectories that we now associate with members of the group: with Barth, Bultmann, Gogarten, Brunner, and with Paul Tillich. In this chapter we will trace the beginnings of the Dialectical theology, its distinctive character and themes, especially in the early writings of Karl Barth, and the emerging differences between the leading members of the group, which resulted in creative new directions that have, in their own right, been influential in the twentieth century. Here we will examine in more detail Barth's early Theology of the Word of God, as well as the mature theologies of Brunner and Gogarten. Subsequent chapters will deal with the extremely important developments in the theologies of Barth, Bultmann, and Tillich and their influence.

THE BEGINNINGS OF DIALECTICAL THEOLOGY

We now can see that the theological revolt against nineteenth-century liberal theology, which is an especially prominent feature of the *Zwischen den Zeiten* group, had its incubation in the political and cultural ferment at the beginning of the century, not least in the response to the horrors wrought by the First World War. But the birth of Dialectical theology as a distinctive movement is inseparable from the leadership of Karl Barth. It was around him that the diverse group of young theologians rallied in the early 1920s. Almost to a person these young pastors and teachers had studied under the great liberal theologians of the turn of the century—Herrmann, Harnack, Weiss, and Troeltsch—and most of them had begun their careers as conventional liberal theologians in either the Ritschlian or Idealist tradition. Both Barth and Bultmann were devoted students of the Ritschlian Wilhelm Herrmann in Marburg. Herrmann had taught them both that Christian faith is not grounded in the relativities of history and that theology need not be parasitical on the other sciences. Barth later confessed: "I soaked Herrmann in through my pores."[3] In 1908 Barth took up the position of editorial assistant for *Die Christliche Welt* (*The Christian World*), the leading journal of Protestant Liberal thought, edited by Martin Rade in Marburg. Barth immersed himself in the atmosphere of Liberal theology and considered himself at the time a committed supporter of the theological tradition from Schleiermacher to Ritschl.

In 1911 Barth became pastor in the village of Safenwil in the Aargau, Switzerland, where he remained for a decade. His early sermons there continued to reflect the liberal tradition of Marburg theology. What was most distinctive about his pastoral experience at the time, however, was his engagement in socialism and the trade union movement. Most of the wage earners in Safenwil were engaged in industrial work in the local mills. They were paid poorly and were not organized. Barth began giving lectures to the Workers' Association. This provoked the local industrialists to attack Barth publicly, but he remained undeterred in his denunciations of economic injustice and in his support of social democracy. In 1915 Barth joined the Social Democratic Party, and he came to be known as "the red pastor of Safenwil." Barth also emerged as a forceful critic of the Christian Church's endorsement of the war in 1914 and of "state religion." Increasingly he became aware that both Christianity and socialism required a new reformation. In this he was supported by a fellow pastor and newfound friend, Edward Thurneysen.

The friendship with Thurneysen was decisive for Barth. In 1914 Thurneysen was installed as pastor in Leutwil, a village near Safenwil, and the two visited each other regularly, engaging in lively conversation, and carried on a weekly correspondence over many years. Thurneysen introduced Barth to several individuals who became important to him at this critical period of his life. One was Hermann Kutter, pastor of the Neumünster in Zürich and a powerful personality and preacher. To Barth, Kutter "represented the insight that the sphere of God's power really is greater than the sphere of the church and that from time to time it has pleased God and still pleases him, to warn and to comfort his church through the figures and events of secular world history."[4] Another figure was Leonhard Ragaz, pastor of the Basel cathedral and professor of theology at Zürich, who was a leader of the Religious Socialist movement in Switzerland beginning in 1906. Ragaz helped Barth to further his practical involvement in socialism, although Barth soon reacted against Ragaz's program because it viewed socialism as an early manifestation of the coming Kingdom of God.

During these active years in Safenwil, Barth became increasingly concerned about his central task of preaching—not *how* to preach but *what* to say week in, week out about God. Reflecting on the period around 1915, Barth writes:

Over and above the group of problems associated with liberal theology and Religious Socialism, I began to be increasingly preoccupied with the idea of the kingdom of God in the biblical, real, this-worldly sense of the term. This raised more and more problems over the way in which I should use the Bible in my sermons, which for all too long I had taken for granted.[5]

Barth agreed with Thurneysen that if they were to see more clearly what was required of them they would have to return to academic theology so that their resources could be widened and deepened. "It was Thurneysen who whispered the key phrase to me, half aloud, while we were alone together: 'What we need for preaching, instruction and pastoral care is a 'wholly other' theological foundation.'"[6] They agreed that they could no longer follow the way marked out by Schleiermacher. And rather than begin again with Kant or Hegel,

in fact we found ourselves compelled to do something much more obvious. We tried to learn our theological ABCs all over again, beginning by reading and interpreting the writing of the Old and New Testaments, more thoroughly than before. And lo and behold, they began to speak to us—but not as we thought we must hear them in the school of what was then "modern theology." . . . I sat under an apple tree and began to apply myself to Romans. . . . I began to read it as though I had never read it before.[7]

Under the apple tree Barth had discovered "the strange new world within the Bible"—a world that had not been opened up to him by his New Testament teachers Rudolf Steck, Adolf Jülicher, and Wilhelm Heitmüller. Out of the notes compiled from his study of Paul's Letter to the Romans there emerged his epoch-making commentary *Der Römerbrief* (1918) (*The Epistle to the Romans*). The first edition did not really cause much of a stir, and Barth proceeded in the next two years to undertake new investigations of Acts, I and II Corinthians, and Ephesians, and to radically rethink his *Römerbrief*. During this time he gave careful attention to Franz Overbeck's radical criticism of the development of Christianity and what Overbeck called "Bismarck-religion" or the confusion of Christianity and German nationalism. Barth also read the works of Overbeck's friend, Nietzsche, and he discovered Dostoevsky, Ibsen, and Kierkegaard. In his novels Dostoevsky pictured rebellious souls tortured by doubt—persons who could not slake their thirst for the eternal, but neither would confuse the awesome belief in a loving God with the moral conventions of a liberal culture. Therefore, they remained alienated outcasts of society. Henrik Ibsen, too, challenged the current bourgeois moralism. In his great plays he dramatized the hypocrisy of conventional behavior, which masked perverse and even devilish motives in seemingly noble actions. No one portrayed the demonic potential of moral idealism with more force than Ibsen in *The Wild Duck* and *The Master Builder*.

What Barth found instructive in Kierkegaard was the "inexorable criticism" that he used "to attack all speculation which wiped out the infinite qualitative difference between God and man." Kierkegaard "was one of the cocks whose voice seemed to proclaim to us from near and far the dawn of a really new day."[8] Barth gave bold expression to his newfound sense of the radical "wholly-otherness" of God in a lecture delivered to a student conference in 1920, entitled "Biblical Questions, Insights, and Vistas":

The Bible has only *one* theological interest . . . interest in God himself. It is this that I call the Bible's otherworldliness, its unhistoricalness, its antipathy to the idea of sacredness. *God* is the new, incomparable, unattainable interest. . . . He is not a thing among other things, but the *Wholly Other*. . . . He it is of whom the Bible speaks.[9]

Adolf von Harnack was present at this lecture and he was shocked and dismayed at Barth's words. His parting comment to Barth was that history teaches that Barth, like the radical Protestant reformer Thomas Münzer, would found a new sect and receive divine inspiration! Harnack feared that Barth's growing popularity would bring theology to a state of affairs worse than it had been with Kierkegaard. This was confirmed in his mind with the appearance of the second edition of *Der Römerbrief* in 1922. The book was a bombshell and it divided the theological world into advocates and detractors. Writing about the impact of the book, Barth later commented:

As I look back upon my course, I seem to myself as one who, ascending the dark staircase of a church tower and trying to steady himself reached for the banister, but got hold of the bell rope instead. To his horror, he had then to listen to what the great bell had sounded over him and not over him alone.[10]

Several of the most eminent New Testament scholars, including Harnack, Paul Wernle, Karl Ludwig Schmidt, and Adolf Jülicher, quickly repudiated Barth's *Romans*. Wernle complained that "no single aspect of Paul's teaching seems to cause Barth discomfort. . . . There remain for him no survivals of the age in which Paul lived—not even trivial survivals."[11] Jülicher called Barth "a bitter enemy of historical criticism" and compared his exegesis of Paul to that of the second-century heretic Marcion. To Jülicher, Barth was proceeding "with the same sovereign arbitrariness and assurance of victory, with the same one-sided dualistic approach of enmity to all that comes from the world, culture, or tradition."[12]

Barth's reply to his critics in the preface to the second edition of *Romans* illuminates the wide gulf that now separated him from the scholarly ideals and theological views of his mentors. Among the Pauline "survivals" that Wernle thought should be dismissed as relics of the past were "Christ the Son of God—Redemption by the Blood of Christ—Adam and Christ—Paul's use of the Old Testament—his so-called 'Baptismal-Sacramentalism'—the Double Predestination—his attitude toward secular authority." Barth found it unimaginable that a commentary on Paul's Letter to the Romans could leave such critical points unexplained or would simply allow them to "remain uncomfortable points." Barth replies:

In contrast with this comfortable dismissal of uncomfortable points it has been my "Biblicism" which has compelled me to wrestle with these "scandals of modern thought" until I have found myself able to undertake the interpretation of them. . . . I have, moreover, no desire to conceal the fact that my "Biblicist" method—which means in the end no more than "consider well"—is applicable also to the study of Lao-Tze and of Goethe. . . . When I am named "Biblicist," all that can rightly be proved against me is that I hold it to be profitable for men to take [the Bible's] conceptions at least as seriously as they take their own.[13]

A number of the younger theologians rallied to Barth's defense, seeing in his *Romans* their own doubts about the theology of their teachers and the new cultural situation. Emil Brunner was among the first to praise Barth for his "naive" (free of all the critical-scientific apparatus) and "unmodern" work on St. Paul. It was the theme of "Wholly Otherness" that Brunner saw as the crucial repudiation of all subjectivism and personal religious experience, which meant the rejection of Schleiermacher, who endeavored "to reconstruct the *content of faith* out of the experience of the faithful."[14]

Bultmann wrote a long and generally appreciative essay on the second edition of Barth's *Romans*, which he thought far superior to the first edition. He, too, saw Barth as fighting on two fronts, against both the *psychologizing* and the *historicizing* of Christian faith. This expressed itself in Barth's polemic against mystical experience and his renunciation of all forms of immanence and pantheism.[15] As Barth had written: "To suppose that a direct road lead from art, or morals, or science, or even from religion, to God is sentimental, liberal self-deception."

What also attracted the younger generation to Barth, and what resonated through most of his writings in the years 1914 to 1922, was his deep sense of the deterioration and crisis of European bourgeois culture—and his prophetic resistance to its values—without embracing pessimism or cynicism. Many of Barth's generation had witnessed the terrors and devastation of the Great War and had returned to the universities only to be told that they had fought the good fight on behalf of Christian civilization. The stock phrases of the time that spoke of defending Christian culture, of making the world safe for democracy, and of Christianizing the social order, sounded trite if not dishonest, because Western civilization appeared to this younger generation to be both impotent and corrupt. The last thing that Christianity should seek to do is accommodate itself to this dying culture; rather, it should stand against it in prophetic judgment without, however, embracing the pessimism of Oswald Spengler's *Decline of the West*. The prophetic "no!" must, as Barth continually insisted, be countered with the divine "yes!" of hope. This, too, was the theme sounded in the most striking postwar writings of Gogarten and Bultmann.

These young theologians of "crisis" shared a sense of living between two worlds, one exhausted if not dead, the other yet to be born. This is the theme of Gogarten's emblematic essay "Between the Times," published in the liberal *Die Christliche Welt* in 1920. He portrays the new generation of theologians as standing "in the middle—in an empty space." They belong "neither to the one nor the other."

Harnack's and Jülicher's dismay over Barth's writings convinced Gogarten that they had not begun to recognize the disintegration in their very midst, and that the new generation had no desire to lift a hand to stem this tide of decline, "since no one enjoys living among corpses."

Was it not you who sharpened our sight for the human element, subjecting everything to history and development? We are grateful that you did. You created the tools for us; now let us use them. Now we draw the conclusion: Everything that is somehow a human work not only has a beginning, but passes away. . . . We see the disintegration in everything. . . . We are so deeply immersed in humanity that we have lost God. . . . None of our thoughts reach beyond the human sphere. Not a single one. We stand not before our own wisdom, but before God. This hour is not our hour. *We* have no time now. We stand between the times.[16]

For these young theologians, living between the times was looking into the abyss. God could be encountered only as the hidden God, not even transparent in his revelation in Christ—indeed, in Christ, God was an even deeper mystery, one that would require an unsettling revision. This is the theme of Bultmann's 1917 Pentecost sermon, "Concerning the Hidden and Revealed God," his response to the radical spiritual change brought about by the First World War. The old pieties and assurances now are gone. Earlier Pentecosts of "brilliant sun and the happy sound of church bells" now had been replaced by a spirit of questioning, of pain, loss, and alarm.

If God is to be known in this time of uncertainty and contending powers, Bultmann reminds his listeners that God will appear "to be wholly other than the picture we have made of him; and we must be prepared to accept his visage even if it terrifies us." God *as God* must be hidden and mysterious, infinitely filled with contradictions and terrors, a God with whom we must wrestle. Yet, this unknown God is at the same time the revealed God—not the God that can be grasped in theological formulas or moral maxims, or glimpsed only in times of light, but the God revealed in demonic times of darkness and brutality. Indeed, it is the "picture of promise and redemption in the picture of the crucified Christ . . . as the embodiment of the hidden and revealed wisdom of God [that] may help us also to understand the mysteries with which we are presently struggling."[17]

Liberal Theology: History and Interpretation

The crucial issue between the new generation of dialectical theologians and the Liberal theology—both the Ritschlianism of Herrmann and Harnack and the Idealism of Troeltsch—concerned the question of historical consciousness, its claims and its limits. For Bultmann, Gogarten, and Barth, this was the crux of the problem and, finally, the issue that was to divide them as well. We already have noted the prominence of this question in Barth's criticism of Jülicher and Wernle in the prefaces to his second edition of the *Römerbrief*.

Bultmann also engaged the issue in an early essay entitled "Liberal Theology and the Latest Theological Movement" (1924), where he addresses the preoccupation of Liberal theology with the issue of faith and modern historical consciousness. The Liberals were confident that critical historical research had proved to be theologically liberating. It had freed belief from the burden of dogmatic tradition, which, it believed, had led to a truer comprehension of the historical figure of Jesus on which faith could now confidently rest. Bultmann, however, now sees the theological claims of Herrmann, Harnack, and Troeltsch as deeply flawed by two conclusions of historical understanding to which they were committed, and which had been exposed so painstakingly and profoundly by Troeltsch. The first flaw

is the belief that historical research can itself "lead to any result which could serve as a basis for faith, for *all its results have only relative validity.*" The widely divergent pictures of Jesus produced by the scholars of the liberal school, and their different assessments as to how much knowledge of the historical Jesus is possible, are evidence to Bultmann of how unstable is a faith based on "historical results."

The real question is evaded by the Liberal theology. This is evident in Troeltsch's insistence that a picture of the historical Jesus is necessary for faith, and that this implies that "there remains an actual dependence on the general sense of historical reliability which results from the impact of scientific research." What Troeltsch did not appear to comprehend is that this contradicts his first principle of historicism, namely, that all the results of historical criticism have only relative validity. Troeltsch's feeble plea is, in effect: "The situation is not really very bad and the results of historic-critical theology are still usable for faith." As we will see, this assumption of Liberal theology strikes Bultmann more acutely in the questions that Harnack addresses to Barth in their 1923 correspondence on the historical-critical method.

At this time, Bultmann and Barth were closely allied on the issue of radical historical research and its assumptions about the historical Jesus and faith. Both fully accepted historical criticism; but both also saw it, as Bultmann expressed it, as "needed . . . because it frees us from bondage to every historical construction . . . and brings us to a realization that the world that faith wills to grasp is absolutely unattainable by means of scientific research."[18] Here we see the influence of their teacher, Wilhelm Herrmann. But both agree that Herrmann carried his insight only halfway, because he continued to believe that there is "a bit of reality which can enter the life of every man, and which is 'perceptible' as the *revelation of God.*" For Herrmann this reality was the "inner life of Jesus." Bultmann concurs with Barth in his rejection of Herrmann's compromise with scientific history: "Barth rejects this answer, not only because he knows that New Testament research has generally led to the concession that we can know little, or almost nothing of the inner life of Jesus, but because Jesus as a man belongs to the psychic historical reality, to the 'world,' and we cannot be helped by such psychic historical perceptiveness."[19]

Bultmann's critics charged that he was saving himself from skepticism by a flight to Barth and Gogarten, but he replied at the time:

I have never felt uncomfortable with my critical radicalism; on the contrary I have been entirely comfortable. But I often have the impression that my conservative New Testament colleagues feel very uncomfortable, for I see them perpetually engaged in salvage operations. I calmly let the fire burn, for I see that what is consumed is only the fanciful portraits of the Life-of-Jesus theology, and that means nothing other than the (*Christos kata sarka*) "Christ after the flesh."[20]

Bultmann's comments direct us to the crucial second error that both he and Barth detect as implied in the historical standpoint of the Liberal theology. Not only had it forgotten that its historical results have only relative validity; it also had failed to remember that *all* historical occasions are "*entities which exist only within an immense inter-related complex.*" Jesus, too, must be so understood within this natural-historical totality. Troeltsch had admitted as much, and Bultmann sees Troeltsch's admission as clear evidence that for him "*Christianity* is understood *as a phenomenon of this world, subject to the laws of social psychology.*" For Bultmann this "is not *theology*, not if God is the subject and the theologian is speaking as a *Christian.*"

Bultmann further insists that Troeltsch is able to propose his social conception of Jesus only *because* Jesus is included in the complex of general historical interrelations; that is, "the belief that *the revelation of God in history can be perceived precisely within this nexus of relations.*" Therefore, it is possible to speak of Troeltsch as proposing a "pantheism of history" analogous to the various "pantheisms of nature." Bultmann points out that Barth and Gogarten are simply being consistent:

There is *no direct knowledge of God, either in nature or history.*

Bultmann illustrates the moral and religious outworking of this "pantheism of history" in the various liberal lives of Jesus that portray him as moral exemplar and spiritual personality; for example, in Harnack's depiction of Jesus's preaching of the Sermon on the Mount. Harnack refuses to see the sermon's demands as a worldly impossibility and therefore as a "stumbling-block." Rather, he presents Jesus's sermon as a norm of ethical activity in the "world," in this present age. This is evident when Harnack asserts: "In contrast to two or three hundred years ago, we today already feel a moral obligation to move in this direction. The more sensitive and therefore more prophetic among us no longer view the kingdom of love and peace as a mere Utopia" (*What Is Christianity?* 1901). It is this "pantheism of history" that Barth now refers to as "religion"—as distinct from faith—religion being a state of spiritual consciousness present in humanity itself.

Gogarten also carried on a prolonged criticism of Troeltsch's theological historicism. In an essay in defense of Barth's *Romans* directed against Jülicher's attack, Gogarten calls on Kierkegaard's argument in the *Philosophical Fragments* regarding the incommensurability between history and the Absolute. Gogarten points out that there are two incompatible ways of conceiving the relationship between God's revelation and history. In the one pursued by Hegel and by Troeltsch, the individual perceives the entire span of historical development as the proper sphere of God's revelation, in which there is posited a "creative synthesis" between the relative and the Absolute. The second and alternative way of understanding the relationship between revelation and history is that proposed by the dialectical theologians. It perceives authentic divine revelation "in God's original action *which does not enter into its own effects and consequences and is not modified by and recognizable in them,* but which must be grasped ever and again in its pure original nature beyond its historical effects and forms. . . ."[21] (Italics added.)

Two antithetical methods are assumed in these two conceptions of the relationship between God's revelation and history. In Troeltsch's case, historical research is required to establish the actual historical facts. This involves the exploration of the historical process in which the Absolute is to be discovered in this sphere of "probabilities and endless approximations." The dialectical method does not follow this path

of historical approximation and probability, because the goal, God's original deed, does not lie there. But if it is at a given place, that is, where it made its original appearance, and is for us, the latecomers, tied to the historical record which brings us its message by that unending passage of time, then there remains for us only the "leap" out of the endless mediacy of history to the place where it is located. But this leap is no greater and no harder for us than it was for the apostles, who lived and walked with Christ.[22]

Troeltsch responded to Gogarten's "Romantic" idea of an "Absolute moment" in an essay entitled "An Apple from the Tree of Kierkegaard." He charges Gogarten with proposing a Christianity wholly personal and private, one that "corresponds to no church or confession or historical form . . . deriving from a sharp radicalism against the world, the nation, the state, culture, and church," but claiming to be the Christianity of Christ.[23] Troeltsch argues that, on the contrary, the Christianity expounded by Jesus, Paul, and Luther all see the need of the Christian community to relate itself, indeed to accommodate itself, in some degree to the world; "only in this way did the church become an entity of historical reality at all," and the churches ever since have had to work out various types of mediation with the world. Troeltsch regards Gogarten's "Absolute moment" as devoid of a publicly accessible content, a dangerous *gnosis*, an inflamed subjective spiritualism.[24]

In reply, Gogarten suggests that Dialectical theology also proposes "a both-and," but not the one envisioned by Troeltsch's "constantly new, creative synthesis." It is, rather, the "both-and" of

faith that believes, dialectically, "in the full presence of the Absolute in the present" but also "in the absolute distance of this moment . . . from God."[25] Gogarten thinks it is folly for Troeltsch to assume that his "creative synthesis" of the Absolute and the relative is a genuine possibility because his purported "synthesis touches neither the relative nor the Absolute."

Strictly speaking, Troeltsch ought not to speak of the Absolute here at all, for the Absolute really means that which is an absolute contrast to all that is conditioned or relative; it is free of all connections. It is then totally inconceivable that the Absolute could have a form possible for a given moment, one that is conditioned by the moment and its situation. It is likewise inconceivable that there could be an approximation of the Absolute, that is, a situation conditioned by something other than the Absolute. The instant one places the Absolute under a condition, that is, the instant one speaks, for example of a form possible for a given moment, he is no longer dealing with the Absolute, but with the conditioned and relative.[26]

Gogarten may be correct that Troeltsch's effort to achieve a creative synthesis of the Absolute and the relative does embrace an implicit pantheism of history. But the reader also will note that Gogarten's appeal to the both-and of faith gives exceedingly little guidance on how the "full presence of the Absolute in the present" can be discerned when faith affirms simultaneously the dialectical "absolute distance" or "otherness" of God in any revelatory, historical moment—unless such guidance is given by some unmediated spiritual intuition or by the pure gracious gift of insight or knowledge. As we will see subsequently, this is the problem that the dialectical theologians seek to address in their later theologies—and which will take them in quite opposing directions.

The irreconcilable differences between the older liberalism and the dialectical theologians on the critical issue of revelation and history are most pronounced in the 1923 correspondence between Harnack and Barth, published in *Die*

Christliche Welt. Harnack had long been troubled by what he had heard and read from Gogarten and Barth, and he believed that theology was taking a dangerous turn toward gnosticism and subjectivism. He expressed his anxious concern in "Fifteen Questions to the Despisers of Scientific Theology"—directed especially to Barth. The questions range over a number of issues, but they all converge on the necessity and the role of historical knowledge in understanding both the Bible and the person of Jesus Christ.

Harnack addresses this central issue directly in two of his questions:

(1) Is the religion of the Bible, or its revelations, so completely a unity that in relation to faith, worship and life one may simply speak of "the Bible"? If this is not so, may one leave the determination of the content of the gospel solely to the individual's heuristic knowledge, to his subjective experience, or does one not rather need here historical knowledge and critical reflection?[27] (14) If the person of Jesus Christ stands at the centre of the gospel, how else can the basis for reliable and communal knowledge of this person be gained but through critical-historical study so that an imagined Christ is not put in place of the real one? What else besides scientific theology is able to undertake this study?[28]

Harnack's concern is that Barth invites both a "subjective" interpretation of the Bible and an "imagined Christ." Barth replies to Harnack's second question as follows:

The reliability and communality of the knowledge of the person of Jesus Christ as the centre of the *gospel* can be none other than that of the God-awakened *faith*. Critical-historical study signifies the deserved and necessary end of *those* "foundations" of this knowledge which are no foundations at all since they have not been laid by God himself. Whoever does not yet know that we *no* longer know Christ according to the flesh, should let the critical study of the Bible tell him so . . . This might turn out to be the service which historical knowledge can render to the actual task of theology.[29]

Harnack simply found Barth's view of biblical revelation "incomprehensible," and concerning

biblical science and our knowledge of the person of Jesus Christ, Harnack protested that Barth had opened "the gates to every suitable fantasy and every theological dictatorship."[30] Harnack's personal charges and the obvious impasse between them provoked Barth to reply again through an extended account of his doctrine of revelation. Although this did not convince Harnack, it clarified the nature of the "chasm" that divided them, and it essentially brought the discussion to a close.

In his reply Barth denies that he wants to be "rid" of critical biblical science; what he opposes is the foregone conclusion that historical criticism can itself discover the truth of the Gospel from above or "*beyond the 'Scriptures'* and *apart from* the 'Spirit'"; that is, apart from what the Protestant Reformers called the Word of God that speaks through the witness of the Scriptures empowered through the Holy Spirit, the *testimonium Spiritus Sancti internum*. Barth insists that one need not *accept* the testimony of Scripture, but one must begin there because the interpreter should take seriously the fact that Christianity had its first beginnings in the testimony of the Scriptures.

According to this testimony, the Word became flesh, God himself became a human-historical *reality* and that this took place in the *person of Jesus Christ.* But from this it by no means follows for me [Barth] that this event can also be an object of human-historical *cognition.* This is excluded insofar as *this* reality is concerned. The existence of a Jesus of Nazareth, for example, which can of course be discovered historically, is not *this* reality.[31]

Here Barth is pressing Kierkegaard's point that in this event the Word became flesh, God the Eternal enters time in the person of Jesus Christ, and that this is an *act of God,* a miracle in the sense that it is not a human possibility, that it is beyond human cognition, that it is not discernible by the methods of historical science.

The historical reality of Christ is not the "historical Jesus" whom an all too eager historical research had wanted to lay hold of . . . but rather the *risen* one. . . . That is the "evangelical, the historic Jesus Christ" and otherwise, that is, apart from the testimony to him, apart from the revelation which must be here believed, "we know him no longer."[32]

It is here that Barth sees the theological role of historical criticism, namely, in "making clear to us *a posteriori* . . . that in the Bible we have to do with testimonies and *only* testimonies." Acceptance of the testimony of Scripture is what Barth calls *faith,* an obedience to a human word which testifies as God's Word addressed to me. Barth is reminding Harnack of the warning of Barth's own mentor Herrmann:

Let no one have any delusions here about the fact that this is an unprecedented event, that here one must speak of the *Holy Spirit* if all the objections Herrmann rammed into our heads against a "mere credence" in historical facts *apart* from this basis of cognition are not to hold good. Therefore I distinguish faith as *God's working* on us . . . from all known and unknown human organs and functions, even our so-called "experiences of God."[33]

The only theological objectivity in which Barth places any confidence is the correlation of the testimony of Scripture with the testimony of the Holy Spirit. It is here that Barth sees the nerve center of all of Harnack's objections, namely, the fact that Barth is content with accepting

the testimonial character of all that which occurs here and there in time and as a result of man. I explicitly *deny* the possibility of positing anything relative as absolute . . . be it in history or in ourselves, or in Kierkegaardian terms, of going from testimony to "direct statement." . . . The fact that eternity becomes time, that the absolute becomes relative, that God becomes man. . . . This can only be *witnessed to* and *believed* because it is revealed.[34]

For this reason *dialectical* thinking is required. The "historical Jesus" reconstructed from the records is not identical to revelation, to the act of God, which cannot be *directly* perceived in history. Yet the connection between God and history is not

severed; the relationship is dialectical, which means that the action of God in the event of Jesus Christ must be understood in the terms that *God has established* and not in our turning it into a premature identity of time and eternity, history and the Absolute. The tension and mystery inherent in holding together the sovereignty of God and the human requires that all human testimony be understood dialectically as both "no" and "yes"— for revelatory truth never can be pronounced directly or as the last word.

The various themes that came to be associated with Dialectical theology largely emerged from the encounters between the young members of the movement and the defenders of the then-dominant Liberal theology. Although these distinctive themes are replete in the writings of most of the members of the *Zwischen den Zeiten* circle, they are most prominently exhibited in the writings of Karl Barth during the early 1920s.

MAJOR THEMES IN KARL BARTH'S THEOLOGY OF THE WORD OF GOD

The Dialectical Method

The theologians of *krisis* took much of their basic orientation from Kierkegaard. Like the Dane, they recognized that the truth is not found in the smooth Hegelian dialectic from thesis to antithesis to synthesis but, rather, in the dialectical tension between truth and truth—a tension never fully resolved. And this is because Christian theology is grounded in revelation; i.e., in the union of the two worlds of eternity and time, for which we have no analogy. Our language about revelation consists of words that attempt to express the intersection of our horizontal line of existence by the vertical line of God's transcendence. So, Barth argues, this relation of time and eternity can be expressed only paradoxically. Theology frequently has attempted to get at the truth immediately, either by means of *dogmatism* or *mysticism*, but all attempts at immediacy must fail. There is, however, a third way—the way of dialectic. Yet the dialectical method never reaches a "solution," a triumphant synthesis or stable position. One who follows this method is like a bird in flight, always on the move.

Our task is to interpret the Yes and the No and the No by the Yes without delaying more than a moment in either a fixed Yes *or* a fixed No; to speak of the glory of God in creation, for example, only to pass immediately to emphasizing God's complete conceal-ment from us in that creation; . . . of the creation of man in the image of God simply and solely to give warning once and for all that man as we know him is fallen man. . . . I need not continue. He that hath ears to hear will understand my meaning.[35]

To the liberal theologian, Barth's dialectic is merely perplexing, for he or she is used to know-ing God *immediately,* of positing continuity between the divine and the human. This is exactly what Barth denies—that we can know the nature of God by starting with our own his-torical or psychic experience. God is not simply a human being writ large. We cannot capture the truth about the eternal God in our own finite for-mulas. We can only witness to the paradoxicality of God's own self-revelation, and dialectic is all that can be expected.

I have done what I could to make you see that neither my affirmation nor my denial lays claim to being God's truth. Neither one is more than a *witness* to the truth, which stands in the center, between every "Yes and No."[36]

The dialectical method is the only way of pre-serving the truth that God is not humanity—that God is beyond the finite realm—and yet is revealed within it. This alone can maintain the "Godness of God," the Wholly Otherness of the divine self-revelation in time.

God as Wholly Other

The rediscovery of the "distance" between God and the creature—hence the "otherness" of God—is the leitmotiv of the crisis theology. It lies at the root of Barth's polemic against rationalism

and mysticism, for both rely upon human resources and human experience for knowledge of God. For Barth the first task of theology is to emphasize the infinite distance between God the Creator and the creature.

God can only be known through God. The finite creation is not a direct revelation of God. On the contrary, the creation *hides* God. This, claims Barth, is the real paradoxical meaning of Romans 1:20.

By calm, veritable, unprejudiced religious contempla-tion the divine "No" can be established and appre-hended. If we do not ourselves hinder it, nothing can prevent our being translated into a most wholesome *KRISIS* by that *which may be known of God.* And indeed, we stand already in the *KRISIS* if we would but *see clearly.* And what is clearly seen to be indis-putable reality is the invisibility of God. . . . And what does this mean but that we can know nothing of God, that we are not God, that the Lord is to be feared? Herein lies His pre-eminence over all gods; and here is that which marks Him out as God, as Creator and Redeemer.[37]

The creation, when clearly seen, will declare the divine "no," will produce that real *krisis* in which we will come to know that from our crea-turely perspective, God is always hidden and un-known. We will discover the Reformed principle: *Finitum non capax infiniti,* the finite cannot con-tain the infinite. God is Wholly Other. God is not given directly in the human heart or in the world of nature. "There is no way from man to God."

There is, however, the way from God to humanity—the way of God's gracious self-revela-tion. God is known only by God, by his revelation in Jesus Christ. What, then, is impossible for us humans has been made possible by God. In Christ, God is revealed, God speaks. But here, too, the God revealed, the *Deus revelatus,* is also the hidden God, *Deus absconditus.* We cannot say that God remains hidden until revealed. In the *krisis* of faith we know that the God revealed in Jesus Christ is, indeed, the hidden God! The knowledge of God in Jesus Christ and God's hid-denness are, paradoxically, one and the same. It is especially in Jesus, as the Christ, that we see the awful hiddenness of God. For this reason, the seeing is not of the normal order of seeing—it requires the eyes of faith, which are a gift of grace. God's revelation is always indirect and veiled and thus requires grace, for it manifests itself in a world where sin and "the flesh" rule. Revelation is a mystery, for it not only signifies the hiddenness of God but also God's becoming manifest in a hidden or nonapparent way. God's revelation is always an "in spite of." It is never transparent. For confirmation we need only to look at the biblical picture of Jesus Christ.

He takes the form of a slave; He moves to the cross and to death; His greatest achievement is a negative achievement. He is not a genius . . . he is not a hero or leader of men. He is neither poet nor thinker: *My God, my God, why hast thou forsaken me?* . . . In Jesus revelation is a paradox. . . . Therefore it is not accessible to our perception. . . . He becomes a scandal to the Jews and to the Greeks foolishness. In Jesus the communication of God begins with a rebuff, with the exposure of a vast chasm, with the clear revelation of a great stumbling-block. . . . To believe in Jesus is the most hazardous of all hazards.[38]

In Christ, God's unveiling is also veiling, and so the individual's relation to God is always that of faith, never sight. The distance, the incommensurableness remains. One does *not possess* revelation as an object, but one is given the gift of faith.

The quest of the historical Jesus is, for Barth, both a futile historical task and a sign of unbelief. In the earthly Jesus we encounter either an apocalyptical fanatic *or* the divine incognito. In either case, God cannot be seen directly in the earthly Jesus. God is revealed in Jesus as the *Christ*, only by an event that breaks the bounds of history. The incognito is lifted by Christ's resurrection from the dead which is a scandal, for it constitutes an *eternal event*, an event that cannot be described historically.

Jesus has been . . . *declared to be the Son of God with power, according to the Holy Spirit, through his resurrection from the dead.* In this declaration and appoint-

ment—which are beyond historical definition—lies the true significance of Jesus. As Christ, Jesus is the plane which lies beyond our comprehension. The plane which is known to us, He intersects vertically from above. . . . In the Resurrection the new world of the Holy Spirit touches the old world of the flesh. . . . *Even though we have known Christ after the flesh yet now we know him so no longer.*[39]

This mysterious "inner two-sidedness" of revelation in Jesus Christ is mere foolishness to the world. The gift of faith alone makes the divine transvaluation, this otherness and mystery of God's being and doing, apprehensible.

The Strange World of the Bible

A strange and unexpected Word of God is what we encounter when we turn and *really* listen to the Bible. This, Barth tells us, we do not wish to do. We prefer to go to the Bible with our own presuppositions, our own worldview, which we then read out of the Bible as its own. And the Bible allows us to do this if we do not really press the question of what lies within the Bible.

The Bible gives to every man and to every era such answers to their questions as they deserve. We shall always find in it as much as we seek and no more: high and divine content if it is high and divine content that we seek; transitory and "historical" content if it is transitory and "historical" content that we seek . . . What is within the Bible? has a mortifying way of converting itself into the opposing question, Well, what are you looking for?[40]

One can find all kinds of edifying things in the Bible—if one does not penetrate too deeply. But on closer inspection one finds that the Bible contains little of real value in the realm of history, morals, and religion. Readers want to know how things happen, what are the natural causes of things. It is on this decisive question of history that the Bible remains silent.[41]

A similar problem is encountered with regard to morals. We look to the Bible for good practical wisdom and for examples of moral excellence—but again we are disappointed.

Large parts of the Bible are almost useless to the school in its moral curriculum because they are lacking in just this wisdom and just these "good examples." The heroes of the Bible are to a certain degree quite respectable, but to serve as examples to the good, efficient, industrious, publicly educated, average citizen of Switzerland, men like Samson, David, Amos, and Peter are very ill fitted indeed. . . . How unceremoniously and constantly is war waged in the Bible.[42]

The Bible often is of little *practical* value, and this is because it is a witness to "the 'other,' new, greater world," because it is not *of* this world.

When we come to the Bible with our questions—How shall I think of God and the universe? How arrive at the divine? How present myself?—it answers us, as it were, "My dear sir, these are *your* problems: you must not ask *me*! . . ."

It is not the right human thoughts about God which form the content of the Bible, but the right divine thoughts about men. . . . We have found in the Bible a new world, God, God's sovereignty, God's glory, God's incomprehensible love. . . . Not human standpoints but the standpoints of God.[43]

What we find in the Bible is the world of God's incomprehensible being and acting, which drives us out beyond ourselves, beyond the Bible as the mirror of our own reflection, to the world of God. It is only when we arrive at this point that we encounter the *krisis*, the awakening to the relativity of all *our* thoughts and expectations. Only then are we prepared to hear of the *last things* that make known the truth that is hidden from the wise of the world. At that point only one possibility remains, but that lies *beyond* all thinking and all things—the possibility:

Behold, I make all things new! The affirmation of God, man, and the world given in the New Testament based exclusively upon the possibility of a new order absolutely beyond human thought; and therefore, as prerequisite to that order, there must come a crisis that denies all human thought.[44]

The strangeness of the Bible is connected with its very revelatory character. Revelation requires that it be received and witnessed to through the mediation of worldliness. But the fact that God chooses to so reveal himself is part of God's veiledness and mystery. That God should reveal himself in the relative and problematical literature of the Bible is comparable to the scandal and mystery of the Incarnation. The worldly character of the Bible, therefore, is no accidental condition that we could hope would someday be removed. The indirectness of its witness is integral to its revelatory character.

The radically human and fallible character of the Bible is one of Barth's most consistent themes.[45] Contrary to what Liberal theology claims, the Bible does not contain universally noble and sublime truths. "The Bible," says Barth, "is the literary monument of an ancient racial religion and of a Hellenistic cult religion of the Near East. A human document like any other."[46] This means that the biblical witnesses are fallible and that their historical and scientific judgments are often erroneous. Moreover, the vulnerability of the Bible extends to its religious or theological content. That the Bible is the word of man is plain enough. And yet, paradoxically, to say that is to speak only half the truth. The Bible is *both* word of man and Word of God. However, the revealedness of the Bible as Word of God can be perceived, through the human limitations and barriers, only by a miracle of grace.

It is evident that for Barth the Bible is not a "content" that we can control. We cannot properly even say that the Bible *is* the Word of God. Rather, we can only go to the Bible *remembering* that the Church has heard God's Word in the Bible and *expecting* that we *will also* hear God's Word—to have faith in a "divine disposing." The Bible only *becomes* God's Word. To say that the Bible is the Word of God is, therefore, not to say that the Word of God is tied to the Bible. God's Word is nothing else than the free disposing of

God's grace. Put more succinctly, for Barth knowledge of the Word of God is not an anthropological problem!

THE BREAKDOWN OF THE DIALECTICAL THEOLOGY

The Dialectical theologians concurred on various crucial matters; for example, on the necessity of a critique of current Liberal theology and bourgeois culture, on all attempts to objectify God or to establish scientific foundations of faith or to identify revelation with church doctrine. Yet these theologians never constituted a coherent school. The group was held together in a loose association around their publication *Zwischen den Zeiten* for, at best, a decade. The correspondence between these allies reveals the fundamental theological disagreements that separated them from the very beginning. The crux of their growing conflict focused on the issues of revelation and history and especially on the place of anthropology in theology. The differences on these matters between Bultmann, Gogarten, Brunner, and Tillich were, on the whole, not fundamental, but they became so for Barth and for Thurneysen. The gulf between Barth and Bultmann and Gogarten is evident in their response to one another's writings as early as 1922.

Bultmann agreed with Barth that it was the first requirement of the interpreter to penetrate to the essence of a text by sympathetic understanding. However, in his review of the second edition of Barth's *Romans,* he rejects Barth's assumption of a historical continuity between the past and present. Barth had refused to allow a second stage of the interpretive task, one that involves the historical responsibility of judging whether what is said in the text is an adequate expression of the true subject matter. In his review, Bultmann contends, on the contrary, that "it is impossible to assume that everywhere in the Letter to Romans the subject matter must have found adequate expression, unless one intends to establish a modern dogma of inspiration, and something like this seems to stand behind Barth's exegesis"—a point

that Barth readily acknowledges. Bultmann insists that when he endeavors to demonstrate how Paul is dependent on Jewish eschatology or Hellenistic philosophy or sacramental practice, he is "thereby practicing not only philological historical criticism." Rather, he is "showing where and how the subject matter is expressed, in order to grasp the subject matter, which is greater even than Paul."[47]

Barth sees Bultmann's twofold interpretive task, however, as a "mix of fire and water." That is, it assumes that one could write *with* Paul in his Jewish-Hellenistic thought world "and then suddenly, when this may get to be too much for me— as if something struck me as especially strange where everything is strange!—to speak 'critically' *about* and *against* Paul."[48] The gulf between the two is apparent here. Bultmann insists that it is not a question of simply taking issue with Paul when things become too "strange" for him, as Barth asserts. Rather, "faithfulness to the author may be demonstrated by sometimes having to correct the material into which we are led by him." And Bultmann recognizes here a deep cultural divide between himself and Barth, a divide that has to do with their respective relationships to history. For Bultmann "Hellenistic mysticism or Jewish legalism is not just a matter of historical interest by means of which I can 'explain' some of the sayings of Paul. Rather, these phenomena represent intellectual attitudes which must draw the scholar into debate with the sources."[49] Barth adamantly refuses to take this second step; it is, he believes, the stance of the spectator, a human effort to separate the Spirit from the spirits. This hermeneutical impasse is, as we will see in subsequent chapters, to divide these two giants of Protestant theology for the rest of their lives.

As the correspondence between Barth and Bultmann reveals, the personal relations between the two remained frank and cordial, despite the growing awareness that theologically they were deeply divided. The same was not true of the relations between Barth and Gogarten. Barth was uneasy about Gogarten from the beginning, and Gogarten increasingly felt that Barth did not give his work proper consideration. Barth often had difficulty understanding what Gogarten was saying and remained skeptical about him. On the other hand, Bultmann and Gogarten increasingly came to recognize that they were pursuing a common course in their efforts to ground theology in an existentialist anthropology through the influence of the philosopher Martin Heidegger. Barth sensed that there would soon be "a great explosion within ZZ." He confessed to Bultmann that he did not see his way "through all that does seem to be up in air between you, Gogarten and me." But that something was "up in the air" was clear to him through his reading of Bultmann's and Gogarten's most recent writings.[50]

When Barth moved to Gottingen in 1922 to take up the chair of Reformed theology, he began preparing lectures for his first dogmatics, and this project continued after his move to the University of Münster in 1925. The work appeared as *Prolegomena zur Christlichen Dogmatik* (1927), and it was now evident that Barth was steering his own course and was distancing himself from the other dialectical theologians. Clearly, the issue was the question of an anthropological starting point. In a review of Barth's "Christian Dogmatics" and in an article of the same year entitled "The Problem of a Theological Anthropology" (1929), Gogarten objected to Barth's theology on the grounds that it lacked a "proper anthropology" as the "center" and "the real problem of theology."[51] For Gogarten, Barth's refusal to develop an adequate anthropological base was closely connected to his failure to investigate the question of the scientific nature of theology which, for Gogarten, meant exploring the relationship between theology and philosophy and all that it involved.[52]

Barth interpreted Gogarten's concern with anthropology as an attempt to ground theology in a conception of human existence. Gogarten had written that "there is no understanding of man without understanding God, but . . . this God again I cannot understand, unless I already understand man.[53] To Barth the word "already" appeared to give priority to an understanding of the human situation—although this may not

have been fair to Gogarten's dialectic at the time—that is, to presuppose some "preunderstanding" with regard to the human, which was now also being proposed by Bultmann's existentialist hermeneutics. All this "starting with the human" was, for Barth, the first step in the direction of a *natural theology*, a path that Emil Brunner already had taken in his new apologetics and his search for a "point of contact" between the Word of God and the human situation. In early 1930 Barth wrote to Bultmann, essentially announcing his theological break with his Marburg friend, as well as with Gogarten and Brunner. He saw a common anthropological starting point emerging in the work of all three.

From my standpoint all of you . . . represent a large scale return to the fleshpots of Egypt. I mean that if I am not deceived, all of you—in a new way different from that of the nineteenth century—are trying to understand faith as a human possibility, or, if you will, as grounded in a human possibility, and therefore you are once again surrendering theology to philosophy. . . . For me there can be no question but that I can only oppose it in the future. . . .[54]

Four of the most prominent colleagues associated with the aims of *Zwischen den Zeiten*—Barth, Bultmann, Gogarten, and Brunner—were by the late 1920s pursuing their own creative yet divergent theological paths. Although the Dialectical theology was to prove only a temporary phenomenon, it was nevertheless the creative incubator of several distinctive theological programs. Each one of these programs was to leave its imprint on theological developments over the next three or four decades. In the remainder of this chapter we will examine the principal themes in the later work of Emil Brunner and Friedrich Gogarten. In Chapter Four we will survey in some detail the development of Karl Barth's theology and its ripening in the massive twelve-volume *Church Dogmatics*. Chapter Five explores the ways in which both Rudolf Bultmann and Paul Tillich constructed their distinctive and influential theologies with the assistance of Existentialist philosophy.

EMIL BRUNNER

The German-speaking theologian who had the widest readership and the greatest influence in the English-speaking world between 1930 and 1950 was, perhaps surprisingly, Emil Brunner (1889–1966) and not Karl Barth, Rudolf Bultmann, or even Paul Tillich. In the 1950s, however, these three were to eclipse Brunner in both repute and influence. It is also noteworthy that Brunner was never held in high esteem in Germany, in part because he did not hold a teaching position there and because his works were banned by the Nazis relatively early in the 1930s.

Emil Brunner was born near Zürich, Switzerland, in 1889. His early schooling was in the *Gymnasium* in Zürich. He then studied at the University of Zürich, where he completed his doctorate in theology. He taught in a high school in Leeds, England, in 1913 to 1914, but the sojourn ended with the outbreak of the First World War. After brief service in the Swiss border militia, he served as vicar in Hermann Kutter's church, the Neumünster, in Zürich and then between 1916 and 1924 was pastor of a small congregation in the mountains of Obstalden in the canton of Glarus. In 1917 he married Margrit Lauterburg, the niece of Hermann Kutter. The associations with Kutter were not coincidental. Brunner's father had been influenced by the theologian, spiritual leader, and Religious Socialist Christoph Blumhardt (1842–1919). Through Blumhardt, the Brunner family was drawn to his two Swiss pupils, Kutter and Leonhard Ragaz, and into Religious Socialism. Like Karl Barth, Emil Brunner was deeply affected by the movement of Religious Socialism. It also was Ragaz, his teacher at Zürich, who introduced Brunner to Kierkegaard. Brunner was attracted to Karl Barth and the *Zwischen den Zeiten* circle largely because these men confirmed the directions of his own thinking, and because Barth and Thurneysen, too, were closely allied to Blumhardt, Kutter, Ragaz, and their movement.[55]

It was during his pastorate in solitary Obstalden that Brunner wrote his first two books, his inaugural thesis *Experience, Knowledge and Faith* (1921) and the provocative *Die Mystik und das Wort* (1924), his critical attack on the theology of Schleiermacher. These books led to his appointment to the chair of systematic and practical theology at the University of Zürich, a position he held from 1924 to 1955. Often ignored is the fact that, in addition to theology, Brunner taught homiletics and pastoral care during this period and regularly preached at the famous Fraumünster church in Zürich. His earliest, widely influential book was *The Mediator* (1927), a study of Christology. It was soon translated into English and was to have a considerable impact on English and American theology. The cultural and political situation in Europe, and the need to address its pressing practical needs, convinced Brunner that theology had "another task" than simply the proclamation of the Gospel; it needed to enter into dialogue with that culture. And that meant engaging philosophy and political thought with the question of anthropology, because every system and ideology presupposes some anthropological foundation.

In developing his distinctive theological anthropology, Brunner was profoundly influenced by the I-Thou philosophy of Ferdinand Ebner and Martin Buber. The latter's influential book, *I and Thou,* had appeared in 1923. Brunner's initial anthropological reflections were outlined in *Man in Revolt* (1935), which he later judged to be his most important contribution to theology. The previous year he had published a small work entitled *Nature and Grace* (1934). As we will see, these two works confirmed Karl Barth's judgment that Brunner had returned "to the fleshpots of Egypt." Barth responded to Brunner with an "angry," unyielding essay, *Nein! (No!).*

Brunner's anthropological explorations focused next on the fundamental question of truth. This culminated in the publication of *Wahrheit als Begegnung* 1937 (translated as *The Divine–Human Encounter*). The book represents one of Brunner's most distinctive and influential contributions to Christian theology, namely, his contrast between the Greek and Western rationalist conception of truth and the biblical Christian understanding of truth as personal encounter

Emil Brunner

and communication. Brunner further developed this theme in an important apologetic work in 1941, entitled *Offenbarung und Vernunft* (*Revelation and Reason*), a prolegomena to his planned dogmatics. The latter appeared in three volumes of 1,200 pages, completed over a period of sixteen years, during which time Brunner was engaged in many other significant ecclesial and ecumenical responsibilities. His *Dogmatics* include *The Christian Doctrine of God* (1950), *The Christian Doctrine of Creation and Redemption* (1952), and *The Christian Doctrine of the Church, Faith and Consummation* (1962). During his entire career Brunner remained deeply engaged by social and ethical questions, and this is reflected in many of his writings, including books such as *The Divine Imperative* (1932), *Justice and the Social Order* (1943), and *Christianity and Civilization*, 2 vol. (1948–1949).

Two features of Brunner's career, not characteristic of the other theologians discussed in this chapter, were his worldwide travels and engagements and his extensive involvement with the Ecumenical movement. He spent much time abroad lecturing, teaching, and on educational and ecumenical missions from his early twenties as a high school teacher in England. He spent 1919 to 1920 at Union Theological Seminary in New York, and during that year he lectured at numerous American seminaries. In 1938 to 1939 he was a visiting professor at Princeton Theological Seminary, and he also made frequent lecture tours to Scandinavia, Great Britain, North America, Asia, and Eastern Europe. In his mid-sixties he spent two years in Japan (1953–1955) helping to build up the International Christian University in Tokyo. This experience, which involved lecturing to non-Christian audiences, confirmed his belief in the necessity of Christian apologetics and the need to seek a "point of contact" with other faiths and ideologies.

The other distinctive feature of Brunner's career was his activity on behalf of the worldwide church and the Ecumenical movement. From the 1930s he participated in numerous ecumenical study groups and commissions that helped to shape the theological bases and the plans for the emerging world Ecumenical Alliance. This was especially true of his involvement in the important study commissions on "Life and Work" and "Faith and Order," which prepared the way for the World Church Conference in Oxford in 1937 that preceded the establishment of the World Council of Churches. These various, worldwide engagements enhanced Brunner's influence over a period of three decades, as did the fact that most of his books were promptly translated into English and other languages. The clarity and ease with which he handled difficult theological themes made these writings attractive to a wide audience. Furthermore, for many persons in the immediate postwar years, Brunner represented a sensible middle way between the old orthodoxy and the theology of Barth on the one hand and a weakened and vulnerable liberalism on the other. It is also true, however, that in contrast to Barth, Bultmann, and Tillich, there never developed a "Brunnerian" school. Therefore, despite his appeal and his influence, he never developed zealous disciples who felt bound to further his particular program. That may, in part, explain why his influence was in rapid decline by the mid-1950s.

Anthropology and the Apologetic Task

Brunner considered anthropology "the cardinal point" of his theology[56] because our knowledge of what it means to be human is the "common concern of both secular and Christian (theological) wisdom." The study of human history appears to confirm the fact that humans can ignore God, but they cannot ignore human life, its meaning, and its purpose. "The question 'What is God?' may be regarded as unanswerable or out of date, or uninteresting, but no one would say the same about the question: What is Man?"[57] All social, political, and cultural beliefs and ideologies presuppose an "anthropology." It is this reality that Brunner articulated in his article, "The Other Task of Theology" in *Zwischen den Zeiten* in 1929, and that led him into his acrimonious dispute with Karl Barth over the former's *Nature and Grace* (1934). Anthropology remained a crucial theme in all the subsequent volumes of Brunner's *Dogmatics*. Contrary to Barth's procedure, the issue for Brunner is (1) whether there is a genuine Christian natural theology, by which he means a revelation of God in the Creation, a teaching that Brunner finds supported both by Scripture and by the great Protestant Reformers, Luther and Calvin; and (2) because the Bible teaches that humanity is created in the *image of God*, this *universal* human fact must be taken with complete seriousness in all theological work and dialogue.

Barth's anathemas in *Nein!* convinced Brunner that his appeal to a "Christian *theologia naturalis*" was widely misunderstood, and that he needed to clarify and defend the *right kind* of general revelation or revelation through Creation. This task was required by the demands of what Brunner calls the discipline of *eristics*, a theological responsibility as important as and correlative to that of *dogmatics*. Brunner prefers to use the term "eristics" rather than "apologetics" because, he believes, the latter too often is associated with the *defense* of Christianity by rational argument as, for example, in the classical proofs of the existence of God. Eristics is not so much a defense as

an *attack*, in the manner of Kierkegaard, on non-Christian ideologies of the day—e.g., scientific positivism or Marxism—by showing that they are contrary to reason or are unscientific or are historically untenable.

While this task is necessary, it must not be confused with or serve as the basis of dogmatics, although Brunner claims that "every living proclamation of the Biblical message . . . is full of eristic apologetic elements."[58] Most importantly, eristics presupposes the revelation of God in the Creation and therefore affords a "point of contact" with non-Christian belief systems. Therefore, it allows for a sharing of the same data, for example, that of the natural sciences. What is operative in eristics is what Brunner calls "the law of closeness of relation":

The nearer anything lies to that center of existence where we are concerned with the whole, that is, with man's relation to God and the being of the person, the greater is the disturbance of rational knowledge by sin; the further away anything lies from the center, the less the disturbance is felt, and the less difference there is between knowing as a believer or as an unbeliever. This disturbance reaches its maximum in theology and its minimum in the exact sciences, and zero in the sphere of the formal. Hence it is meaningless to speak of a "Christian mathematics."[59]

It would be quite appropriate, however, to speak of a Christian sociology, because Christian belief will influence one's presuppositions about the individual and about societal relationships. Whereas a Christian believer's interpretation of the findings of a social science must take full account of all the social data and all logical requirements of that discipline, there is no sociological knowledge without presuppositions. As one moves from mathematics to biology to ethics and human personal relations, the conflict of Christian belief with other ethical systems or assumptions will be greater and more critical. Nevertheless, for the Christian to engage the non-Christian he or she must be fully conversant with the facts and issues in question.

To claim that God is revealed in the Creation is not, Brunner insists, the same thing as saying that humans have a natural knowledge of God. To fail to distinguish the two statements is, in Brunner's judgment, the principal reason for his dispute with Barth. Barth assumed that his own denial of a natural theology entailed denying the reality of God's revelation in Creation. But to say that the "natural man" is in a position to perceive divine revelation in Creation is not to say that the natural man *possesses* a true knowledge of God, because "between the revelation in Creation and the natural man there stands the fact of sin."

According to Brunner, natural theology is not to be identified with the Christian doctrine of God. Rather, it is connected "with the doctrine of Man; for 'natural theology' is an anthropological fact which no one can deny."[60] The history of religions provides incontrovertible evidence that humans through the millennia have devised conceptions of deity. Brunner has been misunderstood here. He does not mean that Christianity shares a "point of contact" with, for example, Hindu or African tribal theism, in the sense that Christian theism shares with these religions some common beliefs about God. Rather, the Christian simply acknowledges the fact of this *theologia naturalis* as inherent in what it means to be a human creature of God, created in God's image and in possession of self-transcendence, conscience, freedom, and responsibility.

Knowledge of God, for Brunner, is intimately connected with the dialectic of human sin as rebellion and apostasy or idolatry—the desire to be "as God." It is the case that "man could not be a sinner if he knew nothing of God, but on the other hand, precisely because he is a sinner . . . he cannot know God aright."[61] In the place of God humanity projects its own idols and imaginings, and is responsible for its own idolatry. "Sin, far from eliminating responsibility, and thus this vestige of the *Imago Dei*, is, on the contrary, a witness to a God—willed responsibility, just as the sinful illusion of idolatry is a witness to the God-given revelation in Creation."[62]

Brunner thus defends a form of natural theology as divine revelation through the Creation, and at the same time agrees with Barth that because of sin humans do not possess a natural knowledge of God. It is God in Jesus Christ who encounters the human person, not the human person who can place him or herself in the presence of God. The initiative wholly lies with God and the divine self-revelation in Jesus Christ. We are now prepared to examine Brunner's influential doctrine of revelation, what he calls the Divine-human encounter.[63]

Revelation as Encounter and Truth

Brunner early conceived of his theology as representing a "third way" between liberalism and orthodoxy. Liberalism typifies the error of subjectivism in theology in that it subjects divine revelation to the norms of human reason and experience. Orthodoxy, on the other hand, tends to a one-sided objectivism whereby it seeks to *control* divine revelation through church authority (Roman Catholicism) or through a doctrine of biblical literalism or verbal inerrancy (certain expressions of Protestantism). With regard to this latter form of objectivism, Brunner makes clear the dialectical character of his third way.

Faith in Jesus Christ is not based upon a previous faith in the Bible, but is based solely upon the witness of the Holy Spirit; this witness, however, does not come to us save through the witness of the Apostles. . . . The Scripture—first of all the testimony of the Apostles to Christ—is the "Crib wherein Christ lieth" (Luther). It is a "word" inspired by the Spirit of God; yet at the same time it is a human message; its "human character" means that it is coloured by the frailty and imperfection of all that is human.[64]

Revelation is the free action of God who, through the person of Jesus Christ, is uniquely made present in the apostolic witness as that is given in the Scriptures and is received by grace through the testimony of the Holy Spirit. Brunner contends that such a view of God's self-revelation is free of the errors of both subjectivism and objectivism. Revelation is a divine action that does not *originate* with the human person—it comes *from* God. In that case, it would at first appear to be a wholly objective phenomenon independent of the human subject. But the biblical witness does not claim such a separation; object and subject are both drawn into the act of revelation. "Revelation is indeed that which becomes manifest to *us* through a definite action of God," but it also "means that we, whose eyes were formerly closed, have now opened them to a certain light. . . . Thus revelation only reaches its goal in the subject, man." Revelation is to be understood, then, as "a transitive event which proceeds from God and ends with man, a light ray with these two poles. There is no point in setting the objective fact of revelation over against the subjective act of receiving the revelation, because the revelation actually consists in the meeting of the two subjects."[65]

What distinguishes Christian *faith* from the knowledge possessed by the natural self is the fact that this encounter of the human person is with the Person of God in Christ. And the authority and truth of this revelatory encounter is grounded neither in human reason or experience nor in the authority of Scripture, as such. "Here . . . we find a completely new conception of the authority of Scripture. We are not required to believe the Scriptures because they are the Scriptures; but because Christ, whom I am convinced in my conscience is the Truth, meets me in the Scriptures." Scripture is not what we call a *formal* authority; rather, it is an *instrumental* authority in that it *contains* "that element before which I must bow in the truth."[66] Furthermore, such a faith in the truth of Christ is, according to Brunner, self-authenticating because it is always mediated through human instruments: the early witnesses as well as the human language and thought forms of Scripture. We trust these witnesses because it is through them that we apprehend what is real and true.

The knowledge of God that is given in this personal encounter is "a special kind" of knowledge but, Brunner insists, it is genuine *knowledge*. Though there can be no appeal to rational proof, and while it is poles apart from our rational and scientific knowledge, it is *not* irrational. Here Brunner's elucidation of revelatory *truth as encounter* is deeply indebted to the work of the philosophers Ferdinand Ebner and Martin Buber and their influential epistemological distinction between rational-scientific knowledge (I and It) and personal knowledge (I and Thou). Brunner discovered in Buber's description of the meeting of the I and the Thou—which he also recognized as Kierkegaard's point of departure—the truth of the biblical understanding of the divine-human encounter and knowledge of God.[67]

According to Brunner, the unique quality of human existence is our "answerability" and "responsibility" before the Other, the divine Self. Our genuine humanity is not to be found in our scientific rationality, as some theologians have claimed, but "in this call to the Creator himself . . . who as a Thou calls us to himself." It is in this personal encounter that "man is transformed from a creature of nature into a responsible, spiritually free creature."[68] From this divine-human encounter there originates both a claim and an assurance, and this is what Christianity means by faith. From the perspective of such faith, a person is understood neither as a mere object nor as a solitary, autonomous subject. It is the very claim to unconditional autonomy that is the root of all egoism and what Christianity calls original sin.

The knowledge that is born of the divine-human encounter, is, according to Brunner, "not knowledge at a distance, *theoria*, but a personal call and a bestowal, by which we ourselves are transformed. The truth that Brunner speaks of here "is not truth of the kind that one *has*." It is, rather, "the kind that one *is*—or better, *in* which one *is*."[69] It is a knowledge that is both cognitive and transformative, in that it restores the human self to its original state, to the condition of personhood in relation to the divine Thou.

An important feature of truth as encounter is the realization that it is a truth that "cannot be *held*, or possessed"; rather it takes possession of the self. It can only be received and is, therefore, a gift of grace. It is a *"being in the truth," not a having* or holding of the truth. This, Brunner points out, is the departure of Kierkegaard's *Philosophical Fragments,* namely "that we do not have the truth because we *are* not in the truth."[70] Whereas the *source* of our knowledge of God thus differs from the sources of our knowledge of other persons, Brunner sees the distinctive form of our knowledge of the divine Thou as analogous to our knowledge of other persons. Although our knowledge of persons can be immediate, it often is also mediated through others. So although our knowledge of God in Jesus Christ always is *mediated* through the earliest witnesses, the written Scriptures, and the fellowship of the Church through the action of the Holy Spirit, we can take confidence that we can know the real historical Jesus Christ. While he rejects the nineteenth-century quest of the historical (*historisch*) man Jesus as both futile and contrary to faith, Brunner also disapproves of the disinterest of Barth and Bultmann in the life of Jesus Christ as portrayed in the New Testament. Concerning this portrayal, as mediated through the early witnesses and the Church, Brunner writes:

This twofold testimony is the objective basis of faith. . . . It is in the providence of God that both have been given to us: the picture of the life of Jesus . . . and the doctrine about him. . . . It is a mistake to contrast "Jesus Himself" with the witness of the Apostles; for the doctrine of the Apostles does not aim at saying anything other than who "Jesus Himself" is, and what "Jesus Himself" means for us.[71]

The twin dangers in Christology are to try to prove or support faith in the uniqueness or genius of Jesus by scientific-historical means or by proof texts (objectivism), or to give up any historical claims and collapse faith into a timeless doctrine (Idealism) or into a subjective truth of self-understanding (Existentialism). In both cases genuine biblical faith as the encounter of divine revelation and human response is misled into a false objectivism or subjectivism. Brunner believes that the

early Dialectical theology of both Barth and Bultmann was a genuine witness to the biblical faith in Jesus Christ, but that their later theologies developed along lines that reflect a false understanding of biblical faith. Brunner charges Barth with moving toward a doctrinal objectivism similar to the older orthodoxy and sees Bultmann embracing a subjective conception of faith that harks back to the legacy of Schleiermacher.

In Brunner's opinion, the proof of Barth's one-sided preoccupation with the "object" of faith is Barth's thirty-year absorption in his gigantic twelve-volume *Church Dogmatics,* with its endless refinements and defenses of, for example, the doctrines of the Virgin Birth, the Trinity, and Election—a work comparable to the intricate and vast medieval *Summae.* Brunner writes of the later Barth:

The *objectum fidei,* the "object of faith" exercized so great a fascination upon him that he had neither interest in, nor understanding of, the identity of subject and object in faith, which was for the Reformers the very central doctrine of Christian faith. . . . In Barth this correlation between God and faith is broken. The insight of Luther that "God and faith belong together" is lost, and accordingly Barth does not deal with faith until near the end of his *Dogmatics,* and makes it clear there that faith has a very subordinate place in comparison with the revelation of God.[72]

Brunner sees the mounting criticism of Barth's *Church Dogmatics* in the postwar decades as paralleling a swing to the other extreme—and to the subjectivism of Rudolf Bultmann's project of "demythologization." (See Chapter Five.) Bultmann's existential interpretation of the New Testament was to dominate theological discussion for twenty years after 1945. Brunner has high praise for Bultmann's work as a historian, and he concurs with Bultmann's concern for a reinterpretation of those aspects of the New Testament message that are enveloped in an antique, mythical world picture, such as its Ptolemaic cosmology. But this, he insists, does not represent anything new in modern theology.

Bultmann's fatal error, according to Brunner, is his interchangeable use of the concepts of the "mythical" and "worldview." For example, Bultmann speaks of the New Testament "cosmological idea of the three-story universe" as comparable with the belief that "the earth is also the arena of the activity of supernatural powers," as if they were analogous statements.[73] This confusion of a prescientific mythical cosmology with worldview allows Bultmann to assert, for example, that "the presentation of God's saving Act corresponds to the mythical world-view." In other words, Bultmann understands such New Testament ideas as the sending of the Son of God in the fullness of time and his atoning death on the Cross as myth.[74] Brunner insists, on the contrary, that Christian theology must draw a real distinction between those elements of a worldview whose truth lies in the sphere of natural science and those that entail a naturalism with regard to any talk about the action of God in the world.

The fact that the earth is not a plate, but a ball, and therefore we can no longer speak of "Heaven" as the "place" where God dwells, is a self-evident truth to anyone with even a smattering of science. But our thought of God and His working in History is a quite different matter, which has nothing to do with natural science.[75]

For Brunner, the crux of Bultmann's problem is a confusion of science with what he calls "the self-understanding of modern man," for the concept of what constitutes our humanity is not a scientific but a philosophical and religious question. And Christians, naturalists, Idealists, and Marxists will hold different views on this subject. Brunner rejects the notion that the "self-understanding of modern man" is any more final and settled than our scientific view of the world. If it were, it would soon become obvious that today this worldview must be that of either Naturalism or Idealism. But, Brunner insists, it is just these philosophies that Christianity must reject. Neither the Naturalist nor the Idealist can, with his or her modern preconceptions, understand a doctrine such as Christ's vicarious atonement—what St. Paul calls "the offense of the Cross"—but that does not prove that it is religiously false. Bultmann's error lies in adopting a contemporary Existentialist concept of authentic existence rather than allowing the existential meaning of the New Testament witness to emerge from the New Testament's own distinctive understanding of true existence—an understanding that Brunner, not surprisingly, finds expressed in his doctrine of "truth as encounter." Brunner's criticisms of both Barth and Bultmann will be repeated by others, as we will see in later chapters. We will then be better able to judge whether or not Brunner does justice to their respective positions.

Brunner was and he remains the foremost Christian exponent of the I-Thou philosophy and the understanding of Christian revelation and truth in terms of the divine-human encounter. It is difficult now to appreciate fully the significance of Brunner's theology in the immediate postwar years, serving, as it did, as a "mediating" position between the various orthodoxies of the right and the liberalisms and modernisms on the left. His "personalistic" doctrine of revelation was attractive because of its emphasis on the Bible's active, "verbal," and personal character, in contrast to the neutral, impersonal, abstract language of philosophical theology. His "personalism" also dominated his treatment of the doctrines of God and Christology. For Brunner, God's personal disclosure in the *Person* of Christ must be the measure of all other philosophical and religious doctrines of God. And God's attributes—omnipotence, unchangeableness, righteousness, and love—all must be understood in terms of God as Person, as the divine Thou whatever reconceptions of the doctrine that might require.

This shows us the confusion that is created when the doctrine of God, instead of starting from this disclosure of His personal Being as Subject, starts from any kind of neutral definition of being, such as that of the theology determined by Platonism, Aristotelianism, and Neo-Platonism.[76]

Brunner's "biblical personalism" also requires that any Christology begin "inductively" with the testimony of Scripture itself. The writings of Paul and the earliest Christian community speak of Jesus in terms of his action, activity, and work, not in terms that focus on the mystery of his being as the God-man. To speak of Jesus is, first and foremost, to speak of his work; only through his work, through his benefits, as the Reformer Melanchthon famously stated, do we know Christ's person. This is confirmed by

the fact that the titles given to Jesus in the New Testament, which are distinctive, are "verbal" and not "substantive" in character; they all describe an event, a work of God, which He does through Jesus in or for humanity. Who and what Jesus *is*, can only be stated, at first at any rate, by what God *does*.[77]

Finally, a word needs to be said about Brunner's writings on the subject of social ethics, for he wrote widely on the subject, especially in the 1930s and 1940s. Brunner's social ethics, particularly in his early and influential *The Divine Imperative*, is shaped by his use of the Reformers' doctrine of the "orders of creation" (*Schopfungsordnung*), such as marriage, the family, the state, and the economy. For Brunner, these social institutions represent "natural orders" that, although corruptible because of the Fall and human sin, are nevertheless intended by God and are, in an imperfect world, meant to serve normative roles for the Christian, as well as for the "natural man." As it happened, however, the experience of the totalitarian control of the institutions of society and culture by National Socialism in Germany caused theologians such as Karl Barth, and later Dietrich Bonhoeffer, to criticize sharply the ethical employment of the orders of creation by both Brunner and Gogarten. Barth charged that it allowed the "German Christians" to give theological legitimacy to the pagan institutions of the Nazi regime. In Chapter Four we will return briefly to both Brunner's and Gogarten's appeal to the orders of creation as we trace the changing course of Karl Barth's theology and his ethical leadership in the "Con-

fessing Church" in its struggle against the German Christians and Nazism.

FRIEDRICH GOGARTEN

Among the influential theologians whom we have identified with the beginnings of Dialectical theology, Friedrich Gogarten (1887–1967) was the least known outside of Germany. However, he did achieve considerable prominence in European and American theology late in his career in the 1950s and 1960s as an influential exponent of "secular" theology. It is to this later development of his thought that we will devote our primary attention in this chapter. Because Gogarten, along with Brunner, wrote extensively on Christian social ethics in the 1930s in the context of the political events associated with the rise of German nationalism and National Socialism, we will briefly characterize this aspect of his thought in Chapter Four.

Gogarten was born in the German industrial city of Dortmund.[78] He began his studies of theology at Jena, was then a student under Harnack at Berlin, and completed his studies at Heidelberg, where Troeltsch was still teaching. He found that neither Harnack nor Troeltsch greatly helped him, and he was drawn to the tradition of German Idealism. His first book, *Fichte as a Religious Thinker* (1914), was a study of the great German Romantic and Idealist philosopher, and Gogarten drew from Fichte and from Idealism his long-standing preoccupation with religion and nationalism and his ongoing critique of the individualism and rationalism of the Enlightenment. By 1917, however, Gogarten had begun his deep immersion in Luther's works and his reading of Kierkegaard. The understanding of revelation that he encountered in these writers was not the immanent "source in us" of the Idealists; on the contrary, it was a confrontation with "an other, one who stands over against us." His book *Religion from Afar* (1917) reflects the new "existential" themes that he had found in both Luther and Kierkegaard.

Gogarten became pastor of a church in a village in Thuringia, where he continued to submerge himself in the writings of Luther. In 1920, at the invitation of its editor, Martin Rade, he published his provocative essay "Between the Times" in *Zwischen den Zeiten*. This resulted in another invitation to address an assembly of the friends of *Die Christliche Welt*—a group of leading liberal theologians and clergy. His address, "The Crisis of Culture," was a sharp attack on the culture-Protestantism that characterized the thought of many of those in his audience. As one commentator remarked: "The 'Friends of the Christian World' had experienced the whip of God."[79] Thereafter, Gogarten was identified as a leader of the "theology of crisis." As we have seen, in his writings of the early 1920s Gogarten's critique of modern individualism is especially directed against theologians such as Troeltsch whom he perceived as a latter-day heir of the Enlightenment. Gogarten's critique of individualism was reinforced by his introduction to the I-Thou philosophy of Ferdinand Ebner, the Jena philosopher Eberhard Griesbach, and Martin Buber. However, Gogarten's own development of the I-Thou theme was distinctive, as we will see. Gogarten's exchanges with Barth during the 1920s demonstrate their growing estrangement, and Gogarten soon found himself directing his theological critique on two fronts: against the Idealists and against the theology of Barth and his followers. In both cases the issue concerned the proper relation between theology and anthropology and the theological understanding of human historicity.

In 1931 Gogarten left his work as a pastor and became professor of systematic theology at Breslau. In 1935 he moved to Göttingen, where he remained until his retirement in 1955. During the 1930s most of Gogarten's writing dealt with the theological interpretation of social ethics, particularly with regard to the immediate political situation in Germany. In this effort he applied his distinctive conception of the I-Thou motif to the Lutheran doctrine of the "orders of creation," as well as to the questions of freedom and authority as they related to his concerns about the dangers of autonomous individualism and secularism. These writings expose Gogarten's deep antipathy to political and cultural liberalism as he saw it

embodied in the culture of the Weimar Republic. The result of this political engagement was Gogarten's brief embrace of a neo-conservative Romantic nationalism and belief in the *Volkgeist*, the folk spirit of the German people and their traditions. The theological ramifications of this chapter in Gogarten's career are briefly discussed in Chapter Four.

In 1938 Gogarten fell seriously ill and he did not produce any significant work for a decade. In 1948 he published two books—*The Preaching of Jesus Christ* and *The Church and the World*—both of which represented a radical reversal of his understanding of modern autonomy and the historical meaning of secularization. His new "theology of secularization" and his defense of Bultmann's important program of "demythologization" cast Gogarten once again into the forefront of theological discussion. The last two decades of his life were extraordinarily productive. To the themes of this late theology and its influence we now turn.

Gogarten's postwar theology of secularization focuses on the modern historicizing of human existence. It represents the convergence of many themes that are present in his early writings, but they now serve a radical new conviction about the theological meaning of modern historical-consciousness, freedom, and responsibility.

The Christian Understanding of the World and Secularization

One theme carried over in Gogarten's postwar theology is his view of history as constituted neither by the meanings read into history by the mind of the interpreter (subjective Idealism) nor by the massing of so-called "objective" facts (scientific positivism). Rather, what constitutes the reality of *human* history is the interpersonal encounters *between* God, the individual, and the neighbor. That is, the reality of history is to be discerned in those everyday events of relationship and not in the great forces and movements of the historical past or present. For Gogarten, it is this radical exigency and particularity of human encounter that prohibits all abstract conceptions of ethical responsibility, such as the Catholic doctrine of the natural law.

Gogarten's utilization of the primal I-Thou relationship is, as mentioned earlier, similar in some respects to Martin Buber's more famous formulation in the contrast between the I-Thou and the I-It relationship. Yet, Gogarten's understanding of the relationship of the Thou and the I is original. It has its source in his reading of the biblical account of Creation and its portrayal of the human creature as both *between* and *in relation to* the Creator and the neighbor. Gogarten draws the contrast between the I of the autonomous and solitary self and the Thou-I of the biblical encounter in which the priority of the *other*—both God and other persons or community—is affirmed as primary. According to Gogarten, each person has or is given her or his being-from-the-other (*Von-dem-Andern-sein*), and so ongoing life always is a being-with-the-other (*Mit-dem-Andern-sein*). Genuine human life is constituted by this openness and responsiveness to the Creator God and to one's fellow creatures—not in a being-in-and-for-oneself (*An-und-für-sich-sein*).

Gogarten's understanding of this primary relationship is the source of his persistent critique of individualism and subjectivism from the 1920s onward. He does not retain the I-Thou terminology perhaps because of the wide and various uses that were given to the term as a result of the popularity of Buber's book, *I and Thou*. In place of the I and Thou, Gogarten adopts the concept of *responsibility* to convey his particular understanding of the biblical meaning of this primary interpersonal relationship. And the concept of responsibility takes on additional significance after 1948 as Gogarten develops the implications of his understanding of secularization for theology. Secularization is now understood by Gogarten as the authentic outcome of Christianity's radical historicizing of human existence, and thus humanity's responsibility for the world.

At the outset it is important to understand that when Gogarten makes the theological claim that the *secularization of the world* has its roots in Christian faith, he is saying something very different from the more conventional statements

then current about *the secularization of Christian faith itself*. Gogarten distinguishes between secularization and secularism. Secularization represents humanity's adulthood, its *freedom from but responsibility for the world*, as the world is given over to humanity's care by God. Secularism, on the contrary, implies an idolatrous sense of responsibility *to* the powers and ideologies of the world—a false surrender of one's freedom and a worship of creaturely powers, such as a political ideology or the state. Both secularization and secularism nevertheless represent ways of understanding the world. By "world" Gogarten means the human world of relationships, of institutions, meanings, and orders. For Gogarten the human world is not simply a natural process; it is the realm of the historical, of ordered human meanings and structures.

Gogarten's argument that the secularization of the world is rooted in the human consciousness that Christian faith introduced into history is elucidated by a prolonged reflection on the writings of St. Paul. The pre-Christian human relationship to the world is fundamentally different from the Christian:

For the pre-Christian man the cosmos is the ultimate, all-embracing reality. Its eternal order is the fundamental problem. The decisive issues for man, therefore, are both *that* and *how* he may adapt himself and his actions to this order. His piety consists in the worship of the order and the powers that support it. . . . Paul identifies pre-Christian piety, with its reverent worship of the gods who uphold the eternal order of the world as that godlessness and wickedness with which men suppress the truth (Rom 1:18). . . . In this piety the world and its powers, regarded by faith as God's creatures, take the place of the Creator and receive the honor that belongs to the Creator alone (Rom 1:23 ff).[80]

The pre-Christian worship of the *creation* (the sun, moon, and other powers of nature) simply means "that one understands himself in terms of the creature." And such an understanding means that the human community "falls into the hands of these powers." Futhermore, these powers are conceived as a kind of law. "They maintain the order of the world. For man to conceive himself in their terms means for him to trust them as the guardians of his life, he must fulfill their law."[81] It is evident that the religious ethos of this pre-Christian world is all-pervading. The entire world is conceived as a sacred cosmos, replete with a profusion of gods, spirits, and powers.

A clarification is here required, however. Although the "worldly powers" are created and are not real gods and do not deserve worship, they do keep the world in its worldly order; they fulfill their task as creatures, and in that sense they are similar to the Lutheran "orders of creation." These powers or orders are not *essentially* hostile to God, for example, as Gnostic dualism teaches, because they are part of God's creation, not the work of some anti-god or evil power. The hostility of these powers toward God must be seen entirely from the human viewpoint: "Their hostility toward God, according to Paul, is not cosmic fate in which man is caught, but it is man's guilt. Man's sin enables the powers to engulf the world. And for Paul sin means that man . . . who is thus placed between God and the world, has decided in favor of the world [the 'powers'] against God."[82]

When the New Testament writers speak of "this world" in negative terms they are referring to the world perverted by human sin and subjected to decay—not to the world as created by God. There is only *one* divine world that human sin has violated by giving the world and its creaturely powers the glory that belongs only to God the Creator. What Christian faith has introduced into history is the secularization of this world by the *desacralizing* of its creaturely powers and orders. The Christian no longer serves and bows in worship before God's creatures. According to Gogarten, this is the original freedom and responsibility bestowed by God on humankind in the Creation that has been forfeited through sin, and that is granted anew through faith in Jesus Christ.

No human being exists simply in and for him or herself. And so, as humans we all fulfill our being only in so far as we can find that being to which or to whom we can *respond*. The original Latin, *spondere*, means "to pledge one's word,"

and we have the alternatives of pledging and of worshiping either the powers of this world or the Creator, because we receive our being either from the world or God. "As long as man is enclosed by the world, his responsibility is defined in terms of that world."[83]

Christian faith thus introduces, first, a new understanding of human *responsibility*, characterized by the awareness that it entails the knowledge that our human being *and* the being of the worldly orders and powers are received from beyond the self and the world, are gifts from God. What is distinctive about Christian faith is that faith both is called forth by God, who reveals the divine trustworthiness, and elicits our responsive obedience. Second, Christian faith is characterized by what St. Paul calls "*sonship*," a theme that is crucial to Gogarten's understanding of Christian secularity. Gogarten points out that the term "son of God" is used by Paul not only for Christ but also for those who believe in him and live in and through him. Unlike a child, the son has come of age and is independent, which entails a new relationship to the world that is appropriate to being a son of God. That independent status includes our human lordship over the world. Gogarten describes this lordship of the sons of God as follows:

First, it means not to be from the world, not to have one's being enclosed by the world like the gentiles, who worship the creature instead of the creator. Second, it means to be responsible for the world in order that it remain God's creation. . . . Both are indissolubly related: we can be sons of God and hence from God and not from the world only when we are "lords of all"; we can only stand before God in filial responsibility . . . when we are no longer in servitude to the "weak and miserable elements of the world."[84]

Human "lordship" over the world means that we and the world receive our being from God. But further, this lordship is not a mere caretakership, for as a "son of God" one must care for the world in gratitude as a patrimony from the Creator. Nevertheless, as one commentator aptly put it, "this filial self-understanding does not interfere with his independence as the mature son, but it surrounds his autonomy with the kind of attentive concern for the heritage which only a grateful heir can experience."[85]

A third feature of Christian faith is the unique gift of *freedom* that characterizes sonship and lordship. St. Paul's Letter to the Galatians speaks of the Christian's freedom *from* the world, but it is not a negative freedom that implies a lack of concern for the world.

This freedom, then, is not the freedom we associate with the free decision or the power over something. It means being opened, being unlocked to another person. . . . Nor is faith the arbitrary or emotional assumption that one has such a freedom. Faith is always an act of obedience, an act of trust in the One for whom one is free.[86]

Because we humans are created in the image of God, we reflect that image in the fact that we belong to God *in* freedom. As God endows humanity with responsibility for the world ("Be fruitful and multiply, and fill the earth and subdue it; and have dominion . . . over every living thing that moves upon the earth." Gen. 1:28), God sets humanity free to undertake its lordship.

If the world is on loan to man as his inheritance, then, as Paul would say, man is a mature son, independent of the world. . . . With the knowledge that the world is granted to the man who has come of age as an inheritance, the relation of man to the world is fundamentally changed. The world no longer rules him. He has become its master.[87]

The Historicizing of Human Existence

Human lordship over the world transforms it from a mythical to a *historical* world. And in this secularized, historical world, Gogarten sees a renewed application of Luther's profound insights into "faith" and "works" and the doctrine of the "two realms." Humanity's independence means that the "works" that humans undertake in the "realms" of science, politics, the economy, or art are to be guided by human reason. The church

(the "realm" of the Gospel and "justification by faith") makes no claim to sovereignty over these worldly orders. They are turned over to human reason without remainder, and faith has no business anxiously intruding itself into the realm of reason's activity, for example, scientific work, fearful that it will destroy faith. Gogarten insists that these worldly "works" have no power over Christian faith. If they did, they would be understood in the pre-Christian sense of mythical "powers" hostile to God. Christian faith remains open, receptive, and trusting in the mystery of God's future. What faith also can do, however, is to make reason aware of its limits, of the danger of extending its sphere beyond concern with particular works in science, politics, and so on.

The dominion of science—and that of politics—is over the data and sphere of its immediate concern and not *over the whole of existence*, what Gogarten calls one's "world-view." In this latter case "it is a matter of an attitude of man toward the world in which, as Heidegger says, he 'can be the one being who gives all being its measure and applies the plumb line.'"[88] That is, when human reason is given over to a religious worship of the world, as often is the case in modern science and political ideology, it undergoes a transformation that is foreign to its original vocation. It no longer is open to the divine mystery but, rather, engages in a new idolatry by making metaphysical or ideological claims ultimate—and *to which* (not *for which*) the human reason becomes responsible and thereby forfeits its freedom and independence. Gogarten refers to this transposition of secularization as "subjectivism," that is, "when human independence toward the world is understood as a kind of world-view."[89] It is the transposing of genuine "secularity" into "secularism." To avoid such a move into secularism, and to remain secular and "responsible for" the world, the modern individual must be responsibly committed to the quest for personal and social wholeness and meaning, and *at the same time* in faith recognize that no human effort will make transparent the world's meaning or its fulfillment. It is this human forgetfulness that is the source of the sin, pathos, and danger of modern secularism.

Without faith there is nothing but naked, bare responsibility of man for the world. This responsibility is naked and bare because in it man depends wholly upon himself and what only he can do. Perhaps man has never been so lonely in this world, so dependent upon himself.[90]

What Christian faith offers this solitary person, burdened with his or her own naked responsibility and anxious about the future, is the assurance that while, as Paul writes, "the very commandment which promised life proved to be death to me" (Rom. 7:10 f), faith "makes all things new." Faith gives courage and tranquility in the face of the open and uncharted future. All forms of tyranny emerge when faith gives way to anxious servitude to some system or ideology. Christian faith thus restores the original relationship of the human being between God and world whereby the individual is enabled to live in genuine freedom *from* the world while taking responsibility *for it*. This is the meaning of the Gospel message regarding the true relationship between faith and history, the crux of the modern problem. Concern over this question drew Gogarten into the controversy over the demythologization of the New Testament that was initiated by Rudolf Bultmann. In his important monograph *Demythologizing and History* (1955), Gogarten specifically addresses this widely debated issue in terms of his own understanding of secularization and the historicization of human existence.

Demythologizing and History

Although Gogarten was critical of Troeltsch's theology, he now was convinced that his teacher was correct in insisting that modern historical consciousness must take for granted the interdependent web of historical events—and that this applies to the study of the Bible and to the Christian tradition as thoroughly as it does to the study of secular events and texts. This is, of course, what has radically affected theological work since the introduction of the modern historical method. No longer, Gogarten asserts, can we interpret the events of the Bible as "historically

factual" if we mean by historicity what is assumed by historical science and, *at the same time*, assert that these events of the "acts of God" are entirely without historical analogy and are not open to historical investigation, because they are "suprahistorical."

According to Gogarten, this is the untenable position that is taken not only by the older orthodoxy but also by Karl Barth. Both the old and the newer orthodoxy criticize Bultmann's application of historical criticism to the mythical outlook (*Weltanschauung*) of the New Testament on the grounds that he denies Scripture's "objective" historical character and severs the historical connection between Jesus and the New Testament *kerygma*, or the preaching about Jesus as the Christ. Bultmann's point* is that the early witnesses to Jesus were not interested in recording the "facts" about Jesus as understood by modern historiography; furthermore, these witnesses used the language of their own prescientific and mythological world picture (*Weltbild*) in their depiction of Jesus as the Christ.

Gogarten uses the demythologizing controversy as an opportunity to attempt to refute the entire notion of God acting "objectively" in history, both as an historical and as a theological problem. In doing this he again calls Luther to his defense. Despite the fact that Luther was not engaged by the modern scientific ethos and its theological implications, he did oppose the metaphysical thinking that dominated the late Middle Ages and that interpreted the Bible in an entirely "objectivist" way. Luther, on the contrary according to Gogarten, drew a distinction between faith that consists merely in regarding as true the facts vouched for by the Bible . . . and the faith that is directed toward the intention of God for man as it is displayed in these facts. The only true faith is that which corresponds to this divine intention.[91]

What is *historically* significant in the New Testament, in Gogarten's view, is a grasping of the redemptive and moral significance of the Gospel

---

* A full analysis of Bultmann's program of 'demythologization' is examined in Ch. five. It is not necessary to examine all the implications of that program here, however, to understand Gogarten's discussion of faith and history.

message, which is its particular depiction of the historical character (*geschichtlichkeit*) or historicity of human existence. It is precisely this emphasis on the historical character of human existence—and not on an essentialist metaphysical conception—that the modern secular world shares in common with the Bible. The Bible, of course, portrays the character of that radical historicity differently, as we have seen. Christian faith understands human sin as crucial to the problem of human autonomy and responsibility, "since man by his sin, namely by worshiping the creature instead of the Creator, has entirely reversed the true nature of the world and has delivered it up to the bondage and vanity of corruption" (Rom. 8:19 ff). But what is crucial for Gogarten in this matter of historicity is "that metaphysical thinking has lost its position of dominance. History is no longer, as it was for a medieval theology of history, 'a process within a stationary—that is to say, a metaphysically conceived world.' . . . It is not the world which is the all-embracing problem, but history,"[92] by which Gogarten means the historicity of human existence.

That the older, static, metaphysical nature of faith has been rendered impossible does not resolve the theological problem, for Gogarten sees modern theology also interpreting faith historically but in an objectivist manner. It sees its primary task as establishing the "real factualness" of the historical events of the New Testament, such as Jesus's birth, life, and resurrection. And this approach insists that such an objective grounding of faith alone can preserve "the 'transsubjective' reality of faith." History in this case is understood as primarily referring to past events, and the task of the historian is that of reconstructing the past.

According to Gogarten, there is another, and a truer, understanding of the historical-theological task.

It arises from the conviction that the actual history—and, one must add, the actual historical character (*geschichtlichkeit*)—of the events recorded in the New Testament is not to be sought in the "objective" and historically (*historische*) ascertainable fact of their having taken place, but in the *kerygma*, the proclamation and witness that in the events of this history, God turns with grace toward mankind and its world.[93]

Gogarten categorically rejects those critics who claim that demythologization and existential interpretation entail a "dehistoricization" of the New Testament and the imposition of a modern scientific or Idealist worldview.

One cannot make the slightest contribution to the clarification of the discussion . . . if one fails to see that the question in dispute between the two parties is not whether the great acts of God "are set before all human existence, indestructibly, indissolvibly and irremoveably." For this is affirmed by both sides. . . . The question which must therefore be decided is, rather, how—in what way—the history of God precedes all the being and doing of man.[94]

The one side insists on "objective factualness." Gogarten, on the contrary, asserts that God's action takes place in the life of a concrete historical person and is accordingly a unique historical event. The event encounters the individual as that which is set before his or her existence in the *kerygma* of the New Testament. And the point is that God's actions in Christ are not "objectively" transparent or retrievable. These actions are given as an ever-present proclamation, not as a report about what *has* happened. It is addressed, ever-anew, to a particular person as God's Word. For Gogarten this does not mean that the person and history of Jesus are replaced by the *kerygma*, which is simply understood as the product of the early Church.

What it does mean is to point out with all possible emphasis that the person and the history of Jesus are present in this *kerygma*, present with the same historical presence as that with which He is present on each separate occasion both with the disciples and with the Church of our own day and the Church of the future.[95]

Whereas God's action in Christ is not reducible to "historical facticity" (what Gogarten refers to as "a miserable rationalization of New Testament history"), neither is faith to be understood as something subjective, because the individual is confronted with the Word of God from beyond the self. And yet, God's Word addressed to the individual person creates a new historical mode of being in the world, a "being-from-the-other and with-the-other." It is this understanding of history that Gogarten insists is inherent in the New Testament itself. The history that the *kerygma* transmits is fundamentally *eschatological;* "It does not arise from the intramundane context, and by the same token its past is not one to which one can look back as one looks back to what has at sometime occurred within the intramundane context and is now past."[96]

Friedrich Gogarten's contributions to twentieth-century theology were significant despite the fact that they were, untypically, associated with two periods of his life separated by several decades: the early writings of the 1920s and those of his mature years from the late 1940s and 1950s. We already have commented on his contributions to the Dialectical theology of crisis; we will, therefore, close the account here by briefly indicating his role in the "theology of secularization" that flourished for a time in the late 1950s and the 1960s. Together with Dietrich Bonhoeffer, whom we will discuss in Chapter Four, Gogarten was instrumental in bringing the subject of secularization to the forefront of theological discussion, and was distinctive in seeing secularity as a consequence of Christian faith itself.

The theme of secularization and its rootedness in biblical faith was popularized in North America by the Harvard theologian Harvey Cox in his highly celebrated book, *The Secular City* (1965). That book builds on a number of Gogarten's basic ideas. Cox, however, focuses his analysis of secularity more particularly on contemporary urban life and technology in a highly interesting and provocative way. Whereas his analysis will strike many today as overly sanguine and simplistic, *The Secular City* provoked a valuable debate on the meaning of secularization for Christianity. Three important motifs developed by Cox essentially expand on themes implicit in

Gogarten's works on secularization. According to Cox, the biblical worldview introduces a "disenchantment" with the world of nature, a "desacralization" of politics, and a "deconsecration" of values. The idolatrous worship of natural powers, social orders, and ideologies is excluded by the biblical doctrine of God's creation and its corollary, humanity's responsibility both to harness nature and to develop provisional and useful social policies and programs for its own use. The following passage is representative of Cox's theme:

> Life for him [the contemporary secular person] is a set of problems, not an unfathomable mystery. He brackets off the things that cannot be dealt with and deals with those that can. . . .
>
> It is characteristic of urban-secular man that he perceives himself as a source of whatever significance the human enterprise holds. . . . Symbol systems, the constellations of meaning by which human life is given value and direction, are seen as projections of a given society. . . . There is nothing timeless or divine about them.[97]

Very likely, Gogarten would be suspicious of Cox's rather too cheerful depiction of the modern urban, technological ethos, and he would see Christianity as speaking more prophetically to this urban context. Gogarten's later theology had a more enduring influence on German theology in the post–World War II period, for example, on the work of theologians such as Gerhard Ebeling and Ernst Fuchs. At the same time, the theology of secularization took a more radical turn in the United States.

In their affirmation of the world of secular culture, some American theologians either denounced or minimized so-called "other-worldly" activities such as prayer, devotions, and churchgoing as distracting Christians from carrying out their responsibilities in and for the "world," such as engaging in politics, civil rights, the war on poverty, and the ecological movement. These latter, it was implied, are the true means of expressing Christian faith and worship. Like Matthew Tindal in the eighteenth century, some of these writers appeared to place "the whole of their religion in benevolent actions," regarding everything "religious" as superstitious impediments to the amelioration of social problems.

Other secular theologians argued that a "secular Christianity" demanded that knowledge and norms of judgment be derived from empirical experience of the world and not from external authorities, such as the Church or the Bible. Although the latter are not to be rejected out of hand, they are authoritative only in so far as they conform to and are consistent with modern empirical and scientific knowledge and experience.

Characteristic of much American secular theology of the 1960s was a deeply felt sense of the absence or the unreality of God. The result was the eruption of various theologies of the "eclipse" or "death of God." The media used the term "death of God" rather haphazardly, when in fact it meant quite different things to the theologians who became identified with the movement. Among the less radical writers, the death of God simply meant that in our modern secular world we have, through our urban, technocratic, and rationalistic culture, diminished the possibilities of experiencing the presence of God. In Martin Buber's influential terms, God had been eclipsed through our loss of genuine I-Thou relationships. In our technocratic culture, the world of the instrumental "It" had taken over, creating a world characterized by transient, purely practical relationships void of genuine mutuality. Hence, God had also become a merely instrumental object, serving our petty subjective needs, insuring Junior's success at school or our safety as we take off in a jet airplane—God the *deus ex machina*, the human problem solver. This spurious God is dead.

In the writings of William Hamilton, Thomas Altizer, and Paul Van Buren,[98] the death of God represented a far more radical critique of the classical Christian doctrine of God, denying the very meaning or reality of such a concept of God. According to Van Buren, the *word* "God," in its classical usage, no longer has any clear or meaningful referent. The word "God" is a vacuous utterance, because it is essentially connected with a metaphysical view of the world that no longer is

credible, namely God conceived as a personal transcendent Being or as the ultimate ground of the natural world. According to Van Buren, our empirical-scientific age regards such a metaphysical conception of God either as confused (i.e., with statements about human ideals or policies of action) or as simply meaningless. Although many contemporary Christians may not have comprehended Van Buren's philosophical argument, many also clearly sensed the difficulty of speaking of God in language that is authentic and intelligible in our secular culture.

The American secular and death of God theologians often touched the deep feelings and the unarticulated convictions of Christians who sensed a dissonance between what their church taught and what they honestly experienced and believed. Many persons also found congenial the emphasis that some of these theologians placed on the historical Jesus as the exemplar of a "this-worldly transcendence." The radical theologians were not interested in exploring the issues posed by the classical christological doctrines, and this was shared by many ordinary believers. Rather, they were drawn to Jesus the man who was authentically open, who was free from anxiety and fear and, most importantly, prepared to live for the neighbor. William Hamilton spoke of "becoming Jesus," by which he meant an imitation of Christ as reflected in a deep identification with the problems and sufferings of one's fellow human beings.

Despite the very real issues that were posed by the American 'secular and death of God' theologians, the movement was short-lived and few, if any, of their writings have proved enduring. The optimism of some regarding secularization and the often-uncritical accommodation of others to a rather outmoded empiricist-positivist philosophy may, in part, explain its brief life. Furthermore, the theological appeal to the historical Jesus as moral exemplar struck some as an ignoring of the lessons of the nineteenth-century "quest of the historical Jesus." Jesus's eschatology and ethics, ironically, represent a spiritual world radically alien to the modern secular ethos embraced by some of these theologians. Finally, many critics would argue that it is a contradiction in terms to attempt to reconceive Christianity without God. The God problem remains a serious issue in contemporary theology, and it may well be in need of radical reconception, a fact that will be made apparent in subsequent chapters. But Christian faith entails a belief in God, although not necessarily the model of God shaped by classical metaphysics.

NOTES

1. Karl Barth, "Nachwort," in *Schleiermacher-Auswahl*, 1968. Cited in Eberhard Busch, *Karl Barth*, trans. John Bowden (London, 1976), p. 81.

2. Ibid.

3. Karl Barth, *Autobiographical Sketch*, 1927. Cited in Busch, op. cit., p. 45.

4. Karl Barth, *Church Dogmatics*, I, (Edinburgh, 1956), pp. 1, 74.

5. Barth, *Autobiographical Sketch*. Cited in Busch, op. cit., pp. 92, 97.

6. Barth, "Nachwort," op. cit., p. 294. Cited in Busch, op. cit., p. 97.

7. Barth, "Nachwort," op. cit., p. 294 f. Cited in Busch, op. cit., pp. 97–98.

8. Karl Barth, *Evangelische Theologie*, 1963. Cited in Busch, op. cit., p. 116.

9. Karl Barth, *The Word of God and the Word of Man* [1924] (New York, 1957), pp. 73–74.

10. Karl Barth, *Christliche Dogmatik* (München, 1927), p. ix. Cited in Paul Lehmann, "The Changing Course of a Corrective Theology," *Theology Today* (October 1956), p. 334.

11. Cited in K. Barth, *The Epistle to the Romans* (London, 1960), p. 11.

12. Adolf Jülicher, *Die Christliche Welt*, 34 (1920). *The Beginnings of Dialectical Theology*, I, ed. James M. Robinson (Richmond, Va., 1968), p. 78.

13. Barth, *Epistle to the Romans*, p. 12.

14. Emil Brunner, "The Epistle to the Romans by Karl Barth," *Kirchenblatt für die Reformierte Schweiz*, 34 (1919). *Beginnings of Dialectical Theology*, pp. 68, 69.

15. Rudolf Bultmann, "Karl Barth's Epistle to the Romans in Its Second Edition," *Die Christliche Welt*, 36 (1922). *Beginnings of Dialectical Theology*, pp. 100–120.

16. Friedrich Gogarten, "Between the Times," *Die Christliche Welt*, 34 (1920). *Beginnings of Dialectical Theology*, pp. 277, 279, 282.

17. Rudolf Bultmann, "The Hidden and the Revealed God," *Die Christliche Welt*, 31 (1917). Reprinted in *Existence and Faith: Shorter Writings of Rudolf Bultmann*, trans. and selected by Schubert M. Ogden (New York, 1960), pp. 24–26, 27, 33.

18. Rudolf Bultmann, "Liberal Theology and the Latest Theological Movement," *Faith and Understanding*, trans. Louise Pettibone Smith (London, 1969), pp. 30, 31.

19. Bultmann, *Beginnings of Dialectical Theology*, p. 115.

20. R. Bultmann, "On the Question of Christology," *Faith and Understanding*, I, p. 132.

21. Friedrich Gogarten, "The Holy Egoism of the Christian: An Answer to Jülicher's Essay," *Die Christliche Welt*, 34 (1920). *Beginnings of Dialectical Theology*, p. 84.

22. Ibid.

23. Ernst Troeltsch, "An Apple from the Tree of Kierkegaard," *Die Christliche Welt*, 35 (1921). *Beginnings of Dialectical Theology*, pp. 312, 313.

24. Ibid.

25. Friedrich Gogarten, "Against Romantic Theology: A Chapter on Faith," *Die Christliche Welt*, 36 (1922). *Beginnings of Dialectical Theology*, pp. 321–322.

26. Ibid., p. 322.

27. H. Martin Rumscheidt, *Revelation and Theology: An Analysis of the Barth-Harnack Correspondence of 1923* (Cambridge, 1972), pp. 29, 48–49.

28. Ibid., p. 31.

29. Ibid., p. 35.

30. Ibid., p. 39.

31. Ibid., p. 44.

32. Ibid., p. 46.

33. Ibid., pp. 46–47.

34. Ibid., pp. 48–49.

35. Barth, *The Word of God and the Word of Man*, pp. 207–208.

36. Ibid., p. 209.

37. Barth, *Epistle to the Romans*, pp. 46–47.

38. Ibid., pp. 97–99.

39. Ibid., pp. 29–30.

40. Barth, *The Word of God and the Word of Man*, p. 32.

41. Ibid., pp. 35–36.

42. Ibid., pp. 38–39.

43. Ibid., pp. 42–43, 45.

44. Ibid., p. 80.

45. Barth emphasized this point in strongly polemical terms in "The Strange New World of the Bible" in 1917, again throughout the *Church Dogmatics*, and in his farewell lectures at Basel in 1962. See his *Evangelical Theology: An Introduction* (New York, 1963), p. 30 ff.

46. Barth, *The Word of God and the Word of Man*, p. 60.

47. *Beginnings of the Dialectical Theology,* pp. 119, 128.

48. Rudolf Bultmann, *Karl Barth–Rudolf Bultmann Letters 1922–1966,* ed. Bernd Jaspert, trans. and ed. Geoffrey Bromiley (Grand Rapids, Mich., 1981) [December 31, 1922], p. 5.

49. Ibid., [April 28, 1927], p. 32.

50. Ibid.

51. Friedrich Gogarten, "Das Problem einen Theologischen Anthropologie," *Zwischen den Zeiten* (1929), p. 505.

52. Friedrich Gogarten, "Karl Barth's Dogmatik," Theologische Rundschau (1929).

53. Gogarten, *Zwischen den Zeiten* (Munich, 1929), p. 496.

54. Karl Barth, *Karl Barth–Rudolf Bultmann Letters,* pp. 49–50.

55. For this and other information on Brunner's life, see "Intellectual Autobiography," in *The Theology of Emil Brunner,* ed. Charles W. Kegley (New York, 1962), pp. 3–20.

56. E. Brunner, "Reply," in Kegley, ibid., p. 331.

57. E. Brunner, *The Christian Doctrine of Creation and Redemption* (London, 1952), p. 46.

58. Ibid., p. 101.

59. E. Brunner, *Revelation and Reason* (Philadelphia, 1946), p. 383.

60. E. Brunner, *The Christian Doctrine of God,* (Philadelphia, 1950) p. 134.

61. Brunner, *Revelation and Reason* p. 65.

62. Brunner, *The Christian Doctrine of God,* p. 135.

63. See the first chapter of E. Brunner's *The Divine-Human Encounter* (Philadelphia, 1943).

64. Brunner, *The Christian Doctrine of God,* p 34.

65. Ibid., p. 33.

66. Ibid., p. 110.

67. Brunner, "Intellectual Autobiography," p. 1.

68. E. Brunner, *Truth as Encounter* (Philadelphia, 1964), p 19.

69. E. Brunner, *The Christian Doctrine of the Church, Faith, and the Consummation* (London, 1962), p. 260.

70. Brunner, *Truth as Encounter,* p. 28.

71. Brunner, *The Christian Doctrine of Creation and Redemption,* pp. 251–252.

72. Brunner, *Truth as Encounter,* pp. 44–45.

73. Brunner, *The Christian Doctrine of Creation and Redemption,* p. 264.

74. Ibid., p. 265.

75. Ibid.

76. Brunner, *The Christian Doctrine of God,* p. 141.

77. Brunner, *The Christian Doctrine of Creation and Redemption,* pp. 271–272.

78. We have no extensive study of Gogarten's life and theological career in English. For biographical information, I am especially dependent on Larry Shiner's excellent essay, "Appendix: Between the Times 1914–1948," in his *The Secularization of History: An Introduction to the Theology of Friedrich Gogarten* (Nashville, 1966).

79. Quoted in John M'Connachie, "The Barthian School, III, Friedrich Gogarten," in *Expository Times* (1931–1932), p. 391.

80. Friedrich Gogarten, *The Reality of Faith,* trans. Carl Michalson and others (Philadelphia, 1959), p. 40.

81. Ibid., p. 41.

82. F. Gogarten, *Despair and Hope for Our Time,* trans. Thomas Wieser (Philadelphia, 1970), p. 15.

83. Ibid., p. 25.

84. Ibid., p. 29.

85. Shiner, *The Secularization of History,* p. 32.

86. Gogarten, *The Reality of Faith,* p. 54.

87. Ibid.

88. Ibid., p. 94.

89. Ibid., p. 95

90. Ibid., pp. 186–187.

91. F. Gogarten, *Demythologizing and History,* trans. Neville Horton Smith (New York, 1955), p. 13.

92. Ibid., p. 20.

93. Ibid., p. 37.

94. Ibid., pp. 67–68.

95. Ibid., p. 75.

96. Ibid., p. 77.

97. Harvey Cox, *The Secular City* (New York, 1965), pp. 63, 72.

98. See Thomas J. J. Altizer, *The Gospel of Christian Atheism* (Philadelphia, 1966); Thomas J. J. Altizer and William Hamilton, *Radical Theology and the Death of God* (Indianapolis, 1966); and Paul M. Van Buren, *The Secular Meaning of the Gospel* (New York, 1963).

SUGGESTIONS FOR FURTHER READING

The Dialectical Theology and Its Background

There are many brief accounts of the beginnings and the distinctive character of the Dialectical theology. However, some of the most informative accounts are to be found in the writings and letters of the participants themselves. The following are recommended:

Busch, Eberhard. *Karl Barth: His Life from Letters and Autobiographical Texts* (Philadelphia: Fortress Press, 1976). Ch. 2–5 give a good account of Barth's crucial role and point of view.

Fisher, Simon. *Revelatory Positivism? Barth's Earliest Theology and the Marburg School* (Oxford: Oxford University Press, 1988). A valuable study of Barth's early theology in the context of Neo-Kantianism.

Jaspert, Bernd, ed. *Karl Barth–Rudolf Bultmann Letters: 1922–1966*, trans. Geoffrey Bromiley (Grand Rapids, Mich.: William B. Eerdmans, 1981). Many of the letters discuss the early collaboration and disagreements between the two men and Bultmann's considerable effort to keep their dialogue going.

Jüngel, Eberhard. *Karl Barth, a Theological Legacy*, trans. Garrett Paul (Philadelphia: Westminster Press, 1986). While concerned with Barth's development, Ch. 1 and 2 give a discerning analysis of the influences on and the issues that absorbed the dialectical theologians.

Robinson, James M., ed. *The Beginnings of Dialectical Theology* (Richmond, Va.: John Knox Press, 1968). This is a valuable collection of primary documents—many written for *Die Christliche Welt* and *Zwischen den Zeiten*—that illustrate the crucial issues between the leading Dialectical theologians and their critics.

Smart, James D., trans. *Revolutionary Theology in the Making: Barth-Thurneysen Correspondence 1914–1925* (Richmond, Va.: John Knox Press, 1964). This correspondence demonstrates the important role of Thurneysen in the movement and his close personal and theological relationship to Barth.

———. *The Divided Mind of Modern Theology: Karl Barth and Rudolf Bultmann 1908–1933* (Philadelphia: Westminster Press, 1967). This is the fullest study in English of the development of the Dialectical theology, and the agreements and disagreements between not only Barth and Bultmann, but also Gogarten, Tillich, and so on. Marred by a bias toward Barth on almost every issue.

Torrance, Thomas F. *Karl Barth: An Introduction to His Early Theology, 1910–1931* (London: SCM Press, 1962). While concerned with Barth's changing theology through the publication of his book on Anselm (1931), this pro-Barth study explores his disputes with Harnack, Bultmann, Brunner, and so on.

Emil Brunner

Cobb, John B., Jr. *Living Options in Protestant Theology* (Philadelphia: Westminster Press, 1962). Ch. 6 is an excellent analysis and critique of some of the major themes in Brunner's theology.

Humphrey, J. Edward. *Emil Brunner* (Waco, Tex.: Word Books, 1976). A reliable survey of Brunner's treatment of the major Christian doctrines: revelation, God, man, Christology, Church, eschatology.

Jewett, Paul King. *Emil Brunner's Concept of Revelation* (London: James Clarke and Co., 1954). A judicious analysis and critique from a conservative perspective of various aspects of Brunner's important writings on revelation.

Kegley, Charles W., ed. *The Theology of Emil Brunner* (New York: Macmillan, 1962). The most thorough analysis and critique of all aspects of Brunner's thought by eminent scholars.

Lovin, Robin W. *Christian Faith and Public Choices: The Social Ethics of Barth, Brunner, and Bonhoeffer* (Philadelphia: Fortress Press, 1984). An excellent analysis of the social ethics of Brunner in relation to that of Barth and Bonhoeffer in the context of the German Church struggle.

Friedrich Gogarten

There is no study in English of Gogarten's life or his entire theological career with its interesting developments from the 1920s to the 1960s. The following will be of some help.

Michalson, Carl. *The Rationality of Faith* (Philadelphia: Westminster Press, 1959). This study of faith and history, although not a study of Gogarten, gives expression to many of Gogarten's ideas in his later writings.

Runyon, Theodore, Jr. "Friedrich Gogarten." In *A Handbook of Christian Theologians*, Martin E. Marty and Dean C. Peerman ed. (Nashville: Abingdon Press, 1965). A brief but helpful overview of Gogarten's career and writings.

Shiner, Larry. *The Secularization of History: An Introduction to the Theology of Friedrich Gogarten* (Nashville: Abingdon Press, 1966). The only extensive study in English of Gogarten's theology, but focusing on the post-1945 writings. An appendix deals briefly with Gogarten's earlier career.

Chapter Four

The Theologies of Karl Barth and Dietrich Bonhoeffer

Dietrich Bonhoeffer at Tegel Prison

This chapter is devoted to the theology of Karl Barth after 1930 and to the theology of Dietrich Bonhoeffer. The judgment of history on the lasting merits and influence of Karl Barth's theology as he developed it in his *Church Dogmatics* over thirty years is, of course, unpredictable. What does appear certain is that Barth's influence on the course of twentieth-century Christian theology is unprecedented, although it is difficult to measure because it is so varied and complex. The import of Barth's work extends far beyond those who identify themselves as "Barthians" or those whose own work reflects his obvious influence. Many twentieth-century theologians have felt obliged to take account of Barth's writings in their own constructive theology. Roman Catholic theologians, for example, have engaged Barth on a variety of issues central to the Catholic theological tradition: natural theology, the use of analogy, Scripture and tradition, and the doctrine of justification. Evangelical scholars long have recognized Barth's doctrine of revelation and Scripture as the most serious challenge to the classical orthodox Protestant doctrines of biblical inspiration and authority and, therefore, to their own foundational doctrines. Some contemporary Evangelical theologians now find in Barth's biblical hermeneutics the most acceptable alternative to an increasingly discredited biblical Fundamentalism and to what they see as the loss of biblical authority in Liberal Protestantism. Contemporary movements such as Process theology, narrative theology, post-liberal theology, and liberation theology all have discovered rich resources in Barth's writings that are relevant to their own interests, or they have recognized that it is essential to engage Barth on crucial points of difference. Karl Barth thus has dominated Christian theology in the twentieth century in a quite unique way, and certainly over a period of time unmatched by other important theologians of the century. For this reason alone, Karl Barth's contribution to Christian thought deserves extended analysis.

In this chapter we will begin by tracing the development of Barth's theology in the 1930s. This is necessary because it will shed light on his distinctive themes and on his method of doing theology, both of which are critical to an understanding of his unique contribution. This development will be followed by an account of Barth's "political theology" and ethics, especially in the writings of the 1930s, for this, too, is closely related to the progression of Barth's mature theology, and it also will afford us an opportunity to compare Barth's social ethics with that of Brunner, Gogarten, and others—and to set the stage for the discussion of Christian social ethics in subsequent chapters.

We will conclude our treatment of Barth with an outline of some of the principal—and often provocative—themes of his multivolumed *Church Dogmatics*, and with some remarks about his work and influence. Dietrich Bonhoeffer was one of the theologians of the younger generation who was, in very significant ways, influenced by Barth, but who also became a critic of Barth's theological method, referring to it as a "positivism of revelation." The term is ambiguous and perhaps it does not convey a just estimate of Barth's biblical hermeneutics; nevertheless, as Bonhoeffer's own writings gained a quite extraordinary readership, his critique of Barth proved significant. It is appropriate, then, to include an account of Bonhoeffer's thought in this context both for its own original merits and also as signaling new theological trajectories that achieve special importance by the 1960s.

KARL BARTH

The Development of Karl Barth's Theology

The point was made in Chapter Three that, in the second and third prefaces to his revolutionary *Epistle to the Romans*, Karl Barth made it clear that this work had proven to be a theological "false start." Between 1922 and 1932 his theology developed in important new directions; and for a long time, scholars have seen these developments as representing a significant break with Barth's earlier dialectical way of thinking. From a certain perspective this is obviously true, especially because his early writings often were resolutely paradoxical and polemical. However, recent scholarship has shown that there are important continuities in the development of Barth's essentially realistic and Dialectical theology. His later writings, contrary to a long-accepted view, also disclose Barth's "modernity," despite his own disclaimers and his ongoing battle with the liberal theological legacy.

Although it is true that Barth rejected much that he had written in the second edition of *Romans*, he nevertheless continued to find value in the "corrective" role that it played in combating what he saw as the subjectivism and the anthropocentrism of the prevailing Neo-Protestant theology. This latter theology continued to speak of a human religious *a priori* immanent in the human subject or in history and by which theology could judge Christianity from *outside* Scripture and the Church. In short, it failed to let God be God. Barth struggled for thirteen years (1922–1935), during his professorships at Göttingen, Münster, and Bonn, with the problem of establishing a theology free of the last vestiges of his own Neo-Protestant subjectivism, because he believed that his own so-called "objective" exegesis in *Romans* did not escape the imposition of existentialist philosophical presuppositions. What he sought was a theology that would stand on its own feet, so to speak, free of the support of other philosophical or anthropological sources.

Barth published his first attempt at a prolegomena to such a dogmatics (*Die Christliche Dogmatik*) in 1927, but the critical reaction convinced him that, while he had sought to avoid grounding theology in an existentialist philosophy, this is how he was read by reviewers such as Friedrich Gogarten. And so, as with the *Römerbrief* twelve years earlier, he began again on a new edition of the *Dogmatik*. This effort coincided with his break with his colleagues associated with *Zwischen den Zeiten* and with his engagement in the political activities in Germany, especially with the rise of the German Christian movement. He entitled the new edition *Die kirchliche Dogmatik* (*Church Dogmatics*) I, 1. The idolatrous triumphalism of the German Christians may have been one reason for the change in the title. In the preface he suggests that the word "Church" replaced the word "Christian" because of the "lighthearted" use to which "the great word Christian" had been put. But, more materially, the reason for the change was Barth's growing conviction that the work of theology is a function of the Church. It is not, he writes, "a 'free' science, but one bound to the sphere of the Church"—and this meant for Barth that he had to "cut out of this second issue of the book everything that in the first issue might give the slightest appearance of giving to theology a basis, support, or even a mere justification in the way of existential philosophy."[1]

Although Barth long had been convinced that theology must begin with the belief of the Confessing Church, his study of the medieval theologian Anselm reinforced this conviction. In the summer of 1930 Barth held a seminar at Bonn that resulted in his book *Anselm: Fides Quarens Intellectum* (1931). What Anselm confirmed in Barth's mind was the conviction that the theologian does not begin outside the faith of the Church and then attempt to show, with the help of philosophy or anthropology, that the faith is true. One begins, rather, with the belief of the Church. And the Anselmian condition necessary for theology is, according to Barth, the following:

The knowledge that is sought cannot be anything but an extension and explication of that acceptance of the *Credo* of the Church, which faith itself already implied. . . . A science of faith, which denied or even questioned the Faith [the *Credo* of the Church], would *ipso facto* cease to be either "faithful" or "scientific." . . . *Intelligere* [understanding] comes about by reflection on the *Credo* that has already been spoken and affirmed.[2]

Anselm asserts, however, that every *theological* statement is an inadequate expression of its object, God, and for that reason theological statements can be made only with symbolic or scientific certainty, which must be distinguished from the certainty of faith. Nevertheless, one criterion can determine whether a theological statement is admissible or not, namely, "the text of Holy Scripture, which," according to Anselm, "forms the basic stability of the *Credo* to which the *credere* and therefore the *intelligere* refer. While it is the decisive source, it is also the determining norm of *intelligere*."[3] Although *intelligere* means a *reflection upon* what already has been said in the *Credo*, this "reflection upon" is not possessed by the believer, nor can the believer seek it outside the *Credo* of the Church, that is, outside of Holy Scripture. Anselm's method is that which Barth now adopts in the writing of the *Church Dogmatics*. He believes that it avoids the errors of both the Neo-Protestants and the orthodox biblical "positivists." One escapes the error of the former by insisting that theological reflection be exclusively on the *Credo* of the Church. The "positivist" error is the belief that the reading and hearing of the written text of Scripture, when assisted by faith, absolves the believer of the task of understanding its meaning and its truth *by human means*. For Barth, as for Anselm, the task of theology is a human reflection on what is given in the written text of Scripture, but only by virtue of a special grace.

For Barth, theology can remain neither an unreflective recital of the biblical text nor a purely historical-critical exegesis of the Bible. Theology must proceed to reflect on the relation between the biblical text and the meaning and truth of the object to which the text points and witnesses. True interpretation thus exists only where the perception of the literal text of Scripture and the understanding of its meaning are one. Furthermore, such an understanding remains dependent upon divine grace, whereby human reason is given the capacity to stand under and be mastered by the Word of God.

Scholars disagree on the question of whether Barth's work on Anselm marks a decisive turning point and change in the method and substance of his theology or whether what he found in Anselm merely confirms an understanding of theology's true task and method that is evident to the discerning reader of Barth's post–World War I writings.[4] We cannot pursue the issue here, but only remark that it appears to be true that Anselm was crucially important to Barth, but also that what he learned from Anselm supported the direction that he had long pursued. From his earliest years in the pastorate in Safenwil, Barth possessed a deep realism with regard to the antecedent order of God's being, which completely determines the order of our knowing. But it is also true that his profound sense of the dialectical character of revelation and theological reflection, so pronounced in the *Römerbrief*, continues in the successive volumes of the *Church Dogmatics*, although integrated with a distinctive use of theological analogy, as we will later see. Before we examine some of the original themes that unfold in the *Church Dogmatics* from the 1930s on, however, it is appropriate first to explore Barth's "political theology" or social ethics, because this was a special preoccupation of his in the political context of the 1930s, and it had a decisive influence on the direction of his theological work. Barth's social ethics is characteristically original. It is, at the same time, an ethics that some acclaim as an authentic and courageous expression of the New Testament witness and that others reject as too idiosyncratic, heedless of the ethical norms required to guide the Christian community in its response to the complex issues of social policy in today's world.

"Political Theology": Barth and the Question of a Christian Social Ethics

On January 20, 1933, Adolf Hitler became chancellor of Germany. Barth was teaching at the University of Bonn at the time, directing a seminar on Calvin's *Institutes* and lecturing on the theology of the nineteenth century. With Hitler and the National Socialists now firmly in power, Barth's activity underwent a marked change. He knew what he had to do: reject and resist National Socialism for, as he wrote, its "policy on religion and the church could only be aimed at the eradication of Christian belief and its expression."[5] Barth realized, however, that the German church, because of the long tradition of alliance between throne and altar, was not prepared to resist this new, aggressive "co-ordination" into the National Socialist state. To his dismay, Barth saw not only some of his pupils but also friends associated with *Zwischen den Zeiten*, particularly Gogarten, approving the religious policies of the Nazis or at least giving tacit approval by refusing to protest against those policies. Barth separated himself from *Zwischen den Zeiten*.

Among his first actions, Barth delivered a lecture on "The First Commandment as a Theological Axiom," warning against the loyalty to "other gods" and the connecting of revelation to other authorities other than the Bible. By April 1933 the National Socialists were demanding the full assimilation of the German churches, and Hitler gave Ludwig Müller full powers over church affairs as Reich Bishop of the Evangelical Church. Shortly thereafter, the "Evangelical Church of the German Nation" was created and published the following "guiding principles":

We see in race, folk, and nation, orders of existence granted and entrusted to us by God. God's law for us is that we look to the preservation of these orders. . . .

In the mission to the Jews we perceive a grave danger to our nationality. It is the entrance gate for alien blood into our body politic. . . . In particular, marriage between Germans and Jews is to be forbidden.

Karl Barth, 1939

We want an evangelical Church that is rooted in our nationhood. We repudiate the spirit of Christian world citizenship. We want the degenerating manifestations of this spirit . . . overcome by a faith in our national mission that God has committed to us.[6]

This was the program of the "German Christians." Barth's first public attack on this Nazi church program was a pamphlet published in *Theologische Existenz Heute (Theological Existence Today)* in June 1933, a copy of which he sent to the Führer, Adolf Hitler. The pamphlet was banned in July 1934, but not before 37,000 copies had been printed. By the end of 1933 an organized opposition to the German Christians began to form. It was first led by the pastor Martin Niemöller and the so-called Pastor's Emergency League, which became the basis of the Confessing Church in Germany. Barth soon joined with Niemöller. The first Confessing Synod of the German Evangelical Church was held in May 1934 in Barmen, with 138 delegates present. Out of this meeting came the famous Barmen Declaration written, in all essentials, by Barth. Characteristic of Barth, the declaration was a theological statement. It consisted of six articles and it was directed to the specific situation in Germany at the time. Each article consisted of a scriptural text, an interpretation, and a statement of what was rejected by the Synod. The declaration affirms the sovereignty of the Word of God in Jesus Christ over against all idolatrous political ideologies.

In view of the errors of the "German Christians" of the present Reich Church Administration, which are ravaging the church and at the same time also shattering the unity of the German Evangelical Church, we confess the following evangelical truths. . . .

1. Jesus Christ, as he is attested to us in Holy Scripture, is the one Word of God whom we have to hear, and whom we have to trust and obey in life and death.

We reject the false doctrine that the church could or should recognize as a source of its proclamation, beyond and besides this one Word of God, yet other events, powers, historic figures, and truths as God's revelation.

To those who opposed Hitler but thought it best that the Church stay out of politics, the declaration stated: "2. We reject the false doctrine that there could be areas of our life in which we would belong not to Jesus Christ but to other lords, areas in which we would not need justification and sanctification through him."

The third article is directed against the Nazi anti-Semitic teaching by rejecting "the false doctrine that the church could have permission to hand over the form of its message and of its order to whatever it itself might wish or to the vicissitudes of the prevailing ideological and political convictions of the day." Articles four and five address the Church's necessary independence of civil authorities and state control of its ministry and work:

4. We reject the false doctrine that apart from this ministry, the church could . . . give itself or allow itself to be given special leaders (Führer) vested with ruling authority.

5. We reject the false doctrine that beyond its special commission the state should and could become the sole and total order of human life and so fulfill the vocation of the church as well, [or that] the church

should and could take on the nature, tasks, and dignity which belongs to the state and thus become itself an organ of the state.[7]

In these latter two articles the declaration does not reject Luther's doctrine of the "two kingdoms," but at the same time places both "kingdoms," the Church and the state, in subordination to the Word of God.

The Barmen Synod and its declaration stand as a courageous witness of the Christian community under political threat and persecution. The declaration is also especially representative of Karl Barth's understanding of political theology and social ethics, an ethics wholly subservient to the Word of God. In the Barmen document one is struck not only by Barth's critique of the Catholic tradition of natural law, but also by his rejection of Brunner's natural theology, Gogarten's use of the "orders of creation," and all secular moral theories based solely on principles of utilitarian or teleological calculation. Barth's social ethics is an ethics of divine command and human obedience as these are apprehended in the hearing of the Word of God in the context of a concrete situation. For Barth, God's command never can be equated with or reduced to a universal natural law, or to a set of rules or ethical axioms. Rather, God's command often will confound and challenge our human notions of ethical reasoning, and of ethics itself. This point was first insisted upon in *Der Römerbrief* and it is echoed throughout the *Church Dogmatics*.

From the final point of view that we must take in Christ, there is no ethics. There is only the activity of God, to which our knowledge of the situation and the action it requires of us must correspond in every moment. . . . For our part, knowledge of God is necessary . . . but that is a knowledge which grasps the situation in the moment, in God, not in a formula which is equally true for today and tomorrow, for here and there.[8]

Within a few months of the composing of the Barmen Declaration, Barth wrote his fiery response, *Nein!*, attacking Brunner's open letter defending a Christian natural theology. Barth's point, again, was that there is no knowledge of God or his will outside of God's revelation in Jesus Christ. It is clear that in Barth's mind the Barmen Declaration is addressed to this larger theological question of the beginning point of theology and to what he saw as the anthropocentric and idolatrous tendencies associated with talk of orders of creation and natural theology.

In Brunner's principal work on ethics, *The Divine Imperative* (1932) (the German title, *Das Gebot und die Ordnungen*, meaning *The Commandment and the Orders*), better conveys the subject of the book), he asserts that we encounter God's commandments not only in the "general laws of creation, of the preservation and furtherance of life . . . [but also] in those existing facts of human corporate life which lie at the root of all historical life as unalterable presuppositions, which . . . relate and unite men to one another in a definite way."[9] Brunner is referring here to those orders and institutions of society such as marriage, the family, and the state. He does not mean to imply that these orders of creation are fixed, because the Christian's responsibility is one of "critical cooperation," a vocation to improve and assist in the perfection of God's Creation.[10] Nevertheless, these orders are, for Brunner, part of God's plan and must be preserved. They can be neither carelessly disregarded nor radically displaced by some utopian human scheme. Brunner feared social revolution as a rebellion against God; Barth, on the other hand, found this deference toward and desire to preserve the social orders as constituting a limitation on the freedom of God.

In his writings on political ethics in the 1930s, Gogarten similarly betrayed a concern to ground the institutions of society—family, vocation, *Volk*, the state—in the human obligation (Hörigkeit) to respond to God in and through these concrete orders of human relations. In Gogarten this reflected the deep influence of Luther's doctrine of the "two realms" and the two uses of the law. For him, as for Luther, the theological use of the law was meant to convict humanity of its failure and sin; the civil use of the law was, however, God's means of maintaining law, order, authority, and peace in a sinful world. As was mentioned in Chapter Three, during the period of the Weimar Republic in the 1920s, Gogarten developed an inordinate fear of the spread of individualism and of political and cultural liberalism, and of social anarchy. This reinforced his belief in the state as an instrument of God for the restraining of evil—a belief that had dire consequences for him with the rise to power of National Socialism and the Nazi state. In his *Political Ethics* (1932), Gogarten speaks of the state as "no greater gift of God on earth because it is the most comprehensive and fundamental of the orders of human life."[11] Although he did not regard the orders of creation as eternally static forms, his political writings of the period reveal a romantic belief in the individual's obligation to listen to the claims of the state and the *Volk* in Germany's present historical context, what he saw as its special "moment" in history. In the community of the German *Volk*, Gogarten perceived a special manifestation of the Thou-I—the "being-from-the-other-and-for-the-other." And in the living morality of the *Volk*, he saw a human law that made claim to the community's obligation and loyalty. For the German Christians, this law of the *Volk* had come to be viewed as the law of God; Gogarten phrased it slightly differently. For him "the law of God is met *in* the law of the *Volk*"; it was not unambiguously the law of God, but it *was* God's law insofar as God's law for the historical situation can only be discerned in the concrete situation and not in some abstract formula.

As was mentioned in Chapter Three, Gogarten briefly joined the cause of the German Christians in 1933 and attacked Barth and the Confessing Church's opposition to the Nazi state. Although he soon broke with the German Christians, especially over their anti-Semitic policies, and while he was never a National Socialist, his ethical writings and actions of this period convinced Barth that Gogarten's Lutheran commitment to the civil law of God was the source of a perilous idolatry, and that it was the inevitable result of his growing insistence on an anthropo-

logical starting point in theology. It was, in Barth's estimation, similar to Brunner's "other task," his apology for a natural theology. Gogarten's writings provoked Barth to publish his 1933 "Parting" in *Zwischen den Zeiten*, signaling the breakup of the Dialectical theology.

In the late 1930s, Barth reflected on his disputes with his earlier colleagues. He was completing the second volume of the *Church Dogmatics* on the doctrine of God, and he was relieved that the earlier polemics were behind him. He now felt he could say "yes" to God's grace rather than have to continue to say "no." He had recently held a seminar on natural theology, and the new volume of the *Dogmatics* was dedicated, once again, to the theme that "God is known only by God." In this volume Barth returns to the subject of Barmen but he points to its larger significance. The Barmen Declaration had not carried the matter as far as was required. In Barth's judgment, the Confessing Church's conflict with the German Christians would not have been a real conflict had it not also been a warfare against natural theology itself in all of its historical manifestations. The situation was similar with regard to ethics. For Barth, the theological matter must always be the priority of God's Word and command, which only then can be followed by ethics. In consequence, he reverses Luther's discussion of "Law and Gospel" and speaks of the Gospel as preceding the Law. The gift of the Gospel issues in a freedom that comes only with the prevenience of grace, a freedom that is bound by no theory of natural law nor by any orders of creation. God's command may, in fact, involve a suspension of "natural" norms and require quite specific, provisional, and even revolutionary action against, for example, unjust civil authority.

According to Barth, the Gospel and the Law are not separable; rather, the Law comes from the Gospel as God's instrument to achieve the divine purpose in Christ, not, however, by some legal rule or axiom, but in the freedom in which God calls a human being to respond in gratitude to his Word in Christ as God's covenant partner. In the *Church Dogmatics*, II, the theme of the freedom to which God calls human beings to serve his Word in Jesus Christ is developed at great length.[12] And this point is the key to his ethics. God's gift of freedom and obedience are one, because God's command is given not as a demand but as a gracious offer. All individual ethical action is, then, justified by God's grace, because it relies on God's Word to discover what one ought to do. This freedom unburdens the individual from the terrors of personal "conscience," or the calculation of some abstract principle, but it also leaves open the perpetually new, concrete hearing of Christ's Word in every new context.

This "actualism" of Barth's ethics has been criticized, because it rejects all appeals to a static rule or to a normative principle, and calls instead for a free, unique action appropriate to the concrete situation. God's command is, therefore, never known *a priori;* it is continually given anew freely *by* God in the situation. This is not, however, to be confused with what later came to be referred to as "situation ethics," because for Barth it is *not the situation* that guides the choice of action but God's gracious, perpetually renewed Word spoken by Christ in the unique situation.

This distinctive character of Barth's ethics is apparent at the time in his disagreements with other Christian ethicists, such as Emil Brunner and Reinhold Niebuhr, on a range of social and political issues. Barth publicly refused to take sides on a number of important political issues in the twentieth century, while his personal actions often were courageous. The reason is that Barth saw most social issues as ambiguous and he refused to generalize. "Before God everything is impure; and therefore nothing is especially impure." Even the so-called orders of creation, though given by God, are to be taken as provisional because God's intentions cannot be equated with the apparent patterns of life reflected in nature or society. As early as 1929 Barth wrote: "These 'orders' were laid down by God at the creation, and even now they are directions intended for my living. But what, for example, works, marriage, family, etc., signify just now in my particular case, as God's 'orders,' I do not know."[13]

Barth's refusal to appeal to any general rules or natural laws is especially apparent in his

post–World War II writings on communism and capitalism and on the Cold War between the East and the West.[14] He was, for example, unwilling to follow Brunner in the latter's attack on communism on the same grounds as his condemnation of National Socialism in Germany. Barth saw communism and capitalism as both "materialistic" ideologies, and despite much criticism, he refused to take a definite side in the conflict, although he recognized the great importance of political democracy. In an open letter Brunner had demanded that Barth explain why he did not condemn communist totalitarianism as he had Nazi tyranny. In Brunner's judgment, communism represented a more thoroughgoing "totalitarian State" than Nazism and was "intrinsically atheistic." Barth's response is highly characteristic. "The church," he writes,

> must not concern itself eternally with various "isms" and systems, but with historical realities as seen in the light of the Word of God and of faith. Its obligation lies, not in the direction of any fulfilling of a natural law, but towards its living Lord. Therefore, the church never thinks, speaks, or acts "on principle." Rather, it judges spiritually and by individual cases.[15]

Barth's call "to stand quietly aloof from the present conflict" between the East and the West was fully developed in an essay entitled "The Church Between East and West" (1949). He urged the Christian churches to avoid partisanship and to embrace a third way of their own, which he called "reconstruction." He saw Western freedom as having degenerated into an unjust individualism and Communist claims to justice as having evolved into a tyrannous collectivism. The church should be free and independent of both of these ideologies and offer the world its own message of freedom and justice. Barth was strongly criticized, as we will see in Chapter Six, by theologians such as the American Reinhold Niebuhr for advocating a Christian neutrality. Whatever the merits of the ethical criticism of Barth on this issue, it is clear that he was not calling for a stance of neutrality but, rather, for an independent witness that would free the churches from being co-opted by either of these powerful political ideologies.

A final illustration of the independence and the contextual character of Barth's ethics is his stand on atomic warfare. Barth had been a peace activist since his early years, but he had not embraced pacifism, nor had he rejected warfare. He had served in the Swiss militia for a brief period during the Second World War. However, in the 1950s he joined with other church leaders in protesting any use of atomic weapons. In 1958 Barth wrote a petition to the Synod of the Evangelical Church of Germany, endorsed by hundreds of signatures, calling upon the Synod to declare its opposition to nuclear war and to the involvement of Christians in atomic weapons research and production.[16] While the Synod did oppose the use of weapons of mass destruction and atomic weapons research, it did not approve the petition as submitted. Nevertheless, Barth and his colleagues had, once again, called upon the Church to witness to a particular moral issue categorically and without compromise. This review of Barth's theological ethics must suffice because we need to turn to other major themes of his mature theology as they were worked out in the multiple volumes of his *Church Dogmatics*.

The Major Themes in Barth's *Church Dogmatics*

It is not surprising that a person with a mind and spirit as gifted and lively as Barth's should, over sixty years of publication, have set out on new and revolutionary paths, but always, in his case, it was within a perspective that remained extraordinarily consistent. The changes in direction were, in Barth's own estimation, "dialectical shifts" of emphasis and corrections.

The Doctrine of the Word of God and Interpretation

We have learned that for Barth dogmatics is to be understood *as a science of the Church*, and, therefore, that it is committed to submitting only

to that which is valid for its object. For Christianity that object is the Word of God as revealed in Holy Scripture. Barth's doctrine of the Word of God in its threefold form is developed in the first volume of the *Church Dogmatics*, properly entitled *The Doctrine of the Word of God*.

For Barth, the reality of the Word of God is given in three forms—as revealed in Jesus Christ, as written in Holy Scripture, and as proclaimed by the Church. These are not three Words; they are one and the same Word of God realized in these three forms. And the first form, the person Jesus Christ speaking and acting, is the ground and source of both the witness of Scripture and the Church's proclamation. The latter two forms of God's Word are not, however, to be understood undialectically in relation either to the words of the Bible or to the Church's proclamation. Both the written Bible and the Church's preaching are human activities and are not, in and of themselves, the Word of God. They are human words and, therefore, possess all of the limitations inherent in anything human.

According to Barth, it is only by God's grace and by the power of the Holy Spirit that the Bible and Church proclamation *become* and, in fact, *are* the Word of God. Holy Scripture is then God's chosen channel by which the divine Word is made known to humanity in the human words of the biblical canon. The absolutely essential role of the written Scriptures in the revelation and proclamation of God's eternal Word, in spite of its being also a human word, leads Barth into a detailed discussion of biblical exegesis and interpretation in *Church Dogmatics*, I, 1, Part II.

For Barth, a Christian dogmatics is not possible without acceptance of the act of faithful obedience to God's revealed Word in Scripture. But because dogmatics is subject to Scripture, it must be corrected continuously by exegesis. By exegesis, Barth now means something quite distinct from an exegesis that simply entails a sympathetic understanding of the meaning of a text by means of a presuppositionless "objectivity," the position that he had proposed in his book on *Romans*. He now calls for a distinctive *theological exegesis*, an exegesis carried out under a quite definite presupposition. This is, firstly, that the reader of the Old and New Testaments remembers that in this book the Church has up to now heard God's Word; and secondly that this reader . . . reads in the expectation that he himself will also for his time hear God's Word. The place of theological exegesis lies right between this remembrance and this expectation. . . . Therefore, *that* exegesis which is the norm for Dogmatics is not an exegesis that is without presuppositions. There is no such thing.[17]

Although Barth had earlier assumed that the biblical exegete could, as in general hermeneutics, leave behind his or her own preconceptions and allow the text to say what it has to say, he now speaks of a theological exegesis that presupposes grace, faith, and prayer.

This new conception of exegesis is developed at length in *Church Dogmatics*, I, 2 in a section entitled "Freedom under the Word of God." Freedom under the Word implies the assumption of responsibility by all members of the Church for the interpretation and application of Holy Scripture. The necessary *form* of such a responsible scriptural exegesis "must consist in all circumstances in the freely performed act of subordinating all human concepts, ideas, convictions to the witness of revelation supplied to us in Scripture."[18] True exegesis of Scripture rests, therefore, on the assumption that the message of Scripture, even in its most problematic and debatable parts, is truer and more important than what we ourselves know. Therefore, biblical interpretation is *not* a conversation *inter pares*: "To try to hold together and accept *pari passu* both the testimony of the Bible which has this content and the autonomy of our world of thought is an impossible hermeneutical programme." Theological exegesis entails, for Barth, the surrender of our human autonomy.

Here, perhaps surprisingly in view of what Barth has just said, he lays down an important, yet problematic, caveat. Subordination to the scriptural text, Barth further insists, does not mean the elimination of our own human resources. Subor-

dination, after all, implies that the subordinate is there and remains there. "It means placing oneself behind, following, complying as subordinate to the superior. . . . It cannot mean that we have to allow our ideas, thoughts, convictions to be supplanted, so to speak, by those of the prophets and apostles." If this were to be done, biblical interpretation would be nothing but a parroting of the words of the text. "Subordination," Barth writes, "must concern *the purpose and meaning indicated in the ideas, thoughts and convictions of the prophets and apostles*, that is, the testimony which, by what they say as human beings like ourselves, they wish to bear. To this testimony of their words we must subordinate ourselves."[19] (Italics added.)

This raises an important question. What can Barth mean when he says that our "ideas and convictions" are not supplanted but that they must remain "subordinate" to the "witness" of the prophets and apostles? Biblical interpretation, he tells us, is not an enterprise *inter pares*. But does not subordination, after all, entail the elimination of whatever ideas one brings to the text? It is not a matter of distinguishing the content (the "meaning") of the text from its form because, for Barth, in contrast to Bultmann, there can be no piercing back behind apparent outmoded forms to the "facts" or "meanings" that lie *behind* the letter of the text. According to Barth, one does subordinate one's ideas and experience in the expectation that what is given in the text will shatter those preconceptions. This is evident in his discussion of the three stages of biblical interpretation. In the first phase of interpretation, the exegete is entirely concerned with the sense of the words of Scripture as such. And the means used for this purpose are those of literary-historical criticism, textual criticism, lexicography, and so on. But even here one must be prepared not to exclude "the idea that what is said . . . might suggest other possibilities than those hitherto known to me." This has to do with the "form" or letter of the text. Our representations of the object pictured in the text must therefore "be determined by its form, not by the laws of form which we bring with us . . . our own presuppositions are not adequate and if we wish to represent it we must be prepared to alter our own ideas of the laws of form."[20]

The second moment of biblical interpretation involves the *act of reflection* on what Scripture declares. Here, again, Barth acknowledges that in the act of reflection on the text "it is quite impossible for us to free ourselves of our own shadow, that is to make the so-called *sacrificium intellectus*."[21] The interpreter inevitably brings to the text "a particular epistemology . . . definite ideas and ideals concerning the relations of God, the world and man . . . and cannot simply deny these. . . . Without such spectacles, we cannot read the Bible at all."[22] This is an interesting admission, but it appears to imply a rather benign notion of philosophical preunderstanding, as if the epistemology, or "definite ideas" used by the interpreter, would not ever play a determinative role. But is this not just the problem? It is not clear how Barth can determine whether or not another interpreter of Scripture is misinterpreting the object of the text unless he, Barth, knows that he has the right interpretive "key" to explicate the true object of the text.

Because Barth readily acknowledges the use of philosophy (in the broad sense of the use of cultural presuppositions) in scriptural interpretation, he lays down a number of principles for the use of any philosophy in the interpretive task. For example, the exegete should be aware that *no philosophy is perfectly fitted* for the explication of Scripture. Luther and Calvin were dependent on Platonism in their scriptural interpretation; the Tübingen school used Hegel, and the Form critical school employed the insights of the phenomenology of Edmund Husserl. Second, no philosophical scheme is more than a hypothesis, provisional and experimental; one may well be converted to a different interpretive scheme. Neither can any philosophy be considered *inter pares* with Scripture as a second absolute. They are all instrumental, some perhaps more useful or valuable than others. "The choice of a particular mode of thought for its serviceableness is the business of grace and therefore cannot be our business."

Finally, Barth asserts that "the use of a scheme of thought in the service of scriptural exegesis is legitimate and fruitful when it is determined and controlled by the text and the object mirrored in the text."[23] The use of a philosophy is somehow chosen by the text. Once again, one must ask: If the philosophical or cultural presuppositions used in the reflective explication or interpretation of a text of Scripture are "determined and controlled by the text," does this not require, in effect, that the exegete "abandon" or set aside the very experience and ideas that Barth has clearly acknowledged as both present and as impossible to eradicate, even though they be recognized as provisional working hypotheses and not absolute? Furthermore, if the use of a hermeneutical key "is determined and controlled by the text," is any philosophical guidance needed, because the text appears to interpret itself? Barth does not attempt to answer the question how one might know when the "legitimate and fruitful" scheme of thought is, indeed, appropriate for a particular text or, as Barth says, when grace is operative in the decision. Because Barth does not satisfactorily clarify these issues, his important reflections on biblical hermeneutics have been the subject of rather broad criticism by theologians as diverse as Rudolf Bultmann, the Jesuit Jerome Hamer, Dietrich Bonhoeffer, and Wolfhart Pannenberg.

The Christological Concentration

In a lecture delivered in 1956 entitled "The Humanity of God," Barth reflected on his theological development since the publication of his revolutionary commentary on *Romans*. He acknowledged that *Romans*, with its emphasis on the "Wholly Otherness" of God, was a necessary corrective to the divine immanence of nineteenth-century theology. But he now sees in the developing volumes of the *Church Dogmatics* "a change of direction," one that represents a "correction" rather than a repudiation of what he had said in *Romans*. This correction is what has come to be called Barth's "Christological concentration." It simply underlines his conviction that God cannot be understood apart from Jesus

Christ and, therefore, from humanity. Nor can humanity be understood apart from God in Jesus Christ. Barth refers to this as his pointing to "the humanity of God" in Jesus Christ the crucified, the God of and for humanity. While Barth never had conceived of God's revelation in abstraction from the person of Jesus Christ, after 1935 Barth's entire theology is focused on Christology. Not only the doctrine of God, but the doctrines of creation, election, anthropology, and reconciliation all are now understood christologically, because God's Godness includes in itself His humanity. In Christ humanity is taken up into the very Godhead itself.

We must not refer to the second "person" of the Trinity as such, to the eternal Son or the eternal Word of God *in abstracto*. . . . According to the free and gracious will of God the eternal Son of God is Jesus Christ. . . . He is the decision of God in time, and yet according to what took place in time the decision which was made from all eternity.[24]

We cannot, then, look at Creation as the work of "the Logos in itself," of a *Deus absconditus*, but only to the work of God as it is seen in Christ. Creation, too, must always be viewed in the light of God's *eternal covenant* in Christ. Barth thus refers to the covenant as "the internal basis of creation." Christian theology does not have the responsibility of showing

how creation promises, proclaims and prophesies the covenant, but how it prefigures and to that extent anticipates it without being identical with it; not how creation prepares the covenant, but how in so doing it is itself already a unique sign of the covenant and a true sacrament; not Jesus Christ as the goal, but Jesus Christ as the beginning of creation.[25]

According to Barth, Jesus Christ, as the only ground and goal of creation, is, therefore, the clue to anthropology. If we want to understand humanity, we need not construct some general anthropological model, nor should we even look to the archetypal image of fallen Adam. Christ alone is the prototype of humanity.

There in the eternity of the divine counsel which is the meaning and basis of all creation . . . the decision was made who and what true man is. There his constitution was fixed and sealed once and for all. . . . No man can elude this prototype. We derive wholly from Jesus not merely our potential and actual relation to God, but even our human nature as such. For it is He who, as the ground and goal of the covenant of grace planned for man, is also the ground and goal of man's creation.[26]

If Christ is the ground and goal of humanity, then sin and evil cannot be the last word about humankind.

In his relation to God a man may become a sinner and thus distort and corrupt his own nature, but he cannot revoke what was decided in Jesus apart from him concerning the true nature of man. . . . And if Jesus forgives his sins and restores his spoiled relation to God, this means that Jesus again controls what originally belongs to Him. . . . He has the freedom and power to do this. . . . And He does just that by making Himself our Savior.[27]

In virtue of the eternal covenant in Jesus Christ, the creation—including humanity—stands essentially in a *positive* relationship to God. That is the first and last word of God. Barth can, therefore, speak of sin and evil as "nothingness" and as the "ontological impossibility," for they are denied by the prior covenant of grace in Jesus Christ.

It [sin and evil] is that which is excluded from all present and future existence, i.e., chaos, the world fashioned otherwise than according to the divine purpose, and therefore formless and intrinsically impossible. . . . That which is ungodly and anti-godly can have reality only as that which by God's decision and operation has been rejected and disappeared, and therefore only as a frontier of that which is and will be according to God's decision and action.[28]

By speaking of the "impossibility" of sin, Barth does not mean that there are no such realities as sin and evil but rather that they exist only *relatively*. Sin is an attempt to evade and escape from grace, but sin cannot finally prevent God from addressing His *Yes* to humanity. "Certainly even as this [sinful] man he has not ceased to be the good creature and the elect of God. Even as a wrongdoer he cannot fall from the hand of God; he cannot, as it were, snatch himself out of the divine grasp."[29]

The Doctrine of Election

The radicalness of Barth's "Christocentric concentration" is most evident in his treatment of the doctrine of election, which he calls "the sum of the Gospel because of all words that can be said or heard it is the best."[30] It is here that Barth parts company with the Protestant Reformers most emphatically. For the Reformers, God's election—coming before Christ—is a mystery. Some are elected to salvation and others to eternal damnation. Why some confess Christ and others remain unbelievers is part of God's inscrutable will, the work of the *Deus absconditus*. For Barth such a conception of predestination, as a mixed message of joy and horror, is intolerable—not because it appears unjust to our human perspective, but because it is contrary to God's eternal covenant of grace in Jesus Christ, for "before Him and without Him and beside Him God does not elect or will anything." According to Barth, Jesus Christ is both the electing God and the elected human.[31] "In Jesus Christ God in his free grace determines Himself for sinful man and sinful man for Himself. He therefore takes upon Himself the rejection of man with all its consequences, and elects man to participation in His own glory."[32]

Here Barth develops a doctrine of double predestination, but one far different from John Calvin's doctrine. According to Barth, predestination takes place in Jesus Christ alone, but it, too, involves a twofold movement. In Jesus Christ, God elected Himself for rejection and death, but also elected sinful humanity for election and eternal life. Here both God's "yes" and God's "no" are heard, but whereas the "no" is addressed to Christ alone as the rejected of God, the "yes" is spoken to humanity whom God in his

original covenant has elected for fellowship with Himself.

> What we have to consider in the elected man Jesus is, then, the destiny of human nature, its exaltation to fellowship with God. . . . It is in this man that the exaltation itself is revealed and proclaimed. For with His decree concerning this man, God decreed too that this man should be the cause and the instrument of our exaltation.[33]

Jesus Christ represents "the original and all-inclusive election," for of none other can it be said that "his election carries in it and with it the election of the rest." Jesus is at once the elect for all and the reprobate for all. It, therefore, follows that for Barth predestination is "the non-rejection of man."[34] Does this not entail a doctrine of *apokatastasis*, of universal salvation? Barth is unwilling to make such an assertion about the freedom of God's grace.

> If we are to respect the freedom of the divine grace, we cannot venture the statement that it must and will finally be coincident with the . . . doctrine of the so-called *apokatastasis*. No such right or necessity can legitimately be deduced. . . . But, again, in grateful recognition of the grace of the divine freedom we cannot venture the opposite statement that there cannot and will not be this final opening up and enlargement of the circle of election and calling.[35]

One thing is certain: Human beings cannot place limits on the lovingkindness of God as revealed in Jesus Christ.

The fact is, Barth insists, that God has declared himself for humanity, for all humanity. What distinction, if any, can be made then between Christians and nonbelievers, if Jesus is at once the elect for all? The difference, for Barth, is not that the Christian is saved and the nonbeliever damned. The Christian and nonbeliever stand together in their common need. It is God who stoops down to both.

> Who is it who really has to stoop down at this point? Not one man to another, a believer to an

unbeliever. . . . He who stoops down to the level of us all, both believers and unbelievers, is the real God alone, in His grace and mercy. And it is only by the fact that he knows this that the believing man is distinguished from the unbeliever.[36]

The person of faith does not arrogantly glory in his or her election. The acknowledgment of God's grace simply makes one aware that he or she is called and chosen to be in Christ, to live the life of truth rather than falsehood. Furthermore, the Christian is called to service in response to the gift of God's grace. "This service, and therefore the blessedness of the elect, consists in gratitude for the self-offering of God."[37] The Christian life is marked above all else by joyful thanksgiving. "The only answer to *charis* is *eucharistia* (thanksgiving). . . . Grace and gratitude belong together like heaven and earth. Grace evokes gratitude like the voice an echo."[38]

It is no wonder that Karl Barth has been called *the* theologian of the Good News. To think of Barth as the gloomy theologian of crisis and judgment is to fail to hear the central theme of his *Church Dogmatics*, namely, the Gospel of God's gracious election. If anything, Barth is criticized today for his optimism. His theology has been referred to as "the triumph of grace"—a triumph that, it is claimed, relativizes evil and divine judgment and leaves no place for real human freedom. It is said that in Barth's theology humanity is "swamped by grace."[39]

There is little question that Barth's theology is open to serious criticism, but it is equally clear that the old stereotype, which portrays Barth as a somber, pessimistic, rather narrowly orthodox theologian obsessed with the transcendent otherness of God, is now impossible for anyone who reads the *Church Dogmatics*. Barth is indeed appropriately called "God's joyful partisan."

The Reception and Critique of Barth's Theology

Few historians of modern theology would reject the judgment that Karl Barth has had a wider and a more enduring influence on theology in the twentieth century than any other thinker. That influence began in the immediate post–World War I years, and it continues in the current discussions between the so-called "postliberal" theologians, who share Barth's basic conception of the nature and task of Christian theology, and their critics, who champion one or another form of a "theology of correlation" between the Christian message and modern philosophy and the sciences. (See Chapter Sixteen.) And yet, despite his extraordinary impact, Barth was and remains a very controversial theologian whose work has been under continuous scrutiny and criticism since the second decade of the twentieth century.

There are, indeed, a number of surprises and ironies that mark Barth's career and writings. While he has had a remarkable influence, his most important writings, the *Church Dogmatics*, are familiar only to a small group of professional theologians. His work, more than that of any other major Christian thinker of the twentieth century, has been both misunderstood and caricatured. Only recently has a more fair and balanced—but also often highly critical—estimate of the method and substance of his work been possible. Both the misrepresentation and dismissal of Barth are due in part to his seeming pleasure in engaging in attacks and polemics, to his creative yet unsuspected "changes of direction," and to the fact that his massive *Church Dogmatics* is too daunting for all but the most dogged reader.

Further ironies that mark Barth's work are the admiration that is felt for his witness during the dark years of National Socialism in Germany, yet also the suspicion that is so widely expressed by Christian ethicists regarding the bases of his social ethics and "political theology." It is also ironic, in view of his severe and sometimes vicious attack on Roman Catholicism, that since the 1950s noted Catholic theologians appear, on the whole, to hold Barth in higher regard than do many of their Protestant counterparts, evidenced in the writings of Hans Urs von Balthasar, Henri Bouillard, and Hans Küng, among others.

Part of the greatness and the power of Barth's theology is that it has challenged other theological positions at their most critical, and often most vulnerable, points. Evangelical Protestant theologians are seriously questioned by Barth regarding their doctrine of revelation and Scripture and, in turn, they have focused their criticisms on Barth's doctrine of Holy Scripture, charging him with confusing revelation with inspiration and with underestimating the threats of modern radical historical-literary criticism of the Bible. Evangelical Calvinists especially have disapproved of his doctrine of election and its implicit, if not fully acknowledged, universalism. Roman Catholic theologians have, of course, felt compelled to respond to Barth's repudiation of natural theology and his understanding of the relations of nature and grace. They also challenge his view of the relationship between Scripture and Church tradition and, of course, his view of the sacraments, his doctrine of the visible Church, which, it is claimed, is minimized if not "dissolved" by Barth's concern to protect the sovereign freedom and action of God in Jesus Christ. We cannot undertake here an analysis of the merits and deficiencies in this considerable body of critical literature.[40] We conclude, rather, by referring to three long-standing and related criticisms of Barth's theology, criticisms that persist in the current discussion of his work: the relationship between theology and philosophy, between revelation and history, and between God and the world.

Barth's doctrine of revelation often has been criticized for what is called its radical divine "actualism." What is meant by this term is that in the event of revelation God alone is active and the human remains only a passive receptor of God's revelatory Word. Critics ask whether such a conception of revelation is even possible considering the fact that revelation is always mediated through finite, human means. This is the point of criticism made initially by both Bultmann and Gogarten. If revelation is a form of knowing, does not this imply that the human agent must, for example, make some discriminating judgments regarding professed revelations, all of which are mediated through some finite means, be it an historical event, a person, or a text? And if such discriminating judgments are required, does not this

involve the exercise of reason and, therefore, some philosophical presuppositions? Is not the connection between theology, as a human science, and philosophy both indispensable and more complex than Barth is willing to acknowledge?

An example of this form of criticism is found in the writings of Wolfhart Pannenberg, whose important contribution to theology in the second half of the twentieth century is discussed in Chapter Eleven. Pannenberg was Barth's student, and he agrees with Barth on many points. But he parts with his teacher on the role of philosophy and the sciences in the theological task and on the uniquely privileged authority that Barth affords the Bible. Barth rightly refers to theology as a human science that investigates its "definite object" by a "self-consistent path," but Pannenberg sees this as resulting in an appeal to faith in the prevenience of God's revelation and in the rejection of any effort of legitimation beyond this confession itself. Pannenberg asserts, on the contrary, that

when the foundation is left to a venture in this way, not only is its scientific status endangered, but also the priority of God and his revelation over human beings, on which, for Barth, everything rests. Barth's unmediated starting from God and his revealing word turns out to be no more than an unfounded postulate. . . . Barth rightly rejects the reduction of the subject-matter of theology to human consciousness, but his use of God and his revelation as an unmediated premise provides no escape from these problems. . . . Barth's apparently so lofty objectivity about God and God's word turns out to rest on no more than the irrational subjectivity of a venture of, faith with no justification outside itself.[41]

The second issue concerns Barth's treatment of the relationship between revelation and history. What Barth often means by history is a "sacred history"; that is, in its most essential sense supernatural and miraculous, a history that is entirely veiled to the scientific historian because it cannot be comprehended or contained within the categories of historiographical science. But for Barth the events of sacred history are at once historical and suprahistorical. They appear to partake of two histories, ordinary empirical history—which is open to common observation—and *Heilsgeschichte*, which is discerned only by faith. But what the relationship is between these two histories and how indispensable the one is to the other are not at all clear. Revelation history appears to be neither solely in heaven nor entirely on earth but in some mysterious limbo between the two. R. R. Niebuhr has raised the question as to whether "sacred history" can properly be called history at all in Barth's theology.

When the resurrection of Christ is thought of as a "sacred event," transcending the historical continuum that conditions all experiential concepts and perception, it has in fact lost its revelatory quality. For that which is said to reveal history must participate to a significant degree in the order of reality it is supposed to illuminate.[42]

The third rather persistent criticism of Barth has to do with his dialectical understanding of the relation between God and the world—that is, with the claim that Barth's view of God's prevenient action in Jesus Christ does not appear to take seriously enough the worldly action of humans; that Barth does not give adequate account of the continuity of the revealing God's activity in the world, a continuity that perseveres between the singular divine revelatory acts. One can see how this form of criticism is closely related to the previous two. This third criticism is especially important to Process theology and to recent theologies of secularization, to political theologies, and to theologies of liberation. It is a criticism that deeply concerned Dietrich Bonhoeffer. It is prominent in one of his earliest works, despite his great admiration for Karl Barth. We will not pursue the matter here because we will explore it in some detail in our discussion of Dietrich Bonhoeffer, to which we now turn.

DIETRICH BONHOEFFER

On April 9, 1945, at the age of thirty-nine, Dietrich Bonhoeffer (1906–1945) was executed by the Nazis at the Gestapo concentration camp at Flossenbürg. The unprecedented horrors produced by the wars and the totalitarian regimes of the twentieth century created a modern age of Christian martyrs. Among them were Christian intellectuals, writers, and theologians, who suffered censorship and muzzling, imprisonment, torture, and death. But perhaps no Christian witness of this century is better known and has been more influential than Bonhoeffer. However, if it had not been for the posthumous publication of his prison letters and papers by his friend and biographer Eberhard Bethge, Bonhoeffer the theologian may long have been forgotten, mentioned occasionally perhaps as the author of a remarkable book called *The Cost of Discipleship* (1937).

Bonhoeffer's adult life was very largely shaped by the rise of National Socialism and Nazism in Germany from 1930 until his death. As Bethge reminds us: "At the age of thirty he was barred from his academic post; when he was thirty-four, the pulpit was closed to him; at thirty-five, written publication was forbidden; and with his imprisonment at thirty-seven, even conversation with his friends was denied him." Yet, as Bethge remarks, as the outer circle of his activities and communication increasingly narrowed, "his acting and thinking gained power," and when "he was silenced for good at thirty-nine, he began to speak more loudly than ever before."[43]

Dietrich Bonhoeffer was born in Breslau, Germany, in 1906. In 1912 the family moved to Berlin, where his father became professor of psychiatry at the University of Berlin. Both of Bonhoeffer's parents came from prominent families: His mother's father had served as chaplain to the emperor and her grandfather was the famous church historian Karl von Hase. Dietrich and his many brothers and sisters grew up in a liberal and cultured home in a pleasant suburb of Berlin. Adolf von Harnack and other distinguished figures were neighbors. Whereas his brothers took up the professions of law and physics, Dietrich decided at sixteen to enter the ministry. After a year of theological study at Tübingen in 1923, he matriculated at the Univerity of Berlin. Ernst Troeltsch had just died, but Bonhoeffer studied under several members of Berlin's eminent theological faculty, including the foremost Luther authority, Karl Holl; the great New Testament scholar Adolf Deissmann; the historian of early Christianity, Hans Lietzmann; and the elderly Harnack, whose church history seminar Bonhoeffer attended in Harnack's home. Bonhoeffer gave the address on behalf of Harnack's former pupils at the memorial service after Harnack's death in 1930.

Bonhoeffer's true interest was in systematic theology, and so he worked principally under Reinhold Seeberg, who held that chair in Berlin. In 1927 Bonhoeffer submitted to the Berlin faculty his thesis, a theological study of the sociology of the Church, entitled *Sanctorum Communio (The Communion of Saints)*. Although he was deeply influenced in different ways by the great learning and the liberality of his Berlin teachers, Bonhoeffer retained his independence and soon found that he was more attracted to the new Dialectical theology, especially to Karl Barth, and its critique of the tradition of Neo-Protestant theology from Schleiermacher to Troeltsch.

Bonhoeffer lived in Barcelona in 1928 as vicar of a German-speaking congregation. On his return to Berlin early in 1929, he worked on his dissertation—a requirement for teaching on a theological faculty. Entitled *Act and Being* (1931), the book was an impressive joining of sociology and theological reflection. Of special note is the fact that, despite the pull toward Barth, *Act and Being* is fundamentally critical of the kind of theology of revelation that characterized the "Wholly Other" God of Neo-Kantian transcendentalism, and which Bonhoeffer detected in Barth's Dialectical theology.

Before beginning his teaching responsibilities at the University of Berlin, Bonhoeffer was granted a leave of absence to accept a scholarship at Union Theological Seminary in New York City. He was not impressed with American theology, but he was fascinated by aspects of American life. He was especially struck by the problems facing black Americans, and he spent a fair amount of time in Harlem. What he did learn at Union through professors Harry F. Ward, Reinhold Niebuhr, and others, and from the work of Union students among the urban poor, was the importance of the Church's engagement with issues of unemployment, poverty, civil rights, and international affairs. The American "Social Gospel" made an indelible impression on Bonhoeffer. As Bethge remarks, "Henceforth a purely desk-bound existence could no longer satisfy him. Previously unquestioned habits of thought and feeling suddenly seemed one-sided and inadequate; they were in need of reappraisal. . . . The later Bonhoeffer of *The Cost of Discipleship* and the church struggle had not forgotten what he learnt in New York."[44]

On his return to Berlin, Bonhoeffer did not confine himself to lecturing in systematic theology at the university; he also served as student chaplain at the Technical University at Berlin-Charlottenburg, taught a confirmation class in a slum area, and opened a club room for unemployed youth in Charlottenburg. In early 1933, with Hitler installed as chancellor of the Third Reich, Bonhoeffer's life took an unalterable turn. He preached a sermon pointing out the dangers of the new "idolatrous" leadership. He joined forces with Hans Asmussen, Martin Niemöller, Karl Barth, and the others in the Confessing Church. However, in October of 1933 he left Germany to take up pastoral duties to a German-speaking congregation in London, in part to make his full break with the German Christians, but also to renew his ecumenical contacts in England, because he had by this time become very active in the "Life and Work" committee of the World Alliance of Churches, the forerunner of the World Council of Churches.

After a year and a half in England, he felt obligated to return to Germany to lead the Confessing Church's newly established seminary for ordinands at Finkenwalde in Pomerania. Here he established a religious community of work and worship, as well as study, and the spirit of this communal experience is reflected in the small book *Life Together*, which Bonhoeffer published in 1939. While at Finkenwalde, Bonhoeffer returned frequently to lecture at Berlin until his authority to teach there was withdrawn by the government officials in 1936. The most important of Bonhoeffer's writings, prior to his arrest and his prison reflections after 1943, was *The Cost of Discipleship* (1937), published within weeks of the closing of the Finkenwalde seminary by the police and the arrest of twenty-seven former Finkenwalde students. In 1938 Bonhoeffer was expelled from Berlin, and it was then that he made his first contact with the leaders of the conspiracy against Hitler. Despite the restrictions placed upon him, and only because of contacts in high places in Berlin, Bonhoeffer was still able to travel abroad often between 1938 and 1943, largely on ecumenical business but also, as later became known, on matters related to the political conspiracy against Hitler. In 1940, Bonhoeffer was forbidden to speak in public and was required to report regularly to the police; seven months later he was forbidden to publish.

When Bonhoeffer returned from a brief trip to the United States in 1939, he became an official member of the political resistance by becoming a civilian employee of the Military Intelligence Service headed by Admiral Wilhelm Canaris, an opponent of Hitler's. General Hans Oster, who served under Canaris, was coordinator of the resistance. Within this inner circle was Bonhoeffer's brother-in-law, Hans von Dohananyi, a former official of the German Supreme Court. It was necessary for this opposition to penetrate into the heart of the Nazi war machine through the Intelligence Service in order to get the information necessary to carry out the conspiracy against Hitler. In late 1942 word of Bonhoeffer's possible involvement reached the Gestapo, and he was arrested a few months later. However, despite two attempts on Hitler's life that had failed in 1943, the Gestapo could not get clear evidence of Bonhoeffer's participation in the plot, that is, until after the third failure in July 1944. It was then that Bonhoeffer was moved from Tegel prison in Berlin, first to the Gestapo prison in the city, then to Buchenwald concentration camp. On April 5, 1945, Hitler ordered the execution of everyone involved in the plots on his life, and Bonhoeffer's name was placed on the list. He was moved to the concentration camp at Flossenbürg on April 8.

On April 9 the SS held a high-treason trial, and Bonhoeffer was executed by hanging on the next morning, along with Admiral Canaris, General Oster, and other members of the resistance. A few days later Flossenbürg was liberated by the American army.

From 1939 until his death, none of Bonhoeffer's writings were published. His *Ethics*, which he considered his most important work, was published posthumously, but only in fragments. What brought Bonhoeffer the theologian to the attention of the world were writings that he had never intended for publication—the letters written to his friend Eberhard Bethge that were smuggled out during his confinement in Tegel prison. These were published in Germany in 1951 and later in England and America as *Letters and Papers from Prison* (1953) and *Prisoner of God* (1954).

Bonhoeffer's Early Writings and the Relationship with Karl Barth

It is clear from Bonhoeffer's earliest writings that he conceived of the task of theology as bound to the life of the Church. His two earliest books, *Sanctorum Communio* and *Act and Being*, are concerned with ecclesiology, the first substantively and the second indirectly. *Sanctorum Communio* is a dense and difficult book, but it is one of the first important attempts to deal with the subject of the Church from *both* a theological and a sociological perspective. It is essentially an effort to bring together the tradition of German sociology of Max Weber, Troeltsch, and Ferdinand Toennies with the theology represented by Barth and the dialectical theologians in an effort to understand the true social character of the Church and its theological implications. He believed that all the Christian concepts—the person, sin, revelation, reconciliation—were fully understandable only in relation to the Church's sociality. Here, as we will see, Bonhoeffer began his engagement with what he knew of the theology of Barth. (His acquaintance with Barth's *Church Dogmatics* went only as far as Volume II, 2.)

Bonhoeffer's two early works reveal not only the deeply social and ethical context of his thinking, but also his suspicion of beginning theology from a Neo-Kantian starting point of epistemology and revelation (Barth) or with the individual's existential situation (à la Heidegger and Bultmann). *Sanctorum Communio* is an exploration of the relationship between the concepts of person, community, and God. It is heavily indebted to Hegel, through Bonhoeffer's teacher Seeberg, and develops as its central theme the concept of "Christ existing as community." It also draws on the I-Thou personalism of the philosopher Eberhard Grisebach, who had also influenced Friedrich Gogarten. Bonhoeffer clearly was seeking a third way that would neither exaggerate the otherworldly transcendence nor the existential immanence of God; and he found the proper focus for theology in the Church, the Christian communion or fellowship. He did not, however, entirely erase the difference between Christ and the Church as some critics allege; for him the formula "Christ existing as community" was not capable of being transposed to mean that the Church is the incarnation of Christ.

In *Sanctorum Communio* Bonhoeffer sees the individual as coming to realization through the ethical encounters with "the other," by being addressed by the "Thou" of "the other," which presents the individual with a limit or "barrier" that elicits a sense of transcendence and responsibility. It is through just such concrete encounters with other human beings that one encounters God: "Every human Thou is an image of the divine Thou. The character of a Thou is in fact the form in which the divine is experienced; every human Thou has its character from the divine Thou."[45]

The relation to God, Bonhoeffer further argues, comes into being in the revelation of God's love in Jesus Christ and this revelation is mediated through the Church, "Christ existing as community." While we are individual persons we also are social beings, members of a community, and a community is a "collective person," it has a personal character. And what characterizes a real community, such as the Church, is not contractual relations but a participation in a social and an ethical responsibility and task. Whereas sin

destroys the human community, Jesus Christ, as the Second Adam, restores true community by way of his own "vicarious action," which "is the life-principle of the new humanity." But Christ's work is not encompassed by his moral influence, for he is humanity's "vicarious representative":

Each man becomes guilty through his own strength and guilt, because he himself is Adam; but each man is reconciled without his own strength and merit because he himself is not Christ. . . . Not "solidarity" which is never possible between Christ and man, but vicarious action is the life-principle of the new humanity. I know, certainly, that I am in a state of solidarity with the other man's guilt, but my dealings with him take place on the basis of the life-principle of vicarious action.[46]

Bonhoeffer proceeds to discuss the empirical Church and the religious community. The former is not identical with the latter. Paradoxically, the Church both is and is not the empirical Church or the religious community. Employing Toennies's sociological distinction between a society (*Gesellschaft*) and a community (*Gemienschaft*), he sees the Church as a society that preaches the Word, administers the sacraments, and so forth, and in so doing truly manifests the Body of Christ, but it is not thereby the religious fellowship. And because this fellowship is not free of egoism and sin, it cannot be equated with the eschatological Kingdom of God. The Church is both a means-to-an-end, a society, and an end itself as the communal life of love and vicarious action. What is noteworthy is that in the *Sanctorum Communio* one sees in germ the leading themes of Bonhoeffer's later theology: the central role of ecclesiology; the concreteness of God in the encounter with others; Bonhoeffer's aversion to transcendental metaphysics; the link between ecclesiology and Christology; and vicarious action as a "being for the other."

In *Act and Being* Bonhoeffer explores the doctrine of revelation through an inquiry into the issues raised by the two then-current approaches to systematic theology: that of the transcendentalists, who emphasized the "otherness" of God and the free divine *action* ("actualism") in revelation; and that of the ontologists or the theologians of being, exemplified principally in the philosophies of Martin Heidegger and the Catholic Thomists. Bonhoeffer proposes that the danger of transcendentalism is that God never becomes objective, whereas ontologists such as Heidegger exclude God as real beyond the self. In the case of the Thomists, God is an object but is objectified in an infallible institution. Bonhoeffer finds the resolution to this problem in his conception of the Church as "Christ existing in community." In this formulation, both God's freedom and transcendence and God's continuous being and presence in the world are secured. *Act and Being* is explicitly addressed to Karl Barth and the dialectical theologians, warning them of the dangers of transcendental philosophy and of their emphasis on the contingent freedom of God, which fail to do justice both to God's presence in the world and to God's freedom *for* humankind. The role of Barth in Bonhoeffer's theological work in these formative years merits brief comment.

Bonhoeffer never studied with Barth. But early he become enamored of Barth's *The Word of God and the Word of Man* and his *Romans*, and he read a good deal of Barth during 1924–1925. He did not meet Barth, however, until his return from the United States in 1931, visiting him in Bonn. They engaged in long conversations and thereafter exchanged letters until Bonhoeffer's last days in prison. To the end, Bonhoeffer regarded Barth as a mentor who always challenged him; and little that Bonhoeffer wrote was not worked through without Barth in mind. Barth, on the other hand, often was suspicious of the directions that Bonhoeffer proposed when he sought out Barth's advice. In later years, Barth greatly praised *The Cost of Discipleship* and *Sanctorum Communio* but, as we will see, he was annoyed by what he called Bonhoeffer's "enigmatic utterances" and the latter's attack upon him in the prison letters. Thus, despite his admiration and obvious concern for Barth's opinion and approval, Bonhoeffer never compromised his own ideas. He criticized Barth, often sharply and

openly, and his crucial differences with Barth, which remained to the end, are clear in *Act and Being*.

Bonhoeffer was grateful to Barth for the latter's resolute emphasis on the majesty of God, the God who is not "at our disposal." Yet he believed that Barth had carried this too far with his Calvinist commitment to the doctrine *finitum incapax infiniti* (the finite is incapable of containing the infinite). Rather, Bonhoeffer followed Luther's christological emphasis on God *pro nobis* (for us), because in Christ the finite *is* capable of bearing the infinite (*finitum capax infiniti*). This Lutheran theme remained preeminent in all of Bonhoeffer's writing. As mentioned earlier, Bonhoeffer sees Barth's "actualism" of revelation as destroying the continuity between God and humanity. For Bonhoeffer, Christian faith no longer can speak of "possibility" or of "dialectical negation" because in Jesus Christ God's self-giving presence is real, incarnate in time and history. For Bonhoeffer, Barth's "actualism" leaves no room for the *being* of the revealed God in the world.

Bonhoeffer's response to Barth is to insist that the being of God's self-revelation continues in the community.

The Christian communion is God's final revelation: God as "Christ existing in community," ordained for the rest of time until the end of the world. . . . There, it follows, revelation is in some way secured or possessed. God's freedom has bound itself, woven itself into the personal communion, and it is precisely that which proves it God's freedom—that he should bind himself to men.[47]

It is his conception of God's freedom *and* final revelation that Bonhoeffer believes overcomes the problem of the relation of God's being and God's action. God's *being* and aseity (self-existence) is in God's vicarious *action pro nobis* (for us) in Jesus Christ within the Church. In Christ, God freely binds himself to the world without losing the divine identity and majesty. Here Bonhoeffer returns to the theme of *Sanctorum Communio* by tying his reflections on God and revelation to his conception of the Christian community. The *being* of revelation is not to be found in a unique event in the past, nor "as an ever-free, pure and non-objective act" which at particular times may deign to explode into time. "No, the being of revelation 'is' the being of the community of persons, constituted and embraced by the person of Christ, wherein the individual finds himself to be already in his new existence."[48]

Does such a conception mean that for Bonhoeffer, as for Hegel, the being of God is only fully incarnate in the spiritual community? The answer is clearly no, because Bonhoeffer, like Barth, takes pains to protect the freedom of God's being— albeit as a co-presence in and for the world. Here Bonhoeffer is moving toward his own distinctive conception of the God-world relationship. As one commentator has remarked, unlike the early Barth,

Bonhoeffer is willing to risk the thought that God and humanity together in Jesus Christ is a greater conception than God alone in himself; God and the world in unity is a greater conception than God *a se*. The world reconciled to God in Jesus Christ *does* add something to God that God did not have before. Through and in Jesus Christ, one can think of God as one who discovers unprecedented delight in the world which he created and reconciled to himself.[49]

Critics have raised questions as to whether in *Act and Being* Bonhoeffer is fair-minded in his criticisms of Barth.[50] The case certainly can be made for Bonhoeffer's seeing a tendency, and a danger, in Barth's theology up to roughly 1931. But as we have learned, Barth himself was not content with his earlier Dialectical theology, as is made plain in his *Christliche Dogmatik*, in his book on Anselm (1931), and, finally, in his *Church Dogmatics*, II, 1 (1940), where he speaks of the "humanity of God." This new emphasis is close to what Bonhoeffer is insisting on in *Act and Being*. It should be said, however, that Bonhoeffer was aware of this new direction of Barth's thought in II, 1, but he does not appear to see it as a critical development since his criticisms persist, and they become more pointed in the prison writings. We

will return to the Barth-Bonhoeffer relationship in the discussion of Bonhoeffer's ethics and his "enigmatic" letters from Tegel prison.

The Christological Concentration

When Bonhoeffer returned from America he began his lecturing career at the University of Berlin. Among the lecture series that he gave were two that are especially significant. One, on "Creation and Sin," was published as *Creation and Fall* in 1933. The second, on Christology, was given in the politically turbulent summer of 1933, and it was to be his last lecture as a member of the Berlin faculty. His own lecture manuscripts from 1931 to 1933 were never discovered, but student notes on the Christology lectures have made possible a reasonable reconstruction of much of what Bonhoeffer said on the subject. These notes were compiled and edited by Eberhard Bethge and published in 1960 (Eng. trans. *Christology*, 1978). The Christology lectures are the link between the earlier works on the Church and the later writing on discipleship and ethics and the prison letters. Indeed, the primary question posed by Bonhoeffer in his last years was: "Who is Christ for us today" in a world come of age? We have seen, however, that Christology was central to Bonhoeffer's conception of the Church ("Christ existing as church") in *Act and Being*, although the attention there is more on the Church as a "collective person" than on the concrete Christ of history. The latter becomes the crux of the 1933 lectures, which consisted of three parts: the present Christ, the historical Christ, and the future Christ. The third part was never delivered.

Bonhoeffer begins with the present Christ in the Church, Christ *pro me*. He rejects both the Ritschlian emphasis on Christ's presence as his influence, which then extends into the community, and a picture of Christ that is outside of history, as in the Idealist theology of the Hegelians and in Wilhelm Herrmann's spiritual depiction of Christ. In all of these cases Jesus is understood in terms of his power and influence, either as cause or as idea, but not as a *living* person. Bonhoeffer further faults the liberal conception of Jesus that focuses on Jesus's actions or his work—that is, only on Jesus up to the cross. For Bonhoeffer this Jesus remains the dead Christ. The presupposition of Christology is Christ as the living person present here and now as word, as sacrament, and as community. All three imply the present historical and social presence of Christ. Bonhoeffer wants to fully accept the orthodox Chalcedonian Christology that affirms Jesus Christ as "truly God and truly human," and to join this with Luther's theology of the Cross, with Christ as both the humiliated and exalted God.

Bonhoeffer insists that Christ's contemporaneity and real presence necessitate the statements that "Jesus is fully human" and that "Jesus is fully God." The question "how" the man Jesus is contemporaneous with us is impossible to express adequately, as is the question of how God can enter time. The only meaningful question is "Who is present and contemporaneous with us here and now?" and the answer is "The one person of the God-man Jesus Christ." "God in timeless eternity is not God, Jesus limited by time is not Jesus. Rather, God is God in the man Jesus. In this Jesus Christ God is present."[51] This Chalcedonian affirmation must be the starting point of Christology. But Bonhoeffer further links this to Luther's emphasis on the scandal of Jesus Christ's humiliation. The issue is not simply the Incarnation but its *form*. "The offense caused by Jesus Christ is . . . his humiliation."[52] And the humanity and the humiliation of Jesus Christ must be distinguished. It is the humiliation of the God-man that is the scandal and the stumbling block of Christianity.

The humiliation of Christ takes form in the fact that Christ "does not enter in kingly robes of a *morphe theou* ("form of God"). . . . He goes incognito, as a beggar among beggars, as outcast among outcasts . . . as dying among the dying."[53] In the Incarnation God truly links himself freely to humanity and "glorifies himself in the incarnate one." Bonhoeffer insists that the humiliation and the glorification or exaltation of Jesus Christ must be understood together. And so, just as the humiliation is a veiling of the God-man, so is the glorification. The incarnate one is the crucified,

and the humiliation and glorification are not distinctive features of the human and divine natures, but modes of God's existence as man. Bonhoeffer writes: "We have seen the exalted one, only as the crucified; the sinless one, only as the guilt-laden; the risen one only as the humiliated. If it were not so, *pro nobis* [for us] would be destroyed and there would be no faith."[54] Here Bonhoeffer engages the important turn-of-the-century discussion about faith and history and the meaning of the historicality of Jesus Christ. It is clear from what has been said that Bonhoeffer insists on maintaining the truths regarding the *one person of Jesus Christ* as enshrined in the Chalcedonian formula. The *docetic* heresy (denying the real humanity in the incarnation) and the *ebionite* or *adoptionist* heresy (denying the eternal Godhead in Jesus the Christ) must be continuously challenged, as must those efforts of modern Liberal theology to separate Jesus from the divine Christ and to interpret Jesus as "declared divine by the community in a burst of enthusiasm."

Bonhoeffer sees in both the humiliation (Christ's taking on "the likeness of flesh") and the exaltation (the resurrection) the crucial events that remain a scandal to historical scholarship but which also threaten to sever the present-historical Christ of the Church's proclamation from the historical person of Jesus of Nazareth. Matters such as the sinlessness of Jesus, the miracles, and the empty tomb accentuate the historical issue for Bonhoeffer. The sinlessness of Jesus, for example, is not simply one position among others that one might take up regarding Jesus Christ; for Bonhoeffer it is central, for it is critical to assert that Jesus entered fully into human sin if Christianity is to claim that he really became human. If not, how can he really help us? But if he does take on our human flesh how, again, can he help us? Bonhoeffer replies by describing what is meant by Jesus Christ taking on the "likeness of flesh":

Christ has taken upon him all that flesh is heir to. But to what extent does he differ from us? First, not at all. He is man as we are . . . he was not the perfect good. At all times he stood in conflict. . . . He became angry, he was harsh to his mother . . . he broke the law of his people. . . . He must have appeared a sinner in the eyes of men. . . . But all depends upon the fact that it was *he* who assumed the flesh with its tendency to sin and self-will. . . . But because it was *he* who does this, these statements appear in a new light. It is really human flesh that he carries—but because *he* carries it, this flesh is robbed of its rights. He pronounces judgment on his doings. . . . He is tempted as we are, but it is his temptation; he is condemned as we are, but because it is *he* who is condemned, we are saved through him. . . . He is really made sin for us. . . . And as such, the one who hears our sins, and none other; he is the sinless one, the holy, the eternal, the Lord, the Son of the Father.[55]

For Bonhoeffer there can be no balancing of the statements of Jesus Christ as sinner and sinless. Jesus Christ is both wholly "in the flesh" like us and condemned, and yet he is without sin.

Christology cannot by-pass this paradox. Simply stating the sinlessness of Jesus fails if it is based upon the observable acts of Jesus. . . . They are not sinless, but ambiguous. . . . We should not therefore deduce the sinlessness of Jesus out of his deeds. The assertion of the sinlessness of Jesus in his deeds is not an evident moral judgment, but an assertion of faith that it is *he* who performs these ambiguous deeds, he it is who is in eternity without sin. Faith confesses that the one who is tempted is the victor . . . the unrighteous one is righteous. . . . Even the sinlessness of Jesus is incognito: "Blessed is he who is not offended in me" (Matt. 11:6).[56]

Similarly, if Christ had proved himself by miracles, the believer would believe in a "visible *theophany* of deity, but that would not have been faith in Christ *pro me*."[57] The believing community sees in the miracle stories signs of the coming Kingdom of God, not "only magic and false claims." But the incognito is not lifted for the unbeliever who, indeed, sees only magic or fabrication.

On the question of Christ's historicality "lies oppressively the stark historical fact of the empty tomb." Is it crucial to Christology? Is it visible evidence that can penetrate the God-man's incognito? Or, if it was not empty, is Christ not raised and exalted and faith futile? Bonhoeffer sees the

account of the empty tomb as the final scandal, because "empty or not empty, it remains a stumbling block."[58] Its historicity is unprovable; the disciples could not convince others that the body was not stolen. Even as the risen one Jesus does not lift his incognito. All that believers can know today of Christ is through their encounter with the humiliated one. Faith and not visible confirmation must be its way. "The church gazes always only at the humiliated Christ, whether itself is exalted or made low."[59]

Bonhoeffer agrees with the radical critics, such as Wilhelm Wrede and Albert Schweitzer, that a credible historical (*historische*) life of Jesus is unrealizable because it is not possible to get behind the faith of the community in the depiction of the *Kyrios Christos*. For theology there is no Jesus other than Jesus the Christ. For Bonhoeffer this means that any *historical* interpretation of the New Testament can only justifiably be undertaken "after serious consideration of the presupposition that Jesus *is* the proclaimed *Kyrios Christos*"[60]—but that implies moving from the historical to the dogmatic plane of exploration. Although dogmatics must be certain of the historicity of Jesus—i.e., that there is an identity of the proclaimed Christ and the Jesus of history— Bonhoeffer questions to what extent dogmatic statements about Jesus Christ must be dependent on historical confirmation. For example, what if, at a later stage of research, certain dogmatic statements appear impossible in the light of new historical conclusions? Bonhoeffer's answer is forthright, but it reveals a failure in these christological lectures on "the historical Christ" to wrestle with the problem as deeply as had scholars of the previous generation. Bonhoeffer points out, with Lessing and Troeltsch, that historical scholarship can never regard a contingent historical fact as the absolute because its absolute necessity cannot be historically demonstrated. But, of course, "the historically (*geschichtliche*) fortuitous fact of the life and death of Jesus must be of basic and absolute significance for the church." Therefore, Bonhoeffer concludes, "historical investigation and its methods are manifestly transcended here." By this he means that historiography *per se* can make neither an absolutely negative nor an absolutely positive judgment. To do so is to "transform history into *historia sacra*," that is, into supra-history. Therefore, as a subject of strictly historical scholarship, Jesus Christ "remains an uncertain phenomenon." Absolute certainty about a historical fact is impossible to acquire *by itself*, but for the church it is constituitive. For the believing community the historical fact of Jesus Christ remains a paradox, which "means that for the church an historical fact is not past, but present; that which is uncertain is the absolute . . . and what is historical is contemporaneous (Kierkegaard)."[61] And so Bonhoeffer leaves the matter with the following persuasion:

Historical access to the historical Jesus is not binding on faith. . . . The Risen One himself creates belief and so points the way to himself as the Historical One. From there faith needs no confirmation from history. The confirmation of historical investigation is irrelevant before the self-attestation of Christ in the present. In faith, history is known in the light of eternity.[62]

Bonhoeffer's treatment of the historical question reveals his familiarity with the sophisticated discussion of the question in the previous half-century, but his own brief discussion and resolution of the issue are not very satisfactory. He sometimes, for example, uses the terms *historische* and *geschichtliche* interchangeably and thereby introduces considerable confusion into the discussion. However, his treatment of Christology offers some profound insights, building on his earlier ecclesiological reflections, and it paves the way for developments in *The Cost of Discipleship* and *Prisoner for God*.

Discipleship and Ethics

The year 1933, and those immediately following, represented a turning point for Bonhoeffer. They involved a deepening of his engagement in the Church struggle in both its political and theological ramifications and a furthering of the

christological concentration of his theology that had been under way for some time. The rise of National Socialism and Bonhoeffer's own course of theological reflection converged. The political situation in Germany gave Bonhoeffer's thinking on Church, Christology, and discipleship an intensity and a greater specificity and concreteness. Work on his influential *The Cost of Discipleship* began during 1933–1934 with meditations on the Sermon on the Mount. He pursued the theme of discipleship in lectures at Finkenwalde during 1935–1937, completing *The Cost of Discipleship* just before the seminary was closed by the police. Costly discipleship had become linked personally with his reflections on Christology and vicarious action.

At this time Bonhoeffer also had undertaken a disciplined reading and exposition of the Bible. He now perceived that historical-critical questions and all the apparatus of biblical scholarship "merely skim the surface of the bible." Furthermore, the Lutheran preoccupations with *sola fide*, and with the "two realms" of the church and the state, and the efforts to relate the "orders of creation" to the new German doctrine of the *Volk* and race, now gave off "the smell of incense offered at the Nazi altar." As Bethge has shown, Bonhoeffer's attitude toward the world now changes markedly. No longer can there be accommodation to the world and to the state, no dual allegiance, nor can there be a withdrawal from the world into an "otherworldly" piety. Discipleship now entails conflict *with* the world *for* the world.

The original German edition of *The Cost of Discipleship*, entitled *Die Nachfolge* (*following after*), is divided into two parts, the first consisting of a profound essay on discipleship based on an exposition of Matthew 5–7 on the Sermon on the Mount. This is followed by an interpretation of Paul's theology directed at countering the Lutheran tendency to separate the Pauline doctrine of justification from the themes of discipleship and sanctification. Now the great enemy of the Church for Bonhoeffer is "cheap grace." Cheap grace can mean many things, for example holding a correct doctrine of grace or proclaiming a conception of God's love and forgiveness of sins without a genuine act of contrition:

Cheap grace means grace sold on the market like cheapjack's wares. The sacraments, the forgiveness of sin, and the consolations of religion are thrown away at cut prices. Grace is represented as the Church's inexhaustible treasury, from which she showers blessings with generous hands, without asking any questions or fixing limits. Grace without price; grace without cost.[63]

It is based on the notion that because Christ has paid the account, "everything can be had for nothing." It is grace without discipleship, repentance, suffering, or a cross. When Luther spoke of God's grace, he assumed its corollary: the cost of his own life in obedience to Christ. When Luther's followers hear grace preached, they leave out its corollary: the obligation of discipleship.

"Grace is *costly* because it calls us to follow, and it is *grace* because it calls us to follow *Jesus Christ.* . . . Above all, it is *costly* because it cost God the life of his Son . . . and what has cost God much cannot be cheap for us."[64] When Christ called his disciples, they dropped their nets and followed him. The response was not a confession of faith but obedience.

The old life is left behind and completely surrendered. The disciple is dragged out of his relative security into a life of absolute insecurity . . . out of the realm of the finite into the realm of infinite possibilities. . . . It is nothing else than bondage to Jesus Christ alone, completely breaking through every programme, every ideal, every set of laws.[65]

Costly grace thus requires an abandonment of the *attachments* of this world and a dying to the old self. "When Christ calls a man, he bids him come and die." One who refuses to obey and stays behind cannot learn how to believe. "*Only he who believes is obedient, and only he who is obedient believes.* . . . Faith only becomes faith in the act of obedience."[66]

Discipleship does not, however, require the seeking out of needless suffering, yet it does involve a "denying of self" that occasions the suffering of temptation, the bearing of the sins and the burdens of others. For Bonhoeffer this means taking literally Jesus's saying about revenge and not resisting evil.

The right way to requite evil, according to Jesus, is not to resist it. This saying of Jesus removes the Church from the sphere of politics and law. The Church is not a national community like the old Israel, but a community of believers without political ties. . . . The Church has abandoned political and national status, and therefore it must patiently endure aggression. Otherwise evil will be heaped upon evil.[67]

Here we can detect Bonhoeffer speaking both to the nationalist German Christian Church but also to the members of the Confessing Church. We also can recognize the extraordinarily radical nature of his ethical stance in the presence of the Nazi menace. He clearly rejects Albert Schweitzer's interpretation of Jesus's ethic as an "interim ethic," one applicable only in view of the immanent coming of the Kingdom of God. Bonhoeffer takes Jesus's words literally; he refuses to interpret these hard sayings as merely rhetorical figures of speech and hyperbole.

Bonhoeffer thus interprets Jesus's command of love as undivided and unconditional. "Love which shows no special favour to those who love us in return. When we love those who love us, our brethren, our nation, our friends . . . we are no better than the heathen and the publicans."[68] What makes the Christian different from the heathen is *perisson* (Matt. 5:47), which means "peculiar," "extraordinary," "unusual." It is "the way of self-renunciation, of utter love. . . . It is unreserved love for our enemies, for the unloving. . . . In every case it is the love which was fulfilled in the cross of Christ."[69] Bonhoeffer sees the approach of a time of widespread persecution of Christians, and he calls upon Christians to prepare for it. "Our adversaries," he wrote in 1937, "seek to root out the Christian Church and the Christian faith because they cannot live side by side with us, because they see in every word we utter and every deed we do . . . a condemnation of their own words and deeds."[70]

These future saints of God will be known by their "unusual" behavior revealed in selfless love, and by their separation not from the world but from the ways of the world. They are called to bear Christ's image. Bonhoeffer is not, however, advancing a conception of Jesus's "moral influence" that, voluntaristically, can be appropriated by his "saints."

To be conformed to the image of Christ is not an ideal to be striven after. It is not as though we had to imitate him as well as we could. We cannot transform ourselves into his image; it is rather the form of Christ which seeks to be formed in us (Gal. 4:19), and to be manifested in us. Christ's work in us is not finished until he has perfected his own form in us. We must be assimilated to the form of Christ in its entirety.[71]

It is through this "assimilation in Christ" that human beings recover their true humanity lost in the Fall. In Christ humanity is divested of its egoism and its individualism and retrieves its solidarity with the whole human community. But to be taken up and borne in the humanity of Jesus, the disciple "too must hear the sins and sorrows of others. The incarnate Lord makes his followers the brothers of all mankind."[72]

The Cost of Discipleship was Bonhoeffer's best-known and most influential book during his lifetime. In writing it he knew that he was taking risks in radically rethinking the Lutheran conceptions of faith and works. The book was bold and provocative. Karl Barth initially was "uneasy" about it, but ten years after Bonhoeffer's death he judged that *The Cost of Discipleship* was the best that had been written on the subject of justification and sanctification as they relate to discipleship.[73]

In *The Cost of Discipleship* Bonhoeffer focused on the exclusiveness of Christ in the life of the Christian. But between 1940 and 1943 his ethical thinking underwent a series of developments. One factor was his move from passive to active resistance against the Nazi regime. At the same time he undertook the writing of *Ethics*, which he considered to be the most important task of his life. It was never finished, but it was posthu-

mously published from largely unfinished essays. These essays and other ethical writing of these last years of his life make clear the movement of his ethical thinking away from his earlier, exclusive focus on the Church and its discipleship and toward a new emphasis on the secular world and its wider range of human activity. The older boundaries of the Church now enlarge, and the accent is no longer on the world as enemy. Christ, Church, and world are brought more closely together. They cannot be isolated, and there is a new sense of the dangers of religiosity. This new sensibility is expressed in a letter written in June 1942:

Again and again I am driven to think about my activities which are now concerned so much with the secular field. . . . I do not want to justify myself, and I observe that I have gone through much richer spiritual periods. But I feel the resistance growing in me against all religiosity, sometimes reaching the level of an instinctive horror—surely, this is not good either. Yet I am not a religious nature at all. But all the time I am forced to think of God, or Christ, of genuineness, life, freedom, charity—that matters for me. What causes me uneasiness is just the religious clothing.[74]

The keynote to these later ethical writings is sounded in a quotation from *Ethics:* "The more exclusively we acknowledge and confess Christ as our Lord, the more fully the wide range of his dominion will be disclosed to us."[75] Christology is bound up with discipleship, but the sphere of the latter is now widened. The unity of Christ and the world requires rethinking. How can the reality of the Church be maintained without a cheap religiosity and the world be affirmed without a cheap accommodation?

No man can look with undivided vision at God and at the world of reality so long as God and the world are torn asunder. . . . But there is a place at which God and the cosmic reality are reconciled, a place at which God and man have become one. . . . This place does not lie somewhere beyond reality in the realm of ideas. . . . It lies in Jesus Christ, the Reconciler of the world. . . . Whoever sees Jesus Christ does indeed see

God and the world as one. He can henceforth no longer see God without the world or the world without God.[76]

It is of interest to note that Bonhoeffer is here developing a deeper understanding of God fully allied with the world that resembles Barth's theme of the "humanity of God" in *Church Dogmatics*, IV, conceived fifteen years later.

Bonhoeffer's new conception of Jesus Christ and the world raises new questions regarding "boundaries." Where, for example, is Christ? Is he bound to the visible Church? What are the boundaries of the Church? Can we think any longer in terms of distinct spheres, one holy and supernatural, the other secular and natural? Bonhoeffer simply rejects this dualism that so often characterized Christianity from its earliest days.

Ethical thinking in terms of spheres, then, is invalidated by faith in the revelation of the ultimate reality in Jesus Christ, and this means that there is no real possibility of being a Christian outside the reality of the world and that there is no real worldly existence outside the reality of Jesus Christ. There is no place to which the Christian can withdraw from the world, whether it be outwardly or in the sphere of the inner life . . . His worldliness does not divide him from Christ, and his Christianity does not divide him from the world. Belonging wholly to Christ, he stands at the same time wholly in the world.[77]

Does the oneness of Jesus Christ and the world erase the boundary of the Church, the space of the visible Church itself? Bonhoeffer defends the visible Church but he now clarifies the limits of its role:

The Church does indeed occupy a definite space in the world, a space which is delimited by her public worship, her organizations and parish life, and it is this fact that has given rise to . . . thinking in terms of spheres. It would be very dangerous to overlook this, to deny the visible nature of the Church, and to reduce her to the status of a purely spiritual force. . . . It is essential to the revelation of God in Jesus Christ that it occupies space within the world . . . [But] the Church has neither the wish nor the obligation to extend her space to cover the space of the world. She asks for no more space than she needs for the purpose of serving the world by bearing witness to Jesus Christ.[78]

The traditional "two spheres" of Lutheran theology has its place, but it is also dangerous, and Bonhoeffer continues exploring other ways of conceiving the Christ-world relationship. In Chapter 3 of the *Ethics*, entitled "The Last Things and the Things Before the Last," he introduces a distinction between the "ultimate" and the "penultimate." Christian ethical reflection often has proposed two alternative solutions to the problem of the relation of the ultimate (God's justification by grace through faith) and the penultimate (the individual's everyday activities and responsibilities). The "radical" solution focuses only on the ultimate, the "last things" of God's grace and justification. It omits any serious concern for the penultimate. Everything worldly and penultimate is seen as the enemy of Christ. Whether it consists in withdrawing from the world or in perfecting it, "it arises from hatred of creation."

The alternative solution is "compromise." "Here the last word is on principle set apart from all preceding words. The penultimate retains its right on its own account, and is not threatened or imperilled by the ultimate."[79] But such a compromise actually springs from a "hatred of the ultimate"; the world must be protected from the ultimate's too dominant encroachment. Bonhoeffer rejects both of these ethical solutions.

For the Christian there is always the "final time," the final word of God's justification by forgiveness alone. But Bonhoeffer now is compelled to give greater place to humanity's penultimate time, although both must be held together. "There is a time when God permits, awaits and prepares, and there is a final time which cuts short and passes sentence on the penultimate."[80] There is a way that all humans must traverse in this world even though it does not lead to the final goal. Therefore, the penultimate remains part of God's will. Bonhoeffer now is asking whether any Christian can live by the ultimate alone, day in and day out. He cites his own experience of being with another associate who has suffered a bereavement. Rather than mouthing pious phrases from the Bible, Bonhoeffer decides to

adopt a "penultimate" attitude, particularly when I am dealing with Christians, remaining silent as a sign that I share in the bereaved man's helplessness . . . and not speaking the biblical words of comfort. . . . Why am I often unable to open my mouth, when I ought to give expression to the ultimate? And why, instead, do I decide on an expression of thoroughly penultimate human solidarity? . . . Does one not in some cases, by remaining deliberately in the penultimate, perhaps point all the more genuinely to the ultimate, which God will speak in His own time?[81]

The penultimate exists for the sake of the ultimate, but it must be stressed that Jesus Christ entered the world of the penultimate, of action, suffering, and responsibility. In Christ the ultimate does not annul or destroy the penultimate. It is here that Bonhoeffer joins the penultimate to the concept of the "natural," an ethical category largely shunned by Protestant theology and left to Roman Catholics. The "natural" "implies an element of independence and self-development"[82] on the part of the person. Because Christ himself entered into the natural life, it is in and through Christ that we, too, "have the right to call others to the natural life and to live the natural life ourselves,"[83] for it embraces the entire human race. Despite the deepening encroachment of the "unnatural," which is the enemy of Christ—in the immediate context this is represented by the Nazi ideology—Bonhoeffer could express his sense of the freedom and the joy of natural life itself, not merely as a means, nor as a natural right, but as a gift of Jesus Christ. Bonhoeffer here is exploring a way to affirm the goodness of the natural world that is an alternative to both the Roman Catholic doctrine of the natural law and the Lutheran doctrine of the "orders" of family, state, and *Volk*.

Bonhoeffer's reflections on ethics break off at this point at the time of his first visit to Switzerland on conspiratorial business in early 1941. But a new line of investigation is taken up again during 1941–1942 when his work for the resistance

was intense. He again seeks to avoid the use of terms such as "orders of creation," but he also wants to speak of Christ's relation to the whole world, not in broad, abstract terms but concretely in terms of the natural human spheres of life. To secure this concreteness he now adopts the word "mandates," and he examines four such "mandates" that he finds present in the Bible: work, marriage, government, and the Church, although he acknowledges that these are by no means exhaustive. Mandates are divinely commanded tasks but they are not orders of being. A mandate is "the concrete divine commission" in which the bearer "acts as a deputy in the place of Him who assigns him his commission."[84] Bonhoeffer stresses that the Church must not claim dominion over the other mandates; nor does government have dominion over the Church or family, nor culture over government or Church. "The commandment of Jesus Christ does indeed rule over Church, family, culture, government; but it does so while at the same time setting each of these mandates free for the fulfillment of its own allotted functions."[85]

One notices the prominence of the words "freedom" and "responsibility" in these late ethical reflections, and they are conjoined with a concept of "deputyship," in an important essay on "The Structure of Responsible Life." Ethical responsibility takes the form of "deputyship," which involves the venture of a free, concrete decision, whether it be the decision of a father acting for his children or the citizen acting for the government. We do not act alone but always with and for others. Bonhoeffer's personal struggle with his participation in tyrannicide against Hitler can be heard in words that he wrote at this time.

Jesus took upon Himself the guilt of all men, and for that reason every man who acts responsibly becomes guilty. If any man tries to escape guilt in responsibility he detaches himself from the ultimate reality of human existence. . . . The origin and goal of my conscience is not a law but the living God and the living man as he confronts me in Jesus Christ. . . . The conscience that has been set free is not timid like the conscience that is bound by the law, but it stands wide open for our neighbor and for his concrete distress.[86]

Bonhoeffer's reflections on freedom and responsibility in relation to the natural spheres of human life bring to fruition two concepts that now dominate his thinking: "life for others" and "worldliness." To be "in Christ" means to share in the life of the world "for other men." "The cross," Bonhoeffer now writes, "is the setting free for life before God in the midst of a godless world; it is the setting free for life in genuine worldliness."[87] Here we have arrived at the point of Bonhoeffer's final ruminations in his prison letters: What would constitute a religionless Christianity in a world come of age?

The World Come of Age and a Religionless Christianity

The letters that were written during his time in Tegel prison after April 1944 contain some of Bonhoeffer's most provocative theological ideas. They reveal continuities with his earlier "Christological concentration," but they also reflect a striking turning point. As Bethge has put it, "the bricks are there and are used. But the old arrangement of the bricks has been altered . . . an extension of the theme that is equivalent to a change in the theme."[88] The letters also reflect a new vitality and calm, a sense that he was undertaking a new book project that would deeply challenge previous theological thinking. Yet he could not have imagined the profound and wide-ranging influence that these letters would have on theological thinking in the second half of the twentieth century and beyond. Here we will discuss this last phase of Bonhoeffer's thought by rehearsing rather schematically several themes in this late correspondence.

The World Come of Age and Religion

In prison Bonhoeffer had been reading Wilhelm Dilthey's important works on the emergence of modernity and the "autonomy of reason," and this affected Bonhoeffer's own rethinking of the "natural" and the "worldly" values of the Enlightenment. Of course, Bonhoeffer was not about to concede to the modern world a thoroughgoing autonomy. The issue for Bonhoeffer was, rather, how Jesus Christ *and* a modern world come of age are to be joined. And the point that he wished to make is that Jesus Christ does not regret or prevent the world from coming of age:

The attacks by Christian apologetic on the adulthood of the world I consider to be in the first place pointless, in the second place ignoble, and in the third place unchristian. Pointless, because it seems to me to be like an attempt to put a grown-up man back into adolescence, i.e., to make him dependent on things on which he is, in fact, no longer dependent, and thrusting him into problems that are no longer problems to him. Ignoble, because it amounts to an attempt to exploit man's weakness for purposes that are alien to him and to which he has not freely assented. Unchristian, because it confuses Christ with one particular stage in man's religiousness, i.e., with a human law.[89]

Bonhoeffer's reflections on the historical development of the world coming of age made him aware of both the failure of Liberal theology in its effort to find a place for religion in the recently secularized world *and* his need to find a nonreligious interpretation of Christianity. Bonhoeffer agrees with Barth that Feuerbach and Nietzsche are sound in their attack on the immature dependency that is found in much of the Christian religion. The time for this type of adolescent religiosity is over:

What is bothering me incessantly is the question what Christianity really is, or indeed who Christ really is for us today. . . . We are moving towards a completely religionless time; people as they are now simply cannot be religious anymore. . . . Our whole nineteen-hundred-year-old Christian preaching and theology rest on the religious *a priori* of mankind. Christianity has always been a form—perhaps the true form—of "religion." But if one day it becomes clear that this *a priori* does not exist at all, but was a historically conditioned and transient form of human self-expression, and if therefore man becomes radically religionless . . . what does that mean for Christianity? It means that the foundation is taken away. . . .[90]

Bonhoeffer characterizes this dispensable form of religion as manifesting itself in two forms: *thinking metaphysically and individualistically.* By metaphysics he means a preoccupation with some "extended world" beyond this one, or the abstract discussion of concepts such as the absolute, the infinite, the divine aseity, and so on. Bonhoeffer is most repelled, however, by what he sees as religion's obsession with the individual's spiritual pulse taking and the saving of one's own soul. He regards this pathetic and pervasive feature of modern religion as unbiblical since religion is relegated to "the sphere of the 'personal,' the 'inner,' the 'private,' that sphere of a person's life that is most isolated and vulnerable." Bonhoeffer finds this preoccupation with the intimate life of individuals, especially by priests and pastors, to be ignoble and prurient, resembling "the dirtiest gutter journalist." He calls it—reminiscent of Nietzsche—"a revolution from below, a revolt of inferiority," a "sniffing-around-after-people's-sins."[91]

Religious people speak of God when human knowledge (perhaps simply because they are too lazy to think) has come to an end, or when human resources fail—in fact it is always a *deus ex machina* that they bring on to the scene, either for the apparent solution of insoluble problems, or as strength in human failure—always, that is to say, exploiting human weakness or human boundaries. . . . I've come to be doubtful of talking about any human boundaries. . . . It always seems to me that we are trying anxiously in this way to reserve some space for God; I should like to speak of God not on the boundaries but at the center, not in weakness but in strength; and therefore not in death and guilt but in man's life and goodness.[92]

God and the Nonreligious Interpretation of Christianity

For Bonhoeffer God must not be conceived either as a metaphysical hypothesis or as an existential or psychological stopgap; God is here neither to help explain for us our philosophical puzzles nor to salve our personal anxieties. To do so is to understand God as present only in our bewilderment and weakness. Therefore, the modern world's coming of age must be seen, in part, as God's chastisement of the Church for its misrepresentation of the Gospel—just as God used Assyria against the Israelites of old. But this coming of age also offers the possibility for a beginning of a new religionless Christianity.

So our coming of age leads us to a true recognition of our situation before God. God would have us know that we must live as men who manage our lives without him. The God who is with us is the God who forsakes us (Mark 15:34). The God who lets us live in the world without the working hypothesis of God is the God before whom we stand continuously. Before God and with God we live without God. God lets himself be pushed out of the world on to the cross. . . . Matt. 8.17 makes it quite clear that Christ helps us, not by virtue of his omnipotence, but by virtue of his weakness and suffering.[93]

Bonhoeffer is exploring here an entirely new conception of God's transcendence. Our relationship to God must no longer be conceived in the traditional terms of a Supreme Being transcendent of the world, absolute in power and perfect in knowledge, goodness, and so on. Rather, God's transcendence is to be understood in

a new life in existence for others, through participation in the being of Jesus. The transcendental is not infinite and unattainable tasks, but the neighbor who is within reach in any given situation. God in human form . . . man for others, and therefore the Crucified, the man who lives out of the transcendent.[94]

God's transcendence is therefore a *this-worldly* transcendence; God known neither speculatively nor mystically, but God encountered in concrete life for others. The Christian life is therefore a "worldly" life, but in the sense that Christians are called to "range themselves with God in his sufferings" for others; "not lording over men, but helping and serving them" by concrete example. This leads us to the final theme in Bonhoeffer's provocative and often enigmatic late writings: discipleship and the secret discipline.

The Secret Discipline

Bonhoeffer's attention to the "world come of age" and a "nonreligious interpretation of Christianity" is intimately related to another theme that is crucial in countering an often-heard claim that Bonhoeffer is proposing a radically new secular form of Christianity similar, for instance, to those proposed by the "death of God" theologians of the 1960s, writers who often refer to Bonhoeffer in their own works. Bonhoeffer, on the contrary, wants to retain the cult and the forms of the visible Church, the life of prayer, and the traditional Christian doctrines: Creation, the Fall, the Trinity, sin, atonement, and eschatology. This is made clear in his brief references in the prison letters to what he calls the arcane or secret discipline (*arkandisziplin*), which must characterize the life of the Christian and the churches in a godless, secular world.

Bonhoeffer adopts the term *disciplina arcana* from the practice of the early Church as it found itself in a pagan environment and required to protect the "mysteries" of Christianity from profanation. Specifically, it referred to the practice of excluding from the Eucharist the nonbaptized and those without catechetical instruction. Therefore, whereas life in the world today means, for Bonhoeffer, concrete action and serving of the neighbor at hand, for the Christian today it also must mean not exposing the "secrets" of the faith to an uncomprehending and indifferent public, nor forcing these "mysteries" upon it. For Bonhoeffer, the consequence for the Christian of being thrown into the midst of the world is the living of a life of humility, of reserve, of silence, which often entails the bearing of a secret discipline by which Christian identity, and the rich treasures of Christian belief and practice, can be preserved from profanation. Bonhoeffer joins this later concern, however, with the equally important demand that every effort be made to interpret Christian faith in a nonreligious way and to shun the repetition of the traditional language of the faith that has been rendered meaningless and has proven an unnecessary offense and a stone of stumbling. Bonhoeffer asks: "What do a church, a

community, a sermon, a liturgy, a Christian life mean in a religionless world?. . . . How do we speak (or perhaps we cannot now even 'speak' as we used to) in a 'secular' way about God? What is the place of worship and prayer in a religionless situation? Does the secret discipline . . . take on a new importance here?"[95]

This question takes on a special poignancy in a sermon that Bonhoeffer wrote for the occasion of a nephew's baptism in May 1944. He recognized that over the child there would be spoken the great but ancient words of the baptismal liturgy, which, again, would drive him back to consider the meaning of these remote and difficult words and doctrines. The sermon closes with the following reflection that nicely summarizes the facets of Bonhoeffer's understanding of the place of the secret discipline:

In the traditional words and acts we suspect that there may be something quite new and revolutionary, though we cannot as yet grasp or express it. That is our own fault. Our church, which has been fighting in these years only for its own self-preservation, as though it were an end in itself, is incapable of taking the word of reconciliation and redemption to mankind and the world. Our earlier words are therefore bound to lose their force and cease, and our being Christians today will be limited to two things: prayer and righteous action among men. All Christian thinking, speaking, and organizing must be born anew out of this prayer and action. . . . It is not for us to prophesy the day (though the day will come) when men will once more be called so to utter the word of God that the world will be changed and renewed by it. It will be a new language, perhaps quite non-religious, but liberating and redeeming. . . . Till then the Christian cause will be a silent and hidden affair, but there will be those who pray and do right and wait for God's own time.[96]

It is clear from these words and others that Bonhoeffer's call for a religionless Christianity did not represent a secularization of the Christian life and the Church. He sees in the traditional words something "quite new and revolutionary," although not now expressible. Moreover, Bonhoeffer calls on Christians to continue to worship and to pray as well as to engage in sacrificial action, as he himself did, though both may be done in secret or be hidden. He is not calling for a dispensing with the great words and doctrines—"the Fall," "atonement," "repentance"—nor even a severe reduction of doctrine, as Bonhoeffer perceived happening in the efforts of Harnack and later of Bultmann. As Bethge rightly insists, for Bonhoeffer the religionless world in itself is *not* Christianity. Furthermore, the failure to speak an authentic Christian word to the world come of age is the fault of the Church that has given its priority to its own self-preservation. However, *if* the Church is to speak authentically to the religionless world it must be done in a worldly, nonreligious way; that is, it must connect in a real way with the life of the secular world. And finally, if the Church cannot speak authentically to the world, then it should undertake an honest reserve and silence, and limit itself to the secret discipline of prayer and unheralded righteous action. Bonhoeffer does, however, make it clear that he looks for a time when Christians will again speak and act in ways that, like Jesus's language, will be "liberating and redeeming."

In the context of Bonhoeffer's meditations on a nonreligious Christianity and the need for a *disciplina arcana*, we have noted that he commended Karl Barth for being the first to attack the entire idea of a human religious *a priori*. But Bonhoeffer also saw—whether fairly or not is debated—that Barth's program in *Romans* and in the *Church Dogmatics* was a substitution of "religion" for "a positivism of revelation"—that is, that Barth was, in effect, saying to the secular world: "'Like it or lump it': virgin birth, Trinity, or anything else; each is an equally significant and necessary part of the whole, which simply must be swallowed as a whole or not at all."[97] And Bonhoeffer sees this move of Barth's as a "restoration" of confessionalism and as unbiblical. Bonhoeffer insists that there are "degrees of knowledge and degrees of significance; [and] that means that the secret discipline must be restored whereby the *mysteries* of the Christian faith are protected against profanation."[98] Bonhoeffer perceives Barth as simply allowing the traditional language of the Church

assertively to replace religion as the presupposition of faith. And so, "in the place of religion there now stands the church." For Barth the "world is in some degree made to depend on itself and left to its own devices" and for Bonhoeffer that is a mistake.[99] Although Barth's emphasis on the free sovereignty of God's Word was an appropriate corrective to a culture-Protestantism, it represents a too confident victory of God's dominion over the world at the expense of the world's autonomy *and* a true *theologia crucis*. A commentator nicely states Bonhoeffer's basic criticism of Barth: "God overwhelms the world and annuls its autonomy. . . . In the unending event of God's coming into and overcoming the world, the world's freedom to be *in its otherness* to God is crushed."[100]

Barth, we know, was annoyed by Bonhoeffer's criticism of him. And the use of the term "positivism of revelation" was unfortunate because it was open to a range of misinterpretations. In turn, Barth's response to Bonhoeffer's criticism strikes one as rather too dismissive. The fact is that Bonhoeffer touched on an aspect of Barth's theology that has concerned other critics.

Bonhoeffer's Legacy

Despite the fact that he died at the age of thirty-nine and that he wrote no great theological tomes as did Barth, Rahner, and Tillich, it may be true that Bonhoeffer's influence will prove to be wider and more enduring. Early attention to his work was related to interests in the emergent theologies of secularization and the "death of God" theologies of the 1960s.[101] In more recent decades, however, his earlier writings have received greater attention and the wholeness and consistency of his thought have required that the more radical and often exploratory prison writings be reexamined in this wider context of his thought.

Bonhoeffer's *The Cost of Discipleship* and *Letters and Papers from Prison* are now modern religious classics. They have had a profound effect on the direction of thinking about Christian spirituality, discipline, and discipleship. His

Christology "from below," especially his theology of the crucified God, has been taken up by such important continental theologians as Jürgen Moltmann and Eberhard Jüngel. Bonhoeffer's insistence on "righteous action" in a world come of age and his reflections on a "worldly," nonreligious Christianity and "secret discipline" have had a deep influence on theologians of liberation and on those who have struggled with oppression and injustice in eastern Europe, Latin America, and South Africa. The liberation theologians have taken up Bonhoeffer's call for the Church to reject its traditional dualism of the Church against the world and to freely but responsibly adopt "penultimate" secular tools and means in the service of the "ultimate." Bonhoeffer's willingness to engage in tyrannicide in the face of a monstrous tyranny is a striking case in point. His concern that Christians must be deeply involved in opposing those forces that deprive human beings of their dignity, freedom, and power is, again, a theme taken up by the theologians of liberation. Finally, Bonhoeffer's prison reflections on the nonreligious "good people" with whom he lived, including members of his own family and his co-conspirators, led him to think deeply about what he called the "unconscious Christianity" of the nonreligious in God's plan of redemption. This question has been taken up anew by theologians, for example, by Karl Rahner in his writings on "anonymous Christianity."

All of Bonhoeffer's writings are marked by a quality of inquiry and testing. In his later years he expressed doubts about much of what he had written in his earlier works, including the well-received *The Cost of Discipleship*. This should alert us to two considerations—first, that it is easy to criticize Bonhoeffer because so much of what he wrote was exploratory and fragmentary. His concepts of "Christ existing as community," of the relationship between God and the world, of the "world come of age," of "religionless Christianity," and of the "secret discipline," all cry out for a fuller, more precise and rigorous examination. Second, Bonhoeffer's theology has proven remarkably rich and suggestive, and his writings remain today a fruitful source for contemporary theological reflection. There is no question, however, that Bonhoeffer's continued attraction is intimately associated with the fact that he witnessed personally to what he wrote. In his "Outline for a Book," written from his prison cell, he divined this great truth. "It [the Church]," he wrote, "must not under-estimate the importance of human example. . . . It is not abstract argument, but example, that gives its word emphasis and power."[102]

A final note: Both Barth and Bonhoeffer severely criticized the Liberal theology of an earlier generation, the theology of "inwardness" and the religious *a priori* that they traced back to Schleiermacher. But it must not be overlooked that both Barth's and Bonhoeffer's responses to this theology were shaped by modernity, by the Enlightenment's preoccupation with human autonomy, and with Romanticism's attention to subjectivity. It is not coincidental that both theologians returned to and wrestled with these themes in their late writings in creative but different ways.

NOTES

1. Karl Barth, *Church Dogmatics*, I, 1. *The Doctrine of the Word of God* (Edinburgh, 1936), p. ix.

2. K. Barth, *Anselm: Fides Quaerens Intellectum*, trans. Ian Robertson (Richmond, 1960), pp. 26–27.

3. Ibid., p. 33.

4. It was the Catholic theologian Hans Urs von Balthasar's book *The Theology of Karl Barth* (1951; Eng. trans. 1971) that established a tradition of Barth interpretation that only recently has been challenged. Von Balthaser interpreted Barth's theology as sharply divided by "two decisive turning-points." The first was his repudiation of liberalism in the Dialectical theology so powerfully expressed in the *Römerbrief* of 1922. The second "turning-point" occurs with the publication of the book on Anselm in 1931. With this book, Barth is freed from "the shackles of philosophy" and discovers a

truly independent theological method that is carried out in the *Church Dogmatics*. In recent years critics have disputed this interpretation of Barth's theological development, most notably Bruce McCormack in his *Karl Barth's Critically Realistic Dialectical Theology: Its Genesis and Development 1909–1936* (1995). McCormack questions the crucial role of the Anselm book and seeks to demonstrate a continuity in Barth's theological development from his first edition of *Romans*, arguing that from at least 1918 Barth's work is informed by a critically realistic "objectivism" and that the dialectical form of his thinking remains a constitutive feature of the writings after 1931.

5. Eberhard Busch, *Karl Barth. His Life from Letters and Autobiographical Texts* (Philadelphia, 1996), p. 223.

6. Cited in Arthur C. Cochrane, *The Church's Confession Under Hitler* (Philadelphia, 1962), pp. 222–223.

7. The citations from the six Barmen articles are taken from the translation in Clifford Green, ed., *Karl Barth: Theologian of Freedom* (Minneapolis, 1991). For accounts of Barth's involvement in the German church struggle, the Confessing Church, and Barmen, see Busch's biography *Karl Barth*; Cochrane's *The Church's Confession Under Hitler*; and Robin Lovin's ethical analysis of Barth's position in the context of these events, *Christian Faith and Public Choices: The Social Ethics of Barth, Brunner, and Bonhoeffer* (Philadelphia, 1984).

8. K. Barth, *Der Römerbrief*, 1st ed., (Bern, 1919), p. 392.

9. E. Brunner, *The Divine Imperative*, (Philadelphia, 1947), p. 210.

10. Ibid., p. 272.

11. F. Gogarten, *Politische Ethik* (Jena, 1932), p. 113.

12. See especially K. Barth, *Church Dogmatics*, II, 2. *The Command of God*, trans. G. W. Bromiley et al. (Edinburgh, 1957), pp. 510 ff.

13. K. Barth, *The Holy Ghost and the Christian Life*, trans. R. Birch Hoyle (London, 1938), p. 21.

14. See Barth's essays in his *Against the Stream: Shorter Post-War Writings* (New York, 1954), and *How to Serve God in a Marxist Land*, ed. Robert McAfee Brown (New York, 1959).

15. Karl Barth, *Against the Stream* (London, 1954).

16. John Howard Yoder, *Karl Barth and the Problem of War* (Nashville, 1970).

17. K. Barth, *Credo*, trans. J. Strathearn McNab (New York, 1936), p. 177.

18. Karl Barth, *Church Dogmatics*, I. *The Doctrine of the Word of God*, Part II, trans. G. T. Thomson and Harold Knight (Edinburgh, 1956), p. 715.

19. K. Barth, *Church Dogmatics*, I, 1. Part II, p. 718.

20. Ibid., pp. 724, 726.

21. Ibid., p. 727.

22. Ibid., p. 728.

23. Ibid., p. 734.

24. K. Barth, *Church Dogmatics*, IV, 1. *The Doctrine of Reconciliation*, Part I, trans. G. W. Bromiley (Edinburgh, 1956), p. 52.

25. K. Barth, *Church Dogmatics*, III, 1. *The Doctrine of Creation*, Part I, trans J. W. Edwards, et al. (Edinburgh, 1958), p. 232.

26. Karl Barth, *Church Dogmatics*, III, 2. *The Doctrine of Creation*, Part II, trans H. Knight, et al. (Edinburgh, 1960), p. 50.

27. Barth, *Church Dogmatics*, III, 2 (1960), 50–51.

28. Barth, *Church Dogmatics*, III, 1 (1958), 102.

29. Barth, *Church Dogmatics*, IV, 1 (1956), 540.

30. Barth, *Church Dogmatics*, II, 2. *The Doctrine of God*, Part II, trans G. W. Bromiley, et al., (Edinburgh, 1957), p. 3.

31. For a full treatment of this theme, see Barth, *Church Dogmatics*, II, 2, (1957), 94–145.

32. Ibid., p. 188.

33. Ibid., p. 118.

34. Ibid., pp. 117, 167.

35. Ibid., pp. 417–418.

36. Barth, *Church Dogmatics*, II, 1 (1957), 95.

37. Barth, *Church Dogmatics*, II, 2 (1957), 413.

38. Barth, *Church Dogmatics* IV, 1 (1956), 41.

39. For a critique of Barth's theology on this point, see G. C. Berkouwer, *The Triumph of Grace in the Theology of Karl Barth* (London, 1956).

40. A good introduction to many of the substantive criticisms of Barth's theology can be found in John Machen's *The Autonomy Theme in the Church Dogmatics: Karl Barth and His Critics* (Cambridge, 1990). The criticisms of Barth discussed by Machen extend beyond the specific theme of divine and human autonomy.

41. Wolfhart Pannenberg, *Theology and the Philosophy of Science*, trans. Francis McDonagh (Philadelphia, 1976), pp. 272–273.

42. R. R. Niebuhr, *Resurrection and Historical Reason* (New York, 1957), p. 87. For another discerning critique of the problem of revelation and history in Barth and other contemporary theologians, see Van A. Harvey, *The Historian and the Believer* (New York, 1966).

43. Eberhard Bethge, "The Challenge of Dietrich Bonhoeffer's Life and Theology," in *World Come of Age*, ed. Ronald Gregor Smith (Philadelphia, 1967), p. 22. For information on Bonhoeffer's life, I am primarily dependent on the biographical accounts of Eberhard Bethge. See his masterful 867-page biography *Dietrich Bonhoeffer: Man of Vision, Man of Courage* (New York, 1970), and his essay "The Challenge of Dietrich Bonhoeffer's Life and Theology." For the English translation of Bonhoeffer's work, see *Dietrich Bonhoeffer Works*, 16 vol., ed. Wayne Whitson Floyd, Jr. (Minneapolis, 1996–). Volumes 1–3, 5 to date.

44. Bethge, *Dietrich Bonhoeffer*, p. 122.

45. D. Bonhoeffer, *Sanctorum Communio. A Dogmatic Inquiry into the Sociology of the Church,* trans. Ronald Gregor Smith (London, 1963), pp. 47–48.

46. Ibid., pp. 52, 69.

47. D. Bonhoeffer, *Act and Being,* trans. Bernard Noble (New York, 1961), pp. 121–122.

48. Ibid., p. 123.

49. Charles Marsh, *Reclaiming Dietrich Bonhoeffer: The Promise of His Theology* (New York, 1994), p. 14.

50. One of the best analyses of the Barth-Bonhoeffer relationship and the latter's critique of Barth is Charles Marsh's study, ibid., on which I am dependent.

51. D. Bonhoeffer, *Christ the Center,* trans. John Bowden (New York, 1966), pp. 45–46.

52. Ibid., p. 46.

53. D. Bonhoeffer, *Christology,* trans. Edwin Robinson (London, 1978). Cited in John W. de Gruchy, ed., *Dietrich Bonhoeffer: Witness to Jesus Christ* (Minneapolis, 1987), p. 118.

54. Ibid., p. 122.

55. Ibid., pp. 119–120.

56. Ibid., p. 120.

57. Ibid., p. 121.

58. Ibid., p. 123.

59. Ibid.

60. Bonhoeffer, *Christ the Center,* p. 72.

61. Ibid., p. 74.

62. Ibid., p. 75.

63. D. Bonhoeffer, *The Cost of Discipleship* (New York, 1959), p. 35.

64. Ibid., p. 37.

65. Ibid., p. 49.

66. Ibid., p. 54.

67. Ibid., pp. 126–127.

68. Ibid., p. 136.

69. Ibid., p. 137.

70. Ibid., p. 135.

71. Ibid., p. 272.

72. Ibid.

73. Barth, *Church Dogmatics,* IV, 2 (1958), 533–534.

74. D. Bonhoeffer, *Gesammelte Schriften,* II, p. 420. Cited by Bethge in *World Come of Age,* op. cit., pp. 70–71.

75. D. Bonhoeffer, *Ethics,* ed. E. Bethge (London, 1955), p. 58.

76. Ibid., p. 8.

77. Ibid., pp. 66–67.

78. Ibid., pp. 67–68.

79. Ibid., p. 89.

80. Ibid., p. 83.

81. Ibid., pp. 84–85.

82. Ibid., p. 102.

83. Ibid., p. 103.

84. Ibid., p. 254.

85. Ibid., p. 264.

86. Ibid., pp. 210, 212.

87. Ibid., pp. 263–64.

88. Bethge, *Dietrich Bonhoeffer,* p. 763.

89. D. Bonhoeffer, *Letters and Papers from Prison,* rev. ed. E. Bethge (New York, 1967), p. 179.

90. Ibid., pp. 152–53.

91. Ibid., pp. 190–91.

92. Ibid., pp. 154–55.

93. Ibid., p. 196.

94. Ibid., p. 210.

95. Ibid., pp. 153–154.

96. Ibid., p. 172.

97. Ibid., pp. 153, 157.

98. Ibid., p.157.

99. Ibid.

100. Marsh, *Reclaiming Dietrich Bonhoeffer,* p. 24.

101. See, for example, J. A. T. Robinson, *Honest to God* (New York, 1963); Harvey Cox, *The Secular City*(New York, 1965); Paul Van Buren, *The Secular Meaning of the Gospel* (New York, 1963); Thomas J. J. Altizer and William Hamilton, *Radical Theology and the Death of God* (New York, 1966).

102. Bonhoeffer, *Letters and Papers from Prison,* p. 211.

SUGGESTIONS FOR FURTHER READING

Karl Barth

Berkouwer, G. C. *The Triumph of Grace in the Theology of Karl Barth* (London: Paternoster Press, 1956). A valuable study by a Dutch theologian, both sympathetic and critical of Barth's doctrine of grace and "universalism."

Bromiley, Geoffrey W. *Introduction to the Theology of Karl Barth* (Grand Rapids, Mich.: William B. Eerdmans, 1979). A simple, direct summary of the interwoven themes of the twelve-volume *Church Dogmatics* that can serve as a helpful guide to the uninitiated.

Busch, Eberhard. *Karl Barth. His Life from Letters and Autobiographical Texts* (Philadelphia: Fortress Press, 1976). The finest biographical study of Barth, full of interesting and illuminating detail.

Ford, David F. *Barth and God's Story: Biblical Narrative and the Theological Method of Karl Barth* (Frankfort: Peter Lang, 1981).

Green, Clifford. *Karl Barth: Theologian of Freedom* (Minneapolis: Fortress Press, 1991). A good selection from Barth's writings with a helpful introduction.

Hartwell, Herbert. *The Theology of Karl Barth* (London: Gerald Duckworth, 1964). A useful, if uncritical, survey of Barth's theology with special attention given to the major themes of the *Church Dogmatics*.

Hunsinger, George, ed. *Karl Barth and Radical Politics* (Westminster Press, 1976). A valuable collection of essays about the influence of Barth's political commitments, especially socialism, on his theology.

————. *How to Read Karl Barth. The Shape of His Theology* (New York: Oxford University Press, 1991). Important among the new efforts to offer a corrective to some earlier readings of Barth.

Jüngel, Eberhard. *Karl Barth, A Theological Legacy* (Philadelphia: Westminster Press, 1986). A collection of essays by an expert that includes an excellent brief account of Barth's life and the beginnings and development of his theology.

Machen, John, S.J. *The Autonomy Theme in the "Church Dogmatics": Karl Barth and His Critics* (Cambridge: Cambridge University Press, 1990). A helpful source of information on Barth's treatment of the theme of divine and human autonomy and the criticisms of Barth by scholars such as von Balthasar, Pannenberg, Rendtorff, and Jüngel.

McCormack, Bruce L. *Karl Barth's Critically Realistic Dialectical Theology: Its Genesis and Development 1909–1936* (Oxford: Clarendon Press; 1995). The finest critical study in English of Barth's theological development contesting the conventional view of a sharp turn by Barth from dialectical to analogical thinking and stressing the continuity of Barth's realistic and Dialectical theology.

Sykes, Stephen W., ed. *Karl Barth: Studies of His Theological Method* (Oxford: Clarendon Press, 1979). A valuable collection of essays on this important theme by British scholars.

Torrance, T. F. *Karl Barth: An Introduction to His Early Theology* (London: SCM Press, 1962). Uncritical and a conventional reading of Barth's "development from dialectical to dogmatic thinking," but still full of valuable insights, emphasizing the Catholic and "scientific" character of Barth's theology, rather than viewing him exclusively within the Protestant context.

von Balthasar, Hans Urs. *The Theology of Karl Barth*, [1951] (New York: Holt, Rinehart and Winston, 1971). A valuable study and critique by a noted Roman Catholic theologian.

Webster, John. *Barth's Ethics of Reconciliation* (Cambridge: Cambridge University Press, 1995).

Dietrich Bonhoeffer

Bethge, Eberhard. "The Challenge of Dietrich Bonhoeffer's Life and Theology." In *World Come of Age*, ed. Ronald Gregor Smith (Philadelphia: Fortress Press, 1967). A brief but informative seventy-page essay dealing with the three periods of Bonhoeffer's life and writing.

————. *Dietrich Bonhoeffer: Man of Vision, Man of Courage* (New York: Harper and Row, 1970). The definitive biography of Bonhoeffer by his close friend and the editor of his writings.

Burtness, James. *Shaping the Future: The Ethics of Dietrich Bonhoeffer* (Philadelphia: Fortress Press, 1985). A fine study of Bonhoeffer's ethics.

deGruchy, John W., ed. *Dietrich Bonhoeffer: Witness to Jesus Christ* (Minneapolis: Fortress Press, 1991). A judicious selection from the whole range of Bonhoeffer's writings, with an up-to-date, helpful introduction.

————, ed. *Bonhoeffer for a New Day: Theology in a Time of Transition* (Grand Rapids, Mich.: William B. Eerdmans, 1997). A very fine collection of papers demonstrating Bonhoeffer's ongoing importance.

Feil, Ernest. *The Theology of Dietrich Bonhoeffer*, trans. Martin Rumscheidt (Philadelphia: Fortress Press, 1985). Considered by many experts to be the best study of Bonhoeffer's thought.

Floyd, Wayne Whitson, Jr., and Charles Marsh, ed. *Theology and the Practice of Responsibility: Essays on Dietrich Bonhoeffer* (Valley Forge, Pa.: Trinity Press International, 1994). New directions in Bonhoeffer scholarship.

Godsey, John D. *The Theology of Dietrich Bonhoeffer* (Philadelphia: Westminster Press, 1960). An early but still valuable exposition of Bonhoeffer's writings and his thought following a chronological order. Not as good on the prison period.

Godsey, John D., and Geffrey B. Kelly, ed. *Ethical Responsibility: Bonhoeffer's Legacy to the Churches* (New York: Edwin Mellon Press, 1981). Includes several valuable essays on aspects of Bonhoeffer's ethics and his influence.

Green, Clifford J. *The Sociality of Christ and Humanity: Dietrich Bonhoeffer's Early Theology* (Missoula, Mont.: Scholars Press, 1975). A fine study of Bonhoeffer's early theological writings.

Klassen, A. J., ed. *A Bonhoeffer Legacy: Essays in Understanding* (Grand Rapids, Mich.: William B. Eerdmans, 1981). A valuable collection of essays on a wide range of issues concerning Bonhoeffer.

Lovin, Robin W. *Christian Faith and Public Choices: The Social Ethics of Barth, Brunner, and Bonhoeffer* (Philadelphia: Fortress Press, 1984). Especially valuable in its comparison of Bonhoeffer's ethics with that of Brunner and Barth.

Marsh, Charles. *Reclaiming Dietrich Bonhoeffer* (New York: Oxford University Press, 1994). An important new reading of Bonhoeffer in the context of modern German philosophy and offering an alternative to post-Kantian conceptions of selfhood.

Rasmussen, Larry. *Dietrich Bonhoeffer. Reality and Resistance* (Nashville: Abingdon, 1972). An insightful study of Bonhoeffer, focusing on his ethics and the conspiracy against Hitler.

Chapter Five

Christian Existentialism

Paul Tillich

In Chapters Three and Four it was noted that the breakup of the movement of Dialectical theology in the 1920s and early 1930s was, in part, brought about by the debate among the members of the group on the legitimacy of grounding Christian theology in an existentialist analysis of the human situation. Karl Barth opposed such an "anthropological" starting point, which, he believed, gave priority to the search for a philosophical "point of contact" between Christianity and the human situation. With the dissolution of the movement of Dialectical theology over this issue there emerged, as we have seen, several creative developments in Protestant thought. Emil Brunner represented one route and Friedrich Gogarten typified another. Karl Barth moved in a third and counter direction, whereas Rudolf Bult-

mann and Paul Tillich were to follow the paths suggested earlier by Søren Kierkegaard and later by the German philosopher Martin Heidegger (1889–1976), that is, theologies correlated with an existentialist hermeneutics. While rightly understood as a twentieth-century movement of thought, the existentialist stance in philosophy can be discerned in many periods of Western thought as a protest against the persistent claims that human existence can be comprehended adequately within some rational conceptual scheme. Existential thinkers have always contended that our finite existence is marked by a radical contingency, uncertainty, and freedom that tells against any abstract rationalism.

In this chapter we will examine the Existentialist theologies of two of the giants of modern

Protestant theology, Paul Tillich and Rudolf Bult-mann. We will also explore the existential themes in the work of an important twentieth-century Catholic philosopher, Gabriel Marcel (1889–1973).

Chief among the precursors of twentieth-century Existentialism are Pascal, Nietzsche, and Kierkegaard.* Pascal (1623–1662) lived at a time of rapid scientific advance, which appeared to him to leave humanity in a state of frightening contingency amidst the spatial and temporal infinities of the physical universe. He saw humans as grand yet pathetic creatures who find themselves in a world into which they have been *cast* without knowing why or to what end.

When I consider the short duration of my life, swallowed up in the eternity before and after, the little space which I fill . . . , cast into the infinite immensity of spaces of which I am ignorant and which know me not, I am frightened, and shocked at being here rather than there; for there is no reason why here rather than there, why now rather than then. Who has put me here? By whose order and direction have this place and time been allotted me? (*Pensées*, 205)

Here Pascal strikes a chord that is heard again and again in existentialist literature. The individual finds him or herself alone, alienated from both the social world and the physical world of nature, which serve only to point up the utter contingency, loneliness, and apparent absurdity of existence.

The events of two monstrous world wars and the appearance of several totalitarian powers within a period of a few decades were important factors in the emergence of Existentialism and its dominant position in continental European philosophy between 1920 and 1950. Existentialism represents, in part, a response to the irrational events of those years. Nevertheless, the sources of the movement are many and stretch back to the beginnings of our history. There are, however, three twentieth-century philosophers who can

* For Nietzsche and Kierkegaard see Vol. I, Ch. 15.

justly be called the creators of twentieth-century Existentialist philosophy: Karl Jaspers (1883–1969), Martin Heidegger (1889–1976), and Jean-Paul Sartre (1905–1980). Heidegger and Jaspers were developing their philosophies independently at approximately the same time after World War I. Heidegger published his most important work, *Sein und Zeit* (*Being and Time*), in 1927; Jaspers' *Philosophie* appeared in 1932. Sartre was a pupil of Heidegger and published his influential *L'Etre et le Néant* (*Being and Nothingness*) in 1943.

In addition to this threesome there are numerous other philosophers and writers who, although perhaps not technically existentialists, consistently expressed existentialist themes in their writings. A list of such twentieth-century figures would include Gabriel Marcel, Albert Camus (1913–1960), and Simone Weil (1909–1943) in France; the Russian writer Nikolai Berdyaev (1874–1948); the Spanish writers Miguel de Unamuno (1864–1936) and Jose Ortega y Gasset (1883–1955); and the Jewish philosopher Martin Buber (1878–1965).

It is not possible, nor is it our purpose here, to attempt a full description of the principal doctrines of any of the major existentialist philosophers. Their doctrines are complex and differ technically in important respects. Nevertheless, Heidegger, Jaspers, Sartre, and Marcel share several concerns, which place them in the same philosophical family tree. What they share are a number of themes that repeatedly appear in their writings. A brief analysis of these key themes will give a general picture of the movement as a whole.

KEY EXISTENTIALIST THEMES

Existence Precedes Essence

Sartre has said that the chief doctrine of Existentialism is that existence precedes essence. This appears clear enough until one examines the words more fully. If one agrees with Kant that there is no determinate difference *in essence* between one hundred imaginary dollars and one hundred dollars in my pocket, but that there is, nevertheless, all the difference in the world in my *existential* financial situation, then there are many philosophers who are not existentialists but who accept Sartre's doctrine.

What Sartre means by this doctrine is that there are no eternal essences, say in the mind of God, that precede the existence of things. If these are essences, they are determined by human, free decision. However, there are many existentialist philosophers who, though holding that "existence precedes essence," would not agree with Sartre. What these philosophers mean by existence precedes essence is simply that existence must not be approached *a priori* but rather through immediate personal experience. One does not, for example, start with an abstract concept of human being and then try to fit experience into one's concept. One begins with the concrete experience of being-in-the-world. This is not to deny that human nature and experience have some common structures or essence; however, it means that if such essences exist they must be discovered *a posteriori* through my experiences and my participation in the experiences of others.

This means, further, that the existentialist begins his philosophizing with problems that arise from her or his own personal existence as a human being. The existential thinker is not a dispassionate observer but a passionate actor whose philosophical reflection emerges from an active engagement in the world. As Feuerbach said: "Do not wish to be a philosopher in contrast to being a man . . . do not think as a thinker . . . think as a living, real being . . . think *in* Existence."[1]

The Critique of Rational Objectivity

What the existentialists distrust about so-called objective reflection is, in the words of Kierkegaard, that it "makes the subject accidental and thereby transforms his Existence into something impersonal, and this impersonal character is precisely its objective validity. . . ."[2] But all significant knowledge must, in the existentialist's view, pose the question "What does this knowledge mean for *me?*" There is nothing wrong with

"objective" knowledge as far as it goes; where it proves dangerous is in its refusal to consider experiences that purely objective modes of analysis and judgment cannot explain or warrant. A good many issues in life can and should be settled only by objective criteria. But there are many questions (and existentially the most significant) that belie logical or empirical resolution and demand the risk of personal decision.

What is more, it is not enough that one know the objective truth but that it be made existentially one's own. A person can believe Christianity is the truth and yet remain personally aloof from it. "Truth," as Kierkegaard said, "consists precisely in inwardness."[3] The only reason we can observe the activities of other creatures with detached objectivity is because we are not personally touched by their lives. Place ourselves in their situation and our frame of reference would significantly alter our understanding of the situation. How, then, can a purely objective investigation ever know the truth of human existence? Is it not the case that we can only understand another way of existence by experiencing that existence existentially? Is it not true that we can only know what it means to love, trust, and die by actually loving and trusting and dying? "One becomes a theologian," remarked Luther, "by living, by dying, and by being damned—not by understanding, reading, and speculating."[4]

Furthermore, what is wrong with a narrowly objective approach to life is that it denies freedom of choice and self-determination. From the scientific point of view everything can be explained deterministically within the cause-effect nexus. But when a person no longer considers her or himself to be self-determining in some important respects, that person comes to view her or himself as a mere product of the environment and loses any sense of individuality; the person becomes other-directed and inauthentic. But deep in the human spirit is a consciousness that one is self-determining and responsible. We know that *we do make ourselves* by our own free choices. No matter how hard we try to escape, we know that we must live with this awful burden of freedom.

Authentic and Inauthentic Existence

Being-in-the-World. According to the existentialists, knowing or understanding is neither subjective nor objective. My being-in-the-world is not the awareness of either an empty ego or of something out there which I observe. Rather, my awareness is a *Dasein*, a "being-there" in a concrete situation. My awareness is always that of being in a situation, being confronted with possibilities. Heidegger would rephrase Descartes' "I think, therefore I am" in terms such as "I think *something, therefore I am in a world.*" My being-in-the-world discloses the givenness, the naked reality of a situation into which I have been thrown. Myself and the world are given together. And my immediate relation to this situation, confronting this world, is not theoretical or objective but existential.

The situation is characterized by what Heidegger calls Care (*Sorge*). For my awareness of the world is never an awareness of mere things, objects, substances in extension, but of things immediately present to my concern. They are present to me as instruments for my use, as objects of practical intention. This does not mean that things do not exist independently of me. What is is there, whether present to my awareness or not. But what is (*das Seiende*) only becomes *an intelligible world* through our human ordering or "projective understanding." Things in themselves are meaningless.

Furthermore, our relation to the world, or human awareness in its primordiality, is not characterized by rational or theoretical conceptualization but by certain moods or feelings. These feelings are not to be judged *merely* subjective. They are modes of real disclosure. Among these feelings, the most important is what Kierkegaard called "dread" and what Heidegger calls "anxiety."

Anxiety. Anxiety is a quality of human existence that the existentialists have analyzed at great length. Anxiety, first of all, should not be confused with fear. Fear, as an affective state, always has something in the world as its object. According to Heidegger, it is for this reason a disclosure of inauthentic existence because it represents a spirit of bondage to the world. Anxiety (*Angst*), on the other hand, is that which discloses to the individual the radicalness of his or her finitude and freedom. Anxiety has no specific object. It is simply the awareness or awakening to the stark reality of one's existence—one's thrownness into the world and one's responsibility for one's finite freedom. Dread or anxiety discloses that we are not at home in the world, that the world is by itself indifferent and without meaning. Genuine dread will necessarily shatter one's contentment and unreflective security, for it will throw the self back upon its own possibilities.

So conceived, anxiety is the necessary precondition of authentic existence, for in anxiety finite freedom becomes conscious of itself and arouses the self to decision and action. Without the experience of dread one never faces the crisis, the break with the world of the everyday. One continues to live a life of inauthenticity, of bondage through busy involvement in "worldly" concern.

Depersonalization. "Worldly" concern leads inevitably to a dehumanized world. Our being-in-the-world is, for the existentialists, "being-with-others" (*Mitsein*). Community belongs to being-in-the-world, for persons are not mere objects to be used as instruments of self-aggrandizement. "Worldly" care, however, transforms our relations with persons into relations with objects. An objectification involves a movement toward depersonalization and an inauthentic "being-with-others." It is what Martin Buber calls the relationship of I and It. It leads to a condition of dominance and dependence, of manipulation and alienation.

Depersonalization, when it becomes a social condition, is characterized by certain features. It is the society of "das Man" or mass man—no longer a community but what Kierkegaard calls a "public" or "crowd"—a collection of other-directed automatons. It is human life leveled down to the average, to the cliché. Life in such a society has no firm position; it is in a state of ceaseless flux, of everywhere and nowhere. The existentialists from Kierkegaard to Marcel have described the condition of mass man with great power and truth. Marcel, for example, describes the modern industrial worker as follows:

Surely everything both within him and outside him conspires to identify this man with his functions—meaning not only his functions as worker, as trade union member or as voter, but his vital functions as well. The rather horrible expression "time-table" perfectly describes his life. So many hours for each function. Sleep too is a function which must be discharged, so that the other functions may be exercised in their turn. The same with pleasure, with relaxation; it is logical that the weekly allowance of recreation should be determined by an expert on hygiene. . . . It is natural that the individual should be overhauled at regular intervals like a watch. . . . The hospital plays the part of an inspection bench or the repair shop. . . . As for death, it becomes objectively and functionally the scrapping of what has ceased to be of use and must be written off as a total loss.[5]

This mechanization of personal existence is powerfully described in Jaspers's *Man in the Modern Age*. Jaspers raises the question whether freedom is still a real possibility in our technological society.

The basic problem of our time is whether an independent human being in his self-comprehended destiny is still possible. . . . Perhaps freedom has only existed for a real but passing moment between two immeasurably long periods of sleep, of which the first period was that of the life of nature, and the second period was that of the life of technology. If so, human existence must die out . . . in a more radical sense than ever before. . . .[6]

It is just this kind of threat that directs the existentialists' attention to what they call the limit-situations of life.

Limit-Situations. There are situations in human existence that we have not chosen and that confront us with the radical openness and alienness of being-in-the-world. These are what Jaspers has called "limit-situations." The most important of these are chance, guilt, and death. They are inescapable conditions of human life

that, nevertheless, resist amelioration. They inject into our life a sickening feeling of danger and insecurity and make us conscious of our fragility and homelessness.

Rationalists have always tried to explain away these situations, but evil, guilt, and death are inevitable realities. Guilt, for example, cannot be escaped. Some try to avoid it by refraining from action. But blood on the conscience is inescapable, if blood on one's hands is not. Whether we act or not, we incur guilt. The authentic person will acknowledge his or her share of guilt and take responsibility for it. It will cause suffering, but the individual will not run away from it or try to deny it.

The same is true of death. Death is inescapable but we constantly suppress the thought of it from our conscious mind. When it is necessary to speak of it, we refer to it euphemistically. We postpone facing this boundary by rationalizing that, although it is certain, it lies in the distant future. Life can proceed as usual. The truth, of course, is that death can come at any moment. Time to determine our goals and to pursue our plans is never certain.

The authentic response to the situation of death is to face the fact that our end can come at any moment and that, therefore, this fact is of momentous consequence. If faced, the fact of death can free us of all postponement; it can set before us the fullness of the present moment and the demand to give our lives a decisiveness and significance here and now before death robs us of this most precious of gifts. To concentrate on death is not morbid. Rather, it is indispensable to achieving freedom and authenticity. It is only by meditating on such limit-situations in life that we can be awakened to decision, to freedom, and, hence, to authentic existence.

It is not surprising that Existentialism has been a subject of special interest to philosophers of religion and theologians, especially Christians, for the themes of freedom, fallenness, evil, alienation, and authentic personal and corporate existence have been integral to the Christian vision of the human story from St. Paul to the present. Our exploration of the thought of the three

Christian existentialist thinkers begins with Gabriel Marcel.

GABRIEL MARCEL

Gabriel Marcel was born in Paris in 1889. His father was a cultured man who held high administrative positions in the Bibliothèque Nationale and the Musées Nationaux. Marcel's mother died when he was four, and he was raised by a moralistic Protestant aunt. He thus grew up in a proper French bourgeois home and attributed his turn toward abstract and idealistic philosophy in the *lycée* and at the Sorbonne to his strict puritanical childhood. Involvement in the horrors of World War I, locating missing soldiers as a member of the Red Cross, helped free Marcel of his love of abstraction and was instrumental in turning him toward a literary career. Most of his adult life was lived as a writer, critic, and freelance intellectual. He converted to Roman Catholicism at the age of forty. Although his new faith had its imprint on his philosophical investigations, he did not consider himself, nor did he wish to be thought of as, a "Catholic" philosopher.

Marcel believed that both Idealism and Empiricism had led us down blind paths and had forced us into metaphysical positions that fail to take account of our true existential situation. Idealism places the mind in a position of an absolute, impersonal observer, when in fact the mind cannot stand outside its own thought and treat it as an object. Because we are engaged *in* being, no purely objective knowledge or judgment of being is possible. The empiricists have also forced us into a philosophical dead end. By dividing the mind from the external world, they have left us in a continuous quandary as to the genuineness of our knowledge of the world outside the ego.

Marcel refuses to split up reality in this way. What is metaphysically indubitable is the self incarnate in a body and present *in* the world. My body is not something that I have or possess; it is not something external to me but simply my mode of presence to the world. I cannot, for instance, think of my body as nonexistent. For Marcel it is the primary given of metaphysics. All

thought takes place *within* existence. Hence existence must be assumed from the start; it is the existential indubitable. The self-being-together-with-the-world is the primary datum of metaphysics. It cannot be proved but it must be assumed.

It is clear that *to be*, for Marcel, means *to participate* in being. For to be is to enter into some sort of commerce with the world. Our existence as given is trans-subjective, which means philosophically that we should not begin our reflection with the Cartesian "I think" but with the "we are," the communion that binds me to others and in so doing gives me my real self.

Marcel acknowledges that this ontological participation can express very different modes of relation. Like the Jewish philosopher Martin Buber, Marcel sees a stage of participation that is characterized by experiencing and utilizing. This is comparable to Buber's I-It relationships. But human beings must be awakened out of this stage into that of authentic ontological communion or genuine personal encounter. In real communion neither the self (I) nor the other (Thou) can be reduced to mere objects, i.e., sums of certain definable characteristics. The self and the other are both irreducible mysteries. What is irreducible is primary and cannot be expressed in terms other than itself. Thus ontological communion or participation is finally nonobjectifiable; it is a mystery.

What has occurred in the modern world is a loss of communion, of participation or the sense of *presence*. Marcel calls this the loss of "ontological weight." We have reduced human relations and tasks to the status of problems to be treated and resolved as objective things. This has led to the widespread depersonalization of life with all its attendant horrors, raising the specter of a *Brave New World*.

In discussing the modes of ontological relation, Marcel distinguishes between the kind of reflection that is appropriate to the sciences and that which is appropriate to reflection on human relations. The distinction is between a problem and a mystery. According to Marcel, a problem is something that is open to solution by the application of certain techniques. It is appropriate to the sciences, because one engages in scientific study from an objective or disinterested stance and achieves a definite solution or result. However, this form of reflection is not capable of dealing with situations in which the self is inextricably involved and where the feelings or attitudes of the person toward the situation are crucial to understanding the true nature of the matter. Questions such as love, suffering, guilt, and death are examples of situations in which the individual cannot remove herself or himself from the situation. Here we are on the threshold of what Marcel calls mystery.

A mystery is a question or a situation in which the data of reflection include the self. Thus Marcel speaks of being, of ontological reflection, as a mystery, because one can never totally extract the self from this reflection on being. Mysteries are existential situations that can never be reduced to neat solutions, nor can they ever be said to be done with. They have a way of ceaselessly renewing themselves. What is distinctive about a mystery is not, however, that it is insoluble. We may never discover a cure for the common cold, but that does not make the cold a mystery. It remains an unsolved problem. What characterizes a mystery is its nonobjectifiability, the fact that it points to the open, transcendent character of being with its ever-deepening implications for our existential experience. Mysteries are "metaproblematic." One approaches problems in a mood of curiosity; one faces mysteries in the spirit of wonder—what Marcel calls ontological humility or reverence.

Marcel believes that humans, as spiritual beings, have an appetite or *exigence* for being, but in our reflection our being always eludes our grasp. Being must be humbly accepted as a continually bestowed gift. What is implied in such reflection is the awareness that one's being must always be a *being with*, a participation, if it is to take on authenticity and know the fullness of being. In the world of mere existence, of *having,* there is a drying up of being—a growing sense of emptiness. Thus authentic *being with* is experienced as fullness. It involves a presentiment of

inexhaustibility, of transcendence, which quickens a person's spirit with joy, faith, and hope. Marcel likens this fullness to the experience of being in love.

I called the experience of fullness like that which is involved in love, when love knows that it is shared, when it experiences itself as shared. From this point of view to fulfil is not strictly speaking to accomplish, if by accomplishment we mean that something is finished or brought to a close.[7]

Our lives are lived in the ever-present possibility of fullness and hope or emptiness and despair. Despair comes when one cannot affirm being—when being is seen as fragmented and barren. Marcel believes that victory over such existential despair comes only through communion or participation in which the presence of being becomes open to the transcendent. Such communion is creative of a hope in being and a fidelity to being.

Marcel's analyses of the phenomenon of hope and fidelity are full of rich insights. Hope, according to Marcel, is not directed at some specific outcome (that is desire), nor is hope dependent on any eventual empirical success. Rather, hope is what gives life its sense of holiness; it is what keeps life open to the transcendent. Hope is expressed in what Marcel calls *disponibilité*, availability, which connotes openness, abandonment of self, welcoming. The person of hope remains open to the "absolute recourse"—he or she does not despair in the face of life's negativities.

Fidelity is also a fruit of genuine participation. Fidelity is a loyalty to other beings and a witness to one's trust or faith in being itself. According to Marcel, fidelity is not a virtue *possessed* by a self; rather it is through fidelity that one acquires a self, i.e., is given unity to one's disparate, immediate states of consciousness. Fidelity actually creates the self. My self is in the making, created in the present by the self's response to other beings. Fidelity is not simply constancy to some principle or to one's own honor. The axis is not the self but the other person. It is, in Martin Buber's terms, the uncoerced presence of an I to a Thou.

Marcel tells us that in every appeal from another there is, in and through it, an appeal to fidelity itself—an absolute fidelity to being. In our relationships of loyalty to other persons we come to exist in a relationship of fidelity to being itself. It is here that we enter into the region of theological reflection. Yet what underlies all theological conceptualization is this existential response of hope and fidelity.

PAUL TILLICH

The intellectual sources of Paul Tillich's rich and monumental theological system are many. They include Platonism, the late medieval Christian mystics such as Jacob Böhme (1575–1624), the German Idealist tradition, especially F. W. J. Schelling (1775–1854), as well as the existentialists from Kierkegaard to Heidegger. For this reason some have questioned whether Tillich can properly be labeled an existentialist. Tillich, however, admits to standing within the Existentialist movement and, although his theology is governed by a clearly worked-out ontological structure, he correlates this structure with our human existential questions and concerns. As we shall see, the existentialist stance dominates Tillich's theological method and system.

Paul Tillich (1886–1965) was born in Starzeddel, Germany, the son of a pastor of the Lutheran Church. He attended school in the old medieval town of Königsberg-Neumark. Tillich believed that this gothic environment and his childhood summers on the Baltic Sea were the principal sources of his lifelong romantic sense of nature and the holy. Tillich studied at several universities, including Berlin, Tübingen, and Halle, receiving the degree of doctor of philosophy from Breslau in 1911, with a dissertation on Schelling. He served as an army chaplain for four years during World War I. After the war he began his teaching career at Berlin and later was professor of theology at Marburg, Dresden, and Leipzig. During these years he served as a colleague of both Heidegger and Bultmann, and he began to develop his own theological system in response to the theology of the young Karl Barth.

Tillich was deeply appreciative of Barth's theology for preserving the sovereign transcendence of God—a truth articulated by thinkers such as Kierkegaard but lost sight of by the liberal theologians. Tillich wished to distinguish himself from both the liberal and conservative critics of Barth who, he felt, failed to grasp the truth and power of Barth's early writings. Nevertheless, Tillich criticized Barth's theology as not truly dialectical but *supernaturalistic*, because it denied that the human self does, paradoxically, contain within itself the existential demand to reach beyond itself. A true *Dialectical* theology

denies, just as does the supernatural way of thinking, that what is a purely divine possibility may be interpreted as a human possibility. But dialectical thinking maintains that the question about the divine possibility is a human possibility. And, further, it maintains that no question could be asked about the divine possibility unless the divine answer, even if preliminary and scarcely intelligible, were not always already available. . . . In his radical opposition to [this] possibility. . . . Barth has made his decision in favor of the supernatural rather than the dialectical interpretation. This is his limitation.[8]

Here we see, in brief, Tillich's commitment to the "method of correlation" between theology and the human situation, a method later followed, for example, in the work of theologians such as Schubert Ogden, Langdon Gilkey, and David Tracy.

In 1929 Tillich became professor of philosophy at the University of Frankfurt at a period when he was deeply involved in the Religious Socialist movement. His efforts to relate Protestant theology in particular to Socialism is evident in writings such as *The Socialist Decision* (1932). He called both for Protestantism's embrace of Socialism and for its criticism of Socialism's profane embodiments at the time. He looked, rather, for what he called a "theonomous" socialist order grounded in a religious faith, such as he found in the prophetic traditions of both ancient Israel and Christianity. We will return to the theme of Tillich's writings on politics and ethics later, for it is an aspect of his thought that often is neglected but that is especially pertinent to more recent explorations in theology.

Tillich's political activity and his opposition to Hitler and National Socialism led to his dismissal from his university chair in 1933. As it happened, the American theologian Reinhold Niebuhr was traveling in Germany that same summer and urged Tillich to come to America. Soon after his departure from Germany, Tillich was invited to be professor of philosophical theology at Union Theological Seminary in New York City. He remained in that position, while also serving as a professor at Columbia University, until his retirement in 1955. He was then given the distinguished position of university professor at Harvard. In 1962 he moved to the University of Chicago, where a special chair of theology was created for him.

Between 1951 and 1964 Tillich published the five parts (in three volumes) of his *Systematic Theology*. Along with Barth's *Church Dogmatics*, this work stands out as one of the foremost pieces of constructive theology of this century. After World War II Tillich produced several more popular books including *The Protestant Era, The Courage to Be, The Shaking of the Foundations, The New Being, The Eternal Now,* and *Dynamics of Faith,* whose influence in both the secular and religious communities was rivaled only by the writings of his colleague, Reinhold Niebuhr.

The Existential Starting Point

In an essay on "Religion as a Dimension in Man's Life," Tillich points out that the modern study of religion has been characterized by the attempt to reduce it to some other natural aspect or condition of human experience. The philosopher tends to equate religion with metaphysics, the sociologist explains religious experience on the basis of certain societal needs and functions, and the psychologist may reduce religion to certain forms of projection and rationalization. Tillich does not deny that these analyses have a place, but he believes that they do not get at the essence of religion as a dimension of the human spirit.

According to Tillich, religion is not a separate endowment of human life that can be set side by side with our rational, moral, and aesthetic faculties. Rather, religion is the *depth dimension* in all of our cultural and spiritual life. What Tillich means by the use of the metaphor "depth" is that the religious dimension of life points to what is ultimate and unconditional in life; i.e., what sustains one's being and gives meaning to one's life.

For Tillich, religion is a person's *ultimate concern*. We are those curious beings who have the capacity to look beyond our immediate and preliminary interests to those concerns that undergird and give meaning to existence.

Man is ultimately concerned about his being and meaning. "To be or not to be" in *this* sense is a matter of ultimate, unconditional, total and infinite concern. Man is infinitely concerned about the infinity to which he belongs, from which he is separated, and for which he is longing. . . . Man is unconditionally concerned about that which conditions his being beyond all the conditions in him and around him. Man is ultimately concerned about that which determines his ultimate destiny beyond all preliminary necessities and accidents.[9]

Like all other creatures, human beings are concerned with those things that condition existence, such as food and shelter. But humans also have spiritual concerns that are urgent and that claim ultimacy. Such concerns can manifest themselves in any of the creative (or destructive) dimensions of life as its depth. It can express itself, for example, in the moral dimension of life as the unconditional seriousness of the demand of conscience, or in the realm of science as the passionate, unflinching search for truth.

The term "ultimate concern" is simply Tillich's abstract translation of the great commandment: "The Lord, our God, the Lord is one; and you should love the Lord your God with all your heart, and with all your soul, and with all your mind, and with all your strength" (Mark 12:29). Tillich acknowledges that not all human concerns that involve this kind of unconditional and total response are conscious, overt commitments. Frequently they are unconscious and hidden. But in any case, the fact of "concern" and the dimension of "ultimacy" point to the *existential* character of religious experience. The object of religious faith and loyalty is always a matter of infinite passion and interest (Kierkegaard). This existential starting point is reflected in Tillich's first formal criterion for any theology: "*The object of theology is what concerns us ultimately. Only those propositions are theological which deal with their object in so far as it can become a matter of ultimate concern for us.*"[10]

This first formal criterion makes it clear that religion and its theological formulations are confined to ultimate concerns. Religion is not involved in the whole range of human preliminary concerns—e.g., the buying of a television set. For that you go to *Consumer Reports*. Nevertheless, Tillich would say that we humans are inveterate idolators and polytheists. That is, we have a proclivity for giving our unconditional trust and allegiance to very finite, limited goods. We humans center our lives around a variety of idols that we worship and on which we depend for our security. Some people make social status or economic power, racial superiority or national pride objects of their ultimate concern. From his own experience with National Socialism, Tillich can testify to the fact that

the extreme nationalisms of our century are laboratories for the study of what ultimate concern means in all aspects of human existence, including the smallest concern of one's daily life. Everything is centered in the only god, the nation—a god who certainly proves to be a demon, but who shows clearly the unconditional character of an ultimate concern.[11]

What do you value most in life? Tillich would say that your answer is your god. Many individuals offer formal worship to God but in fact worship idols. Perhaps the greatest danger facing human beings as spiritual creatures is this tendency to give covert, ultimate allegiance to what deserves only preliminary commitment—to worship what is finite and ephemeral.

This leads to Tillich's second formal criterion for any theology: "*Our ultimate concern is that*

which determines our being or not-being. Only those statements are theological which deal with their object in so far as it can become a matter of being or not-being for us."[12] Here Tillich correlates his existential concern with ontology. Theology not only limits itself to those unconditional, existential human concerns, but it also excludes from its province things that have less than the power of threatening or saving our being. At this point it should be clear that Tillich is speaking of two levels of religion and theology. On the one hand, all persons are religious in that they have some object or objects of ultimate concern through which they seek to find meaning and security in life. On the other hand, most religious commitments are idolatrous in that the object of concern is not truly ultimate and lacks the power to save our being and give a meaning to existence that neither time nor the vicissitudes of life can destroy.

The inevitable result of giving ultimate concern to what is merely temporal is what Tillich calls "existential disappointment." It is the story of "the god that failed" that leaves one empty and insecure. The loss of such meaning and security frequently leads to frantic efforts to find some new ground of assurance and purpose. In *The Courage to Be* Tillich analyzes, with considerable psychological insight, how we humans tend to fluctuate between fanatical commitments to mutable goods and efforts to remove ourselves from freedom's demands for courage by a loss of selfhood through neurosis, drugs, intoxication, or other forms of retreat from reality.[13]

He who does not succeed in taking his anxiety courageously upon himself can succeed in avoiding the extreme situation of despair by escaping into neurosis. He still affirms himself but on a limited scale. *Neurosis is the way of avoiding non-being by avoiding being. . . .* the neurotic personality on the basis of his greater sensitivity to non-being and consequently of his profounder anxiety, has settled down to a fixed, though limited and unrealistic, self-affirmation.[14]

In Tillich's view, every genuine act of religious faith is an act of courage, for it is the free action of a finite creature affirming that which is infinite and ultimate. Hence for us finite creatures, the element of uncertainty and doubt can never be entirely removed—it must be courageously accepted. Tillich distinguishes this act of faith from the traditional notion of belief.

If faith is understood as belief that something is true, doubt is incompatible with the act of faith. If faith is understood as being ultimately concerned, doubt is a necessary element in it. It is a consequence of the risk of faith. . . . The doubt which is implicit in faith is not a doubt about facts or conclusions. . . . One could call it the existential doubt, in contrast to the methodological and the skeptical doubt. . . . It does not reject every concrete truth, but it is aware of the element of insecurity in every existential truth. At the same time, the doubt which is implied in faith accepts this insecurity and takes it into itself in an act of courage. Faith includes courage. Therefore, it can include the doubt about itself.[15]

The "Method of Correlation"

Every theologian is both in faith *and* in doubt, committed *and* alienated, or, as Tillich puts it, inside *and* outside the theological circle. Therefore, theology is always existential and never strictly scientific. "In every assumedly scientific theology there is a point where individual experience, traditional valuation, and personal commitment must decide the issue."[16] It is this existential dimension of theology that distinguishes it from philosophy and the stance of the philosopher of religion.

Whereas both philosophy and theology are concerned with the question of being, the philosopher approaches being analytically. She or he is concerned to analyze the structures and processes of reality in itself. The cognitive attitude is objective and universal. The theologian, on the other hand, approaches being existentially and is concerned with the meaning of being *for us*. Therefore, the theologian "must look where that which concerns him ultimately is manifest . . . that is, the *logos* manifesting itself in a particular historical event"[17] or events. Unlike the philosopher, the theologian stands within a

tradition, a community of faith or theological circle whose symbols express a soteriological answer to our existential questions. Theology follows what Tillich calls the "method of correlation," which seeks to explain the contents of faith through existential questions and theological answers in mutual interdependence. The Christian theologian thus proceeds by making an analysis of the situation out of which the human existential questions arise and then seeks to demonstrate that the symbols used in the Christian message are the answers to these questions. In opposition to Karl Barth, Tillich is emphatic that a Christian theology must be genuinely correlative. The "answers" to our existential situation cannot, however, be simply deduced from the "questions" that emerge from that situation. The answers are provided by the Christian message.

The Christian message provides the answers to the questions implied in human existence. These answers are contained in the revelatory events on which Christianity is based. . . . *In respect to content the Christian answers are dependent on the revelatory events in which they appear; in respect to form they are dependent on the structure of the questions which they answer.*[18] (Italics added.)

Tillich rightly holds that revelation is spoken *to* us and not by us to ourselves. But he is also correct in asserting that we cannot receive answers to questions we never ask. The Christian answers must therefore be couched in a form that speaks to the contemporary situation. In the twentieth century, Tillich affirms, that form is what we call *existential*.

Humanity's Existential Situation

Tillich has remarked that Existentialism (as a philosophical movement) is the good luck of Christian theology. He means by this that contemporary existentialist analysis of the human situation has contributed to the rediscovery of the classical Christian interpretation of human existence: "Existentialism has analyzed the 'old eon,' namely, the predicament of man and his world in the state of estrangement."[19]

As spiritual beings we humans never exhaust our potentialities. To exist (from the Latin *existere*) means to "stand out" of nonbeing or nothingness, but for us this is never absolute, because as finite creatures we always remain threatened by nonbeing. Finite existence is marked by a sense of estrangement from one's essential being. This condition is characterized in the Christian tradition by the symbol of "the Fall" of Adam. In Tillich's opinion, it is imperative that theology "clearly and unambiguously represent 'the Fall' as a symbol for the human situation universally, not as the story of an event that happened 'once upon a time.'"[20] In order to make this clear, Tillich prefers to speak of the Fall as the "transition from essence to existence," thus underlining its universal anthropological significance. So conceived, the Fall is no longer relegated to the past, while at the same time it remains temporal and historical and not merely a speculative idea. If recognized as myth, the story of the Fall in Genesis 1–3 presents us with a rich symbolism describing the conditions and consequences of the transition from essence to existence.

According to Tillich, in Genesis it is humanity's *finite freedom* that is at the root of the Fall and estrangement. We are free, but we are also finite and excluded from the infinity to which our spirit aspires.

Man is free, in so far as he has language. With his language, he has universals which liberate him from bondage to the concrete situation to which even the highest animals are subjected. Man is free, in so far as he is able to ask questions about the world he encounters, including himself, and to penetrate into deeper and deeper levels of reality. . . . Finally, man is free, in so far as he has the power of contradicting himself and his essential nature. Man is free even from his freedom; that is, he can surrender his humanity. . . . Symbolically speaking, it is the image of God in man which gives the possibility of the Fall. Only he who is the image of God has the power of separating himself from God.[21]

What is this essential nature from which humanity is fallen and estranged? Traditionally, theology conceived of this as a prehistorical time before the Fall, a kind of golden age or paradisaiacal existence. Tillich considers such a mythical conception of a prefallen state of perfection as fraught with difficulties. For Tillich essential human nature is not an actual stage of human development but is potentially "present in all stages of [human] development, although in existential distortion."[22] Tillich prefers to speak of this state of essential being in psychological terms as *dreaming innocence*.

Both words point to something that precedes actual existence. It has potentiality, not actuality. It has no place, it is *au topos* (utopia). It has no time; it precedes temporality. . . . Dreaming is a state of mind which is real and non-real at the same time—just as is potentiality. Dreaming anticipates the actual, just as everything actual is somehow present in the potential. . . . in terms of anticipation. For these reasons the metaphor "dreaming" is adequate in describing the state of essential being.

The word "innocence" also points to nonactualized potentiality. One is innocent only with respect to something which, if actualized, would end the state of innocence. The word has three connotations. It can mean lack of actual experience, lack of personal responsibility, and lack of moral guilt. . . . It designates the state before actuality, existence and history.[23]

This state of dreaming innocence drives beyond itself and, in so doing, is experienced as temptation. Temptation is unavoidable because dreaming innocence, contrary to the older dogmatics, is not a state of perfection. Nor is it a state of sinlessness, for every life stands under the conditions of existence.

Orthodox theologians have heaped perfection after perfection upon Adam before the Fall, making him equal with the picture of the Christ. This procedure is not only absurd; it makes the Fall completely unintelligible. Mere potentiality or dreaming innocence is not perfection. *Only the conscious union of existence and essence is perfection.* . . . The symbol "Adam before the Fall" must be understood as the dreaming innocence of undecided potentialities.[24] (Italics added.)

What drives dreaming innocence beyond itself is our unique "finite freedom." We are conscious of the fact that our freedom is bound by our fini-tude. This awareness leads to anxiety, which "expresses the awareness of being finite, of being a mixture of being and non-being, or of being threatened by non-being . . . in man freedom is united with anxiety."[25] We, therefore, see our freedom as a "dreadful freedom" or "aroused free-dom" because we are caught between the desire to actualize our freedom and the command to preserve our dreaming innocence (symbolized in the divine prohibition not to eat from the tree of knowledge).

Man experiences the anxiety of losing himself by not actualizing himself and his potentialities and the anxi-ety of losing himself by actualizing himself and his potentialities. He stands between the preservation of his dreaming innocence without experiencing the actuality of being and the loss of his innocence through knowledge, power, guilt. The anxiety of this situation is the state of temptation. Man decides for self-actualization, thus producing the end of dreaming innocence.[26]

For Tillich, the transition from essence to existence is "the original fact," the "universal quality of finite being" that sets the condition of spatial and temporal existence. Hidden behind the strong ethical theme which dominates the Genesis story of the Fall of Adam, Tillich sees ele-ments of an older mythology of the transcendent Fall of the souls which, while clearly not biblical, does not contradict the biblical account. The myth of the transcendent Fall points to "the tragic-universal character of existence . . . that the very constitution of existence implies the transition from essence to existence."[27]

The cosmic, universal character of the Fall and estrangement raises the question of the relation between Creation and Fall. Tillich's accent on the cosmic, universal, and destined character of the Fall appears to equate the two. Biblical theology has always held, however, that it was the free and rebellious human Fall that changed the universal structure of nature. Tillich rejects this as absurd for, in his view, the structures of nature, including human nature, were always what they are now.

"The notion of a moment *in* time in which man and nature were changed from good to evil is absurd, and it has no foundation in experience or revelation."[28] What, then, of Creation and Fall? Do they coincide? Tillich, himself, raises the ques-tion: "The tragic universality of existence, the ele-ment of destiny in human freedom and the symbol of the 'fallen world' naturally raise the question as to whether sin is made ontologically necessary instead of a matter of personal responsibility and guilt."[29] His answer is resolute: "Actualized cre-ation and estranged existence are identical. Only biblical literalism has the theological right to deny this assertion. He who excludes the idea of a his-torical stage of essential goodness should not try to escape the consequence."[30] Tillich acknowledges that creation is *good* in its essential character and, only when actualized, falls into universal estrange-ment. But it is imperative to remember that for Tillich, as for Hegel, essential goodness is not *per-fection*.* The perfection of humanity's essential being requires the actualization of human poten-tialities. Perfection involves the move from inno-cence through actualized but estranged existence to a condition of *non-estranged existence*. The Fall is a necessary movement in this process.

According to Tillich, the state of existence *is* the state of estrangement. Humans are estranged from the ground of their being, from other beings, and from themselves. Human existence is not what it essentially is and ought to be. Although estrangement is not a biblical term, it is implied in the mythical accounts of the beginnings and spread of sin—e.g., the expulsion from paradise, Cain and Abel, and the Tower of Babel. Tillich believes there is presently good reason to use the term "estrangement" rather than the word "sin."

The term (sin) has been used in a way which has little to do with its genuine biblical meaning. Paul often spoke of "Sin" in the singular and without an article. He saw it as a quasi-personal power which ruled this world. But in the Christian churches, both Catholic and Protestant, sin has been used predominantly in the plural, and "sins" are deviations from moral laws.

* To compare the above account with Hegel's doctrine of the Fall, see Vol. I, Ch. 5.

This has little to do with "sin" as the state of estrangement from that to which one belongs—God, one's self, one's world.[31]

The term "sin" must be kept, nevertheless, for it does express the personal dimension of estrangement, the willful act of turning away. Sin connotes the free dimension of tragic estrangement. "Man's predicament is estrangement but his estrangement is sin . . . a matter of both personal freedom and universal destiny."[32]

Tillich sees human sinful estrangement as characterized by *unbelief, hubris,* and *concupiscence.* Unbelief is the turning away from or separation of the will from the will of God, whereas *hubris* is the other side of unbelief, viz., the turning in on oneself and elevating the self to the center of one's world. Concupiscence is "the unlimited desire to draw the whole of reality into one's self." This is seen in all aspects of human life. It is given classical expression in the unlimited sexual striving of a Don Juan, and in Faust's insatiable search for experience and knowledge. Nietzsche's "will to power" and Freud's "libido" are recent conceptualizations of this classical notion of concupiscence.

In the state of existential estrangement, the individual contradicts his or her essential being. "The attempt of the finite self to be the center of everything gradually has the effect of its ceasing to be the center of anything. Both self and world are threatened."[33] Estrangement means, first of all, a division within the self.

Parts of the self overtake the center and determine it without being united with other parts. A contingent motive replaces the center which is supposed to unite the motives in a centered decision; but it is unable to do so. This is the ontological character of the state described in classical theology as the "bondage of the will."[34]

This self-loss inevitably involves estrangement from other beings and being itself. Tillich describes in detail the ontological conflicts inherent in estrangement and the existential experience of guilt, loneliness, meaninglessness, and ultimately despair that this separation creates.[35]

In the state of estrangement, the individual seeks salvation (*salvus* meaning "healthy" or "whole"). But because our very existence is estranged, we cannot save ourselves. Despite this fact, we continue to seek salvation on our own. Many approaches have been tried—legalism, asceticism, mysticism, to name only a few—but all of these attempts ultimately fail. Yet our very search for a new being points to its presence.

The question of salvation can be asked only if salvation is already at work, no matter how fragmentarily . . . the awareness of estrangement and the desire for salvation are effects of the presence of saving power, in other words, revelatory experiences.[36]

Our situation causes us to ask for the ground and power of all being, and this very question about God implies an answer. Thus we come to the second, or answering, pole of the method of correlation.

Being, God, and Being-Itself

Tillich considers the traditional arguments for the existence of God to have failed as proofs. Rather, they are "expressions of the *question* of God which is implied in human finitude." The continuing value of these arguments lies in the fact that they "analyze the human situation in such a way that the question of God appears possible and necessary."[37] Take, for example, the ontological argument. "It shows that an awareness of the infinite is included in man's awareness of finitude. Man knows that he is finite, that he is excluded from an infinity which nevertheless belongs to him."[38]

Tillich claims that God is the answer to the question implied in human finitude, for God is the ground of all being. *God is being-itself.* Only that which is the ultimate ground and power of all being can save our being from the forces that threaten it. In saying that God is *being-itself,* Tillich wishes to make it clear that "the being of

God cannot be understood as the existence of a being alongside others or above others."[39]

If God is *a* being, he is subject to the categories of finitude, especially to space and substance. Even if he is called the "highest being" this situation has not changed. When applied to God superlatives become diminutives. They place him on the level of other beings while elevating him above all of them.[40]

Logically, God's being is "prior to" the split between essential and existential being. It is therefore a serious error, in Tillich's view, to identify God with existence. Strictly speaking *God does not exist.* In order to argue for the existence of God, Thomas Aquinas was forced to distinguish between a divine existence that is identical with essence and one that is not. But an existence of *God* that is not united with its essence makes God a being whose existence has not fulfilled its essential potentialities. Tillich believes that this is a contradiction in terms. For him "it is as atheistic to affirm the existence of God as it is to deny it. God is being-itself, not *a* being."[41]

What we as finite creatures know is known through our finitude. Hence what we can know and say about God is always symbolic, that is, consists of statements that point beyond themselves—except, in Tillich's view, the statement that God is being-itself. Consider, for example, the statement that God lives.

Life is the actuality of being, or, more exactly, it is the process in which potential being becomes actual being. But in God as God there is no distinction between potentiality and actuality. Therefore, we cannot speak of God as living in the proper or nonsymbolic sense of the word "life." We must speak of God as living in symbolic terms. Yet every true symbol participates in the reality which it symbolizes. *God lives in so far as he is the ground of life.*[42] (Italics added.)

The same would hold true in speaking of God as personal.

The symbol "personal God" is absolutely fundamental because an existential relation is a person-to-person relation. Man cannot be ultimately concerned about anything that is less than personal, but since personality includes individuality, the question arises in what sense God can be called an individual. . . . "Personal God" does not mean that God is *a* person. It means that God is the ground of everything personal and that he carries within himself the ontological power of personality.[43]

The traditional attributes of God, such as omnipotence, eternality, and omniscience, must all be seen as symbolic answers to the question posed by human finitude—answers that serve as the basis for the human courage to be. The popular conception of omnipotence is that "God can do whatever he wants." This, of course, has led to absurd puzzles about whether God can logically will contradictory possibilities and other similar riddles. Tillich suggests that "it is more adequate to define divine omnipotence as the power of being which resists non-being in all its expressions and which is manifest in the creative process in all its forms."[44] Faith in the power of being-itself to overcome the threat of nonbeing is the ground of the courage-to-be despite the fact of finitude.

Eternity is God's omnipotence in respect to time; omnipresence is the power of being-itself in respect to space. God's omnipresence means neither that God is "endlessly extended in space nor limited to a definite space; nor is he spaceless. . . . God's omnipresence is his creative participation in the spatial existence of his creatures."[45] Likewise, to speak of God's omniscience should not mean that God is "all-knowing," that God knows everything past, present, and future. Rather, it is the symbolic expression of faith that nothing falls outside the *logos* structure of being. Chaotic nonbeing cannot overcome the rational character of being-itself.

Existence and the New Being in Jesus as the Christ

As finite creatures we are estranged and threatened with the loss of meaning and even

with the loss of being. Because of this estrangement, we are not able to save ourselves, to create
a new being, or to regain our essential humanity.
The answer to our quest for a new being can come
only as an answer "spoken to" human existence
from beyond it; yet it must reveal itself under the
conditions of existence. Tillich points out that
this quest and answer has expressed itself in the
West in the expectation of a historical Messiah
(Christ) who will actualize the New Being, essential humanity, under the conditions of existential
estrangement. It is here that the ground and
power of being-itself is revealed concretely, overcoming the forces that threaten creaturely existence. Christianity is founded on the claim that
Jesus the Christ is the medium of this final revelation, of the New Being present within the conditions of existential disruption. Where this claim
is absent Christianity does not exist or ceases to
exist manifestly. "Christianity is what it is
through the affirmation that Jesus of Nazareth,
who has been called 'the Christ,' is actually the
Christ, namely, he who brings the new state of
things, the New Being."[46]

According to Tillich, Christianity was born
not with the birth of Jesus but with the event
reported to have taken place at Caesarea Philippi,
where Peter was driven to confess "Thou art the
Christ." The event on which Christianity is
founded thus has two sides: the fact that is called
"Jesus of Nazareth" and the reception of that historical person as the Christ.[47]

The emphasis that Tillich places on the
receptive side of the Christ event has required
that he take a position on the relationship
between Christology and historical research,
which reflects his continuity with such postliberal
theologians as Karl Barth and Rudolf Bultmann
but which also exposes a problem in his own
christological doctrine. Tillich agrees that the old
quest of the historical Jesus has failed because it
attempted to extract a minimum of reliable facts
about Jesus in the Gospels from the layers of theological interpretation, thereby providing a factually certain foundation for Christian belief. Such
a quest is no longer possible because, since the
publication of Schweitzer's *The Quest of the His-*

torical Jesus and the advent of Form criticism, it is
considered impossible to separate Jesus from his
reception as the Christ by the earliest Christian
community.

This situation is not a matter of a preliminary short-
coming of historical research which will one day be
overcome. It is caused by the nature of the sources
itself. The reports about Jesus of Nazareth are those of
Jesus as the Christ, given by persons who received him
as the Christ.[48]

Tillich asserts that it is even inaccurate to
speak of the "historical Jesus," if we mean by that
term the life of a person who stands behind the
Gospel message and can be extracted from it. The
only historical Jesus that exists is what Tillich
calls "the biblical picture of Jesus as the Christ."
All that historical research can do is give us rather
vague "probabilities" about the so-called historical Jesus—but a person's religious faith, his or her
ultimate concern, cannot be based on mere historical probabilities. For this reason Tillich holds
that the risk of Christian faith "lies in quite a different dimension from the risk of accepting
uncertain historical facts. It is wrong, therefore,
to consider the risk concerning uncertain historical facts as part of the risk of faith."[49] In what,
then, does the risk of faith lie? Tillich replies that
"the concrete biblical material is not guaranteed
by faith in respect to empirical factuality; but it is
guaranteed as an adequate expression of the transforming power of the New Being in Jesus as the
Christ. Only in this sense does faith guarantee the
biblical picture of Jesus."[50] Faith should concern
itself only with the transforming power of the
New Being for "no historical criticism can question the immediate awareness of those who find
themselves transformed into the state of faith."[51]

Tillich's position regarding Christology and
the historical Jesus has a kinship with that of
Ernst Troeltsch. While both emphasize the necessity of the historical Jesus for faith, they also reject
the earlier liberal assumption that the "facts about
Jesus" can be established like other facts. Both
Tillich and Troeltsch stress the receptive side of
the event of Jesus Christ through the historical

and contemporary mediation of the Christian community. And for Tillich, the rich, expressionistic "biblical picture of the Christ" always will be received somewhat differently in each concrete, existential, revelatory situation. This cardinal point, shared by Troeltsch and Tillich, has proven more attractive to recent theologies that wish to point to those realities of the "biblical picture of Christ" that are capable of discernment only in the immediate context of present-day social, political, racial, or gender concerns. This point is evident, for example, in the depiction of the blackness of Jesus in African-American theology, in Jesus as liberator in liberationist theology, and in the depiction of Jesus as Sophia and Mother in some feminist interpretation. The common theme here is that Jesus is not the Christ independent of his reception as the Christ—that is, in the concrete terms of his healing and liberating presence.[52]

There is an issue here, however, about which recent theologians may be far less concerned than was Tillich, namely, the real tension between the two poles, the actualized life of Jesus as essential God-manhood and the believing reception of him as the Christ. How does Tillich know, for example, that the Gospel picture of the New Being was, in fact, actualized in a concrete historical existence and was not simply the figment of overly ripe imaginations? To some—for instance, D. F. Strauss and the twentieth-century philosopher George Santayana—this historical question is really irrelevant. It is the *idea* of Christ that is important. But Tillich cannot rest in such a position as this. His doctrine *requires* that the New Being be concretely embodied in a personal historical existence, one such as supports the biblical picture. Tillich wants to reject one clearly mistaken notion: "namely, the mistake of supposing that the picture of the New Being in Jesus as the Christ is the creation of existential thought or experience."[53] The fact is, he asserts, that the biblical picture of Jesus as the Christ "*is the result of a new being; it represents the victory over existence which has taken place, and thus created the picture.*"[54] (Italics added.) Elsewhere, Tillich makes such assertions as that Jesus "surrenders himself

completely" and that "a revelation is final if it has the power of negating itself without losing itself," and that "in the picture of Jesus as the Christ we have the picture of a man who possessed these qualities."[55] How does Tillich know that the biblical picture of Jesus "who possesses these qualities" corresponds to a "concrete historical actualization" without opening the theological claim to historical research? It is imperative to his Christology that the picture of Jesus as the Christ be *factually, historically actualized,* and yet he wishes to insulate this picture from historical criticism. It would not appear that Tillich can have it both ways.

As we have seen, in Chapter One, Rudolf Bultmann's response to the problem of the historical Jesus is similar to Tillich's, although more radical and in some ways more satisfactory. For Bultmann sees the historical Jesus as the "bearer" of the message of the Word of God but makes no claims about Jesus's existential actualization of that message.

For Tillich, Christ is the one who brings in the new eon in his own person, and "those who participate in him participate in the New Being, though under the condition of man's existential predicament and, therefore, only fragmentarily and by anticipation."[56] St. Paul spoke of Christ as the new Adam and of those who were *in* Christ as a "new creature," a "new man." The new Adam or, using Tillich's term, the "New Being in Jesus as the Christ"

is essential being under the conditions of existence, conquering the gap between essence and existence. . . . It is new in two respects: it is new in contrast to the merely potential character of essential being; and it is new over against the estranged character of existential being. It is actual, conquering the estrangement of actual existence.[57]

Tillich stresses the fact that in the New Being of Jesus as the Christ we see human existential estrangement conquered by one who was *fully human*—for only in personal existence, where existence *is* finite freedom, can existence be conquered. This means that Jesus as the Christ is the bearer of the New Being in the *totality* of his being and not in any single expression of it. Tillich rejects the rationalist attempt to emphasize the *words* of Jesus, the pietist emphasis on the *deeds*, and the orthodox focus on the *suffering* of Jesus, to the exclusion of all else. Jesus's whole being is an expression of the New Being, beyond the split of essential and existential being. The conflict between the unity of God and humanity and humanity's estrangement is overcome.

According to the biblical picture of Jesus as the Christ, there are, in spite of all tensions, no traces of estrangement between him and God and consequently between him and himself and him and his world (in its essential nature). The paradoxical character of his being consists in the fact that, although he has only finite freedom under the conditions of time and space, he is not estranged from the ground of his being. There are no traces of unbelief, namely, the removal of his personal center from the divine center which is the subject of his infinite concern. . . . In the same way the biblical picture shows no trace of *hubris* or self-elevation in spite of his awareness of his messianic vocation. . . . Nor is there any trace of concupiscence in the picture. This point is stressed in the story of the temptation in the desert.[58]

Tillich rejects the description of Jesus's conquest of estrangement as his "sinlessness," for it places Jesus above the tensions of finite freedom and thus in a position not truly comparable with our own. Tillich accentuates the seriousness of Jesus's temptations and the genuine marks of his finitude.

In relation to reality as such . . . he (Jesus) is subject to uncertainty in judgment, risks of error, the limits of power, and the vicissitudes of life. . . . Finitude implies openness to error, and error belongs to the participation of the Christ in man's existential predicament. Error is evident in his ancient conception of the universe, his judgments about men, his interpretation of the historical moment, his eschatological imagination.[59]

Jesus's being as the Christ does not remove him from the same finitude, anxiety, ambiguity, and tragedy that we all face as human beings. But the conquest of existential estrangement in Jesus as the Christ

does have the character of taking the negativities of existence into unbroken unity with God. The anxiety about having to die is not removed; it is taken into participation in the "will of God."[60]

Tillich's creative reconception of Jesus the Christ as the New Being is carried forward in his discussion of the Christological dogma. Tillich agrees with Luther that dogmas are "protective" doctrines that were formulated to preserve the substance of the Christian message against heretical distortions. In the case of the christological dogma there always have been two dangers that threaten the truth about Jesus the Christ. One is the denial of the Christ-character of Jesus as the Christ and the other is the denial of the Jesus-character of Jesus as the Christ. These dangers were met in the ancient church by the formulation of the doctrine of the unity of two *natures* in Jesus Christ, his being both "fully God and fully man." Tillich believes that the two-natures doctrine was attempting to protect a genuine truth of Christian faith but that it was doing so with inadequate conceptual tools and therefore the traditional creedal formulation must be replaced.

The assertion that Jesus as the Christ is the personal unity of a divine and a human nature must be replaced by the assertion that in Jesus as the Christ the eternal unity of God and man has become historical reality . . . the New Being is the reestablished unity between God and man. We replace the inadequate concept "divine nature" by the concepts "eternal God-man-unity" or "Eternal God-Manhood." Such concepts replace a static essence by a dynamic relation.[61]

Tillich acknowledges that his relational description does not remove the mystery of the Incarnation and that all metaphysical and psychological attempts to describe this unity must fail.[62]

Tillich's restatement of Christology has certain affinities with that of Schleiermacher, the father of modern Liberal theology—a point noted by Tillich:

He (Schleiermacher) replaces the two-nature doctrine by a doctrine of a divine-human relation. He speaks of a God-consciousness in Jesus, the strength of which surpasses the God-consciousness of all other men. He describes Jesus as the *Urbild* ("original image") of what man essentially is and from which he has fallen.[63]

The universal significance of Jesus as the Christ is expressed in the term "salvation." For Christians he is known as the Savior, the Mediator, and the Redeemer. Tillich points out that the Church has thought of salvation in different ways throughout its history, but that in terms of both its original meaning (from *salvus,* "healed") and our present situation, the most adequate meaning of salvation is "healing."

It corresponds to the state of estrangement as the main characteristic of existence. In this sense, healing means reuniting that which is estranged, giving a center to what is split, overcoming the split between God and man, man and his world, man and himself. . . . Salvation is reclaiming from the old and transferring into the New Being.[64]

Although Christianity derives salvation from the appearance of the New Being in Jesus as the Christ, it does not separate salvation in Christ from the processes of healing that are present throughout all human historical experience. Wherever there is a genuine revelation of the ground and power of being, there is salvation, and history is filled with such authentic revelatory events. "They are saving events in which the power of the New Being is present. It is present in a preparatory way, fragmentarily, and is open to demonic distortion. But it is present and heals where it is seriously accepted. On these healing forces the life of mankind always depends."[65]

What has distorted our understanding of salvation is the belief that it is either total or nonexistent. If this were the case, only a small number of human beings would ever know salvation. "Only if salvation is understood as healing and

saving power through the New Being in all history is the problem put on another level. In some degree all men participate in the healing power of the New Being. Otherwise, they would have no being."[66] Yet it is also true that "no men are totally healed, not even those who have encountered the healing power as it appears in Jesus as the Christ."[67] As humans we remain finite and, to a lesser or greater extent, anxious and estranged. Hence the Christian hope for the ultimate communion of all beings in the eschatological new creation, the Kingdom of God.

What, then, is the peculiar nature of the healing which comes through participation in the New Being in Jesus as the Christ? Tillich replies that Christ

is the ultimate *criterion* of every healing and saving process . . . in him the healing quality is complete and unlimited. The Christian remains in the state of relativity with respect to salvation; the New Being in the Christ transcends every relativity in its quality and power of healing. It is just this that makes him the Christ. Therefore, wherever there is saving power in mankind, it must be judged by the saving power in Jesus as the Christ.[68]

The Spirit's Presence and Morality

The third and final volume of Tillich's *Systematic Theology* (which includes Parts III and IV of his system on the themes of "Life and the Spirit" and "History and the Kingdom of God") was published in 1963, two years before his death. Tillich's discussion of the dimensions of life and their various relations, of the special ambiguities of human life, and of the manifestations of the Spiritual Presence (his symbol of "God present") in the human spirit, in history, in religion, and in culture, is the longest part of the *Systematic Theology.* Here we can focus only briefly on the meaning of life and the Spiritual Presence as it bears on Tillich's mature reflections on ethics.

For Tillich, the power of the Spiritual Presence manifests itself not only in the sphere of religion but also in moments of transcendent and unambiguous cultural and moral creativity. Tillich refers to such moments of Spiritual Presence as "theonomous," in contrast to cultural and moral activity that is either "autonomous" or "heteronomous" (imposed from without). Theonomy is the "self-creation of life under the dimension of the Spirit toward the ultimate in being and meaning."[69]

A theonomous morality is grounded in a love (*agape*) that is a drive toward the reunion of the separated, "participation in the other one through participation in the transcendent unity of unambiguous life."[70] It is a love that is impossible for the human spirit itself but is a creation of Spirit. The contents of our human moral imperative derive from both abstract norms and concrete situations that, because they are ambiguous, lead to oscillation and indecision. But a theonomous morality derives its motivating power from grace, "not a product of any act of good will . . . but given gratuitously without merit."[71] Only such grace or love, the Spiritual Presence, can motivate the moral will by actually giving what is demanded. Because a theonomous morality is a matter of grace, it carries the power of courage.

It is the courage to judge the particular without subjecting it to an abstract norm—a courage that can do justice to the particular. Courage implies risk . . . perhaps because he acts against a traditional ethical norm or perhaps subjects himself to a traditional ethical norm. To the degree that the Spirit-created love prevails in a human being, the concrete decision is unambiguous, but it can never escape the fragmentary character of finitude.[72]

It is clear that Tillich's theonomous morality is skeptical of traditional moral norms and is anti-moralistic. It is a morality that demands courage and risk, one which we must recognize as necessary in our ever-relative context. It is a moral stance that is justified only by the power of grace and a loving forgiveness.

During his years of active engagement in Religious Socialism—between roughly 1920 and 1933 before he immigrated to the United States—Tillich wrote extensively on ethics and social philosophy. It often has been remarked that, by contrast, during his more than thirty years in America he wrote relatively little on ethics, and that he took little interest in American domestic politics. Although it is true that in the last two decades of his life he did devote most of his energies to the completion of his impressive *Systematic Theology*, the record does show that during these American years Tillich wrote numerous significant essays and two books, *Love, Power, and Justice* (1954) and *Morality and Beyond* (1963), devoted to morality and ethics. More importantly, he gave much time to the work of resettling European refugees in America during World War II, to attacking anti-Semitism in numerous talks and publications, to serving as chairman of the Council for a Democratic Germany, which was concerned with opposing Nazi policy and ensuring a democratic postwar Germany, and to other political involvements. He also wrote powerful essays pointing out the dangers inherent in American mass culture and America's growing reliance on and faith in technology and in atomic weaponry.

After World War II Tillich came to believe that the older forms of socialism were no longer relevant to the new context in America, but he also feared that an optimistic, monopolistic capitalism empowered with a new technology was imposing new threats of dehumanization. He called for resistance to these depersonalizing forces. Technology was a sign of human creativity but, like all creative vitality it had proven ambiguous and contained within it "demonic" potential. This expressed itself in a technocratic culture that easily turned means into ends and both nature and persons into objects. Tillich believed that only under a theonomous Spiritual Presence could this confusion of means and ends be overcome. "For the Spirit, no thing is merely a thing," and, therefore, in a theonomous culture there is always a technological self-limitation. Possibilities are seen not only as benefits; "they are also temptations, and the desire to actualize them can lead to emptiness and destruction."[73]

Such "structures of destruction" were present after 1945 in the demonic form of nuclear weapons. Under the impact of the Spiritual Presence, such a destructive use of technology would be "banned," but Tillich warned that no solution for the use of this potentially demonic technology was possible without such a Presence "because the ambiguity of production and destruction cannot be conquered on the horizontal level, even fragmentarily."[74] And, therefore, Tillich did not advocate nuclear pacifism or a unilateral ban on atomic weapons. The fulfillment of a perfect unity and peace could not, Tillich believed, be found within the ambiguities of history, and so the Christian finds ultimate hope in the symbols of the Kingdom of God and Eternal Life as the end or *telos* of history. Nevertheless, such a hope must not involve a retreat from historical engagement; it can only be sustained and realized within it. These are Tillich's final words on Christian hope and the Kingdom of God:

It is not a victory of the Kingdom of God in history if the individual tries to take himself out of participation in history in the name of the transcendent Kingdom of God. . . . For the transcendent is actual within the inner-historical. . . . The more one's destiny is directly determined by one's active participation, the more historical sacrifice is demanded. Where such sacrifice is maturely accepted, a victory of the Kingdom of God has occurred.[75]

Paul Tillich's existentialist reinterpretation of the themes of classical Christian theology is one of the monumental intellectual achievements of the middle decades of the twentieth century. Nevertheless, the very scope and schematic structure of the *Systematic Theology* have raised critical questions from those who believe the concreteness and historicity of biblical faith has been distorted by Tillich's systematic penchant. Paradoxically, it is Tillich's ability to analyze the spiritual malaise of contemporary life and to serve as a guide to many of today's perplexed spirits that has won the plaudits of his theological peers.

A careful reading of Tillich's theology raises a number of questions for the theological critic—a fact evident from even this brief account. At the root of the difficulty is Tillich's use of ontological language and analysis. For example, does he not ontologize the Fall of humanity in such a way that finitude and sin are not properly distinguished, and sin becomes an ontological fate? What does Tillich mean when he asserts that "God is being-itself" is the only nonsymbolic statement about God? As a literal statement it is exceedingly vague—especially in view of the fact that he does not distinguish carefully between being "being-itself," "ground of being," and "power of being," all of which can mean very different things ontologically.

Tillich's conception of God as "Being-itself" has raised further questions as to whether he can maintain the biblical conception of a "personal" God, and this has helped to spark an important debate about the Christian doctrine of God in the latter decades of the century. We earlier pointed to the criticism that Tillich's Christology does not take with sufficient seriousness the need for real knowledge of the historical figure of Jesus when he makes certain theological claims about him. Finally, Tillich has generated an important debate over theological method that harks back to his break with Karl Barth. Many contemporary theologians have pursued one or another form of Tillich's method of correlation as the only responsible way of addressing the religious questions of our largely secular culture. Other theologians believe, however, that such "theologies of correlation" inevitably distort the content of the Christian message, because the theological "answers" that such theologies offer are substantively shaped by the "questions" posed by the secular culture itself. We will see that this issue continues to occupy center stage in the theological debates of the latter decades of the twentieth century. (See Chapter Sixteen.)

RUDOLF BULTMANN

Many younger theologians in the 1950s and 1960s believed that Rudolf Bultmann (1884–1976) had defined the crucial issues that would be at the center of theological discussion in the remaining decades of the twentieth century.

Rudolf Bultmann

1921, Bultmann returned to Marburg as professor of New Testament, and there he remained, becoming professor emeritus in 1951. Few men have led a more active scholarly life after their retirement than did Bultmann. It was only about the time of his retirement from his professorship that Bultmann's program of demythologizing the Bible came to the attention of theologians outside of Germany. He carried on a vigorous debate with his critics and sparked theological investigations in several important directions.

It was remarked earlier that Bultmann, like Tillich, represented a theological position between Ritschlian Liberalism and Barth's Dialectical theology. Bultmann placed himself within the theological movements of this century in the following autobiographical reflection:

This was due largely to the fact that Bultmann the historian had bridged the gulf between historical and philosophical theology as no other theologian had succeeded in doing in this century. Troeltsch, as we have seen, addressed this problem but was not entirely successful in carrying out a constructive synthesis of these two theological disciplines. Bultmann's effort to join the concerns of historical and philosophical theology does not mean that he resolved these problems confronting Christian thought; rather, it means that he helped to free theology from a serious case of schizophrenia and in so doing focused on some of the seminal issues of theology for our time.

Rudolf Bultmann was born in Wiefelstede, Germany, and, like many of the German thinkers we have studied, was the son of an Evangelical-Lutheran pastor. Bultmann began his theological studies at Tübingen but also attended Berlin and Marburg. In these universities he not only studied under the great Ritschlian theologians, Harnack and Herrmann, but also the biblical scholars Gunkel, Jülicher, and Johannes Weiss. In 1912, Bultmann qualified as a lecturer in the New Testament at Marburg. Between 1916 and 1920, he taught at Breslau, where he wrote his influential *Die Geschichte der Synoptischen Tradition.** In

It seemed to me that in this new theological movement, as distinguished from the "liberal" theology out of which I had come, it was rightly recognized that the Christian faith is not a phenomenon of the history of religion, that it does not rest on a "religious a priori" (Troeltsch), and that therefore theology does not have to look upon Christian faith as a phenomenon of religious or cultural history. It seemed to me that, distinguished from such a view, the new theology correctly saw that Christian faith is the answer to the Word of the transcendent God which encounters man, and that theology has to deal with this Word and the man who has been encountered by it. This judgment, however, has never led me to a simple condemnation of "liberal" theology; on the contrary I have endeavored throughout my entire work to carry farther the tradition of historical-critical research as it was practiced in "liberal" theology and to make our recent theological knowledge the more fruitful as a result.

In doing so, the work of existential philosophy, which I came to know through my discussions with Martin Heidegger, became of decisive significance for me. I found here the concept through which it became possible to speak adequately of human existence and therefore also of the existence of the believer. In my efforts to make philosophy fruitful for theology, however, I have come more and more into opposition to Karl Barth. I remain grateful to him, however, for the decisive things I have learned from him.[76]

God's Action and Faith

In Chapter One, we discussed briefly Bultmann's contribution to Form criticism and the significance of that approach to the New Testament sources for our knowledge of the historical Jesus. It was pointed out that, while Bultmann is convinced of an identity between the historical Jesus and the kerygmatic Christ, he rejects all attempts to verify such an identity by historical-critical methods. His refusal to do this is based not only on his conviction that the very nature of these sources makes such an attempted proof impossible but, more important, that it denies the very meaning of faith. To seek such a proof is to be guilty of demanding a sign, a "worldly" security in our own works. What we need is not a proof, but to be encountered by the Word of God in our own existence and to be challenged to believe or reject that Word. What lies behind Bultmann's position at this point is his conviction that the action of God is not susceptible to objectification or empirical confirmation. God's action in the world and upon us as persons is always *existential*, hidden to every eye but the eye of faith. Here Bultmann reveals the patrimony of his Ritschlian teachers in that for them God was not known in himself or in the abstract, but only in the existential judgment of faith.

Bultmann begins his theological reflection with the Kantian doctrine that genuine knowledge is an achievement of both pure and practical reason. Authentic knowledge of the world may be approached both objectively, as is appropriate to the natural sciences, and subjectively or existentially, as is appropriate to our knowledge of persons. According to Bultmann, the objective study of the world and history does not allow for supernatural occurrences and explanations. God cannot be introduced as a factor to explain this-worldly events for

modern science does not believe that the course of nature can be interrupted or, so to speak, perforated, by supernatural powers. . . . The same is true of the modern study of history, which does not take into account any intervention of God or of the devil or of demons in the course of history. . . . Modern men take it for granted that the course of nature and of history, like their own inner life and their practical life, is nowhere interrupted by the intervention of supernatural powers.[77]

To hold to the modern scientific view of the world does not mean, however, that God must be conceived, if at all, as deistical and unrelated to events in this world. Rather, it means that one must give up a *mythological* conception of God's action in the world. Bultmann describes the mythological view of God's action, in terms of miraculous intervention, as follows:

In mythological thinking the action of God, whether in nature, history, human fortune, or the inner life of the soul, is understood as an action that intervenes between the natural, or historical or psychological course of events; it breaks and links them at the same time. The divine causality is inserted as a link in the chain of the events which follow one another according to the causal nexus. This is meant by the popular notion that a miraculous event cannot be understood except as a miracle, that is, as the effect of a supernatural cause. In such thinking the action of God is indeed conceived in the same way as secular actions or events are conceived, for the divine power which effects miracles is considered as a natural power.[78]

The person of faith does not conceive of God's action in this mythological way, for he or she does not view the action of God on the level of secular, worldly events—i.e., as visible and capable of objective proof. Rather, the person of faith thinks of God's act *not*

as an action which happens *between* the worldly actions or events, but as happening *within* them. The close connection between natural and historical events remains intact as it presents itself to the observer. The action of God is hidden from every eye except the eye of faith.[79] (Italics added.)

Bultmann is insisting that the person of faith sees all of nature and history in radical dependence on the transcendent God. Thus, events that can be fully explained in terms of natural, this-worldly causes are seen, nevertheless, as acts of God. An example would be the story of the Israelites crossing the Red (Reed) Sea. This event can be viewed mythologically as the direct, supernatural intervention of God in holding back the waters. On the other hand, the crossing can be explained naturalistically, as due to favorable winds blowing over the low, marshy route of escape and the inability of the heavy Egyptian vehicles to maneuver through the boggy terrain. The latter explanation in no way restricts one from also interpreting the event as an act of divine providence.

Stated in the terms of Martin Luther and made current more recently by Kierkegaard, Bultmann would say that God's action in the world is always *hidden* and *paradoxical*.

Faith insists not on the direct identity of God's action with worldly events, but, if I may be permitted to put it so, on the paradoxical identity which can be believed only here and now against the appearance of non-identity. In faith I can understand an accident with which I meet as a gracious gift of God or as His punishment, or as His chastisement. On the other hand, I can understand the same accident as a link in the chain of the natural course of events. If, for example, my child has recovered from a dangerous illness, I give thanks to God because He has saved my child.[80]*

The meaning given to an event by faith cannot be translated into a general truth for others to accept. It always remains a truth *for the believer.* In Bultmann's view, this is what distinguishes Christian faith from pantheism.

Pantheism is a conviction given in advance, a general world-view, which affirms that every event in the world is the work of God because God is immanent in the world. Christian faith, by contrast, holds that God acts on me, speaks to me here and now. The Christian believes this because he knows that he is addressed by the grace of God which meets him in the Word of God, in Jesus Christ. God's grace opens his eyes to see that "in everything God works for good with those

who love him" (Rom. 8:28). This faith is not a knowledge possessed once for all; it is not a general world-view. It can be realized only here and now.[81]

Christian faith is not faith that God is immanently present in all events and processes of this world, but, rather, a faith that God has acted decisively in Jesus Christ. This faith is not grounded in empirically verified historical facts of the past but in hearing and responding to the *kerygma* ever anew.

God's word is not a general truth that can be stored in the treasure-house of human spiritual life. It remains his sovereign word, which we shall never master and which can be believed in only as an ever-living miracle, spoken by God and constantly renewed. . . . Belief in this word is the surrender of one's whole existence to it; readiness to hear it is readiness to submit one's whole life to its judgment and its grace. . . . The test of whether we have heard it aright is whether we are prepared always to hear it anew, to ask for it in every decision in life.[82]

Bultmann's Christocentrism is reflected in his insistence that for the Christian, the New Testament *kerygma* is where God alone decisively addresses humanity and that the *kerygma* is the source, norm, and substance of all preaching. As one writer has remarked, "what we have in Bultmann is something like a doctrine of the Real Presence in the preaching of the word."[83]

The claim that God acts in a unique and conclusively saving way in the *kerygma* of Jesus Christ is the scandal and stumbling block of Christian faith. Bultmann has no desire to remove this original stone of stumbling from the individuals confronted with the Christian message. However, there is another obstacle to Christian faith that most moderns regard as a serious impediment to belief in the Christian message, and that is the language and worldview in which the Christian message is presented in the New Testament. This stumbling block, Bultmann insists, must be removed so that the New Testament message can be heard for what it really is. Removal of this fortuitous scandal requires demythologization.

---

* This is a central motif in the theology of H. R. Niebuhr, who makes the distinction between "inner" and "outer" history. See Ch. Six.

Demythologizing the New Testament

What modern persons find incredible in the New Testament is its prescientific view of the world and the attendant picture of God acting in a mythological way, i.e., as an otherworldly being intervening supernaturally in the course of worldly events. The New Testament drama of redemption is pictured in the terms of an elaborate cosmological and eschatological *mythos*:

The world is viewed as a three-storied structure, with the earth in the center, the heaven above, and the underworld beneath. Heaven is the abode of God and of celestial beings—the angels. The underworld is hell, the place of torment. . . . The earth . . . is the scene of the supernatural activity of God and his angels on the one hand, and of Satan and his daemons on the other. . . . This aeon is held in bondage by Satan, sin, and death (for "powers" is precisely what they are), and hastens toward its end. The end will come very soon, and will take the form of a cosmic catastrophe. . . . "In the fullness of time" God sent forth his Son, a pre-existent divine Being, who appears on earth as a man. He dies the death of a sinner on the cross and makes atonement for the sins of men. His resurrection marks the beginning of the cosmic catastrophe. Death, the consequence of Adam's sin, is abolished, and the daemonic forces are deprived of their power. The risen Christ is exalted to the right hand of God in heaven and made "Lord and King." He will come again on the clouds of heaven to complete the work of redemption, and the resurrection and judgment of men will follow. Sin, suffering, and death will then be finally abolished. All this is to happen very soon; indeed, St. Paul thinks that he himself will live to see it.[84]

In Bultmann's view, this mythological understanding of the world is impossible in our present day and age. To call upon individuals to accept this form of Christian belief is to ask them to carry out a *sacrificium intellectus* and to isolate their religious beliefs from their daily experience. Bultmann believes that such a demand is neither possible or necessary. It is unnecessary because the Christian message is *not* inextricably tied to this ancient cosmic mythology. As a historian, Bultmann traces the language and worldview of New Testament mythology to the eschatology of late Jewish apocalyptic and the redemption myths of Gnosticism. He believes that a careful examination of these mythological conceptions will reveal a deeper meaning concealed under the mythological cover. Hence, what Bultmann calls for is not elimination of the New Testament mythology, but an *interpretation* of it in terms of its underlying intention. What is this deeper meaning imbedded in the mythical imagery? Bultmann offers the following explanation:

The real purpose of myth is not to present an objective picture of the world as it is, but to express man's understanding of himself in the world in which he lives. Myth should be interpreted not cosmologically, but anthropologically, or better still, existentially. . . . Myth is an expression of man's conviction that the origin and purpose of the world in which he lives are to be sought not within it but beyond it—that is, beyond the realm of known and tangible reality—and that this realm is perpetually dominated and menaced by those mysterious powers which are its source and limit. Myth is also an expression of man's awareness that he is not lord of his own being. It expresses his sense of dependence not only within the visible world, but more especially on those forces which hold sway beyond the confines of the known. Finally, myth expresses man's belief that in this state of dependence he can be delivered from the forces within the visible world.[85]

Mythical imagery is a natural vehicle for expressing transcendent power and action in terms of this world and human life, but what is important is not the imagery but the understanding of existence that the myths enshrine.

Bultmann points out that the process of interpreting the New Testament mythology, of *demythologization*, begins in the New Testament itself, in the writings of Paul, and most decisively with John. This is especially evident in their grasp of the existential significance of the eschatological imagery.

The decisive step was taken when Paul declared that the turning point from the old world to the new was not a matter of the future but did take place in the coming of Jesus Christ. . . . To be sure, Paul still expected the end of the world as a cosmic drama . . . but with the resurrection of Christ the decisive event has already happened. The Church is the eschatological community of the elect, of the saints who are already justified and are alive because they are in Christ, in Christ who as the second Adam abolished death and brought life and immortality to light through the gospel. (Rom. 5:12–14; II Tim. 1:10) "Death is swallowed up in victory" (I Cor. 15:54).

After Paul, John de-mythologized the eschatology in a radical manner. For John the coming and departing of Jesus is the eschatological event. "And this is the judgment, that the light has come into the world, and men loved darkness rather than light, because their deeds were evil" (John 3:19). "Now is the judgment of this world, now shall the ruler of this world be cast out" (12:31). For John the resurrection of Jesus, Pentecost and the *parousia* of Jesus are one and the same event, and those who believe have already eternal life. . . . "He who believes in the Son has eternal life; he who does not obey the Son shall not see life, but the wrath of God rests upon him."[86]

On the basis of this New Testament precedent, Bultmann considers the contemporary task of demythologization to be entirely justified.

If such a hermeneutical procedure is justified, how is it to be carried out? As we have seen, Bultmann believes that the myths are an objectification of our human existential self-understanding and, therefore, should be interpreted existentially. To interpret means to translate, i.e., make understandable, but this in turn presupposes some preunderstanding of the text that we are interpreting. Bultmann contends that every interpreter brings with her or him, consciously or not, certain conceptions and questions that are put to the text—otherwise, the text would remain mute. In this sense there is no such thing as "presuppositionless exegesis." A *prior understanding* of the intention of the text must be assumed. Bultmann maintains that

the formulation of a question arises from an interest which is based in the life of the inquirer, and it is the presupposition of all interpretations seeking an understanding of the text that this interest, too, is in some

way or other alive in the text which is to be interpreted and forms the link between the text and its expositor.[87]

If this be the case, then the real issue in biblical hermeneutics is not whether one comes to the text with certain interpretive principles but, rather, what are the *right* presuppositions. Some types of question are more appropriate to certain types of texts than others, while other kinds of question would be entirely inappropriate to a particular text. If one were studying the evolution of the Federal Reserve System, one would not put musical questions to the documents under examination. Now, all kinds of questions can be asked of the Bible. There are, for example, books on the flora and fauna of the Bible. However, the real question at the heart of the Bible is, What is the truth about human existence?

Now, when we interpret the Bible, what is our interest? Certainly the Bible is an historical document and we must interpret the Bible by the methods of historical research. . . . But what is our true and real interest? Are we to read the Bible only as an historical document in order to reconstruct an epoch of past history for which the Bible serves as a "source"? Or is it more than a source? I think our interest is really to hear what the Bible has to say for our actual present, to hear what is the truth about our life and about our soul.[88]

Some theologians (Barth, for example) would deny that the Bible is about human existence; rather, they would hold that the theme of the Bible is the self-revelation of God. Bultmann, however, rejects this separation between God and human existence and holds that the question of human life and the question of God's self-revelation are inseparable. This relationship is expressed classically in the words of Augustine: "Thou hast made us for Thyself, and our heart is restless, until it rests in Thee." Human life reflects a relation to God in the very question about God, whether put consciously or not. Thus, Bultmann contends that "Man's life is moved by the search for God because it is always moved, consciously or unconsciously, by the question about his own personal existence. The question of God and the question of myself are identical."[89]

If the right questions to be asked of the Bible are concerned with the possibilities of authentic human existence, then it is important to discover a philosophical anthropology that will most adequately conceptualize our human situation and bring to expression the real intention of the biblical texts. Bultmann believes that existentialist philosophy provides us with just the needed conceptual framework to carry out the task of demythologization in our time. More particularly, Heidegger's existential analytic can give new significance to such time-worn terms as "sin," "faith," "spirit," "flesh," "death," and "freedom."

Bultmann's critics, for example, Emil Brunner, have claimed that his use of Heidegger's existential analysis has predetermined the Bible's message by forcing that message to conform to Heidegger's conceptual scheme. However, Bultmann regards this criticism as mistaken, because Heidegger's existential analytic offers no normative pattern of authentic existence. Bultmann replies:

Existentialist philosophy does not say to me "in such and such a way you must exist"; it says only "you must exist"; or since even this claim may be too large, it shows me what it means to exist. . . . (Existentialism) is far from pretending that it secures for man a self-understanding of his own personal existence. For this self-understanding of my very personal existence can only be realized in the concrete moments of my "here" and "now." Existentialist philosophy, while it gives no answer to the question of my personal existence, makes personal existence my own personal responsibility, and by doing so it helps to make me open to the word of the Bible.[90]

Existential analysis can clarify our human situation in the world and even challenge us to exist authentically, but it cannot judge between rival claims to authentic existence. There is, however, a further reason why Heidegger's existentialist philosophy cannot serve as a kind of secular alternative to Christianity. Assuming that Heidegger describes authentic existence in a manner acceptable to Christians, he cannot prescribe how such an existence can be attained.

The question is whether the "nature" of man is realizable. Is it enough simply to show man what he ought to be? Can he achieve his authentic Being by a mere act of reflection? It is clear that philosophy, no less than theology, has always taken it for granted that man has to a greater or lesser degree erred and gone astray. . . . At the same time, however, these philosophers are convinced that all we need is to be told about the "nature" of man in order to realize it. . . . Is this self-confidence of the philosophers justified? Whatever the answer may be, it is at least clear that this is the point where they part company with the New Testament. For the latter affirms the total incapacity of man to release himself from his fallen state. That deliverance can come only by an act of God. . . . Here then is the crucial distinction between the New Testament and existentialism, between the Christian faith and the natural understanding of Being.[91]

It is at this point that Bultmann's program of demythologization has raised the most serious questions from his critics. He has called for a radical demythologizing of the New Testament and yet, as we have seen, he wishes to claim that authentic Christian existence is dependent on the unique and decisive act of God in Jesus Christ in the *kerygma*. Has not Bultmann set a definite limit to his own demythologizing in talking about an "act of God in Christ"? Does not such a limit involve a basic contradiction in his method which vitiates his program?[92] It appears clear that Bultmann wishes to carry out demythologization consistently. This involves demythologizing the event ("act of God") of Jesus Christ *insofar as that event is presented in mythical terms*. However, Bultmann does not consider the action of God in Jesus Christ to be *essentially* mythical. It is here that he parts company with those theologians, such as Fritz Buri, who call for a *dekerygmatizing* of the New Testament and a transformation of New Testament theology into a philosophy of existence.[93] Bultmann underlines this difference in the conclusion of his provocative essay:

We have now outlined a programme for the demythologizing of the New Testament. Are there still any surviving traces of mythology? There certainly are for those who regard all language about an act of God or of a decisive, eschatological event as mythological. But this is not mythology in the traditional sense, not the kind of mythology that has become antiquated with the decay of the mythical world view. For the redemption of which we have spoken is not a miraculous supernatural event, but an historical event wrought out in time and space. . . . For the kerygma maintains that the eschatological emissary of God is a concrete figure of a particular historical past, that his eschatological activity was wrought out in a human fate, and that therefore it is an event whose eschatological character does not admit of secular proof.[94]

Bultmann insists upon the decisive action of God in the *kerygma* and that this points to the real *skandalon* of Christian faith. He also insists that the Christian self-understanding comes only by the action of God as that action is renewed in the preaching of the Word. Such a self-understanding lies outside the possibility of individuals to create for themselves. The action of God in Christ is then a concrete, historical event but *also* an eschatological event; i.e., an event which "does not admit of secular proof" and is hidden to all but the eyes of faith. This explains why Bultmann considers the *historical* (i.e., accessible to scientific research apart from faith) Jesus irrelevant to faith and yet insists on the decisive historical action of God *in* Christ and nowhere else.

The way in which Bultmann proffers a non-mythological interpretation of the event of Jesus Christ, while holding to the historical yet eschatological character of the event, is best seen in his demythologization of the Cross and Resurrection. Bultmann admits that these events are couched in the language of ancient Hellenistic cult-myths, a meaningless language to modern persons. But this mythical form is not required to understand the intention of this message. Bultmann asserts that "in its redemptive aspect the cross of Christ is no mere mythical event but a *permanent historical fact originating in the past historical event which is the crucifixion of Jesus.*"[95] (Italics added.) What is most significant about the cross is not that it happened once but that when it did happen "it created a new and perma-

nent situation in history." The abiding significance of the Cross is that it stands for the judgment of God on human sin and the offer of new life through God's grace. Thus—

to believe in the cross of Christ does not mean to concern ourselves with a mythical process wrought outside us and our world . . . but rather to make the cross of Christ our own, to undergo crucifixion with him. . . . As far as its meaning—that is, its meaning for faith is concerned, it is an ever-present reality.[96]

Bultmann frankly denies that the Resurrection is an empirical fact in the realm of human history. Rather, "the cross and the resurrection form a single, indivisible cosmic event."[97] "Indeed," says Bultmann, "*faith in the resurrection is really the same thing as faith in the saving efficacy of the cross.*"[98] The event of Easter *in itself* is not an event of past history. The Resurrection is an historical event separable from the Cross *only* in terms of the Apostles' faith in the risen Christ, which became the basis of the apostolic preaching. If we ask how we can come to believe in the saving efficacy of the Christ event, the answer is "faith in the word of preaching."

Once again, in everyday life the Christians participate not only in the death of Christ but also in his resurrection. In this resurrection life they enjoy a freedom, albeit of struggling freedom, from sin (Rom. 6:11 ff.). They are able to "cast off the works of darkness," so that the approaching day when the darkness shall vanish is already experienced here and now. . . . Through the word of preaching the cross and the resurrection are made present: the eschatological "now" is here, and the promise of Isa. 49:8 is fulfilled: "Behold, now is the acceptable time; behold, now is the day of salvation" (2 Cor. 6:2).[99]

In the existential response of faith to this message comes a new self-understanding, which is distinctively Christian. It is a summons to die to the old self and all worldly security and to place one's faith in the grace of God. "It means faith that the unseen, intangible reality actually confronts us as love, opening up our future and signifying not death but life."[100]

The message of Christian faith is not then principally concerned with events in the historical past, nor with a hope for some saving eschatological event in the temporal future. The Christian message is the word of God's judgment and God's grace here and now. As Bultmann concludes:

The meaning in history lies always in the present, and when the present is conceived as the eschatological present by Christian faith the meaning in history is realized. . . . Always in your present lies the meaning in history, and you cannot see it as a spectator, but only in your responsible decisions. In every moment slumbers the possibility of being the eschatological moment. You must awaken it.[101]

CONCLUSION

Twentieth-century existentialism afforded theology a contemporary language and an analysis of the human condition that in many respects parallel themes of classical Christianity. Its method of correlation posed those ultimate questions about existence that Christianity perennially has sought to answer. More than this, it offered theology a categorical scheme and style of doing theology that hit a particularly responsive chord in the mid-century "age of anxiety." In stressing the irrational and absurd, in speaking of human fallenness, depersonalization, anxiety, inauthenticity, and the demands of radical decision, Existentialism sounded the modern temper. In using Existentialism as an interpretive tool, Christian theology once again gave evidence of its resilience and its ability to meet the challenge of modern secular culture.

Christian Existentialism has, of course, been criticized from several directions (see e.g. Chapter Nine). It often has been charged with irrationalism, or, as Jacques Maritain charged, with confusing a genuine existential struggle for salvation with philosophical knowledge.[102] It would be difficult, however, to make this charge against the thinkers discussed in this chapter. At the other extreme are those who claim that, through their use of Existentialism, Tillich and Bultmann have distorted the Christian message by foisting an alien philosophy upon the Bible.[103] There may be some justification in this claim but, before merely asserting it, the charge must be tested in specific cases.

A criticism of theological Existentialism that is rather widely held is one that was mentioned earlier and was directed against the Dialectical theology, that is, against its conception of historical revelation. Following Barth, both Tillich and Bultmann wish to assume certain historical facts concerning God's action in Jesus but, at the same time, want to insulate this history from historical-critical research. They want to claim or to assume certain things about Jesus that are immune to any historical examination. Many critics feel not only that this is unwarranted, if Christianity is to continue to claim its historical bases, but also that this disinterest in the problem of the historical Jesus has tended to transform biblical revelation into an ontological abstraction in the case of Tillich, and to cause Bultmann to speak of revelation as a rather contentless or formless call to decision. The problem of faith and history remains one of the unresolved issues in Existentialist theology and a major cause of dissatisfaction with this theology among the younger generation of theologians who were students of Barth, Tillich, and Bultmann.[104]

Many critics also find the existentialist doctrine of God to be problematical in many respects. Buber's Eternal Thou, Tillich's Being-itself and "God above God," and Bultmann's hidden and paradoxical God have evoked positive responses from many believers, but theologians and metaphysicians, such as Maritain, find this kind of theistic discourse experientially evocative but elusive and resistant to analysis, as well as incommunicable to those who do not stand within the circle of faith. Some theologians believe that the contemporary crisis of Christian belief is traceable to the failure of Ritschlianism, Dialectical theology, and Existentialism to ground faith in a reasonably convincing doctrine of God. Thus some of the new generation of Protestant theologians are joining with Catholic theologians in a call for a reformulated Christian *natural* theology, as we will see, particularly in Chapter Ten.

NOTES

1. *Grundsätze der Philosophie der Zukunft* (Zurich, 1843), p. 78. Cited in Paul Tillich, *Theology of Culture* (New York, 1964), p. 89.

2. Søren Kierkegaard, *Concluding Unscientific Postscript* (Princeton, 1941), p. 173.

3. Søren Kierkegaard, *Training in Christianity* (Princeton, 1944), p. 87.

4. Martin Luther, *Lecture on Psalm 5, Luther's Works*, V, (Weimar ed., 1833) p. 183.

5. Gabriel Marcel, *The Philosophy of Existence* (Chicago, 1952), pp. 2–3.

6. Karl Jaspers, *Man in the Modern Age* (London, 1933), p. 241.

7. Gabriel Marcel, *Mystery of Being*, II (Chicago, 1960), p. 55.

8. Paul Tillich, "What Is Wrong with the 'Dialectic' Theology?" *The Journal of Religion*, 35 (April 1935).

9. Paul Tillich, *Systematic Theology*, I (Chicago, 1951), p. 14.

10. Ibid., p. 12.

11. Paul Tillich, *Dynamics of Faith* (New York, 1957), pp. 1–2.

12. Tillich, *Systematic Theology*, I, p. 14.

13. Paul Tillich, *The Courage to Be* (New Haven, 1952); see especially Ch. 3.

14. Ibid., pp. 66, 68.

15. Tillich, *Dynamics of Faith*, pp. 18–20.

16. Tillich, *Systematic Theology*, I, p. 8.

17. Ibid., p. 23.

18. Ibid., p. 64.

19. Paul Tillich, *Systematic Theology*, II (Chicago, 1957), p. 27.

20. Ibid., p. 29.

21. Ibid., pp. 31–33.

22. Ibid., p. 33.

23. Ibid., pp. 33–34.

24. Ibid., p. 34.

25. Ibid., pp. 34–35.

26. Ibid., pp. 35–36.

27. Ibid., p. 38.

28. Ibid., p. 41.

29. Ibid., p. 43. For a critique of Tillich on this point, see the remarks of Reinhold Niebuhr in "Biblical Thought and Ontological Speculation in Tillich's Theology," in *The Theology of Paul Tillich*, ed. C. W. Kegley and R. W. Bretall (New York, 1952).

30. Ibid., p. 44.

31. Ibid., p. 46.

32. Ibid.

33. Ibid., p. 62.

34. Ibid., p. 63.

35. See especially Tillich, *Systematic Theology*, II, pp. 59–86, and Tillich, *The Courage to Be*, Ch. 2–3.

36. Tillich, *Systematic Theology*, II, pp. 80, 86.

37. Tillich, *Systematic Theology*, I, p. 206.

38. Ibid.

39. Ibid., p. 235.

40. Ibid.

41. Ibid., p. 237.

42. Ibid., p. 242.

43. Ibid., pp. 244–245.

44. Ibid., p. 273.

45. Ibid., pp. 276–277.

46. Tillich, *Systematic Theology*, II, p. 97.

47. Ibid., pp. 98–99.

48. Ibid., p. 102.

49. Ibid., pp. 116–117.

50. Ibid., p. 115.

51. Ibid., p. 114.

52. On this comparison, see Mark Kline Taylor, ed., *Paul Tillich: Theologian of the Boundaries* (Minneapolis, 1991).

53. "A Reinterpretation of the Doctrine of the Incarnation," *Church Quarterly Review*, CXLVII (1949), 145.

54. Ibid., p. 146.

55. Tillich, *Systematic Theology*, I, p. 133.

56. Tillich, *Systematic Theology*, II, p. 118.

57. Ibid., pp. 118–119.

58. Ibid., p. 126.

59. Ibid., p. 131.

60. Ibid., p. 134.

61. Ibid., p. 148.

62. Ibid.

63. Ibid., p. 150.

64. Ibid., p. 166.

65. Ibid., p. 167.

66. Ibid.

67. Ibid.

68. Ibid., p. 168.

69. Paul Tillich, *Systematic Theology*, III (Chicago, 1963) p. 249.

70. Ibid., p. 134.

71. Ibid., p. 274.

72. Ibid., p. 259.

73. Ibid., p. 260.

74. Ibid.

75. Ibid., p. 392.

76. Charles W. Kegley, ed., *The Theology of Rudolf Bultmann* (New York, 1966), p. xxiv.

77. Rudolf Bultmann, *Jesus Christ and Mythology* (New York, 1958), pp. 15–16.

78. Ibid., p. 61.

79. Ibid., pp. 61–62.

80. Ibid., p. 62.

81. Ibid., pp. 63–64.

82. Rudolf Bultmann, "How Does God Speak through the Bible," in *Existence and Faith*, ed. Schubert Ogden (Cleveland, 1966), p. 169.

83. Ian Henderson, *Rudolf Bultmann* (Richmond, IN., 1966) p. 47.

84. Rudolf Bultmann, "New Testament and Mythology," in *Kerygma and Myth*, I, ed. Hans Werner Bartsch (London, 1953), pp. 1–2.

85. Ibid., pp. 10–11.

86. Bultmann, *Jesus Christ and Mythology*, pp. 32–33.

87. *Essays Philosophical and Theological* (London, 1955), p. 240.

88. Bultmann, *Jesus Christ and Mythology*, pp. 51–52.

89. Ibid., p. 53.

90. Ibid., pp. 55–56.

91. *Kerygma and Myth*, op. cit., pp. 27, 33.

92. John Macquarrie argues in *The Scope of Demythologizing* that Bultmann imposes this limit upon demythologization and this constitutes the fundamental paradox in his thought. In *Christ Without Myth*, Schubert Ogden (see Chapter Ten) contends that Bultmann sets no limits to demythologizing the New Testament and that in not demythologizing the once-for-all act of God in Christ, Bultmann has failed to carry out his program consistently.

93. For Buri's critique of Bultmann, see "Entmythologisierung oder Entkerygmatisierung der Theologie," *Kerygma und Mythos*, Band II; and "Theologie der Existenz," *Kerygma und Mythos*, Band III.

94. *Kerygma and Myth*, I, op. cit., pp. 43–44.

95. Ibid., p. 37.

96. Ibid., p. 36.

97. Ibid., p. 38.

98. Ibid., p. 41.

99. Ibid., pp. 40, 42–43.

100. Ibid., p. 119.

101. Rudolf Bultmann, *History and Eschatology* (Edinburgh, 1957), p. 155.

102. Jacques Maritain, *Existence and the Existent* (New York, 1966), p. 125.

103. For a critique of Tillich on this point, see R. Niebuhr, "Biblical Thought and Ontological Speculation in Tillich's Theology," and Kenneth Hamilton, *The System and the Gospel* (London, 1963). For a similar critique of Bultmann, see Volumes I and II of *Kerygma and Myth*, op. cit.

104. For an excellent analysis and critique of the problem of historical revelation in Dialectical and Existentialist theology, see Van A. Harvey, *The Historian and the Believer*, (New York, 1966), Ch. V.

SUGGESTIONS FOR FURTHER READING

Existentialism

The literature on Existentialism is immense. The following general studies are recommended:

Barrett, William. *Irrational Man: A Study in Existentialist Philosophy* (New York: 1958).

Blackman, H. J. *Six Existentialist Thinkers* (New York: 1952).

Collins, James. *The Existentialists: A Critical Study* (Chicago: Henry Regnery, 1952).

Heinemann, F. H. *Existentialism and the Modern Predicament* (New York: Harper, 1954).

Kuhn, Helmut. *Encounter with Nothingness: An Essay on Existentialism* (Chicago: Henry Regnery, 1949)

Wild, John. *The Challenge of Existentialism* (Bloomington: Indiana University Press, 1955).

Among the books dealing in general with Existentialism and Christian belief are:

Michalson, Carl, ed. *Christianity and the Existentialists* (New York: Charles Scribner's Sons, 1956).

Roberts, David. *Existentialism and Religious Belief* (New York: Oxford University Press, 1959).

Gabriel Marcel

Cain, Seymour. *Gabriel Marcel* (New York: Hillary House, 1963).

Gallagher, Kenneth T. *The Philosophy of Gabriel Marcel* (New York: Fordham University Press, 1962).

McCown, Joe. *Availability: Gabriel Marcel and the Phenomenology of Human Openness* (Missoula, Mont.: Scholars Press, 1978).

Miceli, Vincent P., S.J. *Ascent to Being: Gabriel Marcel's Philosophy of Communion* (New York: Desclee Company, 1965).

Schilpp, Paul A., and Lewis Edwin Hahn, ed. *The Philosophy of Gabriel Marcel* (LaSalle, Ill.: Open Court, 1984). Essays by noted philosophers on all aspects of Marcel's work.

Paul Tillich

The studies of Paul Tillich's theology are numerous. The following books represent a variety of critical positions:

Clayton, John P. *The Concept of Correlation* (New York and Berlin: de Gruyter, 1980). The best study of this key methodological issue in Tillich's theology.

Gilkey, Langdon. *Gilkey on Tillich* (New York: Crossroad, 1990). A perceptive, sympathetic study.

Kegley, Charles W. *The Theology of Paul Tillich* (New York: Pilgrim Press, 1982). A collection of essays by noted theologians and philosophers.

Kelsey, David H. *The Fabric of Paul Tillich's Theology* (New Haven: Yale University Press, 1967). An excellent analysis of the sources and structure of argument of Tillich's *Systematic Theology*.

McKelway, Alexander J. *The Systematic Theology of Paul Tillich* (Richmond, Va.: John Knox Press, 1964). A helpful survey of the major themes of Tillich's theology. McKelway criticizes Tillich from a Barthian perspective.

O'Meara, Thomas A. and Weissner, C.D., ed. *Paul Tillich in Catholic Thought* (Dubuque, Iowa: Priory Press, 1964).

Pauck, Wilhelm, and Marion Pauck. *Paul Tillich: His Life and Thought Vol. I: Life* (New York: Harper and Row, 1976). The best account in English of Tillich's life. Also see Tillich's autobiographical reflections in *On the Boundary: An Autobiographical Sketch* (New York: Charles Scribner's Sons, 1966).

Stone, Ronald H. *Paul Tillich's Radical Social Thought* (Atlanta: John Knox Press, 1980). A survey of Tillich's writings on social and ethical themes as well as his social and political engagements.

Thomas, J. Heywood. *Paul Tillich: An Appraisal* (Philadelphia: Westminster Press, 1963). A sympathetic yet critical assessment of Tillich's doctrines using the tools of logical analysis.

Rudolf Bultmann

Bartsch, Hans W., ed. *Kerygma and Myth*, Vol. I and II (London: S.P.C.K., 1953 and 1962). A valuable collection of essays on Bultmann's program of demythologization.

Hobbs, Edward C., ed. *Bultmann: Retrospect and Prospect* (Philadelphia: Fortress Press, 1985). A fine collection of essays.

Johnson, Roger A. *The Origins of Demythologizing* (Leiden: E. J. Brill, 1974). Important study of the historical and philosophical background of Bultmann's use of myth and the program of demythologizing.

Kegley, Charles W., ed. *The Theology of Rudolf Bultmann* (New York: Harper and Row, 1966). Essays on the whole range of Bultmann's theology and its significance.

Macquarrie, John. *An Existentialist Theology* (New York: Macmillan, 1955). A comparison of Bultmann and Heidegger.

———. *The Scope of Demythologizing* (New York: Harper, 1960). An excellent survey of the critical responses to Bultmann's demythologizing and attempt to clarify the central issue.

Ogden, Schubert M. *Christ Without Myth.* (New York: Harper, 1961). This book and those by Macquarrie represent the most incisive analyses of Bultmann's theology.

Perrin, Norman. *The Promise of Bultmann* (Philadelphia: J. B. Lippincott, 1969). Excellent brief study, especially good on the issues of New Testament theology.

Schmithals, Walter. *An Introduction to the Theology of Rudolf Bultmann*, trans. John Bowden (Minneapolis: Augsburg Publishing House, 1968). A comprehensive study of all aspects of Bultmann's work as historian and theologian.

Chapter Six

Christian Realism:
A Post-Liberal American Theology

Reinhold Niebuhr

INTRODUCTION

In Chapters Three and Four we spoke of the decline of Liberal theology in Europe between the two World Wars. In America, theological liberalism maintained an important though vulnerable position during the 1920s and 1930s. It was attacked on the right by a vocal and well-organized Fundamentalism and on the left by a naturalistic humanism critical of the exclusive claims of Christian theism but responsive to religious values. Despite the influence of a few theologians, such as Henry Nelson Wieman, and a few apologists such as Shailer Mathews (see Chapter Two) and the popular preacher Harry Emerson Fosdick, Protestant Liberalism's sphere of influence was narrowing.

Out of this situation emerged a new theological movement in America, which, though superficially comparable to European movements often referred to as Neo-Orthodox, could embrace neither the older liberalism (whether Ritschlian or Modernist) nor Barthianism. Rather, it sought to formulate a new liberal theology on a more *realistic* basis. The beginning of what came to be called "American Realistic" theology is frequently associated with the publication of *Religious Realism* (1931), edited by Douglas C. Macintosh, which included an essay by H. Richard Niebuhr entitled "Religious Realism in the Twentieth Century," and with Reinhold Niebuhr's *Moral Man and Immoral Society* (1932). It was the latter book, perhaps more than any other, that launched the American attack on the premises of liberalism.

Though Reinhold Niebuhr was the dominant voice, there were others—some independent of his influence—who, in the early years of the 1930s, were raising serious questions about the ability of Liberal Christianity to meet the intellectual and social realities of the day. In 1931, Henry P. Van Dusen, a young teacher at Union Theological Seminary, was writing about "The Sickness of Liberal Religion."[1] In 1933 an article by John C. Bennett entitled "After Liberalism—What?"[2] appeared in *The Christian Century*. A few years later, in the same journal, Harry Emerson Fosdick, the great defender of liberalism, published his famous article "Beyond Modernism."[3] Liberalism and Modernism were now under attack by some of their most illustrious earlier supporters. The spirit of the new movement was summarized in Walter Marshall Horton's book *Realistic Theology* (1934), written during the economic crisis of the Depression and growing uncertainty about America's role in the world. A few years earlier, Horton had been an eager apologist for a scientific Liberal theology and was closely allied with the Modernism of H. N. Wieman. Now he found liberalism defunct, its doctrines

as dead as the shibboleths of the Gnostics and the Arians though they have only just died and their flesh is still warm. They have not died as a result of any concerted, effective attack upon their validity, but simply as a result of a general change in the intellectual climate.[4]

The root weakness of liberalism, as viewed by the Realists, was its optimistic doctrine of human nature and its naïve vision of the amelioration of evil. Horton now had to confess that orthodoxy had spoken the truth about humanity.

I believe orthodox Christianity represents a profound insight into the whole human predicament. I believe that the basic human difficulty is the perversion of the will, that betrayal of divine trust, which is called sin; and I believe that sin is in a sense a racial disease, transmissible from generation to generation. In affirm-

ing these things, the Christian fathers and the Protestant Reformers spoke as realists, and could have assembled masses of empirical evidence to support their views.[5]

In his article "After Liberalism—What?" John C. Bennett pointed to the extraordinary theological implications of the liberal confidence in humanity itself.

The premise of liberalism is faith in man and his highest values as the clue to the nature of God. This faith in man makes possible confidence in human reason and insight as the basis of authority in religion. It makes possible the emphasis upon the immanence of God. It makes possible the identification of the divinity of Christ with his ideal humanity. It makes possible the optimistic faith in progress which is now under such a cloud. . . . I think that *the best short-cut to an understanding of the present theological situation is to realize that liberalism diverges from orthodoxy and neo-orthodoxy in its various forms in its doctrine of man, and that other differences follow from that.*[6]

As was pointed out earlier, the various forms of Continental Neo-Orthodoxy did not represent a complete break with the liberal tradition in Protestant theology. However, the American Realists sustain much closer ties with liberalism than did Continental Neo-Orthodoxy, in spite of their rejection of the more extreme liberal doctrines. Reinhold Niebuhr may appear to contradict this claim, but a careful reading of Niebuhr shows that he was carrying on his battle on two fronts, against the older liberalism on the one side and the orthodox and Barthian theology on the other.

Niebuhr's realism was always aware of the danger of an uncritical biblicism, which he identified not only with traditional orthodoxy and with American Fundamentalism but also with the theology of Karl Barth. Furthermore, Niebuhr was essentially a theologian of correlation, joining the insights of the Bible with the pragmatic realities of personal and historical experience. His Realist position is well expressed in an essay written in 1931:

In Anglo-Saxon countries the conflict between faith and reason is not insisted upon so sharply, and religious thought still expresses itself in terms less tragic than those upon which the Continent insists. . . . We may need the tragic conception of history and of the futility of moral effort, lest our religion sink into the sands of complacent moral optimism. But on the other hand we will continue to believe that we have a right to express ourselves religiously without completely sacrificing a philosophy of nature and of history which links our faith in God to the facts of common experience.[7]

In later years Reinhold Niebuhr became increasingly experiential and pragmatic in his pronouncements on religious and ethical issues no matter how they may have challenged revered traditional dogmas. What all the Realists sought, however, was a new, chastened liberalism, corrected by the stubborn realism about the human condition and history that was the heritage of classical Christianity and the Protestant Reformers.

The American Realists* saw themselves as continuing the liberal tradition in theology "with a view," in Horton's words, "to carrying over and incorporating into our realistic theology whatever genuine values may be rescued from the wreck, for liberalism still stands for precious truths and values which must not be allowed to die."[8] The spirit of the movement is expressed in Bennett's characterization of himself as "a changed liberal—but still a liberal."[9]

Among those identified with the movement were Walter Marshall Horton (1895–1966), John C. Bennett (1902–1995), H. Richard Niebuhr (1894–1962), and Reinhold Niebuhr (1892–1971). All of these men had distinguished careers as professors of theology and as leaders in the ecumenical movement. They left an indelible impression on a whole generation of churchmen and teachers who occupied positions in the forefront of American Protestantism. Here we will exemplify Realistic theology in the thought of its two most notable representatives: Reinhold Niebuhr and his brother H. Richard Niebuhr.

H. RICHARD NIEBUHR

Like so many of the thinkers we have studied, Reinhold and H. Richard Niebuhr were sons of the manse. Their father, Gustav Niebuhr, was a pastor of the German Evangelical and Reformed Church in Wright City, Missouri, where the two brothers were born. Both Niebuhrs attended their small denominational schools, Elmhurst College and Eden Theological Seminary.

After graduation from seminary, H. Richard Niebuhr served as pastor of a church in St. Louis from 1916 to 1918, during which time he received an M.A. from Washington University. He returned to Eden Seminary as a teacher between 1919 and 1922 but interrupted more than a decade of service to his college and seminary to complete his graduate studies at Yale. Niebuhr received the B.D. degree from Yale in 1923 and the Ph.D., with a dissertation on Ernst Troeltsch, in 1924. Between 1924 and 1927, Niebuhr served as president of Elmhurst College and from 1927 to 1931 as professor of theology at Eden Seminary. In 1931 he returned to Yale to teach in the Divinity School. At the time of his death in 1962, he was Sterling Professor of Theology and Christian Ethics at Yale.

We have underlined the fact that Christian Realism represents an effort to formulate a new

---

* Because of the many associations of the word "realism" in twentieth-century philosophy and theology, some clarification of the term "Realistic theology" is perhaps in order. Realistic theology is not to be confused with either the slightly older "religious realism" associated with D. C. Macintosh and H. N. Wieman (see Ch. Two) or with the metaphysical realism of Samuel Alexander, A. N. Whitehead, and Charles Hartshorne (see Ch. Ten) or with Catholic Neo-Thomist realism (see Vol. I, Ch. 13). Religious realism was realistic in its epistemology and in its view of God (following the empirical, scientific method), and against Idealism and moral subjectivism. Realist metaphysics rejected the Idealist conception of mind and Idealism's dismissal of the spatiotemporal world as merely the phenomenal appearance of a timeless reality. Some of the Realist theologians, notably Horton, Robert Calhoun, and H. R. Niebuhr, were influenced by the new realism in epistemology and metaphysics, but the distinctive mark of Realistic theology was neither its theory of knowledge nor its metaphysics. What chiefly characterized this theology was its realism concerning human nature and human history.

Liberal theology on a *realistic* basis. In that effort it remained open to the best in the liberal heritage *and* the classical Christian tradition, while appropriating some of the more radical insights of the new Continental theology, represented by Kierkegaard and Karl Barth. The complexity of influences that make up Christian Realism is exemplified in the development of H. Richard Niebuhr's theology.

Niebuhr remained deeply committed to the nineteenth-century tradition, which ran from Schleiermacher through Ritschl to Troeltsch. With Schleiermacher and Ritschl he stressed the experiential root of theological reflection—that God cannot be known outside of the personal response of faith. From Troeltsch he gained a radically historical and sociological orientation toward theology. But there were other, newer influences that began to take hold of Niebuhr in the 1930s. Chief among these was the rediscovery of Jonathan Edwards and the European theologians of "crisis"—particularly Paul Tillich, Kierkegaard, and Karl Barth. What Niebuhr found in these writers was a radical monotheism that stressed the priority of God's being and action over the human and their devastating attack on liberal "anthropomorphism." The influence of the new Continental theology is evident in Niebuhr's contribution to D. C. Macintosh's *Religious Realism*, published in 1931. There he wrote:

The anthropocratic and anthropocentric spirit of the nineteenth century is by no means exhausted. But a varied revolt against its dominance has arisen and despite the variety this revolt has a common realistic character. . . . All of these movements of religious realism are united by a common interest in maintaining the independent reality of the religious object. Hence they represent a movement distinctly different from nineteenth century liberal theology which found its center of gravity in the idea of the ethical value of religion. Though realism shares this ethical interest and accepts many of the critical results of liberalism, it has shifted the center of interest from the subject to the object, from man to God, from that which is purely immanent in religious experience to that which is also transcendent.[10]

Niebuhr's first book, *The Social Sources of Denominationalism* (1929), influenced by his study of Troeltsch, exposed those ethnic, economic, and cultural factors that fragment the Christian churches, binding them to narrow ideological commitments and blinding them to some obvious facts. Nevertheless, the book reveals an ambivalent attitude toward the older liberalism, as did Reinhold Niebuhr's books during the same period. Theologically the book represents "a late-flowering of the older Social Gospel in its Christian Socialist aspect."[11]

This new realism and radical monotheism make their appearance in Niebuhr's second book, *The Kingdom of God in America* (1937). It is here that Niebuhr's break with the older liberalism is made clear, most powerfully in his oft-quoted judgment on the Social Gospel: "A God without wrath brought men without sin into a kingdom without judgment through the ministrations of a Christ without a cross."[12] From this point on a single dominant chord runs through Niebuhr's works, namely, the shift of emphasis from the human and the sociological to the sovereignty of God. The thesis of the book is that, despite the sociological and cultural differences that separate the Protestant churches in America, the great common element of American faith is its expectation of the Kingdom of God; and that religion is the key to explaining the American experience. In these first two books Niebuhr helped to change the historiography of American religion.

Along with the other Realists, Niebuhr now finds the root failure of liberalism in its superficial doctrine of human nature and history. It is to this defect that liberalism's inadequate notion of God and salvation are traceable. For Niebuhr, a realistic doctrine of human nature must include recognition of the fact of sin as *disloyalty*—that is, the human failure to worship the true God, while giving one's ultimate loyalty to something other than God. Positively considered, the essence of such sin is *idolatry*, and it is this idolatrous propensity that Niebuhr discovers in liberal anthropocentrism. The theme of radical monotheism—which remains the dominant motif in Niebuhr's theological writings between 1940 and

H.R. Niebuhr

Through the medium of language, with its names and categories, its grammar and syntax, its logic, I have been introduced to the system of nature, that is, to the *system* of nature as *systematized* by society. I classify the events and find their meaning in their relations to each other but do so always with the aid of the a priori categories of my social, historical reason, derived from my companions. To them I look not only for the categorical schemes with which I organize and interpret natural events but also for the verification of my reports of my direct encounters with nature. Hence it is that the concept of nature has a history and that men respond to natural events in varying ways in different periods of social history, on the basis of their different interpretations.[14]

For Niebuhr, awareness of our historical relativity is one of the seminal ideas affecting our present way of thinking. Theology, too, has had to confess its limitations; i.e., that theology cannot describe God as such but only as known in and through human language and experience. Christian faith, then, begins with a revelation that has been mediated through an historical community, the Church. Here Niebuhr joins Schleiermacher with Barth. Theology begins with the faith of the Church, with what persons believe and what they see from the standpoint of the Christian community.

Such a stance is not unique to the Christian vision, for we all stand within some social and cultural matrix that gives orientation and meaning to our experience. Hence, every person should recognize the relativity of his or her apprehension of the truth or the absolute, and that his or her understanding involves an existential factor. Expressed in another way, we should acknowledge that we live by faith. For Niebuhr, such a faith is not to be construed as intellectual assent to the truth of certain propositions but understood as an original, practical relationship of trust, reliance, or confidence. Such a faith is present as much in the scientist's trust in the intelligibility of things as in the daily confidence that we have in one another as persons.

Niebuhr offers the example of the positivist philosopher A. J. Ayer, famous for declaring that all metaphysical and religious statements are

1960—is what marks him off with the other Realists as a postliberal theologian.

During this same period, Niebuhr was consumed with another question that reveals his dependence on and continuity with the nineteenth-century liberal tradition. It is the question of how divine revelation—i.e., knowledge of God—is communicated and validated. In seeking to answer this fundamental theological question, Niebuhr had recourse to Kant, Schleiermacher, and Troeltsch.[13] Thus, Niebuhr's theology can be viewed as a sophisticated effort to mediate the concerns of Ernst Troeltsch and Karl Barth—a fact that sets his theology apart from both the older liberalism and Continental Neo-Orthodoxy, and makes it an important contemporary alternative. To see how Niebuhr attempts such a mediation requires an examination of the central themes of his major works.

Human Faith and Faith in God

Niebuhr begins his theological work with an acknowledgment of his indebtedness to Kant. We do not know things as they exist in themselves. Our knowledge is always conditioned by the point of view that we occupy in space and time.

meaningless and that our moral convictions are simply emotive desires. Yet in his influential book *Language, Truth, and Logic,* Ayer professes his trust in sense experience and the scientific method and acknowledges that we must rely "on senses to substantiate or confute the judgments which are based on our sensations." Niebuhr calls attention to the fact that "this is indeed a faith, an expression of sheer trust in what is not sensibly experienced, since the continuity and unity of sense-experience is not something that is sensed." What we detect in Ayer's discourse is

a kind of structure of faith. . . . He relies on science because he is loyal to human life, not his own merely; and because science is based on sense-experience which he trusts. There are three objects of faith here: sense-experience, science, and human values. And faith moves in a kind of circle justifying reliance on each of these three subjects by reference to the others.[15]

This kind of faith is universal and can rightly be called religious.

This is the faith that life is worth living, or better, the reliance on certain centers of value as able to bestow significance and worth on our existence. It is a curious and inescapable fact about our lives, of which I think we all become aware at some time or another, that we cannot live without a cause, without some object of devotion, some center of worth, something on which we rely for our meaning. In this sense all men have faith because they are men and cannot help themselves, just as they must and do have some knowledge of their world, though their knowledge be erroneous.[16]

We all rely or trust in something, have some object of commitment and loyalty. According to Niebuhr, to have such a faith and to have a god are one and the same thing.

We arrive, then, at the problem of deity by setting out from the universal human experience of faith, of reliance or trust in something. Luther expressed this idea long ago when he asked, "What does it mean to have a god, or what is God?" and answered his question by saying, "Trust and faith of the heart alone

make both God and idol. . . . For the two, faith and God, hold close together. Whatever then thy heart clings to . . . and relies upon, that is properly thy God."[17]

The object of our faith can be almost anything. Some people place their faith in science, in a political ideal, in their nation, in themselves, or in a particular religion. Most individuals are divided and have many competing sources of faith and loyalty. Hence, polytheism is actually the dominant religion of most human beings. But we recognize, unconsciously at least, that such gods are finite, that

none of these beings on which we rely to give content and meaning to our lives is able to supply continuous meaning and value. The causes for which we live all die . . . the ideals we fashion are revealed by time to be relative. . . . At the end nothing is left to defend us against the void of meaninglessness. We try to evade this knowledge, but it is ever in the background of our minds. . . . We know that "on us and all our race the slow, sure doom falls pitiless and dark."[18]

Because we are torn by competing loyalties, we are divided selves; we lack any unified inner history. But even a single, unifying loyalty may prove to be the source of anxiety and disappointment if one's faith is placed in some god whose power, goodness, and absoluteness are uncertain. Such doubt often leads to the worst kind of fanaticism. Faith can be both integrating and liberating only when it is faith in that reality which is the absolute and eternal ground of being—that which will abide when all else passes. Such faith drives us away from reliance on all finite values and expectations and even enables us to say of this reality, "Though it slay us yet will we trust it." "And insofar as our faith . . . has been attached to this source and enemy of all our gods, we have been enabled to call this reality God."[19]

Now, Being or being-itself, which the person of faith addresses as God, can be encountered in other ways as well. We may respond to Being authentically but negatively or cynically. An example of a genuinely religious yet profoundly negative response to Being is that of Bertrand Russell in "*A Free Man's Worship.*"[20] The important point here is that there is no final, objective way of deciding which apprehensions and response to Being are true. Hence, one must begin with revelation, with the way Being has been revealed in personal, existential encounter. Every self begins with faith in the way Being reveals itself to him or to her and, according to Niebuhr, one person's response (e.g., the atheist's) cannot simply assume to be based on more objective information than another's. All such commitments reach beyond the limits of our scientific experience and therefore are personal, existential, and relativistic.

Despite the relativity of all revelation, Niebuhr is concerned to distinguish his view from subjectivism.

Relativism does not imply subjectivism and scepticism. It is not evident that the man who is forced to confess that his view of things is conditioned by the standpoint he occupies must doubt the reality of what he sees. It is not apparent that one who knows that his concepts are not universal must also doubt that they are concepts of the universal, or that one who understands how all his experience is historically mediated must believe that nothing is mediated through history.[21]

The principal reason why revelation is not to be considered subjective is that it is not an individualistic affair. Our apprehension of Being, the way God is revealed, is always to persons in history, i.e., to persons in a social, communal context. Revelation is never given in a vacuum; it is mediated to us through a community that has largely shaped our angle of vision. Thus "every view of the universal from the finite standpoint of the individual in such a society is subject to the test of experience on the part of companions who look from the same standpoint in the same direction."[22] Our faith is not without social corroboration but, Niebuhr argues, "it is not to be gained either from consultation with those who, occupying a differ-

ent point of view, look in a different direction and toward other realities than we do."[23]

The Confessional Method in Theology: Inner and Outer History

Another way of speaking of revelation as personal and communal is to see revelation as "the story of our life," as the existential appropriation of the personal memory of a community. The locus of revelation is in what Niebuhr calls "inner history"—that history in which selves are revealed to one another. Inner history is to be distinguished from "outer history." Outer or external history is impersonal history; it treats its data as objects. "Even when such history deals with human individuals it seeks to reduce them to impersonal parts."[24] In the terms of a Kantian critical idealism, Niebuhr would distinguish external history as the sphere of pure reason from internal history as the sphere of practical reason, or, in Martin Buber's formulation, the relations between the "I" and the "It" from relations between the "I" and the "Thou."

In external history value means a valency or measurable strength that can be reached impartially and objectively by any trained person who has access to the data.

In internal history, however, value means worth for selves; whatever cannot be so valued is unimportant and may be dropped from memory. Here the death of Socrates, the birth of Lincoln, Peter's martyrdom, Luther's reform . . . the granting of the Magna Carta are events to be celebrated. . . . Value here means quality, not power; but the quality of valued things is one which only selves can apprehend.[25]

Revelation is that history that makes life intelligible by giving a key or pattern to one's personal life and to history. The difference between history as lived and history as observed can perhaps best be seen in their different attitudes toward time.

In our internal history time has a different feel and quality from that of the external time with which we deal as exoteric historians. The latter time resembles that of physics. . . . All these time-concepts have one thing in common—they are all quantitative; all these times are numbered. Such time is always serial. In the series past events are gone and future happenings are not yet. In internal history, on the other hand, our time is our duration. What is past is not gone; it abides in us as our memory; what is future is not non-existent but present in us as our potentiality. Time here is organic or it is social. . . . We are not in this time but it is in us.[26]

There are, then, two ways of viewing the same historical event. Take, for example, the accounts of a blind man restored to sight.

Of a man who has been blind and who has come to see, two histories can be written. A scientific case history will describe what happened to his optic nerve or to the crystalline lens, what technique the surgeon used or by what medicines a physician wrought the cure, through what stages of recovery the patient passed. An autobiography, on the other hand, may barely mention these things but it will tell what happened to a self that had lived in darkness and now saw again trees and the sunrise, children's faces and the eyes of a friend.[27]

The difference between these two historical accounts is not at all one of truth and falsehood; it is, rather, a difference of perspective. What is of the utmost importance to one individual may be common or even unobservable to another. This dual nature of history should make it clear that neither external nor internal history is itself superior or inferior. The two perspectives are indispensable and interdependent. Inner history is necessary as long as people seek the meaning of their lives. On the other hand, external history can serve as a needed corrective of internal histories. In the case of the inner history of the Christian community, Niebuhr sees external history as providing two important functions.

In the first place . . . we have found it necessary in the Christian church to accept the external views of ourselves which others have set forth and to make these external histories events of spiritual significance. . . . Such external histories have helped to keep the church from exalting itself as though its inner life rather than the God of that inner life were the center of its attention and the ground of its faith.

Secondly, just because the Christian community remembers the revelatory moment in its own history it is required to regard all events, even though it can see most of them only from an external point of view, as workings of the God who reveals himself and so to trace with piety and disinterestedness, so far as its own fate is concerned, the ways of God in the lives of men.[28]

Revelation is that part of our inner history that illuminates and gives form to the flux of experience. Niebuhr compares revelation to hitting upon a luminous sentence in a complicated book. That one sentence can make sense out of all that came before and will come after. Similarly, Whitehead has written that "rational religion appeals to the direct intuition of special occasions, and to the elucidatory power of its concepts for all occasions."[29] Christianity appeals to just such an occasion.

The special occasion to which we appeal in the Christian church is called Jesus Christ, in whom we see the righteousness of God, his power and wisdom. But from that special occasion we also derive the concepts which make possible the elucidation of all the events in our history. Revelation means this intelligible event which makes all other events intelligible. . . . Such a revelation, rather than being contrary to reason in our life, is the discovery of rational pattern in it.[30]

Revelatory occasions not only give intelligibility to our experiences but give to the mind the "impulsion" it requires to do its work. Here Niebuhr stresses the Augustinian priority of the heart and the will in the act of knowing.

What the revelatory occasion does, first of all, is make the past intelligible. "Through it we understand what we remember, remember what we have forgotten and appropriate as our own past much that seemed alien to us."[31] The elucidatory power of the Christ event involves awareness of one's community with humankind, the breaking down of all barriers of alienation. Hence, while one begins with the particularity of a revelatory occasion, that occasion breaks the bounds of the isolated or tribal self. One begins confessionally but ends with universal identification or humankind.

Secondly, the revelatory event gives us a new standpoint by which to view the present. By using the Christ event as parable and analogy

we gain a new understanding of the present scene; we note relations previously ignored; find explanations of our actions hitherto undreamed of. . . . Not with complete clarity, to be sure, yet as in a glass darkly, we can discern in the contemporary confusion of our lives the evidence of a pattern in which, by great travail of men and God, a work of redemption goes on which is like the work of Christ.[32]

If properly understood, it is essential, in Niebuhr's opinion, to speak of revelation as *progressive*. Just as in our conceptual knowledge we move back and forth from reason to experience and back to reason, so it is with revelation and experience.

By moving back from experience to the categories in our mind we find out more clearly what was in our mind. The reason of the heart engages in a similar dialectic, and it does not really know what is in the revelation, in the illuminating moment, save as it proceeds from it to present experience and back again from experience to revelation. In that process the meaning of the revelation, its richness and power, grow clearer. This progressive understanding of revelation is an infinite process.[33]

Niebuhr contends that it is this capacity of revelation to cast light on the whole range of our experience that validates its claim upon the human mind and heart. The truth of a revelation depends upon its *adequacy*; i.e., its ability to illuminate the widest possible range of experience and to bring this whole range of experience into a meaningful whole. Thus a revelation is validated by its success in overcoming what Niebuhr calls "the evil imaginations of the heart." Evil imagination is characterized by an egoism or isolated subjectivity that cannot transcend its narrow vision. It is the tribal and scapegoat mentality that is unable to see others as real persons.

So all nations tend to regard themselves as chosen peoples. Defeated or victorious they only become more aware of themselves, using both pain and pleasure to fortify themselves in the conviction that all the world is centered in their destiny. Such imagination can never enter into the knowledge of another self; it is always the "I" that is known and never the "Thou." . . . Evil and selfhood are left as mysteries. Solipsism in thought and action or irrational pluralism in theory and practice are the consequences. The impoverishment and alienation of the self, as well as the destruction of others, issues from a reasoning of the heart that uses evil imaginations.[34]

Niebuhr believes that the Christian revelation enables the self to escape both tribalism and the impersonalism of the modern scientific outlook by offering a personalistic vision of our relation to humanity that is universal in scope because it stands in judgment on all egocentric and subjective interpretations of experience.

The moral consequence of this faith is that it makes relative all those values which polytheism makes absolute, and so puts an end to the strife of the gods. But it does not relativize them as self-love does. A new sacredness attaches to the relative goods. Whatever is, is now known to be good, to have value, though its value be still hidden to us. The moral consequence of faith in God is the universal love of all being in him. . . . So faith in God involves us in a permanent revolution of the mind and of the heart, a continuous life which opens out infinitely into ever new possibilities. It does not, therefore, afford grounds for boasting but only for simple thankfulness. It is a gift of God.[35]

Niebuhr rejects the notion that the criteria used by the Christian to validate revelation can also be used as a means of *proving* Christianity and *disproving* other revelatory claims. The theological task of the Christian community is confessional, not apologetic. That is, "it must ask what revelation means for Christians rather than what it ought to mean for all men, everywhere and at all times."[36]

It is this idea of revelation and the task of theology that raises a number of questions in the minds of critics. Niebuhr asserts that the Christian theologian's task is confessional, that he is called to analyze "what Christians see from their limited point of view in history and faith." Yet Niebuhr also insists that the relativity of faith does not imply subjectivism for "it is not apparent that one who knows that his concepts are not universal must also doubt that they are concepts of the universal."[37] But if we are willing to acknowledge that what we see from our relative point of view is also true beyond the limits of our community, then we have moved beyond the circle of confessional theology into philosophical or apologetical theology. This raises the question of whether such a Christian theology can finally avoid engaging in the metaphysical discussion.[38] The alternative would appear to be a theological positivism that Niebuhr would disavow.

Related to the above question is another concerning the adequacy of Niebuhr's fundamental distinction between external and internal history. The problem lies in Niebuhr's ambiguous use of the notion of external history. He often means by the term simply disinterested, value-free history. However, he also includes in this notion all *alien* internal histories that are not disinterested or objective. The fact is that most "external" histories are not disinterested but inner histories of other, alien communities, e.g., the positivist, the Marxist, the Muslim, and so on. . . . This being the case, how can Christians "accept the external views of ourselves which others have set forth and make these external histories events of spiritual significance" when Niebuhr has told us that it is impossible to penetrate into the inner histories of other communities "without abandoning ourselves and our community"?[39]

The point is that Niebuhr's sharp division between external (i.e., alien) and internal history and his consequent relativistic perspectivism may not really be the situation in which the modern believer finds her or himself. In the words of one critic, Niebuhr's

division of history into internal and external history obscures the fact that there are not just two possible perspectives on any given event . . . but a plurality of them. There is a multiplicity of possible inner histo-

ries just as there are a number of possible external histories. . . . It is misleading, then, to place the Christian perspective over against any given other one as if they were necessarily mutually exclusive. Any modern Christian perspective will contain much that is not specifically Christian. . . . The Christian's mind is informed by the physical science, sociology, economics, and psychology of his time, as well as by his own Christian convictions.[40]

The very multiplicity of our perspectives and inner histories makes it possible to distinguish the kind of judgments compatible with certain types of events or questions. It is perfectly possible both to understand another perspective or judgment and to disagree with it or consider it vacuous. This in turn would suggest that Christian theology is not confined to a confessional role.[41] As will become clear, what distinguishes Reinhold Niebuhr's theological method, in part, from that of his brother is his willingness to engage in the apologetic task.

It often has been remarked that H. Richard Niebuhr is "a theologian's theologian." His writings did not attract the wide reading public enjoyed by Reinhold Niebuhr, Tillich, Bonhoeffer, and others. The distinctive features of H. Richard Niebuhr's work are, however, what make him so attractive to many contemporary theologians and likely will ensure his continued importance. One of these features is his empirical and experiential bent reflected in his engagement with Troeltsch, Max Weber, George Herbert Mead, and other social scientists. The recent interest in Troeltsch and in an empirically grounded theology reflect theological interests that were critical to Niebuhr. Another feature of Niebuhr's theology that elicits a positive response is his sophisticated analysis of epistemological issues and theological method, his suspicion of metaphysics and traditional foundationalist claims. Here one can see the affinity of Niebuhr's thought with work in contemporary cultural anthropology and critical theory and with the post-Wittgenstein critique of all comprehensive claims regarding rationality and his defense of the social basis of knowledge; that is, the communal nature not only of language but of logic and rationality itself. Niebuhr's most obvious recent influence can be seen in the emergence of both Narrative theology and the movement identified as Postliberal theology, associated with Hans Frei, George Lindbeck, Stanley Hauerwas, and several younger theologians trained at Yale University (see Chapter Sixteen).

REINHOLD NIEBUHR

Reinhold Niebuhr preceded his younger brother through Elmhurst College and Eden Theological Seminary and then entered Yale University. He completed his B.D. degree at Yale in 1914 with a thesis supervised by D. C. Macintosh, which reveals Niebuhr's attraction to the pragmatism and the experiential approach to truth that he found in the writings of William James. Niebuhr remained at Yale to work for the M.A. degree and, at first, he was excited by Macintosh's lectures in philosophical theology. Soon, however, he became bored with the abstract problems of religious epistemology. This disenchantment and family needs, occasioned by his father's death, prompted Niebuhr to quit graduate study and to accept a call to parish work. In 1915, his Home Mission Board assigned him to a small, newly organized church in industrial Detroit.

Niebuhr's thirteen years at Bethel Church in Detroit had the same resolute influence on him as did Walter Rauschenbusch's experience in the slums of New York. In Niebuhr's case, however, the social realities of industrialism produced a more decisive break with his youthful optimism. What struck Niebuhr with particular force was the moral pretension of the automobile industrialists, particularly Henry Ford, whose five-dollar-a-day wage was widely viewed as a sign of the generosity of the new industrial managers. Few realized that Ford's policy of shortened weeks and enforced vacations through prolonged layoffs led to grossly inadequate annual wages. In 1927 Niebuhr wrote:

I have been doing a little arithmetic and have come to the conclusion that the car cost Ford workers at least fifty million in lost wages during the past year.

No one knows how many hundreds lost their homes in the period of unemployment, and how many children were taken out of school to help fill the depleted family exchequer.

What a civilization this is! Naïve gentlemen with a genius for mechanics suddenly become the arbiters over the lives and fortunes of hundreds of thousands. Their moral pretensions are credulously accepted at full value. No one bothers to ask whether an industry, which can maintain a cash reserve of a quarter of a billion, ought not to make some provision for its unemployed. . . . The cry of the hungry is drowned in the song, "Henry has made a lady out of Lizzy."[42]

During his Detroit years Niebuhr, gained a national reputation as a preacher and writer and "radical," and his close association with secular labor and socialist leaders resulted in criticism from many within the Church. During this period, Niebuhr's thought was still largely in tune with the liberal ethos. He joined and became national head of the pacifist Fellowship of Reconciliation. He played a dominant role in organizing the Fellowship of Socialist Christians which, in its beginnings, was tentatively Marxist in its orientation. It was not until the 1930s that Niebuhr became more critical of the liberal premises that undergirded his own Christian radicalism.

In 1928, Niebuhr became an associate professor at Union Theological Seminary in New York, where he remained until his retirement in 1960. In the 1930s and 1940s, Niebuhr was engaged in an astonishing variety of activities that would have taxed ten ordinary men. He not only taught at the Seminary but was ceaselessly active in public affairs, helping to found political organizations such as the Liberal Party and Americans for Democratic Action. He also helped found publications like *Radical Religion* and *The World Tomorrow*, as well as *Christianity and Crisis*, which he also served as Editor. His name appeared on the masthead of several journals for which he wrote hundreds of editorials and articles. At the same time he kept up a demanding schedule of public speaking before political groups and university audiences and, almost every weekend, he preached in a college chapel.

Intellectually Niebuhr often found himself at considerable odds with his colleagues in the Church, in politics, and in the university. However, this did not embitter him or turn him away from active involvement in organizations and causes devoted to defending human rights and welfare. As John C. Bennett, his friend and colleague of many years, has written:

Niebuhr, after excoriating the illusions of many a liberal rationalist, will be found the next day sitting with these victims of illusion on a committee drafting a political manifesto or planning to rescue someone, perhaps some poor Utopian, from jail.[43]

In 1939, Niebuhr was invited to give the prestigious Gifford Lectures at the University of Edinburgh. The product of those lectures was Niebuhr's magnum opus, *The Nature and Destiny of Man*, which became one of the influential books of the first half of the twentieth century and changed the whole climate of theology in America. In the years following, Niebuhr wrote a dozen important works, including *Faith and History, The Irony of American History, Christian Realism and Political Problems, The Self and the Dramas of History,* and *The Structure of Nations and Empires*.

In all of these books Niebuhr showed himself to be *the* contemporary apologist for Christianity by demonstrating the relevance of biblical faith for understanding the hard realities of our human nature and history. Niebuhr's apologetic does not follow a clearly spelled-out methodology, although his writings reveal a consistent pattern. First, his writing is polemical. In seeking to refute alternative secular views of human nature and history, Niebuhr tends to cite the more extreme and less subtle positions of his antagonists. Moreover, he frequently exaggerates even these extravagant views, which on occasion has led his critics to complain that he is attacking "straw men." Secondly, Niebuhr's apologetic is *dialectical* and open-ended. In showing the weaknesses and limits of alternative doctrines (e.g., Idealism and naturalism or rationalism and Romanticism), he

points to those facets of biblical faith that take into account truths of the human condition either exaggerated or ignored by either alternative doctrine. Niebuhr *points* to the truth of biblical faith without attempting to reduce these often-paradoxical truths to some rationally coherent synthesis. Nevertheless, while remaining irreducible to some simple logic, the interpretation of life that Niebuhr finds in the Bible is not, in his opinion, irrational. It is truer to the *facts of experience* than any alternative analysis.

A third characteristic of Niebuhr's method is his constant joining together of biblical faith and the contemporary situation. Karl Barth had said that theologians should read the Bible and the morning newspaper with the same conscientious regularity. Niebuhr developed this precept into a methodological program. He showed how the Bible illuminates the actual events and moral ambiguities of our present historical experience— from the larger issues of international conflict to relatively smaller issues as diverse as the Kinsey Report on the sexual practices of Americans, price fixing, and White House religious services.

The closest that Niebuhr came to a statement of his method is in an essay entitled "Coherence, Incoherence, and Christian Faith"—in which all three characteristics of his method are evident. Niebuhr begins by attacking those theories that seek to force a simple rational coherence upon experience, thereby distorting some of the facts of human life in order to establish their doctrine. Niebuhr believes that there are four basic perils in any system that attempts to press some rational coherence upon experience:

1. Things and events may be too unique to fit into any system of meaning; and their uniqueness is destroyed by a premature coordination to a system of meaning, particularly a system which identifies meaning with rationality. . . . There are unique moral situations which do not simply fit into some general rule of natural law. . . .

2. Realms of coherence and meaning may stand in rational contradiction to each other. . . . Thus the classical metaphysics of being could not appreciate the realities of growth and becoming. . . .

3. There are configurations and structures which stand athwart every rationally conceived system of meaning and cannot be appreciated in terms of the alternative efforts to bring the structure completely into one system or the other. The primary example is man himself, who is both in nature and above nature and who has been alternatively misunderstood by naturalistic and idealistic philosophies. . . .

4. Genuine freedom, with the implied possibility of violating the natural and rational structures of the world, cannot be conceived in any natural or rational scheme of coherence. . . . The whole realm of genuine selfhood, of sin and of grace, is beyond the comprehension of various systems of philosophy.[44]

According to Niebuhr, the Christian vision of the self and history does not allow for such rational schemes of coherence. Rather,

the situation is that the ultrarational pinnacles of Christian truth, embodying paradox and contradiction and straining at the limits of rationality, are made plausible when understood as the keys which make the drama of human life and history comprehensible and without which it is either given a too simple meaning or falls into meaninglessness.[45]

Niebuhr's critique of rationalism makes him no less aware of the dangers of the opposite tendency—particularly among theologians—of reveling in the incoherences and irrationalities of Christian belief. Christian faith is not without its own wisdom and persuasive realism. However, this cannot be seen nor can it persuade unless the exposition of Christian faith is made vis-à-vis its commerce with culture. Otherwise, Christian belief becomes an esoteric system itself, unrelated to common experience.

There is, in short, no possibility of fully validating the truth in the foolishness of the Gospel if every cultural discipline is not taken seriously up to the point where it becomes conscious of its own limits and the point where the insights of various disciplines stand in contradiction to each other, signifying that the total of reality is more complex than any scheme of rational meaning which may be invented to comprehend it.[46]

Niebuhr believes that it is only in terms of its dialectical relationship to the doctrines and events of secular culture that the truth of Christian faith can be shown with any force or relevance. To scorn the apologetic task is to court a prideful irrelevance.

The Nature of the Self

With some notion of Niebuhr's way of proceeding, we can now examine how he applies this methodology to specific issues—first of all, to the question of human selfhood.

Niebuhr's doctrine of the self emerged out of his own struggle with the social issues of twentieth-century industrial society and his efforts to find some realistic guidance in facing these complex problems. His search convinced him that most analyses of the self, both past and present, were tragically in error in their estimates of human nature. The self and history were viewed either pessimistically, as in Hobbes and Schopenhauer, or optimistically, as in Liberal Christianity and Marxism. In our own century the failure of liberal optimism has turned many to a new historical despair and to a search for solace in some form of mysticism. The extremes were portrayed in Arthur Koestler's *The Yogi and the Commissar*.

Niebuhr rejects all dualistic doctrines of the self that would interpret the person as either a natural object or pure mind or spirit. The self is a union of both nature and spirit, and it is in the tension between our natural creatureliness and our self-transcendence that the self's uniqueness is discovered.

If man insists that he is a child of nature and that he ought not to pretend to be more than an animal, which he obviously is, he tacitly admits that he is, at any rate, a curious kind of animal who has both the inclination and the capacity to make such pretensions. If on the other hand he insists upon his unique and distinctive place in nature and points to his rational faculties as proof of his special eminence, there is usually an anxious note in his avowals of uniqueness which betrays his unconscious sense of kinship with the brutes.[47]

To consider the self either idealistically or from the perspective of a naturalistic behaviorism is to distort our human uniqueness. The attempt to reduce the self to a purely natural object is the danger of *scientism** and is especially evident in the pretensions of modern social science. There is a naïve yet dangerous confusion between descriptive and normative judgments in the work of some scientists—for example, in the Kinsey Report on the sexual behavior of American males and females. The naturalist and materialist have an inadequate doctrine of the self for the simple reason that the unique self-transcendence of human personality remains absurd to naturalistic determinism and, therefore, cannot be seriously taken into account.

However, neither can a rationalistic idealism do justice to the uniqueness and freedom of the self.

The self of idealistic rationalism is both less and more than the real self. It is less in the sense explained by Kierkegaard: "The paradox of faith is this . . . that the individual determines his relation to the universal by his relation to the absolute, not his relation to the absolute by his relation to the universal." In idealism the true self is that reason which relates the self to the universal. But since the true self in idealistic thought is neither more nor less than this universal reason, the actual self is really absorbed in the universal. The actual self is, however, less, as well as more, than reason; because every self is a unity of thought and life in which thought remains in organic unity with all the organic processes of finite existence.[48]

Niebuhr believes that the Christian view of the self allows for a unitary conception of human personality that takes into account both our creatureliness and our capacity for self-transcendence. It is in our self-transcendence that the Christian tradition has located the *imago Dei* in the human person. Self-transcendence is the dimension of the eternal in the human spirit that is reflected in the ability of the self to transcend both the processes of nature and its own rationality.

* Niebuhr has no quarrel with science; what he attacks is scientism; i.e., the metaphysical pretensions of some scientists in claiming to have the key solution to all human problems.

The human spirit has the special capacity of standing continually outside itself in terms of indefinite regression. Consciousness is a capacity for surveying the world and determining action from a governing center. Self-consciousness represents a further degree of transcendence in which the self makes itself its own object in such a way that the ego is finally always subject and not object. The rational capacity of surveying the world, of forming general concepts and analyzing the order of the world is thus but one aspect of what Christianity knows as "spirit." The self knows the world, in so far as it knows the world, because it stands outside both itself and the world, which means that it cannot understand itself except as it is understood from beyond itself and the world.[49]

Self-transcendence is the key to human freedom and hence to genuine selfhood. Nevertheless, the human capacity for infinite self-transcendence must be kept in tension with our awareness of our creaturely finitude. It is this tension which points to both the grandeur and the misery of human life, for we can direct our radical freedom toward both creative and destructive ends. Niebuhr thus rejects any simple identification of human self-transcendence and virtue. It is this unique spiritual capacity that is at the root of Christianity's paradoxically high and low estimate of human nature.

Indeed, it is man's radical and boundless freedom which is the basis of the self-destructive as well as creative powers; and there is no simple possibility of making nice distinctions between human destructiveness and creativity. In the words of Pascal, the "dignity of man and his misery" have the same source. Man stands perpetually outside and beyond every social, natural, communal, and rational cohesion. He is not bound by any of them, which makes for his creativity. He is tempted to make use of all of them for his own ends; that is the basis of his destructiveness.[50]

The human self is that ambiguous creature who finds itself at the juncture of nature and spirit and whose predicament lies in the fact that self-transcendence reveals our finitude encompassed by natural limitations but with infinite expectations and pretensions. It is this equivocal situation that makes the self conscious of its insecurity—what Niebuhr calls *anxiety*.

Man, being both free and bound, both limited and limitless, is anxious. . . . Anxiety is the internal precondition of sin. It is the inevitable spiritual state of man, standing in the paradoxical situation of freedom and finiteness.[51]

Anxiety is the precondition of sin in that it is the internal description of the temptation that leads to sinful self-assertion. However it must not be identified with sin, because there is always the possibility that faith can purge the self of insecurity and anxiety and serve as the spur to further creativity rather than destructiveness. Yet Niebuhr believes that our insecurity invariably leads us to seek to overcome it—to gain some basis of security for the self at the expense of others. Sin emerges out of the self's efforts to secure its safety and enhance its well-being.

Niebuhr is fond of saying that sin is not necessary but it is inevitable. What he means is that sin does not follow from the natural conditions of human life as such (finitude) but that we can point to no human life that is completely free of destructive, egoistic anxiety. It is not our finitude but our efforts to deny or overcome finitude that is the source of human sin. Sin, then, is not of the flesh but of the will and is manifest in our unwillingness to acknowledge our creatureliness and dependence. This egocentricity is expressed in our idolatrous proclivity, i.e., our absolutizing of the relative.

Niebuhr's analysis of the phenomena of human temptation and sin is probably his greatest contribution to anthropology. Even his most severe critics have had to acknowledge that Niebuhr's description of the subtle workings of human pride and sensuality is compelling. Sin, according to Niebuhr, "resides in the inclination of man, either to deny the contingent character of his existence (in pride and self-love) or to escape from his freedom (in sensuality)."[52] For Niebuhr the sin of pride is more basic than sensuality, in part because the latter is a derivative of the former. The sin of pride has many faces, but it shows itself most clearly in the pride of power, of knowledge, and of virtue. Both Nietzsche and Freud have made us more conscious of the fact that the will-to-power is, perhaps, our most powerful drive. Niebuhr sees this rudimentary desire as prompted by two very different responses.

There is a pride of power in which the human ego assumes its self-sufficiency and self-mastery and imagines itself secure against all vicissitudes. It does not recognize the contingent and dependent character of its life and believes itself to be the author of its own existence, the judge of its own values and the master of its own destiny. This proud pretension is present in an inchoate form in all human life but it rises to greater heights among those individuals and classes who have a more than ordinary degree of social power. Closely related to the pride which seems to rest upon the possession of either the ordinary or some extraordinary measure of human freedom and self-mastery, is the lust for power which has pride as its end. The ego does not feel secure and therefore grasps for more power in order to make itself secure. It does not regard itself as sufficiently significant or respected or feared and therefore seeks to enhance its position in nature and society. . . . In the one case the ego seems unconscious of the finite and determinate character of its existence. In the other case the lust for power is prompted by a darkly conscious realization of its insecurity.[53]

It is at the higher and more established levels of human life and history that the sin of pride is most dangerous and just because of the mixture of self-sufficiency and insecurity.

The more man establishes himself in power and glory, the greater is the fear of tumbling from his eminence, or losing his treasure, or being discovered in his pretension. Poverty is a peril to the wealthy but not to the poor. Obscurity is feared not by those who are habituated to its twilight but by those who have become accustomed to public acclaim. . . . The powerful nation, secure against its individual foes, must fear the possibility that its power may challenge its various foes to make common cause against it. . . . Thus man seeks to make himself God because he is betrayed by both his greatness and his weakness; and there is no level of greatness and power in which the lash of fear is not at least one strand in the whip of ambition.[54]

Intellectual pride is closely related to pride of power. Intellectual pride is rooted in the unwillingness to acknowledge that all knowledge is infected with an "ideological" taint, that it is *finite* knowledge, gained from a particular perspective, and that, therefore, it cannot claim finality or infallibility. Intellectual pride usually involves the inability to recognize the limited character of one's own doctrines at the very time that one is excoriating others for their ideological bias. Moral pride, likewise, is revealed in the self-righteousness that condemns others for failing to live up to one's own standards. But, as Niebuhr remarks,

since the self judges itself by its own standards it finds itself good. It judges others by its own standards and finds them evil, when their standards fail to conform to its own. . . . Moral pride is the pretension of finite man that his highly conditioned virtue is the final righteousness and that his very relative moral standards are absolute.[55]

Niebuhr agrees with Luther's insistence that the unwillingness of the sinner to acknowledge himself as sinner is the final form of sin. The person who can justify him or herself neither knows God as judge nor needs God as Savior.[56]

Whereas pride blinds us to the contingent character of existence, that other form of sin, i.e., sensuality, reveals both our inordinate self-love *and* our anxious awareness of and efforts to escape from our limitation.

Sensuality represents an effort to escape from the freedom and the infinite possibilities of spirit by becoming lost in the detailed processes, activities and interests of existence, an effort which results inevitably in unlimited devotion to limited values. Sensuality is man "turning inordinately to mutable good" (Aquinas).[57]

The sensualist often exhibits an unlimited self-love in the search for gratification but, as Niebuhr observes, this inordinate drive may well reveal a desperate effort to escape an insecure and even despised self. Take the example of drunkenness:

The drunkard sometimes seeks the abnormal stimulus of intoxicating drink in order to experience a sense of power and importance which normal life denies him. . . . But drunkenness may have a quite different purpose. It may be desired not in order to enhance the ego but to escape from it.[58]

According to Niebuhr, human sin is "original" in that no one can claim to be freed from the taint of egoism. Yet sin is not necessary in the sense that it is an ontologically essential ingredient in human nature. Our essence is in our self-transcendence or freedom. "Sin," says Niebuhr, "is committed in that freedom. . . . It can only be understood as a self-contradiction, made possible by the fact of his freedom but not following necessarily from it."[59] We alone are responsible for sin through the misuse of freedom. Christianity is, therefore, justly considered "the religious expression of an uneasy conscience."

What Niebuhr sees as one of the marks of modern culture is its denial of the self as sinner and its accompanying "easy conscience." In this denial we moderns have sought all kinds of scapegoats for the evils experienced in history. We find evil everywhere but in ourselves. As Adam blamed Eve and Eve blamed the serpent, so we continue to excuse ourselves by pointing the finger elsewhere. The evils of life are blamed on social forces, cultural lags, poor environments, institutional rigidity, and faulty education.

No cumulation of contradictory evidence seems to disturb modern man's good opinion of himself. He considers himself the victim of corrupting institutions which he is about to destroy or reconstruct, or of the confusions of ignorance which an adequate education is about to overcome. Yet he continues to consider himself as essentially harmless and virtuous.[60]

Christianity, on the other hand, sees sin as resident in the human will, a condition that all the programs of social meliorism will fail to exorcize. Nor can the self restore the self, for it is the will itself that is bound. And when we are the judges of our own actions we are always finally righteous. For Niebuhr the solution to the human problem is to be found only in religious contrition:

The prayer of the Psalmist: "Search me, O God, and know my heart: try me and know my thoughts: and see if there be any wicked way in me, and lead me in the way everlasting" measures the dimension in which our self judgments must take place. We must recognize that only a divine judgment, more final than our own, can complete the whole structure of meaning in which we are involved.[61]

Only when the self knows itself to be under such a divine ultimate judgment will it no longer be confident and righteous in its own self-esteem. The fruit of such humility is a faith that the redemption of our personal and corporate lives is ultimately a gift of grace and not the consequence of our own clever schemes. For the Christian both divine judgment and grace are discerned in the figure of the Cross. To understand Niebuhr's doctrine of Christ and the Cross we must turn to the question of human destiny and history, for it is in our search for meaning in history that the Christ event is especially luminous.

The Dramas of History

Just as the self is found at the juncture of nature and spirit, so is human history a curious mixture of natural coherences and radical freedom. We are both creatures of and creators of history in that history is the realm of both destiny and freedom. When we ignore either of these factors, we are led all too frequently to a historical pessimism or utopianism. There is an irrevocableness about the events of history that should (but, alas! does not) chasten zealous social planners who would reverse social patterns by some simple manipulations.

Actually the past is present to us not only in our memory of its events but in the immediacy of the accomplished events which it places upon our door steps. . . . The problems which arise from the actions of our fathers remind us that past actions are not simply revocable. We can not simply undo what our

fathers have done, even though our fathers might have had the freedom to take another course of action.[62]

But we are not only creatures of history. We are also the creators of history because through memory we can freely act upon the historical past and bring about new configurations of events in the present and historical future. This freedom should save us from a too-easy acquiescence to "inevitable" social structures and authorities. Niebuhr believes however, that it is our radical freedom as creators of history that has led us to make erroneous estimates of our capacity to bend human destiny to our own will. Niebuhr gives as an example the words of the religious humanist Eustace Hayden:

The world today knows nothing more familiar than man's success in imposing his will on the flow of events. No time is wasted by the man of affairs in anxious speculation about the supposed metaphysical controls and rigidities of the universe or human nature. He changes the face of the earth and alters the habits of men.[63]

Niebuhr comments on this kind of voluntarism:

This optimistic creed contains the modern error in baldest form. The optimism is based on the erroneous assumption that the "habits of men" are in the same category of conquerable territory as the "face of the earth" and that there is therefore no difference between the conquest of nature by technical power and the management of historical destiny by the social wisdom which must deal with the "habits of men."[64]

History is not subject to the causal analysis or prediction that is possible in natural science because of the freedom of the human agents in history which creates causalities of endless complexity. To understand fully the forces at work in any complex of events would require knowledge of the hidden motives of the agents involved. Therefore, the meaning of history is not susceptible to a strictly scientific interpretation. Furthermore, no interpretation of history can escape the fact that the interpreter views history from his or her own particular finite locus in history. Every historian has an implicit or explicit framework of meaning through which he or she observes and makes judgments of value and meaning.

When we weigh not the actions and reactions of the atoms of nature, but the ambitions and purposes of our competitors and comrades, we are never disinterested observers. . . . Our judgments of others are mixed with emotions prompted by our strength or our weakness in relation to them. . . . We are involved as total personalities in the affairs of history. Our mind is never a pure and abstract intelligence when it functions amidst the complexities of human relations.[65]

The question of the meaning of the past and the future is always related to the question of the meaning of life itself. There is, then, no widely agreed upon rational solution to the meaning of history. The study of history poses the question of its meaning but does not yield its own meaning.

History in its totality and unity is given a meaning by some kind of religious faith in the sense that the concept of meaning is derived from ultimate presuppositions about the character of time and eternity, which are not the fruit of detailed analyses of historical events.[66]

In the history of Western civilization Niebuhr discerns three dominant approaches to the question of the nature of human history: Greek classicism, the Biblical-Christian vision, and the modern view. Niebuhr believes that both the classical and modern views of history are blind to some obvious facts of human experience and that the Biblical-Christian view gives meaning to the ambiguities of our historicity.

The classical Greeks held an essentially negative view of history in that they conceived of history after the cyclical model of nature. History followed the cyclical pattern of "coming to be" and "passing away." For the Greeks there was "nothing new under the Sun." The world of history, like nature, was considered an inferior realm

of ceaseless change and flux. History itself did not offer the Greeks any hope for meaning. Meaning and fulfillment were possible only through emancipation from the natural-historical cycle of occurrences. This otherworldly, ahistorical form of spirituality is founded on the assumption that there is that divine and rational element in human nature that can be purged of the corruptions of finitude and can raise the mind to the contemplation of that which is timeless and universal. The unique mixture of nature and spirit in the human self is obscured by the Greeks, who are, therefore, prone to view human life either too pessimistically or too optimistically.

The only alternatives are either to reduce the meaning of life to the comparative meaninglessness of the natural order, or to emancipate life from this meaninglessness by translating it into the dimension of pure reason, which is to say, pure eternity.[67]

While classical philosophy was radically pessimistic about finding any meaning *in* history, modern culture shares a common faith in historical development as a redemptive process. As Diderot remarked, for the modern mind posterity has become the object of hope that the other world was for society in the Middle Ages. The idea of historical progress has been a pervasive modern dogma. Niebuhr traces this modern belief to the Renaissance, which saw a convergence of classical and biblical worldviews:

The Renaissance as a spiritual movement is best understood as a tremendous affirmation of *the limitless possibilities of human existence, and to a rediscovery of the sense of a meaningful history.* This affirmation takes many forms, not all of which are equally consistent with the fundamental impulse of the movement. But there is enough consistency in the movement as a whole to justify the historian in placing in one historical category such diverse philosophical, religious and social movements as the early Italian Renaissance, Cartesian rationalism and the French enlightenment; as the liberal idea of progress and Marxist catastrophism; as sectarian perfectionism and secular utopianism. In all of these multifarious expressions there is a unifying principle. It is the impulse towards the fulfillment of life in history. The idea that life can be fulfilled without those reservations and qualifications which Biblical and Reformation thought make is derived from two different sources; from the classical confidence in human capacities and from the Biblical-Christian impulse towards sanctification and the fulfillment of life, more particularly the Biblical-eschatological hope of the fulfillment of history itself.[68]

There are elements in this modern view of history that are salutary when compared with the ahistorical pessimism of classical culture. There is a dynamism, a sense of novelty and indeterminate possibility in the modern view that does justice to our experience as creators of history. Nevertheless, the modern vision of redemption in history is fraught with dangerous illusions. First, we moderns have an unrealistic notion of our freedom and power over history—due to the illusory notion that we can manipulate the conditions of existence. Niebuhr gives the example of Alexis Carrel:

Alexis Carrel in *Man The Unknown* comes to the conclusion that the management of human affairs requires a thorough knowledge of "anatomy and physics, physiology and metaphysics, pathology, chemistry, psychology, medicine, and also a thorough knowledge of genetics, nutrition, pedagogy, aesthetics, ethics, religion, sociology and economics." He estimates that about 25 years would be required to master all these disciplines so "that at the age of 50 those who have submitted themselves to these disciplines could effectively direct *the reconstruction of human beings.*"

This vision of world salvation through the ministrations of an elite of encyclopedists is a nice symbol of the inanity to which the modern interpretation of life may sink.[69]

What is basically wrong with this kind of social utopianism is the erroneous identification of freedom and reason with virtue—the failure to take seriously our human sinful predilections. Niebuhr sees this error in the utopian scheme of the well-known psychologist B. F. Skinner, as set forth in his book *Walden II.* Niebuhr comments that Skinner

admits that he has "managed" the development of the individual components of the harmonious community and that there are, therefore, similarities between him and the notorious dictators of our day. But he feels that there is a great distinction between him and them because he has done what he has done for the good of the community.[70]

This total lack of awareness of one's own limited and egoistic perspective on what is "good" for whole societies of other human beings would be comical if it were not, so common and so dangerous.* Modern individuals will, in Niebuhr's view, go to any extreme to locate the source of evil outside the self.

The modern liberal creed of progress has issued in two major forms of utopianism that imperil the world today. Niebuhr refers to them as "hard" and "soft" utopianism.

Hard utopianism might be defined as the creed of those who claim to embody the perfect community and who therefore feel themselves morally justified in using every instrument of guile or force against those who oppose their assumed perfection. *Soft utopianism* is the creed of those who do not claim to embody perfection, but expect perfection to emerge out of the ongoing process of history.[72]

Hard utopianism is seen most clearly in Marxism, where the messianic pretensions of a party allowed it to identify its purposes so completely "with the very purposes of history that every weapon became morally permissible . . . and every vicissitude of history was expected to contribute to the inevitability of their victory."[73] Its zealous messianism imbues Marxism with an unbridled sense of its own sanctity and righteousness, while its liberal perversion of Christian eschatology enforces its illusion of the coming of a kingdom of perfect righteousness in history. Soft

---

* The humorous aspect of this pretension is illustrated by a straight-faced observation from a medical journal cited in *The New Yorker*: "'Men and women are becoming increasingly equal but there are unfortunately some anatomical differences between them which can never be eliminated.'" The magazine greeted this bit of wisdom with the words: "Goody. Goody."[71]

utopianism escapes the self-righteous fanaticism that justifies the use of any means to achieve its ends. But the soft utopians assume that humanity is progressing toward higher and more inclusive forms of social life. It is apparent that soft utopianism has infected much of modern Liberal Christianity, which has accepted the notion of the progressive triumph of pure love. Liberal Christianity is usually pacifistic,

holding to the conviction that if only all Christians did live perfectly by the law of love, all strife and contention would be progressively eliminated and a universal kingdom of love established. . . . In the words of a typical exponent of the American "social gospel," "The new social order will be based not on fighting but on fraternity . . . not simply because the cooperative fraternal life is the highest ideal of human living but because the spirit and method of cooperation is the scientific law of human progress.[74]

In Niebuhr's opinion, Liberal Christianity, like secular liberalism, suffers from a romantic evasion of the hard, tragic realities of human life. Such sentimentality can lead to fatal consequences when, for example, the soft utopians are prepared "to meet malignant evil with nonresistance, hoping that kindness would convert the hearts of tyrants."[75] In fact, the greatest peril results when a hard utopianism is met by the illusions of a soft utopianism, as in the case of Russia and American democratic idealism. Nevertheless, these bitter enemies share a common faith in historical development as a redemptive process. According to Niebuhr, this "ultimate similarity between Marxist and bourgeois optimism . . . is, in fact, the most telling proof of the unity of modern culture."[76]

Niebuhr has exposed the illusions and failures of secular and sectarian Christian philosophies of history with remarkable perception. What is it that he finds in the Biblical-Christian faith that gives meaning to history while taking account of the mysteries and realities of our historical experience?

First, Niebuhr finds in the biblical concept of the sovereignty of God a number of important

corollaries. Faith in God's sovereignty points to the unity and universality of history under God's rule. History has meaning and purpose, but that meaning is not one that can be discerned by reason—as in Hegel or Marx or Toynbee. It is perceived by faith.

(The) Biblical conception which establishes the unity of history by faith, rather than by sight, is a guard against all premature efforts to correlate the facts of history into a pattern of too simple meaning. It is indeed one of the proofs of the ambiguity of man . . . that he cannot construct systems of meaning for the facts of history, whether of a particular story in it or of the story of mankind as a whole, without making the temporal locus of his observation into a false absolute vantage point.[77]

In the biblical vision, the meaning disclosed in history is set in a mystery— that is, the meaning disclosed is not reducible to a simple rational intelligibility, nor is that meaning fully proven or vindicated in the events of our history. While faith discerns meaning, history remains ambiguous. Meaning is disclosed but not fulfilled.

Biblical faith must be distinguished on the one hand from the cultures which negate the meaning of history in the rigor of their effort to find a transcendent ground of truth; and on the other hand from both ancient and modern affirmations of the meaning of life and history, which end by giving history an idolatrous center of meaning.[78]

Another corollary of belief in the unity of history under the sovereignty of God is the reality of sin and idolatry in human history.

The second contribution of the Biblical idea of divine transcendence to the concept of universal history is contained in the rigor with which the inclination of every human collective, whether tribe, nation, or empire, to make itself the center of universal history is overcome in principle. The God who has chosen Israel promises peril, rather than security, as the concomitant of this eminence. The God who is revealed in Christ brings all nations under his judgment. . . . The scandal that the idea of universal history should be the fruit of a particular revelation of the divine, to a particular people, and finally in a particular drama and person, ceases to be scandalous when it is recognized that the divine Majesty, apprehended in these particular revelations, is less bound to the pride of civilizations . . . than supposedly more universal concepts of life and history by which cultures seek to extricate themselves from the historical contingencies and to establish universally valid "values."[79]

By faith in God's revelation we can discern a meaning in history that both breaks the sinful pretension of our own little systems and points to the fulfillment of that disclosure of meaning "beyond" history. That is, the fulfillment of our history will also represent a transfiguration of history or a new creation. The historical process will not in itself solve the enigmas of history—and this is what distinguishes Christian hope from all utopianism.

Niebuhr holds that the Christian sees history as an *interim*. In Christ the Christian affirms that the Messiah has come and the meaning of life is assured, and yet Christ is crucified in history.

The idea that history is an "interim" between the first and second coming of Christ has a meaning which illumines all the facts of human existence. History, after Christ's first coming, has the quality of partly knowing its true meaning. In so far as man can never be completely in contradiction to his own true nature, history also reveals significant realizations of that meaning. Nevertheless history continues to stand in real contradiction to its true meaning, so that pure love in history must always be a suffering love. But the contradictions of history cannot become man's norms, if history is viewed from the perspective of Christ.[80]

Niebuhr sees in the Cross of Christ meanings that illumine many of the enigmas of our human experience. First, as we have seen, the Cross makes clear the seriousness of human sin. Christ was crucified by the "good" persons and institutions of his day, not by criminals— which points to the fact that even the best in human history is tainted by sin. The Cross also clarifies the charac-

ter of God and his will for humanity. In Christ we see the love of God, which goes beyond his transcendent judgment of all human life by taking the consequences of his divine judgment upon Himself. Niebuhr sums up the wisdom of the Cross in these words:

The climax of the Biblical revelation of the divine sovereignty over history is in the self-disclosure of a divine-love, which on the one hand is able to overcome the evil inclination to self-worship in the human heart and which on the other hand takes the evil of history into and upon itself. These two facets of the divine love establish the two most important aspects of the Biblical interpretation of history. On the one hand there is the possibility of the renewal of life and the destruction of evil, whenever men and nations see themselves as they truly are under a divine judgment, which is as merciful as it is terrible. On the other hand, the life of each individual as well as the total human enterprise remains in contradiction to God; and the final resolution of this contradiction is by God's mercy. From the one standpoint human history is a series of new beginnings. These new beginnings are not the inevitable springtime which follows the death of winter in nature. . . . Life may be reborn, if, under the divine judgment and mercy, the old self or the old culture or civilization is shattered. From the other standpoint human life and human history remain a permanent enigma which only the divine mercy can overcome. . . . Human powers and capacities may continue to develop indeterminately. But a "last judgement" stands at the end of all human achievements; and the "Anti-Christ" manifests himself at the end of history.[81]

The eschatological symbols of the Bible point to the inconclusive nature of history itself and to the fact that the finite mind cannot conceive of the fulfillment of history except in terms of symbols and myths. Nevertheless, if not taken literally the biblical symbols of the end of history can teach us important truths of our historical life. The symbols of a "last judgment" and "Anti-Christ" signify the rejection of all utopian notions of moral progress in history and the idea that history is its own redeemer. Evil is joined with the good until the end of human history. In the light of God's transcendent wisdom and love, all human achievements stand to be finally judged.

Niebuhr believes that despite literalistic interpretations of the "second coming of Christ," the biblical imagery conveys profound truths of the Christian faith. The symbol points to the fact that meaning is fulfilled at the *end* of history and not in some otherworldly realm *above* history. At the same time, it affirms that fulfillment will not come *within* the historical process itself. The symbol affirms that Christian hope is neither ahistorical nor utopian. In similar fashion, the hope of the "general resurrection" points to the uniquely Christian attitude toward history.

On the one hand it implies that eternity will fulfill and not annul the richness and variety which the temporal process has elaborated. On the other it implies that the condition of finiteness and freedom, which lies at the basis of historical existence, is a problem for which there is no solution by any human power. Only God can solve this problem.[82]

The wisdom that is in Christ is a wisdom that comes by faith and not by reason. It is not, says Niebuhr, "a truth which could have been anticipated in human culture and it is not the culmination of human wisdom. The true Christ is not expected."[83] Niebuhr insists that the "wisdom" of God is also the "power" or grace of God in and over us. By this he means that the wisdom of the Cross is not the product of our autonomous reason but a gift of grace. It can be accepted only by those who have come to a realization of the limits of all human systems of meaning, whose self-sufficiency is broken, and who, in humility and contrition, are aware that the wisdom of God is not an achievement but the wisdom of "being completely known and forgiven."

Although the wisdom revealed in Christ is no human achievement, it does become the basis of a new wisdom. The truth of the Gospel does not, therefore, stand in perpetual contradiction to experience. "On the contrary it illumines experience and is in turn validated by experience."[84]

Reinhold Niebuhr often disclaimed the title of theologian. He thinks of himself as a social critic and moralist. Niebuhr's natural milieu is theological ethics and, therefore, any attempt to grasp his apologetic for Christian faith requires some understanding of his contribution to this area of contemporary thought.

Love, Justice, and Power

According to Niebuhr, the Cross reveals not only the wisdom of God but also the norm and law of human life. For in the Cross we discern that perfect, heedless, suffering love (*agape*) of Christ. This pure, heedless love is, in Niebuhr's judgment, the pinnacle of the moral life.

The Christian faith affirms that the same Christ who discloses the sovereignty of God over history is also the perfect norm of human nature. . . . This perfection is not so much a sum total of various virtues or an absence of transgression of various laws; it is the perfection of sacrificial love.[85]

Niebuhr's pragmatism and realism could easily disguise the radical perfectionism of his ethical norm. Against those theologians who would appeal to other less rigorous norms, such as mutual love or natural law, Niebuhr holds to the perfect love of Christ as the ethical norm. The severity that Niebuhr discerns in Christ's love ethic is brought into sharp focus in passages such as the following:

The ethic of Jesus which is founded upon this love is an absolute and uncompromising ethic. . . . The injunctions "resist not evil," "love your enemies," "if ye love them that love you what thanks have you?" "be not anxious for your life," and "be ye therefore perfect even as your father in heaven is perfect," all are of one piece, and they are all uncompromising and absolute.[86]

The absolutism and perfectionism of Jesus' love ethic sets itself uncompromisingly not only against the natural self-regarding impulses, but against the necessary prudent defenses of the self, required because of the egoism of others. It does not establish a connection with the horizontal points of a political or social ethic, or with the diagonals which a prudential individual ethic draws between the moral ideal and the facts of a given situation. It has only a vertical dimension between the loving will of God and the will of man.[87]

If there are any doubts about the predominant vertical religious reference of Jesus' ethic they ought to be completely laid by a consideration of his attitude on the ethical problem of rewards. Here the full rigorism and the non-prudential character of Jesus' ethic are completely revealed. . . . The service of God is to be performed not only without hope of any concrete or obvious reward, but at the price of sacrifice, abnegation, and loss. . . . The sovereignty of God is pictured as a pearl of great price or like a treasure hid in a field which to buy men sell all they have. If any natural gift or privilege should become a hindrance to the spirit of perfect obedience to God it must be rigorously denied: "If thine eye offend thee, pluck it out, and cast it from thee: it is better for thee to enter into life with one eye, rather than, having two eyes, to be cast into hell fire." In all of these emphases the immediate and concrete advantages which may flow from right conduct are either not considered at all or their consideration is definitely excluded. The ethic demands an absolute obedience to the will of God without consideration of those consequences of moral action which must be the concern of any prudential ethic.[88]

Niebuhr believes that the transcendent norm of divine *agape* stands in judgment on all our moral pretensions. Yet this heedless form of love is not totally transcendent of human possibility. In fact the love discerned in Christ clarifies a truth about our human condition and finds validation in our common experience. That truth is that egoism is self-defeating and that giving egocentrism the appearance of normality merely betrays the desperation of an uneasy human conscience.

The law of love is the final law for man in his condition of finiteness and freedom because man in his freedom is unable to make himself in his finiteness his own end. The self is too great to be contained within itself in its smallness. The Gospel observation that "whosoever seeketh to gain his life will lose it" is thus not some impossible rule imposed upon life by Scriptural fiat. It describes the actual situation of the self which destroys itself by seeking itself too immediately.[89]

Niebuhr has been criticized for holding the divine *agape* as his ethical norm because the very radicalness of its disinterestedness raises a question of its moral relevance. Some of these critics would thus prefer to substitute a norm of mutual love. Niebuhr rejects mutual love as a norm because it lends itself to hypocritical forms of ego justification in the guise of unselfish affirmations of the other. *Agape*, he affirms, serves as a check on the subtle forms of egoism in all mutual relations. Niebuhr further argues that mutual love is itself dependent on disinterested love.

Love, heedless of the self, must be the initiator of any reciprocal love. Otherwise the calculation of mutual advantages makes love impossible. But heedless love usually wins a response of love. That is a symbol of the moral content of history. But this response cannot be guaranteed. . . . That is symbolic of the "tragic" dimension of history and a proof that the meaning of life always transcends the fulfillments of meaning in history.[90]

When not replenished with heedless love, mutual love easily degenerates into cool calculation of personal advantage and then into resentment over the failure of genuine reciprocity.

Niebuhr holds that *agape* is the Christian's ethical norm and that it *is* relevant to our history—though not directly as a historical strategy. Rather, its relevance is to be seen in its function as a limit-concept that points to the bounds of what is possible in human experience. Sacrificial love is no simple possibility, but neither is it a human impossibility. It is, says Niebuhr, the "impossible-possibility."

The radicalness of the *agape* norm has led other critics to complain that, although Niebuhr theoretically holds *agape* as his norm, in actual practice his social realism makes constant appeal to such other norms as mutual love and justice.

This, too, is to misunderstand Niebuhr's position, for it fails to recognize the *dialectical* relationship between Niebuhr's norm and historical action. This is made clear in his view of the relationship between love and justice.

According to Niebuhr, love and justice are neither to be confused nor torn asunder. Justice is only an approximation of heedless love, but it is also the *relative* embodiment of love in our social existence. Their relationship is dialectical. On the one hand, love is the *negation* of justice in that

love makes an end of the nicely calculated less and more of structures of justice. It does not carefully arbitrate between the needs of the self and of the other, since it meets the needs of the other without concern for the self.[91]

Justice is not finally normative because of the indeterminate possibilities of unconditional love.

On the other hand, the absolute norm of *agape*—if maintained as an ideal severed from the proximate goals of mutuality, justice, and equality—degenerates into sentimentality and an ineffectual moralism. Justice, says Niebuhr, is love making its way in the world, it is the concrete embodiment of love. Structures of justice are the expression of a love that does not trust its own moral intentions.

A simple Christian moralism counsels men to be unselfish. A profounder Christian faith must encourage men to create systems of justice which will save society and themselves from their own selfishness.[92]

To deny the need for more inclusive structures of justice is to deny the norm of love. Yet, for the Christian, justice is not the end of ethical action because, as Niebuhr remarks, "without the 'grace' of love, justice always degenerates into something less than justice."[93] "Justice without love is merely the balance of power."[94] Justice sets limits upon each individual's interests and thereby achieves a harmony in social affairs. But the balance achieved by justice is only an approximation of genuine brotherhood and needs to be *fulfilled* by

love. Love and justice, then, must be kept in a dialectical relationship, for the norm of love can always raise systems of justice to new heights and wider vistas, but justice can keep love practical, concrete, and unsentimental.

Niebuhr's concern with justice as the embodiment of love in a sinful world led him, during the 1930, to a more realistic and positive attitude toward the uses of power and coercion in ethical strategies and action than was characteristic of the Protestant Liberalism ascendant at the time. It was this issue that caused Niebuhr to break with the pacifists and to maintain that America should enter the war against the Nazi menace. Niebuhr recognized that the achievement of justice was not a simple matter of reason and moral persuasion. Because of the persistence of sinful pride and self-deception, every struggle for justice involves efforts to secure a more equal distribution of power in society. In fact, justice is dependent on a contest and balance of power that can be achieved only by political means. Niebuhr maintains that disproportionate power is always irresponsible power and a cause of injustice. Exponents of Liberal Christianity have generally rejected coercive measures in their ethical strategies and have appealed to various forms of rational and ethical persuasion to change existing injustices. But Niebuhr believes the appeal to moral sentiments, such as good will and philanthropy, reveals the self-deception and ineffectiveness of this form of Christian action to achieve real justice. Philanthrophy, for example,

does not touch the equilibrium of social power and it is therefore something less than justice. It becomes corrupted into the enemy of justice as soon as the next step is taken and it is used by the powerful to beguile the weak from challenging the basic equilibrium of justice.[95]

Liberal Christianity has erroneously equated power as such with evil when, in fact, power can serve the cause of both good and evil. To reject the use of power is to be blind to the power inherent in one's own idealistic notion of what constitutes the common good and in one's own status or interests. The failure to maintain an equilibrium of power through the use of power also supports injustice by leaving power in the hands of a particular group or class. A persistent human sin is the failure to recognize one's own will to power and to work for structures of justice that would set limits on the self's own egoism as an approximation of heedless love of neighbor. Niebuhr sums up his understanding of the interdependence of love, justice, and power in the following passage.

For to understand the law of love as a final imperative, but not to know about the persistence of the power of self-love in all of life . . . results in an idealistic ethic with no relevance to the hard realities of life. . . . To know both the law of love as the final standard and the law of self-love as a persistent force is to enable Christians to have a foundation for a pragmatic ethic in which power and self-interest are used, beguiled, harnessed and deflected for the ultimate end of establishing the highest and most inclusive possible community of justice and order. This is the very heart of the problem of Christian politics: the readiness to use power and interest in the service of an end dictated by love and yet an absence of complacency about the evil inherent in them.[96]

Such an ethic demands the most searching awareness of one's own limits and the fragmentary and tainted character of one's judgments and virtue. Such an awareness can issue in a sense of humility and repentance without disabling a person from engaging in resolute action. However, it does make one aware that his or her actions always stand under a divine judgment and that one is justified not by works but by grace through faith. Such a faith can save us from both self-righteousness and despair. The spirit of such a faith has seldom been expressed more eloquently than by Niebuhr:

Nothing that is worth doing can be achieved in our lifetime; therefore we must be saved by hope. Nothing which is true or beautiful or good makes complete sense in any immediate context of history; therefore we must be saved by faith. Nothing we do, however virtuous, can be accomplished alone; therefore we are saved by love. No virtuous act is quite as virtuous from the standpoint of our friend or foe as it is from our standpoint. Therefore we must be saved by the final form of love which is forgiveness.[97]

Perhaps no theologian in this century (with the possible exception of Karl Barth) has raised more of a furor and has more opponents both within and outside the Christian community than Reinhold Niebuhr. But it is also true that few theologians in our time have had a greater positive influence within the Church *and* in the secular world. Many astute observers lament the fact that, since Niebuhr, Protestantism in America has failed to have a comparable influence on public debate and policy.

We will close our account of Reinhold Niebuhr with a brief analysis of the criticisms levied against his thought, both by his contemporaries and by later critics. Humanists and religious naturalists, like Henry Nelson Wieman, chide Niebuhr for his appeal to a transcendent being and realm of meaning beyond the natural processes and structures of life. Conservative evangelicals criticize him for his critical approach to the Bible. But the largest chorus of criticism comes from religious liberals who censure Niebuhr for what they call his pessimistic view of the self and his suspicion of all redemptive schemes in history. According to these critics, Niebuhr's doctrine of original sin does not allow for a break with sin *in fact* but only as a mere possibility. This relates, in turn, to his understanding of Christian love. Niebuhr's critics assert that his doctrine of the self and God contributes to a "we must live with ourselves as we are" sort of attitude, because human pride and the judgment of God make all human efforts equally suspect.

We already have said that most critics of Niebuhr's ethical norm fail to understand its *dialectical* relation and relevance to history. The charge of pessimism is also suspect. Niebuhr can be interpreted as a pessimist if one is selective in reading his works, but then one must overlook all those passages that speak of human self-transcendence and the "indeterminate possibilities" in history.* Niebuhr admitted that, in terms of the apologetic task, his stress on original sin may have been counterproductive, but he does not reject his realistic analysis of the stubbornness of human sin. In 1965 Niebuhr wrote:

I still think the "London Times Literary Supplement" was substantially correct when it wrote some years ago: "The doctrine of original sin is the only empirically verifiable doctrine of the Christian faith."[99]

With the coming of the 1960s, just as Niebuhr was entering a period of diminishing activity as a writer and commentator on public issues, a veritable sea change occurred both in American political culture and in theology. And it was during the 1960s and after that Niebuhr's Christian Realism came under attack by Christian writers who found his ethical writings and his positions on public policy inadequate, even deeply flawed. This included criticisms of his position on such issues as the Cold War and America's role in the world, on Marxism and social analysis, and on the failure of his anthropology and ethical analysis to address the realities critical to the feminist, black, and Third World revolutions.[100]

Niebuhr did defend a policy of American nuclear deterrence, and he supported America's presence in Vietnam in the effort to resist Communist expansion. It is also true that he was not sufficiently alert to the morally disturbing policies of the United States in Latin America. It is not, however, the case that his views on these questions were inflexible; rather, in his last years Niebuhr's public utterances reveal that his positions on these matters were changing. For example, by 1967 he opposed the war in Vietnam.

A deep conviction, nevertheless, remains with some that Niebuhr's Realism implicitly, if not explicitly, supports a moral pessimism and

inertia, and in other ways remains an inadequate basis for a Christian ethic. Some critics focus on what they see as the too-theoretical and morally enervating concept of power that is so central to Niebuhr's ethical analysis. As one critic writes:

When "power" is conceived, as Niebuhr and other realists conceived it, as an inevitable dynamic of individual and group self-assertion endlessly repeating itself, the particularity of historical process and the shifting history of institutions largely drops out of the picture. . . . Realists assume that all political struggle is reducible to the same core dynamic, that all agents inexorably are drawn to patterns of power-seeking and self-aggrandizement mirrored at the macro-social level by the dynamics of nation states. As a result, realists find little or no moral ground for choosing between sides in such struggles for power.[101]

Niebuhr's defenders respond that Niebuhr was, among all the influential theologians of the twentieth century, more deeply engaged than any others with the day-to-day events in the social, economic, and cultural life of the West, and that the reality of power did not paralyze Niebuhr from continually making difficult, discriminating moral choices. This latter point about power does, however, require further comment. Readers of Niebuhr invariably respond very differently to his analysis of human sin, egoism, and the ambiguities and limits of human action. For some Niebuhr does convey an exhausted, pessimistic "we must live with ourselves as we are" message. Others, including most of those familiar with the full range of Niebuhr's work, find in his depiction of the human situation a profound argument for the self's engagement in uncertain and risky social action and change.

A related criticism is directed at Niebuhr by feminist critics. It focuses on his conception of sin as pride and on his belief that individual interpersonal relations have greater capacity for good than do relations among collective groups, such as corporations and nation-states. This latter belief, feminists have argued, fails to take into account the profound influence of larger social structures on the lives and behavior of private

---

* For instance: "There are no limits to be set in history for the achievement of more universal brotherhood, for the development of more perfect and more inclusive human relations."[98]

individuals and groups, such as families. This fact is very telling considering the prevalence of stereotypes of gender and interpersonal relations, and it is related to what some feminists regard as Niebuhr's male-dominated conception of human nature, of the self, and of sin. Sin as pride, it is argued, is appropriate for describing men who are socialized to be self-assertive. It is not, however, adequate to describe the situation of women, because most women have been socialized to be passive, submissive, and self-sacrificing, and do not take responsibility for their own lives. That is, women do not have a real "self" to assert or to sacrifice. On the contrary, sin for these feminists is a woman's failure to act and to be a genuine free agent. Sin is the forfeiture of a woman's highest potentialities to a life of renunciation.[102]

Third World writers point to Niebuhr's Eurocentric worldview and his often-benign interpretation of European and America imperialism, and hence his blindness to the plight of the dispossessed in Third World countries. Some Latin American liberation theologians simply have denounced Christian Realism as an ideology of the Western establishment. Other Third World theologians acknowledge the socially liberating resources in Niebuhr's analysis of human nature and history, but they believe that his post–World War II political analysis was wholly framed and distorted by his obsession with the conflict between democracy and communism. This is the criticism of M. M. Thomas, the Indian Christian ecumenical leader, who judges that Niebuhr's later political realism did, in fact, become an ideological support for the Cold War. Thomas maintains, in response, that it was "not democracy versus communism, but national independence and social revolution for some kind of egalitarian justice [that] were the priorities of the Third World

which demanded relaxation of the Cold War. . . . It was Niebuhr's ignorance, willful or otherwise, of the political dynamics of the non-Western world that blinded him to these implications and misled him. . . . Out of touch with reality, realism can go wrong."[103]

African American theologians, too, have acknowledged Niebuhr's contribution to racial justice, both through his theoretical writings on power, justice, and equality and through the score of articles that he wrote in the 1950s and 1960s on the desegregation of the schools, on voting rights, and on fair employment for blacks. Nevertheless, some African American theologians detect in Niebuhr's rhetoric of the 1960s a persistent call for black restraint and patience, for prudence and the acceptance of "proximate solutions"—all reflective of Niebuhr's "Realism," which led him to "respond to the increasing restiveness among blacks and to the civil rights movement by overemphasizing their disruptive impact on the white Southern social structure and by cautioning blacks against demanding too much too soon."[104]

There are significant truths in these criticisms of Niebuhr, but the debate continues—and the question remains whether they can and should be balanced by other things that Niebuhr wrote or that are implied in his fundamental analysis of the human condition and the dramas of history. Two things can be said in conclusion. First, Niebuhr was "a prophet among us"—as the historian Arthur Schlesinger, Jr. has written—in his capacity to confront the most complex social, political, and cultural problems of the mid-twentieth century with the wisdom of historical Christianity as no other Christian writer had done. Second, Niebuhr often changed his mind, and he had the courage to acknowledge his errors and his faults.

NOTES

1. *The World Tomorrow*, XIV (August 1931), 256–59.

2. *The Christian Century*, L (November 8, 1933), 1403.

3. Ibid., December 4, 1935.

4. W. M. Horton, *Realistic Theology* (New York, 1934), p. 8.

5. Ibid., p. 56.

6. *The Christian Century*, L (November 8, 1933), 1403.

7. Reinhold Niebuhr, "An American Approach to the Christian Message," in *A Traffic in Knowledge: An International Symposium on the Christian Message*, ed. W. A. Visser 't Hooft, (London, 1931), pp. 55–56.

8. Horton, *Realistic Theology*, p. 15.

9. John C. Bennett, "A Changed Liberal—But Still a Liberal," *The Christian Century*, LVI (February 8, 1939), 179–81.

10. H. Niebuhr, "Religious Realism in the Twentieth Century," in *Religious Realism*, ed. D. C. Macintosh (New York, 1931), pp. 416, 419.

11. Sidney E. Ahlstrom, "H. Richard Niebuhr's Place in American Thought," *Christianity and Crisis*, XXIII, 20 (November 25, 1963), 214.

12. H. R. Niebuhr, *The Kingdom of God in America* (Chicago, 1937), p. 193.

13. For an interpretation of these influences on Niebuhr, see the essay by Hans Frei "Niebuhr's Theological Background," in *Faith and Ethics: The Theology of H. Richard Niebuhr*, ed. Paul Ramsey (New York, 1957).

14. H. Richard Niebuhr, *The Responsible Self* (New York, 1963), p. 80.

15. H. Richard Niebuhr, *Faith on Earth: An Inquiry into the Structure of Human Faith*, ed. Richard R. Niebuhr (New Haven, 1989), pp. 16–17. These 1951–1952 lectures constitute Niebuhr's fullest discussion of the structure of human faith and the self as social.

16. H. R. Niebuhr, *Radical Monotheism and Western Culture* (New York, 1960), p. 118.

17. Ibid., p. 119.

18. Ibid., pp. 121–122.

19. Ibid., p. 123.

20. This is Niebuhr's own illustration given to John B. Cobb, Jr. in a personal conversation. See Cobb, *Living Options in Protestant Theology* (Philadelphia, 1962), p. 289.

21. H. Richard Niebuhr, *The Meaning of Revelation* (New York, 1959), pp. 18–19.

22. Ibid., pp. 20–21.

23. Ibid., p. 141.

24. Ibid., p. 64.

25. Ibid., p. 68.

26. Ibid., pp. 68–69.

27. Ibid., pp. 59–60.

28. Ibid., pp. 84–86.

29. A. N. Whitehead, *Religion in the Making*. Cited in H. R. Niebuhr, *The Meaning of Revelation*, p. 93.

30. H. R. Niebuhr, *The Meaning of Revelation*, pp. 93–94.

31. Ibid, p. 110.

32. Ibid., pp. 123–125.

33. Ibid., p. 136.

34. Ibid., pp. 101–102.

35. Niebuhr, *Radical Monotheism and Western Culture*, p. 126.

36. H. R. Niebuhr, *The Meaning of Revelation*, p. 42.

37. Ibid., p. 18.

38. See Cobb's criticism of Niebuhr on this point in *Living Options in Protestant Theology*, pp. 296 ff. Martin Cook, in *The Open Circle: Confessional Method in Theology* (Minneapolis, 1991), defends Niebuhr against the charge that his theology entails a form of "internalist confessionalism" by pointing to his "radical monotheism," which calls for "a permanent revolution" and the need of the Christian community to accept external views of itself and the "spiritual significance" of these external histories.

39. H. R. Niebuhr, *The Meaning of Revelation*, p. 82. For this line of argument and what follows, the writer is dependent on Van Harvey, *The Historian and the Believer* (New York, 1966), pp. 234 ff.

40. Harvey, *The Historian and the Believer*, pp. 239–42.

41. There is a tension, and perhaps equivocalness, in Niebuhr's epistemological "critical idealism," which is marked by his radical perspectival and relativist stance, and the "realism" of his confessional method that appeals to traditional theological language and concepts. On this question, see the essay by Hans Frei and the response by Gordon Kaufman in *The Legacy of H. Richard Niebuhr*, ed. Ronald F. Thiemann (Minneapolis, 1991). The essays in this book are a fine introduction to the ongoing significance of Niebuhr's subtle writings for contemporary theological reflection.

42. Reinhold Niebuhr, *Leaves from the Notebook of a Tamed Cynic* (Cleveland, 1957), pp. 180–181.

43. Harold R. Landon, ed., *Reinhold Niebuhr: A Prophetic Voice in our Time* (Greenwich, Conn., 1962), p. 58.

44. R. Niebuhr, *Christian Realism and Political Problems* (New York, 1953), Ch. 11.

45. Ibid.

46. Ibid.

47. Reinhold Niebuhr, *The Nature and Destiny of Man*, I (New York, 1951), p. 1.

48. Ibid., p. 75.

49. Ibid., pp. 13–14.

50. R. Niebuhr, *Christian Realism and Political Problems*, p. 6.

51. R. Niebuhr, *Nature and Destiny of Man*, I, p. 182.

52. Ibid., p. 185.

53. Ibid., pp. 188–189.

54. Ibid., pp. 193–194.

55. Ibid., p. 199.

56. Ibid., p. 200.

57. Ibid., p. 185.

58. Ibid., p. 234.

59. Ibid., p. 17.

60. Ibid., pp. 94–95.

61. R. Niebuhr, *Discerning the Signs of the Times* (New York, 1946), p. 14.

62. R. Niebuhr, *Faith and History* (New York, 1949), pp. 19–20. In this section the author is especially indebted to Gordon Harland's excellent systematic presentation of the complexities of Niebuhr's doctrine of history in *The Thought of Reinhold Niebuhr* (New York, 1960).

63. *Quest of the Ages*, p. 210, as cited in R. Niebuhr, *Faith and History*, p. 80.

64. R. Niebuhr, *Faith and History*, p. 80.

65. R. Niebuhr, *Discerning the Signs of the Times*, pp. 7–8.

66. R. Niebuhr, *Faith and History*, p. 118.

67. R. Niebuhr, *Nature and Destiny of Man*, II (New York, 1951), p. 15.

68. Ibid., p. 160.

69. R. Niebuhr, *Faith and History*, p. 90.

70. R. Niebuhr, *The Irony of American History* (New York, 1952), pp. 84–85.

71. R. Niebuhr, *Faith and History*, p. 76.

72. Reinhold Niebuhr, "Two Forms of Utopianism," *Christianity and Society*, Vol. 12 (Autumn 1947), 7.

73. R. Niebuhr, *Faith and History*, pp. 209–210

74. Ibid., p. 207; Niebuhr is quoting from Harry F. Ward, *The New Social Order*, (New York, 1926), p. 104.

75. Ibid., p. 208.

76. Ibid., p. 4.

77. Ibid., p. 112.

78. Ibid., p. 114.

79. Ibid., pp. 113–114.

80. R. Niebuhr, *Nature and Destiny of Man*, II, p. 51.

81. R. Niebuhr, *Faith and History*, pp. 125–126.

82. R. Niebuhr, *Nature and Destiny of Man*, II, p. 295.

83. Ibid., p. 62.

84. Ibid., p. 63.

85. Ibid, p. 68.

86. R. Niebuhr, *Christianity and Power Politics* (New York, 1940), p. 8.

87. R. Niebuhr, *An Interpretation of Christian Ethics* (New York, 1956), p. 45.

88. Ibid., pp. 55–56.

89. R. Niebuhr, *Faith and History*, p. 174.

90. Charles W. Kegley and Robert W. Bretall, ed., *Reinhold Niebuhr: His Religious, Social, and Political Thought* (New York, 1956), p. 424.

91. R. Niebuhr, *Nature and Destiny of Man*, I, p. 295.

92. R. Niebuhr, "Justice and Love," *Christianity and Society*, Vol. 15 (Autumn 1950), 6–7.

93. Ibid., p. 7.

94. R. Niebuhr, "Moralists and Politics," *The Christian Century* (July 6, 1932), p. 858.

95. R. Niebuhr, *Beyond Tragedy* (New York, 1937), p. 186.

96. "Christian Faith and Social Action," in *Christian Faith and Social Action*, ed. J. A. Hutchison (New York, 1953), p. 241.

97. R. Niebuhr, *The Irony of American History*, p. 63.

98. R. Niebuhr, *The Nature and Destiny of Man*, II, p. 85.

99. R. Niebuhr, *Man's Nature and His Communities* (New York, 1965), p. 24.

100. For the fullest account of the many post-1950s criticisms of Reinhold Niebuhr and Christian Realism, and a lively defense of Niebuhr, see Henry B. Clark, *Serenity, Courage, and Wisdom: The Enduring Legacy of Reinhold Niebuhr* (Cleveland, 1994).

101. Beverly Harrison, *Making the Connections* (Boston, 1985), pp. 58–59, 63.

102. On this feminist critique of Niebuhr, see Valerie Saiving Goldstein, "The Human Situation: A Feminist View," *Journal of Religion* 40 (April 1960), 100–112; and Judith Plaskow, *Sex, Sin, and Grace: Women's Experience and the Theologies of Reinhold Niebuhr and Paul Tillich* (Washington, D.C., 1980).

103. M. M. Thomas, "A Third World View of Christian Realism," *Christianity and Crisis*, 46, no. 1 (February 3, 1986), 9.

104. Herbert Edwards, "Niebuhr, 'Realism,' and Civil Rights in America," *Christianity and Crisis*, 46, no. 1 (February 3, 1986), 12.

SUGGESTIONS FOR FURTHER READING

Christian Realism

Bennett, John C. *Christian Realism* (New York: Charles Scribner's Sons, 1941).

Horton, Walter M. *Realistic Theology* (New York: Harper, 1934).

Hutchison, William R. *The Modernist Impulse in American Protestantism* (Oxford: Oxford University Press, 1976). The twenty-page "Epilogue" gives a fine account of the beginnings of Christian Realism.

Lovin, Robin W. *Reinhold Niebuhr and Christian Realism* (Cambridge: Cambridge University Press, 1995). This study of Niebuhr not only examines the theological themes but also touches on some of the background of Christian Realism.

H. Richard Niebuhr

Diefenthaler, Jon. *H. Richard Niebuhr: A Lifetime of Reflections on the Church and the World* (Macon, Ga.: Mercer University Press, 1986). This brief study focuses on Niebuhr's early life and writings on the church and the wider culture.

Fadner, Donald E. *The Responsible God: A Study of the Christian Philosophy of H. Richard Niebuhr* (Missoula, Mont.: Scholars Press, 1975). A study of the role of philosophy in Niebuhr's theology and the distinctive features of his philosophical theology.

Fowler, James W. *To See the Kingdom: The Theological Vision of H. Richard Niebuhr* (Nashville: Abingdon Press, 1985).

Grant, David. *God the Center of Value: Value Theory in the Theology of H. Richard Niebuhr* (Fort Worth, Tex.: Texas Christian University Press, 1984).

Hoedemaker, Libertius A. *The Theology of H. Richard Niebuhr* (Philadelphia: Pilgrim Press, 1979).

Irish, Jerry A. *The Religious Thought of H. Richard Niebuhr* (Atlanta: John Knox Press, 1983).

Kliever, Lonnie D. *H. Richard Niebuhr.* (Waco, Tex.: Word Books, 1977).

Ottati, Douglas F. *Meaning and Method in H. Richard Niebuhr's Theology* (Washington, D.C.: University Press of America, 1982). Good treatment of the problem of method in theology.

Ramsey, Paul, ed. *Faith and Ethics: The Theology of H. Richard Niebuhr* (New York: Harper and Row, 1965). A collection of essays on aspects of Niebuhr's thought. The long essays by Hans Frei on Niebuhr's theological background and theology are essential reading.

Thiemann, Ronald F., ed. *The Legacy of H. Richard Niebuhr* (Minneapolis: Fortress Press, 1991). Essays and responses by prominent scholars on aspects of Niebuhr's thought and legacy.

Reinhold Niebuhr

Bingham, June. *Courage to Change: An Introduction to the Life and Thought of Reinhold Niebuhr* (New York: Charles Scribner's Sons, 1961; 2nd ed., 1972). An early biography full of interesting information on his mature years but not strong on Niebuhr's thought.

Brown, Charles C. *Niebuhr and His Age: Reinhold Niebuhr's Prophetic Role in the Twentieth Century* (Philadelphia: Trinity Press International, 1992). Many Niebuhr scholars consider this the best, most accurate account of Niebuhr's life, thought, and impact.

Clark, Henry B. *Serenity, Courage, and Wisdom: The Enduring Legacy of Reinhold Niebuhr* (Cleveland: Pilgrim Press, 1994). A vigorous defense of Niebuhr the man and thinker against the criticisms directed against Niebuhr since the 1960s.

Durkin, Kenneth. *Reinhold Niebuhr.* Outstanding Christian Thinkers series (Harrisburg, Pa.: Morehouse Publishing, 1989). A study of Niebuhr's books with special attention to theological motifs. Best on the books of the 1930s and 1940s.

Fox, Richard W. *Reinhold Niebuhr: A Biography* (New York: Pantheon Books, 1985; paperback ed., San Francisco: Harper and Row, 1986). A valuable biography in some respects, but questionable in some of its judgments of Niebuhr's character and influence as a teacher and as a thinker.

Harland, Gordon. *The Thought of Reinhold Niebuhr* (New York: Oxford Press, 1960). A fine, systematic exposition of Niebuhr's thought. Sympathetic and uncritical.

Harries, Richard, ed. *Reinhold Niebuhr and the Issues of Our Time* (London: Mowbray, 1986; Grand Rapids, Mich.: William B. Eerdmans, 1986). A valuable collection of essays on various aspects of Niebuhr's thought.

Kegley, Charles W., and Robert W. Bretall, ed. *Reinhold Niebuhr: His Religious, Social, and Political Thought.* Library of Living Theology series (New York: Macmillan, 1956. 2nd ed., edited by Charles W. Kegley. New York: Pilgrim Press, 1984). The fullest collection of studies of Niebuhr's religious and political writings by twenty distinguished critics, with replies by Niebuhr.

Landon, Harold R., ed. *Reinhold Niebuhr: A Prophetic Voice in Our Time* (Greenwich, Conn.: Seabury Press, 1962). Essays on Niebuhr by Hans Morgenthau, Paul Tillich, and John C. Bennett with responses by Niebuhr.

Merkley, Paul. *Reinhold Niebuhr: A Political Account* (Montreal: McGill-Queen's University Press,

1975). Focuses primarily on Niebuhr's socialist period of the 1930s and is critical of Niebuhr's writings and positions after 1945.

Rasmussen, Larry. *Reinhold Niebuhr: Theologian of Public Life* (Minneapolis: Fortress Press, 1989). The most recent of several collections of Niebuhr's shorter writings with a good introduction dealing with Niebuhr's thought and its critics.

Scott, Nathan A., Jr., ed. *The Legacy of Reinhold Niebuhr* (Chicago: University of Chicago Press, 1975). A valuable collection of seven essays on Niebuhr's thought.

Stone, Ronald H. *Reinhold Niebuhr: Prophet to Politicians* (Nashville: Abingdon Press, 1972). Emphasizes Niebuhr's political thought, identifying four distinct periods in his development.

————. *Professor Reinhold Niebuhr* (Louisville, Ky.: Westminster/John Knox Press, 1992). An excellent overview of Niebuhr's life and thought with special attention to Niebuhr's career as a teacher of social ethics.

❧

Chapter Seven

The New Theology
and Transcendental Thomism

Karl Rahner

Nineteenth-century Neo-Scholasticism sets the background for the development of transcendental Thomism in the twentieth century (see Volume I, Chapter Thirteen). In 1879 Pope Leo XIII wrote the encyclical *Aeterni Patris* (*Eternal Father*), "On the Restoration of Christian Philosophy according to the Mind of St. Thomas Aquinas, the Angelic Doctor." Wanting to ensure a coherence between philosophy and Roman Catholic theology, the Pope officially sanctioned the philosophy of Thomas Aquinas as the proper philosophy to carry out this program. He insisted:

Let then teachers carefully chosen by you do their best to instill the doctrine of Thomas Aquinas into the minds of their hearers; let them clearly point out its solidity and excellence above all other teaching.

Let this doctrine be the light of all places of learning which you may have already opened, or may hereafter open. Let it be used for the refutation of errors that are gaining ground.[1]

About forty years later, in 1917, the Code of Canon Law, promulgated by Pope Benedict XV, required that the study of philosophy and theology in all institutes of higher education, including seminaries, must be carried out "according to the arguments, doctrine, and principles of St. Thomas which they are inviolably to hold."[2] Combined with the antimodernism oath (1910) to which all professors and teachers of theology had to swear, the philosophy of Thomas was made the norm and criterion of all theology and philosophy. It was to be the antidote to the spread of modern philosophy within Catholic educational institutions.[3]

These strictures were not merely ideals; they were conscientiously carried out in practice. Non-Thomistic philosophers and theologians were often censured and removed from their teaching positions. Consequently, any dissent from prevailing Neo-Scholastic ideas and teachings had to arise from within the context of Thomistic studies themselves. And that is indeed what happened. The revival of Roman Catholic theology at the beginning of the twentieth century took place through a combination of historical and systematic studies that distinguished between Neo-Scholasticism and historical studies that focused on the development of Scholasticism. It sought to show the limitations of it by arguing that it was very much caught up within the mentality and categories of the post-Enlightenment era against which it sought to argue. The major theological figures of the *nouvelle théologie*, Marie-Dominique Chenu, Henri Bouillard, and Henri de Lubac, as well as the figures of the succeeding generation, such as Karl Rahner, Edward Schillebeeckx, and Bernard Lonergan, all began their theological careers with dissertations or studies interpreting Thomas Aquinas's theology or philosophy.

An unanticipated result took place. These theologians discovered through their research an "historical" Thomas Aquinas to whom they appealed over against the Thomas portrayed by the Neo-Scholastics. Indeed, they depicted a contrasting image of Thomas. Whereas the Thomas of Neo-Scholasticism was primarily a philosopher, their Thomas was primarily a theologian. Whereas the Thomas of Neo-Scholasticism was characterized as an Aristotelian struggling *against* the Neo-Platonism of Augustine, the Thomas of the *nouvelle théologie* was heavily indebted to Neo-Platonism and Augustinianism. Whereas the Thomas of Neo-Scholasticism separated nature and grace into two distinct orders, their Thomas integrated nature and grace through the dynamism of the human desire for God—an Augustinian theme. Whereas the Thomas of

Neo-Scholasticism employed a nonidealist, empirical, and *a posteriori* method, their Thomas was very much aware of the *a priori* elements of knowledge and faith. In order to counter what they considered the sterility of Neo-Scholasticism, the new theology appealed to an authentic Thomas recovered by their historical studies. At the same time, they sought, through constructive philosophical and theological reflection, to link the philosophy and theology of Thomas with modern philosophy and theology.

THE BACKGROUND AND CONTEXT OF THE *NOUVELLE THÉOLOGIE*

Three important movements provide the impetus and background to what came to be called transcendental Thomism. The first is the specific contours that characterized Neo-Scholasticism at the turn of the century, namely its indebtedness to modernity and to the Enlightenment, despite the fact that it arose as a reaction to modernity and as a critique of the Enlightenment. Hence, it acquired features of the very philosophies that it combated. The second movement is the philosophical and theological directions represented by the Catholic theologians Joseph Maréchal and Pierre Rousselot. These two thinkers strongly influenced Roman Catholic theology and provided an impetus for the break with Neo-Scholasticism. The third movement is known as the *nouvelle théologie*. This movement reacted precisely against the features that distinguished the then current Neo-Scholasticism from classical scholasticism, and it was influenced by the philosophical directions pursued by Joseph Maréchal and Pierre Rousselot.

Neo-Scholasticism as a Phenomenon of Modernity

Neo-Scholasticism did not simply attempt to retrieve the theology and philosophy of Thomas Aquinas. It restored Thomas with the polemical intent of contesting modern philosophy and any modern Catholic theology that sought to appropriate modern philosophy. It combated not only Roman Catholic theologians who embraced, from its viewpoint, the rationalism of the Enlightenment, but also those who appeared to adopt the Romantic emphasis on sentiment, feeling, and experience. Even though the Roman Catholic theological reception of Romanticism was a response to the Enlightenment tendencies, Neo-Scholasticism viewed this response with the same suspicion that it showed toward the Enlightenment.

In understanding neo-Scholasticism, it is important, therefore, to ask: (1) What is the Neo-Scholastic view of the Enlightenment? and (2) Why did Neo-Scholasticism object to the theological reception of Romanticism in modern Roman Catholic theology, for example, in the Tübingen School (see Volume I, Chapter Eight), in the same way that it objected to the Enlightenment?

Neo-Scholasticism took issue with the Enlightenment primarily because of the Enlightenment's advocacy of a natural religion and its denial of revelation and the claims of the particular historical religions. By concentrating on the Enlightenment's denial of supernatural revelation, Neo-Scholasticism viewed naturalism and deism as exemplifying this denial. It, therefore, viewed Romanticism not as a reaction to the Enlightenment but as the continuation of the naturalism of the Enlightenment. It was because of this perception that Neo-Scholasticism sought to develop an apologetic and a philosophy of religion that would have as its main purpose a defense of the possibility and existence of supernatural revelation. The discipline of fundamental theology, as a discipline distinct from systematic or dogmatic theology, was developed precisely to combat this denial. It sought to provide an independent rational foundation for supernatural revelation.

To carry this out, Neo-Scholastic fundamental theology assumed some of the same philosophical foundations as the Enlightenment in order to combat it. It developed a philosophy of religion capable of demonstrating the possibility of revelation. Against the denial of miracles and the resurrection of Jesus, it sought to assert their validity within this apologetic fundamental theology. The result was the construction of a natural theology independent of revelation, and a demonstration of the proofs of the existence of God that is prior to faith. In so doing, this Neo-Scholastic theology increasingly affirmed the distinction between nature and grace, as well as the separation of reason and revelation. Grace became a clearly defined and separate superstructure to nature. What in Thomas Aquinas was posited as a preamble of faith came to be developed into a fully constructed natural theology. This natural theology was thorough and proposed historical demonstrations that would convince all—even those without faith.

In the same vein, Neo-Scholasticism combated the influence of Romanticism on Catholic theology. The Romantic view of religious doctrine and belief, as expressive of human feelings and emotions, was viewed by Neo-Scholasticism as entailing a naturalistic interpretation of religious doctrine, as well as a subjective and noncognitive understanding of revelation. The Neo-Scholastics, therefore, fought Romanticism as a naturalistic and subjectivist emptying of religious belief and truth of its objective realism.

Neo-Scholastic fundamental theology thus took its direction from this polemic. Over against the emphasis on experience in both Romanticism and Roman Catholic Modernism, Neo-Scholasticism insisted on the importance of the rational, cognitive nature of religious belief. Over against the emphasis on the metaphorical nature of religious language, the Neo-Scholastics underscored the literal and realistic character of religious affirmations. Against the view that religious experience is basic, whereas the intellectual concepts and ideas used to express that experience are interchangeable, Neo-Scholasticism stressed the necessity of realistic truth, of clear and distinct formulations of religious doctrine. It is in the context of this Neo-Scholasticism that a revival took place. It included Pierre Rousselot's appropriation of the Augustinianism in Thomas Aquinas's work and Joseph Maréchal's attempt to confront

Thomism and modern philosophy in a way that involved not only confrontation but also dialogue.

Pierre Rousselot

One of the most influential figures in the transition to the *nouvelle théologie* is Pierre Rousselot (1878–1915). He began his academic career with a thesis on the intellectualism of St. Thomas.[4] This was followed by a study of the problem of love in the Middle Ages.[5] In 1909, he became a professor of theology at the Institut Catholique in Paris where he briefly taught until 1915, the year he was killed in World War I. Though his teaching career was cut short by his early death, his influence was not. His writings, reedited and published after the war years, were seminal for the new developments in Roman Catholic theology.

Much of Rousselot's influence relates to his analysis of faith, highlighting those aspects of faith that Neo-Scholasticism either overlooked or rejected. In arguing against what they considered to be an irrational sentimentalism implicit in Romanticism's emphasis on religious experience, the Neo-Scholastics sought to produce a rational demonstration of the foundations of faith. They emphasized the independence and autonomy of arguments for the credibility of faith. In so doing, they minimized, even disparaged the mystical and experiential dimension of faith that, in fact, had been so central to the medieval theologians. Developing themes already present in Henri Bergson and Maurice Blondel (see Volume I, Chapter Fourteen), Rousselot's theology moved against Neo-Scholastic theology on several fronts.

First, he addressed the Neo-Scholastic understanding of apologetical and fundamental theology as disciplines that demonstrated the credibility of the Christian faith by a rational act independent of faith. Rousselot, by contrast, sought to show the link between the eyes of faith and judgments about the credibility of faith. The Neo-Scholastic apologetical and fundamental theology assumed that, in order to be rational, these apologetical endeavors had to be based

entirely on reason and must produce arguments for the credibility of Christian faith prior to and independent of human subjectivity. Neo-Scholastic apologetics eliminate the subjectivity of the believer. Rousselot, however, argued that the judgment of credibility is not prior to and independent of an act of faith. Rather, it is intrinsic to the act of faith itself.[6] "We must not imagine a 'judgment of credibility' that constitutes a distinct act. Perception of credibility and belief in truth are identically the same act."[7] Rousselot's argument amounted to a basic critique of the entire Neo-Scholastic approach to apologetics and to faith.

In addition, Rousselot's exposition of faith retrieved two other traditional and interrelated motifs that were neglected in Neo-Scholasticism. The one is the connaturality or unity (or innateness) between the human intellect and the content of faith; the other is the epistemic significance of love. The two motifs are interrelated. Rousselot's basic thesis in *The Intellectualism of St. Thomas* is that "Intelligence, for St. Thomas, is the faculty of the real, but it is the faculty of the real only because it is the faculty of the divine."[8] Rousselot appeals here to an affective habit that grounds love of the desirable good and thereby awakens a new power of seeing. A sympathy and connatural unity exists between this affective habit and the objects of religious desire. The desire and love rooted in this connaturality gives humans a new view: the view of what he calls the eyes of faith. Against the Neo-Scholastic view, Rousselot affirms,

We, on the contrary, hold that love gives us eyes, the very fact of loving makes us see, creates for the loving subject a new species of evidence. Yet we must not imagine that, when it comes to motives of credibility, this evidence is so absolutely personal, as a vision of love, as to be utterly incommunicable.[9]

Joseph Maréchal and Modern Philosophy

Joseph Maréchal (1878–1944) was born in Charleroi, Belgium. In 1895 he entered the Jesuit order and studied philosophy at the Jesuit scholasticate (a college) at the University of Louvain. He earned a Ph.D. in biology and began to teach experimental psychology and philosophy. Except during World War I, when he was sent to England, Maréchal taught courses on philosophical psychology, logic, theodicy, and the history of philosophy from 1910 to 1935 at the Jesuit House in Louvain. In this role he influenced many of the Jesuit theological students sent to Louvain for their graduate studies. His interest in psychology is exemplified by his *Studies in the Psychology of the Mystics*.[10] His major and most influential work, however, was *The Starting-Point of Metaphysics*.[11] Planned as a six-volume study, Maréchal identified each of the six volumes as a *cahier* (student notebook) to indicate their tentative nature. Cahier I deals with the problem of knowledge from antiquity to Ockham. Cahier II deals with rationalism and empiricism in modern philosophy prior to Kant, and cahier III presents an appreciative, though critical, analysis of Kant's philosophy. As a result of these studies, Maréchal was viewed as akin to Modernism and too favorable to Kant. In view of this criticism, Maréchal postponed cahier IV (a study of post-Kantian Idealist philosophy that was eventually published posthumously) and completed the systematic exposition of his philosophy in cahier V. The sixth and final volume never appeared.

Maréchal's work can be seen as the commencement of twentieth-century French and German Roman Catholic engagement with Kant's philosophy, one that would eventually broaden to other countries and continents.[12] Maréchal sought to bring together two philosophical positions: Kant's critique of speculative metaphysics (with a view to its development in Johann G. Fichte) and Maurice Blondel's emphasis on the dynamism of the human intellect (see Volume I, Chapter Fourteen). This Blondelian dynamism rested on the reciprocal bond between the intellect and the will. The two faculties constitute a dynamism of the whole being. Moreover, Blondel underscored the fact that the will or action relates to an absolute or transcendent end. Maréchal maintains with Kant that intellectual concepts do not provide a direct apprehension of the reality of God. However, developing Blondel's position, Maréchal argues that the knowledge of God takes place in a projective act or dynamic movement of the intellect. It is this dynamism of the human intellect that points to the reality of the transcendent or God. Rejecting both a notional and intuitional knowledge of God, Maréchal sought, through the influence of Blondel, to ground the noetic or intellectual character of human knowledge of God in an aspect of knowledge that is not formally noetic and that originates from the dynamism of the human spirit. Such knowledge is initially nonconceptual and provides the presupposition for the knowledge of God.

Maréchal sums up his epistemology as follows: "Hence no activity of our intellect, no intellectual assimilation is possible but in virtue of the deep yearning whose saturating end would be the intuition of the absolute Real."[13] He argues that the human spirit has an orientation or dynamism to desire the immediate knowledge of the transcendent absolute. This intellectual dynamism entails an *a priori* orientation toward transcendence: a dynamism directed toward the most general and unlimited being. It is precisely this openness toward unlimited being that makes possible the knowledge of concrete objects of being. God is understood as the telos of this dynamism insofar as God is interpreted in terms of the pure actuality of God, as pure act, to use the Aristotelian-Thomistic language.[14]

Such an argument seems to imply an identification of being with God, as the critics of Maréchal and of the whole Maréchalian program have argued. Maréchal's major point, however, is epistemological: God is not an object of knowledge as are other objects because God is not an object. How then is God known? The actuality of being and the unlimitedness of being is implicitly affirmed in all knowledge.

If the relation of the data to the ultimate End of the intellect is an *a priori* intrinsically "constitutive" condition of every object in our thought, the analogical knowledge of the absolute Being, as the upper and ineffable term of this relation, enters "implicitly" into our immediate consciousness of every object as an object.[15]

Maréchal posits the knowledge of God (absolute Being) as implicitly presupposed and co-affirmed in the knowledge of every object of thought if that knowledge is not to be empty or absurd. It is the purpose of his critical philosophy, in dialogue as well as in confrontation with Kant, to demonstrate this thesis of philosophy. It is this thesis that has influenced generations of transcendental Thomists.

Critical Issues

Maréchal's position, though widely influential within transcendental Thomism, has been open to question and to criticism. Two major questions have been raised concerning his position on the knowledge of God. The first is whether God is identified with being in general or the unlimitedness of being, which appears to be an implication of Maréchal's claim that the affirmation of unlimited being implies the co-affirmation of God. The second question asks whether Maréchal has sufficiently affirmed the noetic or cognitive character of real, objective contact with God.[16]

The second question shows the distinctiveness of Maréchal's theory of knowledge of God when compared to another critic of Neo-Scholasticism, Dominic De Petter, a teacher of Edward Schillebeeckx. Both Maréchal and De Petter criticize the "conceptualism" of Neo-Scholasticism. Both argue that human concepts do not in themselves apprehend reality in itself, but only grasp individual objects as a part of a totality. Both affirm a nonconceptual basis for the validity of conceptual knowledge. However, Maréchal locates the nonconceptual element of knowledge in the dynamism of the human intellect, whereas De Petter places the emphasis on the dynamic element of the *contents* of knowledge that have a reference to the infinite. That is, a concept brings to the fore an implicit, preconceptual, and unthematized knowledge that the concept thematises, but only incompletely.

Both Joseph Maréchal's emphasis on the dynamism of the intellect and the affirmation of

the transcendent or absolute, and Pierre Rousselot's stress on the connaturality at the basis of his theses on the "eyes of faith" and the credibility of belief, foreshadowed and influenced the *nouvelle théologie*.[17] Their views and those of the *nouvelle théologie*, however, remained in the minority and were contested positions within Roman Catholic theology for some time. Yet, eventually, through the work of Karl Rahner, Bernard Lonergan, and Edward Schillebeeckx, they came to represent the dominant position in theology in the post–Vatican II period.

HENRI DE LUBAC AND THE *NOUVELLE THÉOLOGIE*

The new theology (*nouvelle théologie*) is the term used to describe the revival of Catholic theology in France in the 1940s and the 1950s. Two schools, in particular, exemplify this revival—the Dominican School, Le Saulchoir, located first in Belgium and relocated to Paris, and the Jesuit school at Lyon-Fourvière. Initially, two Dominicans contributed to the revival through their studies of Thomas Aquinas: Henri Bouillard's (1908–1981) study of conversion and grace in Thomas Aquinas[18] and Marie Dominique Chenu's (1895–1990) historical studies on medieval theology, in particular his work on Thomas Aquinas's understanding of theology.[19] Henri de Lubac (1896–1991), a Jesuit professor at Lyon-Fourvière, wrote an influential treatise on the supernatural that became the hallmark of this new theological direction.[20] The original treatise has not been translated into English. In view of the controversies surrounding the treatise, de Lubac later developed and expanded its theses into two volumes, which have appeared in English as *The Mystery of the Supernatural*[21] and *Augustinianism and Modern Theology*.[22] These volumes take into account both the criticisms of his earlier work and those theological writings that were strongly influenced by it, for example, the work of Karl Rahner.

Henri de Lubac entered the Jesuit order in 1914. His initial studies centered on the Church

Fathers. As a co-founder of *Sources Chrétiennes*, a series that made available important patristic texts with critical commentaries in translation, he contributed to the new theology not only through his own writings but also through his editorial work, which sparked renewed interest in patristic theology. De Lubac's criticism of Neo-Scholastic theology is based then upon a return to the Fathers of the church and a retrieval of their theology. During the war de Lubac was very active within the French resistance. Associated with *Témoignage Chrétienne*, his lectures and essays criticized the anti-Semitism and racism of the Nazi movement.[23] *The Drama of Atheist Humanism* (1944) is an important collection of essays, including critiques of positivism, humanism, and the current neo-paganism. Within this political context, de Lubac's critique of Feuerbach and Nietzsche was directed against what he perceived as the philosophical neo-pagan roots of Nazi propaganda.[24]

The Supernatural

Though it is a technical and historical book, de Lubac's *Le Súrnaturel* (1946), more than any other book, exemplifies *la nouvelle théologie*. It argues that much of the malaise of contemporary Christianity is due to the Neo-Scholastic separation of the supernatural from the natural. Neo-Scholasticism affirmed the gratuity of supernatural grace and abstractly contrasted the supernatural with a concept of "pure nature," that is, with an idea of nature independent of any historical dimension. De Lubac charges that such abstract separations lead to a theology of grace that separates grace from life. Such a view sees grace as making us "what we were not."[25] By separating nature and grace, religious doctrine is "elevated" to a distant province above human nature. Such a theology seeks to affirm the transcendence of the Divine, yet its effect is to cut the Divine off from the human, as if God were not the creator of both nature and grace or did not create nature with a view toward grace.[26]

Consequently, de Lubac's argument that nature and grace are integrally related was directed against the Neo-Scholastic emphasis on the extrinsic and gratuitous character of divine grace. Therefore, it had implications for the relation between culture and theology and for the relation between apologetics and theology. De Lubac argued that the loss of a sense of the sacred was due to several causes.[27] First, the Neo-Scholastic duality of the natural and supernatural led to a split between secular knowledge and religious instruction. Theology became a rationalized enterprise of cultured experts, and religious instruction became concerned much more with combating heresies than with exploring the meaning of faith for human life.

The historical argument and the positive thesis of *Le Súrnaturel* is that the Christian tradition views the human person as created in God's image and with a desire for a vision of God. The consequence of the affirmation that humans are created in God's image implies an interpretation of the goal and telos of human nature, namely, a desire for the vision of God. Thomas Aquinas expressed this in terms of Aristotle's discussion of causes. The final end of human nature is the desire for God. The concrete historical world should, therefore, be viewed in terms of this divine destiny.[28]

The crucial point of the debate was the interpretation of Thomas Aquinas and his position on the relation between grace and nature. De Lubac argued that he was retrieving the authentic teaching of Thomas in the face of its misrepresentation by Neo-Scholasticism. He writes:

It is certainly more logical, and closer to St. Thomas himself, than the earlier [view of Neo-Scholastics], because in rejecting the idea of a closed and static natural happiness, it rejects more completely all dualism properly so-called. (. . .) Aware of the insurmountable difficulties raised by the modern notions of a "natural end" and a "natural happiness" . . . a certain number of theologians are today following this line of thought which was first opened by Joseph Maréchal. Though contributing their detailed explanations, they all recognized as he did . . . that in line with the argument of the *Summa Contra Gentiles* the vision of God face to face is the only genuinely final end for any created spirit.[29]

In its reaction to the Enlightenment, Neo-Scholasticism took over the Enlightenment's mechanist conception of nature as a closed system. Thomas, however, did not hold such a static view of nature, nor did he maintain the hypothesis of an essential or pure nature. Instead, Thomas sought to combine two thoughts: that the human person has a natural desire for God and that this end, nevertheless, transcends his or her natural power. A tension thus exists between Aristotle's conception of nature and the patristic view of human nature as created in God's image. A difference exists between other beings of nature, whose ends are proportionate to their natures, and the human spirit with its openness to the infinite. The dynamism of the human intellect that was so predominant in Maréchal and Rousselot, is also present in de Lubac's attempt to interpret Thomas. Maréchal admitted that there was a tension in Thomas's thought and that "he did not always succeed in bringing the elements received from the two different traditions into a perfect unity."[30] The new theology sought to resolve that tension.

Henri de Lubac was a lifelong friend of his fellow Jesuit, Pierre Teilhard de Chardin (1881–1955), who was also under suspicion by church authorities for holding ideas that were close to the *nouvelle théologie* (see Chapter Ten). De Lubac wrote several books defending de Chardin, among which *The Religious Thought of Teilhard de Chardin* and *The Faith of Teilhard de Chardin* are the best known.[31] Although these books primarily seek to present de Chardin's work and to ward off misunderstandings of it, de Lubac is also aware of the deep connaturality between de Chardin's vision and his own. De Lubac's central notion of *desiderium naturale* (natural desire) in *Le Surnaturel* appears in a much more radical and cosmic form in Teilhard's writings. For him the whole universe from its lowest level of matter to spirit expresses this dynamism of the spirit and its movement toward God. The cosmic dimension of Catholicism within de Lubac's work becomes evident in the Christian dimension of the cosmos in de Chardin's evolutionary work.[32]

Interpretation of the Senses of Scripture

Another focus of de Lubac's writings is the interpretation of Scripture. His work on Origen's spiritual understanding of Scripture led to a four-volume study of the senses of Scripture in medieval exegesis. As his work on grace sought to integrate the natural and the supernatural, so do these writings focus on the relation between the literal and spiritual senses of Scripture.[33] De Lubac argues for the integral relation between the literal and spiritual sense. In fact, a large part of his argument is that the four senses of Scriptures (literal, allegorical, moral, anagogical) exhibit not only an interdependence, but also what he calls a dynamic continuity. They engender one another. In his view, the historical and allegorical senses should not be seen as in contrast to one another but, rather, as complementing one another. The one grows out of the other and stands in continuity with it.

De Lubac does not wish simply to criticize contemporary historical-critical and philological interpretation; rather he wants to assert that the historical-critical meaning does not exhaust the meaning of the Scriptures. Therefore, he argues that it is important to appreciate the spiritual senses of Scripture in relation to today's understanding of the literal sense. Just as the supernatural is not extraneous to the natural, neither are the typological and christological interpretations of the Hebrew Scriptures extraneous to its meaning. It is important, therefore, to draw out the meaning of the Scriptures to give life to moral action and Christian hope.

In referring to the classical distich or couplet, "the letter teaches what took place, the allegory, what to believe, the moral, what to do, the anagogy, what goal to strive," de Lubac writes of the fourfold sense:

Without in any way returning to a rudimentary and out-of-date method, especially one that has brought so many abuses, we can use the distich, which long ago summarized both exegesis and theology, to help us retain or perhaps rediscover this salutary truth that an old liturgist saw symbolically expressed by the extinction of the candle flames in reading of the Gospel at the eucharistic celebration. The candles, he said, represent the Doctors of the Church: "And what does it mean that they are extinguished, except that none of the doctors can transcend the words of the Holy Gospel."[34]

This passage indicates the nuance of de Lubac's position. He is not advocating a return to patristic and medieval methods of exegesis nor is he rejecting the historical-critical interpretation, as some postmodern critics might do. Instead, he insists that the scholarly interpretation of the Scriptures does not exhaust the riches of the Scriptures.

In the post–Vatican II situation, Henri de Lubac occupies a pivotal and yet ambiguous position within twentieth-century Roman Catholic theology. On the one hand, his reading of texts, heavily indebted to patristic reading, enabled him to go beyond Neo-Scholastic categories and distinctions. His scholarship spearheaded *la nouvelle théologie*, a movement that despite opposition, came to fruition in Vatican II. On the other hand, as the historical-critical method became more and more dominant in modern Roman Catholic exegesis and theology and, as the spiritual and mystical reading of the Scriptures were practiced less within the halls of the Roman Catholic academy, de Lubac continued to see the importance and value of the traditional approach to Scriptures. No learned exegete can exhaust the meaning of the Scriptures. De Lubac's exegetical approach had a profound influence on Hans Urs von Balthasar (1905–1988) and also has influenced Catholics today who support a postcritical reading of the Bible.

Theological Conflict

Pope Pius XII sought to retard the further spread of the *nouvelle théologie* through the encyclical *Humani Generis* (*Of the Human Race*), issued in 1950. The Pope criticized what he saw as erroneous in the new theology, especially the errors that appeared to correspond to what the Dominicans at Le Saulchoir and the Jesuits at Lyon-Fourvière taught even though he mentioned no theologian by name. This allowed theologians to claim that they did not hold the views condemned in *Humani Generis*. It was apparent, however, that the encyclical contradicted Rousselot's position on credibility and the act of faith and de Lubac's integration of nature and grace. The encyclical also attacked evolutionism and existentialism as fictitious ideologies that refused to acknowledge truth as absolute and immutable. Against the emerging historical criticism within Roman Catholic exegesis and theology, the encyclical argued for the unchangeable nature of Catholic truth. It asserted that the objects of faith "have real objective value and this is unchangeably true, with the result that earlier definitions of faith can never become untrue later."[35]

Despite *Humani Generis*, Henri de Lubac's contributions to theology came to fruition at the Second Vatican Council. There, along with the other members of the *nouvelle théologie*, he became an official *peritus* (the Latin term for "expert") at the Council. However, in the decades following the Council, Catholic theology began to pursue new directions, issues such as secularization, political and liberation theology, and religious pluralism. In this new context, de Lubac became the critic, raising his voice against these directions.

KARL RAHNER

Born on March 5, 1904, in Freiburg-im-Breisgau, Germany, Karl Rahner (1904–1984) followed in the footsteps of his older brother Hugo Rahner and entered the Jesuit order.[36] He spent his novitiate period at Feldkirch in 1922 and did further studies there in 1924 and in 1925. After attending Berchmanskolleg in Pullach (outside of Munich) from 1925 to 1927, he taught Latin to junior Jesuits, and then from 1929 to 1933 he studied theology at Valkenberg, Holland, at a Jesuit school of theology. During these years, Rahner studied Maréchal's writings and was influenced by the father of transcendental Thomism. Rahner was ordained in 1932 in Munich by Cardinal Faulhaber.

Rahner then went to Freiburg to obtain a doctorate in philosophy, and there he took courses with Martin Heidegger, the other major influence on his thought.[37] Although Joseph Maréchal and Martin Heidegger are considered to be the two major influences on him, Rahner describes Maréchal as the more important:

Certainly, I learned a variety of things from him [Heidegger], even if I have to say that I owe my most basic decisive, philosophical direction, insofar as it comes from someone else, more, in fact, to the Belgian philosopher and Jesuit, Joseph Maréchal. His philosophy already moved beyond the traditional neo-scholasticism. I brought that direction from Maréchal to my studies with Heidegger and it was superseded by him.[38]

Karl Rahner's first two books, *Spirit in the World* and *Hearers of the Word*, are philosophical treatises. Whereas the first deals with metaphysics and epistemology, the second develops a philosophy of religion. Together they outline the philosophical presuppositions of his theology, and they anticipate many of the themes of his explicitly theological writings. *Spirit in the World* was written in 1936 as a dissertation. Martin Honecker, professor of Catholic philosophy at Freiburg, did not accept it because, in his opinion, it was more a philosophical argument than a historical interpretation of Thomas Aquinas. Not having obtained a philosophical doctorate, Rahner decided to pursue doctoral studies in theology. He went to Innsbruck where he wrote a theological dissertation on the typological meaning of John 19:34.[39] The following year he was appointed to the faculty at Innsbruck, where he remained from 1937 until 1964, except during World War II when the National Socialists dissolved the Jesuit theological faculty. During this time, he served as a pastor and in Vienna in a diocesan pastoral institute. In 1964, Rahner became the Romano Guardini Professor of Chris-

tian Worldview at the University of Munich. This professorship was located in the philosophy faculty. Professor Michael Schmaus and others in the faculty of theology refused to allow Rahner's students to submit doctoral dissertations in the theological faculty. He then left Munich for a professorship at the Catholic Theological Faculty of the University of Münster in 1966.

Karl Rahner's record of publication over the decades was voluminous, numbering thousands of publications. However, two distinctive characteristics are worthy of note. The first is the quality and the amount of editorial work that he undertook. A few years after he began teaching at Innsbruck, he published a new edition of Viller's classic collection of the writings of the Fathers of the Church that deal with ascetical and mystical topics.[40] He later assumed the editorship of Denzinger,[41] the text that collects official teachings of the Roman Catholic Church. It includes not only conciliar papal statements but also significant decrees of the Roman Congregations. Rahner himself noted that certain theological prejudices often influenced and determined which texts were selected for inclusion in such a handbook of normative church documents. He also published *Lexikon für Theologie und Kirche*, a ten-volume encyclopedia that was the standard German Roman Catholic theological encyclopedia of the post–World War II period, comparable to the Protestant *Religion in Gegenwart und Geschichte*.[42] Along with Edward Schillebeeckx, Hans Küng, and others, he was a founding editor of *Concilium*—an international theological journal that sought to implement the progressive reforms of Vatican II. In addition, Rahner published a theological dictionary[43] and a six-volume theological encyclopedia, *Sacramentum Mundi*, that incorporates much of his own theology.[44] He also initiated a series of disputed questions that consist of small volumes on controversial topics in Roman Catholic theology.[45] In addition, Rahner edited collections of documents of Vatican II and a multivolume commentary on the Council that became the standard reference commentary. This editorial work enabled Rahner's theology to exercise a broad influence on Roman Catholic theology. He was and remains the most influential Roman Catholic theologian of the twentieth century, and many of the texts that he edited remain the standard reference works. The second characteristic of his writings is that most of them have taken the literary form of the essay. The most important of these essays are collected in the twenty-two volumes of *Theological Investigations*. Several other collections of Rahner's writings exist, but *Theological Investigations* remains the major source of his theological work. It was only at the end of his teaching career that he published *Foundations of Christian Faith*—an introductory textbook and a major work, the length of his philosophical dissertation, *Spirit in the World*.

Spirit in the World and *Hearers of the Word*

Spirit in the World offers an interpretation of Thomas Aquinas from the perspective of the questions raised by modern philosophy, especially those raised by Kant and Heidegger.[46] As Rahner acknowledges in his introduction, his exposition of Thomas "has its origin in modern philosophy." The focus of Rahner's interpretation is centered in the analysis of *Summa Theologiae*, I, Question 84, Article 7. Question 84 asks how the soul, when united to the body, can understand corporeal things. Article 7 asks the more specific question of whether the human intellect can understand the intelligible species of a thing without turning to the phantasm, that is, without turning to the imagination.

Rahner observes that for Thomas Aquinas the human intellect has as its proper object that which exists as corporeal, and, therefore, it knows things through the senses and the imagination. The question becomes: How, then, does the human intellect know what is metaphysical or, more specifically, know God, who transcends the senses and is not an object of perception or the imagination? Rahner notes that Thomas, in answering this question, quotes Dionysius to the effect that humans know God either by way of

excess or eminence (transcendence) and by way of negation and remotion, or removal. According to Thomas, three steps are involved in metaphysical knowledge: excess (*excessus*), comparison (*comparatio*), and remotion (*remotio*). Metaphysical knowledge entails more than a comparison between a sensible and a metaphysical object, for metaphysical knowledge also involves the negation or removal (*remotio*) of those characteristics that are valid only in the realm of the sensible and the imagination, but as not valid in the realm of the metaphysical. In addition, this metaphysical knowledge involves a process by which a transcendence or eminence or excess takes place. Metaphysical knowledge involves not simply the negation of the sensible; it involves a transcendence of the being present in the sensible.

A more thorough investigation of this point would show that the analogy of being in Thomas is not merely a construction designed to help towards the conceptual, negative definition of the essence of God, but already has its starting point where the experience of the world is transcended in a pre-apprehension through *excessus* and negation.[47]

This statement reflects Rahner's understanding of the analogy of being. Analogous language about God should not be understood simply as a halfway point between univocal and equivocal language. Instead, analogous language is based upon the experience of the world by which the human intellect experiences through its openness toward infinity an awareness of the limits of the world and its striving toward that which transcends the world.

Rahner develops this epistemological perspective of his dissertation and applies it to the notion of revelation in *Hearers of the Word*, originally given as a set of lectures in 1941 in Salzburg. *Spirit in the World* concentrates on the question of whether humans can have legitimate metaphysical knowledge and can know the transcendent God if all human knowledge is tied to the imagination. *Hearers of the Word* takes up the same question in relation to the possibility of the knowledge of revelation. In the first edition, Rahner contrasts his position with several Protestant conceptions, which, in his view, show an insufficient understanding of revelation.[48] Rahner's proposed solution to this question of the conditions necessary for the possibility of an understanding of revelation is based on his elaboration of Maréchal's conception of the transcendental orientation of the human spirit.

A revised second edition (edited by his student Johann Baptist Metz) drops the polemic against Protestant views on revelation and underscores much more strongly the historical dimension of human existence. This second edition reflects Rahner's own development and the changed ecumenical situation of Roman Catholic theology. Whereas the dynamism of the human intellect is posited as the key to the knowledge of the transcendent (in both editions), the second edition underscores much more strongly Rahner's emphasis on transcendental experience in distinction to propositional, or what he calls categorial, expressions of that experience in concrete doctrines. The second edition brings out much more strongly Rahner's understanding of revelation as transcendental experience rather than as a propositional knowledge.

In short, Rahner's philosophy of religion as a philosophy of the possibility of revelation explicates and develops further the direction that figured so predominantly in both Blondel and Maréchal. This position is the basic view of religious knowledge that undergirds Rahner's many theological essays collected in *Theological Investigations* and in his introduction to Christianity, *Foundations of the Christian Faith*.[49]

The Religious Dimension of Human Experience

Karl Rahner's interpretation of the knowledge and experience of God can be compared to Schleiermacher's understanding of religious experience. Schleiermacher delineates the feeling of utter dependence as pointing to the *whence* of human existence.[50] This experience is a concomitant dimension of experience and the "whence" refers to what religious persons name God. Karl Rahner delineates the experience of self-transcendence in every act of knowing and willing as pointing to the *whither* of human existence. Again, this experience is a concomitant dimension of human knowledge and is both a pre-apprehension and precondition of religious knowledge. The "whither" of the intellectual dynamism is absolute mystery. The search for the meaning of that mystery in history leads Rahner to develop a theological method that could be termed a method of correlation between human transcendental experience and the presence of meaning within history.

The verbal difference between Schleiermacher's "whence" and Rahner's "whither" only touches the surface of the difference. Central to Rahner's interpretation of the religious dimension of human experience is the experience of freedom and responsibility. Rahner seeks to elaborate the relation in terms of a dialectic between dependence and freedom. In the world of finite objects, dependence and autonomy are normally contrasted with one another. However, in relation to the infinite, the more the finite is dependent upon the infinite the freer and more autonomous it is. An example from everyday experience can illustrate Rahner's point. One can say that the more one has learned from a capable teacher, for example, in mathematics, philosophy, or music composition, the more one can become an independent and creative mathematician, philosopher, or composer. One who has learned very little can only slavishly imitate the teacher. The dialectic is the more one has learned, the more independent one can become of the teacher.

A similar dialectical principle is applied to the human experience of the divine presence. This divine presence should not be interpreted only in terms of dependency, but rather has to include freedom and autonomy. This dialectic between dependence and freedom is central to Rahner's interpretation of the experience of the religious dimension of human experience. The presence and experience of divine grace is such that the very experience of the transcendence of the whither of our existence is an experience of freedom and responsibility. Rahner uses a similar dialectic to interpret the christological dogma of Chalcedon so that the human nature of Jesus is both dependent upon God and yet radically autonomous. Rahner insists on this dialectic over against popular or traditional misunderstandings of the Chalcedonian dogma. The latter imagines the divine person as controlling the human nature of Christ and fails to realize that Christian soteriology requires that we are redeemed through Jesus's human act of freedom. The importance of this dialectic of freedom in Rahner's interpretation of the experience of divine grace is perhaps a reason why his theology was instrumental in the development of political theology (e.g., by his student Johann B. Metz) and why his theology influenced the understanding of salvation and grace in Latin American liberation theology (See Chapter Nine).

The Supernatural Existential

Rahner's theology can be described as a form of theology of correlation. Nevertheless, it is not simply a correlation between human experience and religious symbols. The correlation is made complex because Rahner underscores the historical nature both of human experience and of religious symbols. He introduces the category of the "*supernatural existential*" to interpret the source of both human experience and revelation. This notion of "supernatural existential" remains a central and debated concept of Rahner's theology. The intent of the notion can best be seen against the background of the debates within Roman Catholic theology in the 1950s surrounding the *nouvelle théologie*. As we have seen, de Lubac had sought to integrate the natural and supernatural by arguing that the human person has a natural desire for God. The papal encyclical *Humani Generis* rejected such a position for failing to preserve adequately the distinction of nature and grace.

Rahner appropriates Heidegger's notion of the "existential" in order to achieve a resolution or a middle point between the contrasting posi-

tions of de Lubac and Pope Pius XII. "Existential" is the term used by Heidegger to designate those categories that are applicable specifically to human persons, but not to nature. As such, they are contrasted with the Aristotelian categories that were more applicable to the material objects of nature. Historicity and self-understanding belong to the existentials of human existence. Historicity is not simply something that is added to human nature; rather, human persons are determined by their very historicity. Humans do not exist as an abstract essence or a pure nature but as historical persons. Within Rahner's conception, human nature, as historically and concretely created by God, is created with a specific purpose and goal. The supernatural existential characterizes this goal of human nature as *de facto* created and intended by God. Rahner thereby seeks to overcome the impasse between the *nouvelle théologie* and Neo-Scholasticism. Both sides held a view of human nature that overlooked the historicity of human nature. As Rahner affirms:

> It will be permissible at this point to point unhesitatingly at the unlimited dynamism of the spirit. . . . All one must guard against is identifying this unlimited dynamism of the *spiritual nature* in a simply apodeictic [absolutely certain] way with that dynamism which we experience (or believe we experience) in the adventure of our concrete spiritual existence because here the supernatural existential may already be at work.[51]

In addition to using the notion of existential, Rahner appropriates Heidegger's notion of pre-apprehension (*Vorgriff*).[52] He applies both concepts to the issue of the relation between the knowledge of God and the proofs for God's existence. Rahner argues that the traditional proofs of the existence of God presuppose that one demonstrates what one does not know previously. Rahner argues, on the contrary, that only with some pre-understanding or pre-apprehension of God can one have some understanding of what the proofs of the existence of God are about. "A reflective proof for God's existence is not intended to communicate a knowledge in which a previously and completely unknown and therefore also indifferent object is presented to people from without" and, therefore, becomes known only subsequently through proofs.[53]

Rahner explains this pre-apprehension as follows: "Hence this original transcendence's pre-apprehension reaches out towards what is nameless and what originally and by its very nature is infinite."[54] This transcendence is a horizon that is indefinable.

What transcendence moves towards, then, is also indefinable. By the fact that the horizon of the term of transcendence extends beyond our reach and thus offers to knowledge the space for its individual objects of knowledge and love, this horizon or term always and essentially and by its very nature is distinct from anything which appears within it as an object of knowledge.[55]

This pre-apprehension of God is a knowledge of God, but God as the undefined and absolute mystery. Consequently, the quest for meaning still endures. This pre-apprehension is both the condition of the search and the impetus for the search. As the condition for the search it constitutes the *de facto* historical transcendental condition of the possibility for the human person to be open to and to hear God's revelation or, as the title of his second book expresses, it is to be "Hearers of the Word." Rahner's transcendental and existential analysis, therefore, aims to show the conditions of the possibility not merely of metaphysical knowledge of God, but of Christian revelation. The search through history for meaning finds its end in God's revelation in salvation history culminating in Christ and continued in the Church.

Revelation as Transcendental and as Categorical

Whereas traditional Neo-Scholastic theology separates very sharply nature and grace, history and salvation history, religious experience and supernatural revelation, Karl Rahner's constructive theological synthesis seeks to show their fun-damental unity. His interpretation of creation and grace seeks their ontological unity insofar as both creation and grace are constituted by God's self-communication. His notion of "supernatural existential" underscores that the divine creation of the human person is not an abstract ahistorical creation, but rather a historical creation with a specific goal of union with God. The consequence of this ontological vision and this historical unity is that

the history of salvation and revelation is coexistent and coextensive with the history of the world and of the human spirit, and hence also with the history of religion.[56]

Rahner uses the category of "transcendental revelation" to characterize this presence of salvation and revelation throughout the history of the world and of the human spirit. It is this transcendental revelation of God that is the ground or basis of the particular categorical revelation or the explicit history of salvation. Whereas Neo-Scholastic theology had interpreted revelation primarily as a set of propositional truths, Rahner seeks through his interpretation of the distinction between transcendental and categorical to move away from such a propositional view of revelation.

Human persons as spiritual beings are constituted by their basic transcendental experience of God. They then interpret and express that experience in historical language and acts. Consequently, there comes to be an historical and categorical objectification of that transcendental experience. This objectification takes place in and through human history and culture and not alongside of history or independent of culture. When this objectification in history and culture entails an explicitly religious interpretation of that transcendental revelatory experience, it becomes what Rahner calls "categorical revelation." The relation between transcendental experience of God (transcendental revelation) and explicitly religious interpretation of that experience (categorical revelation) is such that the latter is not only an objectification of the former but also an objectification in an explicitly religious interpretation.

Rahner's affirmation of God's universal presence to the human spirit as the divine offer of grace has led to the term "anonymous Christian." This term—originally coined by Johann B. Metz and then accepted by Karl Rahner—has been subject to much debate (see Chapter Fifteen). It should be noted that in relation to the above explanation it could more properly be called "implicitly religious." What Rahner is affirming is the transcendental experience of God that underlies all religious interpretations and objectification of that experience in the so-called world religions. The diverse religions of the world represent differing religious interpretations of the religious dimension of transcendental experience. Because Rahner as a Christian believes that all grace of God is mediated through Christ, he finds some justification in using the term "anonymous Christian." However, at the same time, he concedes that a Buddhist or a Hindu might from their religious perspective want to label him an anonymous Buddhist or Hindu.

Rahner's Theological Method

The specific character of Rahner's theological method can be illustrated by a comparison with Paul Tillich's method of correlation (see Chapter Five). Though they are similar, considerable differences exist between them. One major difference concerns the interpretation of the contemporary human existential pole of the correlation. In Tillich's *Systematic Theology*, the ambiguities of being, reason, existence, history, and life give rise to the questions that find their correlation in the symbols of God, revelation, Christ, the Kingdom, and Spirit.[57] In Rahner's theology, however, the correlation has as its existential pole not so much the experience of ambiguity as the experience of divine grace within the human experience of self-transcendence. Rahner's understanding of this experience has its roots in his understanding of the Thomistic notion of analogy that involves

not only a comparison and negation, but also a transcending eminence. Rahner, therefore, explains the human experience of transcendence in the world not so much in relation to the world understood as a world of ambiguity but, rather, in relation to the world as imperfectly participating in the communication of God's presence. It is this experience of divine presence and grace that underlies the experiential basis of his method of correlation. The difference between Rahner and Tillich can be described as a difference between a Catholic sacramental vision of the world as graced, especially one informed by the *nouvelle théologie*, and a Lutheran vision that is sensitive to the ambiguities and sinfulness of the human condition. The experience of grace is so central to Rahner's theology that a leading commentary on his work is entitled *A World of Grace*.[58] Rahner's theology has been characterized by Rahner himself by a term taken from Gregory of Nyssa: mystagogy, that is, an initiation into the mystery of God's grace.[59]

Karl Rahner's theological method is often referred to as a transcendental method, and the significance of his theological contribution as the turn to the human subject. This description, though correct, overlooks elements that are not taken into account. "Transcendental" is not simply to be equated with the *a priori*, as in the case of Kant, but also takes into account human historicity.[60] Rahner is quite clear that a transcendental analysis of human consciousness is an analysis of a consciousness that is rooted in history. Wolfhart Pannenberg has observed that a Hegelian dialectic of difference in unity is central to Karl Rahner's Christology.[61] This observation is correct insofar as the Hegelian dialectic of unity in difference is central to Rahner's theology. Hegel's notion that differences of degree become essential differences is central to both Rahner's anthropology and Christology. For example, it is central to his understanding of the place of human nature within an evolutionary worldview, and it is crucial for his understanding of the relation between anthropology and Christology.

The Symbol

Rahner affirms that Being is constituted by the presence of Being to itself. Being comes to itself in its expression. To affirm that all being is present to itself appears to many commentators as an Idealist statement.[62] Nevertheless, it is the central ontology of Rahner's theology. This ontology, developed in *Spirit in the World,* is the presupposition of both his transcendental method and his theology. It shows that Rahner is fundamentally more Hegelian than Kantian in his philosophical presuppositions. Rahner writes:

"Being present to itself" is only another way of describing the actuality, that is, the intrinsic self-realization of the being. But then it follows that a being "comes to itself" in its expression, in the derivative agreement of the differentiated which is preserved as the perfection of the unity. For realization as plurality and as possession of self cannot be disparate elements simply juxtaposed in a being, since possession of self (in knowledge and love) is not just an element, but *the* content of that which we call being (and hence self-realization). And it comes to itself in the measure in which it realizes itself by constituting a plurality.[63]

These complex and turgid sentences express the metaphysic by which Rahner correlates the ontological structure of reality and the classic Christian doctrines of God, Trinity, Creation, and Incarnation. An understanding of this quotation and its implications becomes clear through Rahner's notion of a real symbol. A real symbol is differentiated from a sign. Whereas a conventional (traffic light) or natural symbol (smoke) signifies what is other from itself, a real symbol is both an expression of and a self-actualization of reality. An embrace between two persons symbolizes the love between the persons. It is also an expression, intensification, and actualization of that love. The very act of embracing by making explicit the love actualizes it and intensifies it.

In the same vein, God's creation is not simply the making of an external object, but it entails God's very self-communication. Creation entails a self-communication of God. Jesus Christ is spec-

ulatively interpreted by Rahner as the high point of God's self-communication because in Christ, God becomes human as the radical self-communication and symbolization of God. The very difference to God is constituted through the unity with God. To use an analogy, the more a teacher can communicate his or her knowledge to a student, the more the student receives and becomes independent of the teacher. The self-communication of God in Creation means that Creation is an expression of God. The self-possession and self-realization of human nature is a high point of God's self-communication. The radical and perfect expression of this symbolization is the human nature of Christ. Here is the high point of God's self-communication.

Rahner develops this conception of a real symbol to interpret the Trinity, the Incarnation, anthropology, salvation history, the Church, and his controversial concept of anonymous Christianity. The interpretation of being as symbolic leads, for example, not only to Rahner's understanding of Trinity in which the second Person, the Logos, is the symbol of God, but also to his understanding of Christology in which Jesus is the symbol of God.

It follows from what has been said that the Logos, as Son of the Father, is truly, in his humanity as such, the revelatory symbol in which the Father enunciates himself, in this Son to the world—revelatory, because the symbol renders present what is revealed.[64]

This interpretation of Jesus is also applied to the Church. "When we say that the Church is the persisting presence of the incarnate Word in space and time, we imply at once that it continues the symbolic function of the Logos in the world."[65] On the basis of this theology of symbol, Rahner's view of the Church represents a "high ecclesiology" insofar as the church is seen as a continuation of the sacramental and symbolic function of Jesus.

His view of the Church as the continuation of the symbolic function of the Logos also provides the basis for his conception of anonymous Christianity (see Chapter Fifteen). Within this conception the Church is seen as the explicit symbol and intensification of the grace that is universally present throughout the world.

The manifestation of grace which achieves this objective reality in the church is a *manifestation* and a *sign* of that grace wherever it may take effect. In other words, the church as manifestation of grace is a sacramental sign of the grace that is offered to the world and history as a whole (. . .) the message of salvation addressed by God to mankind considered as a unity, as the *archsacrament* or basic sacrament. It embraces the individual and his personal history but is in itself Christ or the abiding continuity of his in history which is the Church.[66]

Christianity is, then, posited as an explicit symbolization of God's grace and presence that is universally present as an offer, which modifies the traditional theological view of no salvation outside the church. The traditional thesis posited salvation on the basis of a baptism by desire; that is, if someone knew that it was God's will, then she would desire to become Christian. Within Rahner's conception, persons through their decisions make a fundamental decision for or against the transcendence that is God. A decision for that transcendence is an implicit affirmation of God and God's grace that is explicitly symbolized and thematized in the Church. God's saving will and offer of grace is universal; therefore, God's grace is implicitly present everywhere, though it is categorically and explicitly symbolized in salvation history and in the Church.

Critical Issues

The most fundamental criticism raised about Rahner's theology revolves around his explicit and intentional attempt to interlink anthropology, theology, and Christology. What Rahner would consider his specific achievement and contribution to theology, others would judge to be its weakness or fault. A second criticism, important though less central to Rahner's explicit intention, concerns the relation between language and

experience as well as between transcendental and hermeneutical analysis.

Regarding the first criticism, the integration between nature and grace, and the view of Christology as perfect anthropology or anthropology as imperfect Christology, is central to Karl Rahner's transcendental and ontological interpretation. Several major criticisms have been made of Rahner's linkage of theology and anthropology. Hans Urs von Balthasar (see Chapter Eight) criticizes Rahner's transcendental and existential approach as an anthropological narrowing of theology. To some degree, as has been noted, von Balthasar's basic objection to Karl Rahner's theology "is an objection not so much to one contemporary theologian (for whom, in fact, he has enormous respect) as it is a protest against the whole tradition of European 'mainstream' philosophy between Kant and Heidegger" because of its focus on human subjectivity.[67] Against such a criticism, one can argue that Rahner develops his transcendental approach quite differently from Kant's insofar as Rahner makes the affirmation of transcendence as constitutive for all cognition. Moreover, Rahner observes that his understanding and interpretation of the human subject is not that of an abstract human subjectivity but, rather, of a concrete historical human subject existing within a specific Christian tradition and history.

Within the Barthian tradition, especially along the directions taken by Hans Frei and George Lindbeck (see Chapters Eleven and Sixteen), Rahner's transcendental approach is criticized for not sufficiently taking into account the particularity and historicity of Christian revelation. This criticism objects that Rahner subsumes the particular under the universal.[68] Defenders of Rahner again counter that his starting point is the historical, concrete experience of persons within the Christian tradition rather than an abstract universal human nature. The correlation between human nature and Christian revelation is not an abstract correlation; rather, it is based upon a specific religious history and tradition.

The second and more philosophical criticism of Rahner's transcendental approach to theology concerns the relation between language and experience. In his study of theology and Wittgenstein, Fergus Kerr, a British Domincan theologian, questions whether Rahner's position presupposes an unthematized experience that is prior to language.[69] Selecting several of Rahner's sentences, he argues that Rahner seems to presuppose that communication comes after language and language after concepts. For example, Rahner writes: "The original self-presence of the subject in the actual realization of his existence strives to translate itself more and more into the conceptual."[70] Hence Rahner's thought appears to presuppose, contrary to Wittgenstein, that there is a religious experience prior to language and conceptualization. Many statements can be found throughout Rahner's writings that appear to reinforce Kerr's critique. However, elsewhere Rahner understands the experience of God as mediated. For example, he speaks of the "immediacy to God as mediated immediacy."[71] Such a reference to "mediated immediacy" illustrates Rahner's understanding of all experience as historically and linguistically mediated.

BERNARD LONERGAN

Bernard Lonergan (1904–1984), born in Buckingham, Quebec, Canada, attended Heythrop College from 1926 to 1929. After receiving a B.A. from the University of London in 1930, he went to the Gregorian University in Rome for theological studies from 1933 to 1937 and then undertook doctoral studies there from 1938 to 1940. Lonergan's doctoral dissertation was on Thomas Aquinas's understanding of grace and freedom.

From 1940 to 1946 he served as professor of theology at Loyola College in Montreal, Canada. After that he returned to the Gregorian University, where he taught for most of his career and where he had the opportunity to educate many clergy and seminary professors from North America. His influence permeates Catholic theology in North America, while his influence in Germany and in France is much less extensive. After his retirement from the Gregorian, Lonergan taught

at Boston College and then at Regis College in Toronto, Canada, where he died in 1984.

Like the other transcendental Thomists, Lonergan's initial writings sought to retrieve and to reinterpret the philosophy and theology of Thomas Aquinas. His first work dealt with the problem of understanding the divine activity in grace. He sought to overcome the classic controversy between the Molinist (mostly Jesuits) who emphasized human freedom along with God's knowledge of the means and the Bãnezian (mainly Dominicans) who emphasized the divine transcendence and the divine "physical predetermination" of the human will. In this scholastic debate about the relation between divine action and human freedom, each appealed to Thomas Aquinas. Lonergan argued that Thomas's conception transcended the *aporia* of both sides of the controversy, and in so doing he developed a conception of divine transcendence and activity as well as of human freedom that would undergird his later philosophical and theological work.[72] Lonergan's next study on Thomas was a series of articles on the notion of *verbum* (word) in which Lonergan establishes that Aquinas's cognitional theory does not emphasize concepts but intellectual operations and activities. He then shows the significance of this difference not only for Aquinas 's theory of knowledge, but also for an understanding of the doctrine of Trinity.[73] Both studies overcome a conceptualist Neo-Scholastic interpretation of Thomas. Both studies, like the work of the other transcendental Thomists, go back to Thomas in order to recover an interpretation of Thomas that breaks out of Neo-Scholasticism. Moreover, these studies already display Lonergan's own constructive work in cognitional theory and its application to theology.

Critical Realism

Central to Lonergan's contribution to philosophy and theology is his account of human knowledge. In both his philosophical and theological endeavors, Lonergan sought to provide a correct account of knowing and to show the implications of that account of knowing for metaphysics and for theology. His writings demonstrate the role that an account of knowledge plays not only within theological method but also within the Christian doctrines of the Trinity, Christ, and grace. Lonergan contrasts two basic accounts of knowing and makes this contrast central to his view of the history of philosophy, religious epistemology, and method in theology. One account understands knowledge according to the analogy of "taking a look." How does one know that something is true? For this account the answer is quite simple: One takes a look. This account assimilates knowledge to looking or perceiving. Such a perceptual account of knowledge, moreover, is a very natural and commonsense account.

In contrast, the other account of knowledge attempts to explain what is involved in knowing the thoughts or feelings of another person or what is entailed in knowing events of past history. In such situations, one cannot simply take a look. One cannot look into the mind of another. Nor can one look into the past. Instead, one relies on data or evidence. Such data or evidence needs to be understood and interpreted. In addition, one needs to come to a judgment about the correct interpretation of the data and evidence. Consequently, knowledge consists not simply of looking or experiencing but includes understanding and judging.

This contrast between knowledge as a looking and knowledge as a reflective judging is crucial to Lonergan's critique of Neo-Scholasticism and of positivistic conceptions of knowledge. It is also central to his own constructive explanation of method within philosophy and theology. The critique of traditional Neo-Scholastic theories of knowledge forms the backdrop to his development of a new understanding of method in theology. Therefore, Lonergan's controversy with the historian of Scholasticism, Etienne Gilson (1884–1978), over the interpretation of the realism of Thomas Aquinas is important for understanding Lonergan's development of method in theology.[74] Lonergan criticizes the realism of the theory of knowledge that Gilson developed in *Réalisme Thomiste et Critique*. In his criticism, Lonergan appeals to the development of the transcendental philosophy of Emerich Coreth, a contemporary Roman Catholic philosopher, especially Coreth's understanding of the role of the horizon of questioning in knowledge. The concept of "horizon" involves the world of meaning that is possible and open to a subject and the necessity of interpretation and judgment. Lonergan also makes the startling claim that Gilson's theory of knowledge is actually much closer to that of Kant than to that of Thomas. It is startling because many would assume that a contrast exists between the epistemology of Kant and Gilson, because Kant is a critical Idealist, whereas Gilson is neither Idealist nor critical, but a Realist. Nevertheless, Lonergan argues that despite his anti-Kantianism, Gilson's theory of knowledge is similar to Kant's on one basic point: the primacy of perception. Gilson maintains that perception is the gateway to the real world, just as Kant asserts that perception is the point of entry to the world of appearances.

In Lonergan's words, Gilson's understanding of Thomas is incorrect because it assumes "that perception is the one manner in which cognitional activity attains objectivity."[75] Although Gilson and Kant assume that objectivity is a matter of perception, they disagree on the matter of fact. Contrary to Kant, Gilson affirms that "de facto we have perceptions of reality."[76] It is this perceptual view of knowledge, a naïve realism, that Lonergan's philosophy consistently strives to overcome. Knowing is not a matter of "taking a look." Here Lonergan appeals to the concept of "horizon":

[A] horizon is prior to the meaning of statements: every statement made by a realist denotes an object in a realist world; every statement made by an idealist denotes an object in an idealist world; and neither of the two sets of statements can prove the horizon within which each set has its meaning, simply because the statements can have their meaning only by presupposing their proper horizon.[77]

The notion of horizon, a concept borrowed from phenomenology, is basic to Lonergan's development of both a theory of knowledge and a method in theology.[78] A horizon involves both a subjective and an objective pole. Subjectively, it refers to the subject's intentionality and possibility of meaning at his or her present development. Objectively, it refers to the worlds of meaning open to the subject. Lonergan's notion of horizon becomes evident in his outline of the diverse ideals of knowledge and in the role of conversion within theology. As the following will show, the ideal of knowledge and the notion of conversion are related to the manner in which human understanding operates.

A New Ideal of Knowledge

Lonergan's major philosophical work, *Insight: A Study in Human Understanding,* written from 1949 to 1953 while at Toronto, sought to show the precise manner in which human understanding develops and operates and thereby to illustrate his account of knowledge.[79] Human understanding is not the intuition of some essence nor, as we have seen, does objectivity amount to taking a look. An analysis of psychological experiences belies the claims of naïve realism. The first chapters of *Insight* draw on mathematics, physics, and common sense to show that human intelligence involves the gathering of data, the setting up of intelligible correlations, the obtaining of a "concrete-identity whole" (which involves the grasp and the interpretation of the data as a unified whole), and the making of reflective judgments. The issue of objectivity becomes not so much an issue of perception as one of judgment. One moves from conditioned judgments to virtually unconditioned judgments. Lonergan argues that objectivity is an issue of judgment in which one decides about whether certain conditions are met. This understanding of objectivity in relation to the condition of knowledge provides the foundational presupposition of his metaphysics. Judgments of objectivity not only affirm that individual objects are distinct from the knower, but they

also point beyond the individual object to the transcendent reality of being.

The principle notion of objectivity solves the problem of transcendence. Through experience, inquiry, and reflection, there arises knowledge of other objects both as beings and as being other than the knower. Hence, we place transcendence not in going beyond a known knower, but in heading for being. . . . In as much as such judgements occur, there are in fact objectivity and transcendence.[80]

Lonergan's attempt to explain concepts of knowledge and meaning in *Insight* is often represented as an effort to incorporate within Roman Catholic philosophy and theology the significance of the Copernican revolution in transcendental philosophy initiated by Kant's critique of knowledge. However, Lonergan's contribution goes far beyond Kant's critique insofar as his analysis is not simply a shift to a transcendental conception of knowledge. Lonergan contrasts two ideals of knowledge, which illustrate a difference in method not only from Neo-Scholasticism but also from German Idealism. Lonergan elaborates on the distinction between the Aristotelian ideal of knowledge and that of contemporary science as a contrast between classic and contemporary modes of theoretical and scientific inquiry. Whereas the classic ideal of inquiry sought certainty and certitude, contemporary inquiry claims only high probability. Whereas the classic mode was concerned with essences and with the changeless, the contemporary mode assumes change, development, and shifting horizons. Whereas the classic view focused on the universal and the formal object of a science, the contemporary interest is in the intelligible correlations within concrete fields or regions of the universe that the particular science studies. Whereas the classical ideal employed logic, often a deductive logic from principles and axioms to a conclusion—often a movement of descent and ascent—the modern scientific ideal moves from data, to hypotheses, to further checking and correction. Whereas the classic conception of knowledge was individualistic and based upon the judgments of the individual scholar's virtue, expertise, and insights, the modern conception of knowledge is collective, collaborative, and constantly open to further revision and development.

It is not only Lonergan's focus on the human subject and the operation of the human intellect in knowledge, but also his differentiation between the two ideals of knowledge that explains the influence of Lonergan's *Insight* on Roman Catholic theologians. Viewed as a crowning achievement in the philosophical analysis of knowledge, *Insight* undermined the Neo-Scholastic vision of theology as a logical and deductive discipline that takes church teaching as its first principles and then seeks to explicate conclusions and applications from them. Instead, it points to the need for the collection of data within the Scriptures and tradition, the interpretation of that data, and the formation of judgments and hypotheses about that data. So pursued, the method of theology can be interpreted in the light of modern canons of knowledge.

The Question of God

Lonergan's turn to the subject, his theory of knowledge, and his contrast between the two ideals of scientific knowledge remain significant contributions that have formed the horizon of contemporary North American Roman Catholic theology. His treatment of the question of God in *Insight* shows how he exploits his approach to deal with the existence and meaning of God. He has taken the orientation of the "turn to the subject" to develop a "transcendental" approach to the transcendent. Lonergan maintains that the shift from Aristotle's physics to modern science entails a shift in the approach to God. In Aristotle's physics, a logical break does not exist between the knowledge of the world and knowledge of ultimate causes. Modern science introduces this break insofar it proceeds from data of this world and moves to verifiable hypotheses. "But God is not a datum—Again between this world and God there is no relationship that can be verified."[81]

It is in Chapters 19 and 20 of *Insight* that Lonergan provides an argument for the existence of

God and his analysis of belief. Lonergan's strategy in approaching God is developed through a set of questions. Could the intelligibility that we assume in the universe be unless it had an intelligible ground? Does not the conditioned character of being require an unconditioned? Lonergan's analysis of human knowledge aims to show that human persons implicitly in their acts of knowledge presuppose that the universe is intelligible. It is from a universe that is not completely intelligible in itself that Lonergan moves to the only ground of the universe's intelligibility, that which in itself is completely intelligible.

His argument for the existence of God proceeds as follows: If reality or the real is intelligible, that is, completely intelligible, then God exists.

If the real is completely intelligible, then complete intelligibility exists. If complete intelligibility exists, the idea of being exists. If the idea of being exists, then God exists. Therefore, if the real is completely intelligible, God exists.[82]

The premises as presuppositions here are the affirmation that being is completely intelligible correlates with the affirmation that complete intelligibility is God. Lonergan writes:

If I am operating in the intellectual pattern of experience, if I am genuine in my acceptance of the domination of the detached, disinterested desire to inquire intelligently and reflect reasonably, then I have no just grounds for surprise if I find myself unable to deny that there is a reality or that the real is being or that being is completely intelligible or that complete intelligibility is unrestricted understanding or that unrestricted understanding is God.[83]

Lonergan's type of demonstration of the existence of God moves from his transcendental analysis of the patterns of human understanding to affirmations of the objectivity of reality and then to affirmations of intelligibility of being and finally to God as unrestricted understanding. He stands in the line of *la nouvelle théologie* insofar as the "immanent source of transcendence in man is his detached, disinterested, unrestricted desire to know."[84] It is from desire that the search for transcendent knowledge springs and that leads to the affirmation of the transcendent.

This achievement of Lonergan's reformulation of the demonstration of God from the perspective of human understanding has not gone without criticism from Lonergan's Roman Catholic peers. Indeed, the sharpest criticisms have come from his own students. David Burrell has argued that one does not have a direct knowledge of complete intelligibility. Hence one cannot affirm that being is completely intelligible because one does not know what a judgment would be like that affirmed that all intelligent questions were completely answered.[85] Similarly, Burrell questions whether the move from a restricted to an unrestricted act of understanding is demonstrative because the unrestricted does not entail the judgment of a restricted act of understanding. Though Lonergan intends to present a strictly philosophical argument, he does not. For as David Tracy argues, he presupposes in his philosophical argument what he has worked out in his theology.[86]

Lonergan has himself admitted that this criticism has a partial validity insofar as he later stresses the need to bring the religious dimension into consideration in the argument for God's existence. He writes:

The trouble with chapter nineteen in *Insight* was that it did not depart from the traditional line. It treated God's existence and attributes in a purely objective fashion. It made no effort to deal with the subject's religious horizon.[87]

It is this religious horizon that Lonergan's subsequent work, especially his analysis of method in theology, seeks to make the centerpiece of his theological argument.

Method in Theology: Functional Specialties

After writing *Insight*, much of Lonergan's theological work consisted of the application of his philosophy to theology. This was carried out through his published Latin treatises on the Trinity[88] and Christology that served as the texts for his lectures at the Gregorian University.[89] Lonergan later developed the theological significance of his approach to human understanding in a major work, *Method in Theology*.[90] Here Lonergan develops the notion of functional specialties that are correlated with the operations of the human mind in terms of the activities of collecting the data, interpreting the data, understanding the data, and making decisions about the data. In *Insight*, Lonergan offers a form of critical realism over against two extremes: on the one hand, a naive realism, or an uncritical empiricism, that considers only empirical data to be determinative; on the other hand, an idealism that considers only the interpretation of meaning as determinative. Lonergan argues that critical realism incorporates both sensation and understanding but also brings the critical element of reflective judgment into play. Such a critical realism interprets objectivity as determined by reflective judgments.

For Lonergan, there are eight functional specialties in theology, namely, (1) research, (2) interpretation, (3) history, (4) dialectic, (5) foundations, (6) doctrines, (7) systematics, and (8) communications (the left and right columns of Chart 1). The eight functional specialties relate to the four levels of consciousness that unfold both in our everyday lives and in every academic pursuit. We move from experiencing to understanding, to judging, and to deciding. The existence of this pattern underlies the method of all disciplines, natural, social, historical, and so on. These four levels of consciousness provide not only a generic pattern but are used by Lonergan to recast the traditional division of theological fields. Using these levels, Lonergan produces the outline of functional specialties in theology as shown in the chart.

The chart shows how these functional specialties, rather than specific content, distinguish the different theological disciplines. The proposed division illustrates how Lonergan explicates a method in theology (as the title of his

CHART I

Functional Specialties	Structure of Consciousness	Functional Specialties
Research	experiencing	Communications
Interpretation	understanding	Systematics
History	judging	Doctrines
Dialectic	deciding	Foundations

book indicates) rather than a specifically theological method. Method is grounded in the meaningful sequence of moves from experience to understanding to judgment to decision. On the level of experience, one inquires as to the relevant data and information for the issue at hand (research). One attempts to understand or to interpret that data (interpretation). On the basis of this understanding one seeks to formulate hypotheses or directions (history). One then has to evaluate different possibilities and hypotheses (dialectic). The circle then turns: In the next functional specialty (foundations), one asks how one stands in relation to the values and possibilities that one has evaluated in dialectic. What proposition does one want to deduce from what one has decided was true and valuable (doctrines)? How are these truths and values of doctrines related to other affirmations (systematics)? How can one communicate with others what one understands, values, and affirms (communications)? Rather than treating the traditional theological curricula as consisting of disparate disciplines, Lonergan organizes them according to functional specialties based upon the different operations of our human understanding.

Conversion

The crucial turning point in Lonergan's division of the functional specialties is at the level of foundations. It is one's decision that provides the foundations for what follows. Lonergan explicates this element of decision with the key concept of conversion and the division of conversion into three types: intellectual, moral, and reli-

gious. Intellectual conversion entails going from the world of immediacy and the direct objectivity of "taking a look" to the horizon that knowing also involves reflection and judgment. Intellectual conversion enables one "to discover the self-transcendence proper to the human process of coming to know, [and] is to break often long-ingrained habits of thought and speech."[91] Moral conversion entails an equally radical self-transcendence through the change of horizons. The criterion of one's decision and choices is no longer personal satisfaction or wants but, rather, values and the good. Consequently, "moral conversion consists in opting for the truly good, even for value against satisfaction when value and satisfaction conflict."[92] Value, rather than satisfaction, becomes the criterion of choice. The final level is religious conversion. It is also a "modality of self-transcendence."

Religious conversion is to a total being-in-love as the efficacious ground of all self-transcendence, whether in the pursuit of truth, or in the realization of human values, or in the orientation man adopts to the universe, its ground, and its goal.[93]

Lonergan describes religious conversion as an affective self-transcendence of falling in love. However, there are different kinds of love. Religious conversion entails a love without conditions, reservations, or limitations. The knowledge of God is given in religious conversion and its unrestricted and unconditional love. In linking love and knowledge, desire and self-transcendence, Lonergan places at the center of his method themes that were initiated at the beginning of the century by Rousselot and the *nouvelle théologie*.

Religion and Theology

Lonergan's influence has been especially strong in the English-speaking world where his conceptions of method have influenced the way many have come to understand the theological task. Neo-Scholasticism, in contrast, had developed a notion of theology as a deductive science. It viewed church teaching as the principles from which doctrinal formulations and systematic expositions were drawn.[94] As early as *Insight*, we can observe Lonergan developing a fundamentally different conception of the scientific method. He emphasizes its procedural nature as a self-reflective and self-critical enterprise. What constitutes science as science is not so much a specific object of knowledge or a particular disciplinary method but, rather, the more generic and ongoing procedure of openness to data, of interpreting and judging that data, and arriving at critical judgments. Such an understanding of theology posits a structural similarity between theology and other disciplines. The same intellectual operations of the human mind that are present in other disciplines, in their effort to achieve understanding, are present in the theological inquiry.

In Lonergan's understanding of theology as an ongoing self-correcting enterprise, the notions of value, meaning, and religion play an important role. The sharp contrast between a theology based upon religion and one based upon God's Word so dominant in twentieth-century German Protestant Neo-Orthodox or Barthian theology, does not have the same valence in Lonergan's method. His *Method in Theology* makes the issues of value, of the good, and of meaning the context for his treatment of religion, as well as the background for topics such as the question of God, self-transcendence, religious experience, the Word, faith, and religious belief. Similarly, the existence of good and evil and other judgments of value raise religious questions about the meaning and intelligibility of the universe. Lonergan argues that

once one grants that the universe is intelligible, "there arises the question whether the universe could be intelligible without having an intelligent ground. But that is the question about God."[95]

Lonergan insists that it is the reflective character of human nature that raises such questions of value and meaning. These questions, in turn, raise the question of God. Here he continues the emphases of the *nouvelle théologie*, interpreting God and religion in relation to human fulfillment and self-transcendence. Lonergan writes:

I have conceived of being in love with God as the ultimate fulfillment of man's capacity for self-transcendence; and this view of religion is sustained when God is conceived as the supreme fulfillment of the transcendental notions, as supreme intelligence, truth, reality, righteousness, goodness.[96]

If religion is formally interpreted in terms of self-fulfillment and self-transcendence, it is through the study of religions and the diversity of religions that Lonergan sees the material and data for the discipline of theology.

Critical Issues

Because Bernard Lonergan's writings are both philosophical and theological, criticism of his contributions have touched on both aspects of his writings. In addition to the specific issue of the adequacy of Lonergan's demonstration of the existence of God, already discussed above, a general criticism is directed against the philosophical presuppositions underlying both his philosophical and theological work. This criticism concerns the formal aspect of his work. Lonergan works out the formal structures of knowledge in *Insight* and seeks to demonstrate a structural universality and invariance in human cognition. Critics argue that the philosophical presupposition of his theory of knowledge does not sufficiently reflect the cultural specifications or particularities of rationality. In response to such criticism, Lonergan argues that any criticism would have to deal with notions of experience, understanding, reflecting, and judging.

A similar criticism, however, has been brought against Lonergan's *Method in Theology.* The division of theology into functional specialties has been criticized for its general and generic quality. Karl Rahner has suggested that it is too general and abstract to be properly theological.[97] Another problem with the functional specialties is the fact that they are divided according to the fourfold operation of the mind, and yet each of these specialties involves diverse functional operations of the mind. Although Lonergan himself concedes this, the question remains: If the functional specialties come into play in every single discipline of theology, how then can they be appealed to in order to justify the division of the disciplines themselves?

A major criticism concerns Lonergan's understanding of foundational theology in *Method in Theology.* Langdon Gilkey and David Tracy argue that Lonergan's treatment of foundational theology is insufficient to provide the critical grounding for religious belief that Lonergan seeks to give it.[98] Tracy notes that for Lonergan the principal role of the functional specialties of dialectics and foundations is to *justify* and to *validate* religious convictions and not simply to explicate or give an account of them. Tracy asks whether Lonergan in fact explicates religious conversion dogmatically or critically.[99] The question remains, with regard to *Method in Theology,* as to what constitutes an account of rationality according to which one can determine what is mediated critically or simply dogmatically.[100]

EDWARD SCHILLEBEECKX

Edward Cornelius Florentius Alfons Schillebeeckx was born on November 12, 1914, into a middle-class Flemish family in Antwerp, Belgium. He entered the Flemish Province of the Dominican Order at Ghent, studied at the Dominican House in Louvain, and was ordained a priest in 1941. In 1943 Schillebeeckx completed his studies at Louvain and began to teach theology at the Dominican House. At the end of the war he went to Le Saulchoir, the Dominican faculty in Paris, to pursue doctoral work. He also attended lectures at the Sorbonne and the Collège de France, as well as at Le Saulchoir where Yves Congar and Marie-Dominique Chenu taught. Schillebeeckx took Chenu as his dissertation adviser, and he maintains that Chenu's commitment to historical studies, and to social problems of justice facing the Church, remain two influences that have permeated his work. His dissertation, completed in 1951, was published the following year in a revised version as *De Sacramentele Heilseconomie* (*The Sacramental Economy of Salvation*).[101] Instead of a projected second volume, he wrote an abbreviated and popular version entitled *Christ the Sacrament of the Encounter with God.* In 1958, he was appointed to the chair of dogmatics and history of theology at the Catholic University of Nijmegen in the Netherlands, where he taught until 1983 when he retired. Schillebeeckx attended Vatican II as an adviser to the Dutch bishops and was influential in drafting the pastoral letter of the Dutch bishops in 1960, though he never served as an official *peritus* at the Council.

Schillebeeckx's contribution to theology covers a wide range of topics, and his basic theological method has changed and developed over time. This shift can be described as a transition from a phenomenological approach to more historical, hermeneutical, and political approaches that involve not only the method but also the content of his theology. Schillebeeckx's earliest writings concentrated on sacramental theology, and his books on the nature of sacraments in general, on the Eucharist, and on marriage were highly influential. In these early writings he used phenomenological categories of personal encounter to explain the efficacy of the sacraments rather than the traditional Aristotelian categories of causality, as was common in Thomist sacramental theology. His later work on Christology and ministry moved toward a more historical and social method. His studies on Christology led to the thorny historical issues concerning the relationship between the historical Jesus and

Edward Schillebeeckx

the Christ of faith, a theme dominant in Protestant theology, as we have seen. As a consequence, he needed to develop a methodology that was historical and interpretive rather than phenomenological. He thus began to approach theology from the reality of the earthly Jesus rather than from the christological formulas. At the same time, he appealed to recent critical theory in his understanding of history, society, and ministry.

Schillebeeckx's early work was influenced not only by the *nouvelle théologie* but also by the phenomenology of Dominic De Petter and Maurice Merleau-Ponty (1908–1961).[102] In analyzing faith within human experience, Schillebeeckx emphasizes that human experience takes place inseparably within a conceptual and linguistic framework. Interpretative frameworks and experience go together. From Maurice Merleau-Ponty, Schillbeeckx picks up language about encounter and dialogue, and the presence of Christ in the sacraments is interpreted within this phenomenological framework. His development of sacramental theology, therefore, uses the phenomenological category of encounter in contrast to the Aristotelian categories of causality to explain the efficacy of the sacraments.

Sacramental Theology

As we have learned, Schillebeeckx took the theses of his dissertation on the sacramental theology of Thomas Aquinas and wrote the more popular and systematic volume *Christ the Sacrament of the Encounter with God*.[103] At the heart of this book is an interpretation of the sacraments in terms of a personal communion between God and persons. His starting point is a Chalcedonian interpretation of Christology in which he views the sacramental life of the church as continuing the sacramental life of Jesus. Just as Christ through his risen body acts invisibly in the world, so he acts visibly in and through his earthly body, the Church, in such a way that the sacraments are the personal saving acts of Christ realized as institutional acts in the Church.[104]

Schillebeeckx's main contribution to sacramental theology consists in his translating scholastic concepts of causality into a more phenomenological or experiential account of the sacraments and their efficacy. He faults Scholastic theology for its mechanical and causal approach:

The consequence of this tendency towards a purely impersonal, almost mechanical approach was that they [the sacraments] were considered chiefly in terms of physical categories. The inclination was to look upon the sacraments as but one more application, although in a special manner, of the general laws of cause and effect.[105]

Schillebeeckx proposes a personalistic approach based upon the category of encounter for, in his view, the sacraments are

culminating moments because they are a special divine contact with a person in a situation which, for the Christian view of life, is decisive. The sacraments bring about the encounter with Christ in exactly those seven instances in which, on account of the demands of a special situation of Christian life, a person experiences a special and urgent need of communion with Christ.[106]

Jesus as Eschatological Prophet

There is a transition and a new focus in Schillebeeckx's work in the 1970s and 1980s with the publication of three major volumes on the historical Jesus and the development of his Christology. This turn can be best described as an increased awareness of historicity in his theology. Although attention to historical studies was always a characteristic feature of his work on sacramental theology, what is significant is how this new historical focus shifts the starting point of his theological reflection. His sacramental work began with the Chalcedonian credal understanding of Christ and its relationship to sacramental theology. Now Schillebeeckx starts out with a reconstruction and interpretation of the diverse strains of tradition within the New Testament. He explores the social and cultural background underlying the development of these diverse trajectories and oral traditions about Jesus prior to their fixity in the Synoptic Gospels. He shows how these trajectories led to the diverse understandings and formulas about Jesus in the New Testament, and how they then led to the christological developments of the ensuing centuries.

Schillebeeckx's investigations into the historical origins of early Christian belief begin with his book *Jesus: An Experiment in Christology* (1974; Eng. trans., 1979).[107] It is followed by *Christ* (1977; Eng. trans., 1980) and the *Interim Report on the Books Jesus and Christ* (1978; Eng. trans., 1981). The latter discusses the controversies that followed the publication of the two earlier books.[108] A third projected volume on Christology did not appear. Instead the volume *Church: The Human Story of God* (1989; Eng. trans., 1990) moves directly to his understanding of Church and ministry.[109]

In tracing the development of the early Christian creeds about Jesus, Schillebeeckx is heavily indebted to the exegetical work of Helmut Koester, professor of New Testament at Harvard Divinity School, where Schillebeeckx was visiting

when he began his work.[110] Following Koester, Schillebeeckx traces four early Christian creeds. One is a Maranatha or Parousia creed that focuses on Jesus's preaching of the coming reign of God. It symbolizes Jesus as the Lord to come and future bringer of salvation. This creed is dominant in the Q source and its community and in Mark's Gospel. A second creed, the "divine man" (*theios anèr*), concentrates on Jesus's miracles. It interprets Jesus in comparison to Greco-Roman miracle workers. The third creed, from the traditions of wisdom, collects Jesus's sayings and interprets Jesus primarily as a teacher of wisdom. One tradition (often called a low tradition because of its less exalted view of Jesus) views Jesus as the messenger or prophet of Wisdom. Another wisdom tradition (called a high tradition because of its more exalted view of Jesus) interprets Jesus as Wisdom herself (Sophia). The Easter creed, prevalent in the Pauline writings, takes as its starting point the death and resurrection of Jesus. It interprets Jesus predominantly as the crucified and risen One.

Though Shillebeeckx is aware that the Gospels represent interpretations of Jesus through the faith of the early Christians, he seeks through a historical reconstruction to get behind these creeds to the historical Jesus. Schillebeeckx departs on two points from Helmut Koester's reconstruction. Whereas Koester gives priority to the Easter creed, Schillebeeckx accentuates the understanding of Jesus as an eschatological prophet. In addition, by so identifying Jesus, Schillebeeckx seeks to make the historical Jesus more theologically significant. He does this by making Jesus's experience of God as *Abba* (which some scholars consider a familiar address rather than the more formal "Father") the basis of these diverse credal trajectories.

In Jesus we are confronted with someone who out of his personal *Abba* experience makes us an assured promise of a "future with and from God" and in his ministry actually proffers it. Apart from the reality of this very original *Abba* experience his message is an illusion.[111]

Schillebeeckx's historical reconstruction also serves a systematic purpose. Each of these creeds can be seen as an interpretation of Jesus that correlates with a different social and cultural horizon within early Christianity. The development to Nicea and Chalcedon represents a specific development of only one of these trajectories. Schillebeeckx can, therefore, affirm that

we have been given to see that the New Testament and later interpretations of Jesus are each one of them set within a very specific horizon of experience and understanding; that as such these are historically contingent and not in themselves the necessary context in which Christological belief in Jesus must be thought out.[112]

Whereas the New Testament writings reveal these diverse Christological trajectories within distinct horizons of experience and interpretation, the history of Christianity shows that one specific model became dominant to the neglect or detriment of other models and trajectories within the synoptic Gospels. Schillebeeckx points out that

from the Council of Nicea onward a particular Christological model—the Johannine—has been developed as a norm within very narrow limits and one direction . . . [and] the course of history has never done justice to the possibilities inherent in the synoptic model; its particular dynamic was checked and halted and the model relegated to the "forgotten truths" of Christianity.[113]

Underlying this historical sketch is an important systematic distinction between surface, conjunctural, and structural levels of history. The surface level consists of the everyday events, facts, and occurrences within history. The conjunctural level consists of larger unities of history, for example, Greco-Roman Hellenism, medieval feudalism, and modern capitalism. These larger units provide frameworks for the interpretation of the surface events. Finally, there are structural features. These are anthropological structures that persist throughout history. Schillebeeckx uses this

threefold distinction to deal with the issues of continuity and change within Christian history. There are not only conjunctural periods of radical change—for example, the shift from a hellenistic to a feudal and then to a modern society—but there are also anthropological structures that endure. The question for Schillebeeckx that is central to this historical inquiry is the identity of Christianity. His writings on Christology point in this direction insofar as he underscores the social and cultural context of the diverse early Christian creeds and their respective trajectories. The question then becomes: What is the relation between these trajectories and our situation today? To answer this question, Schillebeeckx develops a method of correlation.

Method of Correlation

The method of correlation entails for Schillebeeckx a double correlation that is patterned on the Thomistic understanding of the analogy of proportion rather than on the analogy of attribution. The distinction between these two analogies has been a crucial point in the twentieth-century revisions of Neo-Scholasticism. Moreover, Schillebeeckx's use of the analogy of proportion in carrying out his method of correlation illustrates the nuance of his theological method. The analogy of attribution argues in the following manner: Medicine or nutrition is called healthy because it produces the effect of health in humans. Because of the similarity or relation between effect and cause, the cause, nutrition, is called healthy. Applied to the Divine, one can say that God is good or wise because the effects of God's creative activity are good or wise. The analogy of proportion, however, is based upon a similarity of proportion. God's goodness as proportionate to God's being stands in correlation and analogy to the proportion between human goodness and human being. The difference between the two is significant. The analogy of attribution posits a much stronger similitude as the basis of the analogy than does the latter. To the extent that God's being is disproportionate to human being, to that extent God's goodness or wisdom differs from human goodness or wisdom. An analogy exists, not as an identity or similarity, but as a structural proportionality.

How does this double correlation relate to Schillebeeckx's historical concern about the identity of Christianity? First, Schillebeeckx does not affirm that a correspondence exists between our contemporary religious experience and the biblical symbols of faith. Instead, using the example of the difference in the two Thomistic conceptions of analogy, Schillebeeckx argues that a correlation exists between the religious experience and faith of the early Christians and their social cultural context and their expressions of their faith within this context. Likewise, a correlation exists between our experience, formulations, and culture and our religious experiences and faith. What, then, is correlated is a proportional relation existing in early Christianity and in contemporary Christianity.

Schillebeeckx further contours this method of a correlation of proportionality by means of four principles. These point to a fundamental identity or continuity amidst the historical differences and cultural changes. The first is the theological and anthropological principle that God brings salvation to humans. Salvation comes from God to humans. The second is the Christological mediation. Jesus of Nazareth discloses God's plan. Third, the Christian community or the Church continues the story of Jesus. Christian discipleship seeks to continue the message and lifestyle of Jesus. The fourth principle is eschatological fulfillment. The story of Jesus does not come to fulfillment in an earthly order, but looks toward God's Kingdom as an eschatological fulfillment. Amidst all change, the Christian communities, therefore, have a continuity insofar as they seek to serve and to continue the saving presence of Jesus that Jesus disclosed in his preaching and praxis.

The Conflict over Ministry

In the 1980s Schillebeeckx published a set of four articles that were then combined into a book entitled *Ministry: Leadership in the Community of*

Jesus Christ.[114] These writings marked a continuation of his earlier work on the sacraments and the ministry of the Church. Although ministry had become an important topic in contemporary Roman Catholic theological discussions,[115] Schillebeeckx's book nevertheless became his most controversial publication. The book pointed to the enormous historical change in the understanding of ministry in the history of Christianity and underscored the changed pastoral situation in the Roman Catholic Church since Vatican II. One change was the dire shortage of priests (especially in Europe) that left many communities without a Eucharistic minister. Both Schillebeeckx's analysis and his suggested reforms led to controversy. Many welcomed his studies enthusiastically; others criticized them severely.[116] The Vatican Congregation for the Doctrine of the Faith began an investigation. Schillebeeckx was summoned to Rome for a quasi-inquisitorial investigation, and in 1984 an official warning critical of major elements of the book was published and signed by Cardinal Ratzinger.[117] Schillebeeckx's book was so influential and popular that the Committee on Doctrine of the United States Bishop Conference felt compelled to publish in English translation several of the most critical European reviews.[118] In response to these criticisms, Schillebeeckx published a second book, *The Church with a Human Face* (1985).[119] Although this book bore a new title, it contained most of the original book with some changes and many additions.

What, then, were the controversial theses of Schillebeeckx's book *Ministry*? First, Schillebeeckx argued that there was a gradual but radical shift in the understanding of ministry between the first and second millenium. The book begins with a survey of ministry in the New Testament and the early Church in order to show its fluid state, its charismatic and community orientation, and to trace the gradual development of a monarchical episcopate. Schillebeeckx appeals to the sixth canon of the Council of Chalcedon and to early liturgical tradition to make an important point. The Chalcedonian canon declared absolute ordinations invalid; that is, the ordination of an individual independent of service for a particular community. The same canon underlies the practice of ministers returning to the lay state after their service to a community was over. In addition, Schillebeeckx points to Tertullian's statement that "in exceptional situations, the community itself chose its presider ad hoc." The consequence that he will draw from this canon and Tertullian's statement is that the contemporary Catholic Church, with its shortage of priests, should allow communities to delegate laypersons to celebrate the Eucharist.

But this conclusion seems to stand in stark contrast to the understanding of the nature of the priesthood in modern Roman Catholicism. In order to argue for the validity of his point, Schillebeeckx takes pains to demonstrate that several decisive shifts took place from a more functional and ministerial understanding of the priesthood to a more cultic and ontological one. He marks out the points of this shift: The Third and Fourth Lateran Council and the writings of Josse Chitove (1472–1543), which view the priesthood primarily in terms of cult, and the Council of Trent's reaction against the Lutheran emphasis on universal priesthood. Consequently, the opinion emerges that a priest differs from a layperson not only in degree but in essence. Counter-Reformation Roman Catholicism then increasingly emphasizes the unique character of the special priesthood. Later, the French School of Spirituality develops a specific spirituality of the priesthood. Because a priest, in distinction to a layperson, is *Alter Christus*, a priest should develop a spirituality fit for his special status in the church.[120]

The result of this long development is the understanding of the sacrament of orders in such a way so as to underscore that a priest ontologically differs from a layperson. This account views ordination in terms of the unique character of the priest rather than in terms of service to the community. Such an absolute view of ordination works against a reform of the church that seeks to return to the practices of the early Church and would make it possible for laypersons to preside at

the Eucharist in those communities without ordained priests available.

In *The Church with a Human Face*, Schillebeeckx does not change the basic thesis of the earlier book. Rather, he tries to give a more nuanced historical argument by taking into account objections.[121] He also tries, however, to strengthen his argument that ministry has taken different historical forms due to social, cultural, and political factors. He adopts Elisabeth Schüssler Fiorenza's account of the "discipleship of equals" and of the role of the house churches in his treatment of the development of ministry in early Christianity. He argues that

Early Christianity was a brotherhood and sisterhood of equal partners: theologically on the basis of the baptism of the Spirit, and sociologically in accordance with the Roman Hellenistic model for free societies, called *collegia*.[122]

The transition from a discipleship of equal partners to a hierarchical understanding of the Church occurred as a result of many complex societal and cultural factors. There are social and political factors that result from Christianity becoming a state church under Theodosius. This is reinforced culturally as a result of the Neo-Platonic influence of Pseudo-Dionysius's conception of the church as a divine hierarchy.

This pyramidal hierarchical structure of the church community also inspired by the social status-symbols of the existing Graeco-Roman *imperium* is influenced very strongly from the sxith century by the Neoplatonist works of Pseudo-Dionysius.[123]

Schillebeeckx sticks to the historical argument of his first edition. He underscores the changes in the understanding of the Eucharist in the sixth and seventh centuries: from a view linking the celebration of the Eucharist with the Cross of Jesus to one interpreting the sacramental celebration as the making present of the sacrifice of the Cross. In addition, such popular religious practices as the veneration of relics lead to the multiplication of private masses.

While he drops references to laypersons presiding at the Eucharist—the point causing the most controversy—he concludes by arguing for a another type of ministry, one of full-time pastoral work, along with those of the episcopate, presbyterate, and diaconate. Critics acknowledge that Schillebeeckx has argued his thesis in a more nuanced way, but they fault him for not taking into account such a fundamental teaching as apostolic succession.[124]

Critical Issues

The critical discussion and evaluation of Schillebeeckx's theological writings has taken a more specific form than is the case with Karl Rahner or Bernard Lonergan. Because of the very systematic character of their work, their basic methods or conceptions have been criticized—for example, Karl Rahner's attempt to develop theology as anthropology or Bernard Lonergan's delineation of the formal structure of knowledge. Criticisms of Schillebeeckx have focused on more specific and historical issues. Are there only four or are there more basic creeds in the New Testament, or should one focus at all on the precanonical traditions? Is his account of the origin of the resurrection faithful to the New Testament data? Does his historical survey of ministry do justice to the historical material? What these criticisms show is that Schillebeeckx's later work flows less from a specific philosophical conception that undergirds his theology than from specific historical arguments. In this respect, his later work has moved away from a position that could accurately be labeled "transcendental Thomism."

CONCLUSION

In the context of twentieth-century Neo-Scholasticism, the philosophers and theologians discussed in this chapter go back to Thomas Aquinas in order to bring Thomistic theology into conversation with modernity. The *nouvelle théologie* argued against the dualistic split between nature and grace, and between affectivity (feeling, desire) and knowledge. Its return to Thomas Aquinas uncovered a Thomistic philosophy that was heavily Augustinian and was as much Neo-Platonic as Aristotelian. It recovered a Thomistic theology with a more unified vision of nature and grace than was true of Neo-Scholasticism. Influenced by Blondel, Maréchal, and Rousselot, the transcendental Thomists explored the dynamism of the human intellect (which includes the role of the will and affection) and its contribution to human knowledge. Henri de Lubac is the forefather of this important theological direction. Karl Rahner and Bernard Lonergan represent further European and Anglo-Saxon developments of this transcendental Thomism. Edward Schillebeeckx, a generation younger, proceeds farther, moving beyond Thomism and a transcendental phenomenology to a more historical approach to theology. This historical dimension, though present in both Rahner and Lonergan, as we have seen, is developed with greater historical consciousness in Schillebeeckx's Christology, for example. What these theologians share, however, is a commitment to theologies of correlation. They began their careers seeking to correlate Thomistic philosophy with modern philosophy. In their mature works, they seek to correlate Christian faith with modern culture.

NOTES

1. Printed as a preface to St. Thomas Aquinas, *Summa Theologica*, Vol. 1 (New York, 1920), pp. vii–xvi; quotation from p. xvi. For background, see James Hennesey, "Leo XIII's Thomistic Revival: A Political and Philosophical Event," *Journal of Religion*, 58, Supplement (1978), s185–s197.

2. Ibid., p. xvi.
3. For an analysis of the role of ecclesiastical power and politics, see Pierre Thibault, *Savoir et Pouvoir: Philosophie Thomiste et Politique Cléricale au XIXe Siècle* (Quebec, 1972).
4. Pierre Rousselot, *The Intellectualisme de Saint*

Thomas (Paris, 1924; reprint 1936). Translated as *The Intellectualism of Saint Thomas* (New York, 1935).

5. Pierre Rousselot, *Pour L'Histoire du problème de l'amour au moyen âge* (Paris, 1933).

6. Pierre Rousselot, *The Eyes of Faith*, trans. Joseph Donceel (New York, 1990), pp. 21–43.

7. Rousselot, *The Eyes of Faith*, pp. 29–31.

8. Rousselot, *Intellectualisme*, p. 174 (169).

9. Rousselot, *The Eyes of Faith*, p. 61.

10. Joseph Maréchal, *Études sur la Psychologie des Mystiques* (Paris, 1924). Trans. in English Algar Thorold (New York, 1928).

11. Joseph Maréchal, *Le Point de départ de la métaphysique: Leçons sur le dévelopement historique et théoretique de la connaissance* (Paris, 1922–1944). A sixth volume was planned but never appeared. A translation of selections from each of the five volumes has been prepared by Joseph Donceel in Joseph Maréchal, *A Maréchal Reader*, trans. and ed. Joseph Donceel (New York, 1970).

12. For the French interpretation of Kant, cf Rudolf Heinz, *Französische Kantinterpretation im 20. Jahrhundert* (Bonn, 1966); Harold Holz traces Maréchal's influence on twentieth-century German philosophy in *Transcendentalphilosophie und Metaphysik. Studie über Tendenzen in der heutigen philosophischen Grundlagenproblematik* (Mainz, 1966). See also Otto Muck, *The Transcendental Method* (New York, 1968).

13. Maréchal, op. cit., p. 248.

14. On this point, Bernard Lonergan follows Maréchal very closely. See *Insight: A Study of Human Understanding* (New York, 1956).

15. Maréchal, op. cit., p. 223.

16. Edward Schillebeeckx raises this issue. Whereas Rahner was influenced by Maréchal, Schillebeeckx was influenced by De Petter. See the discussion of Schillebeeckx below.

17. For Rousselot's understanding of the dynamism of the human intellect, see Thomas Sheehan, "Pierre Rousselot and the Dynamism of the Human Spirit" *Gregorianum*, 66 (1984), 241–267.

18. Henri Bouillard, *Conversion et grâce chez Saint Thomas d'Aquin* (Paris, 1944).

19. Marie-Dominique Chenu, *Toward Understanding Saint Thomas* (Chicago, 1964), and *La théologie comme science au XIIIᵉ siècle*, 3rd ed., rev. and augm. (Paris, 1957).

20. Henri de Lubac, *Le Súrnaturel: Études historiques* (Paris, 1946). For de Lubac's own discussion of the background, history, and controversy surrounding this work, see his *Mémoire sur l'occasion des mes écrits* (Namur, 1989).

21. Henri de Lubac, *The Mystery of the Supernatural* (New York, 1967).

22. Henri de Lubac, *Augustinianism and Modern Theology* (New York, 1965).

23. Henri de Lubac, *Christian Resistance to Anti-Semitism: Memories from 1940–1944* (San Francisco, 1990).

24. For an analysis of the cultural context and the struggle against Nazi thought, see Joseph Komanchak, "The Cultural and Ecclesial Roles of Theology," *Proceedings of the Catholic Theological Society of America*, 40 (1985), 15–32.

25. Lubac, *The Mystery*, p. 27.

26. See Henri de Lubac, "Apologetics and Theology," in *Theological Fragments* (San Francisco, 1989).

27. "Causes internes de l' atténuation et de la disparition du sens du Sacré," in *Théologie dans l'histoire: II. Questions disputées et résistance au nazisme* (Paris, 1990), pp. 13–30.

28. See Lubac, *Augustinianism and Modern Theology*, and *Mystery of the Supernatural*.

29. Lubac, *Mystery of the Supernatural*, pp. 261–262.

30. Lubac, *Augustinianism and Modern Theology*, p. 435.

31. Henri de Lubac, *The Faith of Teilhard de Chardin* (London, 1965); Lubac *The Religious Thought of Teilhard de Chardin* (London, 1967); Lubac, *The Eternal Feminine: A Study on the Poem by Teilhard de Chardin, followed by Teilhard and the Problems of Today* (London, 1971). See also Lubac, *Teilhard posthume: Reflexions et Souvenirs* (Paris, 1977).

32. Henri de Lubac, *Catholicism: Christ and the Common Destiny of Man* (San Francisco, 1988).

33. Henri de Lubac, *Exégèse mediévale: les quatres sens de l'écriture, Theologie*, Vol. 41–42, 59 (Paris, 1959); Lubac, *L'Écriture dans la tradition* (Paris, 1966); Lubac, *Histoire et esprit: l'intelligence de l'Écriture d' àpres Origene* (Paris, 1950).

34. Lubac, *Theological Fragments*, op. cit., p. 126.

35. Henricus Denzinger and Adolfus Schönmetzer, *Enchiridion Symbolorum*, 23rd ed. (Freiburg, 1963), pp. 3881–3883.

36. Hugo Rahner, four years' Rahner's senior, became an established scholar of early Christianity. Rahner's first published essay in a French journal dealt with Heidegger and was falsely attributed to his brother.

37. A group of Roman Catholic philosophers had at that time studied with Heidegger. They later became influential Roman Catholic philosophers: Johannes B. Lotz, Gustav Siewert, Max Müller, and Bernhard Welte. An important study of Welte's influence on Roman Catholic fundamental theology is Anthony J. Godzieba, *Bernhard Welte's Fundamental Theological Approach to Christology* (New York, 1994).

38. "Karl Rahner at 75 Years of Age: Interview with Leo O'Donovan for *America* Magazine," in *Karl Rahner*

in Dialogue: Conversations and Interviews, 1965–1982, ed. Paul Imhof and Hubert Biallowons (New York, 1986), p. 191.

39. The full title of his unpublished dissertation is *E Latere Christi: Der Ursprung der Kirche als zweiter Eva aus der Seite Christi des zweiten Adam. Eine Untersuchung über de typologischen Sinn von Jo 19:4 (From the Side of Christ: The Origin of the Church as Second Eve from the Side of Christ, the Second Adam).* It has remained unpublished.

40. Marcel Viller, *Aszese und Mystik in der Vaterzeit* (Freiburg, 1939; reprinted in 1989).

41. Heinrich Denzinger (1819–1883) was the first editor. An English translation (of poor quality) is *The Sources of Catholic Dogma* (St. Louis, 1957). For an analysis of the value of the Denzinger volume, see Joseph Schumacher, *Der Denzinger: Geschichte und Bedeutung eines Buches in der Praxis der Neueren Theologie* (Freiburg, 1974). For the currently used edition by Adolfus Schönmetzer, see above note 35.

42. Karl Rahner, *Lexikon für Theologie und Kirche* (Freiburg, 1955–67).

43. Karl Rahner and Herbert Vorgrimler, *Theological Dictionary* (New York, 1965; rev. ed. New York, 1981).

44. Karl Rahner, *Sacramentum Mundi: An Encyclopedia of Theology,* Vol. 1–6 (New York, 1968–1970). An abbreviated one-volume edition was published with the title *Encyclopedia of Theology: The Concise Sacramentum Mundi* (New York, 1975).

45. Karl Rahner and Heinrich Schleier, *Quaestiones Disputatae* (Freiburg, 1960 to present). Several of the volumes of the series were translated into English (New York, 1961–1967). Rahner's essays were combined in Karl Rahner, *Inquiries* (New York, 1964).

46. Karl Rahner, *Spirit in the World* (New York, 1994; original Eng. pub. New York, 1969). The German original was published in 1939.

47. Ibid., p. 402.

48. The first edition was heavily revised and edited by Rahner's student, Johann Baptist Metz. The differences between the two editions should not be traced just to Metz's editorial changes. They also reflect Rahner's own theological and philosophical development. The second edition drops the polemic against Protestant theological conceptions of revelation. It advances a much more consistently transcendental understanding of revelation, and it emphasizes historicity much more strongly. These changes are evident in his other writings at the time.

49. Karl Rahner, *Foundations of the Christian Faith: An Introduction to the Idea of Christianity* (New York, 1982).

50. Friedrich Schleiermacher, *The Christian Faith* (Edinburgh, 1928), # 4,4.

51. Karl Rahner, "Concerning the Relationship between Nature and Grace," *Theological Investigations,* Vol. 1 (Baltimore, 1961), pp. 309–317; quotation from p. 315.

52. Martin Heidegger, *Being and Time* (New York, 1962), p. 32.

53. Rahner, *Foundations,* p. 68.

54. Ibid., p. 62.

55. Ibid.

56. Ibid., p. 153.

57. Paul Tillich, *Systematic Theology,* 3 vol. (Chicago: 1951–1963).

58. Leo O'Donovan, *A World of Grace: An Introduction to the Themes and Foundations of Karl Rahner's Theology* (New York, 1980).

59. For an interpretation of Karl Rahner's theology focusing on the centrality of "mystagogy" and mystical experience, see Klaus P. Fischer, *Der Mensch als Geheimnis: Die Anthropologie Karl Rahners* (Freiburg, 1974).

60. See Francis Schüssler Fiorenza, "Rahner and the Kantian Problematic," in Rahner, *Spirit in the World,* p. xiii.

61. Wolfhart Pannenberg, *Jesus God and Man* (Philadelphia, 1968), pp. 318–319.

62. Cornelius Ernst, the translator of volume one of Karl Rahner's *Theological Investigations,* makes this criticism in his "Introduction" to Vol. 1, pp. v–xix.

63. Karl Rahner, "The Theology of the Symbol," in his *Theological Investigations,* Vol. IV (New York, 1974), p. 229.

64. Ibid., p. 239.

65. Ibid., p. 240.

66. Karl Rahner, *Theological Investigations,* Vol. X (New York, 1973), pp. 14–24; quotation from p. 14.

67. Rowan Williams, in *Analogy of Beauty,* ed. John Riches (Edinburgh, 1986), p. 23.

68. Bruce Marshall, *Christology in Conflict: The Identity of a Saviour in Rahner and Barth* (New York, 1987).

69. Fergus Kerr, *Wittgenstein and Theology* (New York, 1986), pp. 7–16. For a discussion of Kerr and Rahner, see Russell R. Reno, *The Ordinary Transformed. Karl Rahner and the Christian Vision of Transcendence* (Grand Rapids, Mich., 1995), pp. 165–195.

70. Rahner, *Foundations,* p. 10.

71. Ibid., p. 83.

72. Bernard Lonergan, *Grace and Freedom. Operative Grace in the Thought of Thomas Aquinas,* ed. J. Patout Burns (New York, 1971). Originally published as "St. Thomas's Thought on *Gratia Operans,*" *Theological Studies,* 2 (1941), 289–324; 3 (1942), 69–88, 375–402, 533–578.

73. Bernard Lonergan, *Verbum: Word and Idea in Aquinas,* ed. David Burrell (Notre Dame, 1967). Originally published as "The Concept of *Verbum* in the

Writings of St. Thomas Aquinas," *Theological Studies*, 7 (1946), 349–392; 8 (1947), 35–79, 404–444; 10 (1949), 3–40, 359–393.

74. See "Metaphysics as Horizon," *Gregorianum* 44 (1963), 307–318; reprinted in *Collection* (London, 1967). See Lonergan's review of Gilson in *Theological Studies*, 22 (1961), 561.

75. Lonergan, *Collection*, p. 208.

76. Ibid., p. 209.

77. Ibid., p. 214.

78. See Lonergan's essay, "Metaphysics as Horizon," in Lonergan, *Collection*, pp. 202–221.

79. Bernard Lonergan, *Insight* (New York, 1957).

80. Ibid., p. 377.

81. Bernard Lonergan, *A Second Collection* (Philadelphia, 1974), pp. 94–95.

82. Lonergan, *Insight*, p. 673.

83. Ibid., p. 675.

84. Ibid., p. 636.

85. David Burrell, "How Complete Can Intelligibility Be?" *Proceedings of the American Catholic Philosophical Association*, XLI (1967), 252.

86. David Tracy, "Lonergan's Foundational Theology: An Interpretation and a Critique," in *Foundations of Theology*, ed. P. McShane (Notre Dame, 1971), pp. 197–222.

87. Bernard Lonergan, *Philosophy of God and Theology* (Philadelphia, 1973), p. 13.

88. See Bernard Lonergan, *De Deo Trino: Pars Systematica* (Rome, 1964), and *De Deo Trino: Parts Dogmatica* (Rome, 1964). Only a historical section has been translated: Bernard Lonergan, *The Way to Nicea: The Dialectical Development of Trinitarian Theology* (Philadelphia, 1976).

89. Lonergan's lectures on Christology at the Gregorianum (*De Verbo Incarnato*) have not been published in English nor has a shorter monograph, *De Constitutione Christi Ontologica et Psychologica* (Rome, 1956), except in some significant essays, especially "Christ as Subject: A Reply," in Lonergan, *Collection*, pp. 164–197.

90. Bernard Lonergan, *Method in Theology* (New York, 1972). Several important collections of essays are helpful for an understanding of Lonergan's philosophy and method. See Bernard Lonergan, *Collection*; *A Second Collection*. (Philadelphia, 1974); Frederick E. Crowe, ed., *A Third Collection. Papers by Bernard J. F. Lonergan* (New York/Mahwah, N.J., 1985).

91. Lonergan, *Method in Theology*, p. 239.

92. Ibid., p. 240.

93. Ibid., p. 241.

94. See Francis Schüssler Fiorenza, "Systematic Theology: Its History and Method," in *Systematic Theology: Roman Catholic Perspectives*, ed. Francis Schüssler Fiorenza and John Galvin (Minneapolis, 1991), esp. pp. 50–80.

95. Lonergan, *Method in Theology*, p. 101.

96. Ibid., p. 111.

97. Karl Rahner, "Some Critical Thoughts on 'Functional Specialties in Theology,'" in *Foundations of Theology*, ed. Philip McShane (Notre Dame, 1971), pp. 194–96.

98. Langdon Gilkey, "Empirical Science and Theological Knowing," and David Tracy, "Lonergan's Foundational Theology: An Interpretation and Critique," in *Foundations of Theology*, op. cit., pp. 76–101 and 197–222, respectively.

99. Tracy, "Lonergan's Foundational Theology," p. 210.

100. Francis Schüssler Fiorenza, "The Relation Between Fundamental and Systematic Theology," *Irish Theological Quarterly* (1996), pp. 140–160.

101. E. Schillebeeckx, *De Sacramentele Heilseconomie: Theologische bezinning op S. Thomas' sacramentenleer in het licht van de traditie en van de hedendaagse sacramentalsproblematik* (Antwerp, 1952). See also Robert J. Schreiter, "Edward Schillebeeckx: An Orientation to His Thought," in *The Schillebeeckx Reader*, ed. Robert J. Schrieter (New York, 1984), pp. 1–24.

102. The influence of De Petter's attempt to combine phenomenology and Thomism endures and remains important even for Schillebeeckx's later development. Schillebeeckx argues that the knowledge of God entails neither a proper concept (vs. Neo-Scholasticism) nor the subjective dynamism of the spirit (vs. Maréchal), but an "objective dynamism."

103. E. Schillebeeckx, *Christ the Sacrament of the Encounter with God* (New York, 1963).

104. Ibid., p. 59.

105. Ibid., p. 3.

106. Ibid., p. 199 (translation modified).

107. E. Schillebeeckx, *Jesus: An Experiment in Christology* (New York, 1979).

108. E. Schillebeeckx, *Interim Report on the Books Jesus and Christ* (New York, 1981).

109. E. Schillebeeckx, *Church: The Human Story of God* (New York, 1990).

110. Schillebeeckx takes over and adapts the four basic creeds outlined by Helmut Koester in *Trajectories through Early Christianity*, ed. James M. Robinson and Helmut Koester (Philadelphia, 1971).

111. Schillebeeckx, *Jesus*, p. 637.

112. Ibid., p. 570.

113. Ibid.

114. E. Schillebeeckx, *Ministry: Leadership in the Community of Jesus Christ* (New York, 1981).

115. For an excellent survey of the various positions, see Daniel Donovan, *What Are They Saying about the Ministerial Priesthood?* (Mahwah, N.J., 1992).

116. For examples of the criticisms, see Jean Galot's review in *Espirit et Vie* (Langres, France, 1982). See also his book, Jean Galot, *Theology of the Priesthood* (San

Francisco, 1985). For another critical assessment of Schillebeeckx, but one that is closer to him on several points, see Pierre Grelot, *Les ministères dans le peuple de Dieu: lettre à un theologien* (Paris, 1988).

117. Ted Schoof, ed. *The Schillebeeckx Case: Official Exchange of Letters and Documents in the Investigation of Fr. Edward Schillebeeckx, O.P. by the Sacred Congregation for the Doctrine of the Faith, 1976–1980* (New York, 1984). For a treatment of the ecclesial-political situation at the time, see Peter Hebblethwaite, *The New Inquisition?: Schillebeeckx and Küng* (London, 1980).

118. Committee on Doctrine of the United States Bishops' Conference, Washington, D.C., 1983.

119. E. Schillebeeckx, *The Church with a Human Face: A New and Expanded Theology of Ministry* (New York, 1985).

120. A more sympathetic presentation by a Sulpician of this school is Eugene A. Walsh, *The Priesthood in the Writings of the French School: Berulle, de Condren, Olier* (Washington, D.C., 1949).

121. For example, H. Courzel's review in *Nouvelle Revue Theologique*, 104 (1982), 738–748.

122. Schillebeekx, *Church with a Human Face*, p. 47.

123. Ibid., p. 158.

124. This is the criticism of Walter Kasper in *Theologische Quartalschrift*, 166 (1986), 156–188. Kasper's earlier assessment is in "Das kirchliche Amt in der Diskussion," *Theologische Quartalschrift*, 163 (1983), 46–53.

SUGGESTIONS FOR FURTHER READING

Background: Thomism, Maréchal, and Rousselot

Kunz, Erhard. *Glaube, Gnade, and Geschichte: Die Glaubenslehre des P. Rousselot* (Frankfurt: M. J. Knecht, 1969). An excellent analysis of Rousselot's theology with reference to faith and history.

McCool, Gerald A. *Catholic Theology in the Nineteenth Century: The Quest for a Unitary Method* (New York: Seabury Press, 1977). A survey of Roman Catholic theology, especially Neo-Scholastic theology written from a Neo-Scholastic perspective.

———, *From Unity to Pluralism: The Internal Evolution of Thomism* (New York: Fordham University, 1992). A survey of modern Neo-Scholasticism.

McDermott, John. *Love and Understanding: The Relation of Will and Intellect in Pierre Rousselot's Christological Vision* (Rome: Gregorian University, 1983).

Muck, Otto. *The Transcendental Method* (New York: Herder and Herder, 1968). A survey of the major Catholic philosophic thinkers that were influenced by Joseph Maréchal.

Pottmeyer, Hermann-Josef. *Der Glaube vor dem Anspruch der Wissenschaft* (Freiburg: Herder, 1968). An analysis of the relation between faith and reason in Vatican I with attention to background and context.

Rousselot, Pierre. *The Eyes of Faith*, trans. Joseph Donceel (New York: Fordham University Press, 1990). This recent translation contains an invaluable introduction by Avery Dulles.

Van Riet, Georges. *Thomistic Epistemology: Studies Concerning the Problem of Cognition in the Contemporary Thomistic School* (St. Louis: B. Herder Book Co., 1963). Van Riet's volume remains a classic survey of various Thomistic theories of knowledge.

The Nouvelle Théologie and Henri de Lubac

Bouillard, Henri. *Conversion et grâce chez Saint Thomas d'Aquin* (Paris: Aubier 1944). A study of grace and justification in Thomas Aquinas.

Lenk, Martin. *Von der Gotteserkenntnis: Natürliche Theologie im Werk Henri de Lubac*, Vol. 45 (Frankfurt: Knecht, 1993). Uses the issue of natural theology and the knowledge of God in order to interpret de Lubac's contribution to theology.

Maier, Eugen. *Einigung der Welt in Gott: das Katholische bei Henri de Lubac* (Einsiedeln, Switzerland: Johannes Verlag, 1983).

Neufeld, Karl H., and Michel Sales. *Bibliographie Henri de Lubac S.J., 1925–1974*, 2nd ed. (Einsiedeln, Switzerland: Johannes Verlag, 1974). A comprehensive though dated bibliography.

Von Balthasar, Hans Urs. *The Theology of Henri de Lubac: An Overview* (San Francisco: Ignatius Press, 1991). A brief and popular presentation in chronological development of the basic ideas in some of de Lubac's works.

Karl Rahner

Bonsor, Jack Arthur. *Rahner, Heidegger, and Truth: Karl Rahner's Notion of Christian Truth, the Influence of Heidegger* (Lanham, Md.: University Press of America, 1987). This comparison underscores more of the differences than similarities between Rahner and Heidegger.

Carr, Anne. *The Theological Method of Karl Rahner* (Missoula, Mont.: Scholars Press, 1977). A clear exposition of the philosophical and methodological presuppositions of Rahner's theology

Fischer, Klaus P. *Gotteserfahrung: Mystagogie in der Theologie Karl Rahners und in der Theologie der Befreiung* (Mainz: Matthias-Grunewald-Verlag, 1986). An important study because it shows the roots of Rahner's theology in spirituality and mysticism.

O'Donovan, Leo J. ed., *A World of Grace: An Introduction to the Themes and Foundations of Karl Rahner's Theology* (New York: Seabury, 1980). A select group of theologians comment and explain individual sections of Rahner's *Foundations of the Christian Faith.*

Rahner, Karl. *Faith in a Wintry Season: Conversations and Interviews with Karl Rahner in the Last Years of his Life,* ed. Paul Imhof and Hubert Biallowons, trans. Harvey D. Egan (New York: Crossroad, 1990). An informative set of interviews with Rahner about significant aspects of his theology.

Vorgrimler, Herbert. *Understanding Karl Rahner: An Introduction to His Life and Thought* (New York: Crossroad, 1986). Vorgrimler, a student and colleague of Rahner's, gives a popular biographical introduction to his life and work. More descriptive than analytical.

Weger, Karl-Heinz. *Karl Rahner: An Introduction to his Theology* (New York: Seabury Press, 1980). A clearly written popular introduction.

Bernard Lonergan

Boly, Craig S. *The Road to Lonergan's Method in Theology: The Order of Theological Ideas* (Lanham, Md.: University Press of America 1991). The distinctive feature of this analysis is its extensive coverage of Lonergan's works on method and on the Trinity that are in his publications in Latin.

Crowe, Frederick E. *Appropriating the Lonergan Idea,* ed. Michael Vertin (Washington, D.C.: Catholic University of America, 1989). Crowe has not only edited and collected some of Lonergan's work, but he also has consistently expounded the significance of Lonergan's position. These essays explain Lonergan's basic ideas and attempt to show their relevance for diverse topics.

Gregson, Vernon, ed. *The Desires of the Human Heart: An Introduction to the Theology of Bernard Lonergan* (Mahwah, N.J.; Paulist Press, 1988). A collection of essays that interpret Lonergan's theology in relation to the traditional systematic theological treatises with each essay focusing on a specific treatise.

Lamb, Matthew, ed. *Creativity and Method: Essays in Honor of Bernard Lonergan, S.J.* (Milwaukee: Marquette University Press, 1981). This collection of essays, some by students, shows the relevance of Lonergan's theology across diverse fields.

Meynell, Hugo. *The Theology of Bernard Lonergan* (Chico, Calif.: Scholars Press, 1986). A clear exposition of the basic notions of Lonergan's philosophy and theology.

Tracy, David. *The Achievement of Bernard Lonergan* (New York: Herder and Herder, 1970). Written originally as a dissertation, Tracy, a former student of Lonergan's, traces and evaluates his philosophical theology from *Insight* to *Method in Theology.*

Tyrell, Bernard. *Bernard Lonergan's Philosophy of God* (Notre Dame: Notre Dame University Press, 1974). This study is focused on Lonergan's philosophical approach to the question of God.

Edward Schillebeeckx

Bowden, John S. *Edward Schillebeeckx: In Search of the Kingdom of God* (New York: Crossroad, 1983). A popular study of Schillebeeckx's theology. The same book is also published under the title: *Edward Schillebeeckx: Portrait of a Theologian* (London: SCM Press, 1983).

Schillebeeckx, Edward. *I am a Happy Theologian: Conversations with Francesco Strazzari* (New York: Crossroad, 1994). An interview with Schillebeeckx on his life and work.

Kennedy, Philip. *The Knowability of God in the Theology of Edward Schillebeeckx.* (Fribourg: University Press, 1993). It traces the development of Schillebeeckx's position on the knowledge of God, emphasizing the continuities.

Schoof, Ted, ed. *The Schillebeeckx Case: Official Exchange of Letters and Documents in the Investigation of Fr. Edward Schillebeeckx, O.P. by the Sacred Congregation for the Doctrine of the Faith, 1976–1980* (Mahwah, N.J.: Paulist Press, 1984).

Schreiter, Robert J. and Catherine Hilkert, ed. *The Praxis of Christian Experience: An Introduction to the Theology of Edward Schillebeeckx.* (San Francisco: Harper & Row, 1989) It introduces Schillebeeckx's theology through individual presentations of his views on the major theological treatises.

Schreiter, Robert, ed. *The Schillebeeckx Reader* (New York: Crossroad, 1994). A collection of important selections from his work with an introductory commentary.

Chapter Eight

❦

Vatican II and the Aggiornamento of Roman Catholic Theology

Pope John XXIII at the opening of Vatican Council II

The renewal of Roman Catholic theology within the post–World War II European situation took many forms. In addition to the philosophical and speculative renewal represented by the transcendental Thomists (see Chapter Seven) that sought to merge Thomist philosophy with modern philosophy, a renewal based both upon historical research and practical movements began to be shaped in an ecclesial and ecumenical context. A "return to the sources" was taking place in biblical, historical, and liturgical studies. This return or *ressourcement* would provide the foundation for a reform of the Church and for the Second Vatican Council.

YVES CONGAR

One leading theologian of this renewal was Yves Marie-Joseph Congar (1904–1994), a prolific writer of more than 1,600 books, articles, and translations. He was born on April 13, 1904, in Sedan in the Ardennes region of France. He joined the Dominicans in 1925 and was ordained a priest in 1930. He studied at the Dominican House of studies at Le Saulchoir, which at that time was in Belgium. (It later moved to Paris.) The Thomist scholar, Marie-Dominique Chenu, was Congar's adviser. He was made a cardinal by John Paul II a year before his death in 1994.[1]

Congar began his career with the thesis for his licentiate (a European degree giving a person a license to teach) on the topic of the unity of the Church. The majority of his writings consist of books and articles dealing with the structure of the Church, the role of the laity within the Church, and the nature of church reform and tradition. Congar participated in the French revival of Catholicism, in which the Dominican House of Studies at Le Saulchoir played an important role. Chenu's manifesto, "A School of Theology, Le Saulchoir" explains the interest and orientation of the school. Though Chenu's work and that of the school was primarily historical, it was under suspicion and was censured.[2] The concern of the ecclesial authorities was that the historical emphasis of the school constituted a historicist attitude toward theology and history.

True Reform and the Resources of the Tradition

The renewal of theology and of church life in France involved both new academic directions and pastoral initiatives. Academically, there was the call for *ressourcement,* a call for the return to the historical and biblical sources of faith. This return to the sources led to a renaissance in biblical and patristic studies. As a result theologians began to appropriate biblical and patristic categories rather than scholastic categories in their theological work. Hence, the stranglehold of Neo-Scholasticism on theology was broken not so much through a critique that used modern categories as through a return to biblical and patristic categories. This was to be especially true for understanding the image and vision of the Church.

At the same time, movements known as Catholic Action and Mission de France arose in France and Belgium. The Catholic Action movement enabled laypersons to become involved in an organized way in the mission of the Church. The consequence of this involvement was the need to rethink the role of the laity within a church structure that was heavily clerical and hierarchical. The idea of a "Mission de France" had its origin in the increased awareness of the alienation of many in France from their traditional Roman Catholic faith. Whereas previously mission was understood as the missionary movement to foreign or pagan countries, it now came to be realized that the "Christianity" of France was not to be taken for granted, that a need existed for missionary activity within France itself directed at alienated Catholics.

This need for a missionary activity within France was also accompanied by a call for a reform of the Church. Yves Congar wrote several influential essays, among them "Holiness and Sin within the Church"[3] and "Why the People of God Should Ceaselessly Reform Itself."[4] These were eventually combined into a volume, *True and False Reform in the Church,* that took up the clarion call for reforms.[5] Aware of its controversial character, Congar submitted the work to no fewer than sixteen censors before publication and yet it was censored after its publication. In distinguishing between true and false reform, Congar criticized false reform as an adaptation that is innovative but without any reference to the spirit of the Catholic tradition and without drawing on the *ressourcement* of the tradition itself. True reform thus entails "a return to the sources, as they are called, and in view of our present situation to reflect in the spirit of all that the whole tradition teaches us about the sense of the church."[6] Congar concludes the preamble by explaining the aim of his book: "We do not seek a solution in addition to or against the tradition of the Church, but in the very depths of that tradition."[7]

In addition to the notion of *ressourcement,* Congar uses the distinctions between "structure" and "life" as well as between "center" and "periphery" to interpret reform and change within the Church. He suggests that initiatives and change often stem from life at the periphery of the Church, whereas the center, "more specifically, the hierarchy in the church, has as its primary task the continuity of the church, its foundations and principles, and have the task of conserving the form or the essential structure."[8]

The argument for reform points to the historical contingencies of the Church as a historical institution. Congar underscores the relativity of ecclesial institutions in two ways. The first is the transcendent God as the Alpha and Omega of church reform. The Church is ordered to a transcendent God and is relativized in relation to that transcendent God. In addition, an important distinction exists between what the Church should be and what it de facto is:

as the source of all reform movements, this distinction is at the basis of our awareness of the historicity, and, therefore, relativity, of those forms in which the institution is realized. There is no ecclesiology which does not have to assume as a statutory fact that irreducible duality of that which exists in fact and that which ought to exist.[9]

It is this distinction between the Church as it presently exists and as it should exist that forms the basis of the appeal for a reform of the Church that is a critique of the Church for the sake of bringing the existing Church more in line with what it should be.

The Role of the Laity and France's Catholic Action Movement

Congar's own writings on various aspects of the Church, its teaching, and its practices greatly contributed to this reform. One topic was especially significant in the context of the Catholic Action Movement in France in his day. Congar's book, *Lay People in the Church*, theologically supports the renewed emphasis upon the laity in the Catholic Action Movement.[10] Published in 1953, but based on lectures given in 1946 and 1948, the book sought to show the active role of the laity in the Church. The first half of the book begins with the traditional triple division of ministries in its attempt to call for and to justify theologically an increased role of the laity in the Church in relation to the Church's priestly, kingly, and prophetic functions. The second part analyzes the role of the laity in the contemporary church situation in France. This analysis demonstrates the inadequacy of the triple division to describe the ministry of the laity. Congar notes "it became clear that it is not possible rigorously to bring all lay activity under these heads without doing violence to them. Catholic Action, in particular, involves all three."[11] Therefore, Congar sought to explore the role of laity in relation to the Church as community and to the church's apostolic mission.

Church as *Communio*

In developing the role of laity within the context of an understanding of the Church as a community, Yves Congar worked out the central idea of his notion of the Church as *communio*.

The Church is built together by the intercourse of its members one with another in a whole pattern of services, of mutual enlightenment, of taking opportunities, by the habitual use for the benefit of the body of the gifts which each one has received: such a Church cannot be called by any other name than "community."[12]

This notion of the Church as community, more properly called *communio* (see below), becomes the key theological concept of Congar's understanding of the church.[13] This concept came to be called a *communio* ecclesiology. Congar sought to retrieve the centrality of the notion of *communio* within the Fathers of the Church for an understanding of the church within the requisites of Catholic Action. In seeking to retrieve a patristic conception of the Church, Congar was influenced by the work of Johann Adam Möhler of the nineteenth-century Tübingen School (see Volume I, Chapter Eight). In 1984 he published a translation of Möhler's *Einheit der Kirche* (1827) that advocated a spirit-oriented ecclesiology using organic rather than scholastic categories.

In the years after the Second Vatican Council, Congar remained a prolific theological writer. The characteristic feature of his writings was his use of the historical resources of the Christian tradition.

He sought a reform of the present through a return to the tradition.[14] Although his writings touch on many topics, his central focus remained the nature and understanding of the Church. He wrote a major history of the understanding of the Church throughout the centuries that has become a standard work in the field.[15] Beyond his work on the Church and ecumenism, the most influential of his later writings was his three-volume examination of the history of the Christian belief in the Holy Spirit.[16] At a time of renewed interest in the doctrine of the Trinity among theologians, Congar's volumes bring his typical appeal to a historical *ressourcement* to the exploration of the richness and diversity of the understanding of the Spirit within the Christian tradition.

The advocacy of reform through retrieval, as argued in *True and False Reform in the Church*, became the central idea underlying Congar's work. It constituted both the strength and weakness of his program. A reform based upon the tradition could appeal to the best of the tradition in order to criticize distortions and errors of the present. However, such a reform could legitimate itself not only through a critique of these conditions, but also through the retrieval of what it claims to be the authentic tradition. Such a program, although indeed powerful, may not be suited to situations that seriously challenge even authentic aspects of the tradition. Such would be the debate in the post–Vatican II conciliar period. However, in the preconciliar period, Congar's ideas were bold and were viewed with suspicion and censured. Nevertheless, his advocacy of reform through a return to the resources of the tradition became the leitmotiv of Vatican II. The censored book became an inspiration to a future Pope and a Council.

JOHN XXIII

The decision to call the Second Vatican Council is the major contribution of Pope John XXIII (Angelo Giusseppe Roncalli, 1881–1963) during the brief years of his papacy (1958–1963).[17] Pre-viously he had served for twenty-five years as a papal diplomat in Bulgaria, Turkey, and France, and six years as patriarch of Venice. During his stay in France, he came into close contact with the *nouvelle théologie*. As the papal nuncio in France, Roncalli had acquired a copy of Congar's *True and False Reform in the Church*. He relates that he had underlined his own personal copy and had been strongly influenced by its call for church reform. When he became Pope, he convoked Vatican II and insisted that the French theologians associated with the *nouvelle théologie* be invited as experts to the Council. In addition to convening the Council, he set its goal and purpose.[18]

The direction he set for the Council becomes clear not only from the convening statement, but also from the two major encyclicals which he issued: *Mater et Magistra* (*Mother and Teacher*) (1961) and *Pacem in Terris* (*Peace on Earth*) (1963).[19] Both take up the social responsibility of the Church within the modern world.[20] After a recapitulation of Catholic social teaching since Pope Leo XIII's *Rerum Novarum*, the final section of *Mater et Magistra* takes up issues concerning the situation of contemporary agricultural workers and questions of development policy in regard to the emerging nations of the world. Its final section spells out the significance of an education for social justice. The confrontation with both liberalism and socialism has less prominence in this letter than it did in past encyclicals. Instead, strong emphasis is placed on social problems that have a worldwide and global scope in the modern world. *Pacem in Terris* further questions whether the modern technology of weaponry, especially the destructive potential of nuclear weapons, still allows one to justify war, as in the past, as a means of restoring violated rights.[21] The encyclical argues for the interrelation between peace and justice and insists on the importance of the "common good" and the realization of human rights within just political orders, both nationally and internationally, as necessary for the establishment of peace on earth.

Despite the importance of these encyclicals, the convocation of Vatican II is the decisive contribution that Pope John XXIII made to Roman Catholic theology. And in line with the theology expressed in his encyclicals, the Pope gave the Council an explicitly pastoral goal. The Council was to concern itself not so much with doctrinal issues as with pastoral questions. Having announced the idea of a council in January 1959, he officially convoked it on December 25, 1961. Conscious of the postwar crisis in Europe, the Pope linked the Council with the Church's concern for both peace and social justice in the world. The world gave evidence of great technological and scientific progress; humanity was on the edge of a new era. Nevertheless, there were also more alarming "signs of the time"; namely, that this technological progress made possible the instruments of catastrophic self-destruction. At the same time, however, there was an increased desire for peace and a hunger for spiritual values in the midst of spiritual poverty. Pope John XXIII underscores that the Church has as its task to engage vitally in meeting the challenge of these signs of the time. He places the Church in solidarity with humanity. "As we undertake our work, therefore, we would emphasize what concerns the dignity of man, whatever contributes to a genuine community of peoples."[22]

That the Pope's goal was pastoral renewal, rather than the resolution of dogmatic controversies, is made evident in his opening speech on October 11, 1962. He distinguishes between the substance or basic truths of Christianity that permanently endure and the time-conditioned and changing expressions of those truths.

The substance of the ancient doctrine of the deposit of faith is one thing, and the way in which it is presented is another. And it is the latter that must be taken into great consideration with patience if necessary, everything being measured in the forms and proportions of a magisterium which is predominantly pastoral in character.[23]

This distinction between ancient substance and time-conditioned expression reveals a new attitude that goes far beyond the earlier anti-Modernist polemic insofar as it urges change in the face of what is time conditioned. Yet this change should not affect the ancient substance. This affirmation of pastoral renewal and change on the one hand, and unchanging and ancient substance on the other hand, marked not only the spirit of Vatican II, but also its ambiguities. It led to divergent receptions of the Council in its aftermath.

VATICAN II

Vatican II (1962–1965) was the decisive religious, intellectual, and political event within the contemporary Roman Catholic Church. It brought about profound changes within church life, but these changes reflect the ambiguous manner in which the Council's actions were both an innovation and a renewal of the Catholic Church and its theology. The intellectual innovations were advanced in such a way that they did not entail an explicit rejection of the past and its traditions. They sought rather to reaffirm that tradition, while at the very same time incorporating the new, and thus moving the Church in new directions. This double movement is apparent in the Council texts themselves. In the Council's texts one finds both "traditionalist" and "progressive" statements side by side, often within the very same paragraph of a document, without any attempt to resolve the contradictions. For example, Vatican II repeats and affirms the doctrine of Vatican I regarding the primacy and infallibility of the Pope, and at the same time it affirms the collegial structure of the episcopacy and the role of all believers, including the laity. One, therefore, finds within the official documents of the Council two contrasting conceptions of the Church: a hierarchical ecclesiology (reflecting Vatican I) and a *communio* ecclesiology (reflecting the ancient patristic emphasis).

This approach led to profound ambiguity and to the different interpretations of the Church that soon emerged. The Second Vatican Council was indeed seen as an innovation and a change. For some, this change involved the rejection of the past and the opening of new directions. For others, it was not a change that denied the past, but one that returned to the past. Progressives complained about institutional resistance to change, whereas conservatives saw the innovations as the jettisoning of hallowed tradition. What is remarkable is that both progressives and conservatives could appeal to the Council documents to buttress their own opinions.

Vatican II's Understanding of the Church

Several important shifts took place, especially with regard to the basic understanding of the Church and its episcopacy. In the post-Tridentine period, Roman Catholic theology had developed its doctrine of the Church in the context of an anti-Reformation apologetic and polemic. It defended and bolstered those elements of Roman Catholic doctrine and church structures that were explicitly rejected by the Protestant Reformations. Consequently, it emphasized the hierarchical structure and the institutional aspects of the Church. This emphasis reached its high point at Vatican I, which defined the papal authority in the context of the absolute monarchies of its time and with categories that echoed nineteenth-century royalists, such as Joseph de Maistre.[24] (See Volume I, Chapter Thirteen.) The then-dominant Neo-Scholastic conception of the Church not only underscored its hierarchical structure, but also described this structure as monarchical. Vatican II constituted advances in the doctrine of the Church by drawing on earlier biblical and patristic resources.

Communio as the Basic Model of the Church

Gerard Philips, professor at the University of Louvain, secretary of the theological commission, and redactor of the Vatican II document on the Church, calls the notion of *communio* the leading notion of Vatican II.[25] The term *communio* is a technical Latin theological term that translated the Greek word *koinonia*.[26] Its English equivalents are communion, fellowship, participation, or

sharing. Though it is sometimes translated simply as "community," such a translation loses the theological focus of the concept. The notion of *communio* expresses the idea that in *communio* with God, through participation in the Eucharist, a *communio* is constituted among Christians. Such a notion underscores that the participation in the divine through the participation in the Eucharist constitutes the common association and fellowship of Christians. Insofar as diverse local congregations participate in the Eucharist, they are in communion with other congregations. This vision of the Church is a vision of an interlocking *communio* through their liturgical participation in the Eucharist. It locates the center of the Church in the local church's participation in the Eucharist, and it is that participation that unites all local churches.

The Significance of Local Communities

By emphasizing the *communio* character of the Church, the Second Vatican Council thereby reevaluated the significance of local communities in relation to the whole church. *Lumen Gentium* affirmed: "This church of Christ is really present [*vere adest*] in all legitimate local congregations of the faithful which, united with their bishops, in the New Testament are also called churches."[27] The local church is thereby not considered to be a part of the Church; rather, the Church is fully present in each local community in its Eucharistic celebration. In so emphasizing the local church, the Council picks up a theme that is strongly present in Eastern Orthodox theology and its Eucharistic understanding of the Church. It attempts to give a primacy to understanding Church in theological, liturgical, and sacramental rather than in institutional and organizational categories.

Church as the People of God in Pilgrimage

Alongside the notion of *communio*, the metaphor of the Church as the People of God in pilgrimage receives a new emphasis that entails a significant shift in the understanding of the Church. Pope Pius XII's encyclical, *Mystical Body* (1943), described the Church as the Body of Christ. This image of the Church as a historical organism, whose head is Christ, and whose principle of life or soul is the Holy Spirit, returns to the understanding of the Church seized on by Johann Adam Möhler and the Tübingen School. This conception was thought to mirror the Pauline metaphor and to provide a way of understanding the Church in more sacramental and theological than institutional imagery.

Nevertheless, it came under historical and systematic criticisms in the time preceding the Vatican II. New Testament exegesis had shown its historical inadequacy. Paul's image of the mystical union with Christ was quite different from the organic model of the Church as the Body of Christ that was developed in the Romanticism and Idealism of the nineteenth-century Tübingen School. From a systematic perspective, the conceiving of the Church as the Body of Christ minimizes the distinction and difference between the Church and Christ. Sebastian Tromp had made this view influential, for he was not only the principal author of Pius XII's encyclical on the mystical body of the Church, but he also prepared the first draft of the constitution on the nature of the Church for the Council. However, this view, expressed in the first draft, was resoundingly rejected by the Council fathers.

The Second Vatican Council, nonetheless, located the notion of the Body of Christ along with other biblical images of the Church, at the end of chapter one of *Lumen Gentium* and even gave it a special treatment. However, the whole second chapter of *Lumen Gentium* dealt with the Church as the people of God. In describing the Church as "new people of God" and as the "new Israel," Vatican II recalled the idea of a wandering and a pilgrim people, a people living on earth and moving on their way toward holiness.[28] This aspect of the Church as a people in pilgrimage is brought to the fore in Chapter 7 of *Lumen Gentium,* as is evident by its very title, "The Eschatological Nature of the Pilgrim Church and Its Union with the Church in Heaven."[29]

The Church of Christ and the Roman Catholic Church

Along with this emphasis on the Church as the pilgrim people of God, a new understanding of the relationship between the Roman Catholic Church and the Church of Christ is affirmed. The matter of debate was not the issue raised by the Modernist crisis, namely, that historical research on the Gospels had shown that Jesus's proclamation of the Kingdom should be understood within the context of eschatological and apocalyptic expectation, rather than as the foundation of the Church.[30] Instead, what was at issue was the exclusive identification of the Roman Catholic Church with the Church of Christ. Pope Pius XII had affirmed this identification in the encyclical *Mystici Corporis* and in *Humani Generis.* The preparatory committee, lead by Sebastian Tromp, reaffirmed such an exclusive definition.

Many objected to the stark identification of the institutional Church and the mystical Body of Christ in the preliminary draft and in the face of these objections a compromise was reached. Instead of asserting that the Church of Christ is the Roman Catholic Church, the document was amended to read that the Church of Christ "subsists in" the Roman Catholic Church. No two words of the Council have received more attention and commentary than these two. The term "subsistence" probably should not be interpreted in the philosophical sense that it had within scholastic philosophy, because "subsistence" would then mean that the Church of Christ was realized and embodied in the Roman Catholic Church.[31] Instead, the term should be read in the context of other discussions at the Council, especially in relation to the document on ecumenism that the Council was preparing at the same time as the document on the Church.[32] In fact, the two decrees were promulgated on the same day, November 21, 1964.[33] Interpreting the terms used in the document on ecumenism suggests that the ministry of word, sacraments, and leadership continues in the Catholic Church.[34] As Francis Sullivan has interpreted the Council: "To say that it subsists in the Catholic Church means that it is in the Catholic Church that it is to be found still existing with all its essential properties: its oneness, holiness, catholicity, and apostolicity."[35]

The Council was introducing changes in the understanding of the Church insofar as *Lumen Gentium* highlights the significance of *communio*, the importance of the local congregation, the image of the Church as the pilgrim People of God, and the complex relation between the Church of Christ and the Catholic Church. For these innovations go beyond Neo-Scholastic conceptions of the Church by retrieving metaphors and models of the Church drawn from the Scriptures and the Fathers of the Church.

The Church and the Liturgy

A major indication of the Council's new emphasis in its understanding of the Church comes to the fore in the Constitution on the Liturgy (*Sacrosanctum Concilium*), which was the first constitution promulgated at the Council. By so doing, the Council made immediately evident the pastoral and practical nature of its reforms. Its authorization of the use of the "mother language," that is, the vernacular in the liturgy, was a way of publicly affirming that the liturgy was exercised by the whole people of God and not simply by clerics who know Latin (though the Council still retained Latin as the official language of the Latin Church).[36]

Underlying the liturgical constitution is a theological interpretation not only about the liturgy but also about the Church. The constitution begins by elaborating on the relation between liturgical celebration and the nature of the Church.[37] The constitution affirms that the liturgical celebration of the Eucharist is the act by which the Church most reveals itself to be Church.

the Church reveals herself most clearly when a full complement of God's holy people, united in prayer and in a common liturgical service (especially the Eucharist), exercise a thorough and active participation.[38]

In addition, the image of the Church as the people of God, that was to be worked out in the constitution on the Church, was presupposed in this constitution insofar as it emphasized that the subject of the liturgy is the people of God.

All the faithful should be led to that full, conscious, and active participation in liturgical celebrations which is demanded by the very nature of the liturgy, and to which the Christian people "a chosen race, a royal priesthood, a holy nation, a redeemed people" (1 Pet 2:9) have a right and obligation by their baptism.[39]

As this quotation shows, the Council has taken up the theme of the royal priesthood of the faithful—a theme that had been central to the Lutheran Reformation. In these statements the liturgical constitution affirms the theological emphases of the constitution on the Church and the centrality that it gives to the metaphor of the "People of God."

The Tensions and Compromises in the Understanding of the Church

While the Council initiated innovations and renewed its understanding of the Church, it also continued to maintain traditional viewpoints. As a result of the compromises struck at Vatican II, the conciliar texts contain two different conceptions of the Church, and they often stand side by side in the same constitution. One conception is the notion of the Church developed by Vatican I. Its formulations are taken over by Vatican II precisely in those texts that reaffirm the Pope's primacy (both teaching and juridical) and the hierarchical structure of the Church. The other conception is the *communio* by which Vatican II sought to retrieve the idea of the Church held by the ancient church, and that was elaborated on in the historical studies of the theologians of the *nouvelle théologie*. This understanding of the Church as a *communio* highlights the episcopal responsibility for the Church and the collegial structure of its leadership. It likewise calls for participation of the laity in the Church and its diverse ministries. The crucial interpretive question is both historical and systematic. The historical question is: What is the relation between the views of the Church in Vatican I and those in Vatican II? The systematic question is: How does one integrate the hierarchical and *communio* views of the Church that exist side by side within the same document? In view of the normative status of both Vatican I and Vatican II, the historical and systematic questions converge. Both issues become acute in the practical question: How does one implement structures that are both hierarchical and collegial?

The Relation of Vatican II to Vatican I

Three interpretations of the relation exist: Some interpretations argue that the two councils are *complementary;* others propose that the views are *contrasting;* and the third interpretation sees some *unity in difference.* The interpretation that stresses complementarity proposes a consistent doctrinal development. Whereas Vatican I had clearly laid down the parameters for the papacy and its infallibility, it did not complete its work. In this view, Vatican II takes up the unfinished work by developing the role of the bishops and laity in relation to that of the papacy. In this view Vatican II basically complements and supplements Vatican I.

The second viewpoint underscores contrast rather than complementarity. It is the most popular and widespread view. It understands Vatican I and II in terms of contrasting images. Vatican I had a monarchical and hierarchical conception of the Church that was drawn from modern conceptions of sovereignty and was expressed in Neo-Scholastic categories. Vatican II draws its conception of the Church as *communio* from Scripture and the ancient tradition of the Fathers. It emphasizes the local church and the communion of the Church, the collegial responsibility of bishops, and the interconnection between the sacramental and legal structure of the Church. It appeals to a tradition of the ancient church and to ancient traditions of both the East and the West. The contrast exists in vision, in terminology, and

in sources. In this perspective the Second Vatican Council's vision of the Church is not simply a development and complement to Vatican I but, rather, a reform, a change, and an innovation. Where Vatican II took over the formulation of papal primacy in teaching and power, it placed it into a new context. In fact, the *notio praevia* to Chapter 3 of *Lumen Gentium* works as a foreign body in relation to the style and argument of the main body of the text.

The third interpretation argues against viewing the differences between Vatican I and II primarily as a contrast between an ecclesiology centered on papal primacy and one centered on *communio.* Such an interpretation that stresses contrast overlooks the continuities between the two Councils and the new reception of Vatican I within Vatican II. A continuity can be seen in that in both Councils the Church is increasingly viewed as a subject or as a center of action. Whereas Vatican I emphasizes the agency of the papacy, Vatican II underscores the agency of the whole Church. The line of continuity consists in making the agency of the Church the point of action. This agency is elaborated on in Vatican II in the following ways: *Lumen Gentium* refers to the Church as the sacrament of salvation for the world; *Gaudium et Spes,* the pastoral constitution, draws out the concrete consequences of this sacramental function in stressing the Church's solidarity with historical movements furthering the dignity of the human person. The continuity between the Councils does not lie as much in the fact that Vatican II takes over the primacy statements of Vatican I but, rather, in the continued emphasis upon the Church's agency as central to the understanding of the Church.[40]

The Integration of Primacy and Collegiality

Beyond the theoretical issue of relating the ecclesial conceptions of the two Councils, there is the concrete practical issue of how one theologically integrates the office of Peter (papacy) into a church that is understood according to a *communio* structure. Unless the theoretical is integrated with the practical and worked out in the concrete life of the Church, then the theoretical framework of a *communio* ecclesiology remains an empty abstraction. In the wake of the Vatican II, the extension of the collegial and pastoral office of the bishops came to be concretely realized in three ways: in the establishment of the Synod of Bishops, in the increased importance of regional councils, and in the role of the national episcopal conferences. The putting into practice of these three initiatives and their assessment became one of the most acute and controversial issues of the post–Vatican II period.

Pope Paul VI established the Synod of Bishops according to the guidelines of Vatican II and thereby brought to concrete expression the collegial character of the episcopacy in its working communion with the papacy. The decisions of the Synod of Bishops were to be not only consultative but also decisive. The decisions did not serve merely as material for a subsequent papal decision but, rather, expressed the collegial union between the episcopacy and the papacy, as the Pope sought to bring to the fore the whole idea of collegiality.

The second implementation of collegiality was the reestablishment of regional councils of an entire continent or a larger cultural unity that spanned several nations. Although the emphasis on such councils was an implementation of collegiality, this implementation was limited in that such councils or synods should be convened only by Rome or take place under Roman supervision. Such an implementation combined in practice a collegial understanding of the Church with a centralist model of government.

The third implementation of collegiality was the institution of episcopal conferences. The role and significance of these conferences and the relationship between them and the Vatican came to be one of the most controversial issues in the development of the postconciliar ecclesiology.[41] An open debate occurred between many Catholic theologians, canonists, and Roman theologians (especially the congregation for the bishops). The implementation of regional councils and episcopal conferences appears to some to be the legiti-

mate practical consequence of the understanding of the Church as *communio* and the collegial character of the Church, because it translates into canon law and institutional practice the synodal and metropolitan structure of the ancient church.[42] Others fear that such regional councils or episcopal conferences are innovations that limit the traditional authority of the individual bishop over his diocese or seek to establish a regional autonomy of decision making and practice in relation to the universal authority of the Pope.

The Church and Its Relation to the World

The Pastoral Constitution of Vatican II, *Gaudium et Spes* (*Joy and Hope*), is both a high point of the Council and one of the most influential of the conciliar statements. To the extent that the goal of the Council was pastoral and concerned with the renewal of the Church's presence within the world, this constitution brings to expression and concrete application the Council's reflections on the nature of the Church and its mission in the world. The purpose of this document is to provide a comprehensive treatment of the Church's place within the modern world.

Gaudium et Spes does signal an advance in the Roman Catholic understanding of the Church and its social doctrine. Papal social encyclicals from Leo XIII's *Rerum Novarum* to Pope John XXIII's *Pacem in Terris* (*Peace on Earth*) have primarily grounded the Church's social doctrine on the basis of a theological and philosophical anthropology.[43] They have articulated and defended the dignity of the human person and those rights and duties that flow from that human dignity. When the papal encyclicals evaluate economic theories (capitalism or communism) or political systems (liberalism or socialism) or the situation of the world (industrial revolution), they have done so primarily in terms of a theory of natural law that spelled out human dignity and human rights. The appeal to natural law and to human rights was the dominant approach to Catholic social thought prior to Vatican II.

Vatican II takes up a new approach in three ways: (1) It introduces biblical teaching as the basis of social teaching without, however, doing away with the appeal to natural law and reason; (2) it more centrally acknowledges the historical character of social life; and (3) it overcomes a lacuna within previous social doctrine concerning the relation between the vision of society present in the social encyclicals and the theological understanding of the nature of the Church and its mission.[44]

The incorporation of biblical symbols and themes is an important innovation. Until John XXIII's encyclical *Mater et Magister*, the social teaching of the Catholic Church based itself upon what it considered to be the order that God inscribed in human nature. The appeal to revelation was viewed as a corroboration of what was known through human reason and its reflection upon social reality. The Pastoral Constitution employs a different method. It affirms that human nature, society, and dignity cannot be understood apart from the conditions not only of Creation but also of sin and redemption. Moreover, as the third chapter of part II argues, a consideration of Christian eschatology is essential to understanding the meaning of human activity in the world. The consequence is that the Council relates social and political concerns much more directly to the Christian community's religious self-understanding. It also means a weakening of the appeal to natural reason as the basis for public discourse on social and political issues.

The second contribution is the increased awareness of the historical nature of human social life. Traditional natural law appeals to essential and unchanging principles and applies these principles to new situations and conditions. Such an approach did not adequately reflect on the changing historical conditions of social, cultural, and political life. The Council is concerned to describe the distinctive features of the modern world that call for new solutions to new problems. It notes that "the human race is moving from a more static view of things to come to one which is more dynamic and evolutionary, giving rise to

new combinations of problems, which call for new analyses and syntheses."[45]

The third contribution involves the elaboration of the relation between the Church's mission and its social vision. It does so in several ways. The Church is defined as "at once the sign and the safeguard of the transcendental dimension of the human person."[46] Sections 40 to 42 lay out the basis of the church's social mission. The safeguarding of human rights is integral to its religious mission. The religious ministry of the Church is to proclaim and to realize the Kingdom of God. However, God's Kingdom affects or co-penetrates every dimension of human life. The Church's proper mission is constituted through four specific tasks: the defense of human dignity, the promotion of human rights, the cultivation of the unity of the human family, and the explication of the meaning of human life. The religious mission is related to the Kingdom of God in two ways. On the one hand, the Kingdom of God transcends every political authority. Hence the religious mission entails a criticism of political ideology. On the other hand, the Kingdom of God relates to diverse dimensions of social and economic reality, and consequently, the religious mission is related to the right ordering of the social and economic order.

Two other conciliar constitutions further develop the social message of *Gaudium et Spes*. *Apostolicam Actuositatem* (*The Decree on the Apostolate of the Laity*) proposes that the laity have a twofold role: to work for evangelization and to renew the temporal order. This role is based upon an understanding Christ's work of redemption that is primarily related to the salvation of the human being but embraces the "renewal of the whole temporal order."[47] *Ad Gentes* (*The Decree on the Church's Missionary Activity*) explains that the call to work for Christ's redemption includes "the right ordering of social and economic affairs." The Church's missionary activity thus involves collaborating with work to overcome hunger, disease, and ignorance, to establish peace and justice, and to improve working conditions.[48]

Biblical Historical Criticism

The Constitution on Divine Revelation (*Dei Verbum*) displays the significant shift in the Catholic Church's attitude toward historical-critical biblical studies that had taken place in the decades preceding the Council. In 1893 Pope Leo XIII's encyclical, *Providentissimus Deus,* had underscored the dangers of the prevalent "higher criticism" in its approach to the Scriptures. The Pope recognized the discrepancy between the words and outlook of biblical authors and the issues of modern science and, therefore, acknowledged that one could not simply appeal to biblical texts to resolve scientific debates. Nevertheless, he defined "inspiration" in such a way that the human author was little more than an "instrument" in the hands of God. Fifty years after Leo's encyclical, Pope Pius XII's *Divino Afflante Spiritu* (1943) acknowledged that the Scriptures have different literary "forms." Insofar as it acknowledges different literary forms and assigns historical writings to one particular literary form, the encyclical offers an interpretation of the Scriptures that affirms the presence of epic, myth, drama, poetry, legal texts, and so forth alongside the historical in the Scriptures. This encyclical led to a change in biblical scholarship in the period immediately preceding Vatican II. Historical criticism now was widely accepted in Catholic theology in contrast to having been strongly opposed during the anti-Modernist period at the beginning of the twentieth century.

In accepting the importance of historical criticism, Vatican II had to take a stance on several important issues related to the interpretation of the Scriptures: the inspiration and apostolicity of the Gospels, the issue of inerrancy, the historical trustworthiness of the Scriptures, and the sufficiency and primacy of the Scriptures in relation to tradition and the teaching office.

Inspiration and Apostolicity

At the time of the Council, the Roman Pontifical Biblical Commission proceeded on the assumption that the Gospels were substantially historical, but not literally so in every single word. Moreover, it pointed to a development of the material in the Gospels, from Jesus's preaching, to the proclamation by the disciples, to the written Gospels. Vatican II's document on Divine Revelation takes up this same line and, in fact, uses the Commission's statement as a guide. It cautiously affirms the new direction while, at the same time, using traditional categories. For example, it carefully uses traditional categories by referring to the authors of the Gospels as "apostles and apostolic men." At the same time, it clearly distinguishes between the apostles and the evangelists. The apostles preached, gave example, instructed those who were to preach, and were the authors of the Gospels on the basis of that dependency. The evangelists are not the first-generation eyewitnesses but, rather, belong to ensuing generations. The inspiration of the Gospels, therefore, does not entail God's use of the human author as a direct instrumental cause, as Leo XIII had argued, nor does apostolicity mean that the apostles, as members of the Twelve, themselves wrote the Gospels.

Biblical Inerrancy

Concerning the much debated issue of inerrancy, Vatican II breaks new ground insofar as it takes into account historical and literary criticism and the increased awareness of the literary form of the scriptural materials to ascertain their purpose and intent. The Council affirms:

It follows that the books of Scripture must be acknowledged as teaching firmly, faithfully, and without error that truth which God wanted put into the sacred writings for the sake of our salvation.[49]

The Council makes the goal and purpose of the Scriptures determinative. The Scriptures were not written, for example, to be a textbook of the natural sciences. Nor were the Scriptures written to be sources of political history. Instead, the purpose of the Scriptures is human salvation. Therefore, one should not interpret the Scriptures on the basis of a universal principle of inerrancy, but rather should interpret the Scriptures primarily in relation to their affirmation of what concerns salvation.

Historical Trustworthiness and the Notion of Truth

Vatican II states:

> The sacred authors wrote the four Gospels, selecting some things from the many which had been handed on by word of mouth or in writing, reducing some of them to a synthesis, explicating some things in view of the situation of their churches and preserving the form of proclamation, but always in such a fashion that they told us the honest truth (*vera et sincera*) about Jesus.[50]

This passage underscores, first of all, the theological and pastoral purpose of the composition of the Gospels. The writers or editors wrote primarily with a pastoral-theological task of synthesis and explanation with a view to the situation of their church. The English translation uses the term "honest" truth to translate the Latin *vera et sincera,* "true and sincere." That phrase resulted from considerable debate. Whereas some theologians argued for the term "historical truth" in order to affirm the historical nature of the Gospels, others proposed the term "integral truth" in order to avoid a narrowly positivistic understanding of the word "historical." The term "true and sincere" (translated as "honest") was the compromise that stated that the Gospels affirm a truth but avoided a narrowly defined historical and literalist conception of the truth.

Primacy and Sufficiency of the Scriptures

In its polemic against the Protestant Reformation's affirmation of *sola scriptura*—that is, the primacy and sufficiency of the Scriptures—traditional Roman Catholic theology has long emphasized the notion of two sources of revelation, Scripture and oral tradition, and has affirmed the importance of the tradition. The Vatican Council sought to address the one-sidedness of this

polemic. Article 7 refers to Christ as the full revelation and his Gospel as the source. Instead of referring to Scripture and tradition as two sources, the metaphor of "mirror" is chosen. "This sacred tradition, therefore, and sacred Scripture are like a mirror in which the pilgrim church looks at God."[51]

Articles 9 and 10 offer compromise formulations to express the unity and the distinction of Scripture and tradition. Two complementary affirmations, exposing some tension, are stated, but the unity of Scripture and tradition is primarily affirmed. Scripture and tradition flow from "the same divine wellspring."[52] The successors to the apostles "preserve this word of God, faithfully explain it and make it more widely known. Consequently, it is not from sacred Scripture alone that the Church draws her certainty about everything which has been revealed."[53] Although the text here seems close to affirming the two-source theory, it is actually worded much more carefully. It does not attribute a new or additional content to tradition but, rather, a "certainty" about what has been revealed. In regard to the relation between the teaching office of the Church and Scripture, complementary statements again are affirmed. On the one hand, the Council affirms that "the task of authentically interpreting the word of God, whether written or handed on, has been entrusted exclusively to the living teaching office of the Church."[54] On the other hand, "this teaching office is not above the word of God, but serves it."[55]

Religious Pluralism, Freedom, and Ecumenism

The documents of Vatican II display a significant shift in Roman Catholic theological attitudes to religious pluralism, religious freedom, ecumenism, and missionary work. The conciliar document, *Dignatatus Humanae* (literally translated as "The Dignity of the Human Person," but known in English as The Declaration on Religious Freedom) acknowledges religious freedom as a human and civil right in a way that reversed a long-standing theory and practice that opposed the separation of church and state and rejected freedom of religion. Liberalism and liberal society were previously faulted because of their advocacy of these very freedoms. Traditional Roman Catholic theology insisted that because the Catholic Church represented true belief and practice, Catholicism should be established as the state religion and non-Catholic religious expression should not be indifferently tolerated. Pope Pius IX's (1846–1878) condemnations, of which the Syllabus of Errors is the prime example, and Pope Leo XIII's encyclicals, *Immortale Dei* (1885) and *Libertas* (1888), amply demonstrate critical opposition to liberalism and its embrace of religious toleration and freedom. Both popes not only reaffirmed traditional views against the separation of church and state but argued that religious freedom is merely the expression of religious indifference and relativism.

The Council's document begins with the acknowledgment that modern society has become religiously, philosophically, and politically pluralist. This contrasts with Pope Leo XIII's view of society that presupposes the historical tradition of the religious unity of the so-called Catholic Nations in Europe. The document affirms religious freedom as a universal human right. Further, it accepts the political doctrine of the limited function of constitutional government that now has a juridical rather than a sacral function. Its function is juridical, that is, to safeguard human rights and obligations, rather than sacral, or to promote religious truth as an element of the common good. In the declaration, government has the function of protecting and promoting religious freedom (rather than safeguarding a vision of truth, as in the traditional view) as a fundamental right of the human person.

Nevertheless, in response to the concern that such a wholesale acknowledgment of religious freedom as a human right could be misunderstood as governmental indifference, not to mention hostility, to religion, the Council affirms that, in its proper function of caring for the common temporal good, the government should acknowledge and favor the religious life of its citizens. While its first duty is toward the religious freedom of all cit-

izens, its second duty is "to supply conditions favorable to the cultivation of religious life, in such wise that citizens may in fact be enabled to exercise their religious rights and to discharge their religious duties, and that society itself may enjoy the values of justice and peace which ensue upon the fidelity of human persons toward God."[56]

Religious freedom and human rights are acknowledged in both the document on ecumenism and on religious freedom. Non-Roman Catholic Christian communities are no longer labeled as "sects" or "heretical groups" but, rather, are viewed as incorporating real ecclesial elements. *Unitatis Redinintegratio (The Decree on Ecumenism)* views the division among Christians as a scandal and a contradiction of the will of Christ. It describes the principal historical divisions in the Christian family and calls for continual reformation and continual conversion. It affirms, in a new way for Catholic theology, the Christian reality of other Christian churches. In contrast to the traditional Scholastic theology of the day, it explicitly affirms that the Church "subsists in" but is not identical to the institutional church because outside the "visible borders" of the Catholic Church there exist in these other Christian churches and other Christian communities "elements and endowments which together build up and give life to the church itself."[57] The criterion of the ecclesial status is not the Catholic Church itself but, rather, the apostolic fullness.

The Decree on Ecumenism also formulates the notion of a "hierarchy of truths" with its implication that doctrinal truths have a different rank in significance for faith and the Christian life. "When comparing doctrines, they should remember that in Catholic teaching there exists an order or 'hierarchy' of the truths, since they vary in their relationship to the foundation of the Christian faith."[58] The consequence of this decree is that one need not have an agreement on every theological opinion or doctrine as the necessary condition of unity among the churches. A hierarchy of truths implies that an ecumenical consensus need not take place in every detail but, rather, on the more basic and fundamental truths of Christianity.

The Decree on the Relationship of the Church to Non-Christian Religions addresses the relationship between Christianity and Judaism as well as the relation to other world religions.[59] It sought to interpret these religions more positively than previously. On the one hand, it affirms that "other religions to be found everywhere strive variously to answer the restless searchings of the human heart by proposing 'ways,' which consist of teachings, rules of life, and sacred ceremonies. The Catholic Church rejects nothing which is true and holy in these religions."[60] On the other hand, it proclaims that the fullness of truth is found within the Roman Catholic Church. Statements relating to Judaism were of considerable debate during the Council. Positively, the Council revoked the popular notion that one should attribute to the Jews the primary guilt for the death of Jesus, as stated in John's Gospel and read during the Holy Week liturgy. Instead, guilt is attributed to every person as a sinner.

HANS KÜNG

Hans Küng (1928–　) was born on March 19, 1928, at Sursee, in the canton of Lucerne, Switzerland. He went to Rome for graduate studies, studying philosophy from 1948 to 1951, concluding with a licentiate on the atheistic humanism of Jean Paul Sartre. His studies in theology (1951–1955) earned him a licentiate in theology on Karl Barth's doctrine of justification. He then studied at the Institut Catholique in Paris and obtained his theological doctorate with a dissertation comparing the Roman Catholic understanding of justification with Karl Barth's. His early interest in ecumenism remains the enduring interest of his life work, and it marks not only the beginning but also the major part of his contribution to theology. His books on the Second Vatican Council and his many publications on the Church, on church structures, and on papal infallibility show the marks of his early dialogue with Karl Barth. Küng's theological innovations are

Hans Küng

less dependent on thorough philosophical analyses, as is the case with Karl Rahner, than on the influence of Karl Barth's theology and his Neo-Orthodox impulses. Küng's work constantly seeks to retrieve God's Word in the Scriptures as the critical norm by which to judge Catholic institutions and doctrines. Like Karl Barth, he emphasizes the transcendence of God and the distance between the divine transcendence and human religiosity. Hence, in interpreting the Church, Küng will emphasize the human frailty and sinfulness of the Church in contrast to the more traditional Catholic emphasis on the Church as the sacramental continuation of God's presence in Jesus. Küng's proposals for reform of the Church, his critique of the infallibility of the Pope, and his interpretation of Christianity proceed from a theology influenced by Barth's affirmation of the transcendence of God's Word over against all religious institutions.

Justification and the Dialogue with Karl Barth

Hans Küng's *Justification: The Doctrine of Karl Barth and a Catholic Reflection*[61] argues that a basic agreement exists between Karl Barth's exposition of the doctrine of justification in the *Church Dogmatics* and the Catholic teaching about justification (not only of Roman Catholic theologians, but also the doctrine set forth at the sixth session of the Council of Trent). Because Küng deals with such a central point of disagreement between the Reformation churches and Roman Catholic teaching on justification, the book was viewed as a milestone of ecumenical theology. Küng argues that for Catholic theology and the Council of Trent, justification takes place in such a way that nothing, not even the faith preceding justification and sanctification, merits justification. The love of God that takes place in justification belongs on the side of faith and not works.

The general reception of the book was extremely positive. Karl Rahner wrote: "Küng's book has achieved an astonishing result: the consent of a great Protestant theologian to a presentation of a doctrine of justification . . . which cannot be designated as un-Catholic."[62] Ironically, Catholics doubted that Küng's position adequately described Protestant views of justification. Protestants, however, affirmed that Küng's description of the Reformation teaching on justification was correct; however, they wondered whether he had adequately described the Roman Catholic position.[63] In his preface to the book, Karl Barth cautiously follows that line and writes with approval:

if what you present in Part Two of this book is actually the teaching of the Roman Catholic Church, then I must certainly admit that my view of justification agrees with the Roman Catholic view.[64]

Such a rapprochement on the doctrine of justification was indeed impressive. It must be said, however, that the disagreements between Roman Catholic theology and Lutheran theology have indeed traditionally been sharper than those with the Calvinist tradition, represented by Karl Barth. Nevertheless, the book set the direction for further ecumenical studies. In the decades following, consensus statements between Lutherans and Roman Catholics on justification would come to the same conclusion that Hans Küng had pioneered.

Küng's Interpretation of Vatican II

Soon after Pope John XXIII's convocation of Vatican II, Hans Küng wrote a best-seller, *The Council and Reunion: Renewal as a Call to Unity*, which echoed the Pope's call for reform.[65] Translated into many languages, the book helped to set many of the expectations for the Council, its goal, and its achievements. Appealing to Yves Congar's historical research in *True and False Reform in the Church*,[66] Küng outlined the meaning of church reform. He points out that the notions of "reform" and "reformation" should not be understood as beginning with the Protestant Reformation but, rather, that reform has a long tradition within ancient Christianity. In a section on the nature of the Church, Küng argues that the permanent and essential nature of reform within the Church is based upon the nature of the Church as a human and sinful institution.

Küng then proceeds to interpret the Second Vatican Council primarily in relation to ecumenism, and he argues for the interrelationship between reform of the Catholic Church and ecumenism. "The reunion of separated Christians, as conceived by John XXIII, is bound up with a renewal within the Catholic Church to which the coming Council is to make an essential contribution."[67] Küng seeks to combine reform and reunion by focusing on the differences in the understanding of the Church and the need for institutional reform. "The chief difficulty in the way of re-union lies in the two different concepts of the Church, and especially of the concrete organizational structure of the Church."[68] Küng writes that while

the doctrine of justification was the theological lever which started Luther's own development as a reformer and then, in his hands, set the whole Reformation movement going and kept it going . . . the central demand of the reform was reformation: reform of the church in head and members: reform of doctrine, of cult, and the people of the Hierarchy at every level.[69]

The heart of the matter of church reform is the ecclesiastical office, and Küng argues that "the great stone of stumbling is the Petrine office."[70] This task of church reform through reform of institutional structures is now taken up by Küng in a series of scholarly publications.

Structures of the Church

Küng's next two major works deal with the nature of the Church. *Structures of the Church* (1964), published in a series edited by Karl Rahner on disputed questions, raises several historical and controversial issues on the nature of the Church and its structures. The second work, *The Church* (1967), is a comprehensive, systematic treatment of the Church, and was a major postconciliar treatment. Its advantage was that it sought to elucidate the many insights of the Council, but it is also very biblical in its foundation and orientation. Together, these two publications offer a specific vision of the Church. They underscore the collegial nature of the Church and emphasize the importance of charisms or specific "gifts" within the Church. They draw their inspiration less from contemporary social theory about institutions than from the New Testament description of the charismatic pattern and structures of the Pauline communities, in distinction from the deutero-Pauline communities.

These two volumes also display Küng's distinctive theological method.[71] A hallmark of Hans Küng's work is his attempt to place the Scriptures at the center of his theology. How he does so marks a difference between him and the *nouvelle théologie*. Küng notes that the renewal of theology in the latter movement was guided by a return to the Latin and especially the Greek Fathers of the church. Moreover, its exegetical approach employed a spiritual interpretation of the Scriptures. Küng seeks to make the historical-critical reading of the Scriptures normative. He writes:

an examination of the view of the Greek and Latin fathers in the light of the New Testament and thus of

a historical and critical exegesis struck me as unavoidable. This very point had been neglected in the *nouvelle théologie*, and this in turn was connected with the suppression of the French school of exegesis in connection with the struggle against modernism.[72]

As a result, the *nouvelle théologie* replaced historical-critical exegesis with a spiritual or "pneumatic" exegesis. Whereas much of Henri de Lubac's scholarly work involved the historical interpretation and systematic defense of the classic four senses of Scripture, Hans Küng's theological work makes historical-critical exegesis central to his development of critical norms for theology.

Küng appeals to the biblical writings as normative in criticizing the inadequacy of the Hellenistic metaphysical categories of Patristic thought and of Neo-Scholastic theology. This strong methodological emphasis on the primacy of Scripture as a means to criticize the metaphysical categories of the doctrinal traditions sharply distinguishes Küng's work from that of many fellow Roman Catholic theologians who have viewed this approach with a certain caution. He is criticized for an excessive biblicism or a neglect of the classical dogmatic traditions.[73] He is viewed as a "Catholic" theologian who has adopted and made his own Adolf Harnack's program of "de-Hellenization."

On Being a Christian

On Being a Christian (1974) represents a comprehensive statement of Küng's theology and his interpretation of Christianity.[74] The focal criterion of his theology is the "earthly Jesus" or the real Jesus in distinction to the kerygmatic or creedal Christ, or even the historical, reconstructed Jesus.[75] Küng attempts to obtain an understanding of Jesus by interpreting him in relation to four social groups of his period. Each of these groups represents a particular religious worldview with its distinctive beliefs and practices. Küng characterizes them in an "ideal-typical fashion." The Essenes are characterized by their ascetic lifestyle and their monastic withdrawal from society, and the Zealots for their nationalism and their advocacy of violent revolution in order to reestablish the sovereignty of Israel. The Sadducees are seen as representing the Mosaic law, whereas the Pharisees are the advocates of ethical ideals. Because Jesus could have but did not join any one of these groups, his lifestyle and message must, therefore, be understood as "other" than that of these groups. His life and message transcended the practices and beliefs of these groups. Küng takes a further step and relates each of these four groups to a major world religion: Islam to the Zealots, Buddhism to the Essenes, Judaism to the Sadducees, and Confucianism to the Pharisees. Christianity, as defined by Jesus, should expresses Jesus's Otherness.

Küng's interpretation has been equally criticized for its overly stylized characterizations of the religious-social groups of Jesus's environment and the other world religions. One can question whether such a stylized treatment does justice to the historical complexity and diversity of these individual world religions. Though Küng continues to work on the issue of Christianity in its relation to the world religions, and has developed more nuanced interpretations of the world religions, it remains a question whether he has really abandoned his original framework.[76]

In developing a systematic Christology, and in interpreting the development from the earthly Jesus to the early Christian *kerygma* and then to the christological councils, Küng points again to the inadequacy of the metaphysical categories used by these councils. Not only is this terminology foreign to our contemporary culture, but it has an abstract quality that makes it inadequate to presenting Jesus in a living way and for the religious life. Küng proposes to replace metaphysical categories with functional terms. He takes up the terms "Stellvertreter" (representative, placeholder) and "deputy" to describe Jesus's function and significance. Jesus is the representative of God.

Küng's treatment of classic Christology appears to many of his Roman Catholic colleagues to be closer to Albrecht Ritschl's critique of metaphysics and to Harnack's critique of Hellenization (see Volume I, Chapter Eleven) than to the Catholic tradition's acceptance of metaphysics and its awareness of the importance of development in Roman Catholic theology. Küng's Christology became an issue—but not the major issue—in his conflict with Rome. The Congregation for the Doctrine of the Faith asked Küng for clarification about his treatment of Christology. On the one hand, his treatment of the uniqueness and centrality of Christ in relation to other religions made his interpretation of Jesus appear very Orthodox or Neo-Orthodox. On the other hand, his critique of the adequacy of the metaphysical terminology of the christological councils for contemporary Christianity made his work seem very close to the theology of Protestant Liberalism. The issue came to a head, however, not over Christology, but over Küng's analysis and treatment of papal infallibility.

Papal Infallibility, Birth Control, and Religious Affirmations

The conflict between Hans Küng and the Vatican concerning papal infallibility was more than a disagreement about the papacy and the Pope's teaching office.[77] It also involved a fundamental difference about the nature of the Church and the historical character of human language. Küng draws out the implications of the doctrine of justification for the Church itself, and sees the Church as a sinful church. He also brings the issue of birth control to bear on the issue of papal infallibility with a singular syllogistic argument. Küng argues that the Pope's encyclical on birth control (*Humanae Vitae*, 1968) represents an infallible papal teaching. But because, in Küng's view, this encyclical and teaching are obviously mistaken, then the Pope is clearly not infallible. Those critics who agree with the Pope's teaching on birth control obviously do not agree with Küng's syllogism. But more important, even those dissenting on the issue of birth control have countered that in no way can *Humanae Vitae* be considered an infallible doctrine. Therefore, they argue, Küng has not proven his point.

There is, however, a further basic philosophical disagreement concerning the nature of language and how it affects the historicity of doctrine. Hans Küng argues that human language inadequately expresses the truth that it seeks to convey. Consequently, creeds, dogmas, and doctrines are inadequate to the truth that they seek to express, and therefore, they are rightly and continuously subject to reform and reformulation. According to Küng, the doctrine of papal infallibility not only fails to take into account the frailty of the Church, but it also fails to allow for the inability of linguistic formulations to express the truth fully and adequately. (Küng's critics, of course, disagree with his interpretation of the First Vatican Council.[78]) Küng concludes that in place of the notion of infallibility, one should "give preference to the *concept of 'indefectibility' or 'perpetuity' in truth*."[79] By distinguishing between infallibility and indefectibility, Küng can maintain that the Church remains in the truth despite individual errors in ??36?? propositions. "What is meant here then is that the Church remains in the truth and this is not annulled by the sum total of individual errors."[80]

The important relation between language and truth became the point at issue in the ensuing controversy between Küng and the Vatican. The Vatican's Office on Faith and Doctrine issued *Mysterium Ecclesiae* (*Mystery of the Church*) as a response to Hans Küng. This declaration concedes that all doctrines are formulations and as linguistic formulations are incomplete, contextual, and limited.[81] A doctrinal affirmation should be interpreted as a response to a particular question or heresy and not as a general affirmation. Its vocabulary may express a particular culture and philosophy that may need to be reinterpreted in another culture with another philosophical language. The language of doctrinal definitions often presupposes certain worldviews, but those worldviews are not thereby defined. Nevertheless, doctrinal affirmations affirm the truth in a determinate way. They do not merely approximate the truth; they express it in a specific and binding, though historically and culturally conditioned, way. A crucial difference exists here. Whereas Küng emphasizes the degree to which all language approximates the truth, the Vatican declaration underscores the determinate, and hence binding, affirmations of doctrinal truth despite all historical and cultural conditioning.

Philosophical Theology and Comparative Religion

As indicated earlier, the most distinctive contribution of Hans Küng's theological work has been in the areas of ecumenism and church reform. His initial writings, from his dissertation on Karl Barth's doctrine of justification to his comprehensive treatment of the Church and its structures, have more than documented his ecumenical and ecclesiological interests. Nevertheless, Hans Küng also has had a strong interest in philosophical theology, though his writings in this area have attracted less attention and controversy. He worked on a study of Hegel's theology for his qualifying dissertation (habilitation) when he was called to be a professor at the University of Tübingen. He later finished and published this study, which seeks to trace the development of Hegel's interpretation of Christianity and to develop the significance of Hegel's thought for Christology.[82] As a complement to and further development of *On Being a Christian*, Küng published *Does God Exist?* (1978).[83] He answers his question with a straightforward "yes." The denial of God's existence implies that a basic trust in reality is ultimately unjustified, whereas belief in God entails the opposite. Küng formulates the following thesis:

Affirmation of God implies an ultimately justified fundamental trust in reality. As radical and fundamental trust, belief in God can suggest the conditions of the possibility of uncertain reality. If someone affirms God, he knows why he can trust reality.[84]

Küng's basic argument places persons before a fundamental option, whether the fundamental meaning and trustworthiness of reality is ultimately grounded or not. To affirm God is to affirm that such faith and trust is grounded.

After the Vatican withdrew Küng's canonical mission to teach as a Roman Catholic theologian at the University of Tübingen, the subject of his teaching shifted. According to the concordat between the Vatican and the German government, this withdrawal meant that Küng could no longer teach and examine in the Roman Catholic theological faculty in Tübingen. However, he did not lose his tenure as a professor at the University and, consequently, he began to lecture much more on the issues of comparative religion and the world religions rather than on the controversial points of Roman Catholic doctrine. His major books, published after the withdrawal of the canonical mission, reflect this interest. He offers an interpretation of Judaism[85] and has published in collaboration with other authors a comparison between Christianity and other world religions.[86] He also has produced a major interpretation of Christianity that goes beyond *On Being a Christian* insofar as it offers an interpretation of Christianity and its history through the lens of diverse interpretive paradigms.[87] One of his later works reveals a broader ecumenism that seeks to cross religions and cultures as it proposes an ethics for a global context.[88]

Critical Issues

The controversy between the Vatican and Hans Küng underscores some of the critical issues of his theology. If the greatest contribution of his theology, resulting in part from his early dialogue with Karl Barth and Protestant Neo-Orthodoxy, is to underscore the critical function of the Scriptures in relation to church tradition and the critical function of God's transcendence to human institutions and practices, the criticisms of his theology point to the weaknesses of this position. The fundamental question is whether Küng's advocacy of a biblically based theology as rela-

tional and his critique of the metaphysics that underlies the Conciliar christological definitions brings him closer to a Protestant position. Specifically, the question is whether he is closer to Albrecht Ritschl's critique of metaphysics and to Harnack's critique of the Hellenization implicit in Christian doctrine than he is to the traditional Roman Catholic affirmations of the value of tradition, doctrinal development, and metaphysics. In a critical study of the nature of the institution of the Church in German theology, Medard Kehl argues that Küng's theology of the institutional church represents a much more Protestant interpretation that stresses the sinfulness of the Church rather than the classic Roman Catholic emphasis upon the sacramental nature of the Church.[89] Many, of course, would view this emphasis as the strength and contribution of Küng's theology, one that seeks to complement traditional Catholic emphases by incorporating the valid insights of the Protestant Reformation.

JOHN COURTNEY MURRAY AND RELIGIOUS FREEDOM

John Courtney Murray (1904–1967), a North American Jesuit, was born in New York City. He joined the Jesuits and was ordained a priest in 1933. He earned his doctorate in theology at the Gregorian University in Rome. He then spent thirty years as professor of theology at the Jesuit theologate in Woodstock, Maryland. He was an associate editor of *America*, a popular weekly magazine that comments on current religious, cultural, and political events. He also was the editor of *Theological Studies*, the most scholarly and respected Catholic theological journal in the United States.[90] Murray's early writings in the 1940s advocated ecumenism and interfaith cooperation in the postwar reconstruction. However, in the late 1940s and 1950s his scholarly work focused on the relationship between church and state, especially in relation to the North American situation. Several of his essays were critical of traditional Roman Catholic approaches to religious freedom. In 1954, Cardinal Alfred

Ottaviani, prefect of the Congregation of the Faith, had Murray's Jesuit superiors restrain him from publishing on church-state relations. The Vatican congregation considered Murray's writings erroneous, especially his advocacy of religious freedom and his argument that the American constitutional system could be integrated within Catholic doctrine. Murray was rehabilitated at the Second Vatican Council through his influence on the Vatican's document on religious freedom.

In the United States as late as the 1950s, and up to the election of John F. Kennedy as President, it was debated whether the Catholic faith and American religious freedom were compatible. The writer Paul Blanshard objected that Catholics owed their religious obedience—as an ultimate obedience—to a foreign sovereign, the Roman Pontiff, as head of another state, the Vatican. Roman Catholics were very sensitive to this criticism. Many leading figures, Francis Cardinal Spellman and Bishop Fulton Sheen in particular, sought to make the American public aware of the patriotism of Roman Catholics and the practical contributions they had made to the nation. In this context John Courtney Murrray made a distinctive contribution. He argued that this issue was not simply a pragmatic or practical issue but, rather, one needing a philosophical and theological justification. It was his goal and task to provide a theoretical justification for religious freedom that would not simply cohere with liberal principles of tolerance, but would be shown to be compatible with the basic philosophical and theological tenets of Roman Catholicism. His book *We Hold These Truths* (1960), greatly influenced American Liberal Catholic thought. Murray's writings covered the period prior to and during the Council. He died in 1967.[91]

When Vatican II began, Murray was disinvited from attending the first session. Francis Cardinal Spellman of New York invited him to the second session as his personal theologian. He had no role in the first draft of the Declaration on Religious Freedom, but later he became an official *peritus* and had considerable influence on the subsequent drafts on religious liberty through his arguments for the coherence between religious freedom and Roman Catholic theological and philosophical principles.[92] The final statement of the Council on religious liberty, *Dignitatis Humanae*, shows his influence, though in a limited way, for there was considerable debate and opposition to Murray's position. This opposition came not only from the traditionalists, but also from some progressives. In addition, he was opposed not only by canonists but also by French theologians who considered their theological justification of religious freedom to be "more theological" than Murray's use of the language of human rights.[93]

The document went through several drafts. The first two drafts resulted from compromises between August Cardinal Bea's Secretariat for Christian Unity and Cardinal Ottaviani, of the Congregation for the Faith. These drafts sought to establish religious freedom on the rights of conscience. During the third session (September to November 1964), Murray was entrusted with writing two subsequent drafts (*textus emendatus* and *textus re-emendatus*). The argument of both texts corresponds to his previously published arguments. At this moment Murray became very ill and was unable to participate in the preparation of the fifth draft. It was presented to the Council and was accepted on December 7, 1965. Although this final document grounds religious freedom on the right to search after the truth, Murray's principal argument was included in the text but was not the central argument.[94]

John Courtney Murray was convinced that one needed to develop the idea of religious freedom on three levels: philosophical, theological, and practical. A foundation of religious freedom based on each of these three pillars was essential. In taking the practical and de facto existing situation into account, Murray argued that a considerable difference existed between Continental liberalism and North American democracy, and Murray attempted to develop the defense of religious liberty from the point of view of constitutional government.[95] Both he and the North American bishops sought to bring to bear on the Council's deliberations what they considered to be the North American experience of constitutional government. But Murray was not confident that Vatican II had developed, to the degree that he wanted, a foundation for religious freedom that was not only philosophical and theological but was also based on legal and constitutional grounds.

Murray's viewpoint becomes clearer when it is viewed against the traditional modern justification of religious freedom. Murray saw the contemporary situation as divided into two fundamentally different views of religious freedom, both of which differ from medieval and even post-Reformation positions.[96] These two positions, Murray argues, show that the problem of religious freedom involves distinct but related issues: the moral issue of the rights of conscience and the constitutional issue dealing with legal and concrete arrangements. These two views of religious freedom conflict, and they view the moral and legal issues quite differently.

The Two Contrasting Views

The first view argues that from a moral perspective one's conscience should be subjectively formed by norms that are objectively true. A conscience that is correctly formed possesses religious freedom because its freedom is rooted in the objective truth, whereas an unbridled conscience, not acknowledging any norms above itself, lacks rectitude and truth. It has no rights and can make no claim to religious freedom. It is a sincere but erroneous conscience. This view constitutes an advance over traditional thought but, for Murray, it is not sufficient. Murray argues that this

first view represents progress within the tradition, a clearer and less confused understanding of traditional principles—in particular, the distinction between the religious order and the political order, and the limitations of political sovereignty in the order of religion.[97]

However, Murray objects that this first view, which reaches its culmination in Pope Leo XIII's

(1878–1903) teachings, does not go far enough.[98] The social, cultural, and political changes after Leo XIII attest that religious freedom is required not only as a personal right, but also as a legal institution. Religious freedom is not simply a concession to the evil of religious error that should be tolerated, but, rather, entails a genuine moral progress. The increased awareness of human personal freedom finds its correlation in a corresponding political freedom with its more positive encouragement of religious freedom.

The second view of religious freedom takes up this consideration and regards religious freedom primarily as a theological and moral concept. The representatives of this view follow one of two directions: One direction begins with the awareness that free persons need religious freedom and then moves to the juridical issues. The other direction, taking a juridical conception with foundations in theology and philosophy, begins with the legal assumption that persons exist under governments of limited powers, and it then moves to the theological and philosophical issues. The distinctiveness of the latter is that "both religious freedom, as a legal institution, and constitutional government as a form of polity, emerge with equal immediacy as exigencies of the personal consciousness in its inseparable correlation with the political consciousness."[99]

Murray's own proposals can be seen not only as an elaboration of this second view, but also as an attempt to unite the theological and moral with the political and juridical so that they converge to establish both freedom of conscience and freedom of religious expression. Murray illustrates the differences between the two views in relation to the conceptual or definitional question (what something is) and the de facto or judgmental question (whether something is). The second view takes the conceptual and definitional question of religious freedom not as an abstract or *a priori* ideal, but as a concrete experience.

The question, what is religious freedom, is not to be answered a priori or in the abstract. The fact is that religious freedom is an aspect of contemporary historical experience. As a legal institution it exists in the world today in the juridical order of many states.[100]

It, therefore, understands religious freedom as a complex concept involving theological, philosophical, civil, and political elements. Likewise, the definition of the state is a complex concept involving the distinctions between sacred and secular, society and state, common good and public order, and the rule of freedom under the law. In regard to the question of fact, the second view does not seek to justify an ideal instance of religious freedom or constitutional law but, rather, to

affirm the validity of religious freedom . . . as a legal institution, a juridical notion, a civil and human right. Correlatively, it affirms the validity of constitutional government, within whose structure religious freedom in the sense explained, finds its necessary place.[101]

Murray's Contribution

John Courtney Murray developed his contribution by criticizing the traditional Catholic distinction between the thesis or ideal, on the one hand, and the hypothesis or what is allowed in a particular context, on the other hand. The traditional approach viewed religious freedom as legitimate and tolerable in situations that were not ideal. However, the ideal still remained an ideal so that the traditional view held that only Roman Catholics had the right to religious freedom in an ideal situation because they alone possessed the religious truth. The enduring significance of Murray's view is his conviction that religious liberty should not be grounded upon the distinction between the ideal and the practical but, rather, upon an interpretation of society, state, and government that seeks to take into account the American experience of religious pluralism and freedom. Murray argued that one needs to distinguish carefully between the terms "society," "state," and "government." Society is the broadest concept in which state and government are subordinated. The state should be con-

ceived of as narrowly as possible, and the government should be considered as only one element of the state. This distinction between society and the state contrasts with the conception that viewed society as an extension of the state and human rights as assured by the state. The Catholic tradition of natural law holds that human rights and human society have priority over the state. Just as human rights do not derive their justification from the state but from society, so, too, the Church should not derive its justification, existence, and welfare from the state. Just as human rights are divinely given so, too, does the Church have its legitimacy not from the state, but from God. Likewise religious freedom has a legitimacy that does not derive from the consensus of society.

There were and remain many critics of Murray's position not only during his lifetime but also afterward.[102] During his lifetime Murray was often criticized for what his critics considered to be a relativism and historicism, insofar as he did not argue for religious liberty from the ideal but rather from the historical and the factual.[103] But such criticisms overlook the appeal to the natural law in Murray's argument. More nuanced critics have pointed out that a certain tension exists between Murray's natural law argument and his argument from a historical and legal perspective.[104] More recently, under the impact of a renewed political and public theology, Murray's distinction between the spiritual and temporal, the sacred and secular, the natural and supernatural has been questioned, because it does not sufficiently take into account the need for the integration between these spheres. Political and liberation theology will (see Chapter Nine) argue that the Gospel message has important applications in the political realm.[105] Closely associated with this criticism is the role that natural law plays in Murray's doctrine. Aware that civic consensus and religious pluralism coexist in the American situation, Murray argued that the natural law itself provided the philosophical and metaphysical presuppositions for common values and that a Christian, therefore, should approach political issues on the basis of reason and the natural law. This, however, leads to the question of whether society has its unity in certain common values without grounding them in natural law in view of society's diversity of worldviews. It also raises the question as to what extent a Christian should appeal to warrants from the Christian tradition and not simply from the natural or rational law.[106]

HANS VON BALTHASAR

In the aftermath of Vatican II there has not only been a progressive implementation of the Council's actions, but also a critique of those progressive theological developments. Hans Urs von Balthasar (1905–1988) is such a critic. His theological writings are especially critical of Karl Rahner's anthropocentric turn, and he shifted from an initial acceptance to a rejection of Hans Küng's position. Von Balthasar accented this polemical direction of his writings only in the decades following Vatican II. When Hans Küng's dissertation on justification was published, von Balthasar compared Küng to Hercules's cleaning out the stables. He had cleaned out the dung of misunderstandings regarding the positions on justification.[107] Later, when John Paul II declared that Hans Küng was no longer to be considered a Catholic theologian, von Balthasar applied the image of Hercules to the Pope. Pope John Paul II was Hercules, and Hans Küng the dung being removed from the stables of Roman Catholic theology.

Hans Urs von Balthasar was born on August 12, 1905, in Lucerne, Switzerland. He studied German literature at the University of Zurich and began a dissertation on "The History of the Eschatological Problem in Modern German Literature," but interrupted his doctoral studies to become a Jesuit in 1929.[108] Because the order was at that time outlawed in Switzerland, he studied philosophy in the Jesuit Berchmanskolleg in Pullach near Munich, Germany, from 1931 to 1933, where he met the Jesuit philosopher Erich Przywara (1899–1972). He then studied theology at Lyons (Fourvière), France, from 1933 to 1937,

where he was a student of Henri de Lubac. After ordination, he became a chaplain at the University of Basel. There he met Adrienne von Speyr, a mystic and a convert to Catholicism; they become close friends and he resided in her house. Von Balthasar left the Jesuits and together with von Speyr established a secular institute—a group of laypersons who nevertheless took the vows of poverty and chastity. Most of his life was spent in Basel, primarily as a theological writer, publisher (he established Johannes Verlag), and leader of a group called the *Johannesgemeinschaft* (Johannine Community). In 1972, he established, with Joseph Ratzinger, Jean Danielou, and others, *Communio: International Catholic Review* as a conservative counterpoint to *Concilium*, the international theological journal established by Karl Rahner, Edward Schillebeeckx, and Hans Küng. Whereas *Concilium* represented a progressive interpretation of the renewal called for by Vatican II, *Communio* insisted on Vatican II's affirmation of the tradition. Von Balthasar died on June 26, 1988. Pope John Paul II had appointed him to the College of Cardinals just two days before his death.

Von Balthasar's publications are voluminous, covering many diverse historical, spiritual, theological, and practical topics. He differs from the other Roman Catholic theologians of the period insofar as he did not earn a theological doctorate and never occupied a teaching position at a university or taught at a theological school.[109] The lack of an academic training and position is not accidental to the form of his theology. His writings often seek to appropriate resources from literature, poetry, and spiritual and ascetic writings to make them relevant for theology. His appropriation and use of these resources are often both creative and arbitrary insofar as he is more concerned to offer his own individual and speculative interpretation than to confront other scholars' readings of an author.[110] His first major publication was a three-volume study entitled, in translation, *Apocalypse of the German Soul*.[111] As the subtitle of the first volume, *Prometheus: Studies of German Idealism*, suggests, von Balthasar interprets the spirit of modern German culture as Promethean, with its own eschatological mythos. He contrasts the Promethean spirit of modern anthropology with the form and law of the Cross of Jesus.[112] This critique of modern anthropology, from the specific perspective of an interpretation of Jesus, anticipates his later work, for example, his criticisms of the anthropological views of Pierre Rousselot and Karl Rahner.[113] In addition, this critique of modernity is the context for his later interest in and dialogue with Karl Barth's theology and for his return to antiquity and patristic theology. In the years following this publication, much of von Balthasar's writings were dedicated to patristic studies on Maximus the Confessor (whose Christology and theology he studied under the title of "Cosmic Liturgy," and which represents for von Balthasar the counter-pole to a modern view), on Origen and on Gregory of Nyssa.[114]

Analogy of Being and Karl Barth

Hans Urs von Balthasar and Karl Barth shared a friendship and a theological give-and-take over a long period of time in Basel, during which important agreements and disagreements emerged. They shared a disdain for Liberal Protestantism or Neo-Protestantism. Von Balthasar notes: "Barth's reasons for rejecting neo-Protestantism are clear enough: it has moved farther and farther away from Revelation, so that nothing remained of Christianity, but the name itself."[115] Von Balthasar agrees with Barth's interpretation of Liberal Protestantism in terms of a turn toward subjectivity and humanism, because it parallels his own interpretation of the spirit of modernity as Promethean. This agreement sets the stage not only for his criticism of anthropocentrism in contemporary Roman Catholic theology, but also for his own counter-balancing theological aesthetics. He sees a similar loss of the substance of authentic Christianity in the Liberal Catholicism that flourished in the wake of Vatican II, and which seemed to be moving in the same direction as Liberal Protestantism.

The point of conflict between von Balthasar and Barth centers on the analogy of being. Influenced by Erich Przywara's interpretation of analogy, von Balthasar takes issue with Barth's criticisms of analogy and of Catholic theology.[116] In distinguishing between an "analogy of faith" and an "analogy of being," Karl Barth viewed the analogy of being as a fundamental principle of Roman Catholic theology. Calling it an invention of the anti-Christ, he saw it as the main weakness and error of Roman Catholic theology. Von Balthasar defended the analogy of being both against the early and later Barth and some of his own Roman Catholic colleagues.

First, Von Balthasar notes that a shift exists between the "dialectics" of the early Barth of the *Epistle to the Romans* and the "analogy of faith" of the later Barth of the *Church Dogmatics*. (See Chapters Three and Four.) It is in this later view of an analogy of faith that Barth argues that there is a common bond between God and the world, which is created by God. Von Balthasar writes that it is only within the framework of this common bond that

Every real "contra" presupposes a constantly to be understood relationship and thus at least a minimal community in order to be really a "contra" and not a totally unrelated "other." Only on the basis of an analogy is sin possible.[117]

Barth's analogy of faith is a correct analogy, but it represents a truth that needs further development and completion. Von Balthasar argues that in the concrete historical order the analogy of faith does, indeed, correspond to the relation between God and humans. However, this relation presupposes the order of creation and brings the order of creation to its fulfillment. Sin goes against the relation between God and creature, but it does not destroy this relation. Von Balthasar argues that one must correctly understand natural theology, not as a sinful attempt from below to grasp or to control God. Instead, he argues that a natural theology highlights the conviction that God's creation establishes a relation for the sake of communion between God and humanity.[118] With this line of reasoning, von Balthasar picks up a theme from Henri de Lubac and the *nouvelle théologie* that reaffirms the correlation between the natural and the supernatural, which, while distinct, are neither separate nor related only extrinsically.

In his dialogue with Karl Barth, von Balthasar is influenced by Erich Przywara's development of the notion of the polarity between the human and the Divine within a Christocentric framework.[119]

It is in this radically Christocentric framework that Przywara develops his presentation of the analogy of being. Philosophy is not a purely formal framework into which we inject the content of theology. Every concrete philosophy must be measured in terms of its yes and no to the supernatural order of Revelation and the one God in Christ. This Christocentric outlook must be taken into account before one tries to contrast his themes with those of Karl Barth.[120]

He sees this polarity squandered in modern philosophy. The result is that one can neither grasp the transcendent nor ascend to it. The influence of the analogy of being even within the analogy of existence, leads to the development of von Balthasar's theological aesthetics and the notion of an *analogia caritas* (analogy of charity).

Theological Aesthetics

Von Balthasar's development of a multivolume theology of aesthetics represents the systematic culmination of his theological writings.[121] A large part of this theological aesthetics, which has to do with beauty and form, represents a polemic against what von Balthasar regarded as the downgrading of the visual and the aesthetic within traditional Protestant theology. The influence of Kierkegaard's sharp distinction between the religious and the aesthetic spheres in contemporary Protestant theology likewise comes under sharp criticism. In von Balthasar's opinion, the separation of aesthetics from Christian thought is a fateful and negative step. He argues: "For the moment, the essential thing to realize is that, without aesthetic knowledge, neither the theoretical nor the practical can attain to their total completion."[122]

Von Balthasar welcomes Karl Barth's emphasis on divine revelation and views Barth as guaranteeing the objectivity of revelation in contrast to Rudolf Bultmann's existential subjectivism with its consequent loss of objectivity. Nevertheless, in von Balthasar's opinion, Karl Barth does not go far enough. Therefore, his own development of an aesthetics based upon revelation seeks to take up Barth's basic theological impulse but to carry it forward in a more consistent and Roman Catholic theological manner.

At least for the time being, Barth with his contemplation of the objective revelation has not succeeded in really shaping and transforming Protestant theology. Up to the present, and very probably for a long time to come, Protestant theology will continue in dutiful subservience to Bultmann's dualism of criticism on the one hand, and existential, imageless inwardness on the other.[123]

Because von Balthasar appeals to aesthetics, in contrast to what he perceives as the subjectivization of theology in Existentialism and transcendentalism, his aesthetics takes a direction that is the opposite of Kantian aesthetics. For von Balthasar, the aesthetic form is such that it radiates from within itself the very light illuminating its beauty. "The beautiful is above all a *form*, and the light does not fall on this form from above and from outside, rather it breaks forth from the form's interior."[124] Von Balthasar sees his emphasis upon aesthetics and seeing as a means of initiation into Christianity for the positivist and the atheist.

The positivist and atheist, today, has become blind not only to theology, but also to philosophy. When placed before the phenomenon of Christ (the splendor of the glorious and sublime God) such a person should once again learn "to see."[125]

From Theo-Drama to Theo-Logic

In addition to his theological aesthetics, von Balthasar has written what he calls a "Theo-dramatics" in which he offers an interpretation of the *Triduum* (three days) of Good Friday, Holy Saturday, and Easter Sunday. What happens on these three days affect God's very self, hence the title Theo-Drama, used to express the action (drama) in God's very being. In this *Triduum*, von Balthasar emphasizes that the affirmation of the Apostle's Creed that Jesus died and descended into Hell needs to be theologically explained. "What is at stake in theodrama is this: that God acts so as to take upon himself and make his own the tragedy of human existence even to the depths of that abyss."[126]

The "Theo-dramatic" takes up the aesthetic categories of Gestalt, form, and symbol, but it takes them a step further to the categories of play, role, and narrative.[127] Here von Balthasar explores the categories of drama as a means for theological reflection. The move from the aesthetic to the dramatic transforms and elevates the realm of the aesthetic form to that of dramatic action. The form becomes manifest as an action. Von Balthasar uses dramatic categories such as author, actor, director, role, and representation to describe the action. He sees the dramatic structure as explicitly Trinitarian. The author is the father, the actor the Son, the director the Holy Spirit. And humans have a role within the divine drama in response to their mission and calling by God. Representation refers to the representative action of Jesus on our behalf and to the way humans present in their actions the divine drama and represent it for others.

The final installment of his triptych, *Theologik (Theo-Logic)*, also consists of three volumes: *The Truth of the World* (identical to a book published in 1947) gives a philosophical account of the nature of truth, whereas the second and third volumes, *The Truth of God*, and *The Spirit of Truth*, make the transition from philosophy to theology.[128] *The Truth of God* asks how Jesus Christ can express God's truth in human categories. *The Spirit of Truth* develops his understanding of pneumatology (Holy Spirit) and is in large part devoted to the question of the relation between the objective and subjective. He began this final installment at the age of seventy eight, and these volumes dealing with the truth and the logic of theology complete von Balthasar's move from aesthetics through dramatics to logic.

Von Balthasar's triptych expresses his complete system. The theological aesthetics deals with the beautiful, the theo-dramatic is concerned with the good, and the theo-logic deals with the truth. His conception of the beautiful, the good, and the truth is developed in line with a Trinitarian and Christocentric conception of reality.

> Our trilogy of aesthetics, dramatics and logics is built upon the mutual Enlightenment existing between theological categories and the philosophical transcendentals. What one identifies as the qualities of Being encompassing each and every existent (the transcendentals), seem to open up the most appropriate access to the mysteries of Christian theology.[129]

Von Balthasar's triptych further develops the perspective initiated in his early discussions with Erich Przywara and Karl Barth. He seeks to lay the foundation for what he calls an "analogy of charity" (*analogia caritatis*), rather than an analogy of being (*analogia entis*). Von Balthasar argues that the structure and logic of Reality is based upon God's kenosis or self-emptying and love that is manifest in the event of Jesus's crucifixion. God's love that is manifest in the Cross of Christ is the logic of reality. It is his logic that provides an analogy of charity that reveals the beauty, goodness, and truth of reality. Von Balthasar's theological aesthetics thus offers a speculative interpretation of reality from a Christian perspective. The very being of reality in its beauty, goodness, and truth is given a Christian interpretation based upon the Gestalt of Christ.

Critical Issues

Von Balthasar's theology has, in the decades after Vatican II, served both as a resource for criticisms of Vatican II and of the progressive theology following Vatican II. His expositions of the patristic interpretation of Scripture have served as the basis for criticism of the increasing dominance of the historical-critical approach to the Bible. His criticisms of Karl Rahner's transcendental approach to theology as a form of reductionism has become the focal point of theological criticism of recent efforts to integrate Christian theology and modern humanism and secularism. His metaphysical Trinitarian speculation has served as a counterpoint to Hans Küng's attempts to formulate the Christian faith in biblical and relational categories rather than in the terms of traditional metaphysics.

At the same time, von Balthasar's theology has not been free of criticism. His creative and speculative interpretation of Scripture often is seen as arbitrary and lacking sufficient historical grounding. Thus, his theological speculations have often been viewed as Platonic, and his failure to explicate the social and political context of faith has been seen as isolating theology from practice.[130] Moreover, though he makes the identification of the true, the good, and the beautiful central to his theology, he does not provide sufficiently clear criteria as to what constitutes the truth, the good, or the beautiful. Furthermore, he uses the symbolism of male and female in a way that introduces essential gender polarities into theological discussion that owe more to nineteenth-century Romanticism than to theological affirmations.[131]

Major criticisms, however, focus on the Gestalt or form of Christianity that von Balthasar advocates. Because he makes the form and action of Jesus the heart of Christianity, the important issue is how that form and action are depicted.

Balthasar depicts the Gestalt of Jesus so exclusively in terms of his mission of self-abandonment, kenosis, and obedient death that the question has been raised whether his Christology is docetic and reduces the humanity of Jesus to a mere sign or emblem of the eternal infinite divine kenosis. Consequently, von Balthasar's depiction is too conceptual and does not sufficiently take into account the historical. His theological Gestalt of Jesus seeks to produce a theological form or essence that mirrors the eternal kenosis but thereby neglects Jesus's historical existence with his concrete preaching, healings, and deeds that led to conflict and his execution.[132]

JOSEPH CARDINAL RATZINGER

Joseph Ratzinger (1927–) did his doctoral studies in theology at the University of Munich, writing a dissertation on Bonaventure's theology of history[133] under the direction of the famous medieval scholar, Michael Schmaus. He then did a second doctorate, a habilitation, with the fundamental theologian, Gottlieb Söhngen, on St. Augustine's understanding of the notion of the people of God.[134] He served as a professor of theology at the University of Bonn (1959–1963) and the University of Münster (1963–1966). During this time, he was the theological adviser to Joseph Cardinal Frings and participated in sessions of Vatican II. In 1966 he left Münster and joined the faculty at Tübingen (1966–1969), where Hans Küng would be his colleague in systematic theology. He taught at Regensburg between 1969 and 1977 when he left to become the Archbishop of Munich. In June 1977, he was named a cardinal. In 1981 John Paul II appointed him the Prefect of the Congregation for the Doctrine of the Faith.

Joseph Cardinal Ratzinger serves as a fitting end to this chapter on Vatican II. If Yves Congar's reform through *ressourcement* became the leitmotiv for Vatican II, Ratzinger's theological reflections and actions as Prefect of the Congregation for the Doctrine of the Faith have become the symbol of the restorationist movement after

Vatican II. He has himself quite bluntly raised the question.

> Not every valid council in the history of the Church has been a fruitful one; in the last analysis, many of them have been just a waste of time. Despite all the good to be found in the texts it produced, the last word about the historical value of Vatican Council II has yet to be spoken.[135]

Ratzinger leaves the question open and does not explicitly criticize the Council. Nevertheless, he has come, in the eyes of many, to symbolize the forces of restoration. This is not only because of the official positions that he has taken as a prefect in the Roman curia; it also is reflected in his theological writings, which give warnings, illustrate changes, and offer criticisms of the theological directions that flourished in the Second Vatican Council. Four noteworthy themes of these writings are: the understanding of the Church, the relation between the Church and the world, a theological vision centered on the Cross of Christ, and the problem of pluralism and relativism.

From Church as People of God to Church as Body of Christ

When Joseph Ratzinger was a graduate theological student at the University of Munich, the Roman Catholic theological faculty established a prize for the best work on the notion of the People of God in Augustine. Joseph Ratzinger won that prize for what became his dissertation, and it was published as such. The choice of the "People of God" as the topic of the prize was an indication of the emerging theological interest in this metaphor for understanding the Church in contrast to the metaphor of the Body of Christ, which was the central metaphor for Pope Pius XII's encyclical on the Church. The Second Vatican Council would make the image of the pilgriming People of God a central metaphor of its constitution. After the Council, when Joseph Ratzinger collected his essays into a book on the nature of the Church, he entitled the published

volume, *Das Neue Volk Gottes* (*The New People of God*).[136]

Although Ratzinger's own publications contributed to the understanding of the concept of the People of God in the Church Fathers and in contemporary systematic theology, later in retrospect he would suggest that the Body of Christ, rather than the People of God, is the more appropriate metaphor for understanding the Church. He thereby criticizes the directions of theology that not only led to his own theological work, but that also came to fruition in Vatican II. Ratzinger gives the reason for his reversal in a carefully worded statement:

> The emphasis with which the idea of the people of God was seized on during the Council meant that the emotion surrounding this discovery far exceeded what the biblical foundations could bear. Fortunately, the Council documents themselves were able to avoid infection with this emotionalism. But it increased all the more in the period after the Council.[137]

Ratzinger argues that the People of God is not an adequate category for the Church. "Christians are not simply the people of God."[138] By itself the concept does not sufficiently take into account the christological and sacramental understanding of the Church.

> Even when people talk of the people of God Christology must remain the core of what is taught about the Church and as a consequence the Church must essentially be thought of on the basis of the sacraments of baptism, the eucharist, and holy orders. We are the people of God in no other way than on the basis of the crucified and risen body of Christ.[139]

The Optimism and Modernism of Vatican II

The crux of Joseph Ratzinger's criticism of Vatican II is summarized in the following comment: "Today, it is being said with increasing frequency that the Council thereby placed itself under the aegis of the European Enlightenment."[140] Ratzinger suggests that *Gaudium et Spes* understands the "world" and the "Church" as counterparts. Moreover, the Church is depicted as a closed entity with a ghetto mentality that, nevertheless, it is striving (through the Council) to remedy by expressing its solidarity with the whole human family. In one of his rare explicit criticisms of the Council, Ratzinger finds fault with the way the Council urges solidarity with humanity and cooperation with the world as excessively accommodating and optimistic.

The text [*Gaudium et Spes*] and, even more the deliberations from which it evolved breathe an astonishing optimism. Nothing seems impossible if humanity and the Church can work together. The attitude of critical reserve toward the forces that have left their imprint on the modern world is to be replaced by a resolute coming to terms with their movement.[141]

Though Ratzinger would later become known for his critique of liberation theology and the controversy with the Brazilian priest, Leonardo Boff, ten years after the Council,[142] he contrasts the optimistic spirit surrounding Vatican II's accommodation of the modern world with the criticism rightly raised by liberation theology's critique of the modern European Enlightenment and its Eurocentrism and technocratic rationality of domination.[143]

Theology of the Cross or Theology of Incarnation

Because Ratzinger was a *peritus* at the Council and is associated with the theological reform movement that the Council came to incorporate, the question has arisen whether an inconsistency exists between the early reformed-minded Ratzinger and the later curial-official Ratzinger. In fact, a fundamental consistency exists in his basic theological vision. Ratzinger's own theology, represented by his earlier studies of Augustine and Bonaventure, is much closer to the approach of the latter, whereas, as we have seen, contemporary transcendental Thomism has its roots in Thomas Aquinas.

It is in the context of his leaning toward an Augustinian and Bonaventurian vision of theology, that Ratzinger underscores the contrast between a theology of the Incarnation and a theology of the Cross. An incarnational theology is often seen as optimist and sympathetic to human values. It was associated in the 1950s with Teilhard de Chardin and with Karl Rahner, and it brings to expression the Thomistic view that grace does not abolish nature, but perfects nature. A theology of the Cross, on the other hand, underscores the opposition or contrast between the worldly wisdom and divine wisdom. The wisdom of one is folly to the other. Ratzinger's own view of this contrast is:

[A] theology of the incarnation tends towards a static, optimistic view. The sin of man appears quite easily as a transitional stage of fairly minor importance.[144]

Ratzinger suggests that

the theology of the cross, on the other hand, leads rather to a dynamic . . . anti-world conception of Christianity, a conception which understands Christianity only as a discontinuously but constantly appearing breach in the self-confidence and self-assurance of man and of his institutions, including the Church.[145]

Ratzinger warns against producing a simplified synthesis of the two theological traditions. He suggests that they are best seen as polarities that correct each other. Nevertheless, his own approach combines them in a way that does not point, as Rahner does, to the Incarnation and the Symbol of Christ as the culmination of creation and the perfection of anthropology. Instead, he underscores the Incarnation as a kenosis that leads to the Cross. Ratzinger argues that an understanding of the Incarnation "must pass over into the theology of the cross and become one with it," just as the theology of Cross is interpreted as the fundamental reality of the Incarnation.[146] With his theological emphasis on kenosis and Cross, Ratzinger proposes a vision of the Incarnation that is much more closely aligned to that of Hans Urs von Balthasar than to that of Karl Rahner and some of the documents of Vatican II.

In his interpretation of Vatican II and its reception in the modern world, it is clear that, of the two polarities, Ratzinger sees the reception of the Council and its constitution *Gaudium et Spes* as representing an excessively optimistic incarnational theology that does not sufficiently see the evil in the world. Against such a theology, Ratzinger increasingly urges a theology of the Cross and challenges the direction of contemporary Roman Catholic theology that seeks an *aggiornamento* of the Church by opening its windows to the light of the modern world.[147]

Religious Pluralism and Moral Relativism

One of the major problems that the Vatican Council dealt with was the issue of religious pluralism. It issued statements not only on religious freedom, but also on the ecumenical relation to other Christian communites and to other religions. These issues have reemerged more persistently in the aftermath of Vatican II. Pointing to the demise of European governmental systems based upon communism, Cardinal Ratzinger has argued that there is not only a new situation in Europe but a new challenge to the Church. That challenge is no longer Marxism, but relativism. Consequently, Cardinal Ratzinger has shifted from a critique of liberation theology and the dangers of Marxist ideology to a critique of relativism as a false interpretation of the ideological presuppositions of democracy.

After the collapse of totalitarian systems . . . today the conviction has become spread throughout the greatest part of the world that democracy, while not the ideal society, is at least practically the only appropriate governmental system.[148]

Ratzinger argues, however, that relativism has become the prevailing philosophy of modern democratic societies because one assumes that relativism is the philosophical presupposition of democracy.

The notion of truth has been pushed into the zone of intolerance and into what is considered undemocratic. . . . The modern notion of democracy appears to be indissolubly bound together with relativism. Relativism appears as the authentic guarantee of freedom, and, indeed, of its essential core: freedom of religion and freedom of conscience.[149]

Ratzinger seeks to address what he views as the challenge of relativism in several ways. First, he argues that democracy rests not so much on the relativistic conviction of the viability of everyone's own opinion, but rather on the validity of basic human rights and dignity. Only a democracy based upon human dignity and rights can prevent that democratic majority from becoming a tyranny of the majority. Democracies should be based not on an ideology of relativism, but on the inviolability of human rights.

Second, Ratzinger discusses the philosophical and religious theories of some contemporary advocates of religious pluralism, especially John Hick and Paul Knitter.[150] (See Chapter Fifteen.) He sees this religious pluralism as based on the Kantian critique of reason that considers human reason incapable of metaphysical cognition. Such skepticism of metaphysical claims leads not to a genuine pluralism and dialogue, but rather to relativism. Ratzinger argues:

To remove from faith its claim to truth, to stated, understandable truth, is an example of that false modesty. . . . It is a renunciation of that dignity of being a human person which makes human suffering bearable and endows it with greatness.[151]

With this criticism, Ratzinger is arguing that relativism not only robs faith of its claim to truth, but does not provide a vision of human dignity that should be the foundation of democracy. Such skepticism and relativism represent the crisis that the post–Vatican II church faces as it enters the third millennium.[152] Ratzinger affirms that "Pluralism in the interplay of Church, Society, and Politics is a fundamental value for Christianity."[153] However, the Christian faith stands opposed to relativism and skepticism, for faith is "an option for the unconditional authority of the truth and of man's bond to the truth."[154]

CONCLUSION: THE AFTERMATH OF VATICAN II

The period after Vatican II was a period of change. Yet, as we have seen, change was also accompanied by resistance to change. Many of these changes were on the practical and liturgical levels. The changes in the liturgy, debated at the Council and documented in the *Constitution on the Liturgy*, were the most evident and represent all but irrevocable changes. The liturgy of the Mass was changed from the Latin language to the vernacular. A new missal was prepared and eventually published in 1974. In the Sunday liturgy the priest no longer was to stand before the altar with his back to the people but, rather, to face the people. This change in physical posture symbolized important theological changes. It portrayed the Eucharistic celebration not only as the representation of a sacrifice, but also as a sacramental meal. It signified that the Eucharist was offered by the community serving with the priest as its leader rather than by the priest with the community serving merely as witnesses. A revision of the *Code of Canon Law* also was undertaken. The old code, in effect since 1917, was replaced with a new code in 1983 with the purpose of incorporating the theology and spirit of Vatican II into the Church's legal structures.[155]

At the same time, the postconciliar exuberance was accompanied by disappointment that many legitimate expectations were not fulfilled. Though Pope Paul VI (1897–1978) implemented many of the recommendations of the Council, which was brought to a conclusion under his leadership,[156] in 1968 he overturned the recommendation of the commission on birth control.[157] A significant number of priests left holy orders and religious left their communities. A serious decline

in religious vocations took place. Despite the liturgical reforms, church attendance, and to a greater extent the practice of oral confession, declined.

The conflict between innovation and restoration thus remains the hallmark of Vatican II. The Council was inaugurated with the idea that innovation would take place through a retrieval of the tradition. However, after Vatican II innovation and retrieval often came into conflict with one another. The progressive spirit of Vatican II echoed in the work of Hans Küng and John Courtney Murray found its counterbalance in the conservative spirit of Hans Urs von Balthasar and the cautious spirit of Joseph Cardinal Ratzinger. Likewise, the interpretations of Vatican II have been varied.[158] The progressives have stressed the contrast between the preconciliar and postconciliar church and have seen the resistance to change in Rome as responsible for curtailing their creativity and influence. On the other hand, traditionalists see the Council, especially in its statements on religious freedom and on the Church and the world, as surrendering to Modernism, liberalism, and secularism.

In interpreting the significance of Vatican II, it is helpful to be retrospective as well as prospective. Joseph Komonchak has pointed out that one should understand Vatican II against the larger context of modern Catholicism.[159] The development of modern Catholicism that took place in the wake of the French Enlightenment and Revolution understood itself in opposition to and as the antidote for modern liberalism. Unless this background is taken into account, the radical changes and innovations of Vatican II are not understood.

The prospective interpretation is offered by Karl Rahner when he suggests that "the Second Vatican Council is the beginning of a tentative approach by the Church to the discovery and official realization of itself as *world-Church*."[160] The suggestion that the Council represents a shift from a Eurocentric to a world church should not be understood as triumphalist, but rather as a task and challenge. The church has in its history developed from its origins within Israel in Palestine to encompass the modern West. To the extent that the challenge of Vatican II is a challenge to be open to the world, it is a challenge to be open to a world that is becoming less a world identified with European culture and civilization and more a world that is multicultural, multireligious, and multinational.

NOTES

1. For a biographical introduction to his theology and life, see Jean Pierre Jossua, ed., *Yves Congar: Theology in the Service of God's People* (Chicago, 1968); A. Nichols, *Yves Congar* (London, 1989). Yves Congar, *Fifty Years of Catholic Theology*, ed. B. Lauret (London, 1988) contains Congar's reflections on his life and work.

2. Marie-Dominique Chenu, *Une École de théologie. Le Saulchoir* (Tournai, 1937; Paris, 1985).

3. Yves Congar, "Sainteté et péché dans l' église," *La vie intellectuelle*, 15 (1947), 6–40.

4. Yves Congar, "Pourquoi le peuple de Dieu doit-il sans cesse se réformer?" *Irenikon*, 22 (1948), 365–394.

5. Yves Congar, *Vraie et fausse réforme dans l' Église* (Paris, 1950).

6. Ibid., p. 305 (my own translation).

7. Ibid., p. 59 (my own translation).

8. Ibid., pp. 251–252 (my own translation).

9. Yves Congar, "Renewal of the Spirit and Reform," in *Ongoing Reform of the Church*, ed. Alois Muller and Norbert Greinacher (New York, 1972), p. 40.

10. Yves Congar, *Jalones pour une théologie du laïcat* (Paris, 1953), published in English as *Lay People in the Church* (Westminster, 1957).

11. Yves Congar, *Lay People in the Church*, trans. Donald Attwater (London, 1959), p. xxxii.

12. Ibid., p. 324.

13. For a further discussion of the distinctiveness of this notion, see Avery Dulles, *Models of the Church*, expanded ed. (Garden City, N.Y., 1987). See also literature in note 26.

14. Yves Congar, *Tradition and Traditions: An Historical Essay and a Theological Essay* (New York, 1960).

15. Yves Congar, *L' Église. De saint Augustin à l' époque moderne* (Paris, 1970); *Sainte Église; Études et approches ecclésiologiques* (Paris, 1963).

16. Yves Congar, *I Believe in the Holy Spirit* (New York, 1983).

17. General works on his life and work are Peter Hebblethwaite, *Pope John XXIII: Shepherd of the Modern World* (Garden City, N.Y., 1985); and Giancarlo Zizola, *The Utopia of Pope John XXIII* (Maryknoll, N.Y., 1978).

18. See Peter Hebblethwaite, *Pope John XXIII: Shepherd of the Modern World* (Garden City, N.Y., 1985); and Giancarlo Ziozola, *The Utopia of Pope John XXIII* (Maryknoll, N.Y., 1978).

19. See the discussion following the publication of *Mater et Magistra*, Joseph Moody and Justus George Lawler, eds. *The Challenge of Mater et Magistra* (New York, 1963).

20. For the social and cultural context of Modern Catholic social thought, see Paul Misner, *Social Catholicism in Europe: From the Onset of Industrialization to the First World War* (New York, 1991).

21. *Pacem in Terris*, section 127.

22. Pope John XXIII "Message to Humanity," *The Documents of Vatican II*, ed. Walter M. Abbott and Joseph Gallagher (Chicago, 1966), p. 5.

23. "Pope John's Opening Speech to the Council," in *The Documents of Vatican II*, ibid., pp. 710–719.

24. See Herman J. Pottmeyer, *Unfehlbarkeit und Souveranität: Die päpstliche Unfehlbarkeit im System der ultramontanen Ekklesiologie des 19. Jahrhunderts* (Mainz, 1975).

25. Gérard Philips, *L' Église et son mystère au IIe concile du Vatican*, 2 vol. (Paris, 1966).

26. For a traditional understanding of *communio*, see *Ludwig Hertling, Communio: Church and Papacy in Early Christianity* (Chicago, 1992). For the influence of the ecclesiology of Congar and de Lubac, see Yves Congar, *Divided Christendom. A Catholic Study of the Problem of Reunion* (London, 1939), and his *Diversity and Communion* (Mystic, Conn., 1984); Henri de Lubac, *Catholicism: A Study of Dogma in Relation to the Corporate Destiny of Mankind* (New York, 1950); Jerome Hamer, *The Church is a Communion* (New York, 1964). Postconciliar reflections are collected by James Provost, ed., *The Church as Communion* (Washington, D.C., 1978).

27. *Lumen Gentium*, section 26.

28. Ernst Käsemann, *The Wandering People of God: An Investigation of the Letter to the Hebrews* (Minneapolis, 1984).

29. *Lumen Gentium*, sections 48–51.

30. For a survey of the diverse Roman Catholic positions on the foundation of the Church, see Francis Schüssler Fiorenza, *Foundational Theology: Jesus and the Church* (New York, 1984), section II.

31. See Gregory Baum, "The Ecclesial Reality of Other Churches," *Concilium*, 41 (1965), 38.

32. Francis A. Sullivan, "The Significance of the Vatican II Declaration that the Church of Christ 'Sub-

sists in' the Roman Catholic Church," in *Vatican II Assessment and Perspectives: Twenty-five Years After (1962–1987)*, ed. René Latourelle (New York/Mahwah, N.J., 1989), pp. 272–287.

33. On that very day, Pope Paul VI explained in his allocution to the non-Catholic observers that the statements on the Church in the document on the Church should be interpreted in the light of the further explanations in the *Decree on Ecumenism*.

34. See sections 2 to 4 of the *Decree on Ecumenism*.

35. Sullivan, "The Significance," p. 279.

36. *Sacrosanctum Concilium*, section 36.

37. Pedro Romano Rocha, "The Principal Manifestation of the Church," in *Vatican II: Assessment and Perspectives*, op. cit., Vol. 2, pp. 3–21.

38. *Sacrosanctum Concilium*, section 41.

39. Ibid., section 14.

40. Herman J. Pottmeyer, "Kontinuität und Innovation in der Ekklesiologie des II. Vatikanums. Der Einfluss des I. Vatikanums auf die Ekklesiologie des II. Vatikanums und Neurezeption des I. Vatikanums im Lichte des II. Vatikanums," in *Kirche Im Wandel. Eine kritische Zwischenbilanz nach dem Zweiten Vatikanum*, ed. Giuseppe Alberigo, Yves Congar, and Hermann J. Pottmeyer (Düsseldorf, 1982). See p. 106 for the subjectivity of the Pope and p. 107 for the subjectivity of the Church.

41. For literature, see *The Jurist*, 48 (1988). See also H. Müller and Herman Joseph Pottmeyer, *Die Bischofskonferenz: Theologisher und juridischer Status* (Düsseldorf, 1989).

42. *Lumen Gentium*, section 23.

43. For a survey and history of the social teaching, see J.-Y. Calvez and J. Perrin, *The Church and Social Justice: The Social Teachings of the Pope from Leo XIII to Pius XII* (Chicago, 1961).

44. See Francis Schüssler Fiorenza, "The Church's Religious Identity and Its Social and Political Mission." *Theological Studies*, 43 (1982), 197–225; and Francis Schüssler Fiorenza, "Church: Social Mission of," in *The New Dictionary of Catholic Social Thought*, ed. Judith Dwyer (Collegeville, Minn., 1994), pp. 150–171.

45. Pastoral Constitution, section 5.

46. Ibid., section 76.

47. *Decree on the Apostolate of the Laity*, sections, 5–7.

48. *Decree on the Church's Missionary Activity*, section 12.

49. *Dogmatic Constitution on Divine Revelation*, section 11.

50. Ibid., section 19.

51. Ibid., section 7.

52. Ibid., section 9.

53. Ibid.

54. Ibid., section 10.

55. Ibid.

56. Declaration on Religious Freedom, section 6.

57. *Decree on Ecumenism*, section 3.

58. Ibid., section 11.

59. See Miika Ruokanen, *The Catholic Doctrine of Non-Christian Religions according to the Second Vatican Council* (Leiden, New York, 1992).

60. *Declaration on the Relationship of the Church to Non-Christian Religions*, section 2.

61. Hans Kung, *Justification: The Doctrine of Karl Barth and a Catholic Reflection* (New York, 1964). The German original was published in 1957.

62. Karl Rahner, "Questions of Controversial Theology on Justification," *Theological Investigations*, IV (New York, 1974), pp. 189–218, quotation from p. 198. Rahner notes that Küng represents positions that "are not simply taken for granted" but that this is "no reason for doubting the orthodoxy of the general presentation of Catholic doctrine," pp. 189–190.

63. Ibid., p. 192. For example, Rahner says, "This two-fold agreement on the part of Barth is astonishing."

64. Ibid., p. 36. See Hermann Häring and Karl-Josef Kuschel, *Hans Küng: His Work and His Way* (New York, 1979).

65. Hans Küng, *The Council and Reunion: Renewal as a Call to Unity* (New York, 1961).

66. See note 5.

67. Küng, *Council and Reunion*, p. 5.

68. Ibid., p. 188.

69. Ibid., p. 189.

70. Ibid., p. 192.

71. Hans Küng, *The Church* (Freiburg, 1967; New York, 1967); and *Structures of the Church* (New York, 1964).

72. Hermann Häring and Karl-Josef Kuschel, "An Interview with Hans Küng," p.151, in Herman Häring and Karl-Josef Kuschel, ed., *Hans Küng: His Work and His Way* (Garden City, N.Y., 1980).

73. See Catherine LaCugna, *The Theological Methodology of Hans Küng* (Chico, Calif., 1982).

74. Hans Küng, *On Being a Christian* (Garden City, N.Y., 1976).

75. For a clear analysis of the distinction between the "earthly," "historical," and "kerygmatic" Jesus, see Van A. Harvey, *The Historian and the Believer* (New York, 1967).

76. Hans Küng, et al., *Christianity and World Religions: Paths to Dialogue with Islam, Hindusim, and Buddhism* (Garden City, N.Y., 1986).

77. Hans Küng, *Infallible: An Inquiry* (Benziger, 1970; reprint, New York, 1972). See also John J. Kirvan, ed., *The Infallibility Debate* (New York, 1971).

78. John T. Ford, "Infallibility: A Review of Recent Studies," *Theological Studies*, 40 (1979), 273–305; and

"Infallibility: Who Won the Debate?" *Proceedings of the Catholic Theological Society of America* (1976), pp. 179–192.

79. Küng, *Infallible*, p. 165.

80. Ibid., p. 167.

81. "Declaration in Defense of the the Catholic Doctrine on the Church Against Certain Errors of the Present Day," *Origins*, 4 (1973).

82. Hans Küng, *The Incarnation of God. An Introduction to Hegel's Theological Thought as a Prolegomena to a Future Christology* (New York, 1987).

83. Hans Küng, *Does God Exist?* (New York, 1980).

84. Ibid., p. 572.

85. Hans Küng, *Judaism* (New York, 1992).

86. Küng, et al., *Christianity and World Religions*.

87. Hans Küng, *Christianity: Essence, History, and Future* (New York, 1995).

88. Hans Küng, *Global Responsibility: In Search of a New World Ethic* (New York, 1991).

89. Medard Kehl, *Kirche als Institution* (Frankfurt am Main, 1976).

90. For biographical details, see Donald E. Pelotte, *John Courtney Murray: Theologian in Conflict* (New York, 1975).

91. See John Courtney Murray, *We Hold These Truths* (New York, 1960). For a collection of his essays on systematic theological topics, see John Courtney Murray and J. Leon Hooper, *Bridging the Sacred and the Secular: Selected Writings of John Courtney Murray, Moral Traditions and Moral Arguments* (Washington, D.C., 1994).

92. On the North American role at Vatican II, see Vincent Yzermans, *American Participation in the Second Vatican Council* (New York, 1967).

93. John Courtney Murray, *The Problem of Religious Freedom* (Westminster, Md., 1965); reprinted in John Courtney Murray, *Religious Liberty: Catholic Struggles with Pluralism*, ed. J. Leon Hooper (Louisville, Ky., 1993).

94. For a discussion of the diverse drafts of the document on religious freedom and Murray's involvement, see Richard Regan, *Conflict and Consensus: Religious Freedom and the Second Vatican Council* (New York, 1967).

95. John Courtney Murray, "Separation of Church and State," *America*, 76 (December 7, 1946), 261–263.

96. Murray, *Religious Liberty*. Cf Keith J. Pavlischek, *John Courtney Murray and the Dilemma of Religious Toleration* (Kirksville, Mo., Lanham, Md., 1994).

97. Murray, *Problem of Religious Freedom* (Hooper edition), p. 136.

98. Murray has a series of articles on Leo XIII's view of church and state; see *Theological Studies*, 14 (1953), 1–30, 145–214, 551–567, and 15 (1954), 1–33. Due to ecclesiastical censorship, a final installment, "Leo XIII and Pius XII: Government and the Order of Religion," went as far as galley proofs but could not be published.

99. Murray, *Religious Liberty*, op. cit., p. 139.

100. Ibid., p. 140.

101. Ibid., p. 146.

102. See Robert McElroy, *The Search for an American Public Theology: The Contribution of John Courtney Murray* (New York, 1989). Much more critical is George S. Weigel, "John Courtney Murray and the Catholic Human Rights Revolution," *This World*, 15 (Fall 1986), 14–27.

103. For example, A. F. Carillo de Albornoz, "Religious Freedom: Intrinsic or Fortuitous? A Critique of a Treatise by John Courtney Murray," *The Christian Century*, 82 (September 15, 1965), 1122–1126. For some context, see Patrick Allitt, "The Significance of John Courtney Murray," in *Church Polity and American Politics: Issues in Contemporary American Catholicism*, ed. Mary C. Segers (New York, 1990), pp. 61–65.

104. See Edward A. Goerner, *Peter and Caesar: The Catholic Church and Political Authority* (New York, 1965), pp. 191–196. Compare John A. Rohr, "John Courtney Murray's Theology of Our Founding Fathers' Faith: Freedom," in *Christian Spirituality in the United States: Independence and Interdependence*, ed. Francis A. Eigo (Villanova, Pa., 1978), pp. 1–30.

105. Charles Curran, *American Catholic Social Ethics: Twentieth-Century Approaches* (Notre Dame, 1982), pp. 223–225.

106. Ibid., pp. 225–232.

107. See Hans Urs von Balthsar's review of Küng's book on the Church, "The Task Imposed by Our Heritage," *Hans Küng: His Work and His Way*, ed. Hermann Häring and Karl-Josef Kuschel (Garden City, N.Y., 1980), pp. 65–74.

108. For a brief biographical sketch, see Peter Henrici, "Hans Urs von Balthasar: A Sketch of His Life," *Communio*, 16 (1989), 306–350. See von Balthasar's own autobiographical remarks in "A Résumé of My Thought," in David L. Schindler, *Hans Urs von Balthasar: His Life and Work*, Communio Books (San Francisco, 1991). For a bibliography, see Cornelia Capol, *Hans Urs von Balthasar: Bibliographie, 1925–1990* (Freiburg, 1990).

109. His doctoral studies were in literature. He did, however, receive an honorary doctorate from the University of Münster.

110. Karl Rahner has complained that his writing "lacks an academic type of precision" (my translation). See Rahner's view in *Civitas*, 20 (1965), 604.

111. My own translation. The volumes have never been translated into English. Hans Urs von Balthasar, *Apokalypse der deutschen Seele*, 3 vol. (Salzburg, 1937–1939).

112. von Balthasar, *Apokalypse*, Vol. 3, p. 434–435.

113. For his criticisms of this direction, see Hans Urs von Balthasar, *Love Alone: The Way of Revelation* (London, 1968).

114. Hans Urs von Balthasar, *Kosmische Liturgie: Höhe und Krise des griechischen Weltbilds Maximus Confessor* (Freiburg, 1941); *Parole et mystére chez Origène* (Paris, 1957; originally published as a series of articles in 1936–1937), *Présence et Pensée. Essai sur la philosophie religiuese de Grégorie de Nysse* (Paris, 1942). For the importance of his analysis of Maximus the Confessor, see Hans Otmar Meuffels, *Einbergung des Menschen in das Mysterium der dreieinigen Liebe. Eine trinitarische Anthropologie nach Hans Urs von Balthasar* (Würzburg, 1991).

115. Hans Urs von Balthasar, *The Theology of Karl Barth* (Garden City, N.Y., 1972), p. 28.

116. See the third volume of his collected essays; Erich Przywara, *Analogia Entis. Schriften* Vol 3 (Einsiedeln, Switzerland, 1962). See James Zeitz, "Przywara and von Balthasar on Analogy," *The Thomist*, 52 (1988), 473–498.

117. Hans Urs von Balthasar "Analogie und Dialektik," *Divus Thomas*, 22 (1944), 196.

118. von Balthasar, *Theology of Karl Barth*, pp. 191–260.

119. See Berhard Gertz, *Glaubenswelt als Analogie. Die theologische Analogielehre Erich Przywaras und Ihr Ort in der Auseinandersetzung um die Analogia fidei* (Düsseldorf, 1969).

120. Balthasar, *Theology of Karl Barth*, p. 230.

121. For the importance of his aesthetics to his theology, see Louis Dupré, "Hans Urs von Balthasar's Theology of Aesthetic Form," *Theological Studies*, 49 (1988), and Jeffrey Ames Kay, *Theological Aesthetics: The Role of Aesthetics in the Theological Method of Hans Urs von Balthasar* (Bern/Frankfurt, 1975).

122. Hans Urs von Balthasar, *The Glory of the Lord: a Theological Aesthetics*, Vol. 1: *Seeing the Form* (San Francisco, 1982), p. 152.

123. Ibid., pp. 1, 56.

124. Ibid., pp. 1, 151.

125. Hans Urs von Balthasar, *Theologik*, I, (Einsiedeln, Switzerland, 1985), p. xx.

126. *Theo-drama: Theological Dramatic Theory* II (San Francisco, 1988), p 54.

127. Hans Urs von Balthasar, *Theo-drama: Theological Dramatic Theory*, Vol. 4: *The Action* (San Francisco, 1994).

128. Von Balthasar, *Theologik*.

129. Hans Urs von Balthasar, "Epilog," *Theologik*, III (Einsiedeln, 1987), p. 37. English translation by Thomas Norris, in Bede McGregor and Thomas Norris, ed., *The Beauty of Christ. An Introduction to the Theology of Hans Urs von Balthasar* (Edinburgh, 1994), p. 226.

130. Noel Dermot O'Donoghue, "Do We Get Beyond Plato? A Critical Appreciation of the Theo-logical Aesthetics," in *The Beauty of Christ,* ibid., pp. 253–266.

131. Hilary Mooney, *The Liberation of Consciousness. Bernard Lonergan's Theological Foundations in Dialogue with the Theological Aesthetics of Hans Urs von Balthasar* (Frankfurt, 1992).

132. Peter Eicher, *Offenbarung. Prinzip neuzeitlicher Theologie* (Munich, 1977), pp. 340–341. For a general criticism of how such approaches neglect the historical, see Francis Schüssler Fiorenza, "Critical Social Theory and Christology," Catholic Theological Society of Amrica, 30 (1975), 63–110.

133. Joseph Ratzinger, *The Theology of History in St. Bonaventure* (Chicago, 1989).

134. Joseph Ratzinger, *Volk und Haus Gottes in Augustins Lehre von der Kirche* (Munich, 1954).

135. Joseph Ratzinger, *Principles of Catholic Theology: Building Stones for a Fundamental Theology* (San Francisco, 1987), p. 378. The fifth Lateran Council (1512–1517) is given as the example of an ineffective council.

136. Joseph Ratzinger, *Das neue Volk Gottes: Entwürfe zur Ekklesiologie* (Düsseldorf, 1969). See his more recent studies on the Church: *Called to Communion: Understanding the Church Today*, trans. Adrian Walker (San Francisco, 1991); and *A New Song for the Lord: Faith in Christ and Liturgy Today*, trans. Martha M. Matesich (New York, 1996).

137. Joseph Ratzinger, *Church, Ecumenism, and Politics* (New York, 1988), p. 21.

138. Ibid., p. 19.

139. Ibid.

140. Ratzinger, *Principles*, p. 376.

141. Ibid., p. 380.

142. See Harvey Gallagher Cox, *The Silencing of Leonardo Boff: The Vatican and the Future of World Christianity* (Oak Park, Ill., 1988).

143. Ratzinger, *Principles*. The epilogue, "On the Status of Church and Theology Today," pp. 367–393, contains a review of the reception of the Council in the ensuing decade.

144. Joseph Ratzinger, *Introduction to Christianity* (New York, 1978), p. 171.

145. Ibid.

146. Ibid., p. 172.

147. In addition, Ratzinger has developed a distinctive position on eschatology and creation. See Joseph Ratzinger, *Eschatology: Death and Eternal Life* (Washington, D.C., 1988); and *In the Beginning . . . : A Catholic Understanding of the Story of Creation and the Fall (Resourcement)*, trans. Boniface Ramsey (Grand Rapids, Mich., 1995).

148. Joseph Ratzinger, *Wahrheit, Werte, Macht. Prufsteine der pluralistischen Gesellschaft* (Freiburg, 1993), p. 65 (my own translation).

149. Ibid., p. 68 (my own translation).

150. Ratzinger refers to John Hick, *An Interpretation of Religion: Human Responses to the Transcendent* (New Haven, 1989); and Paul Knitter, *No Other Name: A Critical Survey of Christian Attitudes Toward the World Religions* (Maryknoll, N.Y., 1985). For a study of Ratzinger's views on pluralism, see Arthur Fridolin Utz, *Glaube und demokratischer Pluralismus im wissenschaftlichen Werk von Joseph Kardinal Ratzinger* (Bonn, 1989).

151. Joseph Cardinal Ratzinger, *The Nature and Mission of Theology: Essays to Orient Theology in Today's Debates*, trans. Adrian Walker (San Francisco, 1993), p. 92.

152. Joseph Cardinal Ratzinger, *Turning Point for Europe? The Church in the Modern World—Assessment and Forecast*, trans. Brian McNeil (San Francisco, 1994). See also the set of interviews, Joseph Ratzinger and Peter Seewald, *Salt of the Earth: Christianity and the Catholic Church at the End of the Millennium: An Interview with Peter Seewald*, trans. Adrian Walker (San Francisco, 1997).

153. Ratzinger, *Nature and Mission of Theology*, p. 81.

154. Ibid.

155. *Code of Canon Law*, Latin-English ed. (Washington, D.C., 1983). For an interpretation of the Code in relation to Vatican II, see Joseph A. Komonchak, "Vatican II and the New Code," *Archives de sciences sociales des religions*, 31, no. 62 (1986), 107–117.

156. The papal encyclicals *Populorum Progressio* (1967) and *Octogesima Adveniens* (1971) progressively developed the social teachings of the church. For a study of the life and work of Paul VI, see Peter Hebblethwaite, *Paul VI: The First Modern Pope* (New York, 1993).

157. Joseph A. Komonchak, "Humanae Vitae and Its Reception: Ecclesiological Reflections," *Theological Studies*, 39 (1978), 221–257.

158. See Joseph A. Komonchak, "Interpreting Vatican II," *Landas*, 1 (1987), 81–90, for an insightful analysis of three diverse interpretations of Vatican II: progressive, traditionalist, and mediating.

159. Joseph A. Komonchak, "Vatican II and the Encounter Between Catholicism and Liberalism," in *Catholicism and Liberalism: Contributions to American Public Philosophy* (New York, 1993).

160. Karl Rahner, *Concern for the Church: Theological Investigations*, XX (New York, 1981), pp. 77–103. Quotation from p. 78.

SUGGESTIONS FOR FURTHER READING

Yves Congar

Famerée, Joseph. *L'ecclésiologie d'Yves Congar avant Vatican II* (Louvain: University Press, 1992). An important study of Congar's ecclesiology. In chronological order, it analyzes Congar's major writings on the church prior to the Second Vatican Council.

Jossua, Jean Pierre, ed. *Yves Congar: Theology in the Service of God's People* (Chicago: Priory, 1968).

MacDonald, Timothy I. *The Ecclesiology of Yves Congar* (Lanham, Md.: University Press of America, 1984). This study touches upon Congar's ideas concerning reform, the laity, *communio*, and church and world.

Nichols, Aidan. *Yves Congar* (London: Chapman, 1989). A popular introduction that summarizes Congar's views in relation to traditional systematic theological treatises, such as fundamental theology, ecclesiology, and ecumenism.

Vatican II

Abbott, Walter M., and Joseph Gallagher, ed. *The Documents of Vatican II* (Chicago: Follet Publishing House, 1966). A collection of the constitutions and documents of Vatican II with brief introductions and responses. Some explanatory annotation.

Alberigo, Giuseppe. *History of Vatican II: Vol. 1. Announcing and Preparing Vatican Council II Toward a New Era in Catholicism*, English ed. Joseph A. Komonchak (Maryknoll, N.Y.: Orbis, 1995). The first of a three-volume history of the Council. Volume 1 contains a great deal of detail on the practical and organizational preparations for the Council.

Gremillion, Joseph. *The Gospel of Peace and Justice: Catholic Social Teaching Since Pope John* (Maryknoll, N.Y.: Orbis, 1976). A collection of official documents on the social teaching.

———, ed. *The Church and Culture since Vatican II. The Experience of North and Latin America* (Notre Dame: University of Notre Dame Press, 1985).

Horgan, Thaddeus D. *Walking Together: Roman Catholics and Ecumenism Twenty-five Years after Vatican II* (Grand Rapids, Mich.: William B. Eerdmans, 1990).

Küng, Hans, Yves Congar, and Daniel O'Hanlon, ed. *Council Speeches of Vatican II* (London: Sheed & Ward, 1964). A collection of important speeches at the Council that provide key insights to understanding the arguments and debates of the Council.

Latourelle, René. *Vatican II: Assessment and Perspectives: Twenty-five Years After (1962–1987)*, 3 vol. (New York: Paulist Press, 1988–1989). A collection of interpretive essays by an international list of scholars dealing especially with the theological aspects of the Council.

Regan, Richard J., S.J. *Conflict and Consensus: Religious Freedom and the Second Vatican Council* (New York: Macmillan, 1967). Presents an account of the various drafts and editions of the document on religious freedom.

Rome and the Study of Scripture, 7th ed. (St. Meinrad, Ind.: Grail, 1962).

Vorgrimler, Hubert, ed. *Commentary on the Documents of Vatican II*, 5 vol. (New York: Herder and Herder, 1967–1969). This five-volume commentary on the individual documents of the Council has been the standard commentary. Several of the commentators were theologians active at the Council.

Hans Küng

Häring, Hermann, and Karl-Josef Kuschel, ed. *Hans Küng: His Work and His Way* (Garden City, N.Y.: Doubleday, 1980). This book contains a biography and essays on his theology and the debates surrounding it. The bibliography is extensive but only up to 1980.

Hasler, August Bernhard. *How the Pope Became Infallible,* introduction by Hans Küng, (New York: Doubleday 1981). A popularly written condensation of the scholarly—but highly contested—dissertation on the background to Vatican I's definition of papal infallibility.

LaCugna, Catherine. *The Theological Methodology of Hans Küng* (Chico, Calif.: Scholars Press, 1982). LaCugna faults Küng's theological method for its overemphasis on the value of historical criticism and its underemphasis on the significance of the Church's tradition.

Novell, Robert. *A Passion for Truth: Hans Küng and His Theology* (Garden City, N.Y.: Doubleday, 1981). An early and sympathetic study of Küng's theology.

John Courtney Murray

Curran, Charles. "John Courtney Murray." In Charles Curran, *American Catholic Social Ethics: Twentieth Century Approaches,* pp. 172–232 (Notre Dame: University of Notre Dame Press, 1982). One of the best and most concise presentations of Murray's background, basic principles, distinctive contribution, and controversies by a leading North American Roman Catholic ethicist.

Gonnet, Dominique. *La liberté religieuse a Vatican II: La contribution de John Courtney Murray, S.J., Cogitatio fidei; 183* (Paris: Editions du Cerf, 1994).

Hooper, J. Leon. *The Ethics of Discourse. The Social Philosophy of John Courtney Murray* (Washington, D.C.: Georgetown University Press, 1986). A comprehensive analysis of Murray's social ethics with a focus on the philosophical arguments underlying religious freedom.

Love, Thomas T. *John Courtney Murray: Contemporary Church-State Theory* (Garden City, N.Y.: Doubleday, 1975). Underlying Murray's views on religious freedom is a specific view of the nature of state and society in their relation to church. Love analyzes Murray's view of church and state.

Murray, John Courtney. *Religious Liberty. Catholic Struggles with Pluralism,* ed. J. Leon Hopper, S.J. (Louisville, Ky.: Westminster/John Knox Press, 1993). Hopper provides an extensive general introduction to his collection along with introductions to the individual essays and important comments in the footnotes. Valuable not only as a collection of Murray's essays, but as an analysis of his work.

Pavlischek, Keith J. *John Courtney Murray and the Dilemma of Religious Toleration* (Kirksville, Mo.: Thomas Jefferson University Press; Lanham, Md., 1994).

Pelotte, Donald E. *John Courtney Murray: Theologian in Conflict* (New York: Paulist Press, 1975). A good account of the controversies between Murray and more traditional Roman Catholic viewpoints and the Vatican.

Hans Urs von Balthasar

Capol, Cornelia. *Hans Urs von Balthasar: Bibliographie, 1925–1990* Freibourg, Switzerland: Johannes Verlag, 1990). A complete bibliography.

Kehl, Medard, Werner Löser, and Robert J. Daly. *The von Balthasar Reader* (New York: Crossroad, 1982). This collection of selections of von Balthasar's covers a range of theological topics with a helpful and informative introductory commentary.

McGregor, Bede, and Thomas Norris, ed. *The Beauty of Christ. An Introduction to the Theology of Hans Urs von Balthasar* (Edinburgh: T. & T. Clark, 1994). A collection of essays that provides both sympathetic and critical analyses of diverse aspects of his method and theology.

McIntosh, Mark A. *Christology from Within. Spirituality and the Incarnation in Hans Urs von Balthasar* (Notre Dame: University of Notre Dame, 1996). Originally a dissertation at the University of Chicago, it shows the link between von Balthasar's views on spirituality/mysticism and on Christology.

Oakes, Edward T. *Pattern of Redemption: The Theology of Hans Urs von Balthasar* (New York: Continuum, 1994). This study is a narrative and descriptive chronological account of von Balthasar's life and work rather than an analytical examination of his theology.

O'Donnell, John. *Hans Urs von Balthasar* (London: Geoffrey Chapman, 1991). A survey and analysis of Balthasar's contributions to theology that is much more analytical and theological than the volumes by Oakes and Scola.

O' Hanlon, Gerald. *The Immutability of God in the Theology of Hans Urs von Balthasar* (Cambridge: Cambridge University Press, 1990). A study of von Balthasar's understanding of God.

Riches, John, ed. *The Analogy of Beauty: The Theology of Hans Urs von Balthasar* (Edinburgh: T. & T. Clark, 1986). An important collection of essays, including von Balthasar's retrospective on the years from 1965 to 1975.

Schindler, David, ed. *Hans Urs von Balthasar: His Life and Work* (San Francisco: Ignatius Press, 1991). A collection of essays studying his life and thought.

Scola, Angelo. *Test Everything: Hold Fast to What Is Good: An Interview with Hans Urs von Balthasar* (San Francisco: Ignatius Press, 1989). Interviews that touch not only theological issues, but also issues facing the church today.

———. *Hans Urs von Balthasar: A Theological Style* (Grand Rapids, Mich.: William B. Eerdmans, 1991). Another popular though competent brief exposition of the main ideas and his later work.

Joseph Cardinal Ratzinger

Cox, Harvey Gallagher. *The Silencing of Leonardo Boff: The Vatican and the Future of World Christianity* (Oak Park, Ill.: Meyer-Stone Books, 1988). A discussion of the controversy between Ratzinger and Boff.

Nachtwei, Gerhard. *Dialogische Unsterblichkeit: Eine Untersuchung zu Joseph Ratzingers Eschatologie und Theologie* (Leipzig: St. Benno-Verlag, 1986). A study of Ratzinger's theological contributions to eschatology and the discussions about his positions.

Nichols, Aidan. *The Theology of Joseph Ratzinger: An Introductory Study* (Edinburgh: T. & T. Clark, 1988). A basic introduction to Ratzinger's work and theology.

Rollet, Jacques. *Le cardinal Ratzinger et la théologie contemporaine* (Paris: Cerf, 1987). A presentation of Ratzinger's work in the context of contemporary theology.

Segundo, Juan Luis. *Theology and the Church: A Response to Cardinal Ratzinger and a Warning to the Whole Church* (San Francisco: Harper and Row, 1987). Segundo focuses on Ratzinger's treatment of liberation theology.

Chapter Nine

Political Theology and Latin American Liberation Theologies

Gustavo Gutiérrez

POLITICAL THEOLOGY

Political theology arose in the 1960s in Germany. Its leading representatives are Jürgen Moltmann, known especially for his *Theology of Hope*, and Johann Baptist Metz, responsible for reintroducing the term "political theology" into theological discussion. The orientation toward the future, the hope for shaping society, and the intense concern for the public impact of religion, which is characteristic of political theology, corresponded to the mentality of the post–World War II period. Europe had moved beyond the immediate task of reconstruction to a much more theoretical reflection on its past and future.

The theology of hope and political theology mirror many of the characteristics of the 1960s. It

was the era of the Second Vatican Council of the Roman Catholic Church (1962–1965) and the World Council of Churches Conference in Uppsala (1968). The decade was marked by the Prague Spring in Eastern Europe, the beginning of the Christian-Marxist dialogue in Germany under the auspices of the Paulus Gesellschaft, and the civil rights movement and the Kennedy era in the United States—viewed by many as the era of Camelot. For Europe it was a period in which the initial reconstruction after the war was completed and one looked forward to a new future. Political theology and the theology of hope attracted considerable attention, and they were to influence Latin American theology and other liberation theologies. Although Latin American liberation theology was strongly influenced by European political theology, it would follow its own path, offer different interpretations, and, finally, raise objections to political theology.

The Post–World War II Context

Both Johann B. Metz (1928–) and Jürgen Moltmann (1926–) belong to the post–World War II generation of German theologians.[1] When they were teenagers, they were drafted into Hitler's army. This was toward the end of the war when the German military sought to replenish its dwindling manpower by drafting younger and younger recruits. Both were captured and imprisoned. Metz was drafted in 1944 and captured six months before the end of the war. He was sent to prison camps in the United States, first in Maryland, then in Virginia. Moltmann was drafted in 1944, and he was captured by British forces in Belgium. He was imprisoned first in Scotland and then in Nottingham, England, in the Norton prisoner of war camp for three years before his repatriation in 1948. The experience of the war raised decisive questions for each of them: How did National Socialism arise in Germany? What should be the role of the churches in their relation to political society? How can the churches contribute to the prevention of such totalitarian regimes and such a devastating war in the future?

After the war, Metz and Moltmann returned to Germany to pursue their theological studies. Metz, a Roman Catholic, did his philosophical and theological studies at the University of Innsbruck. His philosophical doctorate was on Martin Heidegger and his theological doctorate, written under the direction of Karl Rahner, was on Thomas Aquinas.[2] Jürgen Moltmann, in the Reformed Calvinist tradition, studied at Basel University, where Otto Weber, Hans Iwand, and Ernst Wolfe taught at that time. In 1952 he received his doctorate and became pastor for five years in Wasserhorst near Bremen. Moltmann's doctoral dissertation (1957) dealt with Christoph Pezel, a sixteenth-century Calvinist theologian; his habilitation (a second dissertation qualifying one to become a lecturer) was concerned with the Calvinist doctrines of predestination and preservation.[3] He wrote both under the direction of Otto Weber, who is often associated with Barthian theology.

Two particular currents, one in theology and the other in philosophy, were influential in the development of a political theology that sought both to retrieve biblical eschatology and to encourage the churches to engage in social and political criticism. The theological current came from New Testament studies, especially from the contributions of the New Testament scholar Ernst Käsemann at the University of Tübingen. The philosophical current came from the Christian-Marxist dialogue, especially from the intellectual confrontation with the philosophy of Ernst Bloch.

Eschatology had been brought back as a focus of New Testament studies through the exegetical contributions of Ernst Käsemann, whose work had considerable influence on systematic theologians. A student of Rudolf Bultmann, Käsemann's writings mapped out decisive points of disagreement with Bultmann on important questions, such as the historical Jesus, the Pauline doctrine of justification, and the role of eschatology and apocalypticism within early Christianity. Käsemann argued that Bultmann's existential interpretation of eschatology did not take sufficient account of the apocalyptic significance of the early Christian proclamation of God's reign. Moreover, Käsemann argued that the meaning of the Pauline doctrine of justification has its roots in apocalypticism, thereby pointing out the inadequacy of Bultmann's existential interpretation of Paul.[4] Käsemann maintained that insofar as Bultmann interpreted the Pauline eschatological dialectic of the "now already" and "not yet" as a dialectic of human existence, he narrowed Paul's teaching. That is, he eliminated the worldly elements of apocalypticism and thereby reduced it to an act of individual decision.

Käsemann argues that, although anthropology is indeed important, it is not the center of Paul's theology. The meaning of the Pauline doctrine of justification, contrary to Bultmann, is that Christ becomes Lord of the entire cosmos. Christ becomes Cosmocrator. He is not merely a cultic deity, as the History of Religion school had maintained, nor is he merely Lord of individual believers, as Bultmann implied. In the New Testament writings, and especially in the Pauline writings, the Lordship or dominion of Christ has a worldly dimension that is political, social, and cosmic. It should not be individualized or existentialized.

Complementing this reinterpretation of New Testament eschatology were the beginnings of the dialogue between Christian theologians in West Germany and Marxist philosophers in East Germany, a dialogue that had an impact on political theology. These dialogues led to an exchange and confrontation between Marxist ideas and Christian beliefs. At this same time, Ernst Bloch (1885–1977), who had been a professor of philosophy at the University of Leipzig, emigrated from East Germany when the authorities arrested several of his students. He then became a professor of philosophy at the University of Tübingen. His writings, especially those in which he develops a philosophy of hope, became well-known and influential in West Germany.[5] Ernst Bloch represents a revision of Marxism insofar as he maintains that traditional orthodox Marxism, with its dull and uninspiring materialism, did not sufficiently take into account aspects of the cultural heritage that could serve the Marxist cause.[6] For this reason, he sought a retrieval and a reinterpretation of utopian ideals, religious beliefs, and natural law. Bloch's interpretation of religion in terms of hope and his recovery of the importance of utopian ideals became a focal point of the dialogue between Christian theologians and Marxism. As the title of his major work, *The Principle of Hope*, is echoed in Moltmann's *Theology of Hope*,[7] so, too, is Bloch's critique of the existential interpretation of eschatology echoed in political theology. Referring to Bultmann, Bloch wrote that his existential approach took eschatology "out of the danger area of cosmic history, and away from the figure of Christ, whose position within that area is so explosive, and put it back in the realms of the lonely soul and its solid middle-class God."[8]

Although Moltmann and Metz each were to develop distinctive theological approaches to political theology, there are several striking similarities in their approaches. These common features include (1) their interpretation of the present situation, that is, the cultural and social position of religion in contemporary society; (2) their critique of earlier twentieth-century theologies; and (3) their retrieval of eschatology and its application to social and political life. Despite these common interests, each one goes his own distinctive way. For Metz this involves his conception of fundamental theology and his attention to the role of memory in a philosophy of history. For Moltmann this results in the development of a Trinitarian theology as the key to understanding the messianism of Jesus. However, these similarities do more than mark out their common starting points. They also provide a backdrop against which Latin American theologies of liberation will develop both in dependency upon political theology and in reaction to it.

Interpretation of the Situation: The Privatization of Religion

The war experience was decisive for both Metz and Moltmann as they developed their political theologies. However, their interpretation of the situation in the postwar period appealed directly to analyses of contemporary society that focused on its domination by technocratic rationality, by the market economy of capitalism, and by the secularization of religion. "Since the rise of 'bourgeois society,' and the 'system of needs' in industrial society . . . modern society has been emancipated from the classical concept of religion."[9]

It is the interpretation of modern society as a market economy, that is, as capitalistic, that provides the framework for the interpretation of technocratic rationality and secularization.

Max Weber's notion of the technocratic rationality that robs religion of its relation to nature and the wider world is taken over by Moltmann. He writes

the primary conception of religion in modern society assigns to religion the saving and preserving of personal, individual and private humanity. . . . Now as a result of the fact that all things and conditions can be manufactured by dint of technique and organization, the divine in the sense of the transcendent has disappeared from the world of nature.[10]

In addition, the dominance of the market in capitalism leads to further privatization of religion, because the market economy reduces religion to an item of the market itself. Religion has become an object of individual choice. As an individual consumer chooses which items he or she prefers for his or her private consumption so, too, does an individual choose religion as a matter of private consumption or individual preference. The secularization thesis, as so articulated, does not deny the existence of religious belief in the modern world, as if secularization implied the transition from belief to nonbelief. Rather, secularization reveals that the public social and political dimension of religion has lost its vigor and influence. And this is the loss of a dimension integral to religion itself. As Metz writes,

it seems to be precisely the excessive privateness and intimacy of our talk about God, our persistent contrasting of spiritual and social existence, which widens the gap we see existing everywhere between what is stated by theology and the kerygma to be important and what the Christian actually lives from and what concretely appeals to him.[11]

Moltmann likewise interprets the privatization of religion in terms of religion's loss of its ability to provide the integral substance of a society, its culture and institutions. "This certainly means that the Christian religion is dismissed as the integrating center of modern society and relieved of its duty of having to represent the highest goal of society."[12]

Both Moltmann and Metz refer to the slogan "God is dead." Moltmann traces its use in modernity to the early Romantic poet Jean Paul in his "Address by the Dead Christ from the Heights of the Cosmic System to the Effect that There Is No God" and to the young Hegel, Feuerbach, and Nietzsche.[13] Moltmann's interpretation of the

dictum "God is dead" follows the lead of the young Hegel in his diagnosis of the crisis of the post-Enlightenment era. Hegel refers to the dualism that exists between the emphasis on religious subjectivity in Romanticism and the methodic elimination of God from the scientific rationality of the Enlightenment. Metz, on the other hand, interprets the phrase "God is dead" more in terms of Max Weber's notion of the desacralization of nature due to modern technological rationality.

In interpreting their situation in relation to the dominance of the market economy in modern capitalism and its impact upon the culture of secularized society, neo-Marxist philosophers, especially Georg Lukacs, employed the concepts of "reification" or "objectification." Metz and Moltmann, however, apply these concepts to what happens to religion when, in modern society, religion becomes privatized. Moltmann views this privatization of religion as both a symptom and a result of a market society. Similar to other consummable objects, religion has been "reified"; that is, religion has been reduced to an object of personal consumer choice. An additional cause of this privatization, as Metz has emphasized, is technological rationality with its objectification of nature.

A shift takes place, however, in the interpretation of the contemporary situation in the course of the development of political theology. As a result of the emergence of Latin American liberation theologies, Third World theologies, postmodern criticisms of modernity, and postcolonial analyses of the West, both Metz and Moltmann show an increasing awareness of these directions and currents. They seek to incorporate these critiques of modernity and the situation in the modern West into their own theologies, each in his distinctive manner.

The Critique of a Dominant Existential Theology

Moltmann's critique of earlier twentieth-century theology is above all directed against the Existential theology of Rudolf Bultmann. He labels it a "transcendental subjectivity of man."

To a lesser extent, this charge is directed also against Karl Barth, whose theology Moltmann characterizes as the "transcendental subjectivity of God." Barth's subjectivization is shown in his interpretation of revelation as primarily inter-Trinitarian. Moltmann writes: "yet even here the immanent form of the divine Trinity appears to give the revelation of God the character of transcendental exclusiveness as a "self-contained *novum*."[14] In addition to his critique of these theologians, Moltmann criticizes the dangerous influence of the Lutheran doctrine of the two kingdoms of church and state as it bears on religious and political thought in Germany. In Moltmann's view, this Lutheran distinction of the two kingdoms does not sufficiently resist the privatization of religion; in fact, it reinforces it. As the Hitler period in Germany showed, the Lutheran doctrine did not provide a sufficient basis for resisting National Socialism.

Metz's critique is directed against the transcendental theology of his teacher, Karl Rahner. He faults Rahner's transcendental theology for its failure to deal with significant political issues, for example, its failure to deal with the Holocaust. Although Rahner has written on innumerable topics in his more than twenty volumes of collected essays, there is no reference to the historical, political, and religious significance of the Holocaust. Metz concedes his indebtedness to Rahner, but notes: "I owe everything that I can do theologically myself. I mean the theology taught by Karl Rahner. To be sure, gradually, much too gradually, it dawned on me that even in this theology, Auschwitz was not mentioned."[15]

Metz thus concludes that theology must deal with the Holocaust and with the challenge that National Socialism's dominance in Germany's past raises for the Christian churches and their theologies. It will mean doing theology differently than did the previous generation of theologians. It must deal with these past failures and retrieve the Jewish, biblical, and historical-messianic sources of theology. A transcendental theology that stresses historicity and yet overlooks such historical failures is a theology without history, one written with a view from nowhere.

The Emphasis on Eschatology

Both Moltmann and Metz restore eschatology and make it central to their own theology. Moltmann interprets eschatology by his use of the category of promise, understood as a theological, historical, and performative category. He notes that promise is central not only to Israel's prophetic expectation, but also to Israel's understanding of God. Promise is more than a statement or affirmation. It involves an action, thus there is a performative character to promise.[16] Moreover, a promise announces the coming of what does not exist. Consequently, promises do not simply detect present possibilities, they open up new possibilities and expectations. God's promises create the possibilities of what is to be expected and hoped for. Therefore, Israel's faith in God's promise for the future gives Israel a sense of history and a commitment to the future of history. When history is initiated by promise, then that history has a direction and a tendency, not one constituted by an immanent law of history, but one that points in the direction of God's promise.[17]

Metz similarly argues that "it is impossible to privatize the eschatological promises of biblical tradition. Again and again they force us to assume our responsibilities towards society."[18] The failure of both existential and transcendental interpretations of eschatology is that they overlook this social aspect of Christian eschatology. Metz sees a certain irony in the fact that it is Bultmann who applied Form criticism to the Gospel materials and underscored the social and communal elements of these forms of discourse in the Gospels, but who also should reduce eschatological discourse to a call for an individual existential decision.

Metz's introduction of the term "political theology" has given rise, within a Catholic context, to the false impression that political theology is a return to "political integralism"; that is, to the attempt to impose the Roman Catholic Church's values and morality on society in general. This impression is due to the fact that historically the term "political theology" was used, both in the eighteenth century by the French Roman Catholic Restorationists and in the early twentieth century by Carlo Schmitt, in reference to conservative political programs.[19] To ward off this perception, Metz has carefully described his conception of eschatology and political theology. He introduces the category of "eschatological proviso" that seeks to underscore the critical [see the quote below] aspect of eschatology, because Christian eschatology entails the claim that every historical society is provisional. In Metz's view, the eschatological suggests that eschatology

does not bring about a negative but a critical attitude to the societal present. Its promises are not an empty horizon of religious expectations; neither are they only a regulative idea. They are, rather, a critical liberating imperative for our present times.[20]

For Metz, the central role of eschatology in political theology means that political theology cannot be understood as a restorative attempt to reintroduce within a modern society a Constantinian union or collaboration of the Church and society. Similarly, Moltmann's use of the eschatalogical category of promise points to a political theology that does not entail a progressive view of history and society, as if it were seeking to perfect some innate tendency. Rather it points to the future of God's promise within an open world.

Their common interpretations of the present situation of religion in modern society, their similar criticisms of previous theologies, and their conceptions of political theology as related to the retrieval of eschatology, can all be seen as background and context for the specific and individual contributions of both Metz and Moltmann to political theology in the latter decades of the twentieth century.

JOHANN METZ

Johann Baptist Metz's early publications indicate his indebtedness to Karl Rahner, his teacher. His first publication was his dissertation on Thomas

Aquinas, written under Rahner in Innsbruck. It shows the influence of Rahner's transcendental philosophy and his starting point in anthropology. Metz argues that Thomas Aquinas represents a "Christian Anthropocentrism."[21] By distinguishing between content and *denkform* (form or style of thought), Metz claims that the content of Aquinas's philosophy and theology is cosmocentric, but its form is anthropocentric. The emphasis that contemporary existential philosophy gives to the term "existence" finds its correspondence in Aquinas's emphasis on the soul and its openness to the world. Consequently, Aquinas anticipates and prefigures the turn to anthropocentric philosophy and theology that is exhibited in modern theology, especially in the transcendental Thomism represented by Rahner.[22] Because this anthropocentrism has its roots in Christianity itself, Metz is ultimately making the claim that the Christian view of the world, with its emphasis on history and humanity, is a causal factor in the origin of modernity. Metz's next publications are the editions of Karl Rahner's *Spirit in the World* and *Hearers of the Word*. His edition of *Hearers of the Word* involves a considerable revision of Rahner's original text by bringing to the work much of Rahner's later thought. Especially prominent is Rahner's developed interpretation of revelation as not primarily to be understood in terms of propositional statements but in terms of a transcendental experience.[23]

Before Metz proposed political theology as the agenda that would distinguish his own theology from the transcendental theology of Rahner, he sought to go beyond a purely transcendental analysis of human subjectivity by exploring topics that dealt with the embodiment, sociality, and worldly character of the human subject. He wrote theological essays on the human body in terms of its corporeality and flesh.[24] He sought to articulate a theology of freedom in relation to ideas of sociality.[25] Above all, he was concerned to develop a theology of the world that would evaluate positively the notion of secularization.[26] He transferred Rahner's christological discussion of the autonomy of the human nature of Christ to society itself, and he spoke of the autonomy and independence of the world.

Metz's positive interpretation of secularization, from the standpoint of an incarnational Christology, represented at this time a Roman Catholic parallel to the theological interpretation of secularization proposed by the Lutheran theologian, Friedrich Gogarten.[27] (See Chapter Three.) It also parallels the analysis of secularization in North America, represented by Harvey Cox's best-selling *The Secular City*.[28] By drawing on a christological dialectic for his interpretation of secularization, Metz was able to underscore the autonomy and freedom of the human person in the modern world. In this respect, the early emphasis on the human subject continues and broadens in his political theology. But Metz also praises the desacralization of nature that gave rise to modern technology and sees it as a result of the Christian belief in the goodness of creation. As Metz set out to delineate the contours of his political theology, he began to take a much more negative attitude toward secularization. It now would be viewed as the privatization of religion, a turning of religion into a commodity on the marketplace. Technological rationality would also come under sharp criticism.

The privatization of religion now figures prominently in Metz's definition of political theology as such:

I understand political theology, first of all, to be a critical correction of present-day theology inasmuch as this theology shows an extreme privatizing tendency (a tendency, that is, to center upon the private person rather than the "public," "political society"). At the same time, I understand this political theology to formulate the eschatological message under the conditions of our present society.[29]

In the development of his political theology, Metz accentuates several key themes: the notion of political theology as a fundamental theology, the critique of bourgeois religion, and the importance of remembering the suffering of victims.

Political Theology as Fundamental Theology

Metz's most distinctive contribution is his conception of political theology as fundamental theology. The discipline of Roman Catholic fundamental theology arose as a response to the Enlightenment.[30] The discipline consists of a combination of philosophy of religion, apologetics, and prolegomena to systematic theology. Initially, it was concerned with the demonstration of the possibility and historical fact of a supernatural revelation in the light of the Deists' critique of revelation. It developed other responses to the various critiques of religion in the eighteenth and nineteenth centuries.

Metz advances the thesis that only if fundamental theology is developed as a political theology can it adequately respond to the crisis provoked by the modern European Enlightenment.[31] Metz points out that modern fundamental theology often was understood as an apologetic or defense of specific Christian beliefs. Moreover, many of the disputes that engaged fundamental theology were primarily interconfessional, concerned with the doctrinal differences among the diverse Christian churches. In this sense fundamental theology was a "controversial theology" in that it dealt with the issues and controversies between Roman Catholics and Protestants. Such disputes, however, took place within a horizon that was predominantly Christian and assumed the veracity of the Christian worldview. That is, fundamental theology often defended a Christian belief within a horizon that simply assumed the totality of a Christian view of reality.

Such an approach to fundamental theology, Metz argues, does not do justice to the radically new situation of modernity. The Enlightenment challenge introduced two significant changes in the situation of Christianity and Christian theology.

On the one hand, the identity of faith and religious consciousness, which had hitherto been accepted more or less unquestioningly, ceased to exist. Christian faith found itself confronted with a universal critical concept of religion and challenged to justify itself. On the other hand, the unity of religion and society, which had similarly hitherto been accepted without question, also broke up, beginning in France during the early period of the Enlightenment.[32]

In response to this challenge, Metz proposes that political theology, as practical fundamental theology, should develop a theology of what he calls the "subject." In his view, political theology is a practical fundamental theology only to the extent that it is a theology of the human subject, but one that does *not* consider the human subject apart from social and political praxis, as transcendental theology has done. In using the term "subject" as the key concept of his political theology, Metz seeks to differentiate his position for the notion of "person" in personalist philosophy. In addition, he seeks, at the same time, to avoid misunderstandings and criticisms that political theology overlooks the human person. He seeks, rather, to locate the human person within a social and political context.

I must, therefore, elucidate this essential aspect of political theology and define it more precisely, on the one hand because it is often suspected of obscuring the subject too much in the interests of history and society and, on the other, because the theologies that are often criticized by political theology are also regarded as theologies of the subject (of a transcendental, existential, personalistic, paradoxical and dialectical kind).[33]

In short, Metz's political theology of the subject seeks to provide an alternative to the understanding of the human person in transcendental or existential theologies and to show the inadequacy of their conceptions. To this end, Metz develops the correlation between the idea of God and the idea of the human subject. In the Hebrew and Christian religious traditions, the human subject's identity is that of belonging to a people in the presence of God. "Subject" does not refer to the human self as an isolated individual or monad, but, rather, as a member of a people

standing before their God. This self-understanding as a member of a people in solidarity with other members of that community, and with a hope for liberation, constitutes the *theological* understanding of the human subject. "Experiences of solidarity with, antagonism towards, liberation from and anxiety about other subjects form an essential part of the religious subject, not afterwards, but from the very beginning."[34] That is, solidarity and liberation are not commitments or hopes that are added on secondarily to the constitution of the human subject; they belong to the subject's existence from the very beginning. Therefore, any theological attempt to interpret the human subject needs to take into account this political, social, and redemptive dimension.

For Metz, it is specifically this concern with the interrelation between the religious and the social constitution of the subject that makes political theology a practical fundamental theology. And Metz appeals to the histories of faith in the Hebrew and Christian Scriptures to underline his argument that human persons are constituted as subjects through their relationship with God that is at the same time a political and social relation. Religious experiences of calling, conversion, and exodus show that religion is not a separable or supplementary phenomenon, but rather that it is an active process by which a people comes to itself. The Exodus experience of the Hebrew people, for example, constituted them most clearly as subjects. The biblical understanding of God is "practical" in that it does not disregard but rather constitutes humans as historical and social subjects. The idea of God also entails the idea of responsibility, guilt, and solidarity with victims. It calls for a view of the human subject that leads to a "practical criticism of a culture of hatred and a culture of apathy."[35]

The Critique of Bourgeois Religion

Concurrent with Metz's argument that the constitution of human identity goes hand in hand with its social, political, and religious constitution is his argument against the prevalence of bourgeois religion in contemporary society. "Middle-class" or "bourgeois religion" are the English terms used for "*bürglich* religion" in the translation of his books. Though this is a fitting translation, it does not adequately bring to the fore the meanings that the term "*bürglich*" connotes in the German situation. A good and decent German citizen is at the same time *bürglich*. The term includes a way and style of life and not simply the economic status of a group as does the term "middle class." Metz argues that the prevalence of bourgeois religion is a deformation of biblical religion:

In the Christianity of our time, the message of the religion of the Bible has been largely changed into bourgeois religion. This observation is not intended as a denunciation of the bourgeois. . . . Nor is it primarily a critique of the fact that the church in Central Europe is made up predominantly of so-called petty bourgeois and propertied bourgeois who, especially in this country, make church life what it is. It is much more the expression of an anxiety concerning Christianity, which creates a crisis of identity for itself when it fails to realize and manifest its difference from bourgeois religion.[36]

In defining Christianity in terms of its contrast to bourgeois religion, Metz puts one in mind of the early Karl Barth's critique of religion. In fact, Metz introduces the category of "interruption" to express his interpretation of the contrast of Christianity with bourgeois religiosity.[37] Christianity, Metz asserts, should not be the justification of bourgeois culture but, rather, its critic. Christian communities stand in sharp contrast to and "interrupt" the cultural values of bourgeois society.

Moreover, as Metz further developed his critique of bourgeois society, he has also tended to shift his interpretation of modernity. The counterpart of his critique of modern bourgeois society is his appeal for a polycentric church. And on this theme Metz points to the suffering and poverty of the Third World. By entering into solidarity with this suffering and destitution, the churches of bourgeois society can strive to overcome their own petty and propertied bourgeois obsessions. He proposes a church of the people instead of the Church of the people, thereby concurring with the emphasis of Latin American liberation theologians on the role of base communities. Furthermore, he argues that Christianity should become culturally polycentric. These themes reveal a shift from his early focus on the autonomy of modernity to an emphasis on solidarity with the Third World. The consequences of such a solidarity would transform Christianity from a bourgeois church into what he calls a "basic-community church."[38]

Political theology tries to take into account the irruption of the so-called "third world" and of the non-European world in general into the world of theology. It tries to do this not only pastorally, but in a strictly theological sense, as a challenging to our discourse about God. . . . They [people of third world] call for the formulation of Christian discourse about God under the categories of resistance and transformation. Because of this, political theology began almost from the outset to speak of the church as an "institution of social-critical freedom of faith."[39]

The Memory of Suffering and the Holocaust

As he developed his political theology, Metz did more than simply criticize others for their failure to reflect theologically on the Holocaust. He also argued the need to incorporate Jewish eschatology into the Christian understandings of eschatology. This, moreover, involved relating personal identity and Christian eschatology to the memory of the suffering of and our solidarity with victims of the past.

As a counterbalance to his earlier emphasis on hope, the future, and the "eschatological proviso," Metz has turned his attention to the significance of suffering. He argues that the memory of the suffering of past victims is essential to the meaning of history. Many modern conceptions of history have not only neglected past suffering but also have overlooked that this suffering has abiding significance. He appeals to the Jewish writer Walter Benjamin's use of "dialectical images" in his theses on history and uses the term "dangerous memories" as a practical critique of the historical present.[40] In his essay, "The Future in the Memory of Suffering," Metz writes:

Hence the Christian *memoria* become a "subversive remembrance," which shocks us out of ever becoming prematurely reconciled to the "facts" and "trends" of our technological society. It becomes a liberating memory over against the controls and mechanism of the dominant consciousness and its abstract idea of emancipation. The Christian *memoria passionis* articulates itself as memory that makes one free to suffer for the suffering of others' suffering even though the negative view of suffering in our "progressive" society makes it . . . something increasingly intolerable and even repugnant.[41]

Metz not only adopts the category of suffering as central to his theology, but also gives it a concrete focus with reference to the Holocaust. The catastrophe and suffering of Auschwitz is a suffering that should be practically remembered. Christians must understand their identity in the face of the Jews. This entails overcoming the neglect of the Holocaust in contemporary Christian theology.[42] Metz's critique of Karl Rahner is directed at this forgetfulness (or omission) in the transcendental approach to theology that, Metz argues, does not sufficiently take into account the concrete nature of history.[43] For this reason, Metz introduces the category of "narrative" and appeals to "narrative theology" as the more appropriate approach by which to deal with the concrete reality of historical suffering. Metz's conception of narrative theology is, however, quite different from the narrative theology proposed by the American theologian Hans Frei (see Chapter Eleven). Whereas Frei understands narrative in terms of the internal narrative structure of a text, Metz sees narrative, and the category of story, as the best way to recover the concrete memory of victims of suffering. A narrative theology does not seek a ready-made explanation or a cheap reconciliation or a theoretical solution to the problem of suffering. Rather, it retains the memory and gives voice to the stories of victims, which can serve as a critical and dangerous memory in the present.[44]

Assessment: Political without Politics

Metz's conception of political theology is not without critics. Initially he faced the charge that his political theology was, in effect, an effort either to restore a form of Constantinian Christianity or to secure a form of union between church and state that would even go beyond the advocacy of "Christian Democratic Parties." In responding to these criticisms Metz, as we have seen, introduced his concepts of the "eschatological proviso" and the "negative critique." He proposed that the churches should engage in purely negative criticisms of political programs and policies but that they should not advocate specific political programs. Yet every program and policy is subject to critique in the light of the eschatological hope for harmony among nations, peoples, and even the creatures of nature.

Metz's conception of political theology as a purely negative critique gave rise, however, to an opposite kind of criticism. North American and Latin American liberation theologians argued that a political theology that does not take concrete political stances in fact becomes quite unpolitical. It is the very nature of politics to engage in compromises about policies and pragmatic solutions to issues. To abstain from favoring one particular program over another or from advocating one policy over another, even though both may fall short of the eschaton, is to avoid getting to the heart of what politics is all about.

It is true that Metz's political theology does not sufficiently develop the relationship between political theology and political ethics. He does not, for example, examine theories of justice or of civil society in order to show their relation to a political theology.[45] Metz concedes that there is not a direct and immediate application of Christian faith to political practice. Therefore, political theology itself needs ethical reflection and political ethics

to link faith and practice. Latin American liberation theologians have criticized Metz for this
appeal to ethical theory and the mediating link
between faith and practice. Nevertheless, Metz
has not developed a political ethics that correlates with his political theology. In fact, in his
criticisms of bourgeois society, he insists that
Christian eschatology serves as an "interruption"
of the status quo of society, or offers a critical
"eschatological proviso" on all present societal
and political institutions. However, by emphasizing the centrality of "interruption," he thereby
thwarts efforts to relate political theology to theories of political justice and political society.[46]

This failure to develop a political ethics is
related to the emphasis that both Metz and Moltmann give to the distinction between Greek and
Hebrew thought. Metz characterizes Greek
thought as cosmocentric and metaphysical in distinction to the historical and future orientation of
Hebrew thought. However, as Jürgen Habermas
has argued in a *Festschrift* honoring Metz, the danger of such a position is that it undervalues the
important contributions of Greek thought and
rationality to Western civilization and modern
society.[47]

Jürgen Moltmann

JÜRGEN MOLTMANN

From the time of its publication in 1964, Jürgen
Moltmann's *Theology of Hope* was widely read and
discussed.[48] Some consider it to be his most influential book. In it Moltmann seeks to explore the
foundation of hope in the Bible. Consequently,
Theology of Hope deals extensively with the biblical bases of eschatology and promise in order to
take issue with contemporary philosophical and
theological conceptions of eschatology and history, especially those of Karl Barth, Rudolf Bultmann, and Wolfhart Pannenberg.

A major influence on *Theology of Hope* is
Ernst Bloch's *The Principle of Hope*.[49] One can
view Moltmann's book as a Christian theological
parallel to Bloch's revisionist philosophy of hope.
The Principle of Hope is an encyclopedic narration
of the history of human hopes and utopian con-

sciousness in history and culture, including religion. Bloch argues that hope is not simply a subjective wish or projection of human consciousness but, rather, an ontological possibility.
Consequently, hope relates to the ontological
possibilities and tendencies (also called "laten-
cies") within the world that constitute its multiple open-ended possibilities. The existing world is
a world "latent" with real but not yet actualized or
realized possibilities.

Promise and Hope

Moltmann argues that previous theologies
understood God as an "epiphany of eternal presence." In contrast, the *Theology of Hope* explicates
revelation as promise and history as mission.
Moltmann interprets the revelation of God as an
"apocalypse of the promised future." He, thereby,
contrasts Greek and Hebrew thought. In Greek
thought the world is multiple, corruptible and
changeable, whereas the transcendent Ground is

one, incorruptible, and unchangeable. Whereas the world experiences suffering and struggles, the transcendent God is above suffering and struggle. Moltmann points out that this Greek view has been incorporated into the substance of much Christian theology. Moltmann proceeds to contrast this Greek view with the faith of Israel, a nomadic religion, that begins with faith in a God who accompanies his people, and who makes historical promises to his people. Israel's faithfulness to their covenant with God is rewarded by his faithfulness to his promises to them.

Israel's early faith in God's promises continues in the prophetic and apocalyptic writings, but a universalization of God's promises takes place insofar as these promises concern the whole of humanity and human existence. This promise of a universal eschatological future entails a historicizing of the world and the cosmos. It makes eschatology the universal horizon of all Christian theology. This understanding of eschatology and apocalypticism also provides the background for understanding Jesus and the apocalyptic character of his preaching and the eschatological hope of the early Christian community. The crucial event is the death and resurrection of Jesus because, in the resurrection of Jesus, God shows himself to be faithful to God's promises. God's resurrection of Jesus validates and confirms Jesus's life and already anticipates in history the hoped for eschatological new creation.

The Crucified God and the Doctrine of the Trinity

Moltmann published his second major work, *The Crucified God*, eight years after *Theology of Hope*. The new book complements the first volume and gives a christological foundation and focus to Christian eschatology and hope. The crucifixion of Jesus becomes, for Moltmann, the decisive event and criterion of his theology. Whereas the *Theology of Hope* underscored the fact that God is experienced in the power of the future, *The Crucified God* underscores the fact that God is experienced in suffering. Moltmann

now moves from his emphasis on God's promise of a new creation to an emphasis on God's suffering solidarity with the suffering of humans.

Moltmann views this shift of emphasis in his theology not only as complementary but also as reflecting a shift in the times. The optimism of the 1960s is now tempered by the disappointments of the ensuing years. "The theology of the cross which was meaningful for us then, and gave us firm ground beneath our feet, came to my mind again when the movements of hope in the 1960s met stiffer resistance and stronger opponents. . . ."[50] Nevertheless, a continuity and consistency remain in Moltmann's theology: Just as *Theology of Hope* criticizes political and civil religion, so, too, does *The Crucified God* offer a critique of political religion; now, however, it is more strongly based on a theology of the Cross.

Whereas *Theology of Hope* focused on eschatology and *The Crucified God* on Christology, Moltmann's third major volume, *The Trinity and the Kingdom of God*, offers a fully developed and specifically Trinitarian understanding of God.[51] In *The Crucified God*, Moltmann situates his interpretation of the Cross within a Trinitarian framework and places his understanding of the Trinity within the framework of the Cross. Moltmann seemed to affirm in *The Crucified God* that the Trinity is actually constituted by the event on the Cross. In avoiding that reading by affirming that God is eternally Triune, Moltmann nevertheless asserts that the event on the Cross is internal to God's Trinitarian experience. The distinctiveness of Moltmann's Trinitarian doctrine lies in his affirmation of the implications of the event on the Cross. It is the event of God's suffering love. It gives rise to Trinitarian language and an understanding of God as capable of suffering in God's very being. Moreover, it shows God's relationship to the world as one in which God not only acts upon the world, but is affected in his very being and suffering by the world.

The Trinity and the Kingdom of God makes the Trinitarian framework so central that it could be said that the Trinitarian history of the self-differentiation of God, rather than eschatology, becomes the focal point of Moltmann's theology. *The Trinity and the Kingdom of God* maintains his emphasis on the importance of eschatology for the understanding of the Trinity, but now it develops, in addition, the significance of the Trinity for eschatology and gives special attention to the development of pneumatology (doctrine of the Holy Spirit).[52] The central problem of the book is God's rule and its relation to human freedom: How is the divine sovereignty compatible with human freedom? The solution lies in the doctrine of the Trinity and its relation to God's Kingdom in contrast to a monarchical conception of God.

The development of Moltmann's Trinitarian theology takes place in the context of several currents of German theological reflection on the Trinity. Karl Barth had already identified the Christian Trinitarian God in relation to the revelation of God's true identity in the Cross of Jesus. Karl Rahner had underscored the connection between the immanent (God's eternal being) and the economic (God's activity in the world) Trinity.[53] Eberhard Jüngel, Moltmann's colleague in theology at the University of Tübingen, had argued that the Trinitarian understanding of the Cross reveals the specifically Christian understanding of God. Moreover, he developed this specific Trinitarian notion of God as a response to the atheistic criticism of theism.[54] These developments within Trinitarian theology are the context in which Moltmann's own specific theological view of the Trinity is developed. He is both influenced by these theologians and reacts against them.

In developing the doctrine of God as a doctrine of the Trinity, Moltmann criticizes the separation between the immanent Trinity and the economic Trinity. Instead, Moltmann seeks to link as strongly as possible the immanent and the economic Trinity. He does this by interpreting the Trinity from the specific history of Jesus and by asserting that the history of Jesus is taken up into God's Trinitarian history. The crucifixion and resurrection of Jesus are, therefore, not events that are external to the Trinity but, rather, are internal to the divine Trinitarian life itself. The history of God's relation to the world in Jesus and the Holy Spirit is not a history external to the inner Trinitarian relations, but constitutes them. God's acts *ad extra* (external) are at the same time God's acts *ad intra* (internal).[55]

If we are to speak as Christians about God, then, we have to tell the story of God and to proclaim the story of Jesus as the story of God and to proclaim it as the historical event that took place between Father, Son, and Spirit, that revealed who and what God is, not only for man, but in his very existence.[56]

By so linking the economic and the immanent Trinity, Moltmann attempts to show that the Christian understanding of God differs from views that are more indebted to Greek philosophy. Here Moltmann continues his claim that biblical thought is thoroughly historical in ways that Greek thought is not and proceeds to criticize the classical notion of God's *impassability*, namely, that God is not capable of change or of suffering. In its place Moltmann maintains that God's historical relations to Israel and to the history of Jesus and the Spirit should be understood as internal to the history of God and that God can and does suffer. Consequently, the Cross is not an event of suffering external to God, but is God's very own suffering in solidarity with the active and changing world of suffering. The event of Jesus's crucifixion is, then, an event between the Father and the Son. God suffers the godforsakenness that separates Jesus as Son from the Father. The crucifixion of Jesus implies an understanding of the Trinitarian relationship as a reciprocal dynamic relatedness.

Moltmann contrasts a social doctrine of the Trinity, emphasizing the three persons and their relations to one another, over against a more "monotheistic" Western conception that focuses on the one nature of God. Thereby, he takes issue with the contemporary Trinitarian theologies of Karl Barth and Karl Rahner. Instead, he calls on Eric Peterson's historical work on the political dimension of the Trinity, and he follows much more closely Eberhard Jüngel's systematic approach to the Trinity.[57] As indicated, both Barth and Rahner emphasize the "oneness" over the "threeness" of the Trinity. Barth does not interpret the threeness of persons in terms of "three personalities," as would correspond to a modern understanding of personhood but, rather, of three "modes" of God's being. Likewise, Rahner, following an Augustinian psychological interpretation of the Trinity, argues that if one substitutes the modern concept of person (which emphasizes individual autonomy and self-consciousness) for the classic concept of person (which connotes a way of subsistence), one misunderstands the Trinity. Both theologians agree that the doctrine of the Trinity does not imply three subjectivities.

Moltmann, on the contrary, argues against Barth's and Rahner's overemphasis on the oneness of the Trinity by drawing on Erik Peterson's historical thesis in which he sees monarchical political monotheism as a political theology of the Roman Empire. Moltmann perceives a working out of the Christian doctrine of the Trinity as including a critique of this political theology and the "monarchical" or "patriarchal" system of imperial government that it entails.[58] Consequently, the affirmation of the Trinitarian doctrine, seen in its social and political context, is at the same time a critique by the Eastern Church of the "monarchical" claims to power of the Roman emperor. Moltmann draws a parallel to the present situation and points to the danger in the fact that monotheism can legitimate social and political domination and repression. The belief in a *social* interpretation of the Trinity counters such relations of domination insofar as it portrays the Trinitarian relation as a relation of equality, freedom, and reciprocity. Because the very self of God is constituted by these relationships of equality and love, God's relation to the world is not a dominating lordship, but a loving fellowship. Moreover, God's Kingdom reflects the reciprocal relationship that is the social Trinity.

Moltmann suggests that the Christian belief in the Trinity deals in a very specific way with the problem of suffering and evil. As a result of the link between the economic and immanent Trinity, Moltmann affirms that God suffers, and this suffering of God is important to any theological interpretation of suffering. It does not suffice to argue, as many theologians have done, by appeal to the classical Chalcedonian Christology in which God suffers in his humanity or the humanity of Jesus suffers. Instead, Christian belief affirms that God suffers in God's very self. God's love is not simply a giving generosity that flows in one direction; rather, God's love is such that it is affected by God's Creation, by its history, and by God's involvement in the history of Creation. The experience on the Cross is an experience between the Father and the Son. The Cross is, therefore, not simply a debt, as understood by St. Anselm, to be paid to God by a humanity that owes an infinite debt. Rather, the Cross displays God's loving solidarity with all who suffer. God is present in the very desolation and abandonment of the Cross. The event of the Cross is *dialectical* in that *God* embraces the godless of the world. "God does not merely enter into the finitude of men and women; he enters into the situation of their sin and God-forsakenness as well."[59] In this way, Moltmann radically affirms the presence of the negative and of suffering in God.

A trinitarian theology of the cross perceives God in the negative element and therefore the negative element in God, and in this dialectical way is panentheistic. . . . To recognize God in the cross of Christ, conversely, means to recognize the cross, inextricable suffering, death and hopeless rejection in God.[60]

In his subsequent writings, Moltmann has sought to develop and to apply his messianic vision of Christian eschatology and his Trinitarian theology across the various tracts of theology. Moltmann has not, then, sought to write a systematic theology in the fashion of Karl Barth, Paul Tillich, or Wolfhart Pannenberg. Nevertheless, his many publications cover the traditional themes of systematic theology. In *God in Creation,*

Moltmann develops a theology of creation with an ecological emphasis.[61] Given as the Gifford Lectures of 1984–1985, the book provides a theological foundation for ecology by working out the implications of the presence of God's Spirit in creation. In *The Church in the Power of the Spirit* (1977), Moltmann proposes, as its subtitle indicates, a "messianic ecclesiology" that sketches a vision of the Church as a countervailing society; that is, as a society that stands in contrast and opposition to and critique of the dominant currents of society.[62]

In *The Way of Jesus Christ: Christology in Messianic Dimensions*,[63] Moltmann fills out the Christology of *The Crucified God* insofar as he gives much more attention to the life of Jesus and underscores the role of discipleship. In *The Coming of God: Christian Eschatology*, he returns to some of the early themes of the *Theology of Hope* but now relates them to the classical issues of eschatology, namely, death, immortality, and resurrection.[64] In addition, Moltmann discusses eschatology in relation to various types of millenarianism (political, imperial, ecclesiastical, epochal) in which he deals with issues of civil religion, nuclear war, violence, and the role of Israel. He concludes with a discussion of the universality of salvation.

Critical Issues

Moltmann's political theology has been criticized from opposing standpoints. Latin American liberation theologians have argued that his theology is insufficiently political and have faulted his eschatology. They argue that his conception of eschatology is more Neo-Platonic than Christian to the extent that it presents God's Kingdom mainly as a transcendent reality so that it becomes almost a Platonic ideal standing in contrast to earthly existence. By contrast, the liberation theologians point to the notion of a "realizing eschatology." By this term they suggest that, just as the Kingdom of God is being realized on earth in Jesus's healings and exorcisms, so, too, the Kingdom of God is being realized on earth

whenever justice and love are being realized. Granted that such realizations will always be imperfect and incomplete, they are, nevertheless, actual realizations of God's reign.[65]

From a completely different Protestant sectarian perspective, Arne Rasmusson argues that Moltmann takes far too positive an attitude toward the Enlightenment, with its emphasis on human freedom and autonomy. He interprets Moltmann's political theology as continuing this Enlightenment tradition, despite Moltmann's criticisms of modern technocratic rationality. Rasmussen favors a view of the Church as a contrast or opposition community of discipleship. Despite Moltmann's references to a community of discipleship, Rasmussen does not think he goes far enough in the radical sectarian direction and that he is too indebted to Western modernity and the values of the Enlightenment.[66]

Several other questions have been addressed to Moltmann's version of Trinitarian theology. Richard Bauckham, a sympathetic interpreter, argues that Moltmann's later work has a tendency toward "undisciplined speculation" and "hermeneutical irresponsibility." He writes, "Moltmann freely employs inferences from biblical phrases and metaphors which he sometimes admits . . . cannot be warranted by historical-critical exegesis . . . in his later work Moltmann too often falls back on the mere citation of texts in a pre-critical manner."[67]

The German theologian, Dorothee Sölle, suggests that Moltmann's theology is still caught up in the dilemmas of traditional theism despite his intentions to the contrary.[68] She interprets him as saying that the Father takes the place of the traditional theistic God and hands his son, Jesus, over for suffering. On the other hand, Karl Rahner questions whether Moltmann's affirmation that God suffers in God's very self is really an answer to the thorny problem of theodicy or whether it only sharpens the dilemma of theodicy. Johann Baptist Metz even questions whether, by incorporating suffering into God's very self, Moltmann has, contrary to his intention, actually valorized suffering.[69]

LATIN AMERICAN LIBERATION THEOLOGY

Latin American theologians have acknowledged their indebtedness to the European development of political theology. Nevertheless, they have argued that the situation and context in Latin America differs considerably from that of Europe.[70] The beginnings of Latin American liberation theology stand in a dialectical relation to European theology. On the one hand, many of its theologians studied in Europe. Gustavo Gutiérrez, Leonardo Boff, Juan Luis Segundo, Hugo Assmann, and others all received their theological doctorates at universities in Germany, France, or Belgium. They were, therefore, strongly influenced by European currents, though their own writings stressed their independence from the European tradition—an independence that increased as liberation theology developed. At the same time, the liberation theologians criticize the political theologians for their analysis of the historical situation, their constructive proposals, and their attitude toward politics. As Latin American liberation theology developed, it sought to look for more native and indigenous resources for the execution of its theology. It also provides a different analysis, than do the Europeans, of the situation of religion and the Church within society. Furthermore, they argue that the dominant theological traditions in Latin America differ from those in Europe. Whereas contemporary European theology can be seen as reacting against existential or transcendental approaches to theology, the Latin American theologians are responding critically to Roman Catholic Liberalism. Finally, the liberation theologians offer a quite different interpretation of eschatology and of the political mission of the Christian churches.

The Context: From Development to Liberation

The roots of Latin American liberation theology can be traced back to the 1960s when the term "liberation" emerged in Latin American theology in direct contrast to the concept of "development."[71] Although the idea of development had been around for some time, it was a concept that had itself changed in the course of time. At first it had meant economic and industrial growth in the countries of the Third World; later it began to refer to genuine progress in the well-being of persons and of societies, so as to include social as well as economic and cultural as well as industrial progress. Nevertheless, in Latin America the concepts of development and developmentalism came to have pejorative connotations, especially for Latin Americans. The progress in development was slow, with reversals and failures that were all too evident. Developmentalism was faulted for these failures and reversals precisely because a developmental approach was seen as failing to reach the causes and roots of the problems. Development failed to reform institutions; it left intact the power interests of the elites. It failed to stop the exploitive activities of both national and international groups. In short, developmentalism appeared to many in Latin America as not only not the solution to the problem, but the problem itself.

The demand for liberation arose, therefore, as a critique of developmentalism. Whereas developmentalism sought gradual reform and change within the structures of present institutions, the demand for liberation called for radical institutional change and societal transformation. A pivotal event for Latin American liberation theology, especially for Roman Catholic theology, was the Second General Conference of the Latin American Episcopal Council (CELAM). It assembled at Medellín, Colombia, from August 26 to September 6, 1968, for the one purpose of implementing the Vatican Council's program of pastoral reform and renewal, but in a way that would be specific to the Latin American situation and continent.[72] The bishops took as their starting point the Vatican Council's *Pastoral Constitution on the Church in the Modern World* (*Gaudium et Spes*) as well as Pope Paul VI's encyclical letter of 1967, "On the Development of Peoples" (*Populorum Progressio*).[73] They sought to fashion, for their situation, the church's understanding of its function and mission in the world. The conference was a significant event because it sparked a distinctive ecclesial self-awareness in Latin America inasmuch as the bishops came together as a local church to understand their own particular identity and to underscore their own situation.

A preliminary preparatory draft for the Medellín meeting was circulated that severely criticized the oligarchies of power, capitalism, and violence.[74] Yet this draft was seen by many of the participants as too weak. They criticized it for failing to uncover the roots of social marginality, poverty, and dependency. Nine hundred priests issued a document, entitled "Latin America: A Continent of Violence." It contrasted the violence of the privileged minority to the majority who were hungry, helpless, oppressed, and neglected.[75] It was in this climate that one hundred and fifty bishops and a hundred *periti* (invited experts) met at Medellín and drafted sixteen documents. The final texts are tempered when compared with the preparatory draft and "Latin America: A Continent of Violence." Nevertheless, these documents are important for liberation theology insofar as they go beyond simply calling for further development in Latin America. Instead, they issue a summons to liberation.

The documents offer a typology of three attitudes toward societal and political change. First are the traditional or conservative groups that accept the established order and resist the change of societal structures. Second are the developmentalist or evolutionist groups that aim at an increase in the means of production and technological progress and focus on the economic order. Third are the revolutionary groups who seek the goal of radical social and economic change. The typology illumines the context in which the category of liberation is used in the Medellín documents. Negatively, the documents clearly indicate what the bishops condemn. In the document on peace, for example, they denounce extreme inequality among the social classes, unjust use of power, exploitive trade policies, and situations of injustice that constitute institutionalized violence. The positive use of "liberation" is elaborated on in the specific document on education where the bishops make the call to liberation integral to the mission of the Church. The education document reflects the pedagogical theories of Paulo Freire's *Pedagogy of the Oppressed* and uses them to underscore the liberating function of education.[76]

The Medellín conference and its documents represent the crystallization point for Latin American liberation theology. It was followed a decade later by another conference known as the Regional Synod of Puebla (1979). This conference sought to respond to the developments of the previous decade and to the various critical evaluations that had been made of liberation theology. Pope John Paul II opened the conference and its final document was approved in March 1979. Puebla repeats several themes introduced at Medellín and echoes the call for a "liberative evangelization." And it speaks of the preferential option for the poor as part of the quest for justice—themes that the liberation theologians had worked out in the decade following Medellín. Before we examine the contributions of individual theologians, several common traits of liberation theology should be noted, especially in regard to their interpretation of the situation, their critique of previous theologians, and their interpretation of eschatology as it differs from European political theology.

Interpretation of the Situation: Dependency

The liberation theologians make it clear that northern European political theology interprets the situation in a way that does not correspond to the situation in Latin America. The Latin American situation cannot be characterized by secularization and privatization but rather by dependency and exploitation. The Latin American churches continue to have considerable influence on society; religion is not as privatized as it is in northern Europe or North America. The issue facing the Church in the Southern Hemisphere is not the privatization and secularization of religion but widespread poverty and conditions of dependency.

The idea of dependency is central to liberation theology, not simply as a description of the situation of Latin America but also as integral to liberation itself. Liberation entails a freedom from the conditions of dependency. Although the liberationist's notion of dependency is often attributed to Karl Marx and Marxism, it derives less from Marx and Engels than from the Canadian Neo-Marxist André Gunder Frank.[77] In his inquiries about the unequal level of economic development between the Northern and Southern hemispheres of the Americas, Frank traces the lack of development and socioeconomic inequality to colonial exploitation. Whereas the New England states, for example, lacked natural resources, countries such as Mexico and Peru were rich in these resources. However, the natural resources of these southern countries, their wealth, were exploited by European as well as by northern nations. In writing on the theory of dependency, the distinction is often made between the periphery (South America) and the center (North America). As a result of colonialism, peripheral economies are integrated into capitalism as the suppliers of raw natural resources to the central economies.[78] As a result, the central economies develop manufacturing economies, whereas the peripheral economies do not. Consequently, the poverty of the Southern Hemisphere is related to its dependency on the northern countries. It is this relationship of dependency that the theories and policies of development do not attack or attempt to change.

Previous Theology

Whereas European political theology directed its criticism at the Existential theology of Rudolf Bultmann or the transcendental theology of Karl Rahner, the Latin American liberation theologians are dissatisfied with earlier French Roman Catholic Thomism and with Liberal Catholic social theology. They disapprove of the clear-cut distinctions the latter drew between nature and grace, society and church, clergy and laity. It is important to note that it was not only Neo-Scholasticism but also Liberal Catholic social thought that advocated these distinctions. In order to avoid the integralism of the nineteenth-century Catholic Restoration, Liberal Catholic social thought distinguished clearly between the religious or spiritual realm and the sociopolitical sphere. According to this liberal viewpoint, whenever Roman Catholics engage in social and political issues in a modern society, they should advance their claims not by appeals to divine revelation but by appeal to natural law, which is, as such, rational and open to public discussion. Furthermore, this approach attributes diverse responsibilities to different groups within the Church. Whereas bishops and clergy have the responsibility to proclaim the Gospel and to administer the sacraments, the laity's proper role is to work within the secular world and political society. In short, the clergy have responsibility for the Church, and the laity have responsibility for the world.

Gustavo Gutiérrez, who trained in France, was educated and influenced by the *nouvelle théologie* (see Chapter Seven). As we have learned, this new theological direction sought to integrate nature and grace against the Neo-Scholastic emphasis on their contrast or distinction. It also supported Catholic Action, the lay organization that advocated strong social and political responsibility. Gutiérrez criticizes this theology of Catholic Liberalism, as well as the social philosophy of Jacques Maritain for its distinction between nature and grace that entailed separating the sociopolitical mission of the Church from its religious mission. Moreover, it introduced a "distinction of levels" into the Church, by making the bishops responsible for the Church and the laity for the world. In doing this, these previous theologies deprive the Gospel of its relevance for the world.

Gutiérrez criticizes both Jacques Maritain and Yves Congar for what he views as their distinction between these two planes, missions, and functions of the Church. They appear to see, on the one hand, that there is the task of evangelization, of preaching the Gospel, of proclaiming the faith, and of baptizing individuals. On the other hand, there is the mission to the temporal, historical, and social order. Such a separation of missions into two distinct spheres is a source of differentiation within the Church itself or, as Gutiérrez notes, a source of the distinction between the clergy and the laity:

The functions of the clergy and the laity can be differentiated in like manner. The priest breaks off his point of insertion in the world. His mission is to be identified with that of the Church: to evangelize and to inspire the temporal order. To intervene directly in political action is to betray his function. Lay persons' position in the Church, on the other hand, does not require them to abandon their insertion in the world. In their temporal endeavors, lay persons will seek to create with others, Christian or not, a more just and more human society; they will be well aware that in so doing they are ultimately building up a society in which man will be able to respond freely to the call of God.[79]

Eschatology

The retrieval of eschatology also is central to the Latin American liberation theologians' task. However, it is developed quite differently than is the case in European political theology. In fact, an exchange on eschatology occurred between Latin American theologians and the European political theologians precisely because of the criticisms that the former brought against Metz and Moltmann. The latter are taken to task not only for their inadequate interpretation of eschatology, but also for the consequences that their understanding of eschatology has had on their conception of political theology. The basic accusation is that the political theologians envision God's Kingdom as a contrast image or counterpoint to present society that stands in judgment on all institutions and politics. Both Moltmann and Metz are censured for stressing excessively the transcendence and otherness of the Kingdom in such a way that the eschatological language serves mainly a critical function. It has the effect, for example in Metz's appeal to an "eschatological proviso," of faulting every institution and undercutting support for concrete historical political options and struggles.

Latin American liberation theologians propose a different model of eschatology. It does not interpret the transcendence of the Kingdom of God in categories of complete otherness; rather, it uses categories that relate the imperfect to the perfect. For example, where love, peace, and justice are achieved on earth, there the Kingdom of God is being realized, albeit in an incomplete, fragmentary, and imperfect way. As noted in Chapter Seven, the *nouvelle théologie* pointed to the strong interrelation between the natural and the supernatural in the thought of Thomas Aquinas. The supernatural is not to be understood as standing in contrast to or in opposition to the natural. It represents the fulfillment or perfection of nature. This view of nature and grace has consequences for the conception of eschatology and salvation. And the Latin American liberation theologians point out that supernatural salvation is not an abrogation of but rather a perfection of the natural.

This difference in the interpretation of nature and grace has consequences for the way one relates the eschatological symbols to political practice. In Metz's conception, political theology expresses the "eschatological proviso" as a critique of a political reality by pointing to its provisional nature. A political theology does not, for example, advocate a particular political party or a particular program of reform, because the danger exists that Christianity will be identified with a particular party or program. It would thereby lose its critical function. The Latin American liberation theologies point out that this approach carries with it the danger of becoming "apolitical." One preserves one's innocence or moral purity at the cost of not participating in a political struggle. Gutiérrez writes:

It cannot be denied that despite all his efforts, Molt-mann has difficulty finding a vocabulary both suffi-ciently rooted in human concrete historical experi-ence, in an oppressed and exploited present, and yet abounding in potentialities—a vocabulary rooted in the possibilities of self-liberation.[80]

In a public letter to José Miguez Bonino, Moltmann responds to the criticisms of several Latin American theologians (including Juan Segundo and Gustavo Gutiérrez) that political theology appears to relativize every concrete political decision and practice.[81] He suggests that demand for a correspondence between the King-dom of God and concrete political options or a connection between the Christian faith and social revolution can be found in the work of Ger-man theologians such Karl Barth, Dietrich Bon-hoeffer, Helmut Gollwitzer, Johann B. Metz, and Moltmann himself. He does not see a difference between political theology and liberation theol-ogy on the question of eschatology, despite the fact that almost all of the liberation theologians appear to agree on this criticism of European political theology. At the same time, Moltmann urges a certain caution in regard to the use of Marxist categories of social analysis in liberation theology. He points to the need for a democratic socialism: "Socialism without democracy, eco-nomic justice without realization of human rights, are not hopes among our people."[82] Molt-mann concludes his public letter by underscoring the common goals that both liberation theology and political theology share in their protests against the world's injustices.

GUSTAVO GUTIÉRREZ

Gustavo Gutiérrez, a Peruvian theologian, was born in Lima (1928–). He first studied medicine and obtained a diploma in medicine before taking up studies in philosophy, psychology, and theol-ogy at the Catholic University of Lima. Gutiérrez then went to Europe for further studies at the Universities of Louvain and Lyons. He was ordained a priest of the diocese of Lima in 1959.

While he served as a pastor, Gutiérrez also taught theology at the Catholic University of Lima. He was a theological adviser to, and in that capacity influenced, the Second General Conference of the Latin American Episcopal Council at Medel-lín, which sought to implement the decisions of Vatican II for Latin America.

Gutiérrez's book, *A Theology of Liberation*, is regarded by many as a classic, or even as the Magna Carta of Latin American liberation theol-ogy. His theology not only shares but also illus-trates the common themes of liberation theology as described above. In examining the distinctive themes of Gutiérrez's conception of liberation theology, we will explore his interpretation of the historical Jesus, his understanding of the Church, its nature and its mission, and his view of libera-tion and salvation.

Gutiérrez's Interpretation of the Historical Jesus

Gustavo Gutiérrez, as well as other Latin American liberation theologians, seeks to anchor liberation theology in the Bible and thereby to ground this theology in the biblical or Gospel message. Therefore, he deals with the difficult question of whether one can interpret Jesus's life and mission in a way that shows its social impli-cations and justifies a political mission for the churches.[83] Gutiérrez's basic thesis is that Jesus's preaching, lifestyle, and eschatological message is a religious message and yet one with political implications. Liberation theology is, therefore, faithful to the historical Jesus to the extent that it takes up the political implications of his preach-ing and practice without, at the same time, reduc-ing religion to politics.

The political interpretation of Jesus's life revolves around the time-honored question con-cerning Jesus's relation to the Zealots.[84] It is his-torically acknowledged that Jesus was executed by the Roman authorities and that the title on the Cross, "King of the Jews," indicates the political nature of the crime for which he was executed.[85] The more complex question is whether Jesus was a Zealot or whether he was falsely understood to be one and executed as one. Since H. S. Reimarus (see Volume I, Chapter Two), that claim has often been made. There is speculation that some of Jesus's close associates (Simon the Zealot, Judas Iscariot, Peter, and the sons of Zebedee) may have had some relations with the Zealotic movement. Jesus's preaching of the coming Kingdom of God, his royal entrance into Jerusalem on a donkey, and his violent act of purifying the temple are all actions that, if taken as historical, could be interpreted as evidence of Jesus's political involvement. Certain statements also point in that direction, such as "I have come to bring not peace but the sword" and the "Kingdom of God is to be taken by storm."

Gutiérrez, however, carefully differentiates Jesus from the Zealot movement. Jesus's proclamation of the Kingdom has a universality that transcends the more limited and "national" orientation of the Zealots. Jesus's proclamation calls for a conversion of human hearts and hence it reveals a depth that the Zealots' vision does not have. Moreover, Jesus proclaims a kingdom that is breaking in through his presence and his proclamation as well as through his exorcisms and healings. Although this proclamation has social and political implications, it transcends the political:

The deep human impact and the social transformation that the Gospel entails is permanent and essential because it transcends the narrow limits of specific historical situations and goes to the very root of human existence: the relation with God in solidarity with other persons. The Gospel does not get its political dimension from one or another political option, but from the very nucleus of its message.[86]

The Nature of the Church

Gutiérrez develops his ideas on the mission of the Church not only in relation to his interpretation of Jesus, his preaching and practice, but also in relation to a theology of grace and a theology of history. Gutiérrez takes up and carries forward some of Karl Rahner's major theses on the nature

of the Church as a sacrament but within a more comprehensive view of the relationship between world history and salvation history. Gutiérrez's view of the relation between Church and world brings out the social and political implications of an understanding of the Church as a sacrament within salvation history. He does this by relating the concept of the Church to its salvific mission and purpose rather than to an "ecclesiocentric," or church-centered, view of its mission.[87] The traditional understanding of the word "sacrament" embodies two closely related ideas. Originally the word "sacrament" was used as a translation of the Greek word *mysterion*, and it referred to God's salvific plan for the world, a plan that previously was undisclosed but has become disclosed in Jesus.[88] The Scriptures and the liturgical rites of the early church were characterized by the term "mystery" because in and through them God's salvific plan is made present and revealed to humankind. A second meaning of the term "sacrament" became prevalent as a consequence of Tertullian's more specific application of the term to baptism and the Eucharist. Gradually, however, the two terms became distinct. Whereas "mystery" came to refer to doctrines, the word "sacrament" was used for what is commonly known today as the sacraments, and these were understood as efficacious signs of God's grace.

The Constitution on the Church of Vatican II (*Lumen Gentium*) sought to retrieve the ancient tradition and defined the Church in relation to the divine plan of salvation. It, therefore, described the Church as the "visible sacrament of this saving unity" and the "universal sacrament of salvation."[89] This understanding of the Church as the sacrament of God's saving plan for the world becomes central to Gutiérrez's definition:

As a sacramental community, the Church should signify in its own internal structure the salvation whose fulfillment it announces. Its organization ought to serve this task. As a sign of the liberation of humankind and history, the church itself in its concrete existence ought to be a place of liberation. Since the Church is not an end in itself, it finds its meaning in its capacity to signify the reality in function of which it exists. Outside of this reality the Church is nothing; because of it the Church is always provisional; and it is towards the fulfillment of this reality that the Church is oriented: this reality is the Kingdom of God which has already begun in history. The break with an unjust social order and the search for new ecclesial structures—in which the most dynamic sectors of the Christian community are engaged—have their basis in this ecclesiological perspective.[90]

Gutiérrez has developed Rahner's understanding of the nature of the Church as a sacrament to illuminate the relations between church and world and between salvation history and world history but in a liberation theological perspective. God's grace that is present in the world has its symbolic and explicit presence in the Church and in the history of salvation. It is on the basis of this understanding that Rahner had developed his notion of anonymous Christianity (see Chapters Seven and Fifteen). But it is also on the basis of this understanding that Gutiérrez points to the need for the Church to be a real symbol and a real presence of the love and justice of God's Kingdom that already is present and implicit within the world.

The Meaning of Liberation and Salvation

Gutiérrez seeks to further elaborate on the relation between liberation and salvation, between political action and religious faith, by distinguishing three interrelated but distinct levels: religious faith, utopia, and political action.[91] By these distinctions political action is related to religious faith, but the latter is not reduced to it. First, there is the level of social analysis. This level requires a scientific examination in terms of economic and social analysis and a diagnosis of the issues and problems in terms of structural causes and remedies. But such a level does not suffice and a second level is needed, namely, utopian imagination and hope. Without some image of human nature or some utopian image of the possibilities of a future society, no change is possible. Finally, there is the element of faith that provides

the religious basis for hope. By both distinguishing and interrelating these three levels, Gutiérrez provides a proper role for each in the mediation between his religious faith and social practice. Between the religious belief in the transcendent God revealed in Jesus's life and praxis and the social analysis of society and its ills, there is also a vision of history and humanity with a vision of hope and trust.

Questions

There are various levels of criticism of liberation theology in general and of Gutiérrez's conception of it in particular. On the level of economic analysis, the liberationist theory of dependency has been severely criticized. Gustavo Gutiérrez has, in the fifteenth anniversary edition of *A Theology of Liberation*, acknowledged the need for further work on this question.[92] On the theological level, the basic objection that is raised concerns the relation between liberation and salvation or between economic and social liberation and religious liberation. Wolfhart Pannenberg's criticism and challenge to liberation theology on this issue is typical. He affirms that

there are indeed social conditions of injustice which cry out to heaven and in which there is a need for remedial help and change. That may also be called "liberation," although Christian theology must always remain mindful of the fact that the deepest servitude of human beings is a servitude to the powers of sin and death from which we are freed only by the death of Christ, in faith in God and his kingdom. . . .[93]

Pannenberg further argues that the task of a theology of liberation is to criticize any interpretation of liberation formulated in purely this-worldly categories and to point to the ambivalences inherent in all historical liberation movements.

A related type of criticism contrasts the ethical realism of Reinhold Niebuhr, with its consciousness of human sin (see Chapter Six), with the more optimistic anthropology and ethics of the liberation theologies.[94] From this standpoint, liberation theology's advocacy of social change is undertaken without taking sufficient account of the reality of human sin and the uses of power. Other critics argue that liberation theology gives a one-sided attention to issues of social justice to the neglect of traditional theological issues, such as individual suffering and Christian spirituality. The response of the liberation theologians has been to take up these themes and to discuss them within the perspective of liberation theology itself.[95] For example, Gustavo Gutiérrez tackles the issue of suffering, especially the suffering of the innocent, in his interpretation and analysis of the book of Job.[96] Likewise, he has attempted to relate spirituality to liberation theology but with reference to the spirituality and religious practices indigenous to the Latin American people.[97] In addition, Gutiérrez has written a major study of Bartolomé de Las Casas. During the sixteenth century a debate raged in Spain over the treatment of the Aztecs and the victims of the Spanish conquest. Many defended the conquest pointing to the practice of human sacrifice thus considering the population as savage and barbaric. Bartolomé condemned in no uncertain terms the barbarism of the Spanish conquest. His description of the conquest and its victimization of what is known as the Caribbean and Mexican populations remains a powerful indictment of Western colonialism.[98] In this manner Bartolemé de Las Casas' defense of the native populations in the face of the imperial conquest provides a historical antecedent and model of the defense of the people in liberation theology.

JUAN LUIS SEGUNDO

Juan Luis Segundo (1925–1997) was born in Montevideo, Uruguay. He became a Jesuit in 1941 and did his philosophical studies at the Jesuit house of studies in San Miguel, Argentina. He then went to Europe for advanced theological studies and received a licentiate in theology from the University of Louvain in 1956. He received a doctorate in letters from the University of Paris in 1963, having done a study on the twentieth-century Russian philosopher Nicholas Berdyaev. He

returned to Montevideo where he established the Peter Faber Center for Social and Theological Studies in 1965. The following year he established a monthly journal, *Perspectivas de Diálogo*, the official organ of the center. The periodical was suppressed by the Uruguayan government in 1975, and later the center was closed by the Jesuits.

Segundo's five-volume *A Theology for Artisans of a New Humanity* constitutes a systematic theology, yet one that was written for adult education and from lectures given at the Peter Faber Center.[99] Because Western civilization and Christianity have reciprocally influenced and conditioned one another, Segundo argues that one cannot separate those elements specific to each. In examining this relation, Segundo suggests that a crisis in Western civilization also entails a crisis in religious belief and the Christian image of God and society. In line with other Latin American theologians, he emphasizes a social understanding of God implied in the Trinity as a model for society.[100] He likewise interprets Christology, sacraments, and history in ways to deal with the interrelation between the crisis of religious belief and the crisis of Western society.

There are several distinctive elements of Segundo's work. Two are to be considered here. The first is his concern with scientific worldviews and issues such as ideology, evolution, and technology—and their relation to faith. To explore this dimension of his work, it is crucial to understand his concept of ideology and how it relates to faith. A second element is his delineation of the hermeneutical circle and its application within a liberation understanding of theological method.

Faith and Ideology

Among Segundo's specific contributions is his understanding of the term "ideology" which appears throughout his writings. The first of a multivolume series on Jesus of Nazareth is entitled *Faith and Ideologies*.[101] Segundo's attempt to elaborate the relation between faith and ideology takes place in the same context as does his criticism of political theology, where he charges

Metz and Moltmann with placing faith outside of ideology.[102]

Segundo notes that the term "ideology" is an equivocal word and that he is using it in a sense that differs from its traditional use.[103] Traditional Marxism uses the category of ideology in the pejorative sense of a "false consciousness." An ideology signifies a system of ideas that legitimates the interests of a ruling class while at the same time concealing those interests.[104] Revisionist Marxists, however, use ideology in a more neutral sense. For example, Louis Althusser rejects the notion of ideology as a false consciousness and uses the term to refer to a person's basic system of values, goods, and goals. Althusser writes that "in ideology men do indeed express, not the relation between themselves and the conditions of existence, but *the way* they live the relation between themselves and their conditions of existence."[105] Segundo underscores this dual use of the term:

We have two meanings for the word "ideology." The more *neutral* sense refers to everything that lies outside the precision of the sciences, to the suprascientific or the superstructural realm. . . . The second sense of the term is clearly *negative*. It refers to all the cognitive mechanisms which disguise, excuse, and even sacralize the existing mode of production, thus benefiting those who profit from that mode of production.[106]

The dual meaning of ideology is important for Segundo's own use of the term. When he is using the concept critically or applying ideology-criticism to those mechanisms that disguise and sacralize modes of production, he is using the term in the negative Marxist sense. However, when he develops a more constructive use of the term, then he understands ideology as pointing to that which lies outside of scientific rationality. Consequently, when Segundo speaks of the relation between faith and ideology, he is dealing with the relation between a person's faith and his or her basic system of values, goods, and goals— these are values and goods that lie beyond a purely empirical or scientific rationality. The issue today is, therefore, one of the relation

between faith and ideology that Segundo sees as parallel to the classic distinction between faith and reason or faith and science.

Just as one has contrasted faith and reason so, too, today, one contrasts faith and ideology (even when the term is used in the sense of a system of values). In fact, Segundo argues that this contrast is reinforced on two fronts: On one side, Christian theology contrasts faith and ideology in order to maintain the autonomy and purity of faith. On the other side, especially in Marxist philosophy, ideology is advanced as a system of ideas and values that is "scientific" (a highly inappropriate term for ideology, in Segundo's view). Both Christians and Marxists, therefore, appear to agree that whereas Christianity, as a religion, is faith, Marxism, as a religion, is an ideology. According to Segundo, however, neither a Marxist nor a Liberal can explain his or her existence exclusively in objective scientific terms without reliance on some values that are not scientific.

To further develop his understanding of ideology, Segundo follows Gregory Bateson's *Steps to an Ecology of the Mind*, where Bateson asserts that human reason, in its relationship to human activity, is based upon certain premises. These premises, epistemological and ontological, precede reason. They are what reason is based upon. "The premise is a-rational. Reason works on premises that are not created or verified by reason itself."[107] What Bateson calls ontological and epistemological premises refer to the anthropological structure or foundation that Segundo calls faith. Segundo refers to these premises as an anthropological faith and relates Christian faith to this anthropological faith. Segundo, however, makes a distinction between religious faith as a prolongation of anthropological faith and religious traditions transmitted as culture.

Religious faith is a prolongation of anthropological faith. It makes use of transcendent data provided by a body of testimony concerning meaning and values. The testimony is incarnated in a series of witnesses linked together by their common quest. This approach leads people *first* to accept certain human values and *then* to recognize their sacred or absolute sense. . . . Religious traditions transmitted as culture represent a very different approach. First it seeks to recognize the sacred as such, i.e., as something supernaturally effective; only then, and usually indirectly, does it propose to adopt the value implicit in that sacred set of instruments.[108]

Segundo wants that religious faith, which emerges as a prolongation of anthropological faith, to evaluate religious traditions transmitted as culture. Certain basic values emerge in anthropological faith that are recognized as sacred in "religious faith." A religious tradition and culture continue to exemplify these values. Consequently, the values of anthropological faith as well as the values of religious faith *should* underlie the cultural tradition. If these values are expressed in the culture, then that culture should be transformed so that these values can serve as the basis of the culture and tradition. He points to the Christian tradition as a "process of learning to learn."[109] It learns to ascertain anthropological and religious values in the face of cultural and religious traditions that no longer serve these values. This critical function of religious faith in the face of cultural religious traditions can be seen more clearly in Segundo's interpretation of the hermeneutical circle.

The Hermeneutical Circle

Segundo is extremely aware of the importance of method for theology. He argues that liberation theology is significant for theology and theological method, for it involves—as the title of one of his books suggest—"the liberation of theology."[110] He explains his method by illuminating what he calls the "hermeneutical circle." It is a hermeneutic method or circle with four distinctive steps:

Firstly, there is our way of experiencing reality, which leads us to ideological suspicion. *Secondly,* there is the application of our ideological suspicion to the whole ideological superstructure in general and to theology in particular. *Thirdly,* there comes a new way of experiencing theological reality that leads us to exegetical suspicion, that is, to the suspicion that the prevailing

interpretation of the Bible has not taken important pieces of data into account. *Fourthly,* we have our new hermeneutic, that is, our new way of interpreting the fountainhead of our faith (i.e., Scripture) with the new elements at our disposal.[111]

The first step of this circle takes over the hermeneutical insight (see Chapter Eleven) that the life relation constitutes a pre-understanding. Liberation theology takes up this insight and makes the starting point of liberation theology a particular way of experiencing reality. Specifically, it points to the experience of the reality of the poor in Latin America, an experience that carries with it a certain way of looking at the Christian cultural tradition. This experience then leads to the second step, the examination of that tradition for ideological deformations as well as ideological representations of the class interest of the rich, powerful, and elite. In addition to this ideological critique of the tradition, one also brings an ideological critique to the prevailing interpretation of the Bible for the same end. The final theological step is the rereading of the biblical material from the perspective of the experience of the poor and oppressed. This new rereading not only takes into account the critique of both traditional and prevailing interpretations of the Bible, but it becomes a resource for a new interpretation. This new interpretation shows the relevance of the Bible for the poor and oppressed. In this hermeneutic, the Bible is viewed as the source and fountainhead of religious truth. Segundo's conception of the hermeneutical circle goes back, then, to biblical origins; takes into account experience, ideology, and criticism; and, in the end, demonstrates the abiding truth and significance of God's revealed truth in the Bible.

A Critical Question: The Difference from Feminist Theology

Segundo's interpretation of the hermeneutical circle reveals a significant difference between Latin American liberation theology and feminist liberation theology. The Latin American theologians argue from the primacy of the Scriptures, rightly interpreted, and contrast it with what they see as the ideological deformation of the Scriptures in the traditional reading of the Bible. This primacy of Scripture takes place in various ways. One can appeal to the earthly Jesus as expressing, through his preaching and lifestyle, solidarity with the poor or an option for the poor.[112] The concerns of liberation theology for the poor find their historical and theological foundation, therefore, in Jesus's concern for the poor. That is, one traces a historical trajectory from the prophetic tradition, with its concern for the widow, the orphan, and the poor, to the continuation of this tradition within the New Testament, be it in Luke 4 where the Good News of the Gospel is announced for the poor or in the sharing of goods in the Acts of the Apostles or in the prophetic concern for the poor in the Epistle of James.

Feminist theology, as is evident from a discussion between Elisabeth Schüssler Fiorenza and Segundo, does not share this assumption. Many feminist theologians (see Chapter Thirteen) point to those passages in the New Testament that relegate women to subordinate positions in relation to patriarchal authority and that sanction this subordination as divinely willed. Some feminist theologians also realize that if one is critically aware of recent biblical research, one cannot simply appeal to the historical Jesus as the foundation of a feminist theology. In arguing with other forms of liberation theology, Elisabeth Schüssler Fiorenza argues that one cannot appeal to some pristine golden age of Christianity in the fashion of the liberal theology of Adolf von Harnack. Instead, she argues that conflict can be traced back into the earliest periods of Christianity, as the Pauline writings make plain.[113] The hermeneutical circle, therefore, becomes much more complex within feminist theology. The Scriptures contain not just "Good News" for women, but also "Bad News." Hence the hermeneutical principle cannot be the return to *a* biblical principle, be it the historical Jesus or the prophetic principle, as *the one* criterion of biblical theology and faith.

LEONARDO BOFF

Leonardo Boff (1938–) was born in Concordia, Brazil. He studied in the major seminary in Pétropolis with Father Bonaventura Kloppenberg, a well-known Brazilian theologian. In 1964, he became a Franciscan and went on for further studies in Munich, Germany, where he wrote a doctoral dissertation on *The Church as Sacrament in the Horizon of the Experience of the World*.[114] He later returned to Brazil as a theologian and editor of a theological journal.[115]

The Church as Sacrament of the Spirit

It is Boff's work on the nature and origin of the Church that has become a source of controversy and has brought him into public conflict with church officials. This controversy entails a shift not only in the understanding of the historical origin of the Church, but also in the theological interpretation of the nature and structure of the Church. Boff's treatment of the origin, structure, and sacramental nature of the Church differs decisively from the views of both Karl Rahner and Gustavo Gutiérrez.

Karl Rahner maintained that the Church could be traced back to the historical Jesus as its founder. Moreover, this historical continuity has a theological significance.[116] In Rahner's conception, the Church is a sacrament, and it is a sacrament precisely insofar as it continues the symbolic and sacramental nature of God's presence in Jesus. Not only does a historical continuity exist between the earthly Jesus and the Church, but the sacramental function of the church also continues the sacramental function of Jesus as the sign and presence of an incarnate God. In short, the sacramental understanding of the Church corresponds to the sacramental and incarnational understanding of Christ. Gutiérrez's account of the Church begins with this sacramental view of Christ and the Church, but he extends it by developing its political and social implications. The Church symbolizes the love and peace between God and humanity to the extent that it makes this real in its concrete social and political institutions.

Boff's vision of the Church involves several modifications of this sacramental view. First, Boff takes into account the historical-critical biblical scholarship that had been officially accepted in principle at Vatican II. (See Chapter Eight.) As a consequence of the Second Vatican Council, the results of this scholarship have become much more widely accepted in Roman Catholic theological circles. Historical criticism brought again ("again" because it had been raised originally at the time of Alfred Loisy and Catholic Modernism; see Volume I, Chapter Fourteen) into Roman Catholic awareness the nature of Jesus's eschatological proclamation and recognition that the Christian community historically emerged in the post-Easter period. The beginning of the Church now was understood theologically to be the result of the action of the Spirit on the disciples of Jesus.

The acceptance of this historical and theological thesis led, then, to a further theological thesis: that one should conceive of the Church as the sacrament of the Spirit rather than as the sacrament of Christ. The Church and its structures emerge in the post-Easter "pentecostal" experience of the early Christians. Boff accepts and develops this historical and theological viewpoint. His book *Ecclesiogenesis* maintains that the Church's genesis takes place under the influence of the charisms or "gifts" of the Spirit in the early Christian period. Moreover, he takes one step further: Just as the Spirit created the "Church" in early Christianity so, too, is the same divine Spirit creating the "Church" in the emergence of base communities in Latin America.

The transition from the historical Jesus to the post-Easter origin of the Church and from the sacrament of Christ to the sacrament of the Spirit modifies our understanding of the structures of the Church and the possibilities of changing those structures. To the extent that these structures emerged under the inspiration of the Spirit in the post-Easter situation, they should not be viewed as structures that are permanently instituted by the historical Jesus or that exist by divine right as unchangeable because of that historical fact. Instead, the post-Easter emergence of these structures leaves open the possibility for further action of the Spirit in the life of the Church.[117] Boff also points out that his concentration on the activity of the Spirit stands in a tradition that has its roots in medieval Franciscan theology.

Social Analysis and the Church

Beginning with the Church as the sacrament of the Spirit as his theological horizon, Boff critically applies a social analysis, especially a class analysis, to both the historical and present structures of the Church. He points out that, in Roman Catholic theology, two theological affirmations have traditionally existed side by side. On the one hand, the Church has always affirmed the truth of the "sense of the faithful" as a criterion of theological truth. On the other hand, it has affirmed the primacy of papal and episcopal authority in the transmission of Catholic truth. The history of the Church thus shows a class division between the hierarchy as an upper class and the laity as a lower class. In recent centuries there has been an increasing tendency to give an epistemic privilege to the hierarchy and to minimize the significance of the "sense of the faithful" and the gifts of the Spirit among God's people. Boff writes:

Just as there was a social division of labor, an ecclesiastical division of religious labor was introduced. A group of functionaries and experts was created, responsible for attending to the religious needs of all through the exclusive production of the symbolic goods to be consumed by the now dispossessed people. It is impossible to go into all of the internal conflicts of religious power (e.g., hierarchy-laity, low clergy-high clergy) or all of the forms of ideological consensus that have been created through the centuries that have resulted in the fact that ecclesiastical functionaries today hold a monopoly on the legitimate exercise of religious power. It is clear that a Church so structurally unbalanced is in harmony with the social realm that possesses the same biased means of production.[118]

Boff appeals to Vatican II's understanding of the Church as the people of God, to the post-Easter origin of the Church under the influence of the Spirit, and to the theological vision of the Church as a sacrament of the Spirit in order to counter what he sees as an imbalance of power and knowledge within the Church. In so doing, he takes liberation theology one step beyond its critique of the domination of institutions and powers in the world and brings that critique to the Church in order to criticize those structures of domination and power within the Church itself. This is the reason that his analysis of the Church in terms of power has become the most controversial aspect of his writings. He has been accused of placing a "popular church" in opposition to a hierarchical church.

Future Directions in Liberation Theology

This chapter has singled out three Latin American liberation theologians, Gustavo Gutiérrez, Juan Luis Segundo, and Leonardo Boff, and has described their specific contributions. This should not, however, lead one to overlook the fact that there are many other important and well-known Latin American liberation theologians who have been influential not only in their native Latin America but also in the United States. Jon Sobrino, a Jesuit, has written several influential volumes on Christology, the best known being his *Christology at the Crossroads*.[119] The Brazilian theologian, Hugo Assmann, has produced an interesting book titled *Theology for a Nomad Church*.[120] Clodovis Boff, a Brazilian theologian and the brother of Leonardo Boff, has written on theological methodology and liberation in *Theology and Praxis: Epistemological Foundations*. Ignacio Ellacuría, one of the martyred Jesuits of El Salvador, edited a comprehensive theological encyclopedia from the perspective of liberation theology.[121] Enrique Dussel, an Argentinean philosopher and theologian teaching in Mexico City, has published extensively on the history of the Church and liberation theology in Latin America.[122] José Miguez Bonino, professor

of theology in Buenos Aires, Argentina, and a former vice-president of the World Council of Churches, is the author of an influential survey of Latin American theology. In other writings he has examined the relation between liberation theology and ethics and the relation between liberation theology and pentecostalism.[123] The increase of Pentecostal and Evangelical Christian movements among the Latin American people raises the debated issue about whether Latin America is turning Protestant. The issue of the relation of these popular religious movements to liberation theology as a religious movement is also a subject of considerable interest.[124]

In the latter decades of the twentieth century, many shifts have taken place in Latin American liberation theology. These changes can be seen as a further turning away from a Eurocentric theology. More importantly, it involves a decreasing reaction to political theology and greater attention paid to popular religion in Latin America. Since Latin American theology has from its beginning appealed to the specific experiences of the Latin American poor, the current appeal to popular religion can also be understood as consistent with that original direction.[125] Likewise, the relation between Latin American liberation theology and Christian spirituality has been increasingly explored. Jon Sobrino is at the forefront of this discussion.[126]

CONCLUSION

Both political and liberation theology have been the object of considerable discussion and debate. One issue of continuing concern revolves around the relation between theory and practice. This issue is as much about the *genre* of political and liberation theology as it is a substantive issue about the relation between theology and practice. Johann Baptist Metz is a fundamental theologian; Jürgen Moltmann, Gustavo Gutiérrez, Juan Luis Segundo, and Leonardo Boff all are systematic theologians. Not one of them is an expert in social or political ethics. Often their critics ask for concrete solutions to particular political issues, and they bemoan the fact that they find none in their work. One can reply that this criticism overlooks the fact that their major contributions lie elsewhere. Metz is concerned about fundamental theology; Moltmann has concentrated on eschatology, the Trinity, and the Church. Gutiérrez and Boff are focused on the nature and mission of the Church. Segundo is concerned with theological method and the nature of faith in a modern evolutionary world. Comparisons with a social ethicist such as Reinhold Niebuhr, who is concerned with detailed ethical justifications or specific political options, disregard the fact that this is not the focal point of their various theological endeavors. These political and liberation theologies are much more concerned with the issues of what it means to be Christian and what is the mission of the Church in a world of systemic poverty and exploitation than they are with theories of ethics and justice.

Because of the specifically theological character of political and liberation theology, some of the more fundamental arguments against it have been theological. Joseph Ratzinger and Hans Urs von Balthasar both seek to counter the liberationist's theological vision by appealing to a kenosis Christology.[127] Kenosis Christology takes as its starting point not the Gospel narratives of Jesus's preaching and actions, but rather the hymn in the Letter to the Philippians that speaks of Christ's self-emptying in obedience to the will of the Father. In this view, personal humility, self-denial, and obedience are at the center of the Christian vision. The crucifixion is interpreted as an act of obedience and self-surrender on the part of Jesus, one which all Christians should emulate. That is, personal self-surrender and obedience to God's will, and not a new social structure, are the heart of the Christian Gospel.

Both liberation and political theology have attempted, however, to overcome the one-sidedness of existential Christian eschatology by retrieving the more earthly and social conception of the Kingdom that is found in the Hebrew Scriptures. Their critics, on the other hand, seek to differentiate much more sharply the distinctive

nature of Christian eschatology. As Harvey Cox has pointed out, Hans Urs von Balthasar appeals precisely to the newness and uniqueness of the New Covenant over against the appeal to the Hebrew Scriptures, which characterizes the liberation theologies.[128]

The theological criticisms mentioned above do, ultimately, raise the fundamental question of the relation between Christian ethical reflection on the nature of justice and society and its relation to political ethics.[129] Critics persist in arguing that the political and liberation theologies do not sufficiently develop ethical positions on concrete political and social issues. This criticism is given prominent attention in the Vatican pronouncements on Latin American liberation theology.[130] Issued by Joseph Cardinal Ratzinger, these documents mirror the criticism found in his other writings, namely, that eschatology needs to be linked to political practice through a political ethic.[131] The response of the liberation theologies has, in turn, been directed against a particular kind of ethic, especially an ethic based upon Catholic natural law theory. From their viewpoint, an adequate ethic has to flow from the Gospel message so that there is a link between the Christian proclamation of the Gospel and correct practice. The liberation theologians insist that when one has made social and political decisions based upon a natural law, one is not basing these decisions on the Christian proclamation.

The relation between liberation theology and Christian ethics reaches a critical point on the issue of the use of violence. When is violence ethically justified? Under what conditions can one appeal to criteria for a justified revolution, as is the case in just war theory? The critics of liberation theology require that such ethical considerations be elaborated upon. To some extent, the liberation theologians have sought to underscore the point that one misreads liberation theology if one views it exclusively or primarily in terms of the issue of violent revolution. Moreover, they point out that such a perspective tends to overlook the *de facto* conditions of power and violence in Latin America. As the social and political situation has changed in some countries, this particular issue of violence has receded into the background.

A question often raised concerning the interpretation of political theology and liberation theology is whether these movements are similar to, or a return to, the Social Gospel movement in the United States at the beginning of the twentieth century (see Volume I, Chapter Eleven). An affirmative judgment would be suspect if it overlooked the differences between the contexts of these movements. On a surface level, insofar as the Social Gospel emphasized the social relevance of the Gospel proclamation of God's Kingdom, it shares a common social and political focus with political and liberation theology. As the Social Gospel learned from Albrecht Ritschl's interpretation of the Kingdom and his criticism of individualistic pietism (see Volume I, Chapter Eleven), so, too, do political and liberation theologies underscore the centrality of the proclamation of God's reign and react against all individualistic understandings of it and Christianity. Nevertheless, there are differences between these movements. Political theology is very much aware of the apocalyptic and eschatological dimension of Jesus's preaching of the Kingdom. It attempts to deal with the challenge of Johannes Weiss's discovery of the apocalyptic nature of Jesus's preaching (see Chapter One), which nullifies an interpretation of the Kingdom of God in the optimistic and progressive terms of the Social Gospel. These movements are united, however, in a belief that the Christian faith is social and that Christian discipleship entails caring for the poor, the needy, and the oppressed in the world.

NOTES

1. See Francis Schüssler Fiorenza, "Introduction," in Johann B. Metz and Jürgen Moltmann, *Faith and the Future: Essays on Theology, Solidarity, and Modernity* (Maryknoll, N.Y., 1995), pp. ix–xvii.

2. Johann Baptist Metz, *Christliche Anthropozentrik: Über die Denkform des Thomas von Aquin* (Munich, 1962).

3. Jürgen Moltmann, *Christoph Pezel (1539–1604) und der Calvinismus in Bremen* (Bremen, 1958); and *Pradestination und Perseveranz: Geschichte und Bedeutung der reformierten Lehre "de perseverantia sanctorum"* (Neukirchen, 1961).

4. Ernst Käsemann, "On the Subject of Primitive Christian Apocalyptic," in his collection *New Testament: Questions of Today* (Philadelphia, 1969).

5. See Francis Schüssler Fiorenza, "Dialectical Theology and Hope," *Heythrop Journal,* 9 (1968), 145–163, 384–399; and 10 (1969), 28–46.

6. See Francis Schüssler Fiorenza, "Progress and Eschatology within the Context of Ernst Bloch's Notion of Cultural Heritage," in *Philosophy of Religion and Theology,* ed. David Griffen (Chambersburg, 1972), pp. 104–114; and Francis Schüssler Fiorenza, "Religion and Society: Legitimation, Rationalization or Cultural Heritage," *Concilium,* 125 (1979), 24–32.

7. Ernst Bloch, *The Principle of Hope,* 3 vol. (Cambridge, 1986). It was written in the United States between 1938 and 1947 and first published in East Germany in 1953 and then in 1959 in West Germany.

8. Ernst Bloch, *Atheism in Christianity* (New York, 1981).

9. Jürgen Moltmann, *Theology of Hope: On the Ground and the Implications of a Christian Eschatology* (New York, 1967), p. 305.

10. Ibid., p. 311.

11. Johann Baptist Metz, *Theology of the World* (New York, 1969).

12. Moltmann, *Theology of Hope,* p. 311.

13. Ibid., pp. 165–172.

14. Ibid., p. 56.

15. Johann B. Metz, "Facing the Jews: Christian Theology after Auschwitz," in Metz and Moltmann, *Faith and the Future,* op. cit., p. 40.

16. Christopher Morse relates Moltmann's theology of promise to the theory of speech acts in analytical philosophy of language. See his *The Logic of Promise in Moltmann's Theology* (Philadelphia, 1979).

17. Moltmann, *Theology of Hope,* pp. 102–106.

18. Metz, *Theology of the World,* p. 114.

19. For the history of the concept of "political theology," see Francis Schüssler Fiorenza "Political Theology: An Historical Analysis," *Theology Digest,* 25 (1977), 317–334, and F. S. Fiorenza, "Religion und Politik: Geschichte und Funktion der politischen Theologie," Vol. 27 of *Christliche Glaube in moderner Gesellschaft,* ed. Karl Rahner and Bernhard Welte (Freiburg, 1982), pp. 59–101.

20. Metz, *Theology of the World,* p. 114.

21. Johann B. Metz, *Christliche Anthropozentrik: die Denkform des Thomas von Aquinas* (Munich, 1962); Roger Dick Johns, *Man in the World: The Theology of Johann Baptist Metz* (Missoula, Mont., 1976).

22. Francis Schüssler Fiorenza, "The Thought of J. B. Metz," *Philosophy Today*, 10 (1966), 247–252. For background on Karl Rahner, see Ch. Seven of this text, "The New Theology and Transcendental Thomism."

23. For Rahner's later treatment of revelation, see Karl Rahner and Joseph Ratzinger, *Revelation and Tradition* (New York, 1966).

24. Johann B. Metz, "Caro cardo salutis," *Hochland*, IV (1962–1963), 97–107; and "Zur Metaphysik der menschlichen Leiblichkeit," *Arzt und Christ*, IV (1958), 78–84. See also Francis P. Fiorenza and Johann B. Metz, "Der Mensch als Einheit von Leibe und Seele," in *Mysterium Salutis*, ed. Johannes Feiner and Magnus Lohrer (Einsiedeln, Switzerland, 1967), pp. 584–636.

25. Johann B. Metz, "Freiheit als philosophisch-theologisches Grenzproblem," in *Gott in Welt. Festgabe für Karl Rahner*, ed. J. B. Metz (Freiburg, 1964), pp. 287–314.

26. See his essays in Metz, *Theology of the World*.

27. Friedrich Gogarten, *Verhängnis und Hoffnung der Neuzeit: die Säkularisierung als theologisches Problem* (Stuttgart, 1953).

28. Harvey Cox, *The Secular City* (New York, 1966). For the relation to the German context, see Francis Schüssler Fiorenza, "Das soziale Evangelium und die säkularisierte Stadt," *Stimmen der Zeit*, 91 (1966), 383–388.

29. Metz, *Theology of the World*, p. 107.

30. For the history of the concept of fundamental theology, see Francis Schüssler Fiorenza, *Foundational Theology: Jesus and the Church* (New York, 1984), pp. 252–269, and "Political Theology as Foundational Theology," in *Proceedings of the Catholic Theological Society of America*, 32 (1977), 142–177.

31. Johann Baptist Metz, *Faith in History and Society: Toward a Practical Fundamental Theology* (New York, 1980); Johann Baptist Metz, *The Emergent Church: The Future of Christianity in a Postbourgeois World* (New York, 1986); Johann Baptist Metz, *Followers of Christ: The Religious Life and the Church* (New York, 1978); Metz, *Theology of the World*.

32. Metz, *Faith in History and Society*, p. 15. See Francis Schüssler Fiorenza, "Fundamental Theology and the Enlightenment," *Journal of Religion*, 62 (1982), 289–298.

33. Metz, *Faith in History and Society*, p. 60.

34. Ibid., p. 61.

35. Ibid., p. 62.

36. Metz, *The Emergent Church*, p. 2.

37. Johann Baptist Metz, *Unterbrechungen: theologisch-politische Perspektiven und Profile* (Gütersloh, 1981).

38. See Metz's essay "Transforming a Dependent People: Toward a Basic-Community Church," in Metz, *The Emergent Church*, pp. 82–106.

39. Johann Baptist Metz, *A Passion for God: The Mystical Political Dimension of Christianity* (Mahwah, N.J., 1998), pp. 26–27.

40. See Walter Benjamin, *Illuminations*, ed. Hannah Arendt (New York, 1969). For background and the categories of Benjamin, see Susan Buck Mors's *The Origin of Negative Dialectics: Theodor W. Adorno, Walter Benjamin and the Frankfurt Institute* (New York, 1977), especially pp. 96–111.

41. Metz and Moltmann, *Faith and the Future*, p. 11.

42. See the work of Metz's student on the interpretation of the Holocaust: Jürgen Manemann, *"Weil es nicht nur Geschichte ist"* (Hilde Sherman): *die Begründung der Notwendigkeit einer fragmentarischen Historiographie des Nationalsozialismus aus politisch-theologischer Sicht* (Münster, 1995).

43. Metz writes appreciatively but with reservations in two essays after Karl Rahner's death, "Do We Miss Karl Rahner?" and Karl Rahner's "Struggle for the Theological Dignity of Humankind," in Metz, *A Passion for God*, pp. 92–106 and 107–120, respectively.

44. See his essay "Narrative," in Metz, *Faith in History and Society*, pp. 205–218. An early version is "A Short Apology Narrative," *Concilium*, 9 (1973), 84–96.

45. Francis Schüssler Fiorenza, "Politische Theologie und liberale Gerechtigkeits-Konzeption," in ed. Edward Schillebeeckx, *Mystik und Politik. Johann Baptist Metz zu Ehren*, (Mainz, 1988), pp. 105–117.

46. See Helmut Peukert, *Diskussion zur politischen Theologie* (Mainz, 1969). This volume contains a bibliography of the debates at the time.

47. Jürgen Habermas, "Israel oder Athen: Wem gehört die anamnetische Vernunft? Johann Baptist Metz zur Einheit in der multikulturellen Vielfalt," in J. B. Metz et al., *Diagnösen der Zeit* (Düsseldorf, 1994), pp. 51–64; reprinted in Jürgen Habermas, *Vom sinnlichen Eindruck zum symbolischen Ausdruck* (Frankfurt, 1997).

48. For a collection of the important essays of this discussion, see Wolf-Dieter Marsch, ed., *Diskussion über die "Theologie der Hoffnung" von Jürgen Moltmann* (Munich, 1967).

49. Bloch wrote *The Principle of Hope* in the 1940s during his exile from Nazi Germany in the United States. It became influential primarily through its publication in West Germany in 1959 when it came to Moltmann's attention.

50. Jürgen Moltmann, *The Crucified God* (New York, 1974) p. 7f. Michael Welker, *Diskussion über Jürgen Moltmanns Buch "Der gekreuzigte Gott"* (Munich, 1979).

51. Jürgen Moltmann, *The Trinity and the Kingdom of God,* (New York, 1981).

52. Moltmann, *The Trinity and the Kingdom.* See also Moltmann's *Diakonie im Horizont des Reiches Gottes: Schritte zum Diakonentum aller Gläubigen* (Neukirchen-Vluyn, 1984). Jürgen Moltmann, *History and the Triune God: Contributions to Trinitarian Theology* (London, 1991). Jürgen Moltmann, *Politische Theologie, Politische Ethik, Fundamentaltheologische Studien; Nr. 9* (München/Mainz, 1984).

53. Karl Rahner, *The Trinity* (New York, 1970).

54. Eberhard Jüngel, *The Doctrine of the Trinity: God's Being is in Becoming* (Grand Rapids, Mich., 1976).

55. Moltmann, *The Crucified God,* pp. 294–296.

56. Moltmann, "The Crucified God," in Metz and Moltmann, *Faith and the Future,* op. cit., p. 96.

57. Jüngel, *The Doctrine of the Trinity.*

58. Erik Peterson, *Der Monotheismus als Politisches Problem. Ein Beitrag zur Geschichte der politischen Theologie im Imperium Romanum* (Leipzig, 1935).

59. Moltmann, *The Trinity and the Kingdom,* p. 119.

60. Moltmann, *The Crucified God,* p. 277.

61. Jürgen Moltmann, *God in Creation: A New Theology of Creation and the Spirit of God* (San Francisco, 1985).

62. Jürgen Moltmann, *The Church in the Power of the Spirit: A Contribution to Messianic Ecclesiology* (New York, 1977).

63. Jürgen Moltmann, *The Way of Jesus Christ: Christology in Messianic Dimensions* (San Francisco, 1990). See also his *Jesus Christ for Today's World* (Minneapolis, 1994).

64. Jürgen Moltmann, *The Coming of God: Christian Eschatology* (Minneapolis, 1996).

65. José Miguez Bonino, *Doing Theology in a Revolutionary Situation* (Philadelphia, 1975).

66. Arne Rasmussen, *The Church as Polis: From Political Theology to Theological Politics as Exemplified by Jürgen Moltmann and Stanley Hauerwas* (Notre Dame, 1994).

67. Richard Bauckham, *The Theology of Jürgen Moltmann* (Edinburgh, 1995), p. 167.

68. Dorothee Sölle, *Suffering* (Philadelphia, 1975), pp. 26–27.

69. Johann Baptist Metz, "Suffering from God: Theology as Theodicy," *Pacifica,* 5 (1992), 274–287.

70. See the development of the contrast in Francis Schüssler Fiorenza, "Political Theology and Liberation Theology: An Inquiry into Their Fundamental Meaning," in *Liberation, Freedom, and Revolution,* ed. Thomas B. McFadden (New York, 1975), pp. 3–29.

71. See Francis Schüssler Fiorenza, "Latin American Liberation Theology," *Interpretation,* 28 (1974), 441–457.

72. The texts and papers of this episcopal conference have been translated and published in English by the Latin American Bureau of the United States Catholic Conference, *The Church in the Present-Day Transformation of Latin America,* Vol. I and II, ed. Louis Michael Colonnese (Bogotá, 1970).

73. For a collection of the relevant documents, see Joseph Gremillion, ed., *The Gospel of Peace and Justice* (Maryknoll, N.Y., 1976).

74. See Document 23 in Peruvian Bishops Commission for Social Action, ed., *Between Honesty and Hope* (Maryknoll, N.Y., 1970).

75. Ibid., Document 11.

76. Paulo Freire, *Pedagogy of the Oppressed* (New York, 1970). For a discussion of the applicability of Freire's criticism of the "banking method" of education, see the special issue of *Soundings,* 61 (1978) 228–258.

77. André Gunder Frank, *Capitalism and Underdevelopment in Latin America: Historical Studies of Chile and Brazil* (New York, 1967) and also A.G. Frank, *The Underdevelopment of Development* (Stockholm, 1991). For a broader critique of developmentalism in terms of culture and anthropology, see Katy Gardner, *Anthropology, Development, and the Post-modern Challenge: Anthropology, Culture and Society* (Chicago, 1996).

78. Immanuel Wallerstein, *The Modern World System: Capitalist Agriculture and the Origins of the European World Economy in the Sixteenth Century* (New York, 1974).

79. Gustavo Gutiérrez, *A Theology of Liberation: History, Politics, and Salvation,* rev. ed. (Maryknoll, N.Y., 1988), p. 37.

80. Ibid., p. 124.

81. Jürgen Moltmann, "An Open Letter to José Míguez Bonino," *Christianity and Crisis* (March 29, 1976), pp. 57–63. Reprinted in Alfred T. Hennelly, ed., *Liberation Theology: A Documentary History* (Maryknoll, N.Y., 1990), pp. 195–204.

82. Hennelly, *Liberation Theology,* p. 202.

83. Gutiérrez, *A Theology of Liberation,* pp. 130–135.

84. In his treatment of this issue, Gutiérrez engages especially the exegetical work of Oscar Cullman, *The State in the New Testament* (London, 1957), and *Jesus and the Revolutionaries* (New York, 1970), who notes the parallels but at times downplays their significance.

85. Gutiérrez follows George Crespy, "Recherches sur la signification politique de la mort du Christ," *Lumiere et Vie,* 20, 101 (January–March 1971), 89–109.

86. Gutiérrez, *A Theology of Liberation,* p. 134.

87. Ibid., pp. 143–162.

88. See Romans 16:25–26 and Col. 1:26.

89. The first in *Lumen Gentium,* section 9, the second in *Lumen Gentium,* section 48.

90. Gutiérrez, *A Theology of Liberation,* pp. 147–148.

91. Ibid., pp. 135–140.

92. See Gutiérrez's preface to *A Theology of Liberation*, 2nd ed., pp. xvii–xlvi.

93. Wolfhart Pannenberg, *Christianity in a Secularized World* (New York, 1989), p. 55.

94. Dennis P. McCann, *Christian Realism and Liberation Theology: Practical Theologies in Creative Conflict* (Maryknoll, N.Y., 1981).

95. Gustavo Gutiérrez, *The Truth Shall Make You Free: Confrontations* (Maryknoll, N.Y., 1990). See the essays in Marc H. Ellis and Otto Maduro, *The Future of Liberation Theology: Essays in Honor of Gustavo Gutiérrez* (Maryknoll, N.Y., 1989). Gustavo Gutiérrez and Richard Shaull, *Liberation and Change* (Atlanta: John Knox Press, 1977).

96. Gustavo Gutiérrez, *On Job: God-talk and the Suffering of the Innocent* (Maryknoll, N.Y., 1987).

97. Gustavo Gutiérrez, *We Drink from Our Own Wells: The Spiritual Journey of a People* (Maryknoll, N.Y., 1984).

98. Gustavo Gutiérrez, *Las Casas: In Search of the Poor of Jesus Christ* (Maryknoll, N.Y., 1993). For Las Casas, see also Lewis Hanke, *All Mankind Is One. A Study of the Disputation between Bartolomé de Las Casas and Juan Gines de Sepúlveda in 1550 on the Intellectual and Religious Capacity of the American Indians* (Dekalb, Ill., 1974); and Juan Fried and Benjamin Keen, ed., *Bartolomé de Las Casas in History: Toward an Understanding of the Man and His Work* (DeKalb, Ill., 1971).

99. The five volumes by Juan Luis Segundo are Vol. 1, *The Community Called Church* (Maryknoll, N.Y., 1973); Vol. 2, *Grace and the Human Condition* (Maryknoll, N.Y., 1973); Vol. 3, *Our Idea of God* (Maryknoll, N.Y., 1974); Vol. 4, *The Sacraments Today* (Maryknoll, N.Y., 1974); Vol. 5, *Evolution and Guilt* (Maryknoll, N.Y., 1973).

100. Segundo appeals to suggestive imagery of the "Merciful Trinity," as a model for a more social Christian understanding of God. See also Leonardo Boff, *Trinity and Society* (Maryknoll, N.Y., 1988).

101. Juan Luis Segundo, *Faith and Ideologies*, Vol. 1 of his multivolume *Jesus of Nazareth. Yesterday and Today* (Maryknoll, N.Y., 1982).

102. For a description of this critique, see Alfred T. Hennelly, *Theologies in Conflict: The Challenge of Juan Luis Segundo* (Maryknoll, N.Y.:, 1979), pp. 123–139.

103. Segundo, *Faith and Ideologies*, p. 87. "However equivocal the latter term [ideology] may be, it certainly does not seem to coincide with the meaning that I have given it in this book."

104. For a survey of the concept of ideology, see David McLellan, *Ideology* (Minneapolis, 1986).

105. Louis Althusser, *For Marx* (New York, 1977), p. 233 f.

106. Segundo, *Faith and Ideologies*, p. 97.

107. Ibid., p. 92. See also Segundo's response to Joseph Cardinal Ratzinger: Juan Luis Segundo, *Theology and the Church: A Response to Cardinal Ratzinger and a Warning to the Whole Church* (San Francisco, 1987).

108. Segundo, *Faith and Ideologies*, p. 336.

109. Ibid., p. 338.

110. Juan Luis Segundo, *The Liberation of Theology* (Maryknoll, N.Y., 1976). For the pastoral intent of his theology, see Juan Luis Segundo, *The Hidden Motives of Pastoral Action: Latin American Reflections* (Maryknoll, N.Y., 1978).

111. Segundo, *The Liberation of Theology*, p. 9.

112. Juan Luis Segundo, *The Historical Jesus of the Synoptics*, Vol. 2 of *Jesus of Nazareth. Yesterday and Today*, op. cit.

113. Elisabeth Schüssler Fiorenza, *In Memory of Her*, 2nd ed. (New York, 1994), pp. xii–xxxv.

114. One of the few books of Boff's that has not been translated into English: Leonardo Boff, *Die Kirche als Sakrament im Horizont der Welterfahrung; Versuch einer Legitimation und einer struktur-funktionalistischen Grundlegung der Kirche im Anschluss an das II. Vatikanische Konzil* (Paderborn, 1972).

115. Leonardo Boff, *Liberating Grace* (Maryknoll, N.Y., 1979); *The Maternal Face of God: The Feminine and its Religious Expressions* (San Francisco, 1987); *Trinity and Society* (Maryknoll, N.Y., 1988). Leonardo Boff wrote in association with his brother, Clodovis Boff, *Salvation and Liberation* (Maryknoll, N.Y., 1984).

116. See Karl Rahner, *Foundations of Christian Faith: An Introduction to the Idea of Christianity* (New York, 1982); and his earlier *The Church and the Sacraments* (New York, 1963); Francis Schüssler Fiorenza, "Rahner's Ecclesiology: Jesus and the Foundation of the Church—An Analysis of the Hermeneutical Issues," *Proceedings of the Catholic Theological Society of America*, 33 (1978), 229–254.

117. Leonardo Boff, *Ecclesiogenesis: The Base Communities Reinvent the Church* (Maryknoll, N.Y., 1986).

118. Leonardo Boff, *Church: Charism and Power: Liberation Theology and the Institutional Church* (New York, 1986), p. 113.

119. Jon Sobrino, *Christology at the Crossroads: A Latin American Approach* (Maryknoll, N.Y., 1978); *Jesus the Liberator: A Historical-Theological Reading of Jesus of Nazareth* (Maryknoll, N.Y., 1993); *Jesus in Latin America* (Maryknoll, N.Y., 1987).

120. Hugo Assmann, *Theology for a Nomad Church* (Maryknoll, N.Y., 1975); and *Practical Theology of Liberation* (London, 1975).

121. The English volume is an abridgement of the Spanish. Ignacio Ellacuría, *Mysterium Liberationis: Fundamental Concepts of Liberation Theology* (Maryknoll, N.Y., 1993). See also Teresa Whitfield, *Paying the Price: Ignacio Ellacuría and the Murdered Jesuits of El Salvador* (Philadelphia: Temple University Press, 1994).

122. Enrique D. Dussel, *A History of the Church in Latin America: Colonialism to Liberation (1492–1979)*

(Grand Rapids, Mich., 1981); *History and the Theology of Liberation: A Latin American Perspective* (Maryknoll, N.Y., 1976). See also Enrique D. Dussel and EATWOT Working Commission on Church History in the Third World, *A History of the Church in the Third World* (Maryknoll, N.Y., 1992).

123. José Miguez Bonino, *Christians and Marxists: The Mutual Challenge to Revolution* (Grand Rapids, Mich., 1976); *Doing Theology in a Revolutionary Situation*, (Philadelphia, 1975); *Faces of Jesus: Latin American Christologies* (Maryknoll, N.Y., 1984); *Faces of Latin American Protestantism* (Grand Rapids, Mich., 1997); and *Room to Be People: An Interpretation of the Message of the Bible for Today's World* (Philadelphia, 1979).

124. David Stoll, *Is Latin America Turning Protestant?: The Politics of Evangelical Growth* (Berkeley, 1990); and David Martin, *Tongues of Fire: The Explosion of Protestantism in Latin America* (Oxford, 1991).

125. See Gutiérrez, *We Drink from Our Own Wells.* See also his *The Truth Shall Make You Free: Confrontations* (Maryknoll, N.Y., 1990).

126. Jon Sobrino, *Spirituality and Liberation,* SPI series. Faith and ideology; series 5, year 4 (Manila, Philippines, 1985); *Spirituality of Liberation: Toward Political Holiness* (Maryknoll, N.Y., 1988); *The Principle of Mercy: Taking the Crucified People from the Cross* (Maryknoll, N.Y., 1994).

127. See Joseph Ratzinger's *A New Song for the Lord: Faith in Christ and Liturgy Today* (New York, 1996), pp. 1–55. Ratzinger interprets the themes of exodus and liberation so as not to emphasize "better political structures" but rather the imitation of his exodus that entailed giving up life in order to receive it. Pp. 18–20.

128. Harvey Gallagher Cox, *The Silencing of Leonardo Boff: The Vatican and the Future of World Christianity* (Oak Park, Ill., 1988).

129. See Francis Schüssler Fiorenza, "Politische Theologie und liberale Gerechtigkeits-Konzeption," pp. 105–117.

130. Joseph Cardinal Ratzinger, "Instruction on Certain Aspects of the 'Theology of Liberation'" was issued on August 6, 1984. A copy is reprinted in Segundo, *Theology and the Church,* pp. 169–188. See the three-volume response, *Liberation Theology and the Vatican Document* (Quezon City, Philippines, 1987).

131. See Joseph Cardinal Ratzinger, "Liberation Theology," and Congregation for the Doctrine of Faith, "Instruction on Certain Aspects of the 'Theology of Liberation'" (Vatican City, August 6, 1984). Both are in A. Hennelly, ed. *Liberation Theology,* pp. 367–374 and 393–415. For Ratzinger's own commentary, see Joseph Ratzinger, *Church, Ecumenism, and Politics* (New York, 1988).

SUGGESTIONS FOR FURTHER READING

General

Chopp, Rebecca. *The Praxis of Suffering: An Interpretation of Liberation Theologies* (Maryknoll, N.Y.: Orbis, 1986). A penetrating comparison of Moltmann, Metz, and Bonino in regard to the issue of suffering. The theological method of liberation theology is then compared with a method of correlation.

Dorr, Donal. *Option for the Poor: A Hundred Years of Vatican Social Teaching,* rev. ed. (Maryknoll, N.Y.: Orbis, 1992). A broad survey of Roman Catholic social teaching with an emphasis on the concern for the poor within that teaching.

García, Ismael. *Justice in Latin American Theology of Liberation* (Atlanta: John Knox Press, 1987). In the first section, García elaborates on the centrality of justice and the relation between justice and liberation. A second section discusses the relation of justice to economic and political life.

Haight, Roger. *An Alternative Vision: An Interpretation of Liberation Theology* (Mahwah, N.J.: Paulist Press, 1985). Exposition of the major themes of systematic theology from the perspective of liberation theology.

Hennelly, Alfred T., ed. *Liberation Theology: A Documentary History* (Maryknoll, N.Y.: Orbis, 1990). An important collection of essays dealing with the origin, development, history, and controversies of Latin American liberation theology.

Herzog, Frederick, ed. *The Future of Hope: Theology as Eschatology* (New York: Herder and Herder, 1970). An early collection of essays dealing with the emergence and significance of political theology, especially Jürgen Moltmann's theology.

McCann, Dennis P. *Christian Realism and Liberation Theology: Practical Theologies in Creative Conflict* (Maryknoll, N.Y.: Orbis, 1981).

McGovern, Arthur F. *Liberation Theology and Its Critics* (Maryknoll, N.Y.: Orbis, 1989). A detailed examination and response to the many criticisms of liberation theology.

Torres, Sergio, and John Eagleson, ed. *The Challenge of Basic Christian Communities* (Maryknoll, N.Y.: Orbis, 1982). A collection of essays dealing with the history, practice, and theology of base communities in Latin America.

Johann Baptist Metz

Ancic, Nedjeljko. *Die "Politische Theologie" von Johann Baptist Metz als Antwort auf die Herausforderung des Marxismus* (Frankfurt/Bern: Lang, 1981). A dissertation that examines Metz's political theology as a response to Marxism and its critique of religion.

Ashley, James Matthew. *Interruptions: Mysticism, Politics, and Theology in the Work of Johann Baptist Metz* (Notre Dame: University of Notre Dame Press, 1998). A comprehensive analysis of Metz's political theology that underscores the relation between Metz's emphasis on the mystical dimension of Christian faith.

Columbo, Joseph A. *An Essay on Theology and History: Studies in Pannenberg, Metz and the Frankfurt School.* American Academy of Religion Studies in Religion, Vol. 61 (Atlanta: Scholars Press, 1990). Compares Metz and Pannenberg to the critical theory of the Frankfurt School.

Davis, Charles. *Theology and Political Society* (Cambridge: Cambridge University Press, 1980). A leading theologian, inspired by political theology and critical theory, surveys both and presents his own vision of political theology.

Günther, Titus F. *Rahner and Metz: Transcendental Theology as Political Theology* (Lanham; Md. University Press of America, 1994). A study of Metz's political theology in relation to his mentor and teacher, Karl Rahner.

Hewitt, Marsha. *Critical Theory of Religion: A Feminist Analysis* (Minneapolis: Fortress Press, 1995). Shows the relation between critical theory (especially Walter Benjamin) and political theology (Metz) and feminist theology (Schüssler Fiorenza).

Johns, Roger Dick. *Man in the World: The Theology of Johannes Baptist Metz* (Missoula, Mont.: Scholars Press, 1976). An early study of Metz's political theology.

Jürgen Moltmann

Bauckham, Richard. *Moltmann: Messianic Theology in the Making* (Basingstoke: Marshall Pickering, 1987). A general and basic expository introduction to Moltmann's theology that focuses on his earlier writings.

————. *The Theology of Jürgen Moltmann* (Edinburgh: T. & T. Clark, 1995). An excellent introduction that traces the development from Moltmann's earlier writings to his later writings. It is a follow-up to the previous volume.

Cornelison, Robert Thomas. *The Christian Realism of Reinhold Niebuhr and the Political Theology of Jürgen Moltmann in Dialogue: The Realism of Hope* (Lewis-ton, N.Y.: E. Mellen Press, 1992). A fair and balanced comparison of the two theologians.

Meeks, M. Douglas. *Origins of the Theology of Hope* (Philadelphia: Fortress Press, 1974). An examination of the context and origin of the Theology of Hope.

Morse, Christopher. *The Logic of Promise in Moltmann's Theology* (Philadelphia: Fortress Press, 1979). A sympathetic analysis of Moltman's *Theology of Hope* that relates Moltmann's theology to the categories of speech-acts in analytical philosophy.

O'Donnell, John J. *Trinity and Temporality: The Christian Doctrine of God in the Light of Process Theology and the Theology of Hope* (Oxford: Oxford University Press, 1983). Primarily a study of the doctrine of God as Triune, the author examines Moltmann's development of Trinitarian theology.

Rasmussen, Arne. *The Church as Polis: From Political Theology to Theological Politics as Exemplified by Jürgen Moltmann and Stanley Hauerwas* (Notre Dame: University of Notre Dame Press, 1994). A polemical critique of Moltmann's political theology from the perspective of Hauerwas's vision of the church and society. Rasmussen alleges that Moltmann is insufficiently critical of modernity.

Gustavo Gutiérrez

Brown, Robert McAfee. *Gustavo Gutiérrez* (Atlanta: John Knox Press, 1981). A brief general introduction from a sympathetic North American theologian in the Makers of Contemporary Theology Series.

Ellis, Mark H., and Otto Maduro. *The Future of Liberation Theology: Essays in Honor of Gustavo Gutiérrez* (Maryknoll, N.Y.: Orbis, 1989). A *Festschrift* for Gutiérrez that shows further directions that liberation theology could take.

McCann, Dennis. *Christian Realism and Liberation Theology: Practical Theologies in Creative Conflict* (Maryknoll, N.Y.: Orbis, 1981). A critical analysis of liberation theology from the perspective of Reinhold Niebuhr's realism.

Juan Luis Segundo

Hennelly, Alfred T. *Theologies in Conflict: The Challenge of Juan Luis Segundo* (Maryknoll, N.Y.: Orbis, 1979). A sympathetic analysis that shows the significance and relevance of Segundo's theology within the general framework of Latin American liberation theology.

Hewitt, Marsha. *From Theology to Social Theory: Juan Luis Segundo and the Theology of Liberation* (New

York: Peter Lang Publishers, 1990). A doctoral dissertation that relates liberation theology and social theory.

Nealen, Mary Kaye. *The Poor in the Ecclesiology of Juan Luis Segundo* (New York: Peter Lang Publishers, 1991). A study of Segundo's concept of the Church with special analysis of the option for the poor.

Leonardo Boff

Boff, Clodovis. *Theology and Praxis: Epistemological Foundations* (Maryknoll, N.Y.: Orbis, 1987. Clodovis Boff, the brother of Leonardo, wrote this volume originally as a dissertation at the University of Louvain. It concentrates on theological method.

Cox, Harvey. *The Silencing of Leonardo Boff: The Vatican and the Future of World Christianity* (Oak Park, Ill., Meyer-Stone Books, 1988). A sensitive introduction of the conflict between Boff and Ratzinger as examples of two paradigms of theology and world Christianity.

Chapter Ten

Process Theology

John B. Cobb, Jr.

BACKGROUND

The origins of contemporary Process philosophy and theology have been traced back to the Buddhist doctrines of becoming and the dependent origination of all things, and to the Greek philosopher Heraclitus's doctrine of the eternal flux and becomingness of the world. The more immediate sources of modern Process theology are traceable, however, to two movements of thought in the nineteenth century: the German Romantic philosophy of Friedrich W. J. Schelling (1775–1854) and G. W. F. Hegel (1770–1831),* and to the change in worldview launched by the

Darwinian revolution.** Both of these movements saw development, process, and change as constituitive of reality.

Schelling, for example, insisted that the fact of evil is irreconcilable with belief that the universe proceeds from a being that is perfect, for such a belief would imply that the not-good proceeds from the good. Schelling therefore posited God as the first and the last, but as Alpha God is *not* what God is as Omega. Similarly, a number of late nineteenth-century writers, following the English philosopher John Stuart Mill, insisted that God's goodness and omnipotence are incompatible attributes, and they denied the latter in

---

* On Hegel, see Vol. I, Ch. 5.

** On Darwinian evolution, see Vol. I, Ch. 10.

order to save God's goodness. These writers depicted God as pitting his supreme, though finite, power against alien materials and wringing from them a partial victory. Such a finite theism, Mill argued, is a boon to human moral endeavor—we are, he wrote, "fellow laborers with the Highest." The American philosopher William James (see Chapter Two) proposed a similar "melioristic" type of theism, one in which evil and loss are seen as terribly real. It is a theism that envisiones the ultimate and ideal as not in the beginning, but as the goal of human striving.

Several Process thinkers at the beginning of the twentieth century began their careers as scientists, or with strong empiricist commitments, and directed their philosophical work at countering the mechanistic and materialistic assumptions of the then reigning scientific positivism. Among these writers were C. Lloyd Morgan (1852–1936) (*Emergent Evolution*, 1923), Samuel Alexander (1859–1938) (*Space, Time and Deity*, 1920), and, most importantly, Alfred North Whitehead (1861–1947) and the French philosopher Henri Bergson (1859–1941). Bergson is an important forerunner of contemporary Process thought and, therefore, requires more than passing notice. But before discussing Bergson and those thinkers, primarily Protestant, whose thought is shaped largely by the philosophy of Whitehead, we will discuss the work of the Roman Catholic priest and scientist Pierre Teilhard de Chardin, who developed a theology of evolutionary process during the second quarter of the twentieth century.

PIERRE TEILHARD DE CHARDIN

Teilhard (1881–1955) was born near Clermont in France. He was educated at the Jesuit College of Mongré and entered the Society of Jesus in 1899. After study in philosophy and theology in England, he was ordained in 1911. During this long period of study, which included work in geology and paleontology, he began further work in the latter field at the museum of Paris. His studies were interrupted by service as a stretcher bearer during World War I. He successfully defended a doctoral thesis in paleontology at the Sorbonne in 1922. Teilhard lived and worked in China from 1923 to 1946, concentrating his studies on the stratigraphy and paleontology of northern China and Asia, collaborating in the discovery of *Sinanthropus*. He published over 170 scientific articles and papers. Teilhard was not, however, given the permission of the Church to publish his religious writings. These were published after his death in 1955, although the Vatican then issued a *monitum*, or warning, against an uncritical acceptance of his philosophical and theological views. Teilhard lived in New York for most of the last decade of his life, working for the Wenner-Gren Foundation for Anthropological Research. His most important religious writings include *The Phenomenon of Man* (1955; Eng. trans., 1959); *The Divine Milieu* (1957; Eng. trans., 1960); *Letters from a Traveller* (1962); *The Future of Man* (1959; Eng. trans., 1964); and *Hymn of the Universe* (1965). When these works appeared in rapid succession, Teilhard made a great impression as offering a creative new vision of the unity of science and religion. His rise to influence as a religious writer was mercurial, but interest in his writings has not endured. Both scientists and theologians find his evolutionary vision highly speculative. Nevertheless, for a time his writings did have an influence on important figures such as Henri de Lubac (see Chapter Seven).

Teilhard's grand evolutionary theology portrays the cosmos as constituted by a fundamental energy in the process of development. What we can observe of this process is an evolutionary movement toward greater complexity of energy systems, from elemental particles into atoms and on until we reach complex multicellular organisms. While this process is a continuous, uninterrupted flow, it does reveal three stages or "critical points" in which nature has been marked by profound changes.

In every domain, when anything exceeds a certain measurement, it suddenly changes its aspect, condition, or nature. The curve doubles back, the surface contracts to a point, the solid disintegrates, the liquid boils, the germ cell divides, intuition suddenly bursts on the piled-up facts. Critical points have been reached, rungs on the ladder involving a change of state.[1]

Teilhard sees the first of these critical thresholds as the emergence of inorganic matter when the earth's crust solidified after a long process of cooling. The second stage is the emergence of life, which, after a long development, encircled the earth's surface with a covering or "biosphere." Only five or six hundred thousand years ago did a new phenomenon occur that has radically changed the earth. This was the appearance of mind, or the "noosphere," which involved the critical movement from instinct to thought, the "hominization" of life or emergence of humanity. Teilhard speaks of this as "a mutation from zero to everything."[2] With humanity the universe becomes "personalistic." Humanity is the crown of the present evolutionary process, and its emergence marks a crucial turning point, for henceforth evolution need not proceed blindly but can follow a conscious direction.

This sudden deluge of cerebralization, this biological invasion of a new animal type which gradually eliminates or subjects all forms of life that are not human . . . this immense and growing edifice of matter and ideas . . . seems to proclaim that there has been a change on the earth and a change of planetary magnitude. . . . The greatest revelation open to science today is to perceive that everything precious, active and progressive originally contained in the cosmic fragment from which our world emerged is now concentrated in and crowned by the noosphere.[3]

For Teilhard, the evolutionary pattern has not only moved inexorably toward humanity but will, in the future, exhibit an extension of this process in the direction of a higher consciousness. This is what Teilhard calls "noogenesis," or the growth process of mind or reflective consciousness. He sees human life moving toward greater interpersonal communion, which will lead to the emer-

gence of a new level of complexity-consciousness. The first phase of noogenesis involved a kind of centrifugal force, which exhibited an increase in individuality and personal freedom but a rather slow advance of socialization. Teilhard sees the next phase as centripetal, constituting greater intercommunion and socialization on a planetary scale. This process of unification lies in the future, but Teilhard believes we can know the general direction of the future as extending along lines similar to the past development of complexity-consciousness. Thus it appears quite certain to Teilhard that the "planetization" of humankind will advance toward a new convergence. Teilhard calls this point of convergence the *Omega*, because it constitutes the end of the evolutionary process. At the Omega point all things will reach a suprapersonal unity in God in which agape, or self-transcending love, will reign.

It is not entirely clear whether Teilhard considers the Omega point *as* God or the point at which all things are brought into perfect unity with God. If the former were the case, Teilhard, like Hegel and other process philosophers, would uphold the notion of God's actual growth and dependence on the world. Teilhard's position appears, however, to be more orthodox. The Omega is not only the endpoint of natural evolution but also the divine *Logos* or Word that governs the whole process of cosmic evolution and the power of attraction that drives the process toward its *telos*, or end. Teilhard writes:

To satisfy the ultimate requirements of our action, Omega must be independent of the collapse of forces with which evolution is woven. . . . While being the last term of (evolution's) series, it is also outside all series. . . . If by its very nature it did not escape from time and space which it gathers together, it would not be Omega.[4]

Here the Omega is seen by the Christian as given in foretaste in the person of Christ as the divine *Logos* incarnate. For the Christian

in place of the vague focus of convergence demanded as a terminus for evolution, we now have the well-defined personal reality of the Incarnate Word in whom all things hold together.[5]

A certain ambiguity remains, however, in Teilhard's view of the terminus of the evolutionary process and God's relation to it. Teilhard believes that there are "rational invitations to an act of faith," that the cosmos is moving toward the Omega point. Still he agrees with other process theologians that the future is open and that the direction of the evolutionary process is not divinely determined but is to a great extent dependent on humanity itself. He speaks, for instance, of the superpersonal level of consciousness, by which he means the

superior state which humanity appears destined to achieve *if* it succeeds in totalizing itself completely upon itself, body and soul, by pushing to the end the movement of which it is the historical culmination.[6]

In passages such as these, Teilhard appears, like Whitehead, to conceive of God as offering to humans the attraction and lure of creative advance, but only as a persuasive agency. God and the creatures are interdependent, and the future remains genuinely open. We will see how this theme is developed within a more rigorous and logical metaphysical scheme in the writings of Alfred North Whitehead and by those influenced by him.

HENRI BERGSON

Bergson's philosophical daring made him one of the most widely read and important philosophers of the early decades of the twentieth century. In his early years he came under the influence of the French philosophers of the human spirit and freedom, L. Ollé-Laprune (1839–1898) and Emile Boutroux (1845–1921).* Bergson was professor of philosophy at the Collège de France in Paris from 1900 to 1924. His influential works include *Time and Free Will* (1889), *Matter and Memory* (1896),

* See Vol. I, Chapter 14.

Creative Evolution (1907), and *The Two Sources of Morality and Religion* (1932). In the first two books Bergson explored human psychic experience in an effort to counter the reigning mechanistic doctrine and behaviorist psychology. According to Bergson, a true philosophy must take account of the human experience of time—i.e., duration, memory, and the ego—free of the imposition of scientific abstraction. The consciousness that we humans have of our own selves in flux is, Bergson argues, a far more accurate model of reality itself. For what experience tells us is that we are not discrete, independent entities but, rather, are interdependent beings in a state of flux. The key to reality is what Bergson calls *durée*, duration. *Durée* is concrete, experienced time in contrast to scientific or mathematical time. The latter is homogeneous and is composed of measured units, such as seconds and hours. But we falsify reality by isolating entities into abstract units. Reality is, rather, an interdependent community of durations. Our human predisposition to abstraction can be observed both in the classical metaphysics of Plato and in modern science, neither of which does justice to the unique concreteness and fluidity of reality.

According to Bergson, *durée* is that natural energy that seeks to create against the drag of matter and repetitive recurrence. And so it is that time (*durée*), freedom, and creativity itself constitute, for Bergson, the absolute or final metaphysical reality. In Bergson's metaphysics, God is not a distinct being working on other beings but is, rather, creative evolution itself. Alfred North Whitehead, as well as later Process theologians, were, however, to reject Bergson's identification of creativity with God. For these theists, God is that actual entity that is the ground of all potentials and all creativity and is not interchangeable with creative evolution itself.

ALFRED NORTH WHITEHEAD

Twentieth-century Process philosophy and theology owes its greatest debt to the writings of the English mathematician and philosopher Alfred

North Whitehead. It has been said that his work can best be understood as a full-blown natural theology in the tradition of eighteenth-century rationalism. Just as some of the rationalists of the Enlightenment sought to relate Christian theology to the cosmology of Isaac Newton, so Whitehead and his followers have attempted to develop a contemporary theism congruent with the science of Darwinian biology and Einsteinian physics.

Alfred North Whitehead was born at Ramsgate on the Isle of Thanet in Kent. His father was head of a private school and, after ordination to the Anglican priesthood, was vicar of a large parish near Ramsgate. Life in a largely rural vicarage on the coast of Kent proved to be of lifelong importance to A. N. Whitehead, as was his experience as a young student of the classics and history at the Sherborne school in Dorsetshire, which he attended from 1875 to 1880. In the fall of the latter year, Whitehead began a twenty-year residence in Cambridge, first as an undergraduate scholar and then as a Fellow of Trinity College. At Trinity, Whitehead studied mathematics and was later a mathematics tutor. His most famous student was Bertrand Russell, and from 1900 to 1911 the two collaborated on the writing of *Principia Mathematica*, one of the great works in the field.

Whitehead resigned his senior tutorship at Trinity in 1910 and moved to University College in London where he taught and held various positions. From 1914 to 1924 he served as professor of applied mathematics at the Imperial College of Science and Technology. During these years his interests began to branch out beyond mathematics to more general inquiries on nature, the philosophy of science, and education. In 1924, at the age of sixty-three, he was appointed to a chair in philosophy at Harvard University. In this last phase of his career, Whitehead's thinking about nature and science coalesced into a comprehensive metaphysical philosophy. Important works of this later period include *Science and the Modern World* (1925); *Religion in the Making* (1926); *Symbolism, Its Meaning and Effect*

(1927); *Process and Reality* (1929), which is his *magnum opus;* and *Adventures in Ideas* (1933). Some of Whitehead's students pursued his metaphysical interests, but the philosophical and theological climate between the late 1920s and the 1950s—dominated as it was by analytical philosophy, Existentialism, and Neo-Orthodoxy—was not congenial to Whitehead's metaphysical speculations. Only since the 1960s, and largely among a small, able group of Protestant philosophical theologians in the United States, has Whitehead's metaphysics been appropriated in a significant effort to reconceive Christian theology. This important development will be examined shortly, but to understand it we must first characterize Whitehead's metaphysical doctrines relevant to his theological ideas.

Whitehead's thought begins with the conviction that time and process are constituitive of all reality. Experience shows us that reality is not constituted by static, discreet entities—what Whitehead calls the "fallacy of simple location"—but, rather, is dynamic, organic, and social. The world is a creative process. Moreover, this process is a movement of interrelated and interdependent entities and societies. The world process is an interwoven society of societies, giving and receiving from one another. Whitehead calls this process *concrescence*, or a growing together of many entities and events into a complex unity.

According to Whitehead's metaphysical scheme, the most generalized analysis of the actual, temporal world shows the presence of four factors: The first is *creativity*, whereby the world advances toward novelty or new modes of being. Creativity is not an entity, however, and is real only through those *actual entities*, which exemplify it. Actual entities are the final real things of which the world is made. Nothing is more real. Nevertheless, actual entities are complex and interdependent. They appropriate or *prehend* the past, realize their own peculiar, subjective form or aim, and eventually perish and become an objective datum for some other entity. Although a particular entity is not completely separable from other entities, nevertheless, it is something definite with its own structure that excludes other possible kinds of realization. To account for the determinate and orderly process of the temporal world, Whitehead posits *eternal objects* or pure potentials. He distinguishes between enduring objects that pass away and eternal objects that are abstracted from the concrete object. An example would be a color, which comes and goes but does not perish. Wherever it comes it is the same color. Eternal objects are the real potentialities, patterns, structures, and grades of relevance and value that are displayed in our experienced world. They are entities but in the mode of potentiality. Actual entities incorporate creativity and these eternal potentials in ways that lead to full actualization.

Each actual entity is a process of feeling in which there is a coming together of many elements that are fused into one determinate feeling, or what Whitehead calls the entity's *subjective aim,* or that which seeks its own *satisfaction* and the completion of the process in its own determinate way. This coming together of many elements into one completed subjective aim is, as we have indicated, what Whitehead calls concrescence. One can thus speak of each actual entity as a kind of synthesis of the whole universe from its singular standpoint; it reflects the world in its own unique way. And each actual entity brings to the world its own novelty. When an actual entity is completed it perishes but, as mentioned, it also becomes an object for other entities. This constitutes the actual entity's *objective immortality.* All actual entities know themselves as potentials for the indeterminate future. The world is, therefore, a society of societies, or of entities or actual occasions that fulfill their own subjective aim and become potentials for future occasions.

Whitehead's metaphysics entails, however, a natural theology because the cosmic process requires a fourth component—an everlasting actual entity—God. "God," says Whitehead, "is an actual entity, and so is the most trivial puff of existence in far-off empty space." However, unlike other entities, God is everlasting and does not perish. Unlike Bergson, Whitehead does not believe that creativity itself can account for the actual course of being, and the eternal objects, being in the mode of potentiality, lack causal efficacy or power. According to Whitehead, it is God who grounds the eternal objects in actuality and makes possible their *ingression* or entrance into the ordered process of becoming. God also supplies each entity with its initial aim and serves as the principle of relevance; i.e., as the source of ideal grades of relevance among the eternal objects as they ingress in the order of nature.

Although it is true that God is unique in these respects, God is also the chief exemplification of the metaphysical scheme—not its foremost exception. This means that God is *not* independent, immutable, impassable but rather is to be conceived, like all other entities, as dependent, changing, and thus in some respects temporal and in process. Unless we hold to the analogy of being—i.e., that God is in some sense like us creatures—God, in Whitehead's view, simply cannot be known.

But how do we account for the fact that God is unique both in causal efficacy and as the principle of limitation, concretion, and relevance and, at the same time, truly the chief metaphysical exemplification of that process that is constitutive of all reality? Whitehead's answer, and that of all process theologians, is that God, like other entities, is *dipolar.* Corresponding to the "mental pole" of finite entities is what Whitehead calls God's *primordial nature.* This is the conceptual structure of Deity, which orders, grades, and adjusts the eternal objects and makes them accessible for entry in the temporal world. This primordial nature of God is the original fact in the universe. However, God's primordial nature is lacking or deficient in actuality. As such, the primordial nature of God is unconscious and impersonal.

The other pole of God's being is God's *consequent nature.* This corresponds to the "physical pole" of other entities. God as an actual entity prehends, takes in, and in turn is affected by the concrete entities of the world. God is always receiving new data from the temporal entities, hence is always in a process of becoming. God and the world thus constitute a society of interdependent entities.

God, as well as being primordial, is also consequent. He is the beginning and the end. . . . Thus, by reason of the relativity of all things, there is a reaction of the world on God. The completion of God's nature into a fullness of physical feeling is derived from the objectification of the world in God. He shares with every new creation its actual world; and the concrescent creature is objectified in God as a novel element in God's objectification of that actual world. . . . God's conceptual nature is unchanged, by reason of its final completeness. But his derivative nature is consequent upon the creative advance of the world.[7]

In Whitehead's metaphysics, God is not the only entity involved in creation. Creative advance requires the interdependence of God and the world. For Whitehead, God is better conceived of as the "savior" of the world than as its creator. While all finite entities perish, they do furnish God with new experience for prehension and incorporation into God's consequent nature. Whatever God receives from actual entities never fades away. Hence all perishing entities achieve a kind of objective immortality in God. In turn, God seeks to pour back into the world what is worth saving, to afford entities a new ideal vision of the possibilities of creative advance. However, God is not omnipotent in the traditional theistic sense. God's relation to the world is persuasive, not coercive. Finite creatures are free to reject God's ideal envisagement and lure. There is, then, real loss and tragedy in the world and in God.

In Whitehead's opinion, Christian theism went astray when it joined its vision of God to Aristotle's Unmoved-mover. The Christian God thereafter became the cosmic monarch with no checks on his power and impassive in his relations. It was, Whitehead asserts, "the fashioning of God in the image of the Egyptian, Persian, and Roman imperial rulers. . . . The Church gave unto God the attributes which belonged exclusively to Caesar."[8] It was especially the positing of absolute omnipotence in God—which made God responsible for everything that happens—that made theology such an easy prey of the likes of David Hume. According to Whitehead, if God remains the cosmic monarch, Hume's argument is unanswerable. Furthermore, absolute omnipotence makes no sense of love. Genuine love requires a *free* response, not coercion. Because Christianity affirms the reality of human freedom, God's action in history must be understood to be the persuasion of love and not the coercion of power. Whitehead thus sees in the history of theism an alternative to the image of the imperial ruler, that found "in the Galilean origin of Christianity," an image that "does not emphasize the ruling Caesar, or the ruthless moralist, or the unmoved-mover."[9]

How is one to assess Whitehead's theism? First, it is necessary to recognize the radical character of Whitehead's proposal in the light of two thousand years of Christian history. By introducing the idea of real potentiality in God, Whitehead breaks with traditional Christian theism. He is steadfast in asserting that theology must hold to the analogy of being; that is, that God must be like other creatures in some significant respects or God simply cannot be known. God must exemplify the universal metaphysical scheme and not be conceived of as its sole exception. Therefore, Whitehead attempts to show *how* God *acts* in the world that we actually know—a world that includes temporality and freedom. God and the world mutually act upon one another, so that in a real sense God is continually realizing new potentialities in new moments of experience. Traditional theology envisioned God's essence as absoluteness, perfection, free of all potentiality. It characterized God as omnipotent; Whitehead insists, on the contrary, that omnipotence is incompatible with divine love and real human freedom. God's action in the world is not that of coercive power but one persuasion—the persuasion of love rather than the coercion of power.

In what sense, for Whitehead, does God create the world? Not, it must be understood, in the

Christian understanding of creation *ex nihilo*, creation out of nothing. For Whitehead, God does not alone create things, because God is but one (though the supreme) member of a society of entities, granting these other entitles their own freedom. God is not to be conceived as the absolute efficient cause of the world. "God," Whitehead writes, "does not create the world, he saves it; or, more accurately, he is the poet of the world, with tender patience leading it by his vision of truth, beauty, and goodness."[10] Yet in another sense God *is* the creator because God's primordial nature is immanent in the world as the principle of its order and purpose, in and by which entities can be realized. There can be no actual entity without participation in the primordial nature of God. "In this sense, God can be termed the creator of each temporal entity."[11] Yet to speak of God as creator can be misleading. God is the condition that qualifies all creativity but, of course, "there is no meaning to 'creativity' apart from its 'creatures,' and no meaning to 'God' apart from the creativity and the 'temporal creatures.'"[12]

Whitehead's theism does make real sense of human freedom, and his doctrine saves God from absolute responsibility for evil in the world. Nevertheless, the question remains whether a Christian theology can acknowledge that God's providential presence in the world may prove to be inadequate against the finite forces of evil, or that God's purposes in creation may, in fact, be frustrated. Can the Christian entertain the possibility of such tragedy and loss for God—or is it quite incompatible with Christian theism? We will return to some of these questions later in the chapter.

CHARLES HARTSHORNE

Among the distinguished philosophers of the twentieth century, Charles Hartshorne is the thinker who is most influenced by Whitehead's metaphysics in the development of his own philosophy of religion. Hartshorne (1897–   ) was born in Pennsylvania of Quaker stock, although

his grandfather had become an Episcopalian and his father was a priest of the Protestant Episcopal Church. Hartshorne showed signs of unusual intellectual curiosity and brightness even as a boy. At eighteen he entered Haverford College where he came under the influence of Rufus Jones, a leading Quaker and an authority on mysticism. Hartshorne left college before completing his sophomore year to serve for two years as a hospital orderly in France during the First World War. On his return home he entered Harvard to pursue his interest in philosophy, earning the A.B. (1921), the M.A. (1922), and the Ph.D. (1923) degrees in record time. Hartshorne won traveling awards and spent 1923 through most of 1925 at the universities of Freiburg and Marburg in Germany, attending the lectures of two of the most eminent German philosophers of the period, Edmund Husserl and Martin Heidegger. He returned to Harvard as a research assistant to work on the papers of the American philosopher, C. S. Peirce, which were published in six volumes (1931–1935). He also served as a philosophy instructor and as A. N. Whitehead's assistant for a semester. Hartshorne joined the philosophy faculty at the University of Chicago in 1938 and held a joint appointment in both philosophy and in the Divinity School at Chicago between 1943 and 1955. He completed his teaching career in the philosophy departments at Emory University and the University of Texas. Among Hartshorne's most influential books in the field of philosophical theology are *Man's Vision of God and the Logic of Theism* (1941), *The Divine Relativity: A Social Conception of God* (1948), *Reality as Social Process: Studies in Metaphysics and Religion* (1953), *The Logic of Perfection and Other Essays in Neoclassical Metaphysics* (1962), *Anselm's Discovery* (1965), and *A Natural Theology for Our Time* (1967). He continued to publish books and articles on philosophy and religion well beyond age ninety.

Hartshorne devoted much of his long career as a philosopher to the formulation of a natural theology on the foundations of Whitehead's metaphysics. In this pursuit he addressed theological questions more central to Christian reflection—

e.g., Christology, ethics, and the doctrine of love. Like many theologians in the latter half of the twentieth century, Hartshorne believes that traditional Christian supernaturalism is no longer tenable, but that atheism is not the obvious alternative. For Hartshorne the alternative to classical theism is what he calls *panentheism,* a term coined by the German philosopher K. F. Krause (1781–1832), a student of Hegel's. Panentheism holds that the world is included in God's being and that God and the world are interdependent. However, the world does not exhaust God's being nor does God infringe on human freedom; therefore, God does not know the future and is, in some sense, temporal.

If God is conceived as a sentient being whose purposes are "perfect" or "unsurpassable" as the standard of all other purposes then, Hartshorne asserts, only one of the following theistic possibilities can be true:

I. There is a being in *all* respects absolutely perfect or unsurpassable, in no way and in no respect surpassable or perfectible. (Theism of the First Type; absolutism, Thomism, most European theology prior to 1880.)
II. There is no being in all respects absolutely perfect; but there is a being in *some* respect or respects thus perfect, and in some respect or respects not so, in some respects surpassable, whether by self or others being left open. Thus it is not excluded that the being may be relatively perfect in all the respects in which it is not absolutely perfect. (Theism of the Second Type; much contemporary Protestant theology, doctrines of a "finite-infinite" or perfect-perfectible God.)
III. There is no being in *any* respect absolutely perfect; all beings are in all respects surpassable by something conceivable perhaps by others or perhaps by themselves in another state. (Doctrines of a merely finite God, polytheism in some forms, atheism.)[13]

The first alternative, classical supernaturalism or God as pure act (*actus purus*), envisions a God outside of time, change, or potentiality—a God who, being in all respects absolutely perfect, is in need of nothing and who cannot be affected by anything outside of itself. Such a conception of God appears to Hartshorne manifestly incompatible with the biblical depiction of God, which characterizes God as intimately affected by his Creation. For example, Yahweh, the God of Israel, is depicted as pleased and anguished over the actions of his people, and yearns and wills the return of his disobedient children. In the New Testament God so loves the world that God is willing to give over the divine life to suffering, even unto death. How, then, can traditional theists say that nothing in time can affect God and, at the same time, say that God suffers, sympathizes, and yearns for his creatures? Or how can classical Christian theism say at one and the same time that "God does not suffer or change in any way" and that the "Jesus who suffers and changes is God"? The contradiction, Hartshorne finds, is in the joining of the God of the Judeo-Christian tradition with the God of classical Greek metaphysics. As Hartshorne suggests: "To say that Jesus was God ought to mean that God himself is with us in our suffering, that divine love is not essentially benevolence—external well-wishing—but sympathy, taking into itself our every grief."[14]

The third theistic alternative—that God is not in *any respect* entirely perfect—is not theologically credible, "for one could place no ultimate reliance upon a deity in every way subject to imperfection and alteration."[15] Neither, Hartshorne believes, is atheistic humanism rationally or religiously satisfying, because humanism places too great a trust in human valuation, which cannot stand up under the threat that ultimately human values and achievements come to nothing. Also, Hartshorne finds that while humanism may be sublimely tragic, it fails to answer our profoundest metaphysical questions that cry out for solution; for example, questions about the nature of process, the problems of origins and their conditions, the nature of nature, and so on. It is necessary to look beyond both humanism and supernaturalism to a third alternative that was given rather slight attention until recently. That alternative is *panentheism.* Hartshorne believes, however, that this new attention derives from the fact that panentheism preserves human freedom and spares God responsibility for evil. But the traditional notions of divine omnipotence and impassability must be rejected for a more basic reason than these.

It has become customary to say that we must limit divine power to save human freedom and to avoid making deity responsible for evil. But to speak of limiting a concept seems to imply that the concept, without limitation, makes sense. The notion of a cosmic power that determines all decisions fails to make sense. For its decisions could refer to nothing but themselves. They could result in no world; for a world must consist of local agents making their own decisions. Instead of saying that God's power is limited, suggesting that it is less than some conceivable power, we should rather say: his power is absolutely miximal, the greatest possible, but even the greatest possible power is still one power among others, is not the only power. God can do everything that a God can do, everything that could be done by "a being with no possible superior."[16]

According to Hartshorne's panentheism, God and the world are interdependent. The world is in God, although not coincident with God, because God exceeds the world in certain respects. Nevertheless, God is relative to what happens in the world in that God changes when the world changes. Thus God is not absolutely perfect in *every* respect but is absolutely perfect in *some* respects and *relatively* perfect in others. God's relative perfection (e.g., divine power) means that God is unsurpassable by anything but God. There is nothing illogical, Hartshorne argues, about a being who cannot be surpassed but who can grow in experience. This requires, however, that theology undertake a revision of its conception of divine perfection:

Suppose we define the perfect or supremely excellent or good, as that individual being . . . than which no *other individual* being could conceivably be greater, but which *itself*, in another "state," could become greater (perhaps by the creation within itself of new constituents). Otherwise expressed, let us define perfection as an excellence such that rivalry or superiority

on the part of other individuals is impossible . . . that "the perfect" is the self-surpassing surpasser of all.[17]

God is "self-surpassing" because the divine perfection involves a receptivity to change. But God remains supremely excellent because, while changing, the Divine is never surpassed by any other being except itself.

Hartshorne further believes that only a panentheistic doctrine can make genuine sense of the Christian understanding of God's love, because love is a social category and is meaningless apart from a real relationship of giving and receiving. This notion of divine love is exactly what the orthodox tradition has denied, for it maintains that divine perfection and aseity or necessary existence preclude God's receiving or gaining anything from the world. But love as we know it, Hartshorne argues, is a "*participation* in the good of others, so that some sort of value accrues to the self through the very fact that value accrues to another self."[18] It is this idea of God's love as including desire that is rejected by tradition theism.

They sought to maintain a distinction between love as desire, with an element of possible gain or loss to the self, and love as purely altruistic benevolence; or again between sensuous and spiritual love, *eros* and *agape*. But the distinction between lower and higher forms of love which is alone given meaning by experience—that is, which alone has meaning—is not of this character. Benevolence *is* desire for the welfare of others . . . of course it must be a superrationally enlightened, an all-comprehending, never wearying desire for others' good, that is attributed to God. But still desire, so far as that means partial dependence for extent of happiness upon the happiness of others . . . that is, a wish, *capable of being painfully disappointed or happily fulfilled.*[19]

Hartshorne contends that the older view of God's love also implies a purely egoistic human response to God. "You cannot be motivated by consideration of the value you contribute to another, if that other is so constituted that he can receive no value from any source."[20] Religion has always assumed that humans can give to God, but classical theism has denied it.

Is not the noblest aspect of religious aspiration the wish to have a cause to serve, some value to enrich by our contributions, which is more satisfying as an object of service than mere men? Men die, the race seems destined to die, taking all our contributions back into the nothingness of blind matter again. Besides we often try to help men and fail, with none perhaps ever to know of our attempt, never any to fully understand and appreciate it—none except may-hap God. But now we are told, directly or in effect, that we can do nothing for God, that he certainly will gain nothing from our actions. . . . The whole point of religion is destroyed.[21]

Hartshorne, it must be said here, gives a large place to concrete historical knowledge in religious knowing because our metaphysical knowledge of God is beyond the empirical. Moreover, as essential and true as our metaphysical knowledge is, it is not sufficient because our knowledge must always have a contingent element. "The infinite fullness of the divine life," Hartshorne insists, "is empirical, not metaphysical." For example,

that [God] has an infinitude of contingent features is metaphysical; what these features are is not. . . . Only philosophy, science, and theology drawing upon special experiences of gifted individuals and groups, can together furnish man with his greatest measure of such total knowledge.[22]

In Hartshorne's theology, we are therefore driven to concrete historical experience if we are to know something of the fullness of the divine life.

Hartshorne believes that Jesus is the matchless historical symbol of the panentheistic doctrine. In Jesus our abstract, metaphysical knowledge of God is made concrete and empirical. Hartshorne suggests that

Jesus appears to be the supreme symbol furnished to us by history of the notion of a God genuinely and literally sympathetic (incomparably more literally than any man ever is), receiving into his experience the suffering as well as the joys of the world.[23]

If Jesus is literally divine, as orthodox Christianity teaches, then the panentheist case must be acknowledged by the theologians:

I can only say that if it is Jesus as literally divine who loves men, really loves them, then my point, so far as I can see, is granted. . . . Instead of simply *adding Jesus to an unreconstructed idea of a non-loving God*, should we not take him as proof that God really is love—just that, without equivocation?[24]

Jesus's suffering and love mean not that he is like God but that he *is* God, suffering and loving, in that he points to the very reality of God. If the world can be redeemed only by a suffering of the Son of God, can we deny then that God suffers? Jesus's life also can reveal other truths about God and the world. For example, Jesus's suffering with and for humanity and it with and for him, expresses the social interrelatedness of all life. Jesus's relations with other human beings also reveals the genuine freedom of human response, in that Jesus does not coerce but seeks only to persuade. Above all, Jesus's suffering love teaches us what God's love really is, namely a sacrificial, suffering love. What is present in the Incarnation is not a separation of the two natures of Christ but their perfect union and exemplification.

Hartshorne's theology is realized in the doctrine that God's consequent life is not sheer joy and beauty but also the life of the divine "cosmic sufferer." It has profound implications for Christian ethics, although Hartshorne does not fully explore these connections. Hartshorne's ethics is based on an ontology of love in which *sympathy* as a feeling with the real feelings of the other is central. Ethics is, first, to know how the other really feels. The moral unity of the person, who is always in process, is found in the unity of the person's subjective aim. Our moral integrity is not located, then, in some absolute; rather, it lies in our taking over the decisions of the past, in which we affirm what we have been, and redirect our actions to the new future. Hartshorne's ethics is, in this sense, similar to Existentialist ethics in that ethical decision is the locus of responsibility for the future, because our decisions here and now qualify the future. We really do shape not only our own being but that of the future as well.

The interest in Process theology in the second half of the twentieth century is in very large measure due to the writings of A. N. Whitehead and especially to Charles Hartshorne, whose greatest success as a teacher was with his theological students. Among those students are three theologians whose influence as both teachers and writers has been especially significant in advancing the case for Process theology: Daniel Day Williams (1910–1973), Schubert Ogden, and John B. Cobb, Jr. Williams was both Hartshorne's student and colleague at the Divinity School of the University of Chicago. He later taught at Union Theological Seminary in New York where, for almost a score of years, he introduced Process theology to an academic environment permeated by the influence of Reinhold Niebuhr and Paul Tillich. Williams's most important work of theology is *The Spirit and Forms of Love* (1968). Schubert Ogden and John B. Cobb, Jr. stand among the half dozen most important North American theologians since the 1960s, and they both merit special attention here because of their contributions to Process theology.

SCHUBERT OGDEN

Schubert Ogden's (1928–   ) first book, *Christ Without Myth: A Study Based on the Theology of Rudolf Bultmann* (1961; reissued, 1992), marked him as one of the most gifted and penetrating minds among a rising new generation of theologians in the decades after 1960. Except for a brief mid-career appointment as University Professor of Theology at the University of Chicago, Ogden taught at the Perkins School of Theology at Southern Methodist University as University Distinguished Professor of Theology, until his retirement in 1995. A distinctive feature of his theological work is a continuing dialogue with contemporary German theology joined with a philosophical engagement with the Process meta-

Schubert Ogden

physics of Whitehead and Hartshorne. Therefore, it is not surprising that two of the most decisive sources of Ogden's theological reflection are the existential hermeneutics of Rudolf Bultmann (see Chapters Three and Five) and the Process metaphysics of Charles Hartshorne, which he has developed into a unique coalescence. This integration is evident in Ogden's characterization of the task of Christian theology as "the correlation of the Christian witness of faith and human existence . . . subject to assessment by dual criteria of appropriateness [i.e., normatively Christian] and credibility [i.e., rationally consistent and experientially compelling],"[25] although Ogden recognizes that these criteria of credibility will never meet the test of demonstrative proof.

Among Ogden's other important writings are *The Reality of God and Other Essays* (1966 reissued, 1992); *Faith and Freedom: Toward a Theology of Liberation* (1979; revised and enlarged, 1989); *The Point of Christology* (1982; reissued, 1992); *On Theology* (1986; reissued, 1992); *Is There Only One True Religion or Are There Many?* (1992); and *Doing Theology Today* (1996).

The Task of Christian Theology

Ogden insists that the question of theological meaning and the use of theological language are existential in character, and that Bultmann's solution is, in large measure, the correct one. As Ogden asserts: "To exist as a self at all is possible solely on the basis of faith so that it is true that every human being must acknowledge that the statement 'Unless you believe, you shall not understand,' is true."[26]

To exist as a human being is to exist by faith. Therefore, theological statements must, as Bultmann suggests, be treated as existential statements about our human being and the possibilities of our understanding our human existence. Ogden believes, however, that Bultmann's existentialist solution is unnecessarily one-sided. For example, Bultmann states that for the Apostle Paul "every assertion about God is simultaneously an assertion about man and vice versa," but he then proceeds to say that "Paul's theology can best be treated as his doctrine of man." And yet, as Ogden observes, "if the premise is correct—that for Paul, all statements about God are statements about man *and vise versa*—then one could just as well conclude that Paul's theology can best be represented as the doctrine of *God*."[27] Bultmann is reluctant to do this, however, because his Neo-Kantian philosophical background makes him wary of speaking of God directly and objectively; that is, of misconstruing faith as a form of intellectual cognition. So understood, faith falsifies the reality of God as a living personal God, according to Bultmann. It is to avoid such an objectification of God that Bultmann appropriated the early Heidegger's existential analysis. By so doing he was able to construct his own theological analogies that he considered well-adapted to speaking of the living, nonobjectivized God of the Bible. Ogden, however, finds this move inadequate, because Heidegger's *Being and Time* does not pretend to offer a philosophical *theology*. The result is that "Bultmann has no conceptual resource, comparable to Heidegger's analysis of man, by which God and his action can be directly

spoken of, while at the same time being in no way falsely objectified."[28]

Ogden proceeds to argue that if Bultmann wants to speak of God and God's action in history analogically, rather than mythologically, he must go beyond Heidegger's existentialist analysis and appeal "to a fully developed philosophical theology in which the meaning of 'God' is conceptually clarified in nonmythological terms."[29] This kind of philosophical or metaphysical clarification is, for Ogden, absolutely essential if faith and theology are to make a claim to be cognitively meaningful and true. "Thus," writes Ogden,

not only is it evident that Christian faith alone is an insufficient ground for theology's assertions, but it is also clear that such assertions cannot be established as even meaningful except by establishing a theist metaphysics that is true independently of a specifically Christian faith.[30]

Ogden proposes that Heidegger's existentialist analysis can best be supplemented by Hartshorne's dipolar theism, because Hartshorne's view of God and God's action provides an almost exact theistic counterpart to Heidegger's analysis of human being. By "working out a conception of the divine in strict analogy to personal existence, Hartshorne presents in its fullness what is barely more than postulated" in Bultmann's theology. Hartshorne thus offers "a precise philosophical conceptuality in which God as well as man can be appropriately spoken about in nonmythological terms."[31] Hartshorne accomplishes this by making clear, in a way that Bultmann does not, that all *theological* statements are also existential statements. For Hartshorne there is no ambiguity about the fact that when we speak of God and divine action we also are speaking of the possibilities of our self-understanding. Although the doctrine of analogy may be shown to be inadequate when applied to classical theism—because it has been shown to be logically impossible to join the personalistic view of the God revealed in the Bible with the nonpersonal God of classical Greek metaphysics—Hartshorne has proposed a frankly "anthropomorphic" concept of God, thus challenging the very premises of classical theism. Ogden points out that God must be understood in strict analogy with the human person because, as we have noted, Process metaphysics insists that God must be the chief exemplification, not the exception, to the metaphysical scheme.

When we examine the human self what we recognize is its social character, its relation to and dependence on others. So, too, must we understand the reality of God. Nevertheless,

the word "analogy" reminds us that God is not a self in univocally the same sense as man. . . . So, whereas the human self is effectively related only to a very few others . . . the divine Self is effectively related to *all* others in such a way that there are no gradations of intimacy of the various creatures to it. God is not located in a particular space and time . . . he is directly present to all spaces and times.[32]

Furthermore, while our human self is dependent both for its existence and its actual ongoing reality, for God

there is no existential dependence but only an actual dependence. *That* God is, in some actual state, or other, or in relation to some actual world, is dependent on nothing whatever. . . . The only thing that is contingent is *what* God is, what actual state of a literally infinite number of states possible for him is in fact actualized.[33]

If we are to conceive of God in strict analogy with human action and personhood, we would have to understand God, like the human self, as possessed of a distinctive character or inner intentionality and action that constitutes the divine self. What we observe about the human self is that it is always confronted by two basic possibilities of understanding the self's relation to others and to the world.

Either it can open itself to the world and make its decisions by sensitively responding to all the influences that bear upon it, or it may close itself against its world and make its decisions on the basis of a much more restricted sensitivity.[34]

The Christian faith perceives God as a self whose action is constituted by love, that is, a God who acts

by participating fully and completely in the world of his creatures, thereby laying the ground for the next stage of the creative process. Because his love, unlike ours, is pure and unbounded, his relation to his creatures and theirs to him is direct and immediate. . . . The whole world is, as it were, his sense organ, and his interaction with every creature is unimaginably immediate and direct.[35]

Ogden's dipolar theism requires that every theological assertion about God's action, for example, as Creator or Redeemer, refers not only to its existential meaning for the human self, but also to God's activity.

To say that God acts as the Creator is not merely to say that both I and my world are utterly dependent on his power and love and that I am bound to be obedient to his will as it pertains to myself and my world. That this existential meaning is the *indirect* meaning of the statement is to be readily granted. But what it *directly* says is that the ultimate ground of every actual state of the world is not just the individual decisions of the creatures who constitute its antecedent states, but rather these decisions as responded to by God's own decision of pure unbounded love.[36]

Similarly, to say that God acts as Redeemer is to say more than that I have the possibility of an openness to the world that is expressive of an authentic existence of love.

It is also to say—and that directly—that the final destiny both of myself and of all my fellow creatures is to contribute ourselves not only to the self-creation of the subsequent worlds of creatures, but also to the self-creation of God, who accepts us without condition into his everlasting life, where we have a final standing or security that can nevermore be lost.[37]

There is an analogical sense, then, whereby we can speak of God's actuality as well as human selves as a temporal and historical being, one who acts and is acted upon *in* history and so acts in a direct and not in a merely symbolic or mythological way. "God is not the timeless Absolute . . . who may be said to act only in some Pickwickean sense that bears no real analogy to anything we know as action."[38]

If we carry through our analogy between human actions and the actions of God, we can further understand how we can speak directly of God's distinctive actions in history. We understand a close friend as possessing a distinctive character; that is, the friend is "revealed" in certain, seemingly inherent and natural actions. "That is so characteristic of Richard," we say. In a similar way, Ogden suggests that analogous statements can be made of God. Insofar, then, "as an event in history manifests God's characteristic action as Creator and Redeemer, it actually *is* his act in a sense in which other historical events are not."[39] Many of the world's great religions point to particular historical occasions that are, for that community, uniquely revelatory of the sacred or the Divine. But it is also true, as Ogden claims, that these religions hold conflicting understandings of existence and, therefore, cannot all in fact be true. Nor can they all be genuine revelations or genuine acts of God. The Christian community witnesses to its belief by saying

that Jesus is the decisive act of God . . . that in him, in his outer acts of symbolic word and deed, there is expressed *that* understanding of human existence which is, in fact, the ultimate truth about our life before God; that the ultimate reality with which we and all men have to do is God the sovereign Creator and Redeemer, and that in understanding ourselves in terms of the gift and demands of his love, we realize our authentic existence as men.[40]

Ogden's Later Reflections on Analogy, the Normative Christian Witness, and a Christology of Liberation

Ogden acknowledges that by the early 1970s his theological work embodied several important developments. First, through his encounter with the work of political and liberation theologians, he came to recognize that his notion of credibility was one-sidedly theoretical and metaphysical. "I now saw," he writes,

that, because the self-understanding of faith has moral implications for action and justice no less surely than it has metaphysical implications for belief and truth, the credibility for which Christian witness must always be tested is not only its theoretical, but also—and, in some respects, more urgently—its *practical* credibility.[41]

We will see how this turn to *practice* is worked out in Ogden's christological reflections on liberation. A second development concerns the criteria of appropriateness or the normatively Christian witness. Ogden no longer finds the Protestant or the Catholic appeal to the apostolic witness—whether to Scripture or Scripture and tradition—credible due to the findings of historical research regarding questions of apostolicity and canonicity. Neither does Ogden believe that the "quest of the historical Jesus" as presently carried out is either possible or theologically sound. The true normative witness is the pre-canon witness of the apostles regarding Jesus as God's decisive act. Ogden writes:

I remain confident that the only witness that can be rightly taken as formally apostolic and therefore normative for all other Christian witness is neither the canon of the New Testament nor some canon *within* the canon such as "the kerygma," but rather the canon *before* the canon was constituted by the earliest Christian witness recoverable today by the historical-critical methods now available.[42]

A third important change in Ogden's theology has to do with his rejection of all forms of metaphysical analogy, which entails his principal criticism of Hartshorne's metaphysics. We turn first to this issue, and then to Ogden's christological reflections and his discussion of the normative Christian witness, freedom and liberation and the responsibility of Christian witness.

It is Christianity's claim that in the liberating love of Jesus is found the decisive representation of God's reality. Such a claim implies, however, certain metaphysical assertions, namely, that the ultimate reality called "God" is the strictly universal individual whose boundless love for all things is their primal source as well as their only end.[43] The question remains, of course, how can the Christian justify the claim that ultimate reality or God is boundless love? Is this not, too, a mythological assertion that requires demythologization if it is to remain credible?

As we have seen, the crucial problem with Bultmann's execution of his hermeneutical task is, as Ogden sees it, that Bultmann stops short of a thoroughgoing existentialist interpretation of theological statements when he deals with the subject of Christology. Bultmann claims, for example, that authentic human existence is *factually* possible only in the unique action of God in Jesus Christ. Ogden insists, on the contrary, that Bultmann's interpretation of the New Testament's statements about Christ's redemptive action must also be demythologized and interpreted existentially. However, for Ogden this implies that

the claim "only in Jesus Christ" must be interpreted to mean, not that God acts to redeem only in the history of Jesus and in no other history but that the only God who redeems any history—*although he in fact redeems every history*—is the God whose redemptive action is decisively represented in the word that Jesus speaks and is.[44]

The danger implicit in Bultmann's form of existentialist analysis is not only that it fails to carry through consistently its work of demythologization. More importantly, it reduces the claim about God's action in history simply to the authorizing of our own authentic self-understanding. "It ceases to be a claim about God at all."[45] Hartshorne, on the other hand, explicitly insists that real cognitive assertions about God are implied by the Christian community's christological statements. Thus for Hartshorne the claim

that God is boundless love can be established by a natural theology that employs a proper metaphysical analogy; that is, that "the very nature of ultimate reality . . . can be thought and spoken about in the terms and categories of our ordinary experience."[46]

It is here that Ogden has come to disagree with Hartshorne. Ogden long had followed Hartshorne's commitment to just such a metaphysical use of analogy in speaking about our knowledge of God. However, in his later reflections, developed in *The Point of Christology* (1982), he confesses skepticism about the possibility of generalizing the meanings of our ordinary language so that they may serve as proper metaphysical analogies. Ogden now acknowledges that "unless God is already known, prior to the application of any word, there is no way of establishing that a word like 'love' can be applied to God as a proper analogy as distinct from being a mere symbol."[47] Even the most profound metaphors and symbols about God are no more than just that and, Ogden admits, cannot serve as analogies in the proper sense of giving us *immediate* knowledge of God.

Following the lead offered by Paul Tillich's philosophical theism, Ogden forgoes the use of metaphysical analogy and allows for only two kinds of religious discourse: literal and symbolic. Literal terms

function primarily indicatively to denote the structure of reality itself, and hence to identify what is properly named "God" and to distinguish it from everything else. On the other hand, there are plainly symbolic terms whose meanings in religious discourse are different from the meanings they have in other fields of discourse from which they are borrowed; they function primarily imperatively, to express the meaning of reality for us, and hence to call for the kind of self-understanding and moral action that are authorized by the ultimate reality called "God."[48]

As we have learned from the discussion of Tillich in Chapter Five, Tillich asserts that the only literal statement that can be applied to ultimate reality is the statement that God is "being-itself" although, as Ogden suggests, Tillich often appears to straddle the fence between classical theology's stress on God's Being as absolute and unchanging and an ontology that recognizes in God's actuality the fact of becoming. In any case, Ogden believes that Tillich is correct when he says that a tenable theology entails a literal or transcendental metaphysical statement about ultimate reality. Ogden also believes, however, that it allows for an alternative "kind of transcendental metaphysics—specifically, a neoclassical kind, according to which God is literally becoming as well as being . . . in a word, the genuinely dipolar God."[49]

Ogden thus proposes that it is possible to follow Hartshorne's *panentheism*, and his concept of God as boundless love, without recourse to Hartshorne's questionable doctrine of analogy. But this requires that when speaking, e.g., of the "love of God," such speaking "is not the properly metaphysical function of denoting the structure of ultimate reality in itself." For Ogden, its function is, rather,

the properly religious . . . function of so expressing the meaning of ultimate reality for us as to authorize the kind of existence and action on our part that are appropriate to it. Specifically, the claim that God as ultimate reality is boundless love means primarily that we ourselves are free to exist and act in love in relation to our fellow creatures.[50]

This would appear to be what Bultmann is saying, and Ogden acknowledges that such a move does recognize the important truth in all noncognitivist theories of religious language, namely, that theistic discourse, though not wholly reducible to the noncognitive, symbolic level of linguistic usage, does to a considerable degree function at that level. That said, however, even a *symbolic* metaphysical claim, Ogden insists, "must imply certain assertions about the structure of ultimate reality in itself."[51]

In terms of Hartshorne's and Ogden's dipolar theism, this means that "to assert truly, albeit symbolically, that God is boundless love necessarily implies not only that ultimate reality is individual as well as universal but also that this ultimate reality is acted on by all things just as surely as it acts on them."[52] Ogden further argues that unlike classical metaphysics, "a neoclassical metaphysics can literally assert *all* the conditions that are necessarily implied by the symbolic assertion that God is boundless love."[53] These are manifest in the liberating love of Jesus Christ, who is the decisive representation of God.

Ogden readily acknowledges that a Christology of liberation (i.e., "the freedom we have in Jesus Christ," Gal. 2:4), which he now proposes, will not be credible to anyone who rejects all metaphysical claims, but he believes that it is more credible than a Christology grounded in a classical metaphysics and theology because it offers a convincing representation of divine love. Furthermore, Ogden rejects those many contemporary proposals that call for a Christology that dispenses with metaphysics entirely. For Ogden, Jesus Christ as Liberator *entails* the metaphysical claim that the ground of the freedom that Jesus Christ represents is, in fact, the boundless love of God. This is the case because it is only God who can give human beings the victory through Jesus Christ. It is, Ogden concludes, precisely because of the Christian witness that it is God in Jesus Christ who redeems and liberates that he insists "on the need for a transcendental metaphysics in order to confirm the truth of a christology of liberation."[54]

Although Ogden gives considerable attention to the metaphysical foundations of a dipolar theism and christology, he makes it clear in his most recent reflections on Christology that both the exigencies of our present context and his own central concern are not to offer another revisionary formulation of the person and work of Christ. Rather, Ogden's inquiry is focused on the *point* of all the efforts at christological formulation, especially those related to our situation today. The point of Christology, Ogden contends, is its *existential* point. The reason being that the question that "christology answers is not simply a question about Jesus, but also, and at the same time, a question about the meaning of ultimate reality for us."[55] What is crucial is *what Christology asserts about who we are called to be* by the ultimate reality that determines our existence. Because for Christians the answer to this question is decisively represented through Jesus, it is crucial to determine who Jesus is. This latter task would initially appear to engage Ogden in either the old "quest of the historical Jesus," which was discredited by scholars such as Martin Kähler and Albert Schweitzer (see Chapter One), or in the "new quest," represented more recently by a number of revisionary Christologies, including efforts by students of Rudolf Bultmann such as the New Testament scholar Ernst Käsemann. The "new questers" continue to assert that it is possible to get behind the earliest kerygmatic witness to who Jesus is; that is, to the actual empirical-historical Jesus who can be found in the earliest layer of Jesus traditions.

In one of the most compelling treatments of the entire "quest of the historical Jesus," Ogden rejects the fundamental premise of both the older and the more recent efforts to reconstruct the real empirical-historical Jesus. Ogden asserts

that a quest for Jesus is and would be theologically unnecessary, regardless of any question whether it is also historically possible. This is so . . . because the real subject of the christological assertion is not the historical Jesus, or . . . the *empirical*-historical Jesus, for which the earliest stratum of Christian witness must be used as historical source. Rather, the subject of the christological assertion is correctly identified formally as the *existential*-historical Jesus, for which this same earliest stratum of Christian witness plays the very different role of theological norm.[56]

For Ogden, the question of what the New Testament sources can or cannot tell us about the empirical-historical Jesus is of no theological significance. The earliest stratum of traditions about Jesus are themselves witnesses of faith. Thus the only Jesus that Christians know certainly is Jesus as the Christ of the earliest apostolic witness, and of those later witnesses who conform to it. "We have to allow," Ogden contends,

for the possibility that even what clearly seem to be assumptions about Jesus as he actually was are really assertions about Jesus as he truly is—which is to say, as he is *believed to be* by those who by means of such assertions intend to bear witness to him as the decisive representation of God.[57]

Put another way, all the assertions and claims made about Jesus are not

what *Jesus* had said and done, but rather about what *God* had said and done and was still saying and doing precisely through Jesus. . . . They were all assertions about Jesus as the decisive representation of God . . . as the one through whom the meaning of ultimate reality and the authentic understanding of our own existence are made fully explicit.[58]

The real search is, then, not for the historical Jesus but for the earliest Christian witness of Jesus's significance, a witness that, theologically, is the norm of all christological formulations.

It is crucial, however, that several points be clear regarding Ogden's meaning and intentions here. First, he is not abandoning or underestimating the historical quest; rather, he is seeking to clarify what he considers that quest's only possible and only theologically consequential object. Second, Ogden's Christology is intrinsically *theocentric* in that it attends to what God has done and is doing in and through Jesus, to Jesus's *representation* of the being and meaning of ultimate reality. Third, for Ogden the desideratum of a Christology is its *existential* point, that is, Jesus Christ in his meaning for human beings then and now. This last theme leads us to Ogden's distinctive Christology of *liberation*.

The modern age is, perhaps, marked by no other feature as pronounced as its quest for freedom. It is *the* question that is the linchpin of most other important human questions. Ogden not only regards freedom, in all of its expressions, as *the* contemporary human concern, but also asserts that it is in terms of freedom that a credible Christology today must speak if it is to address the existential questions that are implicit in this theme.

This is not, Ogden clarifies, to confuse the freedom that is given in Christ with secular political freedom, nor, he insists, is it necessary to separate freedom in Christ from responsibility for freedom and equality in the sphere of politics, a position that Ogden finds expressed in some of the writings of Wolfhart Pannenberg. The freedom that the person has in Christ is different from all forms of secular freedom, and yet, Ogden insists, the two kinds of freedom are also inseparable insofar as the moral implications of the freedom that is in Christ includes political responsibility in its widest reaches. It is, therefore, necessary ever to be reminded that "before Christ can be rightly taken as the true model for our own liberating love, he must first be taken as the real presence of the liberating love of God."[59] Nonetheless, "because God's love knows no bounds and excludes nothing from its embrace, there is no creature's good and no creaturely need that is not also a divine need."[60]

Because the two kinds of freedom are as inseparable as they are distinct, Ogden proposes that a credible existentialist interpretation of Christology must include moral responsibility for the political sphere, for it follows necessarily from "the real presence of the liberating love of God." Furthermore, a credible Christology will not sanction what Ogden calls "deideologizing." By this he means "interpreting the meaning of the christological witness so as to disengage it from the economic, social, political, and cultural world"[61]—a disengagement that proves, in fact, to be a sanction for bondage, injustice, and oppression. In the postmodern context, both the practical and the theoretical credibility of a Christology hinge on the genuine link between the liberating love of God and Christian solidarity with those who suffer from want of freedom and justice. Ogden thus concludes his christological inquiry with these words:

So far from in any way sanctioning the want and oppression of the existing order, the assertion that Jesus is the Liberator is by strict implication the demand to do justice—above all, the kind of structural justice that can only be done politically . . . . To do anything less than this is to leave room for the question whether the freedom we have in Christ is not ideological, after all, whatever the conclusion of our christology of reflection.[62]

It is interesting to note how Ogden's essay exemplifies the modern "theologies of correlation." It not only sounds an authentic note of the New Testament imperative ("Why do you call me 'Lord, Lord,' and not do what I tell you?" Luke 6:46), but also reflects the turn to the theme of "praxis" that so dominates the work of many Christian theologians in the decades since the 1960s. We will see a similar turn to application or concrete ethical praxis in the later writings of John B. Cobb, Jr., our final representative of contemporary Process theology.

JOHN B. COBB, JR.

Any account of North American theology in the latter decades of the twentieth century will attend to the influential writings of John B. Cobb, Jr. Akin to the theological work of Schubert Ogden, David Tracy, and Langdon Gilkey, Cobb exemplifies contemporary "theologies of correlation" in that his work is an effort to reconceive Christian theology through an explicit engagement with modern philosophy and the natural and social sciences. Cobb's theology is also similar to Ogden's in that both have sought to carry out their reconception of Christian theology and worldview by a direct appeal to the doctrines of modern Process philosophy, particularly the doctrines of Alfred North Whitehead and Charles Hartshorne. It can be said that Cobb's use of Process philosophy has been both more constitutive of his work and more consistently applied in his writings on an extraordinary range of themes than has been the case with other theologians of comparable influence since the 1960s.

John B. Cobb, Jr. (1925–) was born in Kobe, Japan, where he lived with his missionary parents until 1940. At fifteen he returned to his family roots in Georgia where he finished high school and began college. In 1944 he joined the U.S. Army and, because of his linguistic facility, served in the Japanese language program. This period proved intellectually stimulating and widened his horizons beyond the Protestant pietism of his youth. Upon leaving the Army, Cobb entered the University of Chicago. Later he attended the Divinity School at Chicago where he was drawn to the teaching of Charles Hartshorne, who introduced him to the thought of A. N. Whitehead. It was through Hartshorne's teaching that Cobb was later to say that he "was once again able to take the idea of God seriously."[63]

Cobb's doctoral dissertation explored the question of the possible independence of Christian faith from speculative belief—an exercise that convinced him of the impossibility of a thorough independence. Related issues dealing with faith and philosophy remained at the center of Cobb's work for years. His reconception of Christian faith did, however, undergo changes after the mid-1960s. He was able to speak later of his work before 1965 as dominated by a "Whiteheadian scholasticism." Although the Process categorial scheme that he derived from Whitehead remained foundational in Cobb's later writings, his use of Whitehead's technical language is increasingly moderated, and his own voice becomes more pronounced. Furthermore, his writings, like those of Schubert Ogden, reflect a conscious effort to move from earlier, more abstract analyses of theology to a broader consideration of theology's meaning with regard to the responsibility of Christian witness in specific contemporary contexts; for example, in matters such as ecology, politics, economics, race, and gender. In the late 1960s it was his engagement with the ecological crisis that proved to be a crucial turning point in his career. Much of his writing since the early 1970s has been concerned with the environment and with related issues of political economy. Some of these books, for example, *The Liberation of Life* (1981) and *For the Common Good* (1989), were written in collaboration with both a professional scientist and an economist.

After a five-year stint of teaching at Emory University, Cobb joined the faculty of the newly established School of Theology at Claremont (California). There he remained for over three decades, serving as Ingraham professor of theology and director of the Center for Process Studies, established in 1973 in partnership with his colleague David Ray Griffin. In 1971, Cobb and Lewis Ford, another distinguished Process philosopher, founded *Process Studies*, a journal devoted to the exploration of Process philosophy in all of its ramifications.

The God Who Calls and Human Possibility

The discussion of Cobb's doctrine of God will not go over the Process of metaphysical scheme because we have outlined in some detail Whitehead's metaphysics and theism on which Cobb acknowledges his considerable dependence and concurrence. Cobb's theistic reflections center on the theme of God as the source of all creative novelty, which shows as well the influence of Henry Nelson Wieman (see Chapter Two) on his work. Cobb refers to God as the *source of creative transformation*. In his book *God and the World* (1969) and in later works, Cobb also gives greater attention to God's "consequent nature"; that is, to God's effects on the world and the effects of the world on God. This demands that Cobb give substantial attention to how one might give a credible account of God's "place" in the divine action on the world when the notions of God "up there" or "out there" are no longer plausible. If light can be shed on this question, then some persuasive meaning might be given to how God "acts" in both nature and human history.

The first issue that Cobb addresses is what kind of reality God is if we can neither conceive of God as a physical object among other physical objects nor allow ourselves to be trapped in a dualism that views the physical and the mental as completely different realities. Both of these notions have, of course, been widely discredited.

Contemporary physics and Process philosophy, for example, both offer telling criticisms of older conceptions of the physical. For example, science has shown

the apparently solid, inert objects which give rise to our naive notion of the physical turn out to be composed exhaustively of subatomic entities whose nature is to act and react. . . . The electron can only be understood as a *succession of events*. . . . The building blocks of the universe, the things of which everything else is composed, are energy-events.[64]

If the physical must be understood in terms of "energy-events," the question of its relation to thought must then be revised. Because thought is not a physical reality in the older sense of the word, it is now possible for thought to be understood as an energy event. "My act of thinking receives energy from past occurrences in my body and transmits that energy, appropriately modified, to subsequent events." Thus mind cannot simply to reduced to matter nor regarded only as a by-product of matter. "Thinking has its own unity and creativity. But it need not be regarded as belonging to a completely different order of being."[65] Cobb suggests that if we can think of the notion of energy event as applicable to both unconscious electronic events *and* human thinking we can overcome the older Cartesian dualism, but also think of God in terms of this new conceptuality—God as a special kind of energy event. We naturally think of an electronic energy event solely from the outside. When we think of an energy event in human conscious experience, we think of it from the inside. But Cobb suggests that it is quite proper to think of an electronic energy event as subjective.

We can conceive of it as it impinges upon its successor in the chain of energy-events which we call the electron. But how can we think of that unless we can conceive of the successor in its act of receiving? And if we do that, then we are thinking of the successor as a subject receiving the other event as its object.[66]

Moreover, we can overcome the problematic dualism of subjects and objects "if we recognize that every individual event or entity is, in its moment of immediacy, a subject, usually an unconscious one, which then passes into objectivity in the sense of becoming a datum for new subjects."[67]

Cobb proposes that we use our own experience as the closest analogue for thinking about the reality of God. One can, of course, immediately respond that our subjective experience is dependent on our senses of sight, sound, and so on, and that we cannot expect to believe that God experiences in that same way. Cobb's reply is crucial, because it has to do with a primary claim of Process philosophy, namely, that "human experience is not fundamentally sensory . . . [since] the fundamental data of the human mind or subject are not physical objects outside the body, but energy-events within the body."[68] By this Cobb means that although our experience of the external world is overwhelmingly sensory, the priority of the nonsensory is inferred in human experience. Take our memory of the past and our anticipation of the future. No one seriously is willing to doubt these realities, but sense experience gives no evidence of either. Granted, the experience of the past is sensory-like, but "neither memory nor anticipation is a sensory relation." Certain past visual qualities may be present in memory, but if one "regards them as stemming from a past experience, then he is introducing an element into their interpretation that cannot derive from present sensory experience."[69]

Cobb regards human memory as the best analogy for thinking about God. While past experience appears in present consciousness as if it were reoccurring, what in fact is happening is that "there is immediate experience of one occasion by another occasion which is grasped in a non-sensory way." Although our experience is predominantly sensory, and "we do not think of God as having eyes, there is no reason to deny him the power to enjoy our visual experiences with us."[70]

If we grant that such a conscious, divine energy event—one capable of sharing in both human and subhuman experiences—is reasonable, then, Cobb acknowledges, a second crucial question remains: *Where* can this energy event be? Neither transcendent imagery of God "up there" or immanental imagery of God "in there" are of use, because both either assert or imply spatial relations. One might say that God is nowhere; that is, deny that God can be understood as having a place alongside other places. Or, Cobb points out, because space implies the extension of physical bodies, one can say God is Spirit, meaning that God transcends our categories of space and time, because these categories derive from our sensory experience of the physical world. Although Cobb sees no religious objection to speaking of God as nonspatial, he prefers to say that "God is everywhere." This agrees with the intention of insisting that God is no more at one place than another. But Cobb points out that modern science no longer conceives of spacetime as a fixed, preexistent receptacle; it speaks, rather, of energy events that "have patterns of relations with each other that can only be described as extensive."[71] Those who assert that God is nowhere and those who assert that God is everywhere want, rightly, to deny that God is bound to any limited standpoint within spacetime. But the theological differences implied by these assertions are crucial. Those who say God is nowhere are asserting that God differs from all other energy events. Those who say God is everywhere hold "that God's impartiality toward all is a function of his omni-spatial or all-inclusive viewpoint."[72] The objection to this latter position is that it "goes against the widely held view that two entities cannot occupy the same space at the same time."[73] But this objection applies only at the level of physical objects, and the problem with it, as Cobb points out, is that "if we think of God as related to us in this way, then either God is everything and we are simply parts and pieces, or else we are everything and 'God' is simply another name for the sum total of all the parts. In neither case have we a model by which we can think of both man and God."[74]

Cobb suggests that if the entities about which we are concerned—human beings and God—are thought of as subjects, we can experience both our own subjective spatiotemporal standpoint and also our experience extending out beyond the self's present space, incorporating past occasions and synthesizing them without excluding the genuine subjectivity and aim of these other entities that are also data for our own self's inheritance. "Thus the events occupying the inclusive space and those occupying the included space act upon each other in complex ways, but they have also their distinct individuality and autonomy. They are independent as well as interdependent."[75] And in a similar manner we can think of God's spatial relationship to the world:

> God's standpoint is all-inclusive, and so, in a sense we are parts of God. But we are not parts of God in the sense that God is simply the sum total of the parts or that the parts are lacking in independence and self-determination. God and the creatures interact as separate entities, while God includes the standpoints of all of them in his omnispatial viewpoint. In this sense God is everywhere, but he is not everything. The world does not exist outside God or apart from God, but the world is not God or simply part of God. The character of the world is influenced by God, but it is not determined by him, and the world in turn contributes novelty and richness to the divine experience.[76]

Such a *panentheist* conception of God's relation to the world allows for the independence and integrity of both God and finite creatures *and* also affirms that God is fully present in the world. God is not a Creator outside the world who acts upon the world, either continuously or occasionally, but is not in any requisite way affected by the world.

If the divine creativity is everywhere and yet is, in some respects, independent of the world and at the same time enriched by it, how is God related to those occasions or energy events called human experience? Cobb answers by describing how God, or the One Who Calls us, acts so as to provide each person with possibilities for ever-new creative transformations. Consistent with Whitehead's scheme, each occasion of human experience begins with a given past of experiences that affect the present, but they do not determine how the individual will prehend or use these past experiences. Cobb uses the example of a past moment of anger directed at a friend. In the present moment that anger is part of the given situation. In fact, there is a strong inclination to reenact that anger in a present encounter with this friend—but it is not inevitable. One suddenly may become ashamed of the past anger, which can alter its present and future hold. And so, as Cobb points out, what one does with the anger is, in part, determined by the purpose that he or she entertains. The aim to repay a past grievance may be so dominant as to preclude any response but one of revenge. But other aims or purposes may intervene, in which case the anger may be controlled or displaced.

According to Cobb's Whiteheadian metaphysical scheme, in each new human occasion the concrescence, or unification of feelings that issues in new, novel actions, derives not only from past experiences and from present events in the brain, but also from God's primordial offer of particular potentialities for the new occasion. Cobb describes God's action as follows:

He entertains a purpose for the new occasion, differing from that entertained by the previous human experience. He seeks to lure the new occasions beyond the mere repetition of past purposes and past feelings or new combinations among them. God is thus once the source of novelty and the lure to finer and richer actualizations embodying that novelty. Thus God is the One Who Calls us beyond all that we have become to what we might be.[77]

Now God's offer of new creative possibilities may be rejected—the weight of past experience may be too much. Furthermore, God's action is one of *persuasion* not coercion, for God does not overrule our finite freedom. We do, however, observe individuals of special sensitivity and openness whose lives are directed toward new, creative forms of relatedness, the kind of life to which each one of us is called. The exemplary image of that life is distinctively represented in Jesus Christ.

We will recall that Whitehead's doctrine speaks not only of God's primordial nature, that which orders all human possibilities, but also of God's consequent nature, or God's feeling or prehension of the world—the world's effect on God. Similarly, Cobb affirms that God takes in the whole richness of the world's life, including its miseries and losses, and transmutes them so as to redeem all that can be redeemed. Herein lies the believer's confidence and hope—and the profound sense that everything that we do matters and is used by God. Here is how Cobb describes it:

Regardless of how ephemeral the joys and sorrows of life . . . they are not trivial or insignificant. Even if man destroys his planet in the near future, our efforts now to preserve it are not worthless. Because what we are and do matters to God, our lives are meaningful even when we recognize that in the course of history our accomplishments may soon be swept away. . . . What happens *really* matters only if it matters everlastingly. What happens can matter everlastingly only if it matters to him who is everlasting. Hence, seriousness about life implicitly involves faith in God.[78]

Cobb's panentheism does offer an eschatological hope, but not one that is based on an optimistic faith in inevitable progress, or one that relies on an image of God as a kind of *Deus ex machina*, a God who, irrespective of human responsibility, will inevitably intervene in the last act of the human drama to insure a happy outcome. What human beings most desire, Cobb believes, is a confidence that meaning can be affirmed. Because what we do matters to and endures in God, we can find life meaningful; more than that, we can achieve an egoless peace that passes understanding, even if our own human efforts and accomplishments are defeated and destroyed. We can trust that our own particular efforts and values contribute to and are perpetuated in the larger divine scheme of things. This is what Process theology calls *objective immortality*.

Christ and Creative Transformation

We have noted that the concept of "creative transformation" is central to Cobb's theology and one that he derives, in large part, from both Whitehead and Wieman. As a Christian theologian, Cobb has sought increasingly to make creative transformation constituitive of his thinking about Christology. He confesses that in his early work his Christology was little more than a "Jesusology" in that he was concerned to explain both how God could be said to be incarnate in Jesus and the efficacy or work of Jesus in the world. He resisted using the word "Christ" because he felt that it unnecessarily "confused the Jesus in whom God was distinctly present with God himself."[79] In *Christ in a Pluralistic Age* (1975), Cobb's reflections on Christology reveal a significant development. He now speaks of Christ as the divine Logos. He does so both in relation to the primordial nature of God present as the source of the initial aim by which each subject decides how it will constitute itself, and God as incarnate, as creative transformation in the world.

To speak of Christ as Logos requires, however, that Christian theology understand that the word "Christ" refers to a universal reality, and that reflection on the Logos brings out this characteristic of Christ as creative transformation. If, in fact, Christ as incarnate Logos is creative transformation, then a Christian theology cannot "be satisfied to find Christ only or primarily in its own history . . . it must be discernible in all life."[80] Christ as creative transformation is to be found, then, not only in the "religious" sphere or in the Church but in science, philosophy, art, and social organizations—whenever creative transformation is present. While Christ remains present in those in the Church who may too restrictively confuse Christ's work with that of the Church,

nevertheless, his presence there is diminished. For, as Cobb asserts, "Christ can be most fully present and effective where people believe in creative transformation, understand it rightly, trust it, and open themselves to it."[81] Yet Cobb portrays the work of "Christ" as the incarnate Logos in authentic biblical-prophetic terms. "Indeed," he writes,

the logos is threatening to any given world, for it functions to transcend and transform. That means that the given, familiar forms are subordinate to new ones, that established habits of mind are undercut, that revered teaching is relativized. . . . In short, the function of the Logos is to introduce tension between what has been and what might be . . . to challenge and upset the established order for the sake of the new.[82]

It is essential, Cobb adds, that to name the Logos "Christ" is "also to recognize the cosmic Logos as love." And to affirm this is neither obvious nor easy, for what it entails is a giving up of our own desires and the security we find in our own ways and achievements. Love is first experienced as judgment. Furthermore, creative transformation is not a mere sentiment or emotion. "It is," Cobb maintains, "a way in which the process of becoming is formed and structured."[83]

For Christians the meaning of the Logos as love is incarnated in Jesus because Jesus brought into history a distinctive structure of human existence. It is characterized by an openness and a love of one's neighbors and their need, and a self-transcendence that expresses itself in sensitivity to what is unloving, foreign, and threatening. Cobb sees in Jesus's structure of existence a life that is "peculiarly open to repeated creative transformation," to the entertaining of new possibilities and more inclusive perspectives. In terms of Jesus's work, his creative transformations, present both in his teachings and actions, become for others uniquely revelatory of creative and responsive love. As one recognizes in Jesus the revelation of the truth about reality itself, one becomes more open to being creatively transformed.

Cobb appropriates Whitehead's understanding of the coming-to-be of a structure of existence as a way to envision, in modern terms, the "work" or efficacy of Jesus as the Incarnation of the divine Logos. Refering to St. Paul's use of the image of living or "being in Christ," Cobb introduces the concept of a "field of force" to explain how a past event can exercize a powerful efficacy or influence on future events. Jesus is an entity of the past whose affect on the future is not, like billions of others, simply negligible. "Its repeated reenactment and remembrance has strengthened its field of force."[84] Through memory and attention we participate in Jesus's "field of force."

> To be a field of force is to conform in some measure with the event that generates the field. Thus to be in Paul's sense "in Christ" is to conform in some measure to Jesus. Since Jesus was himself open to creative transformation, to conform to him is to share in that openness. . . . By reversing our self-evaluation he opens us to creative transformation.[85]

Jesus's teachings and deeds are constituted as much by the divine action within him as they are by his own personal past. To employ Schleiermacher's language, which is similar to Cobb's, Jesus never claimed to be the sole mediator of God, yet the Christian's "God-consciousness" and redemption come to realization through the person of Jesus as the Christ. Cobb describes the unique relation of Jesus's words and deeds, his "work," to his "person" in the following way:

> We may think of Jesus' structure of existence in terms of an "I" that is co-constituted by its inheritance from its personal past and by the initial aims derived from God. There is not the normal tension between the initial aims and purposes received from God. There is not the normal tension between the initial aims and purposes received from the past, in that those purposes were themselves conformed to divine aims and thereby involved the basic disposition to be open to God's call in each future moment. Whereas Christ [as the creative-transforming Logos] is incarnate in everyone, Jesus *is* Christ because the incarnation is constituitive of his very selfhood.[86]

The work of Christ in the world is present wherever creative transformation is operative. Yet, as Cobb points out, the powerful efficacy of Christ is especially facilitated where Christ is rightly named; that is, in the community, the Church, which lives consciously in the power of the field of force initiated by Jesus.

> Millions of persons have made decisions to be constituted by the event of Jesus in such a way that its potential for constituting others is increased. . . . Thus the church is the community that is consciously dedicated to maintaining, extending, and strengthening the field of force generated by Jesus.[87]

Theology and "Praxis": Ecological Theology as Example

Earlier it was pointed out that the most decisive turn in John Cobb's theological work occurred in 1969 when he realized he no longer could separate his theological reflections from his deeping involvement in politics and public affairs. And it was the ecological crisis that first made Cobb aware that theology could not be done in isolation from its ethical application, and that effective application was possible only by transforming the sociopolitical context. Indeed, Cobb has come to insist that authentic theory or theology can only be done in deep reflection on and engagement in the social-political context and by transforming it by action. Between 1970 and 1995 Cobb wrote or co-authored six books and well over a score of articles and contributions to books and symposia on very specific issues of public policy. Running like a thread through all of these writings is, however, the issue of ecology. This topic is, of course, a natural expression of Cobb's Whiteheadian concern for nature. In concluding our discussion of Cobb's theology, it is appropriate, then, to focus on what he calls an "ecological theology."

Unlike the theological tradition that derives its framework from Kant's critical Idealism and, therefore, focuses attention on the human world almost exclusively, Cobb's Whiteheadian perspective sees human life as inextricably interconnected with nature and finds intrinsic value in all forms of subhuman natural life. Theologies oriented toward human history and the human self have tended to suppress or ignore the immense time scale of our cosmos when envisioned in terms of billions of years, or the fact that our planet is but a grain of sand in one of a host of galaxies. Process theology, on the contrary, is profoundly conscious of the brief time scale of human life on this planet and the implications of this fact for reflection on God and nature. As Cobb explains:

Process theology intends to think through the meaning for our existence and actions of the space-time scales that scientific cosmology suggests. It affirms there was real value and enjoyment in the aeons of time before high forms of life appeared anywhere in the universe, but that the level and importance of enjoyment increased greatly when on this planet animals and finally humans emerged. . . . It sees that species have risen and perished before and that a similar fate may befall the human species. . . . [And] this would mean the loss of something of peculiar value that is probably unique in the entire universe. Furthermore, there is a danger that, unlike any other species, human beings may involve all high forms of life on this planet in their destruction.[88]

Such a vision of the threat to all of life on this planet should, one would think, elicit alarm and a sense of urgency. Instead, Cobb sees our communities adopting short-term goals in agriculture, resource management, and economic development, policies that are mere palliatives and, in the long run, strategies that will cause greater destruction of our environment. An example is recent so-called "development" programs in some Third World countries that have brought about rapid industrialization, deforestation, the long-term depletion of arable land through large-scale agricultural programs, and the disruption of complex ecosystems that already seriously threaten a sustainable, livable environment. Cobb points out that economic development in the West has

come to be seen as inherently good, and its long-term effect on the destabilization and possible eradication of large segments of the nonhuman world is not seriously considered. Furthermore, we fail to see that as other species are becoming extinct more rapidly with the disruption of the environment, our own civilization, indeed, the human species itself, may face extinction.

Cobb speaks of this narrow horizon of reflection on the human condition as a narcissistic "anthropomorphism." It is a human conceit that fails to appreciate our interconnectedness with and essential concern for the welfare of the nonhuman world. An ecological theology, on the contrary

will not limit its concern for the environment to its role in sustaining human societies. From the point of view of process theologians, justice requires that the rest of the creation should also be treated with respect and be recognized to have reality and value quite apart from usefulness to human beings. Other creatures are of value in themselves and for God.[89]

It is, as we have learned, a critical doctrine of Process theology that all entities, including God, share an interconnected existence with all other entities. There are, of course, differences among entities, in terms of their purpose or subjective aim and the quality and complexity of their feeling. And Cobb, unlike some "deep ecologists," does assert that "human beings do have unique value and worth that is probably not equalled by any other species on this planet."[90] Nevertheless, these differences in gradations of intrinsic value, do not warrant our anthropocentric, exploitive view of the nonhuman world as merely instrumental to our own needs and desires. Each actual occasion in our ecosystem, no matter how seemingly trivial, is made possible by its interconnectedness with other antecedent occasions. This is equally true of more complex entities such as porpoises or human beings. Cobb believes that this sense of participation in one another, in a rich complex of interconnected occasions and communities, is a prereflexive intuition that we humans all share. "No man is an island," the poet John Donne reminds us. And Cobb is dedicated to raising this "prethematized consciousness to full conceptual clarity" with the help of Whitehead's organismic philosophy so that our "awareness of participation in one another will be heightened so that it will again shape our deepest sensitivities and responses to one another," to the point that we will recognize that "we are diminished not only by the misery of the Indian peasant but also by the slaughter of whales and porpoises."[91]

John Cobb's deep conviction about an "ecological model" for doing theology has issued naturally in his practical engagement in concrete scientific, political, economic, and environmental issues over a period of twenty-five years. The range of his interests and explorations is quite remarkable and perhaps unparalleled among Christian theologians working in the latter decades of the twentieth century. He exemplifies well his cardinal doctrine of creative transformation, and this is perhaps best shown in his understanding of Christianity itself in its relation to other religions. It is the theologian's task, he insists, to transform not only our conceptions of nature, the economy, the political order, and our understanding of gender and race, but also the nature of Christian faith itself in its encounter with other religious worldviews. Christianity, like every other entity and community, is in a state of process and it, too, must be renewed as it creatively "prehends" the other rich traditions of spiritual experience. We cannot pursue Cobb's distinctive Christian "theology of religions" here, but we will briefly look at his work in this field in Chapter Fifteen.

CONCLUSION

We close this account of Process theology with some critical observations on issues raised by a Christian Process theology largely derived from the thought of Whitehead and Hartshorne. Brief mention already has been made of the kinds of criticisms directed at Whitehead's dipolar theism.

These criticisms are, on the whole, relevant to most forms of panentheism. Among more recent questions is whether a dipolar or a "dialectical" concept of God can be developed without recourse to a neo-classical metaphysics. For example, some theologians do not think it contradictory to understand God as both changeless and changing. God is unchanging in terms of God's primordial being and purpose but is also changing as the Divine responds to a mutable world of constant modification and development—which, they argue, is basically how God is portrayed in the Bible.[92] Related to this question about the necessity of adopting a neo-classical metaphysics, is the revived historicist argument that all philosophical and theological constructions, whether Aristotelian-Thomistic, modern Neo-Kantian-Ritschlian, or Process neo-classical, presuppose certain epistemological and metaphysical notions that are deeply embedded in the cultural ethos of their time. Theology can be pursued, it is argued, without requiring adherence to one comprehensive metaphysical scheme, such as Whitehead's.

A number of theologians question whether a Christian theism can relinquish the doctrine of creation *ex nihilo* and all that it entails with regard to God's nature. That is, whether Process theology's conceptions of God's temporality and interdependence on the world of finite creatures are compatible with Christian belief. Critical here is Process theology's concept of God's persuasive power. As we have learned, Process metaphysics conceives of God as presenting to the world certain ideal possibilities for its creative prehension. Some critics find this particular formulation of God's agency as encompassed by persuasion to be inadequate. It fails, they argue, to recognize that God's power can be causally efficacious without being wholly determinitive.[93]

Closely related to these concepts of God's interdependence on the world and persuasion hovers the problem of evil. For many critics this is the crucial weakness of Process thought. Although Process theology has advanced Christian thinking about the meaning of freedom and the character of genuine love as involving real relationships of giving and receiving, some look with dismay at the idea that God can only offer the world new possibilities for creative advance. Moreover, they point out, there is slight empirical evidence that maximum persuasive power for good is, in fact, at work in the world. In Process theology, God, of course, is not responsible for the choices of his creatures—only for the ideals through which their creative actions may be coordinated for creative advance. And it is this unburdening of God of responsibility for evil that has made Process theology attractive to many. There remains, however, a significant implication of this doctrine that is raised by Robert Neville. "Suppose," Neville proposes,

evil is chosen only by people, and only in independence of God. Why should we want in the first place to exempt God from responsibility for evil? Because of an antecedent commitment to God's goodness. But to deny God responsibility by denying divine causal agency is not to lend *support* to the doctrine of divine goodness; it only strikes down a counter argument. And the price of this move is to make the actual course of events *irrelevent* to God's moral character;

this goes counter to the religious feeling that God's moral character is *revealed* in events, for better or worse.[94]

The form of Process theology that has developed directly from the philosophies of Whitehead and Hartshorne has not enjoyed a wide following outside of the United States. And yet Process theology has, rather paradoxically, influenced theological thinking in profound ways. While refusing to appropriate the entire Process metaphysical scheme, theologians find its critique of aspects of classical theism—e.g., the latter's often ill-advised concentration on the divine transcendence—to be salutary. Also, Process theology's serious engagement with the sciences; its ecological vision of an interdependent and evolving world; its call for serious human action in and responsibility for the future of the world—on these and other matters the influence of Process theology is deeply and affirmatively felt in contemporary religious experience—and underlines the ongoing importance of Process theology for Christian reflection.

NOTES

1. Pierre Teilhard de Chardin, *The Phenomenon of Man* (New York, 1965), p. 78.

2. Ibid., p. 171.

3. Ibid., pp. 183–184.

4. Ibid., pp. 270–271.

5. Pierre Teilhard de Chardin, *The Future of Man* (New York, 1964), p. 34.

6. Pierre Teilhard de Chardin, *Oeuvres*, VI (Paris, 1962), p. 50; cited in Christopher F. Mooney, *Teilhard de Chardin and the Mystery of Christ* (New York, 1968).

7. Alfred North Whitehead, *Process and Reality* (New York, 1929), pp. 523–524.

8. Ibid., p. 520.

9. Ibid., p. 520.

10. Ibid., p. 526.

11. Ibid., p. 343.

12. Ibid., p. 344.

13. Charles Hartshorne, *Man's Vision of God and the Logic of Theism* (Chicago, 1941), pp. 11–12.

14. Charles Hartshorne, *Reality as Social Process: Studies in Metaphysics and Religion* (Boston, 1953), p. 147.

15. Ibid., p. 155.

16. Charles Hartshorne, *The Divine Relativity: A Social Conception of God* (New Haven, 1948), p. 138.

17. Ibid., p. 20.

18. Hartshorne, *Man's Vision of God*, p. 115.

19. Ibid., p. 116.

20. Ibid., p. 117.

21. Ibid.

22. Ibid., pp. 345–346.

23. Hartshorne, *Reality as Social Process*, p. 24.

24. Ibid.

25. Schubert Ogden, *On Theology* (San Francisco, 1986), pp. 3–4.

26. Ibid., p. 68.

27. Schubert Ogden, *The Reality of God and Other Essay,* (New York, 1966), p. 170.

28. Schubert Ogden, "The Significance of Bultmann for Contemporary Theology," in *The Theology of Rudolf Bultmann,* ed. Charles Kegley (New York, 1966), p. 125.

29. Ibid., p. 126.

30. Ogden, *On Theology,* p. 91.

31. Ogden, *Reality of God,* p. 172.

32. Ibid., pp. 175–176.

33. Ibid., p. 176.

34. Ibid., p. 177.

35. Ibid., pp. 177–178.

36. Ibid., p. 178.

37. Ibid., pp. 178–179.

38. Ibid., p. 180.

39. Ibid., p. 182.

40. Ibid., pp. 185–186.

41. Schubert Ogden, "Toward Bearing Witness," *Religious Studies Review,* 23 (October 1997), 339.

42. Ibid.

43. Schubert Ogden, *The Point of Christology* (San Francisco, 1982), p. 131.

44. Ogden, *Reality of God,* p. 173.

45. Ogden, *The Point of Christology,* p. 132.

46. Ibid., p. 133.

47. Ibid., p. 137.

48. Ibid., pp. 142–143.

49. Ibid., p. 143.

50. Ibid., p. 140.

51. Ibid., p. 145.

52. Ibid.

53. Ibid.

54. Ibid., p. 146.

55. Ibid., p. 41.

56. Ibid., pp. 55–56.

57. Ibid., p. 58.

58. Ibid., p. 59.

59. Ibid., p. 166.

60. Ibid., p. 158.

61. Ibid., p. 94.Ogden's later writings also demonstrate his serious engagement in the inter-religious dialogue. See, for example, his *Is there Only One True Religion or Are There Many?* (Dallas, 1992) and Chapter Fifteen below.

62. Ibid., pp. 166–167.

63. For this and other biographical information on Cobb, I am indebted to David Ray Griffin's illuminating essay on Cobb in *A Handbook of Christian Theologians,* ed. Martin E. Marty and Dean G. Peerman (Nashville, 1984).

64. John B. Cobb, Jr., *God and the World* (Philadelphia, 1969), p. 70.

65. Ibid.

66. Ibid., pp. 72–73.

67. Ibid., p. 73.

68. Ibid., p. 74.

69. Ibid., p. 75.

70. Ibid., p. 76.

71. Ibid., p. 78

72. Ibid.

73. Ibid.

74. Ibid., p. 79.

75. Ibid.

76. Ibid., pp. 79–80.

77. Ibid., p. 82.

78. Ibid., pp. 83–84.

79. J. B. Cobb, Jr., *Christ in a Pluralistic Age* (Phildelphia, 1975), p. 13.

80. Ibid., p. 63.

81. J. B. Cobb, Jr. and David Ray Griffin, *Process Theology: An Introductory Exposition* (Phildelphia, 1976), p. 101.

82. Cobb, *Christ in a Pluralistic Age,* p. 84.

83. Ibid., p. 85.

84. Cobb and Griffin, *Process Theology,* p. 103.

85. Ibid.

86. Ibid., p. 105.

87. Ibid., p. 107.

88. Ibid., p. 146.

89. J. B. Cobb, *Process Theology and Political Theology* (Philadelphia, 1982), p. 132.

90. Cobb and Griffin, *Process Theology,* p. 148.

91. Ibid., pp. 154–155.

92. See, for example, John Macquarrie, *In Search of Deity: An Essay in Dialectical Theism* (London, 1984), Ch. 13 and 17; Keith Ward, *The Concept of God* (Oxford, 1974); and the essays of several evangelical thinkers in *Process Theology,* Ronald Nash, ed., (Grand Rapids, Mich., 1987).

93. See, e.g., Nancy Frankenberry, "Some Problems in Process Theology," *Religious Studies,* 17 (1981). On this same question and others directed at Process theology consult Robert Neville's *Creativity and God: A Challenge to Process Theology* (New York, 1980), which includes critiques of Whitehead, Hartshorne, Ogden, and Cobb. For the advanced student.

94. Neville, ibid., p. 11. For good statements of Process theologians on the problem of evil, see David R. Griffin, *God, Power and Evil: A Process Theodicy* (Philadelphia, 1976); and Schubert M. Ogden, "Evil and Belief in God: The Distinctive Relevance of a Process Theology," *The Perkins Journal* (Summer 1978).

SUGGESTIONS FOR FURTHER READING

Process Theology

Brown, Delwin, Ralph E. James, and Gene Reeves. *Process Philosophy and Christian Thought* (Indianapolis: Bobbs-Merrill, 1971). Essays on aspects of Process theology by process thinkers. A valuable bibliography through 1970.

Cobb, John B., Jr., and David Ray Griffin. *Process Theology: An Introductory Exposition* (Philadelphia: Westminster Press, 1976). Good introduction to the basic concepts of Process theology and to how Christian doctrines can be illuminated by process thought. Bibliographical guide to 1976.

Cousins, Ewert H., ed. *Process Theology: Basic Writings* (New York: Newman Press, 1971). Essays by Process thinkers on various themes important in understanding Process theology. Includes several essays on Teilhard de Chardin.

Process Studies. Published since 1971, this journal is devoted to all aspects and implications of Process theology.

Pierre Teilhard de Chardin

Cuénot, C. *Pierre Teilhard de Chardin: Les grandes étapes de son évolution* (1958). Eng. trans. V. Colimore, ed. R. Hogue: *Teilhard de Chardin: A Biographical Study* (London: Burns Oates 1965). The best study of Teilhard's life in English. Also see, Charles E. Raven, *Teilhard de Chardin: Scientist and Seer* (London: Collins, 1963).

Lubac, Henri de. *Teilhard de Chardin: The Man and His Meaning* (New York: Hawthorne Books, 1965).

———. *The Religious Thought of Teilhard de Chardin* (New York: Desclee Co., 1967).

Lyons, J.A. *The Cosmic Christ in Origen and Teilhard de Chardin: A Comparative Study* (Oxford: Oxford University Press, 1982).

Mooney, Christopher F. *Teilhard de Chardin and the Mystery of Christ* (New York: Harper and Row, 1966).

Tresmontant, Claude. *Pierre Teilhard de Chardin: His Thought* (Baltimore: Helicon Press, 1959).

Wildiers, N.M. *An Introduction to Teilhard de Chardin* (New York: Harper and Row, 1968).

Alfred North Whitehead

Leclerc, Ivor. *Whitehead's Metaphysics: An Introductory Exposition* (New York: Macmillan, 1958)

Lowe, Victor. *Understanding Whitehead* (Baltimore: Johns Hopkins Press, 1962).

Schilpp, Paul A., ed. *The Philosophy of Alfred North Whitehead*, 2nd ed. (Chicago: Tudor Publishing, 1951)

Sherburne, Donald W. *A Key to Whitehead's Process and Reality* (New York: Macmillan, 1966)

Charles Hartshorne

Cobb, John B., Jr., and Franklin I. Gamwell, ed. *Existence and Actuality: Conversations with Charles Hartshorne* (Chicago: University of Chicago Press, 1984). Essays by leading philosophers and theologians with responses by Hartshorne.

Gragg, Alan. *Charles Hartshorne* (Waco, Tex.: Word Books, 1973). A short but helpful introduction.

Hahn, Lewis E., ed. *The Philosophy of Charles Hartshorne* (La Salle, Ill.: Open Court, 1991). Includes an autobiography by Hartshorne, twenty-nine critical essays, responses by Hartshorne, and an extensive bibliography.

James, Ralph E., Jr. *The Concrete God: A New Beginning for Theology—The Thought of Charles Hartshorne* (Indianapolis: Bobbs-Merrill, 1967)

Kane, Robert, and Stephen H. Phillips. *Hartshorne, Process Philosophy and Theology* (Albany: State University of New York Press, 1997).

Peters, Eugene H. *The Creative Advance: An Introduction to Process Philosophy as a Context for Christian Faith* (St. Louis: The Bethany Press, 1966). Especially pp 77–104.

———. *Hartshorne and Neoclassical Metaphysics: An Interpretation* (Lincoln: University of Nebraska, 1970). A discussion of several important themes in Hartshorne's work.

Reese, William L., and Eugene Freeman, ed. *Process and Divinity: The Hartshorne Festschrift* (La Salle, Ill.: Open Court, 1964). Especially pp. 471–527, 533–560.

Viney, Donald Wayne. *Charles Hartshorne and the Existence of God* (Albany: State University of New York Press, 1985). A study of Hartshorne's cumulative case for the existence of God.

John B. Cobb, Jr. and Schubert Ogden

Devenish, Philip E., and George L. Goodwin. *Witness and Existence: Essays in Honor of Schubert M. Ogden* (Chicago: University of Chicago Press, 1989). The introduction is a fine, substantial introduction to Ogden's theology.

Gamwell, Franklin I. "On the Theology of Schubert M. Ogden." In *Religious Studies Review*, 23 (October

1997), 333–340. An excellent, appreciative essay indicating the shifts in Ogden's later writings.

Griffin, David Ray. "John B. Cobb, Jr." In *A Handbook of Christian Theologians*, ed. Martin E. Marty and Dean G. Peerman (Nashville: Abingdon Press, 1984).

Griffin, David Ray, and Thomas J. J. Altizer, ed. *John Cobb's Theology in Process* (Philadelphia: Westminster Press, 1977).

Griffin, David Ray, and Joseph C. Hough, Jr. *Theology and the University: Essays in Honor of John B. Cobb,* Jr. (Albany: State University of New York Press, 1991). This fine collection of essays includes an excellent theological biography of Cobb and a thorough (to 1990) bibliography of Cobb's books, essays, and reviews.

Surin, Kenneth. "Process Theology." In *The Modern Theologians*, II, ed. David F. Ford (Oxford: Basil Blackwell, 1989). The treatment of Cobb and Ogden is brief but the notes and bibliographies refer to some important critical responses to these two theologians.

Chapter Eleven

History and Hermeneutics

Paul Ricoeur

The work and influence of the theologians and philosophers presented in this chapter range from the 1960s to the present. Although significant differences exist among these thinkers, several common threads bind them together. First, they react to the dominant philosophies and theologies of a previous generation, especially what they perceive as the individualism of existential philosophy and theology. Second, they are concerned with history, tradition, and interpretation. Therefore, they modify the distinction made in Neo-Orthodox theology between Word, on the one hand, and history on the other. The criticism of the devaluation of history in both Rudolf Bultmann's and Karl Barth's understanding of revelation is preeminently represented by Pannenberg's development of the concept of revelation as history. The development of hermeneutic theory by Hans-Georg Gadamer and Paul Ricoeur broadens, expands, and corrects the previous existential interpretation advocated by Bultmann. The existential turn purports to be a development of Martin Heidegger's philosophy that, in fact, is contrary to Heidegger's own self-understanding and later development. Finally, on a more profound level, an important shift takes place as to who is the guiding philosophical mentor. Whereas Søren Kierkegaard was the philosophical influence behind the Neo-Orthodoxy of Karl Barth and Rudolf Bultmann, Hegel stands behind the turn toward history in Pannenberg's understanding of universal history and in Gadamer's understanding of the immersion of reason in history.

The chapter begins and ends with two very different theologians. It begins with Wolfhart Pannenberg's criticism of the Neo-Orthodox theology of the Word of God and its separation of faith and reason. It ends with Hans Frei's advocacy of narrative as a retrieval and reformation of Karl Barth's theology over against theologies that seek to correlate faith with anthropology. Between these two theologies is situated the hermeneutical theories of both Gadamer and Ricoeur and the appropriation of their work by David Tracy.

WOLFHART PANNENBERG

Wolfhart Pannenberg (1928–   ) was born in Stettin, Germany, a town to the east of Berlin, now a part of Poland. He began his studies at the University of Berlin concentrating in philosophy and theology. In 1948 he spent a year at the University of Göttingen where he studied with Friedrich Gogarten and Hans Joachim Iwand. A World Council of Churches fellowship then enabled him to study for a year at Basel with Karl Barth and Karl Jaspers. Pannenberg continued his studies at the University of Heidelberg and there was influenced by the Old Testament scholar Gerhard von Rad's interpretation of the history and traditions of Israel.[1] Pannenberg wrote his doctoral dissertation on Duns Scotus's doctrine of predestination with the theologian Edmund Schlink as his director.[2] His habilitation (a second dissertation that qualifies one to teach) at Heidelberg, *Analogy and Revelation,* which remains unpublished, traces the idea of analogy from Greek philosophy to medieval theology.[3] Pannenberg's first teaching position was at the Lutheran theological seminary in Wuppertal where, for three years (1958–1961), he taught together with Jürgen Moltmann. Pannenberg became a professor at the University of Mainz in 1961 where he taught until 1968, when he was appointed professor of fundamental and systematic theology at the University of Munich where he has taught ever since.

Revelation as History

Pannenberg's earliest publications offer criticisms of both Rudolf Bultmann's existential theology and Karl Barth's theology of the Word. He does this through a renewed emphasis on the importance of history—a dimension neglected by these two theologians. Pannenberg's concern for the theological significance of history dates from as early as 1959. In an essay entitled "Redemptive Event and History," he proposes a view of history that became the hallmark of his future work.

History is the furthest horizon of Christian theology. All theological questions and answers have meaning only within the framework of the history which God has in association with mankind, and through mankind, with the whole creation, and which is directed towards a future that is still hidden to the world, but has already been revealed in Jesus Christ.[4]

This view of history received the attention of the international theological world when Pannenberg, with a group of young post–World War II theologians, published a manifesto entitled *Revelation as History.*[5] Although this was a book of technical theology, an article on its significance appeared in the popular news journal *Time*. Most of these young theologians were from Heidelberg, which was then a leading center of German theological education. Gerhard von Rad, Günther Bornkamm, and Hans von Campenhausen were professors there, and the group of young theologians included Wolfhart Pannenberg (systematic theology), Rolf Rendtorff (Old Testament), Ulrich Wilckens (New Testament), Trutz Rendtorff (systematic theology and social ethics), and, later, Martin Elze (early church history). *Revelation as History* contained several essays on the concept of revelation from the perspective of their respective fields. The distinctive way they elaborated on the relation between history and revelation marked a significant departure from the Neo-Orthodox emphasis on such concepts as Word, *kerygma*, and proclamation, and it signaled a new emphasis on the role of history in theology.[6]

Pannenberg's essay in the volume, "Dogmatic Theses on the Doctrine of Revelation," proposed seven systematic theses that summed up and crystallized the position of the group: (1) God's self-revelation is not direct, like a theophany, but indirect and is brought about through God's acts in history. (2) It is at the end rather than at the beginning of history that divine revelation is completely comprehended. (3) Historical revelation is open to all to see and has a universal character. (4) The universal revelation of God's Deity is anticipated in the fate of Jesus. (5) The Christ event is a part of God's history with Israel. (6) The formulation of revelation in the Gentile Christian Church brings to actual expression the universality of God's eschatological vindication of Jesus. (7) "The Word relates itself to revelation as foretelling, forthtelling, and report."[7]

The theses not only assert what many take for granted—for example, that the proclamation of God's Word is empty unless it is linked with what happens in history—but they also raise several controversial questions. These include the indirectness of God's revelation, the openness of revelation to all with eyes to see, and the universality of history. Several of Pannenberg's Lutheran colleagues challenged his view of the relation between faith and historical evidence. In their eyes, Pannenberg's view overemphasized the role of historical evidence and downplayed the role of faith. It seemed to them that he assumed too readily that historical-critical studies could by themselves demonstrate the truth of the Christian faith. The theses also contained other significant themes that Pannenberg would develop further in later publications. A major theme is the tension involved in his dual affirmation that the end of history is already anticipated in the fate of Jesus, and yet that history remains open-ended so that God's revelation is completely understood only at the end of history. Pannenberg would reiterate later that "On this side of the consummation of the truth of God in the history of the world, the sense of the provisional and broken nature of its present actualization among us remains one of the con-

Wolfhart Pannenberg

ditions of the credibility of Christian proclamation and theology."[8]

The Resurrection of Jesus Christ: Historical and Retroactive

Pannenberg continued to develop and publish on the themes found in this inaugural manifesto.[9] His next major publication dealt with Christology. Entitled *Jesus—God and Man*, it is a remarkable achievement for a young scholar because of its mastery of a vast range of exegetical, historical, and systematic materials.[10] In this work, Pannenberg advances several historical and systematic theses that have proven to be significant in subsequent christological reflection, or at least were the subject of considerable discussion. These theses revolve especially around the historical and systematic significance that he gives to the resurrection of Jesus, which is pivotal to his Christology.

Four elements of Pannenberg's treatment of the resurrection should be noted: the historical demonstrability of the resurrection, the historicity of the resurrection, the retrospective or retroactive character of the resurrection in relation to the

Sonship of Jesus, and, finally, the proleptic or anticipatory character of Jesus' resurrection. These aspects of Pannenberg's treatment of the resurrection of Jesus demonstrate the continuities with his longer program on revelation as history.

Historical Demonstrability

Pursuant to his arguments in *Revelation as History* on the relation between faith and history, Pannenberg asserts that the historical events that demonstrate the truth of the biblical revelation in general and the resurrection of Jesus in particular are available to those with the eyes to see them. Furthermore, he takes issue with Ernst Troeltsch's interpretation of the role of analogy in historical understanding, that is, to discern an analogy and correlation between events of the past and the present. (see Chapter One). Pannenberg argues that Troeltsch's canons of criticism do not allow one to take into account historical uniqueness sufficiently.[11] Pannenberg argues against the view that historical investigations are unable to demonstrate the facticity of the resurrection.[12]

Historicity

Pannenberg further shows concretely the role of history in his criticism of a demythologized and existential interpretation of Jesus's resurrection. Against Bultmann's claim that Jesus is risen in the preaching of the *kerygma,* Pannenberg argues for the historicity of the resurrection of Jesus.[13] Through an analysis of the empty tomb traditions, following the work of the Heidelberg church historian, Hans von Campenhausen, and an analysis of the resurrection appearances,[14] Pannenberg argues for the historicity of the resurrection of Jesus and insists that it cannot be reduced to a kerygmatic event. The historicity of the resurrection, Pannenberg argues, roots the *kerygma* in an historical event. The convergence of both traditions—the empty tomb and resurrection appearances—speaks for the historicity of the resurrection in Pannenberg's view. The endeavor to demonstrate the historicity of the

resurrection remains a constant in Pannenberg's work. In the face of Gerhard Lüdemann's recent retrieval of David Friedrich Strauss's view of the resurrection as a subjective vision, Pannenberg has repeated his arguments in favor of its historicity and has vigorously criticized Lüdemann's subjective and psychological interpretation.[15]

The Retroactivity of the Resurrection

Pannenberg also asserts the retroactivity of the resurrection in a creative attempt to take into account the full humanity of Jesus and those New Testament verses that speak of Jesus's inauguration as Son of God at his resurrection. Pannenberg asserts that although Jesus is appointed the Son of God at his resurrection, he is retroactively the Son of God from the beginning of his life. In his book on Christology, Pannenberg is critical of incarnational theories and especially of what he labels as the neo-conservative kenotic Christologies of the nineteenth century that stressed the kenosis (self-emptying) of the divine Logos.[16] These Christologies are unable to overcome the difficulties that the notion of self-emptying and self-humiliation of the Logos causes for the doctrine of the Trinity as well as for an affirmation of the full humanity of Jesus.[17] In asking what it means that this man, Jesus, is God, Pannenberg answers:

It does not mean, naturally, that the universal human nature in Jesus was divine. That would be absurd, an impossible thought. But Jesus as *this* man, as man in this particular, unique situation, with this particular historical mission and this particular fate—as this man Jesus is not just man, but from the perspective of his resurrection from the dead (kata pneuma—"according to the Spirit") he is one with God and thus is himself God.[18]

In addition to specifying the "Sonship" of Jesus retroactively from the resurrection, he further specifies it by proposing that Jesus is the Son of the Father. Rather than follow an incarnational approach that views Jesus's divinity as the Incarnation of the Logos, Pannenberg suggests that Jesus's Sonship be understood as a specific relation to the Father.[19] In so doing, he seeks to take into account the real earthly relation of Jesus to the Father.

The Proleptic or Anticipatory Nature of the Resurrection

The fourth aspect of Pannenberg's treatment of Jesus's resurrection is its proleptic or anticipatory character. The resurrection is not only retroactive but also proleptic or anticipatory. Retroactively, it constitutes the identity of the historical person of Jesus with God the Father rather than on the basis of the Incarnation.[20] What Pannenberg means by the proleptic and anticipatory nature of the resurrection is that the end of history is already anticipated and realized in the event of Jesus's resurrection. A certain tension exists here. On the one hand, Pannenberg underscores that history is open and incomplete so that the meaning and truth of history become manifest only at the end of history. On the other hand, he maintains that its end is proleptically already anticipated in the fate of Jesus, that is, in God's vindication of Jesus through the resurrection.

Theology as an Intellectual Discipline

Throughout his career, Pannenberg has been concerned with the nature of theology, its method, and the validity or truth character of its affirmations. His major work, which culminates and sums up his positions in this regard, has been translated into English as *Theology and the Philosophy of Science*.[21] The English title is unfortunate and misleading, for the German original is *Wissenschaftstheorie and Theologie*. The German word *Wissenschaft* does not mean science; it is a much broader concept, closer to the ancient and medieval Latin *scientia*, meaning an organized body of knowledge. In this book, Pannenberg deals with the relation between theology and theories of organized knowledge or disciplines of knowledge. In discussing the place of theology within the pluralism of disciplines, Pannenberg necessarily takes up various theoretical conceptions of knowledge; i.e., positivism, rationalism, the distinction between the natural and the human sciences, and hermeneutics. He concludes the volume with a brief history of the conception of theology as an academic discipline and with a proposal for his own conception of theology.

Pannenberg maps out a middle path between two theories of knowledge as well as between Protestant Liberalism and Neo-Orthodoxy. With regard to the theories of knowledge, he criticizes positivism for its lack of hermeneutical awareness. Yet he also argues against the hermeneutical theories of Rudolf Bultmann and Hans-Georg Gadamer, contending that they are too focused on an expressive conception of truth and downplay objectivity. In regard to theological conceptions, he rejects, on the one hand, a conception of theology that views it primarily as the study of the religion of Christianity. Because the Christian religion has as its object God, the truth of its affirmation of God must be a prerequesite of theology. In this respect, he takes issue with Ernst Troeltsch's historical conception of theology. On the other hand, he also rejects Karl Barth's exclusive reliance on the positivity of revelation in such a way that it removes theology from the canons of rationality.[22]

Pannenberg seeks a middle way insofar as he locates theology within the context of the science of religion but, at the same time, adopts the conception of a theological hypothesis that is open to verification. Pannenberg writes:

Like philosophical statements, theological statements are offered as hypotheses about the total meaning of experience, but *firstly* from the point of view of the reality which ultimately determines everything given in its still incomplete totality, and *secondly* with reference to the way in which this divine reality has made itself known in religious consciousness.[23]

The question for Pannenberg is how the reality of God can become a theme of experience. He proposes that the reality of God becomes present indirectly through subjective anticipations of the totality of reality. These anticipations are historic models of the totality of meaning. As anticipations they involve hypothesis and can be confirmed or refuted by subsequent experience. Pannenberg, therefore, maintains that "God" as the "all-determining reality," or God as that reality that determines everything, is not directly known as are ordinary objects of experience. Instead, God is indirectly accessible in the human anticipation of the totality of meaning. It is this totality of meaning that the various historical religions have made explicit and have been thematized throughout history. However, since history is not yet complete, this total meaning remains open and its confirmation or refutation is still outstanding.[24]

Pannenberg places theology within the study of the plurality of religions and their history not only to investigate the distinctiveness of Christianity, but also to ascertain the truth of Christianity. Pannenberg insists that an adequate study of religion must include an examination of a religion's truth claims because many religions understand themselves as making such claims. To fail to examine these claims is to fail to take full account of a religion's basic affirmations and self-understanding. Therefore, these truth claims must be advanced within the study of religion itself as hypotheses or claims that are open to consideration, discussion, and verification. To fail to do so is to fail to understand what is intended by religion.[25]

Anthropology as Fundamental Theology

Because the understanding of the human person has become increasingly important in both modern atheism and modern theology, Pannenberg argues that the problems of fundamental theology must be resolved in relation to anthropology.[26] Developments in physics, specifically the principle of inertia and the mechanistic theory of the origin of planets, has meant that the cosmos is no longer the starting point for theology as, for example, in a quasi-experimental demonstration of God as the first cause of the cosmos. Likewise,

the theological appeals to teleology and the argument from design in seventeenth- and eighteenth-century natural theology were gradually abandoned as a result of the general acceptance of the theory of evolution. Anthropology has become the testing ground of the truth of the Christian religion. On the one hand, the moral justification of religion was advanced by Rousseau and by Kant, and a more fundamental anchoring of religion in anthropology was proposed by Schleiermacher. On the other hand, the critique of religion was likewise based on anthropology, as is evident in the critique of Ludwig Feuerbach, Friedrich Nietzsche, and Sigmund Freud. Consequently, Pannenberg argues:

> Theologians will be able to defend the truth precisely of their talk about God only if they first respond to the atheistic critique of religion on the terrain of anthropology. Otherwise all their assertions, however impressive, about the primacy of the Godness of God will remain purely subjective assurances without any serious claim to universal validity.[27]

In Pannenberg's view the assertion of God's Godness in Neo-Orthodoxy plays into the hands of the atheistic reduction of religion and its translation of theology to anthropology. Instead, Christian theology should show the validity of religious affirmations on the basis of an analysis of human nature in its relation to history and the world.

In developing anthropology as a fundamental theology, Pannenberg maintains his focus on human history and its openness. He takes as his starting point Johann Gottfried Herder's anthropology, especially his skepticism about human perfectibility through self-improvement and self-enhancement. Humans do not bring forth their perfectibility out of themselves or their own resources. On the contrary, they are embedded within traditions and thereby are affected by external influences and others persons. Pannenberg interprets Herder's recourse to the notion of the image of God as expressing not only Herder's opposition to the idea of human self-fulfillment through self-perfection, but also his conviction that humans are oriented toward and open to divine providence within history.[28]

Pannenberg reformulates Herder and develops his significance for contemporary theology with the help of a phenomenological analysis drawn from Max Scheler and Helmut Plessner. It is an analysis that underscores "exocentricity" (Plessner's openness of human nature).[29] Pannenberg argues that our human openness to the world has significance for the understanding of the self and for the religious dimension of meaning. This human "openness" not only expresses an openness in every human experience but also points beyond human experience, because, in questioning and searching, humans find no ultimate human satisfaction in their own experiences and creations. It is in this openness and questioning that the meaning of human existence and the question of God comes to the fore.

Pannenberg sums up his argument by carefully limiting its extent:

All that I have been saying does not amount to a kind of anthropological proof of God's existence. The fact that the question of God belongs to the humanity of human beings does not yet signify that a God exists and what kind of God he is. It is only insofar as it is a problem that the question of God cannot be separated from the humanity of human beings.[30]

This anthropological starting point is similar to Karl Rahner's approach (see Chapter Seven), as Pannenberg himself acknowledges. However, Pannenberg develops his anthropology with a specific historical orientation in that he connects the openness of human nature with the incompleteness of history. In his anthropology, Pannenberg seeks to develop further Herder's insight with reference to the formation of the subject in history, his notion of anticipation, and God's Spirit.

Metaphysics and Systematic Theology

At the culmination of his career, Pannenberg began to write a three-volume *Systematic Theol-*ogy,[31] the first volume of which was published in 1988. At the same time, Pannenberg outlined some of the philosophical presuppositions of his systematic theology in two small treatises, one dealing with the relation between metaphysics and the idea of God and the other dealing with the nature of systematic theology.[32] Moreover, he continued to publish essays relating systematic theology both to issues dealing with the philosophy of nature as raised by the natural sciences and to issues regarding the Church raised by ecumenism.[33]

The three volumes of Pannenberg's *Systematic Theology* have a Trinitarian structure. In interpreting the Christian concept of God, Pannenberg follows Gregory of Nyssa insofar as the "infinity" of God's nature is his central category. In Pannenberg's opinion, Gregory's attention to divine infinity accounts for the radical otherness of God in a way that neither Aristotelian not Platonic metaphysics is capable of doing. "In his transcendence beyond everything finite, God is holy and it is precisely because of such transcendence that he is not bound up in any place "up there" or "out there," but can also be present within the world of finite realities."[34] Pannenberg suggests that the idea of God as infinite is more easily reconcilable with "addressing God as Father and as manifest in the Son and through the Spirit,"[35] than Tillich's concept of Being-itself.

In his reflections on the relation between metaphysics and the understanding of God, Pannenberg suggests that a contemporary metaphysics of the Absolute can do justice to modern thought if the Absolute is understood neither in contrast to human subjectivity nor as opposing the independence of the finite, as in some forms of Idealism. The Absolute must be understood as the source and goal, as the condition and perfection of finite consciousness.[36] It is a task that Pannenberg concedes is difficult and complex.

Pannenberg seeks to carry out this task through a critical interpretation that some view as close to transcendental Thomism, especially that of Karl Rahner. As Pannenberg notes, "according to Karl Rahner, an unthematized fore-conception

[*Vorgriff*] of being in its unlimited extension is the condition for grasping any finite essences at all.[37] Pannenberg also agrees with Rahner that this unthematized intuition cannot be grasped conceptually through reflection. But Pannenberg seeks to nuance Rahner's understanding of pre-apprehension or anticipation. He writes:

For there is no particular knowledge or representation of a thing that would be able to conceive in advance the experience of that thing. The infinite horizon, which unthematically precedes all experience of finite entities and concepts, has more the form of an intuitive seeing or a feeling.[38]

Pannenberg develops this point by underscoring that the notion of anticipation must be conceived historically to include both identity with what is anticipated and difference from it. What is presupposed is that the anticipation is of what will appear fully only in the future and yet is anticipated as already present.

Similar metaphysical concerns are present in Pannenberg's systematic theology and relate again to his key concept of anticipation, that is, the integration of experience in relation to history and its future. More specifically, Pannenberg's *Systematic Theology* is concerned with integrating the experience of God, the world, and humanity on the basis of the event of Christian revelation. However, even though he gives precedence to the concept of God in understanding the world, he is at the same time open to a mutual conditioning of knowing. In his own words,

If, in the light of the Christian doctrine of God, the world and human life are seen to be grounded in God, then conversely we have to consider a reformulation of the Christian understanding of God from the standpoint of experience of the world and humanity and the related reflection.[39]

Pannenberg seeks to carry out this goal in his systematic theology. He explicates the doctrines of Creation and reconciliation so as to link the Christian understanding of God as Spirit to our experience of humanity and cosmic reality.[40] The final volume, on the Church and the life of faith of the Christian community, underscores the provisional and incomplete nature of God's truth before the end of history—a constant theme of his theology.

Critical Issues: The Rationality of Faith

Pannenberg develops a theological position that appropriates the philosophical tradition of German Idealism and transcendental reflection. Yet he also seeks to provide an anthropological grounding of Christian belief and to demonstrate the historical and objective truth of Christian claims. The impressive breadth of Pannenberg's theology has resulted in its widespread ecumenical reception.[41] It has been positively appropriated by Roman Catholic theologians. Despite some reservations, Roman Catholic theologians appreciate his emphasis on philosophical theology and his engagement in the task of apologetical and fundamental theology.[42] Also, the importance that he gives to historical demonstration and to the assessment of historical evidence resembles the approaches of Roman Catholic fundamental theology. It is exactly this emphasis on philosophical and historical demonstrations that have made him appear, within the perspective of German Lutheran theology, as too rationalistic and insufficiently attentive to the role of faith.[43] Ironically, what Roman Catholic theologians have welcomed in Pannenberg's theology, German Lutheran theologians have found questionable. His appeal to Hegel's philosophy of history in his critique of Neo-Orthodoxy has led to the charge that he is too Hegelian or Idealist—a critique that overlooks the fact that his notion of eschatology results in a view of history different from that of Hegel. It is also interesting to note that Evangelical theologians, for example, Stanley Grenz and Alister McGrath, have been appreciative of Pannenberg's affirmation of traditional Christian beliefs even when they disagree with his reformulation of some doctrines such as soteriology.[44]

On a fundamental level, however, a tension exists in Pannenberg's theology between his concept of history and his criteria of theological judgment. On the one hand, he argues that history is open and that the Christian belief in God is a hypothesis that is open to verification. On the other hand, the end of history has already been anticipated in Jesus's resurrection. He seeks to reconcile anticipation and openness, but whether he does so adequately remains a question. His theological Idealism tends toward a coherentism in which the best interpretation is that which most adequately deals with the totality and, at the same time, toward a pragmatism by which future practice will reveal the truth.[45] Nevertheless, an historical realism permeates his theology, as does his concern with demonstrating truth. So, on the one hand, the truth of Christianity still remains to be decided in the future development of the religions of the world; on the other hand, this truth has already been anticipated in Jesus.

German Protestant Neo-Orthodoxy lived and thought under the sway of Kierkegaard's contrast between eternity and time and faith and reason. In his reaction to this dualism in German Neo-Orthodoxy, Pannenberg, like Hegel, seeks to reconcile the absolute and history, as well as faith and reason. He postulates the incompleteness and openness of history in a way that provides a tension within his system; nevertheless, he remains one of the more important German systematic theologians in the latter decades of the twentieth century.

HANS-GEORG GADAMER

Hans-Georg Gadamer (1900–) was born in Silesia, a region of Prussia, where his father was a chemist. Gadamer studied humanities and philosophy at the University of Marburg. At that time, the philosophy department was dominated by what is called the Marburg School in which Neo-Kantian philosophy prevailed. Paul Natorp (1854–1924), Hermann Cohen (1842–1918), and Nicolai Hartmann (1882–1950) were the leading representatives of Marburg Neo-Kantianism.[46] In 1922 Gadamer wrote a dissertation, directed by Paul Natorp, on the dialogue poetry of Plato, though he had also studied with Paul Friedländer, a well-known scholar of the ancient classics. His habilitation, for admission as lecturer, dealt with Plato's dialectical ethics and was written under Martin Heidegger's direction.[47] It was completed in 1927–1928 just before Heidegger left for Freiburg. There Heidegger became the successor to Edmund Husserl, the founder of phenomenology and Heidegger's former teacher. In referring to this period, Gadamer mentions the influence at Marburg of both Nicolai Hartmann and Martin Heidegger.[48] Moreover, for fifteen years Gadamer was a member of "Bultmann Graeca," a group consisting of Heinrich Schlier, Gerhard Krüger, and later Günther Bornkamm and Erich Dinkler. The group met every Thursday evening to read the classics of Greek literature.

The influence of Martin Heidegger's philosophy on Gadamer's work is unmistakable. Gadamer's hermeneutics can be viewed as an attempt to develop a theory of interpretation that differs not only from the regnant Neo-Kantianism but also from the existential interpretation of Heidegger, which is also reflected in Rudolf Bultmann's existential hermeneutics. Insofar as Martin Heidegger's later development, after *Being and Time* (1927), focused on language and the meaning of being, it has become evident that the question of being, rather than that of human existence, was at the center of Heidegger's early work. This center was overlooked by interpreters who, in their appropriation of Heidegger's analysis of human existence, developed an existentialism (Bultmann) or a humanism (Sartre). Gadamer's reception and interpretation of Heidegger follow the clear direction of Heidegger's later work.

The Critique of Historicism and Romanticism

The distinctiveness of Gadamer's understanding of the process of interpretation emerges when seen against the background of his understanding of interpretation in Friedrich Schleiermacher, the German Historical School, and the philosopher Wilhelm Dilthey (1833–1911). Although Gadamer is indebted to Schleiermacher for focusing hermeneutics on the process of understanding in general, he disagrees with Schleiermacher's emphasis on the author's intention. It is against the "historicism" of the Historical School of Leopold von Ranke and J.G. Droysen that Gadamer's disagreements are primarily directed. Gadamer also acknowledges Dilthey's concern to elaborate the distinctive process of understanding within the human sciences, but he disagrees with Dilthey's attempt to develop a unique method for the interpretation of the human sciences.

Gadamer sees Schleiermacher's great service in his not viewing hermeneutics as dealing with content, but with the process of understanding. He, therefore, does not limit the task of hermeneutics to interpreting special texts, for example, biblical texts. Instead, it treats the general process of interpreting and understanding. For this purpose Schleiermacher divided hermeneutics into both a technical and a psychological task. The technical or grammatical task analyzes the literary style, grammar, and language of the text. The psychological task seeks to reconstruct the individual author's intent that gave rise to the text. In Gadamer's view, Schleiermacher emphasized the psychological task of hermeneutics and saw the main task of hermeneutics as the avoiding of misunderstanding. Because the interpreter is one individual and the author is another, the possibility of misunderstanding exists and it must be avoided. In Gadamer's view, Schleiermacher accentuates the psychological and downplays the technical task of interpretation—a view for which Gadamer has been criticized by Ricoeur and others.[49] However, such a view allows Gadamer to criticize Schleiermacher for proposing a Romantic hermeneutic that is too individualistic and psychological.

Leopold von Ranke (1795–1886) and J. G. Droysen (1808–1884) not only were great historians but also wrote about historical method.[50] Both scholars insisted that history is an empirical and objective science, one that is grounded in the facts of history, and free of philosophical and speculative assumptions. They argued that history is a distinct science, and they sought to liberate it from what they considered to be Hegel's speculative philosophy of history. Gadamer argues, on the contrary, that it is Hegel, rather than the Historical School, that has the more adequate understanding of history, for Hegel understood the historian's own involvement in history.

> Immediacy to God is for the Lutheran, Ranke, the actual content of the Christian message. Re-establishing this immediacy that existed before the Fall occurs not through the Church's means of grace alone. The historian participates in it insofar as he makes a fallen humanity in history the object of his research and recognizes this humanity in the immediacy to God that it has never entirely lost.[51]

More important than this critique of "immediacy," or overlooking the historian's own involvement in history, is Gadamer's positive thesis. With regard to the cultural and human sciences, Gadamer advances a fundamental thesis that runs contrary to the positivism and scientism implicit in the Historical School. His basic thesis is that the human sciences should be understood in terms of the traditional concept of *Bildung* (formation and education) rather than from the modern ideals appropriate to the scientific method.

We have learned that it was Wilhelm Dilthey who initially perceived the conflict between the human sciences and natural science. Moreover, he saw that, insofar as the human sciences involved interpretation and understanding, they serve different purposes than the natural sciences and that they require a different methodology.

Moreover, historical sciences, as cultural sciences, are themselves embedded within the historicity of all life. However, instead of showing *how* these sciences are immersed in the historicity of life, Dilthey strove, instead, to explain the foundations of the historical sciences and their unique methodology.

In contrast to Dilthey, Gadamer seeks to incorporate Edmund Husserl's phenomenological reevaluation of the life world, as well as Martin Heidegger's hermeneutics of "facticity," or "thereness" of human existence, in order to develop a hermeneutics of human experience. Heidegger's analysis of facticity is subordinate and derivative to a more basic and universal question of the disclosure nature of truth. Heidegger thus relates his analysis of self-understanding as a human existential to a way of being in the world. What and who we are is always in relation to how we understand ourselves and to how we project our possibilities of being. Gadamer takes up this view and develops it further in *Truth and Method* through an analysis of the linguistic nature of human experience and the embeddedness of the human life world within historical tradition. The profundity of his analysis in *Truth and Method* has made the book a classic of hermeneutical theory as well as a major resource for theological reflection in the latter decades of the twentieth century.[52]

Recasting the Hermeneutical Circle

Important to Gadamer's hermeneutics is Heidegger's understanding of the hermeneutical circle that Gadamer develops. In *Being and Time*, Heidegger used the German term *Da-sein* for human persons. The German term stems from the union of two German words, *Da* meaning "there" and *sein* meaning "to be." The conjunction of these two terms into *Da-sein* indicates a certain "thereness," "facticity," or "thrownness" of human existence. We are, so to speak, born in a specific place and thrown into a specific historical constellation in which we live and project our existential possibilities and meaning.

Heidegger develops this concept further in relation to interpretation. He argues that human understanding involves a pre-understanding and pre-involvement with life in which understanding takes place. In a classic statement of the hermeneutical circle,[53] Heidegger maintains that understanding always relates to the whole of our being in the world. In understanding the world, we understand our existence. Therefore, "every interpretation operates with the forestructure that we characterized. Every interpretation which is to contribute some understanding must already have had a life-relation and thereby pre-understanding of what is to be interpreted."[54] Consequently, a hermeneutical circle exists between our pre-understanding and what is to be understood. This hermeneutical circle is intrinsic to the nature of understanding, so much so that it should not be avoided but should be entered into correctly. Heidegger argues:

To see a vitiosum [fault] in this circle and to look for ways to avoid it, even to "feel" that it is an inevitable imperfection, is to misunderstand understanding. (. . . .) What is decisive is not to get out of the circle, but to get in it in the right way. This circle of understanding is not a circle in which any random kind of knowledge operates, but it is rather the expression of the existential *forestructure* of Da-sein itself.[55] [Sentence italicized in original.]

Heidegger's outline of the hermeneutical circle and the necessity of a pre-apprehension or pre-understanding for understanding has had an important influence on German theologians. Karl Rahner, as shown in Chapter Seven, raises the issue of the pre-understanding or life relation by which language about God has its meaning, as well as the fact that the proofs of the existence of God have meaning only in relation to such a pre-understanding. The concept is crucial to Rudolf Bultmann when he asks what is the pre-understanding necessary to understand the Bible as God's revelation. Moreover, it also enables him to argue that no exegesis or interpretation of Scripture is without presuppositions.[56]

Hermeneutics of Belonging: Key Concepts

Several other key concepts are central to Gadamer's hermeneutics and require comment. Concepts such as the classic, temporal distance, *Wirkungsgeschichte* (history of effects), the fusion of horizons, and the relation between understanding and application constitute the core of his hermeneutics. Gadamer's hermeneutics can be viewed, however, as developing the major insight that we always stand within a tradition. Therefore, hermeneutical theory has to take into account the fact that understanding is likened to standing in a river of life that is constantly changing and that we are attempting to understand the changing river of which we are a part.[57] Gadamer also makes the category of *play* central to understanding. Understanding is like playing insofar as a participant in a game seeks to interpret the very movement of the game and the actions of the self and others within the game.

The Classic

A major category of Gadamer's hermeneutical theory is the "classic." Gadamer introduces the concept of a classic in order to overcome what he considers to be the Enlightenment's dichotomy between reason and authority, or reason and tradition. In Gadamer's view, the Enlightenment has a prejudice against prejudice. It allows no prejudgments to stand before critical reason. Taking the term "prejudice" in its root meaning of "prejudgment," Gadamer argues for the legitimacy of a prejudgment in regard to the classics or the inevitable role of tradition. In addition, the notion of the classic serves to resolve a major problem of the Historical School, namely, the historical distance between a work to be interpreted and the interpreter. Whereas the Historical School viewed historical distance as an obstacle to be overcome, Gadamer argues that it serves a positive role, as the notion of a classic shows. The classic serves this purpose insofar as it obtains its authority and legitimacy by its very endurance through time and history. It is the longevity of a work through succeeding generations and ages that makes it a classic. We then approach such a work with the prejudgment that this work has authority.

Gadamer appeals to the enduring value of classics in order, therefore, to rehabilitate the notions of authority and tradition against the Enlightenment's appeal to the dissecting blade of rationality. How does Gadamer understand a classic? A classic is inextricably within history and yet it stands out and above the vicissitudes of history so that it endures, has value, and makes claims.

The "classical" is something raised above the vicissitudes of changing times and changing tastes. (. . . .) When we call something classical, there is a consciousness of something enduring, of significance that cannot be lost and that is independent of all the circumstances of time—a kind of timeless present that is contemporaneous with every other present.[58]

As Jürgen Habermas has noted, "the fundamental drive behind Gadamer's major philosophical work, which ripened through the decades— [is] the drive to clarify for himself and others what the encounter with eminent texts means, what the binding character of the classic is all about."[59]

Wirkungsgeschichte *history of the effects of the classic*

The term *Wirkungsgeschichte* is difficult to translate. Literally, it means the history of effects but is translated as "effective history." A classic does not simply exist in the past; as a classic it endures throughout history. Its history can, in part, be read as a history of the effects of the classic. English literature has been strongly influenced by the King James version of the Bible. It not only has affected literature as such, but also through literature its influence has affected the horizon of many Western traditions and peoples. One also could cite the American Declaration of Independence as a classic that has had its impact on the culture, literature, and laws of the United States of America. This impact is such that when a citizen, born and educated in the United States, reads it, he or she does so not simply as an antiquated document but as a text that informs his or her horizon of understanding. What the concept of *Wirkungsgeschichte* does is make Heidegger's concept of pre-understanding much more complex and historical. We understand classics not only insofar as we have a life relation to the subject matter of these classics, but also insofar as our horizon is determined by these classics.

Fusion of Horizons

The notion of understanding as a fusion of horizons, which could more properly be called an expansion of horizons, is key to Gadamer's criticism of historicism, and it relates to his notion of understanding and application. A historicist maintains that one interprets the past to the degree that one steps out of one's own shoes into the shoes of the original author or situation. Gadamer points out that we bring our horizon (which includes our pre-understandings and even our *Wirkungsgeschichte*) to the text, so that understanding takes place when the text makes a claim upon us and thereby broadens our horizon. To interpret a past text is to understand it, but the understanding of the meaning of the text is inseparable from its application to the here and now.

Understanding always involves something like applying the text to be understood to the interpreter's present situation. Thus we are forced to go one step beyond romantic hermeneutics, as it were, by regarding not only understanding and interpretation, but also application as comprising one unified process.[60]

Gadamer sees his proposal as standing in continuity with the hermeneutical tradition that views philological, legal, and theological hermeneutics as unified in that they regard application as integral to the task of interpretation. The fixed text, be it a law or the Gospel, is understood only when it is applied. In other words, it is understood when its claim (the claim of the law or Gospel text) is applied to a new concrete situation even if in a new and different manner.[61]

It is this crucial link between understanding and application that constitutes Gadamer's major criticism of the adoption of a scientific methodology for the humanities. Because of this link, Gadamer argues that interpretation is a matter of practical reasoning. It involves the Aristotelian virtue of *phronesis* (prudence), which is achieved through experience and education (Bildung), and which enables one to form an appropriate judgment. Such a judgment is not secured by an *a priori* method, but can be concretely manifested only in practice. Moreover, it is not so much an act of an individual subject facing a tradition as it is an event by which the past and present are mediated and the tradition is brought forward. As Gadamer notes:

Understanding is to be thought of less as a subjective act than as participating in an event of tradition, a process of transmission in which past and present are constantly mediated. This is what must be validated by hermeneutic theory, which is far too dominated by the idea of a procedure, a method.[62]

Self-Understanding, the New Testament, and Marburg Theology

Rudolf Bultmann and Hans-Georg Gadamer were both students of Martin Heidegger. In interpreting the New Testament texts, Bultmann made the issue of existential self-understanding central to his interpretation of the New Testament (see Chapter Five). Likewise, his program of demythologizing was not so much a getting rid of mythic elements as it was an effort to interpret them existentially.[63]

From the perspective of his understanding of interpretation, Gadamer raises questions about Bultmann's program of demythologization.[64] He questions whether the central concept of the self-understanding of faith is adequate to describe our relation to the New Testament or whether there is a factor that goes beyond the individual's self-understanding, and even beyond the individual's being, that comes into play. In accordance with his own hermeneutical theory that self-understanding takes place in play, Gadamer underscores the "to and fro" of a dialogue *within* history and tradition. Hermeneutical awareness is not, then, the self-transparency of Hegel's self-conscious absolute knowledge. Rather, the self happens, as an event, just as faith is an event. Consequently, Gadamer expresses his disagreement with Bultmann as follows:

Neither in the work of the theologian nor in the Bible is "demythologizing" a sure guarantee of correct understanding. The real event of understanding goes beyond what we can bring to the understanding of the other person's words through methodical effort and critical self-control. Indeed it goes far beyond what we ourselves can become aware of. Through every dialogue something different comes to be. Moreover, the Word of God, which calls us to conversion and promises us a better understanding of ourselves, cannot be understood as a word that merely confronts us and that we must simply leave as it is. It is not really we ourselves who understand: it is always a past that allows us to say, "I have understood."[65]

Gadamer notes that despite the exegetical fruitfulness of Bultmann's existential interpretation of the Pauline letters and the Gospel of John, in terms of their self-understanding of their faith, "Heidegger's way of thinking led him [Heidegger] in the opposite direction," to the openness of dialogue.[66] Moreover, in sketching out the religious dimension and the question of God in Heidegger's thought, Gadamer notes that Heidegger's concern was how one speaks of God without making God into an object of knowledge. Heidegger posed this question with such a seriousness so that no God of philosophy, or even of theology, could serve as an answer. In pointing to Heidegger's reliance on the poet Friedrich Hölderlin, Gadamer at the same time brings out his own point of view:

Hölderlin's lamentation over the abandonment, his call to the disappeared gods, and on the other hand, his awareness that "we still have access to much of the divine" were like a pledge to Heidegger that the dialogue of thinking can still find a partner even on the eve of the world's complete homelessness and remoteness from the gods. We all take part in the dialogue. And the dialogue continues, for only in a dialogue can a language arise and continue to develop—a language in which we, in a more and more estranged world are at home.[67]

Critical Issues: Gadamer in Dialogue and Confrontation

The influence of Gadamer's hermeneutics on theology and the debates about its validity vary. Several debates with his critics have given Gadamer the opportunity to respond and to refine his position. Some of these debates have become so well known that they are part and parcel of the development of twentieth-century hermeneutical theory. Four of these debates or critical responses will be briefly surveyed. First, Jürgen Habermas has criticized the universality of hermeneutics and has used his critique of ideology against Gadamer's defense of tradition. This criticism has led Gadamer to specify his position more precisely. Second, the debate between Jacques Derrida and Gadamer illustrates the differences between a deconstructionist hermeneutics and a hermeneutics of retrieval. Thirdly, there is an attempt, from a more Enlightenment-oriented position, to defend itself against Gadamer's criticism, for example in the work of Karl-Otto Apel and E. D. Hirsch, Jr. Finally, there is the theological and philosophical appropriation of Gadamer's thought that utilizes some of his key categories and demonstrates their relevance for religious and theological studies.

The Gadamer-Habermas Debate

One of the significant debates has been between the German philosopher, Jürgen Habermas, representing the Frankfurt School and critical theory, and Gadamer, representing a hermeneutical affirmation of cultural tradition. Habermas argues that Gadamer's approach to the interpretation of a tradition and its classics presupposes that language primarily communicates meaning. Yet language, Habermas contends, takes place within social interaction. Consequently, tradition entails not only constellations of meaning but also the lack of meaning. Some traditions may be carried forward not so much by insight as by the effects of domination and power. Gadamer's approach overlooks the extent to which the endurance of the classic is due not simply to its outstanding representation of meaning and truth. It may also result from the endurance of power. An example from religious history illustrates Habermas's critique. One can well ask why it is that Christians today read Augustine's sermons against the Donatists as classics rather than the texts of the Donatists. The endurance of Augustine's sermons and the disappearance of many Donatist texts should not simply be explained by the excellence and truth of Augustine's texts. It must also take into account the effect of power, for example, the use of Roman imperial power to put down the Donatists. History very often is written by the victors, not by the victims. It is the classics of the victors that survive and endure, but that endurance cannot be attributed exclusively to meaningfulness and truthfulness.

Habermas suggests that when a hermeneutical approach seeks to make meaningful and significant what in a tradition appears to us without meaning and significance, it operates on the false assumption that there is there in a particular text meaning rather than a distortion of meaning or a reflection of implicit power. Habermas further illustrates his critique of Gadamer by referring to psychoanalytic theory. Psychoanalysis seeks to interpret a dream or a symbol in a way that uncovers and reveals the hidden structures of power within that dream or symbol. The goal of psychoanalysis is critical reflection into the subconscious forces that determine behavior so that, by bringing them to consciousness, one does not reveal their meaning and truthfulness but, rather, their obsessive force. By applying psychoanalytic theory to a theory of society, Habermas brings his critique of

ideology to bear upon the appropriation of tradition and its classics. Tradition contains not only meaning but also force and domination. It is the point of critical reflection to distinguish between the two. Gadamer's rehabilitation of the prejudice of the truth of classics does not sufficiently make this distinction.[68]

Habermas's criticism has not, however, gone unanswered. Not only has Gadamer himself responded but Paul Ricoeur (see below) has sought to mediate between the two, though he obviously is closer to Gadamer than to Habermas.[69] Gadamer's point is that Habermas's appeal to critical self-reflection overlooks the extent to which the ideals and values to which critical self-reflection appeals are themselves part of a tradition. Consequently, Habermas's critique of his hermeneutical appropriation of tradition is itself rooted in a tradition. Paul Ricoeur seeks to mediate between Gadamer and Habermas. Against Habermas, he argues that critique is rooted in a tradition. Against Gadamer, he argues that there is also a need to take into account the critical element of explanatory modes of thought.

The Gadamer-Derrida Debate

The debate between the French philosopher Jacques Derrida and Gadamer illustrates the difference between deconstruction and hermeneutics in their approach to cultural tradition.[70] Derrida focuses on Gadamer's understanding of the lived experience and rapport that comes from understanding another text or tradition, which entails an enlargement of one's own horizon. Derrida questions, however, whether in such encounters we experience rapport or really experience the interruption of rapport or the breach of understanding.[71] In short, Gadamer sees the experience of interpretation as an experience of the presence of meaning, but he fails, according to Derrida, to realize that one may also have missed what was not said or may detect the absent meaning in the tradition. In response, Gadamer maintains that Derrida does not grasp the role of "otherness" in his hermeneutics.[72] For Gadamer, the point of the fusion of horizons and openness to the authority of the classic is to allow one's understanding to be impacted by the otherness of the tradition. It is the otherness of the tradition that breaks open one's own view and horizons, and allows the otherness of the past to speak and to make claims on the present.[73]

Enlightenment and Hermeneutics

Because Gadamer criticizes Enlightenment rationalism and scientific empiricism as well as the Historical School that emerges from the Enlightenment, it is not surprising that Gadamer is criticized by those sympathetic with that tradition. E. D. Hirsch, Jr., of the University of Virginia, argues that Gadamer conflates meaning and significance. Hirsch argues that the meaning of a text should be limited to its historical-critical meaning and to the authorial intention. He claims that what Gadamer associates with the meaning of the text should be clearly separated from meaning and called the significance of the text.[74] Hirsch wants to reestablish the Enlightenment's affirmation that a text has a singular and fixed meaning that is dependent on authorial intention and historical context. It is the notion of the "significance" of the text that allows for diversity. The question remains, however, whether this distinction does justice to the relation between pre-understanding and understanding. Is not the horizon of a first-century Christian so different from the horizon of a twentieth-century Christian that they do not simply attach a different significance to the text, but understand the meaning of the text differently? Different traditions of culture and science give rise to different horizons so that the same text is understood very differently.

Hirsch's type of criticism suggests that Gadamer's theory of interpretation entails an epistemological relativism, insofar as no one interpretation is acknowledged as the correct and true interpretation. Karl-Otto Apel, a leading German philosopher, makes a similar criticism of

the philosophical conception underlying Gadamer's hermeneutical theory. He argues that Gadamer's hermeneutics seeks to counter both the ideals of objectivity (Dilthey) and of a single specified meaning (the contextualism of the Historical School). Apel argues that Gadamer's downplaying of objectivity has important and negative consequences for ethics in that it undermines the universality of ethical claims.[75]

Theological Appropriation

Several aspects of Gadamer's theory of interpretation have influenced theology. First, the notion of the classic has become a key insight that is developed by David Tracy. As the discussion of Tracy below will show, Tracy appropriates Gadamer's idea of a classic both in his defining of a religious classic and in his understanding of systematic theology as the interpretation of the classics of a specific religious tradition.[76]

Another important theological appropriation of Gadamer is the attempt to retrieve the classical sense of Scripture, especially the concept of the *sensus plenior* (fuller sense). The emergence of historical criticism has tended to conflate the meaning of the Scriptures to the historical-critical specification of the literal meaning. Because Gadamer's analysis argues that the meaning of a text should not be limited to authorial intention, Scripture scholars have appealed to Gadamer to defend the fuller sense of Scripture.[77]

Another theological appropriation of Gadamer is apparent in the debate about the nature of religious studies. Because religious studies emerged in the nineteenth century during the dominance of the Historical School and its emancipation from theological studies, some scholars argue that the canons of the Historical School, such as objectivity, neutrality, and disinterestedness, be applied to religious studies. Gadamer's view of the human sciences and his interpretation of tradition can be applied to religious studies so as to overcome the limitations of classic historicism.[78]

Reception Hermeneutics

A program strongly influenced by Gadamer is what is known as reception hermeneutics, or the Konstanz School. Its leading representatives, Hans Robert Jauss[79] and Wolfgang Iser,[80] have had considerable influence in both Germany and the United States. Reception hermeneutics pays attention to the various receptions of a text, not only synchronically—i.e., in reference to the audience contemporaneous with the original text—but also diachronically—i.e., throughout the history of diverse receptions. Jauss points out that a text is often composed for a specific audience. He shows, however, that classics often transcend the expectations of their audiences and possess a certain shock value. Eventually they become a part of the cultural tradition, and their original shock value is lost on succeeding generations. Jauss uses the example of the differences in the reception of the novel *Madame Bovary.* When first published, it was a scandalous and shocking novel. Today, no one would regard it as such. To understand the novel, one has to understand its original reception as well as the history of its reception. What the classic does is transform the horizons of expectation. The original German title of Jauss's programmatic volume, *The History of Literature as a History of Provocations*, underlines this point. Jauss's hermeneutic takes into account Gadamer's *Wirkungsgeschichte*, yet through the attention he gives to the original audience, he places greater emphasis on historical contextualization.

The work of Jauss and Iser has induced New Testament scholars to pay more attention to the original audience. A distinct approach in the United States, called "audience criticism," has attracted significant interest within New Testament studies. Systematic theologians also have pointed to the origin of the Church less as a foundational act of Jesus, than as a reception hermeneutic's understanding of the meaning of Jesus for the earliest church.[81] Similarly, the interpretation and development of Christian doctrine has been illustrated with reference to Jauss's reception hermeneutics.[82]

PAUL RICOEUR

Paul Ricoeur (1913–) was born in Valence in southern France. Orphaned as a young boy, he was raised by grandparents in the Calvinist Huguenot tradition. He studied metaphysics at the Sorbonne and took his aggregation, or university examinations, in philosophy in 1935. He then taught philosophy in high school in Colmar and Lorient until World War II, during which he was drafted in the French army and became a German prisoner of war for several years. After his release, Ricoeur returned to teaching part-time while he completed the two doctoral dissertations required for a university teaching post. In 1948 he began teaching at the University of Strasbourg and taught there for almost decade. He assumed a chair of philosophy at the Sorbonne in 1956 and taught there until 1967 when he decided to participate in the creation of a new university in Nanterre, a suburb of Paris. There, he was elected dean of the School of Letters. Upset with the student revolutions at the time, he resigned as dean in 1970 and accepted a position at the Catholic University of Louvain. At the same time, he began to teach a quarter-term at the University of Chicago. After three years he returned to Nanterre, which had by then become a part of the University of Paris. He remained there until the end of his career, while continuing to teach at the University of Chicago as the John Nuveen Professor in the Divinity School and as professor of philosophy and a member of the Committee on Social Thought.

The earliest influences on Ricoeur were from the traditions of existential and phenomenological philosophy (Gabriel Marcel, Edmund Husserl, and Jean Nabert). The existentialist phenomenology of Gabriel Marcel (see Chapter Five) had developed out of the early Existentialism in France that had preceded the war. As a prisoner of war during World War II, Ricoeur worked together with Mikel Defrenne on a commentary on Karl Jasper's philosophy entitled *Karl Jaspers et la philosophie de l'existence*. At that time there was a renewed interest in the works of Kierkegaard, Karl Jaspers, and Heidegger's then existentially interpreted *Being and Time*. After the war, Ricoeur wrote a book comparing Gabriel Marcel and Karl Jaspers.[83]

Ricoeur's earliest writings combine elements of the phenomenologies of Edmund Husserl and Jean Nabert. Nabert's work describes existence as a search for meaning. The subject of meaning lies in an originating act of interiority that then exteriorizes itself in signs and thereby becomes capable of analysis. Nabert's stress on the act of being and the process of freedom as a movement from interiority to exteriority influenced Ricoeur. Ricoeur also takes up Husserl's analysis of intentionality and, thereby seeks to analyze the structures and activity of the human will. His phenomenology, therefore, is not so much a phenomenology of perception, as it was for Husserl, as a phenomenology and a philosophy of the will. To elucidate this philosophy of the will, Ricoeur first turned to an analysis of the issues of evil and guilt.

Phenomenology and the Symbols of Evil

Ricoeur's important work on symbol and myth preceded his later work on interpretation and narrative. His original study of the symbol, within the context of his philosophy of will, used the enigmatic expression "poetics of the will" to underscore that only the symbolic language of a poetics can fully express the activity of the will. His *Philosophy of the Will* was to be completed in three volumes. The first volume, *Philosophie de la volonté: Le volontaire et l'involontaire* (the voluntary and involuntary), was translated as *Freedom and Nature*.[84] It investigates the essential structures of the human act of willing prior to examining the concrete issues of evil and transcendence. Ricoeur employs a phenomenological method, called *epoché,* which deliberately prescinds or isolates and brackets out certain aspects of an actual concrete situation of human existence in order to specify, clarify, and illumine particular foundational features of human existence. By carrying out this procedure with regard to the issues of fault, evil, and transcendence, Ricoeur focuses his analysis on the eidetic or equivalent structures of the will itself. The second volume of his *Philosophy of the Will* explores an anthropology attentive to the nature of human finitude and evil. *Finitude et Culpabilité* (finitude and culpability), translated into English in two volumes as *Fallible Man* and *The Symbolism of Evil*,[85] removes the bracketing and analyzes the will itself. *Fallible Man* employs a dialectical method in order to show the polarities of human existence caught between the finite and infinite poles of knowing, acting, and feeling. It points not to evil, but to the fault within which evil can emerge. *Fallible Man* employs a transcendental method of "pure reflection" in that it is concerned with the possibility of the fault rather than an analysis of its concrete historical reality. *The Symbolism of Evil* explores the historical expression of evil and demonstrates the mediational role of myth. The mythic narrative shows how a particular culture and community came to be. This illumines the human confession of fallibility, particularly as it is couched in the symbols and the myths of the ancient Near Eastern traditions. Ricoeur here raises the basic problem of how the interpretation of symbols can relate to broad philosophical and metaphysical issues. The third volume of his philosophical treatment of will, which was to be entitled the *Poetics of Will*, has not been written. It was to deal with the transcendent dimension or the sacred. Later writings on hermeneutical topics do, however, touch on this topic.

Ricoeur's study of symbolic language next led him to analyze the key role that symbols play in psychoanalysis. *Freud and Philosophy: An Essay in Interpretation* not only shows the centrality of the task of interpretation for psychoanalysis;[86] it also depicts how symbols function in diverse realms, such as in poetry, dreams, and religious discourse. Ricoeur points out how Freud saw himself as performing a "Copernican revolution" similar to that of Kant:

Just as Kant warned us not to overlook the fact that our perceptions are subjectively conditioned and must not be regarded as identical with what is perceived though unknowable, so psychoanalysis warns us not to equate perceptions by means of consciousness with the unconscious mental processes which are their object.[87]

Ricoeur concurs with Freud insofar as the Freudian revolution is a form of "anti-phenomenology," or a reversal of the phenomenological approach. Whereas Husserl's phenomenology sought, through bracketing, a reduction to consciousness, Freud actually reduces consciousness insofar as he questions the immediate consciousness as a source of meaning. Freudian analysis entails a twofold process. First, there exists a regressive path that moves from a pretension to conscious meaning to the source of meaning in unconscious desire and then a second stage involving a reappropriation of meaning. It is this combination of suspicion—the questioning of consciousness—and the reappropriation of meaning that provides a prototype to the two movements of hermeneutics.

In the context of his interpretation of Freud, Ricoeur identifies the dual aspect of hermeneutics as a "hermeneutics of suspicion" and a "hermeneutics of retrieval."

Hermeneutics seems to me to be animated by a double motivation: willingness to suspect, willingness to listen; vow of rigor, vow of obedience. In our time, we have not finished doing away with *idols* and we have barely begun to listen to *symbols*.[88]

This statement points to a shift in Ricoeur's understanding of interpretation. In *The Symbolism of Evil* he uses what he calls an "amplifying" or a "recovering" (a term borrowed from Gabriel Marcel) interpretation to point to the surplus of meaning contained in the symbol that interpretation seeks to uncover and to incorporate. Psychoanalysis showed him that in addition, there is a reductive interpretation. Consequently, he explicates the "conflict of interpretations in which an archeology of consciousness is opposed to a teleology of meaning." In an essay published after his

study of Freud, Ricoeur explicates the meaning of hermeneutics in terms of this conflict between the two modes of interpretation, one involving a hermeneutics of suspicion, the other a hermeneutics of retrieval.[89] In the context of this contrast, Ricoeur sought to explicate the significance of semantic innovation and the production of new meaning in symbols. In his *Lectures on Ideology and Utopia*, Ricoeur contrasts ideology as justifying an existing order and utopia that interrupts order through the creative novelty of the utopian imagination.[90] Whereas ideology is the imaginative and symbolic justification of the past, utopia is the symbolic opening toward the future.

The Hermeneutical Turn: From Symbol to Metaphor

Ricoeur's writings after his work on Freud show a significant turn. Through the 1960s Ricoeur's work concentrated on symbols. He wrote at the time: "I shall have a better understanding of man and the bond between the being of man and the being of all beings if I follow the *indication* of symbolic thought."[91] His interpretation of symbols centered, as we have seen, on this double meaning. However, his further study of structural, psychoanalytical, and hermeneutical theory led him beyond his intense focus on symbols to a wider exploration that would include all sign systems.

Ricoeur's turn to metaphor, characterized as his "hermeneutical turn," emerges not only from his study of Freudian psychoanalysis, but also from the impasse encountered in his analyses of fault and guilt. He came to realize that the phenomenon of fault cannot be adequately grasped by a pure phenomenological description. The reason is that fault does not result simply from consciously explicit intentions. To grasp the meaning of fault, Ricoeur was required to turn to the language of the confession of fault as well as the uses of metaphorical and mythic language.[92]

Ricoeur's major work on metaphor, *La métaphore vive*, proposes the basic thesis that the metaphorical function of language is the creation of new meanings in human discourse and requires an appropriate philosophical language to understand them. The French title, *La métaphore vive* (The living metaphor), better expresses his intent than does the English title, *The Rule of Metaphor*.[93] What is important to Ricoeur is the fact that live metaphors do not only have emotive value, but also create new meaning. The question for Ricoeur is this: How can a semantic theory, that is, a theory of meaning, account for the creation of new meaning through the use of metaphor? The question of the creative role and meaning of metaphor becomes central to Ricoeur's theory of interpretation.[94]

Metaphor is living not only to the extent that it vivifies a constituted language. Metaphor is living by virtue of the fact that it introduces the spark of imagination into a "thinking more" at the conceptual level. This struggle to "think more," guided by the "vivifying principle," is the soul of interpretation.[95]

La métaphore vive consists of eight studies. The initial studies discuss the substitutional theory of metaphor that limits a metaphor to a figure of speech and offers criticisms of the theory. After a critical discussion of Max Black's substitution theory and Monroe Beardsley's interaction theory, Ricoeur develops his own *tensional* theory of metaphor and its extension as a model for creativity.

At this time, Ricoeur argues that metaphor is the key to a theory of discourse and meaning. His analysis of metaphor shows that meaning involves the relation between sense and reference and entails a dynamic mingling of operations. The gain in meaning in poetic discourse is due to two factors: the tension between the terms of a metaphorical statement and also the tension between the literal meaning and the metaphorical meaning. The creation of meaning that results from this tension between the literal and the metaphorical is not simply a gain that results from a deeper interpretation. Rather, the gain in meaning derives from the semantic shock to which this tension gives rise. Therefore, the gain in meaning achieved through this tension involves the cre-

ation of meaning. It is in this sense that the problem of interpreting metaphors becomes a model for the task of hermeneutics.

Ricoeur uses Jesus' parables to illustrate his point.[96] The vision that the parables present is a vision that creates a shock, and it is precisely that shock that creates meaning. What manager, for example, pays people who work for one hour the same wage as those who labor for several hours, if he wants his workers to show up early the next morning? What shepherd leaves the whole flock just to find one lost sheep? The meaning that the parables create results from a radically new vision of the world that goes beyond and subverts the hearer's customary views of the world. Ricoeur's theory of metaphor influenced the exegetical work of his colleague, Norman Perrin, and others, especially with regard to the interpretation of the Gospel parables.[97]

Hermeneutics of Objectification: Key Concepts

Ricoeur's developing hermeneutics reveals significant differences with Gadamer's theories. These differences come to the fore especially in the role that Ricoeur gives to the question of textuality and its objectivity. Whereas Gadamer's hermeneutic can be viewed as a hermeneutics of belonging, Ricoeur's theory can be seen as emphasizing hermeneutical objectification. Gadamer stresses that we belong to the horizon of a tradition and the classics that we interpret. The classic is not only an authority to be taken seriously because it has endured the ravages of time; it also influences our own horizons that we bring to it. Moreover, we understand a classic insofar as we apply it to our own life situation.

Ricoeur's approach underscores the objectification that takes place, first of all, in speech that involves a use of particular words and forms and then, secondly, in writing. When a discourse is placed in writing, it becomes further objectified as a text. One can then analyze and scrutinize the meaning of a text independent of the original situation in which it was spoken. The event and the meaning become separated through the act of writing and textuality. The objectification that takes place in speech and writing means that what is said can be analyzed according to its structure. Hence, Ricoeur emphasizes the possibility of bringing structural analyses to the understanding of a text. In referring to this objectification, it should be noted that for Ricoeur the word "text" comprises not only written documents but all cultural productions. Text, Ricoeur writes, means

not only expressions fixed in writing but also mediation exerted by all the documents and monuments which have a fundamental trait in common with the written word. This common trait, which constitutes the text as text, is the fact that the meaning of the text has become *autonomous* in relation to the intention of the author.[98]

The result of objectification is the possibility of the creation of a new reference. Ricoeur points out that insofar as discourse becomes further objectified through becoming a text, it can be read by an audience that is both new and different. As a result, the referents of the text are understood differently. The original textual referent can be replaced with new and other references.

This element of objectification leads Ricoeur to give a specific meaning to the term "distanciation." Whereas Gadamer uses the concepts of temporal distance and *Wirkungsgeschichte*, or a text's effects, to illustrate our belonging to a tradition, Ricoeur suggests that hermeneutics begins when the interpreter is not content to belong to a historical world considered in the mode of the transmission of tradition, but rather interrupts the relation of belonging in order to creatively signify it.[99] As an example of the phenomenological reduction (*epoché*), distanciation refers to a text's independence from lived experience. The textualizing of experience thus makes possible a "distancing," so to speak, of the text from that original experience. It makes possible the analysis of the structure and forms of that text to get at the sense of the text.[100] Understanding the text thus involves the appropriation of the new world opened by the semantic meaning created by the text.

Religious Language and Forms of Discourse

Central to Paul Ricoeur's understanding of language in general and religious language in particular is the relation between the form of discourse and the meaning of discourse. Religious experience and phenomena come to expression in language through specific forms of discourse. The interpretation of religious language, therefore, requires attention to forms of discourse. This basic principle repeats itself throughout Ricoeur's philosophical exposition of religion. An example of this principle is his interpretation of the concept of revelation. In his view, the understanding of revelation has not sufficiently taken into account the diversity of the forms of discourse.[101]

In developing a hermeneutic of the idea of revelation, Ricoeur notes that previous attempts to define revelation have been monolithic. Instead, Ricoeur suggests a pluralistic, polysemic, and analogical understanding of revelation insofar as he points to the diverse literary forms of revelation in discourse. A consistent theme of philosophy, namely, the importance of linguistic structure and form for determined meaning, is applied to the notion of revelation. Ricoeur points to the diverse forms of discourse in Scripture, which include prophetic, narrative, prescriptive, wisdom, and hymnic discourse. Traditional conceptions of revelation overlook this diversity of forms and thereby may reduce revelation to one specific discourse, e.g., prophetic or perhaps prescriptive forms, and fail to appreciate the rich diversity of meanings and uses of revelation.

The same attention to the diversity of literary form and meaning is present in Ricoeur's treatment of Rudolf Bultmann's program of demythologization. His preface to the French translation of Bultmann's *Jesus Christ and Mythology* argues that Bultmann's existential interpretation moves too quickly from language about myth to existential interpretation without pausing to explore the diverse forms of language and the surplus of meaning present in distinct discourses. Furthermore, he points out that Bultmann does not proceed to the significant metaphysical and ontological questions that the program of demythologization implies.[102]

The importance of forms of discourse also comes to the fore in Ricoeur's discussion of the relation between the phenomenology of the sacred and what he calls the testimony or proclamation of the sacred. Here the similarities and differences between phenomenology and hermeneutics are noted. According to Ricoeur, a phenomenology of the sacred has four characteristics: the numinous or sacred power, the hierophanic (manifestation of the sacred), the interrelation of myth and ritual or specific manifestations of the sacred, and the sacred elements of nature, which together characterize a sacred universe.[103] In contrast to these, Ricoeur describes the traits of proclamation: In Hebraic faith, the word goes beyond numinous power; instruction through the Torah outweighs sacred manifestation through image; a historical vision of reality overcomes the repetition and reactualization of ritual; and the ethical dimension of the divine word takes the place of the sacredness of nature. Ricoeur sums up, as follows, his understanding of the function of the religious language of proclamation in relation to the manifestation of the sacred.

> The logic of meaning in all these forms of discourse depends upon the use of *limit-expressions* that bring about the rupturing of ordinary speech. This act of rupturing the ordinary is what I oppose to the language of the sacred universe founded as it were on the correspondence of the macrocosmos and the microcosmos, of humankind, its dwelling place, and the universe, of our mother and the earth. The universality of the sacred, we said, is internally "bound." The paradoxical universe of the parable, the proverbs, and the eschatological saying, on the contrary, is a "burst" or an "exploded" universe.[104]

Narrative and Hermeneutics

In his more recent work, *Time and Narrative*, Ricoeur shows that a phenomenology of time leads to several basic aporia or dilemmas that can be resolved through narrative. "Temporality cannot be spoken of in the direct discourse of phenomenology, but rather requires the mediation of the indirect discourse of narrative."[105] Narrative configures successive events and gives them an identity through plot or story. Narratives thus can entail the construction of an identity both on a social and historical level, such as the identity of a nation or a people, and on the level of an individual life or personal identity.[106] *Time and Narrative* continues what Ricoeur did with metaphor in relation to tropes, or figurative language, but now on a larger scale with the literary genre of narrative. A significant shift also takes place in Ricoeur's use of terms. The term "narrative refiguration" replaces "metaphorical redescription" as the key category he uses to explain his hermeneutical approach. A similar shift in his religious writings can be seen in his use of the term "refiguring the sacred."

Ricoeur hopes to gain several advantages from "narrative refiguration." First, he hopes to avoid the understanding of language as primarily descriptive and linked to reference and to propositions. Refiguration, instead, focuses on the semantic or meaning dimension of the narration itself. Second, he has become more familiar with reception hermeneutics (see above) and seeks to make reception itself more integral to the constitution of the meaning of a text. Third, refiguration underscores the ability of narrative configuration to reveal and to transform, and hence to be applied to life. Narrative provides a transition between description and prescription. In addition to describing actions, narrative provides prescriptive models that lead to ethics.

In his Gifford Lectures at Edinburgh, entitled "Sur l'individu," Ricoeur extends his understanding of narrative to explore the nature of the human self or subject. The lectures deal with the nature of the human person, the identity of the self, and the relation between the self and the other.[107] The question of the human person involves questions about identity and sameness of the self and its cohesion through the changes of a lifetime.[108] He takes as an adversary the critique of personal identity elaborated on by Derek Parfit's *Reasons and Persons* and his claim that "our identity is not what matters."[109] Ricoeur argues for the importance of identity and a narrative conception of personal identity.

The decisive step in the direction of a narrative conception of personal identity is taken when one passes from the action to character. A character is one who performs the action in narrative. The category of character is therefore a narrative category as well. . . .[110]

In addition to his arguments for a narrative identity, Riceour seeks to elaborate on personal identity in relation to ethical aims and moral norms. This brings his hermeneutical theory and his narrative conception of personal identity in relation to the work of John Rawls' on justice and to the issue of the relation between love and justice.[111]

A continuity exists among Ricoeur's latest works in that they all show the interrelation between semantic innovation and productive imagination; they all underscore the creativity of the human imagination through its use of language. His work on metaphor argues that metaphor produces new meaning through new and different predications that bring the disparate or different together. The narrative similarly creates new meaning through the unity of the plot that synthesizes previously disparate elements of the story. Likewise, narrative asserts the unity of the self and its character through the disparate elements of a life story.

Critical Issues

Paul Ricoeur's work covers and relates to a wide range of movements and topics: phenomenology, anthropology, hermeneutics, and narrative. In large part, Paul Ricoeur is his own most serious critic. His awareness of the inadequacies of his early work on phenomenology and symbol led him to the exploration of hermeneutical theory and the study of metaphor. This, in turn, led him to the study of narrative as, perhaps, the best perspective with which to deal with history, time, the self, and identity. Each of these shifts entailed his bringing a new perspective to bear on his earlier work and its shortcomings.

In the field of theological studies, his work has been appropriated by many theologians, especially his colleagues and students.[112] David Tracy's reception of Ricoeur will be discussed below. Hans Frei and his students have criticized Ricoeur's work and its theological reception. Their interpretation of Ricoeur has not, however, focused on the importance that he gives to the structural elements of discourse, or to the relation between forms of discourse and meaning. Rather, they interpret his hermeneutics as too concerned with the question of reference and, therefore, question whether he continues the eighteenth-century mode of interpretation that Hans Frei criticizes. (See the discussion of Frei below.) Others would contend that Ricoeur's hermeneutic reveals a complexity and a diversity of interests that this criticism does not sufficiently take into account.[113]

DAVID TRACY

David Tracy (1939–) is a Roman Catholic theologian who, in dialogue with the transcendental Thomism of Karl Rahner and his teacher, Bernard Lonergan, has sought to go beyond it. He has done this through his positive reception of the hermeneutical theories of both Hans-Georg Gadamer and Paul Ricoeur, and later those of the poststructuralist and postmodern theorists. David Tracy was born in Yonkers, New York. He studied at the Gregorian University in Rome and wrote his dissertation on Bernard Lonergan, who was at that time a professor at the Gregorian. After teaching at the Catholic University of America for several years, he accepted an appointment at the University of Chicago, where he serves as the Andrew Greeley Professor of Theology.

Theological Method and Fundamental Theology

As mentioned, David Tracy was a student of Bernard Lonergan, and his dissertation and first book trace Lonergan's own development. Tracy gives special attention to Lonergan's understanding of the concept of horizon and to the shifting horizons of Lonergan's own diverse writings.[114] Tracy argues that Lonergan's studies on Thomas represent his recovery of the medieval world of theory as horizon and the recovery of interiority, and anticipate the more systematic reflections in Lonergan's later work on understanding and method.[115] (See Lonergan in Chapter Seven, which deals with transcendental Thomism.) The focus of Tracy's dissertation on Lonergan points to his own intellectual concerns and development. In showing that Lonergan's understanding of theory and method led him increasingly to take into account historicity (in engagement with Wilhelm Dilthey) and twentieth-century hermeneutical theory, Tracy is following the path of his own interests. Tracy's own work will develop from a concern with method and theory to an engagement with hermeneutical as well as poststructural theory—with an intensity and expansion that go far beyond Lonergan.

Prior to the publication of Lonergan's *Method in Theology*, Tracy, using a draft version, examined Lonergan's understanding of method and the diverse functional specialties that constitute theology. (See Chapter Seven.) Following his exposition of Lonergan, Tracy examines the adequacy of Lonergan's conception of these functional specialties of theology as they relate to the understanding of both the basis and the task of fundamental theology. Within Roman Catholic theology, fundamental theology has been the discipline that deals with the truth of Christianity and the foundations of Christian theology. It has traditionally two tasks: an apologetic task, to demonstrate the truth of Christianity, and a methodological task, to ground the disciplines of systematic and dogmatic theology.

Tracy appreciates Lonergan's attempt to rethink fundamental theology as a functional specialty. Nevertheless, he registers reservations about his conception. He raises significant questions: Does, for example, Lonergan give too much value to conversion and even presuppose conversion as the basis of fundamental theology? Does he take sufficiently into account the apologetic

task of theology to address the cultured despisers of religion? Does his conception of fundamental theology sufficiently raise foundational and critical questions, or does it presuppose conversion rather than provide a rational demonstration leading to conversion?

The gist of these questions is Tracy's conclusion that "there remains no critical difference between Lonergan's present notion of foundations and his present notion of systematics. . . ."[116] Tracy's basic point is that there are two questions that Lonergan's own method distinguishes but that, as Tracy suggests, Lonergan's present formulation does not sufficiently and critically establish. The question of the meaning of religious language is distinct from the question of the adequacy and truth of religious language.[117]

The first question is a properly fundamental theological question because it deals with the conditions of the possibility of theological meaning. The second is a systematic theological question because it treats the meaning of a religious tradition. These questions lay out a challenge that David Tracy's own theological work takes up. *Blessed Rage for Order* discusses the issues of the first question within the context of his own proposed reformulation of fundamental theology. *The Analogical Imagination* carefully works out the difference between systematic theology and the foundations of theology with reference to social analysis and hermeneutical theory.

The Method of Correlation and Revisionist Theology

In the development of his theological method, Tracy is significantly influenced by his colleagues at Chicago, particularly Langdon Gilkey and Schubert Ogden in systematic theology and Steven Toulmin and Paul Ricoeur in philosophy. Gilkey and Ogden had explored issues of modernity and secularization, and the relation of process thought and theology. Also influential is Stephen Toulmin's work on understanding and the notion of "limit" within religious language, and Paul Ricoeur's work on hermeneutics.

The importance of this Chicago milieu is evident in Tracy's *Blessed Rage for Order*, which speaks to the nature of theology in the contemporary pluralist context that was experiencing not only a crisis of theology but also the crisis of modern secularism and the legacy of Enlightenment rationality.[118] These dual contexts are central for Tracy, though sometimes overlooked by his critics. Tracy proposes that theology must be done in a pluralist and a secularized context but, at the same time, he points to the crisis of the impoverished one-dimensional rationality that underlies secularization. The centerpiece of *Blessed Rage for Order* is Tracy's development of a revisionist model of theological method that employs a critical method of correlation.

It was the widespread influence of Paul Tillich's advocacy of the method of correlation in his *Systematic Theology* (see Chapter Five) that led to its adoption by many theologians in the United States and Europe after World War II. However, these theologians specify the two poles of correlation very differently. Tillich refers to the correlation between the human existential questions and the answers given in the biblical symbols, especially the symbol of Jesus as the Christ. Hans Küng, however, makes the earthly Jesus rather than the Christ symbol the theological pole of the correlation. A leading Roman Catholic feminist systematic theologian, Rosemary Ruether, makes the prophetic principle within the biblical Scriptures the theological pole, whereas for Schubert Ogden that pole is the Jesus *kerygma*. In view of these differences, it is important to examine exactly how David Tracy understands the method of correlation.

Schubert Ogden's conception of correlation provides a context for differentiating Tracy's position.[119] (On Ogden, see Chapter Ten.) Ogden distinguishes quite carefully between the criteria of truthfulness and the criteria of appropriateness as representing a difference between two distinct questions. One is: What is Christianity? The other is: Is Christianity true? Ogden's distinction is often overlooked by critics who think that the second question entails a determination of the identity of Christianity, whereas for him the question is limited to the truth of Christianity. The answer to the question of Christian identity is, for Ogden, the earliest testimony of the New Testament. On this matter of Christian identity, Ogden is influenced by the work of Willi Marxsen, who was professor of New Testament at the University of Münster, and who developed the conception of the Jesus *kerygma* as central to the determination of Christian identity.[120]

David Tracy's understanding of the method of correlation is significantly different from the conceptions of both Paul Tillich and Schubert Ogden. First, he proposes a "mutually critical correlation" as characteristic of his own method. Whereas a common view of Tillich's method is that of a correlation between our question and the biblical answer,[121] Tracy underscores the fact that one has not only to question the New Testament but also to question and to be critical of our own questions. Second, Tracy's interpretation of the two poles of the correlation is much more comprehensive. The first pole is the interpretation of a religious tradition. The second pole is the interpretation of the religious dimension of the contemporary situation.

In developing his method of correlation, Tracy underscores the concept of the "working canon" that includes the diverse literary genre of the New Testament that interpret the event of Jesus for the first pole. The second pole is addressed by the fundamental theological task of interpreting the religious dimension of common human experience. In attempting this task, Tracy follows Toulmin and Ricoeur and points to the role of the "limits" of experience. In explaining human finitude and the religious dimension of experience, Tracy makes use of the conception of "limit."

All genuine limit-situations refer to those experiences, both positive and negative wherein we both experience our own human limits (limit-to) as our own as well as recognize, however haltingly, some disclosure of a limit of our experience.[122]

The distinction between "limit of" and "limit to" is central to express the difference between the experience of the finitude of our human life and the disclosure of a religious dimension or horizon.

That limit-to the everyday also seems to disclose—in the same *ec-stasis*—a limit-of whose graciousness bears a religious character . . . such experiences are more properly described not *as* explicitly *religious* but as disclosive of a "limit," a "religious" dimension or horizon to our lives.[123]

The religious dimension of experience is interpreted not so much as a particular experience *other* than general experience but, rather, as a particular dimension of experience itself. The issue here quite clearly points to significant differences, for example, between Friedrich Schleiermacher's and Rudolf Otto's conception of religious experience: Is there a religious experience separate from other experiences, or is there a religious dimension to all experience? It is clear that Rudolf Otto's *Idea of the Holy* represents the former, whereas Schleiermacher's *Glaubenslehre* typifies the latter. In *Blessed Rage for Order*, Tracy, in line with Karl Rahner and Bernard Lonergan, seeks to the develop the latter answer.

The religious dimension of language is not, I believe adequately described as simply another human activity coordinate to such activities as science, morality, or culture. By its limit-character, a religious dimension is more accurately described by some such phrase as ultimate ground to or horizon of all other activities. . . .[124]

Tracy argues that reflection upon limit questions and situations discloses the reality of a dimension to our lives that, no matter how named or experienced, functions "as a final, now gracious, now frightening, now trustworthy, now absurd, always uncontrollable limit—of the very meaning of existence itself."[125]

Publics and Modes of Argument

In *The Analogical Imagination*, Tracy begins his reflections with a social portrait of the theologian and outlines the three publics of theology: society, the academy, and the Church. These diverse social publics demonstrate the diversity of criteria required for theological argumentation, for these publics relate to different reference groups, modes of argument, ethics, and religious stances. Whereas fundamental theologies relate primarily, but not exhaustively, to the public represented by the academy, systematic theology relates to the Church, and practical theology to society.[126] Tracy is careful to point out that these reference groups are primary to the respective theological disciplines, but should not be exclusive of one another. Likewise, the disciplines differ in terms of their modes of public argument. For example, in regard to fundamental theology, Tracy asserts that

fundamental theologies will be concerned principally to provide arguments that all reasonable persons, whether "religiously involved" or not, can recognize as reasonable.[127]

What is central to fundamental theology is that its discourse is public and available in principle through appeals, with appropriate warrants and arguments, to the experience and rationality of responsible people. Systematic theology is, however, defined through a different orientation:

Systematic theologies will ordinarily show less concern with such obviously public modes of argument. They will have as their major concern the re-presentation, the reinterpretation, of what is assumed to be the ever-present disclosive and transformative power of the particular religious tradition to which the theologian belongs.[128]

Practical theology is defined in relation to the mode of argument appropriate to society. In addition to public modes of argument, real differences emerge with regard to ethical stances. Fundamental theology is concerned "principally with the ethical stance of honest, critical inquiry proper to its academic setting."[129] Systematic theology is characterized by a creative loyalty and critical fidelity to the classical religion of its church. Practical theologies display the ethic of responsible commitment, often a solidarity and involvement in the situation of praxis or practice. Finally, these disciplines differ in their religious stances. Whereas systematic and practical theology assume personal involvement in a particular tradition or praxis, fundamental theologies, although they share that commitment, "in principle abstract themselves from all religious 'faith commitments' for the legitimate purposes of critical analysis of all religious and theological claims."[130]

It is systematic theology that deals with the religious classics of a particular tradition. Tracy describes a religious classic as follows:

Like all classics, religious classics will involve a claim to meaning and truth as one event of disclosure-concealment of the reality of live existence. Unlike the classics of art, morality, science and politics, explicitly religious classic expressions will involve a claim to truth as the event of a disclosure-concealment of the whole of reality *by the power of the whole*—as, in some sense, a radical and finally gracious mystery.[131]

The Theological Reception of Hermeneutical Theory

In developing and applying his theological method, Tracy appropriates and makes central to his endeavors basic categories of Gadamer's hermeneutics. He modifies and supplements these, however, by incorporating several aspects of Ricoeur's hermeneutical theory, namely, the complementarity between modes of explanation and interpretation, the distinction between manifestation and proclamation, and the important interrelation between literary form and content.

The category of the classic remains, nonetheless, central to Tracy's method of correlation, and it has the advantage of allowing him to define each religious tradition in terms of the specific classics of that particular tradition. However, the notion of the classic is not, for Tracy, simply a descriptive term; it is also a normative claim insofar as a classic has specific characteristics. In

a religious classic—which includes texts, but also rituals and exemplary figures such as Jesus—particular norms and limits come to the fore so that a religious classic raises, in an outstanding way, the religious question. The normative claim of the Scriptures within the Christian tradition is special insofar as the Scriptures are the *norma normans*, that is, the "norming norm."

Especially important to Tracy's interpretation of religious classics is the combining of explanatory and interpretive modes, which he takes over from Ricoeur as a corrective to Gadamer. The explanatory modes of interpretation are important because they serve as public corrections for the community in its appropriation of the tradition. Tracy includes the historical-critical, the literary-critical, and the social-scientific as examples of the explanatory mode of interpretation. They stand in a dialectic relation to the interpretive appropriation of texts. They serve the critical function of both explanation and correction.

Theologians employ these methods either to *develop* their enveloping understanding of the tradition through methodical explanation or to argue publicly for the need to correct the tradition at appropriate points.[132]

Tracy also integrates into his theological reception of Ricoeur's hermeneutic, the distinction between event and manifestation, and the relation between form and content. With regard to event and manifestation, Tracy writes:

The realized experience of the truth-character of the religious experience is an experience of its purely given character, its status as an event, a happening manifested *to* my experience, neither determined by nor produced by my subjectivity. Insofar as I honor experience itself, I may accord this experience the status of a claim to truth as a manifestation of a "letting be seen" of what is, as it shows itself to experience.[133]

Tracy proposes that what he calls the "grounding religious event of God's self-manifestation in

Jesus" is expressed in the Jesus *kerygma* of the earliest testimonies and in the Christ *kerygma* of the later writings.[134] The meaning of this event is disclosed in a number of basic literary genres of the New Testament and their correctives. The basic genres are proclamation-confession, gospel narrative, symbols-images, reflective theology, and doctrine (John's Gospel). To these basic genres, Tracy proposes that the genre of apocalyptic (with its intensification and senses of crisis) and of doctrine (with its stability expressive of early Catholicism) are to be interpreted as correctives of basic New Testament genres.[135]

Tracy sees New Testament apocalyptic as an interpretive corrective to the other genres as a "reminder of the explosive intensification and negations" of apocalyptic

as a challenge, for example, to any "private" understanding of the Christian event by forcing a recognition of the genuinely public, political and historical character of all Christian self-understanding, as a challenge to all the privileged to remember the privileged status of the oppressed, the poor, the suffering . . . as a challenge to face the reality of the really new, the *novum*, and the future breaking in confronting every present, exploding, every complacency. . . .[136]

Religion and Ambiguity

Tracy underscores the pluralism of meaning in any classic through the interplay of different explanatory and interpretive modes, different literary genre, and different receptions. Tracy emphasizes that a classic is open to more than one meaning. This accords with Gadamer's understanding of a classic, as Gadamer himself illustrates with reference to music and drama and the plurality of different performances of a musical or dramatic classic. However, Tracy's later writings push the notion of pluralism even further. Just as the poststructuralist and deconstructive critique of classic hermeneutical theory has increasingly emphasized the plurality and ambiguity of all interpretation, so, too, has Tracy's theology

sought to integrate the results of these critiques.[137] Tracy writes:

The development of structuralist and poststructuralist studies of language have exposed as illusory the hope that any fully-preserved unity already lost through hermeneutical analyses of actual language use could be retrieved by studying language as a systematic object—as the structuralists assumed.[138]

Tracy emphasizes not only the plurality of interpretations resulting from different methods and approaches, but also the diversity of religious classics, resulting from diverse religious traditions and from the inherent ambiguity of every religion itself.

We find ourselves, therefore, with a plurality of interpretations and methods. We find ourselves with diverse religious classics among many religious traditions. We find ourselves glimpsing the plurality within each tradition while also admitting the ambiguity of every religion: liberating possibilities to be retrieved, errors to be criticized, unconscious distortions to be unmasked.[139]

This plurality of interpretation calls for an understanding of theology as involving a dialogue and conversation not only among those representing diverse religious traditions but also with diverse methods of explanation and appropriation, and with diverse movements and groups within society.

Critical Issues

The above discussion of David Tracy's achievements in theology have touched on his theological method, his fundamental theology, his advocacy of pluralism and, above all, his understanding of the public character of theology. Owen Thomas has argued that Tracy's conception of the public, and especially his understanding of the role of public criteria within fundamental theology, presupposes a modern, shared conception of reason. Thomas argues that such a theology conceived as a conversation among equals should include the counter-public spheres of discourse that have emerged in feminist, black, and liberation theologies. The question Thomas raises is whether Tracy's appeal to public criteria is sufficiently open.[140] One might suggest that the notions of pluralism, ambiguity, and conversation in Tracy's later work would indicate that he is open to Thomas's suggestions. In interpreting Tracy as closer to Habermas's more public Enlightenment ideal of reason, Thomas overlooks Tracy's reception of the poststructuralist critique and the degree of difference between Tracy and Habermas. Nevertheless, the question Thomas raises remains important. The question remains whether Tracy has changed his understanding of apologetics and fundamental theology. In his criticism of Lonergan, Tracy originally argued from a conception of fundamental theology that was closer to Enlightenment ideals. In his move to accept postmodern and poststructural theories, Tracy has accepted a more contextual and fragmentary understanding of reason, the world, and theology.[141]

Peter Berger, a sociologist of religion, has severely criticized not only David Tracy but also his Chicago colleagues, Langdon Gilkey and Schubert Ogden, whom he lumps together with Tracy under the category of the "Chicago School." Berger's criticism also raises the issue of the public insofar as he accuses Tracy of theological reductionism in his attempt to appeal to the secular publics of modern society.[142] Berger suggests that the centerpiece of Tracy's *Blessed Rage for Order* is the analysis of the religious dimension of common human experience. He views Tracy's affirmation that religious language does not present a new supernatural world but, rather, re-presents the very meaningfulness of the most cherished enterprises of our culture, as theologically reductionistic. In his response to Berger, along with the responses of his colleagues, Gilkey and Ogden,[143] Tracy defends his conception of the supernatural by appeal to the understanding of the supernatural as explicated classically by Aquinas and more recently by Karl Rahner. In this respect, Tracy is drawing in general on the tradition of the *nouvelle théologie* (see Chapter Seven), in which the sharp contrast between the

natural and the supernatural is shown to be inadqate. Tracy further points out that his method of correlation argues from a dual fidelity: to the Christian Scriptures and Tradition and to contemporary experience, but that involves an interpretation of experience that uncovers its religious dimension.[144]

Members of the "Yale School" have also criticized David Tracy's work.[145] George Lindbeck sees Tracy's theology as an example of both expressionism and foundationalism[146] (see Chapter Sixteen). Hans Frei focuses on the question of the role of reference in Tracy's work, as well as in Ricoeur's. He sees their anthropological grounding of religious faith as the reduction of the reference or object of religious belief to an existential way of existing in the world, rather than an affirmation of the reality of *what* is believed. Moreover, he questions, as have others, whether Tracy gives sufficient attention to the historical Jesus.[147] The question, however, is whether such a criticism takes into sufficient account the role that the forms of discourse give to meaning and to religious affirmations. Both Ricoeur and Tracy give considerable weight to narrative structure in their interpretation of religious myth and the Gospel proclamation. Consequently, Ricoeur and Tracy affirm the value of religious myth in a way perhaps similar to that of David Friedrich Strauss. To the extent, however, that Frei's criticism tends to bring their views closer to those of Strauss, and overlooks the hermeneutical and historical differences between them, his criticism may not be valid.

HANS FREI

Hans Wilhelm Frei (1922–1988) was born in Breslau, Germany. Both of his parents were physicians. His father, Wilhelm Siegmund, invented the Frei test, an aid in the discovery of specific venereal diseases. His mother, Magda (née Frankfurther), was a pediatrician. Although the family was Jewish, they had their children baptized in the Lutheran church. Because, however, such baptisms did little to protect one from the Nazis, whose ideology focused on "Jewish blood" rather than on faith, Frei's parents sent him to a Quaker School in England. The entire family fled to the United States in 1938. Financial hardship limited Frei's choice of a school. Because a fellowship to study textile engineering was available, Frei went to North Carolina State University and graduated with a B.S. in 1942. After a lecture by H. Richard Niebuhr at the university, Frei began a correspondence with him and, on Niebuhr's advice, applied to Yale Divinity School where he obtained a B.D. in 1945.

After serving as a pastor in a Baptist church in North Stratford, New Hampshire, he returned to Yale in 1947 for doctoral studies. During this time he married Geraldine Frost Nye in 1948 and became an Episcopal priest. He completed his dissertation, "The Doctrine of Revelation in the Thought of Karl Barth, 1909–1922: The Nature of Barth's Break with Liberalism," in 1956 under the direction of H. Richard Niebuhr. During the writing of the dissertation, Frei taught at Wabash College (1950–1953) and the Episcopal Seminary of the Southwest (1953–1956). He then returned to Yale where he remained until his death on September 12, 1988. He taught in the Yale Graduate School of Religion and, in addition to his academic duties, was master of Yale's Ezra Stiles College.

Hans Frei's place in modern Christian thought, especially through his work on the relation between hermeneutics and history, has led to his recognition as the originator of what is called the new "Yale Theology," or Postliberalism. His theological position is closer to Karl Barth's theology than is any of the others discussed in this chapter. From that perspective, he could be located at the beginning of this chapter as a leading American theologian associated with the reconstruction of Karl Barth's theology. His dissertation explores Barth's conception of revelation in the context of modern theology. The dissertation remains unpublished, though some of its ideas are described in a set of significant essays on the theological background and theology of H. Richard Niebuhr that also deal in part with the

difference between Barth and Ernst Troeltsch on the question of faith and history.[148] Frei has significantly influenced many North American theologians in their appreciation and interpretation of Karl Barth and his relation to nineteenth-century theology.[149]

Hans Frei's writings constitute an important criticism of eighteenth- and nineteenth-century theories of historical reading and interpretation, especially as it relates to the Bible. His criticism is especially directed against the Idealism and rationalism that he sees in these theories of interpretation. In addition, Frei extends this criticism to twentieth-century hermeneutics from Rudolf Bultmann to Paul Ricoeur and David Tracy. In addition to his critique of historical criticism, Frei has argued against both the grounding of theology in a transcendental conception of human nature and current views of the method of correlation. His constructive work can be seen as an interpretive and theological alternative to these criticisms. It centers on the importance of narrative for biblical interpretation and on the understanding of theology as redescription or as "thick" description rooted in the biblical narratives. Because Frei's polemical arguments often serve as a foil for his own systematic propositions, what follows examines first his critique of modern historical criticism and his critique of theologies of correlation. We then will look at his constructive proposals for narrative and redescription.

The Critique of Modern Historical Criticism

In his major work, *The Eclipse of Biblical Narrative*, Frei traces the history of the modern interpretation of the Bible in order to argue that modern biblical criticism and a modern theology based upon that criticism are deeply flawed in their method of interpretation.[150] Whereas the Protestant Reformers interpreted the literal meaning of the Bible in order to grasp the whole Bible as proclaiming Christ through a figural reading, the biblical criticism of the eighteenth and nineteenth centuries proceeded down the wrong path because it confused meaning and reference. Frei attributes this eclipse of the Reformers' realistic reading of the biblical narrative to the use that Enlightenment rationalism and Christian apologetics made of historical criticism. What they did was to falsely identify the literal, realistic meaning of the biblical text with the text's references, that is, with the extratextual actual historical events. Moreover, the meaning of the biblical text was falsely interpreted either in terms of some universal moral truth (rationalism) or historically revealed truth (apologetics).

Frei argues, on the contrary, that the meaning of the biblical text does not derive from the external historical event but, rather, from the internal narrative world of the text itself.

Everything conspired to confine explicative hermeneutics to meaning as reference—to equate meaning with knowledge of potential or actual reality—and to make the primary reference historical rather than ideal. General (not theologically privileged) hermeneutics and biblical-historical criticism grew up together, and historical criticism by and large was the dominant partner.[151]

Frei points out that before the advent of the historical-critical method one interpreted the Scriptures by joining the biblical narratives together to form a whole narrative. Earlier narratives became types and figures of later narratives. These narratives then combined to provide an account of the "real world." Frei argues that the Protestant Reformers, writing before the advent of the historical-critical method, provided such a "realistic" reading of Scripture.

Through the coincidence and even identity between the world being depicted and its reality being rendered to the reader (always under the form of the depiction), the reader or hearer in turn becomes part of that depicted reality and thus has to take a personal or life stance toward it.[152]

With this appeal to premodern interpretation and to the Protestant Reformation, Frei maintains that his proposal retrieves the classical and traditional Christian approach to biblical interpretation before the introduction of the misguided efforts of modern criticism. Although *The Eclipse of Biblical Narrative* does not discuss in detail the major figures of twentieth-century hermeneutics, Frei does believe that most of the major problems that developed in the eighteenth and nineteenth century set the conditions and predicament of twentieth-century hermeneutics.

Hans Frei's method is, however, also indebted to his contemporaries. He published at the time that the New Criticism was in vogue as the reigning literary theory, with its center at Yale University. The New Criticism took serious issue with the psychological, psychoanalytic, or social analysis of literary texts. Instead, it proposed a formal and structural analysis of the text itself.[153] This literary approach studied a text independently of its context and as an autonomous work of art. In addition to the influence of the New Criticism, Frei was influenced by the literary critic Erich Auerbach's analysis of epic literature as "realistic." Auerbach had shown that epic literature is like a realistic novel. Its narrative vision of reality is elaborated through the interaction of character and event within the narrative itself. For Auerbach, the biblical Scriptures even go beyond such epics as Homer's. Whereas the latter can make us forget our own reality, the biblical narratives insist that they indeed are the only real world.[154] Others, for example, Robert Alter, have suggested a similar literary analysis and reading of the Bible. However, in contrast to Hans Frei's proposal, Alter sees literary analysis as a complement rather than an alternative to historical scholarship.[155]

Frei criticizes the historical-critical method not only as a method of interpretation but also in terms of its results. He objects to what the method implies for the subject or agent of interpretation. Because the historical-critical method requires an expertise in the original languages of a text and demands a thorough knowledge of the historical and social context of the writings, the historical-critical method places the authentic meaning of a text in the hands of experts. Frei objects to the fact that historians appear to tell people that they can know Jesus only by engaging in expert study, or by having experts inform them about the results of the academic and historical study of the Bible. Frei counters: "I think most of us have some hunch that we can actually read the Bible, including the New Testament, and that it isn't absolutely essential to have the experts tell us what we can find there."[156] Moreover, Frei proposes a different kind of reading as interpretively and theologically appropriate to Scripture, namely, a theological reading of the literal or realistic sense of the text.

Narrative and Identity

Narrative becomes such a central concept for Frei that he sees it as essential to a Christian reading of Scripture. In Christianity the cultic, moral, and sacramental life directly derive their meaning from the story of Jesus, his life, teaching, death, and resurrection. It is, therefore, "this narrative," Frei insists, "that has a unifying force and prescriptive character in both the New Testament and the Christian community that neither narrative generally nor any specific narrative has in Jewish Scripture and in the Jewish community."[157] The tradition of literal meaning must, however, be understood as a contrast to both the historical-critical analysis of the Bible and fundamentalist biblical literalism, because both share the same basic error:

It was this way for biblical fundamentalists, who saw nothing but identity or correspondence between written text and actual referent, as well as for historical critics, who usually saw a core or residue of such correspondence amidst much that served merely as a detective's clue or source to the "actual meaning." . . . [158]

Although Frei has consistently developed his emphasis on the narrative reading of the biblical text, a subtle shift did take place in his writings. In *The Eclipse of Biblical Narrative,* Frei places a much stronger emphasis on the narrative structure of the text than can be obtained through a literary analysis of the text itself. In his later essays, Frei's understanding of the literal meaning of the text becomes much more the "plain sense" of the text. This leads him to emphasize much more the reading of the text *within* the churches.[159]

Fortunately, Frei has taken his understanding of interpretation beyond the theoretical debate about theories of interpretation and has shown concretely the usefulness of his approach. He does this in *The Identity of Jesus Christ,* which represents Frei's constructive proposal insofar as it develops a Christology based upon Frei's reading of the Gospel accounts. In his interpretation of Jesus's identity in the Gospel narratives, Frei follows his own method of literal reading as he brackets historical-critical questions. What is important for him is not whether the Gospel accounts are historically correct, which is the question that the historical critics ask when they interpret the Gospels. Rather, Frei asks, What is the identity of Jesus, how do the stories indicate the character of Jesus? The narratives of the Gospel point to the identity of Jesus.[160] Because the Gospels are more like novels, their meaning is constituted by what they literally describe rather than by what they refer to objectively. Nevertheless, the narratives of Jesus's life, death, and resurrection attempt through their very narrative character to display both the identity and the presence of Jesus.

The Gospels provide what Frei's colleague, George Lindbeck, has called, an "intratextual" account. They are a redescription or refiguration of Jesus's identity within the framework of the scriptural narrative. What is of utmost concern to Frei is the "patterns" of Jesus's narrated identity rather than the questions about the historical accuracy of the Gospel materials.[161] Frei uses the Gospel narratives to develop a doctrine of Jesus's person and activity. The emphasis is on Jesus as a specific and "unsubstitutable" human being. The intention-action scheme is meant to emphasize Jesus as obedient, Jesus as the crucified human savior. The notion of "pattern of exchange" is used to interpret the work and person of Jesus. This pattern combines Jesus's "unsubstitutable individuality" as savior with the importance of his "universal saving significance."

In describing the genre of the Gospel as a narrative depicting the unsubstitutable identity of Jesus, Frei deliberately sets out to contrast the Gospel stories to myths or mythic stories. For, as George Hunsinger has pointed out, there is an analogy between Frei's understanding of myth and his interpretation of modern theology.[162] In contrast to both mythic and modern interpretations, Frei argues that Jesus is not presented merely as a symbol or as an ideal type. Rather, the very characteristics by which the Gospel narratives portray him show Jesus to have a specific personal identity. Such an argument presents Jesus not only as an historically real individual, rather than a mythic figure, but it also offers an alternative or contrast to the mythic depiction advanced by the modern critic David Friedrich Strauss (see Volume I, Chapter Nine).[163]

Frei distinguishes between two different types of identity-description: an "intention-action description" and a "self-manifestation description."[164] He employs both to show that the narrative description ascribes an identity to Jesus.[165] Jesus's intention-action comes to the fore in the Gospel depiction of the identity of Jesus in his obedience to the mission that God gave him, the power and powerlessness of his situation along with the transition from the one to the other, and the interaction of Jesus's intention-action with God's intention-action. The self-manifestation scheme is used to speak about Jesus's resurrection from the dead.[166]

Against Correlation Theology

Hans Frei's approach to systematic theology resembles the conjunction of critique and construction exemplified in his approach to the interpretation of Scripture. Parallel to his critique of the historical-critical reading of Scripture, Frei argues against the theological use of the method of correlation and the grounding of Christian faith in a general anthropology or concept of human nature. And, similar to his advocacy of

narrative is his proposal for redescription and "thick description" as the proper way of doing theology. Frei's final work, *Types of Christian Theology*, published posthumously by his students, contains the Edward Cadbury lectures that Frei gave in Birmingham, England. These essays present a typology of modern theology by which Frei is able to elucidate his own view in stark contrast with the views of other theologians, some of whom are discussed in this chapter.[167] To the extent that the theological positions of Pannenberg and Tracy and the hermeneutical theories of Gadamer and Ricoeur can be viewed as efforts to go beyond or criticize Neo-Orthodox theology, Frei's constructive view of hermeneutics and theology can be seen as an effort to retrieve and to reformulate Karl Barth's theology.[168]

In developing his typology of modern theology, Frei poses two basic questions that serve as the criteria that enable him to classify and judge these theologies. The first question is: Should theology be understood in terms of its own basis? The second, which is related to the first, concerns the relation between the external descriptions of Christianity and its own self-descriptions, and how the specific self-description is to be related to more general criteria of meaningfulness. In both cases, Frei is concerned that the external description of Christianity not become *the* criterion of the internal self-description, or become the basic standard of theological understanding. This fear underlies Frei's objections to all forms of correlation theology. Therefore, in delineating the nature of theology, Frei asks:

Is theology, as reflection on the ruled us of the Christian community's language, completely internal to that community? Or is self-description here either comparable to another kind of description, though not identical with it, or is it part of some other description? The answer of course depends upon whom you are asking. There are those who say, yes, it is completely internal and there is no use in comparing Christian discourse and its rules with other kinds of discourse. Then there are those who propose that while locating Christian language certainly is not a direct philosophical task since Christianity is a religion, it may be described under the same rubrics in which other religions are described. And here one faces two options.[169]

In delineating his own theological option Frei offers a typology of contemporary constructive theologies. Most typologies lay out two extremes and allow the truth to reside somewhere in the middle. One extreme of Frei's typology is represented by Gordon Kaufman's constructive theology (see Chapter Sixteen) and David Tracy's revisionist theology, both of which are unacceptable to Frei because both allegedly *subject* Christian self-description to philosophical foundations and to external descriptions. Similarly criticized is the type of anthropological grounding of theology pursued in the transcendental Thomism of Karl Rahner and Bernard Lonergan, and Wolfhart Pannenberg's attempt to go beyond what he considers to be the fideism of Neo-Orthodoxy. At the other extreme is D. Z. Phillips (see Chapter Sixteen), who in Frei's opinion does not even allow a subordinate place for philosophy and its criteria of coherence, adequacy, or appropriateness.[170] In the middle of Frei's typology stand Friedrich Schleiermacher and Karl Barth, who subordinate external description to Christian self-description but also allow a role for philosophy. Frei is quite aware that many might read Karl Barth's position as the same as Phillips's, and, therefore, he seeks to show that the inside/outside distinction is much more rigidly maintained by Phillips than by Karl Barth. At the same time, Frei wants to show that his own theology is also much more open.[171] In order to show how his own theology differs, Frei uses the categories of "thick description" and "redescription."

Redescription and Thick Description

Frei's typology can provide the background to understand his own systematic proposals. However, it should be noted that Frei does not develop a systematic theology as comprehensively and systematically as, for example, Wolfhart Pannen-

berg's three volumes. His systematic work on Jesus is much more concerned with explicating the narratives of the Gospel text, in an effort to get at the identity of Jesus rather than to discuss soteriology in terms of an abstract Christology. Likewise, his typology of theological method shows the primacy of the interpretation of the Bible in his theological method.

In describing theology's function, Frei notes that theology involves first- and second-level statements. First-level statements are the communal beliefs that are found in the creeds and confessions. Although they are the basic Christian beliefs and practices, they should not be thought of as constituting the essence of Christianity. In addition, theology has second-level statements and these in turn have two aspects:

Theology is a given Christian community's second-level appraisal of its own language and actions under a norm internal to the community itself. This appraisal in turn has two aspects. The first is descriptive: an endeavor to articulate the "grammar" or "internal logic," of first-level Christian statements. The second is critical: an endeavor to judge any given articulation of Christian language for its success or failure in adhering to the acknowledged norm(s) of Christian language use.[172]

One can illustrate these two levels with the christological creedal formula of the Council of Chalcedon. It affirms that Jesus is one person in whom two natures, human and divine, are united. This creed is, first of all, a statement that this is so about Jesus. In this sense the statement is a first-level theological statement. However, in addition, this formula is also a second-level statement, both descriptive and appraising. On this level the formula is descriptive of the internal logic that makes up the creedal formula. Yet it also has an appraisal function insofar as the formula is composed in response to those unacceptable views that denied either the full humanity or divinity of Jesus. This second-level function of appraisal is also formulated more positively. "The formula is a conceptual redescription of a synthesis of the gospel stories understood as the narratives identifying Jesus Christ."[173]

Frei explains that the categories of nature and person serve primarily to identify Jesus, and this is the grammar of the creedal formula. It serves to describe a unitary subject. The philosophical conjunction of substance/accidence is, however, a metaphysics that is subservient to the "grammar" of the formulae. Consequently, for Frei, it is this grammar of identity that constitutes the *literal sense* of the creedal formula, and this literal sense is primarily ascriptive rather than descriptive. The logic of the formula as a redescription serves the basic literal affirmation. Consequently, what is at stake at Chalcedon for Frei is not the ousia/hypostasis (nature/person) categories themselves, but the identification of Jesus.[174]

In a further attempt to elucidate his method, Frei appeals to the notion of "thick description" used in Clifford Geertz's interpretive anthropology. Rather than interpret the behavior of society in terms of some general principles, functions, or anthropological constants, Geertz provides a thick description, one that describes a society's beliefs and practices in a way that shows the logic of its identity. It is this thick description that Frei advocates. Insofar as such a description leaves room for philosophical categories, but does not allow them to subvert the ascriptive identity descriptions, it avoids both extremes. It neither makes one's own internal self-description wholly dependent upon an internal self-description nor does it avoid all reference to external description. Shortly before his death, Frei published an essay that appealed for a "a kind of generous orthodoxy," one that would include elements of liberalism and evangelicalism.[175] Such an orthodoxy corresponds to Hans Frei's own self-understanding and self-description.

Critical Issues

Several critical issues emerge concerning elements of Frei's thought, especially his appeal to thick description, his critique of historical criticism, and his emphasis on realistic narrative. Frei uses the notion of thick description as an alternative to the various theologies of correlation. The latter allegedly point to an experientially based, general human experience as one pole of the correlation. Frei, however, proposes a very distinctive use of the term "thick description," one closer to the philosopher Wittgenstein's understanding of a language game (see Chapter Sixteen) than to those used by the anthropological and philosophical authors whom he cites. The philosophical and anthropological use of the term relates thick description to an expressive interpretation of human action. For example, Gilbert Ryle (1900–1976), the initiator of the term, uses it to describe the mimics of a young man.[176] To interpret his mimics with a thick description means that one does not merely describe the external actions as isolated and independent actions. Rather, one interprets the young man's mimics precisely as expressing a specific meaning and intention. When an interpretation gets beyond a surface description, then one understands the very meaning of the young man's mimics. The expressive understanding of religious language developed by Friedrich Schleiermacher in his hermeneutics is closer to Ryle's understanding of thick description than is Frei's appeal to the formal structures of narrative. Likewise, Clifford Geertz's interpretation of the religious symbols of a culture involves a thick description, not in terms of the formal structures of those symbols, but insofar as they are embedded within a way of life with its history of traditions and practices.[177] Geertz's use of thick description opposes a structural or functional sociology or anthropology.

Other issues come to the fore concerning Frei's positions on the interrelations among history, truth, and interpretation. One basic question is whether his criticism of the historical-critical method does justice to the actual practice of this method in contemporary scholarship or to contemporary theories of interpretation that attempt to combine explanation and understanding. When a historical-critical exegete studies, for example, Matthew's Gospel, he or she applies source criticism, form criticism, or redaction criticism. Do these methods substitute reference for meaning as Frei's charge against historical criticism maintains? The self-understanding of the advocates of form criticism is that a form critical analysis determines the literary form of the text irrespective of its historical character or reference. Form criticism may decide that a particular text represents a controversy dialogue or a wisdom saying or a legend or a myth. But such form critical analyses are made independent of any historical judgment as to the referent of the text. To declare that a particular passage has a particular literary form says nothing about its historicity. The redaction-critical analyses of the Gospels that interpret the text in the perspective of a specific theological intent seek to show patterns of editorial changes. For example, redaction analysis points to the changes in Matthew and Luke as a result of their drawing on either the Q or second source or on Mark's Gospel, as illustrations of Matthean or Lukan theology. It is the pattern and consistency of editorial changes that characterize the theology of the text. To a large degree, the practice of historical criticism in the twentieth century uses such criticism not in a rationalistic way to determine some eternal truth but, rather, to determine the specificity of what the writings affirm through its various literary and editorial forms and patterns. Whereas Frei's point may be valid in relation to eighteenth- or nineteenth-century forms of historical and literary analysis, it does not apply as aptly to the contemporary practice of exegesis. However, recent scholarly endeavors (e.g., the Jesus seminar) to get behind the texts to the real Jesus do exemplify what Frei is criticizing, especially if the historical reconstructions are to be taken as the meaning of the Gospels.

A final issue is the adequacy of Hans Frei's own proposals for the proper reading of the New Testament materials, especially his charge of reducing the meaning of a text to its reference when the New Testament texts make historical claims.[178] For the meaning of a text is not the only issue. There is also the question of whether the truth claim, or an historical affirmation of a text,

is indeed true or false. When it is determined that the literary form of a text is making a historical affirmation or a historical claim, then the legitimate historical question is whether what is historically affirmed is historically true. Pannenberg interprets the affirmations of Jesus's resurrection to be historical affirmations. He raises the question of historical truth because he interprets the text as making historical claims. Whereas Pannenberg enters the historical debate about the veracity of historical claims, Frei does not. On the basis of his theory of interpretation, Frei offers an interpretive theory that is intratextual and concerned with the structure and narrative of the text as a realistic narrative. However, on the basis of his theological claims, Frei clearly affirms the reality of the resurrection of Jesus. The basic question that Frei's work leaves unanswered is: How does his theory of interpretation as intratextual relate to his theological realism? One might disagree as to whether Pannenberg's attempt to demonstrate the historicity of Jesus's resurrection is sufficiently convincing, but one has to concede that for Pannenberg there is a consistency between his theory of interpretation and his theological claims. Frei leaves the question of the relation between a formal intratextual hermeneutic and a realistic theology open. Two of Frei's students, Ronald Thiemann and Serene Jones, have moved from a purely intratextual understanding to a neo-pragmatic or a rhetorical understanding of interpretation.[179]

CONCLUSION

This chapter has dealt with theologians and philosophers who are quite diverse in their theological positions. Each of them emerged as a significant figure in the two decades after World War II. If one could a draw a thread through all of them, it would be the extent to which they move beyond an existential phenomenology and a transcendental subjectivity. Pannenberg's emphasis on revelation as history, and the openness of history and universal history, goes beyond the existentialism of Neo-Orthodoxy. Gadamer goes beyond the individual self of Bultmann's program of demythologization and shows how the self is located in the play of language, history, and tradition. Paul Ricoeur starts out as a phenomenologist developing a philosophy of will but ends up dealing with hermeneutics and narrative in order to find a more adequate means of understanding the human self. David Tracy, a student of Bernard Lonergan's transcendental philosophy of interiority and consciousness, moves toward the analogical character of the imagination and the conversation required by cultural pluralism. Hans Frei clearly stakes out a position against what he perceives as the grounding of meaning and religion in a general transcendental anthropology.

At the same time, this chapter reveals a certain circle. It begins with Pannenberg. His theological career began with a criticism of German Neo-Orthodoxy and the theology of the Word of God, with its affirmation of the *kerygma* and its emphasis upon the autonomy of the *kerygma* in relation to any historical and anthropological foundation. His whole work can be conceived as an attempt to provide a foundational and systematic theology that grounds the Christian *kerygma* in anthropology and in history. He retrieves elements of classical German philosophy in the service of theology over against the reaction to that philosophy in Protestant Neo-Orthodoxy. Yet the chapter ends with Hans Frei. The aim of his criticism is particularly directed against German hermeneutics and against the academic model of theology imported from Berlin.[180] However, he is also opposed to his North American colleagues for developing a method of correlation that seeks to ground the Christian faith in a general anthropology. Such a procedure, Frei argues, undermines the autonomy of God's Word and often adopts an external description of Christianity as normative for its own self-description.

Karl Barth, as the leading German representative of Neo-Orthodoxy, had criticized the *Anknüpfungspunkt* (point of connection) of the Liberal theology of the preceding generation of theologians. Wolfhart Pannenberg, reacting to Karl Barth's position as a form of fideism, argues for an anthropological grounding of the Christian *kerygma*. Hans Frei seeks to retrieve Karl Barth in the face of those contemporary theologies of correlation that seek to establish a correlation between the particularity of Christian faith and wider human experience. He does this in the face of hermeneutical theories that seek to counteract the emphasis on the proclamation of kerygmatic theology and to take account of a wider, more universal context of human experience. As we will see in Chapter Sixteen, the debate on this crucial issue continues.

NOTES

1. See Wolfhart Pannenberg's autobiographical reflections, "An Autobiographical Sketch," in *The Theology of Wolfhart Pannenberg: Twelve American Critiques, with an Autobiographical Essay and Response*, ed. Carl E. Braaten and Philip Clayton (Minneapolis, 1988), pp. 11–18.

2. Wolfhart Pannenberg, *Die Pradestinationslehre des Duns Skotus im Zusammenhang der Scholastischen Lehrentwicklung* (Göttingen, 1954).

3. German title of 1954 dissertation *Analogie und Offenbarung*. See his later essay entitled, "Analogy and Doxology," in Wolfhart Pannenberg, *Basic Questions in Theology*, I (Philadelphia, 1970), pp. 211–238, which covers some of the material of the habilitation. For an analysis of his habilitation, see Elizabeth Johnson, "The Right Way to Speak about God—Pannenberg on Analogy," *Theological Studies*, 43 (1982), 673–692.

4. Wolfhart Pannenberg, "Heilsgeschehen und Geschichte," *Kerygma und Dogma*, 5 (1959), 218. Translated in English as "Redemptive Event and History," Wolfhart Pannenberg, *Basic Questions in Theology*, I (Philadelphia, 1970), p. 15.

5. Wolfhart Pannenberg et al., *Revelation as History*, ed. Wolfhart Pannenberg (New York, 1968). *Offenbarung als Geschichte*, 2nd ed. (Göttingen, 1963).

6. Wolfhart Pannenberg, "Dogmatic Theses on the Doctrine of Revelation," *Revelation as History*, op. cit., pp. 123–158.

7. Ibid., p. 152.

8. Wolfhart Pannenberg, *Systematic Theology*, II (Grand Rapids, Mich., 1994), p. xvi.

9. Some of these are collected in Wolfhart Pannenberg, *Grundfragen systematischer Theologie: Gesammelte Aufsätze* (Gottingen, 1967). Translated into two volumes (Philadelphia, 1969); Wolfhart Pannenberg, *Basic Questions in Theology*, Vol. I and II (Philadelphia, 1970 and 1971). See his small booklet written at the same time: Wolfhart Pannenberg, *Theology and the Kingdom of God* (Philadelphia, 1969).

10. Wolfhart Pannenberg, *Jesus—God and Man* (Philadelphia, 1968).

11. Ibid., pp. 88–106. Pannenberg picks up on the observations and criticism that Richard R. Niebuhr made on the viability of the argument of historical analogy. See Richard R. Niebuhr, *Resurrection and Historical Reason* (New York, 1957).

12. On this point he is developing one of the central theses of *Revelation as History*.

13. A detailed analysis and comparison of Pannenberg with Bultmann and Ebeling on the resurrection is Klaus Kienzler, *Logik der Auferstehung: Eine Untersuchung zu Rudolf Bultmann, Gerhard Ebeling und Wolfhart Pannenberg* (Freiburg, 1976).

14. Hans Freiherr von Campenhausen, *Der Ablauf der Osterereignisse und das Leere Grab* (Heidelberg, 1952).

15. See Wolfhart Pannenberg, "Die Auferstehung Jesus—Historie und Theologie," *Zeitschrift für Theologie und Kirche*, 41 (1995), 2–12. This was written against Gerd Lüdemann, *The Resurrection of Jesus: History, Experience, and Theology* (Minneapolis, 1994). For contemporary reactions, see Francis Schüssler Fiorenza, "The Resurrection of Jesus and Roman Catholic Fundamental Theology," in *The Resurrection*, ed. Gerald O' Collins, Daniel Kendall, and Stephen Davis (New York, 1997), pp. 213–248.

16. Pannenberg refers to the work of Sartori, Hoffman, Frank, and Gess.

17. Pannenberg, *Jesus—God and Man*, pp. 307–334.

18. Ibid., p. 323.

19. Later, in his three-volume *Systematic Theology*, Pannenberg will develop an incarnational approach to the Christology. See note 31.

20. Pannenberg, *Jesus—God and Man*.

21. Wolfhart Pannenberg, *Wissenschaftstheorie und Theologie* (Frankfurt, 1973); published in English as *Theology and the Philosophy of Science* (Philadelphia, 1976).

22. See Pannenberg's treatment of the debate between Karl Barth and Heinrich Scholz concerning the criteria of knowledge, in *Theology and the Philosophy of Science*, ibid., pp. 326–347.

23. Pannenberg, *Theology and the Philosophy of Science*, p. 341.

24. Ibid., p. 314.

25. See Pannenberg's justification for a theology of religions in "Toward a Theology of the History of Religions," in Pannenberg, *Basic Questions in Theology*, II, pp. 65–118.

26. Wolfhart Pannenberg's development of anthropology can be traced from his early small volume *What Is Man? Contemporary Anthropology in Theological Perspective* (Philadelphia, 1962), to his much more mature and comprehensive treatment in *Anthropology in Theological Perspective* (Philadelphia, 1985). See also Pannenberg's *The Idea of God and Human Freedom* (Philadelphia, 1973), which locates his thought not only in relation to anthropology, but also to Hegel's philosophy of religion.

27. Pannenberg, *Anthropology in Theological Perspective*, p. 16.

28. Ibid., pp. 47–53.

29. See Max Scheler, *Man's Place in Nature* (Boston, 1961), and *On the Eternal in Man* (New York, 1960); Helmut Plesner, *Die Stufen des Organischen und der Mensch* (Berlin, 1928, 1963). See also Arnold Gehlen's *Man in the Age of Technology* (New York, 1980).

30. Pannenberg, *Anthropology in Theological Perspective*, p. 73.

31. Wolfhart Pannenberg, *Systematic Theology*, I (Grand Rapids, Mich., 1991–1997). In English, Vol. I appeared in 1991, Vol. II in 1994, and Vol. III in 1997.

32. Wolfhart Pannenberg, *Metaphysics and the Idea of God* (Grand Rapids, Mich., 1990); and *An Introduction to Systematic Theology* (Grand Rapids, Mich., 1991).

33. Wolfhart Pannenberg, *Toward a Theology of Nature: Essays on Science and Faith* (Louisville, 1993). See his early work on church and ecumenism, Wolfhart Pannenberg, *The Church* (Philadelphia, 1977).

34. Pannenberg, *Introduction to Systematic Theology*, p. 30.

35. Ibid., p. 31.

36. Pannenberg, *Metaphysics and the Idea of God*, pp. 43–68.

37. Ibid., p. 102.

38. Ibid., p. 103.

39. Pannenberg, *Systematic Theology*, II, p. xiv.

40. In this regard, Pannenberg makes suggestive uses of "field theory."

41. For an excellent discussion of the diverse appraisals of Pannenberg's theology, see Stanley J. Grenz, "The Appraisal of Pannenberg: A Survey of the

Literature," in *The Theology of Wolfhart Pannenberg*, op. cit., pp. 19–52.

42. Elizabeth A. Johnson, "The Ongoing Christology of Wolfhart Pannenberg," *Horizons*, 9 (1982), 237–250; and Brian O. McDermott, "Pannenberg's Resurrection Christology: A Critique," *Theological Studies*, 34 (1974), 711–721.

43. Braaten and Clayton, ed., *The Theology of Wolfhart Pannenberg*. See also Braaten's earlier essay, "The Current Controversy on Revelation: Pannenberg and His Critics," *Journal of Religion*, 45 (1965), 225–237.

44. Stanley Grenz, *Reason for Hope: The Systematic Theology of Wolfhart Pannenberg* (New York, 1990); Alister E McGrath, "Christology and Soteriology: A Response to Wolfhart Pannenberg's," *Theologische Zeitschrift*, 3 (1986), 222–236.

45. Francis Schüssler Fiorenza, "Review Essay: Pannenberg, *Systematic Theology*. Volume One," *Pro Ecclesia*, 2 (1992–1993), 231–239.

46. For a collection of autobiographical essays, including relationships with Scheler, Heidegger, and Bultmann, see Hans-Georg Gadamer, *Philosophical Apprenticeships* (Cambridge, 1985). See as well as Gadamer's statement in the Lewis Hahn volume in "Suggestions for Further Reading."

47. Gadamer continued to be occupied with Plato; see Hans-Georg Gadamer, *Dialogue and Dialectics: Eight Hermeneutical Studies* (New Haven, 1980). For the influence of Plato on Gadamer, and in relation to his views during the Nazi period, see Teresa Orozco, *Platonische Gewalt. Gadamers politische Hermeneutik der NS-Zeit* (Berlin, 1995).

48. See the various quasi-autobiographical essays and reminiscences of other leading German philosophers and theologians collected in Gadamer, *Philosophical Apprenticeships*.

49. Schleiermacher's hermeneutics cannot be reduced to authorial intent. See Paul Ricoeur, "Schleiermacher's Hermeneutics," *Monist*, 66 (1977), 181–197; and Yong Huang, "The Father of Modern Hermeneutics in a Postmodern Age: A Reinterpretation of Schleiermacher's Hermeneutics," *Philosophy Today* (1996), pp. 251–262.

50. For a survey of their conception of "scientific" history, see George G. Iggers, *New Directions in European Historiography*, rev. ed (Middletown, Conn., 1984).

51. Hans-Georg Gadamer, *Truth and Method*, 2nd rev. ed. (New York, 1994), p. 186.

52. Ibid.

53. Martin Heidegger, *Being and Time*, trans. Joan Stambaugh (Albany, 1996).

54. Ibid., p. 142.

55. Ibid., p. 143.

56. Rudolf Bultmann, "Is Exegesis without Presuppositons Possible?" in Rudolf Bultmann, *Existence and Faith: Shorter Writings*, trans. Schubert M. Ogden (New York, 1960); and "What Is Hermeneutics," in Rudolf Bultmann, *The New Testament and Mythology and Other Basic Writings*, ed. Schubert M. Ogden (Philadelphia, 1984), pp. 69–93.

57. This is a very Hegelian view—but without Hegel's absolute knowledge!

58. Gadamer, *Truth and Method*, p. 288.

59 Jürgen Habermas, *Philosophical-Political Profiles* (Cambridge, 1983).

60. Gadamer, *Truth and Method*, p. 308.

61. Ibid., p. 309.

62. Ibid., p. 290.

63. Bultmann, *The New Testament and Mythology and Other Basic Writings*.

64. See Gadamer's essays "On The Problem of Self Understanding" and "Heidegger and Marburg Theology," in Hans-Georg Gadamer, *Philosophical Hermeneutics* (Berkeley, 1976), pp. 44–58 and 198–221.

65. Gadamer, *Philosophical Hermeneutics*, p. 58.

66. Hans-Georg Gadamer, *Heidegger's Ways* (Albany, 1994), p. 39.

67. Ibid., p. 195.

68. Jürgen Habermas, "Review of Truth and Method," in Justus George Lawler and Francis Schüssler Fiorenza, *Cultural Hermeneutics: Special Issue of Continuum*, 8 (Spring–Summer 1970).

69. Paul Ricoeur, "Hermeneutics and the Critique of Ideology," in Paul Ricoeur, *Hermeneutics and the Human Sciences*, ed. John B. Thompson (New York, 1981), pp. 63–100.

70. The major thrust of Derrida's philosophy is much more directly aimed against structuralism, as exemplified by his criticism of Saussure's structural approach in the former's *Of Grammatology* (Baltimore, 1974). See Manfred Frank, "Limits of Human Control of Langue: Dialogue as the Place of Difference Between Neostructuralism and Hermeneutics," in *Dialogue and Deconstruction: The Gadamer-Derrida Encounter*, ed. Diane Michelfelder and Richard Palmer (Albany, 1989).

71. Jacques Derrida, "Three Questions to Hans-Georg Gadamer," in *Dialogue and Deconstruction*, pp. 52–54.

72. Hans-Georg Gadamer, "Reply to Jacques Derrida," in *Dialogue and Deconstruction*, pp. 55–57.

73. For an interpretation of the concept of otherness in Gadamer, see James Risser, *Hermeneutics and the*

Voice of the Other: Re-reading Gadamer's Philosophical Hermeneutics (Albany, 1997).

74. Erich Donald Hirsch, Jr., *Validity in Interpretation* (New Haven, 1967); and *The Aims of Interpretation* (Chicago, 1976).

75. Also see Karl-Otto Apel, "Regulative Ideas or Truth-Happening? An Attempt to Answer the Question of the Conditions of the Possibility of Valid Understanding," in *The Philosophy of Hans-Georg Gadamer*, ed. Lewis Edwin Hahn (La Salle, Ill. 1997), pp. 67–94.

76. Tracy seeks, however, to complement Gadamer by appropriating Ricoeur's emphasis on method and explanation as complementary to understanding.

77. Raymond E. Brown, *The Sensus Plenior of Sacred Scripture* (Baltimore, 1955); and more recently, Sandra M. Schneiders, *The Revelatory Text: Interpreting the New Testament as Sacred Scripture* (San Francisco, 1991). Raymond E. Brown appeals to Gadamer in "The *Sensus Plenior* in the Last Ten Years," *Catholic Biblical Quarterly*, 25 (1963), 262–278. See James M. Robinson's reservations in "Scripture and Theological Method: A Protestant Survey," *Catholic Biblical Quarterly*, 27 (1965), 6–27.

78. See Francis Schüssler Fiorenza, "Religious or Theological Studies: The Contest of the Faculties," in *Shifting Boundaries: Contextual Approaches to the Structure of Theological Education*, ed. Barbara Wheeler and Edward Farley (Louisville, Ky., 1991), pp. 119–149; "Theology in the University," *Bulletin of the Council of Societies for the Study of Religion*, 22 (April 1993), 34–39; and "Response to Wiebe," *Bulletin of the Council of Societies for the Study of Religion*, 23 (April 1994), 6–10.

79. Hans Robert Jauss, *Toward an Aesthetic of Reception* (Minneapolis, 1982); *Aesthetic Experience and Literary Hermeneutics* (Minneapolis, 1982); *Question and Answer. Forms of Dialogic Understanding* (Minneapolis, 1989).

80. Wolfgang Iser, *The Implied Reader* (Baltimore, 1974); and *The Act of Reading: A Theory of Aesthetic Response* (Baltimore, 1974).

81. Francis Schüssler Fiorenza, *Foundational Theology: Jesus and the Church* (New York, 1984), Ch. 5.

82. Ormond Rush, *The Reception of Doctrine: An Appropriation of Hans Robert Jauss' Reception Aesthetics and Literary Hermeneutics* (Rome, 1997).

83. Paul Ricoeur, *Gabriel Marcel et Karl Jaspers. Philosophie du mystère et philosophie du paradoxe* (Paris, 1948). Ricoeur's treatment shows more sympathy for Marcel's concept of mystery than for Jasper's notion of paradox.

84. Paul Ricoeur, *Freedom and Nature. The Voluntary and the Involuntary* (Evanston, Ill., 1966).

85. Paul Ricoeur, *Fallible Man*, trans. C. Kelbley (Chicago, 1965); and *The Symbolism of Evil*, trans. E. Buchanan (New York, 1969).

86. Paul Ricoeur, *Freud and Philosophy: An Essay in Interpretation*, trans. Denis Savage (New Haven, 1970).

87. Sigmund Freud, *The Unconcious. Standard Edition of the Complete Works*, trans. James Strachey et al. (London, 1953–1974), p. 118.

88. Ricoeur, *Freud and Philosophy*, p. 36.

89. Paul Ricoeur, *The Conflict of Interpretations: Essays in Hermeneutics* (Evanston, Ill., 1974).

90. Paul Ricoeur, *Lectures on Ideology and Utopia* (New York, 1986).

91. Ricoeur, *The Symbolism of Evil*, p. 355.

92. It should be noted, however, that even before his "hermeneutical turn" he planned a volume to deal with the "poetics" of will.

93. Paul Ricoeur, *The Rule of Metaphor* (Toronto, 1975). As the French title suggests, Ricoeur's approach is critical of the study of metaphor in terms of "dead metaphors."

94. Paul Ricoeur gives a good summary of his positions in *Interpretation Theory: Discourse and the Surplus of Meaning* (Fort Worth, Tex., 1976).

95. Ricoeur, *The Rule of Metaphor*, p. 303.

96. See his analysis of the parable of the sower in Paul Ricoeur, "The Bible and the Imagination" in *The Bible as a Document of the University*, ed. Hans Dieter Betz (Chico, Calif., 1981), pp. 49–75. Reprinted in *Figuring the Sacred*, see note 103.

97. For example, see Norman Perrin, *Rediscovering the Teaching of Jesus* (New York, 1975); and *Jesus and the Language of the Kingdom* (Philadelphia, 1976).

98. Paul Ricoeur, "Phenomenology and Hermeneutics," *Nous*, 9 (1975), 90. See David Pellauer's essay, "The Significance of the Text in Paul Ricoeur's Hermeneutical Theory," in *Studies in the Philosophy of Paul Ricoeur*, ed. Charles E. Reagan (Athens, Ohio, 1979).

99. Paul Ricoeur, "Intellectual Autobiography," in *The Philosophy of Paul Ricoeur*, ed. Lewis Edwin Hahn (Chicago, 1995), p. 36.

100. This objectification also makes possible the dialectical pairing of Wilhelm Dilthey's two operations, explanation and understanding. The explanation of the text takes places through an objectifying analysis (an example of which is A. J. Greimas's textual semiotics).

101. Paul Ricoeur, "Toward a Hermeneutic of the Idea of Revelation," *Harvard Theological Review*, 70 (1977), reprinted in Paul Ricoeur, *Essays on Biblical Interpretation*, ed. Lewis S. Mudge (Philadelphia, 1980), pp. 73–118. See also Paul Ricoeur and André LaCocque, *Thinking Biblically: Exegetical and Hermeneutical Studies* (Chicago, 1998).

102. Paul Ricoeur wrote the introduction to the French translation of Bultmann's *Jesus Christ and Mythology*. This has appeared in English as "Preface to Bultmann," in Ricoeur, *Essays on Biblical Interpretation*, pp. 49–72.

103. See Paul Ricoeur's essay "Manifestation and Proclamation," in Paul Ricoeur, *Figuring the Sacred: Religion, Narrative, and Imagination* (Minneapolis, 1995), pp. 48–67.

104. Ricoeur, *Figuring the Sacred*, p. 60.

105. Paul Ricoeur, *Time and Narrative*, Vol. 3 (Chicago, 1988), p. 241.

106. Ricoeur, *Time and Narrative*, Vols. 1,2,3. (Chicago, 1984, 1988).

107. The original Gifford Lectures included two lectures that are omitted in *Sur l'individu* "The Self in the Mirror of Scriptures" and "The Mandated Self." See Charles E. Reagan, *Paul Ricoeur: His Life and His Work* (Chicago, 1996), p. 78.

108. Paul Ricoeur's *Sur l'individu* (Paris, 1987) was reworked and published in English as *Oneself as Another* (Chicago, 1992).

109. Derek Parfit, *Reasons and Persons* (Oxford, 1986), p. 255.

110. Ricoeur, *Oneself as Another*, p. 143. See also Paul Riceour's essay "Love and Justice," in Ricoeur, *Figuring the Sacred*, pp. 315–329.

111. Ricoeur, *Onself as Another*, pp. 169–239.

112. In addition to David Tracy and Norman Perrin (see note 97), Mary Gerhart, *The Question of Belief in Literary Criticism: An Introduction to the Hermeneutical Theory of Paul Ricoeur* (Stuttgart, 1979); and with Allan Melvin Russell, *Metaphoric Process: The Creation of Scientific and Religious Understanding* (Fort Worth, Tex., 1984); and her "The Restoration of Biblical Narrative," *Semeia*, 46 (1989), 13–29.

113. Among Hans Frei's students, see, for a very critical reading of Ricoeur, Cyril O' Regan, "*De doctrina christiana* and Modern Hermeneutics," in *De doctrina christiana: A Classic of Western Culture*, ed. Duane W. H. Arnold and Pamela Bright (Notre Dame, 1995). A more sympathetic reading is presented by Mark I. Wallace, *The Second Naiveté: Barth, Ricoeur, and the New Yale Theology* (Macon, Ga., 1990); and James Fodor, *Christian Hermeneutics: Paul Ricoeur and the Refiguring of Theology* (New York, 1995).

114. David Tracy, *The Achievement of Bernard Lonergan* (New York, 1970).

115. Ibid., pp. 1–81.

116. David Tracy, "Lonergan's Foundational Theology: An Interpretation and a Critique," in *Foundations of Theology*, ed., Philip McShane (Notre Dame, 1972), p. 216.

117. Ibid., p. 217.

118. David Tracy, *Blessed Rage for Order* (New York, 1975).

119. Schubert Ogden, *On Theology* (San Francisco, 1986).

120. See Schubert Ogden, "Fundamentum Fidei: Critical Reflections on Willi Marxsen's Contribution to Systematic Theology," in Schubert Ogden, *Doing Theology Today* (Valley Forge, 1996), pp. 245–359.

121. This was only one of Tillich's formulations.

122. Tracy, *Blessed Rage for Order*, p.105

123. Ibid., p. 106

124. Ibid., p. 108.

125. Ibid., p. 108.

126. David Tracy, *The Analogical Imagination* (New York, 1981), pp. 56–57.

127. Ibid., p. 57

128. Ibid.

129. Ibid.

130. Ibid.

131. Ibid., p. 163.

132. Ibid., p. 237.

133. Ibid., p. 198.

134. Ibid., p. 264.

135. See also Robert Grant, *A Short History of the Interpretation of the Bible*, 2nd rev. and enlarged ed. with David Tracy (Philadelphia, 1984). Tracy's essay summarizes his views on interpretation.

136. Tracy, *The Analogical Imagination*, pp. 265–266.

137. See his more recent writings: David Tracy, *Plurality and Ambiguity: Hermeneutics, Religion, Hope* (San Francisco, 1987); *Dialogue with the Other. The Inter-Religious Dialogue* (Grand Rapids, Mich., 1990); and *On Naming the Present: Reflections on God, Hermeneutics, and Church* (Maryknoll, N.Y., 1994).

138. Tracy, *Plurality and Ambiguity*, p. 60.

139. Ibid., p. 112.

140. Owen C. Thomas, "Public Theology and Counter-Public Spheres," *Harvard Theological Review*, 85 (1992), 453–469.

141. Francis Schüssler Fiorenza, "Fundamental Theology and Its Principal Concerns Today: Towards a Non-Foundational Theology," *Irish Theological Quarterly* (1996), pp. 118–139; and "The Relation Between Fundamental and Systematic Theology," *Irish Theological Quarterly* (1996), pp. 140–160.

142. Peter Berger, "Secular Theology and the Rejection of the Supernatural: Reflection on Recent Trends," *Theological Studies*, 38 (1977), 39–56.

143. Ibid.

144. David Tracy, Langdon Gilkey, and Schubert Ogden, "Responses to Peter Berger," *Theological Studies*, 39 (1978), 486–507. See also Tracy's later defense of correlation against Linbeck: "The Uneasy Alliance Reconceived: Catholic Theological Method, Moder-

nity, and Postmodernism," *Theological Studies,* 50 (1989), 548–570.

145. This term was first coined by Brevard Childs.

146. George Lindbeck, *The Nature of Doctrine: Religion and Theology in a Postliberal Age* (Philadelphia, 1984).

147. Hans Frei, "The 'Literal Reading' of the Biblical Narrative in the Christian Tradition: Does It Stretch or Will It Break," in *The Bible and the Narrative Tradition* edited by Frank McConnell (New York, 1986). See also the criticism by Cyril O'Regan, "*De doctrina christiana* and Modern Hermeneutics," in *De doctrina christiana: A Classic of Western Culture,* eds. Duane W. H. Arnold and Pamela Bright (Notre Dame, 1995), pp. 217–243.

148. Hans W. Frei, "The Doctrine of Revelation in the Thought of Karl Barth, 1909–1922: The Nature of Barth's Break with Liberalism," 1956. (Microfilm. Ann. Arbor, Mich.: University Microfilms, 1970).

149. Hans W. Frei, "Niebuhr's Theological Background," in *Faith and Ethics: The Theology of H. Richard Niebuhr,* ed. Paul Ramsey (New York, 1957).

150. Hans Frei, *The Eclipse of Biblical Narrative: A Study in Eighteenth and Nineteenth Century Biblical Narrative* (New Haven, 1974).

151. Ibid., pp. 103–104.

152. Ibid., p. 24.

153. For the influence of New Criticism on biblical studies and Neo-Orthodoxy, see Lynn M. Poland, "The New Criticism, Neoorthodoxy, and the New Testament," *Journal of Religion,* 65 (1985), 459–477; L. Poland, *Literary Criticism and Biblical Hermeneutics* (Chico, Calif., 1985).

154. Erich Auerbach, *Mimesis: The Representation of Reality in Western Literature* (Princeton, 1953). See also Hans W. Frei, "The 'Literal Reading' of the Biblical Narrative in the Christian Tradition: Does It Stretch or Will It Break?" in *The Bible and the Narrative Tradition,* ed. Frank McConnell (New York, 1986).

155. See Robert Alter, *The Art of Biblical Narrative* (New York, 1981). Frei's student, Ronald Thiemann, criticizes Alter for moving "too swiftly from realistic narrative to historical reality." Ronald Thiemann, "Radiance and Obscurity in Biblical Narrative," in Garrett Green, *Scriptural Authority and Narrative Interpretation* (Philadelphia, 1987), p. 41.

156. Hans Frei, *Types of Christian Theology* (New Haven, 1992), p. 10.

157. Hans W. Frei. "'Narrative' in Christian and Modern Reading," in *Theology and Dialogue: Essays in Conversation with George Lindbeck,* ed. Bruce D. Marshall (Notre Dame, 1990), pp. 149–163.

158. Ibid., p. 152.

159. This difference can be seen by comparing *The Eclipse of Biblical Narrative* and "The 'Literal Reading'" (see note 154).

160. Hans Frei, *The Identity of Jesus Christ: The Hermeneutical Bases of Dogmatic Theology* (Philadelphia, 1975).

161. Hans Frei's interpretative principles bear a family resemblance to the work of another of his Yale colleagues, Paul Holmer's *The Grammar of Faith* (New York, 1978).

162. See George Hunsinger, "Hans Frei as a Theologian," *Modern Theology,* 8 (1992), 103–128.

163. See also Hans Frei's explicit treatment of Strauss: Hans Frei, "David Friedrich Strauss," in *Nineteenth Century Religious Thought in the West,* ed. Ninian Smart and John Clayton (Cambridge, 1985), pp. 215–260.

164. Frei, *The Identity of Jesus Christ,* p. 127.

165. Hans Frei, "Theological Reflections on the Accounts of Jesus' Death and Resurrection," *Christian Scholar,* 49 (1966), 263–306, especially 277; and Frei, *The Identity of Jesus Christ,* pp. 127–129.

166. See Hunsinger, "Hans Frei as Theologian," p. 111.

167. Hans W. Frei, *Types of Christian Theology* (New Haven, 1992). Unfortunately, Hans Frei died before he could complete the manuscript of this book. His lectures on the typology and several related topics are edited and published by George Hunsinger and William C. Placher. Likewise, an important collection of his essays also was posthumously published: Hans W. Frei, *Theology and Narrative: Selected Essays,* ed. George Hunsinger and William C. Placher (New York, 1993).

168. For a difference in the description of Jesus in relation to his disciples, see David E. Demson, *Hans Frei and Karl Barth: Different Ways of Reading Scripture* (Grand Rapids, Mich., 1997).

169. Frei, *Types of Christian Theology,* pp. 21–22.

170. Pannenberg takes issue with Karl Barth because he sees Barth, in his debate with Schulz, as denying these criteria. (See the treatment of Pannenberg above.)

171. For a relation between this typology and the typologies in *The Eclipse of Biblical Narrative,* see George P. Schner, "*The Eclipse of Biblical Narrative:* Analysis and Critique," *Modern Theology* (1992), pp. 149–172.

172. Hans Frei, *Types of Christian Theology,* p. 124.

173. Ibid., p. 125.

174. Ibid., p. 126.

175. Hans Frei, "Response to 'Narrative Theology: An Evangelical Appraisal,'" *Trinity Journal,* 8 (1987), 21–24.

176. Gilbert Ryle, *Collected Papers 1929–1968* (London, 1971).

177. Clifford Geertz, *The Interpretation of Cultures* (New York, 1973). On the interpretation of thick description in Clifford Geertz, and its difference from

Frei's use of the term, see Francis Schüssler Fiorenza, "Schleiermacher and the Construction of a Contemporary Roman Catholic Foundational Theology," *Harvard Theological Revue*, 89 (1996), 175–194.

178. See Cyril O'Regan, "*De doctrina christiana* and Modern Hermeneutics." in *De doctrina christiana: A Classic of Western Culture*, eds. Duane W. H. Arnold and Pamela Bright. (Notre Dame: University of Notre Dame, 1995), pp. 217–243.

179. Ronald Thiemann, "Radiance," in Garrett Green, *Scriptural Authority and Narrative Interpretation* (Philadelphia, 1987); and Serene Jones, *Calvin and the Rhetoric of Piety* (Louisville, Ky., 1995).

180. It should be noted that the developments in England in the nineteenth century are contrasted with the negative developments in Germany in the same century. Frei sees the dominance of the model of the German academy on contemporary theology as a major weakness. See "The Encounter of Jesus with the Germany Academy," in Frei, *Types of Christian Theology*, pp. 133–146.

SUGGESTIONS FOR FURTHER READING

Wolfhart Pannenberg

Braaten, Carl E., and Philip Clayton, ed. *The Theology of Wolfhart Pannenberg: Twelve American Critiques, with an Autobiographical Essay and Response* (Minneapolis: Augsburg, 1988). An important collection of essays that critically analyzes Pannenberg's theology. Pannenberg's response and the bibliography makes this collection a valuable resource.

Colombo, Joseph A. *An Essay on Theology and History: Studies in Pannenberg, Metz, and the Frankfurt School*, AAR Studies in Religion no. 61 (Atlanta: Scholars Press, 1990). A discussion of the relation to the Frankfurt School that is more applicable to Metz than to Pannenberg.

Galloway, Allan D. *Wolfhart Pannenberg* (London: George Allen & Unwin, 1973). A popular survey in the Contemporary Religious Thinkers Series.

Grenz, Stanley. *Reason for Hope: The Systematic Theology of Wolfhart Pannenberg* (New York: Oxford University Press, 1990). A systematic introduction to Pannenberg's theology from the perspective of a leading Evangelical theologian. It covers the traditional topics of systematic theology.

Olive, Don H. *Wolfhart Pannenberg* (Waco, Tex.: Word Books, 1973). A popular exposition of Pannenberg's early work in the Makers of the Modern Theological Mind Series.

Tupper, E. F. *The Theology of Wolfhart Pannenberg* (Philadelphia: Westminster Press, 1973). A general survey of Pannenberg's early theology.

Worthing, Mark William. *Foundations and Functions of Theology as Universal Science: Theological Method and Apologetic Praxis in Wolfhart Pannenberg and Karl Rahner* (Frankfurt and New York: Peter Lang Publishers, 1996). A comparison of the fundamental theologies of Rahner and Pannenberg.

Hans-Georg Gadamer

Bernstein, Richard J. *Beyond Objectivism and Relativism: Science, Hermeneutics and Praxis* (Philadelphia: University of Pennsylvania Press, 1983). An exposition of Gadamer's hermeneutics in relation to North American pragmatism and neo-pragmatism, philosophy of science, and the critical theory of Habermas.

DiCenso, James. *Hermeneutics and the Disclosure of Truth: A Study in the Work of Heidegger, Gadamer, and Ricoeur, Studies in Religion and Culture* (Charlottesville: University Press of Virginia, 1990). A study that concentrates on the shift in the nature of truth among the philosophers.

Foster, Matthew. *Gadamer and Practical Philosophy: The Hermeneutics of Moral Confidence*, AAR Studies in Religion no. 64 (Atlanta Scholars Press, 1991). An interpretation showing the significance for Gadamer's hermeneutics for practical reasoning and for ethics.

Grondin, Jean. *Introduction to Philosophical Hermeneutics* (New Haven: Yale University Press, 1994). A good exposition of Gadamer's hermeneutic with special attention to its philosophical roots and background as well as to its reception.

Hahn, Lewis Edwin, ed. *The Philosophy of Hans-Georg Gadamer*. The Library of Living Philosophers, Vol. XXIV (LaSalle, Ill.: Open Court, 1997). An important collection of essays. The volume contains an autobiographical statement, essays of exposition and critique, responses to these essays by Gadamer, and a complete bibliography of Gadamer's writings.

Risser, James. *Hermeneutics and the Voice of the Other: Re-reading Gadamer's Philosophical Hermeneutics* (Albany: State University of New York Press, 1997). In view of the emphasis on the Other in postmodern theory, this book demonstrates the role of the Other in Gadamer's understanding of interpretation.

Wachterhauser, Brice R. *Hermeneutics and Truth* (Evanston, Ill.: Northwestern University Press, 1994). An excellent collection of essays dealing with Gadamer's conception of truth and relating his work to Heidegger.

Warnke, Georgia. *Gadamer: Hermeneutics, Tradition, and Reason* (Stanford: Stanford University Press, 1987). In addition to an exposition of the major ideas of Gadamer, she brings his work into dialogue with North American philosophy.

Weinsheimer, Joel. *Gadamer's Hermeneutics: A Reading of Truth and Method* (New Haven: Yale University Press, 1985). An excellent analysis of Gadamer's book.

Paul Ricoeur

Fodor, James. *Christian Hermeneutics: Paul Ricoeur and the Refiguring of Theology* (Oxford: Clarendon Press; New York: Oxford University Press, 1995). A excellent and extensive analysis of Ricoeur's hermeneutics with reference to its significance for theology and its relation to the work of Hans Frei.

Hahn, Lewis Edwin, ed. *The Philosophy of Paul Ricoeur*. The Library of Living Philosophers, Vol. XXII (Chicago and LaSalle, Ill.: Open Court, 1995). An important collection of essays. The volume contains an autobiographical statement, essays of exposition and critique, responses to these essays by Ricoeur, and a complete bibliography of Ricoeur's writing.

Klemm, David E., and William Schweiker, ed. *Meanings in Texts and Actions: Questioning Paul Ricoeur* (Charlottesville: University Press of Virginia 1993). These essays interpret, question, and apply Ricouer's hermeneutic to specific issues.

Reagan, Charles E. ed. *Studies in the Philosophy of Paul Ricoeur* (Athens, Ohio: Ohio University Press, 1979). Important studies on elements of Ricoeur's earlier work.

Reagan, Charles, E. *Paul Ricoeur: His Life and Work* (Chicago: University of Chicago Press, 1996). A biographical account of Ricoeur's life interwoven with accounts of his work and with a selection of interviews.

Van Den Hengel, John W. *The Home of Meaning: The Hermeneutics of the Subject of Paul Ricoeur* (Washington, D.C.: University Press of America, 1982). One of the finest expositions of Ricoeur's early work that shows its roots in a phenomenology of the human subject.

Wallace, Mark I. *The Second Naiveté: Barth, Ricoeur, and the New Yale Theology* (Macon, GA: Mercer, 1990). Written from the perspective of Hans Frei's understanding of interpretation, Wallace compares Karl Barth, Hans Frei, and Paul Ricoeur.

Wood, David, ed. *On Paul Ricoeur: Narrative and Interpretation* (New York: Routledge, 1991). A collection of essays that deal with Ricoeur's later work on narrative.

David Tracy

Downey, John K. *Beginning at the Beginning: Wittgenstein and Theological Conversation* (Lanham, Md.: University Press of America, 1986). A study of Tracy's notion of meaningfulness, truth, and faith within the context of Wittgenstein's philosophy.

Jeanrond, Werner G., and Jennifer L. Rike. *Radical Pluralism and Truth: David Tracy and the Hermeneutics of Religion* (New York: Crossroad, 1991). A collection of essays that honors Tracy's work.

Mueller, John J. *What are they saying about theological method?* (New York: Paulist Press, 1984). A general and popularly written discussion of contemporary theories of method, including Tracy's understanding of theological method.

Ray, Alan S. *The Modern Soul: Michel Foucault and the Theological Discourse of Gordon Kaufman and David Tracy*. Harvard Dissertations in Religion, no. 21(Philadelphia: Fortress Press, 1987). Ray uses Foucault's philosophy as a critical perspective to compare and to interpret Kaufman and Tracy.

Hans Frei

Demson, David E. *Hans Frei and Karl Barth: Different Ways of Reading Scripture* (Grand Rapids, Mich.: William B. Eerdmans, 1997). A comparison of Karl Barth and Hans Frei in their interpretation of the identity of Jesus. Demson sees a greater attention to the relation of Jesus to his disciples in Barth's interpretation.

Demson, David E, and John Webster, ed. *Hans Frei and the Future of Theology*. Special Issue of *Modern Theology*, 8 (April 1992), 101–214. The essays, which are sympathetic, explore the value and significance of Frei's theology. Responses to the essays add value to this collection.

Green, Garrett, ed. *Scriptural Authority and Narrative Interpretation* (Philadelphia: Fortress Press, 1987). A Festschrift honoring Hans Frei with essays by former students and colleagues. A helpful bibliography that includes a listing of major reviews of Frei's writings.

Loughlin, Gerard. *Telling God's Story: Bible, Church, and Narrative Theology* (New York: Cambridge University Press, 1996). A defense of the idea of narrative theology as developed by Hans Frei and George Lindbeck. It expands this defense to show its utility for the Church's use of scripture in its life and liturgy.

Stroup, George W. *The Promise of Narrative Theology: Recovering the Gospel in the Church* (Atlanta: John Knox Press, 1981). An early and general introduction to narrative theology.

Thiemann, Ronald F. *Revelation and Theology: The Gospel as Narrated Promise* (Notre Dame: University of Notre Dame Press, 1984). An outstanding and creative work that combines the basic insights of Frei's theology with elements of contemporary neo-pragmatic philosophy in order to elucidate a key category of theology.

Wallace, Mark I. *The Second Naiveté: Barth, Ricoeur, and the New Yale Theology* (Macon, GA: Mercer, 1990). Written from the perspective of Hans Frei's understanding of interpretation, Wallace compares Karl Barth, Hans Frei, and Paul Ricoeur.

Chapter Twelve

Evangelical Theology

Carl F. H. Henry

BACKGROUND

The twenthieth-century theological movements examined in this volume can be rather easily identified. This is not so in the case of Anglo-American Evangelical theology in the second half of the century. The features that often are associated with contemporary Evangelicalism remain one of the questions most contested by Evangelicals themselves, as well as by scholars who study this important Protestant movement. All authentic Christian theology is, in the most basic sense of the word, evangelical insofar as it claims to address what pertains to the biblical Gospel of God's redemption in Jesus Christ. However, as the word "evangelical" developed

through Christian history, and particularly since the Protestant Reformation, it has taken on a more definite meaning. In the sixteenth century the word was used to refer to those Catholic writers and reformers who called for a return to the beliefs and practices of New Testament Christianity—in contrast to those developments in the medieval Church that were considered unbiblical. The various Christian groups today who, in their own distinctive ways, wish to return to what they view as biblical Christianity and in some cases to the confessions of the Reformation, are often referred to as "evangelical." In parts of Europe and Latin America, however, the word continues to be used merely as synonymous with Protestant, as distinct from Roman Catholic.

Here we are using "evangelical" in a more restricted yet complex sense to refer to a contemporary movement in largely Anglo-American Protestantism, one made up of numerous Christian churches, agencies, and groups that share certain theological commitments.

Historians speak of contemporary Evangelicalism as a mosaic that reveals an organic unity within the complex diversity of its parts. The following statement nicely underscores the diversity that is included under the Evangelical umbrella:

On one side of evangelicalism are black Pentecostals and on another are strict separated fundamentalists, such as at Bob Jones University, who condemn Pentecostals and shun blacks. Peace churches, especially those of the Anabaptist-Mennonite tradition, make up another discrete group of evangelicals. And their ethos differs sharply from that of the Southern Baptist Convention. . . . America's largest Protestant body. Southern Baptists, in turn, have had experiences quite different from those of the evangelicals who have kept the traditional faith within the more liberal "mainline" northern churches. Each of these predominantly Anglo groups is, again, very different from basically immigrant church bodies like the Missouri Synod Lutheran or the Christian Reformed, who have carefully preserved Reformation confessional heritages.[1]

Evangelicalism is, then, a dynamic transdenominational coalition of denominations, church groups, agencies, and independent supporters who share certain commitments, activities, and goals. What appears to unify this extraordinary assemblage is a set of theological convictions that set them apart not only from Roman Catholicism but, more essentially, from the Liberal and Modernist theology that they perceive to characterize many of the "mainline" Protestant denominations. The following convictions are, by and large, shared by contemporary Protestant Evangelicals:

1. The full authority, infallibility, and sufficiency of Scripture in matters religious. Evangelicals trace Christian beliefs or doctrines to Scripture and are wary of appeals to church tradition or reason or personal experience alone.

2. The uniqueness of salvation through Christ's redeeming work on the Cross, often associated with the doctrine of substitutionary atonement.
3. The unmerited, direct gift of God's grace received by the individual's faith through an act of personal conversion.
4. The necessity of a spiritually transformed life.
5. The urgent need to engage in worldwide evangelism.

All of these beliefs are understood to be grounded in the New Testament Gospel and they all are interrelated.

THE FUNDAMENTALIST DEFENSE OF THE FAITH

In our examination of the Princeton Theology (see Volume I, Chapter Twelve), we explored the theological roots of important aspects of twentieth-century American Evangelicalism, especially its belief in the sole authority and sufficiency of Scripture. We noted, however, that in the period between 1880 and 1920 major Protestant denominations in North America were divided over the new historical-critical scholarship on the Bible and over biblical interpretation. The threat of modern historical-critical scholarship and Darwinian evolutionary theory heightened tensions in the churches, which resulted in heresy charges and trials against progressive scholars and churchmen. Efforts also were set in motion to establish a set of doctrinal standards that would characterize orthodox Christian belief and that could be used as a measure against this expanding theological infidelity. The upshot was the adoption by the Presbyterian General Assembly in 1910 of a five-point statement of essential belief, which in the 1920s became the "five fundamentals" that served as the clarion call of the militant movement that came to be known as Fundamentalism. This movement grew into a strange mélange of Presbyterians, Bible Baptists, Dispensationalists, Premillenialists, and other groups prepared to do battle against theological Liberalism and Modernism in the churches.

The fundamentalists' attack sowed religious division just as the mainline denominations were beginning ecumenical efforts to increase Christian unity. The fundamentalists also tended to "separate" themselves from the larger culture, especially those who held fervent premillenial views and who increasingly perceived certain cultural institutions as embodying evil and as their enemy. The fundamentalists came to see themselves as an alienated but "righteous remnant," standing against a world that opposed Christ. As one leader of the movement declared at the time: "If the world loves us it is because we are not following Jesus Christ."[2] The fundamentalists attacked the teaching of evolution in the schools and generated a spirit of anti-intellectualism in sharp contrast to the Princeton Theology. As the movement grew, it spawned a network of nondenominational Bible schools, colleges, and seminaries, as well as summer Bible camps, missionary agencies, and publications. The militant leaders of Fundamentalism who were associated with the traditional denominations joined forces to take control of their churches and to rout the liberals and modernists. A stormy fundamentalist-modernist theological battle ensued.

The most scholarly of the fundamentalist theologians was J. Gresham Machen (1881–1937), who had been a student of Benjamin B. Warfield's at Princeton Seminary. Machen taught New Testament at Princeton for over twenty years. However, after the reorganization of the Seminary in 1927, in an effort to be more theologically inclusive, Machen left and founded Westminster Theological Seminary in Philadelphia in 1927, the purpose being to uphold the "true" Princeton and Presbyterian traditions. Machen helped to establish a new missions board independent of the Presbyterian Church in the United States, and in 1936, he and a small band of followers seceded from the Presbyterian Church to form what became the Orthodox Presbyterian Church.

Machen is, perhaps, best known for his attack on theological liberalism in his book *Christianity and Liberalism* (1923). Though not a typical fundamentalist, his book was widely perceived, especially by his liberal antagonists, as a defense of Fundamentalism. In his book Machen attempts to show that Liberal Christianity is no Christianity at all. He wrote:

The present time is a time of conflict; the great redemptive religion which has always been known as Christianity is battling against a totally diverse type of religious belief, which is only more destructive of the Christian faith because it makes use of traditional Christian terminology. This modern non-redemptive religion is called "modernism" or "liberalism."[3]

Machen wanted all liberals forced out of the Christian churches, but the liberals and the modernists fought back. Any meeting of minds now appeared to be impossible. The liberal counterattack was given special impetus by the famous Baptist preacher, Harry Emerson Fosdick, in a sermon entitled "Shall the Fundamentalists Win?" (1922). The sermon received wide publicity and sympathy because Fosdick focused on the fundamentalists' intolerance and their dogmatic theological tests, which they appeared to want to foist on every Christian. Fosdick contrasted this narrow dogmatism with the tolerance of the vast majority of Christians who felt no need to require tests, such as the inerrancy of Scripture or a particular substitutionary theory of the atonement. Fosdick made it clear that Machen was right: Two irreconcilable views of Christianity were being contested here and much was at stake.

In 1924 a number of sophisticated defenses of a liberal and progressive Christianity appeared, most notably in a book by the dean of the University of Chicago Divinity School, Shailer Mathews (1863–1941), titled *The Faith of Modernism*, and in Fosdick's popular *The Modern Use of the Bible*. At the same time, the political actions of the fundamentalists and their efforts to suppress the teaching of biological evolution were now viewed with alarm by many Americans. In 1925 the famous Scopes "Monkey Trial" was held in Dayton, Tennessee, featuring William Jennings Bryan's misguided effort to discredit evolution. By 1925 the tide had turned against the fundamentalists' advance. And the Monkey Trial was the most vivid portent of the decline.

It soon was evident that the fundamentalists' efforts to take over control of the major American denominations, missionary agencies, and other Protestant organizations had failed. In the late 1920s and in the 1930s, the fundamentalists frequently were caricatured by journalists who portrayed them as backwoods hicks and lowbrow ignoramuses, as well as dangerous fanatics. The journalist H. L. Mencken's description of the fundamentalists characterizes the backlash. They are, he writes,

thick in the mean streets behind the gas-works. They are everywhere that learning is too heavy a burden for minds to carry. . . . They march with the Klan, with the Christian Endeavor Society, with the Junior Order of United American Mechanics. . . . They have had a thrill and they are ready for more.[4]

In fact, a considerable segment of the American Protestant population in the decades of Fundamentalism's advance were religiously conservative and evangelical, and would defend what they understood to be fundamental Christian beliefs even though they were not personnally associated with the fundamentalist cause.

Despite the fact that Fundamentalism was in decline and disarray by 1940, its impact on groups such as the Southern Baptist Convention and on the Holiness and Pentecostal churches was significant and enduring, as was its effect on the growth of independent Dispensationalist churches. Many fundamentalists did, however, remain in the mainline denominations and persevered in their opposition to the accommodation of their churches to modernity and liberalism. As George Marsden has observed, beyond the independent, separatist, Dispensationalist churches,

most of the other groups that had been touched by the fundamentalist experience of the 1920s re-emerged in a new postfundamentalist coalition. Their basic attitude toward culture is suggested by their successful

appropriation of the more culturally respectable term "evangelical."[5]

It is to this "New Evangelicalism" that we now turn.

THE "NEW EVANGELICALISM"

The transformation of the older Fundamentalism—which became the object of derision and repugnance due to its anti-intellectualism, its separatism, and its excessive preoccupation with biblical apocalypticism—began in the immediate post–World War II years. The most significant call for change was made by Carl F. H. Henry (1913–   ), a young professor at Northern Baptist Seminary in Chicago, in a short book entitled *The Uneasy Conscience of Modern Fundamentalism* (1947). Henry criticized his fundamentalist colleagues on many counts. Among his indictments were Fundamentalism's disregard of its environing political culture; its neglect of the earthly needs of humankind; and its sectarian spirit. He insisted that the redemptive message of Christianity has implications for the whole of human life. Henry especially attacked the negative and "loveless" spirit of the fundamentalist movement. He returns to the same charge ten years later:

One of the ironies of contemporary church history is that the more fundamentalists stressed separation from apostasy as a theme in their churches, the more a spirit of lovelessness seemed to prevail. The theological conflict with liberalism deteriorated into an attack upon organizations and personalities.[6]

If Carl Henry was the young prophet, Edward John Carnell (1919–1967) was the young apologist of the new Evangelicalism in the immediate post–World War II years. His *An Introduction to Christian Apologetics* (1948) is considered to be, with Henry's *Uneasy Conscience*, one of the significant catalysts of the new evangelical movement. Carnell served as professor and, from 1954 to 1959, as president of Fuller Theological Seminary in Pasadena, California. His writings in the late 1940s and 1950s included his *Apologetics*, a critique of Niebuhr's thought in *The Theology of Reinhold Niebuhr* (1951), *Philosophy of the Christian Religion* (1952), *Christian Commitment: An Apologetic* (1957), and *The Case for Orthodox Theology* (1959). Among the new evangelical apologists at mid-century, Carnell was the writer who was taken most seriously by the liberal and Neo-Orthodox theologians at the time. Like Henry, Carnell disapproved of Fundamentalism's anti-intellectualism and what he called its "cultic" and schismatic tendency. In an article describing his disaffection with the current fundamentalist outlook, he wrote:

Through a series of subtle internal changes, fundamentalism shifted from an affirmation to a negation. The result was a cunning pharisaism that confused possession of truth with possession of virtue. . . . Having exempted itself from the scrutiny of divine righteousness, fundamentalism often took on the mannerisms of a pugnacious cult. . . . All other elements in the Christian community were considered apostate. It was by a discovery of this pompous theological error that I awoke from dogmatic slumber.[7]

Of considerable moment in the growth of the new evangelical cause was the ministry of the popular American evangelist, Billy Graham, (1918–), who had launched his meteoric career in Los Angeles in 1949. Graham did not attend a seminary, and he never pretended to be a scholar or theologian. Yet he gave his personal support to the evangelical colleges and seminaries that were then attempting to move beyond Fundamentalism. He also played a crucial role in the founding of the biweekly journal *Christianity Today* (1956), conceived both as a counterpoint to the liberal Protestant weekly, *The Christian Century*, and as an organ of intellectually sound evangelical discussion and commentary. The founding editor of *Christianity Today* was Carl F. H. Henry.

Among the theological colleges and seminaries in North America that stand out as centers of the new evangelical theological movement is Fuller Theological Seminary, founded in 1947. It was begun as an alternative to Princeton Theological Seminary, then no longer regarded by conservatives as a genuinely evangelical institution. Fuller remains today the theological center of progressive evangelical scholarship. Its faculty has included some of the foremost new evangelical scholars, including E. J. Carnell, George E. Ladd, Paul K. Jewett, Lewis Smedes, and Jack Rogers. Other important centers of new evangelical thought in North America are Calvin College and Seminary in Grand Rapids, Michigan; Wheaton College in Wheaton, Illinois; Gordon-Conwell Theological Seminary in South Hamilton, Massachusetts; Trinity Evangelical Divinity School in Deerfield, Illinois; and Regent College, Vancouver, British Columbia.

A distinctive feature of post-World War II Evangelicalism is the complex of interrelated institutions that serve and strengthen the evangelical movement. Beyond the seminaries and colleges are organizations such as the National Association of Evangelicals (1942) with its several commissions and agencies, such as the Evangelical Foreign Missions Association, the National Association of Christian Schools, the National Religious Broadcasters, and the Evangelical Social Action Commission.

Evangelical organizations directed toward work with youth and students include Youth for Christ and Young Life, the Inter-Varsity Christian Fellowship, and Campus Crusade for Christ International. And then there is the vast network of evangelical media: television and radio, book publishing, magazines and newspapers that reach millions. The National Religious Broadcasters coordinate several hundred broadcasts both nationally and internationally. The largest operation is Pat Robertson's Christian Broadcasting Network (CBN), which has the capacity to reach most American households and whose International Communications Center can transmit telecasts abroad in over thirty languages. Among religious book publishers, William B. Eerdmans

Publishing Company has played an especially creative role in publishing scholarly books by progressive evangelical scholars while also including the works of other Protestant and Roman Catholic scholars on its lists.

The enumeration of the network of evangelical organizations could be vastly extended, but this sketch gives a sense of its scope and influence.[8] It is with this background in mind that we now can turn to the new Evangelical theology—and it will not come as a surprise that its spectrum of theological positions is richly diverse. One naturally will expect that there are important theological differences within the groups that comprise the contemporary evangelical family; for example, among the Southern Baptists, the Dutch Reformed Confessionalists, the Mennonites, the Wesleyan Holiness movement, the Pentecostals, and the Dispensationalists. Nevertheless, there is a bond that joins many, if not all, of these groups together in an evangelical theological alliance that constitutes a conspicuous "third way" between Roman Catholic theology and the Liberal and Neo-Orthodox theologies that have been so influential in modern European and North American Protestantism since the Enlightenment.

The selection of a few representative theologians from such a complex movement is, for the reasons just suggested, not only difficult but also problematic. Many contemporary Evangelicals point to the literary scholar C. S. Lewis (1893–1963) as having been a formative influence on them. However, Lewis was a brilliant lay apologist and not a theologian or philosopher. The writings of Francis Schaeffer (1912–1984), the founder in 1955 of L'Abri Christian retreat center in Switzerland, also have been influential on a younger generation of Evangelicals from roughly the 1960s through the 1980s. Yet, again, Schaeffer was not a theologian; he was an apologist and culture critic with a broad interest in the arts and the history of ideas.

Since the 1960s, a number of able younger theologians have emerged within the evangelical

orbit and this would include Clark Pinnock, David F. Wells, Stanley J. Grenz, Alister E. McGrath, Miroslav Volf, and William Abraham, among others. It is difficult at this point, however, to judge the continuing influence of their work. The selection of two or three representative evangelical theologians for our deeper exploration here presents a further difficulty. The new evangelical alliance encompasses a wide diversity of Christian churches and groups, but it is not possible to include representative figures from each one. It is necessary, therefore, to limit somewhat our circle of *theological* Evangelicalism. Some evangelical groups can claim influential leaders or preachers, for example, the Dispensationalists and the Pentecostals, but they have not produced theologians of note who have engaged other influential modern theologians. Other contemporary evangelical churches have produced scholars and theologians who have had considerable influence outside their own communities, but often in areas especially distinctive of their tradition. One thinks of the important work of Anabaptist-Mennonite writers, such as John Howard Yoder, on ethics, pacifism, and peace studies. For compelling reasons, two theologians, Gerrit C. Berkouwer and Carl F. H. Henry, will serve as our illustrative theologians here. They represent only the Reformed and Baptist sectors of the movement, but they are appropriate because we can be more confident of the long-term significance of their work, which is completed, because both have played important roles in shaping postwar evangelical thought, and because both were deeply engaged in ecumenical theological discussions. Both are also committed to a "high" doctrine of the Bible's authority as the infallible norm of Christian faith and practice and to the principal orthodox doctrines of classical Protestantism. The chapter concludes, however, with an account of the work of three relatively new evangelical voices from North America and Britain who represent a reaction against the type of theology represented by Carl Henry.

GERRIT CORNELIUS BERKOUWER

G. C. Berkouwer (1903–   ) stands in a venerable, Dutch Reformed theological tradition that emerged in the Netherlands in the late nineteenth century as a protest against the liberal, established state Reformed Church. Thoroughly evangelical and Neo-Calvinistic, this movement seceded from the state church and founded a new denomination called the *Gereformeerde Kerken* (the Reformed Churches) in 1892. The first great theologian and leader of this Neo-Calvinist movement was Abraham Kuyper (1837–1920). Kuyper was educated at Leiden University, a center of theological liberalism, from which he broke through a conversion experience and a study of the great Protestant Reformers. Kuyper not only wrote volumes on theology, politics, and philosophy; he also was a remarkable leader. He founded two newspapers, one of which he edited for many years; led the Anti-Revolutionary Party in Holland; was a long-time member of the Dutch Parliament; and served as prime minister of the Netherlands from 1900 to 1905. Most important, for our purposes, he founded the Free University of Amsterdam in 1880 and was its first professor of theology.

Kuyper's successor in the chair of theology in 1902 was Herman Bavinck (1854–1921), the greatest theologian of this Neo-Calvinist movement. Bavinck completed his doctorate at Leiden, and prior to his appointment at the Free University he was professor of dogmatic theology at the Reformed Seminary at Kampen. His major work is a four-volume *Reformed Dogmatics* (1895–1901). Only a part of volume two on the doctrine of God is available in English. What is significant about Kuyper and Bavinck is the fact that, despite their differences, they established a theological method that followed the tradition of St. Augustine and the Reformers in that they held to the view that faith precedes reason and illuminates and enlarges it. This is in striking contrast to seventeenth- and eighteenth-century Calvinistic scholasticism, for example, to the writings of

Francis Turrentin (1623–1687), that was adopted by the Princeton Theology (see Volume I, Chapter Twelve). Unlike the Calvinist theology that was regnant at Princeton Theological Seminary at approximately the same time, Kuyper and Bavinck did not insist on the priority of theological apologetics or demand that certain reasonable presuppositions or evidential proofs were required before faith could take effect.

G. C. Berkouwer was heir to this Augustinian theological tradition, although he develops it in his own distinctive way to meet a changing theological context. Also, Berkouwer does not follow his predecessors in their assertion that God provides the necessary connection between the mind and natural knowledge as well as theological knowledge; that is, Berkouwer rejects the analogy between natural knowledge and religious faith.

Berkouwer was born and reared in a cultured Dutch Calvinist home and his early education in the classics was at the Christian Gymnasium. He then studied theology at the Free University of Amsterdam. After leaving the university in 1927, he served as a pastor, first in a village in the northern province of Friesland and then in Amsterdam until 1945. This long service as a pastor deeply affected Berkouwer's conception of the role of theology as serving the Christian *kerygma*, or proclamation. His doctoral dissertation was on the relationship between faith and revelation and, as we will see, this idea of *co-relation* is a key to understanding his theology. Berkouwer did not produce a traditional systematic theology; rather, he has written a series of theological monographs on dogmatic themes. These studies have grown into eighteen long volumes, and most of them are translated into English as *Studies in Dogmatics* (1952–1976). An impressive feature of Berkouwer's theological work is his ongoing dialogue with theologians who are not within his own Dutch Neo-Calvinist tradition. His *Studies in Dogmatics* is filled with sympathetic as well as critical commentary on themes in Karl Barth's theology, and his *The Triumph of Grace in the Theology of Karl Barth* (1954; Eng. trans., 1956) remains one of the most trenchant critiques of some of Barth's cardinal doctrines. A consequence of Berkouwer's writings on Roman Catholicism was an invitation in 1961 to be an official observer at the Second Vatican Council in Rome. Two subsequent books on Roman Catholic theology followed: *The Second Vatican Council and the New Theology* (1965) and *Reflection After the Council*, both thoughtful and impressive analyses. Berkouwer's *A Half Century of Theology* (1974; Eng. trans., 1977) is further evidence of his deep and broad engagement with the work of other important twentieth-century theologians.

The *Studies in Dogmatics* cover the full range of classic dogmatic themes from the doctrine of God to eschatology, and it is not possible to explore them all here. We will, rather, focus on a few themes that are both distinctive of Berkouwer's theology and cover topics that are of perennial concern to Evangelicals.

Co-Relationship

Berkouwer does not set forth, in a highly self-conscious way, his method of doing theology as has, for example, Paul Tillich or Emil Brunner. Nevertheless, one can see a guiding theme in Berkouwer's theological approach, namely, the co-relationship between revelation and faith or, more specifically, between the Word of God in Scripture and personal faith. This was the subject of his doctoral dissertation, and the titles of the first three volumes of his *Studies* bear out its importance: *Faith and Justification, Faith and Sanctification,* and *Faith and Perseverance.* Berkouwer's understanding of the co-relation between Scripture and its human reception in faith can, however, be easily misunderstood. It is often pointed out that for a theologian such as Paul Tillich, the subjective and receptive pole of the theological correlation can too readily shape the substance of the object or answer, i.e., Scripture or revelation. And, Berkouwer suggests, Liberal theology has given too large a place to this subjective, existential side of the co-relationship, just as Protestant

orthodoxy, and perhaps even Barth, attend too exclusively to a purely objective and unhistorical conception of divine revelation. Berkouwer also begins by insisting that the Bible is not a source of information, of dogmas or objective facts; it is, rather, the dynamic address and revelation of the living God, which includes the co-relation of a receiving faith. Human faith while decisive is not, however, an autonomous action, nor is it a value in itself. For faith comes from God and only in correlation with the divine Word or revelation does it have any reality. Nonetheless, faith is crucial to any true knowledge of God and God's revelation in Scripture. Berkouwer speaks of faith as both passive, as the work of the Holy Spirit, and active, a dynamic human apprehension of divine truth. Without this authentic co-relationship, revelation (Scripture) would remain either a purely heteronomous, external authority or a purely internal, experiential authority. The former is the danger of Protestant orthodoxy and scholasticism and the latter is the temptation of both pietism and liberalism.

Theology is always a work of faith in creative response to divine revelation in Scripture. But this co-relationship also means that *theology* is always a relative science. Relative, not in the sense of relativism, but relative to the dynamic, ever-renewing and deepening Word of God:

It means that theology is occupied in continuous and obedient listening to the Word. And since listening, unlike remembering, is always a thing of the present moment, theological questions must have relevance and timeliness. Theology is not a complex system constructed for their own entertainment by scholars in the quiet retreat of their ivory towers. It must have significance for the unquiet times; but it can achieve its proper relevance only in obedient attentiveness, not to the times first of all, but to the Word.[9]

Doing theology means that the theologian must be faithfully receptive to Scripture and never the neutral master of Scripture. The doctrine of Holy Scripture is, then, for Berkouwer, as for all evangelical theologians, the cornerstone of the theological task.

In view of his commitment to the Scriptural principle, one might well ask how the Neo-Calvinist Berkouwer regards the great Reformed confessions and catechisms, such as the Belgic and Westminster Confessions and the Canons of Dort. On this question Berkouwer is forthright and clear. The Church must honor its confessional heritage, but it must always ask how the intent of its confessions can deepen the Church's understanding of Scripture's revelation. The Church must never absolutize its creeds and confessions; it must always face new situations that threaten the Gospel and, therefore, it must be ready to formulate Christian truth anew. It is just through such conflicts and challenges that the Church, under the guidance of the Holy Spirit, achieves new insight into the riches of Scripture.

And so there is no reason to make the pronouncement of Chalcedon a final milepost in the history of the Church. . . . For the Scriptures are richer than any pronouncement of the Church. . . . To acknowledge this fact is not to have a relativistic view of dogma but to have a right sense of proportion: the place of dogma is in the Church, which in turn is subject in all of its expressions to the Word of God.[10]

Holy Scripture

The question of the nature and authority of Holy Scripture is, for Berkouwer, the essential prior question for any Christian theology; and it is his conception of Scripture that gives his theological reflections a distinctive place on the contemporary evangelical spectrum. It can be viewed as a "third way" between either a pietistic or a modernist experiential subjectivism on the one hand and a post-Reformation rationalistic objectivism on the other.[11] Berkouwer's principal discussion of this theme is found in a two-volume contribution to his *Studies in Dogmatics* titled *Holy Scripture* (1966–1967; Eng. trans., 1975). These volumes were not well received by Evangelicals who remain committed to the Princeton interpretation of biblical inerrancy (see Volume I, Chapter Twelve). It is, however, commended by many progressive Evangelicals who see it as an alternative to a regressive biblical Fundamentalism.

At the heart of Berkouwer's view of Scripture is his concept of the co-relationship of revelation and faith as understood in terms of St. Augustine's epistemological starting point of faith in search of understanding. When applied to Scripture, this means for Berkouwer that the Christian cannot "discuss Scripture apart from a personal relationship of belief in it."[12] That is, faith is not grounded on some *a priori* conception of the nature of divine revelation and biblical inspiration or inerrancy that serves as the guarantee of Scripture's authority. Rather, "the way of Christian faith is . . . a subjection to the gospel, to the Christ of the Scriptures; and from this alone can a reflection *on* Holy Scripture proceed."[13] Berkouwer points to the conviction of his predecessors, Kuyper and Bavinck, who rejected "the idea that Scripture is the object of the *testimonium* [of the Holy Spirit] apart from its message." To formalize Holy Scripture in such a philosophical way as to afford an *a priori* certainty of its authority is both contrary to the way faith works and is "as nonsensical as to praise a book without reading it."[14]

Following the interpretive principle of the Reformer John Calvin, Berkouwer insists that the authority of Scripture is assured to the Christian through the inner testimony of the Holy Spirit. And the purpose of Scripture is simply to witness to Christ and his salvation. Modern biblical criticism, of course, often loses sight of this kerygmatic and salvific purpose of Scripture. Even so, the theologian should not reject the methods and insights of the historical-critical study of the Bible due to an *a priori* notion of biblical inerrancy. Berkouwer sees the Princeton theologians, for example, as offering "an artificial view of revelation that does not acknowledge with sufficient seriousness that scripture is written in human words and consequently offers the reader legitimate freedom to examine these words and try to understand them."[15] Furthermore, to presuppose an *a priori* conception of verbal inerrancy is to lay down what God's method of revealing his truth must be. This is a human presumption that risks "tarnishing the mystery of Scripture by disqualifying the God-ordained way in which it came to us."[16]

Berkouwer sees the human character of Scripture as neither an accidental or peripheral condition of God's revelation. Rather, it necessitates a close reading of the contents of Scripture and "certain results, be it of natural science or historical research, can provide the 'occasion' for understanding various aspects of Scripture in a different way than before."[17]

Berkouwer appeals to Bavinck's concept of the "organic inspiration" of Scripture to underline the fact that Scripture has a center and a periphery and that Scripture is its own best interpreter. Historical criticism can illuminate the intention of the biblical writers and editors in a way that can be missed if Scripture is read serially in its present canonical order. The intelligibility and accuracy of Scripture is to be found, rather, in its organic message of salvation and not in isolated words or parts. Berkouwer points out that when the Reformers spoke of the "perspicuity" or clarity of Scripture they were referring to the unambiguous lucidity of the Gospel message and were not suggesting the inerrant status of the Bible's human language. Later we will see that the American evangelical theologian Carl Henry takes a very different view of the Bible's inspiration and inerrancy, one much closer to that of the Princeton Theology (see Volume I, Chapter Twelve) and the position especially of B. B. Warfield.

The question of the Bible's inerrancy was an ongoing issue in the Dutch Reformed Church in Holland to the mid-twentieth century, and Berkouwer has responded to this issue in a striking way. He insists that the notion of "error" must be understood in its biblical usage; and the Bible speaks of "error" not as "incorrectness" or "inerrancy" but in terms of sin and deception.

Thus we are quite far removed from the serious manner in which error is dealt with in Scripture. For there what is meant is not the result of a limited degree of knowledge, but it is a swerving from the truth and upsetting the faith (2 Timothy 2:18). . . . It is not that Scripture offers us no information but that the nature

of this information is unique. It is governed by the *purpose* of God's revelation.[18]

The theological use of the word "inerrancy" is, Berkouwer contends, a mistaken formalization and misuse of the biblical idea of erring.[19]

Abstract *a priori* conceptions of biblical inerrancy also fail to take seriously the fact that in revealing the divine purposes to humanity God accommodates revelation to human speech and forms of thought. For Berkouwer, this means taking account of the cultural context in which God's word is given. Here, again, historical scholarship can deepen a reader's understanding of what Berkouwer calls the "goal" or purpose of a particular passage. The universal Gospel message did not come to humanity in the form of "timeless" generalities, despite the fact that believers naturally object to the use of terms such as "time-relatedness" or "time-boundedness" when applied to Scripture, because for them it suggests something relative. Berkouwer appeals to Paul's letters as examples of contextual "time-related" situations that also reveal the goal or purpose of Paul's message. Take the example of Paul's often perplexing statements regarding women. The problem they raise are the result of reading them outside the context of the period in which they were written. But Berkouwer contends that Paul "did not in the least render timeless propositions concerning womanhood." The example of I Cor. 11:10 is instructive. Here Paul states that "the woman ought to have power ("authority") on *her* head (the veil was a symbol of this) because of the angels." This is, indeed, an opaque passage, and, as Berkouwer suggests, "the simple pronouncement that God's Word comes to us here will not suffice. One must take note of the cultural context and intent of the words within that period precisely *in order* to hear the Word of God." But Paul, in this and other passages concerning women, was not rendering

timeless propositions concerning womanhood. Rather, he wrote various testimonies and prescriptions applicable to particular . . . situations against the background of specific morals and customs of that period. . . . The way of God's Word is in the manner of men "in a particular period." It appears clear that numerous and quite varying arguments are used to announce the message precisely for that period in that situation.[20]

Yet recognition of this time-boundedness must move the interpreter on for

obedience to the Word of God is impossible, even an illusion, if it is not a listening discovery of the *meaning* of the words, *of their essential goal*. . . . It is necessary to search out *the meaning and intent of the words* precisely because everything in God-breathed Scripture appears in such an historically human manner. This search saves us from ignoring much of the Bible as hopelessly irrelevant to us because of the changed cultural situation and the changing picture of our times.[20] [Italics added.][21]

In this latter passage it is evident that Berkouwer is contending not only against a rationalistic Fundamentalism that denies the genuinely human form of Scripture but also against Bultmann's effort to demythologize the New Testament worldview of Jewish apocalypticism because he sees it as outmoded and a stumbling block to faith. Bultmann, too, in Berkouwer's view, fails to recognize God's accommodation in offering a universal message of salvation in the human thought-forms and language of the times—and that it is specifically *in and through* these time-bound vehicles and contexts that the *meaning and goal* of God's revelation is discerned.

Berkouwer wisely maintains that the problem of the time-relatedness of Scripture should not be seen as a deep shadow and threat cast over the Church's confession regarding Scripture. Rather, biblical research should be seen as a "searching for the goal and for the Word within the many words."[22] Berkouwer concludes:

One can only walk the road of biblical research in the way of the Spirit and of the message of Scripture . . . in expectation of the reliable Word that testifies of Christ and continues to point the way in its

human and historical form. It is not the way of logical deduction . . . but the way of a continued association with Scripture—Scripture that is *time related* and has a *universal* authority.[23]

Commentators have noted how often Berkouwer speaks forthrightly of Scripture in "functional" and practical terms. They see the root of this usage is his rejection of the docetic notion that Scripture is a book of abstract, logically inferred universal truths, or a body of neutral facts. Scripture is not, he writes, "a metaphysical document, but a living instrument serving God for the proclamation of a message of salvation."[24]

The Doctrine of Providence, Election, and Reprobation

Conservative Reformed theologians contend that Berkouwer deviates most clearly from John Calvin and the Calvinistic standards, such as the Canons of Dort, in his positions on election and reprobation.[25] Berkouwer concurs with Karl Barth that the doctrine of God's providence has nothing to do with natural theology, and that it is a doctrine based solely on faith in the salvation brought by Christ. Berkouwer even objects to his great predecessor Bavinck's speaking of providence as a "mixed article"—that is, as a doctrine known both by natural reason and by special revelation in Scripture—because Bavinck clearly asserts that providence is a confession of faith and not a cosmological theory, such as the pagan conceptions of destiny or fate. Similarly, the philosophical question of human freedom over against nature's necessity is not the same as the question of human freedom and divine providence.

Berkouwer also recognizes the danger in the attempt to *interpret* God's providence in *specific* events of history. "In fear and trembling faith confesses God's Providence over the entire flight of history. . . . But now we see through a glass, in riddles, and our knowledge is made up in fragments."[26] Faith in divine providence does not resolve the puzzles and evils of history but, rather, gives courage and assurance that behind the events of history God's gracious will is mysteriously working.

Berkouwer introduces the concept of "concurrence"[27] in an attempt to indicate that the acts of God and the acts of human beings coincide, and that both human decision and responsibility and God's all-pervading providence are thereby preserved. This, again, is consistent with Berkouwer's method of co-relationship, but it is not proposed as a rational explanation of the relation of human and divine action. Neither is Berkouwer proposing a type of *synergism*, as in the Roman Catholic doctrine of divine and human cooperation in the work of salvation.[28] Synergism, he believes, reduces God's elective decisions by asserting that the human response becomes the *condition* under which election occurs. Such a doctrine is contrary to the Reformed teaching of the *corruptio naturae*, the fallen nature of the human reason and will.

Concurrence, Berkouwer suggests, seeks to confront the question: How do we conceive of divine cooperation in sin? Does it include sin or only human good works? Some Reformed theologians, for instance, Herman Bavinck, argued that God provides the individual with the *ability to sin* but it is the individual who misuses it. Others, such as Abraham Kuyper, insisted that there is a divine energy or power, hence activity, in all things. But this appears to suggest that God cooperates in sin. Berkouwer rejects all such suggestions as products of a purely rational, deductive thinking. God, he insists, cannot be conceived as the *cause* of sin. Berkouwer further rejects a Reformed tendency to fall back on the distinction between the hidden and revealed will of God, as if God's hidden will wills evil while God's revealed will opposes it. To claim this is to question God's oneness and trustworthiness.

Berkouwer openly acknowledges that belief in God's providence and the reality of evil is a mystery, but, more importantly, it is a religious confession of faith and not a philosophical problem.

This inscrutability need not shock us or fill us with a panic which might haunt us for our entire lives. The problem is resolved through confession of guilt and in faith . . . which knows its own responsibility—as it knows the unapproachable holiness of God. He who does not listen in faith to God's voice is left with an insoluable dilemma.[29]

It is in his treatise on *Divine Election* that Berkouwer reveals most clearly his break with the Calvinist orthodoxy of the Canons of Dort. First, he insists that the divine election must not be understood aside from the grace of God in Christ.

Scripture showed us that in the doctrine of God's election the issue is not a *decretum absolutum*, abstracted from Christ, neither a *necessitas rerum* which cannot be changed under any circumstances, nor a dark and irrational power of the *potentia absoluta*. Rather, Scripture points in its doxologies and songs in praise of the free election of God to the deep, unfathomable source of salvation in Jesus Christ.[30]

Election is to be seen as the heart of the good news of Christ's Gospel, and not a hidden and arbitrary decree of a divine sovereign. Here Berkouwer is one with Karl Barth in insisting that God's sovereignty cannot be separated from his love nor his election from Jesus Christ. (See Chapter Four on Barth.)

Berkouwer believes, however, that Barth has objectified the doctrine of the "electing Christ" into a fixed and accomplished state of affairs. He, therefore, rejects Barth's treatment of election as theological speculation. Election can only be properly understood by faith, and in faith "the inscrutable election no longer poses a threat." Because election is election in Christ, the light of the message shines clear in preaching and is understood not as a fixed state "but as a call and summons." "He who travels this way of faith and puts his trust in Jesus Christ alone, will understand that beyond Him there arises no new problem, but that in Him the problem is solved."[31]

There is, then, no hidden God, no *decretum absolutum* that is independent of the *deus revelatus* or God's self-revelation in Christ. The grace revealed in Christ makes known God's deepest intentions—not through logical deduction but by faith.

What of those who do not believe? Has not orthodox Calvinism taught that the decree of election inevitably implies the decree of reprobation (rejection)—that the all-wise God has, from eternity, willed to save some and not to save others? Berkouwer rejects the idea that reprobation is a logical corollary of election and that in their relationship there needs to be an essential symmetry. For Berkouwer it is only possible to see God's reprobation as God's holy response to human sin. He refers to Calvin for support:

When Calvin emphasizes that nothing occurs apart from God's counsel and sovereign act, he begins immediately thereafter to speak so seriously and existentially of sin as the real cause that—happily!—the transition becomes obscure when he suddenly writes that the real cause of sin is not the counsel of God but man's sin. . . . He asks: "Why should man still seek that cause in heaven?"[32]

In Scripture election and reprobation are asymmetrical. Scripture speaks of God's acts of rejection, but it makes little mention of reprobation as an eternal decree. The fatal misconceptions regarding election and reprobation are, for Berkouwer, in seeing them as constituting an eternal causal, deterministic system or a fatalism that robs the message of election of its sense of God's love and assurance.

Election and reprobation must, Berkouwer insists, always be spoken of existentially in the context of the *kerygma*, the dynamic preaching of the good news and summons. In such a context the wrath of God is not parallel with and separate from God's love. Wrath is real and is not to be understood as having been removed by the revelation of Christ's love. Wrath is, indeed, God's divine reaction and opposition to human sin—to what happens on "man's side." Wrath is, therefore, not arbitrary and irrational but fully comprehensible as God's opposition to all obstructions to

divine grace and the Kingdom of God. "It is very remarkable," Berkouwer writes, "that whenever we hear of wrath in the Gospels it is *not a restriction of the Good News* but it is rather a reference to the antagonism against the Kingdom as now revealed or salvation as now proclaimed."[33] Wrath is the instrument of God's grace and love—but this can only be perceived in faith.

The Last Things and Universalism

The Christian doctrine of election is, we have seen, inextricably related to the doctrines of salvation and reprobation, and these are, of course, related to the Last Things or eschatology. Berkouwer has written an expansive two-volume study of eschatology titled *The Return of Christ* (1961, 1963; Eng. trans., 1971). Here, once again, he insists that Christian teaching about the eschaton must not be explored apart from the Church's preaching of the Gospel and faith. That is, biblical eschatology is not to be understood as information about future events that might be considered independently of faith.

Berkouwer notes the intensity of feeling that is especially associated with the contemporary discussion of "universalism," or the question of the ultimate salvation of all persons. And this emotional response is coupled with feelings of abhorrence and even hostility toward the idea of the eternal damnation of one's fellow human beings. For Evangelicals, however, this question remains of critical theological importance, for Scripture speaks not only of God's grace and salvation but also of his judgment and rejection. Berkouwer devotes significant attention to the issue of *apokatastasis*, or universal reconciliation or restoration, and his reflections on the subject have been criticized by fellow Evangelicals.

Contrary to traditional Calvinism, Berkouwer does not dismiss out of hand "universal reconciliation" with God as self-evidently unbiblical and unworthy of investigation. He points to contemporary theologians such as Hans Urs von Balthasar, Karl Rahner, and Karl Barth who, though rejecting universalism as a necessary presumption based on

God's love, nevertheless treat the doctrine with great seriousness because of their sense of the openness of the biblical proclamation on this very question. As Barth has written: "The Church will not preach an *apokatastasis*, nor will it preach a powerless grace of Jesus Christ or a wickedness of men which is too powerful for it."[34] That is, one cannot assume the doctrine of *apokatastasis* if one wishes to respect the freedom of God's grace, but at the same time one cannot dismiss it as impossible *a priori*. Berkouwer cites Barth approvingly: "Strange Christianity, whose most pressing anxiety seems to be that God's grace might prove to be all too free on this side, that hell, instead of being populated with so many people, might some day prove to be empty."[35]

Berkouwer agrees with von Balthasar, Rahner, and Barth that God is to be the judge on this matter, but also that the biblical witness is clear that the last things are related to the Church's *kerygma and* to human faith, trust, and responsibility, including any claim regarding universal restoration. It is *not* a neutral, static postulate "that precedes the dynamics and the appeal of the proclamation and is established by it."[36]

Berkouwer is concerned that, although Barth rejects *apokatastasis* as a doctrine and speaks of it in relation to the Church's proclamation, his doctrine of election in Christ represents such a "triumph of grace" as to raise the question whether he takes seriously enough the "call to faith." "This question," Berkouwer persistently repeats, "presses all the more because Barth, impelled by his conception of the triumph of grace, uses such strong expressions to show how *impossible* unbelief is, and how *powerless* it is to frustrate *what God has from all eternity decided*."[37] For Berkouwer the tension between salvation and reprobation in the New Testament is a matter of profound seriousness, for it

constantly presents an apparent ultimatum that is inextricably connected with this proclamation. . . . The proclamation of the gospel contains a warning against unbelief, and the way of unbelief is portrayed as the way of outermost darkness and lostness.

And such warnings are meant continually "to confront us with the admonition to open our eyes to the light and see the salvation, not to harden our hearts."[38]

Neither can these warnings, however, be abstracted from their context in the New Testament proclamation. "All such threats," Berkouwer asserts, "are not arranged symmetrically beside the gospel, but proceed from it and can be understood only in its light." Nonetheless, "the relationship of [the threats] to the gospel accentuates and illuminates the seriousness of these warnings."[39]

The biblical warnings of judgment and lostness and separation from God are represented in Scripture by the word "hell," a translation of the Greek *geenna* (Gehenna), referring to God's judgment on the Israelite sacrificial abominations carried out in the Valley of Hinnon, south of Jerusalem. Berkouwer points out, however, that hell is often torn from its Gospel relationship and is treated solely as a ruthless threat divorced from God's invitation and love. When hell is so spoken of, out of its New Testament context, it assumes "a magical, terrifying dimension that speaks only of the incalculable, all-consuming wrath of God, and says nothing of His love."[40] The discussion of hell thus becomes preoccupied with a future event and with the numbers of the saved and damned. But all this talk, Berkouwer sees, as a perversion and caricature of the New Testament's proclamation in which "God's full salvation and God's earnest admonition do not limit one another, but are indisoluably related," and where the "many that are first will be last, and the last first (Matt. 19:30), and where the judgment will begin with the house of God" (I Peter 4:17).[41]

The entire context of the references to hell and its threat is its intent to call men back from the paths of darkness lest they prefer it to the light. . . . Mention of judgment always engenders mention of mercy, patience, compassion. . . . This is the radical difference between the gospel's 'threatening' and unevangelical terror. The latter is horrifying but not really serious, for it lacks any real character of appeal. The evangelical reference to judgment—that the Lord is to be feared (II Cor. 5:11)—is a qualified threat, because it is the other side of the invitation, of the abundant riches to which the kerygma attests."[42]

Christ's passion, his descent and abandonment in hell, and his exaltation represent the gracious triumph over the power of darkness and hell and, Berkouwer writes, "the gospel calls us to believe in this triumph, to be comforted by it. This is not a demythologizing of hell; it is more an exorcism of it—*in faith*."[43] Over and over in history the question addressed to Jesus again arises: "Lord, will those who are saved be few?" And Jesus's answer "seems so noncommittal, so evasive": "strive to enter by the narrow door" (Luke 13:23 f). "But," Berkouwer concludes, "this evasiveness is only apparent. This *is* the answer to *this* question . . . *this* question has been answered, once for all time."[44]

The Word of God is not, for Berkouwer, quasiscientific, neutral information; it is always in a dynamic co-relationship with faith, and this has not always been well-received by his evangelical colleagues. This is especially true of traditional Dutch Calvinists who, though a diminishing voice in Evangelicalism, continue to uphold a doctrine of biblical inerrancy, double predestination, and limited atonement. Progressive Evangelicals may, however, also wonder whether or just how Berkouwer's conception of hell differs, for example, from a demythologized or existential interpretation of hell that avoids spatiotemporal objectification. Berkouwer simply refuses to speak of hell in such objectified terms that are removed from the existential hearing and response to the Gospel's proclamation of salvation, warning, and responsibility.

It is widely recognized that G. C. Berkouwer best represents the contemporary evangelical voice of the confessional Neo-Calvinist tradition. He honors his eminent predecessors, such as Abraham Kuyper and Herman Bavinck, by engaging in a lively dialogue with their thought. But he also has reached out beyond this circle of his confession to engage in discussion with most of the leading Roman Catholic and Protestant

theologians of the twentieth century. He has opened new channels of communication with thinkers previously shunned by Anglo-American Evangelicals and, as a result, has also adventured along new paths that have opened the way for a new generation of evangelical theologians to follow. One of them has aptly described Berkouwer's impressive contribution:

> He has become the modern-day example of a biblical theologian within the scope of ecclesiastical confessionalism. For he has tried to get at the *message* of the confessions, and in doing so he has freed theology from the letter of the confessions. Likewise, in working within the framework of a church with a theological tradition, he has, in adhering to that tradition, at the same time set it free from its bondage to dogmatic distinctions that had received almost canonical status. Or, we may say, he has released theology from the tyranny of logic and set it within the freedom of faith.[45]

CARL F. H. HENRY

In the decades between the 1940s and 1970s, Carl F. H. Henry (1913–) stood out as the most influential emissary and theologian of the new Evangelicalism in North America.[46] He was born in New York City, the oldest of eight children of German immigrant parents. Henry was baptized and confirmed in the Episcopal Church. After high school he began work as a reporter, rising to the editorship of a small Long Island newspaper. By then he had left the church, but at the age of twenty he experienced conversion and an evangelical calling through the intervention of several friends. Henry was baptized and joined a Baptist congregation. To pursue theological studies he enrolled at Wheaton College. His Wheaton experience deepened his evangelical commitment and his ties with a number of later evangelical leaders, including Billy Graham.

After receiving the A.B. and M.A. from Wheaton, Henry entered the Northern Baptist Seminary in Chicago in 1938. He was ordained in 1941 and served as a pastor for a short time before returning to Northern Baptist Seminary, where he completed the Th.D. degree and began his teaching career. It was during this time that he participated in the founding of the National Association of Evangelicals (1943). The year 1947 marked two important events in Henry's career. He published *The Uneasy Conscience of Modern Fundamentalism*, "the manifesto of neo-evangelicalism," and he joined the faculty of the newly established Fuller Theological Seminary in Pasadena, California. Fuller's mission was to offer an evangelical alternative to fundamentalist institutions and their anti-intellectual and separatist tendencies. Fuller was to serve as a school for the training of evangelical ministers and missionaries who would remain in the mainline Protestant churches in an effort to counter what was perceived as the latter's disastrous, unevangelical drift into religious modernism.

During Henry's nine years at Fuller, he completed a second doctorate, this one at Boston University with a dissertation on the American Baptist theologian Augustus Hopkins Strong, and eight other books, including several that reveal Henry's active engagement with the wider religious world and culture: *Remaking the Modern Mind* (1946), *The Protestant Dilemma* (1949), and *The Drift of Western Thought* (1951). In 1957 Henry accepted the invitation to be the founding editor of a new journal called *Christianity Today*. As noted, it was to serve as the voice of the best new evangelical thought and commentary on current events and cultural life. Under Henry's guidance, *Christianity Today* gained a large readership, served to unite the Evangelicals in a common cause, and was the impetus for numerous evangelical congresses and symposia. He left the editorship of the journal—"dislodged by cabal" as he later wrote—in 1968 over disagreements regarding the direction and stance of *Christianity Today*.

From 1969 to 1974 Henry was professor-at-large at Eastern Baptist Seminary, after which he served as itinerant lecturer-at-large for World Vision International, a global evangelical social service ministry. During the 1970s and 1980s Henry assisted in the organizing and founding of numerous evangelical enterprises including the Institute for Advanced Christian Studies. The years 1976 to 1983 also saw the publication of his major theological work, the six-volume *God, Revelation and Authority*, to which we now turn.

The Bible, Revelation, and Authority

Carl Henry can best be understood as a theologian of biblical theism and as an evangelical commentator on and critic of modern theological trends. He has not written a systematic theology; that is, one that treats the various Christian doctrines in a coherent and comprehensive way. His six-volume *magnum opus* examines at great length two themes: his conception of biblical revelation, its truth and authority (Vol. I–IV), and his conception of the orthodox understanding of the attributes of the biblical God (Vol. V–VI). All of these volumes include long discussions of modern thinkers, such as Kant, Schleiermacher, Barth, and Bultmann, as well as modern movements, for example, secularization, evolution and science, demythologization, and recent hermeneutical trends.

Here we will give major attention to Henry's position regarding theological method, reason and divine revelation, and the Bible's inspiration, inerrancy, and authority. Henry's biblically based discussion of God presupposes its foundation; that is, what can be said about divine revelation and its authority, about which he gives prior consideration. The doctrine of the Bible thus controls all other doctrines of the Christian faith. Any weakening or surrender of the doctrine of the Bible's inerrancy and authority will, in Henry's estimation, endanger every aspect of Christian belief.

The distinctive theological foundationalism that marks Henry's method can best be called *presuppositionalism*. It is based on the observation that every system of thought presupposes some assumptions or first principles (hypotheses) that themselves cannot be proven but may be rationally justified. This is the case as well, Henry asserts, with modern science and its faith in the evidences of the senses and the trustworthiness of the laws of nature. The truth of any system is then tested by such principles as the law of noncontradiction, the coherency of the principles and parts of the system, and its ability to illuminate and explain the widest range of experience. In his numerous apologetical works, Henry argues that Christian theism is the most compelling first principle and is based not on the proofs of God's existence by the method of natural theology, but is assumed as revealed in the Bible. God is the rational foundation of all other beliefs. Henry writes: "From a certain vantage point, the concept of God is determinative for all other concepts; it is the Archimedean lever with which one can fashion an entire world."[47]

The *presupposition* of Christian theism is, for Henry, biblical revelation:

Divine revelation is the source of all truth, the truth of Christianity included; reason is the instrument for recognizing it; Scripture is its verifying principle; logical consistency is a negative test for truth and coherence a subordinate test. The task of Christian theology is to exhibit the content of biblical revelation as an orderly whole.[48] (Henry's italics)

Biblical revelation, Henry consistently argues, can stand up better than either secular or non-evangelical religious systems of thought, which, he attempts to demonstrate, are contradictory or incoherent in their concepts and, therefore, unreasonable and false.

Henry gives a very large place to reason in theology. "*Human reason,*" he writes, "is a divinely fashioned instrument for recognizing truth; it is not a creative source of truth."[49] Human reason is grounded in the very Logos-being of God. For "the Creator-Redeemer God of the Bible created man in his rational and spiritual image for intelligible relationships."[50] Henry insists that even the Fall of humanity did not nullify reason's capacity to "recognize and elucidate" divine truth. The Fall, rather, "conditions man's

will more pervasively than his reason. Man wills not to know God in truth. . . . But he still is capable of intellectually analyzing rational evidence for the truth-value of assertions about God."[51] What human reason cannot fashion is the *content* of divine revelation; nevertheless, reason can show the rational warrants for Christian belief and demonstrate the inadequacy of objections to the faith.

Henry claims that Barth and Brunner, and the entire legacy of Neo-Orthodoxy and Neo-Protestantism, is largely responsible for dismissing the rational nature of biblical revelation, and for introducing the notion of "truth as personal encounter." What this has done is to oppose personal revelation against propositional revelation. Henry insists, on the contrary, that "God's revelation is rational communication conveyed in intelligible ideas and meaningful words, that is, in conceptual verbal form."[52] Furthermore, revelational truth is not, as some now insist, expressed in a unique symbolic-expressive noncognitive language. The Bible uses a special vocabulary as does every science; nevertheless, revelational truth must obey the logical rules that govern all propositions in any field of endeavor. Nowhere, Henry insists, does biblical revelation depict God's self-revelation in concepts that are imprecise, or that are verbally paradoxical, or are not capable of conveying ordinary intelligible propositions, i.e., cognitive meanings and truth. Henry writes:

The Bible depicts God's very revelation as meaningful, objectively intelligible disclosure. We mean by propositional revelation that God supernaturally communicated his revelation to chosen spokesmen in the express form of cognitive truths. . . . The inspired Scriptures contain a body of divinely given information actually expressed or capable of being expressed in propositions. In brief, the Bible is a propositional revelation of the unchanging truth of God.[53]

If Henry's presuppositionalism must assume God's revelation as the source of truth, and

Scripture as the verifying principle and vehicle, then the question of biblical authority is the crux of Christian theology. It has, of course, always been the cardinal point of Evangelical theology. Henry's six massive volumes attest to this claim that "in every church epoch it is the fate of the Bible that decides the fate of Christianity."[54] Henry laments the compromises of biblical authority that he observes in modern Protestantism, for they not only weaken trust in the Bible's plenary inspiration and inerrancy, but also inevitably, in time, call into question all the crucial Christian doctrines. Scripture cannot be appealed to selectively or read under the control of extra-biblical criteria. Henry addresses the question of biblical authority at extraordinary length in Volume IV of *God, Revelation and Authority*. Some consider it the finest statement on the subject from the conservative evangelical perspective. Henry begins by pointing out that the New Testament makes striking use of the term *exousia*, which conveys the meaning of both authority and power. And the two meanings are coordinate because without authority power becomes ineffectual and power without authority is illegitimate. Therefore, "the first claim to be made for Scripture is not its inerrancy nor even its inspiration, but its authority." At the forefront of the biblical narrative "stand prophets and apostles who claim to be God's chosen and authorized spokesmen."[55] These spokesmen are entrusted with and authorized to publish God's *exousia*.

The Bible's divine authority is grounded, however, in its plenary or full verbal inspiration and its inerrancy, although what Henry means by these terms requires some elaboration, because he has been misunderstood on these matters. The general point, nonetheless, is clear: For Henry an attack on the Bible's inspiration and the inerrancy of the original documents (the "autographs") is an attack on its authority. Neo-Protestant theology wants to retain the Bible's authority without maintaining the orthodox understanding of Scripture's inspiration and inerrancy. For Neo-Protestantism, Scripture's authority is centered in

the inspirations of the believer rather than in the "inspiredness" of the biblical text. The growing Neo-Protestant tendency is, then, "to redefine biblical authority functionally. The result is a refusal to identify Scripture with any fixed intellectual content. The Bible is said to be authoritative merely in the manner in which it operates existentially in the life of the believing community."[56]

Henry argues that orthodox Christianity has always understood inspiration to be a property of the biblical text itself. It does not, however, entail certain conceptions of inspiration that Henry and most Neo-Evangelicals reject. Inspiration does not, for example, imply that the biblical writers were endowed with a special genius; nor does it entail the notion that the writers were inspired by the Holy Spirit to express only the *thoughts* of God but did so in their own autonomously contingent words and cultural expressions. Henry rejects all of these conceptions of scriptural inspiration. "Inspiration," he writes, "is a supernatural influence upon divinely chosen prophets and apostles whereby the Spirit of God assures the truth and trustworthiness of their oral and written proclamation."[57] This, Henry believes, is consistent with the writers communicating the biblical message "in ways consistent with their differing personalities, literary styles and cultural backgrounds" while at the same time being safeguarded from error. Thus Henry accepts the full (plenary) inspiration of the Bible so that the Bible "is in all its parts the very Word of God, completely true in what it says."[58] Divinely revealed and verbally inscripted truth does not, Henry insists, allow for a sundering of thought and words. Whatever form the biblical Words take, for example, various forms of symbolic expression, such as poetry and parable, literally tells the truth about God's being and will.

The matter of the Bible's inerrancy has become a divisive issue in the short history of the Neo-Evangelical alliance. It was especially aggravated by the appearance of Harold Lindsell's *The Battle for the Bible* (1976). In his book, Lindsell

not only defends inerrancy; he extends auto-
graphic inerrancy to the existing received texts of
Scripture. Furthermore, he calls for the rejection
of the historical-critical method of biblical study
in evangelical seminaries and demands that belief
in inerrancy be a test to determine authentic
Evangelicalism from "false Evangelicalism."
Although Carl Henry defends the inerrancy of
Scripture, he does not do so in the sense insisted
upon by Lindsell. Moreover, Henry rejects "Lindsell's elevation of inerrancy over authority and
inspiration as the *first* claim to be made for the
Bible."[59] Henry also is deeply concerned about
the practical consequence of the publication of
The Battle for the Bible:

> The somewhat reactionary elevation of inerrancy as
> the superbadge of evangelical orthodoxy deploys ener-
> gies to this controversy that evangelicals might better
> apply to producing comprehensive theological and
> philosophical works so desperately needed.[60]

Despite these disclaimers, Henry's concern
about the importance of Scriptural inerrancy is
manifest in the extensive consideration that he
gives to the question in *God, Revelation and
Authority*. Due to misunderstandings of his position, Henry accentuates what inerrancy is not. In
addition to the correctives mentioned above, he
points out, for example, that inerrancy does not
claim that the Bible achieves the precision of
modern technology in its reporting of measurements and genealogies, or in its statements
regarding cosmological matters. Nor does it
"imply that only nonmetaphorical or nonsymbolic language can convey truth." What verbal
inerrancy does imply is "that truth attaches not
only to the theological and ethical teachings of
the Bible, but also to historical and scientific
matters insofar as they are part of the express
message of the inspired writings." For example,
the Genesis account of Creation "has implications for God's causal relationship to the cosmos." And so, "while the Bible is not intended to
be a textbook on scientific and historical mat-

ters, it nonetheless gives scientifically and historically relevant information."[61]

Further, "verbal inerrancy implies that God's
truth inheres in the very words of Scripture
. . . and not merely in the concepts and thoughts
of the writers. . . . Thoughts can be properly
expressed only by certain pertinent words." But,
of course, such a doctrine of verbal inerrancy only
implies "that the original writings or prophetic-
apostolic autographs alone are error-free." Here
Henry makes an important distinction that differentiates his position from that of other evangelical theologians, as we will see. He insists that the
verbally inerrant quality of the Bible attaches
"directly to the autographs, and only indirectly to
the copies." This means that Evangelicals must
not attach finality to contemporary versions or
translations of the Bible, and must seriously pursue and honor the best available text. Each version of the Bible, of course, has its virtues and limitations; even "the long-cherished King James
Version is based on manuscripts which are inferior in many details to manuscripts presently
available to us."[62]

Because the Christian community possesses
only somewhat errant copies of the original error-
free autographs, where, in Henry's estimation,
lies the authority of these copies and translations? Henry's answer is interesting. Although he
rejects the Roman Catholic doctrine of papal
infallibility and Hans Küng's notion of the
church's "indefectibility" or perpetuity in the
truth, he does apply the concept of infallibility to
the authority of present-day manuscript copies
and Bible translations. Thus, while inerrancy
applies only to the autographs, infallibility is a
more qualified or conditional perfection of the
copies of those originals:

> Evangelical Christians hold that the Bible as we have
> it unfailingly communicates God's Word, that it can-
> not lead men astray in the knowledge of God and his
> will, and whatever collides with the express teaching
> of the Scripture is fallacious. In short, evangelicals
> apply the term *infallibility* to the extant copies of the

inspired prophetic-apostolic writings rather than to the Roman teaching hierarchy.[63]

It is interesting to note that Henry's confidence in the infallibility of the existing versions of Scripture does not rest on appeal to the inner testimony of the Holy Spirit by which God secures the divine Word against falsity or deception. He appeals, rather, to the judgment of textual scholars, such as F. J. A. Hort, who claim that the biblical text has been restored and preserved "in remarkably pure form."[64]

Henry's critics, such as the biblical scholar James Barr, argue that "far from being a concession to critical methods," Henry's doctrine of the autographs serves as a "useful device for negating them entirely." The reason being that it permits the argument that any discrepancy in a text is due to a textual corruption that was not present in the original inspired texts.[65] Henry rejects this line of criticism but, unfortunately, his response is circular: "The whole science of textual criticism," he writes, "presupposes that the copies are answerable to a normative text" and not just "an older text but a divinely definitive text. If the original autographs were errant, then the recovery of older and more authentic texts would bring us no nearer to the truth of God."[66] This rejoinder, of course, assumes a particular conception of the Bible's inspiration and authority as entailing a particular form of verbal-propositional inerrancy or infallibility.

Henry's immense and weighty treatise on biblical authority, inspiration, inerrancy, and infallibility constitutes not only a protracted dialogue with non-evangelical biblical scholars and theologians but can also be read as an intramural discussion with his colleagues in the evangelical alliance. And this latter discussion highlights the increasing differences within the Neo-Evangelical ranks on the question of inerrancy, a doctrine that has served as something of a test in this theological tradition. Some of the older generation of leaders continue to hold what is called "detailed inerrancy."[67] One is Harold Lindsell, a former teacher at Fuller Theological Seminary,

whose *The Battle for the Bible*, we have noted, provoked an extended controversy and occasioned Carl Henry's strong reproach. For Lindsell, the inerrancy of Scripture applies to the details of biblical geography, chronology and measurements, astronomy, and so on, even if these "facts" may have little or no import for an understanding of the real intent of a biblical passage. Defenders of "detailed inerrancy" also tend to adopt the "domino theory"; that is, that any notion of limited errancy will inevitably slide into unlimited errancy and on into apostasy.[68]

There are a variety of forms of "limited inerrancy" that are defended by contemporary Evangelicals. Basically, the concept suggests that, while the Bible is wholly trustworthy, even infallible with regard to its essential message, there are errors in the Bible even where they relate to the author's intention,[69] for example, prescientific statements regarding historical or cosmological matters. A somewhat different approach holds to the concept of Scriptural inerrancy as it pertains to the Bible's revelatory intention while, at the same time, recognizing things in the Bible that are only accessory to the fulfillment of that intention. These latter are considered "nonrevelatory" matters. The nonrevelatory contents of Scripture are, nevertheless, used by God to communicate divine truth. This position is articulated by Daniel Fuller, a professor of biblical hermeneutics at Fuller Theological Seminary:

Being verbally inspired, the Biblical writers were also supernaturally enabled by God to understand the best way to take certain non-revelational, cultural matters, and without changing them, use them to enhance the communication of revelational truths to the original hearers or readers.[70]

Many Evangelicals now consider the word "inerrancy" to be a stone of stumbling because of the various conflicting and, therefore, potentially misleading ways in which the concept has come to be used. In its place they have adopted the concept of the "complete infallibility" and trustworthiness of Scripture with regard to its teaching on matters of doctrine and conduct. In 1970, David Hubbard, the president of Fuller Theological Seminary, endorsed this way of expressing the evangelical understanding of the Bible's inspiration and authority and incorporated this hermeneutical principle into Fuller's statement of faith. A comparison of the seminary's original statement on the Bible, adopted in 1950, with this revised statement of 1970 is striking evidence of the rather swift development of evangelical thinking on this crucial matter. The two statements read as follows:

The books which form the canon of the Old and New Testaments as originally given are plenarily inspired and free from all error in the whole and in part. These books constitute the written Word of God, the only infallible rule of faith and practice. 1950

Scripture is an essential part and trustworthy record of this divine self-disclosure. All the books of the Old and New Testaments, given by divine inspiration, are the written Word of God, the only infallible rule of faith and practice. They are to be interpreted according to their context and purpose and in reverent obedience to the Lord who speaks through them in living power. 1970

Carl Henry remains opposed to those who explicitly reject the concept of Scriptural inerrancy, because to declare the doctrine irrelevant, he believes, will undermine belief in the truth of Scripture.[71] In *God, Revelation and Authority*, Henry proceeds to detail the unsoundness of the views of numerous respected evangelical scholars, among them G. C. Berkouwer, Donald Bloesch, Daniel Fuller, David Hubbard, Clark Pinnock, and William J. Abraham. By the 1980s, however, the tide was turning against Henry's theological method and his biblical hermeneutics.

A sign of this change is evident in the writings of Bernard Ramm (1916–   ), one of the founding fathers of the postwar evangelical renewal. Late in his career, Ramm has concluded that the older type of Evangelical theology as practiced by Cornelius Van Til, Francis Schaeffer, and Carl Henry is no longer adequate because it has failed to take seriously the intellectual crisis precipitated by the Enlightenment. Commenting on Henry's *magnum opus*, Ramm writes:

In *God, Revelation and Authority*, Carl F. H. Henry sets out his views of revelation, inspiration, and authority against all other options, but his monumental effort stumbles because he glosses biblical criticism.[72]

Ramm contends that the future of Evangelical theology will depend on its willingness and its ability to genuinely interact with modern knowledge without compromising Christian belief. A number of younger evangelical theologians, writing in the closing years of the twentieth century, pointedly criticize Henry's deductive theological method as outmoded and vulnerable to critical demolition because of what they see as his preoccupation with rationalistic, foundational, and epistemological questions. Reason, after all, is often a two-edged sword. They also see Henry as failing to do justice to a host of other central Christian doctrines, and to the contemporary contexts that theology needs to address.

Clark Pinnock, for example, stresses the precariousness of Henry's epistemological foundationalism. Writing about the deficiencies in the older apologetic as represented by Henry, Pinnock comments:

By taking such a strong stand on the vehicle of revelation, on the house of authority, rather than on the saving message it conveys, conservative theology opens itself up to problems that do not touch the gospel directly but could bring their whole edifice down if any were successful. . . . So is it prudent to expose the fate of the whole Christian proclamation to possible refutation just to protect the walls of rational certainty we have built to protect it?[73]

Stanley J. Grenz, in *Revisioning Evangelical Theology: A Fresh Agenda for the 21st Century*, also calls for a reconception of Evangelical theology in light of the failure of the rational-propositional conception of theology that mid-twentieth-century Evangelical theology inherited from Protestant Scholasticism. This tradition was passed on through the nineteenth-century Princeton Theology (see Volume I, Chapter Twelve) and its latter-day disciples, such as Carl Henry. Rather than attempting "minor refinements," Grenz calls for a more radical break with Henry's type of "propositional" theology,[74] and looks to the work of numerous non-evangelical scholars in fashioning his revision of the theological task.

Alister McGrath similarly charges Henry with a discredited foundationalism. He points out that Henry makes an implicit appeal to a rationalist epistemological foundation in his defense of Scriptural authority, for example, in his appeal to the extra-biblical laws of noncontradiction and logical consistency. In so doing, Henry renders Christian theology needlessly vulnerable to the now widely accepted postmodernist critique of Enlightenment rationalism and foundationalism. (See Chapter Sixteen.)

On Henry's "evangelical rationalism," McGrath writes:

Evangelicalism, if it were to follow Henry's lead . . . would set itself on the road that inevitably allows fallen human reason to judge God's revelation, or become its ultimate foundation. This is a road which evangelicalism cannot allow itself to take, even if it did once offer a short-term apologetic advantage within a culture which accepted the Enlightenment world view. . . . Today, evangelicalism is free to avoid the false lure of foundationalism.[75]

NEW THEOLOGICAL SOUNDINGS

Earlier in this chapter we pointed out that the new Evangelicalism was, from its beginnings in the 1940s, a pluralist alliance that was by its very composition precarious. Even Fuller Theological Seminary's reputed theological solidarity early showed signs of fragmenting.[76] This lack of unanimity need not, of course, be viewed as a weakness; it has revealed considerable vitality and power. Yet conservative Evangelicals will claim, with some justification, that Harold Lindsell's prophecy of the "domino effect" has, indeed,

proven true. Evangelical theology in the latter decades of the twentieth century appears to be in a state of significant change and, from many indications, is moving away from the theological tradition of the early luminaries, such as E. J. Carnell and Carl Henry.

Commentators on the present state of Evangelical theology see a clear split between traditionalists and progressives or reformists. The traditionalists give greater importance to the classic Protestant confessionalist heritage and are skeptical of innovation and the progressives' accommodation to modern culture. This trend is evident in the founding of the Alliance of Confessing Evangelicals (ACE), established to bring Evangelicals back to the confessional standards of the Reformation. This traditionalist concern is also reflected in publications such as David Wells's *No Place for Truth* (1993) and *God in the Wasteland* (1994). The progressives however, are more open with regard to doctrinal formulations and the interpretation of the language of Scripture. They maintain the normative authority of Scripture itself as God's Word when conjoined with the illumination of the Holy Spirit in the transformed life of the believer. The progressives are also more open to God's truth wherever it may be found, even in apparently non-evangelical sources—for example, in the theology of a Paul Tillich or in the writings of contemporary Postmodernists. The reformers tend to be critical of what they call the "paleo-Calvinism" of the postwar Evangelicals. Where progressive Evangelical theology is headed is uncertain, and it is difficult to track its labyrinthian maze. We can, nevertheless, indicate some directions that can be observed.

1. For many of the leading post-World War II evangelical theologians, Karl Barth represented the menace of the new modernism. Refuting Barth and other Neo-Orthodox theologians was a major preoccupation of Cornelius Van Til, E. J. Carnell, and Carl Henry. At the close of the twentieth century many evangelical theologians have turned to Barth as the most viable theological alternative between what they see as a moribund rationalist theology represented by Carl Henry on the one hand and various Liberal theologies of "correlation" on the other. The appeal to Karl Barth is evident for example in the later writings of both C. G. Berkouwer and Bernard Ramm, and in the writings of the respected American evangelical theologian, Donald Bloesch.[77]

The attraction of Barth's theology as the paradigm for the future of Evangelical theology is most explicit in Bernard Ramm's *After Fundamentalism: The Future of Evangelical Theology* (1983). The book's title disguises the fact that it is a running commentary on how Barth's theology best answers the Enlightenment's challenge to numerous Christian doctrines. Ramm is convinced that (a) "the Enlightenment was a shattering experience for orthodox theology from which it has never fully recovered"; (b) "neither religious liberalism nor orthodoxy has the right strategy for interacting with the Enlightenment with reference to the continuing task of Christian theology"; and(c) since Barth has been more successful and thorough in dealing with the Enlightenment; (d) "he thereby offers to evangelical theology a paradigm of how best to come to terms with the Enlightenment."[78]

Ramm has learned that those Evangelicals who do not feel the true shock of the Enlightenment simply gloss over its problems and, furthermore, "have not developed a theological method that enables them to be consistently evangelical in their theology and to be people of modern learning."[79] A crucial test for an Evangelical will be, of course, the Bible. Ramm, however, believes that Evangelical theology has tended to emphasize the divinity of the Bible (its inerrancy) while minimizing its genuine humanity and, for that reason, is "written off as obscurantist." Barth affirms the full, unabridged humanity of Holy Scripture as well as its full divinity. "Barth makes no half-hearted affirmation of the humanity of Scripture . . . that is undermined by an overpowering affirmation of its divinity." Ramm thus sees Barth's method as a compelling example of how an Evangelical can encounter the Enlightenment and modern learning and yet retain the full theological integrity of Holy Scripture—and exorcise the evil demon of obscurantism, i.e., inerrancy.[80]

2. Narrative theology is another contemporary theological source that some evangelical theologians appear to have rather cordially appropriated. (See Chapter Sixteen.) In so doing they also appear to have moved beyond the older efforts to guarantee the authority and inspiration of the Bible by deductive claims of inerrancy or by tortured inductive efforts to harmonize, for example, the Gospel accounts. The Bible contains an overarching narrative that is the paradigm story for Christians, and this is the basis of the community's belief in the primacy and authority of Scripture.

Clark Pinnock draws on narrative theology in an effort to articulate his own understanding of the essence and identity of Christianity. "The essence of Christianity," Pinnock writes

is the epic story of salvation that centers upon its chief character, the risen and exalted Lord, Jesus Christ. It is the greatest story ever told, the drama of salvation. . . . Its essence is not law, dogma, theory, not even experience. . . . This story holds together the Bible in all its diversity. It is the overarching story of salvation that renders the character of God for us. . . . People have found their meaning within the story. . . . The truth for Christians lies in this narrative. Their grammar and speech are structured around it. Here is the criterion, the norm, the rule of faith. This is how fidelity is tested. Faith is response to this story and to its promises.[81]

Pinnock proceeds to show that this narrative story is the stuff of the Christian *community's* creeds, liturgies, hymns, prayers, and actions. Therefore, it is not something that the private individual is entitled to alter, for this narrative has created a world of meaning that is encoded in the Bible and has become over two millennia the Christian's language, identity, and lifeview. Pinnock proceeds to compare the older "propositional" theology unfavorably with the promise of narrative theology, since the biblical revelation is mediated primarily through narrative. "The truth of the Christian story simply contains deeper dimensions than bare propositions can exhaust."[82]

3. In their disenchantment with the older Princeton Theology's biblical hermeneutic, some evangelical theologians have found a more adequate method in the Methodist or Wesleyan tradition that appeals to a larger set of authorities while holding to the primacy of the revelation in Jesus Christ. It is referred to as "the Wesleyan quadrilateral."[83] Although John Wesley does not use this term, it does represent a hermeneutical pattern of thinking that can be discerned in Wesley's writings. The "quadrilateral" refers to four norms or sources of theology: Scripture, tradition, experience, and reason. While appealing to all four sources, the Evangelical Wesleyans understand Scripture as the primary source, the "norming norm" of theological work.[84]

Clark Pinnock and Stanley J. Grenz both are attracted to this fourfold hermeneutic in their formulations of the sources for theology.[85] Both also are concerned to counter the tendency in the conservative evangelical tradition to distort revelation by placing undo emphasis on the *inspiration* of the written texts of Scripture at the expense of the receptive dimension of revelation; that is, in the work of *illumination* and *interpretation*. "Revelation," Pinnock notes,

is an earthly and historical event, not a sheer heavenly one. . . . In this way God forms a special history that passes through events and interpretations to endless application. . . . As a cumulative process, revelation does not remain alone. By its very nature it creates secondary forms of itself. It generates vehicles of revelation. . . . There are four such vehicles or sources: Scripture, tradition, experience, and reason. Revelation is the precondition of them all; it occurs and finds itself recorded in sacred writings, passed down through generations, and all the while eliciting a richness of experiential responses and rational reflections. In this way revelation empowers a written form (Scripture), a remembering community (tradition), a process of subjective appropriation (experience), and a testing for internal consistency (reason).[86]

4. What is most apparent in the new appeal to multiple sources of theology is the greater attention now given to the Christian community, the Church, and its rich narrative, that is, to tradition, and to the importance of cultural context. These themes are prominent in discussions that seek to distinguish features of the *modern* age from what is now called the contemporary *postmodern* ethos. Several evangelical theologians have appropriated themes that characterize both Postmodernism and Postliberalism (see Chapter Sixteen) in an effort to re-envision a theology that can offer an alternative to modern, liberal "correlationist" theologies that, they insist, simply reflect the assumptions of the Enlightenment and the older rationalist Evangelical theology. The latter is now perceived—with considerable irony—as an unacknowledged "modernism" in its deep-rooted individualism, rationalism, and naive foundationalism. Since we will discuss both Postmodernism and Postliberalism at greater length in Chapter Sixteen, here we will illustrate rather briefly how recent Evangelical theology reflects an attraction to and an appropriation of themes central to these two contemporary movements. We already have alluded to the critique of rationalism and need not pursue that here.

a.) One theme current in evangelical discussions is the critique of modern individualism. This is given considerable attention in Stanley Grenz's call for a revisioning of Evangelical theology. In addressing the limitations of Evangelical rationalism, Grenz writes:

The problem with evangelical propositionalism is its often underdeveloped understanding of how the cognitive dimension functions within the larger whole of revelation. Therefore, evangelical theologians tend to misunderstand the social nature of theological discourse . . . [and have] been captive to the orientation of the individual knower that has reigned over the Western mindset throughout the modern era. But this orientation is now beginning to lose its grip.[87]

Grenz appeals to Evangelical theology to reconceive its work within the postulate of the *community* of faith. And he calls upon the resources of narrative theology and the work of the Postliberal theologian George Lindbeck to carry out this theological task:

Taking what he [Lindbeck] terms a "cultural-linguistic" approach . . . Lindbeck sees doctrine as providing a "regulative" function. For the individual believer, the believing community provides a cultural and linguistic framework that shapes life and thought. More than being molded by experiences of individuals within it, the communal reality constitutes a central factor in the shaping of the subjectivities and experiences of its members. It provides a constellation of symbols and concepts which its members employ in order to understand their lives . . . and within which they experience their world.[88]

b.) Closely related to the critique of evangelical individualism is a new attention to tradition, a theme that characterizes the writings of both Postliberals and some Postmodern thinkers. Human lives are shaped through the language and the practices of particular communities, i.e., their traditions. Furthermore, these identity-shaping historical traditions are highly particularistic, not universalistic. The British evangelical theologian, Alister McGrath, gives considerable attention to the role of tradition and to its historicist implications for theology. His views find reinforcement in the writings of the philosopher Alastair MacIntyre, an important critic of "the Enlightenment project" of modernity.[89]

Unlike many Evangelicals, McGrath has a deep appreciation of the Christian community's continuity with its unique past.[90] Yet the fact that all thought is historically located and carried by a communal tradition does not imply a relativization of doctrinal belief. It does, however, distinguish communal tradition from the rationalist claim to transcend history and to make universal propositional claims. Tradition entails a more modest, contextualist or "cultural-linguistic" conception of religious meaning and truth. Both McGrath and Grentz support such a contextualist view of *doctrine*. This means that because every society or community is embedded in history, in a particular communal or cultural tradition, the historical context is of determinative importance for the way one perceives the world, speaks, and knows. For McGrath, this means that the Enlightenment ideal of a universal or metahistorical foundation of knowledge and truth is a chimera. One is required, rather, to adopt an historicist epistemology, which recognizes that there are various and different traditions that disagree on what constitutes rationality, evidence, and the conditions and justifications of truth claims. A recognition of these competing frameworks of meaning and truth will explain why the Christian communal tradition and the tradition of the Enlightenment come to very different understandings of the identity and significance of Jesus Christ. Therefore, the demand that the insights and truth claims of the Christian tradition be justified by appeal to the rational framework of the *Aufklärung* is to forget, as Alastair MacIntyre insists, that the quest for a universal framework of rationality, independent of the contingencies of historical context, should be forsaken.

McGrath draws the following postmodernist conclusion from these epistemological reflections:

Considerations such as this tend to suggest that the discipline of doctrinal criticism has its proper sphere within the community of faith. . . . Christian doctrine belongs within the Christian tradition, inextricably interwoven within its various elements. The close interaction between the doctrines, symbols, values, patterns of life, and identity-giving narratives of a community is such that outside perspectives would seem to be intrinsically incapable of making the judgments necessary to evaluate the doctrines. This is not, however, to suggest that the phenomenon of Christian doctrine is immune from outside criticism and evaluation; it is to point out that criticism and evaluation presuppose agreement over the criteria thus to be employed.[91]

Stanley Grenz also seeks to demonstrate how a deep awareness of the "linguistic-cultural" context may require a more radical recontextualization of theology in response to changing historical and cultural conditions. He writes:

The commitment to contextualization entails the implicit rejection of the older evangelical conception of theology as the construction of truth on the basis of the Bible alone. No longer can the theologian focus merely on Scripture as the one complete theological norm. Instead the process of contextualization requires a movement between two poles—*the Bible as the source of truth and culture as the source of the categories through which the theologian expresses biblical truth.* . . . Contextualization demands that the theologian take seriously the thought-forms and mindset of the culture in which theologizing transpires, in order to explicate the eternal truths of the Scripture in the language that is understandable to contemporary people.[92]

Here contextualization may well issue in a theological program that could be viewed as the antithesis of the model proposed by McGrath, whose position appears to be more in line with the narrative intra-textuality of Karl Barth and Postliberals such as George Lindbeck (see Chapter Sixteen). Grentz's proposal, as he acknowledges, is similar to the "method of correlation," classically articulated by Paul Tillich in his *Systematic Theology* (see Chapter Five).

The reconceptions of the evangelical theological task as suggested here by Ramm, Pinnock, Grenz, and McGrath, as well as others, reflects the vitality of Evangelical theology at the end of the twentieth century. The verdict, however, is not yet in on whether these new trajectories are consistent with the modern evangelical tradition; whether they constitute creative ways of insuring its theological substance; or whether they will prove to represent what some see as a disastrous accommodation to the modern tradition of Neo-Protestant theology—that abomination of their evangelical forefathers.

NOTES

1. George Marsden, ed., *Evangelicalism and Modern America* (Grand Rapids, 1984), p. viii.

2. Donald Grey Barnhouse, "The Sin of Credulity," *Revelation*, 2 (December, 1932), 489.

3. J. Gresham Machen, *Christianity and Liberalism* (New York, 1923), p. 2.

4. H. L. Mencken, *Prejudices: Fifth Series* (New York, 1926). For this reference, and for much more on Fundamentalism in twentieth-century America, I am indebted to the works of George Marsden.

5. George Marsden, *Fundamentalism and American Culture: The Shaping of Twentieth Century Evangelicalism 1870–1925* (New York, 1980), p. 195.

6. Carl F. H. Henry, *Evangelical Responsibility in Contemporary Theology* (Grand Rapids, Mich., 1957), p. 43.

7. E. J. Carnell, "Post-Fundamentalist Faith," *The Christian Century* (August 26, 1959).

8. For a thorough discussion of the many institutions, organizations, persons, and trends that make up the new Evangelicalism, see Richard Quebedeaux, *The Worldly Evangelicals* (New York, 1978); and Mark A. Noll, *The Scandal of the Evangelical Mind* (Grand Rapids, Mich., 1994).

9. G. C. Berkouwer, *Faith and Justification* (Grand Rapids, Mich., 1949) p. 9.

10. G. C. Berkouwer, *The Person of Christ* (Grand Rapids, Mich., 1954), p. 91.

11. For an analysis of Berkouwer's "third alternative," see Jack Rogers, "A Third Alternative: Scripture, Tradition and Interpretation in the Theology of G. C. Berkouwer," in *Scripture, Tradition and Interpretation*, ed. W. Ward Gasque and William Sanford La Sor (Grand Rapids, Mich., 1979). I am much indebted to Rogers's essay for my own exposition of Berkouwer's doctrine of Scripture.

12. G. C. Berkouwer, *Holy Scripture* (Grand Rapids, Mich., 1975), p. 9.

13. Ibid., p. 33.

14. Ibid., p. 45.

15. Ibid., pp. 19–20.

16. Ibid., p. 19.

17. Ibid., p. 133.

18. Ibid., pp. 181, 183.

19. Ibid., p. 181.

20. Ibid., pp. 187–188.

21. Ibid., pp. 188–189.

22. Ibid., p. 193.

23. Ibid., pp. 194–195.

24. Ibid., p. 333.

25. See, for example, Alvin L. Baker, *Berkouwer's Doctrine of Election* (Phillipsburg, N.J., 1981) and the citations of critics and defenders of Berkouwer's views.

26. G. C. Berkouwer, *The Providence of God* (Grand Rapids, Mich., 1952), pp. 159, 160.

27. Ibid.

28. G. C. Berkouwer, *Divine Election* (Grand Rapids, Mich. 1960), p. 50.

29. Berkouwer, *The Providence of God*, p. 133.

30. Berkouwer, *Divine Election*, p. 172.

31. Ibid., p. 162.

32. Ibid., p. 189.

33. G. C. Berkouwer, *Sin* (Grand Rapids, Mich., 1971), p. 363.

34. G. C. Berkouwer, *The Return of Christ* (Grand Rapids, Mich., 1972), p. 400.

35. Ibid., K. Barth, "The Proclamation of God's Free Grace," in *God Here and Now* (New York, 1964), p. 82.

36. Berkouwer, *The Return of Christ*, p. 412.

37. G. C. Berkouwer, *The Triumph of Grace in the Theology of Karl Barth* (Grand Rapids, Mich., 1956), pp. 121–122.

38. Berkouwer, *The Return of Christ*, p. 413.

39. Ibid., pp. 414–415.

40. Ibid., p. 416.

41. Ibid., p. 418.

42. Ibid., p. 420.

43. Ibid., p. 421.

44. Ibid., p. 423.

45. Lewis B. Smedes, "G. C. Berkouwer," in *Creative Minds in Contemporary Theology*, ed. Philip Edgcumbe Hughes (Grand Rapids, Mich., 1966), p. 92.

46. Bob E. Patterson, *Carl F. H. Henry* (Waco, Tex., 1983), p. 131.

47. Carl Henry, *Remaking the Modern Mind* (Grand Rapids, Mich., 1946), p. 232.

48. Carl Henry, *God, Revelation and Authority*, I (Waco, Tex., 1976), p. 215.

49. Ibid., p. 225.

50. Ibid.

51. Ibid., pp. 226–227.

52. Carl Henry, *God, Revelation and Authority*, III (Waco, Tex., 1979), p. 248.

53. Ibid., p. 457.

54. Carl Henry, *God, Revelation and Authority*, IV (Waco, Tex., 1979), p. 380.

55. Ibid., p. 27.

56. Ibid., p. 68.

57. Ibid., p. 129.

58. Ibid., pp. 166–167.

59. Carl Henry, "The Concerns and Considerations of Carl F. H. Henry," *Christianity Today*, 25 (March 13, 1981), 19.

60. Carl Henry, "Reaction and Realignment," *Christianity Today*, 20 (July 2, 1976), 30.

61. Henry, *God, Revelation and Authority*, IV, pp. 201–202, 204, 205.

62. Ibid., pp. 205–206, 207, 209–210.

63. Ibid., p. 229.

64. See Ch. 9 of Henry, *God, Revelation and Authority*, IV, ibid.

65. See James Barr, *Fundamentalism* (Philadelphia, 1978), pp. 279–284.

66. Henry, *God, Revelation and Authority*, IV, p. 240.

67. See Robert K. Johnson, *Evangelicals at an Impasse: Biblical Authority in Practice* (Atlanta, 1979). This book has been helpful in sorting out the nuances of the evangelical discussion of inspiration and inerrancy.

68. See, e.g., Harold Lindsell, *The Battle for the Bible* (Grand Rapids, Mich., 1976), Ch. 10; Francis Schaeffer, *No Final Conflict: The Bible Without Error in All That It Affirms* (Downers Grove, Ill., 1975).

69. See, e.g., Dewey M. Beegle, *Scripture, Tradition, and Infallibility* (Grand Rapids, Mich., 1973), passim.

70. Daniel Fuller, "The Nature of Biblical Inerrancy," *Journal of the American Scientific Affiliation*, 24 (June 1972), 49.

71. Henry, *God, Revelation, and Authority*, IV, p. 177.

72. Bernard Ramm, *After Fundamentalism: The Future of Evangelical Theology* (New York, 1983), pp. 26–27.

73. Clark Pinnock, *Tracking the Maze: Finding Our Way Through Modern Theology from an Evangelical Perspective* (New York, 1990), p. 50. See also Donald Bloesch, *Essentials of Evangelical Theology*, II (San Francisco, 1979), p. 268.

74. Stanley J. Grenz, *Reinvisioning Evangelical Theology: A Fresh Agenda for the 21st Century* (Downers Grove, Ill., 1993). See especially Ch. 3, 4, and 5 on revisioning the theological task, the sources of theology, and biblical authority.

75. Alister McGrath, *A Passion for Truth: The Intellectual Coherence of Evangelicalism* (Downers Grove, Ill., 1996), pp. 171–172.

76. See George Marsden, *Reforming Fundamentalism: Fuller Seminary and the New Evangelicalism* (Grand Rapids, Mich., 1987).

77. See Bloesch's *A Theology of Word and Spirit: Authority and Method in Theology* (Downers Grove, Ill., 1992), especially Ch. 9. Bloesch writes: "What Barth propounds is not an apologetic that leaves the fortress of faith to engage in struggle with the world on its own terrain but an apologetic that finds its security precisely in the fortress of faith and calls the world to unconditional surrender. . . . For Barth theology is not simply descriptive . . . but prescriptive, unabashedly presenting before the world the claims of the gospel" pp. 270–271. For a valuable, comprehensive examination of the response to Karl Barth's theology by the Evangelical Fundamentalists and, more importantly, the new Evangelicals, see Phillip R. Thorne, *Evangelicalism and Karl Barth: His Reception and Influence in North American Evangelical Theology* (Allison Park, Pa., 1995).

78. Ramm, *After Fundamentalism*, p. vii.

79. Ibid., p. 27.

80. Ibid., pp. 103, 114.

81. Pinnock, *Tracking the Maze*, pp. 154–155. Also see the importance of narrative in the work of J. W. McClendon, e.g., *Biography as Theology*, 2nd ed. (Philadelphia, 1990).

82. Ibid., p. 183.

83. See Donald A. D. Thorsen, *The Wesleyan Quadrilateral* (Grand Rapids, Mich., 1990); and Thomas C. Oden, *Systematic Theology*, Vol. I: *Living God* (San Francisco, 1987).

84. Donald W. Dayton, "The Use of Scripture in the Wesleyan Tradition," in *The Use of the Bible in Theology/Evangelical Options* ed. Robert K. Johnson (Atlanta, 1985), p. 135 ff.

85. Pinnock, *Tracking the Maze*, Ch. 11, "Sources of the Story"; Grenz, *Revisioning Evangelical Theology*, Ch. 4, "Revisioning the Sources of Theology."

86. Pinnock, *Tracking the Maze*, ibid., pp. 170–171. Stanley Grenz similarly appeals to the multiple sources of theology, which include (1) the biblical message, (2) the rich and diverse theological traditions of the church, and (3) the thought-forms of the historical-cultural context in which Christians live and act. See Grentz, *Revisioning Evangelical Theology*, Ch. 4.

87. Grenz, *Revisioning Evangelical Theology*, ibid., p. 73.

88. Ibid., pp. 77–78. For an excellent discussion of the influence of Postliberalism on Evangelical theology and the reservations of the two movements regarding one another, see Timothy R. Phillips and Dennis L. Okholm, ed., *The Nature of Confession: Evangelicals and Postliberals in Conversation* (Downers Grove, Ill., 1996).

89. See MacIntyre's *After Virtue*, 2nd ed. (Notre Dame, 1984); and *Whose Justice? Which Rationality?* (London, 1988).

90. Alister E. McGrath, *The Genesis of Doctrine: A Study in the Foundations of Doctrinal Criticism* (Oxford, 1990), p. 188.

91. Ibid., pp. 192–193.

92. Grenz, *Revisioning Evangelical Theology*, p. 90.

SUGGESTIONS FOR FURTHER READING

Historical Background

Bebbington, D.W. *Evangelicalism in Modern Britain: A History from the 1730s to the 1980s* (London: Unwin Hyman, 1989).

Marsden, George. *Fundamentalism and Modern Culture: The Shaping of Twentieth-Century Evangelicalism, 1870–1925* (New York: Oxford University Press, 1980).

Noll, Mark A., et al., ed. *Evangelicalism: Comparative Studies of Popular Protestantism in North America, the British Isles, and Beyond, 1700–1900* (New York: Oxford University Press, 1994).

General Studies

Abraham, William J. *The Coming Great Revival: Recovering the Full Evangelical Tradition* (San Francisco: Harper and Row, 1984).

Carpenter, Joel. *Revive Us Again: The Reawakening of American Fundamentalism* (New York: Oxford University Press, 1997).

Dayton, Donald W., and Robert K. Johnson, ed. *The Variety of American Evangelicalism* (Knoxville: University of Tennessee Press, 1991).

Dorrien, Gary. *The Remaking of Evangelical Theology* (Louisville, KY: Westminster-JohnKnox Press, 1998).

Hunter, James Davison. *American Evangelicalism: Conservative Religion and the Quandary of Modernity* (New Brunswick, N.J.: Rutgers University Press, 1983).

Johnson, Robert K. *Evangelicals at an Impasse: Biblical Authority in Practice* (Atlanta: John Knox Press, 1979).

Marsden, George, ed. *Evangelicalism and Modern America* (Grand Rapids, Mich.: William B. Eerdmans, 1984).

———. *Reforming Fundamentalism: Fuller Seminary and the New Evangelicalism* (Grand Rapids, Mich.: William B. Eerdmans, 1987).

McGrath, Alister. *A Passion for Truth: The Intellectual Coherence of Evangelicalism* (Downers Grove, Ill.: InterVarsity Press, 1996).

Noll, Mark A. *Between Faith and Criticism: Evangelicals, Scholarship, and the Bible in America*, 2nd ed. (Grand Rapids, Mich.: Baker Book House, 1991).

———. *The Scandal of the Evangelical Mind* (Grand Rapids, Mich.: William B. Eerdmans, 1994).

Quebedeaux, Richard. *The Worldly Evangelicals* (New York: Harper and Row, 1978).

Ramm, Bernard L. *The Evangelical Heritage: A Study in Historical Theology* (Grand Rapids, Mich.: William B. Eerdmans, 1973).

Smith, Christian. *American Evangelicalism* (Chicago: University of Chicago Press, 1998). Sophisticated and sympathetic analysis of contemporary Evangelicalism and its relation to the culture.

Stone, Jon R. *On the Boundaries of American Evangelicalism: The Postwar Evangelical Coalition* (New York: St. Martin's, 1997).

Thorne, Phillip R. *Evangelicalism and Karl Barth: His Reception and Influence in North American Evangelical Theology* (Allison Park, Pa.: Pickwick Publications, 1995). A valuable study of the responses to Barth by Evangelicals.

Wells, David F., and John D. Woodbridge, ed. *The Evangelicals: What They Believe, Who They Are, Where They Are Changing* (Nashville, Tenn.: Abingdon Press, 1975).

G. C. Berkouwer

Baker, Alvin. *Berkouwer's Doctrine of Election* (Phillipsburg, N.J.: 1964).

Rogers, Jack B. "A Third Alternative: Scripture, Tradition and Interpretation in the Theology of G. C. Berkouwer." In *Scripture, Tradition and Interpretation*, ed. W. Ward Gasque and William Sanford La Sor (Grand Rapids, Mich.: William B. Eerdmans, 1979), pp. 70–91.

Smedes, Lewis B. "G. C. Berkouwer." In *Creative Minds in Contemporary Theology*, 2nd ed., ed. Philip E. Hughes (Grand Rapids, Mich.: William B. Eerdmans, 1969), pp. 63–98.

Carl F. H. Henry

Fackre, Gabriel. "Carl F. H. Henry." In *A Handbook of Christian Theologians*, ed. Dean G. Peerman and Martin E. Marty (Nashville, Tenn.: Abingdon Press, 1985).

Patterson, Bob E. *Makers of the Modern Theological Mind—Carl F. H. Henry* (Waco, Tex.: Word Books, 1983).

Chapter Thirteen

✿

Feminist Theology

Elisabeth Schüssler Fiorenza

INTRODUCTION: THE CONTEXT OF TWENTIETH-CENTURY FEMINIST THEOLOGY

Feminist theology began to emerge as a self-conscious movement in the United States in the 1960s, its earliest exponents being white, middleclass, well-educated women with "liberal" religious leanings. It is worth reflecting on those factors that made this emergence a possibility in North America at a time when the more conservative theological faculties of Europe staunchly resisted questioning about the subordinated roles of women in the Bible and Christian tradition. Naturally the injection of ideas from secular feminism was, and continues to be, a major stimulus

to theological feminism. In the 1950s the impetus to renewed feminist fervor came as a reaction to the attempted redomestication of women after the relative independence they had achieved during the crisis of the Second World War. A celebrated book like Simone de Beauvoir's *The Second Sex* (1953), which, as a subsidiary argument, highlighted the complicity of the Catholic Church in women's oppression, was to exert considerable influence on the first generation of this century's feminist theologians. By making this charge against the Catholic tradition from her secular standpoint, de Beauvoir left future feminist Christians with the task of explaining how, if at all, that tradition could also yield the seeds of its own feminist transformation.

But clearly this secular impetus was as readily available in Europe as in the United States. What was specific to the North American theological environment was the opening up of new opportunities for women for graduate work in theology at precisely this postwar juncture (the 1940s and 1950s), together with the enabling backcloth of American "Liberal" Protestantism's tolerance for theological novelty. There had, too, been the late nineteenth-century forebear and religious feminist precursor, Elizabeth Cady Stanton, whose *The Women's Bible* (1895)[1] had collected and commented upon the startlingly derogatory attitudes to women in the biblical corpus. Given this reforming American Protestant background, it was a suitable irony that many of the outstanding first-generation feminist theologians of the 1960s and 1970s turned out to be Roman Catholic. But they, too, had imbibed that distinctively American ethos of reforming religious energy; and they were further spurred by the events of the Second Vatican Council (1962–1965), which managed to combine scant and condescending remarks about women's "nature" and roles with a vague sense of promise and hope for future reform.[2]

The beginnings of feminist theology in North America also coincided historically with the civil rights movement and the battle for desegregation, and many early Christian feminists were also supportive of that movement. Yet initially they showed surprisingly little consciousness of the specificity and distinctiveness of the oppression of women of color, whether in North America or abroad. Rather the emphasis was, as in the Vatican II documents, on the generic features of "woman" (or of her so-called "femininity"), regardless of the complexifying factors of education, class, or race. Thus, in a pioneering article of 1960 (often cited as the first manifestation of this new feminist theology, and revealingly entitled "The Human Situation: A Feminine View"[3]), Valerie Saiving Goldstein hazarded the suggestion that "feminine" sin sprang not so much from aggressiveness or selfishness, but more characteristically from a *failure* in self-assertion or personal agency. As was common in feminist writing of

this period, Saiving used "feminine" and "female" synonymously, and her daring adjustment to the traditional Christian notion of "man's" sin included all women undifferentiatedly. If this assumption now looks naive, it is not to undermine the creative significance of the questions Saiving was opening up in 1960. At the time they were explosively novel.

It is worth asking at this introductory juncture, however, what "feminism" and "feminist theology" stand for as *generic* terms. This is a surprisingly difficult question to answer simply. Minimally, we can say, following Janet Radcliffe Richards, that (secular) feminism works to alleviate the manifest social disadvantages of women, since "there are excellent reasons for thinking that *women suffer from systematic social injustice because of their sex*."[4] But under that voluminous feminist umbrella, a variety of schools of thought can shelter, and feminist theology, in echoing and complexifying those schools with religious themes, has proved equally multifarious.

We may, however, distinguish roughly, in the secular sphere, between liberal, radical, socialist, and postmodern feminisms.[5] While "liberal feminism" has its roots in the Enlightenment call to "autonomy" and "equality," and urges that these possibilites be extended to women through education and opportunites, it does little to accentuate the *distinctiveness* of women's bodies, experiences, or symbolic imaginations. To do so might indeed undercut the goal of "equality" (intellectual and professional) for which it strives; difference between the sexes is carefully minimized. "Radical feminism," in contrast, has highlighted the nature of the sex war by stressing the differentiating characteristics of women's bodies and sexuality, and what it sees as the pernicious attempts by men to constrain women into the "cage of femininity."[6] Its goal has been less the "equality" of women than their separatist rejoicing in *difference*. "Socialist feminism," slightly differently again, has stressed the *societal*—rather than merely individual—roots of women's oppression, as too of their potential emancipation. In applying a Marxist analysis of "alienation" in the process, it has not omitted to criticize Marx's own blindness to issues of sexual difference. Finally, "postmodern feminism" (a term that itself covers a variety of options in Europe and America) is characterized by its "deconstructionist" aim to undermine imperialist and generalizing claims to truth, specifically male-constructed "truth" about sex differentations. The French forms of postmodern feminism have been profoundly influenced by Freudian psychoanalytic theory and are in revolt against Freud's interpretation of woman as fundamentally marked by loss or incompleteness ("penis envy"). They stress not only the marginalization of women through psychoanalytic theory, but more deeply by the very structure of "phallocentric" *language*. Society's incapacity to recognize the "Other" (woman) is, according to this view, inscribed in the very structure of its linguistic rules. To change this, to subvert language and culture into recognition of its repressed "femininity," is thus a task even more daunting and far-reaching than radical feminism's separatist assertion of women's sexual difference or moral superiority.

Not all the tenets of these "schools" of secular feminism are mutually exclusive, but some clearly are. In particular, the vexed issue of the relation of "sex" and "gender" remains hotly contentious. At the time of Saiving's early article, as we have seen, "feminine" was often used interchangeably with "female" in feminist writing. Saiving assumed that all women were "feminine", but argued that they might need to compensate for those "feminine" traits that trivialized them. The next wave of feminist theory, in reaction, drew a sharp differentiation between "sex" (understood as physiological difference: male or female) and "gender" (societal constructions of appropriate roles for men and women: "masculine" or "feminine") and concentrated on freeing up normative identification of the latter with the former. Postmodern feminisms, however, in yet a further reaction, have re-smudged this distinction for a new reason, pointing out that even physiological difference can be an "effect" of social discourse; and French feminisms, as a further complication, do

not have available to them such a distinction in the French language to start with. Thus even now these terms are not used consistently, and some writers (for the ideological or linguistic reasons just mentioned) use them interchangeably. The differences on this matter bespeak a range of hotly disputed theoretical questions.

Feminist theology, as this chapter will show, has been both dependent on, and critical of, the different "types" of secular feminist theory and their concomitant attitudes to sex and gender. But it has complexified and enriched the debate by introducing the question of God. Are traditional, stereotypical, visions of "masculinity" and "femininity" given their justification in God, or are they rather dissolved and subverted in the Divine? Can biblical and Christian tradition ultimately provide the resources to transcend its own quite evident "patriarchal" bias, or not? It was these issues that were to split emergent feminist theology, entangled as it was with the secular debates about differing feminist ideologies. A discussion of four very different exponents of religious feminism will now illustrate these splits and differing theological options.

MARY DALY: THE MOVE TO "POST-CHRISTIAN" FEMINIST THEOLOGY

The writings of Mary Daly (1928–) have spanned more than one of the feminist and theological options outlined above. But it is her mature work as a post-Christian radical feminist and exponent of primal "goddess" religion that has earned her a reputation as enduring in secular circles as in religious ones, and she remains one of the most important constellating figures of radical feminism. Daly, above all religious feminist writers, challenges the Christian feminist to defend the very possibility of a post patriarchal Christian future; for Daly there is, and can be, no such thing. Although her first pioneering feminist theological work was written as a Roman Catholic and bears the marks of liberal feminist goals (equality and self-transcendence for women[7]), after a transitional phase Daly decisively abandoned the task either of Christian reformation or of "partnership" between the sexes. She then perceived that the "overwhelmingly patriarchal character of the biblical tradition" was unchangeable.[8] The only alternative was a radical one—a self-confessedly lesbian separatism, a subversive women's religion severing all ties with Christian tradition.

Born into a relatively impoverished family, Mary Daly nonetheless received an intensive higher education, accumulating degrees first in American Catholic colleges and universities, and then earning two doctorates at the University of Fribourg in Switzerland, one in theology and the other in philosophy. She was born just a little too early to find (lay Catholic) progress through higher theological and philosophical degrees in America an easy matter as a woman, especially without private funds.[9] It was thus something of an irony that a conservative Catholic faculty in Europe gave her opportunities when comparatively liberal North America did not. The simple reason was that the Swiss state system of university education could not legally debar women from any particular course, not that Fribourg was a budding center of feminist thought. On the contrary, here Daly ingested the most traditional Thomistic education from Dominican priest professors lecturing in Latin. Yet later she admitted that she could never have written her feminist books without this intense intellectual training: "All of these books have drawn upon the athleticism of the mind that I learned then—a kind of intellectual Karate."[10]

In her autobiograhy *Outercourse* (1992), Daly retrospectively describes her theological career as proceeding in "Four Spiral Galaxies," four successive "Moments" in her "Voyage as a Radical Feminist Philosopher." The first is represented by her pioneering book *The Church and the Second Sex* (1968), written as a specific response (and *riposte*) to Simone de Beauvoir's illustrious *The Second Sex*. Daly was spurred to write this book after a particularly significant visit to Rome in the course of the Second Vatican Council. Later she described the scene as follows:

I borrowed a journalist's identification card and went into St. Peter's for one of the major sessions. Sitting in the section reserved for the press, I saw in the distance a multitude of cardinals and bishops—old men in crimson dresses. In another section were the "auditors": a group which included a few Catholic women, mostly nuns in long black dresses with heads veiled. The contrast between the arrogant bearing and colorful attire of the "princes of the church" and the humble, self-deprecating manner and somber clothing of the very few women was appalling. . . . Speeches were read at the session, but the voices were all male, the senile, cracking whines of the men in red. The few women, the nuns, sat docilely and listened to the reading of the documents in Latin, which neither they nor the readers apparently understood. When questioned by the press afterward, the female "auditors" repeatedly expressed their gratitude for the privilege of being present. . . . Although I did not grasp the full meaning of the scene all at once, its multileveled message burned its way deep into my consciousness.[11]

Returning to Fribourg from Rome, Daly set to work in earnest on her new book. Taking up de Beauvoir's charge that the Catholic Church had been a major instrument in the oppression of women, Daly gave both further historical instantiation to that charge and an attempted Christian response. Mercilessly exposing the "history of contradictons" in Christianity's simultaneous "pseudo-glorification" and "degrading" of women,[12] she nonetheless went on to sketch a way forward toward women's "equality" and "partnership" with men in the Church. This involved a typically liberal appeal to a place beyond sex—or gender—differentiation where such equality might be enjoyed:

In the exercise of self-transcending creative activity, inspired and driven forward by faith and hope, sustained by courage, men and women can learn to "set their pride beyond the sexual differentiation." Working together on all levels they may come at last to see each other's faces, and in so doing, come to know themselves. It is only by this creative personal encounter, sparked by that power of transcendence which the theologians have called grace, that the old wounds can be healed.[13]

Within only a few years, however, Daly had rejected most of her own proposals in *The Church and the Second Sex*.[14] Moving into her "Second Spiral," she marked its onset by a dramatic orchestrated walkout from Harvard Memorial Church at a preaching engagement there in 1971.[15] Thereafter, she abandoned interest in reforming the hierarchical organization of the Catholic Church or of canvasing for the ordination of women. Instead, in her celebrated second book, *Beyond God the Father* (1973), which represents this transitional second phase in her thinking, she went straight to the heart of the *symbolic* content of "patriarchal religion." She focused now on a level of oppression more subliminal, and therefore more deep, than the institutional subordination of women in the churches. In a much-quoted passage from the first chapter she wrote:

if God is male, then the male is God. The divine patriarch castrates women as long as he is allowed to live on in the human imagination. The process of cutting away the Supreme Phallus can hardly be a merely "rational" affair. The problem is one of transforming the collective imagination so that this distortion of the human aspiration to transcendence loses its credibility.

Some religious leaders . . . showed insight into the problem to some extent and tried to stress the "maternal" aspect of what they called "God." A number of feminists have referred to "God" as "she." While all of this has a point, the analysis has to reach a deeper level. The most basic change has to take place in women—in our being and self-image. Otherwise there is a danger of settling for mere reform. . . .[16]

These words remain challenging to any of the other feminist tactics for reform within the Christian churches, as we shall see. Daly had exposed the profound indeterminacies in any attempt to ameliorate the plight of Christian women by a superficial adjustment of the God concept at the doctrinal level. Who was to say that the "Supreme Phallus" would not continue to exercise the "collective imagination"? What Daly proposed at this stage (though it was a proposal she was again to adjust within a couple of years) was a

transformation of the concept of God away from "objectifying" and "anthropomorphizing" tendencies altogether:

Why indeed must "God" be a noun? Why not a verb—the most active and dynamic of all? Hasn't the naming of "God" as a noun been an act of murdering that dynamic Verb? The anthropomorphic symbols for God may be intended to convey personality, but they fail to convey that God is Be-ing. Women who now are experiencing the shock of nonbeing and the surge of self-affirmation against this are inclined to perceive transcendence as the Verb in which we participate—live, move, and have our being.[17]

In taking this line Daly was influenced (briefly) by Paul Tillich's existentialist analysis of the threat of "nonbeing," and his call to have "courage to be." (See Chapter Five). However, she expressed dissatsifaction with Tillich's failure to understand the *particular* oppressions of patriarchy.[18] (Later, as revelations about Tillich's sexual life became manifest, Daly's repudiation of his theology took on a more caustic tone.)[19] In *Beyond God the Father*, however, Daly did not give up on men's capacity for transformation alongside that of women. But this is slightly differently expressed than in *The Church and the Second Sex*. Daly now spoke of both sexes moving toward "androgynous being," a state not merely that of women settling for "becoming equal to men in a men's world," but rather of both sexes throwing off the burdens of "inauthenticity, alienation, non-identity."[20] In this quest, however, she (already) saw little help in the earliest forms of Christianity. If Jesus was a "feminist," then "So What?" She wrote: "Fine. Wonderful. But even if he wasn't, *I am*."[21] The subsequent history of Christology (for Daly, "Christolatry") had been so irredeemably sexist that there was little point in trying to reclaim a supposedly pure origin.

It was in her "Third Spiral" that Daly made her "qualitative leap" beyond patriarchy *and* Christianity. In *Outercourse* she describes this as becoming "*Other* than christian" rather than "post-Christian,"[22] and the shift was coincident with her coming out as a lesbian. From now on her radical views about sexuality made any balancing between "feminine" and "masculine" traits—whether in the God concept or in so-called "androgynous" humanity—entirely otiose. Indeed she renounced talk of either. The introduction to *Gyn/Ecology: The Metaethics of Radical Feminism* (1978) makes these new departures plain:

Going beyond *Beyond God the Father* involves two things. First, there is the fact that be-ing continues. Be-ing at home on the road means continuing to Journey. This book continues to Spin on, in other directions/dimensions. It focuses beyond christianity in Other ways. Second, there is some old semantic baggage to be discarded so that Journeyers will be unencumbered by malfunctioning (male-functioning) equipment. . . . Three . . . words . . . which I cannot use again are God, *androgyny*, and *homosexuality*. There is no way to remove male/masculine imagery from God. Thus, when writing/speaking "anthropomorphically" of ultimate reality, of the divine spark of be-ing, I now choose to write/speak gynomorphically. I do so because *God* represents the necrophilia of patriarchy, whereas *Goddess* affirms the life-loving be-ing of women and nature. The second semantic term, *androgyny*, is a confusing term which I sometimes used in attempting to describe integrity of be-ing. The word is misbegotten—conveying something like "John Travolta and Farrah Fawcett-Majors scotch-taped together." . . . The third treacherous term, *homosexuality*, reductionistically "includes," that is, excludes, gynocentric be-ing/Lesbiansim. . . .

The words *gynocentric be-ing* and *Lesbian* imply separation. . . . The primary intent of women who choose to be present to each other . . . is not an invitation to men. It is an invitation to our Selves. The Spinsters, Lesbians, Hags, Harpies, Crones, Furies who are the Voyagers of *Gyn/Ecology* know that we choose to accept this invitation for our Selves. This, our Self-acceptance, is in no way contingent upon male approval.[23]

Daly's move beyond Christianity and into radical feminism clearly not only signaled a new sexual separatism and a concomitant change of mind about "sex" and "gender" (words which Daly uses interchangeably in her later work); it also marked a new phase of creativity in her theological thinking. There are two sides to this. On the one hand there is a ruthless (though deliciously funny) spoofing of central Christian doctrines as wholly contaminated by "necrophiliac," sexist thinking; on the other, an assertion of a more primary "gynomorphic" religious impetus toward goddess worship. Woven into both themes is Daly's repeatedly alliterative undercutting of patriarchal language, an intensive redefinition of terms that propels one, through constant punning subversion of current meaning, into a new "galaxy" of ideas and associations. Daly was to call her collection of postpatriarchal redefinitions her *Webster's First New Intergalactic Wickedary of the English Language* (1987)—"webster" here meaning a "female weaver" and "Wickedary" a "dictionary for witches"![24]

Such play with language is a persistent characteristic of *Gyn/Ecology* and *Pure Lust* (1984), the two substantial works of Daly's "Third Spiral." The former is devoted mainly to an exposé of what Daly sees as the suppression and mutilation of women in patriarchal societies, through such various practices as Indian *suttee*, Chinese foot-binding, African genital mutilation, European witchburning, and contemporary American gynecological management. All of these, claims Daly, are motivated by a "Sado-Ritual Syndrome: the Reenactment of Goddess Murder,"[25] and they reflect "the prevailing religion of the *entire planet*"—"necrophiliac" patriarchy.[26] Deep in the symbolic heart of Christianity is a sadomasochistic drama, the "Veiled Vampirism" of the "Torture Cross," which, according to Daly, replaced an earlier life-giving goddess mythology of the "Tree of Life."[27] Likewise, the doctrine of the Trinity, the most ramified of Christian doctrines, represents the same obliteration of the female:

The triune God is one act of eternal self-absorbtion/self-love. The term *person* is derived from the Latin *persona* meaning actor's mask, or character in a play. "The Processions of Divine Persons" is the most sensational one-act play of the centuries, the original *Love Story,* performed by the Supreme All Male Cast. Here we have the epitome of male bonding, beyond the "best," i.e., worst dreams of Lionel Tiger. It is "sublime" (and therefore disguised) erotic male homosexual *mythos,* the perfect all-male marriage, the ideal all-male family, the best boys' club, the model monastery, the supreme Men's Association, the mold for all varieties of male monogender mating.[28]

The only appropriate response for radical feminist women, then (otherwise known as Spinsters, Hags, and Crones), is to rediscover the psychic power of the goddess mythology that Daly believes underlies Christian trinitarianism and indeed all patriarchal perversion of religion. Daly is not interested in "hypostatizing" the goddess into an actual figure, but rather in releasing "Crone-logically antecedent myths and symbols, which have been stolen and reversed, contorted and distorted, by the misogynist Mix-Masters."[29] *Pure Lust: Elemental Feminist Philosophy* continues the same themes, emphasizing more now the "Elemental Reality" toward which liberated women strive, rather than the rejected Christian patriarchy from which they have escaped. "Pure Lust," explains Daly, is not to be confused with the male "pure lust" of "unmitigated malevolence."[30] On the contrary,

> *Pure Lust* Names the high humor, hope, and cosmic accord/harmony of those women who choose to escape, to follow our hearts' deepest desire and bound out of the State of Bondage, Wanderlusting and Wonderlusting with the elements, connecting with the aura of animals and plants, moving in planetary communion with the farthest stars.[31]

It will be clear that Daly's thought has, in her mature work, definitively abandoned the thought forms of Christianity. It is also clear that her hyperbolic rhetoric aims to subvert and disturb, rather than present a reasoned historical portrait of Christianity in its many manifestations. The latter is not Daly's task. Yet her hilarious caricature of Christianity's core symbolic content leaves its disturbing challenge: how, if at all, is the *Christian* feminist to purify her religious tradition of the taint of the "Supreme Phallus"? What ploys, other than Daly's outright rejection of the tradition, are open to her? And what are the alternatives to Daly's "radical" assertion of women's (all women's) need to dissociate themselves by *separation* from patriarchal culture and language? Daly says little about class and race factors that might restrict some women more than others from even this act of "separatist" rebellion; and she bemoans in *Outercourse* (her "Fourth Spiral," and her last) the current "multiplication of divisions within and among women."[32] Such divisions, however, mark the range of *alternative* possible responses to the acknowledgment of Christianity's patriarchal past. To these alternatives we now turn.

ELISABETH SCHÜSSLER FIORENZA: JESUS AND THE "DISCIPLESHIP OF EQUALS"

Elizabeth Schüssler Fiorenza (1938–) must be counted the most influential New Testament scholar among feminist theologians of the 1980s and 1990s, and her work is to be contrasted with Mary Daly's on a number of scores. While her early work, like Daly's, exhibits commitment to classic liberal feminist goals for women, such as "autonomy," "freedom," and "self-determination" (goals she has never disclaimed), her mature writing is profoundly influenced by the *social* emphases of European "critical" and hermeneutical theory, and by liberation and political theology (see Chapters Nine and Eleven). Her more recent engagement with postmodern thinking is not uncritical, because she fears it may erode faith in personal "agency" just as women are attaining to it,[33] but what she does share with postmodern thought is an appreciation of the deep effect on theological judgment of political and social context, and of the entanglement of "sex/gender"[34] questions with issues of race and class. "Gender" cannot be unproblematically identified with "sex" (as Daly would have it), but neither can they be divorced: The language of "sex" ("maleness" and "femaleness") endures as a recurring myth of "naturalness" onto which different cultural norms are projected in different historical periods. Yet "patriarchy" is not strictly the same enemy as "sexism":[35] the former oppresses not only women, but all those pushed to the bottom of the heap, disadvantaged by race or class or poor education. "Kyriarchy," Schüssler Fiorenza argues in later writings, is thus a better term for the structural enemy, because it is rule by "overlords" rather than (all) "fathers" that is the primary cause of suffering; and "wo/men" (as she now calls them) exist in multiple webs of layered oppression, some of which they manifestly share with oppressed men-folk.[36]

From all this it will be clear why Schüssler Fiorenza is deeply suspicious of separatist feminism (radical feminism of Daly's ilk) or of any feminist theory that smacks of gender "essentialism" (including the psycholanalytic theorizing about the symbolism of women's bodies in French feminism).[37] She is also critical of the anti-intellectualism that has tended to characterize some of Daly's following.[38] Nonetheless she is clear that her work, demanding as it is theoretically, is intended for women and men everywhere, and that its aim is the transformation of both church and society. Like Daly, she is a Catholic by birth; unlike Daly, she has not abandoned that birthright.

Elisabeth Schüssler Fiorenza was brought up in Franconia, a predominantly Catholic part of Germany. She suffered as a child the considerable deprivations and upheavals of the last phase of World War II and its aftermath, an experience not explicitly discussed in her writings but arguably reflected in her abiding concern for the destitute and dispossessed. Her classical *Gymnasium* training after the War, however, was (like Daly's) a rigorous and traditional one, not immediately concerned with the matters of social justice that were later to exercise her. It led on to a highly successful university career at Würzburg in arts and theological subjects, and in the early

1960s she became the first woman there to complete the full range of theological and pastoral options previously reserved for male candidates for the priesthood. Already her feminist thought was developing: Her dissertation at Würzburg was a remarkably daring account of the suppression of women's pastoral gifts even in the progressive ecclesiologies of Rahner and Congar. Published in 1964 as *Der vergessene Partner*,[39] it had a considerable (if underestimated) influence on Daly's *The Church and the Second Sex*. Schüssler Fiorenza's further graduate studies (in Scripture) were completed at Münster, with a dissertation on priesthood in the New Testament, focusing on the Apocalypse. Already in her graduate days she had formulated her views—consistently maintained thereafter[40]—that women should not seek ordination in the Catholic Church unless the full range of ecclesiastical offices were open to them, including the episcopate (and thereby, in principle, the papacy). To incorporate women merely into the lower ranks of a "hierarchical-patriarchal" institution could serve only to shore up its structure.

Looking back on her early theological training, Schüssler Fiorenza has written that she now "marvel[s]" at her "chutzpah" in taking on the question of women's roles and her declaring even the theology of progressive Catholicism (then informing Vatican II) "inadequate" to these issues.[41] She remarks that her work at the time was as yet unformed in its theoretical underpinnings, and yet also remarkably farsighted:

Although my first book did not question hierarchical structures and theoretical frameworks, it had important methodological implications that I could not have articulated at the time. Anticipating feminist and liberation theologies, it assumed that the experience of women and the praxis of church and ministry should be primary for articulating ecclesiology and spirituality. Most important, though lacking theoretical self-consciousness, I nevertheless acted as a theological subject attempting to rethink theological constructions from the marginal location of "lay" woman engaged in the study of theology. I became painfully aware of this marginalization when I applied for one of the two doctoral scholarships available for New Testament students. Although I had completed two advanced theological degrees summa cum laude and published a book, my *Doktorvater* refused to obtain a scholarship for me, explaining that he did not want to waste the opportunity on a student who as a woman had no future in the academy.[42]

Like Daly, then, Schüssler Fiorenza benefited from the most demanding of European doctoral programs; and like Daly, she discovered that her only hope for a developing theological career as a Catholic woman lay in the United States. Initially she held appointments in New Testament alone, a development that proved "fortuitous," because "practical or applied theology is still deemed less scholarly and the field of religious education still regarded as a woman's domain."[43] But it was through the confluence of her detailed New Testament scholarship, her continuing commitment to social and pastoral issues, and her burgeoning involvement with American feminist studies in religion that *In Memory of Her* (1983), her most influential work, was to be created.

Central to Schüssler Fiorenza's theological outlook is an abiding insistence (quite contrary to Daly's later work) that the Christian tradition is capable of feminist reform and readjustment, and that the earliest traditions of Jesus and his followers contain the necessary delineations of such a reform. Writing autobiographically of her work before *In Memory of Her*, she says, "Although I fully shared the trenchant feminist critique of the Christian tradition, I never felt . . . an irreconcilable contradiction between my Christian and my feminist identity. In my experience some Christian teachings had offered a religious resource for resisting the demands of cultural feminine roles. Moreover, I grew up with the notion that all the baptized are the church and are responsible for its praxis."[44] Hence for Schüssler Fiorenza the "solution" of an "Exodus" from the Church (such as Daly advocated and symbolically enacted) was to be resisted. "Sectarianism" was neither a long-

term solution to patriarchal ills, nor even an option for the underprivileged:

Rather than engage in the illusion of Exodus, feminist theology had to find a symbol that encouraged women in biblical religions to choose how and where to attack the many-headed dragon of patriarchy. Those of us who are privileged in terms of race, class and education . . . have to do so in solidarity with those women who must struggle daily against multiple forms of patriarchal oppression and dehumanization in order to survive. Not Exodus but struggle is the common ground for women.[45]

In Memory of Her charts that struggle in the earliest church and finds in Jesus's message and example a subversive "discipleship of equals" that was rapidly compromised as Christianity moved out to confront the Hellenistic world. A "critical feminist theology of liberation," however, is according to Schüssler Fiorenza capable of recovering and redirecting the potential of Jesus's original vision.

The argument here is necessarily undergirded by a sophisticated set of hermeneutical ploys whose discussion constitutes the first section of the book. Schüssler Fiorenza starts with the symbolic example of the New Tesatment story from which her title is taken. In the Markan version of the account of the woman who anointed Jesus with precious oil before his death, Jesus declares that "wherever the gospel is preached in the whole world, what she has done will be told in memory of her" (Mark 14:9). But as Schüssler Fiorenza comments, "the woman's prophetic sign-action did not become a part of the gospel knowledge of Christians. Even her name is lost to us." And the versions in the other Gospels adjust the story to make it "more palatable to a patriarchal Greco-Roman audience": The woman becomes either a faithful friend of Jesus (in John) or a forgiven sinner (in Luke).[46] The task then of a liberating feminist hermeneutic is to reread the biblical text "not only to restore women's stories to early Christianity but also to reclaim this history as the history of women and men."[47] In the case of this poignant example from Mark, we have a "politically dangerous story" in which a woman has grasped with particular acuteness the significance of Jesus as Messiah:

Whereas according to Mark the leading male disciples do not understand this suffering messiahship of Jesus, reject it, and finally abandon him, the women disciples who have followed Jesus from Galilee to Jerusalem suddenly emerge as the true disciples in the passion narrative. They are Jesus's true followers . . . who have understood that his ministry was not rule and kingly glory but *diakonia*, "service" (Mark 15:41). Thus the women emerge as the true Christian ministers and witnesses. The unnamed woman who names Jesus with a prophetic sign-action in Mark's Gospel is the paradigm for the true disciple.[48]

Schüssler Fiorenza is fully aware how contentious such a rereading of the New Testament texts is according to standard historical-critical presumptions. To defend her (necessarily selective) highlighting of some texts over others, and her reading of them that reallocates "agency" to women, she outlines a number of hermeneutical principles.

She consciously rejects the idea of a timelessly true, or "a-historical," hermeneutics: This can serve only oppressive and "androcentric" interests, she says, which are in any case already imposed on the biblical text itself. Hence the text must be read subtly for its "silences," because "the locus of revelation is not the androcentric text but the life and ministry of Jesus."[49] A hermeneutics of "suspicion" must be conjoined with a hermeneutics of "liberation" and "religious agency": "Rather than *abandon* the memory of our foresisters' sufferings and hopes in our common patriarchal Christian past, Christian feminists *reclaim* their sufferings and struggles in and through the subversive power of the 'remembered past.'"[50] Schüssler Fiorenza also throws critical light on recent sociological analyses of early Christianity for their implicit suggestion that the subordination of women in the movement was a

social *inevitability*. On the contrary, she argues, in the earliest period of the Jesus following, "Women who belonged to a submerged group in antiquity could develop leadership . . . because [emerging Christianity] stood in conflict with the dominant patriarchal ethos of the Greco-Roman world."[51] Hence she urges the return to "the historical reality of Jesus" *beyond* the received Gospel texts; but this is not to be on the naive assumptions of earlier such "quests": We cannot rescue a "pristine" Jesus somehow prior to, or separable from, "interpretation." We can only wrestle with the complexity of historical-critical methods to reconstruct the vision of the "Kingdom" that Jesus and his earliest following originally preached. Yet the use of such methods does not involve a (spurious) dispassion: "The Gospels are not transcripts but invitations to discipleship. They are theological interpretation-in-process".[52]

Schüssler Fiorenza does not wish to suggest that Jesus's originality (even in relation to the status of women) lay in a transcendence of Judaism: Such a position would inevitably smack of anti-Semitism. She thus appeals to the book of Judith as a Jewish anticipation of the notion of sexual equality: This "mediates the atmosphere in which Jesus preached and in which the discipleship of equals originated."[53] Relying heavily on the source material ("Q", for *Quelle*) that Matthew and Luke have in common, she then goes on to reconsruct her understanding of Jesus's teaching and its original reception. This is a reconstruction in which her interpretation of the "Q" saying, "Wisdom [Sophia] is justified by all her children" (Luke 7:35), plays a crucial role:

the Palestinian Jesus movement understands the ministry and mission of Jesus as that of the prophet and child of Sophia sent to announce that God is the God of the poor and heavy laden, of the outcasts and those who suffer injustice. As child of Sophia he stands in a long line and succession of prophets sent to gather the children of Israel to their gracious Sophia-God. Jesus' execution, like John's, results from his mission and commitment as a prophet and emissary of the Sophia-God who holds open a future for the poor and outcast and offers God's gracious goodness to *all* children of Israel without exception. The Sophia-God of Jesus does not need atonement or sacrifices. Jesus's death is not willed by God but is the result of his all-inclusive praxis as Sophia's prophet. . . .

This reality of God-Sophia spelled out in the preaching, healings, exorcisms, and inclusive table community of Jesus called forth a circle of disciples who were to continue what Jesus did. Sophia, the God of Jesus, wills the wholeness and humanity of everyone and therefore enables the Jesus movement to become a "discipleship of equals."[54]

In order for Schüssler Fiorenza to sustain this feminist liberative rereading of Jesus's message, his (undeniable) address to God as "Father" (*abba*) has to be downplayed and reinterpreted. Here, an ingenious emphasis on Matthew 23:9 ("Call no one father . . . for you have one . . . father") complements the "Sophia" motif: "The 'father' God is invoked here . . . not to justify patriarchal structures and relationships in the community of disciples but precisely to reject all such claims, powers, and structures."[55]

How then is the depressing descent into patriarchal attitudes, already evident in the New Testament texts, to be explained? Schüssler Fiorenza devotes the rest of *In Memory of Her* to this account, peeling back layers of "androcentric" bias in due order. Here Paul plays an ambiguous role. According to Schüssler Fiorenza, he did not invent, but inherited, the early Christian formula in Galatians 3:28 ("neither male nor female" [in Christ]), a sentiment that is read, in line with her interpretation of Jesus's views, as ruling out "sexual dimorphism, and gender roles based on it."[56] Paul's own assimilation of this theme was, however, affected by the problems of disorder he confronted at Corinth; and in the face of them he fatally introduced into the Christian missionary message the "descending hierarchy, God-Christ-Man-Woman" (see I Cor. 11), a solution not unexpected in the general ethos of the Greco-Roman world, but undermining to the more subversive stress on equality that Paul also embraced

elsewhere.[57] The deutero-Pauline "household codes" (in Colossians, Ephesians, and the Pastorals) take this development yet further, reinscribing a hierarchical order into the "private" sphere of the family, and exhorting Christians to a "love patriarchalism" that inevitably brings a gradual exclusion of women's leadership in its train.[58] In the last section of her book, Schüssler Fiorenza relentlessly charts these developments in a trajectory out into the early patristic materials.

Granted these ostensibly depressing conclusions, it is inevitable that Schüssler Fiorenza would want to give further methodological backing to her insistence that a form of identification with women's *past* (and often unsuccessful) struggles can nonetheless bring new hope and direction to those oppressed today. It is precisely this paradox that has puzzled many of her critics. But in two later volumes (*Bread Not Stone*[59] and *But She Said*[60]), she has further refined the hermeneutical principles of *In Memory of Her* and also plotted her own sophisticated methodology onto the map of current secular feminisms. In *Bread Not Stone*, the rejection of the possibility of "value neutrality" in historiography is made the more explicit,[61] a move that thus claims to leave feminist reinterpretation in no special position of tension with "historical-critical" methods. In the later *But She Said*, the universalizing rhetoric of *In Memory of Her* (talk of a "catholic sisterhood . . . [spanning] all ages, nations, and continents"[62]) receives some modification in the detailed, historicized account of multifarious forms of "kyriarchal" oppression, in which women may participate, or suffer, at various levels.[63] Simultaneously, Schüssler Fiorenza also counters what she sees as a misunderstanding of her proposals as a "naive" construction of "continuity between the early Christian discipleship of equals" and contemporary "women-church, conceived as a feminist movement of self-identified women and men identified with women's struggles." Such readings misapprehend, she says, the "tension between the 'already' and the 'not yet' of the *ekklesia* of women," and fail to understand her rejection of "abstract norm[s]" in favor of "question[s] asked from particular sociopolitical locations and subject-positions."[64]

In *Jesus: Miriam's Child, Sophia's Prophet,*[65] Schüssler Fiorenza has provided further clarification of her systematic christological position. She has insisted that her feminist theology is not "*grounded*" in the "historical Jesus" (such would be a miscontrual of *In Memory of Her*, projecting the desire for "pristine" origins), but rather in "wo/men's struggles for the transformation of kyriarchy."[66] Here the themes of Jesus's death and resurrection become much more developed than in *In Memory of Her*: We should probe behind an Anselmian overlay of talk about "satisfaction for sin," it is urged, and reinvestigate the early Christian formulations of Jesus's resurrection as a "*vindication* of the righteous one."[67] It is not violence or sadism against "wo/men" that is to be justified by one's theology of the Cross, but rather the message of "liberation from oppression" of which the resurrection is "symbolic," and in whose rhetoric of hope "women's experience" was originally implicated.[68] Schüssler Fiorenza has little time for patristic formulations of christological transformation of humanity, however. The Chalcedonian Definiton is read as irredeemably "kyriocentric," given its entanglement of themes of imperial absolutism with those of doctrinal "orthodoxy";[69] and in contrast to the subtle and nuanced retrieval of strands of New Testament christology, no such multifaceted hermenutic, interestingly, is applied to the conciliar christological texts.

Schüssler Fiorenza has provided in her work a compelling vision of "critical feminist liberation" in subtle and dialogical conversation with the New Testament texts. Her hermeneutical sophistication has rescued feminist theology from the easy charge of naive "eisegesis," and her increasing engagement with secular feminist theory has enabled her to plot the distinctiveness of her biblical engagement within the wider feminist spectrum. Moreover, her unwillingness (in contrast to Daly) to advocate a sectarian feminist retreat

from church and society has led her into a deepened engagement with questions of race, class, and other forms of prejudice often inextricably entwined with sexism. The practical "ekklesia of wo/men" has become her central point of hope and reference; on metaphysical questions such as the being and nature of God she is less willing to expatiate, except insofar as Jesus's notion of "Sophia" provides us with a radical adjustment to inherited patriarchal notions.[70] Her work remains firmly based in the practicalities of wo/men's oppression and liberation worldwide, and her influence on emergent Third World theological feminism has been of great significance.[71]

SALLIE McFAGUE: RECONCEIVING GOD AND GENDER

The feminist work of Sallie McFague (1933–   ), in contrast, places its emphasis on linguistic and philosophical discussion of the possibilities of God talk *tout court*, and has had its major impact on (white) liberal Protestantism within North America. Indeed its influence here can scarcely be overestimated. It is, after all, the optimistic embracing of new, feminist, and socially relevant appellations for God (often in some tension with Bible and tradition) that has had so remarkable an effect on the liturgies and thought forms of American liberal Protestantism since the 1970s; and, even though McFague herself rarely discusses liturgy, her theology has provided a blueprint and rationale for such change. Her systematic and philosophical starting point provides an interesting contrast to Schüssler Fiorenza's hermeneutical undertaking, but at the same time another *riposte* to Daly's outright rejection of the future of the Christian theistic tradition.

McFague's work was not originally or primarily conceived as "feminist." She is an American Episcopalian whose first degree was from Smith College, and who then completed three subsequent graduate degrees in theology at Yale. Her earlier writings[72] were on the nature and force of religious language in the culturally plural world of

Sallie McFague

ours; that is, as mainstream, middle-class Christians we have the leisure and the power to attend to these basic but semiremote threats to life as our sisters and brothers oppressed by more immediate and daily threats to survival do not. It has been decisions of those with power and money that have created our ecological crisis as well as escalated the possibility of nuclear war; . . . This essay, then, is a "liberation theology" for life and its continuation, written out of and to the social context of those who control the resources—the money and power—necessary to liberate life.[74]

McFague's feminist contributions, then, arise as protests against the "imperialist, triumphalist metaphors for God"[75] that she sees as endemic to premodern and modern Christianity, and which have also spawned deluded attitudes to the environment and international relations. She does not specifically identify sexism or patriarchy as the *primal* sin. She dubs her theology "postmodern," but not because it is "postmodern feminist" in the sense discussed in the introduction to this chapter. Rather it is postmodern because its "assumptions differ from those of the Enlightenment" in the following respects:

a greater appreciation of nature, linked with a chastened admiration for technology; the recognition of the importance of language (and hence interpretation and construction) in human existence; the acceptance of the challenge that other religious options present to the Judeo-Christian tradition; a sense of the displacement of the white, Western male and rise of those dispossessed because of gender, race or class; and apocalyptic sensibility, fueled in part by the awareness that we exist between two holocausts, the Jewish and the nuclear; and *perhaps most significant,* a growing appreciation of the thoroughgoing, radical interdependence of life at all levels and in every imaginable way.[76] [Italics added.]

From this we can see why McFague acknowledges that her work is "not a feminist theology in the sense that its guiding principle is the liberation of women"; nonetheless she argues that "the fact that I am female is relevant to my perspective

the late twentieth century, and it was her conclusions here that were to inform her views about feminist adjustments to God talk. Although her *theology* in general is strongly in the liberal tradition of American Protestantism, as we shall outline, her feminist commitments are not classical liberal ones. She does not underscore the importance of women's "autonomy," for instance, because she is much more concerned with such goals as "intimacy, mutuality and relatedness"[73] for both women and men. There is a sense that she already takes for granted the achievement of basic societal rights for women, along with a certain level of independence. Thus, unlike Schüssler Fiorenza (who as we have seen is deeply aware of the *multiple* oppressions of the women of color who may draw on her work), McFague, although occasionally signaling support for such constituencies, acknowledges that her work is primarily addressed to the white middle class. Writing in 1987 of her concern for ecological and nuclear issues, for instance, she notes:

I am white and middle-class, writing to a mainstream Christian audience. What joins author and readers is that the ecological and nuclear issues are peculiarly as an author, for it is the form of oppression that has provided me with sufficient disorientation from middle-class, mainstream Christianity both to question it and to risk alternative formulations of Christian faith."[77] On questions of "sex" and "gender", McFague exhibits less subtle theoretical reflection than Schüssler Fiorenza, as this quotation may already suggest. In earlier work she appears not far from the presumptions of Valerie Saiving in accepting certain given stereotypes of "femininity" and then arguing that women need to balance their natural proclivity for such characteristics with complementary "masculine" traits.[78] In later writings a strong distinction is drawn between such stereotypes (what we earlier termed "gender") and physiological difference. However in McFague's usage, somewhat confusingly, "gender" is the term used of the latter, and talk of "femaleness" is apparently deemed unproblematic: We must take care, she says, not to "slip[. . .] in feminine stereotypes under the cover of simple [sic] gender appellation."[79] The more radical suggestion that even physiological differentiation could be affected by cultural "construction" is not considered by McFague.

It is impossible to appreciate the distinctiveness of McFague's contribution as a feminist theologian unless one understands the central tenets of the Protestant liberalism that support her feminism. Unlike Daly, who is in mammoth reaction to a Catholic scholastic training, or Schüssler Fiorenza, who draws significantly on European hermeneutical theory and political thought, McFague's pantheon of theological heroes includes Kant, Schleiermacher, Tillich, and, above all, the contemporary American theologian Gordon Kaufman[80] (on Kaufman, see Chapter Sixteen). Like Kaufman, McFague reads Kant as having established not only the impossibility of speculative metaphysics, but also the *absence* or *unavailability* of God in Godself, and so (as contemporary deconstructionist thinkers also stress) the death of the "presumptuous insistence in Western religious thought on the presence of the divine."[81] Like Kaufman, too, McFague sees in this mysterious absence of God an opportunity to embrace positively the pluralistic and changing world in which Christian theology is now forged. If God is radically mysterious, and thus "all talk of God . . . indirect,"[82] no one religious tradition is privileged over another, except insofar as pragmatic criteria such as "fruitfulness," "helpfulness," or "disclosive power" suggest so. Even that may be a short-lived matter; for by definition theology is a "heuristic" venture, constantly in flux: "Each theologian can only try to identify as clearly as possible the perspective from which she or he reflects, the tradition out of which he or she comes, and the sensibility which prompts one chosen perspective rather than another."[83] All theology is context-bound, fallible, contestible. Consequently, according to McFague,

what we can say with any assurance about the character of Christian faith is very little and . . . even that will be highly contested. Christian faith is . . . most basically a claim that the universe is neither indifferent nor malevolent but that there is a power (and a personal power at that) which is on the side of life and its fulfillment. Moreover, the Christian believes that we have some clues for fleshing out this claim in the life, death, and appearances of Jesus of Nazareth. Nevertheless, each generation must venture, through an analysis of what fulfillment could and must mean for its own time, the best way to express that claim.[84]

It is, however, precisely the minimalist, fluctuating, and indirect nature of what can be said about God in McFague's view that provides her with a confident platform for feminist change. Unlike Daly, who pessimistically rejects Christian tradition as ineradicably patriarchal, or Schüssler Fiorenza, who regards feminist biblical reclamation as a highly complex hermeneutical undertaking, McFague's theological method assumes as normative a constant will-to-change, and an imaginative freedom to shift the "metaphors" for God as new challenges confront the churches. Because theology is "*mostly* fiction,"[85] a problem such as patriarchy can be met with a willed redirection of modes of theistic reflection.

The methodological tool that McFague uses to express the capacity for such redirection is *metaphor*. In *Metaphorical Theology* (1982) she argues that the central (and irreducible) value of a metaphor as a means of conveying theological truth is peculiarly appropriate not only for a contemporary, postmodern sensibility, but true also to Jesus's original mode of communication, and to the great Protestant tradition of anti-idolatry. Here she draws attention to what she sees as a crucial point of connection between metaphor and parable. Jesus spoke in parables, in indirect, allusive speech that called forth commitment to the "Kingdom"; his parables "assume a nonbelieving or secular attitude on the part of their audience; they stress the discontinuity between our ways and the ways of the kingdom; they focus on the dissimilarity, incongruity, and tension between the assumptions and expectations of their characters and another set of assumptions and expectations identified with the kingdom."[86] Likewise, says McFague, with a somewhat bold generalization, the Protestant tradition is less inclined to make "analogical" or "symbolic" statements about God than the Catholic, because such modes of speech assume "a profound *similarity* beneath the surface dissimilarities",[87] whereas "the Protestant sensibility tends to see dissimilarity."[88]

Metaphor, according to McFague, is a form of expression uniquely suited to guarding this sense of dissimilarity between the human and the Divine. "The essence of metaphor," she writes in her later book *Models of God*, "is precisely the refusal to identify human constructions with divine reality."[89] Metaphor takes an idea from one context and applies it in another: It is "a word or phrase used *in*appropriately," and thus it "always has the character of 'is' and 'is not.'" Moreover, in cases (like theology) where we attempt to describe the indescribable, "the idea of metaphor as unsubstitutable is winning acceptance: what a metaphor expresses cannot be said directly or apart from it, for if it could be, one would have said it directly."[90]

It is for these reasons that McFague sees metaphorical theology as the only answer to the charges of "idolatry" and "irrelevance" in contemporary religious language.[91] Religious language can be "revitalized" through new metaphor, thereby gesturing out to the unknown God; it can also, and simultaneously, purge itself of sexism and nonecological sensibilities, because "Language that supports hierarchical, dualistic, external, unchanging, atomistic, anthropocentric, and deterministic ways of understanding . . . is not appropriate *for our time*."[92] McFague makes a further distinction important for her case: Whereas metaphors come and go and regularly become "dead," a *model* is "a metaphor with 'staying power.'"[93]

In *Metaphorical Theology*, McFague devotes her last chapter to a critical assessment of the notion of God as "father." The metaphor of the "father" God is clearly a "model" that has served the Christian tradition for centuries; yet it was, according to McFague (displaying a different emphasis from either Daly or Schüssler Fiorenza) not without value—"a *good* model gone astray."[94] (Italics added.) Surveying the earlier literature of feminist theology on this issue, McFague distances herself from the separatist feminist solution represented by Mary Daly's embracing of Goddess worship in *Gyn/Ecology*. She argues that "Daly's extreme position suggests two significant problems with contemporary Goddess religion in general: its embrace of stereotypical feminine virtues, which becomes a new form of 'biology is destiny,' and its lack of a critical dimension in its elevation of women as savior of self and world."[95] McFague's own proposal at this point is considerably less radical. She does not, even for today, decry the use of "father" for God altogether (and she acknowledges Jesus's own use of "Abba"); but she suggests that we now focus on alternative, maternal images, bearing in mind that none of these images are "meant to *describe* God so much as *to suggest the new quality of relationship* being offered."[96] Her solution at this point is to draw attention to neglected strands of tradition that support "feminine" imagery for God, and which in turn "give credence not to a patriarchal, but to a parental model with shared characteristics of motherhood and fatherhood."[97] She throws out the suggestion in closing that the metaphor of God's "friendship" might, however, prove more fruitful than even this (supposedly) equitable solution.[98]

In McFague's more celebrated *Models of God* (which won the 1988 American Academy of Religion Award for Excellence, an indication of its acclaim and influence), these themes are developed and somewhat recast. The *three* preferred metaphors for God that now come to the fore are "mother," "lover," and "friend," with the underlying perception that the earth be seen as "God's body." Only a shift of imaginative reflection such as this, McFague argues, can rescue us from nuclear nightmare or ecological disaster: "What is needed is attention to the needs of one's own time."[99] God must not be seen any more as possessing "domination and control," but rather as sharing with us in an activity of "co-creation."[100] However, unlike Gordon Kaufman (on whom in other respects McFague's argument is dependent), McFague wishes to defend the continuing use of *personal* metaphors for God. "Does a view of God as personal entail the ideas of separation, dualism, and control?" she asks, and responds that the problem lies not in personal metaphors as such, but in the wrong ones ("king, ruler, lord, master").[101] What is needed is a reassessment of the "destabilizing, inclusive, non-hierarchical vision" that Jesus presented, and a new version of the "Christian paradigm" for today that will be true to these features.[102]

In her choice of "mother" as her first key metaphor for God, McFague evidences a shift from the way she had argued in *Metaphorical Theology*. More aware now of the dangers of merely shoring up oppressive cultural stereotypes by importing the so-called "feminine" into the Divine, McFague argues that she is interested in God as "female" (metaphorically speaking) rather than as "feminine." Here she wishes to draw

attention to the *power* of the maternal image as life-giving:

It is from [the physical act of giving birth] that the model derives its power, for here it joins the reservoir of the great symbols of life and of life's continuity: blood, water, breath, sex, and food. In the acts of conception, gestation, and birth all are involved, and it is therefore no surprise that these symbols became the center of most religions, including Christianity, for they have the power to express the renewal and transformation of life—the "second birth"—because they are the basis of our "first birth." And yet, at least in Christianity, our first birth has been strangely neglected. . . . One reason is surely that Christianity, alienated as it always has been from female sexuality, has been willing to accept the second, "spiritual," renewal of existence in the birth metaphor, but not the first, "physical," coming into existence.[103]

But acceptance of the model of God as "mother" need be no saccharine or sentimental affair, she argues. The maternal God is also "judge," the one who "establishes justice" and promotes an ethic of "care."[104] McFague perceives herself here as still not *ruling out* talk of God as "father," but as destabilizing the oppressive dimensions of that model by shifting attention onto the maternal "bodiliness" of God's relation to the world. Whether she has thereby undermined a "feminine" stereotype or merely given it another form is obviously a question for debate.

McFague's promotion of the model of God as "lover" rescues materials from the mystical strands of Christianity in order to promote the idea of God's care for us as an *erotic* "saving" and "healing." Again the "bodiliness" of the Divine is to the fore in her working out of these themes, although she is careful to stress that what is at stake here is not so much (physical) "sex" but the "value" that God bestows on us by so desiring us.[105] Her reexamination of the model of "friend" admits that the "Aristotelian" tradition of elitist friendship between *equals* cannot of course apply to the God-human relation, but that the Christian tradition of Jesus as "friend" gives the lie to any "exclusive, individualistic, and élitist relationship."[106] The final and underlying model (only briefly sketched in this book), of the world as "God's body," has since become the subject of a further monograph by McFague, in which she extends her analysis of the destructiveness of a divine "mastery" model for the planet's ecological future.[107]

McFague's undertaking as a feminist systematician embracing new imaginative "models" for God is not without paradoxes and points of contention. There is, for instance, a *prima facie* tension between her insistence on the one hand that we can make no "identity" statements at all about God, and her analysis of "metaphor" as involving an "is" statement as well as an "is not." Does not the "is" dimension suggest some (significant, if elusive) *realist* claim about God that the metaphor is attempting to disclose? There is also the puzzle of the coexistence of another two lines of thought, not easily combined: on the one hand the appeal to the "Protestant" sense of a profound "dissimilarity" between God and creation as a justification for the centrality of metaphor, on the other the insistence on the *rejection* of all "dualism" or "hierarchy" between the divine and human worlds. There is also the more puzzling and practical question of whether metaphors and models for God can be changed in the way McFague suggests—by a kind of Promethean act of will; for even she admits at one point that "No one, of course, can create images of God; religious symbols are born and die in a culture for complex reasons."[108] What if the patriarchal God lives on insidiously in the unconscious realm even when "he" has been intentionally and consciously dethroned as an outmoded theological "model"? And what if the insidiousness of patriarchal thought resides not merely in the wrong (albeit changeable) "metaphors" for God, but in a deep-rooted and morphological connection between the male body and the structure of language? It is to these more far-reaching challenges to feminist theology from French Freudian thought that we now, finally, turn.

LUCE IRIGARAY: FEMINIST PHILOSOPHY AND THE CRITIQUE OF FREUD

The inclusion of the French feminist Luce Irigaray (1930–   ) in this chapter may occasion some surprise. Irigaray's interdisciplinary capacities range wide, through psychology, psychoanalysis, philosophy, religion, and literature; but she would never describe herself as a theologian, nor is she a Christian believer. Nonetheless, the influence she has come to wield on English-speaking feminist theologians is profound and still growing;[109] and the questions she raises for theological feminism press at points that none of the other types of feminist theology discussed in this chapter confront in quite the same way. This brief (and necessarily overschematic) treatment of her thought will, therefore, concentrate on just a few areas of her thinking that are currently generative for feminist theology and that represent systematic options not otherwise considered in this survey.

Luce Irigaray was born in Belgium and received her initial tertiary education there; but after gaining a masters degree in philosophy and literature from Louvain, and teaching for a while in high school, she transferred to Paris in 1959 to begin another rigorous set of higher degrees in philosophy, linguistics, and psychoanalysis.[110] It was at the *École freudienne* (the Freudian School of psychoanalysis in Paris) that she was to come into notorious conflict with the thought of the dominant intellectual figure there, Jacques Lacan (1901–1981). Lacan's influential reworking of Freud's psychoanalytic theory accords high significance to the so-called "mirror-phase" of a child's development—the moment when, on seeing himself (*sic*) for the first time in a mirror and recognizing an independent being, the child becomes conscious of his distinction from the mother. This is also the moment, according to Lacan, of the child's primary initiation into what he calls the "symbolic" realm, the "male" sphere of speech and classification (logical distinction, analytic thought, and clarity of expression); it is, moreover, the phallus that supremely represents such order and signification symbolically, in Lacan's view.[111]

Irigaray's second dissertation in psychology (her first was a well-received study of senile dementia) took on Lacan's theorizing about "male" speech and the phallus and subjected it to a daring feminist critique in terms of the history of Western philosophy (*Speculum of the Other Woman*, 1974; Eng. trans., 1985).[112] Without fundamentally undermining Lacan's connection of "masculinity" with philosophical thinking, Irigaray here argues, in her characteristically elusive prose, that such a connection has been wrought at the cost of women's distinctive identity: "In *Speculum* [she writes later of this work] I interpret and critique how the philosophical subject, historically masculine, has reduced all otherness to a relationship with himself—as complement, projection, flip-side, instrument, nature—inside his world, his horizons."[113]

Without explaining her theoretic framework in advance (that would presumably be in itself to bow to the masculine "symbolic"), Irigaray launches first in this book into a deliciously subversive spoof of Freud's lecturing style: "'Ladies and Gentlemen . . . Throughout history people have knocked their heads against the riddle of the nature of femininity— . . . Nor will *you* have escaped worrying over this problem—those of you who are men; to those of you who are women this will not apply—you are the problem.'"[114] Relentlessly she goes on to expose the gendered presumption of Freud's (and no less Lacan's) method: that woman is fundamentally marked by *lack* ("penis envy"); that the social order presumed by psychoanalysis makes little acknowledgment of the significance of the mother; that the "mirror" (*speculum*) held up to a woman detects only a "hole." From here, the second half of the book turns to an exposé of how the generic male has similarly repressed the "feminine" in Western philosophical thought. Thus the allegory of the cave in Plato's *Republic* book VII (in which Plato describes the progress of the mind away from a shackled and delusive life of darkness in a cave toward the light of the sun, which represents achieved rationality, the "Form of the Good") is given an intriguing feminist rereading. With exhaustive textual detail, Irigaray shows how the "cave" here can convincingly be read as the maternal womb from which Plato is demanding that masculinist reason detach itself, simultaneously denying its source. What then is left to the woman who would resist such suppression of her distinctiveness? In Freud's terms, it would seem, as Irigaray puts it, "*Hysteria is all she has left,*" since "the game is controlled by the Phallus's mastery of the sexual economy."[115] But in *Speculum* Irigaray then deliberately elides this despised feminine "hysteria" with the discourses of the Christian mystical tradition, which have also so evidently and *powerfully* chafed at the edges of normal rational thought. Hence a bridge is built between ostensibly repressive psychoanalytical categories for women and the liberative potential of a particular kind of God talk.

In her essay in *Speculum* punningly entitled "La Mystérique" (simultaneously evoking "hysteria," "mystery," and "mysticism"), Irigaray first suggests how woman might thus evade the rule of the Phallus:

La mystérique: this is how one might refer to what, within a still theological onto-logical perspective is called mystic language or discourse. Consciousness still imposes such names to signify that other scene, off-stage, that it finds *cryptic*. This is the place where consciousness is no longer master, where, to its extreme confusion, it sinks into a dark night that is also fire and flames. This is the place where "she"— and in some cases he, if he follows "her" lead—speaks about the dazzling glare which comes from the source of light that has been logically repressed, about "subject" and "Other" flowing out into an embrace of fire that mingles one term into another, about contempt for form as such, about mistrust for understanding as an obstacle along the path of jouissance and mistrust for the dry desolation of reason. . . . This is the only place in the history of the West in which woman speaks and acts so publicly. What is more, it is for/by woman that man dares to enter the place, to descend into it, condescend to it, even if he gets burned in the attempt.[116]

Alluding strongly to a famous passage in Teresa of Ávila's *Life* (Ch. 29, where Teresa has a vision of being pierced by an angel's burning spear), Irigaray goes on to underscore the ironic connection in such mystical literature of woman's apparent self-loss and her unique erotic connection (*jouissance*) with the divine:

How strange is the economy of this specular(riza)tion of woman, who in her mirror seems ever to refer back to a transcendence. Who moves away (for) who comes near, who groans to be separated from the one who holds her closest in his embrace. But who also calls for the dart which, while piercing through her body, will with the same stroke tear out her entrails. Thus "God" will prove to have been her best lover, since he separates her from herself only by that space of her jouissance where she finds Him/herself.[117]

Sometimes, then, Irigaray can write of "God" as if God is a revelatory *gift* to woman in mystical encounter, escaping and undermining rational ("symbolic") attempts to master "Him." But elsewhere (and indeed more famously) she writes, in explicitly Feuerbachian style, of woman's need to project or construct her *own* "feminine" divine. In her essay "Divine Women," in *Sexes and Genealogies* (1987; Eng. trans., 1993),[118] Irigaray argues that "as long as woman lacks a divine made in her image she cannot establish her subjectivity or achieve a goal of her own."[119] For, "If we are to escape slavery it is not enough to destroy the master. Only the divine offers us freedom—enjoins it upon us. Only a God constitutes a rallying point for us that can let us free—nothing else."[120]

What then must the "feminine" Divine look like? For Irigaray this must first and foremost be a matter of the celebration of fleshliness, of earth, of sensuality—a deepened, gendered, perception of the implications of "incarnation"; only from this can arise a new freedom for women to love

one another and to redeem the mother-daughter relationship, especially, from the taint of phallo-centric competitiveness:

Feuerbach claims that we are sick today because God is sick. . . .

In our tradition hasn't God always been sick because he never married? Except in the forms of annunciation our God never speaks to us of the joy, the splendor, the fulfillment that lies in the alliance of the sexes. . . .

This divinity of woman is still hidden, veiled. Could it be what "man" seeks even as he rapes it?

We women, sexed according to our gender, lack a God to share, a word to share and to become. Defined as the often dark, even occult mother-substance of the word of men, we are indeed in need of our *subject*. . . .

To be the term of the other is nothing enviable. It paralyzes us in our becoming. As divinity or goddess of and for man, we are deprived of our own ends and means. It is essential that we be God *for ourselves* so that we can be divine for the other, not idols, fetishes, symbols that have already been outlined and determined. . . . It is equally essential that we should be daughter-gods in the relationship with our mothers, and that we cease to hate our mothers in order to enter into submissiveness to the father-husband. We cannot love if we have no memory of a native passiveness in relation to our mothers, of our primitive attachment to hers, and hers to us.[121]

Irigaray's suggestions about the need for a "feminine" divinity remain, in this essay, somewhat elusive. What is the metaphysical status of this "divine"? Is it, as in McFague's Neo-Kantian view, merely an imaginative construction, devised by contemporary women for particular, pragmatist, ends? It seems not. Elsewhere, when Irigaray writes of the "sensible transcendental" (that is, the divine realm that represents the world of the flesh and the senses), it becomes clearer that she has a more substantial ontological claim in mind, one—like Hegel's—in which new manifestations of Spirit come into being precisely (and only) through human cooperation:

This creation would be our [*sc.* women's] opportunity, from the humblest detail of everyday life to the "grandest," by means of the opening of a *sensible transcendental* that comes into being through us, of which *we would be* the mediators and bridges. Not only in mourning for the dead God of Nietzsche, not waiting passively for the god to come, but by conjuring him up among us, within us, as resurrection and as transfiguration of blood, of flesh, through a language and an ethics that is ours.[122]

This notion of the "transfiguration of flesh" causes Irigaray to recast, if only implicitly for the most part, the specifically *trinitarian* understanding of God in the Christian tradition. Here she is perhaps at her most creative and suggestive theologically—although largely unwittingly. Starting from an analysis of female sexual desire, she insists that even the distinctive morphology of the female genitals bespeaks an inherent relationality and fluidity in female sexuality. The "lips" of the vagina, being dual, mean that the "other" is intrinsically recognized ("the other is part of her"); but women's desire cannot even be constrained by duality: "always at least double, [it] is in fact plural. . . . Woman has sex organs just about everywhere."[123] For Irigaray, the "mucous membrane," especially, achieves a profound significance as a medium "living, porous, fluid . . . to achieve communion as well as difference."[124] What, then, does this analysis of female sexuality have to do with God *as Trinity?* The answer lies in the way it may image, in the sensuous realm, what is true of God eternally: relationality, difference in unity, fluidity of response. Such a connection finally becomes explicit in Irigaray's dense little essay, "Questions to Emmanuel Lévinas." Commenting critically (and perhaps unfairly) on Lévinas's ethics and its response to "otherness," she writes:

He knows nothing of communion in pleasure. Lévinas does not even seem to have experienced the transcendence of the other which becomes an immanent ecstasy. . . . The other is "close" to him in "duality." This autistic, egological, solitary love does not correspond to the shared outpouring, to the loss of boundary of the skin into the mucous membranes of the body, leaving the circle which encloses my solitude to meet in a shared space, a shared breath. . . . In this relation we are at least three, each of which is irreducible to any of the others: you, me and our creation [*oeuvre*], that ecstasy of ourself in us [*de nous en nous*] . . . prior to any "child."[125]

Thus it is that Irigaray's perception of the "fertility of the caress," her analysis of the inherent relationality that female sexuality contributes to the act of love, provides a blueprint of why *divine* love must, also, be "at least three." It is as if the famous moment in Augustine's *De Trinitate,* Book VIII, where Augustine finally rejects the analogy for the Trinity of "the lover, the loved one, and the love that binds" as inadequately bound to "flesh,"[126] is here revisited and redeemed: For Irigaray, bodies, too, indeed bodies precisely as lovers, must bear the imprints of the divine trinitarian nature.

It will be clear that Irigaray's religious thought stands in some interesting points of contrast and tension with the other authors surveyed in this chapter. As we have already noted, there are points of resemblance to McFague's program for reformulating the notion of God, but on closer examination the philosophical presumptions of the two women differ significantly. There is also a superficial parallelism with Daly's thought, granted Irigaray's shared interest in the distinctiveness of women's bodies and thought forms, and the delight they both take in subversive spoofing of the great Western "classics." But on reflection it is clear that Irigaray is no radical feminist in the sense discussed earlier. She is *understanding* of Daly's desire to withdraw into a same-sex group ("may be . . . Mary Daly and others could do little else in their efforts to save their lives, their truth, and their own way"[127]); but she regards this ploy as ultimately a counsel of despair: "Personally I prefer to try everything in an effort to preserve the dimension of a sexual mix because that difference . . . safeguard[s] . . . a notion of the divine not defined as the result of a narcissistic and imperialist inflation of sameness."[128] So

Irigaray is not a "separatist" feminist; nor is she obviously a physiological "essentialist," as is often charged against her. To be sure, her theoretical framework (and her French language, as mentioned earlier) do not distinguish between "sex" and "gender", as did earlier American feminist theory. But as postmodernist influences occasion a re-blurring of those categories in North American feminist theory (a subsuming of "sex" into the historical vicissitudes of "gender"), Irigaray's thought appears the more current: Her talk of female desire, of female bodies, is, after all, talk about their (historically accumulated) symbolic "morphology," not of some *physiologically* determined essence. Elisabeth Schüssler Fiorenza, however, distrusts this interpretation and balks entirely at Irigaray's central interest in *sexual* "difference": "Irigaray's discourse seeks to 'divinize' sexual difference," she charges," . . . whereas my own discourse seeks to demystify the cultural and theological constructs of femininity and masculinity that are dualistic, heterosexist, and essentialist as ideological obfuscations of the multiplicative structures of patriarchal domination."[129] For Schüssler Fiorenza, even Irigaray's concern with sexual "genres" is a sign of "reinscrib[ing] the cultural feminine. . . . Rather than posit a structure of binary male-female domination," she counters, "one must theorize patriarchy as a shifting pyramidal political structure of dominance and subordination, stratified by gender, race, class, sexuality, religion, nation, culture, and other historical formations of domination."[130]

If Schüssler Fiorenza's reading of Irigaray is unsympathetic, the corollary is also true. In an extended review essay of *In Memory of Her*, Irigaray charges Schüssler Fiorenza with obliterating any interest in sexual differentation for the sake of "equality"; that smacks of a covert "identification with the generic masculine," she argues.[131] (She had earlier made a similar critique of de Beauvoir, urging that attaining sexual rights before the law can mean little unless women "can find some value *in being women*. . . ."[132] [Italics added.]) Moreover, Irigaray also finds in Schüssler

Fiorenza's work a "reductive" tendency to subsume "women" under the "socioeconomic" category of "poor among the poor." Whereas Schüssler Fiorenza is committed to "liberation" from poverty and multiple oppressions, Irigaray seeks "respect for the incarnation of all *bodies* (men's and women's) as potentially divine."[133] (Italics added.)

But are these differing viewpoints and emphases inherently incompatible? Schüssler Fiorenza and Irigaray agree, after all, on the crucial significance of the acknowledgment of "difference"; it is just that they construe "difference" *differently*. For Schüssler Fiorenza, the explication of the multiple and complex layers of ("different") oppressions that women, worldwide, confront, leads (ironically, no doubt) to a certain *repression* of concern with "female sexuality"—a subject all too easily hijacked in her view into a dangerous "valorization of the feminine." For Irigaray, conversely, "difference" is fundamentally "sexuate"; and her concern to expound the symbolic, psychoanalytic, and philosophcial ramifications of this insight makes her uneasy about American feminism's consistent concern for "equality", as well as relatively heedless of the entanglements of race and class with problems of sexual justice. Where, then, does this dilemma leave current feminist theory, especially in its impact on theological thinking? And what will be the abiding effects of feminist thought on the traditions of Western Christian theology, granted the different approaches and theoretical presumptions we have by now surveyed? To this speculative question we turn briefly in closing.

CONCLUSION: "DIFFERENCE" IN FEMINIST THEOLOGY

In this chapter the development of theological feminisms from the 1960s to the 1990s has been traced through the lens of four outstanding, and contrasting, exponents. As the different methodological tools and philosophical presumptions of these authors have been described, certain irreducible tensions, or "antinomies," between the varying projects have become evident. Arguably these are tensions that will endure (at least until the "systemic social injustice" suffered by women is finally routed); because the tensions depend on mutually conflicting emphases that feminisms—including theological feminisms, in their distinctive mode—must necessarily confront and negotiate. On the one hand there is what may be dubbed the antimony of "equality and difference," already highlighted as a point of disagreement between the thought of Elisabeth Schlüssler Fiorenza and Luce Irigaray. That is, is feminism to aim primarily for an acknowledgment of women's "equality" with men, or is it more important to explore their "difference"? The answer is surely that *both* must be accounted for; but if one's methodological tools are primarily sociopolitical, on the one hand, or primarily psychoanalytical, on the other, then divergent priorities will inevitably rise to the fore. If the complexifications that religion (rightly) brings to the picture are added to this, the questions of "equality" and "difference" are cast in a new light: "Equality" is not merely secular jostling for "rights," but a vision of "basileia" blessedness before God;[134] whereas "difference" allows the possibility of exploring *both* the complexity of female sexual desire's entanglement with desire for the Divine (something secular feminism would never entertain), *and* the endless variations of combined oppressions that offend against the goal of divine justice.

Another, and overlapping, antinomy that has emerged is that between what may be called "autonomy" and "heteronomy." Feminism in one mode is obviously concerned to enable the independent authority and self-possession of women; yet it also rightly explores the nexus of human dependencies, a factor often overlooked or merely taken for granted by masculinist thought. If, again, these goals have so far been wrenched apart in disparate schools of theological feminism (Schüssler Fiorenza and Daly, in their different ways, stressing the need for women's independence; McFague and Irigaray underscoring dependencies on maternality or earth), it is again unclear whether such a choice should ultimately be forced. Likewise, a third, and final antinomy, between what may be called "locality" and "universality," has caused a more painful theoretical split between those forms of theological feminism that ardently embrace postmodernism and thus tend to eschew the language of universal "women's" rights, and those that continue to resist or moderate this philosophical trend.

Feminist theology, in sum, is no unified movement, although its vociferous detractors like to imagine so.[135] Its primary goals may be as varied as the eradication of systemic social injustice, the raising up of goddess religion, the maintenance of ecological stability, or the elucidation of female desire. As it has turned to address its entanglement with the open sore of racial discrimination in North America (see Chapter Fourteen), so also it has been forced even to reexamine the tenets of liberal Christianity that enabled its inception: If "womanist" theology can unembarrassedly embrace the power of the Cross, for instance, or invoke the possibility of active divine intervention, white feminist theology must pause and take stock once more of its metaphysical presumptions. It is no longer clear that the "absence" of God-self (as in McFague's metaphorical theology) is a foundational tenet of all theological feminism, indispensable as it proved in her particular program of feminist reform.

What all feminist (and womanist) theology has in common, however, is its incisive critical analysis of the patriarchal bias of the traditional Christian symbol system. Once this is acknowledged, no retreat is possible; there is simply a choice between a range of differing methodological responses, such as this chapter has outlined, or else a form of blinkered denial. Just as the latter part of the nineteenth century confronted Western Christianity with unavoidable choices about its relation to historical and scientific method, so the late twentieth century has laid the feminist question, insistently and irrevocably, at the door of Christian theology—for its profound critique and its equally profound renewal.

NOTES

1. A reprinted edition is available: Elizabeth Cady Stanton, *The Women's Bible* (Edinburgh, 1985).

2. The significance of Vatican II for early feminist theology is illuminatingly discussed in Ann Loades, "Feminist Theology," in *The Modern Theologians*, II, ed. David F. Ford (Oxford, 1989), pp. 238–240.

3. Valerie Saiving Goldstein, "The Human Situation: A Feminine View," *The Journal of Religion*, 40 (1960), 100–112.

4. See Janet Radcliffe Richards, *The Sceptical Feminist* (London, 1991), pp. 13–14.

5. Useful surveys of different types of secular feminist theory, drawn upon in this account, are provided in Alison M. Jaggar, *Feminist Politics and Human Nature* (Totowa, N.J., 1983), and Rosemarie Tong, *Feminist Thought: A Comprehensive Introduction* (London, 1989).

6. See Tong, ibid., p. 95.

7. See Mary Daly, *The Church and the Second Sex* (Boston, 1968; 2nd ed., 1975; 3rd ed., 1985). For such language of liberal feminism, see the 1985 ed., pp. 53, 223, etc.

8. Ibid., p. 21 (in the "Feminist Postchristian Introduction," added originally for the 1975 ed.).

9. See Daly's autobiographical *Outercourse: The Be-Dazzling Voyage* (San Francisco, 1992), Ch. 2.

10. Ibid., p. 59.

11. Daly, *The Church and the Second Sex*, p. 10.

12. Ibid., p. 74.

13. Ibid., p. 223.

14. See the new materials added to the 1975 and 1985 editions: ibid., pp xi–xxviii, 5–51.

15. See Daly, *Outercourse*, pp. 137–140.

16. Mary Daly, *Beyond God the Father* (Boston, 1973), p. 19.

17. Ibid., pp. 33–34.

18. See ibid., pp. 23, 103 f.

19. See Mary Daly, *Gyn/Ecology: The Metaethics of Radical Feminism* (London, 1979), pp. 94–95.

20. Daly, *Beyond God the Father*, p. 41.

21. Ibid., p. 73.

22. See Daly, *Outercourse*, pp. 152–153.

23. Daly, *Gyn/Ecology*, pp. xi, xii.

24. See Mary Daly and Jane Caputi, *Websters' First New Intergalactic Wickedary of the English Language* (Boston, 1987).

25. Daly, *Gyn/Ecology*, pp. 107 ff.

26. Ibid., p. 39.

27. Ibid., pp. 79–83.

28. Ibid., p. 38.

29. Ibid., p. 75.

30. Mary Daly, *Pure Lust: Elemental Feminist Philosophy* (London, 1984), p. 2.

31. Ibid., p. 3.

32. See Daly, *Outercourse*, p. 9.

33. Elisabeth Schüssler Fiorenza, *Discipleship of Equals* (New York, 1994), p. 284.

34. For her understanding of "the sex-gender system," see Elisabeth Schüssler Fiorenza, *But She Said* (Boston, 1992), pp. 105–114; also her *Jesus: Miriam's Child, Sophia's Prophet* (New York, 1994), pp. 34 ff.

35. For this point, see Elisabeth Schüssler Fiorenza, "Changing the Paradigms," *The Christian Century* (September 5–12, 1990), pp. 799–800; also her *But She Said*, p. xiv; and Elisabeth Schüssler Fiorenza, ed., *The Power of Naming* (New York, 1996), p. 355, n. 6.

36. For the meaning of "kyriarchy," see Schüssler Fiorenza, *But She Said*, pp. 8, 117, etc. For the use of "wo/men," see Schüssler Fiorenza, ed., *The Power of Naming*, pp. xiii, xxxv, n. 1.

37. See Schüssler Fiorenza, *Discipleship of Equals*, p. 340, for the claim that French feminism, at least in its American reception, tends to "reinscribe the cultural feminine."

38. See Schüssler Fiorenza, "Changing the Paradigms," p. 798.

39. Elisabeth Schüssler Fiorenza, *Der vergessene Partner: Grundlagen, Tatsachen und Möglichkeiten der beruflichen Mitarbeit der Frau in der Heilssorge der Kirche* (Düsseldorf, 1964); see also her *Discipleship of Equals*, Ch. 1, for a section of this dissertation translated into English.

40. See Schüssler Fiorenza, *Discipleship of Equals*, Chs. 2, 6, 10.

41. See Schüssler Fiorenza, "Changing the Paradigms," p. 797.

42. Ibid., p. 797.

43. Ibid.

44. Ibid., p. 798.

45. Ibid., p. 799.

46. Elisabeth Schüssler Fiorenza, *In Memory of Her: A Feminist Theological Reconstruction of Christian Origins* (London, 1983), p. xiii.

47. Ibid., p. xiv.

48. Ibid.

49. Ibid., p. 41.

50. Ibid., p. 31.

51. Ibid., p. 92.

52. Ibid., p. 103.

53. Ibid., p. 118.

54. Ibid., p. 132; for the discussion of Luke 7:35, see, p. 132.

55. Ibid., p. 150.

56. Ibid., p. 212.

57. See ibid., p. 229, and Ch. 6 throughout.

58. See ibid., pp. 233–236, for the contrast with Paul; and part III in general.

59. Elisabeth Schüssler Fiorenza, *Bread Not Stone: The Challenge of Feminist Biblical Interpretation* (Boston, 1984); some of the essays in this book were written before *In Memory of Her*, despite the later publication date.

60. Schüssler Fiorenza, *But She Said*.

61. See Schüssler Fiorenza, *Bread Not Stone*, Ch. 5, countering the influence of Leopold von Ranke; however, interestingly, *In Memory of Her*, p. xvi, claims through feminist scholarship to provide a "more accurate" picture of "Christian beginnings" than previously available.

62. Schüssler Fiorenza, *In Memory of Her*, p. 350.

63. See Schüssler Fiorenza, *But She Said*, Ch. 4.

64. See ibid., pp. 5–6.

65. Schüssler Fiorenza, *Jesus: Miriam's Child, Sophia's Prophet*.

66. Ibid., p. 48.

67. Ibid., p. 112; on atonement and sacrifice, see pp. 104–107.

68. Ibid., pp. 121–122; see the important appeal to Sojourner Truth earlier, pp. 57–59, on the unmasking of "kyriarchal" christology.

69. Ibid., pp. 20–24.

70. In all her work, from *In Memory of Her* on, Schüssler Fiorenza is clear that "Sophia" is not just a balancing complement to a "masculine" notion of God. See, e.g., *In Memory of Her*, pp. 130 ff.

71. Witness the essays from a variety of countries gathered in Schüssler Fiorenza, *The Power of Naming*.

72. See especially Sallie McFague, *Speaking in Parables: A Study in Metaphor and Theology* (Philadelphia, 1975): and her *Metaphorical Theology: Models of God in Religious Language* (Philadelphia, 1982).

73. See Sallie McFague, *Models of God: Theology for an Ecological, Nuclear Age* (Philadelphia, 1987), p. 85. Note also the attack on individualism throughout this work (e.g., p. 86).

74. Ibid., pp. xiii–xiv.

75. Ibid., p. ix.

76. Ibid., p. x.

77. Ibid., p. xiv.

78. See McFague, *Metaphorical Theology*, p. 155, for an explicit appeal to Saiving; and Ch. 5, throughout, for the discussion of gender characteristics.

79. McFague *Models of God*, p. 99.

80. McFague expresses her indebtedness to Kaufman in various places; see, e.g., *Models of God*, pp. 195–196, n. 13.

81. Ibid., p. 196.

82. See ibid., p. 34.

83. McFague, *Metaphorical Theology*, p. viii.

84. McFague, *Models of God*, pp. x–xi.

85. Ibid., p. xi.

86. McFague, *Metaphorical Theology*, p. 15; also see McFague's earlier *Speaking in Parables*.

87. McFague, *Metaphorical Theology*, p. 12.

88. Ibid., p. 13.

89. McFague, *Models of God*, p. 22.

90. Ibid., p. 33.

91. See McFague, *Metaphorical Theology*, Ch. 1.

92. McFague, *Models of God*, p. 13.

93. Ibid., p. 34.

94. McFague, *Metaphorical Theology*, p. 145.

95. Ibid., p. 159.

96. Ibid., p. 166.

97. Ibid., p. 177.

98. Ibid., pp. 177–192.

99. McFague, *Models of God*, p. 14.

100. Ibid., pp. 16, 17.

101. Ibid., pp. 18, 19.

102. See ibid., p. 48.

103. Ibid., p. 105.

104. Ibid., pp. 118, 119.

105. Ibid., pp. 127–128.

106. Ibid., p. 164.

107. Sallie McFague, *The Body of God: An Ecological Theology* (Minneapolis, 1993).

108. McFague, *Models of God*, p. 20.

109. See, e.g., the volume devoted to theology's engagement with French feminism: C. W. Maggie Kim, Susan M. St. Ville, and Susan M. Simonaitis, ed., *Transfigurations: Theology and the French Feminists* (Minneapolis, 1993); and the important essay by Serene Jones, "Divining Women: Irigaray and Feminist Theologies," *Yale French Studies* 87 (1995), 42–67.

110. See Katherine Stephenson, "Luce Irigaray (1930–   )," in *French Women Writers*, ed. Eva Martin Sartori and Dorothy Wynne Zimmerman (New York, 1991), pp. 229–243, for an introductory biographical essay on Irigaray, along with a bibliography.

111. For an introduction to Lacan's thought, see Juliet Mitchell and Jacqueline Rose, ed., *Feminine Sexuality: Jacques Lacan and the école freudienne* (New York, 1982).

112. Luce Irigaray, *Speculum of the Other Woman*, trans. Gillian C. Gill (Ithaca, N.Y., 1985).

113. Luce Irigaray, "The Question of the Other," *Yale French Studies* 87 (1995), 10.

114. Irigaray, *Speculum*, p. 13.

115. Ibid., pp. 71, 72.

116. Ibid., p. 191.

117. Ibid., p. 201.

118. Luce Irigaray, "Divine Women," in *Sexes and Genealogies*, trans. Gillian C. Gill (New York, 1993), pp. 57–72.

119. Ibid., p. 63.

120. Ibid., p. 68.

121. Ibid., pp. 70, 71.

122. Luce Irigaray, *An Ethics of Sexual Difference*, trans. Carolyn Burke and Gillian C. Gill (Ithaca, N.Y., 1993), p. 129; also see p. 32 for another discussion of the "sensible transcendental."

123. See Elaine Marks and Isabelle de Courtivron, ed., *New French Feminisms: An Anthology* (New York, 1981), pp. 102–103, 104.

124. Irigaray, *Sexes and Genealogies*, p. 65.

125. Luce Irigaray, "Questions to Emmanuel Lévinas," cited in Margaret Whitford, *Luce Irigaray: Philosophy in the Feminine* (London, 1991), pp. 166–167.

126. See Augustine, *De Trinitate*, Book VIII. 14: "Let us tread the flesh underfoot and mount up to the soul." Augustine then turns to the famous "psychological" analogies for the Trinity.

127. See Luce Irigaray, "Equal to Whom?" trans. Robert L. Mazzola, in *differences* 1 (1989), 73.

128. Ibid., pp. 73–74.

129. See Schüssler Fiorenza, *Discipleship of Equals*, p. 11.

130. Ibid., pp. 340, 341.

131. Irigaray, "Equal to Whom?" p. 70; see Schüssler Fiorenza's *riposte* in her *Discipleship of Equals*, pp. 10–12.

132. See Whitford, ed., *The Irigaray Reader* p. 31.

133. Irigaray, "Equal to Whom?" p. 64.

134. See again Schüssler Fiorenza, *Discipleship of Equals*, pp. 11–12.

135. Such an attempt to unify, ridicule, and reject feminist theologies is evidenced in some of the essays in Alvin F. Kimel, ed. *Speaking the Christian God: The Holy Trinity and the Challenge of Feminism* (Grand Rapids, Mich., 1992).

SUGGESTIONS FOR FURTHER READING

The following are excellent introductory guides to the various types of secular feminism:

Jaggar, Alison M. *Feminist Politics and Human Nature* (Totowa, N.J.: Rowman & Littlefield, Publishers, Incorporated 1983). This does not cover French feminisms but contains an excellent discussion of liberal, radical, and socialist feminism (Jaggar is an example of the latter).

Tong, Rosemarie. *Feminist Thought: A Comprehensive Introduction* (London: Westview Press 1989). Tong covers more "types" of secular feminism than Jaggar, including "psychoanalytic" and "postmodern" feminisms.

The following are all excellent introductions to forms of feminist theology. Each of them surveys earlier literature in the field:

Carr, Anne E. *Transforming Grace: Christian Tradition and Women's Experience* (San Francisco: Harper San Francisco 1988).

Hampson, Daphne. *Theology and Feminism* (Oxford: Blackwell Publishers 1990). Hampson is a post-Christian (though theistic) theologian, whose work presents an interesting contrast to the thought of Mary Daly. An extremely challenging book for those who wish to remain Christian as well as feminist; comparison with Ruether and Carr is thus worthwhile.

———, ed. *Swallowing a Fishbone? Feminist Theologians Debate Christianity* (London: S.P.C.K., 1996). Hampson is here in debate with a range of British feminist theologians who have chosen to remain in their churches. Lively and provocative essays.

Hewitt, Marsha Aileen. *Critical Theory of Religion: A Feminist Analysis* (Minneapolis: Augsburg Fortress Publishers 1995). This book brings together critical social theory and feminist theology, and is in debate with Schüssler Fiorenza, Daly, and Ruether.

Ruether, Rosemary Radford. *Sexism and God-Talk: Towards a Feminist Theology* (London: Beacon Press 1983).

The following are two well-known collections of feminist theology, both Christian and post-Christian:

Christ, Carol P., and Judith Plaskow, ed. *Womanspirit Rising: A Feminist Reader in Religion* (San Francisco: Harper San Francisco 1979).

Plaskow, Judith, and Carol P. Christ, ed. *Weaving the Visions: New Patterns in Feminist Spirituality* (San Francisco: Harper San Francisco 1989).

The following are two well-known books in feminist (structuralist) biblical theology. Critical interaction with Trible's work may be found in (e.g.) Schüssler Fiorenza, *In Memory of Her*, and Hampson, *Theology and Feminism*.

Trible, Phyllis. *God and the Rhetoric of Sexuality* (Philadelphia: Augsburg Fortress Publishers 1978).
———. *Texts of Terror: Literary Feminist Readings of Biblical Narratives* (Philadelphia: Augsburg Fortress Publishers 1984).

The following are some recent books on Luce Irigaray as feminist philosopher:

Chanter, Tina. *Ethics of Eros: Irigaray's Rewriting of the Philosophers* (London: Routledge 1995). A detailed account of Irigaray's feminist ethics.
Grosz, Elizabeth. *Sexual Subversions: Three French Feminists* (Sydney: Paul & Company Publishers Consertium, Incorporated 1989). Ch. 4 ("Luce Irigaray and sexual difference") and 5 ("Luce Irigaray and the Ethics of Alterity") are helpful treatments.
Whitford, Margaret. *Luce Irigaray: Philosophy in the Feminine* (London: Routledge 1991). The first full-scale, and still authoritative, treatment of Irigaray's feminist philosophy in English.
———, ed. *The Irigaray Reader* (Oxford: Blackwell Publishers 1991). A useful reader as a starting point in getting to know Irigaray.

The following are illuminating treatments of Irigaray (and other French feminists) as conversation-partners in feminist theology:

Jones, Serene. "Divining Women: Irigaray and Feminist Theologies," *Yale French Studies* 87 (1995), 42–67.
Kim, C. W. Maggie, Susan M. St. Ville, and Susan M. Simonaitis, ed. *Transfigurations: Theology and the French Feminists* (Minneapolis: Augsburg Fortress Publishers 1993).
Ward, Graham. "Divinity and Sexuality: Luce Irigaray and Christology," *Modern Theology* 12 (1996), pp. 221–238.

Chapter Fourteen

Black Theology in America

James H. Cone

In the 1960s an event of major significance occurred within American religious life. African American Christians begin to think systematically about the meaning of the Christian faith in light of their ongoing liberation struggle. This chapter will examine the historical, cultural, and social contexts of Black theology, focusing on the ways that these factors shaped its early formation. This chapter will also discuss the central affirmations of Black theology as they are articulated by its most eloquent spokesperson, James H. Cone. Finally, the chapter will describe the most recent development within the arena of African American religious thought, *womanist theology*. However, before moving to these developments in Black theology, we will examine the contribution of the one person in this century most responsible for articulating the relationship between faith and freedom in the American context, Dr. Martin Luther King, Jr.

MARTIN LUTHER KING, JR. AND THE CIVIL RIGHTS MOVEMENT IN THE UNITED STATES

The magnitude of Martin Luther King, Jr.'s (1929–1968) contribution to the development of black theology is formidable. He was one of the many persons, along with Mrs. Rosa Parks, responsible for bringing the black church into the struggle for civil rights. While many courageous people endured hardship and sacrifice for the cause of equality and justice, the one institution that held the greatest potential for change in African American life, the black church, was almost dormant before the 1960s. The revolutionary result of King's life and work was the arousal of this sleeping giant.

Martin Luther King, Jr. was born into a strong and stable family in Atlanta, Georgia. He was reared in relative comfort and security. His father, a minister affectionately known as "Daddy King," was active in the social and political arena, and had led voter registration drives in Atlanta in the 1930s, two decades before the civil rights movement was born. Despite the obstacles of racism, the strong family in which young Martin was raised was a primary source of his central vision. That vision was "the brotherhood of man." Martin Jr. graduated from Morehouse College (1948), received a bachelor of divinity degree from Crozer Theological Seminary (1951) and a Ph.D. from Boston University (1955). He was drawn into the civil rights movement during the period of his first pastorate at the Dexter Avenue Baptist Church in Montgomery, Alabama.

As King's vision became the inspiration for the civil rights movement, the "family" became the basic metaphor for his understanding of reality, and "brotherhood" was an order of relations that, he believed, would overcome the social barriers that divided America. Although one of the major omissions of King's vision was the inclusion of the unique concerns of African American women, his vision was, despite this, such a morally compelling force that it became institutionalized in the civil rights movement. This movement was the embodiment of King's "the beloved community"—an extension of the family—which King sought throughout his life. He described the civil rights movement as having the qualities and characteristics of an "inner church" or a mystical communion, but it was the metaphor of the family that informed both the societal and ecclesial realities of his vision. For King, the civil rights movement was a familial association, in which love and justice reigned. It was also a quasi-ecclesial association having the characteristics of universality, unity, and saving power. However, the movement was not a church. It was, in part, a testament to the failure of American churches to fulfill their divine mandate to prophesy deliverance to the oppressed. Neither was the movement united around a common creed or confession. It was the inevitable progeny of long-standing injustice and racism. And at the end of this long history, King saw a united humanity, and the final destiny of God's created order was a world open to God's saving grace.

King did not separate his political views from his theological perspective. What he saw as the ideal social and political arrangement flowed from what he believed about the activity of God in history. One could say that, for King, a person's theology and politics were two sides of the same coin. Thus, the corollary to his social vision and worldview was his theology. There were several significant influences on his theology; three of them are rooted in the European American and Asian traditions. The decisive influence on King's thought, however, is African American Christianity itself.

The first influence on King was Liberal theology, which he first encountered at Crozer Theological Seminary in Upland, Pennsylvania. In contrast to his rather conservative African American Baptist background, the Liberal theology at Crozer opened for him a radically new way of looking at the world. This Liberal theology emphasized the goodness of the created order despite the evil that people experienced. It saw human sin as primarily the result of ignorance. If sin was synonymous with ignorance, salvation was synonymous with education and knowledge. This theology also emphasized that the spark of God in every human being was the ability to think and to reason. It was this rational capacity that set humankind above the animals and made it, in some sense, like God. Further, the liberal theologians taught that God was active in human history. God's activity, however, was not a revolutionary intervention in and interruption of the natural course of history; rather, God was gently but firmly correcting the course of that history. Liberal theology was, in brief, supremely optimistic. It was confident that human history was headed in the right direction, and that no obstacle could for long hinder the inevitable course of the cause of goodness in God's world.

King drew on the major themes of this liberal theological tradition early in his career as a leader. He, too, believed that the world was inherently good. Believing in the saving power of education and that racism was the result of ignorance, he held that even the most racist individuals would change once their fears were dispelled through education. Furthermore, King emphasized that African Americans were created in God's image. And by virtue of their ability to sit down and reason with their oppressors, they could transcend the instinctual drive to lash out violently at their enemies. King also was convinced of God's activity in human history. God was not a wholly transcendent, distant deity, but a divine presence in the everyday lives and strivings of human beings. In his early career King was certain that the civil rights movement would usher in a new political and social order in which all persons would be judged by "the strength of their character rather than the color of their skin." He was certain that nothing could stand in the way of the cause of goodness in the world, because justice is the natural course of history itself.

The second influence on King's theology was the teachings of Mahatma Gandhi. King was fascinated by Gandhi's campaigns of nonviolent resistance in British-occupied India. The foundation of Gandhi's thought was the concept of *satyagraha*, or love force, the belief that love was not passive but an active force in human affairs. Through nonviolent action, oppressed people could demonstrate that active love and thus break the bonds of colonialism and slavery. King related Gandhi's thought to the central role of love in Christianity and adopted Ghandi's nonviolent method because he was convinced that it would allow the oppressed to resist their enemies without resorting to hate, to love them without surrendering their humanity. King believed that

nonviolent resistance not only gave new self-respect to the oppressed but would also stir the conscience of the oppressor. Thus, nonviolent resistance became the hallmark of the civil rights movement, because it was, for King, the epitome of Christian love, or *agape*.

The third influence on King's theology was the writings of Henry David Thoreau. In his classic work, *On the Duty of Civil Disobedience*, Thoreau had argued that the moral person has the duty to disobey any law that is unjust. Immoral laws are a blight on the political landscape, and the just person is duty bound to oppose them. Further, the person who engages in civil disobedience, Thoreau argued, must be willing to pay the penalty for that disobedience. One of Thoreau's more famous utterances was the statement: "Under a government which imprisons any unjustly, the true place for a just man is also a prison." King drew upon such insights of Thoreau when he looked at the legalized segregation of the American South. Jim Crow laws were unjust and the moral person was obliged to disobey them. This is how he explained Mrs. Rosa Parks's refusal to give up her seat to a white person on a bus. This individual act of civil disobedience led to the collective act of noncooperation known as the Montgomery Bus Boycott of 1955. King, in keeping with Thoreau's insight, was also willing to pay the price for such actions. He was jailed twelve times during his brief life. Civil disobedience and imprisonment were the ways that he chose to express his deepest theological convictions.

Martin Luther King's early theological perspective was significantly affected by these three influences. Liberal theology provided him with the idea of justice as the goal of human history. Gandhi's notion of love-force provided him with the idea of nonviolent action as the chief method for achieving racial justice. And Thoreau's concept of civil disobedience provided him with an effective means of subjecting racial injustice to public scrutiny.

These influences and King's early, rather optimistic, philosophy are epitomized in an article written early in 1957 shortly after the formation of the Southern Christian Leadership Conference, which elected King as its first president. King outlines the five points of his program of nonviolent resistence:

First, this is not a method for cowards; it *does* resist. The nonviolent resister is just as strongly opposed to the evil against which he protests as the person who uses violence. . . . This method is passive physically but strongly active spiritually; it is nonaggressive physically but dynamically aggressive spiritually. . . . A second point is that the nonviolent resistence does not seek to defeat or humiliate the opponent, but to win his friendship and understanding. The nonviolent resister must often express his protest through noncooperation or boycotts, but he realizes that [these] are not ends themselves. . . . The end is redemption and reconciliation. The aftermath of nonviolence is the creation of the beloved community, while the aftermath of violence is tragic bitterness. . . .

A third characteristic of this method is that the attack is directed against forces of evil rather than against persons who are caught in these forces. It is evil we are seeking to defeat, not the persons victimized by evil. . . . The tension is at bottom between justice and injustice, between the forces of light and the forces of darkness. . . . We are out to defeat injustice and not white persons who happen to be unjust. . . . A fourth point that must be brought out concerning nonviolent resistence is that . . . at the center of nonviolence stands the principle of love. . . . We speak of a love which is expressed in the Greek word *agape*. *Agape* means nothing sentimental or basically affectionate; it means understanding, redeeming good will for all men, an overflowing love which seeks nothing in return. It is the love of God working in the lives of men. . . .

Finally, the method of nonviolence is based on the conviction that the universe is on the side of justice. It is this deep faith in the future that causes the nonviolent resister to accept suffering without retaliation. He knows that in his struggle for justice he has cosmic companionship . . . that God is on the side of truth.[1]

In 1967 King's political outlook underwent a drastic change. He spoke out against the war in Vietnam. He began to ask questions about economic justice, and not just racial justice. As long

Martin Luther King, Jr.

as King confined his activities to the area of race relations between white people and black people, he enjoyed the support of a broad coalition of persons interested in social change. However, once he began to question not only the violence of racial segregation but also the violence of international war, he was seen to have stepped out of his proper role. Furthermore, as he raised questions about economic justice, he was perceived as a threat to, not a defender of, "the American Way." The popularity and support he once enjoyed almost instantly vanished, and he found himself largely alone in opposing structural injustice.

Since 1964, the year that King received the Nobel Prize for Peace, he was increasingly reminded that he also had a commission to work harder for world peace beyond national boundaries and allegiances. This meant breaking the silence of his opposition to the Amerian war in Vietnam. This he did before a group of clergy and laity opposed to the war who were meeting at the Riverside Church in New York City. It was one of King's historic addresses, and it included an attack on President Lyndon B. Johnson's war policy and also linked the war and the cause of peace to the wider social evils bedeviling the American nation:

Somehow this madness must cease. We must stop now. I speak as a child of God and brother to the suffering poor of Vietnam. I speak for those whose land is being laid waste, whose homes are being destroyed, whose culture is being subverted. I speak for the poor of America who are paying the double price of smashed hopes at home and death and corruption in Vietnam. I speak as a citizen of the world, for the world as it stands aghast at the path we have taken. I speak as an American to the leaders of my own nation. The great initiative in this war is ours. The initiative to stop it must be ours.[2]

The Liberal theology that had so profoundly influenced King could not address the radical evil he now saw in American society. The sin of oppressors was not simply the result of ignorance; it grew out of the perverse tendency to oppress others. Education alone could not be the answer to human problems if brilliantly trained minds were responsible for the continued exploitation of people throughout the world. King came to realize that Liberal theology was too naively optimistic and too sentimental about the human potential for overcoming evil. After 1967 King also began to focus on the deficiencies of capitalism as a basis for economic justice. He saw the need for a more radical restructuring of the entire American society, including the question of its capitalist economy that allowed for the existence of 40 million poor people in a land of abundance. In his book, *Where Do We Go From Here: Chaos or Community?* (1967), a year before his death, he wrote:

We must honestly admit that capitalism has often left a gulf between superfluous wealth and abject poverty, has created conditions permitting necessities to be taken from the many to give luxuries to the few. . . . The profit motive, when it is the sole basis of an economic system, encourages a cutthroat competition and selfish ambition. . . . A true revolution of values will soon look uneasily on the glaring contrast of poverty and wealth. With righteous indignation, it will look at thousands of working people displaced from their jobs with reduced income as a result of automation while the profits of the employers remain intact, and say: "This is not just." . . . It will look at

our alliance with the landed gentry of Latin America and say: "This is not just." . . .[3]

Gandhi's method of nonviolent resistance remained an important influence on King's theology. But whereas earlier in his career King had emphasized nonviolence as a cure for broken social relations in the United States, after 1967 he extended it to include relations between nations. That is, nonviolence could no longer be limited to personal choice; it had to become public policy. King also realized that for Thoreau's civil disobedience to succeed, it depended upon moral suasion. But for one person to persuade another of the injustice of her or his actions, there must be some common moral ground between them. Both had to respect one another as equal members of the civil order. After 1967, King began to see that America was built on the corrupt social values that perpetuate inequality, and that this corruption made it virtually impossible for the oppressors to be morally persuaded of the injustice of their actions. History now had shown King that oppressors never voluntarily give up power. It must always be seized by the oppressed. These changes in King's theology left him an isolated, prophetic voice on the American political scene. Because of his determination to pursue God's justice beyond the single issue of racial segregation in the South, and to make justice the priority item on the national agenda, he quickly lost popularity. He was harassed by the FBI, he was accused of being a Communist, and former friends, both black and white, turned their backs on him. Yet, in spite of these difficulties, he remained true to his moral convictions.

Out of the challenges of this period in King's life, the fourth, and ultimately, decisive influence on his theology became clear. The pain and disappointment of 1967 left King with nothing to rely on except the one true source of his faith. That source was the African American church tradition. Liberal theology failed him; Gandhi's nonviolent method had been confined to personal relations and was incapable, without modification, of addressing the structural misuse of power; Thoreau's civil disobedience worked only in a situation of moral and political equality, which did not exist between African Americans and European Americans. The bedrock of King's theology was laid in the African American Baptist Church. King's dream had grown out of the spirituality of the African American religious tradition, especially as it was manifest in the preaching tradition of the African American pulpit. This tradition carries a thirst for righteousness, like that of the prophets Amos and Hosea. It bears the perseverance of Sojourner Truth and Frederick Douglass. It inherited its refusal to accept failure from Marcus Garvey and Booker T. Washington. This tradition found its insatiable desire for true knowledge etched in the hearts of Alexander Crummll and W. E. B. DuBois. It found its unshakeable faith in God on the lips of its unnamed witnesses.

King was a product of this tradition, and he was able to articulate, for the nation and the world, the hope which ever burned in the hearts of African slaves and their descendants. Even on the eve of his death in 1968, he was confident. He said, "I may not get to the promised land, but with you I believe that we as a people will get there." He did not put his confidence in what humans could achieve, but in the power of an almighty God to redeem and vindicate his chosen people. King returned to the radicality of the African American prophetic tradition after 1967. This return freed him from the restraints of prior theological influences and left him open to ask hard questions about the possibility of justice in America; questions that arise only from the oppressed community of faith.

THE CONTEXTS OF BLACK THEOLOGY IN AMERICA

The Historical Context

At the present time the most influential historical-theological interpretation of black religion in America is Gayraud S. Wilmore's *Black Religion and Black Radicalism*. Here Wilmore

undergirds the work of two generations of African American theologians. He begins by noting the uniqueness of black religion.

From the beginning the religion of the descendants of the Africans who were brought to the Western world as slaves has been something less and something more than what is generally regarded as Christianity. Under the circumstances, it could not have been otherwise. The religious beliefs and rituals of a people are inevitably and inseparably bound up with the material and psychological realities of their daily existence.[4]

The historical foundations of the African American theological tradition have deep roots in the religious sensibility of the enslaved and dislocated Africans, in early American Christian piety, and in Native American spirituality. This particular aspect of the history of religion in America was largely ignored by scholars for a variety of reasons, including questions about the legitimacy of slave religion as an expression of American religiosity, and a lack of the interpretive tools needed to grasp the intricacies of a very different religious tradition. The fact that slave religion, much like African traditional religion, was not primarily a religion of "the book" was also a factor in the lack of publicly acknowledged scholarship on the subject.

One of Wilmore's basic contentions is that the Middle Passage did not erase the cultural and religious memory of enslaved Africans. Against the backdrop of the Herskovits-Frazier debate on the presence of African cultural retentions among black people in the diaspora, Wilmore observes that

We do know that some of the early preachers to the slaves were not whites, but former African priests or religious specialists of one sort or another who possessed unusual gifts of leadership and persuasion. One source that has been mentioned is the Dahomey, where dynastic quarrels produced such leaders among those sold to the white traders as slaves. Some of the victims were not only the defeated chiefs and their families, but also their priests and diviners. . . . Although compliant priests were retained in order not to incur the wrath of their gods, those who resisted—for example, the priests serving the river gods in what is now the nation of Benin—were sold to the slavers and probably ended up in the New World.[5]

While many slave Christians took the Bible seriously, many felt contempt for "book religion." This was not only because they were dependent on oral instruction; rather, they had confidence in their own traditional ways of religious belief. As Wilmore points out, the "Spirit within" was considered a more reliable guide than the Bible, and some slaves also rejected the Bible because their masters told them that it supported the institution of slavery.

Neither was theology, as it developed in the Western Christian tradition, a major emphasis in slave religion.

The slaves had small concern for doctrinal fidelity, but not because there was no theological or moral content in the religions they practiced in Africa, or in the adaptations they were obliged to make to Christianity. . . . The absence of theological interest among the slaves was due, most of all, to the practical and experiential nature of their religion in which the existence of a Supreme Being, the reality of the spirit world, and the revelatory significance of symbols and myths were all taken for granted and required no explicit theological formulation in the Western sense.[6]

The content of black religion received its basic doctrinal shape under these conditions, and interpretation of the Bible and black belief about God found their peculiar expression in this context.

Wilmore further shows that the slave insurrections in America were empowered by a deep, distinctly African spiritual understanding of reality. He rejects the widespread assumption that revolts such as Nat Turner's in Virginia or Chilembiwe's in Nyasaland were not led by black preachers, because the popular assumption is that they were benevolent "foot-shuffling clowns." The slave preachers, on the contrary, understood the awe-inspiring power of the Spirit, which they had

inherited from their African heritage. The power of the Spirit was not simply the source of interior freedom; it represented as well the God who demanded judgment and blood vengence as a propitiation for human evil, wrongdoing, and sin.[7]

Wilmore does not see otherworldliness as a primary, guiding theme of the slave preachers. He sees it, rather, as an interim strategy to give his people hope in the presence of an often ill-fated decision to strike against their white masters. Although black religion may reflect otherworldly belief, Wilmore argues that "it was not otherworldly-quietistic, but otherworldly-disruptive," because the oppressors were never able to relax their guard in the presence of this kind of otherworldliness. "During slavery it was a way of already living in that *other* world of transcendent freedom."[8]

The major concern that black religion addressed was one of survival and its dominant motif was affirmation and joy.

The overarching question was one of survival—mental and physical—and whatever slaves could appropriate from the conjurer, or later from the charismatic Christian preacher . . . was seized upon as a gift from "de Lawd" who had not seen fit to extricate them from their plight, but nevertheless provided some means of preserving health and sanity in the midst of it. This is not to suggest that slaves did not find joy and consolation in their religion. . . . The dominant motif then of slave religion was affirmation and joy—even carnal pleasure had its prominent place. Such a religion bound men and women to the organic, vitalistic powers of creation. . . . Behind the recognition that in existence there is some radically opposing force, some intrinsic mischief that we must somehow overcome or learn to control, was an even greater recognition that life is good and is to be savored and enjoyed while it lasts.[9]

Christianity, Wilmore writes, would not have appealed to the slaves if it were not vitalized by their African past.

Christianity alone, adulterated, otherworldly, and disengaged from its most authentic implications—as it was usually presented to the slaves—could not have provided the slaves with all the resources they needed for the kind of resistance they expressed. It had to be enriched with the volatile ingredients of the African religious past and, most of all, with the human yearning for freedom that found a channel for expression in the early black churches of the South.[10]

The Cultural Context

There are two formative cultural elements in the development of Black theology: (1) African traditional religions and (2) the sociopolitical, cultural, and quasireligious institution of slavery. These elements formed the building blocks for the construction of a new religious sensibility in a new world. It cannot be emphasized too strongly that the enslavement of Africans in the modern period had no precedent in human history. The social and political structures that regulated and, to a degree, humanized previous forms of slavery in other societies had been eliminated with the emergence of modern forms of social and economic organization. The enslavement of Africans in the seventeenth through the nineteenth centuries was a distinctively modern phenomenon. It is in this context that slave religion, as seen in the narratives of ex-slaves, developed. Dwight N. Hopkins adopts the term the "Invisible Institution." He writes:

The black church begins in slavery: thus slave religion provides the first source for a contemporary statement on black theology. The black church's unique tradition springs from the emerging theology of African American chattel. While white masters attempted to force their Christianity onto their black property, slaves worshiped God secretly. Out of these illegal and hidden religious practices, the "Invisible Institution," black Christianity and black theology arose. Though chained and illiterate, black people dared to *think* theologically by testifying to what the God of Moses had done for them.[11]

These slave narratives are an unusually rich religious and cultural source of African American

Christian thought because they reveal, with startling clarity at times, some of the distinctive theological features of black faith, as well as the culturally specific ways of expressing that faith. Hopkins points out, for example, that

slave theology consistently experienced God dwelling with those in bondage, personal and systemic. The black religious experience prevented any separation between the sacred and the secular, the church and the community. . . . And Jesus assumed an intimate and kingly relationship with the poor black chattel. Slaves emphasized both the suffering human Jesus as well as Jesus' warrior ability to set the downtrodden free. Moreover, the slaves distinguished their humanity from the white slave master. For blacks, God and Jesus called them to use all means possible to pursue religiously a human status of equality. . . . Second, slaves' religious thought accented an original cultural expression. Not only did the slaves wage a political battle for the supremacy of their liberator God, but they also chose to worship this God in their own language and idiom, and in the extraordinary clandestineness of their own black religious community. Thus, God's self was manifested in the specific textures of an African American slave story.[12]

Hopkins describes the distinctive contribution of African religion to the North American slave theology. The African God was a High God. The phrase "God has nowhere or no when" points to the divine omnipresence, as does the use of "the Almighty" speak of the divine omnipotence and the belief that God has the unlimited power to do all things in heaven and on earth. The African slaves also brought with them the belief that God is both transcendent and immanent. Moreover, some African indigenous religions taught that God cares, calling God "the Compassionate One" who cares for the needy and "looks after the case of the poor man." They also speak of God as judge, a God who metes out justice and punishment.

The enslaved Africans in North America also brought with them other aspects of an indigenous theology. As Hopkins points out

African traditional religions shared a belief in a dynamic and interdependent relation between the individual and the community. The latter defined the former. Individualism proved anathema. To be human meant to stand in connection with the larger community of invisible ancestors and God and, of course, the visible community and family. . . . In this theological anthropology African traditional religions also accent the role and importance of the ancestors. The ancestors are connections to the past religious traditions and practices. They are the glue to the sacredness of culture or way of life. . . . The memory and presence of the ancestors helped preserve and teach the cultural heritage of the community.[13]

Slave religion and its development cannot, however, be understood outside of its relationship to the context of European American religion. There are several aspects of this white religious domination that Hopkins notes. First, the practices of the slave master's Christianity sharply limited the access of the African Americans to other encounters with religion. Where blacks were allowed to attend church, they experienced segregation in seating. Nor did the everyday activities of the Christian slave masters differ ethically from that of the non-Christian whites. "The white master of ex-slave Jack White was a 'Mef dis preacher' who whipped his blacks just as often and just as cruelly as other white people did." Hopkins also points out how white theology propagated white institutional control and the subservience of the blacks as the normal expression of Christian belief and practice. The "white folks literally practiced what they preached."[14]

Slavery and its attendant cruelty revealed that absolute power in the hands of human beings results in radical evil. This is why slaves insisted on the assignment of absolute power to God and God alone. Institutional slavery can best be understood then as a cosmic struggle between good and evil, much like Augustine's metaphorical analysis of human existence as the tale of two cities, the *Civitas Dei* and the *Civitas Mundi*.

Through a figural and liberative interpretation of the Moses-Jesus paradigm, and a theological anthropology based on the notion of freedom, the slaves fashioned for themselves a culture of resistance. They defined their own values in light of their concrete circumstances and the divine mandate to obey God's word. They constructed an ethic of integrity and wholeness, rather than a hollow morality that masked slavery and oppression. The desire for survival and the need to worship God resulted in a discourse of solidarity, which, everywhere in the black Christian diaspora, was coded in the songs of Zion, the testimony of the faithful, and the prayers of the righteous.

The Social Context

Black theology is the only theological expression in North America to arise out of an extreme social crisis. Neo-Orthodoxy in Europe and liberation theology in Latin America are other examples. Black theology, however, did not arise at first out of an academic protest, but out of the concrete struggles of African Americans for liberation. Therefore, one cannot understand the development of Black theology without some attention to the social forces that were present in American life at the time.

The 1960s was a period of extreme social unrest, which presented special challenges for the black church. This unrest was due, in part, to the confluence of several forces in American life: a burgeoning economy, an opening of cultural and intellectual institutions, and, ironically, the persistent exclusion of most people of color from participation in this new order. The end of the dominance of the traditional civil rights organizations in the mid-1960s was also a major factor in this social unrest. Civil rights leaders found that the deceptive schemes of urban life in America resisted the traditional approaches for addressing the ills of society. Out of the civil rights movement in the mid-1960s arose the cry for "Black power."

Among the most significant documents in the development of Black theology are the statement

"Black Power" by the National Committee of Negro Churchmen, "The Black Manifesto," and "The Statement on Black Theology" by the National Committee of Black Churchmen.[15] The statement "Black Power," issued on July 31, 1966, addresses power as a theological term. It was unusual to openly associate Christianity with power, despite the fact that Western Christianity has been identified with political, cultural, and economic power since the conversion of Constantine. It was frightening, however, for many Christians, both white and African American, to associate blackness with power. For a host of political, social, and cultural reasons, it raised deep-seated fears. This document recognizes that when power is separated from conscience, evil results.

We realize that neither the term "power" nor the term "Christian conscience" is an easy matter to talk about, especially in the context of race relations in America. The fundamental distortion facing us in the controversy about "black power" is rooted in a gross imbalance of power and conscience between Negroes and white Americans. It is this distortion, mainly, which is responsible for the widespread, though often inarticulate, assumption that white people are justified in getting what they want through the use of power, but that Negro Americans must, either by nature or by circumstance, make their appeal only through conscience. As a result, the power of white men and the conscience of black men have both been corrupted. The power of white men is corrupted because it meets little meaningful resistance from Negroes to temper it and keep white men from aping God. The conscience of black men is corrupted because, having no power to implement the demands of conscience, the concern for justice is transmuted into a distorted form of love, which, in the absence of justice, becomes chaotic self-surrender. Powerlessness breeds a race of beggars.[16]

The statement goes on to address the relationship between power and the four virtues of freedom, love, justice, and truth. These virtues are discussed in relationship to four groups of people: political leaders, the white church, black people, and the media. To political leaders the message is that power and freedom must be held in relationship because it is impossible for anyone to be free without the political power to do so. The National Committee of Negro Churchmen* declared that, while they deplored the violence of the riots in the urban ghettoes, they asked the political leadership to recognize the sources of such actions in the silent and covert violence of the white middle class in its indifference to the conditions of segregation, unemployment, and poverty in the inner cities in the United States. In short, they called upon the political leaders to recognize their failure to use the nation's power to create equal opportunity for blacks "in life as well as in law." This, they asserted, is the real problem and not the anguished cry of black power.

To the white church, the black churchmen declared that the true message of black power in the context of the Christian gospel is that *power* and *love* must be held in relationship because it is impossible to actually live the ethic of love without the power to do so. They point out that the Negro church was created because of the black community's "refusal to submit to the indignities of a false kind of 'integration' in which all power is in the hands of white people." Genuine human relationships require a more equal sharing of power. The issue is not simply one of racial balance but of true interracial mutuality. It is an illusion to oppose love to power; love should be a limiting and controlling element in the exercise of power. A moralistic interpretation of love, devoid of real power, will continue to subvert justice in America.[17]

The churchmen's message to black citizens is that power must be held in relationship to justice because it is impossible to achieve justice in American life without the power to do so. This will, first of all, require the achievement of reconciliation within the black community itself.

---

* The name was changed to the National Committee of Black Churchmen in 1967, and then to the National Conference of Black Christians.

This means

reconciled to ourselves as persons and to ourselves as an historical group. This means we must find our way to a new self-image in which we can find a normal sense of pride in self, including our variety of skin color and the manifold textures of our hair. As long as we are filled with hatred of ourselves we will be unable to respect others.[18]

The churchmen acknowledge that the black churches have preached a distorted, otherworldly conception of God's work and power and that it is imperative that they make the gospel of Jesus Christ more meaningful in the "here and now" of the Church's life, especially in the work for human justice.

We must not apologize for the existence of this form of group power, for we have been oppressed as a group, not as individuals. We will not find a way out of that oppression until both we and America accept the need for Negro Americans, as well as for Jews, Italians, Poles and white Anglo-Saxon Protestants, among others, to have and to wield group power. . . . WE must organize not only among ourselves but with other groups in order that we can, together, gain power sufficient to change this nation's sense of what is *now* important and what must be done *now*. . . . This is more important than who gets to the moon or the war in Vietnam.[19]

The churchmen's statement concludes by commending those in the communications industry who, often courageously, reported on the demonstrations in the South against the "brutalizing system of overt discrimination and segregation." They remind the media, however, that the ability or the failure of Americans to understand the black struggle depends on how the industry's power is related to the truth, and that particular controversies or events not be portrayed as the whole or final truth about the black struggle. "The fate of this country is, to no small extent, dependent upon how you [the media] interpret

the crises upon us, so that human truth is disclosed and human needs are met."[20]

The statement by the National Committee of Negro Churchmen reveals a crucial shift in the direction of the black struggle. The black churchmen who were signatories of the statement on "Black Power" were not prepared to break with Martin Luther King, Jr. At the same time, they did not agree with King's early repudiation of Black power as "a nihilistic philosophy born out of the conviction that the Negro can't win."[21] Furthermore, these black churchmen had now come to recognize, as King had not, that coercive power may, indeed must, be a means of achieving justice for the black community, despite the fears and objections of white Christians. Black church leaders were listening now to the call for Black power by members of the Student Nonviolent Coordinating Committee (SNCC), who were working with Martin Luther King, Jr. in the deep South. The vulnerable unity of King's nonviolent campaigns and his strategic compromises with white political and church leaders was now losing him support in the Black community.

The Black Manifesto

This shift is marked by the appearance of the Black Manifesto. It came out of the creation of the Interreligious Foundation for Community Organization (IFCO) founded by Protestants, Catholics, and Jews to fund the work of radical inner-city organizations. A conflict emerged—at an IFCO-sponsored National Black Economic Development conference in Detroit in 1967— between the Black grassroots community organizers who served on the foundation's board and the wealthy supporters of the IFCO who had "designated projects" of their own. At issue was the independence of the Black community in determining its funding projects and the complicity of the white religious leadership in the ongoing oppression of the Black community.

The Black Manifesto is one of the most important documents in the history of American

Christianity. It was presented by James Forman to the conference in Detroit and adopted on April 26, 1969. On May 4, 1969, Forman presented it to the congregation of the Riverside Church in New York City. The heart of the document is a demand for reparations. It is based on the principle that black people need to build a new society; one based on the economic independence of black people with an ideological overlay of what we would now call Afrocentrism.

We have come from all over the country burning with anger and despair not only with the miserable economic plight of our people but fully aware that the racism on which the Western World was built dominates our lives. There can be no separation of the problems of racism from the problems of our economic, political, and cultural degradation. To any black man, this is clear. . . . The people must be educated to understand that any black man or Negro who is advocating a perpetuation of capitalism inside the United States is in fact seeking not only his ultimate destruction and death but is contributing to the continuous exploitation of black people all around the world. For it is the power of the United States Government, this racist, imperialistic government, that is choking the life of all people around the world. We are an African people. We are concerned actively about the plight of our brothers in Africa.[22]

The tone and tenor of the document reflects the passion of the times, including a socialist agenda, which might be fulfilled through the use of violence, if necessary.

Time is short, and we do not have much time and it is time we stop mincing words. Caution is fine, but no oppressed people ever gained their liberation until they were ready to fight, to use whatever means necessary, including the use of force and the power of the gun to bring down the colonizer. . . . We must also talk of the type of world we want to live in. We must commit ourselves to a society where the total means of production are taken from the rich and placed into the hands of the state for the welfare of all the people. . . . We HAVE an ideology. Our fight is against racism, capitalism and imperialism, and we are

dedicated to building a socialist society inside the United States where the total means of production and distribution are in the hands of the State, and that must be led by black people, by revolutionary blacks.[23]

The Manifesto itself begins with the following description of its rationale for reparations:

We the black people assembled in Detroit . . . are fully aware that we have been forced to come together because racist white America has exploited our resources, our minds, our bodies, our labor. For centuries we have been forced to live as colonized people inside the United States, victimized by the most vicious, racist system in the world. We have helped to build the most industrial country in the world. We are therefore demanding of the white Christian churches and Jewish synagogues, which are part and parcel of the system of capitalism, that they begin to pay reparations to black people in this country. We are demanding $500,000,000 from the Christian white churches and the Jewish synagogues. This total comes to 15 dollars per nigger. . . . We know that the churches and synagogues have tremendous wealth, and its membership in white America has profited and still exploits black people. . . . Underneath all of this exploitation, the racism of this country has produced a psychological effect upon us that we are beginning to shake off. We are no longer afraid to demand our full rights as a people in this decadent society.[24]

The reparations called for in the Black Manifesto were to be used to fund a series of organizations and activities designed to ensure the empowerment of black people. Among them were a land bank, publishing industries, television networks, a research center, a communications training center, the organization of welfare recipients, a black labor strike and defense fund, an International Black Appeal (modeled on the International Jewish Appeal), and a black university.

The reparations demanded in the Black Manifesto were never delivered. However, the importance of this document lies in the fact that subsequent discussion and even rejection of its claims revealed that the differences between the black and white churches were not simply a matter of divergent interpretations of commonly accepted ethical principles. The Black Manifesto linked its calls for reparations to the notion of repentance. The reparations were to be, among other things, a concrete sign of penitence by white churches and Jewish synagogues. The Black Manifesto, with its emphasis on reparations and its relation to repentance, revealed that what separated the black churches and the white churches was not a disagreement on the application of Christian principles, but a disagreement on the nature and content of those principles themselves. The differences were deep, substantive, and theological. The awareness of these differences was the basis of the first preliminary articulation of a distinctive Black theology.

On June 13, 1969, a statement on Black Theology was adopted by the National Committee of Black Churchmen at their annual convocation in Oakland, California. The statement was produced by the NCBC Committee on Theological Prospectus at the Interdenominational Theological Center in Atlanta, Georgia. Within it are the outlines of the themes that would define the discipline of Black theology for the next twenty years.

Black Theology is a theology of black liberation. It seeks to plumb the black condition in the light of God's revelation in Jesus Christ, so that the black community can see that the gospel is commensurate with the achievement of black humanity. Black Theology is a theology of "blackness." It is the affirmation of black humanity that emancipates black people from white racism, thus providing authentic freedom for both white and black people. It affirms the humanity of white people in that it says No to the encroachment of white oppression. The message of liberation is the revelation of God as revealed in the incarnation of Jesus Christ. Freedom IS the gospel. Jesus is the Liberator![25]

The themes of liberation as central to understanding the Christian Gospel, and the liberating work of Jesus Christ, have provided the structural framework for the theological interpretation of black Christianity. However, it was the theological "controversy" around the meaning of forgiveness, repentance, and reparations that led early black theologians to reinterpret the Christian faith.

Reparation is a part of the Gospel message. Zacchaeus knew well the necessity for repayment as an essential ingredient in repentance. "If I have taken anything from any man by false accusation, I restore him fourfold" (Luke 19:8). The church which calls itself the servant church must, like its Lord, be willing to strip itself of possessions in order to build and restore that which has been destroyed. . . . The black community has been brutalized and victimized over the centuries. The recognition that comes from seeing Jesus as Liberator and the Gospel as freedom empowers black men to risk themselves for freedom and for faith. This faith we affirm in the midst of a hostile, disbelieving society. We intend to exist by this faith at all times and in all places.[26]

Out of the social upheavals of the middle twentieth century, African Americans began to think in new and specific ways about the meaning of the Christian faith. It is not that they did not think about what it meant to be a Christian prior to this point, but that they now took advantage of the loosening of some of the institutional barriers in national life. The opening of interracial church organizations and colleges and universities, which had previously been closed to African Americans, gave them access to a public voice not widely available before this time.

In this heated and volatile social context, some of the basic theological issues began to emerge. Although the fuller thematic exposition of the fundamental tenets of Black theology would await later expression, the roots of that development are present here. The social context of Black theology gave it an unmistakable practical character and also gave it a sense of urgency. It was a highly charged, highly focused faith that carried the power of prophetic commitment.

JAMES H. CONE'S BLACK THEOLOGY OF LIBERATION

One of the participants in the framing of the Statement on Black Theology was a young, relatively unknown theologian soon to join the Union Theological Seminary in New York, James H. Cone. He expanded upon the insights of the "Black Theology" statement and began to articulate a systematic theology that would take seriously the African American Christian experience.

James H. Cone (1938-) grew up in the small community of Bearden, Arkansas, and in the nurture of the Macedonia African Methodist Episcopal Church in Bearden. He attended the A.M.E. Shorter College and then Philander Smith, a Methodist college in Little Rock where he experienced firsthand the struggle over integration of Little Rock's Central High School. After college, Cone entered Garrett Biblical Institute (now Garrett-Evangelical Theological Seminary) in 1958. He then completed the M.A. and Ph.D. in the joint Garrett–Northwestern University program in religion. He wrote his doctoral dissertation on Karl Barth's anthropology. Cone taught for a few years at Philander Smith and Adrian College near Detroit, where he especially felt the conflict between his European-centered theological education and the Black struggle of the mid-1960s. During this period he was drawn to the new movement of Black power, but only after King's murder did he fully devote his energies to developing the connection between Black power and the Christian Gospel. The result was his first book, *Black Theology and Black Power* (1969). That same year he was invited to join the faculty of Union Theological Seminary in New York, where he has remained and serves as the Charles A. Briggs Distinguished Professor of Systematic Theology.

Over the next two decades Cone and other black theologians defined, expanded, and enriched the discipline of black theology. Cone's major conversation partners included J. Deotis Roberts, Major Jones, Preston Williams, and Cecil Cone, among others. Cone's other writings include the influential *A Black Theology of Libera-tion* (1970, 1986); *The Spirituals and the Blues* (1972); *God of the Oppressed* (1975); *My Soul Looks Back* (1982); *For My People: Black Theology and the Black Church* (1984); *Speaking the Truth* (1986); and *Martin and Malcolm and America: A Dream or a Nightmare?* (1991).

The Central Affirmations of Cone's Black Theology of Liberation

James Cone's theology is systematically formulated in *A Black Theology of Liberation*. Like other theologians working in a situation of social and political gravity or crisis, Cone's theology is *contextual* and *prophetic*, having to do with the urgent question of what the Gospel of Jesus Christ has to say to the struggle of black people for justice in the United States. Cone is skeptical of theologies that claim to be for all times or all places. It is important to remember that *A Black Theology of Liberation* was written for and to black Christians in the context of the black struggle of the 1960s. Cone was aware at the time that he was not doing theology as defined by the classical European tradition, which, if undertaken, would not have been related to or have made a difference for the liberation of poor blacks. Here his *style* of doing theology is influenced more by Malcolm X than by Martin Luther King, Jr. He followed Malcolm's advice when the latter advised: "Don't let anybody who is oppressing us ever lay down the ground rules. Don't go by their games. . . . Let them know now that this is a new game, and we've got some new rules."[27]

Liberation and the Sources and Norms of Black Theology

A Black Theology of Liberation was Cone's attempt to initiate a new beginning for the discipline of *theology*, one that would empower oppressed blacks; hence, *liberation* emerges as the organizing principle. The book sets out in a systematic way the several doctrinal affirmations of black theology with liberation as the central theme:

Christian theology is a theology of liberation. It is *a rational study of the being of God in the world in light of the existential situation of an oppressed community, relating the forces of liberation to the essence of the gospel, which is Jesus Christ.* This means that its sole reason for existence is to put into ordered speech the meaning of God's activity in the world, so that the community of the oppressed will recognize that its inner thrust for liberation is not only *consistent with* the gospel but *is* the gospel of Jesus Christ.[28]

Cone next addresses the question of what, in Black theology, are understood to be its sources and norm. Because Black theology seeks to relate biblical revelation to the existential situation of blacks in America, it must look to black experience. Revelation is not comprehensible from a black theological perspective without a prior understanding of the concrete manifestation of revelation in the black community and how it is seen in black experience and black history. For Christian faith, revelation is always an event in human history. It is God's self-revelation to humans through an act of human liberation, just as God's self-revelation to Israel was a revelation of what God was doing for the oppressed Israelites. So, for the black community, biblical revelation always must correlate with black historical experience. *"Revelation is a black event—it is what blacks are doing about their liberation."*[29]

The *norm* of Black theology must, similarly, relate to what God is doing in the black struggle for liberation from oppression. For Cone, the norm of Black theology is Jesus Christ; not, however, as understood and interpreted by white experience, but Christ understood as the black messiah, as related to black liberation. He proceeds to develop systematically a Black theology's understanding of revelation, God, the human condition, christology, and eschatology. As we explore each of these themes, we will give prime attention to Cone's own voice.

The Concept of Revelation in Black Theology

Cone sees mainstream theology in America—unlike the theology of the Confessing Church in Germany under Nazism—as silent with regard to God's revelation and the racial oppression against blacks in the United States. Cone agrees with those theologies whose conception of revelation has been influenced by Karl Barth. That is, that God's revelation is not a rational understanding of God's existence and attributes, as natural theology suggests, or an assent to inerrant, infallible biblical propositions, as Fundamentalism contends. Revelation has to do, rather, with God's self-disclosure to humans in Scripture as it makes clear God's will in the present time. But Black theology must go even further, Cone insists.

There is a need to define revelation in such a manner that the definition will, on the one hand, retain the essence of the biblical emphasis and, on the other, be relevant to the situation of oppressed blacks. . . . According to black theology, revelation must mean more than just divine self-disclosure. Revelation is God's self-disclosure to humankind *in the context of liberation.* To know God is to know God's work of liberation in behalf of the oppressed. God's revelation means liberation, an emancipation from death-dealing political, economic, and social structures of society. This is the essence of biblical revelation.[30]

Cone is critical of Rudolf Bultmann's understanding of New Testament revelation on two counts. First, Bultmann talks about the "historicity" of faith but he does not pay sufficient attention to the *context* in which the person sees God's activity. As Cone remarks, "Revelation is not my own individualistic self-understanding; it is the self-understanding of a community which sees God at work in history."[31] Second, and related, Bultmann fails to see revelation as an historical liberation of an oppressed *people*.

God in Black Theology

Black theology presupposes God, of course, but it is concerned to ask the question of God specifically in terms of God's self-disclosure in biblical history *and* the oppressed situation of blacks in America. To speak of God in these terms is doubly dangerous "because the true prophet of the gospel of God must become both 'anti-Christian' and 'unpatriotic,'" because the institutions of the American nation are inextricably joined to what is perceived as Christian. Black theology, therefore, is seriously tempted to give up the word "God," because "the oppressed and the oppressors cannot possibly mean the same thing when they speak of God."[32] Cone, however, rejects this temptation because the black community in America has always looked to its liberation as the work of the Divine.

Every theology is based on certain methodological presuppositions as its starting point; one need only look at the theologies of Karl Barth and Paul Tillich. Black theology begins with the biblical God *as specifically related* to the black struggle for liberation. The black God *is* a God of the oppressed. There are, Cone writes, two hermeneutical principles that are essential in the black analysis of the doctrine of God:

(1) The Christian understanding of God arises from the biblical view of revelation, a revelation of God that takes place in the liberation of oppressed Israel and is completed in the incarnation in Jesus Christ. This means that whatever is said about the nature of God and God's being-in-the-world must be based on the biblical account of God's revelatory activity. . . . (2) The doctrine of God in black theology must be of the God who is participating in the liberation of the oppressed of the land. This hermenuetical principle arises out of the first. Because God has been revealed in the history of oppressed Israel and decisively in the Oppressed One, Jesus Christ, it is impossible to say anything about God without seeing him as being involved in the contemporary liberation of all oppressed peoples. The God in black theology is the God of and for the oppressed, the God who comes into view in their liberation. Any other approach is a denial of biblical revelation.[33]

Anthropology: Freedom and Blackness

Cone sees the doctrine of God as intimately related to a doctrine of anthropology because liberation is a liberation of humanity. Theology implies an anthropology. Most modern theologies

affirm that freedom, and all that that implies, is the essential characteristic of human existence. Cone, however, sees the distinctive feature of anthropology in American Black theology as the relationship between freedom and blackness.

What does freedom mean when we relate it to contemporary America? Because blackness is at once the symbol of oppression and of the certainty of liberation, freedom means an affirmation of blackness. To be free is to be black—that is, identified with the victims of humiliation in human society and a participant in the liberation of oppressed humanity. The free person in America is the one who does not tolerate whiteness but fights against it, knowing that it is the source of human misery. The free person is the black person living in an alien world but refusing to behave according to its expectations. Being free in America means accepting blackness as the only possible way of existing in the world. It means defining one's identity by the marks of oppression. It means rejecting white proposals for peace and reconciliation, saying, "All we know is, we must have justice, not next week but this minute."[34]

Christology: Jesus Is the Black Messiah

Cone's Black theology of liberation is christocentric in that the norm of the Christian Gospel and theology is Jesus Christ. Therefore, he explores here the meaning of Christ's person and work in the context of the black experience. That is, unless Jesus Christ is analyzed in light of this experience, one has to wonder what Christ means for slavery, or the Underground Railway, or contemporary expressions of black power. The identity of Christ is not, then, an abstract question but a present existential one, inseparable from his status as the Oppressed One and his struggle with and for the oppressed. Jesus Christ's identity speaks to the condition of the black community today.

The black community is an oppressed community primarily because of its blackness; hence the christological importance of Jesus must be found in his blackness. If he is not black as we are, then the resurrection has little significance for our times. Indeed, if he cannot be what we are, we cannot be who he is. Our being with him is dependent on his being with us in the oppressed black condition, revealing to us what is necessary for our liberation. . . . If the historical Jesus is any clue for an analysis of the contemporary Christ, then he must be where human beings are enslaved. To speak of him is to speak of the liberation of the oppressed. In a society that defines blackness as evil and whiteness as good, the theological significance of Jesus is found in the possibility of human liberation through blackness. Jesus is the black Christ!. . . . The definition of Christ as black means that he represents the complete opposite of the values of white culture. He is the center of a black Copernican revolution.[35]

The Church's Call and Eschatology

Cone sees the appearance of Jesus as the black Christ as the coming of God's Kingdom in America. The New Testament speaks of the Kingdom as an historical event, and one demanding repentance and decision, that is, the necessity to give up everything for it. The white community fails to see the signs of the times and sees the black revolution as a scandal and a distraction. It does not remember that Jesus compared the Kingdom to a mustard seed, a reality that would have an insignificant beginning but a radical and revolutionary ending. Cone's discussion of the Kingdom leads to his consideration of the Church and eschatology in the context of the black struggle. The Church is the community that responds to God's radical message of the Kingdom. Those threatened by this summons call for "law and order" but, as Cone asserts, the Church "can never endorse 'law and order' that causes suffering."[36] To blacks the message of the Kingdom is Christian freedom, the message that their slavery has come to an end. And the Church's participation in the freedom of the Kingdom means that it does not retreat from the world nor does it accommodate the ways of the world. The black Church exists *in* a racist world but *as* a beacon of liberating hope.

Participation in divine liberation places the church squarely in the context of the world. Its existence is inseparable from worldly involvement. . . . The world is earthly existence, the place where human beings are enslaved. It is where laws are passed against the oppressed, and where the oppressed fight back even though their efforts seem futile. . . . Because the church knows that the world is where human beings are dehumanized, it can neither retreat from the world nor embrace it. Retreating is tantamount to a denial of its calling to share in divine liberation. . . . Christians must fight against evil, for not to fight . . . is to deny the resurrection. Christian eschatology is bound up with the resurrection of Christ. He is the eschatological hope. He is the future of God who stands in judgment upon the world and forces us to give an account of the present. In view of his victory over evil and death, why must human beings suffer and die? Why do we behave as if the present were a fixed reality not susceptible to radical change? As long as we look at the resurrection of Christ and the expected "end," we cannot reconcile ourselves to the things of the present that contradict his presence. It is this eschatological emphasis that black theology affirms.[37]

James Cone's theology is directed at a particular historical context, the black struggle for justice and liberation, and he recognized the risk and danger inherent in such a prophetic and uncompromising theology. He also knew that he would be attacked for it, and he was. His later theological work reveals certain shifts of emphasis over three decades, but he stands by his central theme of liberation as "the organizing principal" and the "central motif" of his reading of the Christian Gospel.[38] The twentieth anniversary edition of *A Black Theology of Liberation* afforded the opportunity to include six critical responses to the book as well as Cone's response.

Cone identifies four themes that critics have addressed and that he concedes *A Black Theology of Liberation* either failed to speak to or that now need to be reconsidered. One obvious omission is the book's silence on sexism. The black womanist theologian Delores Williams directs her response to this issue:

Could Cone affirm the action for black women that logically follows what he and Malcolm X say in the book? . . . If black women said "to hell with sexist black churches" and left them, thereby allowing them to crumble, could Cone validate this action? . . . And I wonder if Cone, who says "I knew racism was a heresy," would also agree that sexism is heresy?"[39]

Other subjects that Cone recognizes as conspicuous by their absence in *A Black Theology of Liberation* are an engagement with Third World theologies, including African theologians, and a serious consideration of socioeconomic issues and class analysis as crucial to any theology concerned with social context. In his later writings Cone has addressed all of these issues, including the role of women.[40] In another important later book, *Martin and Malcolm and America: A Dream or a Nightmare?*, Cone analyzes the religious and political thought of M. L. King, Jr. and Malcolm X in the context of the black revolution of the 1960s. He concludes that by the end of their lives these two leaders were drawing upon one another's views and were coming closer together in their assessment that the social revolution had a wider, international context. It is appropriate to end this section with Cone's concluding words on this theme:

Martin King was right: "The hour is late" and "the clock of destiny is ticking out." We must declare where we stand on the great issues of our time. Racism is one of them. Poverty is another. Sexism another. Class exploitation another. Imperialism another. We must break the cycle of violence in America and around the world. For Malcolm and Martin, for America and the world, and for all who have given their lives in the struggle for justice, let us direct our fight toward one goal—the beloved community of humankind."[41]

Black theology was not the result of an intellectual disagreement between Christians. Rather it was the expression of a community of Christians united in their resistance to oppression and in their commitment to their faith. In its tone and tenor it does not resemble the theologies of Germany or the theologies of Britain. Rather, it reflects in its heart and soul the anguish and hope of Christians for whom freedom is the essence of the Gospel message.

BLACK WOMANIST THEOLOGY: TEXTS, TRADITIONS, AND TRAJECTORIES

The most significant and dynamic development in recent African American theological thought has been the emergence of *womanist theology* in the 1980s. This theological expression is based on the perspectives articulated by Alice Walker's definition of a womanist as found in her book, *In Search of Our Mothers' Gardens*.

Womanist 1. From *womanish*. (Opp. of "girlish," i.e., frivolous, irresponsible, not serious.) A black feminist of color. From the black folk expression of mothers to female children, "You acting womanish," i.e., like a woman. Usually referring to outrageous, audacious, courageous or *willful* behavior. Wanting to know more and in greater depth than is considered "good" for one. Interested in grown-up doings. Acting grown up. Being grown up. Interchangeable with another black folk expression: "You trying to be grown." Responsible. In charge. *Serious*.[42]

Womanist theology is both a critical and a constructive reflection on the Christian faith based on the experience of African American women. Like Feminist theology, it criticizes the patriarchal practices of the churches, the misogynist interpretations of the Bible, and androcentric theological constructions. Like traditional Black theology, it criticizes the racist practices of the churches, white supremacist interpretations of the Bible, and Eurocentric theological constructions. However, Womanist theology is more than a critique of sexism and racism. It is a movement of the Spirit. It celebrates the distinctive historical and contemporary gifts of black women in the churches and in the world.

Womanist theology is then a vibrant movement and its dynamism is continually developing. However, at this point in its history, three distinctive foci have emerged. They are the rereading and reconstruction of the biblical texts, the recasting and reclaiming of the traditions regarding Jesus Christ, and the revision and revitalization of the ethical and moral trajectories of the Christian faith.

Texts: Womanist Interpretations of the Bible

Womanist biblical scholars have turned their attention to the Scriptures of the Christian faith because the Bible is important to the self-understanding of black women, and because the Bible has been used and interpreted in ways that have served to oppress black women. Womanist scholarship has given particular attention to the significance of the story of Sarah and Hagar in the Old Testament. The leading womanist Old Testament scholar, Renita J. Weems, has analyzed that story in her book, *Just a Sister Away: A Womanist Vision of Women's Relationships in the Bible*, in light of the historical and contemporary experience of black women.

For black women, the story of Hagar in the Old Testament book of Genesis is a haunting one. It is a story of exploitation and persecution suffered by an Egyptian slave woman at the hands of her Hebrew mistress. Even if it is not our individual story, it is the story we have read in our mothers' eyes those afternoons when we greeted them at our front door after a hard day of work as a domestic. . . . For black women, Hagar's story is peculiarly familiar . . . Like our own situation, the story of the Egyptian Hagar and the Hebrew Sarai encompasses more than ethnic prejudice. Theirs is a story of ethnic prejudice exacerbated by economic and sexual exploitation. Theirs is a story of conflict, women betraying women, mothers conspiring against mothers. Theirs is story of social rivalry. Hence the similarity of our stories, as black and white women in America, to the story of Hagar and Sarai warrants taking the enormous risk of opening up the deep festering wounds between us and beginning to explore our possibilities for divine healing.[43]

Weems proceeds to discuss the social, economic, and racial dynamics that rendered the relationship between Hagar and Sarah problematic and concludes with instructive insights into black women's historical experience.

The story of the Egyptian slave and her Hebrew mistress is hauntingly reminiscent of the disturbing accounts of black slave women and white mistresses during slavery. Over and over again we have heard tales about the wanton and brutal rape of black women by their white slave masters, compounded by punitive beatings by resentful white wives who penalized the raped slave woman for their husbands' lust and savagery. . . . The painful memory of black and white women under slavery and the web of cruelty that characterized their relations continue to stalk the relationships between black and white women in America even to this day. . . . And for some peculiar reason, when it comes to women, those memories have proven especially hard to erase.[44]

Womanist biblical scholarship also has focused on the Pauline letters, especially those texts that presumably deal with the role of women in the early church and the meaning of slavery in early Christian thought. A leading womanist New Testament scholar, Clarice J. Martin, addresses both of these issues in her study of the *Haustafeln* (domestic codes) in the Pauline letters, as understood in African American interpretation. The slave regulation, "slaves be submissive to your masters" (Col. 3:22–25; Eph. 6:5–8; also Peter 2:18–25), was persistently reinterpreted by black slaves in the eighteenth and nineteenth centuries to imply, contrarily, the message of an empowering freedom under God. The African American slaves and their abolitionist sympathizers simply rejected a literalist reading of the *Haustafeln* slave regulation and reinterpreted it, or used other New Testament passages, in their arguments against slavery. They also argued that the Pauline slave regulation did not exemplify the whole Gospel. "The unmistakable emphasis on the 'universal parenthood of God' and the 'kinship of humankind' was a persistent theme in abolitionist rhetoric" in the slave community.[45]

Martin shows, however, that while the African American interpretive tradition was "marked by a forceful critique and rejections of a literalist interpretation of the slave regulations in the *Haustafeln*," it "was not marked by an equally passionate critique and rejection of a literalist interpretation regarding the subordination of women to men in the *Haustafeln*."[46] It is, Martin remarks, therefore,

appropriate to note that African American women, with women in Western culture in general, have often tasted the pungent fruit of androcentric, hierarchical domination. Black women are no strangers to arguments that the Bible sanctions their submission as wives and women in the domestic and socio-political spheres.[47]

Womanist biblical scholars and exegetes will continue to make their own assessments of previous biblical interpretation. And these exegetical analyses will continue to point to the ways in which the biblical texts both support and challenge the racist and sexist presuppositions of our culture.

Traditions: The Meaning of Jesus Christ in Womanist Theology

In many ways, the most significant and problematic aspect of the Christian tradition for black women is the identity and work of Jesus Christ. This particular theme was the first to receive sustained attention and analysis by womanist theologians. The major works in this area are Jacquelyn Grant's *White Women's Christ and Black Women's Jesus: Feminist Christology and Womanist Response* (1989); Kelly Brown Douglas's *The Black Christ* (1994); and Delores S. Williams's *Sisters in the Wilderness: The Challenge of Womanist God-Talk* (1993).

Jacquelyn Grant examines the historical development of the meaning of Jesus Christ among black women and demonstrates the extraordinary place that Jesus held in the life of Christian black women. Grant points out that the black woman's distinctive experience of Jesus often took priority over the Bible as it did for Sojourner Truth, the black woman preacher. Asked if she preached from the Bible, Sojourner replied: "No honey . . . when I preaches, I has jest

one text to preach from . . . My text is, 'When I found Jesus.'"[48] Grant concisely sketches this distinctive black women's experience of Jesus:

For Christian Black women in the past, Jesus was their central frame of reference. They identified with Jesus because they believed that Jesus identified with them. As Jesus was persecuted and made to suffer undeservedly, so were they. His suffering culminated in the crucifixion. Their crucifixion included rape, and babies being sold. But Jesus' suffering was not the suffering of a mere human, for Jesus was understood to be God incarnate. . . . Jesus Christ thus represents a three-fold significance: first he identifies with the "little people," Black women, where they are; secondly, he affirms the basic humanity of these "the least"; and thirdly, he inspires active hope in the struggle for resurrected, liberated existence. . . . The significance of Christ is not his maleness, but his humanity. . . . [Womanist] Christology must be a liberating one, for both the Black women's community and the larger Black community. A Christology which negates Black male humanity is still destructive to the Black community. We must, therefore, take seriously only the usable aspects of the past.[49]

Grant proceeds to show that the experience of black women is more adequate to develop a Christology that takes into account Jesus's engagement with the tridimensional reality of racism/sexism/classism—that is, that Christ is more likely to be found in the more universal oppressions experienced by black women.

Kelly Brown Douglas explores and reassesses the various ways in which the blackness of Jesus is understood in slave Christianity, among earlier black nationalists, in the writings of Martin Luther King, Jr. and Malcolm X, in Albert Cleage's *The Black Messiah*, and in the theology of James Cone and J. Deotis Roberts. She finds all of these male depictions of the Black Christ to be inadequate because they center their conception in one or another critique of racism alone. Furthermore, she does not see Christ's blackness as the crucial concern; rather, for a black womanist theology, Christ is black in terms of Jesus's commitment "to the Black *community's* struggle for life and wholeness."[50] Important to Douglas's Christology is her "social analysis of wholeness" that proceeds beyond the important focus on racism to the black community's concern for gender, class, and sexual orientation. Thus a black womanist portrayal of the Black Christ will avail itself of a variety of icons and symbols that, for the black community, are living. These will include, among others, portrayals of Christ as seen in the face of black women, such as Harriet Tubman. Douglas writes:

Seeing Christ in the faces of those who were and are actively committed to the "wholeness" of the black community suggests several things. First, it says that the Black Christ is present in the Black community wherever people are engaged in a struggle for that community's "wholeness." Second, it challenges Black people to participate in activities that advance the unity and freedom of their community. It allows them to know that Christ is with them and in them anytime they promote life and wholeness for Black men and women. Third, to portray Christ in the face of Black heroines and heroes signals that it was not who Jesus was, particularly as a male, that made him Christ, but what he did. Essentially, Christ's biological characteristics have little significance to discerning Christ's sustaining, liberating, and prophetic presence. . . . [A] womanist Black Christ will consistently lift up the presence of Christ in the faces of the poorest Black women.[51]

Douglas goes on to show how the womanist Black Christ also offers a critique and a revision of the portrait of Jesus Christ as presented in the Nicene and Chalcedonian creeds, which focus exclusively on the metaphysical being of Christ in relation to God. Douglas does not see these creedal formularies as the basis for *why* Jesus is Christ:

[T]here are aspects of the Nicene/Chalcedonian formulation that appear inconsistent with Jesus as he was present in the Gospels. For instance, this formulation establishes that Jesus is Christ by focusing on God's act of becoming incarnate in him. In so doing, it diminishes the significance of Jesus' actions on earth. . . . The implication is that what took place between Jesus's birth and resurrection—the bulk of the Gospels' report of Jesus—is unrelated to what it means for Jesus to be the Christ. . . . If Jesus did conduct a sustaining, liberating, and prophetic ministry, this would not significantly affect what it meant for him to be Christ. . . . By ignoring Jesus Christ's ministry and focusing on his "being," he is set apart above humanity. He is seen as someone to be worshiped, believed in, but not followed or imitated.[52]

Douglas's womanist understanding of the Black Christ does not begin with an abstract statement of Jesus Christ's metaphysical nature. It begins, rather, with Jesus's ministry as that is narrated in the Gospels. What Jesus concretely *did* becomes the basis of what it means for Jesus to be the Christ. And this makes Christ accessible and relevant to ordinary believers. "That is, Christ can be seen in the faces of others, Black men and women, as they strive in their own historical context to promote life and wholeness."[53]

Delores S. Williams, Paul Tillich Professor of Theology at Union Theological Seminary in New York, also has drawn on Alice Walker's rich definition of a black womanist and has called other black women to turn to the valuable resources of black women's social, religious, and cultural experience on which to construct a new black womanist theology. She refers to those female models whose powerful actions and virtues can and should be used today in building and maintaining the black community and beyond. In so doing, Williams has also exposed the sexist practices that persist in the black church. Her work, *Sisters in the Wilderness: The Challenge of Womanist God-Talk* (1993), is an exploration of black women's experience and oppression and a statement of womanist theology in dialogue with both the male-dominated Black theology of liberation and the white-dominated feminist theology. In this study, Williams explores the issue of Christian doctrine and the primacy of the ministry of Jesus as decisive in the construction of a Christology. Her analysis is based on a suggestive reexamination of traditional, orthodox theories of the atonement in which Jesus is portrayed as a surrogate for condemned humanity. Against the backdrop of black women's historical experience as surrogates for the transgression of others, Williams argues that a womanist Christology must find a more appropriate and usable basis for understanding Christ's redeeming work. Williams finds this source in the sociopolitical thought and action of the African American women's world.

To show black women their salvation does not depend upon any form of surrogacy made sacred by traditional and orthodox understandings of Jesus' life and death. Rather their salvation is assured by Jesus' life of resistance and by the survival strategies he used to help people survive the death of identity caused by their exchange of inherited cultural meanings for a new identity shaped by the gospel ethics and world view. This death of identity was also experienced by African women and men brought to America and enslaved. They too relied upon Jesus to help them survive the forging of a new identity. This kind of account of Jesus' salvific value—made compatible and understandable by use of African-American women's sociopolitical patterns—frees redemption from the cross and frees the cross from the "sacred aura" put around it by existing patriarchal responses to the question of what Jesus' death represents. . . .[54]

In the traditional account of Jesus's crucifixion, the Cross has become "an image of defilement, a gross manifestation of collective human sin." A womanist Christology will not perceive Jesus as conquering sin through death on the Cross. Rather, Jesus will be seen as conquering sin, as in the temptations in the wilderness (Matt. 4:1–11) by resistence. Jesus conquers sin in life, not in death.[55] Williams proceeds to show that God, through Jesus's ministry—his ethical teachings, his healings, his militant expelling of evil forces, his life of prayer—redeems humankind.

Humankind is, then, redeemed through Jesus' *ministerial* vision of life and not through his death. There is nothing divine in the blood of the cross. God does not intend black women's surrogacy experience. Neither can Christian faith affirm such an idea. Jesus did not

come to be a surrogate. Jesus came for life, to show humans a perfect vision of ministerial relation that humans had very little knowledge of. As Christians, black women cannot forget the cross, but neither can they glorify it. To do so is to glorify suffering and to render their exploitation sacred.[56]

Emerging womanist Christologies present significant challenges to traditional understandings of the person and work of Jesus Christ. The point of these Christologies is to reclaim the earthly life, work, and ministry of Jesus as the point of departure for understanding his identity, as well as providing an approachable model for human conduct.

Trajectories: Womanist Moral and Ethical Thought

Womanist theologians have concentrated on the relevance of the Christian faith to the lives of black women and men. This means that the practical aspects of the Gospel are especially important components of Womanist theology. Womanist moral and ethical thought seeks then to revise and revitalize our notions of Christian practice. Among the most significant works in this field are Katie G. Cannon's *Black Womanist Ethics* (1988) and Emilie M. Townes's *Womanist Justice, Womanist Hope* (1993). Both women appeal to personal narrative and to a virtue ethics, as do the proponents of narrative theology and postliberalism (see Chapter Sixteen).

Cannon describes the moral situation of black women in light of the concrete problems of poverty, discrimination, hunger, and disease. She then proceeds to articulate a constructive ethic for black women, in particular, and the black community, in general, by drawing from the life and works of Zora Neale Hurston, Howard Thurman, and Martin Luther King, Jr. She finds within the life and fiction of the writer Zora Neale Hurston a quest for moral virtue particularly suited to the genius of black women. In Hurston's life Cannon sees the virtue of "invisible dignity," and in her fiction Hurston portrays the virtues of "never practiced delicacy," "quiet grace," and "unshouted courage." Cannon writes:

In Zora Neale Hurston's fiction there is evidence of . . . a characteristic of moral agency which is expressed in the "never practiced delicacy" which Black women oftentimes convert into quiet grace. The quality of being dainty, luxurious and feeble in constitution, characterized by modesty with an extreme respect for protocol, was not part of the ethical behavior of the female characters in her writings. Hurston and her literary counterparts acknowledge the raw coarseness of life. They face life squarely, front and center. . . . Cultivating conventional amenities has not been a luxury afforded to Black women. "Quiet" is the qualifying word describing grace as a virtue in the moral agency of Black women. "Quiet" acknowledges the invisibility of their moral character. Black women have never been granted the protective privileges that allow one to become immobilized by fear and rage. The Black woman's very life depends upon her being able to decipher the various sounds in the larger world, to hold in check the nightmare figures of terror, to fight for basic freedoms . . . to resist the temptation to capitulate to the demands of the status quo, to find meaning in the most despotic circumstances. . . . Most of the time this is done without the mumble of a single word, without an eruptive cry to the hierarchical systems that oppress her. . . . Unshouted courage is the quality of steadfastness, akin to fortitude, in the face of formidable oppression. . . . It involves the ability to "hold on the life" . . . to facilitate change, to chip away at the oppressive [sic] structures, bit by bit.[57]

While Cannon recognizes that neither the theologian Howard Thurman nor Martin Luther King, Jr. directly addresses black women's experience, their moral wisdom resonates with Hurston's deepest convictions and can enhance womanist ethics. Especially valuable, Cannon finds, is Thurman's exposition of the *imago Dei* in each human being, declaring her or his inherent worth and sacredness, and inspiring each person's potentiality and liberating transformation. Cannon also finds in King's writings the deep spirituality of Thurman, but given a social concreteness grounded in the quest for justice and equality. Cannon concludes:

In order to sustain the living out of "invisible dignity," "quiet grace," and "unshouted courage" Black women today must embrace the formal features of the theological ethics of Thurman and King because they provide moral resources for the great struggle that *still lies ahead*.[58]

Following on the work of Cannon, Emilie M. Townes pursues a biographical approach in her study of womanist ethics, *Womanist Justice, Womanist Hope* (1993). Townes examines the social and cultural milieu of the years 1892 to 1931 for African Americans, using as her focus of research the social world of Ida B. Wells-Barnett (1862–1931), a social reformer and churchwoman especially active in the antilynching campaigns of the late nineteenth century. Through her study of Wells-Barnett, Townes explores the earlier role of black women's church groups, their spirituality, and their leadership as possible resources for a contemporary womanist Christian social ethic. In Wells-Barnett's life and her distinctive response to such realities as authority by domination, obedience, Christian notions of suffering, liberation, and reconciliation, Townes finds—despite Wells-Barnett's all-too-human faults—a role model and a witness who can encourage and instruct black women today. Like Cannon and Townes, other black women ethicists are drawing upon the indigenous resources within black women's religious experience and also finding in these sources sustenance for reflection and action.

Although of rather recent origin, contemporary Black theology is now a vital movement that will remain so as long as people of African descent interpret their experience in light of their Christian faith. This dynamic story of Black theology also can be seen as developing through several stages,[59] and the present stage, at the close of the century, reveals a number of important trajectories. One is the emergence of Womanist theology that has been explored here. Others include the deeper exploration of the African sources of African American religion, building on the seminal work, Albert Raboteau's, *Slave Religion: The*

"*Invisible Institution*" *in the Antebellum South* (1978). This recent interest informs works such as the volume edited by Dwight Hopkins and George Cummings, *Cut Loose Your Stammering Tongue: Black Theology in the Slave Narratives* (1991), and Hopkins's *Shoes that Fit Our Feet: Sources for a Constructive Black Theology* (1993). Another development is the dialogue between the proponents of a Black theology of liberation and liberation theologians from Latin America, Asia, Africa, and the Pacific Rim.[60] A third lively direction, undertaken largely by the "second generation" of African American scholars, is in the field of biblical studies. The fact that black scholars are engaged in the study of the Bible is not, of course, striking; what is new is the number of black scholars who are bringing to their biblical

research a connection with the concerns of black liberation theology and, in so doing, also challenging the earlier black theologies' use and misuse of the Bible, including the portrayal of black people in the Bible. Exemplifying this new scholarship are the essays in *Stony the Road We Trod: African American Biblical Interpretation* (1991), edited by Cain Hope Felder, and the work of Renita J. Weems and Vincent L. Wimbush.

Since the first sustained attempts to articulate the genius of Black Christianity in the mid-1960s, an impressive body of literature has been developed. Only a sample of that literature has been included in this chapter. However, the major themes in Black theology here explored continue to provide the basic framework for black belief.

NOTES

1. Martin Luther King, Jr., "Nonviolence and Racial Justice," in *Christian Century*, 74 (February 6, 1957), 165–167. Republished in James Melvin Washington, ed., *A Testament of Hope: The Essential Writings of Martin Luther King, Jr.*, (San Francisco, 1986), pp. 5–9.

2. Martin Luther King, Jr., "A Time to Break Silence," in *Freedomways*, 7 (Spring 1967), 8. Republished in *A Testament of Hope*, p. 238.

3. Martin Luther King, Jr., *Where Do We Go From Here: Chaos or Community?* (New York, 1967), pp. 186–188.

4. Gayraud S. Wilmore, *Black Religion and Black Radicalism*, 2nd ed. (Maryknoll, N.Y., 1983), p. 1.

5. Ibid., p. 6.

6. Ibid., p. 11.

7. Ibid., p. 49.

8. Ibid., p. 51.

9. Ibid., pp. 12–13.

10. Ibid., p. 27.

11. Dwight N. Hopkins, "Slave Theology in the 'Invisible Institution,'" in *Cut Loose Your Stammering Tongue: Black Theology in the Slave Narratives*, ed. Dwight N. Hopkins and George Cummings (Maryknoll, N.Y., 1991), p. 1.

12. Ibid., pp. 2–3.

13. Ibid., pp. 6–7.

14. Ibid., pp. 10–11.

15. These documents are published together in James H. Cone and Gayraud S. Wilmore, ed., *Black*

Theology: A Documented History, I, 2nd ed., rev. (Maryknoll, N.Y., 1993), pp. 19–39.

16. "Black Power," in *Black Theology: A Documented History*, I, op. cit., p. 19.

17. Ibid., pp. 21–22.

18. Ibid., p. 22.

19. Ibid., pp. 22–23.

20. Ibid., p. 24.

21. King, *Where Do We Go From Here*, p. 44.

22. "The Black Manifesto," in *Black Theology: A Documented History*, I, p. 27.

23. Ibid., pp. 28–29.

24. Ibid., pp. 30–31.

25. "The Statement on Black Theology," in *Black Theology: A Documented History*, I, p. 38.

26. Ibid., pp. 38–39.

27. Malcolm X, *By Any Means Necessary*, ed. George Breitwan (New York, 1970), p. 155. See *A Black Theology of Liberation*, Twentieth Anniversary Ed. (New York, 1990) p. xiii.

28. James H. Cone, *A Black Theology of Liberation*, Twentieth Anniversary Ed. (New York, 1990), p. 29.

29. Ibid., p. 30.

30. Ibid., p. 45.

31. Ibid., p. 54.

32. Ibid., p. 58.

33. Ibid., pp. 60–61.

34. Ibid., pp. 101–102.

35. Ibid., pp. 120–121.

36. Ibid., p. 130.

37. Ibid., pp. 132, 140.

38. Ibid., p. xix.

39. Ibid., pp. 190–191.

40. See James H. Cone, *My Soul Looks Back* (Nashville, Tenn., 1982), Ch. 4 and 5; *For My People* (Maryknoll, N.Y., 1984), Ch. III, IV, VI–IX; and the articles and bibliography in James H. Cone and Gayraud S. Wilmore, ed., *Black Theology: A Documentary History*, II (Maryknoll N.Y., 1993) pp. 358–398, 428.

41. James H. Cone, *Martin and Malcolm and America: A Dream or a Nightmare?* (Maryknoll, N.Y., 1991), p. 318.

42. Alice Walker, *In Search of Our Mother's Gardens* (New York, 1983), p. xi.

43. Renita J. Weems, *Just a Sister Away: A Womanist Vision of Women's Relationships in the Bible* (San Diego, 1998), pp. 1–2.

44. Ibid., p. 7.

45. Clarice J. Martin, "The *Haustafeln* (Domestic Codes) in African American Biblical Interpretation: 'Free Slaves' and 'Subordinate Women,'" in *Stony the Road We Trod: African American Biblical Interpretation*, ed. Cain Hope Felder (Minneapolis, 1991), p. 216.

46. Ibid., p. 225.

47. Ibid., p. 222.

48. Jacquelyn Grant, *White Women's Christ and Black Women's Jesus: Feminist Christology and Womanist Response* (Atlanta, 1989), p. 214.

49. Ibid., pp. 212, 217, 221.

50. Kelly Brown Douglas, *The Black Christ* (Maryknoll, N.Y., 1994), p. 107.

51. Ibid., p. 108.

52. Ibid., pp. 112–113.

53. Ibid., p. 113.

54. Delores S. Williams, *Sisters in the Wilderness: The Challenge of Womanist God-Talk* (Maryknoll, N.Y., 1993), p. 164.

55. Ibid., p. 166.

56. Ibid., p. 167.

57. Katie G. Cannon, *Black Womanist Ethics* (Atlanta, 1988), pp. 125–126, 144.

58. Ibid., p. 174.

59. See Wilmore, "Introduction," *Black Theology: A Documentary History*, I, pp. 1–21.

60. See the extensive bibliography and the articles in Part V, "The Global Context," in *Black Theology: A Documentary History*, I, pp. 355–440.

SUGGESTIONS FOR FURTHER READING

For a full annotated bibliography of books and articles on Black theology from 1966 through 1992 compiled by Mark L. Chapman, see James H. Cone and Gayraud S. Wilmore, ed., *Black Theology: A Documentary History*, I and II (Maryknoll, N.Y.: Orbis, 1993). Volume I, pp. 441–454; Volume II, pp. 427–440.

The following are secondary works that deal with aspects of Black theology and its development:

Bruce, Calvin E., and William R. Jones, ed. *Black Theology II: Essays on the Formation and Outreach of Contemporary Black Theology* (Lewisburg, Pa.: Bucknell University Press, 1978). These essays represent a second phase of Black theology.

Burrow, Rufus, Jr. *James Cone and Black Liberation Theology* (Jefferson, N.C.: McFarland and Co. 1994).

Cone, James H., and Gayraud S. Wilmore. ed. *Black Theology: A Documentary History*, I and II (Maryknoll, N.Y.: Orbis, 1993). An excellent collection of documents with helpful introductions.

Copeland, M. Shawn. "Black, Hispanic/Latino, and Native American Theologies." In *The Modern Theologians*, 2nd ed., ed. David F. Ford (Oxford: Basil Blackwell, 1997). A good, brief, up-to-date survey, pp. 359–366.

Hayes, Diana L. *And Still We Rise: An Introduction to Black Liberation Theology* (Mahwah, N.J.: Paulist Press, 1996).

Hopkins, Dwight N. *Black Theology U.S.A. and South Africa: Politics, Culture, and Liberation* (Maryknoll, N.Y.: Orbis, 1989). Analyzes both Black theology in the United States and in Africa in relation to one another.

Witvliet, Theo. *The Way of the Black Messiah* (Oak Park, Ill., Meyer-Stone Books, 1987). A thorough critical examination of the Black theology movement.

Young, Josiah Ulysses. *A Pan-African Theology: Providence and the Legacy of the Ancestors* (Trenton, N.J.: Africa World Press, 1992). Young offers a Pan-African theology for the liberation of all poor black people.

The following is a selection of important primary works on Black liberation theology that are not discussed in this chapter:

Cleage, Albert B., Jr. *The Black Messiah* (New York: Sheed and Ward, 1968). Portrays Jesus as a Black revolutionary zealot set on freeing the Black nation of Israel from Roman oppression.

Cone, Cecil W. *The Identity Crisis in Black Theology* (Nashville, Tenn.: The African Methodist Episcopal Church, 1975). The author criticizes other important Black theologians and points to an identity crisis in the movement.

Evans, James H., Jr. *We Have Been Believers: An African American Systematic Theology* (Minneapolis: Fortress Press, 1993). A systematic treatment of African American Christian faith as expressed through its distinctive sources.

Felder, Cain H. *Troubling Biblical Waters: Race, Class, and Family* (Maryknoll, N.Y.: Orbis, 1989). Explores the African presence in the Bible and the themes of the book's title from a Black theological perspective.

———, ed. *Stony the Road We Trod: African American Biblical Interpretation* (Minneapolis: Fortress Press, 1991). A good sampling of recent African American biblical scholarship as it bears on several themes, and illuminating the role of the Bible in the religious experience of Black Americans.

Harding, Vincent. "The Religion of Black Power." In *The Religious Situation: 1968*, ed. D. R. Cutler (Boston: Beacon Press, 1968). An important early essay on the religous aspects of the Black power movement.

Jones, Major J. *Black Awareness: A Theology of Hope* (Nashville, Tenn.: Abingdon Press, 1971). Using Jürgen Moltmann's theme of a theology of hope in relation to Black awareness, the author develops a Black theism beyond a God solely on the side of oppressed Blacks.

———. *The Color of God: The Concept of God in Afro-American Thought* (Macon, Ga.: Mercer University Press, 1987). An historical study of the unique development of the African American concept of God, which, the author argues, is true to the orthodox Christian trinitarian God.

Jones, William R. *Is God a White Racist? A Preamble to Black Theology* (Garden City, N.Y.: Anchor Books/Doubleday, 1973). Jones seeks an adequate theodicy in view of the massive suffering of Blacks and proposes what he calls a humanocentric theism.

Lincoln, C. Eric. *The Black Experience in Religion* (Garden City, N.Y.: Anchor Books/Doubleday, 1974). Valuable collection of essays that illuminates the influence of Black power on Black religion.

Long, Charles H. "Perspectives for a Study of Afro-American Religion in the United States." In *History of Religions*, 11 (August 1971), 54–66. An important article that proposes a History of Religions approach as an alternative to the dominant sociological and theological studies of Black religion.

Rabateau, Albert J. *Slave Religion: The "Invisible Institution" in the Antebellum South* (New York: Oxford University Press, 1978). A valuable study of the role and the distinct features of religion in the lives of the African American slaves, including the impact on them of African traditional religion.

Roberts, J. Deotis. *Liberation and Reconciliation: A Black Theology* (Philadelphia: Westminster Press, 1971). Argues that a Black theology must include consideration of the doctrine of reconciliation along with liberation.

———. *Black Theology Today* (New York: Edwin Mellon Press, 1983). A collection of essays on various aspects of Black theology that illuminates the commonalities and the differences among Black theologians.

———. *Black Theology in Dialogue* (Philadelphia: Westminster Press, 1987). A discussion of Black theology's dialogue with African, Asian, and Latin American theology, and arguing for an interdisciplinary and ecumenical approach to the study of contemporary liberation theology.

Washington, Joseph R. *Black Religion: The Negro and Christianity in the United States* (Boston: Beacon Press, 1964). A provocative book that claims that Black churches lack a sound Christian theological base, hence are more like a folk religion. Calls for Black churches to integrate into white churches to insure their authentic Christian identity.

West, Cornel. *Prophecy Deliverence! An Afro-American Revolutionary Christianity* (Philadelphia: Westminster Press, 1982). Argues that prophetic Black theology and Marxist thought should compliment one another in understanding both the capitalist roots of Black oppression and the liberating dimensions of popular Black religion and culture.

Williams, Preston N. "James Cone and the Problem of a Black Ethic." *Harvard Theological Review* 65 (1972), 483–494. Argues that Cone's first books so emphasize an unqualified acceptance of the Black revolution as to undermine a commitment to Christianity's universal ethic.

Wilmore, Gayraud S. *Black Religion and Black Radicalism* (Garden City, N.Y.: Doubleday and Co., 1972; 2nd ed., 1983, Orbis). Argues that the twentieth century has seen the deradicalization of Black religion and the de-Christianization of Black radicalism. Looking to the work of Martin Luther King, Jr. and Malcolm X, he calls for a reunion between Black religion and Black radicalism.

Chapter Fifteen

❦

Theology of Religions:
Christian Responses to Other Faiths

John Hick

INTRODUCTION

Scholars who study modernity appear to agree that the most disorienting cultural change facing individuals and communities today is the realization that we are living in a radically pluralistic world of competing beliefs and values. And that while the long-term implications of this cultural and religious pluralism are uncertain, they are full of both promise and foreboding.

Modern technology and communications have made us acutely aware of religious diversity, producing what has been called the "shock of difference." On the other hand, this awareness of other cultures and religions also has made us conscious of how much the human family shares in common. We often are surprised at the striking resemblances in the world's religious beliefs, moral values, and ritual practices. And so we also experience a "shock of recognition," of likeness, even kinship. Christian theologians today are, therefore, confronted with giving an accounting for the fact of these religious differences and similarities, that is, with providing a Christian theology of religions. Writing in 1961, the distinguished historian of religions, Wilfred Cantwell Smith, observed that

the time will soon be with us when a theologian who attempts to work out his position unaware that he does so as a member of a world society in which other theologians equally intelligent, equally devout, equally moral, are Hindus, Buddhists, Muslims . . . —such a theologian is as out of date as one who

469

attempts to construct an intellectual position unaware . . . that the earth is a minor planet in a galaxy that is vast only by terrestrial standards.[1]

That time is now upon us, but such an awareness, and especially its significance for Christian belief, has emerged slowly in the West. There was little serious study of the non-Christian religions before the middle of the nineteenth century. It began with the appearance of the new "science of religion" spearheaded by Friedrich Max Müller. (See Chapter One.)

It is worth noting that Max Müller was profoundly convinced that Christianity would be both better understood and better appreciated if it were examined in the same manner as, and compared to, the other great religious traditions of the world. Christianity, he believed, had nothing to fear from such an investigation. Perhaps this is not surprising, because many of the early classics in the comparative field—for example, C. P. Tiele's (1830–1902) *Outlines of the History of Religion to the Spread of Universal Religion* (Eng. trans., 1877), and F. B. Jevon's (1858–1936) *An Introduction to the History of Religion* (1896)—followed a developmental theory of the history of religions that portrayed Christianity as the apex and goal of religious evolution. Typical of many similar works is Allan Menzie's (1845–1916) *History of Religion* (1895)—a popular book in Britain—which speaks of Christianity as "destined to become the faith of all mankind."

This imperial view of Christianity as the "crown" and fulfillment of religious evolution was either implied or explicit in the work of many Christian scholars associated with the new comparative study of religion well into the second decade of the twentieth century. More striking is the fact that between the two World Wars no influential Christian *theologian* gave serious attention to the question of Christianity's relation to the other great world religions.

Since 1945, however, Western culture has undergone profound change. Langdon Gilkey concisely describes it:

Colonies vanished, Europe disappeared as a major power, other non-Western power centers appeared representing other ways of life and other religions. The West no longer ruled the world. . . . Western religion became one among the other world religions.[2]

Gilkey rightly sees that this new pluralistic sensibility about cultural and political institutions and values implicitly includes the notion of a religious "parity." For many today, the presence of diverse religions is perceived positively as a rich cultural mosaic. Yet for Christians the idea of "plurality as parity" constitutes a profound challenge to traditional Christian belief and to theological reflection. As Gilkey suggests, "plurality as parity" demands nothing less than a new theological quest that requires a new theological self-understanding "that includes and supplements what the other [religion] offers instead of rejecting it as false or incorporating it as merely one vista in the panorama shaped by one's own viewpoint."[3]

Religious pluralism today requires a new theological examination at least as challenging as the encounters with modern science and philosophy in the eighteenth and nineteenth centuries. The theologian Karl Rahner states rather compellingly what, for many Christians, is at stake:

Because of Jesus Christ, Christianity understands itself as the absolute religion, intended for all men, which cannot recognize any other religion beside itself as of equal right. . . . [Therefore] pluralism is a greater threat and a reason for greater unrest for Christianity than for any other religion. For no other religion—not even Islam—maintains so absolutely that it is *the* religion, the one and only valid revelation of the one living God as does the Christian religion. The fact of the pluralism of religions, which endures . . . even after a history of 2000 years, must therefore be the greatest scandal and the greatest vexation for Christianity.[4]

In this chapter we examine the way in which both Catholic and Protestant thinkers in the latter decades of the twentieth century have addressed the questions posed by the new dialogue between Christianity and the non-Christian religions. We will select representative thinkers whose work is characteristic of one of the several positions that stand out in this new discussion. While such a typology may tend to exaggerate the features shared by certain writers, distinctive positions have clearly emerged that do identify comparable standpoints of thinkers whose writings have been most influential in addressing this subject.

EXCLUSIVISM

Between approximately 1920 and 1950 much of the writing on Christianity's relationship to the non-Christian religions was traditionalist, and it expressed a position that has since been labeled *exclusivism*. It assumed Christianity's uniqueness, superiority and finality. It held that salvation is found through faith in Christ's singular redemptive work. It appealed to numerous New Testament texts, such as Acts 4:12: "And there is salvation in no one else, for there is no other name under heaven given among men by which we must be saved." In Protestantism the position is expressed with particular force in the writings of the Dialectical theologians, especially by Karl Barth.

You will recall that in Chapter Three Barth contrasts religion, including the Christian religion, with faith in Christ. His discussion of religion appears both in his book on Paul's *Epistle to the Romans* and in a long section of the *Church Dogmatics* I, 2, published in 1938. It constitutes Barth's "*Nein!*" (No!) to religion, which he associates with natural theology, with the idolatrous human claim to know God and to justify the self by its own efforts. It is important to recognize, of course, the context in which Barth wrote this critique of religion as the supreme expression of the human "passion for eternity," namely, the ascendence of the pagan Nazi ideology of Aryan blood and soil. Also, we must recall that human sin and idolatry are not Barth's last word about humanity. Because of God's eternal covenant in Jesus Christ,

humanity stands in a *positive* relationship to God. Nevertheless, Barth's view of religion as human unbelief does not change.

Barth concedes that it is possible to speak of "true" religion but only in the sense that one can speak of a "justified sinner," namely, "as a creature of grace." No religion *is* true. "It can only become true. . . . And it can become true in the way in which man is justified, from without."[5] For Barth, Christianity, too, "stands under the judgment that religion is unbelief." "It is our business as Christians," he insists, "to apply this judgment first and most acutely to ourselves."[6] Barth rejects out of hand the possibility that Christianity can offer empirical evidence that Christianity is a better, truer, or wiser religion than any other. Christianity, looked at historically and candidly, reveals that its institutions, its theology, even its worship manifest as well human "unbelief"—that is, "opposition to revelation"—through human idolatry and sin. The only thing that distinguishes Christianity from all other religions is the Christian's awareness, through God's revelation in Jesus Christ, that he or she is unworthy, unrighteous, and a sinner and that, despite this, God graciously accepts the sinner through Christ's "infinite satisfaction for our sin."

Barth dismisses any effort to compare Christianity with other religions or to find any "points of contact" with another religion. This is demonstrated in one of his rare discussions of the nonbiblical religions. In the section of the *Church Dogmatics* mentioned above, Barth compares Christianity with the Pure Land Schools of Amida Buddhism in East Asia. Many comparativists have pointed to the extraordinary similarity in the teachings of the two religions. Like St. Paul and Luther, the Amida Buddhists teach that good works are of no avail; that salvation comes only through faith in the gracious love of Amida. But Barth sees no "truth" in this Buddhist teaching since, as he writes, "Only one thing is really decisive for the distinction of truth and error. . . . That one thing is the name of Jesus Christ . . . which alone constitutes the truth of our religion."[7] Here Barth makes the contentious, but not illogical, point that there is an enormous difference between similar *doctrines* of grace and "the reality of grace itself." Christianity alone, Barth claims, points to this reality of grace as present in God's unique revelation in and through Christ, and it is this reality alone that allows Christianity to claim to be the "true" religion.

Barth's powerful attack on human religiosity as idolatry was and remains important, but his failure to seriously engage the non-Christian religions has, in the late twentieth century, only accentuated the limitations of Barth's writings on this question. The exclusivist position is articulated more adequately in the writings of the orientalist and missionary theologian to Indonesia, Henrik Kraemer—and Kraemer's position remains compelling to many evangelical Protestants today.

Henrik Kraemer (1888–1965) was born in Amsterdam, Holland. His early education was at the Dutch Missionary High School, and then at Leiden University where he was trained as an orientalist and missionary for the Dutch Bible Society. He served as a missionary in Indonesia during the 1920s and 1930s, and he was an important figure in the International Missionary Council Conferences in Jerusalem (1928) and Tambaran (1938). His book, *The Christian Message in a Non-Christian World*, was written as a study document for Tambaran, and it became a landmark of the exclusivist position. Kraemer served as professor of the history and phenomenology of religions at Leiden between 1937 and 1948, though he was imprisoned by the Germans toward the end of World War II for his work in the resistence movement in Holland. Between 1948 and 1955 he was director of the Ecumenical Institute of the World Council of Churches in Geneva. Among his other writings are *Religion and the Christian Faith* (1956), a response to, but essentially a restatement of his position in *The Christian Message; The Communication of the Christian Faith* (1957); *Why Christianity of All Religions* (1959); and *World Cultures and World Religions* (1960).

Kraemer's writings on Christianity and the non-Christian religions were shaped by two intellectual influences. One is the great Dutch tradition of the comparative and phenomenological study of religion that extends from the early work of C. P. Tiele and P. D. Chantepie de la Saussaye to Gerardus van der Leeuw and Brede Kristensen. Chantepie de la Saussaye and Kristensen were especially important in shaping Kraemer's thinking about the non-Christian religions. The other influence on Kraemer was the Dialectical theology of Karl Barth and Emil Brunner. Kraemer thought Barth's position was too abstract and polemical, in fact not dialectical enough, but that Barth was correct, nevertheless, in presenting the biblical teachings as genuinely *sui generis*. Kraemer judged Brunner's position to be more truly dialectical because of his understanding of Christ as *both* the "Fulfillment" of and the "Judgment" on all religion.[8]

Kraemer considered his distinction between "revelation" and "religion" to be both theological and phenomenological. His study of the great non-Christian religions lead him, perhaps rather surprising for a historian of religion, to the conclusion that all these religions are systems of self-salvation:

Nowhere is there an *Ahnung* (intuition) of God's holiness, of "It is a fearful thing to fall in the hands of the living God," or of the mystery of God's condemning and saving righteousness. Man wants God, but somehow he wants Him in his own way. Therefore . . . the highest flights, the sincerest contrition, remain in the sphere of a lofty moralism and spiritualism. Nowhere do we find a radical repudiation of every possible man-made spiritual world, which is the uncanny power of the gospel.[9]

Kraemer sees a world of difference in the so-called parallels to Christian grace in some of the non-Christian religions because the latter, he insists, lack the sense of "divine forgiveness of sin as the root fact."[10] Kraemer sympathizes with his fellow missionaries who are concerned to find "points of contact" between Christianity and another faith, and he considers it natural for them to want to discover openings for the Gospel in the minds of the Hindu or the Muslim. What he rejects, however, is the notion that one can extract this or that doctrine or practice from its wider context in a religion and abstractly compare it with similar phenomena in Christianity. "Religion," Kraemer argues,

is nowhere in the world an assortment of spiritual commodities that can be compared as shoes or neckties. . . . Every religion is an indivisible, and not to be divided, unity of existential apprehension. It is not a series of tenets, institutions, practices that can be taken one by one as independent items of religious life. . . . and that can be compared with. . . . and grafted upon similar items of another religion.[11]

It was Kraemer's predecessor in the professorship at Leiden, Brede Kristensen, who convinced him of the "totalistic" or "living unity" of religions and that one must be skeptical about apparent similarities. While it is necessary for the phenomenologist to break up a religion into component parts for the sake of analysis, Kraemer nevertheless insists that as "a guide for the adequate apprehension of religion as a living and thriving reality it is less than useless."[12] The result of such an intellectual and abstract comparative approach is an inevitable distortion. One cannot know the real power, value, or function of some aspect of a religion unless, in a living, existential way, one apprehends the totality of life that dominates the entire religion.

Kraemer argues that such a "totalistic" view of religion makes it impossible to demonstrate the superiority or the truth of a religion by religious or philosophical reasoning, because there are no universally agreed-upon criteria by which to decide the question. First of all

the argument of value does not coincide with that of truth. The non-Christian religions can just as well as Christianity show up an impressive record of psycho-

logical, cultural, social, and moral value, and it is wholly dependent on one's fundamental axioms of life whether one considers these non-Christian achievements of higher value for mankind than the Christian.[13]

Kraemer insists that the only way out of this epistemological dilemma is to recognize the inexplicable fact of human consciousness; namely, that prior to all the ideas and valuations that shape our religion or philosophy of life there is a choice and a decision, and an act of faith.[14] For example, an analysis of Ernst Troeltsch's attempt to show the superiority of Christianity (see Chapter One) clearly exposes his implicit value judgments favoring Christianity's superiority over the Asian religions.

Moreover, to speak of Christianity as the "fulfillment" or "crown" of other religions is, for Kraemer, the worst kind of arrogance and imperialism. The Christian attitude toward other religions is, in the last analysis, a paradoxical one, a combination of what Kraemer calls "down-right intrepidity and humility." Humility because the missionary is "the bringer of a divine gift, not something of his making or achievement." Intrepidity, because the Christian missionary "is the bearer of a message, the witness to a divine revelation."[15]

Are there, then, for Kraemer, no points of contact between Christianity and the other world religions? There are, Kraemer suggests, only two such points of contact. One is contact "by antithesis." And this means "by discovering in the revealing light of Christ the fundamental misdirection that dominates all religious life," including much of the religious life of empirical Christianity. There is, finally, only one point of contact and that "is the disposition and the attitude of the Christian missionary," which will express itself "in an untiring and genuine interest in the religion, the ideas, the sentiments, the institutions . . . in the whole range of life of the people among whom one works, *for Christ's sake and for the sake of those people.*"[16]

One senses a candor and a genuine openness and humility in Kraemer's writing that the term "exclusivism" belies. Critics often fail to mention his persistent rejection of any notions of Christianity's superiority. And yet, finally, one is not satisfied with Kraemer's isolation of "Christ's revelation" from the kind of historical scrutiny that he applies to the "culturally shaped" non-Christian religions. There is, as in the case of Barth, something ahistorical, abstract, and *a priori* about Kraemer's work. One senses that he rejects the notion of points of contact because he already has judged Christian revelation to be *sui generis*. His concern not to extract, for example, a Hindu rite from its lived context, paradoxically leads Kraemer to interpret the great religions as abstracted "totalities." This allows him to say, for example, that no other religion shares with Christianity its intuition "of the mystery of God's condemning and saving righteousness." Because a number of non-Christian examples of this intuition come to mind that might counter such a claim, Kraemer's phenomenological approach misses the variability and complexity of many of the non-Christian religions. For example, Kraemer's wholesale labeling of Hinduism as a "mystical monism" simply is not credible. Furthermore, Kraemer's insistence that there are no universally valid or acceptable norms or criteria for judging religious truth claims may or may not be the case, but his *a priori* dictum effectively cuts off dialogue on the question prematurely. In any interreligious dialogue the point is likely to be reached when, as the philosopher Wittgenstein remarks, "the shovel turns," the dialogue reaches bedrock where differences are irreconcilable. But illuminating comparisons and convergences might be discovered long before that point is reached.

The exclusivist position that insists on the "discontinuity" between Christianity and other world faiths, as represented by Barth and especially by Henrik Kraemer, was extraordinarily influential within Protestantism through the 1950s. It shaped the thinking of three important International Missionary Conferences held in Jerusalem (1928), Tambaran (1938), and Willingen (1952).[17] This influence also is reflected in the official pronouncements of the World Council of Churches from its beginning in 1948 until the mid-1960s. The Council, whose membership includes scores of Protestant, Anglican, and Eastern Orthodox churches, was under the directorship of Willem Visser't Hooft until 1966, and he guided the Council's deliberations along exclusivist lines. However, the policy of exclusivism and discontinuity began to be challenged as early as the Tambaran conference the year that Kraemer's *The Christian Message in a Non-Christian World* was published. The central issue raised at Tambaran was whether Christianity's relationship with other faiths should be one of *discontinuity* or a search for points of contact and continuities. Young scholars from India in particular took exception to Kraemer's position and called for a new apologetic approach that would require a genuine dialogue with non-Christian faiths.

A church-centered exclusivism was revived at the World Council's meeting at Willengen in 1952, but by then the world situation had changed markedly. The harmful aspects of earlier missionary collaboration with European colonialism was by then exposed, and the growth and independence of the indigenous Christian churches demanded a new framework of partnership. What these postcolonial churches in India, Africa, and Asia wanted was genuine dialogue with their own people of other faiths. Missionary activity now became identified with Christian "presence" in the Third World, which, for many, meant involvement in nation building, in programs to advance justice and welfare, in peace activities, and even in revolutionary efforts to affect social change—rather than involvement in "proselytizing" and increasing membership in the Church. The meaning of Christian "presence" is epitomized in a World Student Christian Federation document published in 1961:

[Christian presence] is the adventure of being there in the name of Christ, often anonymously, listening before we speak, hoping that men will recognize Jesus for what he is, and stay where they are involved in the fierce fight against all that dehumanizes, ready to act against demonic powers, to identify with outcasts. . . . Presence for us means "engagement." . . . It indicates a priority. First, we have to be there before we can see our task clearly. In one sense of the word presence precedes witness. In another sense, presence is witness.[18]

ROMAN CATHOLIC POSITIONS

The historical and more immediate background of Roman Catholic reflection on a theology of religions presents a different picture. Since the age of the early Christian apologists, the Catholic Church has taught that there is a preparation (*praeparatio evangelica*) for Christ in the pagan religions as well as in the Old Testament. Many of these early Christian apologists—Justin Martyr, Origen, and Clement of Alexandria—taught that the pagan religions and philosophers (Plato and the Stoics are examples) were "schoolmasters" preliminary to but pointing to Christ. Furthermore, the Catholic Church has held that, by virtue of their divine creation, all human beings are able through natural reason (Rom. 1:20) and conscience (Rom. 2:14–16) to know God.

Views Prior to Vatican II

As we have learned in the discussion of Neo-Thomism (Volume I, Chapter Thirteen), belief in a human natural knowledge of God's existence and will was classically formulated by Thomas Aquinas in his *Summa Theologica*, but with a difference. Thomas makes a distinction between what is natural due to its creaturely nature and that which is supernatural due to the gift of God's special, supernatural revelation in Jesus Christ, which is mediated through the divine institution of the Church. The grace of God belongs to the original, natural state of human beings, but this supernatural condition was lost in the Fall. And because the original supernatural quality of life was lost, a special gift of grace is required for the healing or salvation of wounded human nature, so as to restore it to participation in the divine nature. This special gift of grace is not found outside the Church. And so, while the Catholic Church thus continued to uphold the belief in humanity's natural knowledge of God and the divine will, it also maintained the *essential* mediation of the Church, as St. Thomas taught. Therefore, the Church pronounced, on occasion, the doctrine *extra Ecclesiam nulla salus* (no salvation outside the Church).[19]

From the post-Reformation period to the twentieth century, the Catholic Church's position has varied in its emphasis—sometimes relaxing the rigor of the no salvation *extra Ecclesiam* doctrine and at other times stressing the ecclesiocentric view. But the modern Church shows an increasingly positive attitude toward the salvation of non-Christians, holding that those who are ignorant of the teachings of the Church, through no fault of their own, may follow the precepts of the natural law written on their conscience. And these may, through God's grace, receive eternal life. This is essentially the position set forth by Pius XII in his encyclical letter *Mystici Corporis* in 1943. As one commentator has written:

The emphasis lies on the mediation of salvation by the Church, but the idea of "the Catholic unity" is enlarged. The limits of the Church are not visible and strict. Those non-Catholics and non-Christians who are sensitive to God's call in their inner self are in some secret manner latent members of that society to whom the explicit means of salvation are available. . . . In an important way Pius XII widened his perspective from the notion of an implicit membership in the Church to that of an implicit relationship with God in conforming one's will to God's will. A man's implicit membership of the Church now means supernatural faith effected by God through man's intimate direct relationship with his Creator.[20]

There are, the Catholic Church teaches, members of the Church who are saved who are not visible to the manifest Church.

The Catholic theologies of religion immediately prior to the Second Vatican Council generally followed the Thomistic doctrine on the relationship of nature and grace. That is, supernatural grace, through the mediation of the Church, perfects (fulfills) the natural goodness and truth that may exist in the non-Christian. The key word is "fulfillment." The non-Christian religions should be treated with respect because they contain the "seeds" of spiritual and moral truth that prefigure but only become visible and fulfilled in Catholic Christianity. This is the position taken by such distinguished Catholic theologians as Jean Danielou, Hans Urs von Balthasar, and Joseph Ratzinger.[21] These theologians emphasize the natural possibility of salvation, when aided by God's grace, but the non-Christian religions to which such persons may belong contain only signs or prefigurations of grace. They are not themselves channels of genuine salvation. They must, as Danielou expresses it, be "superceded" by Christianity.

There is, however, another tradition of Catholic thought on the non-Christian religions that is identified with the writings of some of the theologians associated with the *Nouvelle théologie* in France. (See Chapter Seven.) Working with the Thomistic distinction, and yet unity, between nature and grace, these theologians, as we have learned, place the emphasis on "grace" rather than "nature," or perhaps more accurately, speak of a "graced nature." By so doing, these writers seek to avoid a split between one form of grace that is an inherent part of human nature and another form of grace that is perceived as a super-added gift required for salvation. These theologians see all of human life as influenced by supernatural grace—a *gratia universalis*.

This inclusive position is associated especially with Henri de Lubac's *Surnaturel* (1946). (See Chapter Seven.) There de Lubac speaks of the supernatural dimension of every person's being as part of their human essence, a return, he contends, to the patristic teaching of a universal gift of grace poured out on the entire creation. Grace

is not then something understood as external to nature and history. Through God's incarnation in Jesus Christ, God has fully entered human life and history, and all humanity is thereby permeated sacramentally by supernatural grace. All human beings, therefore, seek God, though often unconsciously, in the depths of their being.

What Christians and non-Christians share is not an abstract knowledge of God discovered by reasoning from the analogy of nature, but rather a universal human sense of God that St. Augustine spoke of when he wrote that "our hearts are restless, until they rest in Thee." All human beings are, so to speak, "anonymously" participants in the mystery of God's grace. Having taken this new path, de Lubac ends, nevertheless, embracing the classic Catholic position by viewing the non-Christian religions as only partially fulfilling the universal human longing for God. For de Lubac, as for Pierre Teilhard de Chardin, Christ is the "point of convergence" in which the truth in all the other religions is perfectly fulfilled. Karl Rahner, as we have seen in Chapter Seven, follows de Lubac in his effort to overcome the space between the natural and the supernatural. Rahner, however, develops his own distinctive idea of an "anonymous" Christian that breaks new ground in Catholic thinking on this theme.

The Inclusive Way of Karl Rahner

To illustrate contemporary Christian *inclusivism* in the theology of religions, we will explore the position of the Jesuit theologian Karl Rahner (see Chapter Seven). Rahner begins his reflections on this subject from an analysis of the character of individual human existence. All human beings share a common ontological constitution that includes certain "trancendentals" that shape and determine our human nature. We have learned that among these is what Rahner calls the "supernatural existential," the human experience of limitless transcendence, no matter how latent and unexpressed this may be. Rahner further contends that it is experienced as grace, although not necessarily understood *as* grace. This implicit and unavowed revelatory experience is what is explicitly referred to by Christians as the revelation of grace in Christ. Rahner writes that whenever a human being

accepts the revelation, he posits by that fact the act of supernatural faith. But he also accepts this revelation whenever he really accepts *himself completely*, for it already speaks *in* him. . . . Accordingly, no matter how he wants to understand and express this in his own reflective self-understanding he . . . takes upon himself in that yes to himself the grace of the mystery which has radically approached [him].[22]

Rahner here asserts that the radical acceptance of one's being, no matter how it may be explicitly or conceptually expressed, is testimony to the fact that one is a believer: "And anyone who has let himself be taken hold of by this grace can be called with every right an 'anonymous Christian.'"[23]

The relationship between Rahner's concept of the anonymous Christian and the Church's teaching is best formulated in his essay "Christianity and the Non-Christian Religions" (1966). In this essay Rahner outlines his inclusivist theology of religions by examining four critical theses. The first thesis sounds perfectly traditional: "Christianity understands itself as the absolute religion, intended for all men, which cannot recognize any other religion beside itself as of equal right."[24] This affirmed, Rahner proceeds to probe the more complex implications of the fact that Christianity is an historical religion, that it has a beginning in history. "It did not always exist. . . . It has not always or everywhere been *the* way of salvation for men—at least not in its historically tangible ecclesio-sociological constitution." Therefore, one must take seriously the fact that this *absolute religion* comes to human beings in a historical way.

It is therefore a question of whether this moment, when the existentially real demand is made by the absolute religion . . . takes place really at the same chronological moment for all men, or whether the occurrence of this moment has itself a history and thus is not chronologically simultaneous for all men, cultures, and spaces of history.[25]

For Rahner, it follows from the historical reality of Christianity that our understanding of the first thesis must be "delicately differentiated." That is, Christianity can only be maintained as the absolute and only valid religion for humanity as regards its *destination*.

We leave it, however, an open question at what exact point in time the absolute obligation of the Christian religion has in fact come into effect for every man and culture. . . . Nevertheless . . . whether in practice Christianity reaches man in the real urgency of and rigour of his actual existence, Christianity—once understood—presents itself as the only still valid religion for this man, a necessary means for his salvation.[26]

Rahner insists that the thesis regarding the historical character of Christianity contains within it implicitly another thesis "which states that in concrete human existence as such, the nature of religion itself must include a social constitution—which means that religion can exist only in a social form."[27] What this means is that no person encounters the existential reality and demand of a religion outside its social form. The inherently social nature of human beings makes it unthinkable that a person could achieve a salvific relationship to God in a wholly private and interior way "outside of the actual religious bodies which offer themselves to him in the environment in which he lives." Therefore, if human beings can have a genuine saving relationship to God, it must always be "within *that* religion which in practice was at his disposal by being a factor in his sphere of existence."[28]

Rahner states his second thesis as follows:

Until the moment when the gospel really enters into the historical situation of the individual, a non-Christian religion . . . does not merely contain elements of a natural knowledge of God. . . . It contains also supernatural elements arising out of the grace which is given to men as a gratuitous gift on account of Christ. For this reason a non-Christian religion can be recognized as a *lawful* religion.[29]

For Rahner a "lawful religion" is a historical, institutional religion included in God's plan of salvation that can be regarded as a means of gaining a truly salvific relationship to God. Like Christianity itself, lawful religions will not be free of corruption and error. That means that Christians should rid themselves of the either-or notion that they can approach the non-Christian religions with the idea that either everything these religions contain must come from God or that they must be purely human constructions.

The second thesis includes two fundamental points. First, it is *a priori* quite appropriate to believe that supernatural salvific grace is present in the non-Christian religions. This is predicated on the Christian belief in the genuine, universal salvific purpose of God for all human beings. If, on the one hand, we understand salvation as something specifically Christian and offered in *this* life, and if, on the other hand, God truly intends the salvation of all human beings, then, to reconcile these two convictions it is necessary to believe that every human being is really exposed to divine, supernatural grace, whether or not that person accepts this grace. Here we see Rahner's insistence that nature and grace cannot be understood as two chronological phases of an individual's life. Second, Rahner thinks there is no theological reason for believing that God's offer of supernatural grace is ineffective. Where sin existed, grace came in abundance. "Hence we have every right to suppose that grace has not only been offered even outside the Christian Church, but also . . . that grace gains the victory."[30] There are, then, what Rahner calls "lawful religions" that have positive salvific significance in God's providential plan. Because humans are social beings, they must live their

relationship to God within the cultural and religious realities offered to them in their particular historical circumstances.

If Rahner's second thesis is correct, then Christians must not treat a "member of an extra-Christian religion as a mere non-Christian, but as someone who can and must be regarded . . . as an anonymous Christian," someone touched by God's grace and truth. And having experienced the grace of God, this person "has already been given revelation in a true sense before he has been affected by missionary preaching from without." This latter, explicit proclamation of the Christian Gospel does not turn someone abandoned by God into a Christian, "but turns an anonymous Christian into someone who now knows about his Christian faith . . . by objective reflection." And by "the profession of faith which is given social form in the Church" a higher stage of development of a person's Christianity, demanded by his being and intended by God, is achieved.[31] Rahner insists, however, there is no way that one can say, because anonymous Christians genuinely share in God's supernatural grace, that explicit Christian missionary work is superfluous.

Rahner does not expect that the religious pluralism of our modern world will disappear; indeed, it is likely to increase, while secularization deepens hostility toward the Christian Church. Nevertheless, and this is Rahner's fourth thesis, Christians must continue to seek out the anonymous forms of Christianity and, as missionaries, bring them to an explicit and full consciousness of the divine gift and destiny in Christ. The Church in the future "will not so much regard herself as the exclusive community of those who have a claim to salvation, but rather as the historically tangible vanguard . . . and socially constituted expression of what the Christian hopes is present in a hidden reality even outside the visible Church."[32]

Rahner concludes his reflection on the relationship between Christianity and the "extra-Christian" religions with words that, while candid and an authentic expression of the Christian *inclusivist* position, are, nevertheless, perceived by some as not adequate in our increasingly pluralistic context: "Non-Christians may think it presumption for the Christian to judge everything which is sound . . . to be the fruit in every man of the grace of this Christ, and to interpret it as anonymous Christianity. . . . But the Christian cannot renounce this presumption." . . .[33] However one responds to these words, Rahner's inclusivist position is widely recognized as having set the terms of the Catholic discussion of this subject in the latter decades of the twentieth century.[34]

Catholic critics of Rahner—who defend a form of exclusivism or a more traditional form of the "fulfilment" doctrine—claim that Rahner's position inevitably undermines the radical newness and discontinuity of Christ's Gospel when compared to other religions. The effect is to weaken the urgency of conversion to Christ, which, they argue, will undermine missionary endeavor. Henri de Lubac states the criticism this way:

If several ways of salvation really exist, parallel in some manner, then we are faced with a great dispersal, not a spiritual convergence. . . . If we aspire to unity then we have no choice but to search for an axis, a drawing and unifying force which is the Spirit of the Lord animating the Church.[35]

A chorus of pluralist critics cite the paternalistic sound of Rahner's term "anonymous Christian" as being naturally offensive to non-Christians. How, they ask in effect, would Rahner like to be told that he is an "anonomous Buddhist"? A related criticism is that, because Christianity is *a priori* the normative fulfillment of the non-Christian religions, any *genuine* dialogue would likely be undermined from its inception.[36] Furthermore, how can Rahner know in advance that every divine truth is present and fulfilled in Christ without any careful historical study of the evidence from the religions themselves?[37] Rahner and his supporters have addressed these criticisms, but not, as one might expect, to the entire

satisfaction of the critics.[38] To be fair to Rahner, it must be said that he intends his reflection as a dogmatic formulation of Christianity's position *for* Christians. It is not directed to a non-Christian audience. Also, Rahner would be quite willing to abandon the term "anonymous Christian" if a better term could be found, yet one that would also protect the Christian truths it is meant to convey.

THEOLOGICAL DEFENSES OF RELIGIOUS PLURALISM

Advocates of theological exclusivism and inclusivism find support for their positions in the New Testament, the Church Fathers, and in the writings of the great theologians of the Christian tradition. These sources are not as readily appealed to by Christian defenders of a religious pluralism. The Christian call for a religious pluralism first emerges with the Enlightenment and Romanticism, primarily in the writings of the Deists and some heterodox Christians. In the late twentieth-century context, pluralism is the position that holds that the non-Christian religions can be seen as genuine paths of salvation.

Two factors stand out as contributing to a climate of opinion that would support the pluralist case. The first one is epistemological and has to do with a conviction that is the product of modern historical consciousness. It is called historicism and its cultural equivalent is relativism. Today, we are far more aware of the rich variety and individuality of cultures, but, more significantly, we are conscious of how much our own fundamental beliefs and values are shaped by our cultural experiences and assumptions. This is well stated by the foremost advocate of a Christian pluralism, John Hick:

Our beliefs are . . . global conclusions arising from a vast array of influences and considerations—the family and culture and epoch into which we were born, our education and our life experiences, our reading and interaction with others, etc. Much more goes into it [our religious belief] than clearly articulated arguments. . . . This is very obvious at the fundamental level of our adherence to our own religion rather than another. Is it because of carefully weighed arguments that I am a Christian rather than a Muslim or Buddhist? Does it not rather have a great deal to do with the fact that I was born in England rather than, say, in Saudi Arabia or Thailand . . . ? The religion creates us in our own image, so that naturally it fits us and we fit it as no other can.[39]

The second factor is theological and moral. It is well expressed by the historian Arnold Toynbee:

If God loves mankind, He would have made a revelation to us among other people. But, on the same ground and in virtue of the same vision of what God's nature is, it would also seem unlikely that He would not have made other revelations to other people as well. And it would seem unlikely that He would not have given His revelation in different forms, with different facets, and to different degrees, according to the difference in the nature of individual souls and in the nature of the local tradition of civilization. I should say that this view is a corollary of the Christian view of God as being love.[40]

Stanley Samartha

Pluralists agree that not only are our *conceptions* of God or the Ultimate culturally shaped and relative, but the Christian belief in God's infinite love for all human beings implies, as Toynbee suggests, that God will "have given his revelation in different forms." The pervasive character of this pluralist sensibility is reflected in the World Council of Churches' rapid change in policy from one of exclusivism and discontinuity to one of dialogue and even pluralism. The change is marked by the appointment in the late 1960s of the Indian Christian, Stanley Samartha, as the director of the Council's new Department of Dialogue with People of Living Faiths and Ideologies. This new imperative for dialogue was formulated in a World Council of Churches' document, *Guidelines on Dialogue with People of Living Faiths and Ideologies* (1979).

To the member churches of the World Council of Churches we feel able with integrity to commend the way of dialogue as one in which Jesus Christ can be confessed in the world today; at the same time we feel able with integrity to assure our partners in dialogue that we come not as manipulators but as genuine fellow pilgrims.[41]

In a presentation the same year, Samartha enlarged on the meaning of this new Christian witness in dialogue. This witness, he declared, places

another obligation upon both Christians and their partners in dialogue. If Christians speak of "mission" they must be willing to recognize that their neighbors too have their "missions" in the same pluralistic world. The possibility of "mutual witness" to each other cannot be avoided.[42]

Samartha further suggested that the word "mission" itself should be avoided, even abandoned, so that misunderstandings not thwart genuine mutuality.[43]

A thorough pluralism:

means that there are fundamentally different answers to the problems of existence. . . . The mystery of life, the challenge of death, the agony of suffering, the purpose of history, the knowledge of truth . . . —these are fundamental facts of human existence from which no one can escape and to which particular religions have provided particular answers at different times and in different cultures. There are different faiths, there are alternative ways of salvation. . . . In the last analysis, religions should be recognized as having responded differently to the mystery of the Ultimate.[44]

Samartha's religious pluralism is a more qualified one. For while he recognizes the plurality of genuine responses to the Ultimate, he also believes

that in Jesus Christ the Ultimate has become intimate with humanity, that nowhere else is the victory over suffering and death manifested so decisively as in the death and resurrection of Jesus Christ, and that [Christians] are called upon to share this good news humbly with their neighbors.[45]

Two of the most influential defenders of a more thorough Christian pluralism are Wilfred Cantwell Smith and John Hick, and so we conclude the review of this position with a rather extensive analysis of their important work.

Wilfred Cantwell Smith

It was as a specialist in Islamic studies that W. C. Smith (1916–) first made his scholarly reputation. He taught at the University of the Panjab in India and then founded and directed the Institute of Islamic Studies at McGill University in Montreal. He subsequently moved to Harvard University as professor of the comparative history of religion and, for nine years, served as director of its Center for the Study of Religion. Among his many books are *The Meaning and End of Religion* (1962), *Questions of Religious Truth* (1967), *Towards a World Theology* (1980), *Religious Diversity* (1982), and *What is Scripture? A Comparative Approach* (1993). Through both his writings and his personal engagement over several decades, Smith stands out as a major presence in contemporary interreligious dialogue.

In *The Meaning and End of Religion*, Smith seeks to change the way we conceptualize what we call "religion." He shows that the use of the word "religion" has a relatively recent origin in the Enlightenment. And that its adoption transformed the rich and complex human experiences of God or Ultimate Reality into an abstraction, a static and largely intellectual construct. The result is that subsequent interfaith dialogue has been distorted by being conducted almost entirely at the level of conflicting doctrines and truth claims. In place of the term "religion," Smith proposes two concepts: "personal faith" and "cumulative traditions." Personal faith suggests the individual's existential sense of being in a relationship with the Divine, a universally shared dimension of human life:

Wilfred Cantwell Smith

Faith is an orientation of the personality to oneself, to one's neighbour, to the universe; a total response; a way of seeing the world and handling it; a capacity to live at more than a mundane level; to see, to feel, to act in terms of a transcendent dimension.[46]

On the other hand, the concept of cumulative traditions denotes the complex, ever-changing cultural network within which personal faith is shaped, nurtured, and sustained. Smith argues that it is personal faith that should be the fundamental reality in interfaith dialogue because it is what is universally shared and what alone can unite human beings. Moreover, it is, finally, where truth lives. Cumulative traditions are, like cultures, so complex and various that it is impossible to speak of a tradition such as Hinduism as if it were a single religion. The same can be said for the variety of developments in Christianity and Buddhism. Therefore, Smith argues, it is pointless to ask if these multifarious traditions are "true." According to Smith, truth does not reside in "religions" but in persons—in the spiritual integrity and faithfulness of persons. Religions are not in themselves true or false, but they may *become* true in the life of the believer. It is therefore dangerous and impious to suppose that Christianity [or Buddhism or Islam] is true, as an abstract system, something "out there" impersonally subsisting. . . . Christianity, I would suggest, is not true absolutely, impersonally, statically; rather it can *become* true, if and as you or I appropriate it to ourselves and interiorize it, insofar as we live it out from day to day.[47]

The so-called religions are, for Smith, merely the historical-cultural contexts within which men and women have entered into a living relationship with God or Ultimate Reality:

A devout person, whose sense of the presence of God is both vivid and sincere, and of his own unworthiness as he bows in that presence, may plead for God's mercy, and humbly know the quiet transport of its assurance because of his personal and living faith that God is indeed merciful. At that moment the truth of that man's religiousness is perhaps a different matter from the question of the earthly path by which he arrived at his awareness and his faith, or of the community of which he is a member.[48]

Smith's conception of truth as the integrity of personal faith has important implications for the process of interfaith dialogue. First of all, dialogue cannot be undertaken "externally" but only "from faith to faith."

The first great innovation in recent times has been the personalization of the faiths observed so that one finds a discussion of a "they." Presently the observer becomes personally involved, so that the situation is one of "we" talking about "they." The next step is dialogue, where "we" talk to "you." If there is listening and mutuality, this may become that "we" talk *with* "you." The culmination of this process is when "we all" are talking *with* each other about "us".[49]

Smith does not mean to imply that in interpersonal dialogue it will be discovered that all faiths are, at bottom, equally true or adequate, or that the movement of the future is toward convergence into a single world faith. He is uneasy about both a pluralistic relativism and a premature notion of unity. Yet he believes that the various faiths do not reveal "conflicting truth-claims" but rather "divergent paths" that may, through dialogue, be "an invitation to synthesis." In any case, genuine dialogue from "within" is not predicated on converting the other person from error to truth but on understanding the other from the "inside," which can deepen and enrich one's own faith. The Muslim, Buddhist, or Christian remains faithful to his or her vision but also grows in awareness of what is shared and not shared with others. This is the imperative step toward greater mutual understanding, cooperation, and possibly even unexpected convergences.

If religious truth has to do with the Muslim's interiorizing of the teachings of the *Qur'ān* or the Buddhist's appropriation of Buddha's *Dharma*, then, in Smith's view, there is empirical-historical evidence that the Muslim and Buddhist faiths are "true" in the sense that they are liberating or saving. By "saving," Smith means "saved from nihilism, from alienation, anomie, despair; from the bleak despondency of meaninglessness. Saved from unfreedom; from being the victim of one's whims within, or of pressures without; saved from being merely an organism reacting to its environment."[50]

If the cumulative traditions that we call religions were to see truth, not in terms of abstract doctrines but in terms of personal liberation, then there is plenty of objective evidence that various faiths are true. "My submission would be this," Smith concludes:

faith differs in form, but not in kind. This applies both within communities and from one community to another. My observation, as an historian of religion, would be put thus: in so far as he or she has been saved, the Muslim has been saved by Islamic faith (faith of an Islamic form, through Islamic patterns; faith mediated by an Islamic context); the Buddhist by Buddhist faith; the Jew by Jewish.[51]

Smith's form of pluralism is rooted in what he sees as a fundamental Christian supposition. The

Christian can forthrightly say that the Buddhist or the Hindu is saved, and "saved only because God is the kind of God whom Jesus Christ has revealed him to be . . . *therefore* other men do live in his presence. Also, therefore, we [as Christians] know this to be so."[52]

Smith's position is radically theocentric and not christocentric. He points out that God's nature and will is revealed to Christians through the mediation of Christ, and it is here that Christian theology is idolatrous and lags behind the Christian moral imperative that calls for reconciliation and unity. Theology continues to affirm an idolatrous Christian exclusivism because it bases faith on the Church's *doctrine* of Christ's singular mediatorial role. But doctrines are conceptual images of God. The doctrine of the divinity of Christ is, Smith contends, a conceptual form by which Christians come to a knowledge of God. But it is no less a human *form* than a Hindu idol or a Buddhist pagoda. All human images, whether they are made of wood or words, are both dangerous and necessary; dangerous because the image or doctrine is mistakenly elevated to some divine status, "giving it the honour, dignity, deference, due only to God."[53] It follows that it is idolatrous to *identify* one's own religion with God or absolute truth. Yet every human claim to a knowledge of God is mediated through some mundane, human construct. Nevertheless, these human pointers or channels—a work of plastic art, a theological system, a communal rite—are the necessary means by which the Ultimate or God is communicated to and apprehended by human beings. Yet, as Smith puts it: "No such form is either final or complete. No such form is negligible."[54] Christianity can be an "idol" in both respects. Christians rightly see the historical Jesus Christ as the unique means (the perceived form) in and by which God is known. But Christians are also "idolatrous," in Smith's view, when they claim that it is *only* through Christianity (the Bible, the Church's christological doctrines, etc.) that God can be known. Smith believes that working out the theological, and especially the christological, conse-

quences of this new pluralistic perspective, is the major agenda for Christian theologians as we enter the new millenium.

Smith's insistence that interreligious dialogue must be an engagement from "within" and in terms of personal encounter, rather than an objective debate about conflicting doctrines or concepts, is an extremely valuable insight. Yet it has been widely criticized as valuable only as far as it goes and, for that reason, is deficient. When the Muslim or Christian truly commits him or herself to the teachings of the *Qur'ān* or the Bible, he or she does so because he or she believes that these texts describe things as they really are; i.e., they point to an objective reality that is true whether the individual appropriates it or not. In other words, existential truth presupposes a prior truth on which its faith rests. John Hick, a pluralist himself, has summarized well the problem left unresolved by Smith's pluralism:

The truth of Christianity (or Islam or Hinduism) does not consist without remainder in there being true Christians (or Muslims or Hindus). In addition to this it consists, presumably, in the reality, or authenticity, of the knowledge of God which occurs in Christianity, or Islam, or Hinduism. But in that case we still have with us the problem of the at least apparently conflicting truth-claims of different religions. If Christianity cannot become (personalistically) true in a man's life unless it is (propositionally) true that God, as depicted in the New Testament, is real and that Jesus is God's love incarnate; and if, again, Islam cannot become (personalistically) true in a man's life unless it is (propositionally) true that God, as depicted in the Qur'an is real and that God does not become incarnate; and if, again, Vedāntic Hinduism cannot become (personalistically) true in a man's life unless it is (propositionally) true that ultimate reality, Brahman, is non-personal . . . then in order to affirm that all these different faiths can become (personalistically) true in the lives of their sincere adherents it seems that we must be able to affirm that their essential (propositional) beliefs are true. But how can it be true both that there is and that there is not a personal God; both that Christ is God incarnate, and that God does not become incarnate?[55]

While John Hick considers Smith's program of personal dialogue inadequate, due to its failure to face head-on the thorny problem of clearly different conceptual claims regarding the object of faith, he, too, remains committed to religious pluralism. Like Smith, he finds neither exclusive claims to religious truth nor various types of Christian inclusivism adequate responses to our new global awareness. We turn, then, to Hick's distinctive position.

John Hick

Trained both in philosophy and theology, John Hick (1922–) is one of the most prolific and influential writers on the subject of the theology of religions. He also is widely regarded as the thinker who best represents the theocentric-pluralist position. Hick was born in Yorkshire, England, and studied philosophy and theology at Edinburgh, Oxford, and at Westminster Theological College, Cambridge. He served as a Presbyterian minister before taking teaching positions at Cornell University, Princeton Theological Seminary, and Cambridge. It was only after his appointment to the H. G. Wood Professorship in Theology at Birmingham University in 1967 that Hick became absorbed with the question of Christianity's relationship to the other world religions.

In 1982 Hick became Danforth Professor of the Philosophy of Religion, chair of the Department of Religion, and director of Programs in World Religions and Cultures at the Claremont Graduate School in California. Upon his retirement from Claremont, he was appointed Fellow of the Institute for Advanced Research in the Humanities at Birmingham University in England. Hick has written several distinguished books in the philosophy of religion. Among his many works in the theology of religions that focus on the pluralistic hypothesis are *God and the Universe of Faiths* (1973); *God Has Many Names* (1980); *Problems of Religious Pluralism* (1985); *An Interpretation of Religion: Human Responses to the Transcendent* (1989), based on the Gifford Lectures, 1986–1987; *A Christian Theology of Religions: The Rainbow of Faiths* (1995); and the edited works, *Truth and Dialogue: The Relationship between World Religions* (1974), *The Myth of God Incarnate* (1977), and *The Myth of Christian Uniqueness: Toward a Pluralistic Theology of Religions* (1987).

Like all pluralists, John Hick begins with the conviction that God, or the Ultimate, is savingly present, however conceived, in all the great religious traditions. He would insist that this can be maintained on rational, i.e., moral and theological, as well as on Cantwell Smith's empirical-historical grounds.

Hick believes that we are undergoing a revolution in human thought in the late twentieth century. Just as human consciousness was transformed in the sixteenth century from a Ptolemaic to a Copernican vision of the cosmos, so at the turn of the millenium we are undergoing a similar change from a Ptolemaic to a Copernican view of religion. Ptolemaic astronomy conceives of the earth as the center of the solar system and Ptolemaic religion holds that Christianity, Islam, or Buddhism is the center or the truth around which all other faiths revolve. One feature of Ptolemaic religion is that it depends, in large part, on where the believer happens to have been born and raised. Rather than being geocentric, it is ethnocentric. Hick suggests that the problem with both Ptolemaic cosmology and religion is that in the late twentieth century both fail to fit the observed facts. Copernicus rightly shifted the center from the earth to the sun, and a Copernican revolution in religion demands that we shift our religion—be it Christianity, Judaism, or Hinduism—from the center and acknowledge that it is God, the Ultimate, or the Real who is at the center and around whom all the religions revolve.

There are good historical and philosophical reasons for recognizing the need for such a Copernican revolution. First, there are the obvious cultural factors. Because the Eternal can be conceptualized only by means of our human experience, we cannot easily rise above our cultural categories in attempting to conceptualize the Infinite.

Why should religious faith take a number of such different forms? Because, I would suggest, religious faith is not an isolated aspect of our lives but is closely bound up with human culture and human history, which are in turn bound up with basic geographical, climatic, and economic circumstance. It has been pointed out, for example, that "in nomadic, pastoral, herd-keeping societies the male principle predominates; whereas among agricultural peoples, . . . it is the mother-principle which seems important. . . . Among Semitic peoples therefore, whose traditions are those of herdsmen, the sacred is thought of in male terms: God the father. Among Indian peoples whose tradition has been for many centuries, and even millennia, agricultural, it is in female terms that the sacred is understood: God the mother." . . . We must, I think, distinguish between the Eternal One in itself, in its eternal self-existent being beyond relationship to a creation and the Eternal One in relation to mankind and as perceived from within our different human cultural situations.[56]

The point can be made philosophically by reference to the philosopher Immanuel Kant's critique of human reason. Hick agrees with Kant that we cannot know *noumena,* things as they exist in themselves independent of our finite perception of them. Thus, each divine image or *persona* "represents the Eternal One as experienced through the filter of a human religious tradition."[57] The world we perceive is real and not illusory, yet real as *humanely perceived.*

We are real beings in a real environment; but we experience that environment selectively, in terms of our special cognitive equipment. Something similar has to be said about the human awareness of God. God as experienced by this or that individual group is real, not illusory; and yet is adapted to our human spiritual capacities.[58]

Hick reasons that we must distinguish between "the Real" that transcends our human representations and "the Real" as experienced and conceptualized by different human communities, for example, as Yahweh, Krishna, Zeus, Tao, Nirvana, or Brahman. But is not Hick here confusing two quite distinct conceptions of Ultimate Reality? Hick's answer is that throughout human history "the Real" has been brought to consciousness in terms of two basic concepts: the concept of God, or the Real as personal and the concept of the Absolute or the Real as nonpersonal. Hick contends that, although they are different conceptions, they are not mutually exclusive but rather are complementary. "The reality itself is such that it is able to be validly conceived and observed in both of these ways."[59] When schematized in human terms as personal deities, as God or gods, Hick refers to them as *personae;* when schematized variously as absolutes, Hick refers to them as *impersonal.*

With regard to the *personae,* the various gods are, according to Hick's analysis, "different authentic *personae* of the Real."[60] In living traditions such as Hinduism and Buddhism, for example, it is assumed that the gods and the Buddhas are all manifestations of the Ultimate. While the concept of a nonpersonal ultimate represents a very different type of religious experience, Hick finds that the various personal theisms and the various forms of unitive mysticism have

a common effect in the transformation of human existence from self-centredness to a new centredness in the God who is worshipped or in the Absolute that is known as *samadhi* ["to unite"] or *satori* ["enlightenment"]. In each case the transformed state is one of freedom from the anxious, sinful, self-concerned ego, a consequent realization of inner peace and joy, and an awareness in love or compassion of the oneness of humankind, or of all life.[61]

Hick contends that it is this common soteriological affect of both theistic and unitive-mystical religious experience that should be "the basic criterion, then, for judging phenomena." Both of these types of experience facilitate a human moral transformation that "leads on towards the higher ground of positive generosity, forgiveness, love, compassion . . . the transformation of human existence from self-centredness to Reality-centredness."[62] Hick finds this practical, ethical criterion of love or compassion in all of the great religious traditions; and it is this moral ideal that can and has served as the basis of the moral criticism of the doctrines and practices within each of these traditions.[63]

But the question still remains: If the Real *in itself* cannot be humanly perceived and conceptualized, why is such an unknown postulated? Hick answers that "the Real" in itself "is a necessary postulate of the pluralistic life of humanity." That is, if it

is proper to regard as real the objects of worship or contemplation within the other traditions, we are led to postulate the Real *an sich* [as such] as the presupposition of the [true] character of this range of religious experience. Without this postulate we should be left with a plurality of *personae* and *impersonae* each of which is claimed to be the Ultimate, but no one of which can be.[64]

Hick is saying that without the postulate of the Real we would have to regard all the historical reports of religious experience "as illusory or else return to the confessional position in which we affirm the authenticity of our own stream of religious experience while dismissing as illusory those occurring within other traditions."[65] For Hick, neither of these options seem realistic and, therefore, the pluralistic hypothesis is the most adequate; indeed, is inevitable.

Earlier we noted Hick's criticism of Cantwell Smith's pluralism, which showed that Smith did not deal adequately with the truth claims of religion. At the time, Hick himself had not attempted to address this thorny question, and his critics were skeptical of his claims about a common Reality transcending the vast range of human theistic and mystical images or insights. In *An Interpretation of Religion,* Hick offers, as noted above, a practical, ethical criterion for assessing various doctrinal claims. However, he acknowledges that when it comes to conflicting truth claims regarding transhistorical facts—e.g., the state of the soul or self after death, or whether the universe is eternal or had a beginning—we should

be satisfied to recognize that these are questions "to which humanity does not at present know the answers" and that "this ignorance does not hinder the process of salvation/liberation." Therefore, we should live with and tolerate these conflicting convictions.[66]

As a pluralist, Hick does not look to a future convergence of the great living religions into one world faith. He sees value in the rich diversity of cultures and religions, and the fact that these faiths can increasingly influence one another and be enriched by one another. What must be given up, however, is the belief that any of these religions is superior, or absolute, or the only or even the final divine revelation. Hick's hope for the Christianity of the future is, rather

a form of Christianity which reveres Jesus as its supreme teacher and inspirer but does not regard him as literally God incarnate; which seeks to nurture men and women from self-centredness to a new centering in God, thus promoting not only individual but also social and national and international unselfishness; and that sees itself as one major spiritual path among others. . . .[67]

We can conclude this segment by mentioning a few of the types of criticisms that have been directed at Hick's Christian pluralism. Some see his comprehensive pluralism as an ideological product of Enlightenment rationalism, that is, as a form of Western cultural imperialism in disguise. Specialists in the history of religions tend to see Hick's theological scheme as artificially patterned and influenced by his *a priori* theory, rather than based on the empirical particularity of the world's religious traditions. Others argue that, while Hick calls for a discarding of claims to a unique superiority, few of the great world faiths see themselves as one among many ways of perceiving God or the Real. The three monotheistic religions of the Book certainly have traditionally rejected the pluralist position. Christian critics, for example, continue to doubt whether Christianity can give up its belief that divine love and forgiveness are found supremely through Jesus

Christ, or its belief in God's unique incarnation in Jesus Christ, and retain its identity. Moreover, some insist that Hick's conception of a divine love and compassion that seeks the salvation of all humankind is taken from his experience as a Christian and simply is not shared by all faiths, especially by those holding a nonpersonal conception of Ultimate Reality. Hick has addressed these and other criticisms,[68] but not to the satisfaction of some of his critics. Even the critics, however, concur that John Hick has, perhaps more than any other Christian theologian, contributed to the vitality of interreligious dialogue in the latter decades of the twentieth century.

ILLUSTRATIONS OF THE NEW CHRISTIAN INTERRELIGIOUS DIALOGUE

Dialogues between Christians, Buddhhists, Hindus, Muslims, and Jews have produced some remarkable openings on what previously were thought to be irreconcilable differences. One example is the reconception of the Christian doctrine of the divine incarnation in Jesus Christ, which is offensive to both Jewish and Muslim monotheism. Recent interpretations of the Incarnation—for instance, the Islamicist Kenneth Cragg's concept of "divine sending"—has opened up new possibilities of understanding a central doctrinal conflict.[69] Akin are the efforts of Rosemary Reuther and other Christian theologians to rethink the messianic promises of Jesus in light of the dialogue with Jewish colleagues. Jesus preached the coming of the Kingdom of God, which, Reuther points out, is not a *fait accompli* but a Kingdom yet to come. Thus, Reuther contends, Jews proclaimed a Kingdom whose fulfilment *both* Jews and Christians can see as yet-to-be accomplished and the hope of the future. Reuther interprets the meaning of Jesus's messianic role as paradigmatic and anticipatory, but not final and fulfilled. The Jewish Exodus and Christ's Resurrection can both be seen as "paradigms of hope": "In each case, the experience of salvation in the past is recounted as the paradigm for continued hope experienced in the present and pointing to

that final hope which is still ahead of both Jews and Christians." For Reuther, the Resurrection does not supercede the Exodus but reduplicates it. And so, "the Christian can affirm his faith through Jesus in a way that no longer threatens to rob the Jew of his past, eliminate his future, and surround his present existence with rivalrous animosity."[70]

The theologian John B. Cobb, Jr. (see Chapter Ten) has introduced new interpretations of the self, Nirvana, and God that may lead to quite unexpected convergences between and transformations of Christianity and Buddhism.[71] The Buddhist-Christian dialogue is especially interesting because it has engaged thinkers in both traditions on issues that previously were thought to be wholly irreconcilable. Recent discussions between Masao Abe, an influential representative of Zen Buddhism, and several distinguished Christian theologians have, however, made clear that misunderstandings and real differences persist. It is heartening, nevertheless, to see the dialogue continue at the highest levels. A brief look at this particular dialogue will give a sense of the issues and problems.

Masao Abe has attempted to demonstrate convergences between the Mahayana Buddhist doctrine of the Emptiness of all things (*sunyata*), or Ultimate Reality, and the Christian doctrine of *kenosis,* or the radical self-emptying of God, as revealed in the sacrifice and self-denial of Christ on the Cross. Is there a genuine convergence between Buddhist Emptiness and the Christian God? Abe believes so, but for the Christian theologian the question remains: Can Emptiness "will" and "love"? That is, does the relation between Ultimate Reality and the human self involve the freedom of personal agencies, human and divine? The question involves not only the issue of the nature of Ultimate Reality but also the issue of human ethical choice and responsibility for the temporal order. The issue is acknowledged by Abe:

Both Christianity and Buddhism talk about freedom, or liberation from sin, death, or karma. In

Christianity, however, this freedom is the gift of God and is based on the will of God. Liberation from sin and death is the divine work of God. On the other hand, liberation from karma in Buddhism is not based on any kind of will, divine or human. It is realized through the Great Death of the human ego and is based on nothing whatsoever. It is *jinen*, primordial naturalness, an ageless spontaneity which springs from the bottomless depth of Sunyata.[72]

It is evident from subsequent exchanges that, while new insights into possible convergences have been achieved, fundamental issues persist that may not be amenable to simple resolution—given the unyielding metaphysical claims on both sides. For example, Abe must acknowledge that for him Ultimate Reality does not signify a God who is in some sense independent of the world but, rather, "the boundless openness or emptiness that is neither God, human, nor nature, and in which all things, including the divine, the human, and the natural, are all interrelated with and interpenetrated by each other."[73]

The theologian Schubert Ogden (see Chapter Ten) points out that because, for Christianity, God's love for others is "unconditional," it is essential that

no matter what else is or can be real, [God's love] has to have an aspect in which it is independent of everything, actual or possible. . . . We should recognize the important conceptual difference in God's being neither identical with self and world nor separated from them, but related to them and, therefore, also distinct from them.[74]

Ogden has additional questions regarding the moral implications of Buddhist Emptiness and the "dependent co-origination" of all things, for example, with regard to human responsibility for evil actions. Ogden suggests that

if the ultimate metaphysical truth is that everything without exception is interdependent with and interpenetrated by everything else, then each thing simply *is* every other thing, and any real differences between

parts themselves, as well as between parts and the wholes, disappear. But this means, then, that any differences between things sufficient to ground responsible and, therefore, differential thought and action with respect to them is delusive.[75]

Ogden points to Abe's judgment that in human terms the Holocaust should be condemned "as an unpardonable, absolute evil, [but] from the ultimate religious point of view even it should not be taken as an ultimate but relative evil." "But what," Ogden asks, "could Abe mean by this if not that from the ultimate religious point of view, authorized by the emptiness and interdependence of all things, even 'absolute' moral differences cease to make any difference?"[76]

It is clear that the Christian interreligious dialogue has made significant progress in overcoming ignorance and misunderstanding, but also that real differences remain, and it would be a lazy tolerance to deny it. The fact of real difference leads many to seriously question the adequacy of the model that informs a good deal of religious pluralism. That model holds that all religions share a common essence, such as John Hick's "the Real," and that this implies that these religions are equally valid ways to salvation or liberation. Assuming, as we have shown above, that there are *real* foundational differences between Christianity and Buddhism, this does not force Christians into the alternatives of either embracing Hick's essentialism or a thoroughgoing religious relativism or the premises of exclusivism. The experience of real dialogue has demonstrated that, while recognizing genuine uniqueness and difference, there can take place what John Cobb calls "mutual transformation." Over the centuries Christianity has been able to assimilate what is good and true in other traditions—such as Neo-Platonism or Aristotelianism—and thereby has transformed itself. As Cobb suggests: "As the great religious traditions become more aware of one another, there is a tendency for some mutual appreciation to develop among them . . . they learn something from mutual contact." They may, first, "learn to value neglected aspects of their own traditions," but they are in fact transformed by this interaction.

The norms by which they judge themselves and others are enlarged. The universal relevance of their own insights is vindicated as other traditions acknowledge their value. The comprehensiveness and human adequacy of their traditions is enlarged as they assimilate the insights of others.[77]

As Thomas Aquinas deepened Christian theology through his utilization of Aristotle, so can contemporary Christians broaden and deepen Christian thought and spirituality by employing, for example, Buddhist meditation or by learning from the Indian sages Gandhi and Śankara. History demonstrates that Christianity has undergone many creative transformations, and that its future-oriented dynamism gives every evidence that it will continue this broadening and deepening process as it engages in dialogue with the other great world faiths. Our situation, however, has changed in one important respect. As one commentator has correctly observed: "No longer is it possible to say that the other religions will find their fulfilment in Christianity, without at the same time acknowledging that Christianity will also find its own fulfilment through a real meeting with the riches and insights within other religions."[78]

NOTES

1. Wilfred Cantwell Smith, quoted without source in Walter H. Capps, *Religious Studies: The Making of a Discipline* (Minneapolis, 1995).

2. Langdon Gilkey, "Plurality and Its Theological Implications," in *The Myth of Christian Uniqueness: Toward a Pluralistic Theology of Religions*, ed. John Hick and Paul F. Knitter (Maryknoll, N.Y.: 1987), p. 40.

3. Ibid., p. 41.

4. Karl Rahner, "Christianity and the Non-Christian Religions," in *Theological Investigations*, Vol. 5 (Baltimore, 1966), pp. 116, 118.

5. Karl Barth, *Church Dogmatics*, I, 2 (Edinburgh, 1956), pp. 325–326.

6. Ibid., p. 327.

7. Ibid., p. 343.

8. Hendrik Kraemer, *The Christian Message in a Non-Christian World* (New York, 1938), p. 126.

9. Hendrik Kraemer, *Religion and the Christian Faith* (London, 1956), p. 334.

10. Ibid., p. 334.

11. Kraemer, *The Christian Message in a Non-Christian World*, pp. 134–135.

12. Ibid., p. 135.

13. Ibid., p. 106.

14. Ibid., p. 107.

15. Ibid.

16. Ibid., pp. 139, 140.

17. On the various church agencies and conferences that focus on non–Roman Catholic missions, and on the positions of the churches on the non-Christian religions, see the World Council of Churches publication by Carl F. Hallencrentz, *New Approaches to Men of Other Faiths* (Geneva, 1970).

18. "The Christian Community in the Academic World," *The Student World*, 57 (1964), 362.

19. For brief surveys of the Catholic Church's teaching on the salvation of non-Christians and the doctrine of "no salvation outside the Church," on which I have drawn, see Mikka Ruokanen, *The Catholic Doctrine of Non-Christian Religions*, (Leiden, 1992), Ch. 2; and Paul Knitter, *No Other Name: A Critical Survey of Christian Attitudes Toward the World Religions* (London, 1985), Ch. 7.

20. Ruokanen, *The Catholic Doctrine*, ibid., pp. 18–19.

21. Jean Danielou, *The Advent of Salvation: A Comparative Study on non-Christian Religions and Christianity* (New York, 1962); Hans Urs von Balthasar, "Catholicism and the Religions," *Communio*, 5 (1978); Joseph Ratzinger, "Christianity and the World Religions," in *One, Holy, Catholic, Apostolic Church*, ed. H. Vorgrimler (New York, 1968).

22. Karl Rahner, "Anonymous Christians," in *Theological Investigations*, Vol. 6 (Baltimore, 1969), p. 394.

23. Ibid., p. 395. In "Observations on the Problem of the 'Anonymous Christian,'" *Theological Investigations*, 14 (New York, 1976) Ch. 17 Rahner defines this person as "the pagan after the beginning of the Christian mission, who lives in the state of Christ's grace through faith, hope, and love, yet who has no explicit knowledge of the fact that his life is oriented in grace-given salvation to Jesus Christ."

24. Karl Rahner, "Christianity and the Non-Christian Religions," in *Theological Investigations*, Vol. 5 (Baltimore, 1966), pp. 117, 118. In addition to this crucial essay and the one cited in note 23, see "Anony-

mous Christianity and the Missionary Task of the Church," in *Theological Investigations*, Vol. 12 (New York, 1974), pp. 161–178; and "Observations on the Problem of the 'Anonymous Christian,'" in *Theological Investigations*, Vol. 14 (New York, 1976), pp. 280–294.

25. Rahner, "Christianity and the Non-Christian Religions," p. 119.

26. Ibid., p. 120.

27. Ibid., p. 128.

28. Ibid., p. 121.

29. Ibid., p. 124.

30. Ibid., pp. 131, 132.

31. Ibid., p. 133.

32. Ibid., p. 134.

33. Ibid.

34. Paul F. Knitter judges that "the majority of Catholic theologians who are trying to work out a theology of religions endorse the substance of Rahner's theory" and that Rahner was the "chief engineer" of the Vatican II position as stated in the Council's "Declaration on the Relation of the Church to Non-Christian Religions"; Knitter, *No Other Name*, pp. 125, 130. Alan Race sees Rahner as "undoubtedly the major architect of the postconciliar Catholic contribution to the subject" of the Church's relation to the non-Christian religions; Race, *Christians and Religious Pluralism: Patterns in the Christian Theology of Religions*, (Maryknoll, N.Y., 1983).

35. Cited in Race, ibid., p. 53.

36. For these criticisms see, John Hick, *God Has Many Names* (Philadelphia, 1982); and Hans Küng, *On Being a Christian* (New York, 1976).

37. See Maurice F. Wiles, *Explorations in Theology*, Vol. 4 (London, 1979) p. 32. Also see Race, *Christians and Religious Pluralism*, pp. 55 ff.

38. For a good defense but also criticism of Rahner, see Gavin D'Costa, *Theology and Religious Pluralism: The Challenge of Other Religions* (Oxford, 1986), Ch. 4.

39. John Hick, *A Christian Theology of Religions: The Rainbow of Faiths* (Louisville, 1995), pp. 7–8.

40. Arnold Toynbee, *Christianity Among the Religions of the World* (New York, 1957), p. 96.

41. World Council of Churches, *Guidelines on Dialogue with People of Living Faiths and Ideologies.* (Geneva, 1979), p. 11. See the commentary on these guidelines by Kenneth Cracknell, *Why Dialogue?* (London, 1980).

42. Stanley J. Samartha, "The Lordship of Jesus Christ and Religious Pluralism," in Gerald H. Anderson and Thomas F. Stransky, C.S.P., *Christ's Lordship and Religious Pluralism* (Maryknoll, N.Y., 1981), p. 33. See also S. Samartha, *Courage for Dialogue* (Geneva, 1981).

43. Samartha, *Christ's Lordship*, pp. 34–35.

44. Ibid., pp. 35–36.

45. Ibid., p. 36.

46. W. C. Smith, *Towards a World Theology* (London, 1980), p. 113 f.

47. W. C. Smith, *Questions of Religious Truth* (New York, 1967), p. 68.

48. Ibid., pp. 70–71.

49. W. C. Smith, in *The History of Religions: Essays in Methodology*, ed. Joseph Kitagawa and Mircea Eliade (Chicago, 1959), p. 34.

50. Smith, *Towards a World Theology*, p. 168.

51. Ibid., p. 168.

52. W. C. Smith, "The Christian in a Pluralistic World," in *Christianity and Other Religions*, ed. John Hick and Brian Hebblethwaite (London, 1980), pp. 105–106.

53. W. C. Smith, "Idolatry in Comparative Perspective," in *The Myth of Christian Uniqueness: Toward a Pluralistic Theology of Religions*, op. cit., pp. 59–60.

54. Ibid., p. 56.

55. John Hick, "The Outcome: Dialogue into Truth," in *Truth and Dialogue: The Relationship between World Religions*, ed. John Hick (London, 1974), p. 148.

56. Hick, *God Has Many Names*, pp. 51–52.

57. Ibid., p. 84. For an extensive discussion of this point see, J. Hick, *An Interpretation of Religion: Human Responses to the Transcendent* (New Haven, 1989), Part Four.

58. Hick, *God Has Many Names*, p. 106.

59. Hick, *An Interpretation of Religion*, p. 245.

60. Ibid., p. 275.

61. Ibid., p. 278.

62. Ibid., pp. 309, 314.

63. Ibid., pp. 339–340.

64. Ibid., p. 249.

65. Ibid.

66. Ibid., p. 370.

67. Hick, *A Christian Theology of Religions*, p. 126. Ch. 1 offers a brief summary of a Hick's pluralistic hypothesis, whereas Ch. 2–5 present, in dialogue form, Hick's response to a variety of criticisms of his form of Christian pluralism.

68. See note 67.

69. Kenneth Cragg, "Islam and Incarnation," in *Truth and Dialogue in World Religions: Conflicting Truth Claims*, ed. John Hick (Philadelphia, 1974), pp. 126–139.

70. Rosemary Reuther, *Faith and Fratricide* (New York, 1974), p. 256.

71. John B. Cobb, Jr., *Beyond Dialogue: Toward a Mutual Transformation of Christianity and Buddhism* (Philadelphia, 1982).

72. John B. Cobb, Jr. and Christopher Ives, ed., *The*

Emptying God: A Buddhist-Jewish-Christian Conversation (Maryknoll, N.Y., 1990), p. 56. For an additional dialogue on Buddhist Emptiness and the Christian God, see Roger Corless and Paul F. Knitter, ed., *Buddhist Emptiness and Christian Trinity* (New York, 1990).

73. Cobb and Ives, *The Emptying God*, ibid., p. 51.
74. Ibid., p. 130.
75. Ibid., p. 132.

76. Ibid.
77. John Cobb, Jr., "Beyond Pluralism," in *Christian Uniqueness Reconsidered: The Myth of a Pluralistic Theology of Religions,* ed. Gavin D'Costa (Maryknoll, N.Y., 1992), p. 87.
78. D'Costa, *Theology and Religious Pluralism*, p. 124.

SUGGESTIONS FOR FURTHER READING

Anthologies of Important Essays on the Relationship of Christianity to Other World Religions

Hick, John, and Brian Hebblethwaite, ed. *Christianity and Other Religions* (Philadelphia: Fortress Press, 1980).

Thomas, Owen C. *Attitudes Toward Other Religions* (New York: Harper and Row, 1969).

General Studies of Christian Attitudes toward the World Religions

D'Costa, Gavin. *Theology and Religious Pluralism: The Challenge of Other Religions* (Oxford: Basil Blackwell, 1986). Uses the pluralist, exclusivist, inclusivist typology, focusing on the study of John Hick, Hendrik Kraemer, and Karl Rahner. Good bibliography.

———, ed. *Christian Uniqueness Reconsidered: The Myth of a Pluralistic Theology of Religions* (Maryknoll, N.Y.: Orbis, 1992). Essays by noted scholars, including John B. Cobb, Jr., Wolfhart Pannenberg, Lesslie Newbigen, and Jürgen Moltmann, all critical of Christian pluralism.

Knitter, Paul. *No Other Name: A Critical Survey of Christian Attitudes Toward the World Religions* (London: SCM Press, 1985). An excellent survey from Ernst Troeltsch through a variety of Protestant and Catholic positions. Knitter is a pluralist, but he lets the other positions speak for themselves. Helpful notes and bibliography.

Race, Alan. *Christians and Religious Pluralism: Patterns in the Christian Theology of Religions* (Maryknoll, N.Y.: Orbis, 1983). A fine critical discussion of various positions, using the exclusivism, inclusivism, pluralism models. Good bibliography.

For extended statements of important writers on Christian interreligious relations representing distinctive positions, see the following:

Cobb, John B., Jr. *Beyond Dialogue: Toward a Mutual Transformation of Christianity and Buddhism* (Philadelphia: Fortress Press, 1982).

Hick, John. *An Interpretation of Religion: Human Responses to the Transcendent* (New Haven: Yale University Press, 1989). This represents Hick's fullest defense of his "pluralist hypothesis."

———. *A Christian Theology of Religions: The Rainbow of Faiths* (Louisville, Ky.: Westminster/John Knox Press, 1995). An extended dialogue in which Hick responds to the concerns of his critics.

———, and Paul F. Knitter, ed. *The Myth of Christian Uniqueness: Towards Pluralistic Theology of Religions* (Maryknoll, N.Y.: Orbis, 1987). Essays by noted scholars representing various pluralist positions.

Hocking, William E. *Living Religions and a World Faith* (New York: Macmillan, 1940; reprint, 1975). A call for Christianity to broaden and deepen its self-understanding through the encounter with other faiths.

Kaufman, Gordon D. *God-Mystery-Diversity* (Minneapolis: Fortress Press, 1996). A collection of Kaufman's essays on Christianity and religious pluralism and on issues in dialogue with Buddhists.

Kraemer, Henrik. *The Christian Message in a Non-Christian World* (New York: Harper and Row, 1938). An influential Protestant statement of the "exclusivist" position.

Netlands, Harold A. *Dissonant Voices: Religious Pluralism and the Question of Truth* (Grand Rapids, Mich.: William B. Eerdmans, 1991). An excellent study from an Evangelical Protestant perspective.

Newbigin, Lesslie. *The Open Secret* (Grand Rapids, Mich.: William B. Eerdmans, 1978). Defends the uniqueness of Christianity and the necessity of salvation through Jesus Christ.

Ogden, Schubert. *Is There Only One True Religion?* (Dallas: Southern Methodist University Press, 1992). Argues that logically one cannot be an exclusivist or an inclusivist and that pluralism is not the necessary alternative.

Panikkar, Raimundo. *The Unknown Christ of Hinduism* (Maryknoll, N.Y.: Orbis, 1981). An Indian Roman Catholic theologian who represents a theocentric position that calls for a universal Christ in which no single historical form can be the full or final expression.

Rahner, Karl. *Theological Investigations* (New York: Seabury Press, 1966–1979). Vol. 5, Ch. 6, "Christianity and the Non-Christian Religions"; Vol. 6, Ch. 23, "Anonymous Christians"; Vol. 12, Ch. 9, "Anonymous Christianity and the Missionary Task of the Church"; Vol. 14, Ch. 17, "Observations on the Problem of the 'Anonymous Christian'"; Vol. 16, Ch. 4, "Anonymous and Explicit Faith."

Samartha, Stanley J. "The Lordship of Jesus Christ and Religious Pluralism." In *Christ's Lordship and Religious Pluralism*, ed. Gerald H. Anderson and Thomas F. Stransky (Maryknoll, N.Y.: Orbis, 1981).

——. *Courage for Dialogue: Ecumenical Issues in Inter-Religious Relationships* (Maryknoll, N.Y.: Orbis, 1982). In these two works, Samartha presents a theocentric position in which he recognizes God alone as Absolute and, in calling for dialogue, rejects the idea that all particular religions are equally true or that any one can claim to be universal and decisive for all.

Smith, Wilfred Cantwell. *The Meaning and End of Religion* (New York: Harper and Row, 1962).

——. *Towards a World Theology* (Philadelphia: Westminster Press, 1981). In these books Smith lays out the arguments for his distinctive Christian pluralist position.

Examples of Christian Interreligious Dialogue and Reconception

Abhishiktananda, S. *Hindu-Christian Meeting Point* (Bangalore: CISRS, 1969). A French Benedictine monk (later called Swami) who founded an Indian-Christian ashram in South India.

Cobb, John B., Jr. *Beyond Dialogue: Toward a Mutual Transformation of Christianity and Buddhism* (Philadelphia: Fortress Press, 1982).

Cobb, John B., Jr., and Christopher Ives, ed. *The Emptying God: A Buddhist-Jewish-Christian Conversation* (Maryknoll, N.Y.: Orbis, 1990).

Cragg, Kenneth. *Muhammad and the Christian: A Question of Response* (Maryknoll, N.Y.: Orbis, 1984).

Dawe, Donald G., and John B. Carmen, ed. *Christian Faith in a Religiously Plural World* (Maryknoll, N.Y.: Orbis, 1978). Non-Christian scholars respond to a Christian position on interreligious relations.

Ingram, Peter, and Frederick Streng, ed. *Buddhist-Christian Dialogue: Possibilities for Mutual Transformation* (Honolulu: University of Hawaii Press, 1984).

Samartha, S. J., and J. B. Taylor, ed. *Christian-Muslim Dialogue* (Geneva: World Council of Churches, 1973).

——, ed. *Jewish-Christian Dialogue* (Geneva: World Council of Churches, 1975).

——, ed. *Guidelines on Dialogue with People of Living Faiths and Ideologies* (Geneva: World Council of Churches, 1979)

SNC. *Guidelines for a Dialogue between Christians and Muslims* (Rome: Vatican Secretariat for Non-Christians, 1969).

Chapter Sixteen

Christian Thought at the End of the Twentieth Century

Gordon D. Kaufman

This concluding chapter explores some important currents in Christian thought in the latter years of the twentieth century, programs that have not been examined except in passing in earlier chapters on movements since the mid-century. The programs discussed here illustrate rather nicely an important dispute between two fundamental approaches to theology in its response to modernity. The one approach, which we have referred to earlier as "theologies of correlation," follows the direction proposed by Paul Tillich and Karl Rahner. The second approach follows the lead of Karl Barth and is suspicious of attempts to "correlate" the Christian message with modern thought. It questions the assumptions of modernity and seeks to better elucidate the Christian faith through a return to biblical

narrative and the Church's traditions and confession. The five theological programs that we discuss here share the fact that they are more often than not identified as exemplifying some features of what has come to be called postmodernism. Earlier we have seen that other movements of the latter half of the twentieth century, for example, hermeneutical, liberationist, feminist, and African American theologies, also have appropriated postmodernist ideas that are prominent in their work.

The term "postmodern" is now associated with a range of fields, including literature and the arts, cultural studies, social theory, philosophy, theology, and even the history of science. Since the term is sometimes used to refer to the theologies that are examined here, a brief discussion of the distinctive meaning and import of the word "postmodern" is in order.

THE MODERN AND THE POSTMODERN

As the word suggests, the postmodern refers to the time that has followed what we have long spoken of as the modern age. Since the term "postmodern" did not enter fully into our cultural discourse before the 1960s, it would suggest that significant shifts in our cultural and intellectual life have occurred in the latter decades of the twentieth century, and that these changes mark a departure from those features that we have come to characterize as the modern and modernity.

Despite divergent opinions about the appropriate use of the word "postmodern," it has served as a helpful device to mark some interesting cultural and intellectual developments in the late twentieth century. The term is, however, burdened by a lack of precision and questions are increasingly raised about the value of its use, especially in theology. One problem is periodization. Some cultural critics trace the origins of postmodernism to Immanuel Kant, but Kant, of course, is usually considered to be, with René Descartes, the quintessential *modern* thinker. A related problem is how one situates postmodernism vis-à-vis modernism, because there is also little agreement as to what constitutes the modern or modernism. Social historians trace the roots of modernity and the Enlightenment to the Reformation of the sixteenth century. Intellectual historians and philosophers tend to associate the beginnings of modern thought with Descartes, Locke, and Kant, although some trace its origins to late-medieval Nominalism. Literary historians and critics, on the other hand, are generally agreed that modernism in literature and the arts can be dated rather precisely from the 1890s to the 1930s. Efforts to bring some order to this question of postmodernism by introducing terms such as "late modern" and "ultramodern" are not very helpful because they imply that the modern era is still with us. One of the major theorists of

the postmodern, Jean-François Lyotard, readily concedes that "postmodernism is not modernism at its end, but in a nascent state, and [that] this state is recurrent."[1] The most radical of the avowedly postmodern theologians, Mark C. Taylor, also acknowledges that postmodernism is "a notoriously problematic term" and that it "is not simply an additional epoch or era following modernism, [but] is inseparately bound to the modern."[2]

We need not concern ourselves further about these rather inconclusive discussions. We will speak of postmodernism as a contemporary disposition of mind or condition that clearly reveals features that we also associate with aspects of Western culture that we have understood as "modern," but which also discloses some distinctive features. One of these is the heightened sense of radical pluralism, cultural fragmentation, and indeterminacy in the late twentieth century, what postmodernists refer to variously as "the emptiness of the Absolute," "absence," "the loss of self," "the movement toward silence," "the unrepresentable," and "the crisis of legitimation." The deconstructive propensity of postmodern culture often reveals a "will to unmask," a strange mélange of radical relativism, cool insouciance, and apocalypticism. Yet it is also true that the postmodern plunge into immanence and becoming manifests a positive, celebratory, and quasireligious side, which is apparent in the use of terms such as "the feast of becoming," "gay relativity," "anticipation," "holy silence," and a kind of post-Nietzschean "fictive" constructivism. Philosophers and theologians, especially, see the distinctive postmodern break with modern thought in its critique of modern epistemological foundationalism, of representational or referential conceptions of language modeled on science, and its critique of modern autonomy and individualism. Although there is an element of truth in these characterizations, one finds similar critiques of these doctrines in the romantic counter-Enlightenment and in Romanticism itself, for example, in Catholic Traditionalism, and, of course, in various spiritualist and vitalist philosophies in the late nineteenth and early twentieth centuries. We will recognize, however, that several of these critiques of the modern also characterize the postmodern theological trends explored here. We begin with an analysis of the theologian Gordon D. Kaufman's reconception of the theological task. He is sometimes spoken of as a "mediating" theologian or as espousing a "theology of correlation," but he is best understood for proposing a distinctive Christian "theology as imaginative construction," a program that is more radically historicist and pluralist than comparable theologies that seek a mediation between Christianity and modern culture. These features of Kaufman's work are also characteristic of postmodernism. Yet Kaufman remains a quintessential modern theologan in his continuing indebtedness to the Kantian critique of our knowledge of God. This, as we will see, distinguishes Kaufman sharply from the theological postmodernism of the followers of Wittgenstein and the "Reformed epistemology."

GORDON D. KAUFMAN: THEOLOGY AS IMAGINATIVE CONSTRUCTION

Gordon Kaufman (1925–) began teaching at Harvard Divinity School in 1963 and retired as the Edward Mallinckrodt, Jr. Professor of Divinity in 1995. After completing an M.A. in sociology at Northwestern University in 1948, he pursued theological studies at Yale, completing both the B.D. and Ph.D. degrees there. He taught at Pomona College and Vanderbilt University before his appointment at Harvard. His publications in philosophical theology include *Relativism, Knowledge and Faith* (1960); *Systematic Theology: A Historicist Perspective* (1968); *God the Problem* (1972); *An Essay on Theological Method* (1975, 1979); *The Theological Imagination: Constructing the Concept of God* (1981); *Theology for a Nuclear Age* (1985); *In Face of Mystery: A Constructive Theology* (1993); and *God-Mystery-Diversity: Christian Theology in a Pluralistic World* (1996).

Kaufman's Christian theology is both radically theocentric and historicist. It represents a search for an adequate construction of the concept of God and begins with an analysis of our contemporary cultural experience; that is, "in the open marketplace of human experience and ideas."[3] For Kaufman, theology is a public, not a parochial, enterprise. Thus in setting out the proper business of theology in a nuclear age, Kaufman does not simply assume the givenness of the Christian revelation, its traditions, or its ecclesial symbols. He points out that when theologians speak of "God's revelation" they often assume that they are clear about what they mean when they use the words "God" and "revelation." The assumption, of course, begs some important questions. It also fails to take seriously the sociological fact that Christian theological language and concepts are deeply embedded within the culture or cultures in which Christianity, in its various expressions, is found. Kaufman was H. Richard Niebuhr's student at Yale and was influenced by his conception of radical monotheism. From a radical theocentric perspective it is, Kaufman argues, idolatrous to hypostatize, or assume as essential and final, any human theological construction.

Kaufman also sees the advent of the nuclear age, and all that it implies about human power and the fate of the human species and the earth, as demanding a radical reconception of theology, one wholly unanticipated in the previous two millenia of Christian theological reflection. Such a critical reconception of theology, Kaufman proposes, "opens a way for us to take full account of the radical novelty of the historical situation. . . . Our theological work need not be constrained in any way by the limitations of earlier interpretations of Christian symbolism, which had not anticipated this terrifying growth of human powers of destructiveness . . . [these symbols] are in no way binding on us."[4]

It is clear that for Kaufman the theologian's task involves taking seriously the radical nature of our new social and cultural situation and refuses to press into service unauthentic traditional concepts and symbols. This is made clear in his reconception of what he calls the Christian categorial scheme and in the way that he describes the process of theological construction.

Kaufman believes that it is the Christian theologian's task today to formulate a categorial scheme of symbols by which to analyze and criticize the widest range of Christian theologies, institutions, and practices, taking into account the insights provided by, for example, other religious traditions, modern science, and secular worldviews. The four categories that make up Kaufman's Christian categorial scheme are God, world, humanity, and Christ.[5] The first three categories are not uniquely Christian and are important to other monotheistic faiths, e.g., the Jewish and the Muslim. In all of the monotheistic faiths God serves as the ultimate point of reference in terms of which all else is to be understood. The second category, the world, refers to the larger environing context in which human life has emerged and has developed. Modern science, of course, has enlarged our vision of the world beyond the imaginings of earlier periods of human history, including a cosmology of infinite space and time that must be taken into account in any responsible theological reconstruction. The third category, humanity, refers to those creatures living on this planet earth who are self-conscious and "culture-creating beings," but who also are shaped profoundly by their biological history. The distinctive monotheistic faiths believe, moreover, that the world and humanity cannot be understood adequately without reference to how God as lord serves as the relativizer of all our human ideas and ideals, as well as how God serves as the ground and orienting compass for the humanizing of our lives and institutions.[6]

A Christian theological reconstruction adequate to today's world will, however, also include the category of "Christ" who "is believed by Christians to reveal or define . . . who or what God really is, and . . . what true humanity consists in."[7] For Kaufman, the category of "Christ" is

not then simply added to his categorial scheme; for Christ is the paradigm for a Christian understanding of both God and human life.

At this point we can proceed to explore Kaufman's categorial scheme in more detail with reference to his description of the three-step process of theological construction. In doing so we will give special attention to how his Christology informs this process. In brief, Kaufman understands the process of theological construction to proceed as follows:

The first step is the imaginative move beyond the items and objects of experience itself to construct a notion of the context within which all experience falls, a concept of the world; the second step is the further constructive leap which limits and relativizes this concept of the world through generation of the concept of God; finally, there is the third imaginative move which returns again to experience and the world, thoroughly reconceiving them now in the light of this concept of God, i.e., grasping them theologically.[8]

Kaufman insists that the concepts "world" and "God" are correlative, so that experience of the world must materially shape our conception of God, just as God functions to limit and relativize the world. As Kaufman writes: "God can be conceived only through setting him over against everything else of which we can speak and know. For only thus will we be able to see that, in comparison with all else, he is the ultimate reality."[9] In his early writings Kaufman's working concept of the world was Western culture and his prime example of the changing context was the emergent nuclear age. As he suggests, the use of nuclear weapons of mass destruction called for a serious reconsideration of our traditional conceptions of God's omnipotence.

In his later writings Kaufman points to additional factors that must enter into the context in any conceptual construct of the world, namely, our relatively recent biohistorical understanding of human life *and* our radical experience of religious pluralism. Both require that we orient ourselves, not simply by the particular values and customs, institutions and forms of life, characteristic of our own provincial traditions, but instead by a *global consciousness*. We feel a demand on us to move beyond our limited loyalties to American, western, or traditional Christian consciousness and institutions . . . to a universalistic—but pluralistic—human consciousness.[10]

Kaufman's "second movement" of theological reflection is, then, the reconstruction of the concept of God as the ultimate point of reference for understanding and interpreting the world and human experience. It is this ultimacy that distinguishes God from all idols—nation, race, religious tradition. This second reconstructive movement requires us to understand God both as the mystery whom we cannot grasp except through our ordinary language, images, and concepts, and as the one who functions as the supreme relativizer of all things finite. The Western theological tradition has, of course, used human metaphors and models of God—king, lord, and judge, as well as caring father and suffering love. Kaufman remains wary of some of these human and Christian metaphors, as we will see.

While Kaufman rejects parochial appeals to Western symbols and concepts, he concludes, as we have noted, that the most adequate imaginative constructs that point to God as the ultimate reference-point of human concerns are those of God as "relativizer" and "humanizer."

The theologically significant function of the symbol "God" is not that it names an entity or being which we might otherwise ignore or overlook, but rather that it focuses our consciousness and attention on that which humanizes and relativizes us. . . . Devotion to God and service to God are devotion and service to that which gives us our humanity and such fulfilment as may come our way, as well as limits and restricts and judges us when we overreach ourselves or seek that which can only harm and destroy us.[11]

Following Kant and the whole tradition of negative theology, Kaufman rejects all concepts of God that imply that God is an object among other objects. God is not a particular being in or beyond this world. Rather, the word *God* must be understood as a "regulative idea," a construct that is used to order and unify our experience as a whole. In our present evolutionary, ecological, and pluralistic cultural context, the reconception of God no longer can be construed in the older, patriarchal, hierarchic, dualistic, and asymmetrical images of the biblical divine creator, king, and judge. Rather, in our present situation the concept God must be constructed in accord with our ecological vision of a unified, interdependent order. This will mean that "the divine activity which has given us our human being must apparently be conceived now as inseparable from, and as working in and through, the activity of the human spirit itself, as it creatively produces the cultures which make human life human."[12]*

Kaufman insists, however, that we humans do *not* create ourselves, and much that is created is not the work of human thought and intention. We have been brought into being by a complex of factors, powers, and processes, both physical and historico-cultural which is, Kaufman believes, appropriate to symbolize by the concept "God." He thus speaks of a "serendipitous creativity" manifest in the world, a reality or power present in the various novel evolutionary directions, including the human. He writes:

The world . . . is a serendipitous process that has produced a variety of trajectories, one of which has brought into being the historical order. . . . This trajectory appears to represent at least one significant direction in which the cosmic process is moving, and we humans are being drawn beyond our present condition and order by this on-going creative movement . . . *God*, I am proposing, should be understood as the underlying reality—the ultimate creativity, ultimate mystery—that manifests itself throughout the universe.[13]

* Sallie McFague's work on the "models of God" (see Chapter Thirteen) points to Kaufman's understanding of theological construction and his pragmatic criteria as important for her own conception of the theological task.

Here, and in Kaufman's writings since *In Face of Mystery* (1993), one senses a willingness to speak more realistically about God in terms of an ordered "creativity" however "mysterious" and "serendipitous."

The construction of an appropriate God-concept adequate to our cultural situation is, you will remember, only the second step in Kaufman's vision of the constructive and contextual theological task. The third and essential movement is a return again to experience and to the world and, in so doing, to reconceive them in view of the concept of God. As we bring the various aspects of our contemporary lives and culture into relationship to our concept of God, they are

brought under the criticism and judgment of God's absoluteness and humaneness. Our awareness of God's absoluteness will show every point of view . . . every institution, every style of life . . . to be finite and limited and relative; and we will begin to see how frequently we and others falsely absolutize . . . these into idols before whom we bow in worship. As God, the great relativizer of all false absolutes, unmasks these idols of ours, we are enabled better to understand who (or what) God is in our time and place. And we begin to see more clearly the evils that corrupt and threaten to destroy our common life.[14]

As we conceive of God as also *humane*, we bring our lives and institutions into relation with our concept of God, and thereby we are better able to see in what ways they are inhumane, egoistic, and destructive. Our awareness of God is experienced as a demand upon us to humanize ourselves and the inhumane structures of our world.[15]

While the unmasking of the idols enables us to better understand who or what God is, and to recognize the evils that threaten our common life, this third moment of theological construction also enables us to see the demands that are placed upon us to assist in humanizing ourselves and our institutions. It is here, Kaufman believes, that the category of the "Christ" can illumine both our conception of God and human existence in our world today.

Much will depend, however, on what images and concepts from the Christian tradition are used to interpret Christ, because many traditional images of Christ are deeply ambiguous. One powerful tradition depicts Christ sitting on the right hand of God the Father, triumphant and omnipotent, meting out rewards and punishments. Kaufman sees this cluster of images of Christ as supporting a Christian triumphalism that has all to often authorized forms of imperialism and the exploitation of non-Christians. There are, however, other images and concepts of Christ in the New Testament that Kaufman sees as crucial and formative. They are not only authentic to the tradition but also powerfully relevant for orienting human life today toward self-giving, kindliness toward the dispossessed and the needy, and communal reconciliation. These *christic* images "picture Jesus giving himself to others in service and healing, preaching and teaching that women and men should love and respect even their enemies, should do good to those who curse them, should become servants of all."[16] These are the images that can be looked to "both as normative for human being and action and as the definitive revelation of God."[17]

Kaufman is not only forthright in his choice of *christic* images from the New Testament and the Christian tradition; he also is explicit that his Christology, as a reflection on God's special presence in the Christ-event, is not to be understood as limited exclusively to the man Jesus. Kaufman finds in the New Testament—especially in the Pauline writings—texts that speak of "Christ" not only as Jesus Christ but "as signifying the whole complex web of saving and revelatory events within which early Christians found themselves."[18] Although intimately connected with Jesus, these christological texts suggest a new order of relationships that develop after Jesus's death and resurrection.

Though centering on the man Jesus, the Christ-symbol is regarded as referring not only to this solitary figure but also to the larger community of reconciliation that grew up in response to his work—and in principle, thus, it can be extended to all similar communities of genuine healing, love, and justice.

. . . Any community that becomes a vehicle in history of more profoundly humane patterns of life—as paradigmatically epitomized in the christic . . . images of this seminal period—can be understood theologically as helping to constitute (in its own distinctive way) the fullness of Christ in human history.[19]

Here one can also see an instance of Kaufman's concern to open the theological dialogue to the non-Christian communities of faith.

The christic images that Kaufman proposes do not, in his view, only provide a compelling focus for human existence, its devotion and service, but also offer a paradigm of God as ultimate relativizer and humanizer. The adequacy of such claims is not, of course, shown by mere assertion. Kaufman therefore sets out what he considers to be needed to show the adequacy of such a christo-centric paradigm. First, he attempts to show that his wider symbol of Christ provides "sufficiently unified and clear images and concepts to concentrate the attention, interests, and affections of women and men in such a way that they can direct themselves toward God"[20] with some confidence.

Second, Kaufman proposes that the image/concept of Christ conveys a sense of reality and truth since his portrayal of God has been constructed *in relation* to the actual cosmic and historical powers and processes at work in the world, including a history that appears to be drawing the human family toward more profound humanization. These cosmic and bio-historical events are objective realities. And so, Kaufman points out, many persons "when seriously confronting the christic images and meanings, have found them appealing and compelling, revealing something profoundly true about human existence."[21] Third, an adequate image or concept of God must strike those who respond to it with "the conviction that it is *God*, and not some idol" that is revealed in these images. Again, Kaufman suggests that, based on the two criteria of *humaneness* and *relativization*, the *christic* paradigm offers "a conception of the [cosmic, biological, and historical]

forces . . . which draw us out and move us toward a more profound humaneness while simultaneously rendering questionable our proudest achievements" and claims for ourselves. These are the works that "distinguish the True God from all idols."[22]

Kaufman recognizes, of course, that there are no coercive proofs for this Christian theological construction. His claim is a more modest one, namely, that the Christian worldview which he proposes is intelligible; that it is a coherent and comprehensive view; and that it meets the basic warrants of adequacy. For these reasons alone, it should attract the serious attention of contemporary men and women.

While this brief exposition of Kaufman's program for theology at the end of the twentieth century cannot touch on all the significant features of his work, e.g., his dialogue with Buddhism, it does, nonetheless, lay out essential features of his reconception of the Christian theological task. We conclude by suggesting a few lines of criticism that have been raised regarding Kaufman's proposal. First, it is clear that Kaufman gives priority to a radical theocentric critique and analysis over any parochial effort at Christian self-description. The theologian must continually broaden his or her analysis and reconception to encompass the full range of cultural experience and the world faiths in order to construct an ever-more contextually adequate concept of God. This task strikes many as not only daunting but, in fact, an impossible task considering the multiple contending and shifting sources that we face in view of today's knowledge explosion and radical diversity.

This first misgiving is related to another. While Kaufman's God, as the ultimate point of reference, is universal and indispensable, he sees the theological task as radically historicist and culture-specific and, moreover, essentially practical and functional. But has not Kaufman acknowledged that different cultural contexts will reflect different needs and values—and will not these result in different criteria of what is absolute and humane? How, then, is truth or adequacy finally adjudicated in such a historicist framework? Finally, Kaufman rejects, for example, Karl Barth's beginning with the Christian church and its confession, or Paul Tillich's "theological circle," and begins, rather, by insisting that all ideas of God are culturally constructed and subject to critique in terms of the shifting contexts. When Kaufman speaks of God as "an ultimate tendency or power, which is working itself out in the evolutionary process," he speaks in the language of an evolutionary theist—but does not such a vision suggest going beyond the historical particularity commonly understood as constituative of a Christian theism?[23] Kaufman clearly understands himself as a Christian theologian, but does he not also explicitly opt to work within a more capacious theological framework?

RADICAL AND CONSERVATIVE POSTMODERN THEOLOGIES: THOMAS J.J. ALTIZER, MARK C. TAYLOR, AND JEAN-LUC MARION

Earlier it was pointed out that the postmodern condition is characterized by a "deconstructive" impulse, but that it also discloses a recuperative desire for a "reenchantment" of the self and the world. As Paul Ricoeur has noted, "the masters of suspicion and deconstruction 'clear the horizon' through their destructive critique," but they often do so "for a new Truth . . . by the invention of a new art of interpreting."[24] As we have learned (see Volume I, Chapters Nine and Fifteen), this was true of the older masters of suspicion—Feuerbach, Marx, Nietzsche, and Freud—and it is true of many of the postmodern deconstructionists. The new masters of suspicion are predominantly French, and they are reacting against the efforts of structural anthropologists, such as Claude Levi-Strauss, as well as others who, in view of the demise of metaphysics and meta-narratives such as the Judeo-Christian life-world, claim to discover new laws and mythic patterns that give meaning and order to human life. The most important of the French postmodernist writers include the psychoanalyst Jacques Lacan; the historian Michel Foucault; the philosophers Jacques Derrida,

Emmanuel Levinas, and Jean-François Lyotard; the feminist theorists Julia Kristeva and Luce Irigaray (see Chapter Thirteen); and the sociologist Jean Baudrillard. Some Anglo-American postmodernist theologians have been attracted to these French writers, but for others this contemporary Gallic intellectual context has not been at all decisive. While these French writers give postmodernism a certain vogue in the English-speaking world, other thinkers, such as the philosphers Martin Heidegger, Ludwig Wittgenstein, and Alasdair MacIntyre, clearly have been more formative.

The theologians in North America most often identified with postmodernism are Thomas J.J. Altizer,[25] Robert P. Scharlemann,[26] Charles E. Winquist,[27] and Mark C. Taylor.[28] The most prominent postmodern theologian in Britain is Don Cupitt.[29] Only a few of these writers undertake their theological work within a particular ecclesial context, and they all assume the death of God; that is, the death of traditional Christian theism. Among them, Scharlemann insists on the paradigmatic role of the Christ event soteriologically, in that he sees Christ as instantiating the archetype of one who lives for and freely empties himself for the other. This "extantial I," as he calls it, is the symbol of God, "not *what* God is but *where* God is."

Here we will briefly sketch the main lines of thought of three quite different types of theology that are associated with the postmodern. A radical humanistic reconstructive interpretation of Christian symbols is exemplified in the death of God theology of Thomas J. J. Altizer. Deconstructive postmodern theology is illustrated in the works of Mark C. Taylor. The Catholic philospher Jean-Luc Marion proposes a postmodern reconception of God free of the metaphysical categories of being.

Thomas J. J. Altizer

In the 1960s the news media gave quite extraordinary attention to a group of radical theologians who spoke of the "death of God." These theologians meant different things by the term: the eclipse of God by secular culture, the crisis of theistic language in speaking meaningfully about God, Nietzsche's death of the foundations of Western values and morality, and so on. Thomas Altizer was a leader of this movement. Because much of his work predates the the discourse on postmodernity, and the fact that his chief sources are the great modern thinkers, such as Hegel and Nietzsche, and not the French postmodernist writers, Altizer can justifiably be described as a radical "modern" theologian, as well as reflecting certain postmodern themes.

Thomas Altizer (1927–   ) completed both his undergraduate and graduate studies at the University of Chicago and then taught at Wabash College and Emory University before accepting a position at the State University of New York at Stony Brook as profesor of English. While he was a leading figure in "death of God" movement, his conception of the "death of God" was and remains distinct. And while the voices of the other death of God theologians have fallen silent, Altizer continued into the 1990s to pursue his central theological vision in fresh ways. Although he does not have a wide circle of younger disciples pursuing the direction of his program, Altizer has continued to challenge thinking about the nature of theology since the appearance of his first book, *Oriental Mysticism and Biblical Eschatology* (1961). Commentators have remarked that among contemporary theologians Altizer may be the one who has most tenaciously focused on the subject of God, to the neglect of all other theological doctrines and concerns.

Altizer's early engagement with the Oriental religions, particularly with Buddhism, and his effort to clarify the uniqueness of biblical religion in contrast to these religions, is also distinctive, and it predates the more recent turn to this subject by other Christian theologians. Altizer is also original in his being an atheist who continues to see himself as working out a Christian theology that he believes is a more authentic rendering of the biblical Christian gospel. At the same time, he attacks the theologies that have dominated

Christendom and he attempts to subvert them. Furthermore, while he draws heavily on biblical texts and imagery, Altizer's effort to reconceive God calls upon many philosophical and literary sources, primarily Hegel, Nietzsche, Dante, Milton, Blake, and James Joyce. His canon thus includes "heretics" who have attacked the Christianity of Christendom.

A key to Altizer's understanding of the death of God and his Christian atheism is his use of Hegel's dialectic (see Volume I, Chapter 5). Following Hegel's lead, Altizer sees the reality of God's being as involving a dialectical process of negating God's transcendent otherness in the divine Incarnation in Christ and in the community in history—which both Hegel and Altizer see as a positive movement. More striking, this movement entails an ongoing historical dialectic that involves conflict and strife, joy and sorrow, life and death. For Altizer, God is lacking full actuality as pure, transcendent Being removed from world history. In Creation and the Incarnation, God has taken on concreteness and empties himself, actions that negate God as self-contained transcendence. Thus the world and history no longer are alien or estranged from God but joined in the divine immanence. This is what Altizer refers to as the "coincidence of opposites," the joining of God and the world, the finite and the infinite.

For Altizer this divine embodiment in the world is a real historical event in which God's self-negation or emptying (*kenosis*) is the "genesis of God," God becoming God, and also the beginning of history as an irreversable movement. This, Altizer insists, is the biblical vision that supercedes the "eternal return" of the archaic religions. He writes:

The eschatological goal of the original and authentic Christian Word demands that it be an activity or a process of making all things new, of transforming the totality of history so that God may be all in all, therewith annulling all that distance separating the creature and the Creator, and obliterating every opposition between the sacred and the profane, or flesh and Spirit . . . a process of Spirit actually becoming flesh and of flesh actually becoming Spirit: only a real and forward-moving process of Spirit becoming its own other can culminate in an apocalyptic *coincidentia oppositorum*.[30]

For Altizer the death of God means the negating and surpassing of the alien, transcendent God in Heaven. This is accomplished in the Incarnation. God is *in* Christ and *in* his crucifixion without remainder. God does not, then, escape true finitude, embodiment, death. Altizer sees the "atheism" of the radical Christian as "in large measure a prophetic reaction to a distant and nonredemptive God who by virtue of his very sovereignty and transcendence stands wholly apart from the forward movement and the historical presence of the Incarnate Word."[31] It is not surprising that Altizer's theology often is referred to as "christomonistic," as is evident, for example, in this passage: "God *is* Jesus, proclaims the radical Christian, and by this he means that the Incarnation is a total and all-consuming act: as Spirit becomes the Word that empties the Speaker of himself, the whole reality of Spirit becomes incarnate in its opposite."[32]

A final theme that gains prominence in Altizer's later work is apocalypse.* New Testament scholarship has recognized that Jesus's preaching, death, and Resurrection are embedded in an apocalyptic context that, for Altizer, bespeaks an end of God as God and the innocence of an older primordial world. Altizer sees in the modern world the apocalyptic message of Jesus as subsisting in our midst. In *History as Apocalypse,* for example, he offers his own vision of a Hegelian phenomenology of the human spirit or consciousness. He does this by tracing the realization of consciousness in the Western epic tradition from Homer to Israel, and then through Paul, Augustine, Dante, Milton, Blake, and Joyce. For Altizer, Joyce's *Finnegan's Wake* evokes, like no other work, the ending of our form of consciousness.

* See *History as Apocalypse* (1985), *Genesis and Apocalypse* (1990), and *The Genesis of God* (1993).

In so tracing the consequences of Christ's Incarnation and crucifixion as marking the death of God in the cultural history of the West, Altizer reveals both the negation of the transcendent "Other" and the disappearance of human interiority. This historical movement marks the intensification of awareness of Christ's message of apocalypse. It is registered by Spinoza, Newton, the de-Christinization brought about by the French Revolution—but most powerfully in the writings of Blake, Hegel, Nietzsche, and Joyce. The latter call forth "a final and apocalyptic age or aeon," one that Nietzsche especially understood as nihilistic. Yet this nihilism, as Blake realized, "also knows a new creation that can only be the consequence of the final ending of an old totality."[33]

Altizer thus envisions this modern nihilistic voyage as revealing its own *coincidentia oppositorum* in "an apocalypticism which also knows a new creation." Our modern voyage into nothingness is, then, also a voyage into a new totality that subverts the ancient primordial religious world. This is to be seen in Nietzsche's vision of Eternal Recurrence, but perhaps the deepest ground of that reversal was first established by Spinoza's "pure and decisive unification of infinity and finitude," a unification and a totality realized in Hegel's philosophy. This modern voyage into nihilism and anti-Christian atheism is then, for Altizer, this new totality,

a liberating nihilism, and liberating above all in that absolute affirmation or Yes-saying which it alone makes possible, that Yes is the Yes which the Christian knows as the Yes of the gospel, a Yes which faith knows as a total Yes, and a total Yes which is an all comprehending totality. Even if such a totality can only appear and be real to us as a nihilistic totality, both faith and vision finally know totality itself as an absolute Yes and Amen.[34]

One can see that Altizer's theology is a *sui generis* mix of themes common to biblical theology *and* a canon that includes Hegel, Blake, and

Nietzsche, among many others. The critics, of course, find far more of the moderns in Altizer's theology than they do the biblical narrative—at least as that body of Scripture is understood by both modern biblical scholars and the Christian tradition. One doctrine illustrates the problem. Altizer speaks of the divine *kenosis* in Christ as the transcendent God's self-emptying in or merging with the world. It appears, however, that everyone but Altizer interprets the New Testament passages concerned with God's *kenosis* as God's self-emptying in Christ, not in the world *per se*. For Altizer, however, God's Incarnation in the world appears to erase the distinction between God and the world, and especially in terms of the latter's apocalyptic horror. This naturally raises additional questions about Altizer's theology of history and theodicy. If God's death is increasingly actualized in the course of history since Christ's crucifixion, and if that history reveals increasing apocalyptic alienation and darkness what, one asks, is Altizer's analogue to Hegel's "positive" eschatology? That is, what is the nature of the "new totality" that evokes the "Yes-saying" and that subverts the archaic eternal return? This remains opaque.

Mark C. Taylor

Mark C. Taylor (1945–) received his Ph.D. from Harvard, where he studied with Gordon Kaufman. He is the William R. Kenan Professor of Religion and Director of the Center for Humanities and Social Sciences at Williams College, Massachusettes. Early in his career he wrote important studies of Hegel and Kierkegaard, which represented for him something of a dialectic of the "both/and" and the "either/or." Taylor has sought a position between/beyond these two giants and his project is greatly influenced by the deconstructionist philosophy of Jacques Derrida. He also moves beyond Kaufman's historicism to a more radical "playful" historicism. Taylor takes as a given the Enlightenment's critique of religious authority and Nietzsche's pronouncement of the

death of God, that is, the central criticisms of our culture's foundational values and beliefs. For Taylor, the mirror is empty and, as Michel Foucault has said, the self, too, is "erased, like a face drawn in the sand at the edge of the sea."[35] In his most important theological work, *Erring: A Postmodern A/theology*, Taylor outlines the features of what he calls an a/theology, which assumes a condition of being in the middle, neither rejecting the disappearance of God and religious authority nor rejoicing in it like "children unbound from the rule of a domineering father."[36] As with many others, Taylor finds himself "suspended between the loss of old certainties and the discovery of new beliefs," living on the border or the margin.

In *Erring*, Taylor explores the loss of four foundational beliefs: God, self, history, and the book. The secularization of modern culture has brought with it the death of God, and with this loss of divine authority and power the self turns inward for both identity and power—for self-possession and mastery. But "Narcissus, after all, eventually loses himself in the mirror."[37] "The effort to master 'absolute fear' leads to 'absolute terror,' to domination, to deny death." The modern experiment in self-mastery has, not surprisingly, issued in both narcissicism and nihilism. The radical temporality and death of the subject inevitably subverts the identity, possession, and mastery of selfhood.

History, too, attempts to uncover the coherence of time as a whole and is linked to the idea of a providential God. History is Logocentric and Christ is the Logos. However, "Chronos re-asserts itself in the very effort to negate it."[38] Thus history, too, must be recognized as radically relative and nonteleological. Narrative requires a plot, a beginning, center, and telos. But with "the death of Alpha and Omega . . . when it is impossible to locate a definite beginning and a decisive end, the narrative line is lost and the story seems pointless. . . . From the perspective of the end of history, the 'final' plot seems to be 'that there is no plot.'"[39] Taylor sees history as therefore pointing to the closure of the book. The book, with any sense of ending, must now be closed. Taylor writes:

There is no text-in-itself which subsists apart from interpretation. . . . (I)nterpretation is not secondary to a more primary original, but is always an interpretation of that which is itself already an interpretation. . . . There is no more *a* (T)text than there is *an* (A)author. No text, in other words, is author-itative and no author is origin-al. . . . The death of God is the birth of the Word (and, of course, vice versa). This erasure of the "transcendental signified" sets the stage for the infinite play of interpretation. In the absence of any (A)author-itative (S)scripture, "the place we inhabit . . . is always this in-between zone."[40]

In part two of *Erring*, Taylor develops a deconstructive a/theology where, acknowledging the death of God, he interprets the Divine through a radical Christology in which "Jesus is manifested as word, and word is read as writing" or Scripture. Writing is the "divine milieu."[41] Taylor's notion of writing follows French deconstructive criticism in that "writing is the interplay of presence/absence and identity/difference that overturns the polar opposites of classical theology. Along this indeterminate, unrepresentable "middle way," this "'in-between zone,' writing of God repeatedly appears as the unending dissimilation of the word."[42] Everything is relative and evanescent; writing is a ceaseless process. Endless wordplay is the everlasting play of the word that enacts the death of the A/author and subverts every final authority. As scripture, it is always unfinished and erring.

Taylor's "middle ground" of interplay opts neither for Derrida's obsession with "absence" nor Altizer's "total presence." It is not clear whether this ceaseless indeterminacy and the "not" or negativity lead Taylor to a nihilism. For the loss of individual selfhood, he writes, may give rise to "care-less sacrifice" rather than to "anxious mastery." With the end of history life becomes a "serpentive wandering" but, Taylor says, it does not represent a "desperate exile." The death of God, self, and history can, rather, unleash what Taylor

calls "mazing grace" and "the aberrant levity of free play." Play can be called "the absence of the transcendental signified," and this absence negates "both theological presence and the presence of theology." In so doing, "play effectively extends the margin of an a/theology."[43] One must wonder, of course, whether the human spirit (or what kind of human spirit) will find meaning or attraction in Taylor's endless punning, in his call to unending "profitless play" that gives way to "a labyrinthian play of surfaces" and "delight in the superficiality of appearances."

In *Disfiguring: Art, Architecture, Religion* (1992), Taylor chides both modernism and postmodernism for either positing a utopia, a Kingdom as wholly other (Neo-Orthodoxy), or a utopia or Kingdom as wholly immanent and present everywhere (Altizer). Taylor sees the truth of our "apocalyptic" situation as negating such "utopian" thinking and embracing negation. Salvation is not possible. He writes:

The denial of utopia can become utopian and the loss of the dream of salvation can become a salvation. The impossibility of reconciliation means that there is no resurrexit here or elsewhere, nor in the future. The door is closed, closed tightly; there is no upper room.[44]

Some critics see Taylor's ceaseless "erring" and "no resurrexit" as not at all postmodern, but rather an expression of modern despair. Others see his negation of God, self, and history as both ontologically and morally nihilistic and, again, an expression of unrelieved, ultramodern thinking. Taylor, on the contrary, claims to see his deconstructive a/theology as the opening up of new possibilities for "careless sacrifice," the "dissolving of social oppositions," and the experience of "mazing grace."

Jean-Luc Marion: A Conservative Postmodern Theology

The radical theologies of Thomas J. J. Altizer and Mark C. Taylor represent for many readers postmodern theological reflection *in extremis*.[45]

They often use Christian words and images, especially Altizer, but they are used, critics assert, in the way that James Joyce or D. H. Lawrence used words like "epiphany" and "resurrection." The words undergo a semantic shift and they are emptied of their usual Christian meanings. Altizer and Taylor are not, these critics claim, representative of the postmodernist theological deconstruction of modern thought; their programs illustrate, rather, something of the anticlimax of modern thought. The third example of a postmodern project represents a very different approach to Christian theology.

Jean-Luc Marion (1946–   ) is professor of philosophy at the University of Paris X, Nanterre, and is noted for his distinguished work on Descartes. Fundamental to Marion's postmodern theological project is his distinction between metaphysical and theological thinking. He sees metaphysical discourse on God as originating in late medieval Thomistic interpretations of Aristotle, which in turn he sees as initiating what he calls modern ontological theology. Marion's critique of this modern discourse on God is the subject of his book *God Without Being* (1991) (originally published as *Dieu sans l'etre: Hors-texte*, 1982). The book sparked considerable discussion when it first appeared in France.

Marion wants to make it absolutely clear that God "without being" does not imply that God is not or that God does not exist. Furthermore, *God Without Being* is not to be understood as a "correlational theology" in the tradition of Tillich, Rahner, or Tracy. Rather, Marion begins with the revealed God who *only is* as He has embodied himself. Marion begins then, as does Barth, with God's freedom regarding "all determinations, including, first of all, the basic condition that renders all other conditions possible and even necessary—for us humans—the fact of Being."[46] That is to say, God is also *free* of the determinations of onto-theology. Marion joins this theological decision with the philosophical decision to begin with "postmodernity," especially with Derrida's deconstruction. For Marion this means beginning by calling radically into question the

modern metaphysical determinations or attributes of God.

In his studies on Cartesianism, Marion explored the modern construction of the purely metaphysical names and functions that we have imposed upon the conception of God since Descartes. Finally, it was Nietzsche who "not only proclaimed the 'death of God,'" but also "brought the grounds for it to light." These are the conceptual names of God, the metaphysical "idols" "imposed on a God who is still to be encountered." We now can see Nietzsche's death of God as "the death of the death of God" as a metaphysical construction.[47] With regard to this modern onto-theology, Marion asks whether it

is self-evident that the first question comes down to asking, before anything else, whether [God] is? Does Being define the first and the highest of the divine names? When God offers himself to be contemplated and gives himself to be prayed to. . . . When he appears as and in Jesus Christ, who dies and rises from the dead, is he concerned primarily with Being? No doubt, God can and must in the end also be; but does his relation to Being determine him as radically as the relation to his Being defines all other beings? . . . Because, *for us*, as for all beings of the world, it is first necessary "to be" in order . . . "to live and move" (Acts 17:28), and thus eventually also to love. But *for God*, if at least we resist the temptation to reduce him immediately to our own measure, does the same still apply? . . . If, to begin with, "God is love," then God loves before being, He only is as He embodies himself—in order to love more closely that which and those who, themselves, have first to be.[48]

If, as should be the case, theology begins with revelation, it begins with what Marion calls the "gift" of God's self-disclosure as *agape* (love or charity). Both modern metaphysics, as lately represented by Heidegger's *Seinsfrage* (question of Being), but also the onto-theology associated with the interpretations of Thomas Aquinas are, for Marion, "idols" that confine God within the question of Being. He, therefore, calls for a return to the pre-Thomistic theology of the Christian Platonists, such as Pseudo-Dionysius and Bonaventure, for whom Love and the Good take precedence over Being in the order of the divine names.

Marion's theological reflections introduce a notable vocabulary: terms such as "the idol" and "the icon," "vanity," "the gift," "the good," and "the crossing of being." The idol is the human concept that consigns to a sign what the mind itself grasps and that can, thereby, *fix* the Divine. "When a philosophical thought expresses a concept of what it then names 'God,' this concept functions as an idol."[49] Contrariwise,

the icon does not result from a vision but provokes one. . . . Whereas the idol results from the gaze that aims at it, the icon summons sight in letting the visible be saturated little by little with the invisible. . . . [N]ot the visible discerning [*discernant*] between itself and the invisible, hemming in [*cerner*] and reducing it, but the invisible bestowing [*décernant*] the visible. . . . So the icon, as it summons to infinity . . . could not but overabundantly subvert every idol of the frozen gaze[50]

—while bestowing the gift of the other, God as *agape*. This revelatory gift crosses the finite and "distorts the play of being by withdrawing it from Being, by undoing being from the rule of Being. This crossing traces a cross over ontological difference."[51]

The crossing of Being crosses out G⊠d, that is, "demonstrates the limit of the temptation to blaspheme the unthinkable in an idol." The cross indicates "that the unthinkable enters into the field of our thought only by rendering itself unthinkable . . . by criticizing our thought."[52] And that which crosses our thought of Being has the name of *agape*:

To think of G⊠d, therefore, outside of ontological difference, outside the question of Being, as well, risks the unthinkable, indispensable, but impossible. What name, what concept, and what sign nevertheless yet remain feasible? A single one, no doubt love . . . or as St. John proposes- "God [is] *agape*" (I John 4:8).[53]

In the Cross one sees the love of God embodied in the Son. "Only love does not have to be. And G⊠d loves without being."[54]

Marion pursues his theological reflection within an explicit ecclesiological context. He sees the Church's confession and the Eucharist as the places where the presence of God's gift of self-revelation is embodied. Nor, he insists, can or does theology have to justify these iconic gifts. They are, simply, "irreducible to Being and its logic, facts that are only intelligible in terms of the gift."[55] Marion agrees with Heidegger that the logic of philosophy and the logic of theology are not reconcilable. But he shows this by proceeding beyond Heidegger—what he calls the "second idolatry," that is, God according to Being—and offers a postmodernist critique of modern metaphysics and philosophical theology. He also throws down a challenge to modern Thomistic thinking. "If God causes Being," he asks, "wouldn't we have to admit that, for Saint Thomas himself, God can be expressed without Being? . . . If *esse* characterizes God in Thomism, *esse* itself must be understood divinely, thus having no common measure with what Being can signify in metaphysics."[56]

REFORMED EPISTEMOLOGY: THE CRITIQUE OF MODERN FOUNDATIONALISM AND EVIDENTIALISM

A lively discussion has taken place in the United States in the last quarter of the twentieth century that has primarily engaged philosophers of religion rather than theologians. The discussion has to do with what is called "Reformed epistemology," so named because several of its most active proponents are Christian philosophers in the Calvinist or Reformed tradition. The focus of their project is epistemology, specifically the question of the warrants of religious belief. Among the better known philosophers associated with this group are Alvin Plantinga (1932–), professor of philosophy at the University of Notre Dame, Gifford Lecturer, and recognized in philosophical circles for his distinguished work in logic and epistemology. Other noted philosophers associated with the program are Nicholas

Wolterstorff, Gifford Lecturer and the Noah Porter Professor of Philosophical Theology at Yale University; William Alston of Syracuse University; and George Mavrodes of the University of Michigan. Much of the discussion of the issues raised by Reformed epistemology is carried on in the journal, *Faith and Philosophy* and in the deliberations of the Society of Christian Philosophers.

The program of Reformed epistemology is closely allied with the contemporary philosophical critique of what is understood to be the Enlightenment's rationalist and empiricist legacy of epistemological "foundationalism" and "evidentialism." In the past three centuries this legacy has put religious belief on the defensive because of its demand that these beliefs be grounded on evidence. Foundationalism is, from a logical perspective, the view that some of our justified beliefs are mediate beliefs; that is, they are based on and inferred from other immediate or foundational beliefs that are not derived from other beliefs. These latter beliefs are either deductively or inductively established first principles. Descartes, for example, put all beliefs to the test of radical doubt in search of a foundation of truth. His reflections arrived at the famous conclusion, *Cogito ergo sum.* "*I think, therefore I am*" was for Descartes "so certain and so assured" that he could "receive it without scruple as the first principle of the Philosophy for which I was seeking."[57] Descartes was then able to derive all other beliefs inferentially from this basic belief.

Foundationalism insists, then, that our derived or inferred beliefs must be founded on secure basic beliefs or first principles if they are to claim to be warranted, that is, rational. Evidentialism is the claim that the standard of rationality is *evidence* or argument grounded in or provided for by basic beliefs. And basic beliefs, it is claimed, must either be self-evident, such as a logical syllogism, or evident to our senses. Modern foundationalism from Descartes to twentieth-century thinkers such as Bertrand Russell[58] and J. L. Mackie[59] have challenged the rationality of religious belief on these evidentialist grounds. Their argument proceeds along the following lines:(1) Theistic beliefs are not properly basic beliefs because they are neither self-evident nor are they evident to the senses. (2) Because religious beliefs are not basic beliefs they can be rational only if they are warranted by sufficient evidence. (3) Theistic beliefs are not supported by sufficient evidence; therefore, they are not rational and should not be believed. Furthermore, such beliefs support the evil of credulity. As the Cambridge mathematician and "strong" evidentialist, W. K. Clifford, wrote in 1879: "It is wrong always, everywhere, and for anyone, to believe anything upon insufficient evidence."[60] A number of distinguished contemporary philosophers have "deconstructed" the assumptions of this "strong" evidentialism by developing the insight of Ludwig Wittgenstein (see below) that conceptions of meaning and truth are embedded in language that is culture-specific; there is no metalanguage, as the scientific positivists assumed.[61]

Alvin Plantinga

Reformed epistemology accepts as decisive these recent arguments against epistemic foundationalism and evidentialism, but it proceeds to offer its own critique as it applies to the issue of theistic belief. This has been carried out most thoroughly by Alvin Plantinga in a series of monographs and articles. Plantinga begins by attacking the first premise of foundationalism, namely, the claim that religious beliefs are not properly basic. He does this first by showing counterexamples, that is, by showing that many of our commonsense beliefs are nonbasic; for example, that objects exist independent of our perception of them. Plantinga uses the example of our belief that minds other than our own exist. We, of course, assume this, yet it does not meet the classic foundationalist criteria because this belief is neither self-evident, evident to our senses, nor incorrigible, that is, evident by one's own mental states.

Second, Plantinga argues that the classic foundationalist criterion for a properly basic belief is flawed, because the criteria (self-evident,

evident to the senses, or incorrigible) prove to be beliefs. Now, if the foundationalist's criterion of a basic belief were to be believed on the basis of other propositions that are self-evident or evident to the senses or incorrigible, such a person would "be able to provide a good argument whose premises are self-evident or evident to the senses or incorrigible," and the conclusion would be compelling. But, Plantinga argues, "no foundationalist has provided such an argument."[62] The foundationalist's criterion meets none of its own conditions, and hence it is not properly basic; yet the foundationalist believes that it is basic. Plantinga proceeds to point out "that belief in God relevantly resembles belief in the existence of the self and of the external world—and, we might add, belief in other minds and in the past. In none of these areas do we typically *have* proof or arguments or *need* proof or arguments."[63]

Plantinga appeals to the writings of the Protestant Reformer John Calvin (1509–64)* to back up his contention that belief in God resembles many of our commonsense, but unprovable, basic beliefs. For Calvin, belief in God is "implanted in us all [as] an innate tendency, or nisus, or disposition to believe in him." Plantinga submits, with Calvin, that if it were not for sin

human beings would believe in God to the same degree and with the same natural spontaneity that we believe in the existence of other persons, an external world, or the past. . . . The fact is, Calvin thinks, one who does not believe in God is in an epistemically sub-standard position—rather like a man who does not believe that his wife exists.[64]

Critics might well challenge Plantinga's lumping together belief in God and belief in an external world as seemingly equivalent beliefs. But Plantinga is not doing this; he is only saying

---

* Not all who support the general argument of Reformed epistemology see it as necessarily associated with Calvin's theology. They see Calvin's epistemological position as perhaps having a family resemblance to their own epistemological reflections.

that theistic belief *resembles* our other common beliefs. The former beliefs also differ, because not everyone who agrees that these common beliefs are properly basic beliefs also agrees that this is true of theistic belief. Yet those who object to the claim that theistic belief is properly basic actually modify the criterion of classical foundationalism. They say that "P is properly basic for S if and only if P is self-evident or incorrigible or evident to the senses *or is accepted as basic by nearly everyone.*"[65] (Italics added.) Plantinga not only points out that the italicized phrase fails to meet the criterion of a foundationally proper basic belief; he also insists that it is not true that "nearly everybody" takes it as basic. Plantinga, for one, does not. The significant point that he is making here is that there is no agreement on what constitutes an acceptable criterion for proper basic beliefs that might replace a discredited foundationalism.

Plantinga proposes that the appropriate way to arrive at a criterion for proper basicality is inductive:

Accordingly, criteria for proper basicality must be reached from below rather than from above; they should not be presented *ex cathedra* but argued to and tested by a relevant set of examples. But there is no reason to assume, in advance, that everyone will agree on examples. The Christian will of course suppose that belief in God is entirely proper and rational; if he does not accept this belief on the basis of other propositions, he will conclude that it is basic for him and quite properly so. Followers of Bertrand Russell . . . may disagree; but how is that relevant? Must my criteria, or those of the Christian community, conform to their examples? Surely not. The Christian community is responsible to *its* set of examples, not to theirs.[66]

It is clear that Plantinga is proposing a non-foundationalist and pluralist epistemological position that rejects the notion of a single privileged and authoritative criterion of properly warranted or reasonable belief. Does this mean that Plantinga is a relativist or that he believes that theistic belief is irrational? The answer is no.

Plantinga, as well as other critics of classical foundationalism, refuse to equate a necessarily contextual network of arguments and warrants with relativism or irrationalism. They simply recognize that every set of beliefs that claim a rational coherence entails some basic assumptions, or what Nicholas Wolterstorff refers to as "control beliefs,"[67] that make that system of reasonable thought different from others. Contextualism does not imply subjectivism.

How does Plantinga defend theistic belief that may not have a fully developed criterion for proper basicality, or, to put it another way, how can the theist reject other, seemingly irrational, beliefs that claim to be basic—for example, belief in the Great Pumpkin? Plantinga's answer is that belief in God is properly basic while belief in the Great Pumpkin is not *because* theistic belief is not *groundless*: "A belief is properly basic only in certain conditions; these conditions are, we might say, the grounds of its justification and, by extension, the ground of the belief itself. In this sense basic beliefs are not, or are not necessarily, *groundless* beliefs."[68] Calvin, for example, held that God is disclosed in the divine workmanship and order of the universe, and Kant saw the starry heavens above and the moral conscience within the human soul as conditions that serve as grounds for belief in God. The same, Plantinga argues, has not or cannot be said for the Great Pumpkin. As one commentator has pointed out, Plantinga's "parity argument"—i.e., that persons can point to grounds for belief in God just as they can point to grounds for belief in other minds—answers two objections proposed by critics. One is "the objection that belief in God is not relevantly similar to other properly basic beliefs that fall outside the criterion of classical foundationalism and, secondly, the objection that belief in God is too close for comfort to irrational beliefs like belief in the Great Pumpkin."[69]

Theistic beliefs are properly basic because they are formed under "conditions that confer justification on one who accepts them as basic. That is, they are not groundless or gratuitous."[70]

Such *conditions* are not, for Plantinga, the same as *evidence*. Evidence actually consists of beliefs on which other nonbasic beliefs are held. Grounds, however, are the circumstances or the conditions that serve to occasion properly basic beliefs, and that justify them without their being formulated as beliefs. Evidence for a belief means that one holds that belief on the basis of *other* beliefs that support it. Justificatory grounds for belief are not, then, beliefs but *conditions*. The very fact that such properly basic beliefs are held unawares or without deliberation is what makes them basic—although one could point to justifying grounds if asked. Plantinga gives some examples, mostly from Calvin, of such justifying conditions or experiences. Such justifying conditions also are cited extensively and systematically by William Alston in his book, *Perceiving God: The Epistemology of Religious Experience* (1991).* There Alston attempts to show that nonsensory experience of God is so analogous to the rational status of sense experience as to make the former as epistemically respectable as the latter—and that there is no justification for the modern double standard.[71]

Nicholas Wolterstorff

We have discussed the critique of classical foundationalism and Plantinga's defense of properly basic theistic beliefs. We have said little, however, about the related theme that is central to the program of Reformed epistemology, namely *evidentialism*. Nicholas Wolterstorff insists that the "project of Reformed epistemology is to answer the evidentialist critique of Christianity."[72] It is generally conceded that the most powerful philosophical criticism of Christian theism since the Enlightenment is a form of evidentialism that is premised on the epistemological doctrines of classical foundationalism. Wolterstorff and his colleagues are committed to challenging

---

* Alston is not, however, as anti-foundationalist as are some of the Reformed epistemologists, and he does use arguments for realism against some of the nonfoundationalists.

this modern empiricist evidentialism that goes back to John Locke. What is important to the Reformed epistemologists is not, however, simply the critique of classical evidentialism, but the fact that modern Christian apologists have conceded to the critics of Christianity their basic demand for evidence on foundationalist terms. As a result, Christian apologists either seek to marshall evidential proofs, e.g., by appeal to natural theology or the testimony of Scripture and tradition, or, more likely in the twentieth century, seek to reduce Christian claims and doctrines to the point that they are supported by evidence that is acceptable to the modern evidentialist critic. The Reformed epistemologists refuse to follow either course, and much of their polemic is directed not at the critics of Christianity but at its friends and defenders who think that they can make Christianity credible by pursuing one or another type of "evidential" strategy or proofs of Christianity. Here we can illustrate one such Reformed critique of Christian "evidences," Wolterstorff's analysis of the evangelical theologian Clark Pinnock's (see Chapter Twelve) apologetic effort in his book *Reason Enough: A Case for the Christian Faith* (1980).

Pinnock begins his apologetic by stating that his purpose "is to test belief in God from the point of view of its rationality." "I am," he writes, "aiming at a testing of faith in light of knowledge which will enable you [the unbeliever] to take that step of commitment without sacrificing your intellect."[73] Pinnock is not offering demonstrations, that is, deductive arguments from premises that are self-evident. Rather, he is proposing "reasonable probabilities" that may not compel belief but that "do establish the credible atmosphere in which faith can be born and can grow."[74] To what specific kind of evidence does Pinnock appeal? First, his appeal to the unbeliever is to those things that the unbeliever can justifiably accept, such as the evidence of his or her own perceptions. Pinnock contends that it is from such common beliefs or evidences that one can make reasonable inferences to Christian belief. He writes:

"I do not want to make any special demands in the area of knowledge. I have no hidden assumptions, no special philosophy. My contention is that the truth claims of the Christian gospel can be checked out in the ordinary ways we verify the things we know."[75] Christianity, he contends, is the most probable or best explanation of various phenomenon that the believer and the unbeliever commonly recognize and accept.

Having fairly laid out Pinnock's apologetic strategy, Wolterstorff asks what Pinnock understands to be the outcome of this accumulation of "reasonable probabilities." Not, Wolterstorff discovers, a guarded and conditional acceptance of Christianity as a reasonable explanation of some commonly shared experiences such as the design in nature or our basic moral sense or conscience. No, Pinnock expects his unbelievers to convert and commit themselves to Jesus Christ—as he says, "open yourself up to God, confess your failure to live a just and holy life, and determine to follow the Lord Jesus. Act upon the evidence that stands before you and accept the saving offer that is being extended."[76] One is immediately struck by the disjunction here, as if acknowledging that Christian belief is compatible with, or even the best explanation of, certain common experiences or phenomena naturally leads to commitment to Jesus Christ as savior and to the certainty of Christian faith. As Wolterstorff remarks: "Pinnock never explicates the relation between believing with some tentativity that Christianity is the best explanation of various phenomena and adopting a trustful certitude of faith."[77] One is compelled to ask Pinnock, as one must ask John Henry Newman (see Volume I, Chapter Eight): Why does this process of informal inference and probability entail an *unconditional* assent or certitude?

Wolterstorff and his fellow Reformed epistemologists are convinced that evidential arguments such as Pinnock's are, on the whole, wrongheaded and ineffective. The real issue, Wolterstorff contends, is the unbeliever's "*resistence* to the available evidence"; the unbeliever "does not *like* to believe it."[78] Because

Wolterstorff considers resistence to be the crux of the problem, any adequate remedy must be twofold. First, a critique of the objections to Christianity must be undertaken and, in this case, a critique of the modern evidentialist assumptions. The second remedy must be some form of spiritual therapy that can both bring to light the roots of the unbeliever's resistence and relieve the unbeliever of his or her obstinate self-will.

Wolterstorff sees another, and crucial, assumption in evidentialist apologetics, namely, the contention that God asks us to believe only what is rational for us to believe. The reason why this assumption is false is because "intellectual obligations are only one among various types of obligations; and in specific cases they may well be overridden by obligations of other types."[79] Wolterstorff cites the example of an intellectually unsophisticated believer who listens to a powerful attack on Christianity that appears irrefutable. While such a person may no longer be intellectually justified in accepting the faith, Wolterstorff contends that this person may be sustained by other compelling obligations or justifying conditions for his or her faith. In other cases, persons may be required to undergo an agonizing intellectual trial of faith "in which we are asked to endure in the faith in spite of the fact that we find ourselves with adequate reason to give it up."[80]

Wolterstorff acknowledges that the Reformed tradition is *fideist* and not *evidentialist* in its fundamental impulse. The tradition does not accept the contention "that to be justified in believing in God one has to believe this on the basis of evidence provided by one's other beliefs." As Wolterstorff concludes: "We are entitled to reason *from* our belief in God without having first reasoned *to* it."[81]

Reformed epistemology has proven attractive to some Christian thinkers, but it also has numerous critics. Some have argued, for example, that belief in God is not, as Plantinga insists, "properly basic," the reason being that belief in God is an *inferred* belief and that its inferential character is essential to its being considered rational.[82] Other critics find that the Reformed epistemologists' acknowledgment of *fideism* raises a host of questions. One relates to their insistence that theistic belief is so basic that one is required to believe even though such an obligation is not rational. The critics insist that such a purported obligation does absolutely nothing to help the modern troubled seeker who sees no compelling grounds for belief. The critics concede that Plantinga's conclusion about modern foundationalism may give the seeker, or the troubled believer, a *right* to believe, but it does not tell one why he or she *ought* to believe. One critic puts the question to the Reformed epistemologist as follows:

You come in and admit that there are no rational grounds for an obligation to believe, but claim that they [the seekers] nonetheless ought to believe. Why should they pay any attention to you? You tell them they ought to be Christian, others say they ought to be Moslems, others that they ought to be atheists. Unlike you, they don't buy the idea that there are obligations to believe that have no rational basis of any sort. Even if there were, they wouldn't know how to decide among the numerous conflicting claims of obligation in religious matters.[83]

On the other hand, a Wittgensteinian philosopher such as D. Z. Phillips (see below) criticizes Plantinga for being a foundationalist *after all*, because Plantinga does insist that belief in God has *prima facie conditions* or justifications that are subject to successful criticism, and, therefore, to the possible ultimate defeat of belief.[84]

THE WITTGENSTEINIAN TRAJECTORY

Ludwig Wittgenstein

In another century, historians of Christian thought may well judge that the later writings of the philosopher Ludwig Wittgenstein (1889–1951) were the most decisive influence on the way Christian theologians in the latter half of the twentieth century reconceived their task. Without question, a great deal of Christian theology *after* Wittgenstein is pursued in new ways. Here we will briefly summarize the nature of Wittgenstein's later philosophical reflection and its import for theology. Most of this section will, however, show how Wittgenstein's ideas have been employed by two philosophers concerned with the implications of his thought for religion and, more particularly, for Christian theology.

Ludwig Wittgenstein was born in Vienna, Austria, the beneficiary of a wealthy and cultivated family background. He studied engineering in Berlin and Manchester but his interest in mathematics drew him to Cambridge University where he worked with Bertrand Russell. In 1914 he served in the Austrian army on the Russian and then the Italian front, where he was taken prisoner of war. His great work, the *Tractatus Logico-philosophicus*, was completed in 1918 and published in 1921. The *Tractatus* concluded that meaningful language consists of factual propositions that reflect our empirical world. Nonfactual propositions, such as metaphysical claims, lie outside the limits of meaningful language. The *Tractatus* concludes with the aphorism: "Whereof one cannot speak, thereof one must be silent." The *Tractatus* was understood at the time as having reached conclusions similar to those of the Logical Positivists of the Vienna Circle. In fact, as later appreciated, Wittgenstein's ruminations on language and its uses were to lead him far beyond the conclusions of the scientific positivists.

After a period of time as a primary school teacher in Austria, Wittgenstein returned to Cambridge in 1929. He submitted his *Tractatus* for the doctorate, began lecturing in the philosophy faculty, and was appointed professor of philosophy in 1939. During the Second World War he served as a hospital porter. He gave up teaching in 1947 to give full attention to his writings, most of which were not published until after his death in 1951. Among his posthumous works that are especially significant for his reflections on religion are the crucial *Philosophical Investigations* (1953), which reveals his mature thinking on language and its plural uses and meanings; *Lectures and Conversations on Aesthetics, Psychology and*

Religious Belief (1966); *Remarks on Frazer's "Golden Bough"* (1979); and *Culture and Value* (1980). What is the religious and theological significance of these later writings? The answer has to do with his mature understanding of language and its uses, and what this has to say about metaphysical questions, about meaning, understanding, evidence, and belief, especially in a culture dominated by scientific ways of thinking.

There is considerable dispute about Wittgenstein's own religious views and the coherence, if any, of his views on religion in his later work as a whole. Also, there is disagreement as to whether Wittgenstein's disciples have properly understood or appropriated his ideas. Nonetheless, some of his striking ideas with regard to language and meaning are clear. As noted, in the *Tractatus* Wittgenstein claimed that there is one kind of meaningful language or discourse. To depart from it is, literally, to speak nonsense. In the *Investigations*, however, Wittgenstein came to recognize that there are many different kinds of things that can be said. And it is the job of philosophy to analyze language and to discern the forms and boundaries of meaning that separate one linguistic usage from another. Our problems lie in getting these forms of discourse mixed up with one another because this leads to blunders and confusion.

In the *Investigations*, and the other later writings, Wittgenstein explores a pluralist theory of meaning. The meaning of a word is to be understood in terms of its particular use. He illustrates these plural forms of discourse by introducing the concepts of "language games" and "forms of life." Theistic language, for example, is a long-established form of discourse that does a job, that is, conveys certain meanings to those who participate in the theistic "language-game" The participants who live such a "form of life," understand the use of religious discourse. To illustrate his point, Wittgenstein explores the way that the "picture" of the Last Judgment is used by a believer.

Suppose someone were a believer and said: "I believe in a Last Judgement," and I said: "Well, I'm not so sure. Possibly." You would say that there is an enormous gulf between us. If he said, "There is a German aeroplane overhead," and I said "Possibly, I'm not so sure," you'd say we were fairly near.

It isn't a question of my being anywhere near him, but on an entirely different plane, which you could express by saying: "You mean something altogether different, Wittgenstein." The difference might not show up at all in any explanation of the meaning. Why is it that in this case I seem to be missing the entire point?[85]

The answer, Wittgenstein suggests, is that the picture of the Last Judgment is before the believer's mind whenever he or she does anything. The believer can offer no proof, but has what can be called an unshakeable belief. And this shows itself by its regulation over the believer's entire life. As Wittgenstein points out, this commisive or authorizing force of belief in the Last Judgment is

a very much stronger fact . . . because the man risks things on account of it which he would not do on things which are far better established for him. Although he distinguishes between things well-established and not well-established . . . he will treat his belief as extremely well-established, and in another way as not well-established at all.[86]

Participating in a "form of life" involves a use of language that carries with it a certain *ultimacy* for the community, analogous to what Alvin Plantinga calls "basic beliefs." For the community these beliefs constitute what is intelligible and morally compelling, and this is shown by the way the community thinks and lives. The demand for additional justifications or foundations reaches "bedrock" and, as Wittgenstein remarks, "the shovel turns." Belief in God plays such a role in the Christian community. The Christian and the scientific naturalist simply think differently. Wittgenstein would say that they say different things to themselves, they entertain different pictures.

In this regard, Wittgenstein has some interesting things to say about the use of the word "believing" and the question of "evidence." This can be illustrated by his account of belief in a Judgment Day. Wittgenstein points out the odd use of the word "belief" when both the believer and the atheist speak of believing or not believing in a Judgment Day. It appears to be neither a belief such as "Well, that's possible," nor is it a form of knowledge.

If you ask me whether or not I believe in a Judgment Day, in the sense in which religious people have belief in it, I wouldn't say: "No. I don't believe there will be such a thing." It would seem to me utterly crazy to say this.

And then I give an explanation: "I don't believe in. . . ," but then the religious person never believes what I describe. . . . I could say: "I don't believe in this," and that would be true, meaning I haven't got these thoughts or anything that hangs together with them. But not that I could contradict the thing.[87]

When Wittgenstein says that he cannot contradict the believer in the Last Judgment, he does not mean that he cannot understand what the believer is saying. It is, rather, that the expression "I believe that so and so will happen" is used differently than the way it is used in science. And the reasons given look entirely different. This also has to do with what we *normally* think of as evidence, which, for the believer in the Last Judgment, would be irrelevant for the belief. As Wittgenstein points out, anything that science would call evidence would not have the slightest influence on what the believer means by divine punishment.

Suppose, for instance, we knew people who foresaw the future; make forecasts for years and years ahead; and they describe some sort of Judgment Day. Queerly enough, even if there were such a thing, and even if it were more convincing then I described, belief in this happening wouldn't be at all a religious belief.[88]

Religious belief is based on what science would call exceedingly flimsy evidence, or no evidence at all, but neither would indubitable scientific evidence be enough to make the believer change his or her whole way of life or picture of the world. Wittgenstein contends that belief in a Last Judgment is neither what we normally would call a "reasonable" belief nor is it unreasonable, if that were to imply a rebuke. Its justification or "reasons," if we can use these words, are not like meteorological evidence that it will rain tomorrow, or with anything in science. But neither, Wittgenstein asserts, is belief in a Last Judgment a logical blunder. Rather, one must look for an entirely different interpretation, for "whether a thing is a blunder or not—it is a blunder in a particular system. Just as something is a blunder in a particular game and not in another."[89]

Wittgenstein sought to show that there are meanings and beliefs that lie at the very foundation of a person's thinking that the person does not even think of supporting by other grounds. These beliefs represent the "framework" not only of our thinking but of our "form of life." It would, therefore, be foolish to try to explain or criticize the belief from an alien framework; for example, Sir James Frazer's efforts to explain archaic religious rituals in terms of Victorian positivistic notions of scientific error. Errors, or conceptual confusions, are made within the terms and logic of a particular language-game. As Wittgenstein remarks: "Frazer's account of the magical and religious notions of men is unsatisfactory: it makes these notions appear as *mistakes*. Was Augustine mistaken, then, when he called on God on every page of the *Confessions?*"[90] It is *within*, say, a science or a religion that beliefs and actions can be judged logical or illogical.

The Wittgensteinians

Since the 1960s a significant number of philosophers and theologians have taken up Wittgenstein's insights and have pursued his analysis as it bears specifically on the nature and use of religious and theological language and "forms of life."[91] It counts among its most influential practioners the philosophers Norman Malcolm[92] (1911–1990), Peter Winch[93] (1926–1997), and D. Z. Phillips[94] (1934–).

Norman Malcolm

Norman Malcolm explored the traditional discussion of the arguments for the existence of God and points out how they are most often discussed *outside* of their normal context of the religious life. Malcolm has considerable difficulty with the notion of belief in *the existence* of God, "whereas," he writes, "the idea of belief in God is to me intelligible." For instance, Malcolm finds it odd to speak of a person "believing in God" if that person never prays or never thanks God for the blessings of life or never feels the pain of failing to live by the commandments or will of God. Belief *in* God, as Malcolm understands the normal use of the words, entails "some religious action, some commitment, or if not, at least a bad conscience."[95] The traditional proofs of *the existence* of God can, on the other hand, be understood as compelling even to a person devoid of religious sensibility, conscience, or form of life. What, Malcolm asks, would be the marks of such a belief in *the existence* of God?

> Would it be that the man knows some theology, can recite the creeds, is well-read in Scripture? Or is his belief in the existence of God something different than this? . . . What would be the difference between a man who knows some articles of faith, heresies, scriptural writings, and in addition believes in the existence of God, and one who knows these things but does not believe in the existence of God? I assume that both of them are indifferent to the acts and commitments of religious life.[96]

It has been widely accepted in modern philosophy since Hume that Anselm's famous ontological argument for the existence of God is a specious proof, because it is based on Anselm's definitional claim regarding God's "necessary existence." Science has taught us that existential propositions cannot be necessary because they are by definition contingent. In a celebrated article entitled "Is It a Religious Belief that 'God Exists'?" Malcolm, on the contrary, defends Anselm's definition of God *as a necessary existent* by claiming that such a conception of God has long played a meaningful role in the Judaeo-Christian language-game:

In the Ninetieth Psalm it is said: "Before the mountains were brought forth, or even thou hadst formed the earth and the world even from everlasting to everlasting, thou art God." Here is expressed the idea of the necessary existence and eternity of God. . . . In those [Jewish and Christian] complex systems of thought, those "language-games," God has the status of a necessary being. Who can doubt that? Here we must say with Wittgenstein, "This language-game is played!"[97]

D. Z. Phillips

The most influential contemporary Christian philosopher who has applied Wittgenstein's analysis of language and meaning to a theistic form of life is D. Z. Phillips, professor of philosophy at the University of Wales, Swansea, and Danforth Professor of the Philosophy of Religion at the Claremont Graduate School in California. Phillips has authored or edited many books. Among the most important for our purposes are *The Concept of Prayer* (1965); *Death and Immortality* (1970); *Religion Without Explanation* (1976); *Belief, Change and Forms of Life* (1986); *Faith After Foundationalism* (1988); and *Wittgenstein and Religion* (1993).

We noted earlier that one of the characteristics of the work of Christian thinkers in the second half of the twentieth century is a quite explicit stand on the question of the relationship between the Christian tradition and modern philosophy and culture. For some theologians, for example, Thomas Altizer, Christian self-description is strongly shaped by, indeed subordinate to, a broader cultural inquiry and norms. Theologians and philosophers as different as David Tracy and Alvin Plantinga wish to keep Christian tradition and philosophical inquiry related, either in terms of a theology of genuine "correlation," as in the case of Tracy, or in the service of a rational, though nonfoundational, Christian apologetic, as

in the case of Plantinga and Nicholas Wolterstorff. D. Z. Phillips represents a quite different option; namely, a concern to free Christian discourse and theology from any correlation with or subservience to the norms and claims of philosophy of religion as it has been practiced until recently in the Western tradition.

For Phillips, the problem with Christianity's dialogue with philosophy is that the latter has set the rules of the game. This has resulted in an appeal to evidential facts and reasons for belief *external* to the testimony and belief of Christianity itself. This is patent, for example, in traditional inquiry regarding belief in God. Philosophers have assumed that *external* evidence or reasons would, if found, constitute the grounds for theistic belief. But could, Phillips asks, "a philosopher say that he believed that God exists and yet never pray to Him . . . seek His will, or fear and tremble before Him? In short, could a man believe that God exists without his life being touched *at all* by the belief?"[98] Phillips agrees with Malcolm that the answer is "no," because belief that there is a God is not like belief in the existence of a planet, for in the latter case one need not take any interest in it. This, however, is entirely foreign to the question of belief in God, which is not a fact that one can *find out* by an appeal to external methods.

As Phillips insists: "It has far too readily been assumed that the dispute between the believer and the unbeliever is over a *matter of fact*. Philosophical reflection on the reality of God then becomes the philosophical reflection appropriate to an assertion of a matter of fact."[99] But this, for Phillips, is an enormous misrepresentation of the religious concept of God, which should be obvious if we seriously compare talk about God and talk about planets. Philosophy, therefore, can claim "justifiably to show what is meaningful in religion only if it is prepared to examine religious concepts in the contexts from which they derive their meaning"[100]—but this philosophy has refused to do.

The problem here is grammatical. The philosopher either fails or refuses to recognize that there is no meta-language or paradigm of meaning and rationality. As Phillips insists:

Coming to see that there is a God is not like coming to see that an additional being exists. If it were, there would be an extension of one's knowledge of facts, but no extension of one's understanding. Coming to see that there is a God involves seeing a new meaning in one's life, and being given a new understanding. The Hebrew-Christian conception of God is not a conception of a being among beings. Kierkegaard emphasized the point when he said bluntly, "God does not exist. He is eternal."[101]

The believer always speaks of divine love, mercy, wrath, or forgiveness in the context of belief in an eternal God, and it is the *eternity* of the God who is praised or thanked or confessed to that is the crux that gives meaning to all of these divine attributes and all these religious activities.

One implication of this fact is that philosophers who do not believe in God can no longer think of their rejection as the denial of something *with which they are familiar.* Discovering that there is a God is not like establishing that something is the case within a universe of discourse with which we are already familiar. On the contrary, it is to discover that there *is* a universe of discourse we had been unaware of.[102]

Phillips's appeal to Wittgenstein's reflections on language, culture, and meaning *within* various language-games and forms of life prepares the way for his own inquiry into the meaning of such Christian concepts as prayer, death, eternal life, and evil. We will explore Phillips's inquiry into these matters by a brief exposition of his consideration of prayer and the reality of evil.

We have noted that Wittgenstein and Phillips emphasize the *distinctiveness* of religious language and forms of life. This has understandably lead critics to charge that they fail to recognize that religious beliefs are integrally related to what actually surrounds them in human life. Phillips, the critic claims, makes religious language and belief esoteric. This is an odd critique of Phillips because he, in particular, is concerned to explore deeply the way that religious language relates to profound human experiences. He makes this quite explicit in *The Concept of Prayer.* He writes that in his exploration of the meaning of prayer he will *not* treat religious concepts as "*technical* concepts . . . cut off from the common experiences of human life: joy and sorrow, hope and despair."[103]

Phillips begins by addressing some of the puzzles one faces when looking at the experience of prayer. First, prayer is a talking to God, but such a conversation obviously differs from our talking with other individuals. The human participant must, of course, share in a common religious language, for only in using the language can he or she speak to God. But God does not participate *in* any language, and yet God "*is* to be found in the language people learn when they learn about religion"; for example, "to come to see what divine anger means," namely, "to come to view one's life in relation to the will of God."[104] This form of "talking" is then different from talking to another individual, which, in principle, could be a conversation with any person. But this is not true of prayer. Phillips suggests the difference:

In prayer what is said can only be said directly to God. This is an analytic statement, since what is said is God's language as it were. One is lead into difficulties if one thinks of praying as talking to someone who is related to what is said in the ways in which we are related to the language we speak.[105]

That is, in prayer there is a reversal of the positions of speaker and hearer. In ordinary conversation we impart information to the other person, something they otherwise would not know. But we cannot say this of our talking with God because "God does not *come to know* anything."[106] What, then, is the religious person doing when he or she talks to God, for example, in prayers of confession? God clearly does not have to be told that I sinned this morning. "I may rob a temple of its sacred treasurers, trick everyone into thinking I am innocent. . . . But *it does not make sense* to think that God can be a victim of such duplicity."[107] What, then, is happening? Phillips's answer is that genuine prayer allows the believer to come to a new understanding but not in the form of our usual intellectual understanding.

Neither does it mean that what [the believer] understands is God! The position we must try to give an account of is this: man prays to a God whom he does not understand, a fact which to a large extent reflects the nature of prayer, namely, *telling God what we do not understand*. On the other hand, in this very telling, the confession of his own insufficiency, the believer reaches an understanding of himself, he "comes to himself." Consider the situation at the end of the Book of Job. . . . In saying that he does not know, Job is not saying that he could know if he had greater ability. . . . He is saying that things are unknowable. . . . To acknowledge that he did not know was for Job the solution or, rather, the dissolution, of his questions; to see all things in the hands of God . . . [is] a precondition for receiving the understanding or grace which comes from God.[108]

Phillips extends this reflection on the meaning of prayer to the difficult question of prayers of *petition*, to superstition, and to an analysis of evil and theodicy, the justification of God's actions. The close connection between prayer and the reality of suffering and evil demonstrates the direct connections that Phillips makes between belief and ordinary religious activity.

Petitionary prayer and the ever-present threat of evil bring out, for Phillips, the gulf between genuine religious trust and mere superstition. In doing this, he also makes clear why he opposes all theodicies that feel obliged to justify God's actions in the face of evil. Theodicists basically argue that, despite appearances to the contrary, there really is divine purpose and design in the world—seen either in the building of character in the face of trials and suffering or in some future recompense. In either case, the Christian theodicist accepts the skeptics' demand that God be subject to justification; that is, that the evil we see and experience either counts against God or does not count against God *decisively* by reason of arguments that can be set out or by appeals to God's victory in some future time and/or place.

Phillips insists that God does not answer prayer or relieve suffering either by remedying the human situation or by offering explanations, what he calls "higher level planning." As Simone Weil has written, the true answer to prayer is to be released from the "claims of compensation" by the self for the self. That is, prayer reorders the self's understanding:

The instinct for self-preservation makes men ask, "Why is this happening to *me?*" But suffering can also be used to teach one that one is nothing just because it does tempt to put oneself at the centre of one's concern. Simone Weil expresses the point well: "If I thought that God sent me suffering by an act of his will and for my good, I should think that I was something, and I should miss the chief use of suffering which is to teach me that I am nothing." It is therefore essential to avoid all such thoughts, but it is necessary to love God through the suffering.[109]

The believer's understanding consists, in part, in *not* expecting worldly evidences of God's goodness, nor that the meaning of life depends on what happens *in* the world. Phillips calls the latter "the naturalistic fallacy." What the Christian can come to understand in prayer is that he or she does not, again as Simone Weil expressed it, "seek a supernatural remedy for suffering but a supernatural use for it."[110]

Phillips contrasts this authentic use of prayer with examples of superstitious prayer. He cites the case of a man facing a critical danger who prays to God that he will do whatever God wants, if God only will spare him. "Compare that prayer with: 'Yea, though I walk through the valley of the shadow of death I will fear no evil, for thou art with me' (Psalm 23). . . . The two kinds of dependence are radically different."[111] Phillips sees the first prayer as superstitious, like "kissing a rabbit's foot or touching wood."[112] One would, of course, have to know more about the particular case; nonetheless, the test of authentic prayers is that they do play a regular role in a person's life when no crises are present. Prayers offered only in times of crisis "are not characteristic of the *religious* role of prayer in the life of the believer."[113]

Authentic petitionary prayer must, Phillips repeats, express a genuine subordination of the person's desires to the will of God. This alone will reflect the spirit of God within that person—in contrast, say, to the response of the fatalist. One must, however, ask Phillips whether, in authentic prayer, the person is not in fact asking God to do something, namely, to give that person the will and spiritual serenity to subordinate egoistic desires? Perhaps Phillips's conception of petitionary prayer is not as different from more common forms of petition as he appears to think.[114]

A number of related questions have been directed at Phillips's use of Wittgenstein's philosophy. A rather common one, which he has repeatedly sought to refute, is that he understands language-games as so distinctive as to fail to relate religious language and concepts to their wider human cultural contexts, i.e., to other language-games.[115] This charge is related to others. One is that religious beliefs, as conceived by Phillips, can only be understood by believers,[116] or that Christian talk, being but one language-game among innumerable other language-games, must admit to a cultural relativism. This would preclude any objective test or rationale that could evaluate Christianity's comparative adequacy.[117] Phillips has addressed these types of criticisms, whether successfully remains disputed.[118]

The Postliberal theologian Hans Frei is sympathetic to Phillips's wariness about allowing Christian concepts to be judged by external, e.g., philosophical, criteria. Nevertheless, he believes that Phillips is too prescriptive in not allowing conceptual overlaps between Christian and other contexts. For Frei, the matter should be determined case by case. Furthermore, Frei believes that Christian doctrines cannot, without remain-

der, be equated with the way these concepts work in Christian life and nurture. As Frei puts it, the Christian doctrines of God, Jesus Christ, the Church, and so on, "must not be *separated* from *coming to* and *exercizing* faith, but must be *distinguished* from these functions. The internal logic of belief is not identical with the logic of how one comes to be a Christian and live Christian concepts."[119]

Other writers, again sympathetic with much of what Phillips is saying, also are suspicious that what he calls authentic or deep religious belief is not descriptive of religion as widely practiced; rather, these beliefs represent Phillips's own conception of what constitutes genuine or normative religion. This becomes especially evident in Phillips's contrast between religion and superstition. As one writer has observed:

In Phillips' view religious and superstitious belief are differentiated by two constituents. Belief motivated by fear and which presumes a "queer causal connection" between actions the believer performs and divine responses is superstitious. Belief motivated by trust and which does not presume a causal connection between a believer's status and/or actions and the divine status and/or actions is religious. But why is belief motivated by fear superstitious and belief motivated by love or trust religious? Why is a practice that presumes a "queer causal connection" between sins and worldly punishment or between petitionary prayer and miracle superstitions? Phillips makes these connections only by stipulating them, and it is that stipulation that I find unpersuasive.[120]

Phillips's conditions of true belief would appear to dismiss much of the world's religious belief and practice as outside the bounds of authentic or deep religion. This criticism is especially striking because Phillips so often takes his philosophical and theological critics to task for abstracting from the living religious experiences of believers. For some critics this remains a telling criticism.

The value of Phillips's grammatical analysis of Christian belief can, perhaps, serve a different kind of role, one strictly within the bounds of Christian theological discourse itself, because his understanding of Christian concepts does differ from the understandings of other Christians.[121] Phillips would say that whether the understanding of a Christian belief—for example, the being of God—represents the truer or more adequate conception is, first of all, not a matter that can be determined by a popular survey. Further, it is reasonable to believe that authorities knowledgeable about Christian theology could well agree that some conceptions of God are not accurate or adequate representations of what Christian theology understands by the word "God." Some conceptions, for example, are immature and grossly anthropomorphic; others may be incoherent or sub-Christian. Some believers naively compare God with other physical bodies, such as a person writ-large or similar analogies that are equally misleading, even false. Such conceptions, therefore, need clarification and correction. In many instances, it can be argued, Phillips carries out this task admirably, in other instances not so persuasively. But as Phillips himself suggests, in grammatical explorations such as these, one must avoid abstraction and look at specific cases.

POSTLIBERAL THEOLOGY

Among the directions of Christian thought explored in this final chapter, Postliberal theology may prove to be the most influential and enduring. It includes a number of thoughtful explorations of the relationship of Christian belief to its wider secular culture, posing important questions for contemporary theologies of correlation.

Postliberal theology joins forces with both the Reformed epistemologists and with the Neo-Wittgensteinians in their opposition to Enlightenment rationalism, foundationalism, and evidentialism as they are appealed to in both justifying and criticizing theological beliefs. The Postliberals also oppose modern apologetic schemes that are based on appeals to some common ground of religious experience, such as one finds in both Transcendental Thomism and in many forms of Protestant Liberalism.

Postliberalism represents a somewhat loose alliance of theologians, most of whom either were trained or taught at Yale Divinity School. Its origins can be traced to several sources, but the influences of H. Richard Niebuhr (see Chapter Six) and Karl Barth (see Chapter Four) are especially crucial. In their different ways, both Niebuhr and Barth emphasized the narrative character of biblical revelation and the communal context of biblical interpretation. Barth's influence on Postliberalism is mediated through the work of Hans Frei (see Chapter Eleven). As we have learned, Frei's *The Eclipse of Biblical Narrative* (1974) constituted a brilliant historical demonstration of the often pernicious effect that modern Protestant historical-critical scholarship has had on the understanding and reading of the Bible. This "great reversal" turned the Bible into an odd repository of (questionable) historical facts and religious ideas. Interpretation became "a matter of fitting the biblical story into another world with another story rather than incorporating that world into the biblical story."[122] What was lost, according to Frei, was the traditional reading of the Bible as a "realistic narrative." Both Barth and Frei saw a link between the work of the historical critics and the often over-accommodating apologetics of Liberal theology.

While the influence of Hans Frei's work is decisive in the development of Postliberal theology, George Lindbeck's *The Nature of Doctrine: Religion and Theology in a Postliberal Age* (1984) proved to be its rallying cry. The book is a concise articulation of some of the key concerns and convictions of the "Yale School." Since Hans Frei's contributions are detailed in Chapter Eleven, here we will focus first on the work of George Lindbeck. Others associated with Postliberalism are Stanley Hauerwas,[123] Ronald F. Thiemann,[124] William C. Placher,[125] Kathryn E. Tanner,[126] and Charles M. Wood.[127]

George Lindbeck

George A. Lindbeck (1923–   ) began his career as a scholar of medieval thought at Yale where he taught from 1952 to 1993, in the latter years as Pitkin Professor of Historical Theology at the Divinity School. Lindbeck was born in China, the son of American Lutheran missionaries. He attended school in China and Korea before entering Gustavus Adolphus College in Minnesota. He received his B.D. degree from Yale Divinity School in 1943, and then studied with two world-renowned medievalists, Etienne Gilson in Toronto and Paul Vignous in Paris, before completing his Ph.D. at Yale in 1955.

Lindbeck's career took a significant turn in 1962 when he was invited, as a representative of the Lutheran World Federation, to serve as an official observer at the four sessions of the Second Vatican Council (1962–1965) in Rome, called by Pope John XXIII. In the years following the Council, most of Lindbeck's writings were devoted to ecumenical concerns. Only after *The Nature of Doctrine* appeared did his writings focus on his call for a new Postliberal theology, although the continuity with his earlier ecumenical reflections is clearly evident, especially his concern with the issues of religious pluralism. In the foreword to *The Nature of Doctrine*, Lindbeck expresses his dissatisfaction with the way modern theology has understood the Church's doctrines or dogmas, and he perceives this as tied to inadequate conceptions of the nature of religion itself. Although he believes that current theological approaches are no longer helpful, Lindbeck does not suggest that the difficulties can "be solved by, for example, abandoning modern developments and returning to some form of preliberal orthodoxy." Rather, he sees "a third, postliberal, way of conceiving religion and religious doctrine" as called for.[128]

The Nature of Doctrine begins with an exploration of the ecumenical matrix of religion and doctrine, and particularly with the current theories associated with them. Lindbeck calls the first

George Lindbeck

type of theory the *cognitive-propositional*. This type tends to emphasize the cognitive dimension of religion "and the ways in which church doctrines function as informative propositions or truth claims about objective realities." So understood, "religions are thus thought of as similar to philosophy or science as they were classically conceived,"[129] that is, grounded on a correspondence theory of truth that Lindbeck considers untenable in our postmodern context. A second conception of religion and doctrine focuses on what he calls the *experiential-expressive*. "It interprets doctrines as noninformative and nondiscursive symbols of inner feelings, attitudes, or existential orientations."[130] It is the type best identified with Liberal theologies since Schleiermacher.

Neither of these approaches provide a satisfactory conception of religion as it is practiced nor, Lindbeck suggests, can either approach meet the ecumenical goal of doctrinal reconciliation without the acquiescence of one party to the requirements of another. Those who hold a propositional concept of doctrine consider doctrinal truth as always true or always false. And this is because no distinction is made between first-order speech about God or Christ and theological discourse as a second-order form of speech. Lindbeck points out that

this implies, for example, that the historic affirmations and denials of transubstantiation can never be harmonized. Agreement can be reached only if one or both sides abandon their earlier positions. . . . In no way can the meaning of a doctrine change while remaining the same.[131]

Experiential-expressive conceptions of doctrine also are unsatisfactory because the meanings of a doctrine can vary, or the doctrine itself can be altered without changing its meaning. For example, both transubstantial and nontransubstantial doctrines of the Eucharist or Mass can express or evoke similar or quite different experiences of the Divine presence in the sacrament.

The general principle is that insofar as doctrines function as discursive symbols . . . they are polyvalent in import and therefore subject to changes of meaning or even to a total loss of meaningfulness, to what Tillich calls their death. They are not crucial for religious agreement or disagreement, because these [symbols] are constituted by harmony or conflict in underlying feelings, attitudes . . . or practices.[132]

Lindbeck offers an alternative conception of religion and doctrine that is based on recent work in anthropology, sociology, and philosophy. It understands religious belief and practice as neither fundamentally cognitive nor experiential-expressive but, rather, what he calls cultural-linguistic. In elucidating this conception of religion, Lindbeck draws heavily on the work of the cultural anthropologist Clifford Geertz and on Wittgenstein's philosophy of language in which great emphasis is placed

on those respects in which religions resemble languages together with their correlative forms of life and are thus similar to cultures. . . . The function of church doctrines that becomes most prominent in this

perspective is their use . . . as communally authoritative rules of discourse, attitude and action.[133]

Lindbeck argues that theology presupposes a communal network of beliefs and practices that are guided by certain essentials necessary to the identity of the community. These authoritative rules of discourse, for example, those associated with monotheism and the Incarnation, are crucial to the identity of Christianity. "To become a Christian involves learning the story of Israel and of Jesus well enough to interpret and experience oneself and one's world in its terms. A religion is above all an external word, a *verbum externum*, that molds and shapes the self and its world."[134]

There are many rules of belief and practice that can help to shape the "form of life" of the Christian. What is crucial to remember, however, is that church doctrines are rules of speech, that is, are a second-order use of language. Doctrines about God and Christ, for example, regulate the community's belief and activity, but not all regulative doctrines are set in stone. A particular doctrine may not function adequately for one or another community at a particular time or circumstance. This is especially true of religious practices. For example, the "law of love" is held by Christianity as unconditionally necessary, but pacifism, which may have been viewed as mandatory in some circumstances, is not widely held by most churches as unconditionally obligatory. The same might apply to certain rules that have guided sexual ethics that, under changing conditions, may be altered or nullified by new developments in, for example, scientific knowledge. The same may be true of the Church's more strictly theological rules of discourse. "They also can be viewed as unconditionally or conditionally necessary, as permanent or temporary, as reversible or irreversible."[135]

Lindbeck points to the articles of the Apostle's Creed and to the Nicene and Chalcedonian confessions of faith as having been understood as unconditionally and permanently essential, whereas the doctrine of the immortality of the soul could, perhaps, be classified as conditional or even reversible if it could be shown that its necessity is tied to a questionable classical mind-body dualism. A good illustration of his point is the Marian doctrines. They have been understood by Roman Catholics as *conditionally* necessary, because some of them were not always regarded as essential or were even rejected by theologians such as Thomas Aquinas but, nonetheless, are now considered irreversible doctrines.

Lindbeck makes the distinction between a community's "rules of discourse," i.e., its doctrines, and the role of theology as a second-order activity. "There can be great variety in the theological explanation, communication, and defense of the faith within a framework of communal doctrinal agreement," he writes. And "those who agree on explicitly formulated doctrines may disagree sharply on how to interpret, justify, or defend them."[136] Theological explanations and defenses of church doctrine are, therefore, optional theories rather than communally normative. The tasks of theology therefore will vary with historical context.

Lindbeck agrees with Hans Frei, however, that contemporary Christian theology has for a number of reasons lost its compass, the result being a loss of faithfulness to the normative Christian doctrines and to its form of life. From the perspective of a cultural-linguistic Postliberal theology, the issue is not simply grammatical but, more significantly, the matter of *where* the proper, abiding Christian grammar is to be found. For Frei and Lindbeck, with help from Karl Barth, the answer is a return to a "thick" narrative description of the universe of meaning and the form of life that is paradigmatically encoded in the Bible, the story of God's revelation through the history of the people of Israel and Jesus Christ.

What Lindbeck calls for is an *intratextual* hermeneutics, one in which the meanings immanent in the religious language of the Bible itself are attended to rather than reading foreign philosophical or phenomenological meanings into or beneath the biblical text itself. Lindbeck illus-

trates what he means by an intratextual hermeneutics by citing the natural, literary reading of the Western classics:

Masterpieces such as *Oedipus Rex* and *War and Peace* . . . evoke their own domains of meaning. They do so by what they themselves say about the events and personages of which they tell. In order to understand them in their own terms, there is no need for extraneous references to, for example, Freud's theories or historical treatments of the Napoleonic wars. Further, such works shape the imagination and perceptions of the attentive reader so that he or she forever views the world to some extent through the lens they supply.[137]

Lindbeck calls for a reading and interpretation of the Bible that is self-referential, that is, self-interpreting, narratively unified, and typological; i.e., one that uses the figures and events in the Hebrew Scriptures as foreshadowing figures and events in the New Testament. Typology reverses the way the biblical text is read. It does not suggest that faithful believers find *their* story in the Bible's story; rather, that they make the biblical story their story. In so doing, theology redescribes reality from the biblical perspective rather than interpreting the Bible through extra biblical categories. "It is the text, so to speak which absorbs the world, rather than the world the text."[138] The extrabiblical world is thereby shaped for the believer by the overarching, realistic narrative of the Bible.

In language reminiscent of the point made by Karl Barth in his *Epistle to the Romans*, Lindbeck specifies the primary function of the biblical narrative:

It is "to render a character. . . to offer an identity description of an agent," namely God. It does this not by telling what God is in and of himself, but by accounts of the interaction of his deeds and purposes with those of his creatures in their ever-changing circumstances. These accounts reach their climax in what the Gospels say of the risen, ascended, and ever-present Jesus Christ whose identity as the divine-human agent is unsubstitutably enacted in the stories of Jesus of Nazereth.[139]

For Lindbeck, the failure of modern theology may be reversed if it will forego its experiential-expressive effort to find points of contact between Christian belief and universal modes of human religiousness, and return to the Christian community's own identity as it is continually shaped by its reading of Scripture. Theologians, perhaps, will then attend to their primary role of engaging in the second-order task of redescribing the Church's doctrinal heritage by faithfully attending to its communally authoritative, invariant rules of discourse.

Stanley Hauerwas

It is generally acknowledged that Hans Frei and George Lindbeck are the shapers of many of the key features of the Postliberal theological program. Neither, however, paid much attention to the program's significance for Christian ethics. Stanley Hauerwas (1940–) stands out as the most significant Postliberal ethicist. Hauerwas did his graduate work at Yale and his writings, as he acknowledges, show the impress of his Yale mentors and colleagues, especially that of H. Richard Niebuhr, Hans Frei, and Stephen Crites. He also finds Lindbeck's later work highly congenial.[140] Hauerwas taught for some years at the University of Notre Dame before moving to Duke University as professor of theological ethics. He is a prolific writer, having authored or edited a score of books. Among them are *Truthfulness and Tragedy: Further Investigations in Christian Ethics* (1977); *A Community of Character* (1981); *The Peaceable Kingdom* (1983); *Against the Nations* (1985); *Suffering Presence* (1986); and *Why Narrative? Readings in Narrative Theology* (1989).

Hauerwas's writings echo a number of the Postliberal themes: the attack on classical foundationalism, rationalism, universalism, and autonomy, as well as its positive emphasis on particularity, community, and narrative as they bear on ethical reflection. His attention to the role of "story" in the formation of community, biography, and character draws on Frei's conception of "his-tory-like" realistic narrative and on the importance that Frei gives to the particularity and unsubstitutable identity of the person of Jesus. Hauerwas speaks of "stories" rather than narratives, and although he is close to Frei, it does bear mentioning that there are significant differences between the "narrative" theologies of Frei and, for example, Hauerwas, H. Richard Niebuhr's conception of "The Story of Our Life"[141] (see Chapter Six), Stephen Crites's "The Narrative Quality of Experience,"[142] and the work of Paul Ricoeur[143] (see Chapter Eleven).

Hauerwas, like his Postliberal colleagues, insists on underlining the point that

> the emphasis on story as the grammatical setting for religious convictions is . . . to remind us that Christian convictions are not isolatable "facts," but those "facts" are part of a story that helps locate what kind of "facts" you have at all. . . . To emphasize the story character of the gospel is an attempt to suggest that examining the truth of Christian conviction is closely akin to seeing how other kinds of stories form our lives truly or falsely.[144]

Unlike theories, stories are not meant to give explanations, to help a person know the world without changing the person's way of life; they are, rather, meant to help one "deal with the world by changing it through changing yourself."[145] Stories can make a muddle of things intelligible and, in so doing, can shape a self. Thus the narrative shape of experience isn't optional; it is indispensable, because our lives are formed by one or another story. Hauerwas further insists that it is the very shape of narrative that is crucial, because stories do not point to some meaning that is separable from the narrative. The meaning is embedded in the very narrative character of the story. "Stories . . . have no point beyond the story itself."[146] A person's sense of identity is, therefore, shaped by the kind of story that he or she embraces as his or her own. Hauerwas claims that our modern, rational, and liberal story simply "teaches us that we have no story,"[147] hence no sense of identity beyond the autonomous self.

Christian identity, conviction, and action are shaped by the biblical narrative and principally by the particular story of Jesus Christ. "Jesus," Hauerwas writes, "is the story that forms the church."[148] It is not intended to shape the character or ethos of other forms of society, for example, liberal democracy. The Church's story "stands as a political alternative to every nation, witnessing to the kind of social life possible for those that have been formed by the story of Christ."[149]

For Hauerwas, Christian discipleship originates in a virtuous character that is shaped by specific skills that embody a life faithful to Christ. Such an ethic of virtue is not full of quandaries as is a rational ethic of choices based on abstract principles. This does not mean, of course, that the Christian can avoid morally painful tasks. On the contrary, for Christ's summons to be virtuous

necessarily challenges us to face moral difficulties and obstacles that might not be present if we were less virtuous. The coward can never know the fears of the courageous. That is why an ethic of virtue always gains its intelligibility from narratives that place our lives within an adventure.[150]

The key to such a virtue ethic is, then, the communal and narrative context in which a life is shaped and lived.

Hauerwas understands the authority of the Scripture's story as grounded in its practical function in the life of the Christian community:

Claims about the authority scripture are in themselves moral claims about the function of scripture for the common life of the church. The scripture's authority for that life consists in its being used so that it helps to nurture and reform the community's self-identity as well as the personal character of its members.[151]

Hauerwas similarly links the truth of Christian claims to the role that narrative plays in forming beliefs and practices in the ongoing life of the Christian community. The Christian virtues and identity *originate from* the Christian narrative and Christian truth is grounded and tested by the moral community:

The necessary interrelation of narrative and character provides the means to test the truthfulness of narratives. Significant narratives produce significant and various characters necessary for the understanding and richness of the story itself. Just as scientific theories are partially judged by the fruitfulness of the activities they generate, so narratives can and should be judged by the richness of moral character and activity they generate.

Narrative forges a tradition and, Hauerwas contends, "without tradition we have no means to ask questions of truth or falsity."[152]

It is this tendency of some Postliberals to regard Christian truth claims as resting in and as tested by the Church's faithfulness to the Christian tradition itself that has made other Postliberals uneasy. William C. Placher states this concern persuasively:

Assuming that one could argue back from the virtue of the tellers to the truth of their tale, any such argument on behalf of Christian narratives either would fall victim to a strong form of relativism, in which different stories are "true" for different groups, or else would have to claim that the Christian community makes people demonstrably more virtuous than other communities do—[a] claim I would not want to try to defend on empirical grounds.[153]

Ronald Theimann sees another theological problem in a Postliberal functionalist appeal to religious truth; namely, that it is prone to either omit or minimize the essential of Christian faith, i.e., belief in the prevenient action of God. This appears to be a tendency in writers like Hauerwas who place such emphasis on the community's identity formation in its response to a narrative tradition. Although the narrative may presuppose God's prevenience, which seems to be the case in Hauerwas's writings, the point remains that the objective truth about God cannot be determined by either the virtue or the coherence of a community's form of life.[154]

A number of younger evangelical scholars have been attracted to many features of Postliberalism, especially as an alternative to either Fundamentalism or Liberalism.[155] There remains, however, a suspicion, if not a breach, between the two movements on the question of the objective reference or truth claims of biblical revelation. This is apparent in Carl Henry's critique of Hans Frei's position and Frei's response.[156] It is also a concern for younger Evangelicals, as is evident in Alister McGrath's critique of George Lindbeck's *The Nature of Doctrine*. McGrath writes:

Lindbeck, by accident or design, is perhaps somewhat equivocal over whether his cultural-linguistic approach to doctrine involves an affirmation or setting aside of epistemological realism and a correspondence theory of truth. . . . It is at this point that evangelicalism directs one of its most serious criticisms against postliberalism. For evangelicals, postliberalism reduces the concept of "truth" to "internal consistency."[157]

McGrath faults Lindbeck—although the point is disputed—for failing to show that the Christian language-game is adequate to designate the reality of God *outside* its language-game. As for the Christian community holding to the normative role of the Bible, the same, of course, can be said for the role of the Qur'an in Islam, but which one is *right?*[158]

The Reformed epistemologists see a real affinity between their own program and that of Postliberals, such as Frei and Lindbeck. Both movements are committed to reversing the modern theological correlationist's sense of obligation to conform its thought to the methods and results of the modern academy. Both programs hold that theology should challenge the assumptions of modern rationalism and autonomy and should norm their thought and language through fidelity to the language and thought of the Christian community. However, neither school believes that this entails a wholesale repudiation of modern thought and knowledge. The Postliberals advocate an "ad hoc" approach to the encounter with modern philosophy and science.[159]

The Reformed epistemologists, on the other hand, tend to reject such a piecemeal, ad hoc approach to apologetics, and prefer to engage in a more radical alternative form of theorizing, a genuine counterattack, as we have noted above in the writings of Alvin Plantinga and Nicholas Wolterstorff. The Neo-Calvinists see themselves as posing a more fundamental question to the modern academy:

The question is this: Is the regnant self-image of the modern academy tenable? The neo-Calvinist contends that it is not—that it is in fact a piece of self-delusion. Academic learning is not and *could not be* an autonomous, generically human, foundationally structured enterprise whose final foundations, universal theory, and necessary conditions are developed by philosophers.[160]

The Neo-Calvinist counterattack on the fundamental assumptions of the modern academy may easily be misconstrued as implying that the academy and the Church are incommensurable forms of life, but this is not the case. The Neo-Calvinists and the Postliberals both agree that the Church can learn some important things from the secular disciplines. The conformations called for are not one-directional; the Church sometimes must revise its thought and its practice in light of the findings of the sciences. The Neo-Calvinists, however, see the apologetic task as a more constructive and encompassing one. It involves alternative ways of theorizing, rather than a scurrying around in an effort to revise Christian belief in light of new scientific evidence. As Wolterstorff points out, Plantinga's epistemology poses a series of fundamental questions for the academy that the Postliberals, perhaps, have not yet adequately addressed:

Why should the assumption be accepted that evidence is always required? Who says that we may only *reason* to our convictions about God, never simply

reason from them? If one wants to think along foundational lines, who says that beliefs about God may
never be in *the foundations?*[161]

CONCLUSION

The five theological programs explored in this
chapter represent a variety of responses to the
phenomenon of modernity. More particularly,
they suggest different theological positions on the
issue of the relationship between knowledge and
Christian faith, reason and revelation. In the
work of Gordon Kaufman we see a rejection of the
assumed givenness and the binding authority of
Christian revelation and ecclesial tradition.
Rather, Kaufman appeals to a wider cultural and
religious context that, itself, must materially
shape any theology constructed at the end of the
twentieth century. Some forms of liberationist
and political theology also quite explicitly give
epistemological priority to the cultural moment
or context, claiming that the situation is essential
to any discernment as to what Christian revelation or the Gospel means and requires in the present exigence.

Thomas J. J. Alitzer represents a highly distinctive, and some would say idiosyncratic, type
of correlation. While he uses biblical language
and concepts, he interprets them through a
canonical framework of modern writers that
include Hegel, Blake, and Nietzsche. Impartial
critics likely would say that in this case the moderns win out. Both Kaufman and Altizer can best
be understood, perhaps, as radical modernists.
Following the lead of Karl Barth—and with the
help of some postmodernist writers—the Postliberal theologians, on the contrary, refuse to *begin*
by correlating Christian theology with modern
philosophy and science, or with the "religious
dimension" of our contemporary situation, in the
manner of Paul Tillich or Karl Rahner. For the
Postliberal, theology is a discipline of Christian
self-description and re-description within the
community, the Church. So governed, Christian

theology is able to use philosophy in a subordinate and improvised way depending on the specific context.

The Reformed or Neo-Calvinists propose yet
another type of response to modernity in their
call for a more thoroughgoing dialogue with
modernity. This means a more direct engagement
with the assumptions of modern culture as regards
matters such as reason and evidence; that is, on
issues concerning the very foundations and warrants of knowledge. While similarly challenging
the hegemony of modern thought, Christian
thinkers such as D. Z. Phillips and Jean-Luc Marion offer rather different conceptions of the way
that Christian thought should be understood in
its relationship to modernity. We have seen that
Phillips insists that concepts of religious meaning
and truth must be determined from *within* the religious context or form of life itself and not from
the outside. He will not even entertain a subordinate role for philosophy in the theological enterprise. Jean-Luc Marion, too, disallows all strategies of theological mediation or correlation which
employ what he calls modern metaphysical or
onto-theology. He begins with revelation as the
only legitimate foundation for doing Christian
theology. Reason can, of course, examine and
understand Being, but it is wholly incapable of
disclosing God's self-revelation as Love. Theology
must, therefore, forego metaphysics and develop
its own conceptual vocabulary with which to
speak properly about God's revelation.

What do the theological programs here examined tell us about Christian thought at the end of
the twentieth century? Some would say that they
show that Christian thought is both vigorous and
creative. Especially striking are those proposals
that show no defensiveness, neither cowed nor
overwhelmed by the secular challenges of modernity. Indeed, in those writers especially associated
with the work of Wittgenstein, in the Neo-
Calvinist apologists, and in the Postliberals, one
senses considerable confidence but usually tempered by an intellectual modesty. The advocates
of one or another type of "theology of correlation"

reveal a similar assurance and hopefulness that can be seen in their reflections on and engagement with movements of social and economic liberation and justice, the ecology movement, and the interreligious dialogue. Based on what the recent past teaches us, what the future portends for Christian theology at the beginning of the third millennium is quite beyond our capacity to discern. Few observers of the theological scene in the early 1960s, when the era of the theological giants was passing, could have predicted the new theological directions at the century's close. They are, at once, more varied, less grandiose in their visions and claims, more tolerant of religious diversity, but also, and perhaps paradoxically, less expectant but more hopeful.

NOTES

1. Jean-François Lyotard, *The Postmodern Explained*, trans. Don Berry (Minneapolis, 1993), p. 13.

2. Mark C. Taylor, "Reframing postmodernisms," in *Shadow of Spirit: Postmodernism and Religion*, ed. Philippa Berry and Andrew Warnick (London, 1992), pp. 11–12.

3. Gordon D. Kaufman, "The Vocation of Theology," in his *God-Mystery-Diversity: Christian Theology in a Pluralistic World* (Minneapolis, 1996), p. 66.

4. Gordon D. Kaufman, *Theology for a Nuclear Age* (Manchester, 1985), p. 28.

5. On Kaufman's Christian categorial scheme see, *In Face of Mystery* (Cambridge, MA, 1993) Chs. 6 and 7; also, *God-Mystery-Diversity*, pp. 62–64, 143–45.

6. On Kaufman's fullest development of his conceptions of human existence, the world, and God see, *In Face of Mystery* Parts II, III, and IV respectively. On these themes also see, *God-Mystery-Diversity*, Part II.

7. Kaufman, *God-Mystery-Diversity*, p. 63.

8. Gordon D. Kaufman, *An Essay on Theological Method* (Scholars Press, 1979), p. 46.

9. Ibid., p. 52.

10. Gordon D. Kaufman, "A Biohistorical Understanding of the Human," in *God-Mystery-Diversity*, op. cit., p. 78.

11. Kaufman, *Theology for a Nuclear Age*, p. 37.

12. Ibid., p. 40.

13. Kaufman, *God-Mystery-Diversity*, p. 107.

14. Ibid., p. 51.

15. Ibid., pp. 51–52.

16. Kaufman, *In Face of Mystery*, p. 381.

17. Kaufman, *God-Mystery-Diversity*, p. 114.

18. *In Face of Mystery*, p. 382–383.

19. *God-Mystery-Diversity*, p. 117. See also, *In Face of Mystery*, Chs. 25 and 26.

20. *In Face of Mystery*, p. 398.

21. Ibid., p. 42.

22. Ibid., pp. 410–11.

23. See Van Harvey, "Feuerbach on Religion as Construction," in *Theology at the End of Modernity: Essays in Honor of Gordon D. Kaufman* ed. Sheila Greeve Davaney, (Philadelphia, 1991), pp. 249–250.

24. Paul Ricoeur, *Freud and Philosophy: An Essay in Interpretation* (New Haven, 1970), pp. 32–33.

25. See Thomas J. J. Altizer's works *History as Apocalypse* (Albany, 1985); *Genesis and Apocalypse: A Theological Voyage Toward Authentic Christianity* (Louisville, 1990); *The Contemporary Jesus* (Albany, 1997).

26. See Robert P. Scharlemann's works *The Being of God and the Experience of Truth* (New York, 1982); *The Reason of Following: Christology and the Ecstatic* (Chicago, 1991).

27. See Charles E. Winquist's works *Epiphanies of Darkness: Deconstruction in Theology* (Philadelphia, 1986); *Desiring Theology* (Chicago, 1995).

28. See Mark C. Taylor's works *Deconstructing Theology* (New York, 1982); *Erring: A Postmodern A/theology* (Chicago, 1985).

29. See Don Cupitt's works *The Long Legged Fly* (London, 1987); *The Last Philosophy* (London, 1995).

30. Thomas J. J. Altizer, *The Gospel of Christian Atheism* (Philadelphia, 1966), pp. 82–83.

31. Ibid., p. 62.

32. Ibid., p. 68.

33. Altizer, *Genesis and Apocalypse*, p. 22.

34. Ibid., pp. 25–26.

35. As quoted in "The Empty Mirror," in Mark C. Taylor, *Deconstructing Theology*, p. 94.

36. Taylor, *Erring*, p. 5.

37. Ibid., p. 32.

38. Ibid., p. 14.

39. Ibid., p. 73.

40. Mark C. Taylor, "Text as Victim," in Thomas J. J. Altizer et al., *Deconstruction and Theology* (New York, 1982), pp. 67, 73.

41. Taylor, *Erring*, p.15.

42. Ibid., p. 15.

43. Ibid., p. 159.

44. Mark C. Taylor, *Disfiguring: Art, Architecture, Religion* (Chicago, 1992), p. 317.

45. See Graham Ward, "Postmodern Theology," in *The Modern Theologians*, 2nd ed., ed. David F. Ford (Oxford, 1997); Nancey Murphy and James William McClendon, Jr., "Distinguishing Modern and Postmodern Theologies," *Modern Theology*, 5 (1989), 199–212.

46. Jean-Luc Marion, *God Without Being* (Chicago, 1995), p. xx.

47. Ibid., p. xxi.

48. Ibid., p. xx.

49. Ibid., p. 16.

50. Ibid., pp. 17, 24.

51. Ibid., p. 95.

52. Ibid., p. 46.

53. Ibid., pp. 46–47.

54. Ibid., p. 138.

55. Ibid., p. xxiv.

56. Ibid.

57. René Descartes, *Meditations*, in *The Philosophical Works of Descartes*, I (New York, 1955), p. 171.

58. Bertrand Russell, *Why I Am Not a Christian* (New York, 1957).

59. J. L. Mackie, *The Miracle of Theism* (Oxford, 1982). Following David Hume's claim (see Vol I, Ch. 3) that there is no good evidence for a knowlege of God, Mackie's title suggests that it would take a miracle to believe that we can know God.

60. W. K. Clifford, "The Ethics of Belief," in *Lectures and Essays* ed. Leslie Stephen and Frederick Pollock (London, 1886), p. 346. For a fine brief account of the evidentialist argument and the response of Reformed epistemology, see Merold Westphal, "A Reader's Guide to 'Reformed Epistemology,'" *Perspective: A Journal of Reformed Thought*, 7 (November 1992), 10–16.

61. On the contemporary critique of modern foundationalism, see the lucid, brief account in John E. Thiel, *Nonfoundationalism* (Minneapolis, 1994), especially Ch. 1.

62. Alvin Plantinga, "Reason and Belief in God," in *Faith and Rationality: Reason and Belief in God*, ed. Alvin Plantinga and Nicholas Wolterstorff (Notre Dame, 1983), p. 60. For the fullest development of his position, see Plantinga's three volumes on warrant, the first two volumes of which have appeared: *Warrant: The Current Debate* (New York, 1993); and *Warrant and Proper Function* (New York, 1993).

63. Plantinga, "Reason and Belief in God," ibid., p. 65.

64. Ibid., p. 66.

65. Ibid., p. 62.

66. Ibid., p. 77.

67. See Nicholas Wolterstorff, *Reason within the Bounds of Religion*, 2nd ed. (Grand Rapids, Mich., 1984), Part I, 1. This brief work is a fine discussion and critique of foundationalism and what, after foundationalism, constitutes warranted religious belief.

68. Plantinga, "Reason and Belief in God," p. 80.

69. Dewey J. Hoitenga, Jr., "Properly Basic Beliefs: Alvin Plantinga," in his *Faith and Reason from Plato to Plantinga: An Introduction to Reformed Epistemology* (Albany, 1991), p. 186. Hoitenga's explication of Plantinga's position has been helpful in developing my own summary here.

70. Plantinga, "Reason and Belief in God," p. 82.

71. William Alston, *Perceiving God: The Epistemology of Religious Experience* (Ithaca, N.Y., 1991).

72. Nicholas Wolterstorff, "What Reformed Epistemology Is Not," *Perspective: A Journal of Reformed Thought*, 7 (November 1992), 14–16.

73. Clark H. Pinnock, *Reason Enough: A Case for the Christian Faith* (Downer's Grove, Ill., 1980), pp. 17–18, 69.

74. Ibid., p. 18.

75. Ibid., p. 17.

76. Ibid., pp. 121–122.

77. Nicholas Wolterstorff, "Is Reason Enough?" in *Contemporary Perspectives on Religious Epistemology*, ed. R. Douglas Geivett and Brenden Sweetman (New York and Oxford, 1992), p. 144. This essay first appeared in *The Reformed Journal*, 31 (April 1981).

78. Wolterstorff, "Is Reason Enough?" ibid., p. 145.

79. Ibid., p. 147.

80. Ibid.

81. Ibid., p. 149.

82. See Stewart C. Goetz, "Belief in God Is Not Properly Basic," in *Contemporary Perspectives on Religious Epistemology*, op. cit., pp. 168–177.

83. Gary Gutting, "The Catholic and the Calvinist: A Dialogue on Faith and Reason," *Faith and Philosophy*, 2 (July 1985), 255. For a similar type of critique, which argues that Reformed epistemology can give no reason to find a fundamentalist's basic beliefs any less justified than that of any other religious believers, see Terrence W. Tilley, "Reformed Epistemology and Religious Fundamentalism: How Basic Are Our Basic Beliefs?" *Modern Theology*, 6 (April 1990), 237–257.

84. See D. Z. Phillips, *Faith After Foundationalism: Critiques and Alternatives* (Boulder, Colo., 1995), Ch. 4, p. 52.

85. Ludwig Wittgenstein, *Lectures and Conversations on Aesthetics, Psychology and Religious Belief*, ed. C. Barrett (Oxford, 1966), p. 53.

86. Ibid., pp. 53–54.

87. Ibid., p. 55.

88. Ibid., 56.

89. Ibid., p. 59.

90. L. Wittgenstein, "Remarks on Frazer's 'Golden Bough,'" *The Human World*, no. 3, (May 1971), 28.

91. See, for example, the work of George A. Lindbeck, *The Nature of Doctrine* (Philadelphia, 1984).

92. See Norman Malcolm's "Is It a Religious Belief That 'God Exists'?" in *Faith and the Philosophers*, ed. John Hick (London, 1966); "The Groundlessness of Belief," in *Reason and Religion*, ed. Stuart C. Brown (Ithaca, N.Y., 1977).

93. See Peter Winch's *The Idea of a Social Science* (London, 1958); "Understanding a Primitive Society," *American Philosophical Quarterly*, I (1964), 307–324. Winch has influenced religious studies through his examination of understanding and explanation in the social sciences and in religion. His basic argument is that there is no single concept of rationality and that, finally, religion can be understood and explained only from within.

94. See D. Z. Phillips's *The Concept of Prayer* (London, 1965); *Faith and Philosophical Inquiry* (London, 1970); *Religion Without Explanation* (Oxford, 1976); *Belief, Change and Forms of Life* (London, 1986); *Faith After Foundationalism* (London, 1988).

95. Malcolm, "The Groundlessness of Belief," p. 155.

96. Ibid.

97. Malcolm, "Is It a Religious Belief that 'God Exists'?" pp. 55–56.

98. D. Z. Phillips, "Faith, Scepticism and Religious Understanding," in *Faith and Philosophical Understanding* (London, 1970), pp. 63–64.

99. Ibid., p. 65.

100. Ibid., p. 68.

101. Ibid., pp 68–69.

102. Ibid., p. 69.

103. D. Z. Phillips, *The Concept of Prayer* (Oxford, 1981), p. 40.

104. Ibid., p. 51.

105. Ibid., p. 52.

106. Ibid., p. 53.

107. Ibid., p. 55.

108. Ibid., pp. 61–62.

109. Ibid., p. 102.

110. Ibid., p. 103.

111. Ibid., p. 117.

112. Ibid., p. 116.

113. Ibid.

114. On this point see, W. D. Hudson, *Wittgenstein and Religious Belief* (London, 1975).

115. For this and other criticisms, see Phillips, *Belief, Change and Forms of Life* Ch. 1.

116. See Brian Magee, ed., *Modern British Philosophy* (London, 1983), p. 214.

117. See Kai Nielson, "The Challenge of Conceptual Relativism," in *Contemporary Critiques of Religion* (New York, 1971).

118. See Phillips, *Belief, Change and Forms of Life*, Ch. 1.

119. Hans Frei, *Types of Christian Theology* (New Haven, 1992), p. 54.

120. Terrence W. Tilley, "The Philosophy of Religion and the Concept of Religion," unpublished paper given at the annual meeting of the American Academy of Religion, San Francisco, November 23, 1997. I am grateful to the author for permission to quote from his paper.

121. For this line of argument, I am dependent on the work of John H. Whittaker, especially his unpublished paper, "On Grammatical Inquiries and Unsettled Conceptual Contexts," delivered at the annual meeting of the American Academy of Religion, San Francisco, November 23, 1997.

122. Hans Frei, *The Eclipse of Biblical Narrative* (New Haven, 1974), p. 130.

123. See Stanley Hauerwas's *A Community of Character* (Notre Dame, 1981); and *Against the Nations* (Minneapolis, 1985).

124. See Ronald F. Thiemann's *Revelation and Theology: The Gospel as Narrated Promise* (Notre Dame, 1985).

125. See William C. Placher's *Unapologetic Theology: A Christian Voice in a Pluralistic Conversation* (Louisville, Ky., 1989).

126. See Kathryn E. Tanner's *God and Creation in Christian Theology: Tyranny or Empowerment* (Oxford, 1988).

127. See Charles M. Wood's *The Formation of Christian Understanding* (Valley Forge, Pa., 1993).

128. George A. Lindbeck, *The Nature of Doctrine* (Minneapolis, 1984), p. 7.

129. Ibid., p 16.

130. Ibid.

131. Ibid.

132. Ibid. p. 17. The reference to Tillich is to his *Systematic Theology*, I (Chicago, 1951), p. 240.

133. Lindbeck, *The Nature of Doctrine*, p. 18.

134. Ibid., p. 34.

135. Ibid., p. 86.

136. Ibid., p. 76.

137. Ibid., p. 116.

138. Ibid., p. 118. Also see G. Lindbeck, "Scripture, Consensus, and Community," in *Biblical Interpre-*

tation in Crisis: The Ratzinger Conference on Bible and Church ed. Richard John Neuhaus (Grand Rapids, Mich., 1989), pp. 74–101.

139. Lindbeck, *The Nature of Doctrine*, p. 121.

140. See Stanley Hauerwas and William Williman, "Embarrassed by God's Presence," *The Christian Century*, 102 (January 30, 1985), 98.

141. See H. Richard Niebuhr, *The Meaning of Revelation* (New York, 1969), Ch. 2.

142. See Stephen Crites, "The Narrative Quality of Experience," *Journal of the American Academy of Religion*, 39 (September 1971), 291–311.

143. See Paul Ricoeur, *Time and Narrative*, 3 vol., trans. Kathleen McLaughlin and David Pellauer (Chicago, 1984–1988).

144. Stanley Hauerwas with Richard Bondi and David B. Burrell, *Truthfulness and Tragedy: Further Investigations in Christian Ethics* (Notre Dame, 1977), p. 73.

145. Ibid.

146. Ibid., p. 77.

147. Stanley Hauerwas, *A Community of Character* (Notre Dame, 1981), p. 84.

148. Ibid., p. 12.

149. Ibid., p. 115.

150. Ibid., p. 55.

151. Ibid., p. 95.

152. Ibid.

153. William C. Placher, *Unapologetic Theology: A Christian Voice in a Pluralistic Situation* (Louisville, Ky.,

1989), p. 165. I am dependent on Placher for this particular criticism of Hauerwas and its bearing as regards other postliberal notions of truth claims.

154. See Ronald F. Thiemann, *Revelation and Theology: The Gospel as Narrated Promise* (Notre Dame, 1985), pp. 61 ff.

155. See, for example, *The Nature of Confession: Evangelicals and Postliberals in Conversation*, ed. Timothy R. Phillips and Dennis L. Okholm (Downers Grove, Ill., 1996).

156. See *Trinity Journal*, 8 (Spring 1987) for the discussion between Henry and Frei. Frei's response also appears in Hans Frei, *Theology and Narrative*, ed. George Hunsinger and William C. Placher (New York, 1993), pp. 207–212.

157. Alister McGrath, *A Passion for Truth: The Intellectual Coherence of Evangelicalism* (Downers Grove, Ill., 1996), p. 153. A revised form of this essay by McGrath, entitled "An Evaluation of Evangelical and Postliberalism," appears in *The Nature of Confession*, pp. 23–44. See note 155.

158. McGrath, *A Passion for Truth*, p. 155.

159. See Thiemann, *Revelation and Theology*, pp. 43–44; William Werpehowski, "Ad Hoc Apologetics," *The Journal of Religion*, 66 (1986), 282–301.

160. Nicholas P. Wolterstorff, *What New Haven and Grand Rapids Have to Say to Each Other: The Stob Lectures* (Grand Rapids, Mich., 1993), pp. 27–28.

161. Ibid., pp. 43–44.

SUGGESTIONS FOR FURTHER READING

Gordon D. Kaufman

Buckley, James J. "Revisionists and Liberals." In *The Modern Theologians*, II, ed. David F. Ford (Oxford: Basil Blackwell, 1997). Kaufman's theology is discussed along with that of Edward Farley, Schubert Ogden, and David Tracy as exemplifying contemporary theologies of correlation.

Davaney, Sheila Greeve, ed. *Theology at the End of Modernity: Essays in Honor of Gordon D. Kaufman* (Philadelphia: Trinity Press, 1991). Some of the essays in this *Festschrift* explore aspects of Kaufman's theology.

Frei, Hans W. *Types of Modern Theology* (New Haven: Yale University Press, 1992). Frei sees Kaufman's work as representing a Kantian type of academic philosophical theology.

Ray, Alan. *The Modern Soul: Michel Foucault and the Theological Discourse of Gordon Kaufman and David Tracy* (Philadelphia: Fortress Press, 1987). Helps to locate Kaufman's position.

Postmodern Theology

The Postmodern Condition: The following represent a few of the important discussions of this cultural phenomenon:

Calinescu, Matei. *Five Faces of Modernity* (Durham, N.C.: Duke University Press, 1987).

Harvey, David. *The Condition of Postmodernity: An Enquiry into the Origins of Cultural Change* (Oxford: Basil Blackwell, 1989).

Hoesterey, Ingeborg, ed. *Zeitgeist in Babel: The Postmodernist Controversy* (Bloomington: Indiana University Press, 1991).

Lakeland, Paul. *Postmodernity: Christian Identity in a Fragmented Age* (Minneapolis: Fortress Press, 1997). Clearly presents the theological issues raised by postmodern culture and thought.

Lyotard, Jean-François. *The Postmodern Condition: A Report on Knowledge* (Minneapolis: University of Minnesota Press, 1984).

———. *The Postmodern Explained* (Minneapolis: University of Minnesota Press, 1993).

Vattimo, Gianni. *The End of Modernity* (Cambridge: Cambridge University Press).

Discussions of Postmodernist Theology:

Griffin, David Ray. *God and Religion in the Postmodern World*, (Albany: State University of New York Press, 1989). Griffin's own constructive theological response to the postmodern condition.

Griffin, David Ray, William Beardslee, and Joe Holland. *Varieties of Postmodern Theology* (Albany: State University of New York Press, 1989). An introduction to postmodern theologies with responses to Mark C. Taylor, Jean-François Lyotard, Harvey Cox, and Cornel West.

Lakeland, Paul. *Postmodernity: Christian Identity in a Fragmented Age* (Minneapolis: Fortress Press, 1997). Lakeland nicely traces the significance of postmodernism for Christian thought regarding the person, God, and Christ. Also see John E. Thiel's *Nonfoundationalism* below, an excellent guide to movements germane to contemporary Christian theology.

Scharlemann, Robert P., ed. *Theology at the End of the Century* (Charlottesville: University Press of Virginia, 1990). Scharlemann responds to essays by postmodernists Thomas J. J. Altizer, Mark C. Taylor, and Charles E. Winquist.

Tilley, Terrence W. *Postmodern Theologies: The Challenge of Religious Diversity* (Maryknoll, N.Y.: Orbis, 1995). A useful exposition and critique of a variety of postmodern approaches to theology, including the work of Helmut Peukert, David Ray Griffin, David Tracy, Thomas J. J. Altizer, Mark C. Taylor, Edith Wyschogrod, George Lindbeck, Gustavo Gutíerrez, Sharon Welch, and J. W. McClenden, Jr.

Tracy, David. *Plurality and Ambiguity: Hermeneutics, Religion, Hope* (New York: Harper and Row, 1987). This book does not explicitly discuss postmodernism, but it is an excellent essay on the possibilities of theological conversation in a time when traditional modes of interpretation and theorizing

appear spent. Also see William C. Placher's *Unapologetic Theology* below.

Van Huyssteen, J. Wentzel. *Essays in Postfoundationalist Theology* (Grand Rapid, Mich.: William B. Eerdmans, 1997). An interesting effort to move beyond both traditional foundationalism and contemporary postfoundationalism and to open up a public dialogue with philosophy and science.

Ward, Graham. *Barth, Derrida and the Language of Theology* (Cambridge: Cambridge University Press, 1995). An excellent study of Karl Barth's links to and possible engagement with the postmodernist philosophers Emmanuel Levinas and Jacques Derrida.

———. "Postmodern Theology." In *The Modern Theologians*, ed. David F. Ford (Oxford:Basil Blackwell, 1997). A brief overview of postmodernisms and liberal and conservative types of postmodernist theology.

———, ed. *The Postmodern God: A Theological Reader* (Oxford: Blackwell Publishers, 1997). An excellent collection of texts on religion by ten influential French postmodernist writers, including Barthes, Foucault, Derrida, Irigaray, and Kristeva, followed by seven essays on postmodernist religious themes. Includes a helpful introduction by Ward, "A Guide to Theological Thinking in Cyberspace."

Reformed Epistemology

Clark, Kelly James. *Return to Reason: A Critique of Enlightenment Evidentialism and a Defense of Reason and Belief in God* (Grand Rapids, Mich.: William B. Eerdmans, 1990). The latter chapters deal with classical evidentialism, Plantinga's theory, and a defense of Reformed epistemology.

Geivett, Douglas R., and Brendon Sweetman, ed. *Contemporary Perspectives on Religious Epistemology* (New York: Oxford University Press, 1992). Includes a selection of essays on Reformed epistomology and an excellent bibliography of articles and books on the subject.

Gutting, Gary. *Religious Belief and Religious Skepticism* (Notre Dame: University of Notre Dame Press, 1982). Interesting treatments of Plantinga and Wittgenstein with critical analysis.

Hoitenga, Dewey J., Jr. *Faith and Reason from Plato to Plantinga: An Introduction to Reformed Epistemology* (Albany: State University of New York Press, 1991). Argues that Calvin and Plantinga represent the classical Augustinian tradition on the question of faith and reason.

Phillips, D. Z. *Faith After Foundationalism: Critiques and Alternatives* (Boulder, Colo.: Westview Press, 1995). Part I (pp. 3–127) is an extended critique of Plantinga and Reformed epistemology from the perspective of a neo-Wittgensteinian philosopher.

Plantinga, Alvin, and Jonathan L. Kvanvig. *Warrant in Contemporary Epistemology: Essays in Honor of Plantinga's Theory of Knowledge* (Lanham, Md.: Rowman and Littlefield, 1996).

Tomberlin, James E., and Peter van Inwagen, ed. *Alvin Plantinga Profiles*, Vol. 5 (Dordrecht: D. Reidel, 1985). Essays on and "Replies" by A. Plantinga.

Zagzebski, Linda, ed. *Rational Faith: Catholic Responses to Reformed Epistemology* (Notre Dame: University of Notre Dame Press, 1993).

The Neo-Wittgensteinians and Theology

High, Dallas. *Language, Persons and Belief: Studies in Wittgenstein's "Philosophical Investigations" and Religious Uses of Language* (New York: Oxford University Press, 1967).

Hudson, W. D. *Wittgenstein and Religious Belief* (New York: St. Martin's Press, 1975).

Keightly, Alan. *Wittgenstein, Grammar and God* (London: Epworth Press, 1976). Keightly, High, and Hudson above, are older appreciative yet critical studies of the importance of Wittgenstein's philosophy for religion that remain worth consulting.

Kerr, Fergus, O. P. *Theology after Wittgenstein* (Oxford: Oxford University Press, 1986). Kerr and Phillips (see below) represent valuable studies of Wittgenstein and theology and religion.

Monk, Ray. *Ludwig Wittgenstein: The Duty of Genius* (New York: Free Press, 1993). This interesting biography of Wittgenstein deals briefly but accurately with his religious beliefs and his writings on religion.

Phillips, D. Z. *Wittgenstein and Religion* (New York: St. Martin's Press, 1993).

Sherry, Patrick. *Religion, Truth, and Language Games* (New York: Barnes and Noble, 1977). A good study and critique.

Thiselton, Anthony C. *The Two Horizons: New Testament Hermeneutics and Philosophical Description with Special Reference to Heidegger, Bultmann, Gadamer, and Wittgenstein* (Grand Rapids, Mich.: William B. Eerdmans, 1980). Contains a valuable discussion of Wittgenstein and biblical hermeneutics.

Postliberalism

Green, Garrett, ed. *Scriptural Authority and Narrative Interpretation* (Philadelphia: Fortress Press, 1987). A *Festschrift* honoring Hans Frei with a bibliography of his writings and several essays by writers sympathetic to Frei's theological work.

Hauerwas, Stanley, and L. Gregory Jones. *Why Narrative? Readings in Narrative Theology* (Grand Rapids, Mich.: William B. Eerdmans, 1989). Includes some of the seminal essays on narrative theology that are a good background for understanding an important feature of postliberal theology.

Marshall, Bruce D., ed. *Theology and Dialogue: Essays in Conversation with George Lindbeck* (Notre Dame: University of Notre Dame Press, 1990). Contains essays honoring George Lindbeck and a bibliography of his writings.

Phillips, Timothy R., and Dennis L. Okholm. *The Nature of Confession: Evangelicals and Postliberals in Conversation* (Downers Grove, Ill.: InterVarsity Press, 1996). Interesting essays on foundationalism, epistemological realism, biblical authority, and interpretation that bring out the commonalities and differences between these two movements.

Placher, William C. *Unapologetic Theology: A Christian Voice in a Pluralistic Conversation* (Louisville, Ky.: Westminster/John Knox Press, 1989). A lucid, helpful account of the new pluralistic context of theological work which points to many of the sources of postliberal reflection.

———. "Postliberal Theology." In *The Modern Theologians*, II, ed. David F. Ford (Oxford: Basil Blackwell, 1997), pp. 115–128.

Rasmussen, Arne. *The Church as Polis: From Political Theology to Theological Politics as Exemplified by Jürgen Moltmann and Stanley Hauerwas* (Notre Dame: University of Notre Dame Press, 1994). A contrast and critique from a Hauerwas perspective.

Thiel, John E. *Nonfoundationalism* (Minneapolis: Fortress Press, 1994). A clear account of the philosophical and theological critique of modern epistemological foundationalism and the way this critique has influenced movements like postliberalism.

Wallace, Mark I. *The Second Naiveté: Barth, Ricoeur, and the New Yale Theology* (Macon, Ga.: Mercer University Press, 1990). A critical perspective on the new Yale postliberal theology.

Hans Frei

In addition to the discussion of Frei's work in the above, see:

Frei, Hans. *Theology and Narrative: Selected Essays,* ed. George Hunsinger and William C. Placher (New York: Oxford University Press, 1993). Included with these important essays by Frei is a valuable introduction by Placher covering Frei's life and the influences on the development of his thought and an important afterword by Hunsinger on "Hans Frei as Theologian."

Among the journal sources, the most valuable collection of essays on Frei's thought is in *Modern Theology* 8 (1992), 103–204.

George Lindbeck

In addition to the works cited above, see the articles in two symposia on Lindbeck's work:

The Thomist, 49 (1985), 392–472; and *Modern Theology,* 4 (1988), 107–209.

Phillips, D. Z. *Faith After Foundationalism: Critiques and Alternatives* (Boulder, Colo.: Westview Press, 1995). Ch. 15 and 16 are critiques of Lindbeck's *The Nature of Doctrine* from the perspective of a neo-Wittgensteinian.

Acknowledgments

The following publishers and organizations have generously granted permission to use extended quotations from their publications or to reprint photographs.

EXCERPTED TEXT

R. Morgan and Michael Pye, trans. and eds. *Ernst Troeltsch: Writings on Theology and Religion* (Atlanta: John Knox Press, 1977). Reprinted by permission of Gerald Duckworth and Co., Ltd.

Henry N. Wieman, *The Source of Human Good*, (Atlanta: Scholars Press, 1946). Reprinted by permission of Scholars Press.

Dietrich Bonhoeffer, *Letters and Papers from Prison*. Revised enlarged edition translated by Reginald Fuller, Frank Clark et al. Copyright © 1953, 1967, 1971 by SCM Press, Ltd. Reprinted with permission of Simon & Schuster and SCM Press, Ltd.

Rudolf Bultmann, *Jesus Christ and Mythology*. Copyright © 1958 by Rudolf Bultmann, renewed 1986 by Antje B. Lemke. Reprinted with permission of Scribner's, a Division of Simon & Schuster.

Hans W. Bartsch, ed., *Kerygma and Myth, I*, R.H. Fuller (trans), (London: S.P.C.K. Press, 1953). Reprinted with permission of S.P.C.K.

Paul Tillich, *Systematic Theology, I* (Chicago: University of Chicago Press, 1951). Reprinted by permission of The University of Chicago Press.

Paul Tillich, *Systematic Theology, II* (Chicago: University of Chicago Press, 1957). Reprinted by permission of The University of Chicago Press.

H. Richard Niebuhr, *The Meaning of Revelation*. Copyright 1941 by Macmillan Publishing Company; copyright renewed © 1969 by Florence Niebuhr, Cynthia M. Niebuhr, and Richard R. Niebuhr. Reprinted with permission of Simon & Schuster.

Reinhold Niebuhr, *Faith and History*. Copyright 1949 by Charles Scribner's Sons; copyright renewed © 1977 by Ursula Niebuhr. Reprinted with permission of Scribner's, a Division of Simon & Schuster.

Schubert Ogden, *The Reality of God and Other Essays*, 1966; and *The Point of Christology*, 1982. Reprinted by permission of Schubert Ogden.

John B. Cobb, Jr., *God and the World* (Louisville, KY: Westminster Press, 1969). Used by permission of Westminster John Knox Press.

James H. Cone, *A Black Theology of Liberation*, (Maryknoll, NY: Orbis Books, 1990.) Reprinted with permission of Orbis Books.

PHOTOGRAPHS

1	courtesy of Mohr Siebeck, Tubingen
13	courtesy of Verlag C. H. Beck, Munich
33	courtesy of H. N. Wieman
34	Harvard University News Office
62, 100	Karl Barth-Archiv, Basel
96	Gutersloher Verlagshaus/Chr. Kaiser/Kiefel
169, 520	Yale University Divinity School Library Archives
133, 165, 443	Union Theological Seminary
197, 222	courtesy of Crossroad Publishing Company
233	Catholic News Service
247	Continuum Publishing Corp., distributor
273	Orbis Books
283, 341, 343	Augsburg Fortress Publishers
309	courtesy of John B. Cobb, Jr.
320	courtesy of Schubert M. Ogden
387	courtesy of Carl F. H. Henry
417	Joe Wrinn/courtesy of Elisabeth Schüssler Fiorenza
429	courtesy of Sallie McFague
446	Library of Congress
469	courtesy of John Hick
481	Craig Hyde Parker/Harvard University News Office
493	Bradford F. Herzog/Harvard University, The Divinity School

Index

Abe, Masao, 487-88
Abraham, William, 392, 407
Ad Gentes, 243
Alexander, Samuel, 167, 310
Alston, William, 507, 509
Alter, Robert, 371
Althusser, Louis, 296
Altizer, Thomas, 92, 500-03, 504,
    515, 526
    on God's *kenosis*, 501-02, 503
    on God's death, 501, 502
    on apocalypse, 502, 503
Ames, Edward Scribner, 34, 42, 47,
    48
Amida Buddhism, 471
Analogy
    von Balthazar, H. on, 257-58
    Barth, K. on the analogy of faith,
        98-99, 257
    Ogden, S. on, 324-25
    Rahner on, 207
    Schillebeeckx, E. on, 224-25
Anselm, 98-99, 116
Apel, Karl-Otto, 354, 356
apokatastasis, 108
Apostolicam Actuositatem, 243
Asmussen, Hans, 112
Assmann, Hugo, 288, 300
Auerbach, Erich, 371
Augustine, St., 158, 262, 395, 451
Auschwitz, 277
Authority
    question of, 2-3
Ayer, A. J., 169, 170

Balthazar, Hans Urs von, 109, 205,
    213, 255-60, 263, 264, 301,
    399, 400, 476
    and Karl Barth, 257-58
    on analogy of being, 257-58
    on theological aesthetics and
        theo-dramatics, 258-59
Barmen Declaration, 100-101, 102
Barth, Karl, 10, 17, 29, 49, 50, 51,
    52, 62-76, 77, 78, 79, 84, 89,
    96-111, 112, 113, 114, 121,
    122, 127, 128, 133, 140, 141,
    143, 148, 153, 154, 158, 161,

166, 168, 169, 176, 189, 220,
    247-48, 251, 252, 256, 257,
    258, 259, 277, 281, 283, 285-
    86, 292, 341, 342, 345, 370,
    373, 374, 377, 393, 394, 397,
    398, 399-400, 402, 403, 408,
    409, 412, 456, 457, 458, 471-
    72, 493, 505, 519, 522, 526
    criticism of Bultmann, 75-76
    criticism of Gogarten, 75-76
    criticism of Harnack, 70-71
    on Dialectical method, 71-72
    on God as Wholly Other, 72-73
    on the Bible, 73-74
    on the historical Jesus, 73
    the development of his theology,
        97-99
    on social ethics, 99-104
    on the doctrine of the Word of
        God, 104-106
    on interpretation of Scripture,
        104-106
    on the Christological concentra-
        tion, 106-108
    on the doctrine of election, 108-
        109
    criticisms of Barth, 109-111
    and Hans Küng, 247-48, 252
Bateson, Gregory, 296
Bauckham, Richard, 287
Baudrillard, Jean, 500
Beardsley, Monroe, 360
Beauvoir, Simone de, 417, 420
Benedict XV, Pope, 197
Benjamin, Walter, 282
Bennett, John C., 166, 167, 176
Berdyaev, Nikolai, 134, 295
Berger, Peter, 369
Bergson, H., 7, 34, 49, 201, 312
Berkouwer, Gerrit C., 392, 393-401,
    409
    on co-relationship of revelation
        and faith, 394-95
    on the nature and authority of
        Scripture, 395-97
    on providence, election and
        retrobation, 397-99
    on eschatology and universalism,
        399-401

Bethge, Eberhard, 111, 113, 116,
    119, 124, 127
Bible, interpretation of, 13-17, 67-
    71, 73
    Barth on, 73-74, 104-06
    Berkouwer, G. C. on, 395-97
    Black womanist theology on,
        461-62
    Bultmann on, 67-68, 157-60
    Frei, H. on, 370-72
    Gogarten on, 89-91
    Henry, C. F. H. on, 402-07
    Lindbeck, G. on, 522
    de Lubac, H. on, 204-05
    Schüssler Fiorenza on, 425-28
    Vatican Council II on, 244-45
Biedermann, A. E., 7
"Black Manifesto," 453-55
Black, Max, 360
"Black Power," statement of
        National Committee of
        Negro Churchmen, 452-53
Black theology, chapter fourteen,
    historical context, 448-50
    cultural context, 450-51
    social context, 451-53
    and Black Manifesto, 453
    and statement of Black Church-
        men, 455
    of James H. Cone, 456-60
    new trajectories, 465-66
"Black Theology," statement of
        National Committee of
        Black Churchmen, 455
Black Womanist Theology, 460-65
    definition of womanist, 460
    interpretations of the Bible, 461-
        62
    on Jesus Christ, 462-64
    on moral and ethical thought,
        464-65
Blake, William, 501, 502, 526
Blanchard, Paul, 253
Bloch, Ernst, 274, 283
Bloesch, Donald, 407
Blondel, M., 7, 34, 201, 208, 227
Blumhardt, Christoph, 77
Boff, Clodovis, 300
Boff, Leonardo, 262, 288, 298-300